OPERA

Endpaper: Stage setting and design, etching by Stefano della Bella
after a drawing by Lodovico Ottavio Burnacini, Vienna, c. 1666

Imprint:

© 1999 Könemann Verlagsgesellschaft mbH
Bonner Strasse 126, D–50968 Cologne

Art direction	Peter Feierabend
Project management	Kirsten E. Lehmann
Project coordination	Britta Harting
	Sybille Carmanns
Editorial assistance	Evelyn Lampe
Design	Stephanie Weischer
Typesetting of musical excerpts	Kottamester BT, Budapest
Picture research	Barbara Linz
Production	Mark Voges
Reproduction	Typografik, Köln

Original title: Opera. Komponisten. Werke. Interpreten.

© 2000 for this English edition:
Könemann Verlagsgesellschaft mbH
Bonner Strasse 126, D–50968 Cologne

Translation from German	Paul Aston, Peter Barton, Anthea Bell, and Christine Shuttleworth in association with Goodfellow & Egan
Editing	In association with Goodfellow & Egan
Project management	Jackie Dobbyne for Goodfellow & Egan Publishing Management, Cambridge
Project coordination	Nadja Bremse
	Alex Morkramer
Production	Ursula Schümer
Printing and binding	Mateu Cromo Artos Gráficas, Madrid

Printed in Spain

ISBN 3-8290-3571-3

10 9 8 7 6 5 4 3 2 1

OPERA

Composers • Works • Performers

Editor-in-chief **András Batta**

Editor **Sigrid Neef**

KÖNEMANN

Opera in Book Form

This book is not just for opera fans. It is also especially designed for all those who know very little or even nothing about the world of opera. The operatic experience is like a culinary delight: it is the genre for gourmets. *Opera* will make this experience even more appetizing.

This book contains several "layers' – like a musical score. First there are the pictures. A fundamental resource on the richly diverse world of opera was provided by the theatrical science collection of the University of Cologne, especially the pictorial collection with set designs from two centuries, a photographic collection, portraits of singers, old engravings, illustrations and more. We would like to thank the director, Professor Dr. Elmar Buck, for allowing us to use the treasures of this collection, some of which are being shown for the first time, for this publication. Photographs of scenes from performances at renowned opera houses also depict exemplary aspects of the performance and interpretation of the operas discussed in this book.

The texts introduce readers to four centuries of composers and the works that best characterize them. In addition to details about the casts and contents of the various works, the texts also contain information and commentary about individual aspects that are relevant to the given composer, the work, its history or traditional stage performance.

The excerpts from musical scores can be regarded as graphic representations of the music's characteristics; they contain the most well-known themes and motifs, the "hits" of an opera. Sometimes unusual musical or dramatic aspects or associations to other composers can be illustrated by excerpts from musical scores. These are then referred to in the texts.

The Agony of Choice

The world of opera is boundless. The main opera houses draw from a basic repertoire of 50 to 60 works. Then there are also about the same number of pieces that are only performed occasionally. If we include smaller opera houses, the numerous festival, film, and TV productions, as well as the ever-increasing video and CD market, the number of performable operas today includes around 1000 works.

In this book, we have attempted to select and combine the best of the established, international opera repertoire, a few of the rarities that have been forgotten in practice and a tribute to opera-making in the 20th century. Some 338 operas from 124 composers are presented here, to name only two important aspects that went into the selection process. The life accomplishments of the five musical dramatists who indisputably crown the history of opera – Mozart, Puccini, Richard Strauss, Verdi,and Wagner – are represented in their entirety. Special attention was paid to the selection of the repertoire for the 20th century.

Giacomo Puccini → *Turandot:* Arie des Calaf (III. Akt)

Ma il mio mi-stero è chiuso in me, il nome mio nessun sa-prà! No, no, sul-la tua boc - ca lo - di - rò _____ quando la lu - ce splen - de - rà! _____

A Few Tips for Using This Book

Opera is organized according to the composers and the works that it covers. The individual portraits include biographical information, life events, an overview of the composer's works, as well as a brief characterization of the composer in an operatic, historical context. Descriptions of the individual operas follow. Since the book is alphabetically ordered, there is no need for a table of contents. Given its international audience, this book uses the English spellings of composers' names.

In the appendix, readers will find a glossary with definitions of the most important musical terms, a complete register with a list of operas, original performances, and musical scores, as well as an outline of the short essays on the history of opera included in the book. An index of topics and names, a selection of recommended literature on the subject, and a list of photos and illustrations are also included in the appendix.

The authors of the individual entries – also listed in the appendix – are indicated at the end of a text or a double-page spread by their initials. All other texts were written by the editor-in-chief.

Opera is not only the most complex genre of the performing arts; it is also the most enigmatic. This book documents the mysteries and wonders of this captivating art form that become audible when we visit the opera. Because perhaps the most important message of music is that which cannot be expressed in mere words.

Pages 6/7: Curtain design from the theatrical studio of Otto Müller-Godesberg, for the Stadttheater, Barmen, 1905 (TWS)

Pages 8/9: Guiseppe Verdi, *A Masked Ball*, production photograph, production and sets Richard Jones and Antony McDonald, conducted by Marcello Viotti, Bregenz Festival 1999.

Adams, John

b. 15 February 1947 in Worcester (Massachusetts)

From 1966 to 1971, Adams studied music at Harvard University. In 1971, he moved to the West Coast, living initially in Oakland, and then became a professor at the San Francisco Conservatory of Music, where he conducted the New Music Ensemble. At the recommendation of the conductor Edo de Waart, Adams was from 1978 first adviser to and then composer in residence of the San Francisco Symphony Orchestra. In 1985 he married and moved to Berkeley (California), where he has lived ever since as a freelance composer and concert organizer, working with composers such as Robert Ashley, Glenn Branca, Gavin Bryars, →John Cage, Meredith Monk, and →Steve Reich. In Europe, Adams is celebrated for his orchestral works and for the opera *Nixon in China*, but also as a conductor of major orchestras, the Schoenberg Ensemble, the London Sinfonietta, and the Ensemble Modern.

Works: Operas: *Nixon in China* (1987), *The Death of Klinghoffer* (1991), *I Was Looking at the Ceiling and Then I Saw the Sky* (1994); other works include *Phrygian Gates* for piano (1977), *Shaker Loops* for string septet (1978, rev. 1983), *Light Over Water* for synthesizer (1983), *Harmonielehre* (*Harmony Treatise*) for orchestra (1984/85), *Short Ride in a Fast Machine* (1986), *The Chairman Dances* (1986).

*A*dams is one of the second generation of minimalist musicians. Whereas in Steve Reich the minimalism pertains to aspects of form, harmony, and rhythm, Adams creates atmospherically evocative passages by means of quasi-slow-motion deceleration and abrupt harmonic changes.

Nixon in China

Opera in three acts

Libretto: Alice Goodman.
Première: 22 October 1987, Houston (Opera House).
Characters: Richard Nixon, President of the USA (Bar), Pat Nixon, his wife (S), Chou En-lai, Chinese Prime Minister (Bar), Mao Tse-tung, Chairman of the Party (T), Chiang Ch'ing, Mao's wife (S), Henry Kissinger (B), Nancy T'sang, Mao's first secretary (Ms), Mao's Second and Third Secretaries (2 Ms), Wu Ching-hua (dancer), Hung Chang-ching (dancer); citizens of Peking, industrial workers, soldiers of the Chinese People's Army (chorus).
Setting: Peking, 1972.

Synopsis
Act I

The reception of President Nixon and his wife runs wholly according to protocol, whether at the airport (Scene 1), during the first exploratory talks between the Americans and the Chinese (Scene 2) or during a banquet (Scene 3). There is reserve and incomprehension on both sides, at once alarming and funny, but etiquette is preserved.

Act II

The First Lady carries out her cultural itinerary, visiting the sights of Peking, both from the Communist present and the old imperial days (Scene 1). In the evening, the guests are invited to the traditional Peking Opera. There Mao Tse-tung's wife proudly offers them the revolutionary ballet *The Red Detachment of Women* (Scene 2).

Act III

The Americans' last night in Peking. Was the visit historically important? Yes. But Nixon and Mao Tse-tung wonder whether it has brought the dreams of their youth any closer. Mao wanted to carry through the ideal of a great Asiatic revolution, while the American's secret goal in life was a hamburger stall of his own. Only old Chou En-Lai has abandoned all desires, and has nothing more to fear or hope.   *S. N.*

Nixon in China, production photograph with Susan Burghardt as Chiang Ch'ing, production John Dew, sets and costumes Gottfried Pilz, German première at the Bühnen der Stadt Bielefeld 1989.
The revue presented to Nixon and his retinue is a self-portrayal by the Chinese leadership, while at the same time being tailored to the tastes of the distinguished state guests.

I Was Looking at the Ceiling and Then I Saw the Sky
Following the first two stage works, the third collaboration between John Adams and director Peter Sellars was a folk music-inspired "song play" with an eight-piece orchestra. According to librettist June Jordan, it portrays an "earthquake romance" among seven West Coast young men and women in the 1990s: the illegal immigrant Consuelo seeks happiness with gangster boss Dewain (father of her second child), Baptist preacher David hopes for the same with Leila, successful lawyer Rick cannot resign himself to his Boat People origins, and gay cop Mike has difficulty in expressing his feelings to reality TV reporter Tiffany. During an earthquake, churches and inner and outer prisons crumble. Consuelo bids farewell to the consumer paradise and returns to El Salvador. The US première in 1994 was followed by guest performances in Europe, such as those at the Edinburgh and Helsinki Festivals.

Minimalist art and American humor

"Mozart, Verdi, Wagner, Puccini – none had his operas performed at so many theaters within such a short period. And *Nixon in China* is only his first opera!" This was the reaction of astonished contemporaries to the stunning triumphal march of this opera and its composer. Though the material is based on the politically important visit of Nixon to China, it is not a political opera. Adams was much more interested in the encounter of two completely alien cultures and lifestyles. An example of this is the entrance aria of Nixon (arriving at the airport in China), which at the same time wittily takes advantage of the opportunities offered by minimalist music in the constant repetition of the same pattern: "News news news news news news news news news news news a has a has a has a has a has a kind of mystery has a has a has a kind of mystery." Mao's wife, responsible for the destruction of old Chinese culture, has to be imagined as a kind of European operatic diva. The Chinese revolutionary ballet in contrast is packaged in Hollywood sound, becoming ideological kitsch here as in China. Pure minimalist music dominates, mixed with harmonically more varied large ensembles and arias. The uninterrupted musical throbbing is intended by the composer as a critical antithesis to the hectic activities of the protagonists.

Nixon in China, production photograph with (from left to right) Thomas Hammons (Henry Kissinger), Eilene Hannan (Pat Nixon), James Maddalena (Richard Nixon), and Sanford Sylvan (Chou En-lai), production Peter Sellars, Oper Frankfurt 1992.
The use of settings familiar from daily TV news programs in Adams's opera creates a new on-stage atmosphere. The clichés of political protocol match operatic scene types remarkably well. Political scenes also have their arias, duets, and ensembles.

The Death of Klinghoffer

Opera in a prologue and two acts

Libretto: Alice Goodman.
Première: 19 March 1991, Brussels (Théâtre Royal de la Monnaie).
Characters: Captain (B), First Officer (Bbar), Swiss Grandmother (Ms), Molqi (T), Mamoud (Bar), Austrian woman (Ms), Leon Klinghoffer (Bar), "Rambo" (Bbar), British dancer (Ms), Omar (Ms), Marilyn Klinghoffer (A); Ocean Chorus, Night Chorus, Hagar and the Angel Chorus, Desert Chorus, Day Chorus; Palestinians and Jews (chorus).
Setting: The Italian cruise liner *Achille Lauro*, 1985.

Synopsis
Prologue

The dead proclaim a message (chorus of exiled Palestinians and Jews).

Act I

Not far from the port of Alexandria, Palestinian terrorists have hijacked the cruise liner *Achille Lauro*. The passengers, mostly elderly tourists, are herded into a saloon, where Americans, Britons, and Israelis are separated. The voice of nature speaks to all of them, but is not heard (Ocean Chorus). To be a terrorist means to find no peace of mind, like the youngest of them, the music-loving Mamoud. He has to guard the captain, and contact is made between them (Night Chorus).

Act II

The Book of Books tells of Hagar and the Angel. On the advice of his barren wife Sarah, Abraham the Jew made the Egyptian handmaiden Hagar pregnant. Hagar thereupon decided she could bear Sarah's yoke no longer and fled. But the Angel of God ordered Hagar to put up with Sarah's harshness (Hagar and the Angel Chorus). The terrorists bring the Americans, Britons, and Israelis on deck but are undecided as to how to proceed. The sun beats down mercilessly. The Jew Klinghoffer is carried below, chained to a wheelchair. Fear on both sides: who will be the victim, who the perpetrator? A testing time for all, as in the desert (Desert Chorus). Klinghoffer is shot below deck. The captain is ready to sacrifice himself voluntarily: day breaks (Day Chorus). The *Achille Lauro* enters port. The Palestinians have left the ship. Only now does Mrs. Klinghoffer learn of her husband's death. S. N.

The Death of Klinghoffer, production photograph with chorus, production Barbara Bayer, sets Hermann Feuchter, conductor Andreas Kowalewitz, Oper Nürnberg 1997.
Adams's second opera also owed its genesis to the director Peter Sellars, and is based on a real event in comparatively recent history. According to Adams, this is a depiction of a Passion in the tradition of Johann Sebastian Bach. It is not the terrorist hijacking that forms the focus of the action but the choruses that give voice to the dead and the souls of nature and the world. The work has a mystic dimension.

Eugen d'Albert (1864–1932).
Around 1910, d'Albert was considered the most important pianist of his day. He was indeed a remarkable virtuoso, and some recordings by him survive, including one of Liszt's piano sonata in h-minor.

D'Albert began his career as a pianist in London, where he studied at the National Music School under Ernst Pauer, winning the Mendelssohn Prize at the age of 17.

When the great Bayreuth conductor Hans Richter heard him play Schumann's piano concerto at the Crystal Palace in London, he invited the young pianist to Vienna. This was the start of d'Albert's career in the German-speaking countries. He attended Liszt's master classes in Weimar for two years, had his concert début in Berlin, and was already touring Europe widely in the 1880s. Like almost all celebrated pianists of his time, particularly Liszt himself, d'Albert struggled to overcome his fame as a pianist in order to establish himself as a composer. He began his composing career with piano works, his op. 1 in 1883 being a piano suite in Baroque style, which was a novelty in the piano literature of the time. By the 1890s he was working as a conductor, and in 1895 he was appointed opera director in Weimar in succession to Richard Strauss, who was his contemporary. D'Albert was successful in many areas of life as well as music. He conquered the operatic stage, published works by Bach and Beethoven, he had a great liking for women also, who were attracted to him not only because of his musical talent.

The Lowlands, set design (detail) by Franz Gruber, Stadttheater Freiburg im Breisgau 1910 (TWS).
The yearning expressed in the opera for a life free of confusion is projected onto nature in the set design. The untouched upland is a symbol of truth and purity, while the lowlands created by man are the refuge of falsity.

A s a composer, d'Albert aimed at a synthesis of Wagner's dramatic music and the "cantabilitá" of Italian opera. An important aspect for him was the comprehensibility of musical language.

d'Albert, Eugen

b. 10 April 1864 in Glasgow
d. 3 March 1932 in Riga

d'Albert studied in London under Ernst Pauer, in Vienna under Hans Richter, and in Weimar under Franz Liszt, developing into a highly accomplished pianist. From 1895 he worked in Weimar as an opera director, and provided Romantic interpretations of works by Bach and Beethoven.

Works: 21 operas including *Die Abreise* (*The Departure*) (1898, Frankfurt), *Tiefland* (*The Lowlands*) (1903, Prague), *Die toten Augen* (*The Dead Eyes*) (1916, Dresden), *Der Golem* (*The Golem*) (1926, Frankfurt), *Die schwarze Orchidee* (*The Black Orchid*) (1928, Leipzig); concertos, piano works, orchestral and chamber music.

The Lowlands

Tiefland

Musikdrama in a prologue and two acts

Libretto: Rudolph Lothar, after the play *Terra baixa* by Angel Guimerà.

Première First version, in three acts: 15 November 1903, Prague (Neues Deutsches Theater); second version: 16 January 1905, Magdeburg (Stadttheater).

Characters: Sebastiano, a rich landowner (Bar), Tommaso, the village elder, 90 years old (B), Moruccio, a miller (Bar), Marta (S), Pepa (S), Antonia (Ms), Rosalia (A), Nuri (S), Pedro and Nando, shepherds working for Sebastiano (2 T), A Voice (B), The Parson (silent); peasants (chorus).

Setting: A high alpine meadow in the Catalan Pyrenees and a village in a valley, around 1900.

Synopsis
Prologue

A high alpine meadow. Pedro and Nando are two shepherds employed by the rich Sebastiano, and live wholly secluded in the hills with their animals. But Pedro longs for a wife. One day, Sebastiano appears with Marta, his maid, and Tommaso, the village elder. Marta is Sebastiano's lover, but the master now wants to marry her to Pedro, as he wants to marry a rich wife in order to pay off his debts. Sebastiano confesses openly to Marta that he will continue to be her lover. The poor shepherd is to take over the mill in the valley as a wedding present. Marta is outraged at Sebastiano's suggestion, and runs off into the valley. The unsuspecting Pedro learns from the similarly ignorant Tommaso of his good fortune in being allowed to marry the lovely Marta. He leaves his pasture, entrusting his animals to Nando's care and ignoring his friend's warnings about the treacherous lowlands.

Act I

At the mill. Pepa, Antonia, and Rosalia have learnt of the plan to marry Marta to Pedro, and press Moruccio to tell them what is going on. When he remains silent, they turn to the innocent Nuri, who as the confidante of Marta knows all the details and tells them everything quite openly. Pedro is greeted with mockery. The wedding ceremony begins, despite Marta's resistance. Tommaso, who has become mistrustful, wants to know the truth from Sebastiano. Moruccio is indignant: Marta is a hindrance because Sebastiano must marry a rich girl to pay off his debts. Tommaso hurries to the church to stop the wedding ceremony, but it is already over. Pedro solicits the love of his wife in a touchingly naive manner but Marta remains chilly. Only when she recognizes that Pedro has been deceived by Sebastiano and is pure-minded does she turn to him with love.

Act II

At the mill. Nuri's morning serenade wakens the wedded couple. Tommaso urges Marta to be honorable with Pedro. But it is too late: Pedro has learnt the truth about his marriage in town, though without being able to discover the name of his rival. Sebastiano appears with a few peasants and demands that his maid Marta dances for him, upon which Marta admits the truth. His plans for a rich marriage have come to nothing, as Tommaso has warned the bride and her family. He now hopes to return to his former lover and harasses Marta. Pedro challenges his master to a wrestling match and strangles him with his bare hands, as he once killed a wolf that was threatening his herds. He fetches the peasants, makes them witness his act of revenge, and escapes unmolested with Marta into the mountains.   M. S.

The Lowlands, production photograph from Act II, with Marta, Pedro, and Sebastiano (seated), Berlin 1907.
The Lowlands became d'Albert's most popular work in German theaters only after a revision for the production by Hans Gregor at the Komische Oper in Berlin. It was Ernst von Schuch, the manager of the Hoftheater in Dresden, who suggested setting the Catalan subject to music. The librettist made a number of changes, in order to clarify the symbolic significance of untouched upland on the one hand and man-made lowlands on the other – namely, truth and falsehood. The collision of the two worlds leads to archetypal patterns of behavior. Partly realistic and partly idealized, the picture of village life reflects the city dweller's longing for freedom. Basing his work in many respects on Wagner's music drama, d'Albert made use of the dramatic techniques of *verismo*, drew on Meyerbeer's →*The Prophet* (1849), and broke up the otherwise continuous musical structure with discrete musical numbers.

Auber, caricature by B. Roubaud, Paris 1839. Auber was a veritable opera factory. Anyone who managed to turn out such a large number of operas in the 19th century had to be a master of both music and stagecraft, and had to know how to please his public. In this respect, Auber was a real man of the theater. His popularity brought recognition from the imperial court, and from 1857 he bore the proud title of Director of Court Music.

Fra Diavolo, production photograph from Act II with Eberhard Waechter (Beppo) and Karl Dönch (Giacomo), production Nathaniel Merrill, conductor Ivan Pařik, Wiener Volksoper 1986.
As is customary in classic comedies, here we have typical figures acting in typical situations: alongside the simple village beauty Zerline and the honest churl Lorenzo, the rascally scoundrels Beppo and Giacomo.

Auber, Daniel François-Esprit

b. 29 January 1782 in Caen
d. 12/13 May 1871 in Paris

Auber began his composing career as an amateur, his first *opéra comique* being premièred in 1805. From 1820, he produced a new *opéra comique* almost every year, and also wrote about ten works for the Paris Opéra (including *Gustav III*, whose subject matter later became famous through →Verdi's *A Masked Ball*). He and his librettist Eugène Scribe formed a highly successful writing team, remaining unchallenged masters of the lighter kind of French opera from the 1830s to the 1850s. In 1828, the first example of Romantic grand opera, *La muette de Portici*, also resulted from their collaboration.
In 1842 Auber succeeded Cherubini as director of the Paris Conservatoire.

Works: Approximately 50 stage works, of which only *La muette de Portici* (*The Dumb Girl of Portici*) (1828) and *Fra Diavolo* (1830) have found a place in the repertoire, the others passing into oblivion after early sensational success.

*A*uber was effectively the creator of grand opéra, but his style was best suited to the intimate, light-hearted world of the opéra comique.

Fra Diavolo

Opéra comique in three acts

Libretto: Eugène Scribe.

Première: 28 January 1830, Paris (Opéra-Comique).

Characters: Fra Diavolo, a bandit leader (T), Lady Pamela, a traveling Englishwoman (Ms), Lord Cokbourg, Lady Pamela's husband (Bar), Mathéo, an innkeeper in Terracina (B), Zerline, Mathéo's daughter (S), Lorenzo, an officer with the Roman dragoons and Zerline's lover (T), Beppo and Giacomo, bandits (T, B), A Miller (B), A Soldier (T); dragoons, villagers (chorus).

Setting: The vicinity of Naples, around 1830.

Synopsis

The robber Fra Diavolo is terrorizing the country-side. Yet he helps Lorenzo to find happiness. The soldier catches the bandit, receives the bounty on his head, and is thereby able to marry his Zerline.

Act I

The innkeeper's daughter Zerline loves the soldier Lorenzo. He is poor, however, and Zerline is promised to a rich peasant. Lorenzo therefore decides to hunt down the notorious robber Fra Diavolo, on whose head a high bounty has been placed. Just at the right moment an English couple seek protection at the inn. They have been robbed on the road by Fra Diavolo. Lorenzo sets off on his trail. Meanwhile Fra Diavolo turns up disguised as a marquis and makes up to the lady. Lorenzo returns with the regained jewelry and is given a generous reward by the English couple.

Act II

Bedtime. Zerline goes to bed, taking care to put Lorenzo's money away safely. As she does so, she is secretly observed by Fra Diavolo and his cronies Beppo and Giacomo. They decide to kill Zerline and steal the money. In the nick of time, Fra Diavolo is disturbed by Lorenzo. The "marquis" pretends to have come for a rendezvous, and while Lorenzo and the Englishman quarrel about which woman is being unfaithful, the rogues escape.

Act III

Fra Diavolo has agreed with Beppo and Giacomo that they will give him a sign when the others have gone to church. But the two rascals are careless; they are recognized by Zerline and forced by Lorenzo to give the agreed sign. Fra Diavolo is caught. Lorenzo now has enough money to marry his Zerline.   *S.N.*

Fra Diavolo, set design by Franz Moser, Vienna c. 1920 (TWS).

Opéra comique

Unlike the *drame lyrique* imported from Italy, *opéra comique* was considered a homegrown genre in early nineteenth-century France. It grew from the same roots as the German *Singspiel*, but is distinguished by a Gallic lightness of touch. An *opéra comique* consisted of prose dialogue interspersed with airy strophic songs ("couplets"), simple ensembles, and lively choruses. The mood was basically geared to carefree entertainment, which not infrequently turned to frivolous comedy. Any kind of tragic tone was excluded. This approach was only modified around 1870, when the genre was given a deeper psychological motivation. Works of this type, the predecessors of the operettas of Offenbach, were produced en masse in the first half of the nineteenth century.

The bandit as gentleman

The bandit leader Fra Diavolo, who was based on a historical Italian bandit from the time of the Neapolitan king Joseph Bonaparte, is an embodiment of the "noble criminal", a concept later developed in the character of Arsène Lupin and that of the film hero Zorro. His name alone inspires fear: in the imagination of the simple villagers he appears as the archetype of the devil. An echo of this is found in Zerline's tale. M1

At the same time, the bandit Fra Diavolo attaches great importance to his elegance, as becomes apparent in his flirtation with Lady Pamela (duet, Act I). But he can also play the hot-blooded Italian lover (barcarolle, Act II). M2

The Romantic robber story presented in *Fra Diavolo* would have produced a pleasant frisson of horror in the audience, particularly as it did not step outside the boundaries of fairy-tale comedy. P. H.

What qualities made *Fra Diavolo* stand out among hundreds of similar *opéra comiques*? Its strength lies in its memorable melodiousness, which scales the heights not so much in the lyrical passages as in the situations of sparkling cheerfulness. The infectious élan with which the individual numbers follow each other leaves no time for reflection. It draws the listener under its spell and works its effect in a wholly direct fashion. As a backdrop, the setting provides a calm, picturesque counterpoint.

1. Zerline's Couplet

2. Fra Diavolo's Barcarolle

Bartók, Béla

b. 25 March 1881 in Nagyszentmiklós, Hungary
d. 26 September 1945 in New York

After finishing secondary school in Bratislava, Bartók studied the piano at the Budapest Academy under István Thoman, a pupil of Liszt, and composition under Hans Koessler, a friend of Brahms. He had the ability to make a career as a concert pianist but not the personality, choosing instead the role of the performer-composer, whose aim was to give an adequate rendering of his own and others' works. The key experience of his life was the discovery of authentic Hungarian folk music, which he studied in Hungarian villages from 1904. He became acquainted with Zoltán Kodály in 1905, and from this point the two dedicated themselves to the study of folk music, developing and publicizing their shared aesthetic aims for a new Hungarian music. In his own country Bartók's breakthrough as a composer came only after the First World War, in the face of a musically very conservative public. In 1940, he left Hungary for the USA in order to escape fascism. Here he remained until his death in 1945, in poor health and straightened circumstances though still producing works of importance.

Works: Stage works: *A Kékszakállú herceg vára* (*Bluebeard's Castle*) (1911/FP 1918), *A fából faragott királyfi* (*The Wooden Prince*) (ballet, 1917), *A csodálatos mandarin* (*The Miraculous Mandarin*) (pantomime, 1919/FP 1926); piano works, including the famous *Allegro barbaro* (1911); chamber music, including six string quartets; orchestral music, including three piano concertos (1926, 1931, 1945), *Music for Strings, Percussion and Celesta* (1936), and the *Concerto for Orchestra* (1943); choral works, songs, settings of folk songs.

Bluebeard's Castle

A Kékszakállú herceg vára

Opera in one act

Libretto: Béla Balázs.
Première: 24 May 1918, Budapest (Royal Opera).
Characters: A Kékszakállú herceg/Duke Bluebeard (B), Judit/Judith (S), Prologue (spoken), Bluebeard's Former Wives (silent).
Setting: Duke Bluebeard's castle, yesterday and today.

Synopsis

It is asked what the old songs mean; do they tell of external or internal events, do they refer to yesterday or to an everlasting today?

Judith has left her parents' house and her fiancé to follow the gloomy Duke Bluebeard, whom she loves for his suffering. In his dark fortress she finds "seven silent, black doors." In order to understand her beloved wholly and let light into the darkness of existence she presses him to open the doors. The first two doors conceal Bluebeard's torture and armaments chambers, and the third and fourth the treasure vault and magic garden. Now Judith presses Bluebeard to open the fifth door. It grows bright, as the door opens onto the whole kingdom. Bluebeard goes happily to embrace Judith, but she has discovered blood everywhere and wants to know everything. Despite Bluebeard's warning, she opens the sixth door and finds the pool of tears. Finally Judith sees Bluebeard's previous wives behind the seventh door, living in his memory. Judith joins them in the realm of memory. Bluebeard's castle falls dark once again.   S. N.

Bluebeard's Castle, production photograph with Bluebeard and Judith, production Peter Konwitschny, Leipziger Oper 1991.
As woman and man, Judith and Bluebeard embody opposing principles that, in Bartók's pessimistic view, could never be brought into harmony. Their parts also reflect this: in the dark, Bluebeard is passive and immobile, whereas Judith is dynamic and active. At the fifth door, however, she is blind and deaf to the glittering splendor of the male realm.

1.1 Opening Motif

1.2 Debussy, *Pelléas and Mélisande*, Forest Motif

2.1 Light Motif, (Fifth Door)

2.2 Bluebeard's Realm Motif

Lásd ___ ez az én bi- ro- dal- mam, Mesz - sze né - ző szép kö-nyök-lőm. Ugy- e hogy szép nagy, nagy or - szág?

*B*artók created an original musical "voice" which draws on both the central European musical tradition and the folk music of various peoples (particularly Hungarians, Romanians, and Slovaks). Rather than follow fashion, he developed an inspired mixture of the modern and the archaic.

The door to the soul

As a genre, opera did not suit Bartók's artistic character; like Beethoven, he was primarily an instrumental composer. *Bluebeard's Castle* is nevertheless the most important Hungarian opera of the twentieth century. Béla Balázs's symbol-laden text, which has the form and style of a folk ballad, steered Bartók not in the direction of Romantic opera but towards structures of a symphonic type.

The use of motifs and the instrumentation are so graphic and expressive as to involve the visual imagination even in the work's frequent concert performances. The opera begins and ends in F sharp minor with a melody that is both reminiscent of Debussy's dark forest in →*Pelléas and Mélisande* (an important influence), and is yet composed in the style of Hungarian folk song. *M 1*

The tonal antithesis of F sharp – C major – appears when the fifth door is opened and light fills the gloomy castle. What is literally a blinding moment in the drama is depicted musically by grandiose chords and the sound of the organ. Up to the fifth door, the interior of the castle has grown steadily lighter, but it darkens again after this climactic point. *M 2*

"It will remain forever night now, forever ..."

Béla Balázs called his libretto a "ballad of inner life." During the opera's composition, Bartók was inspired by a great unrequited love affair as well as by fin de siècle literary and philosophical ideas (especially Nietzsche), and also by the archaic content of Hungarian folklore, where images constantly alternate between internal and external.

Like Bluebeard, Bartók himself tried to hide his inner life from the world and create an isolated "castle." Access was barred even to those close to him, including his first and second wives. There is a textual reference to Wagner's →*Lohengrin*: "You must never cross-examine me," Lohengrin tells Elsa. "Go and look, but never ask questions. Just look, never ask," Bluebeard instructs Judith. The opera ends as it begins: in the dark. An early (1911) pessimistic vision of the potential tragedy between the sexes.

Ariane et Barbe-Bleue by Paul Dukas, set design by Bernd Steiner, Stadttheater, Bremen 1927 (TWS).
Balázs's source was Maurice Maeterlinck's play *Ariane et Barbe-Bleue* (*Ariadne and Bluebeard*, 1902), which Dukas set as an opera in 1907. Bartók's librettist took over Maeterlinck's male and female protagonists, the idea of the seven doors, and the concealed wives. This Bluebeard does not kill his wives (like his predecessor in the Bluebeard legend and in earlier literary adaptations) but keeps them imprisoned in his castle. Bluebeard can never be satisfied by their unconditional, slavish love, and so is always looking for a new wife. Ariadne promises Bluebeard eternal love. The true meaning of her promise remains concealed from Bluebeard, but love as a symbol and a promise is saved, even if the individual perishes.

Fidelio

Opera in two acts

Libretto: Joseph Sonnleithner (first draft) and Friedrich Treitschke (final version), after Jean-Nicholas Bouilly's libretto *Léonore, ou L'amour conjugal* (*Leonora, or Conjugal Love*).

Première: First version: 20 November 1805, Vienna (Theater an der Wien); final version: 23 May 1814, Vienna (Kärntnertor Theater).
Characters: Don Fernando, minister (Bar), Don Pizarro, prison governor (Bar/B), Florestan, a prisoner (T), Leonore, his wife, under the name of Fidelio (S), Rocco, the jailer (B), Marzelline, his daughter (S), Jaquino, the gatekeeper (T), First and Second Prisoner (T, B); soldiers of the guard, political prisoners, people (chorus).
Setting: A Spanish state prison, some miles from Seville, at the end of the 18th century.

Synopsis
Act I

The prison yard. Rocco the jailer has a great deal to do. The gatekeeper Jaquino is keen to lend a hand because he is in love with Rocco's daughter Marzelline and has already been publicly accepted as a son-in-law. However, Rocco now has an assistant, Fidelio, whose arrival has changed everything. The clever stranger has gained Rocco's favor and Marzelline has fallen in love with him. But Fidelio is a woman, Leonore, who has disguised herself in order to find and free her husband Florestan, a champion of the truth. She believes that he has been unlawfully imprisoned by his opponent Pizarro. When Governor Pizarro hears that his crimes have been discovered, he determines to eliminate all trace of them. The minister must not find Florestan there when he inspects the prison. Florestan knows the truth about Pizarro, and so now languishes in the deepest dungeon. All the towers are to be manned to watch for the minister, whose arrival is to be signaled by a trumpet call so that Pizarro is not surprised in the midst of his fell deeds. At the request of Fidelio and Marzelline, Rocco has meantime released the prisoners into the prison garden. For Leonore, this is an opportunity to look for Florestan. Pizarro is enraged at Rocco's unauthorized action and has the prisoners locked up again. As Leonore has been unable to find Florestan, she obtains permission to accompany Rocco to the underground dungeon. A grave is to be dug there.

Act II

Scene 1: The underground dungeon. Florestan laments his bitter fate – chains as a reward for serving the truth. He sees freedom in a vision. It carries Leonore's features. Rocco and Fidelio dig the grave. Leonore initially does not recognize her

*B*eethoven's only opera is both disparate and magnificent, uniting many musical aims. There is hardly a criticism that has not been leveled at it and hardly an expression of praise that has not been bestowed on it.

husband, but wants to save the prisoner whoever he is. In the end, she casts herself utterly fearlessly between Florestan and Pizarro and reveals herself as Leonore. The murderer is unimpressed by this display of conjugal love. Leonore draws her weapon on Pizarro. Just then, the trumpet signal is heard. Pizarro recoils. The rescued couple rejoice.

Scene 2: The prison parade ground. The minister greets the prisoners like a brother among brothers. Rocco conducts Florestan and Leonore to the light of day. Pizarro is given the punishment he deserves. Marzelline returns to Jaquino. The minister recognizes Florestan as a friend, believed dead. Leonore undoes Florestan's chains, and all join together to praise conjugal love.   *S. N.*

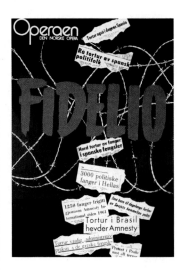

Fidelio, poster, Operaen Den Norske Opera, Oslo.
Though nearly 200 years old, Beethoven's *Fidelio* has never lost its political topicality. After the Second World War, most European opera houses symbolically opened their first peacetime season with this opera.

Fidelio, production photograph with (from left to right) Daniel Kirch (first prisoner), Jürgen Freier (Don Pizarro), Andreas Conrad (Jaquino), Matthias Hölle (Rocco), Brigitte Geller (Marzelline), Miranda van Kralingen (Leonore), Johannes Schmidt (Don Fernando), and chorus soloists, production Harry Kupfer, conductor Yakov Kreizberg, Komische Oper, Berlin 1997.
Harry Kupfer's production sought to bring out the special timelessness of *Fidelio*. He posits the following basic situation: 180 years after the work was written, an operatic ensemble puts on *Fidelio*. "For the singers, who appear in contemporary, almost private clothes, the performance becomes more than just a presentation of the piece handed down to us. Every participant is involved with his character in his own way, so that his identification with it and his commentary on it are absorbed into his interpretation of it."

Politics and love

Fidelio is supposed to be based on a real event that took place during the French Revolution, when a daring woman rescued her aristocratic husband from prison. Jean-Nicolas Bouilly made use of the incident in his libretto *Léonore, ou L'amour conjugal* (*Leonore, or Conjugal Love*), which was set as an *opéra comique* by Pierre Gaveaux and staged in Paris on 19 February 1798. Although Bouilly's libretto sprang from an anti-revolutionary attitude, it was understood by Parisian audiences to be a celebration of the recent political events (even though the action was removed to Spain). Bouilly and the Viennese translator Sonnleithner therefore had to watch out for the censors: one could not afford to be suspected of harboring revolutionary political views.

1. Message of Freedom

Es sucht der Bruder seine Brü - der, und kann er helfen, hilft er gern.

Fidelio – an ode to freedom?

The Viennese authorities had more to fear from the political acerbity of the piece than the Parisians. In Austria in the time of the Emperor Francis I, the notorious state prisons in the fortresses of Spielberg and Kufstein were still untouched by reform. The aristocracy was afraid of the French, who had recently destroyed the Bastille and executed their own king. Sonnleithner had to do his utmost to avoid any temporal reference. Beethoven's attitude of embracing "universal brotherhood" lent the opera an idealistic symbolism from the outset. *Fidelio* was an ardent manifesto against state prisons of all kinds. The action is bound to no time or place. M1

Fidelio, production photograph with Stella Kleindienst as Marzelline (center) and the choir of the Stuttgarter Staatsoper, production Martin Kušej, costumes Gisela Storch, conducted by Michael Gielen, Stuttgarter Staatsoper 1998.
On stage, textual and musical clarity and explicitness can lead to demonstrative gesticulation and banality. In the case of *Fidelio* productions, the danger of this is very great. Beethoven's opera is thus a challenge for every production team.

Fidelio, Hildegard Behrens as Leonore, production Otto Schenk, Wiener Staatsoper 1992.
As a former law student, Hildegard Behrens (b. 1941) probably felt injustice particularly keenly when she sang Leonore. Since the end of the 19th century, the part has usually been sung by Wagnerian heroines.
In the first performances of all three versions, Leonore was sung by the high dramatic soprano Anna Milder (1785–1838), whose idea it was to call the opera *Fidelio* rather than *Leonore*. Theater bills of 1805 and 1806 still announced the opera as *Fidelio, or Conjugal Love*. Beethoven regarded marriage as a sublime ideal, which is how it is presented in his favorite Mozart opera, → *The Magic Flute* (he considered → *Così fan tutte* and → *Don Giovanni* too frivolous). "Man and woman and woman and man attain divinity," is sung here. The figure of Leonore is conceived accordingly, imbued with a profound moral seriousness. Four horns – usually reserved for kings – signal the strength of her determination (Act I). M 7

Symphonic opera or operatic symphony?

Though *Fidelio* has an operatic, action-packed plot, the music is conceived symphonically. Beethoven wrote four large-scale overtures for the four versions of his opera (three *Leonore* overtures and the *Fidelio* overture). The culmination reveals Beethoven's instrumental inclination: at the moment of Leonore's decision to kill Pizarro, a trumpet signal is heard announcing the arrival of the minister. The dramatic resolution is achieved by means of wordless music, rather than by sung words. M 2

A moving moment is provided by the musical depiction of the moment of rescue, in the form of a stirring, hymn-like tune. M 3

The musical roots of the opera can be traced back to a cantata written by the 20-year-old Beethoven on the death of his imperial idol, Joseph II. In this cantata the night of despotism and fanaticism are represented musically, as is the penetrating ray of the Enlightenment: "Then mankind rose to the light, then the earth revolved more happily round the sun." Beethoven used this melody for the second finale of *Fidelio*, where Leonore releases her husband from his chains. It is first heard in the oboe, then passes to the orchestra, and is finally taken up by the chorus. M 4

The Prisoners' Chorus is also symphonically conceived. The most important musical material is again carried by the orchestra, a rising motif like a hand stretching up towards the light. M 5

As if blinded by the sun, the prisoners grope towards the light. Their chorus swells up almost threateningly as a young prisoner sings in praise of freedom, until an older prisoner urges restraint.

The jailer and the others

Though great heroic moments follow one another in quick succession in *Fidelio*, the mundane also has its place, as have ordinary people with their own preoccupations, such as the jailer Rocco, his daughter Marzelline, and the gatekeeper Jaquino. Mention is often made of a dramaturgical hiatus, supposedly caused by Beethoven's inexperience as an opera composer. But how would the opera fare without the "little people"? What standard would then exist by which to measure the deeds of the heroes? And does Leonore's noble attitude not have an ennobling influence on these same ordinary people? In the quartet between Marzelline, Leonore, Jaquino, and Rocco, the voices seek and follow each other as in a canon. An atmosphere of inner consciousness is created, comparable with the slow movement of a string quartet in its clarity and intensity. At this level, too, Leonore performs miracles, as defined by Bouilly: "To give the people a lesson in humanity." M 6

Fidelio, production photograph with Patrick Raftery (Florestan), production Christoph Marthaler, sets and costumes Anna Viebrock, conductor Sylvain Cambreling, Oper Frankfurt 1997.
Originally Beethoven was more interested in concepts than in people. The Florestan of the original version had a heroic aria to sing, which concludes with the manically iterated sentence: "Florestan hat recht getan" ("Florestan did the right thing"). Beethoven's friends, especially Friedrich Treitschke, tried to persuade him that a prisoner starved to exhaustion is no longer capable of heroic deeds. Beethoven was eventually convinced by an alternative text, a vision of spring and freedom that first uplifts the prisoner and then overwhelms him. At this point, the oboe plays a top F three times, a musical image of a man struggling for breath. M 8

2. Trumpet Signal

3. Melody for the Miraculous Rescue

4. Hymn to Freedom

5. Accompanying Motif to the Prisoners' Chorus

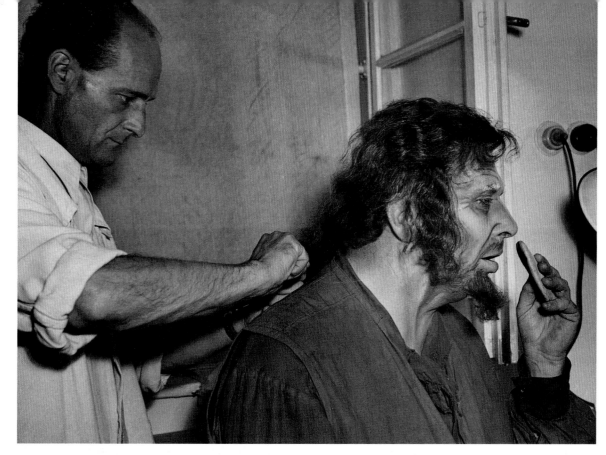

Fidelio, Julius Patzak (1898–1974) was an outstanding Florestan in his day, seen here finishing his makeup before going on at the Salzburg Festival in 1950.

The part of Florestan is taxing and extremely ungrateful. It says a great deal about Beethoven's highhanded attitude to the operatic genre and to the interests of the singer that he gives the male principal only one aria (in the second act, at that), in which the singer has to come in on a high note (g'') after a prolonged symphonic introduction. In the revised versions of *Fidelio*, the figure of Florestan still remained problematic.

6. Amazement Quartet

Mir ist so wun-der-bar, es engt das Herz mir ein; er liebt mich, es ist klar, __ ich wer-de glücklich, glücklich sein.

7. Horn Motif from Leonore's Aria (Act I)

8.1 Florestan's Aria

Und spür ich nicht lin-de, sanft säu-seln-de Luft,

8.2 Obe Melody from Florestan's Aria

Fidelio, set design by Leo Pasetti (Act I, finale) for the production by Anton von Fuchs, conductor Hans Knappertsbusch, Nationaltheater, Munich 1923 (TWS). Both the dramatic context and the text of the Prisoners' Chorus are reminiscent of the young Beethoven's funeral cantata, composed for the death of Joseph II. The cantata contains the words: "Then mankind reached the light." So the prisoners in *Fidelio* sing: "Oh what joy to take a breath in free air," their hands reaching out towards the light.

Fidelio, Wilhelmine Schröder-Devrient was a legendary Leonore in the 1820s.

Vincenzo Bellini, engraving by Antoine Maurin, Paris 1836.
In his tragically brief life, Bellini displayed an exclusive and profound attachment to the Romantic sensibilities of the 19th-century artistic type. In his character, he combined passion and exaltation with a deep sense of melancholy. It is no accident that his work comprises only *opere serie*, that is, serious operas (even *La sonnambula*, which has some features of the *opera semiseria*, or half-serious opera, has no really comic scenes). He lacked the sparkling humor and effervescent gaiety of →Rossini or →Donizetti, and their lightness of touch as composers.

Bellini, Vincenzo

b. 3 November 1801 in Catania (Sicily)
d. 23 September 1835 in Puteaux (near Paris)

Bellini's musical training was initially within the family, then continued under Nicola Zingarelli at the Naples Conservatory, where he became thoroughly familiar with the works of →Haydn, →Mozart, and →Pergolesi. A decisive experience was the performance in Naples of Rossini's →*Semiramide* (1824), after which Bellini devoted himself entirely to the stage. His second opera *Bianca and Fernando* caught the attention of the impresario Domenico Barbaia, who commissioned an opera for La Scala in Milan. This work, *The Pirate* (1827), was the first from the close collaboration between Bellini and the librettist Felice Romani, which generated a string of successes: *La straniera* (*The Stranger*) (1829), *I Capuletti e i Montecchi* (*The Capulets and the Montagues*) (1830), and above all *La sonnambula* (*The Sleepwalker*) and *Norma* (both 1831). The failure of *Beatrice di Tenda* (1833) led to a row with Romani. Bellini subsequently left Italy, traveled to London, and finally settled in Paris, where he became the darling of the artistic world. It was here that he wrote his last opera, *I puritani* (*The Puritans*) (1835), whose première he survived by only a few months, dying at the age of 34.

Works: Operas (all *opere serie*): *Adelson e Salvini* (*Adelson and Salvini*) (1825), *Bianca e Fernando* (*Bianca and Fernando*) (1826, rev. 1828), *Il pirata* (*The Pirate*) (1827), *La straniera* (*The Stranger*) (1829), *Zaira* (1829), *I Capuleti e i Montecchi* (*The Capulets and the Montagues*) (1830), *La sonnambula* (*The Sleepwalker*) (1831), *Norma* (1831), *Beatrice di Tenda* (1833), *I puritani* (*The Puritans*) (1835); sacred vocal music, songs.

*B*ellini's operas are distinguished by a highly developed melodiousness imbued with Romantic pathos, by their sublime dignity, and by their profound sentimentalism. As a great melodist, Bellini had a far-reaching influence on composers both of opera (Verdi and Wagner) and of instrumental music (Chopin and Liszt).

Felice Romani (1788–1865), Bellini's librettist.
Romani originally intended to take up law, but became the most sought after and admired Italian librettist of his day. More than a hundred of his librettos were set to music, a number by Bellini (*The Pirate*, →*La sonnambula*, and →*Norma*), Donizetti (→*The Elixir of Love* and →*Lucrezia Borgia*) and Rossini (→*The Turk in Italy*). Even Verdi's early and unfortunate comic opera →*King for a Day* is based on a Romani libretto.
Written in a smooth, elegant style, Romani's texts reveal strong passions and emotions that matched Bellini's musical and dramatic ideas.
No other Italian composer of the day remained so faithful to a single librettist, and probably no other made such demands on one.

The Capulets and the Montagues, with Wilhelmine Schröder-Devrient (1804–60) as Romeo.
Romeo as a breeches part. Though Juliet is a soprano, the composer rewrote the part for a mezzo-soprano for a performance in Milan. Friar Lawrence was sometimes a baritone, sometimes a tenor. *The Capulets and the Montagues* (1830) is an extreme example of the singer domination of the bel canto period. Anyone looking for Shakespeare here will be disappointed. Romani's libretto offers a conventional love-triangle tale: the mezzo (Romeo) is loved in return by the soprano (Juliet), and the tenor (Tybalt) goes empty-handed. The feigned death of Juliet and the real death of both lovers form the tragic resolution here as in Shakespeare. For the libretto the original Italian novella by Matteo Bandello, which also served as Shakespeare's source, was more important than Shakespeare's text. The real influence of Shakespeare on music drama in the dramaturgical sense began in Italy with Verdi, whose →*Macbeth* (1847) introduced new dramatic ideals into Italian opera. Seventeen years, however, a whole chapter in Italian operatic history, separated these two operas.

Above
Laure Cinti-Damoreau (1801–63), portrait drawing.
Being a prima donna in the 19th century was both a life's ambition and a part to play. The prima donna acted her part everywhere; she was elegant, desired, idolized. Cinti-Damoreau was one of the greatest French prima donnas, who had outstanding success in bel canto roles as well. However, her début was in the breeches part of Cherubino in Mozart's →*The Marriage of Figaro* at the Théâtre Italien in Paris. She was also the female principal in several Rossini premières in Paris (→*Moses and Pharaoh*, *Le comte Ory*, →*William Tell*). From 1834 to 1843 she was a member of the Opéra-Comique. In her later years she enjoyed a reputation as a singing teacher, even writing a manual for singers.

Maria-Felicia Malibran, portrait drawing.
Maria-Felicia Malibran (1808–36) came from the famous 19th-century family of Spanish singers. Her father Manuel García (1775–1832) sang Count Almaviva in the first performance of Rossini's →*The Barber of Seville*. After taking the European theatrical centers of Paris and London by storm, García put together an opera company at the suggestion of Mozart's former librettist Lorenzo da Ponte, who was then living in New York, and organized the US première in that city of Mozart's →*Don Giovanni*. He was praised as a great singer and teacher, and composed more than 100 (now forgotten) operas. Among his best pupils were his own children, Manuel, Maria (-Felicia Malibran) and Pauline (Pauline Viardot, Meyerbeer, →*The Prophet*). Both daughters became prima donnas. Maria's voice ranged from alto to dramatic soprano pitch. She sang Rosine (Rossini, →*The Barber of Seville*) and Norma (Bellini, →*Norma*) with the same perfection, and also Leonore in Beethoven's →*Fidelio*. Maria-Felicia Malibran began her theatrical career in early childhood, singing children's parts from the age of five. Her life was tragically brief, as she died after a riding accident aged 28.

Giulia and Giuditta Grisi, 1833.
Giulia and Giuditta Grisi were prima donna sisters who achieved fame outside their homeland. Giuditta (1805–49) was a mezzo-soprano, and sang Romeo at the première of Bellini's *The Capulets and the Montagues*, while Giulia (1811–69) was fêted both in the great female roles of Bellini, Donizetti, and Rossini, and in the dramatic parts of Meyerbeer and Verdi. With her great vocal range (c'– c''') and acting ability she was a great success with audiences in Paris (Théâtre-Italien) and London (Covent Garden).

La sonnambula

The Sleepwalker

Melodramma in two acts

Libretto: Felice Romani, from the ballet-pantomime *La somnambule, ou L'arrivée d'un nouveau seigneur* (1827) by Eugène Scribe.

Première: 6 March 1831, Milan (Teatro Carcano).

Characters: Count Rodolfo, lord of the village (B), Teresa, a mill-owner (Ms), Amina, an orphan brought up by Teresa (S), Elvino, a wealthy land-owner, betrothed to Amina (T), Lisa, an inn hostess, in love with Elvino (S), Alessio, a villager, in love with Lisa (B), A Notary (T); villagers (chorus).

Setting: A Swiss village in the 19th century.

Synopsis

No one in the village suspects that young Amina is a sleepwalker. This almost leads to disaster. Only when the sleepwalking takes place in public is Amina's innocence recognized and the day saved.

Act I

The engagement of Amina and Elvino is being cele-brated in the village; only the inn hostess Lisa is unhappy, because she too loves Elvino. In the midst of the celebrations a stranger arrives and seeks accommodation in Lisa's inn. He is Rodolfo, the son of the deceased count, who has returned incognito to the place of his childhood. Bewitched by Amina's beauty he pays her compliments, making Elvino jealous. The celebrations are broken off, as a myster-ious ghost is said to be up to mischief in the dark. Lisa visits Rodolfo in his room. They are disturbed by a noise. Lisa flees, leaving her shawl behind. Amina appears in Rodolfo's room, walking in her sleep. Rodolfo realizes what is happening and leaves the room. When the villagers appear to pay their respects to the count, who has now been recognized, they find Amina asleep in his bed. Elvino breaks off the engagement.

Act II

Amina protests her innocence in vain. No one gives any credence to the count's insistence on sleep-walking. Elvino now decides to marry Lisa, at which Amina's foster-mother produces Lisa's shawl, found in the count's bedroom. Elvino now feels cheated by Lisa as well. No one knows what to do. Then Amina appears, sleepwalking, pouring out her love for and loyalty to Elvino. The groom is now convinced of her innocence, the villagers rejoice, and Amina is woken from her trance. Nothing now stands in the way of the marriage.   *S. N.*

La sonnambula, production photograph with Eva Mei (Amina) and Michele Pertusi (Rodolfo), production Mauro Avogadro, sets Giacomo Andrico, conductor Roberto Tolomelli, Teatro Regio, Turin 1998. When Amina wanders into a stranger's bedroom in a trance, her bridegroom Elvino breaks off their engagement. Protestations fail to explain what has happened.

La sonnambula, contemporary illustration. The sleepwalker on the roof – an eccentric-looking notion such as could only occur in the Romantic prima donna period.
The Teatro Carcano opened in Milan in 1803. It wanted to offer a particularly varied season in 1831 to match that of its famous rival, La Scala. The ambitious managers of the Carcano not only succeeded in engaging some of the leading stars of the day, including Giuditta Pasta and Giovanni Battista Rubini, but also commissioned new operas from the composers Gaetano Donizetti and Vincenzo Bellini. Bellini initially wanted to set *Hernani* (after Victor Hugo) to music but finally decided on the subject of *La sonnambula*, which did not run the risk of censorship. The première was one of Bellini's greatest successes.

1. Amina's Great Aria

Ah! non credea mi - rar - ti   si   presto   estin-to, o fio - re

Hysteria as a dramatic resource

In the seventeenth century, especially in England, opera composers provided numerous "mad scenes," written to please famous female singers. The prima donna cult of the Romantic operatic stage demanded that such scenes be even more effective, with coloratura serving a dramatic function, the effortless flights of the voice suggesting a spirit "freed from ballast." Such scenes should preferably be accompanied by flute or cor anglais. When Benjamin Britten caricatured the scene of the crazed Thisbe in the mechanicals' play in →*A Midsummer Night's Dream* (1960), he was writing a parody of a "madness aria" with a touchingly simple flute solo.

The structure of the mad scene is also standardized, and within the customary *scena* form (recitative, slow first part of aria, fast second part), motifs may occur as recollections of past situations.

The structure of the two sleepwalking scenes in *La sonnambula* is clearly distinguished by musical means. In Act I Bellini keeps the scene short, because it only serves to trigger off a conflict. At the end of Act II, however, Amina's sleepwalking unfolds in a great aria scene. This is only superficially a prima donna scene, in that it not only resolves a conflict through the recurrence of motifs (Elvino is finally convinced of Amina's fidelity), but also fully reveals Amina's character. When Rossini described the melody of "Ah! non credea mirarti!" ("Ah! I did not believe I would see you!") as "passionately sad, full of pathos and taste and refined sensibility," he captured this sensitive female figure exactly. *M 1*   *É. P.-L.*

La sonnambula, production photograph with (from left to right) Juan-Diego Flórez (Elvino), Eva Mei (Amina), and Michele Pertusi (Rodolfo), production Mauro Avogadro, sets Giacomo Andrico, conductor Roberto Tolomelli, Teatro Regio, Turin 1998.

Frenzied women on the operatic stage

Sleepwalking appeared on the operatic stage in the early 19th century as a rather mild form of madness. Yet whereas madness, as the loss of human reason, leads to cathartic tragedy, sleepwalking is not an irreversible state and therefore seems harmless and almost ridiculous. Madness and sleepwalking nevertheless have musical and artistic roots in common. Madness was a popular subject even in the 17th century, and in the 19th century, especially in French and Italian operas, its popularity increased. This may be partly explained by certain Romantic preoccupations (the flight from reality, the return to a delightful imaginary world after confrontation with an evil, hostile, and uncomprehending environment), but madness scenes also represent the final stage in the exalted behavior, fuelled by inflamed emotions, that characterizes most operatic figures of Italian Romanticism. The insane were almost always disappointed lovers, and usually female. The flight from reality, where rapture and madness complement one another, implied the mental incapacitation of those led "purely by emotion" – that is, unreasonable, and therefore unpredictable, women.

Norma

Melodramma in two acts

Libretto: Felice Romani, after the tragedy of the same name by Louis Alexandre Soumet (1831).
Première: 26 December 1831, Milan (Teatro alla Scala).

Characters: Pollione, Roman proconsul in Gaul (T), Oroveso, head of the druids (B), Norma, his daughter, high priestess of the druids (S), Adalgisa, a young priestess at the temple (S or Ms), Clotilde, Norma's confidante (Ms), Flavio, friend to Pollione (T), Two Children of Norma and Pollione (silent); druids, bards, priestesses, Gaulish warriors, soldiers (chorus).
Setting: Gaul BC, under Roman occupation.

Norma, production photograph with Maria Callas as Norma, sets Nicola Benois, conductor Tullio Serafin, Teatro alla Scala, Milan 1955.
The figure of Norma is one of the legendary Callas's most famous roles. She managed to bring out the character of a loving and suffering woman, her inner turmoil powerfully expressed by her looks and movements.

Synopsis

Norma, the high priestess of the druids, is secretly in love with the Roman proconsul Pollione and has borne him two children. For his sake, she delays the uprising of the Gauls against the Romans, hoping for peace. Pollione's love for Norma has gone cold, and he is now interested in the young priestess Adalgisa. Norma therefore gives the sign for battle. Pollione is to be sacrificed to the gods as a pledge of victory. He remains faithful to his new love despite threats of death. Impressed by this, Norma accuses herself of treason. Pollione's love for her is rekindled, and they ascend the stake together.

Act I

Gaulish priests and warriors gather in the sacred grove of the druids to await the high priestess Norma, who is to give the signal for the battle against the Romans when the moon goes up. The secret love of the Roman proconsul Pollione for Norma has waned, and he has fallen in love with the young priestess Adalgisa. Norma knows nothing of this, carries out the ceremony, but delays giving the signal for battle, asking the moon goddess for peace in the aria "Casta diva" ("Chaste goddess"). Adalgisa cannot reconcile her love for the enemy Roman with her vows. Pollione urges her to flee to Rome. Adalgisa confides in Norma, though without telling her Pollione's name. The high priestess is moved by the similarity of their two fates. She releases Adalgisa from her vow. When Norma learns of Pollione's treachery, her fury flares up.

Act II

In her passion, Norma tries to kill her children, but proves incapable of such cruelty. She hopes Pollione will repent and realize he should return to her. Her hopes are in vain. She therefore gives the sign for battle against the Romans. In accordance with custom, Pollione is to be sacrificed as a pledge for a successful outcome to the war. Norma struggles with him for a way out, promises him his life if he will renounce his new passion. Pollione remains steadfast. Norma then offers herself as a sacrifice, accuses herself of treason towards her own people and has herself prepared for the stake. In the face of such generosity of soul, Pollione's love for Norma is rekindled. She hands over her children to the care of the druid leader, and goes jointly with Pollione into the flames and death.

S. N.

Opposite
Norma, Giulia Grisi (1811–69) as Norma.
The romantic representation of the mysterious activities of the druids in scenes involving strange cults and barbaric warriors was more important than sticking to the facts. Yet there is a certain mythological verity in the figure of Norma. The druids lived in forests and felt at one with nature. The garland of oak leaves on Norma's head and the sickle in her hand, which she uses to cut the sacred mistletoe from the oak, can be seen as authentic attributes.

GIULIA GRISI.
LA NORMA.

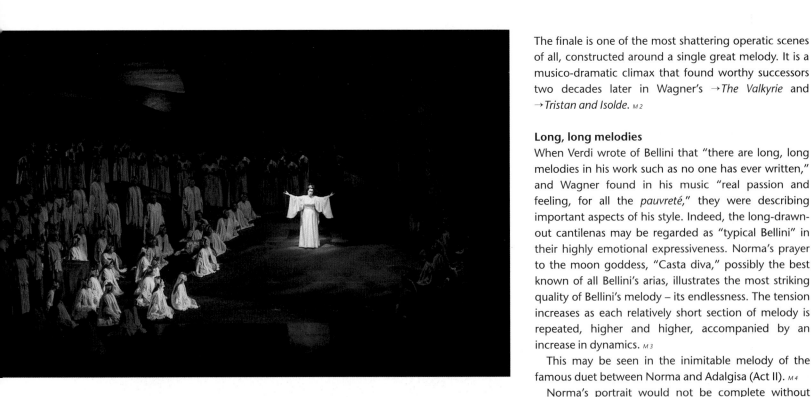

The finale is one of the most shattering operatic scenes of all, constructed around a single great melody. It is a musico-dramatic climax that found worthy successors two decades later in Wagner's →*The Valkyrie* and →*Tristan and Isolde.* M 2

Long, long melodies
When Verdi wrote of Bellini that "there are long, long melodies in his work such as no one has ever written," and Wagner found in his music "real passion and feeling, for all the *pauvreté*," they were describing important aspects of his style. Indeed, the long-drawn-out cantilenas may be regarded as "typical Bellini" in their highly emotional expressiveness. Norma's prayer to the moon goddess, "Casta diva," possibly the best known of all Bellini's arias, illustrates the most striking quality of Bellini's melody – its endlessness. The tension increases as each relatively short section of melody is repeated, higher and higher, accompanied by an increase in dynamics. M 3

This may be seen in the inimitable melody of the famous duet between Norma and Adalgisa (Act II). M 4

Norma's portrait would not be complete without maternal affection. In her disappointment and rage she goes to kill her children – but the knife falls from her hand. Her small *arioso* "Teneri figli" ("Little children") is moving in its simplicity. M 5

Bel canto on the piano: Chopin
Mention is often made of the resemblance between Bellini's operas and the melodic inventiveness of Chopin (1810–49). Bellini did in fact meet Chopin, by whom he was greatly admired, in Paris in 1833. The Pole declared he was delighted with →*La sonnambula* and created a memorial to *Norma* by incorporating the heartfelt melody of the *arioso* "Teneri figli" in his *Étude* in C sharp minor, op. 25, no. 7. M 6

This is one of the best musical examples of sympathetic artistic natures.

Norma, production photograph with Leyla Gencer as Norma, production Margarethe Wallmann, sets and costumes Salvatore Fiume, Teatro alla Scala, Milan 1964.
In the 19th century, historical accuracy was not necessarily wanted in an Italian libretto. Though there are analogies between the events in *Norma* and the revolt of the Gauls and ensuing victory of the Cheruscan leader Arminius over the Romans (the name of the deity Irminsul appears to be derived from Gothic, meaning "Arminius' column"), details of time and place are only hinted at in Romani's libretto.

A woman's love and life
The figure of Norma holds a special place among the great female roles of operatic history. Felice Romani made major changes when adapting Soumet's tragedy. There Norma kills her children. Soumet's models were the mythological figures of Niobe and Medea, Shakespeare's Lady Macbeth, and Chateaubriand's druid priestess Velléda from the epic *Les martyrs, ou Le triomphe de la religion chrétienne* (*The Martyrs, or The Triumph of the Christian Religion*).

Romani enriched this already complex female character with two further aspects: her inextinguishable love for Pollione and her equally profound love for her children. Whereas in Soumet, Norma kills the children in her madness, Romani and Bellini do not go so far. Bellini's Norma is a multi-layered figure with profound emotions: high priestess and mother, abandoned lover and vengeful rival. Her tragic demise is inevitable, the result of inner emotional conflicts stemming from the irreconcilability of her vows, her duty, and her disappointed love. Her death is less self-punishment than a cathartic resolution of otherwise irresolvable conflicts.

Norma, production photograph with Margaret Price (Norma) and Alicia Nafé (Adalgisa), Royal Opera House, London 1987. As Adalgisa confides in Norma, the latter recognizes the similarities between their fates.

2. Catharsis Melody

3. Norma's Prayer

Ca — — sta Di – va, ca - sta Di - va, che i - nar - gen — — ti

4. Duet between Norma and Adalgisa

Mira, o Norma, a'tuoi ginocchi questi ca - ri ___ tuoi pargo -let - ti

5. Norma's *Arioso*

Te - ne - ri, te - ne - ri fi - gli

6. Chopin, *Étude* in C# minor, op. 25, no. 7

7. Oroveso's *Cabaletta*

Si: par-la-rà ter - ri-bi - le   da que-ste quer-cie an-ti - che

8. Battle Chorus

Guerra,   guerra! Le gal - liche sel - ve   quan-te han quer-cie pro - du - can guerrier

Norma, Donzelli (1790–1873) as Pollione, lithograph by A. Ramacci.
In Bellini's operas there are no wholly evil characters. Hellish forces were alien to this composer of "heavenly melodies." Even the sinful Pollione is less a villain than a weak man who becomes heroic through Norma's greatness and their joint death by fire.

Patriotic sounds

The high priest Oroveso, who waits at the head of his oppressed people for the heavenly sign for revolt, is a precursor of the Verdi prophets, army commanders, and freedom fighters in the decade of the *Risorgimento* (Verdi, →*Nabucco*). Here the melodies are like marches, fired by fanatical resolution. M 7

Similarly, the choruses in Bellini's operas do not serve a purely decorative function, but show a nation with a topical message in Italy of the 1830s. The proclamation of the fight against the hated "eagle's lair" and the "city of the Caesars" did not go unnoticed in Milan, the base of the Habsburgs, any more than the stirring, elementary force of the chorus "Guerra, guerra" ("War, war"). M 8

As with many other historicizing Romantic operas, the old subject matter served Bellini only as a pretext for treating contemporary phenomena, though he was less interested in superficial political matters than in expressing both an individual and a collective yearning for a self-determining life, free of prohibitions and regulations – with all its dangers and challenges.   É. P.-L.

Norma, Nicola Rossi-Lemeni as Oroveso at the Teatro alla Scala, Milan 1951/52.
Nicola Rossi-Lemeni (1920–91) was, at Maria Callas's side, one of the greatest exponents of this role. An Italian bass born in Istanbul, he made his début in Venice in 1946 as Varlaam (Musorgsky, →*Boris Godunov*). He had a touch of Slavic hardness in his voice, making him ideally suited to the roles of both Russian ruler and Italian prophet.

I puritani

The Puritans

Melodramma serio in three parts

Libretto: Carlo Pepoli, after the drama *Têtes Rondes et Cavaliers* (*Roundheads and Cavaliers*) (1833) by Jacques Ancelot and Saintine (Joseph-Xavier Boniface).
Première: 24 January 1835, Paris (Théâtre Italien).
Characters: Lord Gualtiero Valton, governor general, Puritan (B), Sir Giorgio, his brother, former Puritan colonel (B), Lord Arturo Talbo, Cavalier, supporter of the Stuarts (T), Sir Riccardo Forth, Puritan captain (Bar), Sir Bruno Robertson, Puritan officer (T), Elvira, daughter of Lord Valton (S), Enrichetta di Francia/Queen Henrietta Maria, widow of King Charles I a.k.a. Dama di Villa Forte (S); soldiers, Puritans, garrison of the castle, ladies (chorus).
Setting: Plymouth, England, around 1650.

Synopsis

In the midst of the preparations for the wedding of Elvira, the daughter of the Puritan Lord Valton, and the Stuart supporter Lord Arturo Talbo, the bridegroom has to carry out a political rescue for his party, thereby coming under suspicion of disloyalty and treason. Elvira loses her mind in consequence. Only when the troubles are resolved does she regain her reason. Elvira and Talbo are happily united.

Part I

At the house of Lord Valton, preparations are under way for the marriage of his daughter Elvira. She was actually intended for the Puritan Riccardo, but on the recommendation of her kindly uncle Giorgio she has been given permission to marry her beloved Arturo, a supporter of the Stuart enemy. During the celebrations Arturo discovers a prisoner, the widow of the executed Stuart king Charles I. Duty prevails over love and Arturo helps the queen escape. Elvira is unaware of the reasons for his leaving the wedding celebrations and becomes deranged.

Part II

At the great house, everyone is concerned about Elvira. The sympathetic Giorgio knows that good news could reawaken her reason, and asks for Riccardo's compassion. Under pressure from Giorgio, he renounces any claim to Elvira's hand and decides to join the Puritan army on campaign.

Part III

Arturo has been sentenced to death, but returns home secretly. He finds Elvira in the house, and in her happiness she regains her reason. However, Arturo is discovered and arrested. Elvira lapses back into madness again. Arturo receives a last-minute pardon. Elvira's reason returns, and the happy couple celebrate their wedding at last.   *S.N.*

I puritani, "Sala d'Arme con loggie" ("Hall of Arms with galleries"), set design (Part I, Scene 3) by Domenico Ferri for the original production at the Théâtre Italien in Paris in 1835.
I puritani involves a sensitive heroine and several right-minded heroes within a military milieu, the action being set in a fortress. The real Bellini lies not in the surroundings but in the emotional lives of those involved.

Bellini in Paris

In the spring of 1833 Bellini left Italy. Initially he went to London, where three of his operas were staged in April to great acclaim. In August, he left for Paris. The French capital was enjoying a great artistic revival at this time, in the interval between the revolutions of 1830 and 1848. In the splendid drawing rooms both of rich émigrés and of the rising and sensation-hungry bourgeoisie, virtuosity was as much admired and fêted as the romantic artistic poses of Paganini, Liszt, and Chopin. In the salon of Princess Cristina Belgioioso, who knew Bellini from his Milan days, the composer met the German lyric poet Heinrich Heine (who left a striking though rather unflattering description of Bellini in his novella *Florentinische Nächte*, or *Florentine Nights*) and cultivated friendships with Chopin, Hiller, and Paër. More important, however, was the support of Rossini, who at this time was no longer writing operas but still a leading figure in Parisian musical life. Always generously ready to help younger colleagues, Rossini secured Bellini an opera commission from the Théâtre Italien.

Meeting place of Italian patriots

Beside the Académie Royale, the scene of great operas such as Rossini's →*William Tell* or Meyerbeer's →*Robert the Devil*, and the Opéra-Comique, with its romantic or fantastic works by Adam or →Boieldieu, the Théâtre Italien offered special musical delicacies from the Italian repertory performed by the most famous Italian singers of the day. Its high standards inspired the already ambitious Bellini. He took to heart Rossini's advice about orchestration, and went on polishing up the libretto and the music to the last minute. At the première, Bellini was not only greeted with a storm of applause by the public but also highly praised by other composers. According to Bellini, Elvira's mad scene, sung by the famous Giulia Grisi, reduced the audience

Right
I puritani, production photograph with Edita Gruberová as Elvira, production
Emilio Sagi, sets Pier'Alli, Teatro Comunale di Bologne, Bologna 1996.
As in almost all Bellini's operas, the credibility and success of the performance
depend on the female principal.

I puritani, production photograph with Luciano Pavarotti (Lord Arturo) and
Joan Sutherland (Elvira), production Sandro Segui, sets Wing Cho Lee,
conductor Richard Bonynge, Metropolitan Opera, New York 1976.
A splendidly cast production. After the masterly first modern interpretation by
Callas in Glyndebourne in 1960, Joan Sutherland's artistry strengthened the
revival of *I puritani*. Pavarotti's magnificent lyric tenor was made for Arturo.

9. Battle Duet (Riccardo and Giorgio)

Suo - ni la tromba, e in -tre - pido io pu-gnerò da for - te

to tears. The heroic duet between Riccardo and
Giorgio, "Suoni la tromba" ("Sound the trumpet"),
not only became a symbol of patriotic struggle but
also served as a basis for the *Hexaméron* piano
variations. At the suggestion of Princess Belgioioso,
six piano virtuosos living in Paris wrote variations on
this popular melody. They were →Liszt, Sigismund
Thalberg, Johann Peter Pixis, Henri Herz, Carl Czerny,
and →Chopin. M 9   É. P.-L.

I puritani, stage photo with Stuart Neill as Lord Arturo, production Graham
Nick, sets and costumes Richard Hudson, Gran Teatro La Fenice, Venice 1995.
At the end of the 20th century there was a great change in the approach to
stage design. Rather than depicting historically accurate locations, sets were
designed as manifestations of emotional energies.

English milieu, French influence, Italian vein

Italian opera composers of this period were fond of using English subject matter (for example, Rossini, in *Elizabeth, Queen of England*, and Donizetti, in *Anna Bolena* and →*Lucia di Lammermoor*). Numerous librettos were based on the novels of Sir Walter Scott, and *I puritani* itself was attributed to him until the real source was identified. Bellini worked on two versions of the opera at once, one for Paris, the other for Naples. In the latter, the individual roles were adapted for other star singers (the part of Elvira, for instance, was intended for the celebrated mezzo-soprano Maria-Felicia Malibran). The

blending of French and Italian operatic styles produced such a heady mix in *I puritani* that it is difficult to imagine how Bellini could have further developed his operatic writing. The French style, with its preference for great tableaux and its prominent use of the orchestra, influenced *I puritani* considerably. Both the rich orchestration, which provides not only a heroic atmosphere but also depictions of nature (sunrise at the beginning of the opera, and the storm scene at the beginning of Part III) and the use of fashionable dance movements in the Paris première bear witness to Bellini's sensitivity to French taste. He sets Elvira's entrance as a happy bride with a *polacca* (a piece in the style of a polonaise), while the aria in which Giorgio begs for compassion, "Se tra il buio un fantasma vedrai" ("If in the darkness you see a spectre"), has waltz features. M 10, M 11

10. Elvira's Bridal Aria

Son ver - gin vez - zo - sa in ve - sta di spo - sa

11. Giorgio's Aria

Se tra il buio un fan - ta - sma ve - dra - i   bian - co, lie - ve

Elvira

The conventions of the Italian "aria opera" are most noticeable in the figure of Elvira. In the first part, she comes on stage with a brilliant *polacca* aria, while her musically and theatrically demanding mad scene occurs in the middle of Part II (certainly a model for Donizetti's →*Lucia di Lammermoor*). Elvira's madness is anticipated in Giorgio's aria at the beginning of this part. The finale consists of the devastated reaction of Riccardo and Giorgio, in which contemplation of Elvira's state of mind brings about a spiritual change in Riccardo.

I puritani, Edita Gruberová as Elvira, production John Dew, conductor Placido Domingo, Wiener Staatsoper 1994.
Not the least important factor in the success of the original production of *I puritani* was its star cast (Giulia Grisi, Giovanni Battista Rubini, Luigi Lablache, and Antonio Tamburini). The opera quickly conquered the major houses of Europe, but once the "classic" bel canto skills of Maria-Felicia Malibran, Giulia Grisi, Lilli Lehmann, and others were no longer available, it passed into oblivion, with other operas by Bellini. Only the bel canto revival of the 1950s and 1960s by singers such as Maria Callas, Joan Sutherland, Renata Scotto, Montserrat Caballé, and later Edita Gruberová led to the rediscovery and reassessment of Bellini's operas.

Above
I puritani, Giovanni Battista Rubini in the role of Arturo, engraving by R.J. Lane after a drawing by Chalon (1836).
Giovanni Battista Rubini sang several tenor roles in Bellini's operas.
Interestingly, Arturo has no great solo scenes, even though his part constitutes an extremely brilliant tenor role. Bellini even wrote a high F into his part, which is something of an oddity in operatic history, being several notes higher than the legendary top C.

I puritani, Marcello Giordani as Arturo, production John Dew, Wiener Staatsoper 1994.
The growing dramatic credibility of Italian operatic practice and venue of the première of *I puritani* (Paris) reinforce the function of the tenor as a heroic, loving *primo uomo*.

A military opera with tears

The finale of Part II in particular demonstrates the inspiration and the compositional care that Bellini put into his characters. Instead of the usual great ensemble finale of Romantic opera, Bellini finished Part II of *I puritani* with the three-part duet between Riccardo and Giorgio. The pleading F major section changes into a muted but tense F minor ("Se tra il buio un fantasma vedrai", "If in the darkness you see a specter"). Giorgio makes it clear to Riccardo that Elvira will not survive Arturo's death and that her death will be on Riccardo's conscience. Riccardo cannot withstand this heartfelt melody in the style of Chopin. Moved to tears, he shows himself ready to abandon any thought of revenge.

É. P.-L.

I puritani, Giulia Grisi (Elvira) and Luigi Lablache (Giorgio) at the King's Theater in London, engraving after a drawing by Chalon, Paris 1835.
The little prima donna Giulia Grisi finds protection with the huge Luigi Lablache, her uncle in the opera. Lablache (1794–1858), the most celebrated bass of his day, was indeed a giant. As Leporello in Mozart's →*Don Giovanni*, for example, he was in the habit of taking the peasant lad Masetto under his arm.

Right
I puritani, Antonio Tamburini (1800–76) as Lord Valton, portrait drawing.
At the Paris première in 1835 Tamburini sang Riccardo. Whereas in Bellini's early operas male roles were often notated for soprano or mezzo-soprano voices, in the manner of castrato operas, by the time of his last opera it was assumed that male characters should be played by "real" men.

Wozzeck, photograph from the production by Ruth Berghaus, sets Hans Dieter Schaal, conductor Christoph von Dohnányi, Opéra National de Paris 1985.
To celebrate the 100th anniversary of Alban Berg's birth and the 50th anniversary of his death, a German team took over the stronghold of French opera for this production.

1. The "Brand"

Wir ar - me Leut!

Berg, Alban

b. 9 February 1885 in Vienna
d. 24 December 1935 in Vienna

Berg wrote his first compositions at the age of 15. He had a fondness for number symbolism both in life and in music, taking his "fate" number (23) from the date of his first attack of asthma (23 July 1900). He read law and music history at the University of Vienna, and from 1904 studied music theory and composition privately with →Arnold Schoenberg. He became acquainted with numerous leading figures of the Viennese artistic world (including Mahler, Karl Kraus, and Adolf Loos), and met Helene Nahowski, who later became his wife. Thanks to a legacy, he was able to give up his work as a civil servant. His first composition to be given an opus number, a piano sonata, dates from 1908. In 1911 he completed his studies with Schoenberg, to whom he remained close throughout his life. He undertook military service during the First World War, initially in Hungary and then at the War Ministry in Vienna. Between 1918 and 1921 he collaborated in the Verein für musikalische Privataufführungen (Society for Private Musical Performances), founded and directed by Schoenberg. In 1922, he published at his own expense, though with assistance from Alma Mahler, a piano extract from the opera *Wozzeck*. In 1923, he was contracted by Universal Edition of Vienna for publication of his works. Berg then turned his attention to the twelve-tone technique (→Schoenberg) and composed the Chamber Concerto. In 1930, he became member of the Prussian Academy of Arts. His last composition, the Violin Concerto dedicated "to the memory of an angel" (Manon Gropius, the daughter of Alma Mahler and Walter Gropius), was written in 1935. He died on 24 December of that year as a result of blood poisoning.

Works: Operas: *Wozzeck* (1922/FP 1925), *Lulu* (1937); orchestral works, including the Three Orchestral Pieces (1915), the Chamber Concerto (1923), and the Violin Concerto (1935); chamber music, including the Lyric Suite for string quartet (1927); piano works, including the Piano Sonata (1908); songs.

Wozzeck

Opera in three acts

Libretto: Alban Berg, after Georg Büchner's play *Woyzeck*.

Première: 14 December 1925, Berlin (Staatsoper).

Characters: Wozzeck (Bar), Marie, his common-law wife (S), Andres, Wozzeck's friend (T), Captain (T), Doctor (B), Drum Major (T), Margret (A), First Apprentice (B), Second Apprentice (Bar), Fool (T), Marie's son (boy S); soldiers, apprentices, women, children (chorus).

Setting: A small German town, around 1820.

Synopsis
Act I
Scene 1: The captain's room, morning. Wozzeck, a poor soldier, is shaving the captain. The captain wants to talk. He philosophizes, and talks about the weather. Wozzeck's only answer is "Jawohl, Herr Hauptmann" ("Indeed, Captain"). But when the captain begins to talk about morality and Wozzeck's child, which he says "was born without the blessing of the Church," the soldier abandons his taciturnity and argues that the poor are not given a chance to act morally: "Look, captain, money, money ... We poor people! I think if we went to heaven, we'd have to help with the thunder!" The captain is taken aback by this.
Scene 2: An open field outside the town. Wozzeck and his friend Andres are cutting willow canes. Wozzeck has visions of disaster.
Scene 3: Marie's small room, evening. The military band marches down the street. Marie waves to the drum major, which elicits spiteful comments from her neighbor Margret. Wozzeck visits his lover and their child briefly, but speaks not of love but of his dismal premonitions.
Scene 4: The doctor's study. Wozzeck has made himself available to the doctor for experiments, to earn a bit of money. He has eaten nothing but beans for months. He talks about his visions. That proves to the doctor that a one-sided diet is conducive to mental disturbance. The doctor hopes the discovery will make him famous and immortal.
Scene 5: The street outside Marie's house, evening. Marie is unable to resist the magnificent Drum Major.

Act II
Scene 1: Marie's room, morning. Marie revels in her youth and beauty and looks at herself in a mirror. The Drum Major has given her some earrings. Wozzeck surprises her, suspects the truth, but restrains himself. He gives Marie money and then hurries away.

Scene 2: The street, daytime. The captain abuses the doctor with his philosophy. The latter has his revenge, predicting that the captain will have a stroke. When Wozzeck crosses their path, they both take out their aggression on him. They allude to the affair between Marie and the Drum Major. Wozzeck is deeply wounded and in despair.

Scene 3: The street outside Marie's house, day. Wozzeck takes Marie to task. She refuses to allow any interference.

Scene 4: A tavern garden, evening. Soldiers, apprentices, women, and girls amuse themselves dancing. Marie and the Drum Major are also there. Wozzeck sees the couple dancing. A fool prophesies a bloody deed.

Scene 5: The barracks, night. Wozzeck cannot sleep. He prays that he will not to be led into temptation. The Drum Major returns, boasting about his new conquest. Wozzeck attacks the Drum Major violently, but is beaten in the fight.

Act III

Scene 1: Marie's room, night. Marie is deeply repentant, and tries to find solace in the Bible.

Scene 2: A forest path beside a pool, night. Wozzeck and Marie are on their way to town. Wozzeck stabs his lover with a knife.

Scene 3: A tavern, night. Wozzeck tries to forget the murder, dances, and amuses himself with Margret. She notices he has blood on his hands. He flees.

Scene 4: The forest path beside the pool. Wozzeck tries to hide the knife deep in the water. He goes further and further into the lake and drowns. The doctor and the captain go past and hear suspicious sounds but do nothing. The doctor only establishes that someone is drowning.

Scene 5: The street outside Marie's house. Children are playing. Marie's body has been found. Everyone runs to see the corpse. The child of Marie and Wozzeck, now an orphan, remains behind, understanding nothing and riding his hobby horse.   *S. K.*

*B*erg was an avant-garde composer with a romantic nature, and the most talented music-dramatist in Schoenberg's circle. His fondness for number symbolism lasted all his life.

Wozzeck, set design by Ludwig Sievert for the original production by Herbert Graf, Opernhaus Frankfurt 1931 (TWS).
The leitmotiv of the opera recurs like a brand, reproaching society. *M 1*
Both play and opera were written in times of crisis. After the Napoleonic wars, thousands of soldiers were left destitute (like the historical figure of the title, Johann Christian Woyzeck). The wretchedness of the proletariat was unimaginable. There was a similar crisis after the First World War. Germany had suffered defeat, and the Austro-Hungarian monarchy had collapsed. The world and its values were awry, distorted, and contradictory. This is how Ludwig Sievert characterizes the basic atmosphere of *Wozzeck* in his sets.

play. The handwritten Gothic "y" he read as "z", so that the play began its public career as *Wozzeck* instead of *Woyzeck*. Only after completing his opera did Berg come across the original title *Woyzeck*. He tried to correct the mistake, but soon gave up the hopeless task. Wozzeck sounds harder than Woyzeck and is therefore better suited to the military milieu.

Magic numbers

It would seem absolutely pointless to ask how many bars a scene or a whole opera consists of, but not in the case of Alban Berg. He was a passionate devotee of number games, and *Wozzeck* is a good example of one. The whole work comprises 1,927 bars. If we discount the six "general pauses" (at the end of Act II and beginning of Act III), the number is 1,921. In 1921 Berg completed the draft score of the opera. The number 21 also plays an important part in individual scenes. The last scene contains 21 bars, and the scene with the doctor 21 variations. Many of them are only one bar long – but these bars contain seven crotchets. Seven also belonged to Berg's magic numbers. *Wozzeck* is Berg's op. 7. *S. K.*

Wozzeck, production photograph with Franz Grundheber (Wozzeck) and Heinz Zednik (the captain), production Adolf Dresen, sets Herbert Kapplmüller, conductor Claudio Abbado, Wiener Staatsoper 1987.
Berg described the captain as "A nonentity … easily moved on the subject of himself." His philosophy consists of definitions such as "Morality: that's when you are moral." He speaks and thinks in commonplaces. He is, moreover, unhealthy; he suffers from asthma and should often cough (Berg carefully notated the musical rhythm of the coughing). "Bloated, fat, thick neck," is how the doctor describes him in Act II. The captain's music similarly has something bloated about it. It also has some very high notes. The theme representing the captain is strongly chromatic, somewhat jaunty, jovial, and grotesque. *M 2*

Woyzeck and Wozzeck

On 27 August 1824, 44-year-old barber Johann Christian Woyzeck was publicly executed. Three years earlier he had killed the woman with whom he lived. Doubts were raised as to whether he was really of sound mind. In scientific circles impassioned debate ensued, the intensity of which was sustained for years. Woyzeck had long been dead when the events and subsequent trial caught the attention of the young doctor and writer Georg Büchner (1813–37). He began to write a play about the "innocent murderer." He died of typhus while still working on it, aged 24.

Some four decades after Büchner's death, the writer and literary scholar Karl Emil Franzos (1848–1904) put together a performable version of Büchner's unfinished

Wozzeck, production photograph with Hildegard Behrens (Marie) and Franz Grundheber (Wozzeck), production Adolf Dresen, sets Herbert Kappmüller, conductor Claudio Abbado, Wiener Staatsoper 1987.
According to Büchner, Marie is between 16 and 18, and strikingly pretty. Her personality is contradictory, but she clearly had the composer's sympathy. There are only two passages in the opera that have an unmistakably tonal and romantic effect: the funeral music in D minor after Wozzeck's death, and part of Act III, Scene 1, when Marie begins to tell her child a story. In the latter, the horn brings out a warm, lilting melody in F minor. Marie's lullaby similarly has a romantic, melodic sincerity. *M 4, M 5*

2. The Captain's Theme

3. The Doctor's Theme

4. Horn Melody

5. Marie's Lullaby

Ei - a po - pei - a, mein sü - ßer Bu', Gibt mir kein Mensch nix da - zu!

Wozzeck, production photograph with Franz Grundheber (Wozzeck) and Aage Haugland (the doctor), production Adolf Dresen, conductor Claudio Abbado, Wiener Staatsoper 1987.
The doctor embodies dry, inhuman science. His theme is constructed from the twelve-note scale. M 3 The doctor's register can be described as "extreme" as particularly deep notes have to be sung at times. Many critics saw him as a prefiguration of the Nazi "doctor" Mengele, but cold-blooded doctors worked not only under the Third Reich. Berg spoke in a letter about a "diabolical" military doctor he had known in the First World War.

Right
Wozzeck, production photograph with Franz Grundheber (Wozzeck) and Hildegard Behrens (Marie), production Adolf Dresen, sets Herbert Kapplmüller, conductor Claudio Abbado, Wiener Staatsoper 1987.
In Act II, Wozzeck gives Marie money. It is everything he has earned from the captain and the doctor, the sum of all his efforts, as it were. Berg wrote a C major chord for this: "How could one better represent the matter-of-factness of the money involved?" he later commented. After this point of calm, Wozzeck hurries on to his Calvary. It is appropriate to mention Calvary, because Wozzeck dies in the 14th scene of the opera, and the way to Golgotha consisted of 14 stations.

Wozzeck, Martin Abendroth as the doctor, Staatsoper, Berlin 1925.
The première under the conductor Erich Kleiber passed into legend. Everyone that had rank and reputation in the contemporary musical world was represented.

Lulu, poster by Dietrich Kaufmann for the two-act production at the Komische Oper in Berlin in 1975.
Joachim Herz took *Lulu* to Walter Felsenstein's legendary Berlin operatic stage. The founder of the Komische Oper himself had never wanted to stage the opera, sensing in it a lack of positive erotic drive.

Spring's awakening
Frank Wedekind (1864–1918), the son of a doctor, first tried his hand at a bourgeois career before breaking into the world of the circus and the theater. His play *Frühlings Erwachen* (*Spring's Awakening*) caused a sensation. "Spring" referred to budding sexuality and all its conflicts. The two separate plays *Erdgeist* (*Earth Spirit*, 1895) and *Die Büchse der Pandora* (*Pandora's Box*, 1902) were only combined into a single tragedy called *Lulu* in 1913.

Lulu

Opera in a prologue and three acts (orchestration of Act III completed by Friedrich Cerha)

Libretto: Alban Berg, after Frank Wedekind's plays *Erdgeist* (*Earth Spirit*) and *Die Büchse der Pandora* (*Pandora's Box*).

Première: Acts I and II: 2 June 1937, Zürich (Stadttheater); three-act version: 24 February 1979, Paris (Opéra).

Characters: Lulu (S), Countess Geschwitz (Ms), A Theatrical Dresser/A Schoolboy/A Groom (A), The Professor of Medicine (spoken)/The Banker (B)/The Professor (silent), The Painter/A Negro (T), Dr. Schön, editor-in-chief/Jack the Ripper (Bar), Alwa, Dr. Schön's son, a writer (T), Schigolch, an old man (B), An Animal Tamer/An Athlete (B), The Prince/The Manservant/The Marquis (T), The Theater Manager (B), A Clown (silent), A Stagehand (silent), The Police Commissioner (spoken), A Fifteen-year-old Girl (S), Her Mother (A), A Female Artist (Ms), A Journalist (Bar), A Manservant (Bar).

Setting: A German city, Paris, and London, at the end of 19th century.

Synopsis
Prologue

The beast in man! An animal tamer presents his menagerie. It includes Dr. Schön (tiger), Alwa (monkey), Schigolch (worm), the professor of medicine (reptile), Countess Geschwitz (crocodile), and Lulu (serpent).

Act I

Scene 1: The professor of medicine has commissioned an artist to paint his wife's portrait. She poses as Pierrot, watched by Dr. Schön and his son Alwa. Called away by social obligations, they leave the painter and model alone. The painter is fascinated by Lulu and makes this blatantly clear. The husband witnesses this and has a heart attack.

Scene 2: Painter and model are married by Dr. Schön. Schön hopes that Lulu's marriage will enable him to break off his affair with her and marry his fiancée. The old man Schigolch comes in and out of Lulu's house. He is an old friend of Lulu, perhaps her father, perhaps a former lover. When Schön realizes that Lulu's husband is blind to her behavior he tells him about her past. The painter commits suicide.

Scene 3: Dr. Schön has introduced Lulu to the theatre and she is now dancing in Alwa's latest work. Schön

and his fiancée are in the audience. On stage Lulu shams a fainting fit, discrediting her patron. She then plays her trump card: she has a suitor who wants to take her with him to Africa. Schön takes fright at the thought of losing her. Lulu forces him to write a letter to his fiancée breaking off his engagement.

Act II

Scene 1: Lulu is now married to Dr. Schön, who is no longer master of his own house. The Countess Geschwitz courts Lulu. Schigolch has settled in, and a schoolboy and athlete are also in attendance. Alwa, too, is at the feet of his father's wife. Schön forces a revolver on Lulu, telling her to do away with herself. In self-defense, Lulu turns the weapon on her husband and kills him. Alwa calls the police.

Metamorphosis (film intermezzo): Lulu has been imprisoned as the murderess of Dr. Schön. The Countess Geschwitz helps her to escape by taking her place in prison.

Scene 2: Schigolch, the athlete, Alwa, and Countess Geschwitz have prepared for Lulu's flight abroad. Lulu returns from prison weakened by illness. Alwa takes on his father's role and becomes her protector.

Act III

Scene 1: Paris. Lulu is on the run. She has attached herself to a marquis, but he is a white slaver and has sold her to Cairo. If she refuses to go, he will hand her over to the police. Neither Alwa nor Countess Geschwitz can help her. The former has lost his fortune speculating, while Geschwitz has spent her money on Lulu's escape. With the police already on their way, Lulu swaps clothes with a groom and slips away. Alwa follows her.

Scene 2: London. Lulu is living with Schigolch and Alwa. They are entirely without means. Schigolch sends Lulu onto the street. Her first client, a Bible-thumping professor and the musical reincarnation of her first husband, the professor of medicine, gives her little money. Countess Geschwitz arrives, having failed to raise money. The second client, a Negro and the musical reincarnation of the painter, wants to have Lulu first and pay afterwards. Alwa intervenes and tries to kill the man, but is himself murdered. Schigolch leaves. Countess Geschwitz stays. Lulu's third client is Jack the Ripper and the musical reincarnation of Dr. Schön. He kills Lulu first and then Countess Geschwitz.

S. N.

Lulu, production photograph showing
Christine Schäfer (Lulu) and John Bröcheler
(Dr. Schön), production and sets Peter
Mussbach, costumes Andrea Schmidt-
Futterer, conductor Michael Gielen, Salzburg
Festival 1995.
The challenge for every production of *Lulu* is
to present the title figure as a real person
while at the same time holding her up as the
embodiment of male fantasies. Peter
Mussbach's production was a co-production
with the Berlin Staatsoper.

Lulu, set design by Ruodi Barth for the
production by Werner Düggelin, Düsseldorf
1984 (TWS).
According to Wedekind and Berg, man is a
badly domesticated animal. That is why the
characters are introduced by an animal
tamer. A bourgeois comedy then follows this
prologue. In Ruodi Barth's set design, the set
for a vaudeville stage remains visible behind
the bourgeois set.

Earth Spirit

Man should be capable of recognizing natural laws provided he studies hard and thinks logically. This rational view of the world formed the basis of school teaching in the last third of the nineteenth century. The facts of life, however, were not taught. It was not acceptable to talk about instinct and sexuality in middle-class society. Around the turn of the century, there was a reaction against this naive and optimistic rationalism. Sigmund Freud formulated the concept of

Lulu, production photograph with Karan Armstrong (Lulu) and Erik Saeden (Schigolch), production Götz Friedrich, sets Timothy O'Brien, conductor Colin Davis, Royal Opera House, London 1981.
The American soprano Karan Armstrong (b. 1941) was a celebrated Lulu in London and Berlin.

Lulu, production photograph with Christine Schäfer (Lulu) and Tom Fox (Animal Tamer), production and sets Peter Mussbach, costumes Andrea Schmidt-Futterer, conductor Michael Gielen, Salzburg Festival 1995.
A vaudeville setting for the bourgeois comedy was reinforced musically at the Salzburg Festival by means of a jazz ensemble that played stage music alongside the Berlin Staatskapelle.

the subconscious to explain the apparently irrational factors that influence human behavior. At the same time, the figure of the femme fatale appeared in literature, a symbol of sexuality, an instinct that cannot be understood logically or rationally but that ultimately governs everything in human life. That is the true "spirit" of the earthly world, the *Earth Spirit* of Wedekind's play.

Lulu

Who is Lulu, then? We learn virtually nothing of her origins and childhood. Every man calls her by a different name. The professor of medicine in Wedekind's play calls her Nelly (in the opera, he hardly says a word). To the painter she is Eva (Eve), and to Dr. Schön Mignon ("pet"). "Lulu" is apparently the name Schigolch has given her. She appears in different clothes in every scene, sometimes having to change quickly several times. Thus she appears in varying guises – the eternal woman, as it were, who dominates men and ultimately becomes their victim. That idea is brought out particularly clearly in Berg's opera. The last three of Lulu's "clients" are reincarnations of the professor of medicine, the painter, and Dr. Schön – her three dead husbands. It is puzzling that Lulu loses her appeal in Act III. She is not much older nor grown ugly. Yet her magic is extinguished. As if she had gone out of fashion, like a suit, a dress, or a work of art.

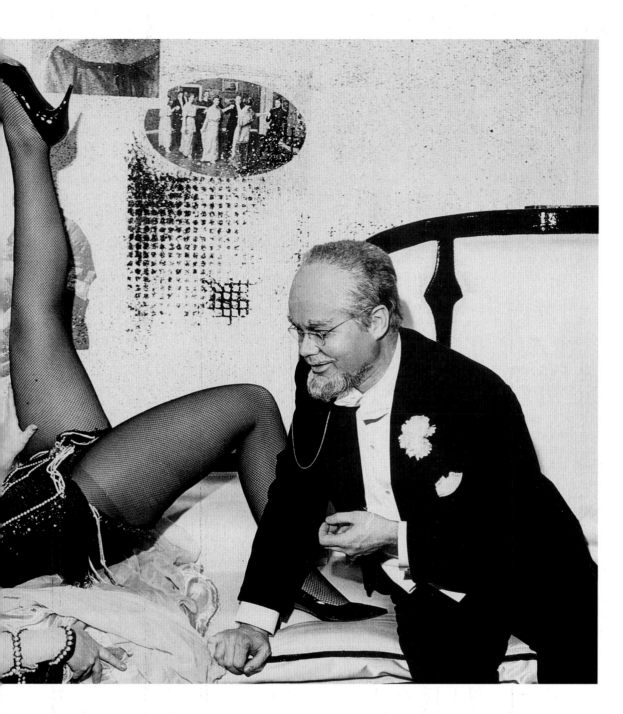

Lulu, production photograph with Edda Moser and Dietrich Fischer-Dieskau, production Gustav Rudolf Sellner, sets Filippo Sanjust, conductor Karl Böhm, Deutsche Oper, Berlin 1968.
The part of Lulu requires a Wagnerian soprano with the figure of a bar dancer. Anyone wanting to sing the part needs a soprano voice of dramatic power and coloratura ability, such as that of the German singer Edda Moser (b. 1938).

Twelve

Berg composed his second opera on the basis of the twelve-note scale, a compositional technique developed by Berg's teacher and friend →Arnold Schoenberg in the early 1920s. Although Berg had already used twelve-note thematic patterns in his works (→*Wozzeck*, the doctor's theme, →M 3), he adopted Schoenberg's procedure only one step at a time, and from the first sought solutions of his own that did not strictly conform to Schoenberg's rules. In *Lulu*, he set up a system of several basic rows from which others were derived. Thus each figure in the opera has a row of its own. Particularly characteristic is the row allocated to Geschwitz with the dominance of fifths. Of course, other means are also used for characterization, especially instrumental color. The color of the vibraphone is associated with Lulu, while the athlete is linked with piano clusters.   S. K.

Lulu, production photograph with Christine Schäfer (Lulu) and Gerd Wolf (the theatre manager), production and sets Peter Mussbach, costumes Andrea Schmidt-Futterer, conductor Michael Gielen, Salzburg Festival 1995.

Passage

Passaggio

Messa in scena

Libretto: Edoardo Sanguinetti.
Première: 6 May 1963, Milan (Piccola Scala).
Characters: She (S), chorus (A, B).

Synopsis

The 'stations' in a woman's life: personal and political passions, career, incarceration, torture, persecution, prostitution.   *S. N.*

A stage mass

Models for Berio's main character, succinctly called "She," were the Jewish journalist Milena Jesenská (1896–1944, in Ravensbrück concentration camp), who features in literary history as a friend of Franz Kafka, and Rosa Luxemburg (1870–1919). The notable feature of this stage work, described by Berio as a "stage mass" and containing references to Biblical texts, is the chorus, which has to speak in Italian, English, French, German, and Latin. Its function is to reveal the audience to be part of "the people," following the protagonist's Passion with dull impassivity, spiritually unmoved and lacking in sympathy. Berio's concern was not so much to abolish the separation of stage and auditorium as to give meaning to the operatic genre at a time when, according to Berio (citing Brecht), a conversation about trees is almost a crime because it keeps silent about so many atrocities.

Berio, Luciano

b. 24 October 1925 in Oneglia (now Imperia, in Liguria)

Berio began his music studies very early under his father's guidance, continuing under Ghedini at the Milan Conservatory and under →Dallapiccola during a study visit to Tanglewood in 1951. In 1954 he and Bruno Maderna founded an electro-acoustic studio (Studio di Fonologia Musicale di RAI) in Milan, which he directed until 1961. From 1956 to 1960 Berio was editor of the periodical *Incontri Musicali,* and until 1960 he conducted a concert series of the same name. From 1960, he was in demand as a teacher in Europe and the USA, living in America until 1972. From 1958 Berio worked with the Italian semiotician and author Umberto Eco on a series of so-called "open works," which included the various compositions known as *Sequenze,* in which he explored with wit and imagination new ways of using traditional instruments. From 1950 to 1966 he was married to the American singer of Amish origin Cathy Berberian, and during this period produced works for her enormously expressive and adaptable voice, notably *Circles* (1960), *Sequenza III* (1966), and arrangements of folk songs. The *Requies* for orchestra of 1983–84 was dedicated to her memory, following her death in 1983 at the age of 57. From 1993 to 1994 Berio was Charles Eliot Norton Professor of Poetry at Harvard University, and worked with the leading symphony orchestras in the USA and Europe. A noteworthy event was his *Sinfonia* of 1968 for eight vocal soloists (the Swingle Singers) and orchestra, dedicated to →Leonard Bernstein and the New York Philharmonic, by whom it was first performed. In this work, truth and beauty are reconciled with comprehensibility, the wit of the philosopher with popular wit.

Works: Stage works: *Allez-Hop!* (1952–59), *Passaggio* (*Passage*) (1963), *Opera* (1970, rev. 1977), *La vera storia* (*The True Story*) (1978/FP 1982), *Un re in ascolto* (*A King Listens*) (1984), *Outis* (*No One*) (1997); ballets, orchestral works, solo concertos, chamber music, electronic music.

*B*erio is one of the most important, versatile, and at the same time successful composers of his time. His music proclaims cheerful intelligence, and the idea of a serene, contemplative farewell.

Passage, production photograph from the third scene with Giuliana Tavolaccini, production Luciano Berio, Edoardo Sanguineti, and Virginio Puecher, sets Nicola Benois, conductor Luciano Berio, La Piccola Scala, Milan 1963.
The large stage at La Scala was traditionally a stronghold of established art. It was quite different at the Piccola Scala. Here new works were given their first performance.

Mimic tale of a flea

Berio's first opera was a "mime tale" ("racconto mimico") called *Allez-Hop!*, from 1959, based on a text by Italo Calvino (for mezzo-soprano, eight mime actors, ballet, and orchestra). The action takes place in an imaginary world. A flea has escaped from the state circus and lands at an official political reception. It irritates the politicians so much that they are driven to declare war. When the war is over and peace returns, the world seems so tedious to the owner of the flea circus that he now deliberately releases one of his performers. So the whole business starts all over again. Even in his first opera, Berio's desire to speak about the serious conflicts of the world is clear, though he does it not in a pontificating manner or with a deeply gloomy tone, but with wit and irony.

Meditation, dream, and morality play: Opera

Berio called his third stage work *Opera*, the Latin for "works," implying that several pieces are present at the same time. The first version was first performed at the Opera Santa Fe in New Mexico in 1970, while the première of the second version took place in 1977, at the Teatro della Pergola in Florence. In this work singers and actors have equally important roles, while a chorus recalls the death of Eurydice and thus the Orpheus legend. Scenes depicting the sinking of the *Titanic* and dying in an intensive care unit at a modern specialist clinic are linked. According to Berio, this is "a meditation, a dream, and to some extent also a morality play about the subject of the end."   *S. N.*

Passage, production photograph with Evelyne Mandak, Juilliard School of Music, New York 1963.
Berio became familiar with the German philosopher Walter Benjamin's concept of "passage" through his friend, the linguist, writer, and cultural philosopher Umberto Eco. The program of his opera matches this. Passage is change, dangerous and at the same time unavoidable and necessary.

The True Story, production photograph with Milva (a street-singer), production Luis Pasqual, sets and costumes Roberto Plate, Opéra National de Paris 1985. In Act I, Berio retells Verdi's →*Il trovatore* in paradigmatic situations that exemplify elemental conflicts and feelings. In Act II, events of Act I are apparently repeated, but while the texts are almost the same, the music and the settings are quite different. Berio asks: "Where is the real story, then? In the first or second part?" His answer is: "I don't know. Perhaps in an imaginary, even truer part." This idea of a "truth" that is not easily determinable was taken up by Japanese film director Akira Kurosawa in his cult film *Rashomon* of 1950.

The True Story

La vera storia

Opera in two acts

Libretto: Italo Calvino.

Première: 9 March 1982, Milan (Teatro alla Scala).

Characters: Ada (Ms), Leonora (S), Ugo (T), Ivo (Bar), The Condemned Man (B), The Commandant (Bar), Priest (T), Two Street-singers (Ms, A), Four Passers-by (actors); vocal ensemble and chorus, mimes, dancers, acrobats.

Synopsis
Act I

During a festival, a tyrant has a man taken prisoner and executed. Out of revenge, the sister of the murdered man abducts a son of the commandant but is unable to kill him, instead bringing him up as her own son. The ruler dies and his second son takes over. The brothers know nothing of each other, but both fall in love with the same woman and fight one another to death and ruin.

Act II

During a festival – or is it an uprising? – a man is taken prisoner and executed. A child is abducted – for love or revenge? Why do two men fight? For a woman, for love, or is all an excuse? But for what? *S. N.*

The True Story, rehearsal photograph with Milva, Teatro alla Scala, Milan 1981. Italy's superstar Milva contributed significantly to the success of both the première and the production at the Bastille Opera in Paris in 1985.

Right
The True Story, rehearsal photograph, Teatro alla Scala, Milan 1981. Fiesta or revolt? A man is arrested in the middle of a crowd ... What appears to be unambiguous becomes questionable when repeated in a different form.

A King Listens

Un re in ascolto

Azione musicale in two parts

Libretto: Italo Calvino.
Première: 7 August 1984, Salzburg (Kleines Festspielhaus).
Characters: Prospero (Bbar), Producer (T), Friday (spoken), Female Protagonist (S), Soprano I, Soprano II, Mezzo-soprano; Three Singers (T, Bar, B), Nurse (S), Wife (Ms), Doctor (T), Lawyer (B), Singing Pianist; Accordionist, Mime, Messenger, Stage Designer and Assistants, Dressmaker, A Woman to be Sawn in Half, Acrobats, Clown (silent); chorus.

Synopsis
Part I

A modern Prospero looks for salvation on a lonely island – a theatrical impresario who has chosen the refuge of art in the midst of life's storm. He overhears that a director wants to weld many mutually antagonistic personalities into an artistic whole. Great harmony seems to prevail, only to be shattered. Harmony arises accidentally. It cannot be forced.

Part II

Prospero lies dying. The artists dependent on him busy themselves around him playing their false games, but now and then true feelings also surface. Prospero takes his dream of completion with him to the grave.

S. N

Above
A King Listens, production photograph with Ronald McIntyre (Prospero) and Graham Valentine (Friday), production Graham Vick, Opéra National de Paris 1991.
In the original production, Götz Friedrich staged Berio's "musical action" (title role Theo Adam, conductor Lorin Maazel) with crude realism, as a reflection on art. In fact it is a work of farewell, "musical contemplation" about the end. The "addio" effects that are so typical of Berio's music and the use of quotations as reminiscences were brought out only in a later production, a co-production by the Royal Opera House, London (1990) and the Bastille Opera, Paris (1991).

A King Listens, photograph from the production by Graham Vick, Opéra National de Paris 1991.

Berlioz, Hector

b. 11 December 1803 in La Côte-St.-André
d. 8 March 1869 in Paris

Berlioz had his first great success in 1830 with what is still his most popular work, the *Symphonie fantastique*. In spite of a number of important state commissions and some extensive concert tours as a conductor, he was forced to earn his living as a journalist and librarian. As a music critic, he kept a sharp eye on the activities of his contemporaries. His manual of instrumentation still counts as obligatory reading for every composer. He was a close friend of Liszt and Chopin while all three lived in Paris.

Works: Operas: *Benvenuto Cellini* (1838), *Béatrice et Bénédict* (*Beatrice and Benedick*) (1862), *Les troyens* (*The Trojans*) (1863); orchestral works, including the *Symphonie fantastique* (1830), *Harold en Italie* (*Harold in Italy*) (1834); dramatic works including *Roméo et Juliette* (*Romeo and Juliet*) (1839) and *La damnation de Faust* (*The Damnation of Faust*) (1846); choral works, including the *Grande messe des morts* (*Requiem*) (1837), the *Te Deum* (1849), and *L'enfance du Christ* (*The Childhood of Christ*) (1854).

Beatrice and Benedick

Béatrice et Bénédict

Opéra comique in two acts

Libretto: Hector Berlioz, after Shakespeare's comedy *Much Ado About Nothing*.
Première: 9 August 1862, Baden-Baden (Neues Theater).
Characters: Béatrice/Beatrice (S), Bénédict/Benedick, a Sicilian officer (T), Héro/Hero, Beatrice's cousin (S), Claudio, Hero's lover (Bar), Léonato/Leonato, governor of Messina, Hero's father (spoken), Don Pedro, a general in the Sicilian army (B), Ursule/Ursula, Hero's attendant (Ms), Somarone, the choirmaster (B); A Messenger, A Lawyer, Two Servants (spoken); musicians, singers, people of Sicily, the governor's retinue (chorus).
Setting: Messina, the 16th century.

Synopsis

Whereas Hero and Claudio are certain that they love each other, Beatrice and Benedick think they hate each other. A trick by friends reveals their true feelings, and the couple are joined in a love-hate relationship.
Act I
Scene 1: The townspeople are awaiting the arrival of Don Pedro's victorious army. Hero is waiting for Claudio in order to marry him. Beatrice is waiting for Benedick in order to quarrel with him. Bridegroom Claudio and Don Pedro hope to bring Benedick round to the idea of marriage – in vain.
Scene 2: For choirmaster Somarone, the wedding provides an opportunity to show off. He tries out a wedding composition.
Scene 3: Claudio, Don Pedro, and Leonato encourage Benedick to believe that Beatrice loves him. This unexpected news awakens in Benedick tender feelings for Beatrice, which he has hitherto repressed.
Scene 4: The happy bride Hero had tricked Beatrice in a similar fashion. She herself revels in anticipation of her forthcoming wedding.
Act II
Scene 1: The choirmaster Somarone improvises a drinking song in preparation for the wedding. It proves to be as wretched as the wedding song.
Scene 2: Beatrice is deeply moved by the news of Benedick's love for her, and remembers how worried she was when he left for the war. She loves him in return, but has kept her feelings hidden out of pride. She watches Hero's happiness with envy. The friends' wedding celebrations are already under way when Beatrice and Benedick begin to quarrel once again, though now each recognizes the signs of love in the words of the other. As Hero and Claudio sign the wedding contract, the quarrelsome pair join them, after a few misapprehensions have been cleared up.   S. N.

"Le Tannhäuser demandant à voir son petit frère" ("Tannhäuser demands to see his younger brother"), caricature of Berlioz's *The Trojans* from *Charivari* magazine, 25 November 1863.
Rarely has any composer been so often the butt of ridicule as Berlioz, whose avant-garde views and experimental genius provided ample material for petit bourgeois critics. In terms of critical reception, he fared particularly badly in the field of opera. His first opera, *Benvenuto Cellini* (1838), was a flop, *Beatrice and Benedick* was given a cool reception, and only three acts of →*The Trojans* were performed during the composer's lifetime. That was two years after the scandal of the Paris production of Wagner's →*Tannhäuser*, which prompted Berlioz's numerous opponents to make unfavourable comparisons.

Berlioz was, without doubt, an avant-garde visionary. Despite his successes, he remained an outsider in the musical world, a composer whose bold innovations would be recognized only after his death.

Swansong – as comedy?

Looking back at Berlioz's life's work, with its long chain of remarkable achievements and unsuccessful experiments, it seems somewhat disconcerting that his last completed score was an *opéra comique*, his only attempt at the genre. The laughter in Berlioz's story of Beatrice and Benedick is somewhat bitter and uncomfortable, in that it is the laughter of a man who stands outside his time and who refuses to bow to external pressure, either of convention or of fashion. In relation to *Beatrice and Benedick*, the *opéra comique* label thus requires substantial reinterpretation. Though Berlioz's comic opera fulfils the formal criteria of the genre, in terms of content it has nothing in common with the *opéras comiques* of →Auber and →Halévy, which were produced and consumed by the dozen in Paris during the period between 1820 and 1850. The very choice of a Shakespearean subject suggests that Berlioz had something other than an ordinary comic opera in mind.

"Malvenuto Cellini" ("Unwelcome Cellini"), caricature by Banger, Paris 1838. Berlioz's operatic firstborn, *Benvenuto Cellini*, was indeed called "malvenuto" ("unwelcome") at the time of its first performance in 1838. It was the greatest and most painful fiasco that Berlioz was to experience in his eventful life. The overture was warmly received by the audience – Berlioz was a born symphonist – and is still often played today, but otherwise every number in the opera was booed. *Benvenuto Cellini* is an effective opera, rich in comic situations and sublime moments. At its heart is the problem of the creative artist. There are some inspired crowd scenes, with a particularly memorable carnival scene.

Individual music

The music of *Beatrice and Benedick* cannot be compared with the clichés of contemporary *opéras comiques*. It is much richer in detail and subtler than other works of the time. The extended overture, the main part of which recurs in the closing duet at the end of Act II, suggests an approach that values sophisticated wit above common comedy. *M 1*

Beatrice and Benedick, production photograph with Hélène Perraguin (Beatrice) and Tibère Raffalli (Benedick), production Pierre Barrat, Opéra Lyon 1991.
In the final decades of the 20th century, Opéra Lyon specialized in reconstructed fragments of stage works, rarely performed works, and first performances. Under the musical direction of conductor Kent Nagano, these performances often attracted international attention.

1. Closing Duet (Beatrice and Benedick)

A similar tone characterizes the male voice trio in Act I and Benedick's rondo. In addition to the humor and the technical brilliance, Berlioz managed to bring out the dramatic aspects. This is particularly noticeable in Beatrice's great aria (Act II). The heroine is oppressed by alarming memories, and the scene develops into a splendid monologue, which would not have been out of place in *The Trojans*. *M 2*

2. Beatrice's Great Aria

Il m'en souvient, il m'en souvient, le jour du dé - part de l'ar - mé - e, Je ne plus m'ex-pli - quer L'é - tran - ge sen - ti - ment.

However, probably the finest jewel in the opera is the duet between Hero and Ursula. The anticipation of love is combined with virginal innocence, culminating in a moving nocturne under a shining starlit sky. *M 3*   *P. H.*

3. Duo-nocturne (Hero and Ursula)

Nuit   pai - sible et se - re - ne!   La lu - ne douce rei - ne, Qui plane en sou - ri - ant,

The Trojans

Les troyens

Grand opéra in five acts

Libretto: Hector Berlioz, after Virgil's *Aeneid*.

Premières: Acts III–V: 4 November 1863, Paris (Théâtre-Lyrique); concert performance Acts I–II: 7 December 1879 (10 years after Berlioz's death), Paris (Théâtre du Châtelet).

Characters: Énée/Aeneas, Trojan hero, son of the goddess Venus (T), Ascagne/Ascanius, Aeneas' son (S), Panthée/Panthous, Trojan priest, friend of Aeneas (B). In Troy: Cassandre/Cassandra, Trojan prophetess, Priam's daughter (Ms), Chorèbe/Corebus, Asian prince, betrothed to Cassandra (Bar), Priam, King of Troy (B), Hécube/Hecuba, his wife (S), Hélénus/Helenus, Trojan priest, Priam's son (T), Polyxène/Polyxena, Cassandra's sister (S), Ghost of Hector, Trojan hero, Priam's son (B), A Greek Soldier (B), Andromaque/Andromache and Astyanax, widow and son of Hector (silent). In Carthage: Didon/Dido, Queen of Carthage (Ms), Anna, her sister (A), Narbal, Dido's minister (B), Iopas, a poet at Dido's court (T), Hylas, a young Phrygian sailor (T or A), Two Trojan Soldiers (2 B), Mercure/Mercury (B), A Priest of Pluto (B); Trojans, Greeks, Tyrians, Carthaginians, nymphs, satyrs, fauns, sylvan spirits, invisible spirits (chorus).

Setting: Troy and Carthage, during the time of the Trojan War.

The Trojans, set design (detail) by Franz Angelo Rottonara, Cologne 1898 (TWS). The design for the palace at Carthage by the famous Viennese set designer Rottonara shows him to have been at something of a loss. While there are obvious influences from the original Paris production, the Viennese concept mixes classicism (antiquity) and Romantic exoticism (Dido's realm was on the coast of North Africa).

Synopsis

After a ten-year war, the victorious Greeks finally murder the inhabitants of Troy. Only Aeneas manages to escape with a few people, guided by the ghost of Hector. Aeneas is expected to found a new race in distant lands. His journey takes him to Carthage, where he finds happiness with Queen Dido. But the ancestral shades drive him on. Abandoned, Dido takes her own life, and as she dies has a vision of the truth: only misery comes of loveless action. The victims of the Greeks will return one day as bloody perpetrators and in turn destroy Carthage.

Act I

After ten years of besieging Troy, the Greeks have suddenly vanished, leaving behind a great wooden horse. The Trojans celebrate victory. Only Cassandra fears the enemy's cunning and warns against premature rejoicing. But the Trojans turn a deaf ear to her.

Act II

The Trojans consecrate the wooden horse as a tutelary deity and set it up in the city. But Greek soldiers are hidden inside. Troy falls, and its inhabitants are murdered. Venus saves her son Aeneas, and the ghost of Hector commands him to found a new homeland in Italy. Cassandra and the Trojan women choose suicide rather than captivity.

Act III

Under the rule of Queen Dido, the people of Carthage enjoy prosperous lives. Although feeling lonely after the death of her husband, Dido has rejected an offer of marriage from the Numidian king, and therefore expects war. The Trojans drop anchor in port and ask Dido for permission to stay and for her protection.

Act IV

Carthaginians and Trojans go hunting together. A storm approaches. Dido and Aeneas seek shelter in a cave, whither the goddess of love, Venus, sends her messengers. The god Mercury reminds Aeneas not to forget his duty. Dido's minister Narbal warns her about Aeneas' destiny, and discourages her from attempting to defy the will of the gods. The advice comes too late for Dido. The Queen of Carthage and hero of Troy find themselves in love.

Act V

The ghost of Hector reminds Aeneas of his destiny. The hero decides in favor of duty rather than love. When Dido learns that Aeneas has left her, she casts all souvenirs of her lover onto a pyre, before throwing herself onto his sword. In a vision, she sees mighty Carthage destroyed by Rome.

S. N.

The Trojans, set design by Philippe Chaperon for the original production at the Théâtre Lyrique, Paris 1863.
Berlioz's contemporaries were not only alarmed by the colossal scale of the work; its very essence offended them, as it did not adhere to the conventions of French opera. A grandiose panoply of antiquity was intended here, whose basically classical spirit had nothing in common with the customary superficial entertainment.

Ars poetica in dramatic form

It has often been observed that every one of Berlioz's works contains autobiographical references. Whether it involves the metalworker Cellini, the brooding Faust, or the youthfully ardent Romeo, its protagonist will always be a personification of the composer's own ideals. In *The Trojans*, Aeneas' divine mission to found a new empire determines the course of the action. To new shores! This idea was part of the philosophy of Romanticism, which hoped to build a new world on the ruins of the old. In Aeneas' case, the hope is only realized through renunciation. That creates the unity of the action. A man (or artist) with a mission cannot be diverted from his goal either by his own happiness or by thoughts for the welfare of others – that is the bottom line of Berlioz's opera. The contradictory element in the actual realization of this thesis is that the composer's aesthetic principle rested not on his efforts to create a new kind of music but on his return to a century-old tradition. It was a tradition derived from the operas of Gluck, which had injected new life into French dramatic music in the 1770s. Just as Gluck's reforms had effected a return to classical ideals, Berlioz now sought to repeat the change of direction, though in new historical circumstances.

Once again, the aging composer conjured up his models. Besides Gluck, whom Berlioz had always regarded highly and whose works he had edited from time to time, they included Spontini, the classicizing master of Napoleon's imperial France, and of course Mozart and Shakespeare. In the company of this pantheon he felt worthy of Virgil and his grand theme. As his farewell, he wanted to found the music drama of the future. And Wagner? It is astonishing and at the same time typical that, in 1861, after concerts of Wagner's music in Paris, and with Wagner himself, Berlioz wrote an article in which he outlined the principles of the new music drama. Like all other operatic reformers, he declared war on convention, on the tyranny of singers, and on euphony: let there be drama instead of opera! The prototype was ready in his workshop, awaiting a first performance. It was *The Trojans*. *P. H.*

The Trojans, set design by Franz Angelo Rottonara, Cologne 1898 (TWS).
Queen Dido's bedroom, where in Act V she bids farewell to the world in a sublime monologue.
Romantic sensuousness and the rapture of Berlioz's own personality are absent. Even the nocturnal love duet has clear melodic lines and classical proportions. The protagonists move through the drama like shadow figures behind a white screen. The color of mourning is white rather than black. This is where the discrepancy between the late Romantic stage set and Berlioz's musical language arises.

Rounding off a tradition

Just what does this attachment to tradition in *The Trojans* consist of? It is the total rejection of coloratura and of concessions to the singers. The vocal parts are simple, and often somewhat uncharacteristic. For Berlioz, creating a general atmosphere was more important than any form of dramatic or musical showiness, and the orchestra was equally involved in this. The whole opera is thus marked by an epic long-windedness, which appears both in the preference for slow tempos and in the combining of musical numbers into large tableaux. The division between recitative and aria is also blurred. Yet the result is far from tedious. Berlioz was merely attempting to establish standards that were at variance with the prevailing norm. Though *The Trojans* is often compared with the operas of Wagner, it is in fact the antithesis of the Wagnerian music drama, in that it seeks not to change the language of music but to round off a tradition.

Musical highlights

The first half of *The Trojans* is dominated by the prophetic figure of Cassandra. All her scenes, but particularly her extensive duet with her fiancé Corebus, are marked by dark resolve, which reaches a climax in the furious finale of Act II with the mass suicide she has ordered. Cassandra's insight contrasts with the illusions of the Trojans, who feel liberated after the long siege. Not only in the brash, energetic introduction but also in the Trojan march (finale of Act I) does this optimism surge forth. Always sensitive to the spatial effects of music, Berlioz sets up three stage orchestras in this scene, which repeat the march theme at varying distances. M4

The march is followed by the appearance of the ghost of Hector – a turning point in the action and an ominous change of mood – who reveals Aeneas' mission to him. In this subtly worked out scene, four muted horns provide an incomparably mystical atmosphere.

After the groans of the dying Trojans, the happy voices of the Carthaginians ring out. The prosperity of the country is conveyed by a procession of architects, sailors, and laborers, which is musically embedded in a national song. The melody of the latter radiates sublime calm and thus constitutes a contrast to the rousing Trojan march. M5

Only Queen Dido is unhappy. She feels unfulfilled by her work for the common good. She longs for love (duet, Dido and Anna). The arrival of the Trojan refugees is announced by their musical insignia, the march, though it is now in the minor key, which wholly accords with the yearning, melancholy mood of the queen. They are greeted by the Carthaginians as comrades in arms, and this lends the finale military élan.

Berlioz the symphonic composer is also in evidence (Act IV, Scene 1). The interlude entitled Royal Hunt and Storm is an orchestral insert accompanied by a minutely detailed stage pantomime. Dido and Aeneas first come together in a nature idyll in which a hummed chorus (a manifestation of mythological presences) enriches the orchestral palette. The second scene of Act IV, with its lengthy ballet, leads unswervingly to the final duet. This is preceded by two substantial ensembles, which feed Dido's growing love for the Trojan hero. (Berlioz was inspired here by a painting by Pierre Guérin.) Aeneas tells of his sad fate. When the lovers are left alone, the decisive avowals burst from overflowing hearts. The motifs in the text are borrowed from the dialogue between Jessica and Lorenzo in Shakespeare's *The Merchant of Venice*. The intoxicating power of the night is praised. Berlioz wrote an exquisite nocturne, whose melodies soar in endless lines, as endless as it is hoped this newfound love will prove to be. M6

Act V brings a sober day and the tragic conclusion. Aeneas has remembered his mission. Abandoned, Dido says farewell to her happiness and to life, not in a concise aria as in Purcell's version of the story (→*Dido and Aeneas*) but in a long chain of contrasting mental states. In the last two scenes of the opera, the music pours out in a flood that is only occasionally checked –

6. Love Duet (Dido and Aeneas)

Nuit d'iv - resse et d'ex - ta - se in - fi - ni - e!

Blon - de Phoe - bé,   grands   as - tres de   sa   cour

7. Dido's Farewell Aria

A - dieu,   fiè - re ci - té,   qu'un généreux ef - fort   si promptement é - le - va flo - ris - san - te.

for example, by the austere chorus of the ceremony of mourning.

The jewel of the piece is an aria in which Dido says farewell to her city, her homeland, and her companions. Words issue forth as if broken, like a psychograph translated into music. The musico-dramatic genius displayed in this aria is indeed worthy of the tradition of French classicism. M 7   P. H.

The Trojans, engraving for Act I (Dido grants Aeneas asylum), Théâtre de l'Opéra-Comique, Paris 1892.
Berlioz had read Virgil's *Aeneas* extensively from his youth. He used the first four books as the basis for his opera, placing the destruction of Troy (which is narrated by Aeneas in Virgil's poem) directly on the stage. This produced a structure that could easily be divided into two parts: the first two acts are set in war-torn Troy, the last three in prosperous Carthage. Even so, for Berlioz this work (composed 1856–58) was a single entity, though he never saw it on stage in its entirety.

Bernstein, Leonard

b. 25 August 1918 in Lawrence (Massachusetts)
d. 14 October 1990 in New York

After training as a music scholar, pianist, and conductor, Bernstein taught at the Boston Institute of Modern Art from 1941 to 1942, worked as an assistant to Koussevitzky at the Berkshire Music Center, and wrote his first compositions. After a successful substitution for Bruno Walter at the New York Philharmonic Orchestra on 14 November 1943, he was signed up as second conductor from 1945–48. Guest appearances with famous orchestras ensued, then professorships at the Berkshire Music Center and, from 1951 to 1956, at Brandeis University in Waltham. From 1955 Bernstein also took responsibility for TV programs in which he displayed his ability to talk about art to a broad public in a vital and media-sensitive fashion. He was principal conductor of the New York Philharmonic from 1956 to 1966. In the 1960s he established closer ties with Europe, working for prolonged spells with the Vienna Philharmonic, and also undertook engagements with the Israel Philharmonic Orchestra and as guest conductor with all the great orchestras of the world. As a world-renowned conductor, a highly individual composer, and a writer, he left a permanent mark on international musical life.

Works: Stage works: *On the Town* (1944, New York), *Trouble in Tahiti* (1952, Brandeis University), *Wonderful Town* (1953, New York), *Candide* (1956, New York), *West Side Story* (1957, Washington, New York), *1600 Pennsylvania Avenue* (1976, New York), *A Quiet Place* (1983, Houston); theater music, ballets, film music, orchestral works.

Candide, photograph from the production by Jonathan Miller and John Wells, sets Richard Hudson, conductor John Mauceri, Scottish Opera, Glasgow 1988. Convinced of Dr. Pangloss's notion of living in the best of all possible worlds, the protagonists are driven by the chaos of war into distant lands, where they have to learn the difference between philosophy and reality. Snobbishness, prostitution, murder, and fanaticism are what the world has to offer. The trio attempt to resist all evils.

Bernstein's compositions spring from the music of the American metropolis, blending European art music, Jewish music traditions, and Afro-American jazz with great personal energy and melodic inventiveness. The result is a style all his own.

Voltaire and Bernstein: from musical to opera

Candide haunted Bernstein for 35 years. It began life as a musical, first performed on 1 February 1956 in New York. The libretto by American writer Lillian Hellman is based on Voltaire's famous novel *Candide, ou L'optimisme* of 1759. A second version as a musical, first performed in 1973, again in New York, was followed by an operatic version staged at the Barbican Centre in London on 13 December 1989, with the composer at the rostrum. This was incidentally Bernstein's last recording. *Candide* failed to make it as a musical, and even the opera was not a success, though Bernstein was very fond of the work.

The plot tells of the adventures of Candide and Cunigonde, who are brought up by their teacher, philosopher Dr. Pangloss, in the belief that they live in the best of all possible worlds. A war destroys their homeland, they have to flee, and they lose contact with each other. In Lisbon, Pangloss and Candide fall victim to the Inquisition, and only the famous earthquake of 1755 saves them from death. Meanwhile, Cunigonde earns a crust as a courtesan with two patrons, the Grand Inquisitor and a Jewish banker. Candide and Cunigonde meet up once more and reach Eldorado, become unimaginably rich, and then lose all their money again. Pangloss becomes a galley slave, and Cunigonde walks the streets. Candide buys his mentor's freedom from the galley, and with what remains of his wealth acquires a patch of land on the fringes of a city. Here he will live with Cunigonde and Pangloss, devoid of any illusions, on the principle that "Il faut cultiver notre jardin" ("One should cultivate one's own garden").

This last sentence of the novel, which has become famous, remains enigmatic and has been a subject of controversy since 1759. One view is that Pangloss's thesis of the best of all possible worlds is culpably naive and taken to absurd lengths in the novel. The other interpretation is that all misery and suffering can lead to a happy conclusion.

Musically, *Candide* is a cross between a musical and an opera, which is why the work has proved difficult to integrate into the repertory. There are very few singers who can manage the demanding vocal parts and the equally demanding dramatic requirements. An example of this is Cunigonde's aria "Glitter and be gay," a breakneck coloratura number. M 1

1. Cunigonde's Bravura Aria

Ha   ha   ha ha ha ha!   Ha ha ha ha ha __ ha ha ha!   Ha   ha   ha ha ha ha!   Ha ha ha ha ha __ ha ha ha!

An American opera

In 1980 journalist Stephen Wadsworth asked Bernstein for an interview, tempting the busy musician with an offer to write a libretto for him. Bernstein agreed, and Wadsworth complied with Bernstein's request for a libretto about middle-class Americans. *A Quiet Place* is an opera in three acts, and was first performed on 17 June 1983 in the Jones Hall in Houston. The story takes place in twentieth-century America. A mother of two dies after a car accident. When the remaining members of the family meet – the father and his son and daughter, now grown up – it is clear that they no longer have anything in common. Hatred and irritation have long replaced love. Then a letter from the dead mother arrives, asking the children to love and feel sympathy for their father. At first they comply only through obedience, but gradually obedience is replaced by their own conviction.   S. N.

Candide, production photograph with (from left to right) Konstanze Esser (Cunigonde), Fred Hoffmann (Candide), and Peter Anton Ling (Dr. Pangloss), production Holger Klembt, sets and costumes Andreas Rank, conductor Myron Romanul, Staatstheater, Mainz 1996.
Bernstein's *Candide* is a treasure in terms of both music and libretto, a witty, sparkling comedy with a philosophical undertone and a satirical bite that is as topical today as it was in Voltaire's time.

Left
A Quiet Place, production photograph, production Stephen Wadsworth, conductor Leonard Bernstein, Wiener Staatsoper 1986.
Dinah's death conjures up conflict-charged memories: son Junior had a relationship with François, now the husband of daughter Dede. Father Sam becomes aware both of his alienation from his children and of his failings as a husband. But the pleas of the dead mother and some frank admissions bring the members of the family closer together again.

Bizet filled the framework of the opéra comique with such lively and passionate music that he became the precursor of late nineteenth-century "verismo."

The Pearlfishers, production photograph with Nadir, Leïla, and Zurga, Staatsoper, Berlin 1934.
The Pearlfishers belonged to a new genre of opera that owed its genesis to the opening of the Théâtre Lyrique in 1851 and the ambitions of its director Léon Carvalho. To meet the challenge of a new age, the crowd scenes and stage effects were reduced in the *drames lyriques*, and the conflicts between the protagonists given greater emphasis.

Bizet, Georges

b. 25 October 1838 in Paris
d. 3 June 1875 in Bougival (near Paris)

Bizet studied composition under →Halévy at the Paris Conservatoire, later marrying his daughter. Halévy's nephew was the librettist for *Carmen*. After initial attempts at instrumental composition, including the remarkable Symphony in C, Bizet turned entirely to the stage. Fourteen complete stage works – operas, operettas, and incidental music – have survived. After moderate success with his earlier works, his great triumph with *Carmen* (1875) came as something of a surprise, though Bizet did not live long enough to see the work become internationally famous.

Works: Operas: *Les pêcheurs de perles* (*The Pearlfishers*) (1863), *La jolie fille de Perth* (*The Fair Maid of Perth*) (1867), *Djamileh* (1872), *Carmen* (1874/FP 1875); incidental music for *L'arlésienne* (*The Girl from Arles*) (1872), Symphony in C, choral works, piano works, songs.

The Pearlfishers
Les pêcheurs de perles

Opéra in three acts

Libretto: Michel Carré and Eugène Cormon.

Première: 30 September 1863, Paris (Théâtre Lyrique).
Characters: Leïla, priestess of Brahma (S), Nadir, a pearlfisher (T), Zurga, head pearlfisher (Bar), Nourabad, high priest of Brahma (B); pearlfishers and their wives (chorus).
Setting: The island of Ceylon, in ancient times.

Synopsis
Nadir and Zurga once vowed to renounce love for the sake of their friendship, because both had fallen in love with the same woman. When this woman, now ordained a virgin priestess, returns Nadir's love, friendship triumphs. Zurga saves the lives of the two lovers, bringing about his own ruin.
Act I
With singing and dancing the pearlfishers invoke the gods' blessing for their dangerous work and appoint a new leader, Zurga. Nadir returns after a long absence, and renews his old friendship with Zurga. Both men profess to have been true to their common vow – to renounce a woman with whom they were both in love, in order to preserve their friendship. A priestess of Brahma arrives, specially appointed by the pearlfishers to pray constantly for the favor of the gods. When the veiled woman makes her vow of chastity, Nadir recognizes the voice of his beloved Leïla. She too senses his presence, but nevertheless goes through with the ritual.
Act II
Leïla is installed by the high priest Nourabad in her new domain, an inaccessible temple ruin. Nadir scrambles up a cliff face in order to reach her. Love

French taste
Bizet's most important model was →Gounod, an older friend as well as a musical model for the young composer. Gounod taught Bizet clarity of melodic line as well as a sense of orchestral color. *The Pearlfishers* shows that Bizet proved to be not only an apt pupil but also a prospective master, as is evident in the most popular piece in the opera, Nadir's "Romance" (Act I). M1

The gently lilting melody, which is particularly effective in a tenor voice, is imbued with sweet melancholy. Despite its simplicity, it is memorable, bearing witness to Bizet's inspired inventiveness. Similar qualities are found in Leïla's cavatina (Act II).

The duet between Leïla and Nadir (the main number of Act II) in no way follows the form of a classical love duet. Both psychologically and musically, it is some time before both voices are in harmony, but in the end Nadir's love overcomes Leïla's sense of duty. The drama overcomes Leïla's sense of duty. But the lovers are discovered and condemned to death. Zurga takes pity on his friend and the unknown priestess, but when she is unveiled he recognizes the woman he once loved, and feels tricked by Nadir.

Act III

Scene 1: Zurga is torn between his feelings of friendship for Nadir and rage at his treachery. He has Leïla brought before him. She pleads for Nadir, thus rekindling Zurga's jealousy. He orders them both to be burnt at the stake. He then notices a necklace Leïla is wearing, and realizes that she is the woman who once saved his life. He now considers it his duty to save Leïla and his friend from death.

Scene 2: The fishermen have gathered for the execution of Leïla and Nadir. But Zurga announces that the camp is on fire, and all rush off to save it. Zurga releases the lovers, telling them that he himself started the fire, in order to allow them to escape.   *S. N.*

The Pearlfishers, production photograph with Edith Leinbacher (Leïla) and Jean-Luc Chaignard (Nadir), production Torsten Fischer, conductor Bertrand de Billy, Wiener Volksoper 1994.
Even though the libretto cannot be considered a theatrical masterpiece, it is economical in construction, with each of the three main characters describing his/her situation in an aria and each singing a duet with the others. The small ensembles culminate in a trio (Act III) in which the major motifs of the plot – love and self-sacrifice – are expressed.

of this moment is encapsulated in a heartfelt though simple melodic figure. *M 2*

A more important role is allocated to the duet between Nadir and Zurga, whose hymn-like melody, resembling a solemn march, functions as a recurring motif. It recalls the friendship of the two men and at the same time conjures up the figure of the divinely pure Leïla, with whom both are passionately in love. *M 3*   *P. H.*

The Pearlfishers, set design (detail) by Heinz Grete, Nuremberg 1930/31 (TWS).

Exoticism

The story of *The Pearlfishers* was originally set in Mexico, which would have meant American Indians rather than Asian Indians. Then the story was moved to Ceylon, but Bizet put less emphasis on specifically Asian features than on the directness of a "non-European" environment. The boisterousness of the religious dances (the introduction to Act I and the *chœur dansé* of Act III), the lofty severity of the Brahma ceremony (Act I), and the somber atmosphere of the funeral march (during the preparations for the execution in Act III) are all part of this.

1. Nadir's Romance

Je crois entendre en-co — — re ca-ché sous les pal-miers

2. Duet between Leila and Nadir

Ton cœur n'a pas com-pris le mien, Au sein de la nuit par-fu-mé — e

3. Duet between Nadir and Zurga

Oui, c'est el-le, C'est la dé-es-se plus char-mante et plus bel-le,

Carmen

Opéra comique in four acts

Libretto: Henri Meilhac and Ludovic Halévy, after the novella by Prosper Mérimée.

Première: 3 March 1875, Paris (Opéra-Comique).

Characters: Carmen, a gypsy (Ms), Don José, a corporal (T), Micaëla, a girl from Don José's village (S), Escamillo, a bullfighter (Bar), Le Dancaïère and Le Ramendado, smugglers (2 T), Frasquita and Mercédès, gypsies (2 S), Zuniga, a lieutenant (B), Moralès, a corporal (Bar), Andrès, a lieutenant (T), Lillas Pastia, an innkeeper (Bar); people of the street, children, cigarette factory girls, soldiers, gypsies, smugglers, bullfighters.

Setting: Spain, the 19th century.

Synopsis

An amorous passion upsets the even tenor of the life of dutiful soldier Don José. Carmen's love of independence comes into conflict with his possessiveness. Don José acts like a true soldier and kills the anarchic element in his life – the gypsy Carmen.

Act I

Outside the tobacco factory in Seville, the military guard is on duty. Micaëla, a peasant girl, comes to find her Don José, a corporal. The factory bell rings, and the girls come streaming out to where the men are waiting. The gypsy woman Carmen stages a dramatic entrance, admired by all the men. Only Don José stands unimpressed to one side, and Carmen attempts to provoke him by throwing him a flower. The peasant lad in Don José is confused by her impudent sexuality, but he regains his equilibrium in a conversation with Micaëla. Suddenly uproar breaks out in the factory, where Carmen has injured another worker in a quarrel. Lieutenant Zuniga orders Don José to take Carmen away to prison. She tempts him with the prospect of becoming her next lover; he lets her escape and is himself arrested.

Act II

Lillas Pastia's tavern is a meeting place for a gang of smugglers to which Carmen also belongs. After a month in prison, Don José has just been let out. Carmen waits for him. The famous matador Escamillo passes down the street, feted by all. He drops in at Lillas Pastia's and is fascinated by Carmen. However, she is grateful to Don José. As promised, she sings and dances for her liberator. When Don José hears the bugle sounding the last post, he vacillates between love and duty. Surprised by Lieutenant Zuniga, who is on Carmen's trail, Don José threatens his superior with his weapon. The smugglers pull the combatants apart. There is now only one way open to Don José: to remain with the smugglers and join their enterprise.

Act III

The smugglers rest at night in the mountains. Carmen is already tired of Don José. She and her friends read their fortunes with cards, where Carmen finds her premonition of an early death confirmed. Some of the smugglers, including the girls, go ahead to divert the customs officials. Don José remains to guard the rest of the goods. Escamillo comes looking for Carmen and gets into a knife fight with Don José. Carmen steps between them and Escamillo invites her to the next bullfight in Seville. Micaëla is then discovered hiding in a crevice in the rocks – she is looking for Don José. His dying mother wants to see him again. Though Don José is reluctant to leave the smugglers, he follows Micaëla, but threateningly warns Carmen he will return.

Act IV

The bullfight is a great popular occasion and a triumph for Escamillo. Carmen has become his bride, enjoying the applause in the arena. Don José waits for Carmen at the entrance to the ring. She courageously approaches him; he first asks for her love, and then demands it. She throws at his feet the ring he once gave her, tries to go past him into the ring, and runs into his knife.   S. N.

Carmen, portrait drawing by Hanns Haas, Berlin 1922.
In a trance: Barbara Kemp as Carmen. In the following year, she became the wife of the composer Max von Schelling. She remained with the Berlin Hofoper company until 1931.

Carmen, production photograph (Act IV) from the production by Franco Zeffirelli, conductor Carlos Kleiber, Wiener Staatsoper 1978.
Six years after the première, *Carmen* was being performed in 15 cities across three continents. The march of success was already unstoppable. In 1907, the public rioted outside the theater in São Paulo, causing several deaths, because some people were unable to get tickets for the performance. Since 1908, more than 50 complete recordings have been issued. To this day Bizet's work is one of the most reliable box office successes. Strangely, the public did not recognize the work's stature immediately, and Bizet was hard hit by the fiasco of the first performance. However, that he died of a broken heart as a result is nothing more than a sentimental legend. In the following months, he worked at an oratorio and on a revision of the opera for a planned Viennese staging in the autumn. He succumbed to a weak heart on 3 June 1875, his death coinciding to the minute with the curtain that fell on the 33rd performance of his *Carmen*.

The Czech soprano Emmy Destinn (1878–1930) as Carmen.
At first sight, more of a tipsy turn-of-the-century bourgeoise than a wild gypsy. Carmen holds the fatal card. The photograph conveys something of the solitude of the great operatic heroine. But can the fiery Carmen, who inflames the air around her and who is always at the center of attention, ever be lonely? In the card-reading trio, she recognizes the inevitability of her common destiny with Don José. Carmen accepts the card's prediction of death with tragic seriousness, even dignity. Her quiet song conveys a premonition of her end.

Carmen, photograph from the film by Francesco Rosi, with Julia Migenes as Carmen, conductor Lorin Maazel, Orchestre National de France, France/Italy 1983.
Thanks to Bizet's opera, *Carmen* has become a concept, the image of a beautiful but wild woman in a Spanish ambience combining exoticism and folklore – an excellent subject for films.

X-rated

It is difficult to judge whether the cool public reception of the first performance of *Carmen* was due to the opera's subject or to the music itself. In the end both provided the grounds for rejection. With a gypsy girl as the main character, one who lures a soldier away from the army, sings and dances in disreputable places, takes up with smugglers, and is finally killed on stage by her former lover, Bizet's work certainly stands apart from the conventions of *opéra comique*. The milieu was described as lawless and the main character accused of indecency. As a result, the press demanded that minors be denied entry to performances of *Carmen* for moral reasons. The truth of course is that Bizet managed to create an archetypal figure, whose effect is comparable with that of Don Giovanni, Hamlet, or Faust. In the twentieth century, Carmen acquired special status as the embodiment of a woman who makes her own decisions.

Carmen and death

According to the music, Carmen is sentenced to death from the outset. A leitmotiv of pathos and admonition is associated with her figure. $_{M4}$

With its augmented seconds that are at once exotic and threatening, this motif is heard in two versions. One appears in the introduction to the opera, while the other accompanies Carmen's first entry, having the effect of a clap of thunder. $_{M5}$

When the gypsies consult the cards about the future (trio), Frasquita and Mercédès dream of happiness, but Carmen is confronted with the prospect of death. This moment is perhaps the most profound in the whole opera, as Carmen comes into contact with the forces that rule her. $_{M6}$

Femme fatale

Carmen has often been seen, inappropriately, as a femme fatale. She is not like Richard Strauss's Salome or Berg's Lulu. It is not she who conquers men: they run after her. Perhaps she feels that a relationship can consist of something more than sexual attraction. Yet when she recognizes that Don José wants to possess not only her body but also her soul, she needs to escape. Her relationship with Don José may be different from previous relationships, but for Carmen it is just as unacceptable. Whereas Don José perishes as a result of his desire, Carmen is destroyed in the encounter with her emotions.

The fearless heroine

Carmen knows neither past nor future. She lives entirely in the present. Love for her is not a program for life but a passing mood. The essence of her life is change, which is what Don José hates above all things. For Carmen, there is no either/or, only a both/and. Waiting for Don José, she flirts unashamedly with Zuniga and Escamillo. One is like the other; anyone can have his turn, provided he is prepared to wait. Carmen wants nothing for keeps, neither man nor object. (Indeed, it is her throwing away the ring José gave her that provokes her murder.) Whereas Don José seeks happiness in constancy, Carmen finds it in fickleness. The social motive is unimportant in her case: she is not a revolutionary, but is a social outsider. Her actions, therefore, cannot be measured by the prevailing moral standards. Like a natural phenomenon, Carmen has her own laws.

Opposite
Carmen, production photograph with
Giulietta Simionato as Carmen, Teatro alla
Scala, Milan 1959.
Giulietta Simionato (born 1910) was the most
memorable Carmen of the second half of the
20th century. Thanks to the huge range and
unique timbre of her voice and her wonderful
vocal technique, she sang all roles from
coloratura alto to dramatic mezzo-soprano.
She gave her operatic heroines human
features: her Carmen was a portrait of a
woman full of passion, kindness, and
Mediterranean temperament – a being
without compare in all operatic literature.

Carmen, poster by Josef Fenneker, Duisberger
Oper, Theater am Königsplatz, 1935.
Carmen was among the few operas not to
require scenic updating after the First World
War, at a time when opera was losing its roots
in society. The figure of Carmen and her
tragic story are at once so modern and so
timeless that one easily forgets the operatic
aspect in the momentum of the drama.
The Carmen in this poster does not look in
the least like an opera singer, but like a
proletarian woman of the 1920s, depicted in
the style of Käthe Kollwitz.

4. Carmen's Fate Motif

5. Carmen's Musical Portrait

6. Trio: Frasquita, Mercédès, and Carmen

En vain, pour é - vi - ter les ré - pon - ses a - mères,   En vain, tu mê - le - ras!

Don José

Though the opera is dominated by the powerful character of Carmen, the story is actually about Don José. Initially he is a shy lad, whose life is built on his relationship with his mother. The planned marriage with Micaëla is only an extension of his childhood idyll. Then repressed sexuality erupts in him, depriving him of both rank and honor. As he hurries off to Carmen after being released from prison, he sings a little song to himself (off stage), like a child lost in a dark wood, humming to give himself courage. The duet with Carmen in Act II manifests separation rather than fulfillment. The famous "Flower Song" is only a component of this duet. Don José produces the flower Carmen threw him, as a pledge of his love. *M 7*

Duel or love duet?

There are three dialogues between Carmen and Don José. Duet is hardly the appropriate word, as none of them follows the conventions of either French or Italian love duets in which the voices of two people unite as one. The dialogues mark three stages in the events – seduction, conflict, and tragic solution – and show that at no stage in the drama are Carmen and Don José spiritually united.

To depict the debilitating process of love, Bizet dispenses with the traditional stock of *opéra comique* techniques. The *seguidilla* with which Carmen attempts to seduce Don José in Act I is a provocative song that allows for a duet only in the recitative middle section. *M 8*

At this point, Don José shows no will of his own: he can only respond, only obey Carmen. It is similar to the great duet in Act II, which begins with a ditty sung by Carmen, accompanying herself with castanets. *M 9*

Above
Carmen, Ludwig Suthaus (1906–71) as Don José.

Below
Carmen, Emmy Soldene as Carmen, c. 1880.

Emmy Soldene, one of the earliest singers to tackle Carmen, and Wagnerian tenor Ludwig Suthaus, both with cigarettes. Although the score does not state that Carmen and Don José should smoke on stage, it became a custom, at least in casting photographs, to show the two protagonists with cigarettes. But were cigarettes really involved? Carmen worked with hundreds of other women in a tobacco factory making Spanish cigars. The cigar is a prominent motif in the story by Prosper Mérimée (1803–70) that served as the literary source for the libretto. The narrator of the story is a traveling French intellectual who visits Andalusia and makes the acquaintance of both Carmen and Don José in bizarre circumstances (and picks up their story from that point). He attracts the attention of the robber Don José by offering him a cigar. He himself puffs away doughtily during the narrative (the smoking being, as it were, a French attribute), and brings the condemned Don José a cigar as a last gift in prison. The narrator has the cigar to thank that he ever heard the distressing story of Carmen and Don José.

Bizet's inspiration was to have trumpets sounding the last post at the barracks during this melody. Don José speaks only when roused by his sense of duty. He protests his love clumsily and Carmen mocks him. Then follows the "Flower Song" with its passionate confession of love. The popularity of the aria often makes one forget that Carmen responds to this moving confession with the words "You don't love me!" Yet her response continues in a soaring confession, addressed not to Don José but to freedom. This forms the core of the scene, and Don José can only answer Carmen's enthusiasm with desperate sighs. This "love duet" ends like scarcely any other in operatic history: Don José decides to leave Carmen. Only with the unexpected arrival of Zuniga do events suddenly take a different course. In the closing duet (Act IV), Don José takes the initiative for the first time, for the sole reason that Carmen has nothing more to say to him. Only in hopelessness does the man find his way to express his passion in accordance with the situation. There are no more long melodies, just short phrases and desperate screams. *M 10*

As Escamillo's victory is cheered in the arena, Don José kills Carmen.   *P. H.*

7. Don José's Flower Song

La fleur que tu m'a-vais je - tée Dans ma pri - son m'é -tait res - té - e ; Flé - trie et sè - che cet - te fleur Gar-dait tou - jours sa douce o - deur.

8. Carmen's *Seguidilla*

Près des rem - parts de Sé - vil - le, Chez mon a - mi Li - las Pas - tia

9. Duet between Carmen and Don José (Act II)

La____ la_ la____ la___ la____ la_ la____ la____

10. Duet between Carmen and Don José (Act IV)

Mais, moi, Car-men, je t'aime en -co - re, Car - men, hé-las ! moi, je t'a - do - re !

Carmen, Erico Caruso as Don José, self-caricature 1910.
Don José as Bizet never imagined him. The caricature is evidence of the artistic talent and developed sense of self-mockery possessed by the "real" Caruso. Don José is anything but a corpulent toy soldier. He is naive and innocent. In the first half of the story his part is that of a lyric rather than a dramatic tenor. Was Don José an attractive man? He must have been, to have appealed to a woman like Carmen.

Opposite
Carmen, production photograph with Agnes Baltsa (Carmen) and Jon Buzea (Don José), production by Jean-Pierre Ponnelle, conductor Rolf Reuter, Opernhaus, Zürich 1981.
Carmen's Latin temperament is an important aspect of her character. How to go on portraying this temperament on stage with the same intensity night after night is a secret of the great exponents of this role, one of whom is the Greek mezzo-soprano Agnes Baltsa.

Below
Carmen, production photograph (Act IV) with Marilyn Schmiege (Carmen) and Neil Wilson (Don José), production Harry Kupfer, guest appearance by the Komische Oper of Berlin at the Vienna Festival in 1992.
Man and woman face to face, without glamour or exoticism. What is the tragedy of Don José? It is not as a man that he fails at Carmen's side, but because his previous existence, deeply rooted in social convention, governs his consciousness. To Carmen, he still smells of uniform and uniformity. She therefore opts for Escamillo, the peripatetic matador. Escamillo and Carmen are similar beings: they live dangerously, dice constantly with death, and escape it unscathed. Only once is Carmen unable to evade it – when death appears in the form of blind jealousy.

The recitative version

Neither the first performance nor even Bizet's death put an end to the evolution of *Carmen*. Its original form, a sequence of prose dialogues and musical numbers, proved unsuitable for performances outside France. Even for the first Viennese performance, Ernest Guiraud had to supplement it with recitatives. Thus, what was once an *opéra comique* took on the appearance of *grand opéra* and in this form became famous worldwide. Only in France was the original version still performed. Walter Felsenstein's legendary production at the Komische Oper in Berlin in 1949 was the first production outside France to return to the dialogue version.

Micaëla and Escamillo

Alongside the central couple, the librettist created two "rivals" in Micaëla and Escamillo. The girl symbolizes Don José's past, the matador Carmen's future. They are both acting personalities and also symbols of different codes of behavior, incorporating respectively the innocent side of Don José's character and the unalloyed sensuality he can never attain. In her almost kitsch purity, Micaëla's predecessors are found in Gounod's lyric operas. Even when she plucks up courage to save Don José, she remains a somewhat shadowy village girl. *M 11*

Escamillo is more of a figure from the world of *opéra comique*. Bizet gave him only a single *couplet*, a one-stanza song. The composer knew very well that its vigorous tune would make him popular, but he thought little of such popularity. "They want their trash, and will get it," was his contemptuous remark about the most successful number of his opera. *M 12*

The musical environment

The drama of Carmen and Don José is embedded in a vivid musical environment. Such atmospheric inserts as

11. Micaëla's Aria

Je dis   que rien ne m'é-pou-van - te, Je   dis,   hé - las ! que je ré - ponds de moi ;

Carmen, set design by Ludwig Sievert for Act I of the production by Hans Meissner, Opernhaus Frankfurt 1936 (TWS). The main square of Seville with Carmen (center) and Don José (seated left). Many great stage designers and directors are reluctant to forego the picturesque atmosphere and potential splendor of *Carmen*. Ludwig Sievert's detailed set can be regarded as the forerunner of the famous Zeffirelli production. The spectacle of a crowd scene suggests the genre of grand opera rather than of *opéra comique*, yet a naturalistic, folklore depiction is bound up with the Spanish atmosphere that pervades the score.

the chorus of street urchins, the brilliant smuggler's quintet or the great ensemble in march tempo in Act III are orientated to the conventions of *opéra comique*. Yet they should not be regarded simply as concessions to a spectacle-hungry public. They provide a background that is caught up in the fate of the individual with either indifference or pity. How this relationship is achieved is shown in the gypsy song in Act II, which is entirely in Carmen's idiom but develops into an effective ballet scene. M 13

Spanish local color

Remarkably, Carmen's gypsy song, a thoroughly "Spanish" melody, is Bizet's own invention, like nearly all the other apparently "authentic" music in the opera. Asked if he would like to make a study tour to Spain, the composer said: "That would only confuse me." He did not want to imitate exotic Spain but to imagine it, and this gave his music a captivating atmosphere. Music scholars have nevertheless found three melodies to be of Iberian origin. The most famous is found in Carmen's first song, the habanera that brilliantly depicts her thoroughly untrammeled temperament. This came from the pen of Sebastian de Yradier, and with its contrast of graceful chromaticism and radiant diatonicism ideally suits Bizet's style. M 14

Another invented song was arranged for the opening of Act IV. The only true folk song in the opera is the little song with which Carmen attempts to provoke Zuniga in Act I. M 15   *P. H.*

Carmen, photograph from the film by Francesco Rosi, with Julia Migenes (Carmen) and Placido Domingo (Don José), France/Italy 1983.
1983 was a Carmen year in film history. Carlos Saura made a dance film to flamenco music based on Mérimée's story, featuring Laura Sol and Antonio Gades; Jean-Luc Godard updated motifs from the Carmen story for his melodramatic thriller *Prénom Carmen* (*First Name Carmen*); and Francesco Rosi presented Bizet's opera with the attractive singer Julia Migenes (who began her career as a showgirl on Broadway) in the title role and Placido Domingo and Ruggero Raimondi in the principal male roles.

12. Escamillo's *Couplet*

To - ré - a - dor, en gar - - de! To - ré - a-dor! To - ré - a-dor!

13. Gypsy Song

Les tringles des sistres tin - taient A - vec un é-clat mé-tal - li - - que Et

sur cet é - tran - ge mu - si - - que Les zin - ga - rel - las se le - vaient.

14.1 Habanera (Minor Strophe)

L'a - mour est un oi - seau re - bel - le, Que nul ne peut ap - pri - voi - ser.

14.2 Habanera (Major Strophe)

L'amour est en - fant de Bo - hême, Il n'a ja - mais, ja-mais con - nu de loi.

15. Carmen's Folk Song (Act I)

Tra la la la la la la la, Cou-pe-moi, brû-le - moi, je ne te di - rai rien!

Boieldieu, François Adrien

b. 16 December 1775 in Rouen
d. 8 October 1834 in Jarcy (near Paris)

Boieldieu's first *opéra comique* was performed in Rouen in 1793. In the following years he established himself in Paris with a number of successful operas, becoming acquainted with Méhul and →Cherubini.
After holding a court post in St. Petersburg from 1803 to 1810 he returned to Paris, where he was appointed teacher of composition at the Conservatoire in 1817.

Works: Of his more than 30 operas, some of them in collaboration with Cherubini, Auber, and Hérold, only a few have remained in the repertory, for example, *Le calife de Bagdad* (*The Caliph of Baghdad*) (1800), *Le petit chaperon rouge* (*Little Red Riding Hood*) (1818), and above all *La dame blanche* (*The White Lady*) (1825).

*B*oieldieu ranked with Auber in the 1820s as the uncrowned king of opéra comique. His work shows the influence of Italian opera and the German "Singspiel".

The White Lady, illustration (detail) by Émile Vernier (1829–87), Paris.
In the scene in Act II that changes the course of events, the good-natured ghost Anna behaves "à l'écossaise." The harp belongs to Celtic culture, and is accordingly associated with the White Lady. This instrument is traditionally used in opera for mysterious apparitions.

The White Lady

La dame blanche

Opéra comique in three acts

Libretto: Eugène Scribe, after Sir Walter Scott.

Première: 10 December 1825, Paris (Opéra-Comique).

Characters: Gaveston, steward of Castle Avenel (B), Anna, his ward (S), George Brown, an English officer (T), Dikson, a tenant (T), Jenny, his wife (S), Marguerite, an old servant of the Count of Avenel (S), MacIrton, Justice of the Peace (B), Gabriel, an employee of Dikson (B); villagers (chorus).

Setting: A Scottish village, in the mid-18th century.

Synopsis

In a world ruled by force, good people have to resort to subterfuge. Anna pretends to be the castle ghost in order to help her childhood friend secure his inheritance. Now the White Lady can reside at the ghost-free castle as Countess Avenel.

Act I

Tenant Dikson celebrates the birth of a son, but the godfather is unable to attend. Soldier George steps in, and Dikson grants him right of hospitality.

Dikson owes his happiness to a ghost that haunts Castle Avenel, the so-called White Lady, whose commands he need only obey. This evening she has summoned him to the castle, because the estate is to be auctioned the following day. George goes to the castle instead of the apprehensive Dikson.

Act II

The castle steward, Gaveston, has brought the estate to the brink of ruin, so as to be able to acquire it himself. He allows George to stay at the castle only reluctantly. Gaveston's poor ward Anna recognizes the soldier as a childhood friend, the abducted Julien, the son of the deceased Count Avenel. She appears to him in the night as the White Lady, and tells him that he must outbid Gaveston the following day. At the auction Gaveston outbids all the tenants, but is then outbid by George, who is in fact penniless and therefore at serious risk of imprisonment.

Act III

The villagers greet their new lord in the Hall, while Anna recalls her childhood with Julien. When Gaveston demands that George pay up, the White Lady appears and hands to the soldier the hidden treasure of the Avenels and a document certifying his identity as Count Julien Avenel. Gaveston unveils the ghost, to find his own ward. Count Julien makes Anna his countess.   *S. N.*

The White Lady, Henriette Sontag as Anna, Vienna 1826.
In the 19th century, *The White Lady* was a great success. Within a few months of the Paris première it had been taken up by numerous other European opera houses. The celebrated German singer Henriette Sontag (1806–54) was fond of the title part. She was a notable performer in both dramatic and coloratura roles, being equally at home in the German and Italian repertories. Her début was in Boieldieu's opera *Jean de Paris* in Vienna in 1822. She sang the title role in the première of Weber's →*Euryanthe*, and the soprano solo in the first performance of Beethoven's Symphony no. 9.

Scotland, a romantic place

The land of warring clans and haunted castles, Scotland became fashionable in the early nineteenth century through the novels of Sir Walter Scott. With their dramatic effects and fascinating local color, his stories captivated composers. Operas based more or less closely on Scott's novels appeared on the stages of Europe with remarkable frequency. First off the mark, always with an eye for the coming fashion, was Rossini, with *La donna del lago* (*The Lady of the Lake*) of 1819. He was followed by his younger Italian colleague Donizetti, with →*Lucia di Lammermoor* and →*The Puritans*, both in 1835. The trend was also seen in France, with Auber's *Leicester* (1823) and Boieldieu's *The White Lady* (1825). That the story of *The White Lady* takes place in Scotland is only noticeable now and then, an example being the Scottish "national anthem" which reminds George of his lost homeland (Act III). Boieldieu took the tune from a Scottish ballad. M 1

An auction on the operatic stage

In *opéra comique*, musical numbers are linked by prose dialogues. Boieldieu adhered to the tradition, but also composed dramatic recitatives. The tension is increased in the auction scene that forms the finale of Act II. This is a real rarity as an operatic scene, and would reappear in Stravinsky's late opera →*The Rake's Progress*. Hesitation and resolution, underhandedness and courage, despair and triumph – all these elements are dramatically and intricately interwoven.   P. H.

1. Scottish "National Anthem"

Chan - tez, chan - tez, joy - eux mé - nes - trel,

2. Anna's Aria

Je vous revois, je vous revois, sé - jour de mon en - fan - ce!

3. George's Cavatina

Viens, gen - til - le da - me, viens, gen - til - le da - me,

Above
The White Lady, production photograph with Sandra Zeltzer (Jenny) and Steven Cole (Dikson), production Jean-Louis Pichon, costumes Frédéric Pineau, Opéra-Comique, Paris 1999.
At the beginning of the opera, Jenny and Dikson celebrate the birth of a son.

Left
The White Lady, production photograph with Jaïl Azzaretti (Anna) and Gregory Kunde (George), production Jean-Louis Pichon, costumes Frédéric Pineau, Opéra-Comique, Paris 1999.
The protagonists are not folk characters, but rather the usual uncomplicated figures of *opéra comique*. This is particularly true of Anna, who as a proper heroine puts all the others in the shade. Her aria (beginning of Act III) anticipates Elisabeth's hall aria in Wagner's →*Tannhäuser*. M 2
George would appear to be cast in the mold of the thoughtless soldier, but in his cavatina (Act II) the qualities of a sensitive young man shine through. M 3

An unfinished masterpiece

Borodin worked on the opera, with a number of interruptions, from 1869 to his death in 1887. Even so, *Prince Igor* remained unfinished, Borodin having completed only a quarter of the orchestration. After his death, Rimsky-Korsakov and Glazunov completed the score from sketches, and it is their version that is performed throughout the world. The Soviet Russian musicologist Pavel Lamm planned to publish a more authentic version in 1947, incorporating music composed by Borodin that had not been used by Rimsky-Korsakov and Glazunov, and restoring the original order of the scenes. The new version was never

published. In 1974, composer Yury Fortunatov and music historian Yevgeni Levashov revisited Lamm's research and produced a version for performance in Vilnius, Lithuania, based on Lamm's research. It was performed again at the Deutsche Staatsoper in Berlin and published there in 1978. In 1993, a new improved version orchestrated by Yury Falik was performed at the Mariinsky Theater in Leningrad (St. Petersburg). *M.P.*

Borodin, Alexander Porfir'yevich

b. 12 November 1833 in St. Petersburg
d. 27 February 1887 in St. Petersburg

Borodin was the illegitimate son of a Tartar prince and a burgher's daughter from St. Petersburg. He received a sound education, learning foreign languages and music (cello, piano, and flute), and later studied at the Medico-Surgical Academy in St. Petersburg, graduating as an MD in 1858. He also studied chemistry (in Heidelberg and elsewhere), and was appointed to a chair in chemistry in St. Petersburg, where his chemical discoveries made him an authority of international renown. He was actively committed to social questions, advocating among other things the emancipation of women in Russia. Throughout his life composing remained a secondary occupation. He belonged to the group of composers known as "The Russian Five" or "The Mighty Handful," champions of a specifically Russian style of music. The group also included Balakirev, Cui, →Musorgsky, and →Rimsky-Korsakov. His compositions began to be popular in western Europe from 1880. He was also a friend of Franz Liszt.

Works: The opera *Knyaz' Igor'* (*Prince Igor*) (1869–87, incomplete/FP 1890); two symphonies (a third unfinished), the symphonic poem *In the Steppes of Central Asia*, two string quartets, chamber music, songs.

*B*orodin was a self-taught composer of genius. His music combines national Russian and exotic oriental stylistic characteristics.

Left above
Prince Igor, title page of the first edition of the score, 1880.

Russian heroic opera or musical heroic epic?

Borodin's grandiose torso cannot be categorized according to Western operatic genres. In 1869 he was introduced to the subject of Prince Igor by Vladimir Stasov, a leading critic and aesthete, who drew up a scenario consisting of narrative episodes, descriptions of landscape, and lyric reflections. Borodin himself wrote the libretto, after careful study of the historical and literary sources. He did not produce a complete libretto – a fact that later hampered attempts to create a final version of the opera – but worked up music and words simultaneously. During the years in which he worked on the opera, he gradually moved further away from Stasov's historical drama ideal and closer to the epic.

Far left
Prince Igor, photograph from the production by Harry Kupfer, Det Kongelige Teater, Copenhagen 1976.
Borodin's *Prince Igor* was classified by music scholars as an old Russian heroic epic, and as such eked out a mean existence on the world's stages. That changed only when producers stopped emphasizing exotic display at the expense of the inner essence of the work. Among the first to do so were Harry Kupfer with his production in Copenhagen and Christian Pöppelreiter a decade later at the Staatsoper in Berlin. Whereas Kupfer hoped for a reconciliation of the enemies – in his version, the opera ends with the marriage of Vladimir and Konchakovna – Pöppelreiter focused on irreconcilable power politics.

Left
Prince Igor, production photograph with Therese Waldner as Yaroslavna, production Günter Könemann, sets Csaba Antal, Badisches Staatstheater, Karlsruhe 1995.
Russian roles are no longer reserved for Slav singers. International opera houses are including an increasing number of new productions and musical interpretations of Russian national operas in their repertories.

Prince Igor

Knyaz' Igor'

Opera in a prologue and four acts

Libretto: Alexander Borodin, after the anonymous Russian epic *Slovo o polku Igoreve* (*The Lay of the Host of Igor*).

Première: 4 November 1890, St. Petersburg (Mariinsky Theater).

Characters: Igor Svyatoslavich, Prince of Novgorod-Seversk (Bar), Yaroslavna, his second wife (S), Vladimir Igorevich, Igor's son from his first marriage (T), Vladimir Yaroslavich, Prince Galitsky, brother of Yaroslavna (B), Konchak, Polovtsian khan (B), Konchakovna, Konchak's daughter (A), Ovlur, a baptized Polovtsian (T), Skula and Yeroshka, gudok players (B, T), Yaroslavna's Nurse (S), a Polovtsian Girl (S); Gzak, Polovtsian Khan (silent); Russian princes and princesses, boyars and boyarïnyas, elders, Russian warriors, girls, crowd, Polovtsian khans, Russian prisoners, Polovtsian guards (chorus); Polovtsian girls, slaves, Polovtsian warriors (ballet).

Setting: The town of Putivl' and the Polovtsian encampment, 1185.

Synopsis (version by Nicolai Rimsky-Korsakov and Alexander Glazunov)

Prologue

Prince Igor's camp. The prince intends to risk a campaign against the Polovtsians. The sun darkens, but Igor ignores this bad omen. He bids farewell to his wife Yaroslavna, entrusting his empire to Prince Galitsky, his wife's brother. Amid paeans of praise, he and his men set off to war. Only the two gudok (rebec) players Skula and Yeroshka fear death more than the disgrace of cowardice. They hide, remaining in safety in the town of Putivl'.

Act I

Prince Galitsky holds festivities in order to win the people's favor and thereby usurp Igor's throne. Skula and Yeroshka already treat him as the new ruler. Girls beg the lecher to release an abducted friend, but Galitsky mocks them and chases them away. Yaroslavna is worried about Igor, having received no news from him. The girls beg Yaroslavna to protect them from Galitsky. Galitsky drives them out, dismisses his angry sister, and imagines himself already on Igor's throne. Boyars bring Yaroslavna the sad news that the Russian army has been defeated and Igor taken prisoner.

Act II

In the Polovtsian camp, the cool of evening brings the girls out to sing and dance. The khan's daughter

Prince Igor, Igor and Khan Konchak, costume designs by Konstantin A. Korovin, 1909.

Konchakovna and Igor's son Vladimir exchange vows of love. Igor paces restlessly up and down. He regrets the rash campaign and yearns for his beloved wife. Yaroslavna has sent Ovlur to Igor. He is a baptized Polovtsian living in Putivl'. Ovlur is supposed to help the prince escape, but Igor does not want to act dishonorably, since Khan Konchak is treating him like a guest. Konchak offers the Russian the hand of friendship. United, they would be unbeatable; they could use their combined force to conquer nations. Igor rejects the proposal. To cheer the depressed prince and win him over to his plan, the khan summons his most beautiful girls. They caress the downcast prince, while Polovtsian men display their military prowess.

Act III

The hordes of the cruel Khan Gzak return from a campaign of plunder in Russian territory. Igor resolves to escape. Vladimir hesitates to follow his father. Konchakovna begs him to stay or to take her with him. Igor leaves without his son. Konchak spares Vladimir, hoping to catch the old falcon with the young one.

Act IV

Yaroslavna mourns for Igor. But the prince's escape has been successful. Ignorant of this, Skula and Yeroshka sing a satirical song about Igor. Then they notice Igor's standard flying over Putivl'. They ring the bells, summon the populace, and proclaim Igor's return. "The sun stands high in the heavens – Prince Igor is in Russian country again."   S. N.

A political message

Though more than 800 studies have been written about the legend of Igor's campaign over two centuries, it has not yet been agreed when the legend arose, when and in what part of Russia the unknown author lived and what his origins were, why he immortalized the unwarranted campaign of an unimportant prince (Igor was the ruler of a tiny principality), and why the Polovtsians – and not the Tartars, who ruled Russia for 200 years – constitute the enemy. In the 19th century, the legend of Igor was still highly topical. It was seen as a patriotic call to the Russian aristocracy to unite against the common enemy, which had to be sought within the Russian empire, where the powerful showed themselves unworthy of patriotic ideals. Russia could only progress, according to the nationalists, to whom Borodin belonged, with a tsarist house intellectually revived by political reforms, an enlightened aristocracy, and a (still non-existent) bourgeoisie. In *Prince Igor*, the question "What for?" is much more important than the question "Against what?" This was why Borodin opted for the Igor legend in his search for a national operatic theme.

Historical facts

The Polovtsians, a nomadic Turkic-speaking people, migrated from Siberia in the eleventh century to the Volga, where they first clashed with Russian armies. Konchak was one of their most famous military leaders. In the late twelfth and early thirteenth centuries the Polovtsians pushed forward still further under pressure from the Tartars. Part of them settled in the Carpathian Basin.

The eclipse of the sun reported in *The Lay of the Host of Igor* did indeed take place on 1 May 1185, at 3.25 p.m. In 1185, Prince Igor advanced on the Polovtsians. He was initially an ally of the Polovtsians and married the Khan Konchak's daughter. In the first battle he was victorious, but was defeated in the second on the River Kayala, where his army was destroyed. He himself fled to the Russian Grand Prince in Kiev.

Russia and the Orient

The musical and dramatic uniqueness of Borodin's opera lies in the confrontation of two fundamentally different worlds – old Russia and the exotic Orient. In his depiction of Russian atmosphere, Borodin's dose of archaism is far stronger than Glinka's of 30 to 40 years earlier. Borodin composed in the spirit of old folk songs, and used the modes and the characteristic melodic features of old Russian church music. M1

Borodin drew not only on folk music and church music but also on urban romances of the nineteenth century. The romance style is bound up with the subject of love. It characterizes above all the character of Vladimir, but also recurs in a thrilling melody sung by Igor (aria, Act II) and one sung by Yaroslavna (lament, Act IV). M2

The music of the Polovtsians, like all Borodin's oriental music, is magical, at times conveying heady

Prince Igor, set design by Heinz Grete, production Richard Meyer-Waldens, conductor Richard Lert, Nationaltheater, Mannheim 1925 (TWS).
If there were a genre of "Russian grand opera," *Prince Igor* would be its most splendid example. Borodin wanted to write history in operatic form, and wove a magical musical legend from large-scale scenes depicting different peoples.

1. Chorus of Boyars

Нам, княгиня,   не впервы-е   под сте-на-ми   го - род-скими   у во-рот встре-чать вра-гов

eroticism, at others earthy barbarism. In contrast to the Russian sphere, the oriental melodies make much use of melismatic writing. *M 3, M 4*

Borodin's interest in the Polovtsians and other oriental people was awakened on the occasion of a scientific conference in 1874 in Kazan, the "gateway" to the East. The University of Kazan contained the greatest research center for oriental studies. Borodin's democratic views are surely reflected in his depiction of the "barbarian" Polovtsians as being in no sense more primitive or less honorable than the Russians. In his way, Khan Konchak is as great a soul as Igor, and Konchakovna is as attractive a female figure as Yaroslavna. Polovtsians and Russians are of equal rank, only endowed with different temperaments and customs. *M. P.*

Prince Igor, production photograph, Mariinsky Theater, St. Petersburg 1993. Under Valery Gergiev, probably the most famous conductor of the post-Gorbachov era, the neglected Mariinsky Theater in St. Petersburg has reestablished its reputation. The musical standard is high, the stage sets traditional.

2. Igor's Aria

Ты од - на, го - луб-ка ла - да, ты од - на ви - нить не станешь,

серд-цем чут-ким всё пой-мёшь ты, всё ты мне про-стишь.

3. Polovtsian dance (female melody)

4. Polovtsian dance (male melody)

Prince Igor, Fyodor Ivanovich Shalyapin as Prince Galitsky, 1910 (left), and as Khan Konchak, 1930 (right).
The celebrated Russian bass Shalyapin (1873–1938) was one of the greatest character players of 20th-century opera. From Moscow to New York his appearances were a sensational success, whether on the operatic stage or concert platform, and his fairy-tale fees kept pace with his reputation. He was born in a suburb of Kazan, in conditions of dire poverty. He did not become famous overnight, but had to fight hard and with great determination for recognition on the stage, which was always his great love. His dark, Slavic voice was without compare. He often sang very quietly, with perfect diction. His facial features were soft and good-humored, suitable for the great variety of masks with which he conjured his dramatic characters into credible existence. Shalyapin's unique interpretations of the bass roles of →Glinka, →Rimsky-Korsakov, →Musorgsky, and Borodin gave American and European operagoers their first experience of Russian opera, which had been terra incognita until the turn of the century.

Britten, Benjamin

b. 22 November 1913 in Lowestoft
d. 4 December 1976 in Aldeburgh

Britten came into contact with music at a very early age through his mother, who was an amateur singer. He studied under Frank Bridge, to whom he later paid tribute in the orchestral piece *Variations on a Theme of Frank Bridge* (1937). Through Bridge he got to know the compositions of Béla Bartók and the Second Viennese School (→Schoenberg, →Berg, and Webern). In the early 1930s, Britten studied at the Royal College of Music in London, where he developed not only his compositional skills but also his extraordinary ability as a pianist. It was during this period that he produced his op. 1, a Sinfonietta (1932). His acquaintance with →Berg's →*Wozzeck* (through a radio broadcast in 1934) was of decisive importance to him. In the later 1930s, he dedicated himself to film music and composed his first vocal works. In 1939, he and his lifelong companion the singer Peter Pears, an inspiring artistic personality, emigrated to the USA, but returned permanently two years later. During the war years, Britten composed several important works, including the opera *Peter Grimes* (1944) for Sadler's Wells Theatre. Its rapturous reception in 1945 made Britten England's leading musical dramatist. In the years that followed, further operas appeared in regular succession. From 1947, Britten composed mainly for the English Opera Group, from which the Aldeburgh Festival, which he and Pears founded in 1948, also benefited. Many of his works were first performed in Aldeburgh, where he lived until his death. In the 1960s he and Pears cultivated close personal friendships with Soviet Russian artists such as the cellist Mstislav Rostropovich, the pianist Sviatoslav Richter, and the composer →Dmitry Shostakovich. Some now legendary recordings of songs and chamber music followed. In 1973, following a heart operation, Britten had a stroke, which darkened the last years of his life. He had to give up his work as a performer, but remained active as a composer until his death.

Works: Operas: *Paul Bunyan* (1941), *Peter Grimes* (1945), *The Rape of Lucretia* (1946), *Albert Herring* (1947), *The Beggar's Opera* (adaptation, 1948), *The Little Sweep* (an independent part of the children's opera *Let's Make an Opera*, 1949), *Billy Budd* (1951, rev. 1960), *Gloriana* (1953), *The Turn of the Screw* (1954), *A Midsummer Night's Dream* (1960), three church parables: *Curlew River* (1964), *The Burning Fiery Furnace* (1966), and *The Prodigal Son* (1968), *Owen Wingrave* (television opera, 1970–71), *Death in Venice* (1973); orchestral and choral works, chamber music, songs, theater and film music, a ballet (*The Prince of the Pagodas*, 1956–57).

*B*ritten ranks with Henry Purcell as one of the foremost composers in the history of English music. His music is highly suggestive, not avant-garde, and always in the service of drama and poetry.

Above right
Peter Grimes, production photograph (Act I, Scene 2) with Janice Watson (Ellen Orford) and Iain Goosey (John), production Peter Stein, conductor Carlo Rizzi, New Theatre, Cardiff 1999.

Right
Peter Grimes, photograph from the original production with Peter Pears as Peter Grimes, production Eric Crozier, costumes Kenneth Green, conductor Reginald Goodall, Sadler's Wells Theater, London 1945.
The role of Grimes was tailored for the great English tenor Peter Pears (1910–86), as were all the great tenor roles in Britten's operas. Pears had great influence on the creative work of his lifelong companion, and the two of them founded the Aldeburgh Festival together. Pears was knighted in 1978.

The rebirth of English opera

Peter Grimes was the first English opera since Purcell's →*Dido and Aeneas* to find a place in the international repertory. As a composer, Britten had no English tradition to follow. It was up to him to create modern English opera from his own resources. Although strongly influenced by →Alban Berg's →*Wozzeck*, particularly in the choice of an unheroic title character, Britten adhered to traditional operatic structures in the arrangement of his material. Musical numbers – arias, ensembles, and choruses – alternate with recitatives that carry the plot forwards. The musical language is characterized by the combination of traditional and modern stylistic elements, its transparency deriving from the absolute dominance of melody. Though the two principal figures are Grimes and Ellen, the subject matter of the opera is psychological terror as directed against an oddball. In contrast to the verse narrative by George Crabbe on which the libretto is based, the opera presents Grimes's behavior as illogical. He behaves as if he were guilty, although he is not. Yet the music offsets the hero's failure of nerve: its expressive power and grandeur transform him into a richly contradictory character.

P. M.

Peter Grimes, production photograph with Neil Shicoff as Peter Grimes, production Christine Mielitz, conductor Mstislav Rostropovich, Wiener Staatsoper 1996. Peter Grimes is a loner, rejected by the community, a martyr above all to his own nature. Directors used to interpret his character as sadistic and obsessive and give him the external features to go with it. Today the view is different: the American tenor Neil Shicoff (b. 1949) features as a man who is aware of his mental sickness. He loves and injures at the same time. This interpretation corresponds to the highly expressive vocal part.

Peter Grimes, production photograph (Act III, Scene 2) with John Daszak as Peter Grimes, production Peter Stein, sets Stefan Mayer, conductor Carlo Rizzi, New Theatre, Cardiff 1999.
Peter Stein's production conveys the story with an intense realism that includes Ellen Orford, Captain Bulstrode, and Bob Boles among the outsiders in this fishing town.

Peter Grimes

Opera in a prologue and three acts

Libretto: Montagu Slater, after the poem *The Borough* by George Crabbe.

Première: 7 June 1945, London (Sadler's Wells Theater).

Characters: Peter Grimes, a fisherman (T), Boy (John), his apprentice (silent), Ellen Orford, a widow, the schoolmistress (S), Captain Balstrode, a retired merchant skipper (Bar), Auntie, landlady of "The Boar" (A), First and Second Niece, the main attractions of "The Boar" (2 S), Bob Boles, fisherman and Methodist (T), Swallow, a lawyer (B), Mrs. Sedley, a widow of a clerk at the East India Company (Ms), Rev. Horace Adams, the rector (T), Ned Keene, apothecary and quack (Bar), Dr. Thorp (Crabbe in some sources) (silent), Hobson, a carter (B); townspeople, fishermen (chorus).

Setting: The Borough, a small fishing town on the east coast of England, around 1880.

Synopsis
Prologue

The fisherman Peter Grimes has been summoned to an inquest investigating the circumstances of his apprentice's death. Even though he is cleared, the townspeople continue to regard him as a murderer. The coroner, Swallow, forbids Grimes to employ another apprentice. Ellen Orford attempts to calm the furious Grimes.

Act I
Interlude I ("Dawn")

Scene 1: Despite the court order, Grimes intends to take another boy from the orphanage as an apprentice, and is supported in this by Ellen Orford. Captain Balstrode gives Grimes a friendly word of advice, urging him to lead a normal life and accept things as they are. Grimes is not willing to do this.

Interlude II ("Storm")

Scene 2: As usual, the inhabitants of the Borough congregate in "The Boar." A storm rages outside. When Grimes comes to fetch his new apprentice, he is greeted by a shocked silence. Ellen once again goes to him, bringing the boy with her.

Act II
Interlude III ("Sunday morning on the beach")

Scene 1: Some weeks later, during the Sunday morning service, Ellen notices that the coat of Grimes's new apprentice John is torn and that the boy has bruises on his neck. She reproaches Grimes for his uncontrollable temper and his acts of violence, but is unable to stop rumors about Grimes's bullying of his latest apprentice. At the end of the service, the men set out for Grimes's hut, to see how he is treating the boy.

Interlude IV: Passacaglia

Scene 2: In Grimes's hut near the cliff edge. Grimes warmheartedly sings a song to the boy, but at the same time accuses him of telling Ellen lies. When he notices the crowd approaching, he opens the door and pushes the boy out. The boy falls over the cliff and dies. The rector and Swallow find an empty, tidy hut, and go away relieved. Only Balstrode looks over the cliff and sees what has really happened.

Act III
Interlude V ("Moonlight")

Scene 1: Some days later. Rumors are flying that Grimes has killed his latest apprentice. Ellen and Balstrode want to help Peter. The outraged townspeople demand retaliation.

Interlude VI ("Fog")
Scene 2: Some hours later. (The orchestra is silent except for a foghorn – a tuba off stage – accompanied by distant sighs from the chorus.) Grimes is alone, and on the brink of madness. He calls out his name for one last time, and is answered by silence. Ellen can no longer calm him. Balstrode advises Grimes to take his boat out and sink it and himself. Rumors fly again. Someone has seen a boat sinking out at sea. Life in the Borough returns to normal. *P. M.*

Right
Peter Grimes, production photograph (Act III, Scene 2) with John Daszak as Peter Grimes, production Peter Stein, sets Stefan Mayer, conductor Carlo Rizzi, New Theatre, Cardiff 1999.
The last option: the sea. The human world pushes the outsider into nature, which takes him with total indifference.

Britten's sea

The sea in Britten's *Peter Grimes* is quite unlike Claude Debussy's gleaming watery miracle (the symphonic sketch *La mer*), or the splendidly colorful elemental force depicted by Italian composers, "il mare azzurro." This is not just for the obvious geographical reason that the sea on the east coast of England is often foggy and threatening. Decent citizens do not want anything to do with this disaster-bearing element. They reject the uncomfortable, the unclassifiable, the deviant from the norm, both in nature and in society. Being an outsider, Grimes was bound to be sacrificed sooner or later.

Above
Peter Grimes, set design by Kenneth Green for the original production, Sadler's Wells Theatre, London 1945.

Right
Peter Grimes, set design by Ruodi Barth for the production by Friedrich Schramm, conductor Ludwig Kaufmann, Staatsoper, Wiesbaden 1959/60 (TWS).
In contrast to the set of Ruodi Barth, Kenneth Green's set for the original production almost seems to portray an idyll. It was some years before 20th-century stage sets put romantic clichés behind them.

Britten's interest in George Crabbe's poem *The Borough* (1810) derived partly from the fact that Crabbe was a fellow countryman in a very specific sense: both he and Britten came from Suffolk. The action is set in Aldeburgh, where the composer later settled and where the Britten archives are still held. Britten loved his home county so much that when he emigrated to the USA he chose to live in Suffolk, Virginia, even though he had been offered a comfortable flat in downtown New York. When he read in a newspaper article on George Crabbe in 1941 that "to think of the figure of Crabbe is to think of England," he was overwhelmed by such strong feelings of homesickness that he returned permanently to England at the end of the following year. The expressive power of the music of *Peter Grimes* – especially the orchestral interludes (four of which Britten later published as an independent orchestral series entitled *Four Sea Interludes*) and the choral numbers – derives from Britten's feeling for what is English.   *P. M.*

Peter Grimes, production photograph with René Kollo as Peter Grimes, production Tim Albery, conductor Andrew Davis, Bayerische Staatsoper, Munich 1991.
Peter Grimes is often sung by leading Wagnerian tenors such as René Kollo (born 1937), who has sung all the Wagnerian roles at Bayreuth. Although the role of Grimes cannot be called heroic in the Wagnerian sense, it is so taxing that it can only be mastered by singers with considerable staying power.

The Rape of Lucretia, photograph from the first German production, Bühnen der Stadt Köln, Cologne 1948.
The tension between the sensuality and hypocrisy of the Etruscans on the one hand and the debasement of morality among the Romans on the other is a literary leitmotiv. The story, which may be traced back to Livy and Ovid, was taken up by Shakespeare in a youthful poem and further developed in *Macbeth* and *Cymbeline*. Obey's play, on which Ronald Duncan based his libretto for Britten's opera, was originally written for a French theatrical ensemble (the Compagnie des Quinze, led by Jacques Copeau). Obey quotes widely from Shakespeare, and introduced male and female choruses, represented by a man and a woman. Britten and Duncan, however, changed the nature of the chorus. While its commenting role derives from the function of the chorus in ancient Greek drama, its text is more suited to a Christian Passion. Britten's Lucretia is the female version of the innocent lamb of God.

The Rape of Lucretia

Opera in two acts

Libretto: Ronald Duncan, after the play *Le viol de Lucrèce*, by André Obey.
Première: 12 July 1946, Glyndebourne, Sussex.

Characters: Male Narrative Chorus (T), Female Narrative Chorus (S), Collatinus and Junius, Roman generals (B, Bar), Prince Tarquinius, son of the Etruscan tyrant Tarquinius Superbus (Bar), Lucretia, wife of Collatinus (A), Bianca, Lucretia's old nurse (Ms), Lucia, Lucretia's servant (S).
Setting: Roman encampment/Lucretia's house in Rome, around 500 BC.

Synopsis
Prologue
A report of Rome's misery under Tarquinius' rule.

Act I
Scene 1: An army camp outside the gates of Rome on a sultry night. Collatinus, Junius, and Tarquinius are drinking, and complaining about unfaithful women. Only Lucretia, Collatinus's wife, enjoys the reputation of utmost virtue. Tarquinius decides to bring down this paragon of virtue by seducing her.

Interlude Depiction of Tarquinius' ride to Rome

Scene 2: Lucretia sits with her nurse and servant at the spinning wheel. Tarquinius enters and asks for lodging for the night.

Act II
Scene 1: The Etruscans have wrought terrible destruction on Rome. But what is external devastation compared with the inner wasteland? The Romans still have a last bulwark against the immoral Etruscans: the virtuous Lucretia. But Tarquinius forces his way into Lucretia's bedroom. She defends herself in vain, and is overwhelmed.

Interlude Chorale on the sufferings of Christ when virtue is "beset by sin"

Scene 2: Bianca and Lucia happily sing to the new day, only to learn with horror what has happened. Lucretia demands to see her husband, and bids farewell to life. Though Collatinus declares his trust in and love for her, Lucretia feels the only way of proving her innocence is suicide. She stabs herself. The general consternation and mourning (passacaglia) culminate in a Christian promise of redemption (Epilogue).

S. N.

Chamber opera: virtue from distress

The work is Britten's first chamber opera, written for eight vocal soloists and 13 instrumentalists. He wrote the title role for Kathleen Ferrier, an "angel" with an extraordinary contralto voice. As there were few operatic ensembles in England at the time (1946), Britten conceived his work for a small touring group. The group (Glyndebourne English Opera Company) was directed by the young Rudolf Bing, who later became successful as a director at the Metropolitan Opera in New York. The company later evolved into the English Opera Group, for whom Britten became resident composer, and which gave the first performances of most of Britten's works.

P. M.

Right
The Rape of Lucretia, photograph from the original production, with Kathleen Ferrier (Lucretia), Anna Pollak, and Margaret Ritchie, production Eric Crozier, sets and costumes John Piper, conductor Ernest Ansermet, English Opera Group, Glyndebourne 1946.
Kathleen Ferrier (1912–53), who used her contralto voice like a perfect instrument, began her artistic career as a singer of lieder. Lucretia was her operatic début, but by that stage she had only a few years to live. Besides her concert activities, only a few sublime static roles are associated with her, above all Gluck's Orpheus (→*Orpheus and Eurydice*). Undoubtedly Ferrier's character and her incomparable voice were a major inspiration for Britten's purest female figure (a rarity in his operatic oeuvre).

Left
The Rape of Lucretia, production photograph with Laureen Livingstone (Lucia) and Judith Pierce (Bianca), production Anthony Besch, sets John Stoddart, Scottish Opera, Glasgow 1976.
A splendid morning follows the night of crime and the rape of the virtuous Lucretia. Lucia and Bianca arrange flowers in a scene that precedes the appearance on stage of the humiliated Lucretia. The flower scene has dramatic and symbolic significance. The contrast between this scene and the scene that follows is eloquently described by Britten's music.

Albert Herring

Comic opera in three acts

Libretto: Eric John Crozier, after the short story *Le rosier de Madame Husson* by Guy de Maupassant.
Première: 20 June 1947, Glyndebourne, Sussex.

Characters: Lady Billows, an elderly, impatient and demanding autocrat (S), Florence Pike, her house-keeper (A), Miss Wordsworth, head teacher at the church school (S), Mr. Gedge, the vicar (Bar), Mr. Upfold, the mayor of Loxford (T), Superintendent Budd, a policeman (B), Sid, a butcher's boy (Bar), Albert Herring, an assistant in the greengrocer's (T), Nancy Waters, the baker's daughter (Ms), Mrs. Herring, Albert's mother (Ms), Emmy, Siss and Harry, pupils from Loxford school (2 S, boy soprano or S).
Setting: Loxford, a small market town in East Suffolk, April and May 1900.

Albert Herring, costume designs for Miss Wordsworth and Albert Herring by Josef Fenneker for the production by Werner Kelch, Städtische Oper, Berlin 1950 (TWS). Britten's musical and theatrical parody of English social habits and characters enjoys international popularity: Miss Wordsworth, the headteacher, and the as yet virtuous Albert Herring.

Synopsis
Act I

Scene 1: Lady Billows's breakfast room. A committee of local dignitaries is holding a meeting to choose a May Queen. Unfortunately there is not a single virtuous girl in Loxford that can satisfy the demanding Lady Billows. As a possible solution Superintendent Budd proposes Albert Herring, a chaste, virtuous lad who is completely under his mother's thumb.

Scene 2: Mrs. Herring's greengrocery. Sid the butcher's boy taunts the greengrocer's boy Albert. He boasts about the pleasures of the chase and flirts with Nancy. The committee announces that Albert has been elected May King. When Albert tries to resist, his mother intervenes: Lady Billows is offering a prize of 25 sovereigns.

Act II
Scene 1: The vicarage garden. Miss Wordsworth is rehearsing a welcome song for the May King. Sid spikes the lemonade set out for Albert with a large shot of rum. Miss Wordsworth delivers a patriotic speech, but gets her pages in a muddle and the phrases come out in the wrong order. (Here Britten parodies a series of well-known patriotic songs.) Albert is too shy to correct her, but like a good lad drinks his lemonade. (The orchestra comments with a fantasia on Wagner's Tristan chord, →*Tristan and*

Albert Herring, set design by Rolf Christiansen for the production by Reinhard Lehmann, conductor Heinz Dressel, Städtische Bühnen, Freiburg im Breisgau 1951/52 (TWS). Musically speaking, the chamber opera *Albert Herring* is as variegated and as irregular as the houses of an old English market town. The story unfolds in the hands of 13 singers (including the children) and only 12 instruments. Britten's technical virtuosity, his skill in assembling very diverse singing ensembles, and his wicked sense of parody are abundantly evident here. In Albert's "love potion" he quotes Wagner's Tristan (→ *Tristan and Isolde*), and when Superintendent Budd talks of rape, the Lucretia motif from Britten's earlier chamber opera (→ *The Rape of Lucretia*) is heard in the orchestra. Britten's treatment of recitative is similarly witty. The various characters often sing at the same time, each speaking in his or her own style. The result is recitative ensembles that sparkle.

Isolde, a symbol of a magic potion that dissolves common sense and inhibitions.)

Scene 2: In Mrs. Herring's greengrocery. Albert returns tipsily to the shop, having decided at last to rebel against his mother. When Sid and Nancy drop by, Albert also leaves the shop. Mrs. Herring finds the shop empty.

Act III

Scene 1: The shop, the following afternoon. Everyone is worried about Albert. When someone brings in a wreath of orange-blossom that has been crushed by a cart, Mrs. Herring even thinks her son is dead. Then Albert appears and describes the joys of drinking the night away. The local dignitaries disavow their protégé. Only Sid and Nancy celebrate Albert's liberation.   P. M.

A Midsummer Night's Dream, poster, Komische Oper, Berlin 1961. Walter Felsenstein's 1961 production at the Komische Oper in Berlin made Britten's opera internationally famous. (The American première took place in San Francisco in the same year.) Shakespeare's original play was, of course, enlivened by musical performances, the text containing references to songs, fanfares, and other musical effects. During the Restoration period, several of Shakespeare's plays were staged with song and dance interludes and sometimes with entire masques. In 1692 *A Midsummer Night's Dream* appeared in a version entitled *The Fairy Queen*, with music for its masques provided by Henry Purcell. Decades later, Shakespeare's sparkling comedy featured on the program as a sort of Baroque musical. Britten's decision to write an opera based on it was thus not without precedent.

A Midsummer Night's Dream

Opera in three acts

Libretto: Benjamin Britten and Peter Pears, after William Shakespeare.

Première: 11 June 1960, Aldeburgh, Suffolk (Jubilee Hall).

Characters: Oberon, King of the Fairies (counterT or A), Tytania/Titania, Queen of the Fairies (coloratura S), Puck (spoken), Theseus, Duke of Athens (B), Hippolyta, betrothed to Theseus (A), Lysander and Demetrius, both in love with Hermia (T, Bar), Hermia, in love with Lysander (Ms), Helena, in love with Demetrius (S), Bottom, a weaver (Bbar), Quince, a carpenter (B), Flute, a bellows mender (T), Snug, a joiner (B), Snout, a tinker (T), Starveling, a tailor (Bar), Cobweb, Peaseblossom, Mustardseed, Moth, fairies (4 boy S); chorus of fairies (S or boy S).

Setting: A wood near Athens and Theseus' palace, mythological times.

Synopsis

Act I

A wood near Athens, deep twilight. The fairy realm is in uproar because the royal couple have quarreled. Titania refuses to hand over to Oberon a nobly born Indian boy. To punish her, Oberon orders Puck to gather a magic herb, the juice of which, sprinkled on someone's eyelids, will make that person fall passionately in love with the first creature they see. Athenian craftsmen meet in the wood to rehearse a play that they have written themselves and which they intend to perform as a wedding gift for Duke Theseus. Hermia has fled from Athens with Lysander, to avoid having to marry Demetrius. Demetrius is on her trail, however, followed by Helena, who is in love with Demetrius. Oberon orders Puck to sprinkle Demetrius' eyes with the juice, to make him love Helena. But Puck mistakes Lysander for Demetrius and bewitches him. Lysander sees Helena, falls in love with her, and abandons Hermia. The fairies make a bed for Titania. Oberon himself sprinkles the potion on the eyelids of his obstreperous wife.

Act II

The wood at night. Not far from the camp of the sleeping Titania, the craftsmen are rehearsing their piece. Annoyed by the simple fellows, Puck makes fun of them and places an ass's head on the weaver Bottom. The others flee in alarm. Titania awakes, and her gaze falls on the ass-headed weaver. She makes him her lover. Oberon discovers the confusion Puck has sown among the young Athenians. He intervenes to put things right, sprinkling Demetrius' eyes with the juice so that he falls in love with Helena. Lysander and Demetrius quarrel over the once-spurned Helena, and turn their backs on Hermia, whom they formerly yearned after. Oberon now commands Puck to chase the four lovers through the wood until they are exhausted.

Act III

The wood, early morning. Oberon frees Titania from the spell. The weaver recovers his human shape and is found by the craftsmen. The couples think the events of the night were a dream, and resume their proper pairings – Lysander and Hermia, Demetrius and Helena. In Theseus' palace, the wedding of Theseus and Hippolyta takes place. The duke gives his permission for the weddings of the escaped lovers. The craftsmen are permitted to perform their play. The happily reconciled royal fairies congratulate the ducal couple of Athens.   *S. N.*

KOMISCHE OPER

EIN SOMMERNACHTSTRAUM

VON BENJAMIN BRITTEN

A Midsummer Night's Dream, production photograph with Rudolf Asmus (Bottom) and Ella Lee (Titania), production Walter Felsenstein, sets and costumes Rudolf Heinrich, conductor Kurt Masur, Komische Oper, Berlin 1961. Britten and Pears reduced Shakespeare's original text by half. The opera opens in Act II of the play, in the wood. The characters are arranged according to a precise sound scheme: the two pairs of lovers are cast as conventional soprano/tenor and mezzo-soprano/baritone pairings, accompanied by woodwind and strings; the fairies all sing in the upper register, with Oberon as a countertenor, Titania as a coloratura soprano, and the four fairies as boy sopranos, accompanied by harps, harpsichord, celesta, and percussion; and the craftsmen get the low notes as befits their social status, accompanied by brass and bassoon.

Music of unreality

In *A Midsummer Night's Dream*, all is achieved through tonal color. In this way, Britten creates a fairy-tale atmosphere, calls up historical (Baroque) associations, and characterizes both humans and fairies. The usual orchestral palette is supplemented by various percussion instruments, two harps, and a harpsichord. The role of Oberon was specially written for the internationally acclaimed countertenor Alfred Deller. The three groups of characters – fairies, lovers, and craftsmen – are distinguished musically. The dream world created in Act I gives way to the court of Theseus (Act II, Scene 2). A prelude, interlude, and postlude symbolize bewitched sleep (Act II), while a ritornello (Act I) portrays the wood. M 1

The themes are based on twelve-note rows, including the interlude constructed on a hunting motif, which provides the transition from wood to court in Act III. The marvelous atmosphere of the sleep music is based on four simple chords derived from a twelve-note row, which is continuously developed and varied. M 2

The night theme is borrowed from Britten's *Nocturne* for solo tenor and orchestra of 1958, which ends with a sonnet by Shakespeare. *P. M.*

1. Wood Noises

Slow and mysterious

2. Sleep Chords

A Midsummer Night's Dream, production photograph with Lillian Watson (Titania) and James Bowman (Oberon), production Christopher Renshaw, sets and costumes Robin Don, conductor Roderick Brydon, Royal Opera House, London 1986.
The choice of a countertenor for Oberon, the king of the fairies, a supernatural being who is neither man nor woman, is unique, adding a touch of the Baroque to the piece. The first Oberon was Alfred Deller. Puck does not sing, but is a boy acrobat.

Above left
Billy Budd, production photograph (Act II) from the original production by John Cranco, sets and costumes John Piper, conductor Benjamin Britten, Royal Opera House, London 1951.
Britten himself directed the première, with Peter Pears in the role of Captain Vere and Billy sung by Theodor Uppman. The work was well received in London, though its roots lie in the Slavonic rather than the English operatic tradition, its spiritual predecessors being Janáček's →*Kát'a Kabanová* and Shostakovich's →*Lady Macbeth of the Mtsensk District.*

Below
Billy Budd, Theodor Uppman (Billy Budd) and Peter Pears (Captain Vere) in the original production, conductor Benjamin Britten, Royal Opera House, London 1951.
At the core of the opera is the struggle between the forces of good and evil, embodied by Billy Budd and Claggart, respectively. But the main character is Captain Vere. Neither noble nor evil himself, he is exposed to the current of passions and thus becomes a weapon for use by either force. Only belated reflection brings him to his senses.

Billy Budd

Opera in four acts (1951), revised in two acts (1960)

Libretto: E.M. Forster and Eric Crozier, after the story by Hermann Melville.
Première: 1 December 1951, London.

Characters: Billy Budd, able seaman (Bar), Edward Fairfax Vere, captain of HMS *Indomitable* (T), John Claggart, master-at-arms (B), Mr. Redburn, first lieutenant (B), Mr. Flint, navigation officer (Bar), Lieutenant Ratcliffe (B), Red Whiskers, a press-ganged seaman (T), Dansker, an old seaman (B), Donald, a sailor (Bar), Novice (T), Novice's Friend (Bar), Squeak, a ship's corporal (T), Bosun (Bar), First and Second Mates (2 Bar), Maintop (T), Arthur Jones, press-ganged seaman (Bar), Four Midshipmen (boys' voices), Cabin Boy (spoken); officers, seamen, powder monkeys, drummers, marines (chorus).
Setting: On board HMS *Indomitable*, during the French Wars of 1797.

Synopsis (four-act version)
Prologue

Old Captain Vere reflects on his life and his search for spiritual peace. Why did he side with evil during an incident in 1797?

Act I

The main deck and quarterdeck of HMS *Indomitable*. Unrest prevails among the sailors. Tension grows when two officers sentence a recruit to be lashed for a small transgression. A cutter brings on board three men press-ganged from a passing merchantman. One of them protests against being recruited by force, the second accepts his lot, while the third, Billy Budd, is curious about the job. He is made foretopman. Billy soon becomes popular with the rest of the crew. Only the master-at-arms Claggart dislikes

him, and is all too ready to spy on him at the officers' request, on the grounds of suspected mutinous tendencies.

Act II

Scene 1: Captain Vere's cabin. The captain discusses the forthcoming battle with the officers. Though he fears the "French spirit" could spread to the Royal Navy, he trusts his crew.
Scene 2: The berth deck. Billy catches Squeak rummaging in his kitbag. Rage causes Billy's only weakness to surface, his stammer. A fight breaks out, and Claggart intervenes to protect Squeak, who was acting on Claggart's orders. The master-at-arms now tries to induce the recruit to provoke Billy.

Act III

Scene 1: The main deck and quarterdeck. Dense fog prevents the engagement with the French. Claggart attempts to throw suspicion on Billy by making vague denunciations of him to the captain, who summons Billy to his cabin.
Scene 2: Captain Vere's cabin. Vere recognizes that Billy is innocent and good, and that Claggart is evil. He brings the two men face to face. Billy is so shocked by Claggart's malice that he strikes out at him and kills him. Although Vere is aware that justice has been done to Claggart, he allows the death sentence to be passed on Billy.

Act IV

A bay of the gundeck, and the main deck and quarterdeck, dawn. The sailors are ready to mutiny to help Billy. However, he has accepted his fate and suffers himself to be led out to execution.

Epilogue

Old Captain Vere finds peace by reflecting that, although he failed to save Billy's, Billy has "saved" him.

S. N.

Opposite right
Billy Budd, production photograph, production Francesca Zambello, sets Alison Chitty, conductor Robert Spano, Royal Opera House, London 1995.
Melville's novel is based on a real incident that took place aboard an American warship in 1842. By moving the events to the 18th century, Melville places his story within the context of the French Revolution. Like →*Peter Grimes*, *Billy Budd* is a "sea opera." The atmosphere of the sea – which in Zambello's production seems to wash into the hull of the ship – provides the background for this story of persecution and injustice. The lack of female parts does not prove to be a disadvantage, but in fact adds to the work's appeal. Once again, Britten shows himself to be a master of melody and of prosody.

Death in Venice, production photograph with Robert Tear as Gustav von Aschenbach, production Colin Graham, sets Tobias Hoheisel, conductor Graeme Jenkins, Glyndebourne Festival 1992.
Though at first sight the story may seem to be about an aging writer's homosexual love, at a deeper level it deals with the conflict between beauty and passion, Apollo and Dionysus. The casting of Tadzio as a dancer draws attention to his Dionysiac appeal, checked neither by language nor reason. The bundling of several characters into one role reinforces the sense of there being a single origin for all Aschenbach's temptations. As the whole story is seen through Aschenbach's eyes, the part makes enormous demands on the singer. Britten's last opera might be called a dramatic

Death in Venice

Opera in two acts

Libretto: Myfanwy Piper, after the novella *Der Tod in Venedig* (*Death in Venice*) by Thomas Mann.

Première: 16 June 1973, Snape, Suffolk (The Maltings).

Characters: Gustav von Aschenbach, a novelist (T), The Traveler, also The Elderly Fop, The Old Gondolier, The Hotel Manager, The Hotel Barber, The Leader of the Players, The Voice of Dionysus (B bar), The Voice of Apollo (counterT); young men and girls, hotel guests and waiters, gondoliers and boatmen, street vendors, touts and beggars, citizens of Venice, choir in St. Mark's, tourists, Dionysius's followers (chorus); choral soloists including a Danish woman, Russian mother, an English woman, a French girl, a strawberry-seller, a lace-seller, a newspaper-seller, a strolling player (S); a French mother, a German mother, a Russian nanny, a beggar woman (A); a hotel porter, two Americans, two gondoliers, a glass-blower, a strolling player (T); ship's steward, Lido boatman, Polish father, German father, Russian father, hotel waiter, tourist guide in Venice, restaurant waiter, gondolier, priest in St. Mark's, English clerk in the travel bureau (Bar and B); the Polish mother, her son Tadzio, his friend Jaschiu, his two sisters, his governess, other boys and girls, strolling players, beach attendants (ballet).

Setting: Munich and Venice, around 1910.

Synopsis
Act I
Scene 1: "A cemetery in Munich." The writer Aschenbach is looking for a way out of his psycho-logical and creative crisis. An unknown traveler suggests he travel south.
Scene 2: "On the Boat to Venice." One of the passengers, an old fop, catches Aschenbach's attention and arouses disgust. Aschenbach foresees disaster.
Scene 3: "The Journey to the Lido." On his way by gondola to the hotel on the Lido, Aschenbach becomes calm again, but the sight of a black gondola arouses forebodings of death.
Scene 4: "The First Evening at the Hotel." Aschenbach has a splendid view of Venice from his room. His spirits are lifted by the beauty of the city and the beauty of the Polish boy Tadzio, who is staying in the same hotel with his mother and sisters.
Scene 5: "On the Beach." Aschenbach watches Tadzio playing with other children and reflects on beauty.
Scene 6: "The Foiled Departure." Aschenbach decides to leave Venice, but he loses his luggage and is forced to stay. His initial moroseness is soon overcome by the pleasure of seeing Tadzio again.
Scene 7: "The Games of Apollo." Observing the boys' games, Aschenbach admits to himself that he loves beauty in general and the boy Tadzio in particular.

Act II
Scene 1: "The Hotel Barber's Shop." Here Aschenbach hears the rumor that cholera has broken out and visitors are leaving Venice.
Scene 2: "The Pursuit." Aschenbach secretly follows the Polish family and hopes that they will not leave Venice.
Scene 3: "The Strolling Players." Strolling players enter the hotel, but refuse to give Aschenbach information about the epidemic.
Scene 4: "The Travel Bureau." The danger of an epidemic is confirmed.
Scene 5: "The Lady of the Pearls." Aschenbach decides to warn Tadzio's mother of the epidemic, but when she appears, he remains silent: he is afraid of losing the boy.
Scene 6: "The Dream." Aschenbach has a dream: in a struggle between Apollo and Dionysus, Dionysus triumphs.
Scene 7: "The Empty Beach." Once again, Aschenbach is absorbed in his contemplation of beauty.
Scene 8: "The Hotel Barber's Shop." Aschenbach has himself rouged and his hair dyed, like the elderly fop on the boat.
Scene 9: "The Last Visit to Venice." Deluding himself into thinking the boy has encouraged him, Aschenbach follows the family into the city again. It becomes clear to him that the inclination to sensual beauty has led him to the abyss of passion.
Scene 10: "The Departure." Aschenbach learns that the family are preparing to leave Venice. In the moment of his death, he has a vision of beauty, represented by the boy Tadzio.   *P. M.*

Busoni, Ferruccio

b. 1 April 1866 in Empoli (near Florence)
d. 27 July 1924 in Berlin

Busoni created a stir even as an eight-year-old *wunderkind*. He studied in Graz, where the family settled, and traveled throughout Europe as a celebrated pianist. In 1888 he embarked on a teaching career, which took him to Helsinki, Moscow, and Boston. In 1894 he adopted Berlin as his main residence, but was active at the Vienna Conservatory in the years 1907–08 and at the Liceo Musicale in Bologna from 1913 to 1919. With the outbreak of the First World War he moved to Zürich, where he remained until he was offered a master class in composition in Berlin in 1920. Busoni was equally successful as a performer, teacher, and composer. His *Entwurf einer neuen Ästhetik der Tonkunst* (*Sketch of a New Aesthetic of Music*) of 1907 influenced many composers, not least →Arnold Schoenberg.

Works: Stage works: *Die Brautwahl* (*Choosing the Bride*) (1912, Hamburg), *Arlecchino, oder Die Fenster* (*Harlequin, or The Windows*) (1917, Zürich), *Turandot* (1917, Zürich), *Doktor Faust* (1925, Dresden); orchestral music, chamber music, vocal music, piano works, adaptations.

*B*usoni put forward interesting aesthetic ideas and cultivated a highly artificial style, with occasional ironic allusions to the language of Romantic music. Borrowings and parody distinguish his intellectual musical thought.

Above
The young Busoni c. 1874.
His full name was Ferruccio Dante Michelangiolo Benvenuto Busoni. This name became an agenda, in that as a composer Busoni felt he was strongly rooted in the tradition of European art, as confirmed by the sheet music in the photograph (Haydn, Mozart, and Beethoven). Busoni was a true European. He was born near Florence of a German mother and Italian father, and chose Berlin as his home.

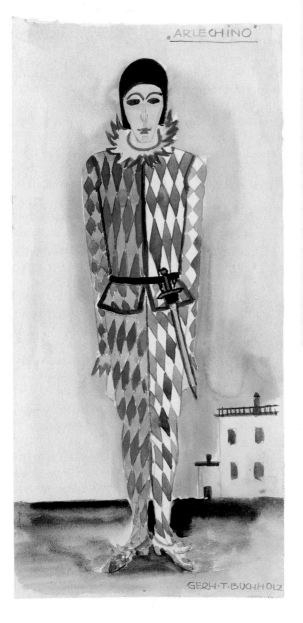

Harlequin or *The Windows*
Arlecchino, oder Die Fenster

Theatrical capriccio in one act

Libretto: Ferruccio Busoni.
Première: 11 May 1917, Zürich (Stadttheater).
Characters: Arlecchino/Harlequin (spoken), Colombina/Colombine, his wife (Ms), Leandro, a knight in love with Colombine (T), Ser Matteo del Sarto, master tailor (Bar), Annunziata, his wife (silent), Cospicuo, an abbot (Bar), Bombasto, a doctor (B); two sbirri (policeman), a carter, a donkey, people at the windows (silent).
Setting: Bergamo, in the 18th century.

Synopsis

Tailor Matteo sits outside his house, sewing and reading Dante's *Divine Comedy*. Meanwhile his wife Annunziata betrays him inside with Harlequin. Bold as brass, Harlequin jumps out of the window right in front of the tailor, and tells him the barbarians are at the city gate. Taking advantage of the tailor's confusion, Harlequin steals his key, locks him inside, and makes off. Harlequin also warns the doctor and the abbot of the supposed danger, and they hide in the tavern. Harlequin disguises himself as an officer and orders the tailor to go off and defend the town. A rendezvous between Harlequin and Annunziata is interrupted by Harlequin's wife Colombine. She takes her revenge by becoming involved with the knight Leandro. Harlequin stabs Leandro, dumps the body outside the tavern, yells "Murder!" and hides. When Leandro's body is discovered, the abbot calls for help, but none of the faces peering out of the windows come to assist. The corpse is finally placed on a donkey cart, where it joins in the farewell song with the abbot, the doctor and Colombine. Harlequin makes off with Annunziata. When the tailor returns from the war that has not taken place, Annunziata has disappeared, supposedly having gone to Vespers. Matteo resumes his reading of the *Divine Comedy*. M. S.

Harlequin, costume design for Harlequin by Gerhard T. Buchholz, Wiesbaden 1926 (TWS).
While the tailor is reading Dante, Harlequin seduces his wife (musical allusion to Mozart's →*Don Giovanni*). Busoni explored classical and at once quite pragmatic ideals in his stage works and his writings. For example, elemental situations should only be implied, in order to avoid the danger of ridiculousness. "A love duet on stage is not only indecent but also untrue ... There is no worse sight or sound than a small man and a large lady cooing at each other tunefully and holding hands," remarked Busoni in his essay *Über die Möglichkeiten der Oper* (*What You Can Do in Opera*, 1921). The self-restraint explains his choice of *commedia dell'arte* stories and Chinese fairy tales. In *Harlequin* and *Turandot* feelings always appear in quotation marks.

Turandot

Chinese fable in two acts

Libretto: Ferruccio Busoni, after the play of the same name by Carlo Gozzi.
Première: 11 May 1917, Zürich (Stadttheater).
Characters: Altoum, emperor (B), Turandot, his daughter (S), Adelma, her confidante (Ms), Calaf (T), Barach, his follower (Bar), The Queen Mother of Samarkand, a mooress (S), Truffaldino, head eunuch (T), Pantalone and Tartaglia, ministers (2 B), Eight Doctors (4 T, 4 B), A Choir Leader (Ms); the executioner, a priest, slaves, soldiers (silent); Altoum's retinue, women, eunuchs, people (chorus); wailers (girls' voices); dancers.

Setting: China, once upon a time.

Synopsis
Prince Calaf woos the lovely Princess Turandot, the daughter of the emperor of China. However, she asks her suitors three questions. Anyone who is unable to answer is beheaded. Unlike his predecessors, Calaf answers the questions correctly. Turandot is not at all pleased by the prospect of marriage, but Calaf gives her a chance. If she can guess who he is, she will be free again. Turandot's confidante Adelma had once hoped to marry Calaf. Out of revenge, she betrays Calaf's origin. But the prince does not have to keep his promise. Turandot now loves him and marries him.   *M. S.*

Turandot, set design by Friedrich Schleim, production Dr. Schüler, conductor Joseph Rosenstock, Staatstheater, Wiesbaden 1927/28 (TWS).
Busoni had already written incidental music to Gozzi's *Turandot* in 1905. Max Reinhardt's exemplary performance of *Turandot* with Busoni's incidental music in 1911 prompted the composer to return to the subject. In his opera Busoni followed Gozzi's *commedia dell'arte* of 1764 fairly closely, taking over the figures of Truffaldino, Pantalone, and Tartaglia. Apart from the subject and the Chinese background, this version has little in common with the later, far more popular →*Turandot* of Puccini (1926).

Masked opera
In 1912 Busoni saw a *commedia dell'arte* performance in Bologna and a marionette show in Rome. These were decisive experiences for both the subject and the style of his later operas. He initially considered a "marionette tragedy with music." The libretto of *Harlequin* was written before the First World War, but the composition was delayed by a tour of America, so that the score was not ready until 1916. The first performance had already been agreed with the Stadttheater in Zürich, but Busoni wanted to combine *Harlequin* with a second short opera, *Turandot*. The two works were premièred together. Performances in other European locations followed, but the works only really began to attract attention again in the 1960s and then mainly *Harlequin*. As Busoni is neither avant-garde nor conservative, his works are considered rarities. In fact, the influence of *Harlequin* on the epic theater of Kurt Weill and Bertolt Brecht is greater than is generally assumed.   *M. S.*

Doktor Faust

Opera in two preludes, an intermezzo, and three scenes

Libretto: Ferruccio Busoni.

Première: Version by Philipp Jarnach: 21 May 1925, Dresden (Sächsisches Staatstheater); version by Antony Beaumont: 2 April 1985, Bologna (Teatro Comunale).

Characters: Poet (spoken), Doktor Faust (Bar), Wagner, his famulus (Bar), Mephistopheles, first a man in black, then a monk, a herald, a court chaplain, a courier, a night watchman (T), The Duke of Parma (T), The Duchess of Parma (S), Master of Ceremonies (B), Gretchen's Brother, a soldier (Bar), A Lieutenant (T), Three Students from Kraków (T, 2 B), A Theology Student (B), A Law Student (B), A Student of Natural Philosophy (Bar), Six Students in Wittenberg (4 T, 2 Bar), The Shy One (B), Five Spirit Voices (Beelzebub, Megaeros, Asmodus, Gravis, Levis) (2 T, Bar, 2 B), Three Female Voices (S, Ms, A); apparitions, including demons, Solomon

Doktor Faust, production photograph with James Johnson as Faust, production Werner Herzog, sets and costumes Henning von Gierke, Teatro Comunale di Bologna 1985. Busoni's *Doktor Faust* never managed to establish a place in the repertory, but it had enough appeal to continue to attract directors, such as the film director Werner Herzog in 1985. Busoni finished the fair copy of the score leaving only a few gaps. Current versions include those by Busoni's pupil Philipp Jarnach (1925) and the English conductor Antony Beaumont (1984).

and the Queen of Sheba, Samson and Delilah and a black female slave, John the Baptist and Salome and an Executioner, Helen of Troy, a naked boy, a child, six soldiers, two torchbearers (silent); churchgoers, soldiers, courtiers, huntsmen, Catholic and Lutheran students, country folk (chorus).

Setting: Wittenberg and Parma, in the late Middle Ages.

Synopsis

Prelude I: Faust tries in vain to acquire magic powers. Three students from Kraków present him with a magic book, the *Clavis Astartis Magica*, which would show him how to attract superhuman energy.

Prelude II: The magic book helps Faust to requisition a servant from hell. Mephistopheles knows how to please Faust. As a sample of his ability, he destroys the creditors waiting outside the scholar's door. As the Eastertide bell rings, Faust signs a pact with the devil, who promises to give him everything he wants in return for his soul.

Intermezzo: In Wittenberg Minster, a soldier asks God to show him the man who has seduced his sister and driven her to suicide. Hearing the prayer, Faust desires the soldier to be rendered harmless. Armed men burst into the cathedral and kill the soldier, believing him to have murdered their captain.

Main play

Scene 1: The duke of Parma has invited Faust – now a famous magician – to his wedding. With Mephistopheles' help, Faust impresses the guests – especially the duchess – with his tricks. He changes day into night, and conjures up biblical characters at will. The duchess falls under Faust's spell and flees with him, while Mephistopheles reassures the duke in the guise of the court chaplain.

Scene 2: In a tavern in Wittenberg, Faust is drawn into an argument between Protestant and Catholic students. After the combatants have calmed down, they want to hear more of Faust's experiences with women. Faust recalls his love for the duchess. Mephistopheles arrives with tidings of the death of Faust's former beloved, and bringing him her "last remembrance," a stillborn child. The Devil turns the baby into a bundle of straw. He sets it alight, and the figure of an ideal woman emerges from the flames – Helen of Troy. Faust tries to grasp the figure, but it fades. He sees that life is transitory, and his actions senseless. Childhood memories are reawakened, inspiring a desire to start again. But the three students from Kraków tell him he is to die at midnight.

Scene 3: A winter's evening. Students are celebrating the appointment of Faust's former famulus Wagner as rector of the university. On the steps of his former residence, Faust discovers a beggar woman with a child, an apparition of the duchess. She hands the dead child to him. In despair, Faust hurries to the Minster, but the dead soldier blocks his way. He manages to reach the crucifix, but cannot summon up a word of prayer. Mephistopheles transforms the image of the crucifixion into a mirage of Helen. In the moment of death, Faust gives the dead child his soul, and a young man arises in its place. Mephistopheles is left with only the soulless shell of Faust.

M. S.

Doktor Faust, set design by Walter Gondolf, Hanover 1967/68 (TWS).
Faust's magic chamber of science. Who is this man? This question has preoccupied poets, composers, and literary scholars for centuries. For Busoni, an artist of "Faustian temperament," the question was particularly important. It was not the usual trio of problems that worried him (guilt, forgiveness, and redemption) but the inner driving force: human will. His protagonist declares for him: "I, Faust, an eternal will."

Busoni's masterpiece

"From childhood, one play thrilled me, where the devil has something to say" (from the prologue to the opera, 1922). Busoni described himself as a Faustian type, and was correspondingly inspired by Liszt's symphonic masterpiece, the *Faust-Symphonie*. He was already thinking of setting the Faust story in 1906, and planned to write an opera about Leonardo da Vinci, the "Italian Faust," in collaboration with Gabriele d'Annunzio. He wrote a libretto between 1910 and 1914, and continued to work on the opera until his death in 1924, putting into practice his theories about music drama: "The stage shows gestures from real life, the false is writ large upon its brow … And if you laugh at it, as at reality, it strengthens its solemnity, considered as pure play … So my play appears alive, though its puppet origins are clear" (from Busoni's prologue to the opera, 1922).

Busoni made no attempt to provide a continuous plot, but gave the music free rein. The source was not Goethe's *Faust*, but a puppet theater version of the popular play of Dr. Faustus. Existing compositions were combined with newly written music so as to bring out the music's own meaning, rather than use it merely as the servant of word and stage. Busoni hoped that "The work will generate a school, which will prove fruitful over decades" (from the epilogue to the opera, 1922). Alas, it was not to be – the opera did not give rise to any "school." But an echo of Busoni's aesthetic ideas is to be found in neo-Classicism, and in the "anti-operas" of the late twentieth century (for example, in plots by Kagel, Ligeti, Stockhausen, and others, which mix mystery plays and stage happenings).   M. S.

Doktor Faust, sketch by Karl Dannemann, Berlin, 1925 (TWS).

Doktor Faust, production photograph with Horst Hiestermann (Mephistopheles), Tomas Möwes (Faust), and Lia Frey-Rabine (the duchess of Parma), production Willy Decker, sets Wolfgang Gussmann, conductor Georg Schmöhe, Opernhaus Leipzig 1991.
Busoni is a precursor of late 20th-century operas in that *Doktor Faust* is a mixture of mystery play and stage happening.

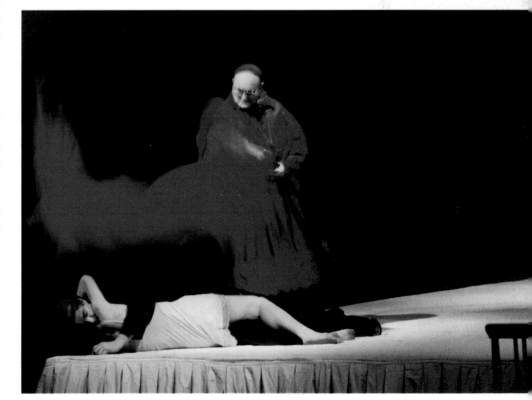

Cage, John

b. 5 September 1912 in Los Angeles
d. 12 August 1992 in New York

The son of an inventor, Cage studied arts at Pomona College, then architecture and piano in Paris. In 1931 he returned to the USA, taking composition lessons from Arnold Schoenberg in Los Angeles from 1934 to 1937. In 1941 he was appointed professor of experimental music at the Chicago School of Design by László Moholy-Nagy. In New York in 1942 he became acquainted with Max Ernst, Piet Mondrian, André Breton, Marcel Duchamp, and the dancer Merce Cunningham, with whom he arranged many of his avant-garde events. Though Cage's works from the 1930s to mid-1940s may sound odd – he emphasized silence, and favored noise-generating equipment such as the "prepared piano" and (from 1939) electro-acoustic sound generators – they still make use of preplanned structures and are still characterized by a certain subjectivism of approach. In the second half of the 1940s Cage moved to "non-intentional" art, in which things speak for themselves – a move that bore important aesthetic consequences. Disenchanted with what he saw as the excesses of civilization, which had culminated in Auschwitz and Hiroshima in the Second World War, he turned to the study of Eastern philosophy. He studied at Columbia University, firstly under the Indian Gita Sarabhai and then under the renowned Japanese Zen philosopher Daisetz T. Suzuki. Basic Zen philosophy subsequently guided both Cage's life and his art, though with an admixture of Henry Thoreau's anarchism and the ideas of the futurologists Fuller and McLuhan. Chance operations based on the use of the Chinese fortune-telling book *I Ching* became the basis for Cage's "non-intentional" art. The first sample of this came with the Concerto for Prepared Piano and Chamber Orchestra in 1951. His aesthetic principle of "nothing" and "chance" made Cage the leading stimulus and force for renewal in music in the second half of the twentieth century.

Works: Stage works: various theatrical pieces including *Theater Piece* (1960) and *Europeras 1–5* (1987–1991); orchestral works, including Concert for Piano and Orchestra (1957–58) and *Atlas Eclipticalis* (1961–62); piano works, including *Music of Changes* (1951) and *Winter Music* (1957); vocal music, including *Song Books* (1970); works for indeterminate resources, including *Variations I–VII* (1958–66); also nearly 300 compositions are listed in the catalogue of his works, including writings, paintings, installations, films.

Europera

Première: *Europera 1 & 2*: 12 December 1987, Frankfurt (Städtische Bühnen); *Europera 3 & 4*: 17 June 1990, London (Almeida Theatre); *Europera 5*: 12 April 1991, Buffalo (University of New York, Department of Music, Slee Hall).

Europera 5, production photograph with Marcia Parks, production Björn Kruse, sets and costumes Frank O. Sulzer, Staatstheater, Oldenburg 1994.
Cage's principle that nothing should relate to anything else except by chance gives the participants a truly coauthorial responsibility. They have to invent three-dimensional situations depending on the particular time and place of performance.

Cage is regarded as the most consistent modernizer of music in the second half of the 20th century. By using chance operations in expression, structure, and dramaturgy, he seeks to sweep away every appearance of subjectivity in art in a Zen sense and thus overcome the human ego's striving for dominance over animate and inanimate nature.

More than just a parody of opera?

The title is a synthesis of Europe and opera, and Cage explains: "Europeans have showered their operas on us for centuries – and now I'm giving them the whole lot back at once." *Europera 1 & 2* were commissioned by the Alte Oper in Frankfurt. The complex simultaneity of the scenes and musical events arises through the linking of up to 12 actions unfolding in parallel. (In *Europera 3, 4, & 5* Cage dispensed with the scenes altogether, making the action entirely musical.) The link follows the motto "Nothing relates to anything else except by chance," and at the same time turns this on its head: "In the universe everything is both cause and effect." The events in the plots, set pieces from current European operas, are arbitrarily arranged, as is the music from 64 operatic scores. Coordination is via monitors with digital timings. *Europera 1* lasts 90 minutes, *Europera 2* only 45. The 19 soloists have to sing their mostly well-known arias to unrelated accompaniments. At the same time a tape prepared by Cage plays 101 opera extracts. (The number 101 is an allusion to *The Thousand and One Nights*.) Parts and costumes do not match because they too are controlled by chance, like the stage sets and lighting. As in modern art, the familiar models of opera and operatic performances are treated as forms of "objets trouvés," opera stories as a reservoir of current thoughts and feelings, broken up by new, chance constellations. In *Europera 3 & 4*, lasting 70 and 30 minutes respectively, the concept is varied. In *Europa 3* six singers perform the concert events, in which six gramophones and cassette players are used and two pianists swing into action. (In *Europera 4* there are only two singers.)

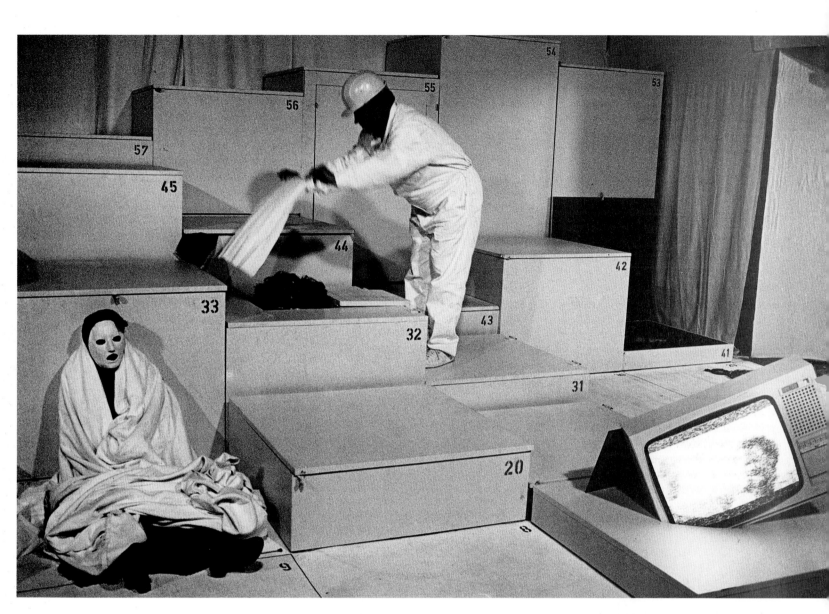

Europera 5, production photograph with Marcia Parks, production Björn Kruse, sets and costumes Frank O. Sulzer, Staatstheater, Oldenburg 1994.
A successful combination of boringly unambiguous everyday objects and ambiguous processes.

Right
Europera 1 & 2, photograph from the original production, sets Roberto Goldschlager and Andrew Culver, Opernhaus, Zürich 1991.
Familiar musical models and pictorial motifs are quoted and defamiliarized.

"Objets trouvés" from 100 operas are heard either on tape or live. Only two singers and a technician feature in *Europera 5*, which lasts 60 minutes. A pianist has to perform chance operations, an empty television screen flickers pointlessly, the bell of a gramophone sticks up without making a sound. Did Cage want to draw attention to an old culture full of subjectivity and emotion, or the mental condition of educated Europeans and their spiritual baggage?   *S. N.*

Catalani, Alfredo

b. 19 June 1854 in Lucca
d. 7 August 1893 in Milan

Born into a family of musicians, Catalani began his studies in Lucca (his teachers including Fortunato Magi, an uncle of Puccini), continued them in Paris, and completed them in Milan under Antonio Bazzini. In Milan, he became a member of the Scapigliatura literary society, and joined the ranks of the post-Verdi generation centered on Arrigo Boito and Franco Faccio. Through them, he became familiar with the music of →Richard Wagner. His graduation piece for the Conservatory, the one-act opera *La falce* (*The Scythe*) of 1875, made him famous and financially independent. The second opera, *Elda*, of 1880, was only a modest success, and was followed by *Dejanice* in 1883 in Milan, which was a fiasco. The success of his fourth opera, *Edmea*, encouraged Catalani to revise *Elda*. It was performed as *Loreley* in Turin in 1890, to general acclaim. In 1886, Catalani succeeded Ponchielli as professor of composition at the Conservatory in Milan. He died at the zenith of a brilliant career.

Works: Operas: *La falce* (*The Scythe*) (Egloga orientale,1875), *Elda* (dramma fantastico, 1880, revised as *Loreley* 1890), *Dejanice* (dramma lirico, 1883), *Edmea* (1886), *La Wally* (dramma lirico, 1892); orchestral works, piano pieces, songs.

Catalani is seen as a representative of Italian neo-Romanticism and a forerunner of "verismo." He was a friend of Toscanini.

La Wally, production photograph, Bremen 1985.

Right
La Wally, production photograph with Joanna Povracková (Wally) and Vera Ehrensperger (Walter), Theater Hof 1995.
The figure of Wally is of a woman hiding her sensitivity behind male toughness. In the original novel, she is called "Vulture Wally" by the villagers, after she rescues a vulture chick from the rocks and presents it to her father. Wally is brave and selfless, vindictive and defenseless, and falls victim to intrigue – but also instigates a murder attempt herself. The unique feature of this woman in the adaptation by Catalani and Illica is that she accepts responsibility for her fate and shoulders it without self-pity. In Italian *verismo*, it was an attitude otherwise reserved for men.

La Wally

Dramma lirico in four acts

Libretto: Luigi Illica, after the novel *Die Geyer-Wally* (*Vulture Wally*, 1875) by Wilhelmine von Hillern.
Première: 20 January 1892, Milan (Teatro alla Scala).

Characters: Stromminger, a landowner (B), Wally, his daughter (S), Afra, a tavern owner (Ms), Walter, a zither-player (S), Giuseppe Hagenbach, a huntsman from Sölden (T), Vincenzo Gellner, the factor (Bar), Messenger (B); Tyroleans, huntsmen, young people, children from Sölden and Hochstoff, strolling players (chorus, extras, ballet).
Setting: The Tyrol, around 1800.

Synopsis

Wally, the daughter of a rich landowner, secretly loves Hagenbach the huntsman, and escapes into the mountains in order not to have to marry the factor Gellner. When she returns, Hagenbach humiliates her publicly. Wally commissions Gellner to kill Hagenbach, but then changes her mind and saves Hagenbach, once again fleeing into the mountains. Only when Hagenbach comes to profess his love for her is she willing to return to the village. On the way home, Hagenbach is carried away in an avalanche. Wally throws herself after him.

Act I

The mountain village of Hochstoff in the Ötz Valley. The factor Gellner loves the daughter of the rich Stromminger and offers himself to her father as a son-in-law. But Wally loves the huntsman Hagenbach. Her father gives her a choice: either marry Gellner or leave the house. Wally retreats into the mountains.

Act II

Sölden village green. After her father's death, Wally, now rich, comes to a festival at Sölden. Gellner persuades her that the huntsman loves the owner of the tavern, Afra. Wally insults Afra. Hagenbach knows nothing of Wally's love, but feels obliged to protect Afra from Wally. He ridicules Wally, but is then struck by love for this unapproachable girl. She meanwhile promises Gellner her hand, on condition that he murder Hagenbach.

Act III

The same night, both Wally and Hagenbach have severe pangs of conscience. Having returned home, Wally wants to warn Hagenbach about Gellner, but a storm prevents her from setting out for Sölden. Hagenbach, however, is undeterred, and sets out for Hochstoff to ask Wally to forgive him for his impertinent behavior and at the same time to confess his love for her. On the way he is attacked by Gellner and thrown into a ravine. Wally saves him, still believing him to be promised to Afra. Once more she takes to the mountains.

Act IV

On the Murzoll. Wally lives alone in the mountains and wants never to return to the village. Hagenbach climbs up to her and is finally able to tell her of his love. All obstacles to their happiness seem finally to be removed, when an avalanche carries the huntsman into an abyss. Wally then throws herself after him.   S. N.

1. Wally's Farewell Aria

Eb - ben?.. Ne andrò lon - ta - na, co - me va l'e - co del-la pia cam - pa - na

là, fra la ne - ve... bian - ca!___ là fra le nu - bi d'or!_

2. Tyrolean Huntsmen's *Ländler*

3. Walter's Yodeling Song

vi - ve mu - ta - - ta___ la fan - ciul - la in fior!_____

Ah!_____ ah!___ ah!___ ah!___ ah!___ ah!_____ mu - ta - ta in fior!

Edelweiss and Tyrolean yodelers

In its musico-dramatic structure, *La Wally* is orientated towards the late nineteenth-century French operatic model, like Puccini's →*Manon Lescaut* (Puccini was younger than Catalani). There are also points of contact with *verismo*. Gellner's utterances of embittered passion in his two solos in Acts I and II are comparable with those of Canio or Beppo in →Leoncavallo's →*I Pagliacci*. Although the idiom is Italian, the rich, colorful harmony is closer to rustic Tyrolean. Examples of musical Germanisms are the quasi-quotations in the Tyrolean-style waltz or *ländler* melodies of the "kiss" dance, or the edelweiss yodeling song in Act I. The Tyrolean flavor provides local color here. M 2, M 3   J. K.

La Wally, production photograph with Mara Zampieri as Wally, production Tim Albery, Bregenz Festival 1990.
One distinguishing feature of the Bregenz Festival is that it makes a point of putting on rarely performed works.

Puccini's rival?

Catalani had much in common with Puccini, including a feeling for "sweet melancholy," for an elegiac, sensitive overall mood, and for orchestral preludes preceding each of the acts. Toscanini thought very highly of Catalani's talent, the development of which was cut short by his premature death. Catalani composed one of the finest soprano arias in the literature: "Ebben, ne andrò, lontana" ("And so, I'll go, far away"). M 1

Cerha's compositions draw on non-European folklore and music, neo-classicism, the compositional techniques of Anton Webern, and serialism.

Baal, photograph from the first German production with Hubert Bischof (Baal) and Beatrice Niehoff (Sophie), production Kurt Horres, conductor Hans Drewanz, Staatstheater, Darmstadt 1981.
The first German production was more pointed in its criticism and more contemporary in style than the original Viennese production.

Right
Baal, photograph from the original production with Theo Adam as Baal, production Otto Schenk, conductor Friedrich Cerha, Wiener Staatsoper 1981. Cerha's "stage work" progresses like a monodrama. The subject had interested him for 15 years.

Cerha, Friedrich

b. 17 February 1926 in Vienna

Having begun writing music when he was only nine years old, Cerha went on to study composition with Alfred Uhl at the Vienna Music Academy and graduated with a thesis on *Turandot* material in German literature in 1951. The war put an abrupt end to his childhood. He was called up in 1943, but played an active part in the Resistance. Shortly after the war, and before completing his education, he was a mountain guide in the Tyrol. From 1956, he took part in holiday courses in Darmstadt, and in 1956–57 won a scholarship to Rome. In 1958 he and Kurt Schwertsik founded die reihe, an ensemble for the performance of new music. In the 1950s he conducted the Camerata Frescobaldiana, and from 1959 worked as an occasional lecturer at the Vienna Academy. In 1969 he was appointed professor extraordinary, a post that in 1976 became a chair for the composition, notation, and interpretation of new music until 1987. He has performed as a conductor at international festivals and leading opera houses since 1969. Empathizing closely with →Alban Berg's sound world, he orchestrated the incomplete third act of Berg's opera →*Lulu* in 1977–78.

Works: Stage works: *Baal* (1981, Salzburg), *Netzwerk* (*Network*) (1981, Vienna), *Der Rattenfänger* (*The Ratcatcher*) (1987, Graz); orchestral works, including the cycle of seven pieces *Spiegel* (*Mirror*) (1960–68), choral works, chamber music, songs, music for radio.

Baal

Stage work in two parts

Libretto: Friedrich Cerha, after the Bertolt Brecht's play *Baal*.

Première: 7 August 1981, Salzburg (Kleines Festspielhaus).

Characters: Baal (Bar), Ekart (B), Johannes (T or high Bar), Emilie (Ms), Young Woman (Ms), Johanna (S), Sophie (S), Baal's mother (A); small roles in double casting: S, A, 2 T, 2 Bar, B, 2 spoken.

Setting: The present.

Synopsis
Part 1

Businessman and publisher Mech has organized a soirée during which the poet and songwriter Baal will be presented. He behaves as extravagantly as the

splendid company expects of a true artist. Drunk, he snubs publisher and critic alike, and the gathering snubs him in return. Mech's wife Emilie tries in vain to intervene. While Baal complains about his life as a free artist, his friend Johannes confides in him his vision of a virginal girlfriend. Emilie is fascinated by Baal, who arranges to meet her at the beerhouse. There, Baal meets Johanna, the girlfriend of his friend Johannes. Baal entertains the assembled company – mostly truckers –with the ballad of Evelyn Roe, a prostitute who sold her body in her search for the Holy Land and died, since when, excluded from both heaven and hell, she lingers in no-man's-land, tortured by unfulfilled longings. To amuse himself, Baal humiliates Emilie by demanding she allow a trucker, Horgauer, to kiss her. In the meantime, Johanna has yielded to Johannes, who consequently feels cheated of his vision of virginity, and leaves her. Baal enlightens Johanna about the inconstancy of all flesh, thus rendering her totally miserable. Two sisters thrust themselves into Baal's arms and bed. Baal finds a loyal partner in Sophie. He takes a job as a cabaret singer, but upsets the public with smutty couplets, so the police are called in. He evades arrest by escaping through the lavatory window. Having agreed to meet his friend Ekart in a dive, he has just enough time to entrust Sophie to him before he is arrested by the secret police. In prison, he promises his mother to start a new, more respectable life when he is released.

Part 2

Baal has carried out his resolution and become a lumberjack, though without abandoning his alcoholism. When he discovers that Sophie is expecting their child he brutally rejects her, so that she seeks refuge with Ekart. In a hospital bar, he recognizes his own image in the wretched creatures around him, and escapes with Ekart into the country, where he rapes a young woman who was actually looking for Ekart. He meets his mother and endeavors to reassure her with dreams of the life of a great writer. She dies in his arms. Back in the beerhouse, he has to produce a new song to pay for her burial. There he also meets the disheveled Johannes, who is being pursued in his dreams by the drowned corpse of Johanna, who has committed suicide. Baal then makes amorous advances to his friend Ekart, but when he finds the latter tenderly engaged with a waitress, he beats him up. He then escapes, finishing up in a bar. As ever, he tries to force the girls to dance but is beaten up by the local lads and thrown out. Pursued by the rural police, he finds refuge in a lumberjacks' hut. The end is nigh, he senses, and fearing a lonely death, begs the rough lumberjacks to stick by him. They troop out. With his failing strength, he crawls out of the hut and "dies like a dog" in the forest.

S. N.

Cerha and Brecht

Cerha wrote the libretto of *Baal* using all four versions of Brecht's play. Cerha attempts to achieve the maximum possible sound continuum by running together the various sections. The opera is strongly influenced by two works, namely →*Wozzeck* and →*Lulu* by Alban Berg. This is of course no accident, since it was Cerha who completed the orchestration of the third act of *Lulu* from Berg's sketches. As a musical exploration of Brecht, *Baal* caused quite a stir at the Salzburg Festival.

However, both the work and the first production were controversial. Composer and director alike were accused of tailoring Brecht's anarchic play to bourgeois norms of respectability. As Baal, Theo Adam made every effort to create a credible portrayal of an egocentric who destroys both himself and others with crude violence. A number of well-meaning critics defended Cerha's opera as a successful attempt to treat Brecht like a "classic," in that everything disturbing and open to attack is eliminated by the reconciliatory musical idiom.   *M.S.*

Left
Baal, photograph from the original production with Theo Adam as Baal, production Otto Schenk, sets and costumes Rolf Langenfass, conductor Friedrich Cerha, Salzburg Festival 1981.
In singing Baal, Theo Adam had to reinvent himself. He usually looks noble in whatever part he sings, perhaps appearing so naturally, whereas here he had to act the dissolute anarchist.

Right
Baal, photograph from the first German production with Hubert Bischof (Baal) and Beatrice Niehoff (Sophie), production Kurt Horres, sets and costumes Andreas Reinhardt, conductor Hans Drewanz, Staatstheater, Darmstadt 1981.
In the first German production, Kurt Horres treated Cerha's adaptation of Brecht as a contemporary opera about an aging dropout from the generation of 1968 – an opera about the difficulties of remaining an outsider.

Louise, Emmy Destinn as Louise, 1906.
The story of a great stage success apparently began, like so many, in a restaurant in Paris, where the composer and his artistic friends were contemplating a modern story about Paris. It had to be wholly in the spirit of the new century, the century that promised them a "magically beautiful" life. Charpentier succeeded in capturing this contemporary spirit. The first performance was a sensational success, with the unknown Marthe Rioton making her début in the title role. (Rioton entered music history on the strength of that performance alone, as she left the stage for good two years later.) *Louise* was also the beginning of a great career for Mary Garden, as she stood in for the lead singer in Act III of the 33rd performance. At the Berlin première in 1906 the role of the young Parisian dressmaker was sung by the already famous Czech soprano Emmy Destinn. In the same year the opera also opened in Vienna under Gustav Mahler. Toscanini conducted the first performance at Milan's La Scala in 1908. A film version of *Louise* appeared in 1938, which used the opera's plot and some of its most successful musical numbers, and with Grace Moore in the title role. The public waited in vain for a recording during the composer's lifetime as a result of Charpentier's excessive royalty demands. Perhaps the 95-year-old Charpentier foresaw that his second opera, *Julien* – a continuation of *Louise* – would prove a fiasco.

Louise

Roman musical in four acts

Libretto: Gustave Charpentier.

Première: 2 February 1900, Paris (Opéra-Comique).

Characters: Louise, a worker in a sewing factory (S), Her Mother (Ms), Her Father (Bar), Julien, a poet in love with Louise (T); people from the streets: a Rag Picker (B), a Young Rag Picker (Ms), a Sleepwalker (T), a Newspaper Girl (S), a Street Sweeper (Ms), a Milkwoman (S), a Coal Collector (Ms), an Apprentice (Bar), an Arab Street Vendor (S), Two Policemen (2 Bar), Irma (S), Camille (S), Élise (S), Marguerite (S), Blanche (S), Gertrude (A), Madeleine (A), Suzanne (A), a Painter (B), Two Philosophers (T, B), a Sculptor (Bar), a Songwriter (Bar), a Singer (T), a Poet (Bar); dressmakers, bohemians, people of Montmartre (chorus).

Setting: Paris, around 1900.

Synopsis

Paris is paradise for some, hell for others. To the working girl Louise it promises happiness and love. Her parents on the other hand hate the city; they are afraid of it.

Act I

Factory girl Louise is courted by the young poet Julien, but her parents mistrust the artistic world and forbid her to have anything to do with him.

Act II

Louise is working as a dressmaker in Montmartre. Her parents believe she is safely out of sight. But Julien tracks her down and brings her a serenade. Louise runs off with him.

Act III

For weeks, Louise has been living happily with Julien high above the rooftops of Paris. Julien's friends call her "the muse of Montmartre." Her mother comes to take her home on the pretext that her father is ill and wants to see her, promising that she can return to Julien at any time.

Act IV

More weeks have gone by. Despite her mother's promise, her parents have kept Louise at home. They lament their lot – hard work and an ungrateful daughter. In a quarrel, Louise's father curses Julien and shows his daughter the door. Louise escapes into the city. Her father curses Paris: the city has robbed him of his daughter.   *S. N.*

Charpentier, Gustave

b. 25 June 1860 in Dieuze (Moselle)
d. 18 February 1956 in Paris

As the son of a poor baker, Charpentier was able to study music only with communal assistance. Though he began his career with orchestral works, his greatest success was the opera *Louise*, a success that was not matched by its sequel, *Julien*. After these two operas he composed little, but was known for his charitable activities. He was founder of the Conservatoire Populaire Mimi Pinson, thereby creating a monument to the heroine of the novel *Scènes de la vie de bohème* by Henri Murger (and of the operas based on Murger's novel by →Puccini and →Leoncavallo).

Works: Operas: *Louise* (1900), *Julien* (1913); symphonic works, songs.

*C*harpentier's opera "Louise" introduced an unfamiliar tone of realism into the French theater.

Independence and sewing machines

The fin de siècle celebration of the new was in fact a legacy of Romanticism, the culmination of laborious attempts to change the world. Charpentier saw the task as being fulfilled in contemporary art. At the same time, one must ask whether this included a valid perspective on the future. Louise's double loyalty – to her parents and to her lover – is an insoluble problem for modern man, who in a rapidly changing world longs for stability as well as renewal. Symbolism and realism: Charpentier plays on both sides at once. The transition between these spheres is carefully managed throughout. A peaceful, petit bourgeois evening scene, accompanied by a clinking of soupspoons heard in the music, passes seamlessly into a quasi-surrealist picture of morning in Paris. The scene in the dressmaking factory on the other hand is realistic, with the humming and whirring of machines.

The end of an age

The unity of *Louise* is due in no small part to a consistent use of certain characteristic themes. The introduction to Act I is built on an effervescent and energetic theme, which reappears in various guises in the course of the opera as a sign of youth. *M 1*

Similarly, Julien's love is expressed by the recurrence of a passionate melody, while the gloomy figure of Louise's father is portrayed by low notes in the strings. The climax of the opera is Louise's famous aria, which is followed by the love duet (beginning of Act III). The tenderness and devotion conveyed by the aria give it considerable appeal. *M 2* This scene shows most convincingly the two aspects of Charpentier's music. It contains highly wrought emotions typical of Wagner's →*Tristan and Isolde* (a parallel which is underlined by textual and musical allusions), but the accumulated emotional tension is discharged quite differently. Here it runs over into a grandiose waltz – a self-assured continuation of the French tradition. This ambiguity shows that *Louise* does indeed stand between two worlds: it forms the conclusion of the golden age of French opera in a new era, the already proclaimed classical modern period. *P. H.*

1. Paris Theme

2. Louise's Aria

De - puis   le   jour   où je me suis don - né - e,   *(Echo by Oboes)*

Louise, poster for the original production by G. Rochegrosse, Opéra-Comique, Paris 1900. Charpentier described his *Louise* as a "roman musical," a musical novel, and indeed he put great emphasis on depicting the world in detail. The world is Paris, the mighty metropolis of modern life, an artificially created environment for human suffering and joy, yearning and despair. In this opera, Paris is given a voice of its own that is fresh, industrious, and seductive. It is the voice of bohemianism.

*C*harpentier was, with
Lully, the most
important French composer
of stage and church music
under Louis XIV. His music
unites French splendor and
declamation with Italian
"cantabilità."

Medea, production photograph (Act III) with Lorraine Hunt as Medea and
members of Les Arts Florissants, production Jean-Marie Villégier, conductor
William Christie, co-production of the Opéra-Comique, the Théâtre de Caen,
and the Opéra du Rhin, Paris 1994.
Les Arts Florissants played a leading role in reviving Baroque theatrical
traditions, which featured in this 1994 Paris production of *Medea*.

Charpentier, Marc-Antoine

b. 1634 in Paris
d. 24 February 1704 in Paris

Charpentier's life is poorly documented by comparison with those of contemporaries such
as →Lully, partly due to the fact that he never worked for the king. He probably studied in
Rome under Giacomo Carissimi (a seventeenth-century composer of dramatic church
music and oratorios), which would explain the Italian influence in his compositions. He
worked as *maître de musique* for various aristocrats. As a composer, he was a successor to
Lully. When Lully's collaboration with Molière came to an end, Charpentier composed
music for Molière's *comédies-ballets*. His sole *tragédie lyrique*, *Médée* (*Medea*), of 1693,
could be staged only after Lully's death, as Lully was in sole possession of the royal privilege
for staging operas. In the 1680s Charpentier occupied various posts as a director of church
music. The peak of his career was his appointment as *maître de musique* of the Sainte-
Chapelle in Paris, where he remained very active both as a composer and as a performer
until his death in 1704.

Works: Stage works: *Médée* (*Medea*) (tragédie-lyrique, 1693), short operas including
Les plaisirs de Versailles (*The Pleasures of Versailles*) (1680s), *Les arts florissants* (*The Flourishing
Arts*) (1686), *La descente d'Orphée aux enfers* (*Orpheus' Descent into the Underworld*) (1687);
also pastorales, *divertissements*, *intermedi* (musical interludes), and incidental music;
extensive (and partly unknown) sacred choral music, including 11 Masses, 10 Magnificats,
4 Te Deums, 84 psalm settings, and 204 motets and further sacred compositions;
instrumental music (principally for use in church).

Medea
Médée

Tragédie mise en musique in a prologue and five acts

Libretto: Thomas Corneille.

Première: 4 December 1693, Paris (Académie Royale
de Musique).

Characters: Prologue: La Victoire/Victory (S), La
Gloire/Glory (S), Bellonne, goddess of War (A), Two
Shepherdesses (2 S), A Shepherd (T), Leader of the
People (B); people of the banks of the Seine, shep-
herds (chorus). Main plot: Créon/Creon, King of
Corinth (B), Créuse/Creusa, his daughter (S), Cléone,
her confidante (S), Médée/Medea, princess of
Colchis (S), Nérine, her confidante (S), Jason, prince
of Thessaly (T), Arcas, his confidant (T),
Oronte/Orontes, prince of Argos (Bar),
L'Amour/Cupid (S), An Italian Girl (S), Two Spirits
(S), Two Corinthians (counterT, T), Two Argians
(counterT, B), La Jalousie/Jealousy (T), La
Vengeance/Vengeance (B), Three Prisoners (S, A,
counterT); Corinthians, Argians, the entourages of
Creon and Orontes, Cupid's captives, demons,
spirits, guards (chorus).

Setting: Corinth in antiquity.

Synopsis
Prologue
An allegory paying homage to King Louis XIV as a
bringer of peace.
Before the opera begins
Medea has fled her homeland, where she helped the
foreigner Jason to steal the Golden Fleece of her
ancestors. She has followed Jason and borne him
children.

Act I
An open square in Corinth. Jason and Medea have
found asylum in Corinth. Medea is tortured by
doubts as to whether Jason is still faithful to her. She
swears vengeance if she discovers for certain that
Jason loves Creusa, the daughter of King Creon of
Corinth. Jason intends to give Creusa a splendid
robe in thanks for their asylum. He confesses his
love for Creusa to his confidant Arcas, who warns
him of Medea's fury. The prince of Argos, Orontes,
puts himself and his soldiers at Creon's service in the
battle with the Thessalians, hoping for Creusa's
hand in return. Jason and Orontes decide to join
forces in the battle.
Divertissement: Corinthians and Argians prepare for
the campaign.

Act II
A hall in the palace. Creon banishes Medea from the
country, explaining that her presence is generating

political tension. Only her children may remain under his protection. Medea is willing to leave only if Jason goes with her. Creon needs Jason's help in the war, and so encourages his affair with Creusa, in the hope that this will keep him in Corinth. Jason is torn between his debt to Medea and his love for Creusa. Creusa meanwhile evades Orontes' advances.
Divertissement: Cupid's captives sing of the pleasures and pains of love.

Act III

A cave. Medea reassures herself that she retains her old magical power of ruling the demons. Orontes offers Medea asylum for herself and Jason in Argos after the war, but Medea tells him of Jason's love for Creusa. Medea calls upon demons to assist her plans for revenge, and prepares a poison with which to saturate the robe that Jason intends to give Creusa.

Act IV

A courtyard in the palace. Dressed in her new robe, Creusa arouses Jason's desire. Orontes sees Medea's suspicions confirmed. Before going into exile, Medea tries to force Creon to marry Creusa to Orontes. When Creon rejects her imperious demands, Medea demonstrates her magical powers by making him insane with fear.

Act V

Medea's palace. Creon has committed suicide after killing Orontes. The Corinthians lament the death of their king. The poison in Creusa's robe takes effect, and Creusa dies in Jason's arms. In the triumph of vengeance Medea tells Jason she has killed their children. Jason collapses. Medea commands demons to destroy her palace and set fire to the city.

An essay by the younger generation

The librettist Thomas Corneille was the younger brother of Pierre Corneille, the father of French neo-classical tragedy. Not wanting to be completely over-shadowed by the figure of his brother, he sought to prove his dramatic abilities with the Medea theme, which had already been treated by Euripides, Seneca, and Pierre Corneille. Thomas Corneille's version begins with neither the marriage of Jason and Creusa (Euripides) nor the banishment of Medea (Corneille), but with an uncertain, dramatically open situation – Medea's suspicion that Jason could be deceiving her. In this version Medea is a more human figure than she is in the libretto's classical and neo-classical predecessors. As a human being – a wife and a mother – she wants to retain her husband's love, and only when she fails to do this does she resort to her superhuman powers.

Medea, production photograph with René Shirrer (Creon) and Esther Hinds (Medea), production Robert Wilson, conductor Michel Corboz, Opéra National de Lyon 1984.
American Robert Wilson is one of the most important theatrical directors of the 20th century. He began his career in France, and *Medea* in Lyons was one of his early operatic productions.

Left
Medea, production photograph (Act V) with Lorraine Hunt (standing) and Monique Zanetti (lying), production Jean-Marie Villégier, conductor William Christie, Paris 1994.
The notable feature of the figure of Medea is that Corneille and Charpentier brought out in her not only the sufferings of the abandoned wife but also the rage and vengefulness of the enchantress. The scene in which Medea summons up demons and creates a death-robe by black magic (Act III, last scene) is one of the most effective moments in the history of Baroque opera. In this magnificent madness scene the model of the French prima donna is created, and indeed the part of Medea was sung at the first performance by the prima donna Marthe Le Rochois.

Above
Medea, photograph from the production by Liliana Cavani, sets Ezio Frigerio, Opéra National de Paris 1986.
Ezio Frigerio had a particular talent for combining Baroque style and contemporary attitudes in productions of power and pomp and collective rituals.

Below
Medea, title page of the first edition, Paris 1797.
The last decade of the 18th century witnessed a revival of classicism in Europe (Mozart, →*La clemenza di Tito*), as an expression of the restoration of the ancien régime after the French Revolution. Luigi Cherubini was considered a leading exponent of this classicism. Paradoxically, François-Benoît Hoffman, who wrote the libretto of *Medea*, which is based on Euripides and Pierre Corneille, also wrote librettos for Étienne-Nicolas Méhul (1763–1817), the star of the operatic composers of the Revolution. *Medea* made Cherubini famous. Though he cast his monumental opera as an *opéra comique* with spoken dialogues, he provided extensive continuous sections of music. In this he was following his model, →Gluck. As the central character, Medea herself is on stage almost throughout. All her emotions – from radiant happiness to raging hatred – are depicted by means of subtle, almost symphonic techniques.

Medea on the operatic stage

By the twentieth century, the Medea operas had passed into oblivion (despite numerous attempts to revive Cherubini's). This may be related to the fact that there were no Medea operas in the oeuvres of the composers who were valued in the nineteenth century (Gluck, Mozart, Weber, Meyerbeer, Verdi, and Wagner). At the turn of the century, destructive female figures such as Salome and Electra (→Richard Strauss) did appear on stage, but Medea was not among them. Posterity had to wait for Maria Callas's interpretation of Cherubini's heroine in 1953, and the rediscovery of Marc-Antoine Charpentier's →*Medea* as part of the French Baroque repertory by the early music movement (William Christie and his *Les Arts Florissants*, 1985). Both *Medea* operas followed operatic ideals that never caught on. A third Medea opera is Bellini's →*Norma*, which is a variant of the same material (and another opera to mark the end of an era, in this case that of bel canto). Whereas in the Medea operas of both Charpentier and Cherubini the eponymous heroine ultimately surrenders herself to evil forces, Norma manages to overcome her desire for revenge at the last minute, spares her children, and mounts the stake with her treacherous lover. In Bellini, romantic feeling overrides the classical principle of enforcement.

M.S.

Cherubini, Luigi

b. 14 September 1760 in Florence
d. 15 March 1842 in Paris

The son of a theater musician, Cherubini gained the support of the Grand Duke of Florence (later Emperor Leopold II), and from 1778 to 1782 studied under Giuseppe Sarti in Bologna and Milan, who introduced him to polyphonic. He was initially active as a church composer, but soon turned to opera with great success. From 1784 to 1788 he worked in London, where he was appointed court composer, and then resolved to try his luck in Paris. As director of the small Queen Marie Antoinette Theater, he witnessed the political and social upheaval brought about by the Revolution. This affected his experience of life, his music, his themes, and the way they were set. In 1795 he helped to found the Paris Conservatoire, where he worked as an inspector. Commissions from European opera houses took him abroad regularly. He was eventually appointed professor of composition at the Paris Conservatoire in 1816, and from 1821 to 1842 was its director. He also worked as *surintendant de la musique du Roi*, until the office was abolished in 1830.

Works: Operas (selection): *Il Quinto Fabio* (*Quintus Fabius*) (1780, Alessandria), *Armida abbandonata* (*Armida Abandoned*) (1782, Florence), *Adriano in Siria* (*Hadrian in Syria*) (1782, Livorno), *Mesenzio, re d'Etruria* (*Mesenzio, King of Etruria*) (1782, Florence), *L'Alessandro nelle Indie* (*Alexander in India*) (1784, Mantua), *La finta principessa* (*The False Princess*) (1785, London), *Giulio Sabino* (*Julius Sabinus*) (1786, London), *Ifigenia in Aulide* (*Iphigenia in Aulis*) (1788, Turin), *Démophoön* (*Demophon*) (1788, Paris), *Lodoïska* (1791, Paris), *Eliza, ou Le voyage aux glaciers de Mont St. Bernard* (*Eliza, or The Journey to the Glaciers of Mount St. Bernard*) (1794, Paris), *Médée* (*Medea*) (1797, Paris), *La punition* (*Punishment*) (1799, Paris), *Les deux journées, ou Le porteur d'eau* (*The Two Days, or The Watercarrier*) (1800, Paris), *Anacréon, ou L'amour fugitif* (*Anacreon, or Fugitive Love*) (1803, Paris), *Faniska* (1806, Vienna), *Les abencérages, ou L'étendard de Grenade* (*The Abencérages, or The Granada Standard*) (1813, Paris), *Ali-Baba, ou Les quarante voleurs* (*Ali Baba, or The Forty Thieves*) (1833, Paris); secular and sacred vocal music, orchestral works, chamber music.

*T*hough Cherubini was for a long time regarded as a mouthpiece for the French Restoration, he was rather a champion of ethical principles, which he considered to be endangered by revolutionary terror and arbitrary and egotistical urges.

Medea

Médée

Opera in three acts

Libretto: François-Benoît Hoffman.

Première: First version: 13 March 1797, Paris (Théâtre Feydeau); second version: 6 November 1802, Vienna (Kärntnertor Theater).

Characters: Créon/Creon, King of Corinth (B), Dircé/Dirce, his daughter (S), Jason, leader of the Argonauts, betrothed to Dirce (T), Médée/Medea, his disowned wife (S), Néris/Neris, her confidante (A or Ms), Two Companions of Dirce (S, Ms), Captain of the Royal Watch (B), Captain of the Argonauts (T), Two Children of Jason and Medea (silent); Argonauts, priests, soldiers, servants, Corinthians (chorus).

Setting: Corinth in antiquity.

Synopsis
Before the opera begins
Medea once helped Jason to steal the Golden Fleece from her homeland Colchis. She fled with Jason and bore him two children. The family found asylum in Corinth and lived there happily until Jason repudiated Medea so he could marry Dirce, the daughter of the Corinthian king Creon.

Act I
On the morning of her wedding, Dirce is seized by fear of Medea's revenge. To calm her down, Jason brings the Golden Fleece over to his bride as a sign that all ties have been severed. Creon begs the gods to protect the young couple. Then a veiled woman seeks admission. It is Medea. She reminds Jason of their past happiness. In vain: he pushes her away. Medea swears revenge.

Act II
Medea refuses to hand over her children to Jason and Dirce. Her bid to escape with them is frustrated by the palace guards. The populace are afraid of the foreign woman and threaten to kill her. She asks Jason to grant her protection in Corinth for one day, after which she will leave. With great diplomacy, Neris achieves a compromise: Medea may spend this last day with her children. Meanwhile, Medea carries out part of her plan of revenge, and sends Dirce a poison-bearing veil to wear at her wedding.

Act III
Neris has brought the children to the temple. Medea vacillates between maternal affection and the rage to destroy. Then the lament is heard for Dirce – the magic veil has already taken effect – and this rekindles her hatred. Overcome by passion, she rushes into the temple, stabs the children, and presents herself to the horrified populace, brandishing the bloody weapon. Then she curses Jason, and vanishes in a dragon chariot, leaving fire in her wake. M. S.

Medea, Maria Callas, Teatro all Scala, Milan 1953.
This role gave Callas her international breakthrough. Though her performance led to the "rediscovery" of the opera, *Medea* nevertheless failed to find a secure niche in the 20th-century repertory, in spite of excellent recordings and continuing scholarly interest.

The Watercarrier

Les deux journées, ou Le porteur d'eau

Opera in three acts

Libretto: Jean-Nicolas Bouilly.

Première: 16 January 1800, Paris (Théâtre Feydeau).

Characters: Count Armand, a parliamentary leader (T), Constance, his wife (S), Mikéli, a Savoyard watercarrier (B), Daniel, his father (B), Antonio, Mikéli's son (T), Marcellina, Mikéli's daughter (S), Sémos, a rich tenant in Gonesse (B), Angelina, his daughter (S), Two Officers (2 B), An Officer of the Guard (silent), Two Italian Soldiers (2 B), A Girl (S); inhabitants of Gonesse, soldiers and countrymen (chorus).

Setting: Paris and the village of Gonesse, 1647.

Synopsis
Act I
Mikéli's living room in Paris. Mikéli's son Antonio intends to marry the rich tenant's daughter Angelina the next day. As proof of the equality of all people and the necessity for magnanimity, he relates how a nobleman once saved a Savoyard from freezing to death and was later repaid for his kindness when the Savoyard released him from prison. Antonio himself was once saved from starvation by an unknown nobleman. Antonio's father Mikéli is a noble soul. He intends to save Count Armand and his wife Constance from persecution by Mazarin. He hides them in his house, dressed as a watercarrier and Savoyard woman, so that even in a house-to-house search they will not be discovered. Antonio recognizes in the count the man who once saved his life.

Act II
The square outside the guardroom at a Parisian city gate. Dressed in the clothing of Mikéli's daughter Marcellina and accompanied by Antonio, the countess endeavors to pass through the city gate early in the morning. Initially she is turned back, because the description in the pass does not correspond to her appearance. But then the officer who carried out the house-to-house search at Mikéli's the previous day intervenes; he incorrectly identifies the countess as the watercarrier's daughter, and lets her through. Mikéli follows as usual with his water barrel on the cart. When questioned about the aristocratic couple, he sends the pursuers off in the wrong direction, so that the count can get out of the barrel unseen and escape from Paris.

Act III
A rural location outside Gonesse. Antonio has delivered the count and countess to his father-in-law. During the wedding celebrations, the villagers present the bride Angelina with doves as a symbol of peace, but Italian soldiers enter the village and are quartered with Sémos. The count has to hide in a hollow tree. His wife Constance brings him food, but is watched by the soldiers as she does so and is seized. Her cries for help lure Armand out of his hiding place. In the last minute, Mikéli, accompanied by French soldiers, is able to save the pair from death: with the help of Parisian citizens, he has been able to get a pardon from the queen for the popular noble couple. Now nothing stands in the way of the wedding celebrations of Angelina and Antonio. *S. N.*

A rescue opera

Jean-Nicolas Bouilly's libretto is based on a true incident from the period of the Jacobin terror, when an official was saved from the guillotine by a watercarrier. The incident served as a "lesson in humanity," as Bouilly pointed out in his *Récapitulations* (*Memoirs*) of 1836, rather than a criticism of the Revolution. He therefore moved the action to 1647, when Cardinal Jules Mazarin ordered the arrest of members of the aristocratic party under Prince Louis Condé II. The first performance of Cherubini's *Watercarrier* was a brilliant success. The work remained in the repertory of the Opéra-Comique repertory until 1830, but was revived in 1842. It was a success outside France as well, becoming part of the standard repertory in German-speaking countries. Interest waned after the turn of the century, despite attempts to adapt and update it, and in the twentieth century *The Watercarrier* passed into oblivion.   M. S.

To sing of magnanimity …

The basic concept of the opera is the idea of humanitarianism, according to which every being in need must be helped irrespective of his origin or status. With its portrayal of heroic courage and self-sacrifice on the part of the rescuer, and horror and mortal fear on the part of the victims, the story presented the composer with a wealth of human emotions and consequently an opportunity to create subtle musical characters of a predominantly moral and enlightened nature. Cherubini's *Watercarrier* was highly regarded both by →Beethoven and later by →Weber. As a rescue opera, Beethoven's →*Fidelio* derives from *The Watercarrier*, and indeed the libretto of *Fidelio* was based on another libretto by Jean-Nicolas Bouilly, *Léonore, ou L'amour conjugal* (*Leonora, or Conjugal Love*), which had been set to music by Pierre Gaveaux and staged in 1798 in Paris. The extent to which Cherubini served as a model for the composers of his time, with his elaborate orchestration, use of strophic folk songs, and effective deployment of graphically dramatic stylistic resources, is indicated by the choice of the same material for settings by Jean-Frédéric-Auguste Lemière, Simon Mayr, Thomas Attwood, and Paolo Fabrizi.

The Watercarrier, production photograph with Eliane Lublin (Constance), Charles Burles (Armand), Françoise Garner (Marcellina), Jean-Philippe Lafont (Mikéli), Annick Dutertre (Angelina), and Tibere Raffalli (Antonio), production Bernard Sobel, sets Bernard Thomassin, conductor Pierre Dervaux, Opéra-Comique, Paris 1980.
In France under the Emperor Napoleon and during the Restoration, Cherubini was known as the composer of the classicistic *Medea* rather than of the *Singspiel*-like *Watercarrier*. In the early 19th century, Cherubini's rescue opera had more success on German and Austrian stages. Beethoven himself thought highly of it (there are musical similarities between *The Watercarrier* and →*Fidelio*). However, the operatic world gradually forgot the exciting story, and it was hardly performed at all in the 20th century, particularly in its native France. This is why the revival at the Opéra-Comique aroused such interest, though Bernard Sobel's production provoked a mixed reaction from the critics.

Portrait of Adrienne Lecouvreur (1692–1730) by Legnay, after a drawing by C. A. Coypel.
Adrienne was one of the most famous and outstanding French actresses of her time and a member of the Comédie-Française. She was the lover of Count Maurice of Saxony (1696–1750), the illegitimate son of Elector Augustus the Strong of Saxony. Maurice lived in Paris and was a marshal of the French army. His affair with Adrienne ended before the actress died. After her premature death, the rumor spread that she had been the victim of intrigue. Eugène Scribe and Ernest Legouvé constructed the plot of the play *Adrienne Lecouvreur* (1849) around this rumor.

Cilea, Francesco

b. 23 July 1866 in Palmi
d. 20 November 1950 in Varazze (near Genoa)

Cilea embarked on a composer's career against the wishes of his father, a distinguished lawyer. From 1881 to 1889 he studied piano and composition at the Naples Conservatory. The success of his graduation piece, the opera *Gina*, resulted in a contract with the Milan music publisher Sonzogno. In 1894 he was appointed professor of piano at the Naples Conservatory, becoming its director in 1916. His principal work was the opera *Adriana Lecouvreur*, which was enthusiastically received at its première in 1902 and has remained in the repertory throughout the twentieth century.

Works: Operas: *Gina* (1889), *La Tilda* (1892), *L'arlesiana* (*The Woman of Arles*) (several versions dated 1897, 1910, and 1937), *Adriana Lecouvreur* (1902), *Gloria* (1907), *Il matrimonio selvaggio* (*The Wild Marriage*) (1909); orchestral works, piano works.

Adriana Lecouvreur, production photograph with Neil Shicoff (Maurizio) and Vesselina Kasarova (Princess de Bouillon), production Andrei Serban, sets Chloé Obolensky, Opernhaus Zürich 1994.
The Bulgarian mezzo-soprano, one of the most sought-after singers of the 1990s, made her début in a bel canto role with the Princess de Bouillon. Paired with the multi-talented tenor Neil Shicoff, noted both for his singing and for his acting abilities, she proved to Zürich audiences that, nearly a century after it was written, Cilea's *Adriana* can hold its own on the stage beside → *Tosca* and → *Salome*.

Adriana Lecouvreur

Opera in four acts

Libretto: Arturo Colautti, after the play *Adrienne Lecouvreur* by Eugène Scribe and Ernest Legouvé.

Première: 6 November 1902, Milan (Teatro Lirico).

Characters: Adriana Lecouvreur, of the Comédie-Française (S), Maurizio, Count of Saxony (T), Prince de Bouillon (B), Princess de Bouillon (Ms), Michonnet, stage director of the Comédie-Française (Bar), Abbé de Chazeuil (T), Mlle Jouvenot, Mlle Dangeville, Poisson, and Quinault, members of the Comédie (S, Ms, T, B), The Majordomo (T); Athenaïde, Duchess of Aumont, The Marquise, The Baroness, A Chambermaid (silent); ladies, gentlemen, extras, stagehands, servants (chorus).

Setting: Paris, March 1730.

Synopsis
Actress Adriana Lecouvreur loves Count Maurizio of Saxony and is loved in return. The Prince de Bouillon also loves an actress, Adriana's rival La Duclos, and fears she is being unfaithful to him. In fact it is his own wife who is unfaithful. Count Maurizio had become involved with the Princess de Bouillon for political reasons. When he now tries to end their relationship, the spurned lady defends herself. She sends the happy actress a bouquet of poisoned flowers for her birthday. Adriana dies in the arms of her lover.

Act I
The foyer of the Comédie-Française. The celebrated actress Adriana Lecouvreur confesses to her admirer Michonnet that she loves the young sergeant Maurizio. Maurizio is in reality the Count of Saxony. Before the performance in which she is to play the role of Roxane in Racine's tragedy *Bajazet*, she gives Maurizio a bunch of violets. However, the new affair is overshadowed by an old one: the count has not yet terminated his relationship with the Princess de Bouillon. The Prince de Bouillon also has a mistress among the actresses, Mlle Duclos, who, during the performance, attempts to convey to the count an invitation from the Princess to a secret rendezvous at her house. However, the note is intercepted by the Prince, who thinks La Duclos is deceiving him, and he invites all the artistes in the theater to the house after the performance.

Act II
Maurizio and the Princess de Bouillon meet at the cottage of the actress La Duclos in the grounds of the Grange Batelière. He is grateful to the Princess for her political help, but rejects her love. To allay her suspicion that he has a new lover, he gives her Adriana's bunch of violets. The prince and his guests

arrive, determined to prove the infidelity of La Duclos, but they find the count alone. With Adriana's help, the princess manages to leave the villa by a secret door.

Act III

During celebrations at the Palais Bouillon, Adriana and the princess recognize each other as rivals. In reply to provocation by the princess, Adriana recites a monologue from Racine's *Phèdre* – an allusion to the princess's immorality. The guests cheer the actress with enthusiasm, while the embittered and insulted princess notes the message of the monologue.

Act IV

On her birthday, one of the presents Adriana receives is the bunch of violets that she once gave to Maurizio. The flowers are poisoned, sent by her rival, the princess. Adriana assumes that the violets are a farewell gift from Maurizio, and with deep melancholy she breathes in their fatal scent. Coming to profess his love, Maurizio arrives too late: Adriana dies in his arms.

S.N.

*C*ilea was close to "verismo," but his operatic music is more lyrical and melancholic, less full of passion and excess. The opera "Adriana Lecouvreur" became more famous than its creator.

Adriana Lecouvreur, set design by Eduard Löffler, Teatro Municipal, Rio de Janeiro 1943 (TWS).
Scribe's original play is a sharp piece about intrigue, with well-observed cameos of the theatrical world, a "historicizing" representation of the Baroque, and a pointed wit that sometimes lifts the whole into the realm of comedy. Cilea similarly makes use of comedy, namely the French *opéra comique* style of late Romanticism, following the examples of →Massenet and →Puccini. In the group scenes Cilea strikes a quick conversational tone that is often tinged with humor. Yet the underlying atmosphere is serious and even sentimental.

Melodious visiting cards

In keeping with contemporary practice, Cilea made use of reminiscence motifs and leitmotivs, most of them highly memorable melodies, which he linked loosely together. Each of the principal characters was given a musical profile: Count Maurizio (one of Enrico Caruso's great roles) was given a soaring, youthful, passionate cantilena *M 1*, while the princess was characterized by a dark, strongly rhythmic hatred motif. *M 2* For Adriana,

Cilea reserved his best and most tender melody. It is introduced at the very beginning of the opera, in the first scene of Act I, in a kind of entry aria, and is associated with the title role right through to the end of the work. *M 3* Thus the solemnity of the aria text contributes directly to the characterization of a high-minded female figure: "Io son umile ancella del Genio creator" ("I am the humble servant of the creator spirit").

Adriana Lecouvreur, production photograph with Mara Zampieri as Adriana, production Andrei Serban, Opernhaus Zürich 1994. Born in 1941, Mara Zampieri prefers the roles of less well-known fin de siècle Italian opera composers, such as Catalani, Zandonai, and Cilea.

1. Maurizio's Aria

La dol - cis - si-ma ef - fì - gie sor - ri - den - te   in te ri - ve - do del - la ma-dre ca - ra; nel   tu - o   cor

2. The Princess's Outburst of Emotion

con l'im-pe - to   ar - den - te   di chi sen - te   pri - ma - men - te   di - schiuder -si   il   co - re...

3. Adriana's Entry Aria

I-o son l'u - mile an - cel - la del   Ge - nio cre-a - tor: ___   ei

m'of - fre   la fa - vel - la, io la dif - fon - do a - i cor...

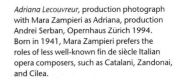

Cimarosa, Domenico

b. 17 December 1749 in Aversa (near Naples)
d. 11 January 1801 in Venice

Cimarosa trained as a violinist, pianist, and singer at the Conservatory of Santa Maria di Loreto in Naples, subsequently taking lessons from the celebrated Niccolò Piccinni. After his first successful operatic première in Naples in 1772, other important Italian opera houses opened their doors to him, including those of Rome and Venice. In 1779 he was appointed royal organist in Naples. In 1787, following an invitation from the court of the Tsarina Catherine II, he succeeded Sarti in St. Petersburg. In 1791 he left for Vienna, where he acquired the position of court *Kapellmeister* which Mozart had been refused. After the death of Leopold II in 1793 Cimarosa returned to Naples, where he was much admired until the uprising against the Bourbons in 1799. A patriotic hymn, written as a protest against the French occupation of Naples, resulted in his being imprisoned for four months. Though he was not poisoned by royalists, as it was rumored, he did nonetheless die shortly after being released, little over 50 years old.

Works: 65 operas, bearing various generic descriptions, such as *dramma giocoso, dramma per musica, commedia per musica, farsa per musica,* and *intermezzo in musica.* The first opera, *Le stravaganze del conte* (*The Count's Eccentricities*) was a *commedia per musica* (1772); the last, a *dramma tragico per musica* called *Artemisia,* from 1801, remained unfinished. The most famous opera is *Il matrimonio segreto* (*The Secret Marriage*) of 1792. Other works include oratorios, Masses and other sacred works, 32 one-movement piano sonatas, and chamber music.

The Secret Marriage

Il matrimonio segreto

Dramma giocoso per musica in two acts

Libretto: Giovanni Bertati, after the comedy *The Clandestine Marriage* (1766) by George Colman senior and David Garrick.
Première: 7 February 1792, Vienna (Hoftheater).

Characters: Geronimo, a rich merchant (B), Elisetta, his elder daughter (S), Carolina, his younger daughter (S), Fidalma, Geronimo's sister, a rich widow (Ms), Count Robinson (B), Paolino, a young clerk employed by Geronimo (T).
Setting: Bologna, in the 18th century.

Synopsis

Carolina, the daughter of the merchant Geronimo, is expected by her father to become the wife of Count Robinson, but is already secretly married to Paolino. After some turmoil, Carolina has no choice but to confess everything to her father. The latter gives his reluctant blessing only because the count declares he is willing to marry Geronimo's elder daughter Elisetta.

Act I

The rich merchant Geronimo would like to marry off at least one of his daughters to a nobleman. But the younger one, Carolina, is already secretly married to Paolino, one of Geronimo's clerks. Attracted by the generous dowry, Count Robinson presents himself as a suitor. Unluckily, he plumps for Carolina, spurning the willing Elisetta.

Act II

Count Robinson informs Geronimo that he wants to marry Carolina. Geronimo refuses to give his paternal blessing. Only the count's offer to forego half the dowry finally convinces him. Moreover, Geronimo's sister Fidalma has set her mind on marrying Paolino, but is turned down. The two rejected women, Fidalma and Elisetta, conspire together against Carolina, suggesting to Geronimo that he send her to a convent. At this the clandestine couple confess their secret to Carolina's father. He decides to grin and bear it, so that in the end the count marries Elisetta and Fidalma goes empty-handed.   *S. N.*

The Secret Marriage, photograph from the production by Peter Baumgardt, sets Peter Werner, Staatstheater am Gärtnerplatz, Munich 1988.
One of the few productions of *The Secret Marriage* to set the old story in the here and now.

A gallery of laughs

Giovanni Bertati transplanted the English plot into the world of *opera buffa* and the *commedia dell'arte*. Geronimo, for example, resembles Pantalone in his tyrannical manner, his sense of superiority, and his cunning, and his hardness of hearing gives rise to comical misunderstandings. The other figures, too – the jealous and quarrelsome Elisetta and her widowed and love-hungry aunt Fidalma – all belong to the repertory of stock characters of traditional Italian comedy.

On the scales of music history

Cimarosa was one of a number of very successful eighteenth-century composers in whose hands *opera buffa* flourished, others being Baldassare Galuppi, Pasquale Anfossi, Giuseppi Sarti, Niccolò Piccinni, and Antonio Salieri. It was a genre in which Cimarosa also competed with Mozart. Of his many comic operas, only *The Secret Marriage* has been a lasting success, but even this does not rank with Mozart's →*Marriage of Figaro* and →*Così fan tutte*. The plot is based on *buffa* stereotypes and the music has no depth, but there is nonetheless a lightness of touch and lots of charm.

Vocal caricatures

The work testifies to an assured hand and mature compositional skills, and its large number of ensembles demonstrates a receptiveness to contemporary fashions. Cimarosa had a good sense of musical caricature: his frequent use of the technique of rapidly repeated notes to represent empty chatter anticipates the *buffa* style of Rossini and Donizetti.

The Secret Marriage was the most spectacular success of his whole career. According to contemporary reports, after the second performance at the court theater in Vienna, Emperor Leopold II insisted on the whole thing being repeated from beginning to end. With Mozart's operas, *The Secret Marriage* is one of the few eighteenth-century comic operas still in the repertory today.

J. K.

Above
The Secret Marriage, production photograph (Act I) with Carlos Chausson (Geronimo) and Malin Hartelius (Elisetta), production Jonathan Miller, sets John Conklin, conductor Adam Fischer, Opernhaus Zürich 1996.
An archetypal situation of satirical comedy: the ennobled bourgeois and the daughter who is left cold by 'noble' thoughts and simply dreams of love.

The Secret Marriage, production photograph with Antti Suhonen (Count Robinson) and Efrat Ben-Nun (Elisetta), production Hennig Brockhaus, conductor Asher Fisch, Deutsche Staatsoper, Berlin 1994.
Every comedy conceals an undercurrent of tragedy. And happy endings are not happy for everyone: there are also losers.

The Secret Marriage, poster for the production by Giorgio Strehler, Teatro alla Scala, Milan 1949.

Left
The Betrothal, the first of a series of paintings by William Hogarth entitled *Marriage à la mode*, 1743–45 (National Gallery, London).
Cimarosa's *opera buffa* was the earliest opera to be inspired – even if indirectly – by this series of paintings, the others being two important 20th-century operas, Strauss's →*Der Rosenkavalier* and Stravinsky's →*The Rake's Progress*. The sharp satire of Colman and Garrick's comedy *The Clandestine Marriage* was aimed at the habits of the nouveaux riche middle class and the impoverished aristocracy. Similar social constellations were not unknown in Italy.

Cimarosa is one of the most important composers of comic opera in Italy in the late 18th century, with a light touch and effervescent style.

Right
The Barber of Baghdad, production photograph with Constanze Nettesheim (Margiana) and Willy Wörle (Nureddin), Staatsoper, Berlin 1935.
The love duet occurs relatively late, in the final third of the opera. Though the female protagonist, Margiana, has only a few minutes of solo singing in the opera, her role is not in the least unimportant. One of Cornelius's innovations was to follow the traditional love duet with a second that is interrupted by the song of the barber, who is keeping watch on the other side of the street – a musico-dramatic gem.

Cornelius was an adherent of the New German School led by Franz Liszt. His models were the Frenchman Berlioz and the Hungarian Liszt, but his music is nevertheless much more intimate. It has the tone of Weber and Mendelssohn.

Cornelius, Peter

b. 24 December 1824 in Mainz
d. 26 October 1874 in Mainz

Even before Cornelius emerged as a composer of songs in 1853, seven years after completing his musical training, he was already known to readers of the periodical *Neuer Zeitschrift für Musik* (*New Music Journal*) as one of the most ardent representatives of the New German School. He exercised his many talents throughout his life, which included providing German translations for →Hector Berlioz, writing texts himself, working as an actor, and composing vocal music. After an unsuccessful first performance of his opera *The Barber of Baghdad* in 1858, conducted by Liszt, he left Weimar for Vienna. In 1867 he was appointed a professor of composition at Vienna's newly founded Royal Music School.

Works: Operas: *Der Barbier von Bagdad* (*The Barber of Baghdad*) (1858, Weimar), *Der Cid* (*The Cid*) (1865, Weimar), *Gunlöd* (unfinished); choral music and songs.

Condemned to flop

Peter Cornelius was 28 when he first visited Franz Liszt at the Villa Altenburg in Weimar in 1852. He had to climb a lot of steps to reach Liszt's study. He counted them: if it was an even number, the meeting would bring luck, if odd … thought the young composer, who also had no mean talent for literature. There were 21 steps: a bad omen. Six years later, it was the infamous reception of Cornelius's *The Barber of Baghdad* conducted by Liszt that induced Liszt to leave his position as court music director in Weimar.

The son of a thespian couple, Cornelius went to live in Berlin with his uncle, the famous painter Peter von Cornelius, after the early death of his father. He was immediately at home in the artistic atmosphere surrounding Liszt. Thanks to Cornelius's excellent French, Liszt took him on as his secretary, and Cornelius lived at Liszt's house in the Altenburg. He translated into German Liszt's articles and also the texts of some of his French songs. Liszt wanted to make a church composer of him, so Cornelius composed several Masses, all of which proved unsuccessful.

In 1854 Cornelius retreated to a cottage in the Thuringian Forest, where he translated the libretto of Berlioz's *Benvenuto Cellini*, and composed his own comic opera *The Barber of Baghdad*. Liszt was less than enthusiastic about the idea – comedy played little part

The Barber of Baghdad, production photograph with Ivar Andersen (Abul Hassan) and Willy Wörle (Nureddin), Staatsoper, Berlin 1935.
A delightfully comic scene. The loquacious barber Abul Hassan drives his customer Nureddin mad with his non-stop babble. The long shaving scene is musically interesting, in that the barber flies rapidly and rhythmically through a vast amount of text while the lovelorn Nureddin interjects only a few melodic phrases of few words. Then the situation is reversed, as the barber checks his speech and Nureddin grows increasingly angry about the wasted time. The song of Abul, a dance parody, was described by Cornelius and his Weimar friends as the "shaving minuet."

The Barber of Baghdad

Der Barbier von Bagdad

Komische Oper in two acts

Libretto: Peter Cornelius, after a story from *The Thousand and One Nights*.

Première: 15 December 1858, Weimar (Hoftheater).

Characters: The Caliph (Bar), Baba Mustapha, a cadi (T), Margiana, his daughter (S), Bostana, a relative of the cadi (Ms), Nureddin (T), Abul Hassan Ali Ebn Bekar, a barber (B), Three Muezzins (B, 2 T), A Slave (T), Four Armed Men (2 T, 2 B); Nureddin's servants, friends of the cadi, people of Baghdad, wailing women, the caliph's retinue (chorus).

Setting: Baghdad, in ancient times.

Synopsis
Act I

Nureddin is in love with Margiana, the cadi's daughter. With no hope of winning her hand in marriage, he mopes about, lovesick. When Bostana, a friend of Margiana, tells Nureddin that his beloved will be waiting for him at a rendezvous when the muezzin summons the faithful and her father will be in the mosque at prayer he is transformed into a happy young man. So as to look as handsome as possible, Nureddin places himself in the hands of the best barber around, Abul Hassan. Talking rather than working, the barber embarks on a dramatic campaign of beautification, and asks Nureddin about his love. When Abul proposes himself as an escort, Nureddin resorts to cunning: he diagnoses a grave illness in the barber and orders him to rest in bed.

Act II

Margiana and Bostana wait for Nureddin in pleasant anticipation. In the meantime, the bridegroom selected by her father, the rich Selim from Damascus, has had a chestful of treasure sent as a wedding gift. The cadi has scarcely left the house to go to prayer when Nureddin appears. The barber has secretly followed him and keeps watch on the house. The cadi returns unexpectedly, and beats a slave for breaking a vase. Nureddin rapidly vanishes into the treasure chest. The barber presumes his protégé is in danger, and summons passers-by to enter the house with him. He discovers that Nureddin is in the chest, and accuses the cadi of murder. The caliph comes to mediate, has the chest opened, and passes sentence: since, as the cadi declares, the chest and its contents belong to his daughter, she may keep it. Everyone is generously invited to the wedding. The caliph takes the faithful barber into his service. *M. S.*

The Barber of Baghdad, set design (detail) by Josef Fenneker for the production by Werner Jacob, conductor Paul Drach, Duisburger Oper 1936.

Although the plot is set in Baghdad, Cornelius's music is not exotic in the manner of German *Singspiel* from →Mozart to →Lortzing. Cornelius was using a different operatic genre. There are no spoken dialogues here, and the libretto is through-composed. The impression is that in *The Barber of Baghdad* Cornelius aimed to transplant Berlioz's operatic ideals to German soil. At Liszt's initiative and under his direction, Berlioz's works had been performed frequently in Weimar during the 1850s.
Yet oriental tones are not entirely absent. In the orchestral introduction to Act II, Cornelius paints the midday scene in Baghdad in music. The libretto contains still more exotic color (Cornelius was an excellent linguist and outstandingly literate), with comic-sounding Turkish or Arabic names and deliberately effusive turns of phrase.

in the creative output of this otherwise amusing sophisticate. Nevertheless, he agreed to sponsor the work at its public presentation. Misreading the situation – which was in fact the result of intrigues against Liszt by the court theater director Franz von Dingelstedt – Cornelius concluded that the work's public failure was due to poor quality. Several revisions and reorchestrations were unable to save the work, because the problem lay not in the music or the libretto but in the public's aversion to the New German School. It was not until Hermann Levi returned to the original version for a performance in Munich on 15 October 1885 that the work finally found acceptance. The revival of the original version in Weimar on 10 June 1904 was also successful, and the work has been in the repertory of smaller opera houses since the middle of the century. *M. S.*

Dallapiccola, Luigi

b. 3 February 1904 in Pisino (now Pazin, Croatia)
d. 19 February 1975 in Florence

Even as a child, Dallapiccola felt the effect of politics on his life; in 1917 his father, a teacher and the headmaster of an Italian secondary school, was deported to Graz, where he was interned as an undesirable alien until the end of 1918. After training in Graz and Florence, and making a number of international study tours which at one point took him to the Berkshire Music Center in the USA, Dallapiccola became professor of piano at the Florence Conservatory, where he taught until 1967. A key artistic experience in his career was hearing a performance of the song cycle *Pierrot lunaire* by (and with) →Arnold Schoenberg in Florence in 1924. The rejection of comfortable complacency evident in that work corresponded to Dallapiccola's own ideas. Marked by his experience of two world wars, Dallapiccola was deeply opposed to Fascism, adopting an ethically committed outlook, and his example influenced younger composers.

Works: Stage works: *Volo di notte* (*Night Flight*) (1940, Florence), *Il prigioniero* (*The Prisoner*) (1950, Florence), *Job* (1950, Rome), *Ulisse* (*Ulysses*) (1968, Berlin); ballets, film music, vocal music, orchestral works.

The Prisoner, production photograph with Thomas de Vries as the Prisoner, production Joachim Griep, sets and costumes Joachim Griep, conductor Reinhard Seifried, Oldenburgisches Staatstheater 1996
The account of moments in the life and sufferings of a prisoner, chosen by Dallapiccola as the subject of a one-act opera, becomes a parable for the helplessness of a human being pursued even into his inmost illusions by an invisible power – and then destroyed.

*D*allapiccola was one of the first innovators to breathe new life into Italian music, which had become ossified in tradition.

The ultimate disappointment – presented in music

After the Second World War, serialism was the modern, contemporary technique for a new generation of composers, from Dallapiccola to Pierre Boulez. Their music was organized in rows of twelve or fewer notes, arranged in a certain order. In *The Prisoner*, Dallapiccola employed the twelve-tone technique in the service of dramatic expression. The Prisoner, frankly expressing his true feelings, sings in harsh twelve-tone melodies. His prayer before his supposed escape contains all twelve tones, and forms a strange, freely constructed, dissonant melody. M1 However, the Grand Inquisitor, who pretends to befriend the Prisoner, sings an *arioso* melody in regular meter, accompanied by pleasing tonal chords. M2

Other musical methods also assume great significance. The scene of the Prisoner's flight, when between hope and fear he seeks the way to freedom, is based on a contrapuntal Baroque musical form, the *ricercare* (meaning "to search"). The chorus also plays an important part; in writing its *intermezzi*, the composer had in mind "fanatical Spanish choral works of the 16th century, the color of blood."

The Prisoner

Il prigioniero

Prologue and one act

Libretto: Luigi Dallapiccola, after the novella *La torture par l'espérance* (*Torture by Hope*) by Philippe-Auguste Villiers de l'Isle Adam, and Charles de Coster's novel on the subject of Till Eulenspiegel.

Première: concert première: 1 December 1949, Turin (Radiotelevisione Italiana); stage première: 20 May 1950, Florence (Teatro Communale).

Characters: The Mother (S), The Prisoner (Bar), The Jailer (T), Fra Redemptor (silent, R), Two Priests (T, Bar), The Grand Inquisitor (T); chamber chorus (on stage), large chorus (off stage).

Setting: A prison of the Inquisition in Saragossa, in the second half of the 16th century.

Synopsis

Prologue, in front of a black curtain. A mother is waiting for her son, who has been imprisoned by the Inquisition. She has forebodings of his imminent death, having seen King Philip II, the man responsible for the cruelties of the Inquisition, appear as the figure of Death in a dream.

Scene 1

An underground cell with a straw mattress and a rack. The prisoner meets his mother here. He is full of hope as the jailer has addressed him as "brother", and he sees this as a sign that he is soon to be freed.

Scene 2

The same cell, after the prisoner's mother has left. The jailer visits the prisoner again, bringing him news of a rebellion in Flanders that has undermined the power of Philip II. As if to confirm what he has said, he leaves the cell door unlocked when he goes out, and the prisoner escapes.

Scene 3

Underground vaults. The prisoner is making his way through underground passages, and has to hide several times, but he is not discovered.

Scene 4

A large garden. When the prisoner finally reaches a garden, and at last sees the starry sky again, he is greeted by the word "brother" – uttered by the jailer, who is really the Grand Inquisitor. The hope of freedom was the last of the tortures devised for him. He is led to the stake.

S. N.

Torture by hope

Dallapiccola read Villiers de l'Isle-Adam's story *La torture par l'espérance* (*Torture by Hope*) in 1939, and immediately connected it with Victor Hugo's depiction of King Philip II of Spain in *La légende des siècles* (*The Legend of the Centuries*). The cruel Philip II, fanatically intent on converting heretics, suggested to the composer associations with Hitler and Mussolini. Dallapiccola drafted the libretto in late 1943 and early 1944, began composing the music in 1944, and completed the score, after several lengthy interruptions, in 1948.

Intellectually, the opera is close to the *Canti di prigionia* (1941) and the subsequent *Canti di liberazione* (1955). *Il prigioniero* arose out of a contemporary political situation (the establishment of Fascist dictatorships in Europe), but it takes the torments of political prisoners as its subject in an archetypal approach modeled on, and referring to, Dante's *Divine Comedy*. In Dante's work, all who enter the underworld are warned to abandon hope. This theme, transcending historical periods, is the unique feature of Dallapiccola's opera. The dramatic idea of turning every state of affairs into its opposite – "La speranza … l'ultima tortura" ("Hope … the last torment") – is also given convincing musical structure. Dallapiccola worked with

twelve-tone rows (→Schoenberg), which are linked to certain ideas and change their form – to retrograde, to inversion, or to retrograde inversion – as situations and feelings turn into their opposites. Self-contained forms (*ricercare*, *ballata*, aria) keep the musical structure transparent.

S. N.

1. The Prisoner's Prayer

Si - gno - re, A - iu - ta- mi a cammi - na - re

2. Aria of the Grand Inquisitor

Sul - l'O - ce - a - no, sul - la Schel - de, con il so - le, con la piog - gia, con la gran - di - ne e la ne - ve

Pelléas and Mélisande, production photograph with François le Roux (Pelléas) and Frederika von Stade (Mélisande), production Antoine Vitez, conductor Claudio Abbado, sets and costumes Yannis Kokkos, Wiener Staatsoper, Vienna 1988.
Playing beside the well: Mélisande loses her wedding ring. At that moment Golaud falls from his horse. The scene by the well reveals the childishly innocent affinity between Pelléas and Mélisande, the source of their feelings for each other. They themselves do not know whether these feelings should be called love.

*A*s a composer indebted to both Impressionism and Symbolism, Debussy sought freedom of expression. He set particular store by tonal color.

Debussy, Claude

b. 22 August 1862 in Saint-Germain-en-Laye
d. 25 March 1918 in Paris

Debussy studied piano and composition at the Paris Conservatoire. After three years in Rome, he lived in Paris as a freelance composer, cultivating contacts with men of letters and painters. These friendships refined his taste and had an enduring influence on him. The opera *Pelléas and Mélisande*, in which he found his own musical language in the 1890s, is central to his early works. In his later years he tried to write a second opera, *The Fall of the House of Usher*, after Edgar Allan Poe, but it remained a fragment.

Works: As well as his one full-length opera, *Pelléas et Mélisande* (*Pelléas and Mélisande*) (1902), he composed the scenic cantata *L'enfant prodigue* (*The Prodigal Son*), incidental music for the mystery play *Le martyre de Saint-Sébastien* (*The Martyrdom of St. Sebastian*), many songs, piano works (*Pour le piano, Estampes, Images* I–II, *Préludes* I–II), chamber music, orchestral works (*Prélude à l'après-midi d'un faune, Nocturnes, La mer, Images*), and ballets (*Khamma, Jeux*).

Pelléas and Mélisande

Pelléas et Mélisande

Drame lyrique in five acts (15 scenes)

Libretto: Maurice Maeterlinck.
Première: 30 April 1902, Paris (Opéra-Comique).
Characters: Arkel, King of Allemonde (B), Pelléas and Golaud, Arkel's grandsons, half-brothers (high T, B), Yniold, Golaud's son by his first marriage (S), Geneviève, mother of Golaud and Pelléas (A), Mélisande (S), A Shepherd (B), A Doctor (B); serving-women, beggars (silent R); sailors' voices (chorus).
Setting: The kingdom of Allemonde in legendary times.

Synopsis

Golaud brings the mysterious Mélisande home to his castle to be his wife. His brother Pelléas wishes to leave the castle, but remains, feeling attracted to Mélisande, and she too is drawn to him. Golaud murders Pelléas. Mélisande bears a child by Golaud, and dies.

Act I

Scene 1: A forest. Golaud, who has lost his way while hunting, comes upon the weeping Mélisande. He cannot comfort her, but takes her with him.
Scene 2: A hall in the castle. Golaud has written his younger half-brother Pelléas a letter, asking Pelléas to intercede for him with King Arkel: after a sea voyage of six months, he wishes to bring his new, second wife Mélisande home. His mother Geneviève reads Arkel the letter. Pelléas himself, summoned by a dying friend, wants to leave the castle. Although King Arkel had plans for Golaud to marry a different woman, he agrees to his choice of bride, and allows him to return home. However, he forbids Pelléas to leave.
Scene 3: A room in the castle. Geneviève shows Mélisande her new home. Mélisande does not like the gloomy atmosphere of the castle and its grounds. Voices are heard from the departing ship. The sound brings Mélisande and Pelléas together.

Act II

Scene 1: Beside a well in the castle park. Pelléas shows Mélisande the Well of the Blind; its waters bestow the power of sight. It also opens the eyes of Pelléas and Mélisande to their feelings for each other. Mélisande drops Golaud's ring into the well.
Scene 2: A room in the castle. At the moment when Mélisande dropped Golaud's ring into the well, Golaud himself fell from his horse and was injured. Mélisande is nursing him. He discovers the loss of the ring. She lies to him, telling him that she lost it in a grotto. He sends her away to look for the ring, the pledge of his love.
Scene 3: A grotto. At Golaud's request, Pelléas goes with Mélisande to search for the ring. The lie is a

barrier between them, and there is misfortune all around them as well, for disease and famine are rife in the kingdom. They meet three emaciated old beggars and flee in horror.

Act III

Scene 1: A tower. Mélisande is combing her long golden hair, and as she does so she expresses her yearnings in song, drawing Pelléas to her. They give themselves to each other in an exchange of glances and gestures; Pelléas wraps Mélisande's golden hair around him. Golaud finds them playing this game, and reproaches them for their childish behavior.

Scene 2: An underground vault. Golaud threatens Pelléas with the horrors of darkness and death.

Scene 3: A terrace near the exit from the vault. Shaken by the terrors of death, Pelléas is glad to see the outside world and the sunlight. Golaud forbids him to have anything more to do with Mélisande, for fear of harming her pregnancy.

Scene 4: Outside the castle. Golaud uses his son Yniold, the child of his first marriage, to act as a spy for him. Holding the boy up to a window, he asks what Mélisande and Pelléas are doing in the room inside. Yniold is reluctant. He fears his father, and at the same time senses his distress. Golaud learns everything yet nothing from the child: Pelléas and Mélisande are merely sitting opposite one another, sad and silent.

Act IV

Scene 1: A room in the castle. Pelléas asks Mélisande to meet him in the park for a last farewell.

Scene 2: A room in the castle. Arkel tries to comfort Mélisande and fill the gap in her life left by Pelléas. She is disconsolate. Golaud openly reveals his jealousy and rage, seizing Mélisande by her golden hair.

Scene 3: Beside a well in the park. Yniold is playing alone. He hears the sheep coming home, as they do every day. Then they fall silent. The Shepherd is taking them not to their stable, but off to be slaughtered. The child has forebodings of death. Pelléas says goodbye to Mélisande. For the first time, they express their love for each other in words. Golaud appears and kills Pelléas. Mélisande flees.

Act V

A room in the castle. Mélisande gives birth prematurely to a girl. Golaud tries in vain to justify the murder he has committed. To King Arkel, the child is the pledge of the continuance of his family and the triumph of life. Mélisande pities her daughter, who must live. She herself dies.

S. N.

Pelléas and Mélisande, set design (section) by Ottomar Starke, Munich 1909 (TWS). An opera in which, outwardly, almost nothing happens. Such an observation sounds like adverse criticism, but in the case of *Pelléas and Mélisande* it is high praise, proving that the opera's creator realized his intentions fully. Debussy dreamed of an opera in which outward events are merely hinted at. What is not seen on stage is complemented by the music and the power of imagination. The sea, the forest and the castle, the well, the grotto, and the tower, are as important in the dramatic world of this work as the human characters.

Below
Pelléas and Mélisande, Edith Mathis as
Mélisande, Bayerische Staatsoper, Munich
1973/74.
The attractive personality of Edith Mathis
(b. 1938) endowed the part of Mélisande
with lifelike feminine characteristics. Born in
Switzerland and living in London, the singer
gave some outstanding performances in
the 1960s and 1970s, particularly in lyric
soprano roles. Her singing of Mozart's
parts for women and of lieder were
particularly fine.

Pelléas and Mélisande, Mary Garden as
Mélisande, portrait print, Paris 1902.
The career of Mary Garden (1877–1967) took
off rapidly, and she was already a popular
singer at the Opéra-Comique when she
created the part of Mélisande, a role of an
entirely new kind for her. A sensational
appearance in Gustave Charpentier's →*Louise*
had made her name overnight. In 1907 she
went to America, where she became a
member of the Chicago opera company,
and later its director.

Pelléas and Mélisande, production photograph with Frederica von Stade as
Mélisande, production Antoine Vitez, conductor Claudio Abbado, Wiener
Staatsoper 1988.
Mélisande is a cross between a siren and an angel, a fateful figure without
being aware of it, both Desdemona and Lorelei. The American mezzo-soprano
Frederica von Stade (b. 1945) gave the impression of being a fairy-tale figure
in the production by Antoine Vitez in Vienna.

Hidden conflicts

Pelléas and Mélisande appears to be a simple tale of a love triangle. Its true character lies in what remains unexpressed. Golaud, the husband, is a man of reason, and cannot understand his wife Mélisande. Pelléas suffers from indecision; he constantly wishes to be gone, and yet he stays. He has childlike and innocent feelings for Mélisande. Only at the last, fatal moment does he dare to reveal his love to her. The strangest figure in the opera is Mélisande, a lost, spoilt child, and at the same time a *femme fatale*. Her origin remains obscure, and her constant fears have no foundation. She was intended to be like a shimmering light that irradiates the dark lives of the men, but is then extinguished, never to return.

Only very occasionally do the voices assume a true melodic contour, as in the song Mélisande sings while she combs her hair, which is heard without accompaniment. Here Mélisande gives full expression to her nature. M 1   P. H.

1. Mélisande's Song

Mes longs che - veux des - cen - dent jusqu'au seuil de la tour; Mes che - veux vous at - ten - dent tout le long de la tour, ___ Et tout le long du jour, Et tout le long du jour.

Pelléas and Mélisande, set design showing the three protagonists by Hans Strohbach, production Hans Strohbach, conductor Eugen Szenkar, Vereinigte Stadttheater, Köln 1927/28 (TWS).
Maurice Maeterlinck was the same age as Debussy, and by the turn of the century was already famous as an author. His characters live in a dreamlike world. They constantly feel vulnerable to tragic dangers threatening them, not from the outside, but from within themselves. They are fated, according to Maeterlinck, "always [to encounter] a third person, mysterious, invisible, but ever-present, so that it could be called a sublimated figure." That "third person" is Death.

Delibes, Léo

b. 21 February 1836 in Saint-Germain-du-Val
d. 16 January 1891 in Paris

Delibes studied with Adolphe Adam at the Paris Conservatoire. His first stage work, an operetta, was performed in 1855, and was followed by further compositions, produced at Offenbach's Bouffes-Parisiens and the Théâtre-Lyrique. Delibes led something of a double life; besides his daily duties as an organist, he was a sophisticated man of the theatre, holding the posts first of co-répétiteur at the Théâtre-Lyrique, then of chorus master at the Opéra. After 1881 he taught at the Conservatoire. He wrote no new works in the last years of his life.

Works: The only works by Delibes still in the repertory are his ballets *Coppélia* (1870) and *Sylvia* (1876), and his *opéras comiques Le roi l'a dit* (*The King has Spoken*) (1873) and *Lakmé* (1883).

*T*he music of Delibes was widely popular because of its ease and charm.

Lakmé

Opéra in three acts

Libretto: Edmond Gondinet and Philippe Gille.
Première: 14 April 1883, Paris (Opéra-Comique).
Characters: Lakmé, a priestess of Brahma (S), Nilakantha, her father, a priest of Brahma (B), Gérald and Frédéric, English officers (T, Bar), Ellen and Rose, English girls (2 S), Mrs. Bentson, their governess (Ms), Mallika, Lakmé's maid (Ms), Hadji, Nilakantha's servant (T); Englishmen and Englishwomen, Brahmins, Indian street people, Chinese and Indian traders, worshippers, crowd (chorus).
Setting: India in the 19th century.

Synopsis

The worldly love of the Indian priestess Lakmé for an Englishman is sanctified by her courage and self-sacrifice. Her European lover, who cannot understand her foreign culture, is left to mourn and admire her.

Act I

Nilakantha, priest of Brahma and a sworn enemy of the English colonizers, has left his daughter Lakmé in charge of the sacred garden during his brief absence. Although the place is forbidden to Europeans, a group of English visitors enters the sacred precincts. Gérald falls in love with Lakmé, and she returns his feelings.

Act II

Nilakantha is angered by the desecration of the garden, and seeks the guilty man, but Lakmé remains silent. The priest disguises himself as a beggar, and forces Lakmé to attract attention in the market place by singing. Gérald falls into the trap and gives himself away. Nilakantha tries to kill him, but he is not mortally wounded.

Act III

Lakmé has hidden Gérald in a hut in the forest, where she has nursed him back to health. His friend Frédéric tells Gérald that it is time for him to return to his military duties. Lakmé realizes that they can never hope for a future together. She places her lover beyond her father's reach by giving him a cup of holy water to drink, while she herself takes poison. Nilakantha is appeased, since his daughter has atoned for her shame in death. S. N.

Lakmé, Marie van Zandt as Lakmé in the year of the opera's première, Paris 1883.
The charm of the opera *Lakmé* derives from the contrast between the radiant beauty of the eponymous heroine and the oppressive atmosphere of her surroundings, and similarly the great success of its première was due to the singer Marie van Zandt, who shone in the title role. During her short but meteoric career, the American-Dutch soprano was an outstanding singer of Mozart (Cherubino, Zerlina), and a virtuoso performer of operas by Rossini and Bellini (Rosina in →*The Barber of Seville*, Amina in →*La sonnambula*). She inspired not only Delibes but also Massenet, who wrote the part of the capricious Manon for her.

Exoticism

The tragic tale of Lakmé was rather a curious production for the Opéra-Comique, where audiences expected more cheerful pieces. Eight years earlier, however, the same theater had given the première of a great tragic opera, Bizet's →*Carmen*, to which *Lakmé* is indebted both dramatically and musically. A common factor in the two works is an exotic setting outside the bourgeois experience of the audience.

The story of *Lakmé* has its roots in the intellectual soil of the colonial age, an era when Europeans increasingly came into contact with non-European cultures, which were seen as providing artistically intriguing backgrounds. In the last third of the nineteenth century anything that offered the charms of exoticism could expect to be a great success. The composer was not expected to immerse himself in the music of the region concerned. Authenticity was not required; exotic references and a touch of the foreign, alarming, or adventurous were sufficient. These expectations on the part of the audience were often fulfilled by the setting alone, as in Bizet's →*The Pearl Fishers*. The India depicted in *Lakmé* makes no claims to authenticity either. The singing of the Brahmans in the introduction to the first act, and the series of dances in the second act (obligatory for any French operatic composer), acquire local color merely from a few turns of harmony. The beautiful, dreamlike duet between Lakmé and Mallika deserves special mention; it suggests something of the inner peace and proximity to nature of the Indian way of life. M 1

1. Duet: Lakmé and Mallika

Dô - me é-pais le jas - min A la ro - se s'as - sem - ble.

The Bell Song

The same dreamlike calm is heard in the famous Bell Song. It is heard in the middle of the second act, and is far from being merely an enchanting interlude, since it performs an important dramatic function. Lakmé's father has put her on show and is using her as exotic bait; her voice, soaring to breathtaking heights, is to lure the guilty man to reveal himself. There is extraordinary tension in this scene: Lakmé's heart is torn between keeping faith with the commandments of her religion, and her burgeoning love for the stranger who is guilty of entering the sacred garden. M 2

A multicultural opera

In the many exotic operas of the time, a clash between two cultures was seldom at the heart of the action, as it is later in Puccini's →*Madame Butterfly*. *Lakmé*, however, is an exception. The noble daughter of the Indian priest is presented as being not beneath the Englishwomen, whose presentation verges on caricature, but morally above them. "My heaven is not yours; I do not know the gods you worship," Lakmé confesses to Gérald, cogently summing up a basic cultural problem. Development of a true mutual understanding remained an unfulfilled wish in the nineteenth century. Dreams are a key concept in the opera. The two lovers experience their relationship as if in sleep, but reality brings them down to earth from the heaven of which they dream, and causes their tragic end.   P. H.

Lakmé, Franz Egenieff as Nilakantha, Komische Oper, Berlin c. 1906.
The story of Lakmé was remarkably bold and modern for the early 1880s, 40 years before Gandhi's freedom movement.

2. Lakmé's Bell Song

Ah ! ah ! ah ! ah ! ah ! ah !   ah ! ah ! ah ! ah ! ah ! ah ! ah !   ah !

Dessau's work was regarded as a model of ethically inspired composition in postwar Germany, uniting modern musical techniques and traditional structures with masterly skill.

Dessau, Paul

b. 19 December 1894 in Hamburg
d. 28 June 1979 in Königswusterhausen (near Berlin)

The son of a synagogue cantor, Dessau began his musical education early, and was already performing in public as a violinist at the age of eleven. He studied at the Klindworth-Scharwenka Conservatory in Berlin, and embarked on a career as a music director in 1912. From 1925 to 1933 he worked at the Städtische Oper, Berlin; he then emigrated to Paris and became a friend of René Leibowitz, through whom he became acquainted with the twelve-tone technique. In 1939 he emigrated to the USA, living first in New York and then in Hollywood. His first collaboration with Bertolt Brecht was in 1942. He settled in Zeuthen, near Berlin, in 1948. He and his wife, the internationally famous director Ruth Berghaus, made their house a meeting place for outstanding artists, including the writers Heiner Müller and Karl Mickel, and the composers →Hans Werner Henze and →Luigi Nono. Dessau was among the most important composers of East Germany, and many young artists took him as their model.

Works: Stage works: *Die Verurteilung des Lukullus* (*The Judgment on Lucullus*) (1951, Berlin), *Puntila* (1956/FP 1966, Berlin), *Lanzelot* (*Lancelot*) (1969, Berlin), *Einstein* (1974, Berlin), *Leonce und Lena* (*Leonce and Lena*) (1979, Berlin); vocal works, orchestral works, chamber music.

Paul Dessau and Bertolt Brecht, c. 1940.
Paul Dessau was one of the composers to whom Bertolt Brecht turned most frequently in his later years for settings of his song texts and for incidental music for his plays; others were Kurt Weill and Hans Eisler.

The Judgment on Lucullus

Die Verurteilung

Opera in twelve scenes

Libretto: Bertolt Brecht.
Première: first version: *Das Verhör des Lukullus*, 17 March 1951, Berlin (trial performance, Deutsche Staatsoper); second version: *Die Verurteilung des Lukullus*, 12 October 1951, Berlin (Deutsche Staatsoper).
Characters: Lukullus/Lucullus, a Roman general (T); figures on frieze: The King (B), The Queen (S), Two Children (2 S), Two Legionaries (2 B), Lasus, cook to Lucullus (T), Man with cherry tree (T); witnesses in the shadow court: The Fishwife (A), The Courtesan (Ms), The Teacher (T), The Baker (T), The Farmer (B), Tertullia, an old woman (Ms); Three Women's Voices (3 S, in the pit), Judge of the Dead (high B), Five Officers (3 T, 2 B), Teacher of a class of children (T), Two Shades (2 B), Woman's Voice commenting (S, in the pit); Court Spokesman, Three Ushers, Two Young Girls, Two Merchants, Two Women, Two Plebeians, A Driver (spoken); crowd, soldiers, slaves, shades (chorus); children's chorus.

The Judgment on Lucullus, production photograph from the première, with Alfred Hülgert (left) as Lucullus, production Wolf Völker, conductor Hermann Scherchen, Berliner Staatsoper 1951.
The controversial, pacifist message of the opera was well received, and it was a brilliant success.

Setting: Rome and the underworld in antiquity.

Synopsis

As a Roman general, Lucullus has conquered the East, defeated seven kings, and added to the riches of the city of Rome. A magnificent funeral procession accompanies his body to the grave. Slaves carry a frieze showing his conquests. After his funeral on the Appian Way, the living return to their everyday occupations. The soldiers from the procession arrange to visit a brothel. A Teacher tells his pupils about the deeds of the great conqueror. Lucullus himself must wait in the anteroom of the underworld before he can be allowed in. Once so powerful, he is not used to being placed on the same footing as common people. He protests, but in vain. An Old Woman is called to judgment first, and she is soon permitted to join the shades. The court asks Lucullus about his life, and when he is asked whether he has done mankind more good or more harm, he can find no one to speak for him. The Judge of the Dead orders the frieze to be brought in, and calls the figures on it as witnesses. A King whose kingdom Lucullus conquered, a Queen raped and murdered by his soldiers, two Children who died in the sack of cities, and a Courtesan all give evidence against Lucullus. He justifies the destruction of 53 cities by citing the honor and glory of Rome. But what is Rome? The trial is taking so long that the Judge of the Dead calls for an adjournment. Newly arrived shades, once common people, throng the anteroom, complaining of their wretched lives in Rome. To hasten proceedings, a Fishwife represents all mothers in accusing Lucullus. Thousands have died as legionaries in his campaigns, she says. The Cook raises his voice in his master's defense, saying that he is grateful to Lucullus for allowing him to pursue cookery as an art. A Farmer praises Lucullus for bringing a rare species of cherry tree back to Italy from his campaigns. Yet a single man would have been sufficient to bring back the cherry tree, and Lucullus sacrificed thousands. Judgment goes against him: he is damned.

S. N.

An opera about a trial

Bertolt Brecht wrote a radio play entitled *Das Verhör des Lukullus* (*The Interrogation of Lucullus*) at the time of the invasion of Poland by German troops in the fall of 1939. It was first broadcast in Berne on 12 May 1940. Dessau met Brecht in the USA during the emigration, and Brecht asked him to suggest the play to Igor Stravinsky as an opera libretto. Stravinsky turned it down, but Dessau himself liked both the subject and the construction of the play. When he and Brecht returned from the USA, they offered their joint work to the Deutsche Staatsoper, Berlin. There were arguments with the cultural bureaucracy, and the authors changed not only the title but also the closing scene, which now ended definitively with the condemnation of Lucullus (originally, the outcome of the trial was left open). The opera refers to ideas beyond the events which inspired its composition, for the central concepts of the fear of death and the desire for fame are of general relevance. The music is striking and memorable, colorful in its instrumentation and harmony, and rich in associations, with allusions to works by J.S. Bach and Handel. One solo, the Fishwife's accusation, became famous and popular. The work was a landmark in the development of an independent form of German opera in the postwar period. The successful première of *The Judgment on Lucullus* in Berlin induced Hermann Scherchen to give the official première of the opera's first version, *The Interrogation of Lucullus*, in Frankfurt am Main in 1952. The Leipzig production of 1957 made the work internationally famous, and it was successfully performed at the Théâtre des Nations Festival in Paris in 1958.   *S. N.*

The Judgment on Lucullus, photograph from the production by Ruth Berghaus, sets Hans-Joachim Schlieker, conductor Hartmut Haenchen, Berliner Staatsoper, Berlin 1983 (photograph 1998).
Ruth Berghaus directed the opera five times, including her productions of 1960, 1965, and 1983. The 1983 production remained in the repertory for over a decade, and was very successful again on its revival in 1998, with Reiner Goldberg as Lucullus and Barbara Bornemann as the Fishwife.

Below:
The Judgment on Lucullus, photograph from the production by Ruth Berghaus, Berliner Staatsoper 1983 (photograph 1998). The children killed in Lucullus's wars are ever present on stage.

Doctor and Apothecary, fresco design by Moritz von Schwind for the foyer of the Wiener Oper, 1866.
Archetypal figures from the *commedia dell'arte*: the *dottore* (Krautmann), the *capitano* (Sturmwald), and the girl (Leonore) who loves another.

*D*ittersdorf was the founding father of German comic opera. He was influenced by the north German Singspiel, adopted Italian techniques, and employed stylistic methods from the Viennese tradition.

Dittersdorf, Karl Ditters von

b. 2 November 1739 in Vienna
d. 24 October 1799 at Schloss Rothlhotta (near Nové Dvory/Neuhof, Central Bohemia)

As a child, Dittersdorf had played in the instrumental ensemble of a Benedictine church in Vienna. When he became page to Field Marshal Prince Josef of Hildburghausen he received a sound education of which the musical part was provided by Giuseppe Bonno, who helped him to gain a place in the orchestra of the Vienna Court Opera. Dittersdorf went on a successful tour of Italy as a violin virtuoso before succeeding Joseph Haydn as *Kapellmeister* to the Bishop of Grosswardein. Among the most important events in his life were his appointment to the papal Order of the Golden Spur, and his elevation to the nobility. He declined the offer of a position as imperial court *Kapellmeister*, since he was already running his own theater in Johannisberg. His stage works were later overshadowed by the operas of Mozart, and with the exception of *Doctor and Apothecary* did not hold their place in the repertory.

Works: Over 40 operas, including *Amore in Musica* (*Love in Music*) (1767, Grosswardein), *25000 Gulden oderlm Dunkeln ist gut munkeln* (*25000 Guilders or Gossiping is Easier in the Dark*) (1785, Vienna), *Doktor und Apotheker* (*Doctor and Apothecary*) (1786, Vienna), *Betrug durch Aberglauben* (*Deception by Superstition*) (1786, Vienna). *Die Liebe im Narrenhause* (*Love in the Madhouse*) (1787, Vienna), *Hieronymus Knicker* (1789, Vienna), *Das rote Käppchen* (*The Red Cap*) (1788, Vienna), *Das Gespenst mit der Trommel* (*The Ghost with the Drum*) (1794, Oels), *Don Quixote der Zweyte* (*Don Quixote the Second*) (1795, Oels), *Die lustigen Weiber von Windsor* (*The Merry Wives of Windsor*) (1796, Oels); oratorios, masses, cantatas, orchestral works.

Doctor and Apothecary
Doktor und Apotheker

Comic *Singspiel* in two acts

Libretto: Johann Gottlieb Stephanie (the younger).
Première: 11 July 1786, Vienna (Burgtheater).
Characters: Stössel, an apothecary (B), Claudia, his wife (Ms), Leonore, their daughter (S), Rosalie, Stössel's niece (S), Krautmann, a doctor (B), Gotthold, his son (T), Sturmwald, a former army captain with a wooden leg and a patch over one eye (T), Sichel, a surgeon (T), Gallus, a patient's servant (T), a Superintendent of Police (B).
Setting: Vienna, around 1780.

Synopsis
Act I
The apothecary Stössel, who is at daggers drawn with Dr. Krautmann, will not allow his daughter Leonore to marry Krautmann's son Gotthold, and arranges a marriage between her and the former army captain Sturmwald. Stössel's niece Rosalie is involved with the surgeon Sichel. One night, Gotthold and Sichel lure Stössel out of the house and climb in through the window to see the girls. The two young couples decide to marry without their families' consent, but in their excitement they wake Stössel's wife Claudia. Stössel comes home drunk, with Sturmwald. The two young men take refuge in the laboratory, Claudia locks the girls up, and Sturmwald promises to keep watch. But he falls asleep, giving Sichel and Gotthold the chance to steal his wooden leg and his uniform, and to lock him in the laboratory.
Act II
A farcical scene is acted out for Stössel's benefit: Gotthold, disguised as a notary, pretends to marry Leonore to "Sturmwald", really Sichel. As they are about to begin the wedding breakfast, the real Sturmwald wakes up. Claudia exposes the masquerade and mocks Stössel and Sturmwald. Meanwhile, a patient treated by Stössel instead of Krautmann has died. Krautmann intends to take Stössel to court as a quack. Claudia suggests that if Krautmann withdraws his complaint, Stössel will refrain from laying charges against Gotthold for abduction. Everyone agrees to these terms, and the young people can marry.

M. S.

Popular – by imperial decree
At the instigation of the imperial opera company, Johann Gottlieb Stephanie, director of the Burgtheater in Vienna, commissioned Dittersdorf to write a German opera. Emperor Joseph II wanted a successful work with which to revive the tradition of German *Singspiel*. However, borrowings from Italian opera were inevitable. The librettist conceived the plot and characters to suit these requirements, and the *buffo* figures of Stössel

Doctor and Apothecary, Carl Seydel as Sichel, Munich 1925.
An age-old recipe for comedy: the man dressed in women's clothes.

Right
Doctor and Apothecary, photograph from the production with (left to right) Santucci, Krause, and Anders, Landestheater, Dessau. The opera's comic elements still appeal to singers and directors.

and Krautmann were depicted in a musically relaxed manner. The work's easy accessibility and comic situations, together with succinct, graceful melodies and small but telling effects were to guarantee its success. The construction of the first act finale is of some interest; it shows traces of the influence of Mozart's second act finale in → *The Marriage of Figaro*. Mozart's opera had received its première not long before Dittersdorf's *Doctor and Apothecary*, but was not nearly as successful as Dittersdorf's *Singspiel*, which brought the composer three more commissions to write operas.

M. S.

Doctor and Apothecary, production photograph with Gabriele Prahm as Claudia, production Kornelia Repschläger, Südostbayerisches Städtestheater, Landshut 1992.
Dittersdorf's music mingles the effervescent Italian *opera buffa* style with Austrian folk elements.

Below
Doctor and Apothecary, photograph from the production by Hans Hartleb, sets Ludwig Hornsteiner, conductor Meinhard von Zallinger, Bayerische Staatsoper, Munich 1961.
Krautmann and Stössel accuse each other publicly of being quacks. A tried and trusted recipe for comedy is to mock medical men.

*D*onizetti was a versatile dramatist who produced a remarkably extensive body of work. He showed great powers of musical invention, and had a sure touch with effective dramatic situations.

Elisa Orlandi as Jane Seymour in *Anna Bolena*.
Anne Boleyn's bloodthirsty husband King Henry VIII (B) is unfaithful to her with her lady in waiting Jane Seymour, whom he wishes to make his queen. Only Anne stands in his way – but not for long. Henry has her first thrown into prison and then executed for a secret but entirely harmless meeting with the friend of her youth, Lord Percy (T). In her cell, she goes mad, and sings a prayer for herself, her rival and the king to a beautiful tune. *M 1*

Closing scene from *Maria di Rohan* with Eugenia Tadolini (Maria, Contessa di Rohan), Carlo Guasco (Riccardo, Conte di Chalais) and Giorgio Ronconi (Enrico, Duca di Chevreuse), from the drawing by J. Cajetan, engraved by J.W. Zinke for the *Wiener Theaterzeitung*, mid-19th century.
A typical operatic scene, showing the singers in the première of Donizetti's *Maria di Rohan*: the soprano (Maria) and the tenor (Riccardo) are in love, the baritone (Enrico) feels betrayed, and kills the tenor in the last act.

Adelaide Gambaro as the Roman nobleman Maffio Orsini in *Lucrezia Borgia*. Even in the stylized world of opera she seems a strange hybrid – the alto as transvestite: the role is a breeches part, but the singer wears a woman's dress and a moustache.

Donizetti, Gaetano

b. 29 November 1797 in Bergamo
d. 8 April 1848 in Bergamo

Donizetti's musical education, which he received from Johannes Simon (Giovanni Simone) Mayr, was an unusually thorough one for Italy at the time. He began his career by writing orchestral and chamber music, cantatas, sacred music, and songs, but after the première of his opera *Zoraida di Granata* (*Zoraida of Granada*) (1822, Rome), which attracted the attention of the famous impresario Domenico Barbaia, he devoted himself chiefly to opera. His international breakthrough came with *Anna Bolena* (*Anne Boleyn*) (1830, Milan). Further successes followed: *L'elisir d'amore* (*The Elixir of Love*) (1832, Milan), *Lucrezia Borgia* (1833, Milan), and the enthusiastically received *Lucia di Lammermoor* (*Lucy of Lammermoor*) (1835, Naples) established his reputation. Not all his operas were successful at their first performances (although that is no indication of their musical quality); the première of *Maria Stuarda* (*Mary Stuart*) (1834, Naples) was a fiasco. After *Pia de' Tolomei* (1837, Venice), *Roberto Devereux* (1837, Naples), and *Maria di Rudenz* (1838, Venice), Donizetti left Italy when *Poliuto* (1848, Naples), was banned by the censors; he had also suffered a severe blow at this time, with the early death of his wife. Like →Rossini and →Bellini, he moved to Paris, and was so immediately successful with *La fille du régiment* (*The Daughter of the Regiment*), and *La favorite* (*The Favorite*) (both 1840) that Hector Berlioz spoke of a "positive war of invasion." Donizetti's health deteriorated at the beginning of the 1840s. In spite of some periods of creative inspiration and success – for instance, with *Linda di Chamounix* (*Linda of Chamonix*), which had its première in Vienna in 1842 and *Don Pasquale* in Paris in 1843 – the last decade of his life was marked by the course of the syphilis that finally killed him. Donizetti became mentally disturbed, and spent his last years first in a sanatorium, later with friends in Bergamo, until death released him.

Works: Over 70 operas, about two-thirds of them *opere serie* or *opere semiserie*; solo cantatas, many sacred works, a large number of songs, orchestral works, and chamber music (including 18 string quartets).

Maria Stuarda, production photograph with Agnes Baltsa as Elizabeth, production Grischa Asagaroff, conductor Adam Fischer, Wiener Staatsoper 1985.
Subjects from British history were very popular in the bel canto era. The struggle between Queen Elizabeth I and Mary Stuart for the same man (the Earl of Leicester) offered a series of conflicting states of mind very suitable for great monologues, scenes and arias. The basic mood of this work, as in most of the *opere serie* of the period, is one of melancholy. In her private life, the powerful Queen Elizabeth is the loneliest woman in the world.

1. Anne Boleyn's Prayer

Cie-lo, a' mieilun - ghi spa - si - mi con - ce - di alfin ri - po - so

Typical roles of Romantic opera

Stage characters were linked to certain types of singers and their forms of musical expression: the part of the innocent, suffering heroine who breaks into delirious coloraturas was as well suited to a virtuoso soprano as was the role of lover to the tenor, who might be a lyric or perhaps a heroic tenor, but was always passionate. Baritones and basses could appear as evil intriguers or fatherly friends (only the talents of the famous Giorgio Ronconi, who sang in many of Donizetti's operas and was the first Zaccaria in Verdi's →*Nabucco,* led to some extension and variation in the parts for this vocal register). When →Igor Stravinsky wrote of his collaboration with W.H. Auden as the librettist of his opera →*The Rake's Progress*, "We began with a hero, a heroine, and a villain, and decided that they should be sung by a tenor, a soprano, and a bass," he was ironically echoing the old distribution of roles usual in Romantic opera with respect to content, music, and vocal range. É. P.-L.

Left
Achille Basini as Don Alfonso in *Lucrezia Borgia*.
In *Lucrezia Borgia,* which has perhaps the most hair-raising libretto in operatic literature, the historical characters are adapted to suit the usual vocal registers. The notorious poisoner Lucrezia Borgia does indeed practice her dreadful art, but she is careful to have an antidote for her own son. He does not recognize her as his mother, and even falls in love with her. The villain of the piece is her fourth husband, Don Alfonso I, the Duke of Ferrara (bass), who correctly sees the young mercenary soldier Gennaro (tenor) as his rival in love.

The Elixir of Love, production photograph from Act I, Wiener Staatsoper 1980. Donizetti had already written several comic operas before composing *The Elixir of Love* in 1832. They included the amusing comedy *Le convenienze ed inconvenienze teatrali* (*The Usages and Misusages of the Stage*, better known as *Viva la Mamma!*, 1827); however, his first major venture into the field of comic opera was with *The Elixir of Love*. The Italian village background, typical motifs of impromptu comedy, and simple melodies reminiscent of folk song give the piece its charm and contribute to its popularity. The legend that the opera was composed within two weeks has now been disproved; its composition took Donizetti six weeks.

Setting: A village in the Basque region, early in the 19th century.

Synopsis

The young peasant Nemorino is in love with the rich and beautiful Adina, who is also being courted by Sergeant Belcore. To alleviate his sufferings, Nemorino buys an "elixir of love" (in fact only a bottle of good wine) from the "miracle doctor" Dulcamara. When Adina discovers that Nemorino has had to enlist as a soldier in order to buy the elixir, she is touched; she recognizes Nemorino's true love for her, buys his freedom, and the couple are happily united.

Act I

At the merry harvest festival, the simple young peasant Nemorino tells of his love for the beautiful, rich Adina. Adina reads the villagers the old story of Tristan and Isolde, making fun of the effects of the love potion used by Tristan to win Isolde's heart. Sergeant Belcore enters, to the rousing sound of a military march, and woos Adina passionately. Adina, flattered, ignores the shy advances of Nemorino. The villagers' curiosity is aroused by the arrival of an itinerant quack doctor, Dulcamara, in his showy carriage. The doctor is selling remedies which he claims will cure every disorder, and of course he has a magic potion to help with Nemorino's unrequited love. It is only a bottle of good Bordeaux, but it soon takes effect, and the now cheerful Nemorino is no longer shy with Adina, who agrees to marry Belcore out of pique.

Act II

Nemorino is in despair: the elixir has not had the hoped-for effect. He allows Belcore to enlist him as a soldier so that he can afford a second bottle of the expensive potion, paying the miracle doctor with his enlistment bounty. Meanwhile, a rumor is spreading through the village that Nemorino is heir to his rich uncle, who has recently died. All the girls are suddenly chasing him, but since Nemorino has not heard the rumor himself, he puts their conduct down to the effects of the elixir. Adina learns that Nemorino has enlisted in order to get money to buy the magic potion. She is touched by his true love for her, and buys him out of the army. Both at last confess their love for each other, and Dulcamara too is happy at the end of the opera: he can now do very good business with his "elixir of love."

E. P.-L.

The Elixir of Love, Otto Edelmann as Dulcamara, Theater an der Wien 1954. Outrageous charlatan or clever psychologist? The itinerant Dr. Dulcamara spices up dull village life with his aggressively clownish character as well as his elixir: he can be both positive and negative, *dolce* (sweet) and *amaro* (bitter), "as you like it".

The Elixir of Love

L'elisir d'amore

Melodramma giocoso in two acts

Libretto: Felice Romani, after *Le philtre* (*The Philtre*) by Eugène Scribe.
Première: 12 May 1832, Milan (Teatro della Canobbiana).
Characters: Adina, a rich and capricious landowner (S), Nemorino, a simple young peasant, in love with Adina (T), Belcore, sergeant of the village garrison (Bar), Dottor Dulcamara, an itinerant quack doctor (B), Giannetta, a young peasant girl (S); peasants, soldiers (chorus).

The Elixir of Love

"Elisir di sì perfetta, di sì rara qualità ..." ("What an excellent, what a rare elixir! ..."), sing Adina, Nemorino, and the villagers, commenting on the magic potion that once brought Tristan and Isolde together. Early in Donizetti's *The Elixir of Love* Tristan and Isolde's story is read and interpreted with ironic amusement. Only Nemorino really believes that the potion will work – and work it does, although not by magic, but by bringing about a change of heart in the main characters. Dulcamara's "magic potion," really a good red wine, is not a cheap deception (for Nemorino literally pays a high price for his two bottles), nor indeed just an item out of the box of tricks of *opera buffa*; it genuinely assists the leading characters to throw off their inhibitions and admit their true feelings.

É. P.-L.

The Elixir of Love, production photograph with Roberto Alagna (Nemorino) and Angela Gheorghiu (Adina), production Frank Dunlop, costumes Jacques Schmidt, conductor Evelino Pido, Opéra National de Lyon 1995.
The Elixir of Love is a mixture of several old recipes for comedy, but its delicate depiction of the psychology of love, and its study of desire, are very modern.

The figure of Adina, a rather flirtatious, capricious young woman in Scribe, also acquires more sensitivity as handled by Romani and Donizetti. At first she rejects Nemorino, and is flattered by Belcore's compliments, but when she buys Nemorino out of the army with her money, she shows her true love for him. Her aria, "Prendi, per me sei libero" ("Take this, you will be free through me"), another innovation introduced by Romani and Donizetti, has melodic simplicity and dignity, and is comparable to Bellini's cantilenas. *M 3*

The Elixir of Love, production photograph with Mirella Freni (Adina) and Luciano Pavarotti (Nemorino), production and sets Jean-Pierre Ponnelle, conductor Reynald Giovanetti, Hamburgische Staatsoper 1977.
A star cast, high musical standards, and a production observing the spirit of the score were the outstanding features of this staging of *The Elixir of Love* in Hamburg in 1977. Ponnelle's great productions of *Figaro* and his filmed versions of operas by Mozart and Rossini also fell into this period. They were attractive and faithful to the works themselves, setting them in their original periods without trying to update them. Nonetheless, he liberated the most popular works on the operatic stage from old production clichés.

Above right
Andrea Rost as Adina in the wardrobe of the Metropolitan Opera House, New York, in 1996.
Even in the wardrobe, the Hungarian soprano is "singing herself into" the part. Andrea Rost has been singing in the great opera houses of the world since the early 1990s.

A bitter-sweet comedy

This rustic idyll sometimes assumes greater seriousness, and one senses deeper significance in the village comedy. The characters may have their roots in *opera buffa*, but Donizetti's music rounds them out and gives them greater complexity. Nemorino ("the little nobody") describes himself as a fool, but even at his most ridiculous and in a state of intoxication, he arouses sympathy. His love for Adina is deep and genuine. The "magic potion" brings him to understand the importance of expressing his feelings. His famous aria "Una furtiva lagrima" ("A furtive tear"), which was not in fact in Scribe's original libretto but was introduced into the opera by Romani and Donizetti, is a great tenor showpiece, and also expresses a new maturity and intensity. But Donizetti does not let even this lyrical moment pass without light relief: he alternates between the serious and the comic, and the aria "Una furtiva lagrima" is introduced by the unusual combination of harp, bassoon (an instrument generally used for comic effects), and pizzicato strings. *M 2*

Even Dulcamara (whose name means "bitter-sweet", suggesting the flavor of his magic potions) is more than the stereotype of an itinerant quack. The eloquent, cunning figure of a doctor had been a stock figure of Italian comedy ever since the *commedia dell'arte*. Donizetti had already created a similar character in his one-act opera *I pazzi per progetto* (1830). Dulcamara, a very rewarding role for great bass buffos, attracts the attention of the whole village with his entrance aria

The Elixir of Love, Alfred Piccaver as Nemorino, Vienna 1916.

2. Nemorino's Romance

U-na fur-ti-va la-grima __ negl' oc-chi suoi spun-tò

3. Adina's Aria

prendi, per me sei li-be-ro: re-sta nel suol na-ti - o

"Udite, udite o rustici!" ("Listen! Listen, you country folk!") and the delightful trumpet solos that accompany it. With the wisdom of a man of experience, he then uses his wiles to help the undecided make up their minds and so find happiness. Such aspects of the opera make *The Elixir of Love* deeply moving, for all its wealth of comic situations – and show it to be a comedy where there is always the suggestion of "a furtive tear." É. P.-L.

Right
The Elixir of Love, Luciano Pavarotti as Nemorino, Wiener Staatsoper 1984.
In his younger days Pavarotti was the ideal Nemorino, with all the warmth of the Italian sun in his golden voice. His singing of the folk-like melodies of Nemorino's part is inimitably natural.

Below
The Elixir of Love, production photograph with Roberto Alagna (Nemorino) and Angela Gheorghiu (Adina), production Frank Dunlop, sets Roberto Plate, conductor Evelino Pido, Opéra National de Lyon 1995.
The Elixir of Love can easily be produced in a setting other than that of its original period and village background. It is an opera in which there is no essential local color to be preserved, and a comic opera is more easily updated than a tragedy, since it employs more immediate dramatic expression.

Lucia di Lammermoor

Lucy of Lammermoor

Dramma tragico in two acts (also in three acts, seven scenes)

Libretto: Salvatore Cammarano, after the novel *The Bride of Lammermoor* by Sir Walter Scott.
Première: 26 September 1835, Naples (Teatro San Carlo).
Characters: Lord Enrico Ashton (Bar), Lucia, his sister (S), Sir Edgardo di Ravenswood (T), Lord Arturo Bucklaw (T), Raimondo Bidebent, priest and tutor to Lucia (B), Normanno, captain of the Ravenswood guard (T), Alisa, companion to Lucia (Ms); ladies and gentlemen attached to the house of Ashton, inhabitants of Lammermoor, pages, soldiers, and servants at Ashton (chorus).
Setting: Scotland in the late 17th century.

Synopsis

Lord Enrico Ashton is planning to marry his sister Lucia to Lord Arturo Bucklaw. However, Lucia loves Edgardo, her brother's sworn enemy. Deceived by a forged letter which makes her believe Edgardo is unfaithful to her, she agrees to marry Bucklaw, whom she does not love. When Edgardo, who is innocent of the charge, curses her, Lucia goes mad, kills her bridegroom on the wedding night, and dies. Edgardo commits suicide.

Act I

Scene 1: Lord Enrico Ashton is pursuing his arch-enemy Edgardo Ravenswood, whose ancestors were robbed of their property by the Ashtons in the past. In the political and tactical interests of the Ashton family, Lucia is now to marry Lord Arturo Bucklaw. When Ashton discovers that she is secretly in love with Edgardo, he swears revenge.
Scene 2: Lucia tells her companion the tale of a Ravenswood who once killed his beloved; since then, she has appeared as a ghost near the well in the park. Alisa takes this story as a bad omen, and warns Lucia against a similar fate. Nonetheless, Lucia keeps her assignation with Edgardo. Edgardo has to leave on a political mission; they say their farewells, swearing eternal love and constancy.

Act II

Scene 1: Enrico has shown Lucia a forged letter which makes her believe that Edgardo has been unfaithful. In despair, she agrees to marry Arturo.

Scene 2: As Lucia signs the marriage contract, Edgardo appears and curses the unhappy girl.

Act III

Scene 1: Enrico and Edgardo determine to settle their feud with a duel, but postpone the fight until next morning.

Scene 2: The merry wedding festivities end abruptly when the guests are told that Lucia has killed her bridegroom. Lucia, who has gone mad, appears before them in her bloodstained gown, with a dagger in her hand. She imagines that she is marrying Edgardo, dreams of his forgiveness, and wishes herself dead.

Scene 3: Edgardo hides in the ancestral vault of the Ravenswoods, waiting for Enrico. When he learns of Lucia's madness and death, he commits suicide. *É.P.-L.*

Edgardo gets a word in too

At the première, the famous prima donna Fanny Tachinardi-Persiani sang the title role, a fact which certainly contributed to the huge success of *Lucia di Lammermoor* but was also at the root of the disfiguring changes and cuts that became typical of later productions. For instance, by transposing the great mad scene downward, Fanny Tacchinardi-Persiani was able to make a better effect with her high notes. She thus ultimately made this dramatic scene, and indeed the entire role of Lucia, into a brilliant vehicle for a singer. Even the close of the opera – Edgardo's suicide – now lost its point. In accordance with the conventions of Romantic opera, the work should have ended with the great mad scene and death of the eponymous heroine. However, Donizetti did not follow that convention, thereby endowing the character of Edgardo with new qualities. The passionately enamored and often quick-tempered young hero displays movingly tragic characteristics in his aria "Tu che a Dio spiegasti l'ali," in which he describes Lucia as a transfigured angel, anticipating the pathos and dignity of Verdi's great tenor heroes. *M 4 É.P.-L.*

Lucia di Lammermoor, Adelina Patti (opposite, above) and Marie von Marra (above) as Lucia.
This opera features in several novels (for instance Tolstoy's *Anna Karenina* and Flaubert's *Madame Bovary*) as the quintessence of Romantic opera, because of its tense drama and the expressive force of the music. The part of Lucia was important to many prima donnas. Adelina Patti (1843–1919), one of the most sought-after prima donnas of the 19th century, made her début as Lucia in New York at the age of 16. Her elder colleague, Marie von Marra (1822–78), who sang Lucia in Vienna during Donizetti's own lifetime, has been a comparatively neglected figure in operatic history.

Opposite, below
Lucia di Lammermoor, set design by Adolph Mahnke, production Hans Strohbach, conductor Kurt Striegler, Sächsisches Staatstheater, Dresden 1937/38.
The romantic setting of a Scottish castle with a well, by moonlight. The works of Sir Walter Scott (1771–1832) were very popular as the basis for operatic libretti in the 19th century. They offered both the historical background that replaced classical and mythological subjects in Romantic libretti, and plots full of excitement, adventure, and conflicting love tangles. His *The Bride of Lammermoor* (1819) was set to music no less than six times between 1827 and 1834.

Lucia di Lammermoor, Giovanni Pancani as Edgardo, lithograph, 1841.
Edgardo is a part for the lyric tenor *par excellence*. The role portrays him as a young man inexperienced in courtly intrigues.

4. Edgardo's Farewell Aria

Tu che a Dio spie - ga - sti l'a - li,   o bel-l'alma in - na - mo - ra - ta

Lucia di Lammermoor, production photograph with Alexandra von der Werth as Lucia, production Christof Loy, sets and costumes Herbert Murauer, conductor Francesco Corti, Deutsche Oper am Rhein, Theater der Stadt Duisburg 1999.
The young soprano Alexandra von der Werth was enthusiastically received as the ideal embodiment of Lucia, not only for the limpid clarity of her voice and her attractive appearance but for her convincing acting in the part; her posture and her small gestures suggest the stress Lucia suffers from living in a male society.

Lucia di Lammermoor, production photograph from the finale of the second act with Edita Gruberová (Lucia) and Alfredo Kraus (Edgardo), Wiener Staatsoper 1987.
The famous sextet at the end of Act II is regarded as a focal point of the opera, with the emotions of the individual characters merging in a wonderful ensemble. When Edgardo suddenly appears at Lucia's wedding, time seems to stand still. Edgardo and Enrico, who is now tormented by pangs of conscience, begin to sing the moving melody of the sextet, and are then joined by Lucia and her tutor Raimondo, and later (complementing rather than developing the musical texture) by Alisa and Arturo. *M 7*

The unhappy Lucia

The unique beauty and elegance, the fiery flow and sweeping passion of Donizetti's melodies, have often been highly praised. One of the finest examples is Lucia's story of the ghost that haunts the well. The melody begins simply, in a nocturne-like rhythm, and is enriched by stirring coloratura passages as Lucia's agitation increases. The audience discovers at this point that she is very sensitive, indeed highly strung, and is tormented by dark fears and forebodings. *M 5*

Except in her great love duet with Edgardo in Act I, the eponymous heroine of the opera never appears

5. Lucia's Coloraturas (Aria, Act I)

e l'on - da pria si lim - pi - da di ___ san - gue ___ ros - seg - giò

6. Mad Scene, in Three-Four Time

Spar - gi d'a - ma - ro pian - to il mio ter - re - stre ve - - lo

7. Melody of the Sextet (Act II)

Chi mi fre - na in tal mo - men to?.. Chi tron - cò del - l'i - re il cor - so?

Lucia di Lammermoor, production photograph with Joan Sutherland as Lucia, production Franco Zeffirelli, Royal Opera House, Covent Garden, London 1959.
Confronting the audience with the depiction of madness is a considerable challenge to great singers. This photograph shows Joan Sutherland (b. 1926) in the outstanding production by Franco Zeffirelli (b. 1923).

Elisabetta o il Castello di Kenilworth (1829) for glass harmonica and harp accompaniment. The same accompaniment had originally been intended for Lucia's mad scene, but it was later changed to flute and harp. The ethereal tonal color and ecstatic passages for these two instruments are used to express Lucia's character in music.

É. P.-L.

Below
Lucia di Lammermoor, production photograph with Andrea Rost as Lucia, production Andrei Serban, conductor Bruno Campanella, Opéra National de Paris 1996.
Situations of extreme drama in Romantic bel canto operas often end in derangement and madness. From both the musical and the dramatic viewpoint, mad scenes have offered great prima donnas the opportunity for a rewarding finale; in this case the soprano is Andrea Rost of Hungary (b. 1962). Composers writing operas in early 19th-century Italy had to bow to the often tyrannical demands of great star singers.

happy, content, or well balanced. Derangement is the almost inevitable outcome of her increasingly extreme state of mind. Lucia never finds peace and inner contentment until she invokes death. Her apparently calm words "Spargi d'amaro pianto" ("Cover with bitter tears" *M 6*) become more and more disturbed by sudden harmonic changes, chromatic figures, and passionately distorted passages. The customary coloraturas of a traditional mad scene become an essential component of her musical portrait. Donizetti had already used flute and harp accompaniment earlier, in Anna Bolena's mad scene, and he set Amelia's aria in

The Daughter of the Regiment

La fille du régiment

Opéra comique in two acts

Libretto: Jules Henri de Saint-Georges and Jean-François-Alfred Bayard.
Première: 11 February 1840, Paris (Opéra-Comique).
Characters: Marie, a young *vivandière* (S), Tonio, a young Tyrolean (T), La Marquise de Birkenfeld (Ms), Sulpice, a Sergeant (B), Hortensius, the Marquise's major-domo (B), Duchess de Crakentorp (A), A Peasant (T), A Corporal (B), A Notary (spoken); French soldiers, Tyrolean peasants, Bavarian courtiers (chorus).
Setting: In the Tyrolean mountains near the Swiss border, at the end of the Napoleonic wars, around 1815.

Synopsis

Marie, found as an infant by the soldiers who have brought her up, is the darling of the regiment, and follows her protectors as a *vivandière*. A young Tyrolean joins the army for love of her. Marie's mother, a marquise, finds her daughter and takes her away to her castle, where she plans to educate and marry her in accordance with her rank, but Marie remains true to her soldiers.

The Daughter of the Regiment, Elisabeth Leisinger (1856–1934) as Marie.
The idea of a woman in the army was a very comical one in the 19th century. The costume and little drum were so characteristic of this part that all singers who took the part of Marie were provided with the same uniform, creating a positive army of daughters of the regiment.

Act I

Marie was found as an infant by soldiers, who brought her up, and was adopted by the regiment. She now lives happily with them, following the drum in all their manoeuvers and battles as a *vivandière*. She is in love with the young Tyrolean Tonio; when he learns that only a member of the regiment may marry Marie, he joins the company. The Marquise of Berkenfeld claims that Marie is her niece, and takes her away to her castle, intending to bring her up there in a manner befitting her noble birth.

Act II

Marie has been living in the castle for a year, but cannot settle down in her new life, although the Marquise confesses that she is her mother and not her aunt. Marie is to marry the son of a duchess, and the guests invited to the wedding arrive. However, Marie remembers the happy days when she lived with her soldiers. The regiment arrives in the nick of time, just as the bridegroom's mother, the Duchess of Crackentorp, is about to sign the marriage contract. Tonio, who has now risen to the rank of lieutenant, reveals Marie's past as a *vivandière* to the distinguished company. The wedding plans fall through, and the indignant guests leave the castle. However, the Marquise now gives Marie and Tonio permission to marry, with her blessing. *S.N.*

Salut à la France

The success of this work (in which Donizetti uses spoken dialogue, as is usual in French *opéra comique*) was certainly connected with its simple, idealistic picture of military life. It became traditional to perform the opera on 14 July, the anniversary of the storming of the Bastille. Marie's "Salut à la France" became almost a second French national anthem. *M 8*

8. Marie's Aria

Sa - lut à la Fran - ce, à mes _ beaux jours, à l'es-pé - ran-ce, à mes _ a - mours!

9. Tonio's Aria

Pour   mon   â -   me Quel _ des - ti - a _____

10. Rataplan

Ra-ta-plan, ra-ta-plan, ra-ta-plan, ra-ta-plan, plan, plan, plan, plan,

The Daughter of the Regiment, photograph from the production by Giancarlo del Monaco, sets and costumes Toni Businger, conductor Marcello Panni, Opernhaus, Zürich 1988.
For the climax of the opera, the director provided a carefully composed stage tableau resembling a historical painting.

The Daughter of the Regiment, caricature by Johann Christian Schoeller from the *Wiener Theaterzeitung*, 1840.
The dream of the petite bourgeoisie in 1840: "I wouldn't mind serving with that regiment!"

peculiar logic of the libretto of a Romantic opera; various other dramatic aspects also look forward to what was to be the most successful stage genre of the nineteenth century. Everything is seen from the point of view of the bourgeoisie, even of the petite bourgeoisie: the army, patriotic feelings, the aristocracy. And the dénouement distinctly resembles operetta: a bourgeois love match is shown to be better than an aristocratic marriage of convenience. Even the Marquise, Marie's mother, finally gives way, moved to tears, and gives the young couple her blessing, in almost the same way as the aristocratic characters of Emmerich Kálmán's operetta *Csárdás Princess*, 70 years later.

The Daughter of the Regiment, production photograph with Daniela Lojarro (Marie) and Maurizio Picconi (Sulpice), production Giancarlo del Monaco, sets and costumes Toni Businger, conductor Marcello Panni, Opernhaus, Zürich 1988.
In this opera, Marie is not only fighting to be allowed to choose her own rank in society; her military career also gives her confidence in her feminine identity.

The Daughter of the Regiment was also popular for its two rewarding leading roles, although the part of Tonio calls for a tenor with confident top notes, particularly in the aria "Je suis soldat" ("I am a soldier"). M 9

Marie was one of the famous roles of such renowned coloratura sopranos as Jenny Lind, Adelina Patti, and Toti dal Monte. The figure of the *vivandière* is attractive in terms of the drama too, for instance in the "singing lesson" in the second act. Marie is to be given an education befitting a lady of quality, and sings first a demure little song which seems to her very insipid. However, when her friend Sergeant Sulpice quietly strikes up the theme of the fiery "Rataplan" that reminds her of her former happy life with the regiment, she forgets all about her aristocratic surroundings and enthusiastically joins in his song, to the growing indignation of the Marquise. The humorous situation is full of changes of mood, reminiscent of scenes in French operettas in the style of Offenbach or Hervé. M 10   É. P.-L.

The secret of a success

Mendelssohn is reported to have said that he wished he had written *The Daughter of the Regiment*. Its huge success – by 1950 it had been performed 1000 times at the Opéra-Comique in Paris – does not derive solely from its dramatic and musical structure. Some operas turn out to be epoch-making works without the composers actually intending it. In *The Daughter of the Regiment*, Donizetti brilliantly satisfied the French taste in opera: the decorative aspects and the atmospheres of different ways of life and social classes as they encounter one another. Here we have a military review with soldiers playing music on the appropriate instruments (bugles, piccolos, and Turkish crescents), there is a bucolic scene with pastoral overtones, and then there is the landed aristocracy, parodied in affectedly archaic music. It is all kept simple, easily understood, accessible. Indeed, *The Daughter of the Regiment* might be described as a folk opera on the grounds of its popular tone. Ten years before the birth of operetta, Donizetti had written a piece in which the sudden twists and turns of the plot anticipate those of operetta, lacking even the

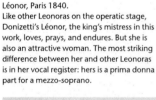

La favorite

The Favorite

Opéra in four acts

Libretto: Alphonse Royer, Gustave Vaëz, and Eugène Scribe, after *Le Comte de Comminges* (*The Count of Comminges*), by Baculard d'Arnaud.
Première: 2 December 1840, Paris (Opéra).
Characters: Alphonse XI, King of Castile (Bar), Léonor de Guzmán, his favorite (S or Ms), Fernand, a young novice (T), Balthazar, superior of the monastery of Santiago de Compostela (B), Don Gaspar, an officer of the king (T), Inès, Léonor's confidante (S), A Nobleman (T); ladies and gentlemen of the court, pages, guards, monks, novices, pilgrims (chorus).
Setting: Castile, in the middle of the 14th century.

Synopsis

The young novice Fernand does not know that Léonor, whom he loves, is in fact the king's favorite. Fearing excommunication by the Pope, the king plans to end his liaison, and marries Léonor off to Fernand. When Fernand discovers the truth about her, he returns to his monastery, where Léonor seeks him out, confesses her love for him, and begs his forgiveness. She dies in Fernand's arms.

Act I

Fernand, the young novice, is leaving his monastery because of his love for a beautiful woman, who will not divulge her identity. He does not know that she is the king's favorite Léonor. Fernand hopes to win fame as a soldier, in order to be worthy of Léonor's hand.

Act II

Fernand has distinguished himself as a soldier, and Léonor, who loves the young officer, asks the king for her freedom. The king, however, wishes to make her queen. Abbot Balthazar brings news that the Pope is planning to excommunicate adulterers.

Act III

King Alphonse agrees to the marriage of Léonor and Fernand, but keeps the truth about his bride from Fernand. Only after the wedding ceremony does the young man discover that he has married the king's mistress. Deeply disillusioned, he returns to his monastery.

Act IV

As Fernand is about to take his vows, the exhausted Léonor appears. She was innocent of the king's intrigues, and begs forgiveness. Fernand's love is rekindled, but it is too late: Léonor dies in his arms.

É. P.-L.

A hit tune stolen by the composer from himself
The history of the way in which *La favorite* was written is particularly complicated, for Donizetti used material from no less than four of his earlier works. It was not until the rehearsals, for instance, that he added to the score Fernand's captivatingly lovely aria "Spirito gentil" ("Gentle spirit"), a gem among Romantic arias, taken from his unfinished opera *Le duc d'Albe*. M 11

A social tragedy at court
A story full of love tangles and courtly intrigues against a historical background was typical of French grand opera. However, the tale of the triangular relationship between Léonor, Fernand and the king describes three people whose real tragedy is that their social rank will not allow them to display their emotions – indeed, explicitly forbids them to do so. The result turns out to be profoundly tragic for Léonor, who had once believed the king would marry her; he failed to keep that promise, and now she is merely tolerated but not respected as the royal mistress. The figure of the woman who has gone astray appears elsewhere in Donizetti's works, in *Rosmonda d'Inghilterra* and *Linda di Chamounix*, and in works by other composers too, from Bellini's →*Norma* to Verdi's →*La traviata*, Massenet's →*Manon*, and Puccini's →*Manon Lescaut*. In a society that regards constancy and submission as the highest of feminine virtues – the period of the action of a particular opera is of no significance – a woman has no right to determine her own fate. If she tries to do so nonetheless, she must pay for it. She may go mad or die, and will then be accepted retrospectively, earning the hypocritical sympathy of the bourgeoisie, or the no less hypocritical forgiveness of the Church. In the second act, particular emphasis is placed on Léonor's fate and

La favorite, Rosine Stolz as Léonor disguised as a novice in the monastery.
Rosine Stolz was a "favorite" in real life too, although not a novice in a monastery. The famous mezzo-soprano founded her career on an outstanding interpretation of Halévy's →*La juive* in 1836. Donizetti wrote the role of Léonor especially for her and it made her name. She became the mistress of Léon Pillet, director of the Paris Opéra. In 1857, theatrical and press intrigues forced her to retire from the stage, and she went to Brazil, where she became the mistress of the Emperor, Don Pedro, who engaged her for his operatic company at a staggering salary.

Below
La favorite, Fiorenza Cossotto as Léonor at the Teatro alla Scala, Milan 1964/65.
Léonor was the first title role sung at La Scala, Milan, by Fiorenza Cossotto (b. 1935), and it made her internationally famous overnight. She and Giulietta Simionato were the leading Italian mezzo-sopranos of the 1960s and 1970s. She won plaudits in the annals of operatic history for her wonderful vocal timbre, her perfect singing technique, and the ease with which she could master different registers. Besides singing the great mezzo roles, she also took the outstanding alto parts of the Italian operatic repertory.

11. Fernand's Aria

Spiri-to gentil, ne' so-gni mie-i bril-la-sti un dì, ma ti perde-i:

La favorite, production photograph with Dagmar Peckova (Léonor de Guzmán) and Egils Silins (Balthazar), production Andreas Rochholl, Theater Basel 1994.
La favorite is a contemporary story disguised as a historical incident, an earlier operatic variant of *La traviata*.

the impossibility of her ever winning social acceptance: although there is no harmony between her and the king, they both watch a long, courtly ballet with pretended cheerfulness until the news of the papal threat of excommunication reaches them. The scene leads to an agitated finale. The conventional ballet interlude, an established component of French opera, is inserted into the course of a tense drama portraying the feelings of two disappointed, embittered people with unique clarity.

É. P.-L.

Don Pasquale

Dramma buffo in three acts

Libretto: Giovanni Ruffini and Gaetano Donizetti, after *Ser Marcantonio*, by Angelo Anelli.

Première: 3 January 1843, Paris (Théâtre Italien).
Characters: Don Pasquale, an old bachelor (B), Ernesto, his nephew (T), Norina, a young widow, loved by Ernesto (S), Dottor Malatesta, A Physician (Bar), A Notary (Bar); servants (chorus).
Setting: Rome, the 19th century.

Synopsis

The young widow Norina and her suitor Ernesto, nephew of the rich and elderly Don Pasquale, thwart Don Pasquale's plans to marry. With the aid of the cunning Dr. Malatesta, Norina assumes another identity, and stages a fake marriage in which she torments the old man.

Act I

The elderly bachelor Don Pasquale is waiting impatiently for Dr. Malatesta, who has promised to find him a bride. Don Pasquale plans to marry in order to disinherit his nephew. Ernesto is deeply disappointed. Wishing to help Ernesto and the widow Norina, with whom Ernesto is in love, Malatesta concocts a plan: he will introduce Norina to Don Pasquale as his own virtuous young sister Sofronia, and stage a false marriage guaranteed to cure the old man of his dreams of love.

Act II

Ernesto is about to leave on his travels. Malatesta introduces his alleged sister to Don Pasquale, who is immediately enchanted by "Sofronia's" beauty and modest behavior (carefully rehearsed in advance). A marriage ceremony is performed at once. Ernesto, to whom the doctor has disclosed his plan, offers to act as witness. No sooner has the contract been drawn up by the pretended notary than Norina/Sofronia changes into a termagant. She turns the entire household upside down, and begins spending Don Pasquale's money freely.

Act III

Bills keep arriving at Don Pasquale's house, and Norina tries her elderly husband's patience further by announcing that she is going to the theater. When Don Pasquale forbids her to go, she boxes his ears and sweeps out, intentionally dropping a note as she leaves. The humiliated Don Pasquale reads it, and finds that his "Sofronia" has made an assignation. He plans to get revenge, with Malatesta's aid, and most of all he wants to be rid of his wife again. It would be possible, says Malatesta, if he agrees to the marriage of Ernesto and Norina. Don Pasquale gives his consent. When the whole intrigue is revealed, he can only take it with a good grace, and he forgives both the lovers and the doctor.

É. P.-L.

Don Pasquale, photograph from a production with Marian Pop (Malatesta) and Sebastian Reinthaller (Ernesto), Wiener Volksoper 1996. Dr. Malatesta is the moving force behind the action in this chamber work; he is omnipresent, whether in the foreground or the background.

Don Pasquale, production photograph with Oleg Bryjak (Don Pasquale) and Ludwig Grabmeier (Malatesta), production Tobias Richter, conductor Francesco Corti, Deutsche Oper am Rhein, Düsseldorf 1998.
Even in a surrealistic setting, the famous patter duet between Malatesta and Don Pasquale makes its usual frenetic effect.

Don Pasquale, production photograph with Erich Syri (Don Pasquale) and Karl Adolf Appel (Notary), production Venjamin Smechov, conductor Wolfram Koloseus, sets and costumes David Borovski, Nationaltheater Mannheim 1993. The pretend marriage makes Don Pasquale aware that he is not merely a victim of his own egotism, but in a way a tragic hero, for he learns that solitude is the only way of life open to him.

Right
Don Pasquale, production photograph with Elena Brilova (Norina) and Ludwig Grabmeier (Malatesta), production Tobias Richter, conductor Francesco Corti, Deutsche Oper am Rhein, Düsseldorf 1998.
Malatesta gives Norina her final instructions before she begins to act her part.

A corpulent Don Pasquale

Donizetti was lured to the Théâtre-Italien in Paris by the prospect of working with a dazzling cast. Giulia Grisi, who had already sung Elvira in the première of Bellini's →*I puritani*, was to take the part of Norina; the trio of male leads consisted of three legendary singers: the tenor Giovanni Mario, the baritone Antonio Tamburini (known as "Rubini the baritone"), and in the title role the bass Luigi Lablache, who had delighted the Parisian public as Riccardo in *I puritani* as well as in other parts, and was equally famous for his vocal equipment and his girth. "Like a monstrous beetle that wants to open its wings and fly away, but cannot," Théophile Gautier described him in the wedding scene, when the portly Don Pasquale squeezes himself into his fine clothes from days gone by.   *É. P.-L.*

Don Pasquale, photograph from the production by Stefano Vizioli, conductor Riccardo Muti, Teatro alla Scala, Milan 1993/94.
The chorus has a small but very interesting role in this work; it accompanies Ernesto's famous serenade and lends the number a magical character. Conversely, it makes a great deal of noise at the wedding ceremony: a bad omen for the old bachelor embarking on married life for the first time.

Comedy in the shadow of old age

Donizetti and his librettist, Giovanni Ruffini, turned the story on which the plot is based into a kind of society game for four, with constant alternation between typical *opera buffa* situations (for instance the scene of the pretended wedding, in which the marriage contract is read out in recitative), and perfectly serious, indeed realistic scenes. The game is amusing only on the surface; it has a number of cruelly sober aspects, and the "players" are presented in a variety of ways, in line with this approach. There is no doubting Norina's love for Ernesto – yet she constantly surprises the audience with her ability to change, and her readiness to achieve her goal of marriage to Ernesto through lies and deception. The "rehearsal" with Malatesta of her conquest of Don Pasquale is very amusing, but in the third act, when she deliberately provokes Don Pasquale to quarrel with her, she goes too far: boxing his ears is an unnecessary insult to an already humiliated man. She seems to be ashamed of it, showing some pity and humanity – but then she takes her leave of Don Pasquale, already addressed as "little grandfather", with a light waltz melody almost reminiscent of operetta ("Via, caro sposino" – "Come, dear little husband"). *M 12*

Ernesto too shows deep feeling, not only in the tone of resignation in his aria "Cercherò lontana terra" ("I will travel far away," Act II *M 13*), which is accompanied by a melancholy trumpet solo, but also in his famous serenade, "Com' è gentil la notte a mezzo April!" ("How lovely is the night in mid-April!" Act III *M 14*), which is apparently intended to deceive the eavesdropping Don Pasquale but really reveals Ernesto's true emotions.

Don Pasquale, Ludwig Mantler (Don Pasquale) and Franz Egenieff (Malatesta), Komische Oper, Berlin 1906.
Malatesta explains that it would be best for Don Pasquale to give up his young "wife". The patter duet between the two low men's voices is the most popular number in the opera. *M 16*

Above
Don Pasquale, production photograph with Janet Perry (Norina) and Alexander Malta (Don Pasquale), Staatstheater am Gärtnerplatz, Munich 1972.
The tragedy of the action is suggested on stage: in the decade of the discovery of alienation in human relationships, Norina and Don Pasquale wear modern costume. Do not the elderly men in many famous *opera buffa* arouse our sympathy, as losers? Might not Donizetti's last comedy be described as the tragedy of Don Pasquale? Stefan Zweig's reworking of the subject for Richard Strauss (→*The Silent Woman, 1935*) gives an unambiguous and resigned answer to such questions.

12. Norina Mocking Don Pasquale

Via, ca - ro spo - si - no, non far - mi il ti - ran - no

13. Ernesto's Sadness

Cherche - rò lon - ta - na ter - ra do - ve ge - mer sco - no - sciuto;

14. Ernesto's Serenade

Com'è gen - til ___ la notte a mezzo April!

15. Don Pasquale in Melancholy Mood

16. Patter Duet (Don Pasquale and Malatesta)

A-spet-ta, a - spet - ta, ca-ra spo - si - na: la mia ven - det - ta già s'avvi - ci - na

Don Pasquale, production photograph with (left to right) Paolo Montarsolo (Don Pasquale), Urban Mahnberg (Ernesto), and Hellen Kwow (Norina), production Franz Marijnen, sets Santiago del Corral, conductor Stefan Soltesz, Hamburgische Staatsoper 1987.
The amorous Don Pasquale does not yet know who is behind the white veil. In this Hamburg production, the part was taken by a born comedian among basses.

The wrong treatment?

Even Dr. Malatesta, the cool, calculating puppetmaster who pulls the strings, is sometimes genuinely moved by Don Pasquale's plight. He proves to be not merely an intriguer, but an experienced figure who hopes to prevent the unhappy marriage of an old man and a young woman. Malatesta keeps protesting that his "cure" is applied in the patient's own interests. But from what "sickness" must Don Pasquale be cured? International literature and opera alike are full of foolish elderly men who fall in love with young women. Sometimes their feelings are depicted as tragic, sometimes as comic or grotesque. King Mark in Wagner's →*Tristan and Isolde*, Hans Sachs from the same composer's →*The Mastersingers of Nuremberg*, King Philip II in Verdi's →*Don Carlos*, are all characters depicting the loneliness of the old, while works in the *opera buffa* style, from Pergolesi's →*La serva padrona* and Haydn's →*The Apothecary*, to Rossini's →*The Barber of Seville* and Donizetti's *Don Pasquale* itself mock the late flaring up of love in the old. These two opposites in the depiction of love in old age have one thing in common: they question love and above all sexuality in old people. Sensuality is regarded as the domain of the young. When the old, like Don Pasquale, fall in love, they become objects of mockery and derision, and must be "cured". Many risqué plays and comic operas deal with the subject of old men who are tricked, cuckolded, and made to look ridiculous. The theme derives from the social dictates which decree that a rich old suitor does in fact have a better chance than a poverty-stricken young man of marrying a young girl. Such unions have probably seldom brought happiness. Donizetti's ability to depict both realistic situations and genuine human reactions to them within the framework of *opera buffa* is evident in the resigned farewell in A minor, "E finita, Don Pasquale" ("It's over, Don Pasquale), after Norina has boxed the old bachelor's ears. Even the happy ending of the opera cannot quite reconcile us to Don Pasquale's loneliness. M 15   É. P.-L.

Don Pasquale, production photograph with (left to right) Michael Volle (Malatesta), Julia Borchert (Norina), Erich Syri (Don Pasquale), and Karl Adolf Appel (Notary), production Venjamin Smechov, conductor Wolfram Koloseus, Nationaltheater Mannheim 1993.

Don Pasquale, photograph from a production at the Nationaltheater Mannheim 1931/32. A classic scene of comedy: the old bachelor's house is being turned upside down on the orders of the new mistress as Don Pasquale's troubles begin.

Dvořák, Antonín

b. 8 September 1841 in Nelahozeves (Mühlhausen, near Prague)
d. 1 May 1904 in Prague

Dvořák first became familiar with the music of the classical composers during his studies at the Prague Organ School; later, as an orchestral musician, he played works by →Robert Schumann, Franz Liszt and →Richard Wagner. The Austrian state stipend awarded to him for the years 1875–1878, through the good offices of Johannes Brahms and Eduard Hanslick, opened up Dvořák's path to an international career. His subsequent travels took him as far as the USA, where he was director of the National Conservatory of Music in New York from 1892 to 1895. From 1891 onward he was active as a teacher, and he was director of the Prague Conservatory from 1901 to 1904. Although most of his major works were orchestral and chamber music, in *Rusalka* he wrote an opera that became famous beyond the borders of his native land.

Works: Operas: *Alfred* (1870/FP 1938, Olmütz), *Král a uhlíř* (*The King and the Charcoal Burner*) (1871, Prague), *Trvdé palice* (*The Stubborn Lovers*) (1874/FP 1881, Prague), *Vanda* (1875, Prague), *Šelma sedlák* (*The Cunning Peasant*) (1878, Prague), *Dimitrij* (1882, Prague), *Jakobin* (*The Jacobin*) (1889, Prague), *Čert a Káča* (*The Devil and Kate*) (1899, Prague), *Rusalka* (1901, Prague), *Armida* (1904, Prague); symphonies, chamber music, choral works, songs.

Rusalka, Gabriela Beňačková-Čáp (Rusalka) and Yevgeny Nesterenko (Water Sprite), production Otto Schenk, costumes Silvia Strahammer, conductor Vaclav Neumann, Wiener Staatsoper 1987.
Rusalka, the Prince's bride, laments her fate to the Water Sprite. As in the later Czech music of Janáček, nature and the relationship between man and natural creatures play an important part. The music depicting the water and the forest is of great significance, and forms the most original stratum of the score. For Rusalka, nature means the familiar world of her earlier life, a childhood world. The spokesman for that world is the Water Sprite. His vocal register and the part itself are reminiscent of the great Russian bass roles, yet he has softer, warmer melodies.

The Czech water nymph

On vacation in 1899 on the island of Bornholm, Jaroslav Kvapil was inspired to write an opera libretto which reflected the mystic *fin de siècle* mood of the time, but did not appeal to Oskar Nedbal, Josef Bohuslav Foerster, or Josef Suk. It was through the director of the Prague National Theater, František Šubert, that the libretto came into Dvořák's hands. He was immediately enchanted by its lyrically impressionistic subject matter, and he composed his opera between April and November 1900.

Drawing on his experience in the many works he had composed, he employed every stylistic method that seemed suitable for depicting two opposing worlds: the world of soulless but sympathetic elemental beings, and the world of humans with their souls and their fluctuating emotions. In the process, Dvořák drew on the entire expressive repertory of his century, leaving no emotion, however slight, musically ignored. Classical procedures, the use of motifs, forms of lied and aria are synthesized through impressionistic tonal coloring and expressionistic gesture. In this way the composer succeeded in conveying the irrational world of his subject convincingly to the audience, and his opera won international admiration.   M.S.

The music of Dvořák shows influences of Classical forms, and a leaning toward Liszt and Wagner. However, he developed his own unmistakably individual style through the inclusion of folk elements and impressionistic techniques.

Rusalka

Lyrical fairytale in three acts

Libretto: Jaroslav Kvapil, after the fairytale *Undine*, by Friedrich de la Motte Fouqué, the fairytale *Den lille Havfrue* (*The Little Mermaid*), by Hans Christian Andersen, and the play *Die versunkene Glocke* (*The Sunken Bell*) by Gerhart Hauptmann.
Première: 31 March 1901, Prague (National Theater).
Characters: Prince (T), Foreign Princess (S), Rusalka (S), Water Sprite (B), Witch (Ms), Gamekeeper (T), Scullion (S), Huntsman (T), Three Wood Nymphs (2 S, A); Prince's retinue (extras); wood nymphs, guests at the castle, water nymphs (chorus); wood nymphs, guests at the castle (ballet).
Setting: The place and time of fairytale.

Synopsis
Act I
In the depths of the forest, the Wood Nymphs are dancing by night on the banks of the lake, teasing the Water Sprite. Only Rusalka is unhappy. She longs for a

human form and a human soul, in order to win the love of the young Prince whom she saw recently swimming in the lake. The Water Sprite warns his favorite nymph of the dangers, but in vain. Rusalka turns to a Witch for help, who grants her wish on condition that she will be mute in the human world, warning that if her lover proves unfaithful she will be accursed and an outcast. Rusalka fearlessly agrees. When the Prince goes hunting by the banks of the lake, her silent beauty captivates him, and he takes her back to his castle.

Act II

By the pool in the castle grounds. The Prince's mute bride seems strange and uncanny to the castle servants. Although the Prince loves the beautiful and mysterious girl, her strange nature makes him uneasy. A Foreign Princess who has been invited to the wedding seizes this opportunity to make open erotic advances to the bridegroom.

Rusalka flees to the lake and tells the Water Sprite her sorrows. When the Prince courts the Princess passionately, the Water Sprite draws Rusalka down into his domain, and threatens the faithless bridegroom.

Shattered by the loss of his true love, the Prince lapses into mental derangement.

Act III

By the banks of the lake. Now homeless, and banished from her sisters, Rusalka seeks out the Witch again. The Witch can only help her if she kills her faithless lover, but Rusalka cannot and will not bring herself to do so. The Prince's Gamekeeper and Scullion also come to ask the Witch for a remedy to cure their master of his deep depression, saying that he was forced into marriage by an evil being whose magic caused him to fall sick. The angry Water Sprite drives them away.

Once again, the nymphs tease the Water Sprite, but he tells them of Rusalka's sad fate. The Prince looks for Rusalka on the banks of the lake; she is hovering above it in the form of a will o' the wisp. He begs her for a kiss, and she grants him one, but this proof of her love brings him death. *S.N.*

Rusalka, production photograph from the third act: the closing scene of the opera with Gabriela Beňačková-Čáp (Rusalka) and Peter Dvorsky (Prince), production Otto Schenk, sets Günther Schneider, conductor Vaclav Neumann, Wiener Staatsoper 1987.
The moving conclusion of the opera: Rusalka must renounce her Prince and human love, and so returns to the realm of elementary beings. The Czech word "Rusalka" is of Russian origin, and means "enchanted and enchanting feminine creature." Rusalka is related to those creatures described in various fairy tales, myths, and legends as nymphs, sirens, undines, nixies and mermaids.

Danton's Death, production photograph with Peter Weber (Danton) and Wolfgang Glashob (Robespierre), production Gernot Friedel, sets H. Hauser, conductor Isaac Karabtchevsky, Theater an der Wien 1992.
In 1939, Einem saw Georg Büchner's play *Dantons Tod* on stage for the first time. Fascinated by the expressive power of the drama, and personally affected as he was by Hitler's dictatorship, he and Boris Blacher wrote a libretto, and he began composing the music on 22 July 1944. To make his score as musically authentic as possible, Einem studied the texts and melodies of French Revolutionary songs. Effective choral scenes, parlando passages supporting the text, and Einem's clear-cut construction of character and situation ensured that the opera (in six scenes) was a resounding success at its première on 6 August 1947, during the Salzburg Festival. Einem was the first living composer to have an opera given its première at that festival.

*E*inem's stylistic principle is the integration of *different historical techniques.*

Einem, Gottfried von

b. 24 January 1918 in Berne
d. 12 July 1996 in Waldviertel, Lower Austria

At first Einem was largely self-taught; he then studied with Boris Blacher, and developed his own restrained musical language. He began his career in 1938 as co-répétiteur at the Berlin Opera and assistant at the Bayreuth Festspielhaus. During the Nazi period he was imprisoned several times. After the war Einem held a number of important posts, for instance at the Salzburg and Vienna Festivals. He taught at the Musikhochschüle in Vienna from 1963 to 1972, and from 1964 was a member of the Berlin Academy of Arts. From 1965 to 1970 he held office as president of the Austrian Academy of Music.

Works: Operas: *Dantons Tod* (*Danton's Death*) (1947, Salzburg), *Der Prozess* (*The Trial*) (1953, Salzburg), *Der Zerrissene* (*The Man at Odds with Himself*) (1964, Hamburg), *Der Besuch der alten Dame* (*The Visit of the Old Lady*) (1971, Vienna), *Kabale und Liebe* (*Cabal and Love*) (1976, Vienna), *Jesu Hochzeit* (*The Wedding of Jesus*) (1980, Vienna), *Tulifant* (1990, Vienna); ballets, incidental music, songs, orchestral works, chamber music.

Danton's Death

Libretto: Boris Blacher and Gottfried von Einem, after Georg Büchner's drama of the same name.
Première: 6 August 1947, Salzburg (Salzburg Festival).
Characters: Georges Danton (Bar), Camille Desmoulins, deputy (T), Jean Hérault de Séchelles, deputy (T), Robespierre (T), St. Just, member of the Committee of Public Safety (B), Herman, president of the Revolutionary Tribunal (Bar), Simon, the prompter (Bbuffo), Young Man (T), First and Second Executioners (T, Bar), Julie, wife of Danton (Ms), Lucille, wife of Desmoulins (S), A Lady (S), A Woman, Simon's wife (A).
Setting: Paris, 1794.

Synopsis
Robespierre's Terror and the desperate situation of the people create an atmosphere of crisis which the dictator's advisers feel is dangerous. Some way must be found of eliminating the opposition that has grown up around Danton. As the people are behind Danton, and Desmoulins is to be spared as a personal friend of the dictator, the only way is to spread rumors that Danton is a royalist. When Robespierre hears of the opposition offered by Desmoulins, he agrees to his arrest too. Danton's brilliant defense speech before the Tribunal cannot save either himself or his fellow opponents of the Terror.

S.N.

The Trial

Der Prozess

Libretto: Boris Blacher and Heinz von Cramer, after Franz Kafka's novel of the same name.
Première: 17 August 1953, Salzburg (Festspielhaus).
Characters: Josef K. (T), Franz (B), Willem (Bar), Bailiff (Bar), Frau Grubach (Ms), Fräulein Bürstner (S), Bailiff's Wife (S), Leni (S), Passerby (Bar), Boy (T), Investigating Magistrate (Bar), Court Usher (B), Student (T), Thug (B), Albert K. (B), Advocate (Bar), Lawyer (B), Manufacturer (Bar), Three Men (2T, B), Deputy Director (T), Hunchbacked Girl (S), Titorelli (T), Chaplain (Bar), Three Young Men (2T, Bar), First Gentleman (spoken), Four Speakers (spoken).

Setting: Uncertain.

Synopsis

One day in the year 1919, Josef K. is informed that he is under arrest, but may still move around freely. By night, in the street outside the building where he lives, a Passerby suddenly hands him a summons to his first investigation. Josef K., a bank signatory, has no idea of the reason for any of these incidents and suddenly he feels guilty. Seeking an explanation, he realizes that everyone he talks to knows more about his situation than he does himself. He becomes desperate and tortured by feelings of hopelessness. Finally, in the cathedral, he asks the prison Chaplain for help, but the Chaplain can no longer do anything for him; two thugs take him away for execution.   *S. N.*

The influence of Brecht
Einem's concentration on moods and contrasts, and his intention to make the language of the opera as easily understood as possible, shows the latent influence of Brecht. Rhythmic and melodic accessibility made the work a great public success.

Kafka, Brecht, Einem

Einem's opera *The Trial*, from Franz Kafka's novel of 1925, was the background to a scandalous event. In 1947, Einem, as advisor to the Salzburg Festival, was asked by Caspar Neher to support Bertolt Brecht, who was then in Zurich, stateless after his return from the USA, holding only a fixed-term residence permit and waiting to be granted Austrian citizenship. Neher wanted Brecht to be commissioned to write the libretto for the opera *The Trial*, although nothing came of the plan because of Brecht's insistence that the text take priority over the music. Meanwhile, Einem was using his contacts with influential people to get Brecht's application for citizenship granted, and it was finalized in April 1950. Einem's actions had serious consequences: the rumor that he was a Communist and therefore unfit to work for the Salzburg Festival led to his dismissal. Although burdened with this scandal, Einem completed his two-part opera *The Trial* in the summer of 1952.   *M.S.*

The Trial, set design by Alfred Siercke, production Günther Rennert, conductor Leopold Ludwig, Hamburger Staatsoper 1953 (TWS).
In the cathedral: the key scene of both the novel and the opera.

The Visit of the Old Lady

Libretto: Friedrich Dürrenmatt, after his tragi-comedy of the same name.
Première: 23 May 1971, Vienna (Wiener Staatsoper).
Characters: Claire Zachanassian, née Wäscher, a multimillionairess (Ms), Her Seventh Husband (silent), Her Ninth Husband (T), Butler (T), Toby and Roby (silent), Koby and Loby, blind men (2T), Alfred Ill (Bar), His Wife (S), His Daughter (Ms), His Son (T), Mayor (T), Pastor (Bbar), Teacher (Bar), Doctor (Bar), Policeman (Bbar), First and Second Women (2 S), Hofbauer (T), Helmesberger (Bar), Stationmaster (Bbar), Locomotive Driver (B), Conductor (T), Journalist (spoken), Cameraman (B), Voice (T).
Setting: Güllen, in the present day.

Synopsis

Claire Wäscher and the businessman Alfred Ill were once lovers. Made pregnant and abandoned by Ill, Claire went away to seek her fortune. Years later, she returns to the poverty-stricken and debt-ridden town of her youth as the wealthy Claire Zachanassian. She promises the town a huge sum of money in return for the life of Ill. When she leaves, the coffin she brought with her is no longer empty. Ill has paid with his life.

S. N.

The Visit of the Old Lady, photograph of a scene from a production by Otto Schenk, sets Günther Schneider-Siemssen, conductor Horst Stein, Wiener Staatsoper 1971 (photograph 1977).
The most striking musical features of Einem's opera, besides the large choral scenes, are the *arioso* passages, which almost suggest parody, and the composer's strong sense of what is effective on stage, including sound effects.

Einem and Dürrenmatt

Einem's masterpiece is based on Dürrenmatt's tragi-comedy *Der Besuch der alten Dame* (*The Visit of the Old Lady*) written in 1955. Dürrenmatt had convinced himself that Einem's musical language was right for his play, and wrote the libretto himself. Einem's language is basically tonal, and he employs an approach reminiscent of Mahler's "folk" effects to do justice to the grotesque subject. He provides each character with its own distinct musical identity, the sounds of different bells give acoustic structure to the course of the action, and the organization of the speaking parts assumes musical features. Close thematic relations, imitation, and variation establish the inner coherence of the opera, ensuring that it is easily understood. As a result, the work has been very successful.

M.S.

The Visit of the Old Lady, production photograph with Patricia Johnson as Claire Zachanassian, production Otto Schenk, costumes Leo Bei, conductor Horst Stein, Wiener Staatsoper 1971 (photograph 1977).
Otto Schenk produced the opera in the early 1970s with Christa Ludwig in the title role. In the revival of the production six years later, Patricia Johnson also proved herself a powerfully expressive character singer.

Right
The Visit of the Old Lady, production photograph with Anton Wendler and Karl Terhal as Koby and Loby, production Otto Schenk, costumes Leo Bei, conductor Horst Stein, Wiener Staatsoper 1971 (photograph 1977).
On the old lady's orders, Koby and Loby were blinded for giving false evidence in her paternity claim against her former lover Ill. Since then, they have rendered her all kinds of services as her blind retainers.

Interior of the Hungarian National Theater in Budapest, c. 1840.
The first Hungarian national theater, where Ferenc Erkel became music director in 1838, staged both spoken drama and opera, and before the 1848 Revolution it fulfilled an important political function. The beautiful Budapest opera house, which opened in 1884, no longer exists.

Erkel, Ferenc

b. 7 November 1810 in Gyula (Hungary)
d. 15 June 1893 in Budapest

Erkel was born in southern Hungary, near the present border with Romania. His family came from Pressburg (now Bratislava); most of them were musicians and teachers. Erkel received his basic musical education in Pressburg between 1822 and 1825, and in Klausenburg (now Cluj) between 1828 and 1834. The young musician attracted public attention mainly as an outstanding pianist (he gave the first performance in Hungary of Chopin's E minor concerto). In 1834 he moved to Pest, where he gave concerts and conducted operas, and was appointed musical director of the first Hungarian National Theater in 1838. His greatest success as a composer came in the 1840s, when he wrote two operas, including *Hunyadi László*, which is very popular in Hungary, the patriotic choral song *Admonition*, and the national anthem. He founded the Hungarian National Philharmonic Society in 1853, became opera director at the National Theater in 1873, and in 1875 was appointed director of the Academy of Music founded by himself and Franz Liszt. The Budapest opera house opened in 1884 with compositions by Erkel. Hungary's defeat in the Wars of Liberation of 1848–49 was a severe blow to him, both personally and as an artist. For some years his inspiration seemed to flag, and he never again achieved the originality and verve of his early compositions. His last operas were written in collaboration with his sons, who were also important figures in the musical history of Hungary in the late 19th century.

Works: Operas: *Bátori Mária* (1840), *Hunyadi László* (1844), *Erzsébet* (*Elizabeth*) (1857), *Bánk bán* (1861), *Sarolta* (1862), *Dózsa György* (1867), *Brankovics György* (1874), *Névtelen hősök* (*Unknown Heroes*) (1880), *István király* (*King Stephen*) (1885); choral works, incidental music, musical interludes for popular plays, songs, piano works.

The unluckiest of national composers

Ferenc Erkel was perhaps the unluckiest of the national composers of the Romantic era. Although he wrote nine operas, including the two outstanding works *Hunyadi László* and *Bánk bán*, his name is almost unknown outside Hungary. He did not succeed in making the history and music of his country popular on the international operatic stage. Some of his great contemporaries, such as the Hungarian-born cosmopolitan Franz (Ferenc) Liszt and the innovative French composer Hector Berlioz, who saw the highly successful *Hunyadi László* in Pest, promised Erkel their support, but nothing went further than the planning stage. No doubt the language barrier played a part, and even more so the composer's isolation, for he never left Hungary.

The father of national Hungarian music

The subjects of most of Erkel's operas are taken from Hungarian history. Since Hungary was ruled by the hated Habsburgs during Erkel's lifetime, the construction of national identity was a matter of great importance to Hungarian patriots, including Erkel. Hungary was a country still in the feudal age, with countless villages and small country towns distributed over the steppes and in the valleys and mountains of the Transsylvanian Alps. The capital, Budapest, formed by the amalgamation of three existing towns (Buda, Pest, and Altofen), was not founded until 1873. The majority of the population of Buda and Pest were still predominantly German-speaking around the middle of the nineteenth century. There had been a national theater since 1837, but the capital had to wait until 1884 to acquire its own opera house. Erkel's was certainly pioneering work.

"A new day breaks, O Hungary!" *(Hunyadi László)*

The action of the opera takes place in 1456–57 in Nándorfehérvár (now Belgrade), in Temesvár (now Timosoara), and in Buda. King László V (T) is under age; his uncle Ulrik Cilley (Bar) is acting as regent for him. Cilley hates the Hungarians, and sees the Hunyadi (Corvinus) family as dangerous rivals. He discredits László Hunyadi (T) and tries to murder him, but is killed himself. The young king, in a mood of indecision, swears the Hunyadi family an oath not to avenge the death of his uncle the regent, but a few months later he breaks this promise, and has László Hunyadi executed in Buda. Up to this point the opera follows history, although in one respect it diverges into fiction: the king has his eye on Hunyadi's beautiful fiancée Mária (S). Her father, the governor-general Palatine Gara (Bar), who is hungry for power, is a political rival of the Hunyadis. He promises the king his daughter's hand if László Hunyadi is executed. An important and moving part is played by the hero's anxious mother, Erzsébet Szilágyi (S). In the years leading up to the March 1848 revolution, the opera *Hunyadi László* fulfilled a function similar to that of Verdi's operas in the Risorgimento. In the first act, for instance, after the death of Cilley, who was hostile to the Hungarians, a patriotic chorus announces: "The intriguer is dead! … A new day breaks, O Hungary!" Similarly, the Hunyadis will not allow the German soldiers in the royal retinue access to their fortress. All this was political dynamite at the time, and duly took effect. Erkel's great creative achievement was to integrate the popular music of Hungary seamlessly with the "number opera" on Italian and French models, introducing a Hungarian national opera composed to a very high level.

Hunyadi László, a contemporary colored engraving.
This scene shows the finale of the second act. The king and the national hero are swearing an oath to each other. Erkel brought the Hungarian background to life with such decorative scenes, and with fine dance music suggesting folk themes.

Hunyadi László, Anne de la Grange as Erzsébet, lithograph by Miklós Barabás. In 1850 the famous French coloratura soprano Anne de la Grange made guest appearances at the National Theater in Budapest, singing roles by Rossini, Bellini, and Meyerbeer. Audiences insisted on hearing her in a Hungarian part, and she sang the role of Hunyadi László's mother Erzsébet. For the occasion, Erkel wrote a breathtaking coloratura aria for her, known in the world of performance as the "La Grange aria". During her guest appearance in Budapest, Anne de la Grange was portrayed in national costume by one of the most famous painters of the 19th century.

*E*rkel was the father of national Hungarian opera, composer of the national anthem, and the founder of many musical institutions.

1. Bánk bán's Confession of Love for his Native Land

Ha-zám,   ha-zám,   te min de-nem,   tu-dom, hogy é - le-tem ne - ked kö-szön-he-tem.

"My land, my land is all to me!"

This quotation is from the great aria sung by the eponymous hero of *Bánk bán* (Act I, м 1). A confession of love for his native land, it is a gem of Hungarian bel canto. It presented the idea of a sovereign Hungarian state, comforting the Hungarian people in the days when they were ruled by foreign powers (including some periods in the twentieth century), and sometimes inspiring them to public demonstrations. The action is set at the beginning of the thirteenth century, the period of the Crusades. Hungarian noblemen unite in opposition to the German queen Gertrud (Ms) and her adherents, who are despoiling and plundering the land and the people in the absence of King Endre II (Bar). Only the Hungarian Palatine Bánk bán (T) hesitates, for he has sworn eternal loyalty to the king. But when the queen's nephew Otto

(T) assaults the honor of Bánk bán's wife Melinda (S) with the aid of Gertrud, and drives Melinda to madness, Bánk bán kills the queen. When the king, on his return, calls the Hungarian nobles to account, Bánk bán admits to his deed, but the death of his wife breaks his strength and courage. This is an outline of the nationalist Hungarian play by József Katona, written in 1815, on which the opera is based. Austrian censorship banned its production until 1860. In the opera, Bánk bán's tragedy is contrasted with the frivolous world of the foreign rulers, and the wretched condition of the oppressed Hungarian population. Erkel used melodies from the *verbunkos* folk music of the nineteenth century for Hungarian atmosphere, and with instrumentation for dulcimer, viola d'amore and flute (in the second and third acts) created an enchanting national musical world.

La vida breve

The Short Life

Drama lírico in two acts

Libretto: Carlos Fernández Shaw.
Première: 1 April 1913, Nice (Théâtre du Casino Municipal).

Characters: Salud, a girl from Granada (S), Salud's Grandmother (Ms), Paco (T), Sarvaor, Salud's uncle (B or Bar), Carmela, Paco's bride (Ms), Manuel, Carmela's brother (Bar), a Singer (Bar), Four Women Peddlers (3 S, Ms), Blacksmith's Voice (T), Peddler's Voice (T), Distant Voice (T); smiths, people of Granada, wedding guests (chorus); wedding guests (ballet).
Setting: Granada, around 1900.

Synopsis

Act I

Scene 1: The courtyard of a house in a poor quarter of the city of Granada. A scene of everyday life, with the rhythmic hammering of smiths, and the singing and talking of workers. Salud's grandmother is feeding the birds in the courtyard; she is anxious about her granddaughter's future. Salud is expecting her lover, Paco, and falls into despair when he is late. On arriving, Paco succeeds in calming the girl, although she has good reason to doubt his love. Salud's uncle Sarvaor indignantly tells her grandmother that Paco is about to marry a girl of his own social class.
Scene 2: A musical interlude. Day is ending and night falls over Granada.

Act II

Scene 1: A small street outside Carmela's house. The inner courtyard is visible through large open windows. The wedding of Carmela and Paco is being celebrated. Watching the merry festivities from outside, Salud laments her sad fate. Paco senses that Salud is somewhere near, and cannot enjoy himself; he appears distracted.
Scene 2: The inner courtyard. Salud enters the house of the happy bride, followed by her grandmother and her uncle. She publicly accuses Paco of faithlessness. Paco denies everything, and she says she wishes he would kill her. He repulses her in horror. She goes toward him for the last time, sinks to the ground at his feet, and dies. The wedding party ends in general consternation.   *S.N.*

The musical style of de Falla has an individuality all its own, and the characteristic harmonic and instrumental coloring derived from authentic Andalusian folk music lends it particular charm.

La vida breve, costume designs by Wera Schawlinsky, Cologne 1946/47 (TWS).
A mysteriously magical atmosphere permeates de Falla's first opera. The tragedy of the emotions and fates of the characters derives from gypsy folklore, while the music has its roots in the Spanish dance tradition. With this work, the 28-year-old de Falla proved himself a Spanish national composer of remarkable gifts.

de Falla, Manuel Maria
(de Falla y Matheu, Manuel Maria)

b. 23 November 1876 in Cádiz
d. 14 November 1946 in Alta Gracia (Córdoba, Argentina)

In 1904 Falla took private tuition from Felipe Pedrell to supplement his training at the Madrid Conservatory. He won the opera prize in the competition held by the Real Academia de Bellas Artes in Madrid in 1905 with *La vida breve*, and immediately gained recognition as a composer. In 1907 he took up a position as a piano teacher in Paris, where he became friendly with →Ravel, →Debussy, Dukas and Albéniz. He went to live in Granada in 1914. In 1939 he went on a concert tour of Argentina, and never returned to Europe.

Works: Stage works: *La vida breve* (*The Short Life*) (1905/ FP 1913, Nice), *El retablo de maese Pedro* (*Master Peter's Puppet Show*) (1923, Seville/Paris); ballets, incidental music, vocal music, orchestral works, chamber music.

Spanish gypsy honor

La vida breve was written as an entry for an opera competition, in much the same way as Mascagni's →*Cavalleria rusticana*, written in Italy a decade and a half earlier. In both cases the subject is honor and constancy, and the story ends tragically. The ballad element is more conspicuous in Spanish than in Italian national opera.

In *La vida breve*, de Falla was referring to the Spanish *zarzuela* form (a mixed dramatic form containing singing, dancing, and dialogue in the Spanish style), but he took it further, creating an independent Spanish opera. The story of the abandoned girl, which moves quickly towards its tragic ending, is given extra depth by many textual and musical symbols, beginning with the comments of a smith's journeyman: "Unhappy the man born to a sad fate / Unhappy the man who is anvil, not hammer." The grandmother's feeding of the birds, the ending of the day (in the musical interlude), and fading flowers are metaphors standing for the brevity of life.

There is similar symbolism in the first of the two scenes of the second act, in which Salud watches the rich people at the wedding. Once she has penetrated their circle, there can be nothing but death for her. Here, de Falla makes use of Andalusian folk music, not so much in the melody as in the use of typical instruments (such as castanets and guitar), in his harmonic coloring, and above all in his handling of the singing voices. There are no operatic arias and ensembles; instead, a kind of recitation intermingles with songs and dances. In line with the ballad or epic character of the work, the chorus acts as a musical backdrop and remains in the background, although it takes an active part in the opera at the climactic moment.   *M. S.*

La vida breve, production photograph, production and sets Herbert Wernicke, Theater Basel 1995-96.
This was one of the few productions to resist the lure of allowing folklore to mute the action with pretty effects, stripping it down to its essentials: the overwhelming power of collective rituals to which individuals are subject.

Master Peter's Puppet Show

El retablo de maese Pedro

Opera in one act

Libretto: Manuel de Falla, adapted from an episode in Miguel de Cervante Saavedra's novel *El ingenioso hidalgo Don Quixote de La Mancha* (*The Ingenious Knight Don Quixote of La Mancha*).

Première: concert première: 23 March 1923, Seville (Teatro San Fernando); stage première: 25 June 1923, Paris (the house of the Princesse de Polignac).

Characters: Don Quixote (B or Bar), Master Peter, a puppet master (T), El Trujamán, his barker and narrator (boy S); Sancho Panza, The Landlord, a Student, a Page, Man with lance and halberd (silent). Characters in the puppet play: Carlo Magno/Charlemagne; Melisendra, his daughter; Don Gayferos, her husband; Don Roldán, a knight at the court of Charlemagne; Marsilio, King of the Moors; An Enamored Moor; heralds, knights and guards at the court of Charlemagne, a captain and soldiers in the service of King Marsilio, executioners, Moors.

Setting: The stable of an inn in Aragonia, with a puppet theater illuminated by candles, at the end of the 16th century.

Master Peter's Puppet Show, production photograph with Karsten Mewes (Don Quixote) and Eberhard Büchner (Master Peter), production Hartmut Lorenz, conductor Simone Young, Deutsche Staatsoper, Berlin 1993. Originally de Falla intended to have both the framing action and the puppet play acted by marionettes, placing the singers in the orchestral pit. However, as early as the 1920s it became usual to give singers and actors the framing action, and use professional puppeteers to execute the main action. The success of the concert première aroused interest in this very individual work, which has been successful all over the world.

Synopsis

Master Peter volubly announces the performance of a play about the rescue of the fair Melisendra. The curious spectators take their seats, among them Don Quixote and his companion Sancho Panza. Master Peter picks up the puppets, the curtain opens, and the narrator begins.

Scene 1: A hall in Charlemagne's palace. Don Gayferos is playing chess with the knight Roldán. Charlemagne angrily urges his son-in-law to go and rescue his wife Melisendra, Charlemagne's daughter, from the power of the Moorish king Marsilio.

Scene 2: A tower of Marsilio's citadel in Saragossa. Melisendra looks longingly into the distance, remembering her loved ones. A young Moor tries to kiss her; when she cries out for help Marsilio arrives in haste, and orders the Moor to be punished. At this point Don Quixote intervenes in agitation, protesting against the introduction of subplots. Master Peter calms the knight, and the narrator continues.

Scene 3: A square in Saragossa. The young Moor is punished with 200 lashes.

Scene 4: The Pyrenees. Gayferos is riding through the mountains.

Scene 5: The tower of Marsilio's citadel. Melisendra addresses the unknown knight from the tower, asking him for news of Gayferos. Gayferos reveals his identity, and they make their escape.

Scene 6: The square in Saragossa. The couple's flight is discovered, and Marsilio has the alarm bells rung. Don Quixote indignantly interrupts the play again, saying that the Moors do not ring bells, but play drums and shawms. Master Peter tries to soothe the agitated knight by staging an spectacular scene showing the pursuit of Melisendra and Gayferos by the Moors. His thrilling performance inflames Don Quixote's chivalrous feelings. Drawing his sword, he wreaks havoc among the puppets, and dedicates his victory over the Moors to his adored Dulcinea. The destruction of the puppets has deprived Master Peter of his livelihood. *S.N.*

Famous outsiders

During the war years, the Princesse de Polignac, the daughter of the American sewing machine manufacturer Singer, commissioned works from several composers, including Igor Stravinsky and de Falla. The results included two works which lie outside the European operatic tradition: Stravinsky's *Renard* and de Falla's *Master Peter's Puppet Show*. After moving to Granada in 1914, de Falla had turned to the intensive study of Andalusian folklore, for instance in the *canto jondo* and the old puppet show tradition, and here he worked closely with the poet Federico García Lorca. This was the background to *Master Peter's Puppet Show*, a work which had a legendary première. The guests invited to attend included Paul Valéry, Pablo Picasso, and Igor Stravinsky. Wanda Landowska played the harpsichord part, and de Falla conducted the Andalusian Orquestra bética de cámara founded by García Lorca. Andalusian folk music is present here as harmonic color and sound, rather than in the melody.

Man as a puppet – the saving grace of laughter

With the catastrophe of the First World War, a general sense of artistic uneasiness in portraying human beings as the creators and masters of their own destiny became perceptible. Reference to the old tradition of the puppet play was a way of showing mankind in the grasp of uncontrollable powers, and also of providing a faithful depiction of human beings and the world without abstaining entirely from laughter. *S. N.*

Master Peter's Puppet Show, photograph from the production by Lorenz, sets and costumes K. Kavrakova-Lorenz, puppets K. Tiefensee, conductor Simone Young, Deutsche Staatsoper, Berlin 1993.
De Falla tried to keep the elements of this opera apart: the singing and acting are performed by the singers, while the marionettes illustrate the story. The visible presence of puppeteers was intended to exclude illusory factors, as usual in the Spanish popular theater.

Below
Master Peter's Puppet Show, photograph from the production by Pierre-Jean Valentin, sets and costumes Pit Fischer, conductor Peter Seibel, Hamburger Staatsoper 1980.
Musically and dramatically, the pursuit of Melisendra and Don Gayferos by the Moors makes an effective scene. Here, de Falla was playing on the popularity of chases in Spanish street theater.

Martha, production photograph with Krisztina Laki (Lady Harriet), Waltraud Meier (Nancy), and Jörn W. Wilsing (Lord Tristan Mickleford), production Vicco von Bülow, Württembergisches Staatstheater, Stuttgart 1986.
As the opera opens, Lady Harriet and Nancy very obviously demonstrate their boredom.

Martha or *The Market at Richmond*

Romantic comic opera in four acts

Libretto: Friedrich Wilhelm Riese, from an idea by Jules Henri Vernoy de Saint-Georges.

Première: 25 November 1847, Vienna (Kärntertor-theater).

Characters: Lady Harriet Durham, maid of honor to Queen Anne (S), Nancy, her confidante (Ms), Lord Tristan Mickleford, her cousin, supervisor of the royal pages (B), Plumkett, a rich tenant farmer (B), Lyonel, his foster brother (T), Judge at Richmond (B), Three Maidservants (A, 2 S), Three Manservants of Lady Harriet (2 B, T), Clerk of the court (silent), Farmer (B), Farmer's Wife (S); manservants, maidservants, huntswomen in the royal retinue, farmers and their wives, country folk (chorus).

Setting: England around 1710, during the reign of Queen Anne.

Synopsis

Lady Harriet, maid of honor to the queen, and her confidante Nancy are bored; to amuse themselves, they masquerade as maidservants. At Richmond Fair the supposed maids, under the false names of Martha and Julia, are hired by the farmer Plumkett and his foster brother Lyonel. Their total lack of skill infuriates the farmer, and only Lyonel, who has fallen in love with Martha, can save them from punishment. The two women conclude their adventure by escaping. During a hunt, the royal retinue stops to rest in a woodland tavern, where Plumkett and Lyonel recognize their runaway maidservants among the queen's maids of honor, but no one believes their story. Lady Harriet herself accuses Lyonel of delusions, and he is arrested. However, Lyonel's true identity is brought to light by a ring he has inherited; he is really the son of a nobleman who had fallen into disfavor, but has already been rehabilitated. There is now no obstacle to his marriage to Harriet, but the angry Lyonel rejects her offer of reconciliation. Lady Harriet enlists the help of the courtiers, staging a play set at Richmond Market in which she and Nancy again hire themselves out to Plumkett and Lyonel. Moved, Lyonel forgives her. Plumkett and Nancy also marry.   *S. N.*

Below
Martha, Adelina Patti (1843–1919) as Lady Harriet. The song "Letzte Rose des Sommers" ("The Last Rose of Summer", from an Irish melody in a collection by Thomas Moore, sung by Lady Harriet in Act II) became an evergreen operatic favorite. *M 1*

Flotow, Friedrich von

b. 27 April 1812 on the Teutendorf estate (Mecklenburg)
d. 24 January 1883 in Darmstadt

After studying with Reicha in Paris from 1828 to 1830, Flotow, who came from an aristocratic landowning family but wished to devote himself to music, had a success with his first opera, *The Wreck of the Medusa*. The July Revolution in Paris sent him back to Germany. In France he wrote several pieces for the German-spoken operatic stage. From 1855 to 1863 he was court director in Schwerin. He returned to Paris in 1863. His most famous opera is *Martha*, followed by *Alessandro Stradella*. Although all his stage works were successful, only *Martha* established itself in the international repertory.

Works: 25 stage works, including *Alessandro Stradella* (1844, Hamburg), *Martha* (1847, Vienna), *Die Grossfürstin Sophie Katharina* (*Grand Duchess Sophia Catherine*) (1850, Berlin), *Indra* (1852, Berlin), *Rübezahl* (1853, Frankfurt am Main), *Die Witwe Grapin* (*The Widow Grapin*) (1859, Paris), *Pianella* (1860, Paris), *Zilda* (1866, Paris), *Am Runenstein* (*At the Runic Stone*) (1868, Prague), *Der Schatten* (*The Shadow*) (1870, Paris).

1. The Last Rose of Summer

Letz - te Ro - se,   wie   magst   Du   so   ein - sam hier   blühn?

*F*lotow followed the French style, and created a work of the "Spieloper" type, melodious and easily accessible.

The recipe for success

When Flotow received a commission from the Vienna court opera, after the sensational success of his *Alessandro Stradella*, he decided to work with the librettist Friedrich Wilhelm Riese, and chose a subject that had already been set to music, the ballet-pasticcio *Lady Harriet,* or *The Servant of Greenwich.*

The plot attacks the decadence of aristocrats who are merely intrigued by the idea of the harsh realities of everyday rural life. The dramatic device of a "play within a play" lends the story humor, staging an incident that went wrong for a second time, in the hope of setting matters right.

In his musical technique, Flotow sought clarity of structure and harmonics, and he successfully depicted the world of the nobility in the French operatic style, while illustrating the life of the countryside with dances, cantabile melodies, and songs in the style of *opéra comique* in the manner of Auber. In fact the work was only a moderate success at its première, but it was very successfully produced by Liszt in Weimar in 1848, and eventually achieved great popularity, not least because of its wealth of melody.   *M.S.*

Above
Martha, set design by Anatoli Gelzer for the Bol'shoy Theater, Moscow 1873.
In spite of this stylized old English street scene, and Plumkett's song about porter, there is little local color in the music.

Martha, photograph from the production by Vicco von Bülow, conductor Wolf-Dieter Hauschild, Württembergisches Staatstheater, Stuttgart 1986.
Harriet denies her love for Lyonel and has him arrested.

Gershwin, George

b. 26 September 1898 in Brooklyn (New York)
d. 11 July 1937 in Beverly Hills (California)

Gershwin was familiar with the light music of the big cities of America from an early age, and developed an exciting style that made his publisher Dreyfus decide to launch him on Broadway. When Paul Whiteman heard Gershwin's music, he advised him to write "symphonic jazz." One of the results was the *Rhapsody in Blue* (1924). Always seeking a new kind of sound, Gershwin made ethnomusicological studies in the southern States for his folk opera *Porgy and Bess*. He was acquainted with the avant-garde techniques of European art music (he knew Schoenberg personally), and made a major contribution to the musical presentation of the "American way of life". Gershwin died of a brain tumor at the height of his fame.

Works: Stage works (selection): *Blue Monday* (1922), *Lady, be Good!* (1924), *Oh, Kay!* (1926), *Funny Face* (1927), *Strike up the Band* (1930), *Girl Crazy* (1930), *Of Thee I Sing* (1931), *Porgy and Bess* (1935); orchestral works (including *Rhapsody in Blue*, 1924, and *An American in Paris*, 1928), songs, music for revues, film scores.

Above
Porgy and Bess, production photograph from the guest performance given by the Everyman Opera Company of New York, with William Warfield (Porgy) and Helen Colbert (Clara), conductor Alexander Smallens, Titania Palast, Berlin 1953.
After giving five performances to enthusiastic audiences at the Wiener Volksoper, the Everyman Opera Company went on to West Berlin, and fascinated the German public with 13 delightful evenings at the Titania Palast. In the postwar period, *Porgy and Bess* was the best possible advertisement for American culture, and indeed for America itself. Toward the end of its tour, the *Porgy* company gave guest performances in the Soviet Union, a most unusual event at the time of the Cold War. The company returned to the USA in 1956, and was dissolved a little later, since it could not find a permanent theater.

Porgy and Bess, photograph from the production by Götz Friedrich, sets Hans Schavernoch, conductors Andrew Litton and Wayne Marshall, Bregenz Festival 1998. Later productions of *Porgy and Bess* made it clear that the European attitude to America had become more critical. Less emphasis was now laid on the folklore element, and more on the theme of the harsh battle for survival.

George Gershwin: America at last, if rather late in the day, found a genuinely national composer. He created a musical idiom based on differences of class and race: popular national music of very high quality.

Porgy and Bess

Folk opera in three acts

Libretto: DuBose Heyward, after his novel *Porgy* and Dorothy Hartzel Heyward's play.
Première: 10 October 1935, New York (Alvin Theater).
Characters: Porgy, a crippled black man (Bbar), Bess, a young black woman (S), Sportin' Life, a dope peddler and smuggler (T), Crown, a high-earning but brutal stevedore (Bar), Jake, a fisherman (Bar), Clara, his wife, mother of a baby boy (S), Robbins, a young fisherman (T), Serena, his wife (S), Peter, an old black honey seller (T), Maria, his wife (A), Jim, Mingo and Nelson, black fishermen (Bar, 2 T), Lily and Annie, black women (2 Ms), Strawberry Woman (Ms), Crab Man (T), Simon Frazier, a black lawyer (Bar), Undertaker (Bar); Scipio, a young black (spoken), Mr. Archdale, a white lawyer (spoken), Autopsist (spoken), Detective (spoken), Policeman (spoken); residents of Catfish Row, fishermen, children, stevedores (chorus).
Setting: Charleston, South Carolina, around 1870, after the American Civil War.

Synopsis

"Oh, I got plenty o' nuttin, an' nuttin's plenty fo' me ..." is the crippled Porgy's attitude to life. He has harnessed a goat to his soapbox cart, and drives it around the Negro neighborhoods of Charleston. Secretly, he watches and admires the attractive Bess, but she is mistress of the brutal Crown, and beyond the cripple's reach – until she unexpectedly seeks shelter in Porgy's shack in Catfish Row. Crown has killed a fisherman in a fight, and is on the run from the police. Porgy is overjoyed to be able to offer the girl refuge. Bess is now living with the poorest of the poor, and rejects the advances of the dandified Sportin' Life, who has up till now sold her some "dream powder" and would like to lure her away to New York. The neighbors in Catfish Row sense that Porgy and Bess are transformed by love, and accept Bess into their community. In relaxed mood, the lovers join the traditional fishermen's picnic party on Kittiwah Island. Crown, the murderer, greets Bess's decision to stay with a cripple with a scornful laugh. During the party he forces her to join him in his hiding place, and Porgy returns to Catfish Row alone. Days later, Bess returns to his shack, sick and

delirious, begging him to protect her if Crown comes after her. During a violent storm, while the women, children and old people are praying to Jesus to protect all the fishermen out at sea, Crown reappears. He has survived the storm, and is not prepared to have Bess stolen by a cripple. But when Crown tries to break into his shack with a knife, Porgy overcomes his rival; he wrestles Crown to the ground with his strong arms, and kills him. Finding the body of Crown, the police try to trace the murderer, but in vain, and take the cripple away with them as a witness. The local people claim not to have seen or heard anything; they are all behind Porgy, and he soon returns to Catfish Row, to the delight of his friends and neighbors. But Bess has gone. Sportin' Life has shaken her confidence by pretending that Porgy will never be back, and she has left the shack. "Oh, Bess, oh where's my Bess?" Porgy asks again and again. However, he is not about to give up. He sets out in his goat cart to look for Bess in the distant city of New York, singing, "Oh Lawd, I'm on my way."

S. N.

An American note: the difficulty of choice

It was not inevitable that, out of the wide diversity of American folklore, Gershwin would choose the Afro-American strand as the inspiration for his score. He might, with more historical justification, have chosen North American Indian folklore as more genuinely American, or the hybrid musical traditions of the white population. His choice was determined by a literary factor – the novel and play *Porgy*, by DuBose Heyward and his wife – and by Gershwin's own enthusiasm for jazz, which (although it is not folk music in the strict sense of the word) had a great influence on twentieth-century American art music.

Porgy and Bess, photograph from the production by Götz Friedrich, sets Hans Schavernoch, conductors Andrew Litton and Wayne Marshall, Bregenz Festival 1998.
A fierce storm is raging, and the women, children, and men who have stayed on shore pray for themselves and for the fishermen out at sea. While the storm is shown as real, it is also a metaphor for life at a time of catastrophe.

A popular piece and a national opera

Gershwin himself said that he thought the music of *Porgy and Bess* so wonderful that he could not believe he had written it. Although he was able to get DuBose Heyward, the author of the novel, to write the libretto, while his own brother Ira provided the requisite lyrics, he still wanted authentic experience, and spent the summer of 1934 on Folly Island, near Charleston. This vacation yielded results in the shape of the rhythmic patterns and specific intonation of the recitative in the opera. The work was completed in the late summer of 1935. Staging it presented problems, since there were not enough black opera singers available, and night-club singers had to be recruited. The première was a successful attempt to create a typically American opera with American influences.

Musical or opera?

The opera's subject and musical language – a synthesis of elements from traditional and light music – are now considered typically American. Gershwin, who had already won fame as a composer of Broadway musicals, wanted to appeal to a wide audience, beyond the élite circle of classical music lovers. As a result he integrated the main theme, the constantly threatened love between Porgy and Bess, into the everyday life of an ordinary urban quarter, presenting the lives of its inhabitants episodically. The through-composed succession of scenes and the musical plasticity of the score are structurally reminiscent of *verismo* (→Mascagni), but with his individual synthesis, Gershwin created a new type of folk opera. Reviewers, expecting clear distinctions between genres, criticized it for being too close to the musical, and although the public loved some of the numbers, which became hits, demand for tickets was only moderate, and for financial reasons the opera had to close after 124 performances. Only after Gershwin's death did it really become successful, at first mainly in America but then in Europe too. In 1943, for instance, *Porgy and Bess* was staged in Copenhagen as a kind of protest against the occupation of Denmark by the Nazis, who managed to close down this production of the "negro opera" only after several performances had taken place. The breakthrough to wide popularity came with Otto Preminger's film version of 1959.   *M. S.*

Porgy and Bess, production photograph from the guest performance given by the Everyman Opera Company of New York, with William Warfield as Porgy, Titania Palast, Berlin 1953.
The ecstatic Porgy would happily embrace the whole world. Since the music of Gershwin's opera has its roots in Afro-American folk themes, and most of the individual numbers take the simple form of songs, there is much less stylistic distance between the emotions to be expressed and the musical effect itself than in traditional European opera. Both the protagonists and the chorus (which plays a prominent part) reveal their feelings in elemental and even explosive fashion. In spite of their violent and often bloody arguments, all the members of this community of black people living in South Carolina around 1870 breathe to the same rhythm. They live their hard lives to the full, and express their passions in song. Indeed, song is the reality of their world, and is one reason why *Porgy and Bess* is so immediate and gripping on stage.

1. "Summertime": Clara's Lullaby

Sum - mer - time _____ an' the liv-in' is eas - y, _____ Fish are jum-pin', __ an' the cot-ton is high. _____

2. Jake's Lullaby

a wo - man is a some - time thing, _____ Yes, a wo - man is a some - time thing.

3. Porgy's Banjo-Song

Oh, I got plen - ty o' nut-tin', _____ An' nut-tin's plen-ty fo' me.

4. Sportin' Life's Song

There's a boat dat's leav-in' soon for New York, ___ Come wid me, ___ dat's where we be-long, sis-ter. ___

5. Porgys and Bess's Love Theme

Bess, you is my wo-man now, __ you is, __ you is! An' you mus' laugh an' sing an' dance for two in-stead of one. ___

6. Duet: Porgy and Bess

I wants to stay here, but I ain't wor-thy, You is too de-cent to un-der stan'

Porgy and Bess, photograph from the production by Götz Friedrich, sets Hans Schavernoch, conductors Andrew Litton and Wayne Marshall, Bregenz Festival 1998. The chorus is presented as a living community. The street people never stand still to sing as an ensemble, but are constantly on the move.

7. Porgy's Lament

Bess, oh where's my Bess, _____ Won't some-bod-y tell me where ___ ?

8. Porgy's Final Song

Oh ___ Lawd, I'm on my way. I'm on my way to a Heav'n-ly Lan' _____

Giordano, Umberto

b. 28 August 1867 in Foggia (Apulia)
d. 12 November 1948 in Milan

The son of a pharmacist, Giordano became a musician against the wishes of his parents. He studied at the Naples Conservatory until 1890, with some interruptions. When he submitted a one-act opera, *Marina*, to a competition organized by the publishing house of Sonzogno in 1889, the first prize was won by Mascagni with →*Cavalleria rusticana*, but the publishers commissioned Giordano to write a full-length opera. The result was *Mala vita* (1892), an extreme example of the *verismo* style then becoming fashionable. Giordano's greatest and most enduring success was with *Andrea Chénier*, in 1896, and he consolidated his reputation with his next opera *Fedora* (1898). It was said in Italy at the time that "Fedora fè d'oro" ("Fedora makes money"), and Giordano's fame, lasting into his old age, was indeed founded on this work and its predecessor.

Works: Operas: *Marina* (around 1889), *Mala vita* (*Low Life*) (1892), renamed *Il voto* (*The Vow*) (1897), *Regina Diaz* (1894), *Andrea Chénier* (1896), *Fedora* (1898), *Siberia* (1903), *Marcella* (1907), *Mese Mariano* (*The Marian Month*) (1910), *Madame Sans-Gêne* (1915), *La cena della beffe* (*The Dinner of the Mockers*) (1924), *Il re* (*The King*) (1929); some orchestral works, piano works, songs, ballet music, incidental music.

Andrea Chénier

Dramma di ambiente storico in four acts

Libretto: Luigi Illica.
Première: 28 March 1896, Milan (Teatro alla Scala).
Characters: Andrea Chénier (T), Carlo Gérard (Bar), Maddalena de Coigny (S), Bersi, a mulatto woman (Ms), La Contessa de Coigny (Ms), Old Madelon (Ms), Roucher (B), Pietro Fleville, a novelist, holding a pension from the King (B or Bar), Fouquier Tinville, the Public Prosecutor (B or Bar), Mathieu, nicknamed Populus, a sansculotte (Bar), The Abbé, a poet (T), An Incroyable (T), Master of the Household (B), Dumas, President of the Committee of Public Safety (B), Schmidt, jailer at St. Lazare (B); crowd, consisting of people of all classes and all professions (chorus).
Setting: France, during the French Revolution of 1789–94.

Synopsis

In the turmoil of the French Revolution, the poet Andrea Chénier, once a supporter of the Revolution, is now himself persecuted by the Revolutionaries. The aristocratic Maddalena de Coigny takes refuge from her Revolutionary pursuers with him, and they fall in love. However, Chénier is arrested and

Left
Andrea Chénier, production photograph with Pilar Lorengar (Maddalena) and Stefano Algieri (Chénier), production Nicolas Joël, sets and costumes Hubert Monloup, conductor Rico Saccani, Opéra Lyon 1989.
Ideas inflame but sometimes burn humanity: Chénier, a supporter of the Revolution, is condemned by the Revolutionary Tribunal. Only the love between Maddalena and Chénier burns brighter than death.

*G*iordano was a composer in the "verismo" style, and like many of his contemporaries, such as Mascagni, Leoncavallo, Catalani, and Cilea, became internationally famous for a single work.

Andrea Chénier, set design by Kurt Söhnlein, production Peter Eber, conductor Ernst Richter, Landestheater, Hannover 1955/56 (TWS).
As well as being a tragic and sensitive love story, the opera depicts the Revolution itself in a series of episodes. Giordano uses musical quotations as illustrations, such as the Rococo gavotte in the first act, symbolizing a foundering world, and fragments of such famous Revolutionary songs as "Ça ira", the "Carmagnole," and the "Marseillaise." He intended to create a realistic picture of the time, and one that would not be without its bitter ironies.

condemned to death by the Revolutionary Tribunal. Maddalena follows her lover to prison in order to die with him.

Act I

In the château of the Countess de Coigny in the provinces of France, there is increased tension between the aristocrats and the Third Estate of society on the eve of the French Revolution. Gérard, chamber valet to the Countess, leaves his post and joins the Revolutionaries. The poet Andrea Chénier also declines to offer his services to the nobility, and is admired by the Countess's daughter Maddalena for his courageous and honest stand.

Act II

Paris, in the summer of 1794. Gérard has made a great name for himself during the Revolution, and Chénier has also joined the revolutionary side. At first popular with the Revolutionaries, he has now fallen out of favor. Maddalena, pursued as an aristocrat and in danger, seeks refuge with Chénier. Both under threat, they take courage from each other and swear eternal love. Gérard appears, summoned by a spy; he is now Chénier's rival in love. The poet forces him to fight a duel, and wounds him. At this point Gérard recognizes Chénier and is prepared to let him escape, so that Maddalena will have someone to protect her from the danger of the Jacobin Terror. He tells the guards, when they arrive, that he did not know his assailant.

Act III

In the Hall of the Revolutionary Tribunal. Chénier is arrested, and accused of being an adherent of the aristocracy. Gérard intends to protect him, but then discovers the love between Chénier and Maddalena, whom he loves himself. He tells Maddalena that she must give herself to him to save Chénier's life, and she is prepared to comply. Moved by such self-sacrifice, Gérard now defends Chénier, but in vain, for the Revolution devours its children, and the poet is condemned to death.

Act IV

The prison of St. Lazare, on the night before 25 June 1794. The last service Gérard can render his friends is to bribe the jailer to let Maddalena take the place of a mother condemned to death, so that the lovers can die together.   S. N.

A new trend in opera: politics and passion
Luigi Illica, who was Puccini's customary librettist, provided Giordano with a libretto that is partly a drama of love and jealousy and partly a historical and political thriller, and that derives from his own careful study of historical and literary sources rather than being an adaption of a drama already in existence Libretti took on more and more independent literary characteristics in the 19th century. Illica's libretto paved the way for a series of similar operas, the most famous being Puccini's →*Tosca* (1900) and Giordano's own *Fedora*.

Andrea Chénier, set for the première by Constantino Magni and Mario Sala: a street in Paris (Act II), Milan 1896 (TWS).
A typical stage set of the historicizing period. The monumental architecture, neo-Classical funerary monument, and broad flights of steps are characteristic not of the Rococo age but of the taste of the late 19th century. The view of Paris with the Seine in the background is almost idyllic. Only the lampposts, their shape suggesting gallows, clearly indicate that this attractively designed place can become a violent battlefield where antagonists settle accounts.

Andrea Chénier, production photograph with Stefano Algieri (Chénier) and Jean Philippe Lafont (Gérard), production Nicolas Joël, sets and costumes Hubert Monloup, conductor Rico Saccani, Opéra Lyon 1989.
Friends or enemies? The poet who pays homage in his work to the ideals of a peaceful, humane order of society; the former chamber valet, now a man with a political career, who must acknowledge himself the slave of an illusion now destroyed. At least they are not competing against each other but side by side.

Andrea Chénier, production photograph with Eva Marton (Maddalena) and Piero Cappuccilli (Gérard), conductor Riccardo Chailly, Teatro alla Scala, Milan 1985. Even the discriminating audiences of La Scala, Milan, acclaimed an extraordinary event when Eva Marton, Pietro Cappuccilli, and José Carreras all appeared on stage together.

Revolutions devour their children

Giordano describes his opera as a "historical drama". *Andrea Chénier* is a work imbued with political disillusion. Not only are the protagonists of the opera disappointed by the atrocities of the "glorious" French Revolution, they are all destroyed by its dictatorship. All they have left is love. It is through love that Maddalena and Chénier find freedom, but, tragically, only in their free decision to die together. The ecstatic closing duet, sung at dawn before their execution, depicts the union of the lovers in their readiness to face death, and is a *liebestod* like that of Tristan and Isolde. M 1 The story of André Chénier reflects disappointed bourgeois feelings. There were three more revolutions in France after 1789 (in 1830, 1848, and 1870), but the ideals of liberty, egality, and fraternity were never attained. What still remained sacred? Chénier's answer: love alone.   J. K.

A poet in the shadow of the guillotine

André Chénier (1762–94) was a major French literary figure, and one of the many victims of the Jacobin reign of terror. As a journalist and poet, he had originally been an enthusiastic supporter of the ideas of the Revolution, but he opposed the Jacobins over the king's execution, was accused of being a royalist, and was then condemned to death. Giordano represents the eponymous hero of his opera as a sensitive poet. In Chénier's two arias, poetry and elevated feelings are transfigured by great melodies. M 2, M 3

Andrea Chénier, Lotte Lehmann (Maddalena) and Tino Pattiera (Chénier) at the Wiener Staatsoper, 1925.
The two lovers and Gérard have melodious and rewarding roles in Giordano's opera. The first Andrea Chénier, Giuseppe Borgatti, was the outstanding Italian Wagnerian singer of his day (Wagner's influence can be detected in the score of this opera). Later, almost all the great tenors specializing in Italian roles sang the part, from Enrico Caruso to José Carreras. Tino Pattiera, a *Heldentenor* of Dalmatian origin, was a favorite with the public between the two world wars, as was Lotte Lehmann, celebrated for her singing of Wagner and Richard Strauss. Pattiera was particularly successful in Dresden, where he was a member of the opera company until 1941, and in Vienna, where he settled after the war, also making a great name for himself as a singing teacher.

1. Closing Duet (Maddalena and Chénier)

La no-stra mor-te è il tri-on-fo dell' a-mor!

2. Chénier's Aria (Act I)

Un dì al-l'az-zur-ro spa-zio guar-dai pro-fon-do,

3. Chénier's Aria (Act IV)

Come un bel dì di mag-gio che con bac-chio di ven-to

e ca-rez-za di rag-gio si spe-gne in fir-ma-men-to,

Andrea Chénier, production photograph with Katia Ricciarelli as Maddalena, production Otto Schenk, conductor Nello Santi, Wiener Staatsoper 1981.
In spite of several similarities between →*Tosca* and *Andrea Chénier*, which had the same librettist, Giordano's heroine Maddalena de Coigny is no Tosca who can kill for love, but a gentle, insecure woman. She seeks protection from Chénier, who could do with some help himself. This realization leads to their romantic but hopeless love. "Viva la morte! Insieme!" are the last words they utter, in an impassioned duet intended as an apotheosis of love.

Andrea Chénier, production photograph with Gabriela Beňačková-Čáp (Maddalena) and Piero Cappuccilli (Gérard), production Otto Schenk, conductor Riccardo Chailly, Wiener Staatsoper 1981.
Many details of *Andrea Chénier* anticipate *Tosca*, which was written four years later. The moving force in the dramatic action is Gérard; a political symbol and Chénier's rival in love, he is an ambiguous figure. He takes the crucial step from oppressed servant of an aristocrat to convinced revolutionary, and then, in abusing his newly won power, assumes characteristics similar to those of Puccini's Scarpia. However, Gérard is no out-and-out villain; feelings of love and friendship overcome his desire for revenge.

Glass, Philip

b. 31 January 1937 in Baltimore

Glass studied at the University of Chicago and the Juilliard School of Music in New York, and was a pupil of Darius Milhaud in Aspen, Colorado, and of Nadia Boulanger in Paris. His encounters with the great Indian musician Ravi Shankar and the famous tabla player Alla Rakha were of crucial importance to him. In the mid-1960s, Glass withdrew all his previous compositions, most of them written in the post-serial style, and applied the meditative principles of Indian musical practice to his own writing. The results include the use of an additive series of tiny melodic cells based on a fundamental beat, the addition or subtraction of these particles, his apparently static harmony, and the extreme reduction of his methods, in the spirit of minimalism. The aim of music-making, as he saw it, was no longer to provide variety and information, but to steer the listener in the direction of the river of time by the constant repetition of series of uniform phrases. From 1968 onwards, Glass performed this music with his own ensemble. He won international fame in 1976 with his opera *Einstein on the Beach*, inspired by Robert Wilson, which together with his Gandhi opera *Satyagraha* and *Akhnaten* forms a trilogy on the subject of the transformation of the world by spiritual powers. Glass became a cult figure, and established artists such as the pop musician David Bowie and the director Achim Freyer identified with his work. Freyer's productions of Glass's operas in Stuttgart in the mid-1980s were notable European events, and the music for Godfrey Reggio's three cult films *Koyaanisqatsi* (*The World Turned Upside Down*, in the Hopi Indian dialect, 1988), *Powaqqatsi* (*Enchanter of the World*, or *Life in Transformation*), and *ANIMA MUNDI* (*Soul of the World*, 1991), and also his music for Paul Schrader's film *Mishima* (1985), made Glass a figure transcending the boundaries of race, nation, and generation. Such works as *A Descent into the Maelstrom*, produced by the Australia Dance Theater, *In the Upper Room*, with Twyla Tharp, and *Glass Pieces*, with choreography by Jerome Robbins for the New York City Ballet, have been major artistic events, together with Glass's symphonically conceived *Nature Portraits* for orchestra, comprising *The Light* (1987), *The Canyon* (1988), and *Itaipu*, for chorus and orchestra (1988).

Works: Stage works: *Einstein on the Beach* (1976), *Satyagraha* (1980), *The Photographer* (1982), *Akhnaten* (1984), *1000 Airplanes on the Roof* (1988), *The Fall of the House of Usher* (1988), *The Making of the Representative of Planet 8* (1988), *The Voyage* (1992), *Die Ehen zwischen den Zonen 3, 4 und 5* (*The Marriages between Zones 3, 4 and 5*) (1997), *Monsters of Grace* (1998); a piece of music-theater *Hydrogen Jukebox* (1991); operas on film: *Orphée* (*Orpheus*) (1993), *La belle et la bête* (*Beauty and the Beast*) (1994); symphonies, concertos, string quartets, piano pieces, incidental music, film scores.

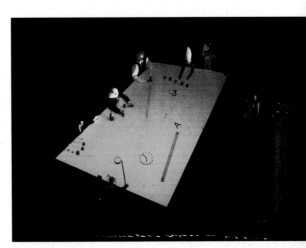

Einstein on the Beach, photograph from the production by Achim Freyer, sets and costumes Achim Freyer, conductor Michael Riesman, Württembergisches Staatstheater, Stuttgart 1988.
Achim Freyer's production was a highly regarded dramatic event.

Einstein on the Beach

"Opera" in four acts

Libretto: Robert Wilson and Philip Glass.
Première: 25 July 1976, Avignon (Théâtre Municipal).
Performers: 4 main performers, 2 women soloists (S, A), male soloist (T), speaking parts, dancers, chorus.
Setting: Everywhere, in the present day.
Synopsis
Act I
Scene 1: Railroad train: limited movement from place to place on the earth.
Scene 2: Lawcourt (with bed): our own judgments, prejudices, and those of others pass sentence on us.
Act II
Scene 1: First dance – airfield with space ship: ideas for new dimensions open up.
Scene 2: Night train: transitional time in which different spaces merge.
Act III
Scene 1: Lawcourt/penitentiary: how our own ideas and those of others can fetter us.
Scene 2: Second dance – airfield with space ship: liftoff from all that holds us fettered. The universe and the space-time machine open up.
Act IV
Scene 1: Building/train: "This is the time for space."
Scene 2: Bed (without lawcourt): freeing ourselves from our own, inhibiting ideas.
Scene 3: Spaceship. Arrival inside the space-time machine: letting body and spirit alike fly free. Freedom or catastrophe, a nuclear holocaust.   S. N.

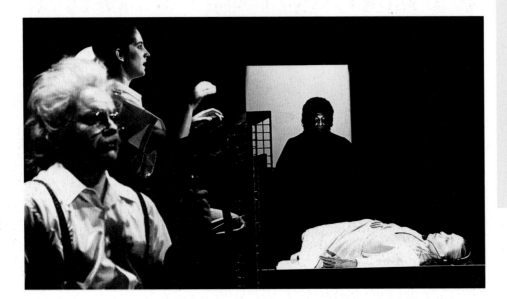

Einstein on the Beach, photograph from the production by Robert Wilson, conductor Philip Glass, Oper Frankfurt 1992.
The opera is a poetic study of Albert Einstein – as scientist, humanist, amateur violinist, and founder of modern nuclear physics, appearing first as the character familiar from textbooks, and then as a kind of Everyman.

Satyagraha

M.K. Ghandi in South Africa

Opera in three acts

Libretto: Philip Glass and Constance de Jong.

Première: 5 September 1980, Rotterdam (Stadsschouwburg).

Characters: Mohandas Karamchand Gandhi (T), Miss Schlesen, his secretary (S), Mrs. Naidoo, an Indian colleague (S), Kasturbai, Gandhi's wife (Ms or A), Mr. Kallenbach, a European colleague (Bar), Parsi Rustomji, an Indian colleague (B), Mrs. Alexander, a European woman friendly to Gandhi (A); mythical figures: Arjuna (T), Krishna (B), Duryodhana (silent); legendary historical figures: Leo Tolstoy, Rabindranath Tagore, Martin Luther King (silent); soldiers of two enemy armies, *satyagrahi* (those endeavoring to achieve enlightenment), Europeans, Indians, police officers (chorus).

Setting: The legendary battlefield of Kuru in mythical times, and South Africa in 1896-1913.

Synopsis
Act I "Tolstoy"

Scene 1: The Kuru Field of Justice, which is both a mythical battlefield and a plain in South Africa. Two armies face each other, ready to do battle. Like the legendary hero Arjuna, Gandhi asks himself if he has the right to fight. The god Krishna tells him that a human being can do no more than make sure he knows the motives for his actions. If his motives are pure, he may fight, for there will then be no victories and defeats, no friends or enemies, only the truth.

Scene 2: On the "Tolstoy Farm" in 1910. Gandhi has founded a cooperative in South Africa, in line with the ideas of Tolstoy, the Russian writer, philosopher, and peace campaigner. Here he practices *satyagraha*, the taking of action for pure motives.

Scene 3: "The Vow." In the open air, 1906. The South African government has reinforced its policy of racial discrimination with the "Black Act." The Indians vow common resistance, in the spirit of *satyagraha*.

Act II "Tagore"

Scene 1: "Confrontation and Deliverance," 1896. The outskirts of a European settlement in South Africa. The Europeans fear for their privileges. Gandhi is stoned; put to the test in this way, he offers passive resistance. A European woman rescues him.

Scene 2: "The Indian Opinion," 1906. Gandhi intends to spread his ideas through the newspaper *Indian Opinion*.

Scene 3: "Protest." Out of doors, 1908. Gandhi and his adherents vow to conduct their struggle without hatred in their hearts. They burn their certificates of registration so that they will be on a par with the outcasts and imprisoned.

Act III "King"

"The Newcastle March." A mythical battlefield, and at the same time a plain in South Africa, 1913. Gandhi's ideas are spreading. The Newcastle March is successful. Government and police are both powerless: no resistance is offered, there is no focal point to be attacked – and one can hardly imprison thousands. Gandhi states what he has learned: *satyagraha* must be newly acquired every day. Yet every human being who aspires to it may be sure of the aid of the Enlightened Ones.   *S. N.*

Glass is the most successful representative of American minimalism, particularly with his operas written in that style. They show actions taking place at the same time, instead of in chronological order in the traditional way. As a result, yesterday, today, and tomorrow may appear simultaneously and be of equal value.

Satyagraha, photograph from the production by Achim Freyer, sets and costumes Achim Freyer, conductor Dennis Russel Davies, Württembergisches Staatstheater, Stuttgart 1981.
Achim Freyer, originally a painter, first began designing sets in collaboration with Ruth Berghaus. He made very skillful use of the principle of the scenic metaphor, and with his wife Ilona has been a congenial designer for Glass's works.

"Opera"

The director Robert Wilson (b. 1941) and Philip Glass made history with *Einstein on the Beach*, which they described as an "opera" not in the usual generic sense, but simply meaning "work." They liberated the old operatic genre from its traditional fetters; there are no fully formed texts (the singers chant numbers, solfeggio syllables, and nonsense words). The images and metaphors conjured up, however, are very powerful, and so is the music that develops the temporal dimension. Interludes called "knee plays" open and close the work and link the acts together. According to Wilson and Glass, the word derives from the play of the knee-joint which links two similar elements together. Glass followed up his success with this work by writing *Satyagraha* and *Akhnaten*, two further operas about people whose ideas have changed the world. The basic idea of the trilogy, according to Glass, is that the world can be altered by the power of thought.   *S. N.*

Satyagraha: beyond the terrorism of the consumer society

Glass's interest in Gandhi's life and teachings coincided with his turning to Indian music in the middle of the 1960s. Convinced of the relevance of the teachings described by Gandhi (1896–1946) as *satyagraha* ("holding to the truth"), he followed his Einstein opera with a portrait of Gandhi. Tolstoy, Tagore, and Martin Luther King, after whom the three acts are named, are historical representatives of this principle, spiritual models drawn from different times, cultures, and religions, and acting with different aims in mind, but united in being motivated by love and pity. The first scene in the opera is based on the *Bhagavad Gita* ("Song of the Sublime"), one of the central sections of the *Mahabharata*, and other Sanskrit texts deriving from Hindu religious traditions also feature, so that the characters both represent historical figures and interpret sacred writings. Here, as in the entire work, Glass aims to merge ancient wisdom with the tasks facing us in the present day. The music and the subject are unusually congruent. The repetition of sound patterns leads to tonal areas that rest and then shift, following the idea of *satyagraha*, to become one with cosmic energies. By comparison with *Einstein on the Beach*, the sound is softer. Glass used a string ensemble and a massive chorus. There is a constant melodic and harmonic pattern to each act, and sometimes to a single solo or ensemble, engendering change and tension by means of increasing or decreasing harmonics.

The work was acclaimed by people receptive to the idea of passive resistance: adherents of the peace movement, opponents of nuclear power, those inspired by religious motives to seek something outside the terrorism of the consumer society. This was the theme emphasized in the very successful and highly praised production by Achim and Ilona Freyer in Stuttgart in 1981. The production went on to be given in Utrecht, Scheveningen, and Amsterdam, and was taken to New York in 1981. *Satyagraha* is an unusual opera not only in its use of unfamiliar methods, but more particularly for its ethical and religious dimension. It is surely no coincidence that Richard Attenborough's film on Gandhi came out in the same year.   *S.N.*

The Fall of the House of Usher

Libretto: Arthur Yorinks and Philip Glass, after Edgar Allan Poe.

Première: 18 May 1988, Cambridge, Massachusetts.

Characters: Roderick Usher (T), Madeline Usher, his sister (S), William, his friend, the narrator (Bar), The Doctor (spoken); servants, spirits (spoken).

Setting: Somewhere in England, on a day in the fall, late 19th century.

Synopsis

Roderick and his invalid sister Madeline, the last of the Usher family, live in fear, surrounded by threatening shadows and indissolubly united to their property, which has absorbed the negative energies of all preceding generations and is now radiating them out again. At the urgent request of Roderick, his old school friend (and narrator of the opera) makes haste to visit the brother and sister. But there is nothing he can do; he can only watch as Madeline mysteriously dies, reappears, and drags her brother away to the realm of the dead with her. He is barely able to save himself in time from the collapsing house.   *S. N.*

Dreams outside book learning
Edgar Allan Poe's story has fascinated poets, dramatists and composers for over a century, among them →Claude Debussy, Heiner Müller, and Pierre Boulez. Philip Glass and Arthur Yorinks created an atmosphere full of suspicions, half-truths, truths, and lies. We do not know for sure whether incest, homosexuality, murder, or supernatural powers are involved, or whether the last of the Ushers are bearing the burden of their ancestors' guilt. The unfolding of the tonal surfaces corresponds to the dramatic structure, suggesting the constant presence of inescapable shadows.

The Fall of the House of Usher, production photographs with Antje Herzog as Madeline Usher, production Henry Akina, conductor Brynmor Llewelyn Jones, Berliner Kammeroper 1993.
The Wiener Kammeroper brought the work to Europe with its production of 1990, followed by Münster (1991), and by the Berliner Kammeroper (1993), which has made a name for itself by staging such works.

Akhnaten

Opera in three acts

Libretto: Philip Glass, in collaboration with Shalom Goldman, Robert Israel, Richard Riddell, and Jerome Robbins.

Première: 24 March 1984, Stuttgart (Württemberg Staatsoper, in the main theater).

Characters: Akhnaten (counterT), Nefertiti, his wife (A), Queen Tye, his mother (S), Horemhab, general and future Pharaoh (Bar), Aye, Nefertiti's father and adviser to the Pharaoh (B), High Priest of Amon (T), Six Daughters of Akhnaten and Nefertiti (6 female voices), Narrator (spoken) in the roles of Amenhotep (son of Hapu), The Scribe, and The Tourist Guide; funeral party, people of Thebes (chorus).

Setting: Thebes and Akhetaten, around 1365–48 BC, and in the present day.

Synopsis
Act I
Thebes, in Year 1 of the reign of Akhnaten. The funeral procession of the late Pharaoh Amenhotep III is setting out to escort him to Ra. His son Akhnaten ascends the throne.
Act II
Thebes and Akhetaten, in Years 5–15 of the reign of Akhnaten. Akhnaten overthrows the powerful polytheistic priestly caste and proclaims the supremacy of the One God, Aten. He builds Aten a temple and a city, Akhetaten.
Act III
Akhetaten, Year 17 of the reign of Akhnaten, and the present day. In his devotion to his god, and for the love of his wife Nefertiti and mother Tye, Akhnaten withdraws from all earthly concerns and is overthrown. In the ruins of Akhetaten (modern Amara), indifferent tourists listen to the account of Akhnaten given them by an indifferent tourist guide. Meanwhile, in the cosmic train of the dead, Akhnaten joins his father's funeral procession. *S. N.*

Akhnaten: a modern man
Akhnaten, the heretic who sat on the Pharaonic throne, has come down to us through the ages not as a pale figure of myth; according to Glass he was a modern man on an ancient throne. The music of this opera is harsher in sound than its two predecessors, and decidedly mechanical in effect. The production by Achim and Ilona Freyer presented the heretic king as a bringer of light. In the first performance in America, in Houston in 1984, David Free played him as a capricious hermaphrodite.

Akhnaten, production photograph from the première, production Achim Freyer, sets and costumes Achim and Ilona Freyer, conductor Dennis Russel Davies, Württembergisches Staatstheater, Stuttgart 1984.
After *Einstein on the Beach* (1976) and his Gandhi opera *Satyagraha* (1980), Glass created the last opera of his trilogy, a tribute to the spiritual forces that change the world, at the suggestion of Achim and Ilona Freyer.

Glinka, Mikhail Ivanovich

b. 1 June 1804 in Novospasskoye (Smolensk administrative district)
d. 15 February 1857 in Berlin

Glinka spent his childhood on the family estate, where he gained early impressions of both folk music and salon music with a folk flavor, sources that inspired him later. He had private music lessons in piano, violin, and Italian song. From 1818 he lived in St. Petersburg, and for a short while pursued a career in the civil service. His travels during the years 1830-33, both in Italy, where he met →Bellini and →Donizetti, and in Germany, where he met Mendelssohn, as well as his studies of music theory in Berlin, led to an increase in compositional activity during those years. The première of his first opera in St. Petersburg was a great success. He was music director of the imperial chapel from 1837 to 1839, but after the poor reception of his second opera he withdrew from the society life of the Russian nobility, and thereafter lived mainly abroad, in Spain, France, Poland, and Germany.

Works: Operas: *Zhizn' za tsarya* (*A Life for the Tsar*, originally *Ivan Susanin*) (1836), *Ruslan i Lyudmila* (*Ruslan and Lyudmila*) (1842); symphonic works, incidental music for Nestor Kukolnik's play *Prince Kholmsky*, two Spanish overtures (*Jota aragonesa* and *Souvenirs d'une nuit d'été à Madrid*), the orchestral fantasy *Kamarinskaya*, many songs and romances, piano pieces.

*G*linka is regarded as the father of Russian national music in the fields of opera, song, and instrumental music. He was a model for later Russian composers.

The "fathers" of Russian opera

Glinka is revered as the father of Russian national opera, and he did indeed usher in a new era in Russian music in 1836 with *A Life for the Tsar*. However, he was not the first Russian operatic composer. The real creator of Russian opera had been active several decades earlier, at the court of Catherine the Great; he was Vassily Pashkevich (1742–97). Between 1779 and 1791 he wrote seven operas on Russian libretti, most of them comic operas, and including three with libretti by Catherine herself. Pashkevich was music director at one of the first private theaters to be opened to the public in Russia, Karl Knipper's Free Theater in St. Petersburg. Dmitry Bortnyansky (1751–1825), active at court in the same period, was a pupil of the contemporary Italian operatic composer of that time, Baldassare Galuppi, and composed operas to French libretti to suit the taste of the tsar's court, which had close ties with the Western ruling classes, in particular the French aristocracy.

The first opera to be based on a play by Beaumarchais, Paisiello's *The Barber of Seville*, had its première at the court of Catherine the Great, where lively interest was also shown in the second, controversial part of the Beaumarchais trilogy (*Le mariage de Figaro* (→Mozart, *The Marriage of Figaro*). The third important contemporary Russian composer of the Classical era was Yevstigney Ipanovich Fomin (1761–1800), who wrote comic operas to texts by a range of authors from Catherine the Great to Voltaire.

The Bol'shoy Theater, St. Petersburg, drawing by V. Sadovnikov, c. 1930.
St. Petersburg symbolized Russia's connections with Western Europe. Founded by Peter the Great as a counterpoise to Moscow, the "pearl on the Neva" became the Russian equivalent of Versailles. Glinka's first opera had its première at the Bol'shoy Theater here in 1836. After a fire – a very frequent occurrence in 19th-century theaters – the St. Petersburg opera house was rebuilt and renamed the Mariinsky Theater in 1860. The Mariinsky now entered upon a period richer in tradition than that of any other Russian opera house. Premières given here included →*Boris Godunov* (Musorgsky), *The Stone Guest* (Dargomïzhsky), and *The Demon* (Rubinstein), and also Verdi's →*The Force of Destiny.*

Glinka in a St. Petersburg salon of the poet Nestor Kukolni, drawn by N. Stepanov, around the middle of the 1830s. Glinka is at the piano, playing music from his operas for the art-loving guests. The drawing represents a group portrait of the guests rather than an actual situation; there can be no doubt that in real life they would have listened more attentively to the father of Russian national opera.

Alexey Nikolaievich Verstovsky (1799–1862) was active in Moscow; he hoped to create a Russian operatic tradition in line with that of Carl Maria von Weber's →Der Freischütz, and attempted to realize it in large-scale Romantic or magical operas. Glinka's appearance on the scene of Russian operatic history was therefore not entirely unheralded. The fact that he was nonetheless regarded in the nineteenth century as the father of the national opera may be ascribed to his outstanding gifts, and to the development of a characteristically Russian technique of declamation for the operatic stage.

The biggest opera house in the world

The plans for the biggest opera house of the nineteenth century were never executed. Compared with that monumental architectural dream, even the Palais Garnier in Paris would have seemed a modest structure. In 1890 Tsar Alexander III commissioned the architect Viktor Schroeter to build him a private theater. This gigantic palace was to be at the disposal of the imperial family for grand state occasions, but the tsar's sudden death brought the idea to an abrupt end, and his family had to content itself with the Mariinsky Theater before being toppled from power in 1917.

The Bol'shoy Theater, Moscow, 1856. The first Bol'shoy ("great") Theater was opened in 1776, two years before the Teatro alla Scala in Milan. The history of the theater is one of repeated destruction by fire and subsequent rebuilding. The first rebuilding began in 1825, the second (by Alberto Cavos) in 1856, and the third after an air raid in 1942. After the October Revolution of 1917, the Bol'shoy became the leading opera house of the Soviet Union. Throughout the towns and villages of that huge country, people dreamed of going to the Bol'shoy once in their lives, but for many it remained an unfulfilled dream. The Bol'shoy Theater had a representative selection of mainly Russian and Soviet operas in its repertory, and was also the scene of political meetings (the plan for the electrification of the Soviet Union was agreed here).

A Life for the Tsar (Ivan Susanin)

Zhizn' za tsarya

Opera in four acts and an epilogue

Libretto: Yegor Rozen.
Première: 9 December 1836, St. Petersburg (Main Theater); première with new libretto by Sergey Gorodetsky: 21 February 1939, Moscow (Bol'shoy Theater).
Characters: Ivan Susanin, a peasant from the village of Domnino (B), Antonida, his daughter (S), Bogdan Sobinin, a militiaman and Antonida's fiancé (T), Vanya, Susanin's adopted son (A), Head of a Polish Army Detachment (B), Polish Messenger (T), Russian Officer (B); Russian peasants, militiamen, Polish courtiers, knights (chorus); Polish courtiers (ballet).
Setting: The Russian village of Domnino, Poland, and Moscow, 1612-1613.

Synopsis

Act I

The peasants assemble in Domnino, forming a militia to defend the country against invaders. Antonida, the daughter of the peasant Susanin, dreams of her fiancé Sobinin, who is fighting far away. Susanin encourages the people to resist. A party of Russian soldiers, with Sobinin among them, brings the good news that Moscow has been liberated. The nobility have agreed on a candidate for the tsar: Mikhail Fyodorovich Romanov.

Act II

In King Sigismund's palace, the Polish nobles are celebrating their conquests in Russia with feasting and dancing (a polonaise, a krakowiak, a waltz and a mazurka). A messenger brings news that the Russians have recaptured Moscow. Sigismund sends a troop of soldiers out to track down the young tsar and take him prisoner.

Act III

Vanya, Susanin's adopted son, wishes to join the Russian defenders and serve the fatherland like his foster father. The villagers greet Antonida and Sobinin, the bridal couple. Susanin invites them all to the wedding. Suddenly a Polish search party bursts into Susanin's house. The Poles order the master of the house to show them the way to the tsar's hiding place. Susanin pretends to be willing, but succeeds in sending Vanya away, unnoticed, to carry a warning to the tsar. Then Susanin sets out at the head of the Poles. When the wedding guests arrive, they find only the bride Antonida, weeping bitterly.

Act IV

Sobinin sets off with his men to rescue Susanin. Vanya makes haste to the nearby monastery in the forest, to warn the tsar. Meanwhile, Susanin leads the Poles into an impenetrable and marshy forest. As day breaks, the Poles realize that they have been deliberately led astray, and kill Susanin. But they themselves then perish at the hands of Sobinin and his men.

Epilogue

Preparations for the coronation are in progress in Moscow. Antonida, Sobinin, and Vanya are among the rejoicing crowds. They mourn for Ivan, and describe his heroic deed. The people acclaim the new tsar and the liberation of Russia.   M. P.

A Life for the Tsar, production picture (watercolor) by G. Gagarin for the third act of the opera, with Ivan Susanin (center), the bridal couple of Antonida and Sobinin, and Polish soldiers in the background. Glinka gave both the Russians and the Poles music of a national character. The Russian world is represented musically in a variety of ways, while the Polish soldiers and courtiers are depicted by simple Polish dance rhythms (mazurka, polonaise, krakoviak). The confrontation of two hostile nations – presented in musical as well as dramatic terms – is at the heart of the drama, in the same way as in Musorgsky's →*Boris Godunov.*

History, legend, and politics

The action of *A Life for the Tsar* is set towards the end of the "time of troubles", when the Russian nobles had set aside their long disputes over the succession to the throne and united to repel their foreign conquerors, Poland and Sweden. Folk memory preserved the names of several legendary heroes of that time. The most famous of them was Ivan Susanin, a simple Russian peasant, who saved the young tsar at the price of his own life, and led an entire Polish army to its death. The legend of Susanin was revived at the beginning of the nineteenth century, made its way into the visual arts and literature, and was told on the operatic stage and in the concert hall. In 1815, an opera by Catterino Cavos entitled *Ivan Susanin* had its première in St. Petersburg, and was very successful. Incidentally, it had a happy ending. Glinka was not, however, inspired by this opera (he was only eleven years old at the time of its production), but by a ballad by Kondraty Rileyev, a poet and member of the Decabrist movement, who used the figure of Susanin to symbolize the independence of the Russian people. Kondraty Rileyev, a nobleman, was the leader of the uprising of 14 December 1825, and was condemned to death and

executed on the tsar's orders. It is one of the curious paradoxes of Russian history that he, of all people, should have been the author of the epic ballad on which the opera later given its première as *A Life for the Tsar* was based. Glinka was not a political composer, and there is no doubt of his loyalty to the court. On the other hand, his position in the artistic life of St. Petersburg brought him into contact with many leading representatives of the discontented Russian intelligentsia, and he had close friends among them. However, he subordinated everyday politics to the grand idea of a national opera. In the 1830s the subject of Susanin was taken up by Tsar Nicholas I's police state, and put to the service of the official state ideology. It even acquired new political topicality with the suppression of the Polish revolt of 1830–31, Nicholas I and his court ideologists being undeterred by the fact that while the Poles had indeed invaded Russia in 1612, Russia was occupying Poland in 1830. For the tsar and his court, the simple statement that a Russian peasant was always ready to sacrifice his life for his divinely appointed ruler was of overriding importance.

A Life for the Tsar, Maria Stepanova in the role of Antonida (artist unknown). The village atmosphere and peasant characters, the didacticism of the plot, and the folk element in the music (with reminiscences of Russian peasant music and urban folklore merging into a unified musical style) are notable features of this opera, in a way that was also characteristic of other, later Romantic national composers of Central and Eastern Europe (→ Smetana, → Dvořák, → Moniuszko, → Erkel). However, the folk elements are highly idealized: the peasant girl Antonida wears expensive national costume, Susanin's wooden hut is neat and clean like a house in a fairytale, and, above all, the Russian protagonists are all brave and heroic. There are no villains here: the opponent is a collective one, in the form of the enemy nation.

An opera for the tsar

It took two years to write the opera. The original title of the work was *Ivan Susanin*, and Glinka devised the scenario himself. Several authors contributed to the text, but Baron Rozen, secretary to the tsarevich, provided the final version. He ensured that Susanin, as depicted on stage, did not bear too much resemblance to a genuine serf. The legendary hero became an ideal subject: a model peasant. It is not surprising that Tsar Nicholas I liked the opera very much. He attended rehearsals, summoned Glinka to see him, addressed him in familiar terms like a friend of distinguished birth, and gave him a valuable ring on the occasion of the première. It was during rehearsals that Glinka changed the title from *Ivan Susanin* to *A Life for the Tsar*, dedicating his opera to Nicholas – who has gone down in history as "the policeman of Europe."

The "Slav'sya" chorus

"Hail to the tsar, hail to Russia!" The famous chorus which features in the finale of the opera was several times considered for adoption as the Russian or Soviet national anthem. With its lapidary simplicity, and the polyphonic writing inspired by Russian folk songs, it is an extremely effective number. Its musical theme stands for the imaginary "holy figure" of the tsar, here identified with the fatherland of Russia itself. M 1

A Life for the Tsar, Osip Afanasievich Petrov, the first Ivan Susanin. Osip Petrov (1807–78) was the greatest Russian bass of his time. His unique voice was discovered by chance at a market in Kursk by the director of the St. Petersburg opera house. It was unusually deep and had a great range (incredible as it may sound, he could sing down to low B, although his top note, high G sharp, was also rather low). He made his début in St. Petersburg in 1830 as Sarastro (Mozart, →*The Magic Flute*), but was particularly famous for his singing in the new Russian operas, where he was the first to take many of the great bass roles such as Glinka's Ivan Susanin and Ruslan.

1. "Slav'sya" Chorus

Славь - ся, славь-ся, свя-та - я   Русь

2. Susanin's Farewell Aria (Act IV)

Ты прийдешь, мо - я заря! Взгляну в ли-це тво - е

The Russian bass

The role of Ivan Susanin was the first of a series of great Russian bass parts in the operatic repertory, including the mighty figures of Boris Godunov (→Musorgsky), Dosifey and Ivan Khovansky (→Musorgsky, *Khovanschchina*), Prince Galitsky and Khan Konchak (→Borodin, *Prince Igor*), Ivan the Terrible (Rimsky-Korsakov, *The Maid of Pskov*), and old Prince Yury of Kitezh (→Rimsky-Korsakov, *The Legend of the Invisible City of Kitezh*). These heroes generally belong to the paternal generation, and in fact often have children of their own. However, the weight and authority of their roles is determined less by family and personal relationships than by their political and social rank, their station in life, and their charisma. Russian bass roles are reserved, in particular, for outstanding figures: tsars, popular leaders, saviors of the fatherland. Paternal feelings play only a subsidiary part. The heroic bass role expresses the great social interest in messianic ideas felt by Russian intellectuals in the nineteenth century. Their music, usually solemn in nature, corresponds to those ideas. The tone of Ivan Susanin's farewell aria, sung as he is about to die (Act IV), is echoed in the music for other and later bass parts, such as those of Prince Igor, Dosifey, and Prince Yury of Kitezh. M 2

A Life for the Tsar, set design by Andrey Roller for the première in 1836. A model house for model peasants! The set for the third act: the interior of a typical but much idealized Russian peasant dwelling.

A Life for the Tsar, photograph from the production by Alfred Kirchner, costumes Joachim Herzog, conductor Vladimir Fedoseyev, Opernhaus Zürich 1996.
Western European productions tend to approach Russian opera respecting its national character, but also seeking to express ideas of more general relevance. Alfred Kirchner made this very Russian opera a notable theatrical event by emphasizing phenomena transcending its period.

These great Russian bass roles have been interpreted by equally great Russian bass singers. Osip Petrov (1807–78) was the first Susanin and the first Ruslan. Three decades later, he sang the part of Varlaam in the première of →*Boris Godunov*. Among the outstanding singers of the next generation of basses was Fyodor Stravinsky (1843–1902), father of the composer Igor Stravinsky, a member of the Mariinsky Theater ensemble in St. Petersburg. He was followed by Fyodor Shalyapin (1873–1938), who began his career in Savva Mamontov's private theater in Moscow, and became an international star. A great Russian (and then Soviet) bass of the next generation was Mark Reisen (1896–1995), as of 1930 a member of the Bol'shoy Theater company in Moscow, who continued singing until the 1970s, and lived to a great age. His successors, Yevgeny Nesterenko, Alexander Vedernikov, and other bass singers, were among the last in the line of descent. At the end of the twentieth century the Russian bass, a unique phenomenon in the world of opera, seems to be a species in decline.   M. P.

Above
A Life for the Tsar, production photograph with Boris Shtokolov (Ivan Susanin) and Larissa Dyadkova (Vanya), production Roman Tikhomirov, conductor Viktor Fedorov, Mariinsky Theater, St. Petersburg 1974 (photograph 1978). For a long time there were few departures in Russia from the convention that makes *A Life for the Tsar* a historical and legendary tale of the past, with very little relevance to the present.

A Life for the Tsar, production photograph with Matti Salminen (Ivan Susanin) and Elena Mosuc (Antonida), production Alfred Kirchner, conductor Vladimir Fedoseyev, Opernhaus Zürich 1996.

Ruslan and Lyudmila, production photograph with N. Ognovenko (Ruslan) and L. Netzebko (Lyudmila), Mariinsky Theater, St. Petersburg 1996.
Valery Gergiyev, principal conductor of the Mariinsky Theater, aroused this Russian opera house from its Sleeping Beauty slumbers. His conducting of *Ruslan and Lyudmila* made the production a great event.

Ruslan and Lyudmila, Fyodor Stravinsky as Farlaf. Fyodor Stravinsky (1843–1902) was the father of the world-famous composer →Igor Stravinsky, and the leading bass at the Mariinsky Theater in the generation of singers preceding Shalyapin. He sang there for quarter of a century, taking 64 bass parts, both heroic and comic, and participating in 1200 performances.

Ruslan and Lyudmila

Ruslan i Lyudmila

Opera in five acts

Libretto: Mikhail Glinka and Valerian Shirkov, from the poem of the same name by Alexander Pushkin.
Première: 9 December 1842, St. Petersburg (Main Theater).
Characters: Svetozar, Grand Prince of Kiev (B), Lyudmila, his daughter (S), Ruslan, a knight of Kiev and betrothed to Lyudmila (B or Bar), Ratmir, a Khazar prince (A), Farlaf, a Varangian knight (B), Finn, a good enchanter (T), Naina, a wicked enchantress (Ms), Gorislava, a captive of Ratmir (S), Bayan, a bard (T), Chernomor, a wicked enchanter, a dwarf (silent), Head of a Giant (male voice chorus, T, B); Svetozar's retinue, knights, nobles, maids, nurserymaids, wetnurses, pages, armed guards, cupbearers, guests, crowd, Moors, dwarfs, slaves of Chernomor, maidens of the magic castle, nymphs and water sprites (chorus and ballet).
Setting: Russia in legendary times, and the fairytale East of the past.

Synopsis
Act I

The bard is singing of the deeds of times long past, warning of the vicissitudes of fate. But the wedding guests in the hall of the Grand Prince Svetozar call for songs of a more pleasing nature. The bride Lyudmila takes leave of her father cheerfully, and comforts her rejected suitors Ratmir and Farlaf. Svetozar blesses Ruslan and Lyudmila. Then a thunderclap is heard, and darkness falls. When it clears away, Lyudmila has disappeared. Her father promises half his kingdom and his daughter's hand to anyone who can bring Lyudmila back. Ruslan and Ratmir set off, while Farlaf hatches dark plots.

Act II

In his search for his lost bride, Ruslan meets the old enchanter Finn. As a young man, Finn had courted the beautiful Naina and was rejected. He had acquired magical powers in long years of study, and so won Naina's love at last. But they had both grown old, and Finn now fled in horror from the woman he had once desired so much. Since then Naina has persecuted all lovers vindictively. Finn tells Ruslan how to find Lyudmila, who has been abducted by the dwarf Chernomor. Naina, however, favors Ruslan's rival Farlaf, and promises to help him. Ruslan has to fight the Head of a Giant, and is victorious. The dying Head tells its secret: its owner was a brother of the dwarf Chernomor and was killed by him; giving Ruslan a sword, the Head demands vengeance.

Act III

Persian maidens in Naina's magic castle promise refuge from the cold world outside, enticing knights to stray from the path of virtue. Ruslan and Ratmir fall victim to their wiles. Naina's maidens so cloud Ratmir's mind that he fails to recognize Gorislava, whom he had formerly loved and abandoned. Ruslan too falls into the trap. His love for Lyudmila fades, and he believes himself in love with Gorislava. Finn exposes Naina's deceptions, and sets the knights on the right path again; Ratmir recognizes the faithful Gorislava as his true love, and unites himself with Ruslan in bonds of friendship.

Act IV

The captive Lyudmila resists the enticements of Chernomor, and thinks of her beloved Ruslan. The thieving dwarf challenges Ruslan to fight, first casting a spell on the captive Lyudmila to send her into an enchanted sleep; he then faces Ruslan and is defeated. But Lyudmila is still in her trance, and nothing can wake her. A smile plays around her lips. Ruslan is a prey to despair and jealousy. His friends Ratmir and Gorislava preserve him from madness and advise him to return home.

Act V

Ratmir watches over Ruslan while he is sleeping. Meanwhile, Lyudmila is abducted by Farlaf. Ruslan follows the abductor. Finn tests Ratmir's friendship, giving him a magic ring which will awaken Lyudmila. Farlaf brings the sleeping Lyudmila home to Kiev, where he claims her hand and the throne. But he cannot break the dwarf's spell; only Ruslan (to whom Ratmir has given Finn's magic ring) can bring Lyudmila out of her trance. Ratmir and Gorislava, Ruslan and Lyudmila have withstood the trials of their love and friendship. "The walls of the banqueting hall fall away," and the people unite with the princely couple, now matured by their sufferings, to praise their common homeland. *S. N.*

Unexpected vocal registers

The operagoer hearing *Ruslan and Lyudmila* for the first time will find that in many respects it sounds rather strange. The reason may be the unconventional allocation of parts to certain vocal registers, which is entirely different from what one expects in both Italian and French opera. The young knight Ruslan is not a heroic tenor, but a heroic bass or baritone. The tenor parts are taken by two ageless character figures, the enchanter Finn and the bard. The soprano part of Lyudmila cannot be described as either dramatic or lyric, while Gorislava is a genuine lyric soprano role. Ratmir is sung, strikingly, by an alto, the witch Naina is a comic mezzo, and her protégé Farlaf is a *buffo* bass. The only heroic bass part – the type given to the title role in *Ivan Susanin* – is a small one here, and is sung by Lyudmila's father the Grand Prince of Kiev.

M. P.

Right
Ruslan and Lyudmila, production photograph with N. Ognovenko (Ruslan) and L. Netzebko (Lyudmila), production Lotfi Mansouri, conductor Valery Gergiyev, Mariinsky Theater, St. Petersburg 1996.
The Grand Prince of Kiev blesses his daughter Lyudmila and her bridegroom Ruslan. The directing and acting of this production were conventional, but musically Gergiyev made it outstanding.

Below
Ruslan and Lyudmila, Chernomor, the evil dwarf, costume design by Valentina Chodassevich, Bol'shoy Theater, Moscow 1937.
The evil dwarf Chernomor with his long beard is not a singing part, but he has a striking leitmotif: a whole-tone scale that sounds strange and dissonant in the context of Classical and Romantic music. His brother is no less strange, and consists only of a giant head. The part is sung by an entire male voice chorus.

Above
Ruslan and Lyudmila, Finn, the good enchanter, costume design by Valentina Chodassevich, Bol'shoy Theater, Moscow 1937.
Finn, the good enchanter, is a sympathetic character. In his comic ballad he tells how he studied hard to rise from his station as a simple shepherd and win the hand of the lovely Naina. But while he eagerly pursued his studies, Naina became a repulsive old witch, and now it is she who pursues him with her love.

Gluck, Christoph Willibald

b. 2 July 1714 in Erasbach (Upper Palatinate)
d. 15 November 1787 in Vienna

Gluck was the son of a forester, and grew up in Bohemia. He studied music at Prague University, and began his career by writing occasional pieces for noble patrons, and working as a church organist (1727–34). He had early experience as an orchestral musician, which acquainted him with works by Vivaldi, Albinoni, Lolli, Pollarolo, and Porta, and acquired a taste for opera from performances given in Prague. Around 1735 he traveled to Vienna and then to Milan, where he spent four years as a pupil of Giovanni Battista Sammartini. His first opera, *Artaxerxes*, had its première at the Teatro Ducale, Milan, in 1741. Between 1745 and 1752 he visited a number of the musical centers of Europe. He composed a pasticcio for the reopening of the Haymarket Theater, London, entitled *La caduta dei giganti* (1746), and gave a concert there together with Handel. As resident composer with Mignotti's Italian opera company, he had his operas produced in Vienna, Hamburg, Copenhagen, Paris and Prague. In 1752 he settled in Vienna where, as an acknowledged master, he regularly received commissions from the imperial court opera for Italian opera and *opéras comiques*. His collaboration with the librettist Ranieri de' Calzabigi and the choreographer Gaspari Angiolini began in 1761. It was in reaction to the routine operatic writing of his time that Gluck developed his ideas for the reform of the genre. Between 1773 and 1779 he was back in Paris, where his reform of the typically French *tragédie lyrique* gave rise to much controversy, leading to outright hostility between the "Gluckists" and the "Piccinnists". In the last decade of his life, Gluck divided his time between Vienna and Paris, and enjoyed a very high reputation.

Works (mainly for the stage): Opere serie (selection): *Artaserse* (*Artaxerxes*) (1741), *Demofoonte* (*Demophoön*) (1742), *Il Re Poro* (*King Poros*) (1743), *Ipermestra* (*Hypermestra*) (1744), *Ezio* (1750), *La clemenza di Tito* (*The Clemency of Titus*) (dramma per musica 1752), *Le Chinoises* (*The Chinese Girls*) (Azione teatrale, 1754); *opéras comiques* (selection): *Le Chinois* (*The Chinese*) (1756), *L'île de Merlin, ou Le monde renversé* (*Merlin's Isle, or The World Turned Upside Down*) (1758), *L'ivrogne corrigé* (*The Reformed Drunkard*) (1760), *Le cadi dupé* (*The Cadi Deceived*) (1761), *La rencontre imprévue* (*The Unexpected Meeting*, or *The Pilgrims of Mecca*) (1763); reform operas (Italian and French): *Orfeo ed Euridice* (azione teatrale per musica, 1762) and *Orphée et Eurydice* (tragédie-opéra, 1774) (*Orpheus and Eurydice*), *Alceste* (*Alcestis*) (tragédie-opéra, 1767, 1776), *Paride ed Elena* (*Paris and Helen*) (dramma per musica, 1770), *Iphigénie en Aulide* (*Iphigenia in Aulis*) (1774), *Armide* (*Armida*) (drama heroique, 1777), *Iphigénie en Tauride* (*Iphigenia in Tauris*) (tragédie-opéra, 1779), *Echo et Narcisse* (*Echo and Narcissus*) (drama lyrique, 1779); ballets (selection): *Don Juan, ou Le festin de pierre* (*Don Juan, or The Stone Guest*) (1761), *Semiramide* (*Semiramis*) (1765); *Seven Odes and Songs from Klopstock* (1786), *De profundis* for chorus and orchestra, eight sonatas for two violins and basso continuo (1746).*

Gluck is one of the great reformers of operatic history, and took an important step toward the ideal of "music drama" in his operas.

found itself at the time to the music, and introduced reforms there too. He replaced the conventional *recitativo secco* (recitative accompanied by harpsichord alone) with orchestrally accompanied recitative of great dramatic power, sometimes heightened to an *arioso* style to suit a particular dramatic situation. Gluck conceived his works not as a linear series of scenes, arranged according to the entrance and exit of the characters, but as larger units sometimes embracing half an act or a whole act, with the chorus and ballet playing an active dramatic part.

Tragedy with a happy ending

Gluck's reform operas had considerable influence on the operatic history of the following decades, but they could not save *opera seria*. His innovations had no effect on the essential aspects of the genre: the heroes of classical mythology were not banned from the stage, and comic elements remained strictly out of bounds, reserved for opera buffa only. Above all, Gluck failed to break with the principle of the *lieto fine* (the eighteenth-century term for a happy ending). All in all, *opera seria* remained an institution calculated to please courtly society. The great conflicts on which the action of the operas turns are experienced and suffered by the characters, yet the tragedy is resolved by the gods rather than the characters themselves.

"Sir Gluck," the Classical composer

Gluck was highly esteemed by his contemporaries, and even by the aristocracy. After his death, his title of "Imperial and Royal Court Kapellmeister" to Maria Theresia and later to Joseph II of Austria was not bestowed even on as great a composer as Mozart, who had to be content with the title of "Imperial and Royal Chamber Composer." E.T.A. Hoffmann, in his story *Ritter Gluck* (*Sir Gluck*), published in 1809 as one of the *Fantasienstücken in Callots Manier* (*Fantasy Pieces in the Manner of Callot*), still presented Gluck's music as typical of the old, elevated style. Gluck was in fact a knight, having received the Order of the Golden Spur, like the young Mozart later, from the Accademia Filharmonica in Bologna. Hector Berlioz and Richard Wagner found Gluck's ideas of reform congenial, and regarded him (rather than Haydn or Mozart) as the archetypal Classical composer. His works display perfect equilibrium between darkness and light, simplicity and pathos, love and hate, the static and the dynamic. Even the flow of passions does not break the formal bounds. This perfect balance in his various works caused Winckelmann, Goethe, and the contemporary French philosophers to praise the "classical" proportions of Gluck's music (referring in this case to the classical architecture of ancient Greece).   *T. Sz.*

Combating the tyranny of singers

The dominant operatic genre throughout Europe in the eighteenth century was the *opera seria* (→Handel). However, the genre was so much at the mercy of the expertise and the wishes of prima donnas and castrati that a composer, if he wanted to be successful, quite often had to write his arias and ensembles, and even change the course of the action, to suit the whims of his star singers. Gluck's reform of opera consisted of restoring its obedience to the laws of drama, in a manner similar to the Greek tragedy on which he drew. He traced the reasons for the crisis in which *opera seria*

Alcestis, set design by Theo Lau, production Boris Pilato, Musiktheater im Revier, Gelsenkirchen 1964-65 (TWS). Undoubtedly the large-scale choral scenes of an opera by Gluck linger in the mind most memorably. Gluck was not merely reviving the example of Greek drama in opera, with the new musical methods available to him: the chorus also stands for the community, society, mankind. It sings of strong and universal emotions: grief, joy, and anger. Last but not least, it is possible that without the example of Gluck's choruses, Beethoven could never have written the "Ode to Joy" in the finale of the Ninth Symphony.

Below
Orpheus and Eurydice, set design by Jean-Pierre Ponnelle, Cologne 1977 (TWS). The first opera in history (*Euridice*, by Jacopo Peri), the first true masterpiece of the genre (→*Orfeo*, by Monteverdi), and the first reform opera (→*Orpheus and Eurydice*, by Gluck) all place the fate of the mythical musician and the power of music at the center of the action. These are disguised self-portraits: the artist is alone with his art, his fate is bound up with his work, he can win or lose only through his art. This design presents a melancholy picture of the loneliness of Orpheus.

1. Mourning Chorus

Ah, se in - tor - no a quest' ur - na fu - ne - sta, Eu – ri - di - ce, om - bra bel – la,

2. Lament of Orpheus

Che fa - rò senza Eu - ri - di - ce? Dove an - drò senza il mio ben?

Orpheus and Eurydice, production photograph with Lucia Popp (Orpheus) and Eva Minton (Eurydice), production Jean-Pierre Ponnelle, conductor Jesus Lopez Cobos, Oper Köln, Cologne 1977.
Jean-Pierre Ponnelle's pictorially poetic productions opened a new chapter of 20th-century theatrical history; Gluck's *Orpheus and Eurydice* in Cologne was among them. In Ponnelle's typical manner, this set links man-made buildings and cultivated nature, both of them in a state of dilapidation, intermingling with each other in a way that is a visual metaphor for the genre of opera itself.

The opera of grief

Eurydice is mourned twice in Gluck's opera. The profound, final pain of parting is expressed in dark colors (Act I). Fate seems implacable. In the finale (Act III) the tragedy is one of the human conscience: Orpheus knows that he himself, and not the gods, is responsible for the loss of Eurydice. Despite his despair, Orpheus remains an artist even in his grief: his famous lament for Eurydice brings the ideals of neo-Classical beauty to perfection. M 1, M 2

Orpheus and Eurydice

Orfeo ed Euridice

Azione teatrale in three acts

Orphée et Eurydice

Tragédie opéra in three acts

Libretto: Italian version for Vienna by Ranieri de' Calzabigi; French version for Paris by Pierre-Louis Moline, after Calzabigi.
Première: 5 October 1762, Vienna (Kaiserliches Hoftheater); 2 August 1774, Paris (Académie Royale).
Characters: Orfeo/Orphée/Orpheus (A, in Paris T), Euridice/Eurydice/Eurydice (S), Amore/Amour/Cupid (S); shepherds, shepherdesses, nymphs, Furies, blessed spirits, heroes and heroines (chorus and ballet).
Setting: The world above and the underworld in mythical times.

Synopsis (identical in both versions)
Act I

A cypress grove near the tomb of Eurydice. Orpheus is mourning for Eurydice, accompanied by the nymphs and shepherds. He implores the gods to give him back his beloved. Cupid tells Orpheus that Zeus, moved by the singer's grief, will allow him to bring Eurydice back from the underworld, but on one condition: Orpheus must not look at Eurydice while he is in the realm of the dead, or she will be lost to him for ever.
Act II
Scene 1: Tartarus. The Furies bar Orpheus from the underworld. He calms them for a few moments by singing and playing his lyre, and so makes his way into the realm of the dead.
Scene 2: The Elysian Fields. Orpheus finds Eurydice, and they both set off to return to earth.
Act III
Scene 1: A dark grotto in the underworld. Eurydice cannot understand why her beloved Orpheus will not look at her. She doubts his feelings: if he no longer loves her, she would rather stay with the dead. In his despair, Orpheus breaks the command of Zeus, and turns to Eurydice. She sinks dying into his arms.
Scene 2: The temple of Cupid. The god of love prevents Orpheus from killing himself, and as a reward for his steadfast love he gives Eurydice back to the singer again. The couple are reunited once more, and all praise the power of love. T. Sz.

Orpheus and Eurydice, production photograph with Jochen Kowalski as Orpheus, production Harry Kupfer, conductor Hartmut Haenchen, sets Hans Schavernoch, costumes Eleonore Kleiber, Komische Oper Berlin 1987. Harry Kupfer's production transfers the ancient myth to the 20th century; Orpheus is holding the modern version of a cult instrument, the guitar. This updated version won the 1989 Laurence Olivier Award for the best production of the year.

The voice of Orpheus

The history of Gluck's *Orpheus and Eurydice* is one of the strangest of success stories. The première in Vienna won only moderate acclaim. It was not until a few years later, with its first performance in Parma in 1769, that the work really began to conquer the world. In the process, the part of Orpheus underwent a daring metamorphosis. In accordance with the customs of the time, it was sung by an alto castrato at the Vienna première, and by a soprano castrato in Parma. By 1774 the work had had performances in London, Bologna, Munich and Stockholm, and the register of the part of Orpheus always depended on which of the two star castrati of Europe was singing the title part: Gaetano Guadagni (alto) or Giuseppe Millico (soprano). The composer decided on a third version for the first performance in Paris, where Orpheus was sung by a tenor; French audiences did not care for castrati on the operatic stage. After Gluck's death and the end of the castrato era in opera, the three versions existed side by side, and were selected to suit particular singers or the tastes of directors. In 1859 Hector Berlioz prepared an edition of the opera for the contralto Pauline Viardot-Garcia, since when the part has frequently been performed by a female contralto. Those of the 20th century include Kathleen Ferrier, Marilyn Horne, and Janet Baker. The role has also on occasion been sung by a baritone (for instance, Dietrich Fischer-Dieskau). Since the early years of the 19th century, parts for the original castrato voice have often been sung by countertenors. It seems almost symbolic that Orpheus, son of a Muse and the incarnation of music and musicians, can be sung on stage in any human vocal register.   *T. Sz.*

Orpheus and Euridice, set design by Eduard Löffler, production Georg Hartmann, conductor Franz von Hässlin, Friedrichtheater Dessau 1925 (TWS). The closing scene of the opera takes place, in Calzabigi's words, in "a dark grotto forming a winding labyrinth, enclosed by rocks that have fallen from the stony cliffs, and are entirely covered with tangled undergrowth and wild plants." A scene similar to Mozart's trials by fire and water (→ *The Magic Flute*) with a negative outcome? This time the trial of love does not succeed. Why not? Because Eurydice doubts the love of Orpheus. Is Eurydice herself unworthy of her husband in the concept of Calzabigi and Gluck? Or does the tragedy show that even exceptional human beings cannot live up to the gods' commandments? But love conquers all; Amor intervenes, and brings about a happy ending.

Alcestis, photographs from a production of the French version, with Anna Caterina Antonacci as Alcestis, production Achim Freyer, conductor Thomas Hengelbrock, guest performance given by the Staatsoper Berlin at the Vienna Festival 1993.
The story of Alcestis is a kind of reversal of the Orpheus myth. Until the very end, the plot steers a course that should exclude any possibility of a happy ending. The setting of the action is also permeated by inexorable tragedy. The fundamental atmosphere is conveyed by the use of dark minor keys – the music of the underworld – and the cries of the birds of death that accompany the dialogue between Alcestis and the gods of Hades.

Alcestis

Alceste

Tragedia/tragédie opéra in three acts

Libretto: Italian version for Vienna by Ranieri de' Calzabigi; French version for Paris by Bailli Le Blanc du Roullet.
Première: 26 December 1767, Vienna (Kaiserliches Hoftheater); 23 April 1776, Paris (Académie Royale).
Characters: Admeto/Admète/Admetus, King of Thessaly (T), Alceste/Alceste/ Alcestis, his wife (S), Eumelo and Aspasia, their children (2 S, in French version silent), Evandro/Evandre/Evander, confidant of Admetus (T), Ismene (Italian version only) (S), High Priest of Apollo (T), Hercule/Hercules (French version only) (B), Apollo (T), Herald (B), Oracle (B), Infernal Deity (B); courtiers, citizens, ladies in waiting to Alcestis, priests of Apollo, gods of the underworld (chorus and ballet).
Setting: Thessaly in mythical times.

Synopsis (Viennese version)
Act I

Scene 1: A square in front of the palace of Admetus. King Admetus is dying. The people are urged to ask the gods if anything can be done to help him.
Scene 2: The temple of Apollo. The oracle announces that Admetus may live if someone else dies in his place. Alcestis is prepared to sacrifice herself for her husband.

Act II

Scene 1: A grove consecrated to the gods of the underworld. Alcestis begs the gods to accept her sacrifice, and they agree. First, however, she wishes to take leave of Admetus and her children.
Scene 2: A hall in the palace of Admetus. Unexpectedly restored to health, Admetus now learns that the price of his life is the death of Alcestis. In despair, he implores the gods not to accept her sacrifice.

Act III

The forecourt of the palace. Alcestis's sacrifice cannot be reversed. Husband and wife say their last farewells, and Alcestis dies. Admetus is about to follow her into death, when Apollo appears, bringing Alcestis with him, and reuniting the couple in honor of their faithful married love.

Synopsis (Paris version)

Thanatos and Eros, Death and Love, are engaged in a dispute. King Admetus must die, but according to an oracle he can be saved if someone else will die for him. His wife Alcestis is ready to make the sacrifice, but Admetus cannot live without her, and intends to follow her into death. His guest, the hero and demigod Hercules, having witnessed the strength of their married love, rescues Alcestis from the underworld. Eros has defeated Thanatos. *S. N.*

One opera, two works
The Paris version of *Alcestis* is so different from the Viennese version that they have to be regarded as separate works. Gluck changed the extent and order of the scenes, left out dance movements and replaced them with newly composed music. The figure of Alcestis's confidante Ismene is cut from the French version, but instead – following the drama on the same subject by Euripides – Hercules appears, doing battle for Alcestis with the gods of the underworld.

Noble simplicity
"I believed I ought to exercise the greatest care, in order to achieve a fine simplicity. I therefore avoided making a great show of difficulties, at the expense of clarity, and indeed I have never set store by innovations if they did not spring naturally from the situation and the expression of it." In his foreword to *Alcestis*, dedicated to Grand Duke Leopold of Tuscany in 1769, Gluck set out his aesthetic principles. Consequently, *Alcestis* is regarded as the prototype of the reform opera as conceived by Gluck.

3. Alcestis's Prayer

O __ fu - ne - sta Dea, __ Nu - me fa - tal, non io pla - car __ dell' im - mor - tal cor - ruc - cio vo' il
re - o ri - gor, non io vo' __ non vo' pla - ca - re del cor - ruc - cio il reo ri - go - - - re!

4. Alcestis's Farewell

Il gri - do del do - lor __ che spez - za i vo - stri cor non
può pla - car __ al - fin __ l'or - ri - bi - le de - stin?

Death, the fundamental theme

In spite of the happy ending of the story, Gluck wrote some of the saddest and most tragic music in operatic history for *Alcestis*. Between the overture – which prepares the audience for the tragic atmosphere of the piece, in accordance with Gluck's new operatic aesthetics and contrary to earlier custom – and the appearance of Apollo in the finale, there is nothing to divert attention from the tragic course of events. The subject is one of the most important fundamental questions of human existence: helplessness in the face of death, and grief at the loss of a beloved person. The pleading of Alcestis for her husband's life, and her farewell (Act III) to her husband and children, are deeply moving moments. M 3, M 4

T. Sz.

Iphigenia in Aulis

Iphigénie en Aulide

Tragédie-opéra in three acts

Libretto: Marie François Bailli de Roullet, after Jean Racine's *Iphigénie*.
Première: 19 April 1774, Paris (Opéra, Palais Royale).
Characters: Agamemnon, King of Mycenae and commander in chief of the Greek against Troy (B), Clitemnestre/Clytemnestra, his wife (S), Iphigénie/Iphigenia, their daughter (S), Achille/Achilles, King of Thessaly (counterT), Patrocle/Patroclus, his friend (B), Calchas, High Priest of the temple of Diana in Aulis (B), Arcas, captain of Agamemnon's bodyguard (B), Three Greek Women (3 S) and A Greek Man (T) in Iphigenia's retinue, Fourth Greek Woman (S); Greek officers and soldiers, Greek crowd, guards, Thessalian warriors, women of Argos in the retinue of the queen and Iphigenia, women of Aulis, slaves from Lesbos, priestesses of Diana (chorus and ballet).
Setting: The Greek camp on the shore at Aulis, just before the beginning of the Trojan War.

Synopsis

The Greek army is at Aulis, ready to leave for Troy and avenge the abduction of beautiful Helen. However, they have no wind, and are becalmed; it is Diana's revenge on Agamemnon, who once killed one of her sacred stags. She demands that the Greek commander sacrifice his own daughter Iphigenia, who is expected to arrive at the army camp in order to marry Achilles. In despair, Agamemnon tries to prevent his daughter's arrival, but in vain. On the way to the marriage altar, Iphigenia and her mother Clytemnestra hear of the will of the gods. Achilles protects his bride with his Thessalian troops, but the Greeks continue to demand the performance of the sacrifice. Iphigenia bows to the divine decree. Clytemnestra begs Jupiter for aid, and Achilles mobilizes his men against the Greeks.

At this point the gods intervene: Iphigenia's virtue, her mother's tears, and the courage of Achilles have rendered the sacrifice unnecessary. The winds are beginning to rise, and there is nothing now in the way of the departure of the Greek army. Everyone pays homage to the gracious goddess Diana. *S. N.*

Struggle for the approval of Paris

Not content with his reforms of Italian opera, in the 1770s Gluck turned to the transformation of the French *tragédie lyrique* genre (→Lully, →Rameau), thereby laying the foundations for the French heroic grand opera of the nineteenth century. He did not have it all his own way in Paris. The première of *Iphigenia in Aulis* gave rise to one of the most famous scandals in operatic history. Part of the public thought Gluck could do no wrong, another part supported the Italian Niccolò Piccinni (1728–1800), who had set the same mythological subject to music. The result was the famous dispute between the Gluckists and the Piccinnists.

Opera was not the only point at issue; the interests of various artistic policies were also at stake. However, the noble power of Gluck's music, and the patronage of Queen Marie Antoinette (Maria Theresia's daughter) brought victory for the German composer within a few years. *T. Sz.*

Iphigenia in Aulis, set design by Gustav Wunderwald, Berlin 1914 (TWS).
In its striking conflicts, dramatic contrasts, and characters this work anticipates features of both French Romantic and later German opera. Gluck's aesthetic of opera had a great influence on Richard Wagner and his concept of music drama. In token of his admiration, Wagner revised Gluck's *Iphigenia in Aulis* in 1847, including it in the repertory of the Dresden Opera. However, he changed the original ending: in his version Diana rescues Iphigenia, and makes her priestess of her temple in Tauris. Despite his arbitrary alterations, Wagner did much for the revival of Gluck's music in Germany.

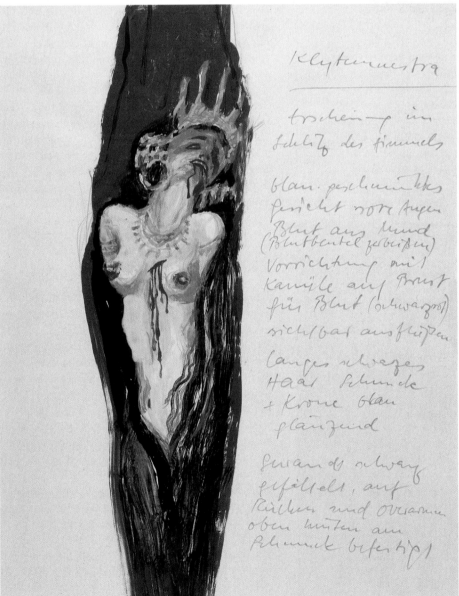

Iphigenia in Tauris

Iphigénie en Tauride

Tragédie in four acts

Libretto: Nicholas François Guillard, after Claude Guimond de la Touche's *Iphigénie en Tauride*.
Première: 18 May 1779, Paris (Opéra, Palais Royale).
Characters: Iphigénie/Iphigenia, High Priestess of the temple of Diana in Tauris (S), Oreste/Orestes, her brother (T), Pylade/ Pylades, a Greek prince, friend of Orestes (counterT), Thoas, King of the Scythians (B), Diane/Diana (S), Two Priestesses (2 S), Servant in the temple precincts (B), A Scythian (Bbar), Four Priestesses (2 S, 2 A); Greeks, priestesses, Eumenides, Scythians, bodyguard of Thoas (chorus); Scythians, Eumenides, shade of Clytemnestra (ballet).
Setting: Tauris (now the Crimea) in archaic times.

Synopsis

A storm in Tauris threatens to destroy the temple of Diana, and Iphigenia, the High Priestess of the goddess, is distraught. In a dream, she has seen her father Agamemnon being murdered and her mother Clytemnestra handing her a sword so that she, Iphigenia, can kill her brother Orestes. Iphigenia implores Diana to let her die and be reunited with her family in the kingdom of the shades, thus escaping the tyranny of Thoas, King of Scythia, who is forcing her to offer human sacrifices. Warned by an oracle, Thoas fears all strangers who arrive on the island, and has them killed in honor of the goddess. This is to be the fate of the two Greeks recently washed up on shore: Orestes and his friend Pylades. Brother and sister recognize one another only at the last minute, when Iphigenia is about to plunge the sacrificial knife into her brother. She now refuses to carry out the orders of Thoas. Pylades manages to escape, fetches their Greek companions, and there is a fight between the Greeks and the Scythians. Diana orders the fighting to stop, and tells the Scythians to restore her statue to Greece. Orestes is forgiven for his sin of matricide, and will return to Mycenae with Iphigenia to rule there. The anger of the gods is mollified by suffering. *S. N.*

Iphigenia in Tauris, set design and costume design for Clytemnestra by Achim Freyer for his production at the Bayerische Staatsoper, conductor Karl Richter, Munich 1979 (TWS).
The history of the interpretation of *Iphigenia in Tauris* is an interesting one. It was no coincidence that around 1900 Richard Strauss created his own famous version of the subject of the house of the Atrides (→ *Elektra*). In the era of Sigmund Freud and depth psychology, an opera where the course of the action consists of the fulfilment of an anxiety dream was bound to arouse interest. Late 20th-century interpreters have also laid emphasis on the terrible abysses in the human soul.

Karoline Bettelheim (1845–1926),
Goldmark's muse when he was writing
The Queen of Sheba.
According to an anecdote, the idea of an
opera on the subject of the Queen of Sheba
arose from a casual remark made by the
principal director of the Vienna court opera.
He is said to have commented of Karoline
Bettelheim, formerly Goldmark's favorite
piano pupil and a member of the opera
company, "That girl! What a face! She could
be the Queen of Sheba!"

Below
The Queen of Sheba, Amalie Materna, the
queen in the Viennese première, with her
seductive veil, studio photograph.
After singing soubrette roles in operetta,
Amalie Materna (1844–1918) made her
début as an opera singer in Vienna in 1864 in
the title role of Meyerbeer's →*The African
Woman*. She was an active member of the
Vienna court opera until 1897, and was one
of the first outstanding singers of Wagner's
roles for women, creating the parts of
Brünnhilde (1876) and Kundry (1882)
at Bayreuth.

The Queen of Sheba, Leo Slezak as Assad.
"Assad's Romance" – the most famous number
in the opera – is a showpiece for star tenors
(it was sung by Caruso, and in recent decades
by Nicolai Gedda and Siegfried Jerusalem).
At the end the singer is required to pluck a
very quietly sung high C out of the air. M 3

Goldmark, Karl

b. 18 May 1830 in Keszthely (Hungary)
d. 2 January 1915 in Vienna

The son of a Jewish cantor, Goldmark grew up in straitened circumstances, with a large family of brothers and sisters. After thorough study of the violin in both Hungary and Austria, he played with various Hungarian and Austrian theatrical companies as a violinist during the early decades of his life. He took an active part in the Hungarian Wars of Liberation (1848–49), and then settled in Vienna in 1851. He began his professional career as a composer in the 1850s, writing pieces of chamber music. His most important early success was the première of the overture *Sakutala* with the Vienna Philharmonic (1865). However, his real breakthrough came only in 1875, with the première of his first and still best-known opera, *The Queen of Sheba*. The opera made him one of the most popular and highly regarded composers of the Austro-Hungarian monarchy.

Works: Operas: *Die Königin von Saba* (*The Queen of Sheba*) (1875), *Merlin* (1886), *Das Heimchen am Herd* (*The Cricket on the Hearth*, meaning "the little housewife") (1896), *Götz von Berlichingen* (1902), *Ein Wintermärchen* (*A Winter's Tale*) (1908); choral works with orchestra, songs, symphonic works, chamber music, piano works.

The Queen of Sheba

Die Königin von Saba

Opera in four acts

Libretto: Salomon Hermann Mosenthal.
Première: 10 March 1875, Vienna (Hofoper).
Characters: King Solomon (Bar), High Priest (B), Sulamith, his daughter (S), Assad, favorite of Solomon (T), Baal-Hanan, the palace overseer (Bar), The Queen of Sheba (Ms), Astaroth, her slave girl (S), Voice of the Temple Guard (B); women, maidens, maidservants, slave girls, bodyguards, soldiers of Solomon, slaves of the Queen of Sheba, companions of Baal-Hanan, crowd, priests, Levites, singers (chorus, ballet, extras).
Setting: Jerusalem and the border of the Syrian desert, in Biblical times.

Synopsis
Act I
A hall in King Solomon's palace. Solomon is awaiting the visit of the Queen of Sheba, and has sent his favorite, Assad, to meet his guest. But Assad returns from his successful mission distraught, and avoids the company of his future bride Sulamith. He confesses to the king that a wonderful woman seduced him under the cedars of Lebanon. When the Queen of Sheba arrives, and lifts her veil during her welcome, Assad recognizes her as that woman. However, she denies the incident, and Solomon reminds Assad that his wedding to Sulamith is to be celebrated the next day.
Act II
Scene 1: A fantastic garden, by night. The queen, who has now fallen in love with Assad, cannot bear the thought that he is to marry Sulamith the next day. With the aid of her slave girl, she entices Assad into the garden, and he is captivated by her yet again.
Scene 2: The Temple. During the wedding ceremony, the queen arrives with wedding presents. Assad halts the ceremony, throws his wedding ring away, and declares that the queen is his goddess. The righteous Jews demand the death penalty for such blasphemy. Solomon reserves the right to pronounce judgment.
Act III
A banqueting hall. The king is holding a feast in honor of his guest, and the queen asks his mercy for Assad. In doing so, she reveals her secret love, and Solomon resists both her pleas and her threats. Only when Sulamith, in the purity of her heart, pleads for Assad does the king let leniency prevail. Assad is to be banished to the desert.
Act IV
The desert. Assad is tempted yet again by the queen, now on her way home. But this time he rejects the temptress, and dies, purified, in the chaste arms of his bride Sulamith.

S. N.

*G*oldmark proves a typical representative of the "fin de siècle" Austro-Hungarian historical style with his opera on the subject of the Queen of Sheba, a musical equivalent of Hans Makart's lavishly exotic paintings.

Anticipating the Art Nouveau

The exotic setting, the visual and musical orientalism, and the late Romantic *sfumato* orchestral technique give this opera a tone that anticipates Viennese art nouveau. The title role of the Queen of Sheba in particular expresses the atmospheric opulence of the style. Act II is set in a "fantastic garden of cedars, palms, and rose trees … a fountain in the foreground, left … Night. The moon is rising." The queen wears "a robe and veil as fine as gossamer and shot with silver, enveloping her whole figure." Assad, a kind of oriental Tannhäuser, is torn between the erotically enchanting queen and his virginal bride Sulamith. His passion takes musical expression in an exotically colored leitmotif. M 1

The plain and sober world of Solomon's court stands counter to that of the Queen of Sheba. Mosenthal used old Hebrew texts for the ceremonies in Solomon's temple, introducing elements of Jewish customs, and Goldmark gave the chorus that is sung by the Jews a psalmlike character. M 2

1. Assad's Aria

O zau-ber-haf-ter Traum, der mei-ne Seel' __ er-füllt, _____ der mei-ne Seel' _____ er-füllt

2. Sacred Chorus

E-wig e-wig währt sei-ne Gü-te, e-wig, e-wig wahrt sei-ne Gü-te, sei-ne Gü-te.

3. Assad's Romance

Ma-gi-sche Tö-ne, be-rau-schen-der Duft, _____

küs-se mich, mil-de A-bendluft

The Queen of Sheba, set design by Carlo Brioschi (watercolor).
The historic set for the second scene of Act III (the Temple) was one of the finest works by Carlo Brioschi (1826–95), a Viennese theatrical designer of Italian origin, who designed and executed the sets for the première of *The Queen of Sheba* with his famous colleagues Hermann Burghart and Johann Kautsky. The exotic set design was modeled on drawings of the finds uncovered by Austen Henry Layard during his excavations in the Tigris region. The set contains both Assyrian and Egyptian stylistic elements. The visual effect, reflecting Goldmark's opulent music, was of an Orient intended to be historically faithful, although it must in fact be described as eclectic.

Goldschmidt, Berthold

b. 18 January 1903 in Hamburg
d. 17 October 1996 in London

Goldschmidt studied at the universities of Hamburg and Berlin, where he was a pupil of →Franz Schreker among others. As early as 1925 he was awarded the Mendelssohn State Prize for composition. From 1926 to 1927 he was co-répétiteur at the Dessau Provincial Theater and the Berlin State Opera, and from 1927 to 1929 he held a post as Kapellmeister at the Darmstadt Provincial Theater. In 1931 he was invited to be guest conductor of the Leningrad Philharmonic. With the advent of radio orchestras he embarked on a new field of activity, as conductor of radio music in Berlin. He was also appointed artistic adviser to the Berlin-Charlottenburg Municipal Opera until 1933. In 1935 he emigrated to England, where he found work with the European Service of the BBC. Goldschmidt was chiefly active as a conductor, and in 1964 he conducted the first performance of an edition of Mahler's unfinished Tenth Symphony prepared by himself and Deryck Cooke.

Works: Der gewaltige Hahnrei (*The Magnificent Cuckold*) (1932, Mannheim), *Beatrice Cenci* (1951); ballets, radio music, vocal music, orchestral works, chamber music.

*G*oldschmidt's music emphasizes rhythmic and cantabile elements, and the influence of Stravinsky, Hindemith, and jazz can be detected in it. He achieves emotional nuances in his music for the stage and other media by the use of Romantic harmonic methods.

The Magnificent Cuckold, set design for the première by Eduard Löffler, production Richard Hein, conductor Joseph Rosenstock, Nationaltheater, Mannheim 1932 (TWS).
Crommelynck's successful play *Le cocu magnifique* was produced in the Soviet Union in 1922 by the epoch-making theatrical genius Vsevolod Meyerhold, and was brought to Germany in 1930 during a tour by Meyerhold's company. The director Erich Maria Rabenalt recommended it to Goldschmidt as a libretto. Stylistically, Goldschmidt's music was notable for its lucid instrumentation, precise rhythms, and cantabile style, and thus there was every prospect of the opera's being a success. However, the bold nature of the subject displeased the conservative authorities, and changes had to be made to the libretto. In spite of the disapproval of the Nazis, the Jewish composer's opera was well received in Mannheim. However, the political situation meant that it had only four performances.

The Magnificent Cuckold

Der gewaltige Hahnrei

Musical tragicomedy in three acts

Libretto: Berthold Goldschmidt, after the play *Le cocu magnifique* by Fernand Crommelynck.
Première: 14 February 1932, Mannheim (Nationaltheater).

Characters: Bruno (T), Stella, his wife (S), Petrus, a sea captain and Stella's cousin (B), Oxherd (B), Estrugo, Bruno's clerk (T), Young Man from Osterke (T), Meme, a wetnurse (A), Policeman (Bar), Cornelie (S), Florence (A); peasants, musicians, policemen (chorus).
Setting: Flanders.

Synopsis

Bruno has no reason to doubt his wife Stella's fidelity, but he suffers from pathological jealousy which keeps him constantly looking for clues to any indiscretion on her part. In fact, the Oxherd does make advances to Stella while Bruno is away, but thanks to the courageous intervention of the wetnurse he does not achieve his aim. A visit from Stella's cousin Petrus fuels Bruno's jealousy; he provokes the young man for no reason and throws him out. Stella is at her wits' end. She decides to pretend to be unfaithful in order to free her husband from his delusions. However, she only makes matters worse, since Bruno sees through her ruse and now thinks she is concealing her real lover from him. Taking the initiative himself, he faces Stella with all the men in the village. She complies with his wishes yet again, but he thinks it is only to divert attention from a genuine lover. In disguise, he pays court to Stella himself; sure enough, she falls in love with the stranger, and cannot resist him. When the village women attack him as a supposed adulterer, he lays all the blame on Stella, and the hostility is turned against her. Only the Oxherd comes to her aid, and asks for her love in return. Bruno comes to the conclusion that he has been Stella's real lover all along, and attacks him. Stella leaves her pathologically jealous husband and places herself under the Oxherd's protection. Obviously there is no helping Bruno. *M. S.*

The Magnificent Cuckold, production photograph with Günter Neumann (Bruno) and Yvonne Wiedstruck (Stella), production Harry Kupfer, conductor Yakov Kreizberg, sets Hans Schavernoch, costumes Reinhard Heinrich, Komische Oper Berlin 1994. During the National Socialist period in Germany, Goldschmidt's music was regarded as "degenerate." After the banning of the opera, it lapsed into oblivion for five decades. A concert performance was given in London in 1982. In the early 1990s there was a revival of Goldschmidt's music in general, and a series of performances of his opera. It was also revived in Berlin in 1994 in this production by Harry Kupfer, with Expressionist-Cubist sets.

A grotesque tale

Man as the author of his own fate is an ancient subject of European culture, and one that was called into question by the First World War. In 1920 Crommelynck expressed his doubts about mankind's creative genius in the form of a grotesque tale; its moral is that you become what you most fear to be. Bruno fears that his wife will betray him, and when he finally becomes a "great cuckold" it is entirely his own doing. The story is also a parody of bourgeois marriage, in which the union of two people is reduced to "the mutual use of their sexual organs" (as Immanuel Kant put it). *S. N.*

The Guaraní, photograph from a production by Werner Herzog, conductor John Neschling, Oper Bonn 1994.
The first performance in Germany was a great occasion for lovers of operatic rarities, comprising as it did a fine soprano part (Cecilia), a good tenor role (Pery), and a rewarding role for a baritone (Gonzales). There are no South American samba rhythms, but as a whole the music (except for the part of Pery) is of a light, dance-like character, even at the most passionate moments. Perhaps this is the reason for the curious description of its genre as "opera ballo" – "dance opera."

Gomes, Antônio Carlos

b. 11 July 1836 in Campinas (Brazil)
d. 16 September 1896 in Belém (Brazil)

Gomes was given his first music lessons by his father, a bandmaster, while he was quite young, and appeared publicly as a composer and pianist at an early age. After studying at the Conservatory in Rio de Janeiro, he immediately attracted attention with two operas written in rapid succession. Emperor Pedro II of Brazil gave him a stipend, which enabled him to study at the Milan Conservatory, and it was in Milan that he composed his masterpiece, the opera *The Guarani*, which was enthusiastically received at La Scala. Verdi and Boito also commented favorably on the young Brazilian's talent. He composed five more operas, and in 1880 returned to Rio de Janeiro, where he settled and was held in high esteem. After the abolition of the monarchy he lost the official support he had enjoyed, and moved to Belém, where he was director of the Conservatory for several years. He died there, an embittered and lonely man.

Works: Operas: *A noite do castelo* (*A Night in the Citadel*) (1861), *Joana de Flanders* (*Jeanne of Flanders*) (1863), *Il Guarany* (*The Guaraní*) (1870), *Fosca* (1873), *Salvator Rosa* (1874), *Maria Tudor* (*Mary Tudor*) (1879), *Lo schiavo* (*The Slave*) (1889), *Condor* (1891); and the oratorio *Colombo* (Columbus) (1892, to celebrate the 400th anniversary of the discovery of America).

*T*he Brazilian national composer Gomes is regarded as a successful representative of the school of Italian opera founded by his older contemporary, Verdi.

The Guaraní

Il Guarany

Opera ballo in four acts

Libretto: Antonio Enrico Scalvini and Carlo d'Ormeville, after the novel *O Guarany* (*The Guaraní*), by José Martiniano de Alencar.

Première: 19 March 1870, Milan (Teatro alla Scala).

Characters: Don Antonio de Mariz, an old Portuguese hidalgo (B), Cecilia, his daughter (S), Pery, chieftain of the Guaraní Indians (T), Don Alvaro, a Portuguese adventurer (T), Gonzales, Ruy-Bento, and Alonso, Spanish adventurers (Bar, T, B), The Kazike, chief of the Aimoré Indians (B), Pedro, an armed man in the service of Don Antonio (B); adventurers of various nationalities, men and women of the Portuguese colony, natives of the Aimoré tribe (chorus).

Setting: Brazil, near Rio de Janeiro, in 1560.

Synopsis

The noble hidalgo Antonio has a beautiful daughter, Cecilia, with whom the Portuguese Don Alvaro is in love. However, Cecilia loves the Guaraní chieftain Pery, who once saved her life, and who returns her love. But her father intends to marry her to Don Alvaro. The Spanish adventurers Gonzales, Ruy-Bento, and Alonso have been taken in by Antonio as his guests; they plan to get possession of Antonio's silver mine and abduct Cecilia. Pery overhears them plotting, puts Ruy-Bento and Alonso to flight, and disarms Gonzales. The "noble savage" grants the European his life, on condition that the foreigner leaves the country, and Gonzales appears to comply. Pery goes to Don Antonio to warn him. Antonio's palace is now attacked by the Aimoré Indians. The Portuguese successfully defend themselves, and only Cecilia and Pery are taken prisoner. Enchanted by Cecilia's beauty, the chieftain of the Aimoré wants to make her his wife – and his cannibal tribe welcome Pery as the wedding breakfast. The festivities begin with ceremonial dances. At the last moment, Antonio and Alvaro come to the rescue, but Alvaro is mortally wounded in the fighting. Hoping to seize the silver mine, the Spanish adventurers occupy Antonio's palace, but Pery knows of an underground passage giving access to the palace. To save Cecilia, he is prepared to abjure his own faith and be baptized, and only now will Don Antonio agree to betroth his daughter to the Indian. He then blows up the palace, with himself and the Spaniards inside it.

S. N.

A cosmopolitan national opera

Composers of the nineteenth century (Weber, Glinka, Smetana, Moniuszko, and Erkel) presented their native lands to an international public by writing national operas, often with the political intention of portraying a struggle to achieve independence. National coloring was conveyed by the scene of the action, almost always by the language, by elements of folklore, and by local color in the music. The Brazilian national opera *The Guaraní* is an exception. It has a Brazilian subject, but it was composed to an Italian libretto, and had its première at the Teatro alla Scala. Exotic folklore plays little part; the Spaniards, Portuguese, and Indians all employ the same musical idiom. Gomes created a work that was both Brazilian and cosmopolitan. As a protégé of the Emperor of Brazil, Pedro II, who was of Portuguese descent, he set the "noble savage" Pery and the Portuguese, as representatives of good, against the villainous Spaniards. The Guaraní chieftain, unlike the Aimoré Indians, is well disposed toward the colonizers and intent on reconciliation. This political statement is rooted in the period when the opera was written, but history ignored Gomes: his dream of friendship and brotherhood between the different ethnic groups of Brazil remained merely Utopian. Nonetheless, his opera is still performed in Brazil today.

The Guaraní, production photograph with Veronica Villaroel (Cecilia) and Placido Domingo (Pery), production Werner Herzog, conductor John Neschling, Oper Bonn 1994. The lovers, Cecilia and Pery, embody the idea of peaceful coexistence between the whites and the Indians in Brazil. However, the couple are persecuted by extremists on both sides. Musically, Gomes produced a synthesis of bel canto opera with French grand opera. Indians and colonists alike sing in the European style.

Gounod's lyrical style brought a new note into French opera. Meyerbeer had emphasized the political and general in his grand operas; individual figures and their emotions now moved to the center of the music and the stage.

Gounod, Charles

b. 17 June 1818 in Paris
d. 18 October 1893 in St. Cloud

The son of a well-known painter, Gounod began his musical studies early. His teachers at the Paris Conservatoire included Halévy. His first operas (for example, *Sappho*, 1851) were not very successful, but he made his name with *Faust*, which had its première at the Théâtre Lyrique in 1859, was performed ten years later at the Opéra, and was soon being staged all over Europe. Further operas followed in the 1860s, with varying degrees of success. In his later years, Gounod turned to sacred music.

Works: Sapho (Sappho) (1851), *La nonne sanglante (The Bleeding Nun)* (1854), *Le médecin malgré lui (The Doctor Despite Himself)* (1858), *Faust* (1859), *Philémon et Baucis (Philemon and Baucis)* (1860), *Die Königin von Saba (The Queen of Sheba)* (1862), *Mireille* (1864), *Roméo et Juliette (Romeo and Juliet)* (1867), *Le tribut de Zamora (The Tribute of Zamora)* (1881); 16 masses, sacred choral works, and songs.

Faust, production photograph with Francisco Araiza as Faust, production Götz Friedrich, sets Andreas Reinhardt, conductor Rafael Frühbeck de Burgos, Opernhaus Zürich 1997. The challenge in all productions of *Faust* is to represent a medieval scholar in his historical environment, without omitting reference to the situation of modern scientists and their "fall from grace" in producing the nuclear bomb.

Faust

Opéra in five acts

Libretto: Jules Barbier and Michel Carré, after the drama of the same name by Johann Wolfgang von Goethe.
Première: 19 March 1859, Paris (Théâtre Lyrique).

Characters: Faust (T), Marguerite (S), Méphistophélès (B), Valentin, a soldier, Marguerite's brother (Bar), Siébel, a young man in love with Marguerite (S), Marthe, Marguerite's neighbor (Ms), Wagner, a soldier (B); girls and women, citizens, students, soldiers, apparitions, angels (chorus).
Setting: A small German town in the 16th century.

Synopsis

The aged Faust, doubting that there is any point in his knowledge or his life, sells his soul to the Devil in return for the youth, wealth, and love that he hopes will make him happy. However, he ruins a young girl and kills her brother. Although the powerful and learned Faust cannot save his own soul, the weak and ignorant Marguerite escapes the powers of darkness.

Act I

Faust has grown old. He doubts the purpose of his life's work, and strikes a bargain with the Devil, Méphistophélès: he will sell his soul in return for youth, riches, and good fortune in love.

Act II

Students, soldiers, and citizens take refuge from their drab everyday lives in drink and other pleasures. The soldier Valentin must go to war. He leaves his sister Marguerite, whom he idolizes, to the care of his friend Siébel, who loves her. Méphistophélès amuses himself by stirring up the feelings of the crowd and unleashing their worst instincts. Faust is inflamed by desire for Marguerite.

Faust, set design (Walpurgis Night) by Hein Heckroth, production Wolf Völker, conductor Gustav Kozlik, Essen 1928/29 (TWS).

Act III

Siébel brings Marguerite a bouquet of flowers. However, Méphistophélès outdoes him with a gift of valuable jewels, and having prepared the ground in this way, introduces Faust to Marguerite. While Méphistophélès diverts the attention of the neighbor Marthe, Faust pays court to Marguerite. He wins the girl's love and trust.

Act IV

Marguerite, once regarded as the quintessence of virtue, has now become an object of public contempt: she has had a child by Faust, but he has abandoned her. Her brother returns from the war, and learns of his sister's fate. Marguerite seeks comfort in prayer, but Méphistophélès prevents her from making her peace with God. Faust now wishes to return to Marguerite, but Méphistophélès also prevents their reunion. In a serenade, he pretends to be courting Marguerite himself, but he is really singing a mocking song. Faust and Valentin fight a duel, and the Devil guides Faust's blade. Valentin is killed; dying, he curses his sister.

Act V

Méphistophélès takes Faust to the celebrations of Walpurgis Night, when spirits and the elements are unleashed. At the height of the festivities, the image of Marguerite appears to Faust. His conscience smites him. Marguerite has killed her child, and is to be executed for infanticide. With the aid of Méphistophélès, Faust tries to rescue the condemned woman from the clutches of the law, and they appear in the prison, but Marguerite will not go with him. She dies. While Méphistophélès proclaims that she is damned, the angels assure us that she is saved. In an apotheosis, "the prison walls give way, and Marguerite's soul rises to Heaven."   *S. N.*

Gounod's *Faust* is an opera about the loss of values in general. The only entirely consistent character is Valentin, a narrow-minded petit bourgeois. The love between Marguerite and Faust, full of emotion in itself, is brought about by a demonic power, and is thus in principle sinful and flawed. The riches linked with the power of Méphistophélès (his "Golden Calf" aria, the "Jewel Song", the dialogue with Marthe) play a part similar to the central role of wealth in Balzac's novels. The idea of the world as fundamentally flawed was all too close to the daily experience of French citizens in the era of Napoleon III. Perhaps this attractively disguised picture of their own times contributed to the success of Gounod's *Faust*.

The melodist

All musical settings of literary works represent a fundamental reinterpretation of the original, and *Faust* is no exception. The grandiose style of French opera is a long way from Goethe's classical simplicity, and Gounod retained many traditional elements of grand opera, such as the waltz and the soldiers' chorus. M1, M2

In some scenes, however, he relaxed the principle of the strict number opera, and his countrymen often labeled him a "German" for that reason. The introduction and the scenes in church and in prison break the chain of musical numbers following one another in sequence.

Gounod's instrumentation is in many respects more demanding than was usual in the French opera of his time. Yet he is first and foremost a fine melodist, realizing his melodic ideas with lavish generosity even in the recitatives. Not only the three principals but also subsidiary figures such as Valentin and Siébel are given delightful melodies. M3, M4

Marguerite

Gounod's chief inspiration was the figure of Marguerite. Innocence, ruin, and transfiguration: the dramatic metamorphosis of a pure, vulnerable spirit is central to the opera. Gounod's Marguerite is not a heroine; she is more of a child, accepting the beautiful jewels and the courteous attentions of Dr. Faust with the same pleasure. She lives an isolated life in the oppressive atmosphere of a small town, and is regarded by her brother as an angel. Profoundly devout, she nonetheless has a young girl's healthy fantasies, and abandons herself guilelessly to her first experience of love. The climax in the depiction of her innocent character is the "Jewel Song", written in waltz time, complemented by the simplicity of the love duet and the shattering tragedy of the church scene. M5

When Marguerite recognizes the demonic element in Faust, she is in a tragic dilemma: religious devotion and sin clash within her tormented soul. However, the conflict is not carried through to its end, but is resolved

Faust, Nellie Melba (1861–1931) as Marguerite, c. 1900.
The famous Australian soprano Nellie Melba had a remarkably long and successful international career between 1887 and 1926.

1. Waltz

2. Soldier's Chorus

Faust, set design for Act I by Franz Angelo Rottonara, Wiesbaden 1899 (TWS).
On the operatic stage, Faust's study imitates Goethe's literary model: vaulted, with high Gothic arches. Mysterious sounds on the lower strings and chromatic melodies provide musical illustration of the shadows and Faust's gloomy thoughts. However, this French Faust hears no angelic voices, but a chorus of peasant girls and reapers. Worldly existence beckons him. He appears as an aging man in the opera, but his singing voice (tenor) is full of youthful power, and he expresses his readiness to die in a captivating march melody.

in an episode of transfiguration comparable to the old appearance of a *deus ex machina*. Marguerite's apotheosis is the product of the composer's own religious feelings rather than of well-constructed drama.

Faust

Although Faust has the title role, he tends to retreat slightly into the background in the opera. His character is largely ambiguous. On the one hand, his pact with the Devil makes him the real agent in the tragedy of Marguerite's ruin and Valentin's death. On the other, Faust also has honorable feelings which come clearly to the fore in his soulful cavatina and his passionate duet with Marguerite. *M 6*

Faust is a problematic hero: he abhors the shameful machinations of his accomplice Méphistophélès, but nonetheless accepts them without protest.

Méphistophélès

The Devil seems to be a character who has strayed into a lyrical opera by mistake. His real domain is *opéra comique*, where his elegantly evil figure would find its appropriate environment. He is less a demon than a rogue. His famous arias – the "Golden Calf" rondo and the serenade – are really lighthearted interludes in which Gounod was able to develop his liking for caricature to good effect, thus ensuring the popularity of the opera. The first of these arias makes a rousing impression, while the second is of a rather exotic character. *M 7, M 8*   *P.H.*

Faust, Fyodor Shalyapin as Méphistophélès, 1906.
Méphistophélès can assume other forms, and gives evidence of his diabolical powers in the church scene and at the Walpurgis Night celebrations.

3. Valentin's Prayer

A - vant de quit - ter ces lieux, Sol na - tal de mes aï-eux,

A toi, Seigneur et Roi des cieux, Ma sœur je con - fi - e.

4. Siébel's Couplet

Fai - tes - lui mes a - veux. Por - tez mes voeux !

5. Marguerite's "Jewel Song"

Ah !_____ je ris de me voir si bel - le en ce mi - roir!

6. Faust's Cavatina

Sa - lut ! de meu - re chaste et pu - re, Sa - lut ! de meu - re chaste et pu - re,

ou se de - vi - ne La pré - sen - ce d'une âme in - no - cente et di - vi - ne !

7. "Golden Calf" Rondo

Le veau d'or est toujours de - bout! On en - cen - se Sa puis - san - ce, On en -

cen - se Sa puis - san - ce D'un bout du monde à l'autre bout !

8. Serenade

Vous qui fai - tes l'en - dor - mi - e, N'en - ten - dez - vous pas, N'en - ten - dez - vous pas,

O Ca - the - ri - ne, ma mi - e, N'en - ten - dez vous pas Ma voix et mes pas ?

Mireille

Opéra in five acts

Libretto: Michel Carré, after the epic poem *Mirèio* by Frédéric Mistral.
Première: 19 March 1864, Paris (Théâtre Lyrique).

Characters: Mireille, a rich farmer's daughter (S), Vincent, a poor basket weaver, in love with Mireille (T), Taven, a sorceress (Ms), Ourrias, a bull tamer, Vincent's rival (Bar), Vincenette, Vincent's sister (Ms), Maître Ramon, Mireille's father (B), Maître Ambroise, Vincent's father (B), Ferryman (B), Andreloux, a shepherd (Ms or boy S); people of the towns and countryside of Provence, pilgrims, farmhands, souls of the drowned (chorus).
Setting: The south of France in the 19th century.

Synopsis

Mireille and Vincent are destined for each other, but their love is subjected to harsh trials, and will be fulfilled not in this world but the next.

Act I

Mireille, daughter of a rich farmer, and the poor basket weaver's son Vincent are in love. A wise woman has foretold sorrow for them, and they vow that if one of them is in danger, the other will go on pilgrimage to Saintes-Maries-de-la-Mer.

Act II

The peasants are making merry in the arena of Arles, dancing the *farandole*, Mireille and Vincent among them. The rich farmer favors the bull tamer Ourrias as a husband for his daughter, and curses Mireille when he learns of her attachment to Vincent.

Act III

Vincent and Ourrias meet in the *Val d'enfer*, the "valley of hell." Vincent is struck down by his rival and severely wounded. But Ourrias, tormented by his conscience, drowns while he is crossing the river Rhône.

Act IV

Midsummer Eve festivities are being celebrated at Ramon's farm, where the people are dancing the *musette*, an old rustic dance to bagpipe accompaniment. Mireille envies a shepherd playing a pipe his carefree existence. When she hears that Vincent has been wounded, she sets off immediately on pilgrimage to Saintes-Maries. On the way, she has to cross a desert, and collapses with exhaustion. Only the sound of a shepherd's pipe gives her new strength.

Act V

Vincent, restored to health by the witch, is waiting for Mireille at the place of pilgrimage, in keeping with their vow. Exhausted, Mireille drags herself as far as the church, and dies in ecstasy in Vincent's arms.
(A version abbreviated by Gounod omits the third act, and the two last acts are merged together.)   S. N.

Mireille, production photograph with Maryse Castets (Mireille) and Rita Gorr (Taven), production Robert Fortune, Opéra-Comique, Paris 1995.
A prophecy of misfortune is the dramatic prelude to the unhappy love story between a poor basket weaver and the rich farmer's daughter Mireille: Taven's gesture in this scene expresses both comfort and the imminence of danger.

Mireille: from peasant girl to heroine

Mireille is a star vehicle in the true sense of the term, a work in which the singer of the title role has to be on stage almost continuously, except in the third act. The eponymous heroine first appears as a naïve peasant girl, and matures slowly into a great heroine who accepts her tragic fate. Her solo numbers – the lilting waltz arietta, the cavatina in which she vows constancy, and her great aria in the desert – are landmarks in this process. *M 9, M 10, M 11*

Beside the rather pallid figure of Vincent, it is Mireille who impels events in the opera forward. When she takes up the struggle against her father, selflessly seeking to bring her lover aid, her strength seems to go beyond the boundaries of lyrical opera. However, Gounod's music preserves a fundamentally transparent, emotional character, and never breaks into over-dramatic gestures. Mireille's piety reinforces her determination in her suffering, and in this she resembles Marguerite (→ *Faust*). It was certainly as a result of Gounod's own religious feeling that he concluded the opera, on a note of sacred rapture, with Mireille's transfiguration.   *P. H.*

Mireille, set design by Marcel Jambon for Act IV, Opéra-Comique, Paris 1901.
In every respect, *Mireille* stands alone in the history of French opera. The setting (in Provence) plays an important part. All the locations can be found on the map, including the arena at Arles, where the peasants are dancing the *farandole*.

9. Mireille's Arietta

O lé - gère   hi - ron - del - - - le,

10. Mireille's Cavatina

A toi, mon â - me,   Je suis ta fem - me! Mal - gré leur blâ - me Je t'ap - par - tiens!

11. Mireille's Aria

En mar - che, en mar - che, en marche, ain - si que Ma - gue - lon - ne!

Romeo and Juliet

Roméo et Juliette

Opéra in five acts

Libretto: Jules Barbier and Michel Carré, after the play of the same name by William Shakespeare.
Première: 27 April 1867, Paris (Théâtre Lyrique).
Characters: Roméo/Romeo, of the House of Montaigu/Montague (T), Juliette/Juliet, of the House of Capulet (S), Frère Laurent/Friar Laurence (B), Mercutio, friend of Romeo (Bar), Stéphano/Balthasar, Romeo's page (S), Benvolio, friend of Romeo (T), Capulet, Juliet's father (B), Tybalt, Capulet's nephew (T), Gertrude, Juliet's nurse (Ms), Grégorio/Gregory, servant of the Capulets (Bar), Paris, a young count and Juliet's intended husband (Bar), the Duke of Verona (B), Frère Jean/Friar John (B); courtiers and nobles, guests at the ball and the wedding, retinue of the duke, armed men, servants, crowd (chorus).
Setting: Verona in the early 15th century.

Synopsis

The children of two feuding families, the Montagues and Capulets, meet and fall in love. They are married by Friar Laurence. After a violent street fight, Romeo is banished from the city. Several tragic misunderstandings ensue, and the lovers commit suicide together.

Prologue

The chorus anticipates the events to come.

Act I

A great ball is being held at old Capulet's house. The company includes some uninvited guests: Romeo and Mercutio, members of the Montague family, the enemies of the Capulets. Romeo approaches a beautiful, unknown girl, and falls in love with her. To his horror, he discovers that she is Juliet, the daughter of his arch-enemy. The Montagues are recognized, and have to flee.

Act II

Romeo waits in the garden under Juliet's balcony, hoping to catch a glimpse of her. The Capulets are still pursuing him, but he manages to hide from them. He and Juliet declare their love for each other, and determine to marry in spite of the enmity between their families.

Act III

Friar Laurence, Romeo's confessor, blesses the secret marriage of Romeo and Juliet in his cell. He hopes their union may resolve the feud. Romeo's page Stéphano (Balthasar in Shakespeare's play), taunts the Capulets with a mocking song – a provocation on enemy territory, outside the Capulet house. Tybalt tries to drive him away, but Mercutio comes to the boy's aid. The two men fight. Romeo tries to settle the quarrel, but Tybalt stabs Mercutio, and Romeo himself now enters the fight and kills Tybalt.

The Duke of Verona condemns Romeo to banishment for life.

Act IV

Before leaving, Romeo spends the night with Juliet. Capulet intends to marry his daughter to Paris the next day, but Friar Laurence has devised a ruse. Juliet will take a sleeping draft; she will be thought dead, and laid to rest in the family crypt. At the appointed hour, however, when she wakes from her deathlike trance, Romeo will be there to take her away with him. Juliet agrees to this bold plan. The wedding guests arrive, but in the middle of the ceremony Juliet collapses, apparently dead.

Act V

Juliet lies in the crypt, seemingly dead. Friar Laurence's messenger has failed to find Romeo, who believes Juliet has really died, and takes poison in order to be reunited with her in the grave. As Romeo is dying, Juliet wakes from her trance. After one more brief dream of life together, Romeo dies, and Juliet follows him.

Romeo and Juliet, the balcony scene with Adelina Patti and Jean de Reszké at the Paris Opéra in 1888, illustration.
This opera is not as colorful as →*Faust*, and is perhaps less poetic than →*Mireille*, but with its clarity of outline and depiction of an emotionally charged atmosphere, it may be regarded as Gounod's most consistent score. It is not surprising that it became the composer's most popular opera in France. The whole story is based on a series of duets representing the development of two people, leading them from careless attraction, to a responsible concept of love, and at last to the inevitable ending in death.

The finest melodies

Juliet's waltz arietta stands in the line of descent from Marguerite's "Jewel Song" in →*Faust* and the arietta in →*Mireille*. M 12 The second act contains a wonderful nocturne. M 13

Romeo's cavatina is a tenderly drawn portrait of a young man enraptured by his burgeoning emotions, and conducting himself with true heroism as he senses the danger to his happiness. The situation and the moving tone bring this little aria close to Faust's cavatina. M 14

The third act is much more dramatic than its predecessors. There is a fine finale in which the bitter hatred between the Montagues and Capulets flares up again, and Romeo expresses his despair. The sublime dignity of this arching melody shows how dramatically Gounod could write even when he was exercising restraint. M 15

Act IV is introduced by a great duet. The orchestra gives expression to the lovers' tender meeting. A passionate melody is heard when they unite in a silent kiss, illustrating the consummation of their happiness even without words. M 16

The text of their love duet is taken almost literally from Shakespeare, while the musical structure, a melody of extreme despair, is one of the most moving passages in Gounod's score. M 17

The closing duet expresses the lovers' suffering. As in the final scene of →*Faust*, memories come back to both their minds. There are references to melodies from earlier duets, the love theme and the dialogue of the lark and the nightingale, and the bitter-sweet story of a doomed love affair appears as if in flashback. At the end of the opera, not only the lovers but also love itself is transfigured.   *P.H.*

Romeo and Juliet, production photograph with Francisco Araiza as Romeo, production Bernard Uzan, sets and projections Annelies Corrodi, conductor Serge Baudo, Opernhaus Zürich 1990.
This Zurich production "projected" the city into the love story between the children of two feuding families, making the intermingling of individual stories and the structure of society immediately present on stage.

12. Juliet's Arietta

Je   veux   viv - - re   Dans   ce   rê - - - ve
qui   m'en - - iv - - - re;   Ce   jour   en - - cor,

13. Nocturne

14. Romeo's Cavatina

Ah !   lè - ve-toi, so-leil !   fais pâ-lir les é - toi - les   Qui, dans l'azur sans voi - les,   Bril-lent au fir - ma - ment.

15. Finale

Ah !   jour   de deuil   et   d'horreur   et   d'a-lar - mes,   Mon   coeur   se brise   é - per-du   de   dou-leur !

16. Love Theme

17. Duet: Romeo and Juliet

Non !   non, ce n'est pas le jour !   Ce n'est pas l'a-lou-et - te !   C'est le doux ros-si - gnol   confident   de l'a - mour !

Spanish fan with motifs of the Garnier opera house by Scalbert Lefebvre (TWS). A souvenir of the Grand Opéra, Paris. This little jewel – a triptych from the final phase of the golden age of opera – shows a ball at the Palais Garnier: on the left, a meeting place where the ladies of high society display their fashions on the magnificent stairway; on the right, masked guests in carnival mood; and in the center, the curtain rises. The Palais Garnier, the main subject of this scene, is the embodiment of the Empire under Napoleon III.

The Paris Opéra: the Palais Garnier

After the failure of an attempt to assassinate Napoleon III outside the old Paris Opéra in 1858, the emperor decided to have a magnificent new opera house erected elsewhere in the city. Charles Garnier, the architect of this great opera house, was only 36 when he won the competition with his plans in 1861, fending off the challenge of many famous architects. In all, 171 designs were submitted. The empress, who favored another architect, asked Garnier indignantly when he showed his plans, "What is this supposed to be? It's in no style at all, not Louis XIV, not Louis XV, not Louis XVI." Garnier replied, "Madame, it is Napoleon III." The construction of the vast building took almost 15 years, and was carried out during the Empire, but the opening ceremony in 1875 took place under the Republic. On the eve of the inauguration of the opera house, Garnier was made a Chevalier of the Légion d'Honneur. Apart from the Budapest opera house, which was built on the Paris model (1884), there is scarcely another such theater in the world described by the elegant term of "palace". But the Palais Garnier was never the property of kings or princes; it is a palace of the bourgeoisie.

Above
Postcard showing Gounod and the Paris Opéra.
Two symbols of the city of Paris: Gounod and the Opéra on a postcard. The new opera house opened in 1875, though not with one of Gounod's works (at the time he was working as a chorusmaster in London). The inaugural evening was devoted to the memory of →Halévy and →Meyerbeer, both of whom had been dead for over ten years. Bizet never saw a première of one of his works in this fine opera house; he died in 1875. The composer hero of the Romantic generation was Gounod, who enjoyed successful revivals of his earlier operas at the Paris Opéra for another 18 years, until his death in 1893.

Right
Charles Garnier in 1868, engraving by M. Devaux from the portrait by P. Baudry.
Charles Garnier during the building of "his" opera house.

Opposite
The *grand escalier d'honneur* – the magnificent stairway of the Paris Opéra, 1878.
The people of Paris take possession of their palace with awe and admiration.

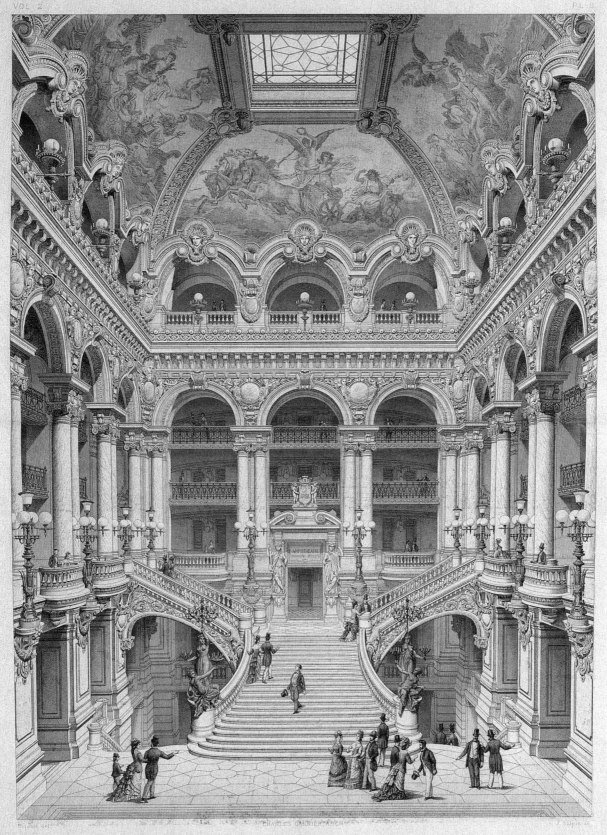

LE NOUVEL OPERA
DE PARIS

GRAND ESCALIER D'HONNEUR

La Juive, Marie-Cornélie Falcon as Rachel, engraving c. 1835.
The young opera star Marie-Cornélie Falcon (1812–97) sang the part of Rachel with great success at the première of the opera. She made history, for the dark soprano tones of her dramatically expressive voice created a new type of vocal register, later known as a "soprano Falcone."

La Juive, photograph from the production by John Dew, sets and costumes Gottfried Pilz, conductor Rainer Koch, Stadttheater Bielefeld 1989.
This production by John Dew made Halévy's *La Juive* an exciting contemporary piece of music drama.

Halévy, Jacques Fromental

b. 27 May 1799 in Paris
d. 17 March 1862 in Nice

Halévy came from a Jewish family of German origin. He studied with →Cherubini at the Paris Conservatoire, and was later chorusmaster at the Paris Opéra. He became professor of composition at the Conservatoire in 1840; his pupils included →Gounod, →Bizet, and →Saint-Saëns, the major French composers of the second half of the 19th century. In spite of his many successes, he felt that he was overshadowed by →Auber and →Meyerbeer.

Works: Over 40 operas, including *La Juive* (*The Jewess*) (1835), *Guido et Ginevra* (*Guido and Ginevra*) (1838), *La reine de Chypre* (*The Queen of Cyprus*) (1841); choral works and songs.

*P*robably Halévy's best work, "La Juive", is a perfect example of the grand opera style. It was among the most frequently performed works in the operatic repertory of its time.

La Juive

The Jewess

Opéra in five acts

Libretto: Eugène Scribe.
Première: 23 February 1835, Paris (Opéra).
Characters: Eléazar, a Jewish goldsmith (T), Rachel, his daughter (S), Emperor Sigismond (silent), Léopold, Prince of the Empire (T), Princess Eudoxie, the emperor's niece (S), Cardinal Brogni (B), Ruggiero, the city provost (B), Albert, an officer in the imperial bodyguard (B), Two Men of the People (T, B), Imperial Herald (B), Imperial Major Domo (B), Imperial Officer (T); courtiers, citizens, Jews, priests, officers, soldiers (chorus).
Setting: Konstanz, Switzerland, 1414.

Synopsis

The Christian Cardinal Brogni committed a crime when he burned the two sons of Eléazar the Jew. Later, Eléazar rescued Brogni's daughter, but has concealed her from her father. Brogni's later attempts at reconciliation cannot prevail against Eléazar's anger, which grows even greater as he faces persecution. Brogni reaps the reward of his wicked deed. When Eléazar's supposed daughter Rachel dies on Brogni's orders, the Jew at last reveals that she was Brogni's own child.

Act I

The victory of Imperial Prince Léopold over the Hussites is being celebrated in Constance. Only the Jewish goldsmith Eléazar disturbs the peace of the festive day with his loud hammering; as a punishment, he and his daughter Rachel are to be executed. But Cardinal Brogni pardons the Jews. In the past, as leader of the city council in Rome, he had Eléazar's two sons executed, and he has suffered the blows of fate since that time: his wife and daughter were killed by looting soldiers. Brogni has become a cardinal, and is now prepared to make his peace with Eléazar, but the Jew is unwilling. He rescued Brogni's daughter and has brought her up as his own child, keeping her from her real father, and waiting to take his revenge.

Act II

Rachel loves Samuel, who is really Prince Léopold pretending to be a Jew, and spends Passover with him in her father's house. Emperor Sigismond's niece Eudoxie orders a gold chain from Eléazar for her wedding to Léopold the next day. During the Passover festival, Rachel notices some mistakes made by Léopold in the ritual, and questions him. He confesses that he is a Christian, and Eléazar curses him.

Act III

During the wedding of Léopold and Eudoxie, Eléazar delivers the chain that Eudoxie had ordered. Rachel recognizes the bridegroom as her lover, and publicly accuses him of a forbidden relationship with herself,

La Juive, production photograph with James O'Neil (Eléazar) and Gidon Saks (Cardinal Brogni), production John Dew, sets and costumes Gottfried Pilz, conductor Rainer Koch, Stadttheater Bielefeld 1989.
On the surface, Scribe's subject – the conflict between Eléazar and Cardinal Brogni – is remarkably like that of Lessing's Enlightenment drama *Nathan der Weise* (*Nathan the Wise*). In both works, religious hatred engenders extreme situations. However, there is one major difference: Eléazar is not a wise man like Nathan, since he can neither forgive nor contemplate reconciliation. Scribe, a true professional among librettists, intended to shock the audience; Lessing, a humanist, wished to teach his fellow men.

Below
La Juive, Leo Slezak as Eléazar, Wiener Hofoper 1911.
The part of Eléazar was written for the celebrated tenor Adolphe Nourrit, who imbued the role with extraordinary psychological depth. Eléazar is Halévy's most original creation, a man of genuine stature, depicted in all his complexity and with all his contradictory instincts – he is a fanatical rebel and honorable rabbi, a clever businessman and a concerned father. His aria in the fourth act sums up his dilemma: is it right for him to sacrifice Rachel in order to take the revenge he longs for? This extraordinarily gentle melody, in which an age-old melancholy seems to linger, became very popular, and with good reason. M 1

a Jewess. Brogni has Léopold, Rachel and Eléazar thrown into prison.

Act IV

Eudoxie tries to save Léopold's life, and asks Rachel to take all the blame on herself. In her love for Léopold, Rachel agrees. Brogni, wishing to save Rachel, urges Eléazar to renounce his Jewish faith. Eléazar indignantly refuses, and avenges himself on the Cardinal by revealing that Brogni's daughter was rescued years ago, by a Jew, and is still alive. But neither pleas nor threats can induce him to say more.

Act V

Eléazar and Rachel are led to their execution: they are to die in a cauldron of boiling water. Thanks to Rachel, Léopold is reprieved, and condemned only to exile. Eléazar gives Rachel his permission to convert to Christianity. However, she stands by the man she believes to be her father. At the moment of Rachel's death, Eléazar reveals the truth to Brogni. S. N.

Religious motivation for intrigues

France was unusually progressive over the Jewish question after the Revolution. The subsequent separation of church from state removed any grounds for official discrimination against Jews, and Jewish capital, now free of all restrictions, played a considerable part in the country's rapid economic development. In intellectual circles, Jewish artists and scientists had equal rights. *La Juive*, then, was written at a time when anti-Semitism was not an issue. As in other libretti by Eugène Scribe, the opera makes use of such abstract moral questions as revenge and reconciliation, pure love and devastating deception, as vehicles to move the drama along at a rapid speed.

1. Eléazar's Aria

Ra - chel, quand du   Sei - gneur   la grâ - ce tu - té - lai - re

Handel, George Frederick

b. 23 February 1685 in Halle
d. 14 April 1759 in London

Handel learned to play the organ, harpsichord, violin, and oboe, and studied counterpoint and composition with the organist Friedrich Wilhelm Zachow in his native town of Halle, where he himself became organist in 1702. He was then appointed *Kapellmeister* to the Hamburg Opera, where he stayed until 1707, before spending the next three years, until 1710, in Italy. His early operas were produced in Italy, and he also performed on the organ and harpsichord while he was there. He then entered the service of the Elector of Hanover, and received a stipend to visit London, where he settled in 1712. He regularly composed Italian operas for the English public until the end of the 1730s, becoming part of the newly formed Royal Academy of Music in 1719. From 1739 he composed oratorios on Biblical subjects to English texts, and became celebrated as a national English composer.

Works: His dramatic oeuvre is extensive, comprising 46 operas, the first of which, *Almira*, had its première in Hamburg in 1705, and the last, *Deidamia*, had its première in London in 1741. The operas composed between these two include *Agrippina* (1709), *Rinaldo* (1711, 2nd version 1731), *Acis and Galatea* (1718), *Radamisto* (1720), *Tamerlano* (*Tamerlane*) (1724), *Rodelinda, regina de' Longobardi* (*Rodelinda, Queen of the Lombards*) (1725), *Orlando* (1733), *Alcina* (1735), *Giustino* (*Justin*) (1735), and *Serse* (*Xerxes*) (1738) and *Deidamia* (1741). His most famous opera was *Giulio Cesare in Egitto* (*Julius Caesar in Egypt*) (1724). About a third of all Handel's operas are now lost, or extant only in fragmentary form. He composed 30 oratorios, including *Saul* (1739), *Israel in Egypt* (1739), *Messiah* (1742), and *Jephtha* (1752). Other works include cantatas, anthems, works for organ and harpsichord, concertos and concerti grossi, suites, including the *Water Music* (1717) and *Music for the Royal Fireworks* (1749), sonatas, and songs.

Agrippina

Dramma per musica in three acts

Libretto: Vincenzo Grimani.
Première: 26 December 1709, Venice (Teatro di S. Giovanni Grisostoma).
Characters: Agrippina, Empress of Rome, wife of Claudio (S), Claudio/Claudius, Emperor of Rome (B), Nerone/Nero, Agrippina's son (S), Ottone/Otho, a general (A), Poppea/Poppaea, loved by Otho (S), Pallante/Pallas, a courtier (B), Narciso/Narcissus, a courtier (T), Lesbo, Claudius's servant (B), Giunone/Juno (A).
Setting: Rome, AD 54.

Synopsis

Agrippina married her second husband, Claudius, only to become empress, and she is intriguing for her son Nero to succeed to the throne. She is prepared to use any method to hand: slander, deception, or treachery. Her strength prevails and she achieves her aims; her weaker opponents withdraw from politics.

Act I

In the apartments of Agrippina and Poppaea. A square on the Capitol.

Agrippina receives news that her husband Claudius is dead. She hopes to have her son Nero crowned emperor, and is already letting him act in public as heir to the throne. Her plans are thwarted, for Claudius has been saved by Otho, one of his generals, and out of gratitude has named Otho his successor. The beautiful Poppaea is courted by Claudius, Nero and Otho, but loves only Otho. Agrippina slanders Otho to her, and achieves her aim in persuading Poppaea to reject him. In her anger, Poppaea flatters the emperor, and Agrippina now stirs up Claudius's jealousy of Otho.

Act II

A street outside the imperial palace. Poppaea's garden. Agrippina's apartments.

Too late, Poppaea sees through Agrippina's scheming, and plans revenge. However, Agrippina makes use of her advantage, inducing Claudius to name Nero as successor to the throne instead of Otho.

Act III

A room in Poppaea's house. An imperial hall.

Poppaea uses a trick to make Claudius aware of the machinations of Agrippina and her son. Agrippina talks her way out of trouble. Otho publicly declares that he will reject the imperial crown out of love for Poppaea. Claudius acts magnanimously, gives Otho Poppaea's hand in marriage, and crowns Nero as the next emperor of Rome.

S. N.

Agrippina, production photograph with Lisa della Casa and Costanza Cuccaro, Zurich 1970.
The masks of the Roman women Agrippina and Poppaea conceal two Venetian ladies of refinement. Although Agrippina is motivated solely by ambition, she is not a female monster, but an attractive and confident woman. Poppaea can actually arouse the sympathy of the audience: she uses sex as a weapon, but is capable of feeling genuine love.

A topical opera

To Italy, suffering from the effects of the Spanish War of Succession, the action of this opera was full of topical allusions, addressing the subjective reasons for the lust for power and changes of government. Cardinal Vincenzo Grimani was an experienced diplomat who also wrote libretti. He himself supported the Habsburgs in the War of Succession, while Pope Clement XI was on the side of France and Spain. The rivalry between Nero and Otho in the opera reflects that situation.

Great depths of decadence are reflected in the dreadful story of Agrippina, a mother who, in her ambition for power, did not shrink from sleeping with her own son Nero, and was then forced to die by his command. Nero was the most bloodthirsty of all the tyrants of the Roman period; here, the opera and reality agree on the immorality of the powerful.

The other characters in the opera are a different matter. Poppaea was really an ambitious courtesan whose husband Otho offered her to Nero for purposes of sexual titillation. The historians Tacitus and Suetonius gave extensive accounts of the real persons and events involved. Grimani made an almost cynical libretto out of this bloodthirsty subject; it was one of the best texts Handel ever set.

Nero's Rome in Venice

Handel's opera *Agrippina* inevitably invites comparison with a "sequel" that had in fact appeared on the operatic stage decades earlier (1642), Monteverdi's →*The Coronation of Poppaea*. In Monteverdi's opera, Nero and Poppaea occupy the foreground, and Agrippina does not appear at all. Despite some comic minor characters and situations, Monteverdi's opera is much darker than Handel's. There are similarities, however, in the depiction of a period when instinct had free rein, uninhibited by any taboos, a situation that would later have been regarded as unimaginably amoral in the heroic and sublime world of *opera seria*. The intellectual background to both operas was not a fictional Rome but the real city of Venice, a rich and mighty seaport.

Agrippina, production photograph with Janice Hall (Poppaea) and Claudio Nicolai (Otho), production Michael Hampe, sets and costumes Mauro Pagano, conductor Arnold Östman, guest performance of the Oper der Stadt Köln at the Schewetzingen Festival 1985.
The so-called Early Music movement, aiming to provide historically accurate performances of works from earlier centuries, led to two major productions of *Agrippina*, one in the Baroque theater in Schwetzingen in 1985, and one at the Göttingen Festival in 1991 (with the Capella Savaria, conducted by Nicholas McGegan).

*H*andel composed music to texts in three languages (German, Italian, and English), and reflected the diverse musical styles of his time in his compositions. With Johann Sebastian Bach, Handel is the last and greatest figure of the Baroque period.

Rinaldo

Dramma per musica in three acts

Libretto: Giacomo Rossi, on a scenario by Aaron Hill, after the epic poem *La Gerusalemme liberata ovvero Il Goffredo (Jerusalem Liberated)* by Torquato Tasso.

Première: first version: 24 February 1711, London (Haymarket Theater); second version: 6 April 1731, London (Haymarket Theater).

Characters: Goffredo, leader of the Christian army (A), Almirena, his daughter (S), Rinaldo, a Christian hero (S), Eustazio, Goffredo's brother (A), Argante, King of Jerusalem, Armida's lover (B), Armida, Queen of Damascus, an enchantress, (S), A Christian Magician (A), Herald (T), A Woman (S), Two Sirens (2 S).

Setting: Jerusalem, around 1100, during the siege of the city in the First Crusade.

Synopsis (first version)

Jerusalem must be conquered, as the symbol of the pure Christian faith. But Goffredo is offering his own daughter to his commander Rinaldo as a reward, and therefore secular feelings are also involved, resulting in love tangles, while magical forces take shape and gain power.

Act I

The besieged city. Pleasure gardens with fountains and a bird cage.

Goffredo, leader of the Christian army, promises his commander Rinaldo the hand of his daughter Almirena, if he conquers Jerusalem. An armed confrontation with King Argante of Jerusalem lies ahead. Armida, an enchantress and Queen of Damascus, determines to stand by her lover Argante in his fight against Rinaldo. She abducts Almirena, whose father can do nothing against her magic powers. Goffredo turns to a magician for aid.

Act II

The sea shore, with a boat. A pleasure garden in Armida's magic castle.

Goffredo is on his way to the magician, with his brother Eustazio and Rinaldo. Armida succeeds in deceiving Rinaldo and luring him away from his companions. He too is now a prisoner in Armida's castle. The enchantress falls in love with him, while Argante is inflamed by passion for Almirena. But the two Christians remain steadfast.

Act III

A wild mountain landscape, with Armida's castle. Armida's garden. The besieged city.

The Magician gives Goffredo and Eustazio a magic wand with which they destroy the castle and liberate Rinaldo and Almirena. Armida and Argante flee, but are later taken captive by the victorious Christian army. Armida and Argante convert to the Christian faith; Rinaldo and Almirena will marry. *S. N.*

Rinaldo, costume design for the magician by Maria-Luisa Walek, production Jean-Louis Martinoty, sets Heinz Balthes, Badisches Staatstheater, Karlsruhe 1981.
The magician with his warlike talisman. Handel's attempts to win the favor of the English public began with *Rinaldo*, and continued for 30 years.

Rinaldo, photograph from a production by Frank Corsaro, sets Mark Negin, Metropolitan Opera House, New York 1984.
Leading opera stars performed at the Metropolitan Opera House in the 20th century. To sing here was a distinction in itself, showing that an artist belonged to a select circle. Productions at the Met, however, remained conventional in style.

1. Rinaldo's Aria

Ca – – ra spo – sa, a – man – te ca – ra, do – ve se – i? ____

do – ve se – i? deh! ri – tor – na a' pian – ti mie – i!

The recipe for success in London

In the eighteenth century, London was the largest and richest city in Europe, with lively musical activity in its churches, palaces, and concert halls. Handel was the first foreign composer of standing to make his career in London. For Handel's first London opera, Aaron Hill, the manager of the Haymarket Theater, devised a scenario that was part fairytale, part historical. He wanted to surprise the audience with a variety of stage effects, and accordingly Handel made particularly prominent use of brass instruments, writing seven independent orchestral movements, as well as the overture. Although it took Handel a very short time to write the score, *Rinaldo* is one of his most brilliant and stirring operas. He and Hill engaged the best Italian stars, including the fine bass Giuseppe Maria Boschi, who had already sung the Emperor Claudius in ›*Agrippina*. The opera was a great success, and a music publisher of the time with good business sense, John Walsh, made a fortune by publishing some of the individual arias translated into English. "Cara sposa" ("Dear beloved," Rinaldo's aria at the end of Act I) is one of the opera's most famous and popular numbers. M 1   J. M.

Rinaldo, production photograph with Samuel Ramey as Argante, production Frank Corsaro, sets Mark Negin, Metropolitan Opera House, New York 1984.
Frank Corsaro's production brought the brilliance and opulence of the Baroque period even into the details of the costumes: the King of Jerusalem appears here as an exotic counterpart to the Christian commander Rinaldo.

Acis and Galatea

Masque in one act

Libretto: John Gay, with additions by Alexander Pope, John Dryden, and John Hughes.
Première: 1718, Cannons (Edgware).
Characters: Galatea, a nymph (S), Acis, a shepherd (T), Coridon, a shepherd (T), Damon, his friend and companion (T), Polyphemus, a giant (B); nymphs and shepherds (chorus).
Setting: The period of Greek mythology.

Synopsis

Acis and Galatea are in love, but the giant Polyphemus, also in love with Galatea, intends to take her by force. Acis prepares to do battle, but he is killed. Nature, mankind and the gods all mourn the shepherd, who is transformed into a spring. S. N.

Opera in the English style

According to the account of a contemporary journalist, Handel composed a masque, or "little opera," at Cannons, the seat of the Earl of Carnarvon, basing it on an episode from Ovid's *Metamorphoses*. The traditional masque of the English court consisted of prose dialogues, songs, and dances, and provided the opportunity for a society game with masked participants (›Purcell). *Acis and Galatea* is distinguished from the Italian type of opera not so much by criteria of genre as by its English text; the germ of Handel's oratorios is discernible for the first time here. The chorus of soloists plays a more important part than in any other opera by Handel. (Not even the cantata *Acis, Galatea, and Poliphemus,* composed in Naples in 1708, is comparable.) The mourning chorus at the beginning is reminiscent of Greek tragedies, and anticipates the reform operas of ›Christoph Willibald Gluck. M 2

The music shows what a great influence Purcell's opera ›*Dido and Aeneas* had exerted on Handel. It is clearly perceptible in the unusually prominent role of the chorus, and in similarities between Galatea's mourning aria and Dido's aria of farewell. M 3   J. M.

2. Mourning Chorus

Mourn, all ye mu – ses! weep, all ye swains!

3. Galatea's Mourning Aria

(Orchestra)

Must I my A – cis still be – moan, in – glo – rious crush'd

be – neath that stone, in – glo – rious crush'd ____ be – neath that stone

Right
Pietro Metastasio (Pietro Antonio Domenico Bonaventura Trapassi, 1698–1782), colored engraving by Johann Ernst Mansfeld the Elder (1739–96), from a painting by Johann Nepomuk Steiner (1725–93).
Metastasio was court poet in Vienna; his most successful literary activity was the writing of libretti for *opere serie*. His texts were probably set more often than those of any other librettist in operatic history. Some of them were set by 60 to 70 composers during the 18th century. There are at least 40 different operatic versions of *Artaserse*, his best-selling libretto. Handel composed scores for revisions of several of Metastasio's libretti.

Below
Caricature of the singers Bernardi Senesino, Francesca Cuzzoni, and Berendstadt, contemporary engraving.
The caricaturist shows the famous castrato Senesino towering above the equally celebrated prima donna Francesca Cuzzoni, like Gulliver in Lilliput (in Jonathan Swift's famous novel of the same period, published in 1727). Castrati were tall and corpulent (perhaps as a result of a lack of male hormones), but the audience for opera was ready to dispense with realism on stage in return for outstanding voices and fine singing – as indeed it still is.

How to transplant Italian opera to foreign soil

Create an exciting operatic world for bored aristocrats and sensation-hungry members of the middle classes, a world full of intrigues both on and off stage, with artistic battles and victories. First, acquire sufficient money for your project. Get credit from the royal treasury, and induce as many aristocrats as possible to contribute by subscribing. Give your business the elegant title of the Royal Academy of Music, and then you have only to engage the right artists. This was what happened in London in 1719. In eighteenth-century opera, there was no copyright. Every libretto, indeed, every aria, was fair game for composers, and it was quite usual for several of them to write an opera jointly (or simply to put one together out of other people's material). Alternatively, a composer might create a "new" opera consisting of arias and scenes he had already composed for other purposes. In the theatrical practice of the eighteenth century, such a work was called a pasticcio. Handel himself was a natural artistic improviser, given to incorporating his earlier arias into whatever work he was writing at the time, or sometimes composing new numbers for new versions of his old operas. For example, Almirena's aria "Lascia ch'io piango," a gem of his Handel's operatic oeuvre, was originally written for his allegorical oratorio *Il trionfo del Tempo e del Disinganno* and then inserted into the second version of →*Rinaldo* of 1731. M 4

P. METASTASIVS
ROMANVS.

Victory
In the Royal Academy of Music's fifth season, Bononcini suffered a severe blow. On 20 February 1724 the opera →*Julius Caesar* had its première. It had taken Handel what for him was an unusually long time to compose, and it turned out to be his finest heroic opera. The leading performers included Senesino, Cuzzoni, Boschi, and Durastanti (in her last stage role). The brilliant heroic part of Julius Caesar was sung by a castrato. The opera was given 13 performances in its first season, and from that time on, although some of Bononcini's works were performed occasionally, he was in effect ousted from the direction of the Royal Academy.

The rivals

The Royal Academy of Music began its activities on 2 April 1720 with the première of Giovanni Porta's opera *Numitore*. The second production was Handel's →*Radamisto*. The composer Bononcini was especially successful in the Royal Academy's second and third seasons. His *Astaro*, first staged on 19 November 1720, was given 24 performances, a sensational number for the theatrical conditions of the time. The secret of his success was that Bononcini – a well educated and imaginative composer – wrote music that was more easily accessible than Handel's. The beguiling melodies of his arias are short, simple, and easy to remember, and thus became "hits" sooner than Handel's arias, with their greater weight, frequent surprises, and demanding accompaniment. Thus the first seasons at the Royal Academy were a great success for Bononcini. In time, however, the more discriminating public began to tire of the facility of Bononcini's music, and turned, at first slowly, then more obviously and with increasing speed, to Handel. In January 1723, the fourth season of the Royal Academy, Bononcini could no longer compete with the successful première of Handel's *Ottone*. One reason was the deployment by Handel of a "miracle weapon" in the form of the newly engaged super-star, the soprano Francesca Cuzzoni. This young woman, who was short, plump, and far from beautiful, was one of the outstanding women singers of the period, and exerted an irresistible influence on those who heard her. J. M.

4. Almirena's Lament

La - scia ch'io pian - ga mia cru - da sor - te, e che so - spi - ri la li - ber - tà,

Engraving of the Haymarket Theater opposite the old Royal Academy of Music, c. 1780.
The Haymarket Theater in London (near Trafalgar Square) was sometimes known as the King's Theater and sometimes as the Queen's Theater. The great operatic battles of the 18th century were conducted in this building.

Contemporary illustration for *The Beggar's Opera* by John Gay and Johann Christoph Pepusch.
The most dangerous competition Handel was to encounter was from a piece that was not a real opera at all – *The Beggar's Opera* of 1728. It anticipated the much later genre of operetta with its irreverent social criticism, and parodied serious opera by inserting musical interludes in the form of songs. John Gay (1685–1732) replaces the kings and noble lords and ladies of *opera seria* with a cast of rogues, beggars, and whores (cf. →Weill, *The Threepenny Opera*). Some of the music was taken from folk song, some from popular works by famous English composers such as Purcell and Handel. Pepusch (1667–1752), born in Berlin, the son of a German minister, composed only the overture himself, and harmonized the songs. This ballad opera constituted an attack on Handel's Italian operatic style, and the authors also wanted to offer the middle-class English public enjoyable light entertainment. It was with *The Beggar's Opera* that the Theater Royal opened in Covent Garden in 1732; the present theater on the site is London's Royal Opera House.

Alessandro Scarlatti (1660–1725)

Scarlatti, descended from a Sicilian family of musicians, enjoyed international fame, something of a rarity in the musical life of Baroque courts. The leading representative of what was called the Neapolitan school, he was regarded as the composer who brought Italian Baroque opera to its ultimate perfection. He preferred the genre of *dramma per musica* (a synonym for *opera seria*), with an elevated and serious subject, usually from classical mythology, for which he regularly supplied a happy ending. An opera by Scarlatti lasted an average of three hours and contained 40 to 60 arias, most of them short. These included duets, which were described as "arie à due" – arias for two voices. Scarlatti composed 69 operas, and was thus far more prolific than Handel as a writer of opera. His generally unified style is distinguished for its inexhaustible and expressive melodic ideas, an amusing lightness of touch, and depth of emotional feeling. Scarlatti was an imaginative musician, and in spite of the monotonous alternation of recitative and aria typical of the genre at the time, he achieved some notable dramatic effects.

Alessandro Scarlatti (1660–1725), portrait with sheet music, 18th century, Bologna, Accademia Rossini.

Pietro Metastasio (1698–1782)

Although not a composer of opera, Metastasio was a key figure in operatic history as the uncrowned king among librettists of the century. At the time, the libretto itself was far more important than its musical setting, and remained in existence much longer. While operatic libretti had a wide distribution, entire operas – that is to say, complete with their music – were imported or exported only in exceptional cases. Metastasio wrote 27 libretti for three-act heroic operas, and a series of smaller dramatic works, such as the popular *azione teatrale* or *festa teatrale*, and the *serenata*, which was chiefly performed at aristocratic weddings. Metastasio reformed opera libretti, rational-

izing and standardizing them; he "purged" the action of the intervention of transcendental powers (and also, unfortunately, of its comic elements), eliminated bombastic linguistic excrescences, and introduced technical stage effects as a dominant factor. He may be said to have standardized the number and characteristics of the various roles, also defining the types and the function of arias within individual scenes. (This was partly in response to the financial demands of the time for productions of opera to be inexpensive, using as few singers as possible, and cutting down on expensive props.) Metastasio's reforms did undoubtedly result in some impoverishment of the genre – for example, by introducing a degree of schematic rigidity. On the other hand, his libretti are distinguished by density of action, a high literary standard, well devised dramatic construction, and moving situations of a nature particularly suitable for setting to music. He came close to the spirit of the Enlightenment in his creation of the character type of the understanding, gracious ruler. The influence of Metastasio was still felt in the time of Mozart.

Johann Adolf Hasse (1699–1783)

According to contemporary critics, Hasse's works were the perfect embodiment of Metastasio's principles. He had a long and friendly relationship with the king of librettists, and almost half his 63 operas are direct or indirect settings of libretti by Metastasio. He was the outstanding composer of the courtly and aristocratic *opera seria*. Hasse lived and worked in three of the major musical centers of his time: Dresden, Venice, and Naples. In Italy, he was known as "Il Sassone" ("The Saxon"), a token of recognition accorded to no other foreign composer in that country.

Below right
Johann Adolf Hasse (1699–1783), engraving from a portrait by Rotar.

Antonio Vivaldi (1678–1741), caricature by Pier Leone Ghezzi (1674–1755), 1723.

Below
Stefano Dionisi as Farinelli, photograph from the film *Farinelli*, director Gérard Corbiau, France 1995.
The art of the castrato is one of the mysteries of opera. In spite of the high soprano or alto registers of castrati, their voices are said to have sounded stronger, more radiant, and more masculine than a modern female voice.

Antonio Vivaldi (1678–1741)

Posterity tends to forget that the epoch-making figure in the revival of Italian instrumental music in the Baroque era, the inexhaustible genius of the concerto, turned his talents to opera in the second half of his life, from 1713 onward. More than 20 operas by Vivaldi are extant, although they are little known today. While he did not achieve the same importance in the genre as he did in the field of instrumental music, and his contemporaries often voiced strong criticisms of the real or alleged deficiencies of his operas, he was undoubtedly one of the most sought-after Italian composers for the stage. Vivaldi was also an impresario. The great merit of his operas is the high musical level of the arias. In his early works, he wrote arias reminiscent of the concerto: the singing voice stands in the same relation to the orchestra as an instrumental solo, and the central section of the aria resembles an instrumental *ritornello*. This structure was superseded by the simple and much more usual *da capo* form in Vivaldi's later operas.

Farinelli (Carlo Broschi), lithograph by J. Wagner after the painting by Jacopo Amiconi.
The celebrated star Farinelli against a classical Greek background (on Parnassus?). He is ignoring the presence of his half-naked Muse.

The king of singers: Farinelli

Opera flourished between 1720 and the French Revolution of 1789. Never before or after were so many operas composed, nor was opera so constantly the subject of heated and even violent discussion. It was a golden age for singers, particularly castrati. Caffarelli, Senesino, Ranuzzini, and other castrati were admired by crowned heads as the greatest stars of the eighteenth century. The king among them, who might be described as the Paganini of singing, was Carlo Broschi, better known as Farinelli (1705–82). He ruined Handel's prospects in London between 1734 and 1737 by joining the rival operatic company, and left the capital as a millionaire. He then went to the royal court of Spain, where he provided luxurious music therapy for King Ferdinand VI, who suffered from depression and insomnia, soothing the king every evening with his delightful singing (favorite numbers were arias by Hasse). He was the "nightingale" of the oppressive court, where he remained until the king's death in 1759, a colleague of the equally brilliant harpsichordist Domenico Scarlatti (nephew of Alessandro). Later, Farinelli moved to Bologna, where he lived as a rich and famous man; his guests there included Gluck and Mozart, Emperor Joseph II, and Casanova.

Radamisto

Opera seria in three acts

Libretto: Nicola Francesco Haym, adapted from the libretto of Benedetto Domenico Lalli for the dramma per musica *L'amor tirannico*, by Francesco Gasparini.
Première: first version: 27 April 1720, London (Haymarket Theater); second version: 28 December 1720, London (Haymarket Theater).

Characters: Radamisto, son of Farasmane (A), Zenobia, Radamisto's wife (S), Farasmane, King of Thrace (B), Tiridate, King of Armenia (B), Polissena, his wife, Farasmane's daughter (S), Tigrane, Prince of Pontus (S), Fraarte, Tiridate's brother (S).
Setting: Thrace and Armenia, around AD 50.

Synopsis
The lives and love of Radamisto and Zenobia are threatened by the Armenian King Tiridate, who goes to war hoping to gain possession of Zenobia. But she is faithful to Radamisto, and Tiridate's wife Polissena also remains devoted to her unfaithful husband. Tiridate is overcome by a mutinous army commander. Magnanimity wins the day, and the couples are reunited. The work celebrates married love.

Act I
The tent of the King of Armenia. An army camp. A square outside Radamisto's palace.
Polissena laments the inconstancy of her husband Tiridate, King of Armenia. He has fallen in love with Zenobia, the wife of Radamisto, heir to the throne of Thrace, and has attacked Radamisto's country. Meanwhile, Tiridate's military commander Tigrane is paying court to Polissena, but she rejects him.

Radamisto and his father Farasmane are taken captive by the Armenians, and are offered their lives if they will surrender. Farasmane, Radamisto and Zenobia will not give way, and are prepared to die. Tiridate gives orders for father and son to be killed, but his commander Tigrane fails to carry out this command.

Act II
The banks of the river Arax. Tiridate's garden. A royal hall.
Radamisto and Zenobia have escaped. Zenobia, exhausted, begs her husband to kill her. He cannot bring himself to do so, and she throws herself into the river. Radamisto thinks Zenobia is dead, but Tigrane has rescued her, and now she is in the power of Tiridate. Radamisto tries to liberate her, but Polissena comes between the two men – one of them her husband, the other her brother – and prevents violence. Radamisto now resorts to a ruse. He disguises himself, and spreads the rumor of his own death.

Act III
The court outside the royal palace. Inside the palace. Tiridate's temple.
Tiridate is pressing his attentions on Zenobia, and offers her the crown of his kingdom. Since Radamisto is believed dead, Tiridate is not guarded, and Radamisto is able to pounce on him unexpectedly. Once again, Polissena intervenes. Radamisto is to be executed. Tigrane has mutinied against Tiridate, and prevents the death sentence from being carried out. Farasmane is reinstated as King of Thrace, and Radamisto, happily reunited with Zenobia, refrains from taking revenge. Tiridate repents, and returns to his wife Polissena.

S. N.

Radamisto, photograph from a production by Drew Minter, conductor Nicholas McGegan, sets Scott Blake, Deutsches Theater, Göttingen 1993.
Radamisto was the first opera that Handel composed for the Royal Academy of Music. In the third act, the librettist and composer assemble all the protagonists of this Baroque opera, to draw the threads of the plot yet more closely together before their final resolution.

The two duets between Radamisto and Zenobia, placed at two very prominent points in the opera (the ends of the second and third acts), are also extremely beautiful. Handel set great store by the brilliance of the singing parts and by his instrumentation. Here, the orchestral writing is dominated by flute, trumpets, and horns, as well as oboes and bassoon. M 6, M 7   J. M.

Below
Handel and King George I of England on a musical trip on the Thames, colored steel-engraving from the painting by Edouard Hamman (1819–88).
Handel was on friendly terms with the German-born royal family of Great Britain. This was not always politically advantageous to him; on several occasions the aristocratic opposition tried to annoy the court with operatic scandals.

Left
Radamisto, photograph from a production by Drew Minter, conductor Nicholas McGegan, sets Scott Blake, Deutsches Theater, Göttingen 1993.
The 20th-century Handel revival in Germany began at Göttingen, and was later taken up by Handel's birthplace of Halle, where the Handel Archive is now located. The Göttingen Handel Festival continues to be at the center of international interpretations of the composer's work. Research by the conductors John Eliot Gardiner and Nicholas McGegan has led to a number of outstanding productions.

A heroic opera

Radamisto is a heroic Baroque opera, with all the blood and terror of that genre. But the true subject of the opera, as Handel's own contemporaries pointed out, is married constancy.

The love of Radamisto and Zenobia, triumphant over all adversity, runs in counterpoint to the fate of Polissena. She is the true heroine of the piece, for she is capable of remaining faithful to a tyrannical and faithless husband in spite of all inducements. He even owes her his life. The great hit of the opera was the aria "Ombra cara di mia sposa" ("Dear shade of my wife," Act II), in which Radamisto laments the supposed loss of Zenobia. This lament inspired Handel to write one of his most enchanting cantilenas. The composer himself thought highly of it, for he mentioned it subsequently to his biographer John Mainwaring as being – with the aria "Cara sposa" ("Dear beloved") from →*Rinaldo* – his best aria. M 5

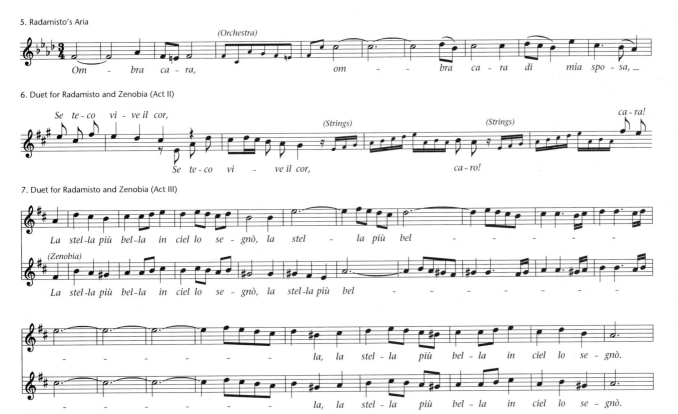

5. Radamisto's Aria

Om — bra ca — ra, (Orchestra) om — bra ca — ra di mia spo — sa, —

6. Duet for Radamisto and Zenobia (Act II)

Se te — co vi — ve il cor, (Strings) (Strings) ca — ra!
Se te — co vi — ve il cor, ca — ro!

7. Duet for Radamisto and Zenobia (Act III)

La stel — la più bel — la in ciel lo se — gnò, la stel — la più bel —
(Zenobia) La stel — la più bel — la in ciel lo se — gnò, la stel — la più bel —

— la, la stel — la più bel — la in ciel lo se — gnò.
— la, la stel — la più bel — la in ciel lo se — gnò.

Julius Caesar

Giulio Cesare in Egitto

Dramma per musica in three acts

Libretto: Nicola Francesco Haym, adapted from a libretto of the same name by Giacomo Francesco Bussani.

Première: 20 February 1724, London (Haymarket Theater).

Characters: Giulio Cesare/Julius Caesar, first Emperor of Rome (A), Curio/Curius, a Roman tribune (B), Cornelia, widow of Pompeo/Pompey (A), Sesto/Sextus, son of Cornelia and Pompey (S), Cleopatra, Queen of Egypt (S), Tolomeo/Ptolemy, King of Egypt, Cleopatra's brother (A), Achilla/Achillas, army commander and adviser of Ptolemy (B), Nireno/Nirenus, confidant of Cleopatra and Ptolemy (A); Caesar's retinue, conspirators (chorus).

Setting: Egypt, 48 BC, during Caesar's campaign against Pompey.

Synopsis

Julius Caesar conquers all his opponents and escapes from all political attacks; he is vulnerable only to the temptations of the heart. The most powerful man in Europe is in thrall to an unimportant Egyptian princess.

Act I

The plains of the Nile. Cleopatra's apartments. Caesar's camp. A hall in Ptolemy's palace.

Caesar has won a great victory over his rivals for power in Rome, and has now pursued the fugitive Pompey to Egypt. At the request of Pompey's wife and son, Cornelia and Sextus, he is ready to be reconciled with his old enemy, but the Egyptian ruler Ptolemy sends him Pompey's head as a present. Ptolemy is contending with his sister Cleopatra for the throne, and hopes to win the support of Caesar. However, Caesar is not grateful. Ptolemy now plans to murder Caesar with the help of Achillas, promising Cornelia to his general in return. Cleopatra approaches Caesar, disguised as a maidservant. She bewitches him with her charms, and he promises her his protection. Ptolemy holds a banquet in Caesar's honor, planning to have him murdered, but the attempt fails. Instead, Cornelia and Sextus force their way into the palace of Ptolemy to avenge Pompey's death, but this attack also fails. Sextus is thrown into a dungeon, and Cornelia is held captive in Ptolemy's seraglio.

Act II

The apartments of Cleopatra. A garden in the seraglio. Cleopatra's pleasure garden. A garden in the seraglio.

Cleopatra wins Caesar's love in a tryst, which is disturbed by the murderers of Pompey. To escape, Caesar jumps into the sea, and is believed dead. Achillas insists on the reward Ptolemy has promised for his services: he wants Cornelia. She rejects him scornfully. Achillas changes sides, and goes over to the Romans.

Act III

A forest near Alexandria. The port of Alexandria. Cleopatra's apartments. A royal hall. The port of Alexandria.

Ptolemy defeats Cleopatra and her Roman allies, and orders his sister's execution. Achillas, mortally wounded in the battle, gives his ring to Sextus as he dies; it confers authority to command. Caesar has come on shore from the sea alive, takes over command, defeats Ptolemy, and sets Cleopatra on the throne of Egypt.

S. N.

Musical originality

Julius Caesar is still Handel's most popular opera. Its wealth of musical characterization, consistently high musical standard, and clear, noble emotional expression make it a true masterpiece. Caesar's great *recitativo accompagnato* (accompanied recitative), in which he meditates on the meaning of life, singing alone before the mortal remains of his noble opponent Pompey ("Alma del gran Pompeo," Act I, Scene 7), his powerful hunting aria with brilliant horn obbligato ("Va tacito," Act I, Scene 9), Cleopatra's heart-rending lament ("Piangero," Act III, Scene 3), and Sextus's archetypal revenge aria ("La giustizia," Act III, Scene 5) are among the greatest moments of all operatic writing. *M 8, M 9, M 10*

The scoring, with four horns, recorders, transverse flutes, and divided bassoon parts, also makes this the richest of Handel's operatic scores, with wonderful solo passages for violin and oboe as well as the horn solo mentioned above. A high point is the scene in the cedar grove (Act II, Scene 1), where the uniquely delicate coloring of harp, theorbo, and viola da gamba (in the incidental music) mingle with the rest of the orchestral sound. Moreover, Handel had moved a long way from the monotonous sequence of *da capo* arias. Instrumental movements, accompanied recitative, cavatinas, choruses, duets (especially the beautiful "Son nata a lagrimar" for Cornelia and Sextus, Act I, Scene 11, finale), and a series of ensembles make *Julius Caesar* a work of unequaled variety within the *opera seria* tradition. *M 11*   J. M.

Julius Caesar, set design by Leo Pasetti, production Max Hofmüller, conductor Hans Knappertsbusch, Nationaltheater, Munich 1923 (TWS).
Leo Pasetti was one of the most important stage designers of the 20th century. His set designs were inspired by the spirit of the music, the bright, contrasting colors lending the sets a touch of Expressionism, a style of painting particularly suitable for Handel's lively Baroque music.

8. Caesar's Hunting Aria

Va   ta - ci - to e na - sco - - sto, quand' a - vi - do è di pre - da,   l'a - stu - to   cac - cia - tor, _____

(Horn)

quand' a - vi - do è di   pre - da,   l'a - stu - to   cac - cia - tor;

9. Cleopatra's Lament

Pian - ge - rò,   pian - ge - rò   la   sor - te   mi - a,

10. Sextus's Revenge Aria   (Orchestra)

La   giu - sti - zia ha già sull' ar - co pron - to stra - le,   pron - to stra - le al - la   ven -

det - - - - - - - - - - ta,

11. Duet for Cornelia and Sextus

Son na - ta a la - gri - mar,   e il dol - ce mio con - for - to, ah, sem - pre pian - ge - rò;

A favorite with the public

Julius Caesar is still the most popular of Handel's operas. Even in the composer's lifetime, there were three revivals in London, with 38 performances in all. Between 1725 and 1737, audiences at the Hamburg Opera acclaimed the musical heroes of Roman history. The opera was revived again in Göttingen in 1922, and has been a staple of the international repertory ever since.

Tamerlane

Tamerlano

Dramma per musica in three acts

Libretto: Nicola Francesco Haym, adapted from a libretto of the same name by Agostino Piovene, after the tragedy *Tamerlan, ou La mort de Bajazet* (*Tamerlane, or The Death of Bajazet*) by Jacques Pradon.
Première: 31 October 1724, London (Haymarket Theater).
Characters: Tamerlano/Tamerlane, ruler of the Tartars (A), Bajazete/Bajazet I, Sultan of Turkey, Tamerlane's captive (T), Asteria, Bajazet's daughter (S), Andronico/Andronicus, a Greek prince and ally of Tamerlane, lover of Asteria (A), Irene, Princess of Trebizond, betrothed to Tamerlane (A), Leone/Leo, confidant of Tamerlane and Andronicus (B), Zaida, confidante of Asteria (silent).
Setting: Prusa (now Bursa), the capital of Bithynia, in 1403.

Synopsis

The intrigues of Tamerlane to gain the love of Asteria, who is attracted to Andronicus, set off a series of murder and suicide attempts. Only when Bajazet sacrifices himself to protect his daughter is evil averted. The Tartar ruler is moved to mercy, and all ends happily.

Act I

A courtyard in Tamerlane's palace in Prusa. The apartments of Bajazet and Asteria. The palace courtyard.
The Mongol leader Tamerlane has annexed the Turkish empire, and taken Sultan Bajazet and his daughter Asteria prisoner. The Greek Prince Andronicus, who loves and is loved by Asteria, is living at Tamerlane's court. For political reasons, Tamerlane has become betrothed to Princess Irene of Trebizond, whom he does not know, but he is now paying court to Asteria. She and her father reject him. Tamerlane knows of the love between Asteria and Andronicus, and resorts to cunning, slandering the Greek to her. Irene of Trebizond, incognito at Tamerlane's court, observes all that is going on.

Act II

Arcades outside Tamerlane's apartments. The throneroom.
Having deceived Asteria, Tamerlane now turns his attentions to Andronicus. Asteria has decided to appear to fall in with Tamerlane's marriage plans, but only in order to assassinate him. She has not let Andronicus or her father Bajazet into her confidence, and both are deeply distressed. Irene of Trebizond appears, disguised as her own ambassador, and reminds the Mongol leader of his promise to her, but in vain. His wedding to Asteria is arranged. Bajazet threatens his daughter that he will commit suicide, a tragedy she can avert only by confessing her plan to assassinate Tamerlane, who falls into a rage.

Tamerlane, production photographs with Axel Köhler as Tamerlane, production Peter Konwitschny, Operhaus Halle 1990.
Peter Konwitschny, who was once assistant to Ruth Berghaus at the Berlin company, developed the art of reducing musical scenes to their essence, becoming one of the outstanding opera directors of the 20th century. His production of *Tamerlane* was a masterly probing of the characters' states of mind.

Act III

A courtyard in the seraglio. The imperial hall in the palace, with preparations for a banquet.
Bajazet and Asteria prepare to die a shameful death, and provide themselves with poison. Tamerlane humiliates Asteria by making her wait on him at a banquet as his slave. She takes her chance to drop poison into a goblet, and offers it to Tamerlane. Irene prevents this murder attempt, reveals her identity, and wins Tamerlane's favor. Asteria is now to be handed over to the slaves to be raped, and Bajazet poisons himself before Tamerlane's eyes, reminding the tyrant as he dies of all that Tamerlane has on his conscience. Asteria awaits death, and Andronicus no longer wishes to live. But Bajazet's suicide has caused a change of heart in the raging tyrant. Tamerlane shows mercy: he marries Irene, and allows Andronicus to marry Asteria.   *S. N.*

A hero in the tenor register

In 1724, Handel engaged a new singer for the Royal Academy of Music: the celebrated Francesco Borosini. He was the first major Italian tenor to be heard in London. He was also useful over the composition of the opera itself, since he introduced Handel to its subject in the form of an opera by Francesco Gasparini. He also seems to have provided the idea of the tragic conclusion (Bajazet's suicide and monologue, skillfully constructed by Handel as a hybrid form between recitative and *arioso*). The very fact that the tragic protagonist Bajazet was cast as a tenor lends this opera a certain status, for this was the first really important tenor part in all operatic history. After the countless heroic tenors of Romantic opera, it is difficult for us to understand today why the parts of male heroes in *opera seria* were taken by soprano castrati and women sopranos, or sometimes by alto castrati, but until *Tamerlane* tenors were thought unsuitable for such roles. At the time, the bass was regarded as a vocal register in its own right, but the tenor was considered only a paler version of the soprano register.   *J. M.*

Rodelinda

Roderlinda, regina de Longobarde

Dramma per musica in three acts

Libretto: Nicola Francesco Haym, adapted from a libretto of the same name by Antonio Salvi, after the tragedy *Pertharite, roi des Lombards* (*Perctarit, King of the Lombards*) by Pierre Corneille.

Première: 13 February 1725, London (Haymarket Theater).

Characters: Rodelinda, Queen of the Lombards (S), Bertarido, King of the Lombards and husband of Rodelinda (A), Grimoaldo, usurper of Bertarido's throne (T), Garibaldo, Duke of Turin, in rebellion against Bertarido and a friend of Grimoaldo (B), Eduige, sister of Bertarido, betrothed to Grimoaldo (A), Unulfo, a Lombard nobleman, adviser to Grimoaldo and secretly a friend to Bertarido (A), Flavio, son of Rodelinda and Bertarido (silent).
Setting: Milan, in the 7th century.

Synopsis

Grimoaldo has usurped the throne of Lombardy, and has rejected his own betrothed in order to marry Queen Rodelinda. His friend Garibaldo emulates him; he too abandons all virtue and compassion, and plans to seize Grimoaldo's throne. Only the persecuted outcasts remain loving and constant, refraining from revenge, and they save Grimoaldo from his treacherous friend. The wicked man repents, and happiness returns. *S. N.*

Marriage glorified

Although Handel was a confirmed bachelor, despite showing a lively interest in women all his life, particularly pretty singers, he wrote music celebrating married love in particularly poetic tones in his operas. They depict the wife as heroine. Here, as in →*Radamisto*, the constancy of marital love triumphs. *Rodelinda* is often compared with Beethoven's →*Fidelio*, since both works culminate in a rescue scene. Beethoven, like Handel, never married.

Rodelinda, set design by Hans Strohbach, Grosse Volksoper Berlin 1924 (TWS).
This watercolor in pastel shades conveys the essential character of *Rodelinda* even better than the final set. Handel liked depicting nature in his music, even in his later oratorios, and there are some enchanting natural scenes in *Rodelinda*.

RODELINDE. Hans Strohbach

Orlando

Opera seria in three acts

Libretto: Anonymous adaptation of a libretto by Carlo Sigismondo Capece, after the epic poem *Orlando furioso (Roland Deranged)* by Ludovico Ariosto.
Première: 27 January 1733, London
Characters: Orlando (A), Angelica, Queen of Cathay (China) (S), Medoro, an African prince, in love with Angelica (A), Dorinda, a shepherdess (S), Zoroastro, a magician (B).
Setting: The time and place of the action are undefined, though Ariosto's Orlando is attached to the court of Charlemagne, suggesting a period around AD 800.

Synopsis

The magician Zoroastro wishes to guide his friend Orlando on the path of truth and chivalrous heroism. However, Orlando is involved in an unhappy love affair with Princess Angelica, who flees with her lover Medoro, Prince of the Moors. To protect the fugitives, Zoroastro clouds Orlando's mind, and in his madness he threatens to commit dreadful deeds. Freed from madness again by Zoroastro, Orlando acknowledges the truth, abjures love, and devotes himself entirely to a life of chivalry; Angelica and Medoro, like all true lovers, can now enjoy their happiness undisturbed. *S. N.*

Orlando and *Alcina* – the similarities

Both operas ignore any real historical background, and derive from an episode in Ludovico Ariosto's *Orlando furioso*. In both, an enchanter or enchantress plays a crucial part (if in very different ways). And finally, both operas need very effective stage production. *Orlando*, with only five characters, is more of a chamber piece, while *Alcina*, which has seven solo voices, chorus, and ballet, is an opera on a large scale, almost a spectacular. The influence of Henry Purcell on Handel is most clearly perceptible in *Orlando* and *Alcina*, as it is, of course, in the masque →*Acis and Galatea*.

Zoroastro and Alcina – precursors of *The Magic Flute?*

Zoroastro and Alcina are reminiscent of Sarastro and the Queen of the Night in Mozart's →*The Magic Flute*. Their vocal registers reinforce this impression: Zoroastro is a bass (a rare phenomenon in *opera seria*) and Alcina a coloratura soprano. Zoroastro hopes to liberate the young knight Orlando from his self-centered erotic delusions, winning him back to the virtuous path of chivalry. Alcina, on the other hand, works black magic, and is ready to destroy everything out of jealousy.

Alcina

Dramma per musica in three acts

Libretto: Anonymous adaptation of the libretto for Riccardo Broschi's *L'isola di Alcina (The Island of Alcina)*, after Cantos vi and vii of the epic poem *Orlando furioso (Roland Deranged)* by Ludovico Ariosto.
Première: 16 April 1735, London (Covent Garden Theater).
Characters: Alcina, an enchantress (S), Ruggiero, a knight (S), Morgana, Alcina's sister (S), Bradamante, betrothed to Ruggiero, disguised as Ricciardo (A), Oronte, Alcina's general (T), Melisso, confidant of Bradamante (B), Oberto, son of the paladin Astolfo (S); ladies, pages, maidservants, young knights, magical apparitions, spirits (chorus).
Setting: Alcina's magic island.

Synopsis

The beautiful enchantress Alcina is holding Ruggiero under a spell in her realm. He is saved by the faithful love of Bradamante, and Alcina's magical realm disappears. *S. N.*

Alcina, production photograph with Eva Mei as Alcina, production Jürgen Flimm, sets Erich Wonder, conductor Nikolaus Harnoncourt, Vienna Festival 1997.
Recent productions have endeavored to remove the operas of Handel from the world of myth and fairytale, projecting them into other periods to allow the sense of a genuine music drama to unfold. One such example was this joint production of 1997 for the Vienna Festival and the Zurich Opera House. The designs for the production, by Erich Wonder, provide a congenial setting for Handel's music drama.

Alcina, production photograph with Sonia Theoduridu, production, sets and costumes Herbert Wernicke, conductor Michael Hofstetter, Theater Basel 1996.
Without making a great display of it, Wernicke stood back from the conventions of the scholarly Handel tradition in this production, depicting the characters' states of mind in an extraordinarily poetic and imaginative manner.

Below
Alcina, production photograph with Hedwig Fassbender and Anette Markwander, production, sets and costumes Herbert Wernicke, conductor Michael Hofstetter, Theater Basel 1996.

A magic opera with a ballet

The internal logic of *Alcina* is very different from that of *Orlando*. While the wise enchanter Zoroastro in *Orlando* watches with steadfast benevolence over the activities of mortals, the enchantress (who has the title role in *Alcina*) acts as a woman driven by passionate desire. The conflict in *Orlando* arises from the knight's choice between love and dispassionate chivalry; Ruggiero, on the other hand, is torn between sensual love (Alcina) and pure love (Bradamante). Alcina might be described as a combination of Zoroastro and Orlando in one person, although in feminine form; she has the gift of magic powers, but is beside herself with passion. One particular circumstance played a crucial part in determining the opera's external structure: for the third, 1734/35 season of the Academy, the impresario John Rich had engaged a French ballet company to appear with his theatrical ensemble, which had moved into the now renovated Covent Garden Theater. This was Marie Salle and her troupe, and their presence explains why each act of *Alcina* includes a ballet that fits into the action organically.   J. M.

Alcina, costume design for Alcina by Maria-Luisa Walek, production Hans Hartleb, sets Heinz Balthes, Badisches Staatstheater, Karlsruhe 1978 (TWS).
Alcina has been revived by later generations because of its fine soprano role for the eponymous heroine. The modern popularity of the piece is due to the great singer Joan Sutherland, who sang in the triumphantly successful production of the opera – which had not been performed on stage for 120 years – by Franco Zeffirelli in London in 1957. Since then, *Alcina* has been an established part of the international operatic repertory. In the last 20 years alone, there have been at least eight outstanding stage interpretations of the opera, including the Karlsruhe production of 1978.

Xerxes

Serse

Dramma per musica in three acts

Libretto: Anonymous adaptation of a libretto by Silvio Stampiglia.
Première: 26 April 1738, London (Haymarket Theater).
Characters: Serse/Xerxes, King of Persia (S), Arsamene, his brother (S), Ariodate, a prince and general (B), Romilda, his daughter, loved by Arsamene (S), Atalanta, her sister (S), Amastre, betrothed to Xerxes (A), Elviro, servant of Arsamene (B); servants, sailors, priests (chorus).
Setting: Abydos on the Hellespont, 480 BC.

Synopsis

King Xerxes, in love with Romilda, fails to win her after many attempts, for she prefers his brother Arsamene. Arsamene's slave Elviro plays a considerable part in resolving the conflicts, through his comic behavior and his cunning. Finally, Xerxes returns to Amastre, who loves him faithfully, and Romilda and Arsamene are married. *S. N.*

Larghetto

Of Handel's three last operas, *Xerxes* met with the least understanding and most adverse criticism from posterity. Yet in the last 75 years this work has been the most frequently performed of all his operas. The "largo" (described merely as "larghetto" in the original score) became one of the best-known of evergreen classics, sung by many great singers and arranged for all kinds of different instruments. *M 12*

Xerxes contains both tragic and comic situations. It may have been the great success of →*The Beggar's Opera*, by Gay and Pepusch, that encouraged Handel to give comic and popular elements a prominence unusual for *opera seria*.

Xerxes, production photograph with Ann Murray as Xerxes, production Martin Duncan, sets and costumes Ultz, conductor Ivor Bolton, Bayerische Staatsoper, Munich 1996.
Musically, Handel's tone changes constantly from serious to comic in *Xerxes* – entirely in keeping with the capricious nature of the title character. With this opera, his last at the Haymarket Theater in London, Handel came back almost full circle to his early work and the satirical overtones perceptible in →*Agrippina*.

Left
Xerxes, costume design for the army commander Ariodate, by Ute Frühling, Karlsruhe 1983 (TWS).
Since the arias in this opera are quite long, and the plot unfolds slowly, costume has a particularly important function.

12. Larghetto (Xerxes's Aria)

(Orchestra)

Om - - bra mai fù   di ve - ge - ta - bi-le ca-ra ed a - ma - bi-le   so - a - ve più,

Giustino

Dramma per musica in three acts

Libretto: Anonymous adaptation of a libretto by Pietro Pariati.
Première: 16 February 1737, London (Covent Garden Theater).
Characters: Anastasio/Anastasius, Emperor of Byzantium (S), Arianna, his wife (S), Leocasta, the emperor's sister (A), Amanzio, the imperial general (A), Giustino/Justin, a peasant (A), Vitaliano, a tyrant of Asia Minor (T), Polidarte, his general (B), La Fortuna/Fortune (S), Voice from within the tomb (B); crowd, courtiers, sailors (chorus).

Setting: Byzantium, Asia Minor, sometime during the 4th to 5th centuries AD.

Synopsis

The goddess of Fortune promises the peasant Justin fame, wealth, and a crown if he goes out into the world. On his way he encounters the imperial court in Byzantium, but he abstains from all intrigues, follows the path of virtue, and protects and liberates the persecuted and those in danger. As a result he wins fame and honor, but suffers loneliness and distress. Just as Justin begins to doubt Fortune, she comes to his aid: chance helps him to win the promised crown.   S. N.

The chorus as catalyst
In Handel's late opera *Giustino*, the protagonist is the most important figure singing with the chorus, in this case a collective term for various different groups. Of the 42 numbers in the opera, 12 are choruses or instrumental movements, a fact that betrays French influence (the *tragédies lyriques* of Lully and Rameau often included large-scale musical tableaux). On the other hand, it is also clear in this work that Handel was turning towards oratorio. After 1733 he progressively came to prefer this more English genre to opera, and was very successful with it.

Deidamia, set design by Helmut Jürgens, production Heinz Arnold, Staatsoper, München 1959 (TWS).
The Baroque stage designed in neo-Classical style. The intention of this set was to provide a visual illustration of both the way in which Baroque opera was typical of its time and the timelessness of Handel's fine music. The rediscovery of Baroque opera toward the end of the 1950s went hand in hand with a burgeoning interest in authentic interpretations of early music.

Deidamia

Melodramma in three acts

Libretto: Paolo Antonio Rolli.
Première: 10 January 1741, London (Theater Royal, Lincoln's Inn Fields).
Characters: Deidamia, daughter of King Lycomedes (S), Nerea, her friend, a princess (S), Achilles, disguised in women's clothing under the name of Pyrrha (Ms), Ulisse/Odysseus, King of Ithaca, going under the name of Antilochos (T), Phoenix, King of Argos (Bar), Lycomedes, King of Scyros (B), Nestor, King of Pylos (silent); companions of Deidamia, masters of the ceremonies, courtiers (chorus).
Setting: The island of Scyros in the Aegean Sea, before the beginning of the Trojan War.

Synopsis

An oracle has foretold that the boy Achilles will die young on the battlefield, a hero. To spare him such a fate, his parents send him to a friendly prince to be brought up in girl's clothing. But another oracle predicts that the Greek army will not defeat the Trojans without Achilles, and Odysseus goes in search of the missing youth. Meanwhile, the prince's daughter Deidamia has discovered the hero's secret, despite his female clothes. Achilles and Deidamia are in love, but neither his parents' cunning nor the love of Deidamia can save Achilles, for he himself is attracted to weapons and war. Deidamia's marriage to Achilles brings not love and happiness, but a parting from her beloved.   S. N.

The failure of a masterpiece
The theater in Lincoln's Inn Fields was not a lucky one for Handel. It was the stage on which Pepusch and Gay's → *The Beggar's Opera* was performed 26 times in succession in 1728, and that work's success was the direct reason for the failure of the first Royal Academy of Music. Handel's activity here ended after only three months, *Deidamia* having won merely lukewarm approval from the public, and having had only three performances. Its failure was undeserved, for it is an outstanding setting of an unusually good libretto. Handel was in his element in this work, depicting the title role of Deidamia in particular with versatility and a wealth of ideas. In the character of the cunning and kindly Odysseus, Handel created an opposite pole, evenly matched with her dramatically.   J. M.

Hartmann, Karl Amadeus

b. 2 August 1905 in Munich
d. 5 December 1963 in Munich

Hartmann first attended a teachers' training college before studying at the Akademie für Tonkunst (Music Academy) in Munich from 1924 to 1929, where he began a friendship with Hermann Scherchen. In 1928 he was one of the founders of the "Die Juryfreien" concert series. Between 1933 and 1945 there were no performances of Hartmann's music in Germany. At the Geneva Chamber Music Competition in 1936 he was awarded first prize for his String Quartet no. 1. In 1942 he began to study under Anton Webern in Vienna. He founded the "Musica viva" concert series in 1945, which he continued to run until his death; this series provided an audience for music banned by the Nazis and created a forum for young composers.

Works: Stage works: *Das Wachsfigurenkabinett* (*The Waxworks' Museum*) (five short operas, 1929–30), *Simplicius Simplicissimus* (1935/FP 1949, revised version 1957); eight symphonies, concertos, two string quartets, piano works, *Friede Anno 48* (*Peace Anno 48*) for soprano, mixed choir and piano (after Andreas Gryphius), *Gesangsszene* (*Song-scene*) for baritone and orchestra (after Jean Giraudoux).

Simplicius Simplicissimus

Three scenes

Libretto: Hermann Scherchen, Wolfgang Petzet, and Karl Amadeus Hartmann, after a novel by Hans Jakob Christoffel von Grimmelshausen.
Première: Concert première: 2 April 1948, Munich (Bavarian Radio); stage première: 20 October 1949, Cologne (Theater der Stadt, Kammerspiele); première of the revised version: 9 July 1957, Mannheim (Nationaltheater).
Characters: Simplicius Simplicissimus (S), Hermit (T), Governor (T), Mercenary (Bar), Captain (B), Peasant (B), Lady (dancer), Narrator (spoken); peasants, chorus, and speaking chorus.
Setting: Central Germany, the time of the Thirty Years' War.

Synopsis
Introduction
A narrator tells of the numbers killed in the Thirty Years' War.
Scene 1
A peasant boy tending his sheep falls asleep under a tree and dreams that its branches are groaning under the weight of people sitting on them. He is woken by a mercenary. The village has been destroyed and its inhabitants – including the boy's parents – killed.
Scene 2
The orphan meets a hermit in the forest who calls the boy "Simplicius Simplicissimus" because of his naïveté. The hermit teaches the child joy and how to live in harmony with nature. Nearing death, the old man digs his own grave and passes away peacefully. Simplicius is once more alone.
Scene 3
In the governor's palace the soldiers are enjoying a banquet, and they welcome Simplicius as a kind of court jester. Simplicius remembers his dream and, wiser now, interprets it as meaning that the generals and the rich are on the uppermost branches, with the merchants and soldiers below them, while the peasants are forced to slave away at the roots. A peasant army storms the palace and massacres everyone. Simplicius manages to escape. Once again, the narrator recounts the number of the dead.   *S. N.*

Simplicius Simplicissimus, poster (linoleum print: Plakat-Wurm) from the Munich production by the Bayerischen Staatsoper at the Theater am Brunnenhof, 1951.
A poster and a set design (opposite) which visualize society as a tree. The familiar image of society or the social hierarchy as a tree is central to *Simplicius Simplicissimus* as the visual expression of social relationships and power structures. Hartmann, however, did not use the symbol as a static element but exploited it as a dramatically powerful motif. When Simplicius first sees the tree in a dream it has the impact of a generalized and abstract truth; it is only as the result of his painful experiences of life that this truth is able to provide him with tangible insights of his own.

Simplicius Simplicissimus, set design by Helmut Jürgens, production Heinz Arnold, Bayerische Staatsoper, Munich 1960.
The symbol of the Tree of Society conceals other motifs, which have been brought out in the various productions of *Simplicius*. The tree can be seen as a symbol of life, with its protective crown of foliage, or as a veteran stripped bare by storms – a living creature, centuries old, the witness of the universal processes of life and death by which all human destinies are limited.

A confession of beliefs

In his *Autobiographischen Skizze* (*Autobiographical Sketch*) Hartmann emphasized the confessional nature of his art, in particular that of the opera *Simplicius Simplicissimus*. For Hartmann 1933 marked the beginning of distinctly negative social developments in Germany – the "victory of the idea of tyranny." He recognized that at that moment in history a confession was required of him, namely an expression of his belief that, in spite of everything, man remains free: that he can, unimpeded by all external forces and oppression, choose a path that will allow him either to contribute to life or to destroy it. Put simply, his belief was: for the individual's conscience there can be no such thing as "simply obeying orders."

Hartmann portrayed the experience of "inner emigration" (a term describing the predicament of artists who chose to stay in the Third Reich) in compelling terms. The Hermit figure in *Simplicius* makes the point that it is possible to lead a morally distinguished life and do good works in the face of adversities presented by the outside world. His death forms the focus of the opera, as he passes away peacefully in his sleep surrounded by an inferno of destruction. Later generations of composers travelled to India and studied Asiatic religions to understand this approach (for example, →Cage, →Glass, →Reich, and →Stockhausen). Simplicius is a type of Everyman. The two framing scenes of the work mirror each other by depicting murder and mayhem being committed by both oppressors and victims: violence is thus seen to breed violence. The plot is linked to the process of obtaining insights, a process illustrated by Simplicius's dream of the tree and its interpretation. Thus, *Simplicius* is not a traditional opera driven only by a plot. If realism is an intellectual attitude that seeks to unmask the structure rather than the surface of a set of historical conditions, then Hartmann's *Simplicius* is realistic – though not in the sense of a work which is strikingly naturalistic. Neither is it a history play. The Thirty Years' War did not end with the Peasants' Revolt: that had taken place a century earlier. The conflict between professional soldiers and a peasantry intent on defending itself was meant as an historical paradigm referring to events in the 20th century.

Quotations, associations

Genre pieces are particularly prominent in this work, including marches, dances, chorales, the street-ballad couplet, and allusions to Jewish folk music (the viola solo in the overture). There are also quotations from and allusions to works by →Bach, →Stravinsky, and →Prokofiev, which, along with the Jewish melody, testify to the composer's solidarity with music that had been outlawed by the Nazis. The quotation from the "Florian Geyer Song" underscores musically the connection between Simplicius's fate and those of many other people.   *S. N.*

Hartmann created music characterized by the intensity of its expression of suffering and inwardness. Never completely silenced by Nazi Germany, it was later recognized as evidence of his unusual ethical integrity and became a model for the next generation of composers. His use of musical quotations was highly individual: they are a reminder of the forgotten and the excluded, and function as a dialogue with the positive spirits of all ages and cultures.

PROSPECT NACH DEM GARTEN UND WALD GEGEN SÜDEN.

View of the Esterházy palace from the park side to the south, 1784 (Hungarian National Museum).
Shown here on the left-hand side of the drawing is the promenade in front of the opera house and the route taken to the great musical events. Inside the opera house, the nobility sat in the boxes while the rest of the audience sat in the area directly in front of the stage, to which entrance was free.

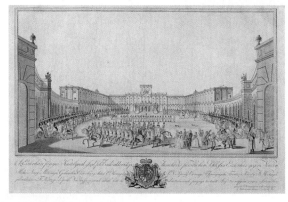

A parade with musicians in the grounds of the Esterházy palace, 1784 (Hungarian National Museum).
In 1760 Haydn entered the service of the Esterházy family. "His" prince, Nikolaus I, the "Ostentatious," inherited the estate at Eisenstadt in 1762 at the age of 48, and immediately began building a pleasure palace some 50 km (30 miles) east (on what is now the Austrian-Hungarian border), in the middle of a marshy area surrounding the Neusiedler See. This magnificent building, with its huge park in the French style, was completed in 1766.

Haydn, Joseph

b. 31 March 1732 in Rohrau
d. 31 May 1809 in Vienna

Haydn was born into a poor family, but after an early discovery of his talent he was given a good education. He became a singer (1740) in the boys' choir of St. Stephen's Cathedral in Vienna, and later studied with the most famous singing teacher of his day, the composer Nicola Porpora. He was then appointed head of Count Morzin's private orchestra in Lukavce (Bohemia) where he composed his first symphony (1759). In 1761 he entered the service of the Esterházy family, and was a highly regarded house composer and director of music at their palace at Eszterháza until 1790. His works were published in Vienna and brought him an international reputation without requiring him to leave the Esterházy residence for any length of time. After his retirement from service with the Esterházy family, he was invited to compose symphonies for performance in England and even to stage his work in London. His two trips to England (1790–92 and 1794–96) brought him enormous artistic, social, and financial success. It was here he composed his 12 London Symphonies. After returning from England he settled in Vienna, and, following the example of Handel, wrote two great oratorios, *Die Schöpfung* (*The Creation*, 1798) and *Die Jahreszeiten* (*The Seasons*, 1801). In his later years he was celebrated as Austria's national composer (he wrote the Austrian imperial anthem which is today the German national anthem).

Works: The Italian operas are the most important of Hadyn's stage works; without exception they were composed for the Esterházy court opera. Complete surviving operas: *La canterina* (*The Singer*) (intermezzo in musica, 1766), *Lo speziale* (*The Apothecary*) (dramma giocoso, 1768), *Le pescatrici* (*The Fisherwomen*) (dramma giocoso, 1770), *L'infedeltà delusa* (*Faithlessness Confounded*) (burletta per musica, 1773), *L'incontro improvviso* (*The Unexpected Meeting*) (1775), *Il mondo della luna* (*The World on the Moon*) (dramma giocoso, 1777), *La vera costanza* (*True Constancy*) (azione teatrale, 1779), *L'isola disabitata* (*The Desert Island*) (1779), *La fedeltà premiata* (*Faithfulness Rewarded*) (dramma pastorale giocoso, 1780), *Orlando Paladino* (*Sir Roland*) (dramma eroica-comico, 1782), *Armida* (dramma eroica, 1783), *L'anima del filosofo, ossia Orfeo ed Euridice* (*The Philosopher's Soul, or Orpheus and Eurydice*) (dramma per musica, 1791/FP 1951); the only surviving *Singspiel*: *Philemon und Baucis, oder Jupiters Reise zur Erde* (*Philemon and Baucis, or Jupiter's Travels on the Earth*) (a puppet opera, 1773).

Main works: 104 symphonies, 84 string quartets, piano trios and other chamber music, 52 piano sonatas, oratorios, and sacred works.

Haydn, as the eldest of the trio of Classical Viennese composers – with Mozart and Beethoven – heralded a new epoch in music.

An opera paradise

In the 18th century the small opera house at the Esterházy palace possessed the most up-to-date stage equipment, none of which, unfortunately, has survived. Operas were also performed at the puppet theater opposite. The *Beschreibung des Hochfürstlichen Schlosses Esterháss im Königreiche Ungern* (*Description of the Princely Palace of Eszterháza in the Kingdom of Hungary*) of 1784 gives the following account this bizarre theater: "The stalls resemble a grotto; the walls, niches, and openings are all covered with diverse materials, stones, shells, and snails, and when it is illuminated it makes for a most curious and impressive sight. The theater is relatively spacious, the decorations are pretty, and the puppets are very well made and splendidly attired. Not only farces and comedies are performed there, but also *opera seria*: the immortal Maria Theresia bestowed her

approval on the opera *Alceste* which was performed there, and admired the quick changes of scenery which almost escape one's notice."

Nikolaus I, the "Ostentatious"

In 1760 Haydn entered the service of one of the most important Hungarian noble families. The founder of this princely dynasty, Pál Esterházy (1635–1713) had enjoyed an artistic education and was a composer himself, and "in addition" led successful campaigns against the Turks in the 1680s. His successors inherited these cultural interests, especially Nikolaus I, known as the "Ostentatious." In 1762, at the age of 48, he inherited the estate at Eisenstadt, and immediately commissioned a design for a pleasure palace some 50 km (30 miles) east of Eisenstadt (at what is now Fertőd on

This scene probably depicts an opera being performed at Eszterháza between 1766 and 1790, gouache (Deutsches Theatermuseum, Munich).
The opera being performed seems to be on an exotic theme. The quality of the set and the figure of the angel in the clouds (top right) show the high technical and artistic standards of the Baroque theater. The depiction of the orchestra is of special interest. The conductor (perhaps Haydn himself) sits at the harpsichord to the left surrounded by the bass instruments (cello, double bass, and bassoon); these instruments provided the foundations for the music (the so-called "basso continuo"). In addition there are two oboists, and six or seven violinists and viola players. The usual orchestra of the day also included two French horns; as they are not pictured it is likely that – as was customary – the musicians are here playing a second instrument.

the border between Austria and Hungary), in the middle of a marsh surrounding the Neusiedler See. This magnificent building with its French park was completed in 1766, and in the years that followed two theaters were built there.

Haydn, the composer and conductor of operas
Though Haydn was first and foremost a composer of instrumental music, opera formed a significant part of his *oeuvre*, especially during his years of service at Eszterháza. The statistics are astonishing: in the small palace opera house there were 1200 performances in a period of 30 years, 88 of which were premières – some of Haydn's own work. Haydn not only performed the work of his contemporaries – Anfossi, Cimarosa, Gazzaniga, Guglielmi, Traëtta, Paësiello, Piccinni, Sarti, and Gluck – but also adapted them to suit local conditions. For this reason, a number of Haydn's arias have survived as inserts in operas by other composers. His operas reflected the taste at the imperial court, but did not influence it. While the instrumental music produced under Nikolaus I achieved a high standing on account of Haydn's originality, the Esterházy palace was far from the center of Europe to be able to compete with the imperial capital at Vienna, or with Paris, London, and the leading Italian cities.   T. Sz.

Below
The prince's opera house at the Esterházy palace, groundplan and elevations, engraving after Joseph von Fernstein from the *Beschreibung des Hochfürstlichen Schlosses Esterháss im Königreiche Ungern* (*Description of the Princely Palace of Eszterháza in the Kingdom of Hungary*), 1784 (Hungarian National Museum).
"There are alternating performances of Italian *opere serie* and *buffe* and German comedies every day, which the Prince always attends and which generally keep to the hour of six in the evening. What pleasures are here provided for both the ears and the eyes! When the orchestra suddenly begins to play the soul is pierced by the most touching delicacy one moment and the impassioned power of the instruments the next. The great musician, Herr Haiden, is the prince's *Kapellmeister* and it is he who directs the orchestra. The lighting is sublime and the stage sets most impressive – Gods slowly descend on clouds only to disappear again in an instant from whence they came, and what is at first a graceful garden becomes next an enchanted forest only to be then transformed into a magnificent hall." (*Description of the Princely Palace of Eszterháza*)

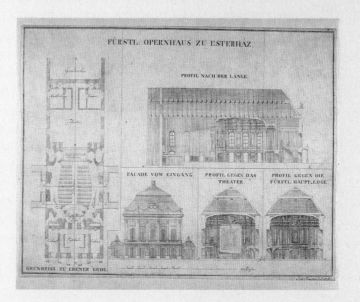

The Desert Island, photograph from the production by Alexander Schulin, conductor Francesco Corti, Staatsoper Unter den Linden, Berlin 1996.
The Desert Island was composed in 1779 to a libretto by Pietro Metastasio. An *azione teatrale*, or piece for a courtly celebration, it is unique among Haydn's operas. It appeared in selections for piano from 1909, several decades before the complete edition of Haydn's works. Its revival in 1996 was marked by the use of parody as a distancing device.

Right
The Desert Island, photograph from the production by Alexander Schulin, conductor Francesco Corti, Staatsoper Unter den Linden, Berlin 1996.
This piece was composed in homage to Haydn's patron Prince Nikolaus (Haydn himself called it an "operetta"), on the occasion of the prince's name-day on 6 December. A fire in the Esterházy opera house meant that it was staged in the palace's puppet theatre.

Opera: a life-long dream

Haydn is said to have told his first biographer, Georg August Griesinger, that he should have written more vocal music instead of string quartets, sonatas, and symphonies – he would then have become the best opera composer of his day. One can only speculate as to why he never did this. Haydn lived in relative isolation and it was not until he was 60 years old that he saw opera productions outside his own country (for example, in London). Perhaps he had allowed himself to be too restricted by traditional forms of opera; perhaps he really had too little time to devote himself as intensively to stage music as he did to instrumental music; or perhaps he was less gifted at this genre than Mozart and Gluck. The candor with which Haydn was able to estimate his position in the world of opera is therefore all the more admirable.

In December 1787 (only weeks after the première of Mozart's →*Don Giovanni* in Prague) Haydn replied to a request from Prague to submit an opera he had already completed. His letter is both modest and perceptive: "All my operas [are] too closely associated with our staff (at Eszterháza in Hungary) and would never achieve the desired effect which I have calculated according to our locality. It would be altogether different were I to

have the inestimable good fortune of composing a completely new work for [your] theater. But even then I should have to be very bold, for it would be most difficult to stand alongside the great Mozart."

Opera by the book

Although he was an innovative composer, Haydn never managed to throw off the musical and dramatic conventions of *opera seria* and *opera buffa*, the dominant operatic forms of his day. He chose his libretti and themes according to the subject matter that was fashionable at the time, never confronting his librettists with the sorts of demands made by Mozart and Gluck. Haydn's operas are largely *drammi giocosi*, in other words comic operas, charming stories involving situation-comedy or frivolous psychological predicaments, in which the comic dialogue (*secco* recitative) is interspersed with amusing, intimate, or touching arias and ensembles. The set pieces owe much to the comic operas of Paësiello (→Mozart, *The Marriage of Figaro*) and →Cimarosa. The style of Haydn's operas also shows the influence of contemporary song styles, which combines with the sensitivity and breezy humor of his music. His two most popular comic operas, *Lo speziale* (*The Apothecary*), after a comedy by Carlo Goldoni, and *Il mondo della luna* (*The World on the Moon*) still appear frequently in today's repertory, although they are generally in an abridged form. T. Sz.

The World on the Moon, production photograph with Karl-Friedrich Dürr (Bohnsack), Josefin Hirte (Clarice), Anat Efraty (Flaminia), Tom Allen (Astradamus), and Jan Konieczny (Prospero), production Ulrich Greb, sets and costumes Birgit Angele, conductor Francesco Corti, Württembergisches Staatstheater, Stuttgart 1995.
This comic opera from 1777 is in fact set in Venice and not on the moon. Two cunning suitors who want to marry the daughters of the amateur astrologer Bohnsack convince the old man that the Emperor of the Moon has invited him to visit. The second act is then set on what purports to be the moon and ends with the youths' victory.

Orpheus and Eurydice, production photograph with Eva Mei (Spirit) and Roberto Saccà (Orpheus), production Jürgen Flimm, conductor Nikolaus Harnoncourt, co-production of the Vienna Festival and the Opernhaus Zürich, 1995.
Orpheus and Eurydice does not fit into any of the traditional operatic categories from Haydn's day. In the year Mozart died, Haydn began to follow his younger friend in the field of dramatic music by brilliantly combining styles for dramatic purposes. The opera contains richly colored *opera seria* arias (especially for the part of the spirit), and choral pieces in the manner of Gluck and Handel. The influence of Mozart himself (for example, →*Don Giovanni*) is felt in the depiction of the underworld.

Orpheus and Eurydice

L'anima del filosofo, ossia Orfeo ed Euridice

Dramma per musica in five acts

Libretto: Carlo Francesco Badini.
Première: 9 June 1951, Florence (Teatro della Pergola).

Characters: Orfeo/Orpheus, a Thracian singer (T), Euridice/Eurydice, betrothed to Arideo/Aristaeus (S), Creonte/Creon, a king, Eurydice's father (B), A Spirit, messenger of the Sibyl (S), Plutone/Pluto, lord of the underworld (B), Four Followers of Creonte (4 B), A Warrior of Aristaeus (T), A Bacchante (S); cherubs, virgins, men, unhappy spirits, Furies, bacchantes (chorus).
Setting: Mythological.

Synopsis
Previous history: Creon has promised the hand of his daughter Eurydice to Aristaeus. She, however, is in love with the singer Orpheus.

Act I
Scene 1: A deep forest. Eurydice has fled from marriage to a man she does not love, but is threatened by savages who are about to sacrifice her to the gods. Orpheus soothes them with his song and Eurydice is saved.
Scene 2: When Creon learns of this incident, he agrees to the marriage of Orpheus and Eurydice.

Act II
Scene 1: An idyll. Orpheus and Eurydice are celebrating their wedding. When Orpheus leaves his bride alone for a moment, one of Aristaeus's warriors tries to overpower her. Eurydice flees but treads on a poisonous snake, is bitten and dies.
Scene 2: In the royal palace. A messenger brings Creon a declaration of war from Aristaeus, because he has broken his promise. Creon swears revenge for the death of his daughter.

Act III
Scene 1: Eurydice's grave. Orpheus, Creon, men, and virgins are grieving for the deceased.
Scene 2: Creon tries in vain to cheer Orpheus.
Scene 3: A cave at the entrance to the underworld. Orpheus turns to the wise Sibyl for help. She sends him a spirit who advises him to seek solace in philosophy, and who will accompany him into the underworld to search for Eurydice.

Act IV
Scene 1: While wandering through the underworld they pass unhappy, tormented spirits.
Scene 2: At the gates to Pluto's kingdom. Orpheus's song moves the lord of the underworld; he allows Orpheus to take Eurydice back to the land of the living – on one condition: that he resists the temptation to turn and look at Eurydice until they have reached daylight.

Act V (incomplete)
Scene 1: Orpheus has not kept his promise and has lost Eurydice forever. Dispirited, he wanders aimlessly along the seashore. A group of bacchantes attempt to seduce him, but he rejects them. They force him to drink what they call a "potion of love" (in fact, poison), and Orpheus is redeemed by death.   *T. Sz.*

A mysterious opera

The original title of the opera – *L'anima del filosofo*, that is, *The Philosopher's Soul* – is puzzling. It may be related to the philosophical interests of the librettist Carlo Francesco Badini; indeed, in the opera the spirit does recommend the consoling powers of philosophy to Orpheus. But perhaps the philosopher refers to the singer Orpheus, and the soul is identical with Eurydice? Or is it a story of self-knowledge, gained with the assistance of a guiding spirit? In this respect, Orpheus's descent into hell is reminiscent of Dante's *Divina commedia* (*Divine Comedy*): in both, an artist figure is led into the kingdom of shadows.

Haydn received the commission for the opera in 1791 when he was almost 60 years old and had made a momentous decision to go to London. He perceived the opportunity to explore new avenues in opera composition. The peculiar form of the title was fitting, as Gluck's →*Orpheus and Eurydice* was considered the greatest operatic version of this famous myth.

Unfinished – why?

The London impresario John Gallini had wanted to open the King's Theater on the Haymarket with a new work by Haydn. The theater had burned down in 1783 and had been rebuilt with the support of the Prince of Wales (later King George IV). Intrigues at court (especially the rivalry between George III and the Prince of Wales) meant that the king denied Gallini the right to open the theater, and this seemed to seal the opera's fate. It is doubtful whether Haydn would have kept to the tragic finale that we know today: the customs of the age and the traditions of *opera seria* would have ruled out a tragic ending.   *T. Sz.*

Orpheus and Eurydice, production photograph with Cecilia Bartoli as Eurydice, production Jürgen Flimm, conductor Nikolaus Harnoncourt, co-production of the Vienna Festival and the Opernhaus Zürich, 1995.
Haydn's last opera lay forgotten for a long time. The composer himself saw only an incomplete edition of the work in 1806. For 150 years this version of the Orpheus story was silent. The stars of the première in Florence in 1951 (Maria Callas, Boris Christoff, and Tygge Tyggeson under Erich Kleiber) should have been able to rescue the work from obscurity, but it was not to appear on the stage again for another 16 years (in a new production with Joan Sutherland and Nicolai Gedda at the Vienna Festival Weeks in 1967). The most recent revival (1995) can be attributed to the efforts of the Early Music movement. The highly successful production by Jürgen Flimm at the Zurich opera house, conducted by Nikolaus Harnoncourt, as well as the CD recording (conducted by Christopher Hogwood, with Cecilia Bartoli in the dual role of Eurydice and the spirit!), have helped this remarkable and moving opera to attain the acclaim it deserves.

Boulevard Solitude, photograph from the production by Jean-Pierre Ponnelle, sets and costumes Jean-Pierre Ponnelle, conductor Klaus Tennstedt, Bayerische Staatsoper, Munich 1974.
Ponnelle rehabilitated this work more than 20 years after it was first performed (he designed the set for the original production). Henze took the title of his version of the *Manon* story (→Auber 1856, →Massenet 1884, and →Puccini 1893) from the film world, Billy Wilder's film *Sunset Boulevard* being the inspiration for *Boulevard Solitude*. A sense of detachment, cooled emotions, and a filmic editing technique spoke of 1950s' ideals of objectivity.

*H*enze's work is characterized by a plurality of styles – from late Romantic orchestral techniques through to an individualistic approach to serialism and naturalism. His operas make use of the formal richness of the traditional genre, combining it with elements that are his own.

Boulevard Solitude, production photograph with Janet Williams as Manon Lescaut, production Nicolas Brieger, Oper Frankfurt 1998.
Henze's Manon adaptation is about a lack of feeling rather than an excess of passion, which was the traditional theme of the opera. This presents singers who have had a traditional training with a difficult task, and productions of this opera have been problematic as a result.

Boulevard Solitude

Lyric drama in seven scenes

Libretto: Grete Weil and Walter Jockisch, after the novel *Manon Lescaut* by Abbé Prevost.
Première: 17 February 1952, Hanover (Landestheater).

Characters: Manon Lescaut (S), Armand des Grieux, a student (T), Lescaut, Manon's brother (Bar), Francis, Armand's friend (Bar), Lilaque (père), a rich old gentleman (buffo T), Lilaque (fils), his son (Bar), A Prostitute (dancer), A Servant to Lilaque (fils) (mime), Two Drug Addicts (dancers); newspaper boys, beggars, prostitutes, policemen, students, travelers (ballet).
Setting: France, in the present day.

Synopsis

The student Armand meets Manon Lescaut in the railway station of a large French city and persuades her to stay with him rather than go to her boarding school. They both live happily in a Paris garret, until Manon is persuaded by her brother to offer herself to the wealthy Lilaque. Lescaut steals from his sister's new admirer, who then throws her out of the house. Manon returns to Armand but he has become a drug addict. Lescaut arranges a match between his sister and Lilaque's son, but when Armand visits Manon they are surprised by the elder Lilaque and Manon shoots him dead. She is sent to prison and ends her relationship with Armand. When Armand waits for her at the prison gates she walks by without so much as a glance at him.

Henze, Hans Werner

b. 1 July 1926 in Gütersloh

After studying with Wolfgang Fortner and René Leibowitz, Henze worked as director of music for Heinz Hilpert's Deutsches Theater in Konstanz. After a period as artistic director of ballet at the Staatstheater at Wiesbaden (1950–53) Henze decided to settle permanently in Italy. As a composer he was always interested in opera, a form that he never considered old-fashioned – unlike representatives of the post-war avant-garde – but rather saw as a relevant forum in which to discuss both topical and universal questions. By reserving the freedom to use whatever stylistic means were necessary to express verbal and non-verbal content, he diverged from avant-garde trends without sacrificing his popularity with the public.

Works: Operas: *Das Wundertheater* (*The Theater of Miracles*) (1949, Heidelberg; 1965 Frankfurt/Main), *Ein Landarzt* (*A Country Doctor*) (1951, Hamburg, as opera for radio), *Boulevard Solitude* (1952, Hanover), *Das Ende einer Welt* (*The End of a World*) (1953, Hamburg, as opera for radio), *König Hirsch* (*The Stag King*) (1956, Berlin), *Der Prinz von Homburg* (*The Prince of Homburg*) (1960, Hamburg), *Elegie für junge Liebenden* (*Elegy for Young Lovers*) (1961, Schwetzingen), *Der junge Lord* (*The Young Lord*) (1965, Berlin), *Die Bassariden* (*The Bassarids*) (1966, Salzburg), *La Cubana, oder Ein Leben für die Kunst* (*The Cuban, or Life in the Service of Art*) (1975, Munich), *We Come to the River* (1976, London), *Pollicino* (1980, Montepulciano), *Die englische Katze* (*The English Cat*) (1983, Schwetzingen), *Das verratene Meer* (*The Betrayed Sea*) (1990, Berlin), *Venus und Adonis* (*Venus and Adonis*) (1997, Munich); ballets, symphonies, concertos, chamber music, and vocal works, including *Voices* and *Das Floss der Medusa* (*The River of Medusa*).

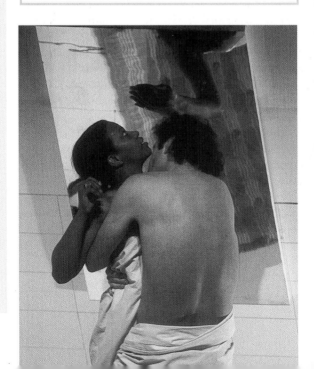

Boulevard Solitude, production photograph with Martin Kränzle as the king from the production by Nicolas Brieger, costumes Jorge Jara, Oper Frankfurt 1998.
Besides emotional frigidity the opera deals with what philosopher Hannah Arendt described as a fundamental evil of the age: social hypocrisy and conformity. These issues have been brought out in productions.

The Stag King

König Hirsch

Opera in three acts

Libretto: Heinz von Cramer, after the tragicomedy by Carlo Gozzi.
Première: Abridged version: 24 September 1956, Berlin (Städtische Oper); original version: 7 May 1985, Stuttgart (Württembergisches Staatstheater, Grosses Haus); second version, entitled *Il re cervo, or The Errantries of Truth*: 10 March 1963, Kassel (Staatstheater).
Characters: The King (T), The Girl (S), Governor (B-bar), Scollatella, a female role that may be shared (coloratura S), Scollatella II, III and IV (soubrette, Ms, A), Checco, a dreamy lad (buffo T), Coltellino, a shy murderer (buffo T), Lady in Black (A), Inventors (clowns singing ad lib.), The Stag (silent), The Parrot (dancer), Two Statues (2 S or 2 boy S), Voices of the Forest (S, Ms, A, T, B), Spirits of the Wind (dancers), Cigolotti (spoken, second version); women, hunters, soldiers, animals, apparitions (extras and chorus).
Setting: A Mediterranean landscape, a Venice set between forest and the sea, in an undefined period.

Synopsis
Act I

The interior of a castle. The young king, who has been raised in the forest, has just been crowned and now wishes to marry. A date for presenting eligible young women to the king is set. Scollatella wants to be queen more than anything and flirts enthusiastically with the man she believes to be the king; it is, however, the governor, and he is determined to have the throne for himself. When one young woman refuses to take part in the presentation, he accuses her of attempting to murder the king. The king, however, has already fallen in love with the girl and leaves the palace in a state of confusion.

Act II

A forest. The governor orders the shy Coltellino to murder the king, but Coltellino begins hunting other things and the governor decides to take matters into his own hands. Because the animals of the forest have not accepted their former companion, the king, he assumes the form of a dead stag. The governor witnesses this transformation and takes over the king's body.

Act III

A great square from which streets radiate like the rays of a star. Looking like the king, the governor has imposed a tyranny on the land. The real king, in the form of a stag, comes to the city to look for the girl he loves. The governor tries to kill the stag, but falls down dead himself. The stag king is restored to his human form and marries the girl to the jubilation of the people.   *S. N.*

The Stag King, production photograph from the first production of the original version, with Julia Conwell (Girl) and Toni Krämer (King), production Hans Hollmann, sets Hans Hoffer, conductor Dennis Russell Davies, Württembergisches Staatstheater, Stuttgart 1985.
The Stag King is a fairy-tale opera, a counterpart to 1950s' ideals of objectivity. The work is Baroque in attitude (thunderstorm scene, forest setting), and is densely layered; it is a synthesis of the most diverse forms of traditional opera, including the symphonic.

The Young Lord

Der junge Lord

Comic opera in two acts

Libretto: Ingeborg Bachmann, after the fairytale *Der Affe als Mensch* (*The Ape as Man*) by Wilhelm Hauff.
Première: 7 April 1965, Berlin (Deutsche Oper).
Characters: Sir Edgar (silent), His Secretary (Bar), Lord Barrat, nephew of Sir Edgar (T), Begonia, the Jamaican cook (Ms), The Mayor (Bbar), Hasentreffer, a lawyer (Bar), Scharf, a financial adviser (Bar), Professor von Mucker (buffo T), Baroness Grünwiesel (Ms), Frau von Hufnagel (Ms), Frau Hasentreffer, judiciary advisor (S), Luise, ward of the baroness (S), Ida, her friend (coloratura S), A Chambermaid (S), Wilhelm, a student (T), Amintore La Rocca, the circus director (T), A Lamplighter (Bar), Herr La Truiaire, a teacher of manners and dancing master (silent), Meadows, the butler (silent), Jeremy, a Moor (silent), A Teacher (silent), A Street Sweeper (silent), Two Men with Paint and Brushes (silent); circus people (dancers): "Rosita, girl of the air," a small tightrope walker from Sicily, Brimbilla, a juggler from Istria, Vulcano, a fire-eater from Milan, Adam, the ape; ladies, gentlemen, well-to-do young men and women from Hülsdorf-Gotha, townsfolk, children (chorus); military band, dance band (extras).
Setting: Hülsdorf-Gotha, 1830.

Synopsis

Act I

In order to pursue his studies without distraction, Sir Edgar moves into a house on the main square, but he is constantly interrupted by the town's dignitaries. It is here that Luise, the ward of Baroness Grünwiesel, meets the student Wilhelm. On the main square an itinerant circus is advertising its performances. Sir Edgar offers the performers accommodation in his house.

Act II

Strange cries are heard emanating from Sir Edgar's house. The dignitaries who rush to the scene are calmed by Sir Edgar's secretary, who tells them that the man of the house is giving his nephew, Barrat, language lessons and will soon be presenting him to society. The day has arrived, and everyone is gathered in Sir Edgar's house, where they find an eccentric young man. He is courted by all present as Sir Edgar's nephew. During the ball it appears that an engagement between Luise and Barrat may be developing. But Barrat's dance becomes frenzied; he threatens Luise and throws her across the room before tearing the decorations from the walls. Sir Edgar fetches his whip: the much-admired nephew is revealed as Adam, the ape from the wandering circus. Luise, contrite, returns to Wilhelm. M.S.

The Young Lord, photograph from the production by Günter Krämer, sets and costumes Andreas Reinhardt, conductor Dennis Russell Davies, Bayerische Staatsoper, Munich 1995.
Librettist Ingeborg Bachmann added the young couple of Luise and Wilhelm to Hauff's parable, and gave them a touch of the Biedermeier. Henze chose a style reminiscent of Mozart and Rossini, which contrasts strongly with that of the Darmstadt School. This roused the indignation of critics, but the opera was nevertheless a great success with operagoers.

The Bassarids

Die Bassariden

Opera seria with intermezzo in one act

Libretto: W.H. Auden and Chester Kallman, after Euripides.
Prèmiere: 6 August 1966, Salzburg (Grosses Festspielhaus).

Characters: Dionysos/Dionysus, who also sings A Voice and A Stranger (T), Pentheus, King of Thebes (Bar), Kadmos/Cadmus, his grandfather, founder of Thebes (B), Teiresias/Tiresias, an old blind visionary (T), A Captain of the Royal Guard (Bar), Agaue/Agave, Cadmus's daughter and Pentheus's mother (Ms), Autonoe, her sister (S), Beroe, an old slave, formerly the wet nurse of Semele and Pentheus (Ms), A Young Woman, a slave in Agave's household (silent), A Child, her daughter (silent); characters for the intermezzo *The Judgment of Calliope*: Venus (Ms), Proserpina (S), Calliope (T), Adonis (Bar); servants, musicians, bassarids (maenads, bacchantes), citizens of Thebes, the guard, servants (chorus).
Setting: The Royal Palace at Thebes and Mount Cytheron, in antiquity.

Synopsis

First movement

The aging founder of Thebes, Cadmus, has transferred the rule of his kingdom to his grandson, Pentheus. The procession of Dionysus into Thebes sows discord: Agave doubts Dionysus's divine origins; Cadmus, determined to live in peace with the gods, is non-committal; while Tiresias hurries off with many others to Mount Cytheron to worship the god. Pentheus denounces the cult of Dionysus and extinguishes the fire on the grave of Semele, Dionysus's mother. But the temptations of Dionysus cannot be resisted, and even Agave follows his voice to Cytheron.

Second movement

Pentheus orders that prisoners are to be taken on Mount Cytheron; through interrogation and torture they are to reveal what has been happening on the mountain. But the prisoners are in a trance and are incapable of uttering a word.

Third movement

Part 1: Pentheus's attempts to establish the truth have failed; worse still, the flame on Semele's tomb has been reignited by an earthquake. Once again, everyone makes their way to Cytheron. Only a stranger remains behind. It is Dionysus himself, who shows Pentheus the events on Cytheron in a mirror.
Intermezzo: A mythological garden, with scenery from a Rococo theater. Agave as Venus, Autonoe as Proserpina, Tiresias as Calliope, and a captain as Adonis perform *The Judgment of Calliope*, whose theme is the victory of intoxicated sensuality.

Part 2: Pentheus is greatly shaken and, following the advice of the stranger, makes his way in disguise to Cytheron in order to observe incognito all that happens there. Here he sees respectable citizens transformed into raging bassarids and maenads. The stranger betrays Pentheus's hiding place and the king is killed by a mob led by Agave.

Fourth movement

The procession of bassarids moves triumphantly into Thebes. Agave brings the head of the king, certain that she has killed a lion. Cadmus reveals the truth: she has killed her own son. Dionysus sends her into exile, burns the palace down, and summons his mother Semele, in order to ascend with her to Olympus. Fearful and intimidated, the people worship at the feet of the new god. *M. S.*

Opera in symphonic form

When Henze began to work with the symphonic form at the start of the 1960s, the poet W.H. Auden drew his attention to Euripides's tragedy, which had already exercised a fascination for Egon Wellesz in 1931 and Giorgio Federico Ghedini in 1948. It was the symphony, therefore, with its four traditional movements, which inspired the grand formal conception of this opera. Dionysus is characterized by striking chromatic phrases, while Pentheus is portrayed diatonically. Connections are created by 12-tone modes, and the movements are designed to follow each other without a break. Stylized dances serve to depict sensual abandon, and Dionysus's seductive powers are developed in an adagio with a fugue. The intermezzo aspires to associations with the satyr plays of antiquity, in order to provide some relief for a plot that moves inevitably towards cataclysm. *M. S.*

The Bassarids, production photograph with Horst Hiestermann and chorus, production Christine Mielitz, sets and costumes Gottfried Pilz, conductor Markus Stenz, Oper Hamburg 1994.
Most directors of the *Bassarids* have concentrated on exploring the work's mythological meaning. This approach has resulted in intelligent productions, but ones that have been unpopular with audiences because they are unrelated to the present. Christine Mielitz, a director with an international reputation, was determined to choose another path by foregrounding the political aspects of the work that are relevant to contemporary audiences.

We Come to the River

Actions for music

Libretto: Edward Bond.

Première: 12 July 1976, London (Royal Opera House).

Characters: General (Bar), Adjutant (B), Major Hillcourt (spoken), Sergeant-Major (Bar), Sergeant (T), Deserter (T), Emperor (Ms), Governor (Bar), Gray-Haired Minister (B), Doctor (Bbar), Drummer (drummer), Rachel (coloratura S), May (Ms), Young Woman (S), Old Woman (Ms), Wife of the Second Soldier (S), Four Officers (2 T, Bar, Bbar), Eight Soldiers (4 T, 3 Bar, B), Seven Wounded Soldiers (2 T, 2 Bbar, 3 spoken), Three Ministers (T, Bar, Bbar), Three Officials (T, Bar, Bbar), Three Men (T, Bar, Bbar), Two Orderlies (Bar, B), Two Murderers (2 T), Four Women (2 S, 2 Ms), Six Young Ladies (3 S, 3 Ms), Six Young Girls (3 S, 3 Ms), Three Prostitutes (3 Ms), Ten Madmen (3 T, 4 Bar, 2 S, drummer), Eight Madwomen (2 S, 3 Ms, 3 spoken), Thirteen Victims (3 S, 3 Ms, 2 T, 2 Bar, 2 Bbar, B), Three Children (3 boy S); servants, soldiers (extras).

Setting: An imaginary empire, in the present day.

Synopsis
Part I

1. Victory. A people's uprising has been bloodily crushed. The general dictates the victory dispatches. Soldiers are getting drunk, and a deserter waits to be sentenced. **2. The court martial.** Without giving him a chance to explain, the general condemns the deserter to death. **3. The long night.** There is a reception in celebration of the victors. In the guardroom, the deserter explains his motives to the firing squad. The general learns from his doctor that he will go blind. **4. The battlefield.** In the gray of dawn, the general goes to the battlefield and sees for the first time the suffering he has caused. Two women, one young and one old, are searching the corpses for valuables; the young woman is hoping to find her husband. At that moment he is shot: he was the deserter. **5. The governor.** The new governor is being honored with a military parade. The general is in a state of distraction. **6. The liquidation.** He returns to the battlefield and is arrested by pursuing officers. **7. At the river.** The general, under arrest, sees the old woman shot by soldiers as she tries to cross the river with her grandchild.

Part II

8. The Madhouse. The general has been placed in an asylum. A soldier gains entry and asks for advice on how to assassinate the governor. The governor also comes to see the general. The empire is threatening to fall apart, and he wants the general to help save it with his prestige. The general rejects both requests:

he is no longer amongst the powerful, but he is not yet a victim. **9. The assassination.** The soldier shoots the governor, but he and his family pay with their lives. **10. The emperor.** The young regent behaves in an esoteric manner, and sees himself as the executor of Buddha's will; he orders the blinding of the general. **11. The blinding.** Blind, the general is able to see: he sees his victims and empathizes with them. The inmates of the asylum fear the blind man and stab him to death. The general reaches the river: he dies.

S. N.

A play on three levels

The action takes place at three locations simultaneously. One represents a level of contemplation, a second is reserved for social action and the third tells the story of the general. The complexity of the scene-changing is aided by a clear musical structure: song, aria, and madrigal are used, and hymns are sung alongside the "Charleston" and the gavotte. Occasionally these elements are used to parody events; a coloratura aria, for example, is used as an ironic comment on a cozy scene, while a waltz accompanies the firing squad. The development of the 12-tone series is subtle, and is not fully realized until the general's fate has been fulfilled. *We Come to the River* is an important and courageous work, and its message – that we are all both perpetrators and victims – was immediately understood by audiences. In spite of the enormous challenges represented by the scene changes, there have been several successful productions, including those at smaller theaters such as Nuremberg.

M. S.

We Come to the River photograph from the production by Michael Hampe, sets John Gunter, conductor Wolfgang Gayler, Oper Nürnberg 1981.
The Nuremberg team took Henze's work seriously, the cast working with great commitment and empathy to create what proved to be an entirely convincing – and ultimately exemplary – production.

The English Cat

Die englische Katze

A story for singers and instrumentalists

Libretto: Edward Bond, after Honoré de Balzac's *Peines de coeur d'une chatte* (*Confessions of an English Cat*).
Première: 2 June 1983, Schwetzingen (Schlosstheater).

Characters: Lord Puff, tomcat, President of the Royal Society for the Protection of Rats, also a Serenade Singer (T), Arnold, tomcat, his nephew, also a Serenade Singer (B), Mr Jones, tomcat, money-lender, also Mr Fawn, tomcat, member of the RSPR, also a Judge, dog, also a Serenade Singer (Bar), Tom, tomcat, also a Serenade Singer (Bar), Peter, tomcat, Tom's friend, also Mr Keen, tomcat, member of the RSPR, also Defense Counsel, dog, also a Minister, sheep, also Lucian, fox, also a Serenade Singer (T), Minette, cat (S), Babette, cat, her sister, also The Moon, also a Member of the Jury, bird (Ms), Louise, mouse, member of the RSPR, also a Star, also a Member of the Jury, bird (S), Miss Crisp, cat, member of the RSPR, also a Star, also a Member of the Jury, bird (S), Mrs Gomfit, cat, member of the RSPR, also a Star, also a Member of the Jury, bird (S), Lady Toodle, cat, member of the RSPR, also a Star, also a Member of the Jury, bird (Ms), Mr. Plunkett, tomcat, member of the RSPR, also a State Attorney, dog, also a Serenade Singer (Bbar).
Setting: London, 1900.

Synopsis

Mrs Halifax, chairwoman of the board of the Vegetarian Society, has ordered her aged tomcat Puff to contribute to the survival of his species by marrying the young country cat Minette. This marriage guarantees Puff the presidency of the RSPR, the Royal Society for the Protection of Rats, an organization to which the orphaned mouse, Louise, who is under the protection of the cats, also belongs. Puff's nephew, Arnold, who is heavily in debt, uses all the means at his disposal to prevent the marriage, in order to come into Puff's inheritance. After the wedding, Minette's acquaintance with the roving tomcat Tom is conveniently used by Arnold to accuse the couple of adultery. Tom loves Minette, and stands by her during the divorce proceedings that reveal his true identity: he is the son of a missing lord, and therefore the heir to a fortune. But this news comes too late: he is unable to prevent Minette being drowned in the Thames. He joins forces with Minette's sister Babette, intending to sign over his entire fortune to her. While signing the contract he is stabbed to death by a member of the RSPR, his cause of death being given as suicide. His fortune is claimed by the Society. Disillusioned, Louise, the mouse, leaves the cats.   S. N.

Below
The English Cat, photograph from the original production with Inge Nielsen and Martin Finke, production Hans Werner Henze, sets and costumes Jakob Niedermeier, conductor Dennis Russell Davies, Württembergisches Staatstheater Stuttgart, Schwetzingen Festival 1983.
Written between March 1980 and May 1983, Henze's opera did not stint on social criticism: it exposed the bigotry and hypocrisy of society while combining humor with political commitment. The style of the work was influenced by Offenbach, Verdi, Rossini, and Donizetti Pate, but also included elements from the songs of Kurt Weill. Henze followed the formal traditions of 18th-century *opera buffa*, and aimed at the greatest possible transparency of musical language. The work was immediately accepted by large and small stages alike.

Left
The English Cat, photograph from the original production with Inge Nielsen (center), production Hans Werner Henze, sets and costumes Jakob Niedermeier, conductor Dennis Russell Davies, Württembergisches Staatstheater Stuttgart, Schwetzingen Festival 1983.

Above left
The English Cat, photograph from the production by Hans Werner Henze, sets and costumes Jakob Niedermeier, conductor Dennis Russell Davies, Württembergisches Staatstheater Stuttgart, 1983.

The Betrayed Sea, photograph from the original production with (from left to right) Andreas Schmidt (Ryuji), Stephanie Sundine (Fusako), and Clemens Bieber (Noboru), production Götz Friedrich, sets Hans Hofer, conductor Markus Stenz, Deutsche Oper, Berlin 1990.

The short novel *Gogo No Eiko* (*The Sailor Who Fell from Grace with the Sea*) by Yukio Mishima was much discussed in Germany in the second half of the 1980s. It explored the problem of teenage delinquency without a trace of far-eastern exoticism. Henze did not directly quote from Japanese melodies in this opera, composed between 1986 and 1989, but he did give the work a symphonic dimension, and included naturalistic elements such as street noises and the sound of jackhammers, a wrecking ball, and bulldozers in order to portray the reality of the protagonists' lives with greater force.

The Betrayed Sea

Das verratene Meer

Music drama

Libretto: Hans-Ulrich Treichel, after the novel *Gogo No Eiko* (*The Sailor Who Fell from Grace with the Sea*) by Yukio Mishima.
Première: 5 May 1990, Berlin (Deutsche Oper).
Characters: Fusako Kuroda, a 33-year-old widow, owner of the "Rex" fashion boutique in Yokohama (S), Noboru, her 13-year-old son, also called "Number Three" (T), Ryuji Tsukazaki, second officer on the freighter "Rakuyo-Maru" (B), First Mate (T); Noboru's gang and friends: Number One, the leader (Bar), Number Two (counterT), Number Four (Bar), Number Five (B); ship's officer, crew, harbor workers, manager of "Rex," three saleswomen.
Setting: Japan, in the 20th century.

Synopsis

The widowed boutique-owner Fusako lives with her 13-year-old son Noboru in Yokohama. While visiting a ship she falls in love with second officer Ryuji Tsukazaki. Her son considers the sailor a hero of the seas. But Ryuji has had enough of sea travel; he proposes to Fusako and quits the service to work as a fashion seller. Noboru is a member of a gang and has boasted to his friends about Ryuji; he is now disillusioned and sees that Ryuji is no hero. The gang hates the generation of their parents, and considers how to do away with their fathers. In their eyes, Ryuji is a coward. The boys now sit in judgment over Ryuji – as they had done earlier over a cat that they then tortured to death. While Fusako dreams of a happy family life, the boys lure Ryuji to a hideout and kill him.

HM. S.

The Betrayed Sea, photograph from the original production with (from left to right) Martin Gantner (Number One), Ralf Lukas (Number Four), Friedrich Molsberger (Number Five), David Knutson (Number Two), and Clemens Bieber (Noboru), production Götz Friedrich, sets Hans Hofer, conductor Markus Stenz, Deutsche Oper, Berlin 1990.

The Deutsche Oper in Berlin produced this commissioned work as a co-production with La Scala in Milan. The three main figures are each characterized musically: Fusako by strings, the sailor by dissonant phrases on wind instruments, and Noboru, the son, by "piano lesson music" (Henze), bolstered by percussion.

Venus and Adonis, photograph from the original production by Pierre Audi, sets and costumes Chloé Obolenski, conductor Markus Stenz, Bayerische Staatsoper, Munich 1997.
In *Venus and Adonis* Henze joined past and present by means of parallel plots: just as Venus and Adonis become matched, so is there a relationship between the prima donna and the young tenor. This technique may be seen as similar to the use of parallel montage in film. In order to highlight the difference between the two time-frames, the singers perform their recitatives and dance-songs in modern clothing, while the characters representing the archaic era dance boleros. There are also shepherds who comment on events through madrigals in the style of Gesualdo, Marenzio, and Monteverdi. Corresponding to the three levels within the plot – song, dance, and commentary – there are three orchestras named after mythological characters.

Venus and Adonis

Venus und Adonis

Opera in one act for singers and dancers

Libretto: Hans-Ulrich Treichel.
Première: 11 January 1997, Munich (Bayerische Staatsoper).
Characters: Singers: The Primadonna (S), Clemente, a young opera singer (T), Heroic Baritone (Bar), Six Madrigalists, shepherds (S, Ms, A, T, Bar, B); dancers (mime and actors): Venus, Adonis, Mars, a Mare, a Stallion, a Wild Boar.
Setting: Rural settings, both in the present and an antique past.

Synopsis

A tenor and a heroic baritone both court the prima donna and become rivals. Their feelings are revealed in the form of mythological characters and events, which are observed and commented on by shepherds from antiquity. The well-known tragic story of Venus and Adonis provides the focal point. In mythological terms the tenor is Adonis. Surprised by Venus in his sleep, he responds to her affection, just as the tenor does with the prima donna. Thunder and lightning usher in misfortune. Adonis is killed by a wild boar, as the heroic baritone murders the tenor. Hans Werner Henze himself comments: "Three concert singers experience strong erotic conflicts; their emotional outbursts are repeatedly taken up and expressed by their dancing 'Doppelgänger' – who are bearers of the plot and called variously 'Venus,' 'Adonis,' and 'Mars' – until a catastrophe occurs which explodes the form of the whole work."

S. N.

Murder, Hope of Women, set design by Ludwig Sievert for the production by Ernst Lert, Opernhaus Frankfurt 1922 (TWS). Ludwig Sievert's set design corresponded in style to the Expressionism of the libretto.

Immoral operas

In a play written in 1907 for the Garden Theater of the Kunstschau in Vienna, the painter Oskar Kokoschka had questioned bourgeois sexual morality. Hindemith continued in the same vein in his opera. In Franz Blei's *Vermischten Schriften* (*Miscellaneous Writings*) he found the story of Nusch-Nuschi. The work's use of random quotations from Wagner, ironic allusions to the operatic tradition, and the rejection of dominant sexual morality by puppet-like figures made the work highly controversial.

A s a young composer, Hindemith enjoyed provoking his audiences without ever neglecting the precision of his craft. A unique and original organisation of tonal material without breaking with tonality, and the stylistically assured integration of historical forms, are the formal characteristics of his work.

Hindemith, Paul

b. 16 November 1895 in Hanau am Main
d. 28 December 1963 in Frankfurt am Main

After graduating from the Hoch Conservatory in Frankfurt, where he studied composition and counterpoint with Arnold Ludwig Mendelssohn and the violin with Alfred Rebner, Hindemith worked as leader of the Frankfurt Opera orchestra from 1915 to 1923. He played an important part in establishing the music festivals of Donaueschingen and Baden-Baden, and in 1927 was appointed professor of composition at the Berlin Hochschule für Musik. In 1934 he lost this position, and the boycott of his work by the Nazis forced him into exile. After concert tours in the United States he lived for a short while in Switzerland, before settling in the USA in 1940. From 1951 to 1957 he held a professorship at the University of Zürich.

Works: Stage works: *Mörder, Hoffnung der Frauen* (*Murder, Hope of Women*) (1921), *Das Nusch-Nuschi* (*The Nusch-Nuschi*) (1921), *Sancta Susanna* (1922), *Tuttifäntchen* (1922, Darmstadt), *Cardillac* (1926), *Hin und Zurück* (*There and Back*) (1927, Baden-Baden), *Neues vom Tage* (*News of the Day*) (1929, Berlin), *Lehrstück* (*Didactic Play*) (1929, Baden-Baden), *Wir bauen eine Stadt* (*Let's Build a City*) (1930, Berlin), *Mathis der Maler* (*Mathis the Painter*) (1938), *Die Harmonie der Welt* (*Harmony of the World*) (1957, Munich), *The Long Christmas Dinner* (1961, Mannheim); orchestral works, chamber music, songs.

Murder, Hope of Women

Mörder, Hoffnung der Frauen

Opera in one act

Libretto: Oskar Kokoschka.
Première: 4 June 1921, Stuttgart (Württembergisches Landestheater).
Setting: Sloping ground which rises to a tower with a barred iron gate, in antiquity.

Synopsis

Warriors resist the order of their commander to march. A woman and a girl claim the area as their own, and this results in confrontation. The latent tension is discharged in conflict between the protagonists: the man brands the woman, she wounds him with a knife. The warriors lock their leader in the tower. Men and girls enter a state of sexual ecstasy. Only the woman is drawn to the commander: during the act of love the man regains his dominance while the woman becomes weaker. The woman is killed by a push from the man, but as she falls she grabs a torch and sets the place alight. Warriors and girls rush to their leader, who crushes them "like flies." At the first crow of the cock it is he alone who hurries off through the alleyway of fire.   *S. N.*

The Nusch-Nuschi

Play for Burmese marionettes in one act

Libretto: Franz Blei.
Première: 4 June 1921, Stuttgart (Württembergisches Landestheater).
Setting: The lands of the Burmese emperor Mung Tha Bya.

Synopsis

On the orders of his master Zatwai, Tum-Tum is to kidnap a woman from the emperor's harem – but all four women follow him to become Zatwai's lovers. Suspecting something is afoot, Tum-Tum searches for a new master. Kamadewa, the god of desire, predicts good fortune for Tum-Tum because he has helped the emperor's wives to achieve pleasure; he then disappears, leaving the animal he was riding on – Nusch-Nuschi, a creature that is "half rat, half cayman." A drunken general takes fright at Nusch-Nuschi, but Tum-Tum comes to his assistance, and in return is taken into the general's service. The emperor's four wives are enjoying themselves with Zatwai, but a court hearing is convened and Tum-Tum is accused of kidnapping. He pleads that he was obeying the orders of his master – but that now means the general rather than Zatwai. The emperor commands that the general be castrated. Returning empty-handed, the executioner reports that it had already been done. Kamadewa appears in triumph. An old beggar is the only reminder of the transience of earthly love and desire.   *S. N.*

Sancta Susanna

Opera in one act

Libretto: August Stramm, *Sancta Susanna, Ein Gesang der Mainacht* (*Sancta Susanna, A Song of a May Night*).
Première: 26 March 1922, Frankfurt (Opernhaus).
Setting: In a monastery church, on a May night.

Synopsis

Concerned, Sister Klementia observes the young nun Susanna collapsed in front of the altar to the Virgin in a state of prayer-induced ecstasy. The scents and sounds of spring waft in through the window of the church, as do a woman's groans of pleasure. Klementia then recalls a similar spring night, when Sister Beate stripped herself naked and kissed the image of Christ – an act for which she was walled up. Sensual desire awakens in Susanna too. She undresses and removes the loincloth from the statue of Christ. The nuns gather. The sinner demands her own punishment, but then resists the sentence being carried out.   S. N.

Sancta Susanna, production photograph with Beate Blandzija as Susanna, production Siegfried Schoenbohm, conductor Klauspeter Seibel, Oper Kiel 1992.
Even today every performance of *Sancta Susanna* is a challenging undertaking reserved for an audacious few.

Banned operas

August Stramm's *Gesang der Mainacht* (*Song of a May Night*, 1913) tempted Hindemith to write his third short opera which completed his "erotic" triptych. The composition was completed on 5 February 1921, after little more than two weeks' work. In free harmony, reminiscent of Debussy, Hindemith arranged his material around a symmetrical axis: the musical motif of a cross. The work was felt to be so shocking at its première that the Catholic Women's Union established a vigil for penance, and various organisations held public talks on promoting morality. Alexander Zemlinsky's successful staging in Prague in 1923 did nothing to modify the hostility of the public and the Church. In 1958 Hindemith withdrew all three works. *M 1*   *M. S.*

1. Susanna's Ecstasy

So hel - - fe mir mein Hei - land ge - gen den eu - - ren.

News of the Day

Neues vom Tage

Comic opera in three parts

Libretto: Marcellus Schiffer.
Premiere: First version (described here): 8 June 1929, Berlin (Krolloper); second version, in two acts, translated by Rinaldo Küfferle as *Novità del giorno*: 7 April 1954, Naples (Teatro San Carlo).

Characters: Laura (S), Eduard (Bar), The Handsome Herr Hermann (T), Herr M. (T), Frau M. (Ms), a Hotel Manager (B), a Registrar (B), a Tour Guide (B), a Chamber Maid (S), a Head Waiter (T), Six Managers (2 T, 2 Bar, 2 B); chorus.

Synopsis

Laura and Eduard want a divorce and hire "the handsome Herr Hermann" to provide the necessary pretext, but Eduard forgets his role and attacks Hermann. The case causes a furore. To pay the fine, Eduard and Laura act out scenes from their marriage for money in cinemas, circuses, theaters and variety clubs, in the course of which they become reconciled. But they are doomed to remain what they always have been and what they were made to be: a quarelling couple.   S. N.

Topical opera

First performed in 1929 in the legendary Krolloper under the conductor Otto Klemperer, *News of the Day* belongs to the "topical opera" genre. The subject of the work is the power of the press and the helplessness of love turning sour within the confines of marriage. Tragicomic attempts at liberation are acted out, as are the absurd entanglements that result. According to the famous musicologist Alfred Einstein in 1929, the work was a case of "topical art" and "eternal art" coming up against each other.

Below left
News of the Day, production photograph with Karan Armstrong (Laura) and Andrzej Dobber (Eduard), production Günter Krämer, conductor Manfred Mayrhofer, Oper Köln 1999.
With its polished, witty libretto, well-written and amusing music, and its ever relevant themes Hindemith's opera has attracted directors such as Günter Krämer, who has made a name for himself by his consistently startling and intelligent productions.

Cardillac

Opera in three acts (four scenes)/ in four acts

Libretto: First version: Ferdinand Lion, after E.T.A. Hoffman's story *Das Fräulein von Scuderi* (*Mademoiselle de Scudéry*); second version: Paul Hindemith, after Lion. **Première:** First version: 9 November 1926, Dresden (Sächsisches Staatstheater, Opernhaus); second version: 20 June 1952, Zürich (Stadttheater).
Characters in the first version: Cardillac, a goldsmith (Bar), His Daughter (S), An Officer (T), The Gold Merchant (B), A Cavalier (T), A Lady (S), The Leader of the Prévôté (high B), The King (silent), The Prévôté; cavaliers and ladies of the court (silent); crowd (chorus).
Characters in the second version: Cardillac, a famous goldsmith (Bar), His Daughter (S), His Servant (T), An Opera Singer (S), An Officer (B), A Young Cavalier (T); characters in Jean-Baptiste Lully's opera *Phaéton*: Clymène (A), Phaéton (T), Le Soleil (B); The Rich Marquis (silent); singers, dancers, theater staff, crowd, guards (chorus).
Setting: Paris, the end of the 17th century.

Synopsis (first version)
Act I

Scene 1: A square in Paris. The citizens of Paris have been shaken by a series of murders. The victims are all customers of the famous goldsmith Cardillac. A lady is so fascinated by his artworks that she will only give herself to a suitor if he brings her a piece from Cardillac's workshop.
Scene 2: The lady's bedroom. Overcoming his fear, the Cavalier has purchased a piece of valuable jewelry and brings it to his lover: as he embraces her, he is stabbed by a masked man.

Act II

Cardillac's workshop. Cardillac's gold merchant suspects a connection between the goldsmith and the mysterious murderer. Frightened and mistrustful he visits his client, but Cardillac is not happy with his gold and goes off to look for new material to work with. Cardillac's daughter loves an officer but cannot make up her mind to leave her father and follow him. The king and the court pay Cardillac a visit and admire his jewelry. At first Cardillac is proud and feels flattered, but he subsequently becomes increasingly rude and abrupt, and eventually throws the king and his entourage out. Left on his own, he admits that he would have had to kill the king if he had bought anything. Cardillac light-heartedly gives the officer permission to marry his daughter. But when the officer snatches a gold chain from him, throws the money down on the table and leaves, Cardillac hurries after him in order to retrieve the piece of jewelry.

Act III

A street at night. The officer has made sure he is prepared for an attack and successfully fends off Cardillac's attempt at murder. The gold merchant

Cardillac, set design by Theo Lau for the production by R. Schubert, Musiktheater im Revier, Gelsenkirchen 1964 (TWS). Lynch law: the murderer is about to be punished at the hands of the crowd (second version). The opera *Cardillac* is dominated by an atmosphere of impending catastrophe which was "translated" into Expressionist imagery in the set design. Its tilting and collapsing streets are the very picture of a city lacking stability or security. The set was an allusion to the time of the opera's composition (the 1920s), but it also borrowed from the style of contemporary German Expressionist cinema.

has observed the incident and sounds the alarm. Cardillac flees. The police arrive and a crowd gathers. The merchant names Cardillac as the murderer, but the officer directs suspicion at the accuser himself: the merchant is arrested. Cardillac's daughter confesses the truth to the officer. The crowd celebrates the arrest of the supposed murderer and praises Cardillac. But the goldsmith's speech is strange; he becomes somewhat entangled in contradictions when answering questions, and finally reveals himself to be the murderer. He is lynched by the mob.

Synopsis (second version)

The scenes are slightly different. A man has been stabbed in front of Cardillac's house. An officer calms the enraged crowd. In spite of the threatening rumors, a singer asks her lover for a diadem made by Cardillac. He brings it to her, but as they embrace he is stabbed by a masked man and the diadem is seized.

Cardillac's servant woos the daughter of his master in vain. The servant suspects the truth and believes that Cardillac is the murderer, yet he himself is suspected and arrested.

An opera company is looking for jewelry for a performance of Jean-Baptiste Lully's opera *Phaéton* and finds what it requires at Cardillac's workshop. The singer recognises her diadem and chooses it for the performance.

The servant escapes from prison. During the performance of *Phaéton*, officers and the servant observe the events on stage from behind the scenes. The servant warns the singer about Cardillac, but she feels sorry for the goldsmith and gives him back the diadem after the performance. The officer seizes it from him. Cardillac attacks the officer at the stage exit but is restrained by the servant. Cardillac manages to flee, and the servant is now arrested as the murderer. In the meantime, the singer has taken the diadem and given it to Cardillac's daughter as a wedding present. When Cardillac sees the diadem on his daughter he is beside himself; he reveals himself to be the murderer and is killed by the enraged crowd.   *S. N.*

A subject of revision and criticism

In revising his opera after the second world war, Hindemith distanced himself from the possibility of any empathy for the murderer. He condensed the relationships, concentrated on logical characterization, and, above all, he "modernized" the characters: the king became a marquis, the lady a singer. The performance of Lully's *Phaéton* in the context of the opera was a masterful *coup*, which provided for a "stage within a stage." The audience is treated to the film-like effect of witnessing a murder about to happen on stage: there is no camera to be sure, but the end result is nonetheless just as convincing. Hindemith also reduced the percussion section, as well as arranging the vocal parts more melodically, though without losing sight of his original score. Of the 18 numbers from the first version, he retained 14.

The work was extremely well received at the time of its première, but after 1953 Hindemith would approve no further performances of the first version. It was not until much later that the second, revised version was widely accepted, and even then it failed to attain the same popularity as its forerunner.   *M. S.*

Cardillac, set design by Ludwig Sievert for the production by Hans Esdra, Opernhaus Frankfurt 1928 (TWS).
A murder attempt: Cardillac and the officer outside the tavern (first version). E.T.A. Hoffmann's crime story *Das Fräulein von Scuderi* (*Mademoiselle de Scudéry*) fascinated writers and composers alike. Lucien Dautresme had already composed an opera on the theme, which was premièred in Paris in 1823, and Mario Cesarini filmed Hoffmann's tale in 1911. In accordance with the story's setting, Hindemith restored the musical vocabulary of the 18th century. He made use of the traditional "number opera" format, arranged the material of the work by key, combined both complex and simple structures, and reduced the orchestra. Although he retained the large percussion section, the wind instruments perform in solo pieces, and the strings are used only sparingly.

Cardillac, production photograph with Doris Soffel, production and sets Jean-Pierre Ponnelle, conductor Wolfgang Sawallisch, Bayerische Staatsoper, Munich 1985.
In the lady's bedroom (Act I, Scene 2) the lover looks forward to an amorous rendezvous, but in fact meets his death at the hands of a murderer. The threatening mood of the work was conveyed by the sharply pitching vertical lines of Jean-Pierre Ponelle's sets.

Mathis the Painter

Mathis der Maler

Opera in seven scenes

Libretto: Paul Hindemith.
Première: 28 May 1938, Zürich (Stadttheater).
Characters: Cardinal Albrecht von Brandenburg, Archbishop of Mainz (T), Mathis, a painter in his service (Bar), Lorenz von Pommersfelden, dean of Mainz Cathedral (B), Wolfgang Capito, the cardinal's counsellor (T), Riedinger, a wealthy citizen of Mainz (B), Hans Schwalb, leader of the rebellious peasants (T), Truchsess von Waldburg, an army commander (B), Sylvester von Schaumberg, one of his officers (T), Count Helfenstein (silent), The Count's Piper (T), Four Peasants (2 T, 2 B), Ursula, Riedinger's daughter (S), Regina, Schwalb's daughter (S), Countess Helfenstein (A); Catholic and Lutheran citizens, peasants, mercenaries, students, brothers of the Order of St. Anthony, demons (chorus).
Setting: Mainz, Königshofen, the castle of Martinsburg, and the Odenwald forest in the 1520s, during the Peasants' Revolt.

Synopsis

Confronted with the misery of war during the Counter-Reformation, the painter Mathis joins the peasants. In spite of temptations, he does not abandon his art. After the completion of the Isenheim altarpiece and the death of his beloved Regina, a peasant girl, Mathis himself reaches the end of his life.

Scene 1

The monastery of the Order of St. Anthony in Mainz. The wounded peasant leader Schwalb seeks refuge with his daughter in a monastery, the cloister of which is being decorated by the painter Mathis. The monks tend to Schwalb's wounds and Mathis becomes attracted to Regina. When soldiers arrive at the monastery, Mathis gives the peasant leader his horse so that he can escape. The military commander threatens to lodge a complaint with Mathis's master, Cardinal Albrecht.

Scene 2

A hall in the Martinsburg castle in Mainz. The dispute between Catholic and Lutheran citizens is brought to an end by Cardinal Albrecht. Mathis has returned to his employer and is greeted with joy by Ursula Riedinger, who is in love with him. Her wealthy father promises Albrecht financial assistance to promote the arts if he is able to prevent a planned book burning. But the liberal Albrecht is overruled by the dogmatic dean of the cathedral. Mathis is accused of supporting the enemy, but thanks to Albrecht he escapes punishment. Albrecht asks only that Mathis live for his art. Convinced by the peasants' cause, however, Mathis quits the cardinal's service.

Scene 3

Riedinger's house on the market place in Mainz. Riedinger's hidden books are discovered and taken away to be burned. Albrecht's counsellor Capito advises him to convert to Protestantism, so as to be able to pay off his debts; a marriage with Ursula Riedinger would then be possible. But Ursula loves Mathis. Mathis however rejects the bourgeois life, preferring to fight for the downtrodden.

Scene 4

Königshofen, a small square with damaged houses. The peasants have taken over in Königshofen; they murder the count and humiliate his wife. Mathis argues with the peasants over their violent behavior. Schwalb, accompanied by Regina, calls the peasants to order: it is not Mathis who is the enemy but the approaching army. The peasants lose the battle, Schwalb is killed, and Mathis escapes execution only through the intervention of the countess. He leaves the battlefield with Regina.

Scene 5

The cardinal's study in the castle of Martinsburg. Albrecht cannot agree to a marriage for purely material reasons. When Ursula Riedinger attempts to convert him to Protestantism, he recognises that she is not acting out of love for him, but out of a profound faith. He decides to remain true to his own beliefs.

Scene 6

The Odenwald forest, a region with massive trees; the last rays of the sun. Distressed by the horrors she has witnessed, Regina is unable to sleep. Mathis tells her a story of angels playing music. Reality and fantasy merge as Mathis experiences in a vision the temptations of St. Anthony. Albrecht appears as St. Paul, and encourages Mathis to return to his creative life.

Scene 7

Mathis's workshop in Mainz; night. Mathis has just completed the Isenheim altarpiece when Regina, who has been cared for by Ursula, dies. Her death is a signal to Mathis of his own impending end. He rejects a face-saving invitation from Cardinal Albrecht and begins to put his meagre possessions in order.   M. S.

Costume design with a motif from the Isenheim altarpiece by Charlotte Vocke, Gelsenkirchen 1952 (TWS).
Little is known of the life and work of the painter of the Isenheim altarpiece, Matthias Grünewald (orginally Mathis Gothart Nithart). He was probably born around 1480 in Würzburg, and was for a time in the service of Albrecht of Brandenburg in Mainz-Aschaffenburg. He painted the magnificent winged Isenheim altarpiece for a monastery church before the advent of the Reformation. The Order of St. Anthony resident in Mainz claimed a number of cures for erysipelas (also known as "St. Anthony's fire"), a highly dangerous infection in the Middle Ages. Grünewald was a contemporary of Albrecht Dürer and Lucas Cranach the Elder. He died in 1528.

Mathis the Painter, production photograph with Jorma Hynninen as Mathis, production Götz Friedrich, sets and costumes Peter Sykora, conductor Jiri Kout, Deutsche Oper, Berlin 1993.
The fundamental idea behind the work and behind Götz Friedrich's production is that Mathis is a painter who is both a creator and a creature acting within a certain self-defined world of images. This same world is also a reaction to the chaos that surrounds him in everyday life.

Hindemith's "Ars poetica"

After several failed attempts to use the works of well-known writers as the basis for his libretto, Hindemith wrote his own text, at first concentrating on the figure of the 15th-century printer Johann Gutenberg. Not until after Hitler came to power did he turn to the Mathis theme, completing the first draft of the libretto in September 1933; the first sections to be completed were the prelude and interludes, which were premièred in 1934 as the symphony *Mathis der Maler*, conducted by Wilhelm Furtwängler. After re-working the libretto several times he completed the score on 27 July 1935. *Mathis* is one of Hindemith's most important works and is based on a profound examination of the role of the artist in society. Hindemith organized the opera with the aid of Baroque forms such as the chaconne or concerto grosso. Modal passages (with original quotations from the *Altdeutschen Liederbuch*, the *Old German Songbook*, edited by Böhme in 1877) are integrated whole into his expanded tonality. The prelude to the opera, with its quotation from the song "Es sungen drei Engel" ("There sang three angels"), achieved particular popularity. Linear melodies and an easily comprehensible libretto contributed the work's popular appeal, although its success was initially hindered by its suppression under the Nazis. M 2   M. S.

Mathis the Painter, production photograph with Hubert Hofmann as Mathis, production Oscar Fritz Schuh, conductor Hans Schmidt, Hamburgische Staatsoper 1967.
The difficulty in staging this conceptually and musically important work consists in portraying a medieval painter executing his art. A similar problem exists in Puccini's →*Tosca*. Hindemith's notion of the artist as prophet often leads singers to adopt a missionary-like stance, but this is to obscure the composer's intention. What Hindemith had in mind was the responsibility of the modern individual for his own actions.

2. "There Sang Three Angels"

Mathis the Painter, production photograph with Jorma Hynninen as Mathis, production Götz Friedrich, sets and costumes Peter Sykora, conductor Jiri Kout, Deutsche Oper, Berlin 1990.
The hero is pictured here in front of his painting. The correspondence between the painter and the figure on the canvas symbolizes Hindemith's concept of the truth of artistic creation – as does the interplay of costumes, set design, and direction.

Mathis the Painter, set design by Heinz Grete for a production by Rudolf Hartmann, conductor Alfons Dressel, Städtische Bühnen, Nuremberg 1951 (TWS).
A number of scenes in *Mathis* seem more like legend than reality, and lend the opera an oratorio-like quality. At the time *Mathis the Painter* was being composed and first performed, other prominent composers such as Schoenberg, Bartók, Stravinsky, and Honegger were reminding audiences of their duty to humanity through compelling oratorios. Their music aimed to create a unity out of the disparate elements of nature – God, humanity, and art.

Hölszky, Adriana

b. 30 June 1953 in Bucharest

A Romanian German born in Bucharest, Adriana Hölszky studied composition with Stefan Niculescu at the Bucharest School of Music. After settling in West Germany in 1976 she became a pupil of the renowned Yugoslavian avant-garde composer Milko Kelemen in Stuttgart and studied electronic music under Erhard Karkoschka. Between 1977 and 1980 she was a concert pianist in the Lipati Trio, founded by Antonio Janigro, during which time the trio won prizes at international chamber music competitions in Florence (1978) and Colmar (1980). Composition and chamber music courses at Siena, Darmstadt, Salzburg, Bayreuth, and Cambril brought her recognition. Amongst the awards she has received is the highly regarded Rome Prize of the Villa Massimo in 1992. In 1980 Hölszky became a teacher of music theory and aural development at the Hochschule für Musik in Stuttgart. As a composer she takes full advantage of her background as an Eastern European raised in a multilingual and multicultural environment: her music is characterized by an openness to contemporary styles, as well as a great sensitivity toward the varying depths of language. She works with sonority, noise, and electronic sampling techniques such as serialism, at which she is highly talented and which she is able to use in an imaginative and humorous way. Her breakthrough came in 1988 with the première of her "song-work on a woman's life," *Bremer Freiheit*, at the Munich Biennale, a festival initiated and directed by →Hans Werner Henze. Adriana Hölszky's works can be heard at the most important international music festivals, and she holds seminars in composition all over the world (for example, in Tokyo, Kyoto, and at the Paris IRCAM in 1992, in Athens and in Boston in 1994). In 1998 she was appointed director of composition at the Hochschule für Musik und Theater in Rostock.

Works: Operas: *Bremer Freiheit* (*Bremen Freedom*) (1988), *Die Wände* (*The Walls*) (1995), *Der Aufstieg der Titanik* (*The Rise of the Titanic*) (tragedy, 1997), *Der Unsichtbare Raum* (*The Invisible Room*) (1997); orchestral works, chamber music, vocal compositions.

Bremen Freedom

Song-work on a woman's life

Libretto: Thomas Körner after the play by Rainer Werner Fassbinder.
Première: 4 June 1988, Munich (Biennale, by the ensemble of the Stuttgart opera).
Characters: Geesche Gottfried (Ms), Miltenberger, her first husband (Bar), Timm, her father (B), Geesche's mother (A), Gottfried, her second husband (T), Johann, her brother (Bar), Zimmermann, a friend (T), Rumpf, a friend (T), Father Markus (B), Bohm, a cousin (Bar), Luisa Mauer, a friend (S).
Setting: Germany, in the present day.

Synopsis

Geesche lives a normal woman's life, is humiliated and blackmailed by her husbands, and regarded as a tool by her father, mother, and brother. She is plagued by her children and female friends, and exploited by her male friends. She sets out to establish some order in her life. One after the other they all die: husbands, children, father, mother, brother, friends. Then poison is discovered in her coffee – and it is Geesche's turn to die.   S. N.

Bremen Freedom, photograph from the original production by Christian Kohlmann, sets and costumes Birgit Angele, conductor Andras Hamary, Munich 1988.
Both musical and dramatic actions are revealed as linked events that condition one another; this corresponds to the composer's own ideas of "associative sound motifs" and "imaginary actions in sound."

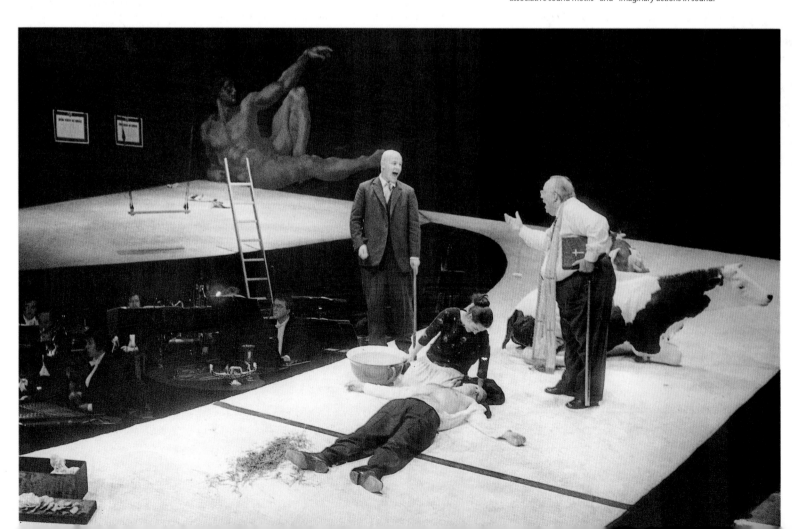

"Radicalist"

The subtitle "Song-work on a woman's life" is an allusion to one of the shrines of bourgeois sentimentality, Robert Schumann's *Frauenliebe und -leben* (*Life and Loves of a Woman*) after Adalbert Chamisso, a hymn to those wives who selflessly served the husbands to whom they had been entrusted. Ironically it was Chamisso himself who wrote the epitaph for the historical figure of Geesche: "I waged war, as everyone should and does, on hostile powers. I only did what you all do." The idea of a private war in the form of acts of crime against a society which was itself seen as criminal is familiar enough from Kleist's *Michael Kohlhaas*, Dostoyevsky's *Raskolnikov*, and Charlie Chaplin's film *Monsieur Verdoux*. Fassbinder and Hölszky merely presented the female version of the story. The real Geesche was beheaded in 1831 on Bremen's cathedral square, and until 1932 the worthy citizens of Bremen would spit in moral outrage on the stone onto which her head had fallen – until one night an anti-fascist trickster blocked off the cross chiselled into the stone with heavy wooden beams. Only then was the offensive item removed – after a century of male indignation.

Opera in the style of a telegram

Hölszky's "song-work" is in the tradition of the Grand Guignol, the Paris theater famous for its horror plays. In the space of ten short scenes, nine murders take place, one after the other, without any detailed psychological explanation. When Geesche is finally led away, she simply remarks: "Now I'm about to die," and sings the chorale "Welt, ade – ich bin dein müde" ("Adieu, world – I am weary of you") which she has already sung nine times, once for each of her victims. Hölszky works with associative sound motifs: "falling chains" for Geesche, an alarm bell for her father, "a lion's roar" for her first husband, and the sound of a toy trumpet for her brother. There are "imaginary actions in sound" (even the instrumentalists are to sing, growl, and make comments and various other acoustic contributions, in order to achieve a distancing effect), overlapping layers, composed aural surfaces, a percussion that creaks and cracks, and sounds which oscillate. The mixture of the frightful and the faithful, horror and cheerfulness, succeeds brilliantly, avoiding any trace of sentimentality or hypocrisy in its depiction of distorted relationships – something that has been a characteristic of modern opera since Alban Berg's legendary →*Wozzeck* of 1925.

The original production of the work (directed by Christian Kohlmann and conducted by Andras Hamary) was restaged at the Vienna Festival in 1989 and at the Helsinki Festival in 1991. Bremen finally gave its own production in 1994.

No literary operas

Thomas Körner is the ideal librettist. He adapted a play by Jakob Lenz for Friedrich Goldmann's opera *Hot* in 1973, and undertook librettos for →Paul Dessau's 1978 version of Georg Büchner's *Leonce and Lena* as well as

for →Mauricio Kagel before joining forces with Adriana Hölszky. The literary origins of the Körner's librettos are present only in their titles, so that the music can take on its own unique dimension. This was certainly the case with Hölszky's opera *The Walls*, adapted from Jean Genet's 1961 novel *Les paravents* and first performed in 1995 at the Theater an der Wien under the director Hans Neuenfels, with the conductor Ulf Schirmer and designer Reinhard von der Thannen. Once again the work was an enormous success, and even went on to be staged by the city of Oldenburg's small opera company in 1996. The opera tells the story of the Arab Said in a distorted colonial world; as an anarchistic loner, Said seeks to shatter the order of the dead, and finds himself as a result caught between two fronts (the walls of the title), becoming first a victim, and then a villain.

Opera without singers

The "tragedy" *The Invisible Room*, commissioned by the Oper der Stadt Bonn and first performed there in 1997, is an opera without singers: "The work seeks to foreground events in sound." In 1984 Luigi Nono had declared an absolute ban on images for his "tragedy of hearing" →*Prometheus*, and in this spirit Adriana Hölszky banned singers from her stage, in order to transform the tragedy of everyday events into something the audience must simply listen for. Director Hans Neuenfels had the following comment to make: "Hölszky's music, her capacity to 'listen for,' smooths nothing out, beautifies nothing, waters nothing down, and overtrumps nothing: the hissing cat plays on the same level as the howling dog." S. N.

The Walls, production photograph with Helmut Wildheber (Si Slimane), Elisabeth Reichardt (Arabic mourner), and Jutta Geister (prostitute), all seated at the front, production Hans Neuenfels, sets and costumes Reinhard von der Thannen, conductor Ulf Schirmer, Theater an der Wien 1995.
Adriana Hölszky's adaptation of Jean Genet's play *The Walls* marked her international breakthrough: the opera was staged by the innovative director Hans Neuenfels.

*H*ölszky takes thought patterns and stylistic conventions to paradoxical extremes, a tendency that has been described as "radicalist." Her material blends humor with the thrills of crime, and is concerned with the private transgressions of everyday conflicts on the brink of the 21st century.

Honegger, Arthur

b. 10 March 1892 in Le Havre
d. 27 November 1955 in Paris

Honegger was a Swiss citizen of German descent, who, after studying in Zürich and Le Havre, spent most of his life in Paris. Here together with →Milhaud, Auric, →Poulenc, Durey, and Tailleferre he was a member of the group known as "Les Six," whose spokesman was the poet Jean Cocteau. Honegger was a conductor and accompanist, critic and publisher, composition teacher and composer. Of his 186 pieces, 33 were for film and as many again for radio plays and the stage. He first achieved international recognition in 1921 with a stage presentation of an oratorio *Le roi David* (*King David*) and then again in 1923 with the seven-minute symphonic piece *Pacific 231*. In addition to the five great symphonies written between 1930 and 1951, he considered his *Antigone* from 1927 to be his greatest achievement. It nevertheless proved to be less popular than the dramatic oratorio *Jeanne d'Arc au bûcher* (*Joan of Arc at the Stake*).

Works: Opera: *Judith* (1925), *Antigone* (1927), *Le roi David* (*King David*) (stage presentation of an oratorio, 1921), *Jeanne d'Arc au bûcher* (*Joan of Arc at the Stake*) (dramatic oratorio, 1935); operettas, including *Les aventures du roi Pausole* (*The Adventures of King Pausole*) (1930); music for plays, choral works, works for orchestra and piano, chamber music, and five symphonies.

Judith

Opéra sérieux in three acts

Libretto: René Morax.
Première: First version: 11 June 1925, Mézières im Waadt (Théâtre du Jorat); second version: 13 February 1926, Monte Carlo (Opéra).

Characters: Judith, an Israelite (Ms), Her Servant (S), Holopherne/Holofernes, an Assyrian general (Bar), Bagoas, his servant (B), Ozias, governor of the Judaic fortress of Bethul (Bar), A Guard (T), A Soldier (T), Three Voices (S, T, Bar), Female Slave (dancer); women, people and soldiers of Bethul, an Assyrian leader, soldiers, priests (chorus); crowd, soldiers (speaking chorus).
Setting: Bethul at the time of the conquest of Nebuchadnezzar II.

Synopsis

Bethul is besieged by a powerful Assyrian army under Holofernes. The people of Bethul are prepared to surrender, but still hope for a miracle from God. The Israelite Judith decides to make her way into the encampment of the enemy, trusting in God to save her. After various challenges she finally succeeds in killing the drunken Holofernes in his sleep. She is acclaimed by her people as their savior, and together they sing a song of praise to the Almighty.

S. N.

Biblical opera
Honegger took up the biblical idea of a self-sustaining event that occurs when people step beyond their own limits and manifest divine strength. This notion applies to the people of Bethul in this opera as well as to Judith herself. The musical focus of the work is formed by the impressive choral sections, on account of which this adaptation of the Judith story has been described as an "operatic oratorio."

Honegger's genius "felt itself drawn to music that was related to the craftsmanship of the cathedral and the factory. In his work, the world of machines alternates with that of altarpieces, buttresses, and church windows." (Jean Cocteau)

Judith, production photograph with William Oberholtzer (Holofernes) and Susan Maclean (Judith), production Elmar Fulda, conductor Lukas Höfling, sets and costumes Ruth Schaefer, Theater Bielefeld 1995.
Honegger's "biblical opera" has again and again proved itself to be an opera that speaks to our own time. The opera does not attempt to illustrate the story told in the Bible, but rather investigates the way a person can develop and retain inner strength despite being overwhelmed by circumstances. Thus Holofernes appears both as a real person and as a metaphor for violence.

Antigone

Tragédie musicale in three acts

Libretto: Jean Cocteau.
Première: 28 December 1927, Brussels (Théâtre de la Monnaie).

Characters: Antigone (A or Ms), Ismène/Ismene, her sister (S), Créon/Creon, King of Thebes (T), Eurydice, his wife (Ms), Hémon/Haemon, his son, in love with Antigone (Bar), Tirésias/Tiresias (B), A Guard (T), A Messenger (B), Four Leaders of the Chorus (S, A, T, B); people of Thebes (chorus).
Setting: Thebes, in mythological times.

Synopsis

In spite of their good intentions, Oedipus's sons quarrel over the throne, Polynices allying himself with the enemies of Thebes in order to topple Eteocles. Both brothers fall in battle. Oedipus's brother-in-law seizes the vacant throne and forbids the burial of the traitor Polynices on pain of death. But his sister Antigone places love and humanity above Creon's reasons of state, and buries her brother. For this she must die, and Creon, impervious to the pleas of his own son Haemon, who is in love with Antigone, has her walled up alive. Not until the visionary Tiresias curses him does Creon have second thoughts, but it is too late: his son has hanged himself next to the body of his beloved, and his wife Eurydice has also commited suicide. *S. N.*

Hidden emotions

In 1922 Jean Cocteau staged a version of the Antigone story in his famous "dramaturgie simple" at the Théâtre de l'Atelier; this production caused a sensation, and not only in artistic circles: the emotional coolness of his interpretation allowed a more intimate contact with the ancient source material which, because of its theme of the conflict between love and duty to the state, was highly relevant at the time. Honegger developed his dramaturgical structure, a symphonic opposition of musical themes and motifs, from the underlying polarity between Antigone and Creon. *Antigone* was staged in Essen just weeks after its première in 1927, where it caused a scandal, as it did again in 1954. This work has appeared a number of times in the international repertoire – for example, in a production in 1961 in Hamburg, with Helga Pilarczyk in the title role. *S. N.*

Joan of Arc at the Stake

Jeanne d'Arc au bûcher

Dramatic oratorio with a prologue and 11 scenes

Libretto: Paul Claudel.

Première: Concert première: 12 May 1938, Basel (Grosser Musiksaal); stage première: 13 June 1942, Zürich (Stadttheater).

Setting: Rouen, 30 May 1431.

Synopsis

Joan of Arc is shown at the moment of her death in the flames. Entering into a dialogue with St. Dominic and the Virgin Mary the spirit of the girl returns to examine incidents from her life. Joan recognizes the nature of the world and frees herself from all earthly bonds.   *S. N.*

Oratorio or opera?

Joan of Arc at the Stake is, in fact, a mixture of drama, opera, and oratorio. At the beginning of the German occupation of France it was an immediate success; from 1941 it was performed in over 40 cities by an ensemble that was especially formed for the purpose. One of Honegger's greatest achievements was the integration of the speaking voice into the musical flow of events. The inclusion of three saxophones, various types of clarinet, and the ondes martenot in the orchestral section is also unusual. Honegger's dramatic oratorio is now a standard with larger opera companies. The German première took place in Berlin in 1947. Roberto Rossellini's production at the Teatro San Carlo in Naples in 1950, with Ingrid Bergman in the title role, caused a sensation (conductor Gianandrea Gavazzeni). A 1984 production in Munich, with Andrea Jonasson as Joan, was also a great success (director August Everding, conductor Silvio Varviso). Of all the adaptations of the Joan of Arc story, that of Arthur Honegger has a special quality which can be felt in all its productions, however much they may vary: at the moment of death the truth of a life becomes apparent, and the act of dying becomes the last great attempt to lend expression to this truth.   *S. N.*

Above
Joan of Arc at the Stake, set design by Paul Haferung, Essen 1948 (TWS).
Honegger's *Joan* as a type of mystery play: in post-war Germany, this uncompromisingly antifascist opera must surely have been seen as the promise of redemption.

Left
Joan of Arc at the Stake, production photograph with Inge Lange as Joan, production Rudolf Kempe, conductor Arthur Honegger, Bayerische Staatsoper, Munich 1953.
With Inge Lange as Joan, the Munich production became a superb theatrical event.

Right
Joan of Arc at the Stake, production photograph with Ingrid Bergman as Joan, production Roberto Rossellini, Teatro San Carlo, Naples 1950.
The film director and his female protagonist created unforgettable scenes from one of the great themes of European art: the re-examination of one's life from the standpoint of imminent death.

Below
Roberto Rossellini and Ingrid Bergman, Teatro San Carlo, Naples 1950.

Bottom
Joan of Arc at the Stake, set design by Heinz Dahm, Saarbrücken 1961 (TWS).
In 1961 it was not only the antifascist aspect of the opera that was considered interesting, but also the resistance to seemingly all-powerful institutions such as the church.

In the face of death

Honegger's *Joan of Arc at the Stake* has become a favorite in theaters all over the world, in spite of its unusual genre. One of the reasons why *Joan* has fascinated actresses such as Ingrid Bergman and directors like Roberto Rossellini is the central theme of the work: the idea of recalling one's entire life at the moment of death is one of the oldest themes in European art. This dramatic moment usually provides an opportunity to reflect upon the various phases of one's life. Honegger approaches this issue quite differently. At the moment of death life expresses itself only in order to free itself from all earthly shackles. The moment of death becomes a heroic deed, before which all the military victories of this resolute and courageous girl pale. *S. N.*

Hansel and Gretel, postcard.
The date of its première (23 December 1893) explains why *Hansel and Gretel* is traditionally staged as a Christmas fairy tale and therefore as "entertainment for the entire family." The opera's plot and its memorable words and melodies do indeed appeal greatly to children. *Hansel and Gretel* seemed to provide Humperdinck with an opportunity to be something other than a mere imitator – a means of finding his own path and avoiding being overshadowed by the figure of Richard Wagner. *Hansel and Gretel* was an alternative both to Wagner's dramas and to Italian *verismo* (Alexander Ritter, Ludwig Thuille, and Wagner's son Siegfried were also exponents of the operatic fairy tale), and it was for this reason that it found acceptance amongst the most prominent conductors of the day. The première in Weimar was conducted by Richard Strauss, and Felix Mottl, Hermann Levi, and Gustav Mahler came to be fond of driving the orchestra in "The Ride of the Witches." The great conductors who succeeded them (such as Karajan and Solti) also included *Hansel and Gretel* in their repertory.

Humperdinck, Engelbert

b. 1 September 1854 in Siegburg (Rhineland)
d. 27 September 1921 in Neustrelitz (Mecklenburg)

The son of a school headmaster, Humperdinck learned to play the piano at an early age. His gift for composition was already evident at the age of 14, but in spite of this his parents insisted that he study architecture. From 1872 he began music studies at Cologne Conservatory (composition, piano, cello, and organ); in 1874 he destroyed most of his juvenilia. His professional confidence was bolstered by receiving several prizes in composition competitions, and by winning a Mozart scholarship under Joseph Rheinberger and Franz Lachner. He undertook a study tour of Italy, where he met Richard Wagner, later helping him in his preparations for the première of →*Parsifal* in Bayreuth (1881–82). His international breakthrough came in 1893 with *Hänsel und Gretel* (*Hansel and Gretel*). His second great success was achieved when the fairy-tale opera *Die Königskinder* (*The King's Children*) was staged at the Metropolitan Opera in New York in 1910. He held teaching posts in various countries and at a number of institutions, and was a critic for newspapers in Bonn and Frankfurt. In 1900 he settled in Berlin where as a highly regarded professor of composition and a member of the Academy of Arts he received international recognition and acclaim.

Works: Hänsel und Gretel (*Hansel and Gretel*) (1893), *Die Sieben Geisslein* (*The Seven Little Kids*) (1895), *Die Königskinder* (*The King's Children*) (as melodrama 1897, as operatic fairy tale 1910), *Dornröschen* (*Sleeping Beauty*) (1902), *Die Heirat wider Willen* (*The Reluctant Marriage*) (1905), *Bübchens Weihnachtstraum* (*The Christmas Dream*) (musical nativity play, 1906), *Die Marketenderin* (*The Vivandière*) (1914), *Gaudeamus: Szenen aus dem deutschen Studentenleben* (*Gaudeamus: Scenes from German Studentlife*) (1919); choral works, songs, music for plays, orchestral works, chamber music.

1. Dance-song (Hänsel and Gretel)

Brü - der-chen, komm tanz mit mir, bei - de Händ-chen reich ich dir,

ein - mal hin, ein - mal her, rund her-um, es ist nicht schwer!

2. Gretel's Evening Prayer

A - bends, will ich schla - fen gehn, vier-zehn En - gel um mich stehn

Hansel and Gretel

Fairy tale in three acts

Libretto: Adelheid Wette, after the fairy tale of the same name by the Brothers Grimm.
Première: 23 December 1893, Weimar (Hoftheater).
Characters: Peter, a broom-maker (Bar), Gertrud, his wife (Ms), Hansel and Gretel, their children (Ms and S), Sandman (S), Dew Fairy (S), Gingerbread Witch (Ms or T), Echo (4 S, 2 A); cake children (children's chorus); 14 angels (ballet).
Place and time: That of fairy tale.

Synopsis
Scene 1: A small, humble room in the house of the broom-maker. The mother and father are out searching for money and food. The children are supposed to be making themselves useful by darning stockings and making new brooms. But Hansel and Gretel are hungry, their only comfort being a pot of milk, which is to be used for a rice dish. Full of anticipation, they tumble about and forget their work. The mother returns home tired and empty-handed and sees the work undone; she scolds the children and reaches for the broom in order to punish them. In doing so she knocks the milk from the table. She sends the children into the forest to pick strawberries, telling them not to return home until the basket is full. The father has been more fortunate and returns drunk but laden with groceries. But the children are in danger from the Gingerbread Witch from Ilsenstein. The parents rush into the forest to find them.

Hansel and Gretel, production photograph with Nigel Robson as the witch, production Richard Jones, sets John MacFarlane, conductor Vladimir Yurovsky, Welsh National Opera, Cardiff 1999.
The witch: a bizarre part for a mezzo-soprano – and a wonderful opportunity for a comic tenor!

Scene 2: A forest with Ilsenstein in the background. While looking for berries the children have wandered close to the witch's lair. Hansel's basket is full, and Gretel has woven a wreath of flowers: the children begin to play again. Time passes, it becomes dark. Hansel has forgotten the way home. All of a sudden the beautiful, cozy forest seems threatening and full of danger. The children seek shelter under a tree. The sandman brings them sleep while 14 angels watch over them.

Scene 3: The dew fairy wakes the children. They are hungry again; what should they see but a little house made entirely of gingerbread, perfect for breakfast. However, they are captured by the witch who imprisons them both. Hansel is to be fattened up, but the witch intends to eat Gretel on the spot. When the witch tells Gretel to look in the oven to see how the gingerbread is doing, Gretel pretends not to understand. The witch shows her how to do it and crawls inside the oven; Gretel slams the door shut. After the witch has been consumed in the oven, it explodes. Gingerbread children appear, but they are stiff and mute. Hansel and Gretel hear them begging to be set free. Gretel caresses the children and they come alive; Hänsel helps them to move their rigid limbs. The gingerbread children thank Hansel and Gretel, who in turn thank their 14 guardian angels. The parents arrive and joyfully embrace the children. All join together in song, mocking the witch and thanking the angels. *S. N.*

Hansel and Gretel, set design by Ludwig Sievert for the production by Lothar Wallerstein, Opernhaus Frankfurt 1926 (TWS).
At the beginning of the 20th century, the motif of the gloomy forest – such as that of *Hansel and Gretel* – was subjected to psychological research that brought new insights to familiar fairy tales, but also deprived them of some of their immediacy and naïveté. Humperdinck's opera has not been negatively affected by having this psychological spotlight cast upon it. The fairy tale as well as the opera can of course be interpreted as representing the drama of puberty. The quasi-religious motif of the guardian angels – the personification of the individual's self-protecting thoughts and deeds – represents an inconvenient obstacle to this rationalistic interpretation. But a transformation is currently taking place here, too, with the recent appearance of a veritable flood of research on the motif of the guardian angel.

*H*umperdinck's operatic fairy tales tended toward the philosophical and the religious, a precedent that composers of a later generation were to follow.

The story of the opera: a fairy tale in itself
Although the figure of Gertrud, the mother of Hansel and Gretel, is by no means positive, the woman whose ideas form the basis for the opera was herself a mother. Adelheid Wette, the composer's younger sister, had wanted to surprise her husband on his birthday with a "nursery play." She asked her brother to provide the songs, which led to the most popular number from the later opera, "Brüderlein, komm, tanz mit mir" ("Little brother, come, dance with me"). The play was enthusiastically received by the family. Some months later Wette entered the history books when she developed her idea by writing the libretto for *Hansel and Gretel*.

A familiar fairy tale told differently
In adapting the Grimm brothers' version of *Hansel and Gretel*, Adelheid Wette reinterpreted some aspects, omitted others, and added some elements of her own. In the story told by the Brothers Grimm it is the evil stepmother who drives the children out of their house. When the witch is destroyed, the cold-hearted stepmother dies at the same instant: two events that are independent from each other and yet parallel. Adelheid

Wette portrayed a mother whose unjustified anger is the result of fatigue and desperation. Yet she is able to reflect immediately on her actions and express her regret: "The good pot is now lying in pieces! Well, rashness always brings ruin!" Instead of being a woodcutter the father is a broom-maker, an occupation that allows for multiple meanings: brooms for sale and for sweeping, brooms for punishing, and finally brooms for the witches to ride.

A pious leit motiv in the brutal realm of the fairy tale
All this is secondary compared with the motif of the 14 angels, whose actions are anticipated in the overture by a hymn-like melody that unfolds fully in the forest scene (Scene 2, close), portraying the pantheistic forest as a temple of God. While the opera's other motifs occur only in specific situations, the theme of the "evening benediction" extends throughout the work. It can be heard in Gretel's evening prayer in Scene 1, it represents the pleas of the children when they take fright in the dark forest in Scene 2, and it forms the basis of the apotheosis of the finale in Scene 3. *N 2*   *S. N.*

Hansel and Gretel, costume design for the witch by Hans Strohbach, Cologne 1930 (TWS).
The witch is the most eccentric figure of the opera – visually as well as musically – and not just because of the diabolical "Ride of the Witches." Humperdinck wrote a peculiar mixture of song and speech for the character. The melodies have a pentatonic coloring and the brief motifs are constructed from a limited number of notes.

Janáček, Leoš

b. 3 July 1854 in Hukvaldy
d. 12 August 1928 in Ostrava

After studying the organ and other areas of music in Prague, Leipzig, and Vienna (1874–80), Janáček founded an organ school in Brno in 1881. He was the conductor of the Philharmonic Society there from 1881 to 1888, and from 1884 edited the music journal *Hudební listy*. In 1887 and 1888 he composed his first opera, *Šárka*, and began to collect folk songs from Eastern Moravia. (He published his first collection of folk songs with František Bartoš in 1890.) Janáček's life was punctuated by tragic events: his son died in 1890 and his daughter in 1903. His marriage to Zdenka Schulzová was characterized by crisis, and he drew artistic inspiration from love affairs with a number of women from a circle of artists and musicians (Kamila Urválková, Kamila Stösslová, Gabriela Horvátová). Despite the celebrated première of *Jenůfa* (Brno, 1904), international fame did not come until it was first performed in Prague at the National Theater in 1916. From 1919 he was director of the newly established Prague Conservatory, and from its nationalization in 1920 until his death he led a masterclass at the Brno branch of the Conservatory.

Works: Operas: *Šárka* (1888/FP 1925), *Počátek románu* (*The Beginning of a Romance*) (1891/FP 1894), *Její pastorkyňa* (*Her Stepdaughter*, later *Jenůfa*) (1904), *Osud* (*Fate*) (1904/FP 1958), *Výlety páně Broučkovy* (*The Excursions of Mr Brouček*) (1917/FP 1920), *Káta Kabanová* (1921), *Příhody lišky bystroušky* (*The Cunning Little Vixen*) (1924), *Več Makropulos* (*The Makropulos Case*) (1926), *Z mrtvého domu* (*From the House of the Dead*) (1930); orchestral works (*Taras Bulba*, 1915–18, *Sinfonietta*, 1926), piano works, chamber music, two ballets, publications of folk songs and their adaptations, choral works, sacred music (*Mša Glagolskja, Glagolitic Mass*, 1926).

*J*anáček was recognized as an important musical dramatist only toward the end of the 20th century. His music represents the fusion of a contemporary western European musical vocabulary with Czech and Moravian folk songs. His interest in Czech and Moravian characteristics led to the creation of a carefully constructed and unique vocal style.

Jenůfa, Martha Mödl as the Kostelnička, Wiener Staatsoper 1964.
The Kostelnička is a highly expressive role, which a number of dramatic sopranos, such as the great Wagnerian Martha Mödl (b. 1912), have been drawn to in the latter part of their careers. Jenůfa's stepmother is an unforgiving, strong-willed woman – an impregnable authority figure compared with the gentle Jenůfa. Her emotional collapse is therefore all the more agonizing when she too is forced to bow to fate.

Jenůfa (Her Stepdaughter)

Jenůfa (Její pastorkyňa)

Opera from Moravian peasant life in three acts

Libretto: Gabriela Preissová, after her drama *Její pastorkyňa* (*Her Stepdaughter*).
Première: 21 January 1904, Brno (National Theater).
Characters: Grandmother Buryjovka, a retired mill owner and now housekeeper at the mill (A), Kostelnička Buryjovka, a widow, her daughter-in-law (S), Jenůfa, the Kostelnička's stepdaughter (S), Števa Buryja, grandson of Grandmother Buryjovka (T), Laca Klemeň, Števa's half-brother (T), Foreman (Bar), Mayor (B), His Wife (Ms), Karolka, their daughter (Ms), Barena, a housemaid at the mill (S), Jano, a shepherd boy (S), Aunt (A); musicians, villagers, recruits (chorus).
Setting: A village in the hills of Moravia, in the second half of the 19th century.

Synopsis
Act I

Outside the mill. Jenůfa awaits the return of her lover, Števa, from the recruitment muster. She is worried about the drafting of the village men: if Števa is conscripted then they will not be able to marry, and she is secretly expecting his child. Števa's half-brother, Laca, is also in love with Jenůfa, but is ignored by the girl. Števa is not called up and returns drunk and in a mood to celebrate. In the opinion of the Kostelnička, Jenůfa's feared and respected step-mother, he behaves scandalously, and to Jenůfa's dismay she postpones the marriage for a year. When Laca makes advances to Jenůfa, she angrily rebuffs him; in his rage, Laca wounds her face with a knife.

Act II

Six months later, in the Kostelnička's house. No one suspects that Jenůfa has had a child, as the Kostelnička has kept the girl concealed in her house and spread the story that Jenůfa has left on a journey. The stepmother reproaches herself for her strictness: Števa no longer wants to marry the disfigured Jenůfa and has become engaged to Karolka, the daughter of the mayor. Laca, however, still loves Jenůfa. The Kostelnička fears that he will abandon his intention to marry her when he learns of the

The honor of Czech peasants
The dramatic idea of *Jenůfa* (the most frequently performed Czech opera after Smetana's →*The Bartered Bride*) is unusual for Janáček but not unique. His protagonists are almost without exception antiheroes, fallible human beings ruled by prejudice, fear, and volatile emotions. The spiritual background is gloomy, and the action naturalistic. The village in *Jenůfa* is a far cry from the idyllic atmosphere of folkloric and Romantic national operas of the 19th century. Here, folklore has a

child; although greatly troubled by her conscience, she drowns Jenůfa's son in the millstream while Jenůfa lies in bed with a fever. She makes Jenůfa and Laca believe that the child died a natural death. Jenůfa reluctantly agrees to marry.

Act III

Two months later in the Kostelnička's house. On the morning of the wedding of Jenůfa and Laca, guests arrive, including Števa and Karolka. As the Kostelnička is about to give the couple her blessing, word reaches them that the body of an infant has been found in the millstream under the ice: Jenůfa is accused of infanticide. The Kostelnička confesses her guilt and is arrested. Jenůfa alone forgives her. Števa and Laca feel equally responsible for the tragedy. Karolka calls off her engagement to Števa. Jenůfa releases Laca from his obligations, but he stands by her and they both decide to begin a new and better life.

S. N.

different function. The articulation of motifs modeled on folk songs is expressive, and serves to heighten the opera's psychological effect. The music is not divided up into individual numbers; rather, scenes follow one another in an unbroken musical stream. The melodies are shaped by Moravian dialect and influenced by the underlying tone of Moravian folk songs (although Janáček did not actually use a single folk song), making *Jenůfa* one of the key works of Czech *verismo*.

The interational career of *Jenůfa* began with its première at the Wiener Hofoper in 1918. The title role was sung by Maria Jeritza, Vienna's star performer, whom Janáček loved and admired (her Czech origins were a factor in his regard for her). The list of singers who have interpreted the role of Jenůfa is almost endless: during Janáček's lifetime alone the opera was staged more than 70 times. The 1999 production in the Royal Theater in Copenhagen with its fields of grain stretching out into infinity rendered the stage almost unrecognisable: it could almost be a photograph of a scene taken from nature itself …

T. Sz.

Jenufa, production photograph with Gitta-Maria Sjöberg as Jenufa, production David Radok, sets Tazeena Firth, conductor Jan Latham Koenig, Det Kongelige Teater, Copenhagen 1999.
The most recent productions of *Jenufa* have placed less emphasis on its criticism of social prejudices, preferring to concentrate on the way a great capacity for love – such as that of the heroine – is developed and maintained.

Left
Jenůfa, Waldemar Kmentt as Laca, Wiener Staatsoper 1964.
In *Jenůfa* the male roles take a back seat. Laca, the country lad, does not become a worthy partner for Jenůfa until the final duet. Laca is a character part rather than a heroic tenor role, and was sung by the famous Austrian tenor Waldemar Kmentt (b. 1920).

Kamila Urválková, 1903.
Muse and model in one: Janáček's friend, Kamila Urválková.

Fate

Osud

Opera in three acts

Libretto: Leoš Janáček and Fedora Bartošová.

Première: 25 October 1958, Brno (National Theater).

Characters: Živny, a composer (T), Míla Válková (S), Míla's Mother (A), Dr. Suda (T), Lhotský, a painter (B), Konečný (Bar), Miss Stuhlá, a teacher (S), A Poet (T), Two Ladies (2 S), Mrs Major (S), Her Child (child S), Miss Pacovská (S), A Student (T), An Old Slovak Woman (A), Mrs Rat (A), A Young Widow (A), An Engineer (T), Fanča, a girl (S), Two Young Men (T, B), Doubek, the son of Míla and Živny (boy S, T in Act III), Žán and Vána, servants (silent), Verva, a student (Bar), Součková and Kosinská, students (S, A), A Waiter (T); female teachers, students, schoolgirls, spa guests, students at the conservatory (chorus).

Setting: Moravia, at the end of the 19th and beginning of the 20th century.

Synopsis
Act I

A summer morning in the park of the spa town, Luhačovice. The guests at the spa are conversing happily. The darling of this society is the beautiful Míla. The composer Živny, her former lover and the father of her child, turns up unexpectedly. While the merry group leave on an outing, Míla and Živny meet. They are still in love. Míla's mother alone had been responsible for their separation as she had not wanted to entrust her daughter to Živny. When the rest of the company returns from their outing, Míla and Živny have already left.

Act II

Four years later, in Živny's study. Míla, Živny, and their son Doubek are now living together. Míla's mother is making life difficult for them. She doubts Živny's competence as a composer and a husband. When Míla and the composer look through his still unfinished operatic score together, Míla recalls the beginnings of their love and wonders whether her desires and plans have been fulfilled. Míla's mother accuses her son-in-law of having made her daughter unhappy. Deranged, she leaps from the balcony; Míla tries to stop her and is dragged to her doom.

Act III

Eleven years later, on a hot summer's day, in the great hall of the Conservatory. The students are preparing the première of the new opera. They do not understand the pathetic tone of the work, and the rehearsal becomes a parody. They ask Živny to explain his piece. In so doing, the composer becomes increasingly agitated, since he identifies with the hero of his opera. In the meantime, a violent storm has arisen. When the heroine of the opera dies, the composer's son, who is amongst the students, cries out the name of his mother. It becomes clear that the work is about Živny's own fate. Distraught, the composer leaves: the work will forever remain unfinished.

T. Sz.

Art reflecting life

Although this opera was never performed in the artist's lifetime, numerous incidents in it reflect Janáček's psychological crisis at about the time of his 50th birthday. The cause of his depression was not only creative, for he also had a family crisis to contend with: the death of his 21-year-old daughter Olga in February 1903. After the completion of *Jenůfa*, Janáček, for whom composing was often an escape from everyday life, sought a means of giving voice to his anguish. Six months after Olga's death he traveled to Luhačovice, a fashionable Moravian spa town, in order to rest and gather his strength. It was here that he met his future muse, Kamila Urválková, the wife of the administrator of the Czech imperial forests. (Some 14 years later he would meet the last great love of his life, Kamila Stösslová, in the same place.) This attractive, 27-year-old woman had originally wanted to be an actress, but her wealthy and respectable family intervened, putting an end both to her artistic plans and her plans to marry Ludvík Celansky, a conductor and composer popular in the 1890s. Celansky later immortalized the story of their love in an opera performed in the National Theater in Prague in 1897, under the title *Kamila*. Janaček was fascinated by the beauty and youth of Kamila Urválková and her fate inspired him to create this opera – although he retained a sceptical view of married life (Act II).

T. Sz.

The Excursions of Mr. Brouček

Výlety páně Broučkovy

Opera in two parts (nine scenes)

Libretto: Part 1: Viktor Dyk, and František Serafin Procházka; Part 2: after Svatopluk Čech.

Première: 23 April 1920, Prague (National Theater).

Characters: Mathias Brouček, a landlord in Prague (T), Mazal, a young technician/Mazalun, head constructor/Amalka's husband (T), Sacristan of St. Vit's Cathedral/Lukristan/The Bell-Ringer (B-bar), Málinka, the sacristan's daughter/Lunamalis/Amalka (S), Würfl, publican at the Vikárka/President Würflun/Koska, the councillor (B), Piccolo at the Vikárka/Minister of Culture/A Student (S), Fanny Novak, Brouček's housekeeper/Minister of Nutrition/Frantischka, the bell-ringer's housekeeper (A), Tram conductor/Minister of Transport/Miroslav, a guard (T), The President of the Society of Publicans/Vaček, of the iron hand (Bar); customers of the Vikárka/representatives of the Republic of the Moon and Prague citizens from 1420.

Setting: Prague, the night of 12–13 July 1920; Prague and the moon in 1420.

The Excursions of Mr. Brouček, set design by Rochus Gliese (moon scene) for the production by Wolf Völker, conductor Joseph Keilberth, Prinzregententheater, Munich 1959 (TWS).
Mr. Brouček on the moon. The petit-bourgeois figure of Brouček was the forerunner of the good soldier Schweik in Jaroslav Hašek's novel of the same name. Brouček made his creator, Svatopluk Čech, the most popular Czech writer of his day. In his opera, Janáček deliberately painted the figure in an unsympathetic light. In 1918 he wrote: "There are as many Broučeks amongst us as there are Oblomovs amongst the Russians. I want such a person to appear repulsive to us, so that with every step we destroy him, throttle him – especially the Brouček in ourselves – so that he may be reborn in the pure spirit of the martyrs of our people."

Synopsis
Part 1

Scene 1: Outside the Vikárka inn. Brouček is a regular customer and frequently meets the sacristan of the cathedral of St. Vit here. Málinka, the daughter of the sacristan, comes to fetch her father. The young technician, Mazal, who is courting

Málinka also comes into the inn. Brouček sometimes drinks more than his thirst requires; he then falls asleep and has strange dreams.

Scene 2: On the moon. In the first of his dreams, Brouček reaches the moon where he encounters the inhabitants who are people from his everyday life. Mazalun (Mazal) appears as the inventor of a rocket that can reach the earth. But Lukristan (the sacristan), the father of Lunamalis (Málinka) refuses to give him his daughter's hand. Brouček flies off with Lunamalis in a helicopter.

Scene 3: The center of government for the Republic of the Moon. The alien visitor is taken to the headquarters of the lunar republic. During a reception in his honor he is shown paintings and exposed to the scent of flowers. He ignores all that, however, and takes out a piece of sausage from his pocket to chew on, much to the horror of the moon-dwellers. Despite his behavior, Lunamalis (Málinka) falls in love with him. Although Brouček learns that moon-dwellers die from physical contact, he embraces Lunamalis, who dissolves into nothing. Brouček wakes up.

Scene 4: The last guests have left the inn. Málinka also leaves for home, accompanied by Mazal. Brouček dreams on.

Part 2

Scene 5: On the Barandor Hill near Prague. Brouček sets off for the moon in a spaceship.

Scene 6: Prague Old Town Square, 1420. Instead of landing on the moon, Brouček finds himself in his own city at the time of the Hussite wars. The bell-ringer (the sacristan) at first believes him to be a spy of Emperor Sigismund. Brouček pretends that he is a Frenchman.

Scene 7: The house of the bell-ringer. The people are preparing for the decisive battle of the Hussite wars. The bell-ringer introduces Brouček to his daughter Amalka (Málinka) and her husband (Mazal). Brouček becomes involved in a political debate with them, but then he crawls into bed while the others go off to battle.

Scene 8: Prague Old Town Square. Brouček tries to hide but is recognized by returning soldiers. He is accused of slander and of spreading false doctrines. Only Amalka tries to defend him; this only makes things worse: he is charged with immoral behavior and condemned. He is dragged away to the stake and forced into a barrel.

Scene 9: Outside the Vikárka inn. When Brouček regains consciousness his predicament does indeed prove to be critical: he has fallen into a barrel. Würfl hears his piteous cries and frees him. Brouček is able to see that he has returned to his own time, and immediately begins to boast of his exploits.

(This is one of the many existing versions of the story; the characters and their names are also subject to variation.)

T. Sz.

1. Tavern Waltz

2. Moon Motif

3. Hussite Chorale

Kdy   vzej - de   v zla - tém   pla - me - ni? _____

The Excursions of Mr Brouček, sets by Rochus Gliese (the Vikárka inn) for the production by Wolf Völker, conductor Joseph Keilberth, Prinzregententheater, Munich 1959 (TWS). The inn scenes are dominated by waltz-like dance motifs which represent the jovial simplicity of the hero. The mystical atmosphere of his dream about the moon is depicted by Impressionistic colorings, while the scenes involving the Hussite wars are characterized by archaic choral and hymn motifs. *M 1, M 2, M 3*

Kát'a Kabanová

Opera in three acts

Libretto: Leoš Janáček, after the play *Groza* (*The Storm*) by Alexander Ostrovsky.
Première: 23 November 1921, Brno (National Theater).

Characters: Savël Prokofjevič Dikoj, a merchant (B), Boris Grigorjevič, his nephew (T), Marfa Ignatěvna Kabanová (Kabanicha), a rich merchant's widow (A), Tichon Ivanyč Kabanov, her son (T), Katěrina (Kát'a), his wife (S), Váňa Kudrjáš, a teacher, chemist, and engineer (T), Varvara, Kabanicha's foster-daughter (Ms), Kuligin, friend of Kudrjáš (Bar), Glaša and Fekluša, servants (2 Ms), A Passerby (T), A Woman in the Crowd (A); citizens (chorus).
Setting: The town of Kalinow on the Volga, the mid-19th century.

Synopsis
Act I
Scene 1: The banks of the Volga. Boris Grigorjevič is hopelessly in love with Kát'a Kabanová who is already married. But he is financially dependent on his uncle Dikoj. Kát'a Kabanová is unhappy in the house of her mother-in-law, who makes her life difficult. Even her husband bends to his mother's will. Kabanicha orders her son to go to the market at Kazan for two weeks.

Scene 2: A room in the Kabanov house. Kát'a confesses her love for Boris to Varvara, though she tries to resist her feelings. Varvara promises to help. Tichon is ready to leave, but Kát'a desperately tries to prevent him from going. She knows that if she stays on her own, she will not be able to resist temptation. Tichon rides off.

Act II
Scene 1: A study in the Kabanov house. Varvara is getting ready for her nightly rendezvous with Kudrjáš, and gives Kát'a the key to the garden with the message that Boris is waiting there for her.

Scene 2: A rocky grove on the banks of the Volga. Both couples spend a few happy hours together.

Act III
Scene 1: A ruin on the banks of the Volga. Kudrjáš, Dikoj, Kabanicha and Kát'a seek shelter from a thunderstorm. Kát'a is tortured by her conscience. The raging of the elements increases her fear. When she sees Tichon returning, she kneels before him and confesses to having spent the past ten nights with Boris. Then she runs out into the storm.

Scene 2: A lonely spot on the banks of the Volga. Kabanicha wants to punish Kát'a severely. Varvara and Kudrjáš decide to flee to Moscow. Kát'a is half mad with fear and desperation. Boris is sent by his uncle to Siberia. The lovers take leave of each other, then Kát'a throws herself into the river. Beside Kát'a's corpse Tichon dares to say a word against his mother for the first time, accusing her of murder. *T. Sz.*

Kát'a Kabanová, production photograph with Nancy Gustafson as Kát'a, production Joachim Herz, conductor Ulf Schirmer, Wiener Staatsoper 1991.
Kamila Stösslová, Janáček's last great love, can be recognized in the figure of Kát'a Kabanová: it is no coincidence that Janáček emphasized the love motif at the expense of the psychological and socially critical elements of Ostrovsky's play. The opera has a single central figure: Kát'a, who battles with the elementary power of her love and with her conscience.

Kát'a Kabanová, production photograph with Clarry Bartha as Kát'a, production Stein Winge, sets and costumes Timian Alsaker, conductor Hans Wallat, Deutsche Oper am Rhein, Düsseldorf 1996.
The opera's mood is defined by a prevailing sense of alienation and loneliness. In the Düsseldorf production, the moment of Kát'a's spiritual isolation was heightened by a stage design which "trapped" the heroine in a courtyard before the gaze of the onlookers.

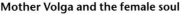

Center left
Kát'a Kabanová, production photograph with Clarry Bartha (Kát'a) and Christian Papis (Boris Grigorjevič), production Stein Winge, sets and costumes Timian Alsaker, conductor Hans Wallat, Deutsche Oper am Rhein, Düsseldorf 1996.

Center right
Kát'a Kabanová, production photograph with (from left to right) Louise Winter (Varvara), Nancy Gustafson (Kát'a), and Ryland Davies (Tichon), production Nikolaus Lehnhoff, sets Tobias Hoheisel, conductor Andrew Davis, Glyndebourne Festival 1988.
In Nikolaus Lehnhoff's production the winter cold dominated as the psychological basis for the opera's events.

Below
Kát'a Kabanová production photograph with Louise Winter (Varvara) and Nancy Gustafson (Kát'a), production Nikolaus Lehnhoff, conductor Andrew Davis, sets Tobias Hoheisel, Glyndebourne Festival 1988.

Janáček, Russophile

Janáček was fond of Russian literature from an early age. The influence of works by Tolstoy, Gogol, Dostoyevsky, Ostrovsky, Turgenev, and Chekhov is shown in his operas, which have "Russian" themes. Works by these writers also inspired numerous instrumental pieces. Janáček considered himself a type of pan-Slavic nationalist – perhaps in order to counter the German orientation of the citizens of Brno. He spoke excellent Russian, gave his children Russian names, traveled to the empire of the tsars several times, and founded a "Russian Circle" in Brno which was active until the end of the First World War. *Kát'a Kabanová* was Janáček's first opera with a Russian theme – a confessional love ballad to Russian culture and the Russian soul.

Mother Volga and the female soul

The expressive description of nature in *Kát'a Kabanová* is given a marked psychological role in contrast to the more illustrative nature-music of Janáček's earlier operas. The emotions of the protagonists are conveyed by nature, in particular by the Volga. The river is a constant presence from the beginning of the first act through to the love scene and the suicide at the end of the opera. At the high point, during the thunderstorm, the raging elements reinforce Kát'a's rising anxiety, which approaches madness in its intensity. *Kát'a Kabanová* is one of the greatest creations of musical Expressionism, and one of the most outstanding works in Janáček's *oeuvre* as well as in the musical history of the 20th century.

T. Sz.

The Cunning Little Vixen

Príhody lišky bystroušky

Opera in three acts

Libretto: Leoš Janáček, after a tale by Rudolf Těsnohlídek.
Première: 6 September 1924, Brno (National Theater).
Characters: The Forester (Bar), The Forester's Wife (A), The Schoolmaster (T), The Parson (B), Harašta, a tramp (B), Pásek, an innkeeper (T), Pásková, his wife (S), Frantík and Pepík, two boys (2 boy S), Bystrouška ("Little Sharp Ears"), the vixen (S), Fox (S), Lapák, the dachshund (Ms), Cock (S), Chocholka, the hen (S), Badger (B), Woodpecker (A), Owl (A), Jay (S), Mosquito (T), Frog (child S), Cricket (child S), Grasshopper (child S), Fox Cubs (S, A), Hens (S, A); fly, dragonfly, hedgehog, squirrel, forest animals (pantomime); voices in the forest, forest animals, villagers (chorus).
Setting: A forest and a Moravian village, at an undefined time.

The Cunning Little Vixen, costume designs for animals by Ruodi Barth for the production by Bohumil Herlischka at the Opernhaus Düsseldorf, 1972 (TWS).
Janáček loved the sounds of nature, and actively researched and collected them. He often sat for hours in his garden listening to birds calling, the sounds of insects, and the wind in the trees, writing down descriptions of different types of birdsong. These experiences found their way into the score for *The Cunning Little Vixen*, which is without doubt Janáček's most Impressionist work. *M 4*

Synopsis
Act I
Scene 1: A forest. Summer. Midday sun. In the quiet before a storm the forester is dreaming of the gypsy Terynka. When he wakes up he sees a fox cub whose look reminds him of Terynka's eyes. He grabs it with both arms and takes it back to his house. The vixen calls in vain for its mother.
Scene 2: Courtyard of the lake forestry. Autumn. Afternoon sun. The cub is unhappy in the forester's house; his wife dislikes the creature and the forester's sons constantly torment it. Because it once tried to defend itself it is kept on a leash like a dog. The cub chews through its lead and flees back into the forest.

Act II
Scene 3: The forest, outside the badger's set. Late afternoon. The forest animals joyfully greet the return of the cub, which has grown up into a vixen. Because she needs a home, she turns the badger out.
Scene 4: Pásek's inn. The VIP room, with the bar next door. Noise from the inn. In the inn the parson, forester, schoolmaster, and teacher are drinking and talking about Terynka, to whom they all feel attracted. They accuse the forester of wanting to set the gypsy girl up in the village – but what else are they to expect from someone who keeps a fox beside his chicken coop, and then lets it escape?
Scene 5: The forest, on a moonlit night. The drunken schoolmaster sees a sunflower, behind which the vixen is hiding, and believing it to be Terynka he pours out declarations of love. When the forester discovers the vixen he fires two shots at it and chases it away.
Scene 6: The vixen's den. In the beautiful summer moonlight, the vixen's female instincts awaken and she accepts the advances of the little fox. But just as the couple want to disappear into the conquered badger's set, the owl makes their love known throughout the forest. Now they have no choice but to be officially married by the woodpecker. The animals celebrate the wedding in song and dance.

Act III
Scene 7: The edge of the forest on an autumn afternoon; there is a clear sky. The tramp Harašta is getting ready for his marriage to Terynka, and sets off into the forest to catch birds. On the way he finds a dead hare, which according to the forester is the work of the vixen. He sets a trap, but the vixen and her cubs laugh at him: they know all about traps. Harašta watches the fox cubs playing and thinks what a fine wedding present for Terynka a fox-fur would make. Harašta shoots and hits the vixen.
Scene 8: Pásek's inn, the garden near the bowling alley. The schoolmaster and the forester are listening sadly to the merry sounds of the wedding of Harašta and Terynka. Mrs Pásková compliments Terynka on the fine fox-fur she has received from Harašta for her wedding present; the forester realizes that his cunning little vixen has been killed. Deeply moved, he heads off into the forest.
Scene 9: The forest (as for Scene 1). It has been raining. Full of grief the forester returns to the place where he once met Terynka and where he caught the vixen. But when he catches sight of a fox cub that looks just like his vixen, his soul is gradually permeated with the peace of the forest and the eternally renewing power of nature. *T. Sz.*

4. Wedding Dance of the Forest Animals

The Cunning Little Vixen, production photograph, Wiener Volksoper 1992. In later years Janáček regarded the forest as the symbol of a sad, solitary, and intimate world. The hopeless love of the forester for a radiantly beautiful young girl, and the way in which this ageing man comes to terms with the passing of life, convey a sense of resignation and the wisdom that comes with age.

A Czech midsummer night's dream – with overtones of resignation

Janáček found the characters of the forest animals quite by chance in the Brno magazine *Lidové noviny*, where a humorous novel by Rudolf Těsnohlídek with drawings by Stanislav Lolek was serialized from April 1920. This was the inspiration for the composer's *The Cunning Little Vixen*. But it is not a comic opera; Janáček was nearly 70 when he composed it, and something of the experience of old age can be glimpsed in the piece. It is once again a young woman who is the central figure of the opera: Terynka, the gypsy who brings turbulence into everyone else's life. Remarkably, she never appears on stage herself. The vixen stands in for her, and the

fate of both figures is closely connected. The vixen must die so that Terynka can receive her fur as a wedding present; thus the forester finally loses both his love and the vixen that symbolized that love. But it is precisely this mysterious connection between the animal and human world which prevents the composer – who at the time he wrote the opera was in love with Kamila Stösslová, a woman 38 years his junior – from becoming sentimental. The forester is full of humor and worldly wisdom, a figure who is capable of laughing at himself. He awakes in a calmer state of mind after his midsummer night's dream.

T. Sz.

The Makropulos Case

Več Makropulos

Opera in three acts
Libretto: Leoš Janáček, after the comedy by Karel Capek.
Première: 18 December 1926, Brno (National Theater).
Characters: Emilia Marty, a famous opera singer (S), Albert Gregor (T), Dr. Kolenatý, a lawyer (Bbar), Vítek, his clerk (T), Kristina, Vítek's daughter (Ms), Jaroslav Prus (Bar), Janek, his son (T), A Stage Technician (B), A Cleaning Woman (A), Hauk-Šendorf, a diplomat (T), A Chambermaid (A); male voices behind the scene (male chorus).
Setting: Prague, 1922.

Synopsis
Act I

The room of Vítek the clerk in Dr. Kolenatý's chambers. The dispute between the Prus and Gregor families has been a source of income for several generations of the Kolenatý family of lawyers. The object of the case is an enormous fortune. Josef Ferdinand Prus died childless and intestate in 1827, having given verbal instructions to the president of the Theresianum in Vienna that one of their students, a young man by the name of Ferdinand Karel Gregor, should inherit his estate at Loukov. His instructions have not been carried out. The Gregor family has pursued litigation into the second generation, and now seems about to lose the case definitively. Thanks to Emilia Marty, however, a celebrated prima donna, affairs take a different turn. Emilia makes a statutory declaration that the claims of the Gregor family are justified, on the grounds that Ferdinand Karel Gregor was the illegitimate child of Josef Ferdinand Prus and Elian MacGregor, a singer at the Vienna court opera. Proof, she states, can be

provided by a document to be found in the Prus household. Kolenatý leaves to investigate. Albert Gregor woos Emilia but is rebuffed. When the lawyer returns he confirms Emilia's statement, and therefore the validity of Gregor's claims.

Act II

The empty stage of a large theater. Emilia's admirers – Vítek, Gregor, and the diplomat Hauk-Šendorf – visit her after the performance. Janek Prus is amongst them, although he is engaged to Kristina, Vítek's daughter. Emilia Marty reminds Hauk-Šendorf of the Spanish singer Eugenia Montez, who was his lover 50 years earlier. Prus senior tells of finding letters by Elian MacGregor amongst his papers; he believes Elian to have been identical with one Elina Makropulos. Emilia offers to buy the letters from Prus. When he refuses she tries to persuade Janek to steal the documents from his father. This conversation is overheard by Prus, who drives his son off and reaches an agreement with Emilia: if she will spend a night with him, she can have the papers.

Act III

Emilia's hotel room. Prus is disappointed with the night spent with Emilia, but keeps his word and gives her the papers. Janek has in the meanwhile committed suicide as he could not tolerate the idea of a liaison between Emilia and his father. Prus is distraught, but Emilia is completely unmoved by the news. Dr. Kolenatý is worried: the police suspect fraudulence as the signature of Elian MacGregor on the papers from the Prus household is by the same hand as the dedication to Kristina on the photograph of Emilia Marty. While Emilia is getting changed, the men search through the papers lying on her desk. The initials of the signature are always E.M.: Elina Makropulos, Elian MacGregor, Elsa Müller, Ekaterina Miskin, Eugenia Montez and now: Emilia Marty. Remarkably, all these signatures are in the same handwriting. Emila then tells them the story of her life. She was born Elina Makropulos in 1585. Her father, a Greek alchemist and physician to Emperor Rudolf II, had discovered the elixir of eternal life and tried it out on his daughter; he was murdered soon afterwards. In the centuries that followed, she lived in various countries under different names. She had left the document containing the secret of the elixir in the house of her only true love, Josef Ferdinand Prus, and she had intervened in their affairs in order to get the document back and extend her life again. Now she has realized that her life is unhappy and pointless, and no longer wants to continue it. She hands the document to Kristina who throws it in the fire. Emilia dies relieved and content.

T. Sz.

The Makropulos Case, production photograph with Anja Silja (Emilia) and Kurt Schreibmayer (Albert Gregor), production Christine Mielitz, Wiener Staatsoper 1993.
The text by Karel Čapek (1890–1938) was not ideal for a libretto in the conventional sense, but the composer was fascinated by the remarkable figure of Emilia. This cold, cynical, and remote woman does not develop her humanity until late in the story, but from her he was able to develop a heroine full of contradictions. This picture shows a strange scene in an even stranger story: Emilia and Albert Gregor, grandmother and (illegitimate) grandchild.

The Makropulos Case, set design by Ruodi Barth for Walter Pohl's production at the Staatstheater Wiesbaden, 1961 (TWS).

A set design featuring a fantastically exaggerated lawyer's chamber. With its musical settings of long legal texts and its use of the sounds of cars and telephones, *The Makropulos Case* belongs to the "topical opera" typical of the 1920s. Janáček developed a new musical style, for which the most important source of inspiration was the circle of composers around Arnold Schoenberg.

Though Janáček did not write 12-tone music for *The Makropulos Case*, he did allow chromaticism freer rein than in his earlier operas, using it to express tension and criminal activity. The action occurs as rapidly as in a prose drama, the "numbers" (arias and ensembles) of earlier opera being replaced by an almost unbroken flow of conversational recitative, which is kept from becoming dry by a highly varied instrumentation. Indeed, the recitative possesses considerable charm as a result of its unusual melodic style. *M 5*

5. Quotation From the Will

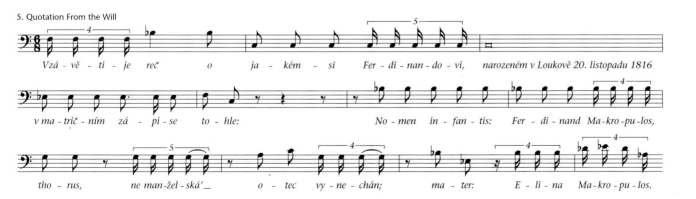

Vzá - vě - ti - je reč   o   ja - kém - si Fer - di - nan - do - vi,   narozeném v Loukově 20. listopadu 1816

v ma - trič - ním zá - pi - se to - hle: No - men in - fan - tis: Fer - di - nand Ma - kro - pu - los,

tho - rus,   ne man - žel - ská'   o - tec vy - ne - chán;   ma - ter: E - li - na Ma - kro - pu - los.

From the House of the Dead, set design by Eduard Löffler, Mannheim 1930 (TWS). Janáček's *From the House of the Dead* has often been described as a "black opera." Only at the very end, when the captive eagle soars up into the sky, does a feeble ray of light fall upon the suffering characters.

From the House of the Dead

Z mrtvého domu

Opera in three acts

Libretto: Leoš Janáček, after the novel *Zapiski iz myortvogo doma* (*Memoirs from the House of the Dead*) by Fyodor Dostoyevsky.

Première: 12 April 1930, Brno (National Theater).

Characters: Alexandr Petrovič Gorjančikov (Bar), Aljeja, a young Tartar (T), Luka Kusmič (Filka Morozov) (T), Tall Prisoner (T), Short Prisoner (Bar), The Governor (Bar), Old Prisoner (T), Skuratov (T), Čekunov (Bar), Drunken Prisoner (T), Prisoner-Cook (Bar), Prisoner-Blacksmith (B), Priest (Bar), Young Prisoner (T), Prostitute (Ms), A Prisoner (Don Juan and the Brahmin in the pantomime) (Bar), A Prisoner (Kedril in the pantomime) (T), Šapkin (T), Šiškov (B), Čerevin (T), First Guard (T), Second Guard (Bar); prisoners (pantomime and chorus).

Setting: A Russian prison on the Irtysh in Siberia, the middle of the 19th century.

Synopsis
Act I

The prison yard on an early winter's morning. The early morning activities of the prisoners are interrupted by a loud argument. The camp atmosphere is already tense, as a new prisoner is expected, about whom it is known only that he is "a political." The new man, Alexandr Gorjančikov, is welcomed by the governor with a hundred lashes. This injustice is accepted with equanimity: it is an everyday matter in the camp. The prisoners care for an eagle with injured wings. They see in it a symbol of their own fate. Skuratov recalls his life in Moscow and, almost insane, he dances until he collapses. Luka tells how he killed the former governor.

A trip to hell

"In every creature, a spark of divinity." This is the motto from the title page of Janáček's last opera, written at the very end of his life (he did not live long enough to see the première). "This bleak opera is weighing me down. I have the feeling of descending ever further into the depths of mankind, to the most wretched of us all. And this is a hard road ..." he wrote in November 1927, nine months before his death. In contrast to the novel, the opera has no central figure. The events begin and end with the arrival and departure of Alexandr Gorjančikov, but the emphasis is not on his experiences and thoughts: the opera's subject is rather the range of experience, sin, suffering, cruelty, and human behavior under degrading conditions that he encounters. "Truth does not exclude beauty," Janáček said at the end of his life, with an eye on the future of the opera. Although the dark side of human nature had been given artistic expression in literature decades earlier (especially by Dostoyevsky and Zola), it required a catastrophe such as the First World War to open the world of opera to social problems of this sort. Ten years before the composition of *From the House of the Dead*, Puccini had composed a proletarian tragedy (→*Il tabarro*). Prague was the second city to stage a production of Alban Berg's →*Wozzeck* after its Berlin première of 1925. The Prague production of *Wozzeck* – which Janáček enthusiastically attended – took place at the time the Czech composer was working on his pessimistic final opera. Janáček, too, discovered that the fate of the individual concealed an abyss. In this sense his opera is dramatically riveting – in spite of its fundamentally narrative tone – from the dark winter's morning of the opening scene to the hymn to freedom at the close of the opera. M6   T. Sz.

From the House of the Dead, costume designs by Rudolf Schulz, Hanover 1958 (TWS).
Pictured here are prisoners both with and without faces. The unusual subject matter forced the composer to develop new dramatic and musical methods, unlike those used in his earlier operas. *From the House of the Dead* is a "men's opera": apart from the prostitute in Act II there are no female characters. Furthermore, the eroticism that had earlier been so important to Janáček appears only in a repugnant form (in the scene with the prostitute and in Šiškov's tale). Other novelties include the central role given to the chorus and chamber-music style of orchestration.

6. Freedom Motif (Final Chorus)

Svo - bo - da, svo - bo - dič - ka!

Act II

The banks of the river Irtysh with a view of the steppe; a year later, in summer. The prisoners are scrapping ships. Gorjančikov has become friends with the Tartar boy Aljeja. It is a holiday. A priest blesses the camp and holds a service. The prisoners have rehearsed two pantomimes (*Kedril and Don Juan* and *The Beautiful Miller's Wife*), and perform them on a stage they have hammered together from ships' timbers. As they return to their cells, an insane prisoner attacks Aljeja.

Act III

Scene 1: The prison hospital at night. Gorjančikov sits on Aljeja's bed. Luka Kusmič lies dying. The prisoners exchange memories. Šapkin tells of being tortured. Šiškov tells how he murdered his wife Akulka when he learned that she had been the lover of Filka Morozov, and that she continued to love him despite being married. Luka dies. Only at this point does Šiškov look closely at his face and sees that it is Filka Morozov. Gorjančikov is called to see the governor.

Scene 2: In the prison yard the governor, drunk, apologizes to Gorjančikov before the other prisoners and tells him he is to released. Aljeja says goodbye to Gorjančikov. As he leaves the prisoners release the eagle. For a moment a ray of hope seems to flicker – but the enforced labor begins again and the horrors of camp life go on.   T. Sz.

Kagel, Mauricio

b. 24 December 1931 in Buenos Aires

As a student in Buenos Aires, Kagel studied music (clarinet, cello, piano, and conducting – he was self-taught as a composer), literature (Jorge Luis Borges was one of his teachers), and philosophy (particularly Spinoza). In 1949 he became artistic adviser to the group Nueva Musica. His first compositions were written in 1950, the year in which he became a co-founder of the Argentinian film federation. He wrote film reviews and compositions for films and radio plays, and worked as a répétiteur and conductor at the Teatro Colón. In 1957 Kagel went to Europe and settled in Cologne. From 1958 he took part in the Darmstadt summer courses for New Music, where he taught from 1960. From 1964–65 he was Professor of Composition at the State University of New York at Buffalo; in 1968 he was Director of the Scandinavian Courses for New Music in Göteborg, and from 1969–75 Director of the Cologne New Music courses. In 1970 Kagel's *Sur scène* (*On Stage*) was the first work to be performed on the experimental stage of the Bayerische Staatsoper in Munich, where he would later became a regular presence. He became Professor for New Music Theater at the Musikhochschule in Cologne in 1974, and in 1989 Composer in Residence of the Cologne Philharmonic. His *Staatstheater* (*State Theater*) was first performed in 1971 in Hamburg; it became a model for a whole generation of artists in its portrayal of the comedy and absurdity of the music business. *Die Erschöpfung der Welt* (*The Exhaustion of the World*), first staged in 1980 in Stuttgart, was equally influential.

Works: Operas (selection): *Sur scène* (*On Stage*) (1962), *Staatstheater* (*State Theater*) (stage composition, 1971), *Mare nostrum* (discovery, pacification, and conversion of the Mediterranean by an Amazonian tribe, 1975), *Die Erschöpfung der Welt* (*The Exhaustion of the World*) (stage illusion in 11 scenes, 1980), *Aus Deutschland* (*From Germany*) (lieder opera, 1981); other stage works: *Die Frauen* (*The Women*) (theatrical piece for women, with voices and instruments, 1964), *Prima vista* (for slides and an indeterminate number of sound sources, 1964), *Tremens* (scenic montage of a test for two actors and electrical instruments, 1965), *Acustica* (music for experimental sound sources, loudspeakers, and from two to five players, 1970), *Klangwehr* (*Sound Corps*) (for a marching military band, 1970), *Zwei-Mann-Orchester* (*Two-Man-Orchestra*) (for two one-man orchestras, 1973), *Bestiarium* (sound fables for two stages, 1976), *Déménagement* (*Moving*) (silent play for stage workers, 1977); radio plays, solo and orchestral works, chamber music.

State Theater

Stage composition in nine pieces

Première: 25 April, 1971, Hamburg (Staatsoper).

Performers: 1. *Repertoire. Theatrical Concert Piece* (at least five participants: instrumentalists or actors), 2. *Rehearsals. Music for Loudspeakers* (pre-recorded tapes), 3. *Ensemble for 16 Voices* (four each of sopranos, contraltos, and tenors; two baritones and two basses), 4. *Debut for 60 Voices* (chorus: 15 sopranos, 15 contraltos, 15 tenors, 15 basses), 5. *Season. "Singspiel" in 65 Scenes* (16–76 participants: male and/or female singers), 6. *Program. Instrumental Music in Action* (five to seven players, mainly percussionists), 7. *"Contredanse." Ballet for Non-Dancers* (seven male and female performers), 8. *Free-Passage. Gliding Chamber Music* (at least two players from each of the wind, string, and percussion sections), 9. *Stalls. Concert Mass Scenes* (10–76 participants and sound sources of various types).

Synopsis

1. *Repertoire*: Actors and instrumentalists produce sounds on non-instruments such as bicycle pumps, zippers, alarm clocks, cellophane paper, plates, wire brushes, squeaky toys, and bottles, attempting to outdo each other. 2. *Rehearsals*: The pre-recorded tapes can be played to any one of the other pieces. 3. *Ensemble*: 16 soloists, representatives of the main voice types (from coloratura soprano to *basso profundo*) demonstrate the power of their voices (in nonsense syllables). They form traditional as well as unconventional couples, and occupy old positions in the musical hierarchy as well as developing new ones. 4. *Debut*: 60 choral soloists make their debut in familiar roles ranging from beggar woman to king. 5. *Season*: Individual groups attempt to produce vocal novelties while sound effects are produced; random quotations from the current season's productions constantly intrude. 6. *Program*: Everyday objects and toys are used as percussion instruments. 7. *"Contredanse"*: Non-dancers attempt to perform demanding roles from classical ballet. 8. *Free-Passage*: For the imagination. A small number of instruments struggle to produce a small number of sounds for a vast repertory of imaginary opera scenes. 9. *Stalls*: The choir and soloists together produce the same series of chords, while performing gymnastic exercises.

S. N.

*K*agel, one of the wittiest
and most imaginative
composers of the 20th
century, is both a rationalist
and a mystic; he combines
the high spirits of a clown
with the seriousness of the
Enlightenment. His ability to
invent new sources of musical
sound and theatrical-musical
action is virtually endless.

Exercises for limbering up body and soul

State Theater was written as a commission for the
director of the Staatsoper in Hamburg, the composer
Rolf Liebermann. Kagel used the work to demonstrate
and dramatize the processes of making and listening to
music, its comic elements being derived from both
over- and understatement. The main theme is a critique
of the established opera business according to Kagel's
own maxim: "The music industry is unintentionally
comical." The disintegration of state theater into
specialized branches is carried to extremes, exposing
certain predominant forms of behavior, such as the
sense of superiority among vocalists and instrumentalists. *State Theater* is also a type of social criticism, a
depiction of the state as theater. In contrast to others of
his generation, such as Nono or Henze, Kagel does not
launch a direct attack on society; he is rather a master
of subtle criticism.

S. N.

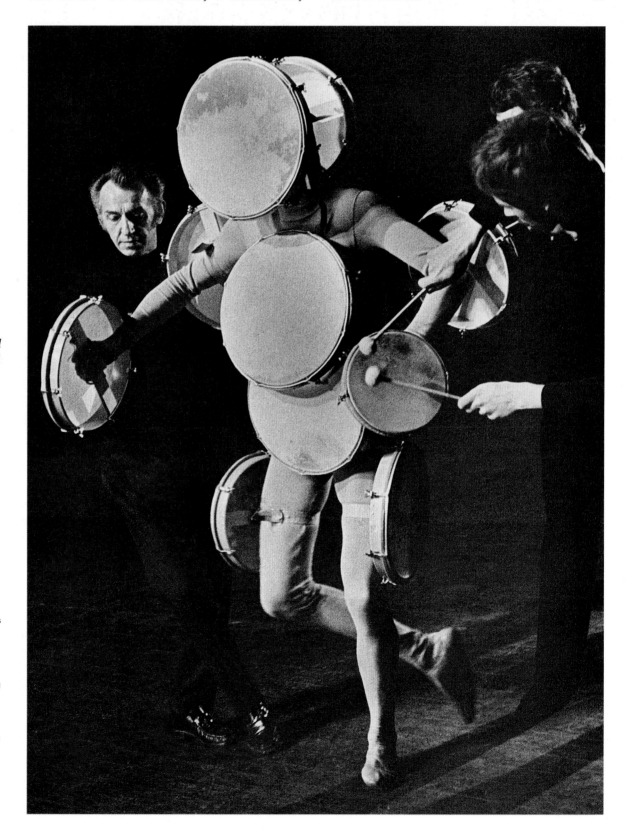

The Exhaustion of the World, photograph from the original production with Jutta Meyer zur Heide, Benno Ifland, and Jan Geerd Buss, production Mauricio Kagel, sets Helmut Stürmer, conductor Bernhard Kontarsky, sound-maker: Mauricio Kagel, Württembergisches Staatstheater, Stuttgart 1980.
While opera flourished in Frankfurt under the direction of Gielen (1977–87), who produced spectacular new interpretations of old works, the Stuttgart Opera was also making an equally impressive name for itself with a number of premières. Among these was The Exhaustion of the World, performed by Kagel himself.

The central work of a negative theology

Kagel, an exiled Argentinian, is at home in the Judeo-Christian tradition. Following his philosophical mentor, Spinoza, he developed a "negative theology," which is demonstrated in The Exhaustion of the World. Kagel described the work as a stage illusion in 11 scenes. The titles and sequence of the scenes provide the action: I. On the origins of some of the Lord's acts and curses. II. The creation of the stage set as a parable. III. The zoological garden of God. IV. A flood, The Flood, before The Flood. V. Hymn and procession of the images of God. VI. Chronicle of procreation and change. VII. Appetite and faith. VIII. Lamentations. IX. Funeral dance with thanksgiving. X. Tableau de concert. XI. God's mincing machine; Finale. The text that opens the opera and provides its title is taken from the psychoanalyst Tilmann Moser, who described his Prayers Before Dawn as God's poisoning: "Finally God exhausted / the heavens / and the earth. / The earth was desolate / and barren. / Smog lay on the waters, / and the spirit of God / swam in the sewer." The Exhaustion of the World was first performed in 1980, after six years' work, by the combined forces of the Stuttgart Theater and Opera, and South German Radio. The première was directed by Kagel himself and was enthusiastically received, being considered a counterpart to Penderecki's rappresentazione opera Paradise Lost, which had been premièred the year before at the Stuttgart Opera. Penderecki's adaptation of John Milton's epic poem affirmed the Christian tradition.

The Exhaustion of the World presented a critical view that acknowledged radical doubt, and even desperation: hope from hopelessness, according to Kagel. The Exhaustion of the World is not only an anti-cosmogony; it is a piece about music. Man's first creative stimulus and pleasure came from making music; even where there is not so much as the sound of a pipe there is the praise of God, murmured in ecstasy. The "Zoo of God" ispopulated with musical animals (a hippopotamus with two guitars as a mouth, a cow with a bell as an udder), which mate using genitals made from instruments.

An Argentinian in Germany

Kagel called his great opus *From Germany*, first performed in 1981 at the Deutsche Oper in Berlin, a "lieder opera." The texts, images, and music of German Romanticism provide the subject matter, and are recalled with profound understanding and considerable empathy. Kagel takes Romanticism and its metaphors literally; his "lieder opera" contains 27 scenes with more than 70 lieder texts by Heine, Hölderlin, Goethe, Eichendorff, Chamisso, and others, and is full of fantastic characters and events. Here, too, Kagel showed himself to be a master of perplexing references and images. But can an Argentine really do justice to German Romanticism, which is after all a very specific national legacy? Perhaps this question is best answered by Friedrich Schiller, who once said: "That which has been earned, can be owned."

S. N.

Below
From Germany, production photograph; production, sets and costumes Herbert Wernicke, conductor Jörg Henneberger, Theater Basel 1997. This Swiss production of an opera by an Argentinian about an essentially German subject (the Romantic movement) not only managed to convey the work's distinctive flavor, but also revealed its freshness, beauty, humor, playfulness, and poetry. It showed the universal character of Romanticism as well as its national limitations. This can be partly explained by the production's rejection of taboos and prejudices, as old texts were given new and even naïve interpretations.

From Germany, photograph from the production by Herbert Wernicke, conductor Jörg Henneberger, Theater Basel 1997. The desire for love and the pain of love, music as an expression of erotic fascination or as erotically motivated action, the tension between Eros and Thanatos (love and death) – these are the themes of German Romanticism which Herbert Wernicke brought to his production of Kagel's "lieder opera," embellishing it with light and transparent imagery, and with wit and irony, but also with a deeper meaning. The ambiguity of Romanticism and of Kagel's interpretation was somewhat overshadowed by the director's approach, and his tendency to place the work's hidden aspects center stage.

Kodály, Zoltán

b. 16 December 1882 in Kecskemét (Hungary)
d. 6 March 1967 in Budapest

As the son of a stationmaster whose profession required him to move often, Kodály did not receive regular musical tuition until a relatively late age, though music was both encouraged and performed in the family home. He was captivated by folk music at an early stage in his career, an interest that was to become a defining influence in his artistic development. In Budapest he studied Hungarian and German in the department of humanities at the university, and composition with Hans Koessler at the Music Academy. He wrote his doctoral thesis on the verse structure of Hungarian folk songs (1906). His first public appearance as a composer was in 1906, with *Sommerabend* (*Summer Evening*) for orchestra, and together with Béla Bartók, his friend and supporter in the struggle for a new Hungarian music, he edited a collection of folk songs. Around 1910 Kodály was regarded as being as avant-garde as Bartók, and the premières of their works were equally controversial. His earliest works (String Quartet no. 1, piano music, Cello Sonata) were influenced by contemporary French music (especially by →Debussy) and by Hungarian folk music. From 1908 he taught a composition class at the Budapest Academy of Music, and was a highly esteemed teacher of generations of Hungarian composers. Kodály's pupils continued his program of a "hundred year plan" for developing a choral culture and music for schools.

Works: Two "Singspiele": *Háry János* (1926), and *Székely fonó* (*The Spinning Room*) (1932); unaccompanied choral works (mixed choirs, children's choirs, male choirs), choral works with orchestra (including the masterpiece *Psalmus Hungaricus*, 1923), songs, adaptations of folk songs, symphonic works, chamber music, works for piano.

Kodály is the Hungarian national composer of the 20th century. His work as an academic and a teacher were just as important as his compositions.

Háry János, Hungarian Hussars, costume design by Tivadar Márk, Hungarian State Opera 1952.
The hussars may seem like toy soldiers in the fairy tale of *Háry János*, so unrealistic do their miraculous feats appear, but the chorus of soldiers and the recruitment music (Intermezzo, M 1) radiate the nation's self-confidence and pride, which was still intact after 450 years of foreign domination. In *Háry János* Kodály wanted to use adaptations of Hungarian folk songs in order to make the country's folk tradition familiar to an international audience. This goal was ultimately achieved not through the opera but through the now famous orchestral suite, which contains the opera's best numbers.

Háry János

Singspiel in a prologue, four adventures, and an epilogue

Libretto: Béla Paulini and Zsolt Harsányi (prose), folk songs (verse).
Première: 16 October 1926, Budapest (Royal Opera).

Characters: Háry János (Bar), Örzse, his fiancée (Ms), Emperor Franz (spoken), The Empress (S), Napoleon (Bar), Marie-Louise, the emperor's daughter and Napoleon's wife (Ms), Marzci, the coachman of Marie-Louise (B), Ebelasztin (T); General Crucifix, General Dufla, Countess Melusina, Baroness Estrella, Hungarian sentry, Russian sentry, Little Mother, First Hussar, Second Hussar, Third Hussar, First Artilleryman, Second Artilleryman, Footman, Guard, Steward, Village Mayor, Student, Innkeeper, First Peasant, Second Peasant (spoken); generals, Hungarian and French soldiers, Ruthenian girls, members of the court (chorus).
Setting: Nagyabony, Vienna, and northern Italy, c. 1810, at the time of the Napolenonic Wars.

Synopsis
Prologue

In the inn at Nagyabony, the retired soldier Háry János is once again telling of his adventures.

First adventure

János served as a hussar in the imperial army on the border with Russia. His fiancée Örzse had followed him there. One day, the Russian sentry refused to let the daughter of Emperor Franz I, Marie-Louise, cross the border. Háry János went immediately to her aid, and pushed the guard's hut containing Marie-Louise and her husband Napoleon across to the other side of the border. The road to Vienna was now clear! In gratitude, Marie-Louise took the burly hussar with her to Vienna to serve in her father's bodyguard. Örzse was allowed to go with him.

Háry János, the Hungarian Münchhausen
At the request of the Universal publishing house in Vienna, Kodály himself described the message behind *Háry János*: "Every Hungarian is a dreamer. He flees from the sad reality of the centuries … into the world of illusions. Yet Háry János's boasting is more than a dream: it is also poetry. The authors of heroic tales are themselves no heroes, but they are the spiritual kin of heroes. Háry János may never have done the deeds he talks about, but the potential was always there. János is a primitive poet, and what he has to say he concentrates in a single hero: himself. After we have listened to the heroic feats he has dreamed up, it is tragically symbolic that we see him again in a grubby village inn. He appears happy in his poverty: a king in the kingdom of his dreams."

Second adventure

At the royal court, János – now a sergeant – reins in a wild horse and cures the ageing emperor's gout. The nobleman, von Elbelasztin, is jealous of János and hands the emperor Napoleon's declaration of war, which he has until now carried in his jacket pocket. Emperor Franz hurriedly promotes Háry János to the rank of captain, and sends him as a trusted officer against Napoleon.

Third adventure

János attains the rank of colonel, defeats Napoleon near Milan and takes him prisoner. In recognition of his service, the Austrian General Crucifix awards him his own rank. When Marie-Louise sees Napoleon quaking with fear, she rejects him, and declares she wants to marry the new general: but Örzse objects.

Fourth adventure

Marie-Louise has separated from the cowardly Napoleon. Emperor Franz gives his approval to a marriage with János, and offers to give him half his empire as a dowry. János turns down the emperor's daughter and his offer of half the empire in order to return with Örzse to his homeland. Emperor Franz grants him early retirement from the army.

Epilogue

After returning home, the couple marry and live happily until Örzse's death; there is now no longer a living witness to János's heroic deeds. But who would ever doubt the truth of his tales?   *S. N.*

Háry János, Háry's room in the castle, set design by Gusztáv Oláh for the original production, Royal Opera, Budapest 1926 (Hungarian National Library, Theater Collection).
Háry János's room in the Vienna palace is given a Hungarian peasant's stove. The set design by Gusztáv Oláh retains the folk and oriental elements of Hungarian Art Nouveau. The humorous and ironic mood of the fairy tale, which is often taken to absurd lengths, has left its mark on this imaginative design. Gusztáv Oláh (1901–56) was one of the dominant personalities at the Budapest Opera for more than 20 years, and some of his designs have only recently passed out of use.

Below
Háry János, the double-headed eagle of the Habsburgs with a built-in mechanism for moving the wings, costume design by Tivadar Márk, Budapest State Opera
The double-headed eagle of the Habsburgs was an especially painful symbol for Hungary: it dominated the Hungarian coat of arms from 1745 (the accession of Maria Theresia) until the revolution of 1848. In a satirical scene in the Vienna palace, Háry's fiancée Örzse (a popular pet name for Elizabeth) feeds the double-headed eagle with corn while singing a sad Hungarian folk song. *M 2*

1. Intermezzo ("Verbunkos")

2. Folksong

Ti-szán in-nen, Du-nán túl, túl ___ a Ti-szán, van egý csi-kós nyá - jas - túl.

Korngold as a boy, c. 1908.
Korngold was one of the most talented musicians of the 20th century. His father, the famous music critic Julius Korngold, introduced his son to the very best academics and performers. Gustav Mahler was delighted with the child's talent, and recommended study with Alexander von Zemlinsky. Felix von Weingartner conducted the 12-year-old's pantomime at the Hofoper in Vienna, and one of his piano trios was premièred by Bruno Walter, Arnold Rosé (the leader of the Vienna Philharmonic), and the cellist Friedrich Buxbaum. His orchestral works were conducted by the greatest conductors of the day. Korngold had his first operatic premières at the age of 19 (*The Ring of Polycrates* and *Violenta*) and he was only 23 when his major work, *The City of the Dead*, was premièred simultaneously in Hamburg and Cologne.

The City of the Dead

Die tote Stadt

Opera in three scenes

Libretto: Paul Schott (Julius Leopold Korngold, and Erich Korngold), after the novel *Bruges-la-morte* (*Dead Bruges*) by Constantin Rodenbach, and *Le Mirage* (*The Mirage*) (1897) by Georges Raymond.
Première: 4 December 1920, Hamburg (Stadttheater) and Cologne (Opernhaus).

Characters: Paul (T), Marietta, a dancer, also the apparition of Marie, Paul's dead wife (S), Frank, Paul's friend (Bar), Brigitta, Paul's housekeeper (A), Juliette, a dancer (S), Lucienne, a dancer (Ms), Gaston, a dancer (mime), Victorin, a stage director (T), Fritz, the Pierrot (Bar), Count Albert (T); nuns, participants in the procession, dancers (chorus).
Setting: Bruges, the end of the 19th century.

Synopsis
Scene 1

Paul's room. Paul has built a "temple of memories" to his dead wife Marie in her former room, and lives a life of self-denial in Bruges, the "city of the dead" and symbol of the past. One day the dancer Marietta enters his life; she is touring with a company performing Meyerbeer's "Robert le diable." Marietta is the image of Paul's dead wife Marie. Paul invites Marietta to his house. With a song (now known as "Marietta's Song") and an erotic dance she flirts with him, but sees that he is obsessed with the memory of his dead wife. Marietta rushes off to her rehearsal. Confused, Paul imagines he hears Marie's vows of love, but the figure that utters them immediately changes into that of the dancing Marietta. He has a vision:

Scene 2

An abandoned quay in Bruges at night. Paul watches Marietta return home from the performance surrounded by high-spirited admirers who parody a scene from Meyerbeer's work. Paul brusquely interrupts this game. Marietta says goodbye to the others and turns her attention to Paul to try to banish the shadow of death with her seductive charms.

Scene 3

Paul's room the next morning. After a night spent together, Marietta believes she has cured Paul's obsession. A church procession goes past the house, and once again Paul is drawn into the vortex of death. Outraged, Marietta drapes the locks of Marie's hair from the "temple of memories" around her neck and begins an orgiastic dance. Paul strangles her, putting an end to his vision. In reality, only a few minutes have actually passed. Marietta returns once again to fetch the umbrella she had left behind. Paul feels liberated from his obsession and tells his friend Frank that he will now put his life in order and leave the "city of the dead."   *S. N.*

Korngold, Erich Wolfgang

b. 29 May 1897 in Brno
d. 29 November 1957 in Hollywood, Los Angeles

By the age of 11, this son of the music critic Julius Leopold Korngold had already had a number of successful performances. He studied in Vienna with Robert Fuchs and →Alexander von Zemlinsky, and quickly came to the attention of the music world. In 1921, a year after the triumphant première of his *The City of the Dead* in Hamburg, he was appointed to a position at the Hamburg Stadttheater. Ten years later, Korngold was called to a professorship at the Vienna Academy of Music, a position he gave up in 1934 in order to emigrate to America. Whereas in Europe his style was dismissed as "overblown," in Hollywood's film studios his dramatic gifts as a composer were positively received. Together with Max Steiner, he developed the so-called "Hollywood Sound." His work for Hollywood brought Korngold into disrepute in Europe, so that after 1945 he was unable to build on his earlier successes. The last part of his life was divided between Europe and the USA.

Works: Der Schneemann (*The Snowman*) (pantomime, 1910), *Der Ring des Polykrates* (*The Ring of Polycrates*) (1916, Munich), *Violanta* (1916, Munich), *Die tote Stadt* (*The City of the Dead*) (1920, Hamburg and Cologne), *Das Wunder der Heliane* (*The Miracle of Heliane*) (1927, Hamburg), *Die stumme Serenade* (*The Silent Serenade*) (1946/FP 1954, Dortmund); operettas.

The City of the Dead, production photograph with John Vickers as Paul, production Götz Friedrich, conductor Heinrich Hollreiser, Wiener Staatsoper 1985.
The first recording of *The City of the Dead* was made in 1975 – 55 years after the première – under the direction of Erich Leinsdorf, with Carol Neblett as Marietta and René Kollo as Paul. The moving story of Paul became part of the operatic repertory in Vienna, Korngold's own city, in 1985.

A forgotten hit

Puccini heard *The City of the Dead* while he was on a visit to Vienna and enjoyed it greatly. The libretto follows the premises of what was then the new discipline of psychoanalysis, and, to a degree, uses the illusion of the stage to depict the contours of a pathological obsession. Reality and dream are detached from one another, and the whole given a measure of ambiguity by the insertion of a scene from Giacomo Meyerbeer's opera →*Robert le diable.*

Korngold's style reveals the talents that were later to make him a successful composer of film music. The music proceeds on two levels; one is symphonically dominated and conveys emotional content, while the other is dramatic and pushes the events of the story forward. But neither the skillful dramatic construction nor the well-crafted parts were able to preserve the work from obscurity. As an opera in the real sense of the word it was considered too pathetic for the tastes of the interwar period; and after the Second World War, a time when either canonical works or absolute abstraction were the order of the day, it was considered too antiquated. All attempts at resurrecting the piece have been greeted with interest, but the opera has never been able to establish itself in the operatic repertory for any length of time.

Only a few opera fans know that it contains one of the finest of all melodies – the blissfully dreamy duet between Paul and Marietta. *M 1*   *M. S.*

*K*orngold's music is marked by rich, almost sentimental melodies, combined with colorful instrumentation.

The City of the Dead, set design by Johannes Schroeder, production Saladin Schmitt, Vereinigte Stadttheater Duisburg/Bochum 1931/32 (TWS).
Portraying a medieval city as a dead and ghostly place, a forsaken realm of past joys, and then reanimating it with color, processions, and the ringing of bells, clearly indicates that Korngold's opera is not simply a tale of a nostalgic and resigned romance.

1. Duet (Paul and Marietta)

Glück, das   mir ver - blieb,   rück zu mir, mein   treu - es Lieb.   A –   bend   sinkt im Hag, _ bist mir Licht und   Tag.

Krenek, Ernst

b. 23 August 1900 in Vienna
d. 22 December 1991 in Palm Springs

After studying under Franz Schreker in Vienna and Berlin, Krenek worked as artistic adviser at the Staatstheater in Kassel from 1925 to 1927. Here, his second opera *Orpheus und Eurydike* (*Orpheus and Eurydice*) was premièred in 1926, composed after a libretto by the painter Oskar Kokoschka. After the international success of his *Zeitoper* (opera of its time) *Jonny spielt auf* (*Jonny Strikes Up*), Krenek settled as a rich man in the well-to-do Viennese suburb of Hietzing. In 1938 he emigrated to the USA, where he had professorial posts at Vassar College (Poughkeepsie, NY) and at Hamline University (St. Paul, MN). In 1966 he moved to Palm Springs. It was in the US that he changed his name from Křenek to Krenek. In the last years of his life he spent the summer months in the "Schoenberg House" in Mödling, Austria.

Works: Operas: *Der Sprung über den Schatten* (*The Leap Over the Shadow*) (1924), *Orpheus und Eurydike* (1926), *Jonny spielt auf* (*Jonny Strikes Up the Band!*) (1927), *Der Diktator* (*The Dictator*) (1928), *Das geheime Königreich* (*The Secret Kingdom*) (1928), *Schwergewicht, oder Die Ehre der Nation* (*Heavyweight, or The Honor of the Nation*) (1928), *Leben des Orest* (*Life of Orestes*) (1930), *Karl V* (*Charles V*) (1938), *Tarquin* (1950), *Dark Waters* (1950), *Pallas Athene weint* (*Pallas Athene Weeps*) (1955), *The Belltower* (1957), *What Price Confidence?* (1962), *Der goldene Bock* (*The Golden Ram*) (1964), *Das kommt davon, oder Wenn Sardakai auf Reisen geht* (*Sardakai*) (1970), *Kehraus um St. Stephan* (*Cleanout at St. Stephen's*) (1990); television opera, operetta, ballet, orchestral and vocal works, chamber music.

Jonny spielt auf

Jonny Strikes Up the Band!

Opera in two parts (11 scenes)

Libretto: Ernst Krenek.
Première: 10 February 1927, Leipzig (Stadttheater).

Characters: Max, a composer (T), Anita, an opera singer (S), Jonny, a black jazz-band fiddler (Bar), Daniello, a virtuoso violinist (Bar), Yvonne, a hotel chambermaid (S), The Manager (B buffo), The Hotel Director (T), Railway Employee (T), Three Policemen (T, Bar, B); Chambermaid, Groom, Nightwatchman, Policeman, Two Chauffeurs, Shopgirl, Porter (silent); hotel guests, travelers, members of the public, voice of the glacier (chorus).
Setting: A large central European city, Paris, and the Alps, in the 1920s.

Synopsis
Part 1

The composer Max goes on a glacier walk with Anita, a singer, during which she distracts him from

his gloomy thoughts by assuring him of her love. But Anita becomes frightened at the lonely wastes on the glacier, and urges their return to the hotel where she goes off to prepare for a performance of his opera. As she leaves, the jazz violinist Jonny makes advances to her, but the violin virtuoso Daniello comes to her aid. He manipulates the situation in order to have a romantic adventure with Anita, but is puzzled when she returns to Max the next day. To satisfy Daniello's request for a keepsake, Anita gives him a ring. In the meantime, Jonny has played a trick on Daniello, swapping his valuable violin for Anita's banjo. Daniello reports the theft to the hotel director who suspects Yvonne, who is the chambermaid and Jonny's girlfriend. Yvonne is fired but is immediately taken into Anita's service.

Part 2

Daniello plans revenge. He persuades Yvonne to make sure the ring that Anita gave him falls into Max's hands. The plan seems to work: Max is unhappy about Anita's absence that night, and now believes that the ring is proof of her unfaithfulness. He determines to throw himself from the glacier, but the voice of the glacier admonishes him, telling him to turn back. Over the hotel loudspeaker he hears one of his songs performed by Anita, and is once again overcome with feeling for her. Jonny retrieves Daniello's violin, which Anita is unknowingly carrying around, in order to play it during a performance to be broadcast on the radio. Daniello recognises the sound of his instrument, but before the police arrive Jonny hurries to the railway station where he sees Max. The couple are off to America, where Anita has a concert date. He hides the instrument in their luggage. As the chief suspect, Max is arrested. But Yvonne has witnessed everything and steps forward to provide Max with an alibi. Daniello tries to prevent her, and in the ensuing commotion he falls under a moving train. Jonny promises Yvonne that he will put everything right. He helps Max to escape from the police station and brings him as quickly as possible to the railway station, where he just manages to catch the train departing with Anita for the New World. As the hero of the day – and of his age – Jonny, the man and artist of the future, strikes up a melody on Daniello's violin. *M. S.*

*K*renek is one of the first 20th-century composers who could be called "postmodern." He was exemplary in his free use of a wide range of compositional techniques, was as familiar with Expressionism as he was with Romanticism, and incorporated into his music elements of both jazz and electronic music.

1. Jonny's Way

Oh,   ma bell',   nicht so schnell,   gib   mir ei - ne   kiss!

2. Locomotive Motif

Jonny spielt auf, costume design for Jonny by Lothar Schenck von Trapp, Darmstadt 1927/28 (TWS).
In the *Zeitoper* of the 1920s, a mythical America was presented as a symbol of modernism. The figure of Jonny embodies the New Man, who will sweep away Europe's old and exhausted culture and the burdens of its tradition (represented in the opera by the decadent violinist and the brooding composer) with his vigor and instinctive musicality. *M 1*

Opposite
Jonny spielt auf, set design by Paul Schönke for the production by Ernst Legal, Staatliches Theater, Kassel 1927/28 (TWS).
Fashionable dance music and the musical interpretation of the sounds of a railway station *M 2* were critical elements in this most successful of all *Zeitopern*. The ghostly realism of this design for the station scene by Paul Schönke – bereft of people but otherwise accurate in all its details – betrays some of the current fears about the technological age. The death of the violinist Daniello under the wheels of a train was therefore all the more significant.

Opera of its time

The modernism inherent in the term "Zeitoper," or "opera of its time," consisted in everyday settings (the mountains, the hotel and the railway station), in the integration into the work of mundane events (the radio performance by the black jazz musician), and in the presence of technology (the railway station).

At the time of the work's composition, radio had only just been discovered by the well-to-do. In addition to that, jazz musicians were an indispensable part of modern hotels and other establishments in the 1920s and 1930s. It was precisely this openness toward the spirit of the age that led to Krenek's success, but it also caused some to doubt his seriousness, even though the artistic nature of his style, apparent even in the jazz sequences, classifies it as "high brow" music.

In spite of these misgivings, the public's enthusiasm for *Jonny* was of a type usually reserved for operettas: *Jonny spielt auf* was performed 500 times in a single season. By 1930 the work had been staged at 70 theaters, before it came to be scorned by the Nazis as "degenerate art." *M. S.*

Below
Kurt Weill, *The Tsar Has His Photograph Taken*, set design by Johannes
Schroeder, Vereinigte Stadttheater, Duisburg 1929 (TWS).
The *Zeitoper* of the 1920s was a musical production that aimed to have the
realism and relevance of a newspaper report. Other terms used to describe the
genre included "musical comedy," "operatic revue," "comic opera," "jazz
opera," "contemporary opera," and *Zeitoper*-revue. Cars, radios, and
telephones were often seen or heard on stage, and the action moved at a fast,
film-like pace. In Paul Hindemith's opera *Hin und Zurück* (*There and Back*), the
action did in fact oscillate back and forth. In his comic one-act opera *The Tsar
Has His Photograph Taken*, Kurt Weill satirized armchair revolutionaries; their
carefully planned assassination of the Tsar of all the Russias (the last of the
Romanov dynasty had in fact been murdered ten years before by the
Bolsheviks) fails miserably.

Above
Jonny spielt auf, set design by Lothar Schenk von Trapp for the production by
Renato Mordo, conductor Karl Böhm, Hessisches Landestheater, Darmstadt
1927–28 (TWS).
A backdrop using the collage technique of the 1920s. In the mid-1920s, many
Europeans scarred by their experiences of the First World War came to see
America as a kind of Promised Land. Just how quickly this cult of America
developed into an independent fashion is demonstrated by this backdrop,
which represents a snapshot of the so-called "American way of life." But this
homage to the USA has relatively little to do with Krenek's opera: Jonny's lack
of sexual, moral, and musical inhibitions symbolized the demise of an old
culture rather than the triumph of the New World. Jonny was the herald of a
new, primitive, and barbaric agè. The conclusion of this *Zeitoper* – by far the
most popular of its type – is more puzzling than programmatic: is the "dance"
Jonny plays a dance of joy or of death?

Right
Max Brand, *Maschinist Hopkins*, set design
by Johannes Schroeder for the première,
Duisburger Staatsoper 1929 (TWS).
Max Brand owed the "machine music" for his
opera *Maschinist Hopkins* (1929) to the
Futurist movement. Heinrich Strobel, a critic
in Berlin, commented that "people were
trying from every angle to redefine the
concept of opera. They were fed up with
productions which were always set in distant,
fantastic worlds; people were gripped by
modern life and it was that they wished to see
on stage."

Above
Paul Hindemith, *News of the Day*, set design by Traugott Müller for the original production by Ernst Legal, conductor Otto Klemperer, Krolloper (Staatsoper am Platz der Republik), Berlin 1929 (TWS).
Paul Hindemith's opera →*News of the Day* is a satire on the media age. The work features open-plan offices with clattering typewriters, the visual chaos of advertising signs, a marital crisis, and the symbolic destruction of a 3000-year-old statue of Venus (a carefully preserved European cult object!).

Right
George Antheil, *Transatlantic*, set design by Ludwig Sievert for the original production by Herbert Graf, conductor Hans-Wilhelm Steinberg, Opernhaus Frankfurt 1930 (TWS).
The *Zeitoper* was short-lived: like the ship in the 1930s' opera *Transatlantic*, it seemed to disappear for good. In the 1990s, however, it experienced something of a revival, when the popular American composer John Adams based his operas →*Nixon in China* and →*The Death of Klinghoffer* on recent political events.

The Dictator

Tragic opera in one act (two scenes)

Libretto: Ernst Krenek.
Première: 6 May 1928, Wiesbaden (Staatstheater).

Characters: The Dictator (Bar), Charlotte, his wife (S), The Officer (T), Maria, his wife (S); Courier, Groom, Orderly, Detective (silent).
Setting: Any country, after the First World War.

Synopsis

When the Dictator declares war on a small country, he is criticized by his wife Charlotte for causing blood to be spilled unnecessarily. Her words have no effect: the Dictator proposes a toast to his own power, and keeps his gaze fixed on Maria in the sanatorium opposite as she tends her husband, who has been blinded in the war. Maria wants to kill the person responsible for this suffering. But instead of taking action, she allows herself to become involved in an argument with the Dictator; she loses and submits to him. Charlotte observes the scene from the wings. As Maria is about to surrender herself to the Dictator, Charlotte shoots but hits Maria. Standing by Maria's body, the blind man asks his wife if her act of revenge has been carried out. M.S.

The Dictator, production photograph with Karl-Friedrich Dürr (The Dictator) and Ulrike Sonntag (Charlotte), production Brian Michaels, conductor Manfred Schreier, Württembergisches Staatstheater, Stuttgart 1990. Krenek called *The Dictator* a tragic opera, but not without irony: it paradoxically merges a marital and a political crisis.

The Secret Kingdom photograph from the production by Brian Michaels, conductor Manfred Schreier, Württembergisches Staatstheater, Stuttgart 1990. Krenek's operatic triptych is a series of variations on extraordinarily absurd events, which take place so illogically and implausibly they could almost be real. The 28-year-old composer's message seems to have been that the world is unfathomable and therefore terrifying. *The Secret Kingdom* forms the slow, lyrical central "movement" of Krenek's cycle of three one-act operas. These works were first performed in 1980, in Minneapolis, and were resurrected in various European opera houses in the early 1990s. The composer lived long enough to see the generous and appreciative way in which his cycle was received.

The Secret Kingdom

Das geheime Königreich

Fairy-tale opera in one act (two scenes)

Libretto: Ernst Krenek.
Première: 6 May 1928, Wiesbaden (Staatstheater).
Characters: The King (Bar), The Queen (S), Fool (Bar), Rebel (T), Three Singing Ladies (S, Ms, A), First Revolutionary (T), Second Revolutionary (B), Guard (T); rebels, dancers, ladies-in-waiting (chorus).
Setting: That of fairy tale.

Synopsis

There is unrest in the kingdom: the people are in open revolt. The king hands over his royal insignia to his fool. In the meantime, the queen is turning her attention to a handsome prisoner, a rebel, who is interested in the crown only so as to hand it over to the people.

The queen uses all the means at her disposal to deprive the fool of his clothing and insignia, and releases the rebel from jail. The rebel immediately whips up the people and storms the palace, so that the queen, the fool, and the king – in the fool's motley – are forced to flee. The rebel overtakes the queen and forces her to give up her insignia, which she attempts to deny him, disrobing seductively. As he throws himself at her, she is changed into a tree.

The king wishes to die; because he is not recognised by two rebels who seek to kill the king for the bounty placed on his head, he decides to do away with himself. As if by magic, the woods light up: the king recognises the beauty of nature and passes away peacefully. M.S.

Heavyweight or the Honor of the Nation

Schwergewicht, oder Die Ehre der Nation

Burlesque operetta in one act

Libretto: Ernst Krenek.
Première: 6 May 1928, Wiesbaden (Staatstheater).
Characters: Adam Ochsenschwanz, a boxing master (B), Evelyne, his wife (S), Gaston, a dancing master (T), Professor Himmelhuber (Bar), Anna Maria Himmelhuber, his daughter (Ms), Journalist (T), Government Official (T), Ottokar, Ochsenschwanz's servant (silent), Chambermaid (silent).
Setting: The training room in the house of the boxing master, in the present day.

Synopsis

The boxer Ochsenschwanz is angered by his wife's dancing lessons with Gaston, as he thinks they are having an affair. Evelyne is indeed more interested in Gaston than in dancing; observing a secret kiss between the two, Ochsenschwanz loses his composure, wrecks a table, and locks up his wife, while Gaston hides in a neighboring room. At that moment the student Anna Maria Himmelhuber slips quietly into the room to request an autograph from Ochsenschwanz. Discovered by Gaston, she disguises herself as a boxing dummy in order to hide from her father, Professor Himmelhuber, who has arrived to award the famous boxer an honorary doctorate. The boxer is flattered and sets about proving his skill by

punching the dummy. The professor recognizes his daughter and promptly charges Ochsenschwanz with abuse of a minor. Furious, the boxer takes to his training machine, which Gaston switches on so that he can escape with Evelyne. Ochsenschwanz is trapped in the machine and forced to continue exercising. Even the government official who arrives with an invitation to attend the Olympic Games dares not switch the machine off for fear that he might disturb the boxer.   *M. S.*

Heavyweight, or The Honor of the Nation, production photograph with Karl-Friedrich Dürr as Adam Ochsenschwanz, production Brian Michaels, costumes Katrin Scholz, conductor Manfred Schreier, Württembergisches Staatstheater, Stuttgart 1990.

Below
Heavyweight, or the Honor of the Nation, set design by Egon Wilden, Hagen/Eberfeld-Barmen 1928/29 (TWS).
Training and fitness equipment are seen to unite America and Europe in an international enthusiasm for sport. As an intellectual himself, Krenek wished to register his outrage at the claim of a diplomat that sportsmen had done more for Germany's international standing than had the nation's intellectual elite. An operetta, *Heavyweight* is characterized by a transparent conversational style which was well received by the public.

Charles V

Karl V

Stage work with music, in two parts

Libretto: Ernst Krenek.
Première: First version: 22 June 1938, Prague (New German Theater); second version: 11 May 1958, Düsseldorf (Deutsche Oper am Rhein).
Characters: Karl V/Charles V (Bar), Juana, his mother (A), Eleonore, his sister (S), Ferdinand, his brother (T), Isabella, his wife (S), Juan de Regla, his father confessor (spoken), Henri Mathys, his physician (spoken), Francisco Borgia, a Jesuit, former majordomo to the queen (T), Alarcon, Alba, Frundsberg, and Lannoy, captains of the king (4 spoken), Chancellor (spoken), Pizarro (T), A Spanish Free Spirit (spoken), François I/Francis I (T), Frangipani (T), Pope Clement VII (spoken), A Cardinal (spoken), Martin Luther (Bar), Moritz of Saxony (spoken), A Follower of Luther (T), A Protestant Captain (spoken), Sultan Soliman/Suleiman (B), His Court Astrologer (T), Four Spirits (2 S, Ms, A), Four Clocks (2 S, 2 A); the voice of God, alumni of the monastery, clerics, Spanish heretics, German mercenaries, Spanish ladies, nuns, German and Spanish people, voices of the dead (chorus).
Setting: Europe, 1558.

Synopsis

Charles V confesses to the young monk Juan de Regla the errors of a life spent caught between external forces and his ethical and religious idealism. While Juan slowly begins to understand Charles V, the Jesuit priest Borgia – the personification of a dutiful conscience – insists on a confession of guilt.

Part 1

In order to find inner peace at the end of his life, Charles V visits the young monk Juan de Regla at the monastery of San Yuste. Called to account by the voice of God, he seeks to reveal the divided nature of his existence – symbolized by his coat of arms – in a confession encompassing his entire life. In his youth Charles V had hoped for the spiritual renewal of the Christian world, but after Luther's break from the Roman church he had begun to doubt the possibility of lasting unity within the church. National interests had also stood in the way. Despite being married to Charles's sister Eleonore, the French king, Francis I, had refused to enter into negotiations for peace, even supporting the Turks in their hostilities against Charles. Furthermore, Rome had plundered by German soldiers, leading to a serious conflict with the Pope and strengthening the Protestant cause.

Charles had been ruthless in his persecution of heretics until the death of his wife, which taught him to appreciate the suffering of others. This caused him to waver in his resolve to use bloody measures to defend his religion. At this point in his narrative, Charles V is overcome with emotion and sinks unconscious to the floor.

Part 2

Charles V's heartfelt outburst awakens doubts in Juan, which the Jesuit Francisco Borgia seeks to crush by pointing to the unchanging nature of belief and morality. He accuses Charles of religious laxness. Juan pities Charles, but Borgia accuses him of allowing emotion to interfere with the execution of duty. When Charles regains consciousness, he goes on to explain that he had wanted to achieve the goals of his youth. After Luther's death, he had enforced the conversion of all German Protestants to Catholicism, but this turned the people against him and strengthened the position of his religious opponent, Sultan Suleiman. These events compelled his abdication. Juan accepts Charles's actions had been motivated by external circumstances, but Borgia still insists on a confession of remorse from the dying man.   M. S.

Above right
Charles V, photograph from the production by Otto Schenk, sets and costumes Xenia Hausner, conductor Erich Leinsdorf, Wiener Staatsoper 1984.
Charles V is Krenek's most important opera. A dense and complicated composition, it is a philosophical opera in the manner of Hans Pfitzner's →*Palestrina*. The reputation of *Charles V* is also evidence for the increasing influence of Krenek's work on the world of opera. After its première in Prague, *Charles V* was not performed again until a production in Essen in 1950. Today, however, *Charles V* is a staple of the international operatic repertory.

Below left
Charles V, photograph from the production by Otto Schenk, sets and costumes Xenia Hausner, conductor Erich Leinsdorf, Wiener Staatsoper 1984.
Though commissioned by the Wiener Staatsoper, *Charles V* was not premièred there, because of the invasion by German troops. For his 1984 Vienna production, Schenk could not merely stage the piece as an historical drama and pretend that nothing had happened in the interim. In spite of its historical setting both the work and the production developed into a debate on the rights and wrongs of hegemonic assertions of power.

Europe, 1933

With the deterioration of the political situation in Germany around 1930, Krenek began to have doubts about what might be termed his "neo-Romantic" style. He wanted to play an active part in political life as an artist and intellectual. He had already taken up a clear position against every form of tyranny in his one-act opera *The Dictator*. Because it offered him an effective platform from which to criticize the events of his day, he responded with great enthusiasm to the suggestion of the conductor Clemens Krauss that he write an historical piece for the Wiener Staatsoper. The idea of equating a Christian empire with the ideology of the Christian state of Austria in 1933 required detailed historical study. Krenek wanted to send out a clear signal that he opposed any aspirations of the Third Reich to annex Austria. The opera was written between July 1932 and May 1933. Three months before its première, troops from fascist Germany marched into Austria. In a second version dating 1954, Charles's moment of remorse was removed from the conclusion. In order to portray the connection between past and present, the action takes place on two levels at the same time, a technique that was inspired by Baroque drama and influenced by the epic theater of Kurt Weill and Bertold Brecht, as well as by the use of the flashback technique in films. The use of dodecaphony in the work was new; Krenek felt this was the only communicative medium appropriate to this type of subject matter, although he by no means abandoned traditional structural methods. *M. S.*

Charles V, set design by Paul Haferung for the production by Hans Hartleb, conductor Gustav König, Städtische Bühnen, Essen 1950 (TWS).
The focus of the set for this production was a free adaptation of an historic painting – the *Adoration of the Trinity (La Gloria)* by Titian (c. 1554), which was commissioned by Charles V. He treasured the picture above all else, and even had it at his side in the San Yuste monastery. In his will he referred to the painting as "The Last Judgment."

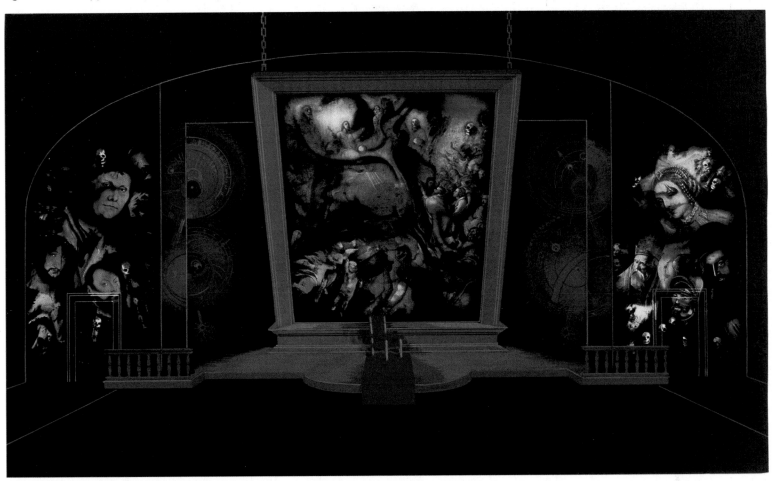

An opera about history

Charles V (1500–58), whose portrait was painted twice by the artist Titian, was one of the most important rulers throughout European history.

In order to consolidate the power of his empire, he was forced to fight against France, against the Reformation movement, and against the independent German princes. He dreamed of a single *Monarchia universalis* but at the end of his life, as a lonely monk in the monastery of San Yuste in Spain, he had to acknowledge that the age of universal power was coming to an end.

Krenek saw in Charles V a great conciliatory figure of the sort Europe desperately needed at a time of increasing National Socialist tendencies. But Krenek additionally wanted to examine the problems of political responsibility, and especially the way in which the actions of a ruler can be justified by reference to historical circumstances. He wanted to portray the multiplicity of history in the sense of Leo Tolstoy's great novel *War and Peace*, and he therefore chose that most complex of musical methods, the 12-tone technique: *Charles V* was consequently the first opera in musical history to be composed strictly according to the 12-tone technique.

Leoncavallo, Ruggiero

b. 8 March (or 23 April) 1850 in Naples
d. 9 August 1919 in Bagni di Montecatini

The son of a police official, Leoncavallo studied composition in Naples (under Lauro Rossi) and then literature at Bologna University. Inspired by his study of literature, he developed an interest in the music dramas of →Wagner, under the influence of which he wrote his first opera, *Chatterton*. Of his projected historical trilogy, only the first part, *I Medici* (*The Medici*), was completed. As a café pianist Leoncavallo traveled throughout Europe and beyond as far as Egypt. His years of wandering ended when he met the publisher Giulio Ricordi, who commissioned an opera from him. Ricordi was unhappy with the result, *I Medici*, and the two men parted company. Leoncavallo subsequently transferred allegiance to Ricordi's rival, Sonzogno, and within five months he had composed the opera *Pagliacci* (*Players*), a work that marked the start of his international career. One of the first composers to become seriously interested in gramophone recordings, Leoncavallo wrote the famous song *Mattinata*, which was recorded by the great opera singer Enrico Caruso in 1904. Three years later he directed the recording of *Pagliacci* – the first time a complete Italian opera had been captured by this new technology! His later operas were also successful, and by the time he died he was a fashionable composer who was much in demand – though he had come a long way from his original intention to transfer the Wagnerian *Gesamtkunstwerk* to Italian soil.

Works: Operas: *Chatterton* (1876), *Pagliacci* (*Players*) (1892), *I Medici* (*The Medici*) (1893), *La Bohème* (*Bohemian Life*) (1897), *Zazà* (1900), *Il Rolando* (*Roland from Berlin*) (1904), *Maia* (1910), *Zingari* (*Gypsies*) (1912), *Edipo Re* (*King Oedipus*) (1920), *Prometeo* (*Prometheus*) (unpublished, unperformed); nine operettas, songs, choral, orchestral, and piano works.

Pagliacci, set design by Johann Kautsky, Berlin 1904 (TWS).
This set design by Johann Kautsky shows how long it took to develop a stage design that was capable of meeting the aesthetic demands of fin de siècle opera. Instead of a simple and sparse stage suitable for the small wandering troupe of players, Kautzky created an idealized little theater. Decorative and fabulous sets were still standard features of the operatic stage at a time when operatic naturalism (*verismo*) was undergoing an upsurge in popularity. Most sets were built in studios and delivered to the theater from there; they were often generic designs created for use in the kinds of scene that were traditionally required by opera.

Below
Pagliacci, set design by Helene Gliewe, Städtische Bühnen Mönchengladbach/Rheydt, 1937/38 (TWS).
Surrounded by ruins and lit by pale moonlight, this small, improvised stage outside the city precincts resembles a place of execution. The Constructivist elements of the set (popular with designers since the 1920s) together with the Expressionist components (the garish colors) are highly effective, and create the sense of a universal location where only the rituals of death can occur.

Pagliacci

Drama in a prologue and two acts

Libretto: Ruggiero Leoncavallo.

Première: 21 May 1892, Milan (Teatro dal Verme).

Characters: Canio (in the play, Pagliaccio), the principal in a troupe of players (T), Nedda (in the play, Colombina/Columbine), Canio's wife (S), Tonio (in the play, Taddeo), a hunchbacked clown (Bar), Beppe (in the play, Arlecchino/Harlequin) (T), Silvio, a villager (Bar), Two Villagers (T, B); boys, peasants, musicians (chorus).

Setting: Close to Montalto, in Calabria, between 1865 and 1870 on the feast of the Assumption (15 August).

Synopsis

The players have set up their stage in the village square. The clown Tonio confides his philosophy of life and art to the public: the dualism of appearance and reality, art and life, mask and man, is blurred by the truth of performance and the impossibility of sharing feelings. Canio announces the evening's performance: a play about love and jealousy. His pretty young wife Nedda is wooed by the misshapen Tonio. The villagers laugh about this, but Canio warns them that although he may play the dumb Pagliaccio he is not to be joked with in real life. When Tonio becomes too persistent, Nedda drives him off with a whip. The hunchback's love now turns to hatred. He reveals to Canio Nedda's love for a young villager, Silvio. Canio seeks revenge, and Silvio only just manages to escape his rage. In the course of the evening's performance, Nedda plays Columbine, who deceives Pagliaccio (Canio) with Harlequin. Canio is overwhelmed by his passion, and demands to know the name of the young villager. When Nedda/Columbine refuses to reveal it, he stabs her, and when Silvio runs to help her he too is killed. Tonio sends the audience home: the play is over ...

S. N.

Pagliacci, set design by Otto Reigbert for the production by Walter Felsenstein, conductor Fritz Zaun, Städtische Bühnen, Cologne 1933 (TWS).
This production of *Pagliacci* was set at the time of the Depression (the 1930s) in a proletarian setting. The contrast between the shabby tent of the players beneath an ordinary streetlamp and the beautifully ordered Renaissance houses of a small Italian town highlights the relationship between the *commedia dell'arte* and the ageless (and ever relevant) drama of jealous lovers. It also makes clear Nedda's motivation for seeking to escape from this oppressive world.

*L*eoncavallo is one of the most prominent and successful representatives of Italian "verismo." At the turn of the century he was regarded as a rival of Puccini.

Right
Pagliacci, Franco Corelli as Canio, Teatro alla
Scala, Milan 1955–56.
Because of the dramatic power and heroic
timbre of his voice, the Italian *Heldentenor*
Franco Corelli (b. 1921) is considered by
many to be the greatest Italian tenor of the
1950s and 1960s. He made his debut in 1951
in the role of Don José (in Bizet's →*Carmen*),
and within a few years had sung at all the
major opera houses of the world (La Scala,
The Met, the Wiener Staatsoper). He was
Birgit Nilsson's partner in the *Turandot*
productions of around 1960, which were
known as "the Battle of the Giants."

Below
Pagliacci, production photograph with
Placido Domingo as Canio, production
Jean-Pierre Ponnelle, conductor Adam
Fischer, Wiener Staatsoper 1985.
"Tu sei pagliaccio!" ("You are a clown!"):
even if he is suffering as a man, the clown
must entertain his audience. This has been a
popular theme in all artistic genres from
Watteau to Fellini. In his famous monologue
"Vesti la gubba" ("Put on your costume"),
Leoncavallo's Canio reveals the isolation of
the artist unable to find his place in society,
who is compelled from within to dwell in an
imaginary world as the hero of his own story.

A foreword set to music

Throughout the history of opera, composers have announced their aesthetic programs to the public either, like Lully and Gluck, in the form of a foreword to a published score, or, like Wagner, Busoni, and others, as a separate explanatory publication. Leoncavallo set his aesthetic program to music, and attached it to *Pagliacci* as a prologue. Tonio confides to the audience the "poet's intention" of presenting real people with real feelings within the framework of the *commedia dell'arte*. But in the loveliest melody in this prologue – an Andante triste – Leoncavallo indicates that the composer himself is hiding behind the clown's mask. M 1

Melancholy clowns

In the most famous number of the opera, "Ridi, Pagliaccio" ("Laugh, Pagliaccio") – a phrase which has since become a common expression – Canio reveals his pain: he is playing out his life on stage in the role of a cuckolded husband. M 2

What is presented in *Pagliacci* as an inescapable fate, in Goldschmidt's →*The Magnificent Cuckold* of 40 years later becomes a parody of an ancient bourgeois foible: the idea of regarding the world solely in terms of ownership.

As the leading player, Canio is domineering and

sometimes brutal, but he is essentially a resigned man, and probably much older than his beautiful wife Nedda. In spite of his tyrannical attitude, he loves her desperately. When the villagers taunt him with Tonio's advances to his wife, Canio responds with a magnificently sad cantabile, M 3 and concludes with a confession that Puccini quoted almost word for word ten years later (*Tosca*, →Cavaradossi's "Picture Aria," Act I): "Adoro la mia sposa!" ("I adore my wife!"). M 4

Nedda fears the possessive love of her husband and is sick of the itinerant life. She wants to be free, like a bird. Her *ballatella* (a small ballad) is a brilliant piece with superb instrumentation. The sublime orchestration of the work is a clear indication that Leoncavallo belonged to the generation of Italian Wagnerians. M 5

"The tenor wants to go to bed with the soprano, but is prevented from doing so by the baritone." George Bernard Shaw's witty description of nineteenth-century operatic plots does not apply to *Pagliacci*. Here the cuckolded husband is a tenor, while both the rejected and the successful lover are baritones. The hunchback Tonio loves Nedda, but is almost in awe of her at the beginning of the opera. After the *ballatella* he speaks to Nedda "con dolcezza" ("gently"), and the last three fading chords are "dolcissimi … con espressione dolorosa" ("very gentle … and painfully expressive"). After his humiliation, however, Tonio becomes not only angry but also vengeful. M 6

Left
Pagliacci, rehearsal photograph with Ileana Cotrubas (Nedda), Placido Domingo (Canio), and Jean-Pierre Ponnelle, production Jean-Pierre Ponnelle, conductor Adam Fischer, Wiener Staatsoper 1985.
Rehearsing a murder. Director and set designer Jean-Pierre Ponnelle (1932–88) was able to play by heart on the piano all the operas he staged, and had the unique capacity for getting the maximum effect from every chord and every word. This picture shows him as a tireless and omnipresent director.

Right
Pagliacci, Caruso as Canio, self-caricature, Vienna 1911.
Caruso as Canio: Caruso sang this role more than 100 times, immortalizing himself in a skillful self-caricature. According to tradition, he and his predecessor Fernando de Lucia (the first Canio) were responsible for putting the final words of the opera – "La commedia è finita!" ("The play is ended!") – into the mouth of Canio. Leoncavallo's manuscript score shows that this was not the composer's intention. He wanted the piece to end the way it began – with Tonio turning to address the fictitious as well as the real audience.

Below
Pagliacci, production photograph with Ileana Cotrubas (Nedda), Placido Domingo (Canio), and Matteo Manuguerra (Tonio), production Jean-Pierre Ponnelle, conductor Adam Fischer, Wiener Staatsoper 1985.
The murder. Together with →*Cavalleria rusticana*, *Pagliacci* established the genre of the one-act shocker at the turn of the century. From the →*Cavalleria rusticana* (Mascagni, 1890) to →*Il tabarro* (Puccini, 1918) the heart-stopping finale is an indispensable part of the dramatic arsenal.

Nedda's real lover, Silvio, is also somewhat melancholy. He approaches her "mestamente e con amore" ("sadly, affectionately"). Is he aware of the tragic nature of their love? M 7. The love duet in which Silvio persuades Nedda to elope with him is rooted in the second act of Wagner's →*Tristan and Isolde*. It has a dreamlike quality and a profound sense of withdrawal from the world. The culmination of the duet strongly resembles the night hymn of Tristan and Isolde (→Night love-hymn). Even the text has a similar meaning: "Tutto scordiam!" ("Let us forget everything!"). M 8

1. Tonio's Prologue

Un ni - do di me - mo - rie in fon do a - ll'ani - ma can - ta - va un gior - no,

2. "Laugh, Pagliaccio"

Ri - di Pa - gliac - cio, sul tuo a - mo - re in - fran - to!

3. Canio's Cantabile

Un tal gio - co, cre - de - te - mi,___ è me - glio non gio - car - lo con me, miei ca - ri;

4. Canio's Love Motif

A - do - ro la mia spo - sa!...

5. Nedda's Ballatella

Stri - do - no las - sù, ___ li - be - ra - men - te...

6. Tonio's Gentle Chords

7. Silvio's Melancholy

8. Love Duet (Nedda and Silvio)

Tut - to scor - diam! ___ Tut - to scor - diam! ___

64

J. V. Dupleßis inv.   *L. Desplaces scul.*

ACTE SECOND

Marschner, Heinrich

b. 16 August 1795 in Zittau
d. 14 December 1861 in Hanover

Though he had no musical education, Marschner wrote the ballet *Die stolze Bäuerin* (*The Proud Peasant*) in 1810, aged 15. Having begun to study law in Leipzig, he attended courses given there by Kirnberger and Türk and undertook his first concert tours, finally deciding on a musical career. In 1816 he acceped the position of music teacher to Count Zichy in Pressburg (Bratislava), and was appointed *Kapellmeister* to Prince Krasatkowitz. In 1820 →Weber successfully produced *Henry IV and d'Aubigné* in Dresden. Marschner settled in Dresden, and worked as a stage composer and conductor. He left in 1826, after failing to secure Weber's former post as royal *Kapellmeister*. He assumed direction of the orchestra at the Leipzig Stadttheater in 1827, and in 1831 became conductor at the Hoftheater in Hanover. After he retired in 1859 he lived in Paris.

Works: Operas: *Titus* (1816), *Saidar und Zulima* (*Saidar and Zulima*) (1818), *Das stille Volk* (*The Silent People*) (1818), *Heinrich IV und d'Aubigné* (*Henry IV and d'Aubigné*) (1820), *Der Kyffhäusserberg* (*Mount Kyffhäusser*) (1822), *Der Holzdieb* (*The Wood Thief*) (1825), *Lukretia* (*Lucretia*) (1827), *Der Vampyr* (*The Vampire*) (1828), *Der Templer und die Jüdin* (*The Templar and the Jewess*) (1829), *Des Falkners Braut* (*The Falconer's Bride*) (1832), *Hans Heiling* (1833), *Das Schloss am Ätna* (*The Castle on Mount Etna*) (1836), *Kaiser Adolph von Nassau* (*Emperor Adolph von Nassau*) (1845), *Austin* (1852), *Sangeskönig Hiarne, oder das Tyrsingsschwert* (*Hiarne, the King of Song, or The Sword of Tyrsing*) (1863); music for plays, songs, choral and orchestral works, chamber music.

arschner is a true German Romantic with his masterful descriptions of nature and his sensitivity towards the supernatural. He developed an effective technique of dramatic declamation and was capable of subtle orchestration. He is the most important German opera composer between Weber and Wagner.

Hans Heiling, design for a fresco for the Wiener Hofoper (lunette) by Moritz von Schwind, 1866.
This fairy-tale opera had fairy-tale origins: early in 1831 Marschner received a libretto from an anonymous correspondent which so gripped him that he immediately began to set it to music. The librettist was later revealed to be the baritone Eduard Devrient from the Opernhaus in Berlin, who had sung the role of the Knight Templar in Marschner's successful opera *The Templar and the Jewess*. Devrient had already offered the libretto to Mendelssohn, but the composer had rejected it, fearing it was too close to →Weber's *Der Freischütz*. Marschner was not deterred by such considerations.

Hans Heiling

Romantic opera in a prologue and three acts

Libretto: Eduard Devrient.
Première: 24 May 1833, Berlin (Royal Opera House).
Characters: The Queen of the Earth Spirits (S), Hans Heiling, her son (Bar), Anna, his beloved (S), Gertrude, her mother (A), Konrad, the baron's chief huntsman (T), Stephan, the village blacksmith (B), Niklas, a peasant (spoken); earth spirits, peasants, wedding guests, musicians, huntsmen (chorus).
Setting: The underground kingdom of the earth spirits, and a village surrounded by woodland.

Synopsis
Prologue

Hans Heiling is the offspring of a union between the Queen of the Earth Spirits and a mortal. His desire for the peasant girl Anna drives him into the realm of the mortals, in spite of his mother's warnings. He will return if Anna proves to be unfaithful. Heiling takes with him gifts for Anna and a book of magic spells, for his supernatural powers will fail him in the world of men.

Act I

Scene 1: Heiling's abode. Gertrude, Anna's mother, thinks Heiling is a good catch because he is rich. She

An "intermediate" work?

Although the score was completed in 1832, the work was not successfully premièred until 1833, but productions at all the leading opera houses of Europe soon followed. Richard Wagner's artistic program was strongly influenced by *Hans Heiling*, as a result of which Marschner has tended to be portrayed by music historians as a "forerunner" of Wagner, and his work has been accorded the position of an historical rarity. In reality, however, *Hans Heiling* is an individual and highly original work – particularly in its melodrama scenes. *M. S.*

Hans Heiling, production photograph with Roland Hermann in the title role, production Nikolaus Lehnhoff, conductor Massime de Bernart, Opernhaus Zürich 1979.
Nikolaus Lehnhoff's production at the end of the 1970s focused on a psychological interpretation of the characters.

visits the suitor with her daughter, who obeys her reluctantly: she is in love with the huntsman, Konrad. Anna notices strange things about Heiling, and this feeling is confirmed when she discovers his book of magic spells and observes its pages turning by themselves. She asks Hans to destroy it. He does as she asks, and, as a sign of his love, he presents her with a golden chain. Overjoyed, Anna wants to show it off and asks Hans to accompany her to the village festival. He goes against his will and only on condition that she refrains from dancing.

Scene 2: Outside the village tavern. The peasants are celebrating the feast of St. Florian. The baron's chief huntsman, Konrad, is in the company of his fellow hunters, and stories about dwarves and trolls are exchanged. Konrad asks his secret love Anna for a dance, but Heiling reminds her of her promise. They argue, and Anna goes with Konrad into the tavern.

Act II

Scene 1: A wild and rocky part of the forest. Returning home, Anna enters a remote part of the forest. Suddenly, she sees a crowd of earth spirits led by their queen, who prophesies misfortune if Anna marries Hans Heiling, the ruler of the underground spirits. Horrified, Anna faints. Konrad finds her and carries her home.

Scene 2: Gertrude's hut. Anna no longer wants to marry Heiling, but Gertrude is reluctant to give her to Konrad because he is poor. When Heiling brings the jewelry to the house as a dowry, Anna hides behind Konrad, and tells him that Heiling is an earth spirit. Konrad tries to throw him out but Heiling stabs his rival and runs off with a mocking laugh.

Act III

Scene 1: A desolate rocky valley. Heiling calls the earth spirits together, and claims that he is satisfied with Konrad's death. But Konrad has only been injured and is to marry Anna that very day. Beside himself with rage, Heiling swears revenge. The dwarves and gnomes pledge their support.

Scene 2: A chapel on the forest cliffs. The marriage ceremony of Anna and Konrad is taking place. According to the custom of the time , after the ceremony the bride is made to search for the bridegroom. Hardly has Anna been blindfolded when Heiling appears. Anna is resigned to her fate, begging only for Konrad's life. Konrad tries to kill the earth spirit, but Heiling cannot be harmed. Before Heiling can take revenge, the Queen enters. Hans Heiling is forced to give up his hope for mortal love and reconcile himself to his fate as an earth spirit. Peace returns once more. *S. N.*

Hans Heiling, Josef Alois Prokop as Hans Heiling.
Marschner wrote the title role for the author of the libretto, the baritone Eduard Devrient, perhaps as a gesture of thanks.

Martinů was a Czech emigrant, always proud of the music of his homeland, the customs of Bohemia, and the craft of the musician. He was also influenced by contemporary composers such as Stravinsky, Milhaud, and Honegger.

Martinů, Bohuslav

b. 8 December 1890 in Polička (eastern Bohemia)
d. 28 August 1959 in Liestal (Switzerland)

After a brief period of study with Josef Suk in 1922, Martinů moved to Paris in 1923, where he studied with Albert Roussel and remained until 1940. He lived in the USA from 1941 to 1946, when he left for two years to take up a professorial post in Prague. In 1948 he returned to America, to an academic appointment at Princeton University, a position he held until 1957. The last years of his life were spent in Switzerland.

Works: Over 15 operas, including: *Voják a tanečnice* (*The Soldier and the Dancer*) (1928, Brno), *Trojí přání, aneb vrtkavosti života* (*Three Wishes or The Moods of Life*) (film opera, 1929/FP 1971, Brno), *Hlas lesa* (*The Voice of the Forest*) (radio opera, 1935), *Divadlo za branou* (*The Suburban Theater*) (1936), *Veselohra na moste* (*Comedy on a Bridge*) (radio opera, 1937, Prague), *Dvakrát Alexandr* (*Alexander Twice*) (1937/FP 1964, Mannheim), *Julietta: Snář* (*Julietta: The Book of Dreams*) (1938, Prague), *Ženitba* (*The Marriage*) (television opera, 1953, New York), *Mirandolina* (1959, Prague), *Řecké pašije* (*The Greek Passion*) (1961, Zürich), *Ariane/Ariadna* (*Ariadne*) (1961, Gelsenkirchen).

Julietta

Lyric opera in three acts

Libretto: Bohuslav Martinů, after the play *Juliette, ou La clé des songes* (*Juliette, or The Key of Dreams*) by Georges Neveux.
Première: 16 March 1938, Prague (National Theater).
Characters: Julietta (S), Michel (T), Commissar, also a mailman and forest ranger (T), Man in Helmet (Bar), Man at Window (B), Small Arab (Ms), Old Arab (B), Bird Seller (Ms), Fishmonger (Ms), Three Men, one in blue and two in gray clothing (female V), Grandfather "Youth" (B), Grandfather (B), Grandmother (A), Old Lady (Ms), Fortune-Teller (A), Dealer in Memories (Bbar), Old Sailor (B), Young Sailor (Ms), Hotel Boy (Ms), Beggar (Bar), Prisoner (B), Official (T), Train Driver (T), Nightwatchman (spoken), Policeman (silent); townsfolk (chorus); a group of figures dressed in gray (extras).
Setting: A small town by the sea.

Synopsis:

In his search for a girl whose love song he has heard while traveling, Michel arrives at a small harbor town. No one can help him, as no one has any memory, and so he decides to leave – but the railway station has disappeared. Julietta, whom he has been looking for, now appears. They are to meet in the forest where everything will be explained. The fortune-teller of the past and the dealer in memories reduce the time he has to spend waiting. He is finally alone with Julietta when a horn sounds and she runs off. He shoots at her with a revolver. Depressed, he then boards a ship in order to leave, but finds himself in the Central Office of Dreams. There, he is once again captivated by Julietta's voice, and the story begins anew.   M. S.

Julietta set design by Ruodi Barth for the production by Walter Pohl, conductor Ludwig Kaufmann, Staatstheater/Grosses Haus, Wiesbaden 1958/59 (TWS). The Wiesbaden theater was enthusiastic about this rarely staged work by Martinů even while the composer was still alive. The set design shown here is by the prolific Ruodi Barth, one of the most influential set designers in German theater in the post-war period.

The Greek Passion

Řecké pašije

Opera in four acts

Libretto: Bohuslav Martinů, after the novel *Christ Recrucified* by Nikos Kazantzakis.
Première: 12 June 1961, Zürich (Stadttheater).
Characters: Manolios, a shepherd (T), Katerina, a widow (S), Grigoris, a priest (Bbar), Fotis, a priest (Bbar), Kostandis, a café owner (Bar), Yannakos, a pedlar (T), Lenio, the fiancée of Manolios (S), Panait, a blacksmith (T), Patriarcheas, a village elder (Bbar), Ladas, a village elder (spoken), Michelis, son of Patriarcheas (T), Nikolios, a shepherd boy (S), Andonis, the village barber (T), Old Woman (A), Despinio (S), Old Man (B), Banner Carrier (silent); villagers, refugees (chorus, children's chorus).

Setting: Lykovrissi, a Greek village on the slopes of Sarakina, during the Turkish occupation.

Synopsis

Manolios, who has been chosen by Grigoris to portray Christ in the coming Passion play, begins to take on the characteristics of the part: he separates from his fiancée Lenio, preaches contemplation, has visions, and causes the wicked widow, Katerina, to repent.

When refugees arrive asking for help, he shows them to a place on Mount Sarakina where they build a village. An old man asks to be walled up so that they may be protected from evil. Gradually, the actors in the Passion play begin to identify with their roles including Panait, who is playing Judas. During the wedding celebrations for Lenio and Nikolios he kills Manolios, who has Christ's part.

M. S.

The Greek Passion, production photograph, Wiesbaden May Festival, guest performance from Prague, 1988 (TWS).
By condensing the plot, the focus of this work is different from that of the novel on which it is based: the religious and visionary aspects come to dominate rather than the political themes. Echoes from Greek folklore and Orthodox church music lend the work authenticity. The characterization and the situations that develop are entirely credible. The use of the chorus is appropriately archaic and the story unfolds naturalistically, allowing the surreal dream sequence in Act III to seem even more startling. Martinů insisted that the work's première should be directed by his patron Paul Sacher.

Mascagni, Pietro

b. 7 December 1863 in Livorno
d. 2 August 1945 in Rome

The gifted son of a baker, Mascagni began to study music and to compose at an early age, and was already working on his first opera at the age of 13. In 1882 he was accepted into the Milan Conservatory where he studied for two years under →Ponchielli and Saladino. He then left the Conservatory and became a double bass player at the Teatro dal Verme. After working as *Kapellmeister* for various traveling companies, he finally settled in the small town of Cerignola in Puglia, where he worked as a music director. When in 1889 he saw an advertisement for a competition for one-act operas organized by the Milan music publisher Sonzogno, he threw himself into the composition of *Cavalleria rusticana*, with which he won first prize out of 70 entries, even though he had to share it with two other composers. Within a year the opera had made him internationally famous. This success paved the way for a busy career as a conductor, which he was to pursue throughout his life. In 1895 he was appointed director of the Conservatory in Pesaro, and from 1903 he held the same position in Rome. Although he went on to compose 12 further operas, these neither had the originality nor attained the popularity of his first one-act work. He accepted the title of National Composer under Mussolini's fascist regime, which caused many of his colleagues (including Toscanini) and friends to abandon him.

Works: Operas: *Pinotta* (c. 1880/FP 1932), *Guglielmo Ratcliff* (*William Ratcliff*) (1885/FP 1895), *Cavalleria rusticana* (*Rustic Chivalry*) (1890), *L'amico Fritz* (*Friend Fritz*) (1891), *I Rantzau* (*The Rantzau*) (1892), *Silvano* (1895), *Zanetto* (1896), *Iris* (1898), *Le maschere* (*The Masks*) (1901), *Amica* (*Friend*) (1905), *Isabeau* (1911), *Parisina* (1913), *Lodoletta* (1917), *Il piccolo Marat* (*Little Marat*) (1921), *Nerone* (*Nero*) (1935); songs, sacred and secular choral works, mostly unpublished orchestral and piano works, chamber music.

Cavalleria rusticana, photograph from the production by Liliana Cavani, sets Dante Ferretti, conductor Massimo de Bernart, Teatro Comunale di Bologna, Bologna 1997.
Santuzza feels excluded from the Easter Mass and from the congregation because of her "immoral" love. The beautiful spring Sunday makes her isolation seem even bleaker.

1. Intermezzo Melody

Mascagni had a great gift for melody and a dramatic talent that was capable of providing the "vita italiana" with convincing musical expression.

The Italian national opera?

Cavalleria rusticana is a thrilling opera, although it has its faults in terms of form and dramaturgy, and cannot be said to be a milestone in the history of opera. It is no more passionate than Verdi's →*Il trovatore*, and its exotic color and naturalism do not make it any more original than Bizet's →*Carmen*. Nevertheless, a new *fin de siècle* fashion, *verismo* – the frank and honest portrayal of everyday reality – is associated with this one-act opera. *Cavalleria rusticana* became one of the most popular works of the musical stage.

The melodies have long since become a firm part of Italian musical culture; the most famous of them (from the Intermezzo) is even sung by the gondoliers in Venice. M 1 And there is not a single important tenor in the field of Italian opera who has not sobbed at least once during Turiddu's heart-breaking departure from his mother. →M 11

If one opera were to be selected as "the" Italian national opera (a purely whimsical notion – after all, opera itself is an Italian invention!) it would have to be *Cavalleria rusticana*. Why? Largely because the plot is taken directly from the life of the people: there is love, jealousy, and deadly revenge ("vendetta"). The setting – a Sicilian village on Easter Sunday – is also typically Italian, with its focus on the church as the center of community life.

Cavalleria rusticana

Rustic Chivalry

Melodramma in one act

Libretto: Giovanni Targioni-Tozzetti and Guido Menasci, after the folk play of the same name by Giovanni Verga.
Première: 17 May 1890, Rome (Teatro Costanzi).
Characters: Santuzza, a young peasant woman (S), Turiddu, a young peasant (T), Lucia, his mother (A), Alfio, a coachman (Bar), Lola, Alfio's wife (Ms), Woman (spoken), Lady (spoken); villagers (chorus).
Setting: A village in Sicily, Easter Sunday around 1880.

Synopsis

Before going off to become a soldier, Turiddu had been in love with Lola. Returning home he finds she has become Alfio's wife. The old passion still burns in him, and he seeks comfort in the arms of Santuzza, whom he promises to marry. She loves Turiddu, and gives herself to him. Lola grudges her friend this happiness and competes with Santuzza for Turiddu's favor, ultimately luring him into her web. Santuzza fears for her "honor" and feels excluded as a sinner from attending church on Easter morning. She confides in Turiddu's mother, but is offered no help. Rejected by Turiddu, Santuzza betrays his relationship with Lola to Alfio. Alfio challenges the adulterer to a duel. Sensing the worst, Turiddu asks his mother to care for Santuzza. He dies, a victim of Alfio's revenge.   *S. N.*

Cavalleria rusticana, production photograph with Violeta Urmana (Santuzza) and José Cura (Turiddu), production Liliana Cavani, conductor Massimo de Bernart, Teatro Comunale di Bologna, Bologna 1997.
One does not need to be able to understand the text of the duet between Santuzza and Turiddu to feel that it is a love song; the dominant mood is indeed that of Santuzza's love. *M2, M3, M4*
Although Turiddu rejects Santuzza with increasing anger, Mascagni did not provide him with his own characteristic material. Could it be that Turiddu's former affection for Santuzza has not completely died?

2. Santuzza's Declaration of Love

La tu - a San-tuz - za   pian-ge e t'im-plo - ra;

3. Santuzza's Doubt

No,   no, Tu - rid - du, ri - mani, rima-ni an - co - ra, _ ab-bando-nar - mi dun-que tu vuo - i?

4. Santuzza's Entreaty

Ah, _ no, Tu - rid - du, _ ri - ma - ni, ri-ma-ni an-co - ra, _ an - cor!

Cavalleria rusticana, set design by Otto Müller-Godesberg, Koblenz 1923 (TWS). The eternal setting for *Cavalleria rusticana*: white walls and clear blue skies, the entrance to the church and the southern Italian street scene. Even the Mediterranean climate has been immortalized in the vocal parts.

The melodies in their dramatic context

Although the melodies of *Cavalleria rusticana* have become famous purely as melodies, each of them serves an important dramatic purpose. The first vocal number, for example, is – what else? – a siciliana, which reveals Turiddu's blind love for Lola, ᴹˢ while the dignified opening chorus expresses feelings associated with spring, as well as the rituals of an Italian Sunday in the country.

Crowds are filing through the church doors: the church welcomes the righteous but sinners must remain outside – or so it seems to Santuzza and Lucia, Turiddu's mother, after Santuzza has given herself to Turiddu without receiving the blessings of the church. There are only a few dramatic dialogues in the opera. The brevity of the opera meant that Mascagni could only hint at the origins of the story, but this technique lends the opera a certain impetus and helps to limit situations that might become overheated or pathos-laden. The coachman Alfio introduces himself (opening song with choral

5. Turiddu's Siciliana

O Lo-la, bian-ca co-me fior di spi-no,   quan-do t'af-fac-ci-tu, s'af-fac-cia il so le

refrain): a cheerful, rather vulgar man. M 6 After Alfio's song, which is constructed from short motifs, there follows a large, expansive melody from the Easter choir, begun by Santuzza. M 7

The audience does not learn until the middle of the story what it is that is about to take place between five Sicilian villagers on this Easter Sunday. Santuzza confesses her love for Turiddu to Mamma Lucia (in the form of a romance), but also reveals his faithlessness and the adultery of his liaison with Lola. The simple melody at the start of her tale is based on a folk song, M 8 and its sad apotheosis is one of the most beautiful melodies in the operatic repertory. M 9

Santuzza's romance is followed by a short dialogue with Mamma Lucia – that is, the aria precedes the dialogue rather than the other way around as was customary. The great duet between Santuzza and Turiddu is also unusually structured, in that it incorporates Lola's song, sung from backstage. This entirely independent song contrasts sharply with the duet on which it intrudes, arousing a renewed sense of desperation in both Santuzza and Turiddu. Lola's song became so popular that it was even printed on postcards beneath Mascagni's portrait.

Before the impending catastrophe, Turiddu sings a drinking song whose good cheer contrasts with the tragic events to follow, thereby enhancing their dramatic effect. M 10 Turiddu takes his leave of his mother with an ominous request that she take care of Santuzza if he dies. This monologue is almost entirely spoken, with the sudden expression of desperation "translated" into a magnificent melody. M 11

Postcard with Mascagni's portrait and a musical quotation (Lola's song).
Pietro Mascagni is pictured here around the turn of the century, when he was at the height of his fame. With Verdi and Puccini Mascagni is still one of Italy's most popular composers. His 5000 mostly unpublished letters are kept in a parish church in the small town of Bagnara di Romana, where he spent the summers with his companion Anna Lolli.

6. Alfio's Song

Il ca-val lo scal-pi-ta, i so-na-gli squil-la-no, schioc-ca la fru-sta. Ehi là ____

7. Melodies of the Easter Choir

In-neg-gia-mo, il Si-gnor-non è mor-to,

8. Santuzza's Romance

Voi lo sa-pe-te, o mam-ma, pri-ma d'an-dar sol-da-to

9. Santuzza's Sad Apotheosis

(Orchester)

Pri-va dell' o-nor mi-o, dell' o-nor mi-o ri-man-go:

10. Turiddu's Drinking Song

Vi-va il vi-no spu-meg-gian-te nel bic-chie-re scin-til-lan-te co-me il ri-so dell' a-man-te mi-te in-fon-de il giu-bi-lo!

11. Turiddu's Farewell

voi ___ do-vre-te fa-re da ma-dre a San-ta,

Massenet, Jules

b. 12 May 1842 in Montaud
d. 13 August 1912 in Paris

At the turn of the century, Massenet was considered France's leading opera composer. His style had its roots in the lyrical traditions of the 19th century, and he did a great deal to familiarize French audiences with the music of Wagner and Liszt. His work can be thought of as a series of "romantic depictions of life." The 11th son of an officer, Massenet studied at the Paris Conservatoire under →Ambroise Thomas and →Gounod. In 1878 he himself became teacher of composition at the Conservatoire, his most successful students being →Gustave Charpentier and George Enescu.

Works: Almost 30 operas, including *Hérodiade* (*Herodias*) (1881), *Manon* (1884), *Werther* (1892), *Thaïs* (1894), *Cendrillon* (*Cinderella*) (1899), *Le jongleur de Notre-Dame* (*The Minstrel of Notre-Dame*) (1902), *Don Quichotte* (*Don Quixote*) (1910).

Manon, production photograph with Dagmar Hermann (Rosette), Dorothea Frass (Javotte), and Ruthilde Boesch (Poussette), Wiener Staatsoper (Theater an der Wien) 1949. Massenet put the finishing touches to *Manon* in The Hague, in the house in which the Abbé Prévost had written his Manon novel over 150 years earlier. The effect of this geographical proximity to the source of the story was heightened by Massenet's desire to create a monument to the French Rococo era and the contradictory world of the *ancien régime*. The gavotte, which can be heard in the introduction and which then dominates as a theme in the carnival of Act III, is evidence of this desire. M 1 Manon's aria in Act III also has a Rococo character. M 2 Love, on the other hand, reveals itself in open, Romantic melodies. M 3, M 4, M 5

Manon

Opéra comique in five acts

Libretto: Henri Meilhac and Philippe Gille, after the novel *L'histoire du chevalier des Grieux et de Manon Lescaut* by Abbé Prévost.
Première: 17 January 1884, Paris (Opéra-Comique).
Characters: Manon Lescaut (S), Le Chevalier des Grieux (T), Count des Grieux, his father (B), Lescaut, Manon's cousin (Bar), Guillot de Morfontaine, a wealthy playboy (T), De Brétigny, a nobleman (Bar), Poussette, Javotte, and Rosette, actresses and friends of Manon (2 S, Ms); travelers, guests, swindlers, churchgoers, soldiers, salespeople, crowd (chorus).
Setting: Amiens, Paris, and the road to Le Havre, in the mid-18th century.

Synopsis

Manon and des Grieux bring each other both happiness and unhappiness: together they experience true love but also poverty and the decadence of luxury. They come together, abandon each other, and come together again, and in the process bring about their mutual destruction.

Act I

Accompanied by actresses, two rich Parisians, Guillot and de Brétigny, are waiting for their lunch in a tavern in Amiens; they observe the arrival of a coach. Manon, an enchanting young woman who has been sent by her family to be educated in a convent, alights from the carriage escorted by her cousin, Lescaut. Guillot immediately begins to court her, but the innocent girl does not respond to his advances. It is only when the similarly inexperienced des Grieux enters and falls in love with her, that her passions begin to be aroused. They both flee in Guillot's carriage to Paris.

Act II

The young lovers are living in reduced circumstances, and Manon feels oppressed by their poverty. Des Grieux wants to make their union legal and writes to that effect to his father. For weeks de Brétigny has been wooing Manon, trying to persuade her to accept him and his fortune. He has informed des Grieux's father of his son's activities, and the father now wishes to fetch his son back. Manon does not give in to de Brétigny, but neither does she warn des Grieux. When des Grieux is overpowered by his father's messenger and taken away, Manon leaves the apartment they have shared.

Act III

In the Cours-la-Reine park in Paris a carnival is in full swing. Amongst the pleasure-seekers are Manon and her circle: Guillot, de Brétigny and the actresses.

She is their uncrowned queen and is happy. She then learns that the unfortunate des Grieux has decided to devote himself to the service of God and is preparing for the priesthood. Secretly she leaves her company and hurries to St. Sulpice, where des Grieux's youth and rhetorical skills are holding remorseful churchgoers spellbound. Manon speaks to him, swearing her love. In vain he seeks to maintain his distance and keep to his chosen path of inner tranquility: his love for Manon gets the better of him.

Act IV

Manon and des Grieux are again living together, but she cannot survive without luxury. Des Grieux has exhausted the inheritance from his mother. Manon persuades him to visit the Hôtel de Transylvanie, an infamous gambling den. Des Grieux wins against Guillot who accuses him of cheating. Both Manon and des Grieux are arrested.

Act V

Des Grieux is released on the intervention of his father, but Manon is to be transported overseas as a thief. Des Grieux's rescue attempt fails, and he has just enough money left to bribe the guard to let him hold Manon in his arms once again. They remember the happy moments of their love, before Manon, weakened by her experiences in prison, dies.   S. N.

Massenet's style was in the lyrical tradition of the 19th century and assured him of considerable success during his lifetime. Within a short time of his death, however, his works began to be dismissed as sentimental and old-fashioned. It was not until the end of the 20th century that his music came to be appreciated once again.

1. Gavotte

2. Manon's Aria (Act III)

Pro - fi - tons bien de la jeu - nes - se, Des jours qu'a - mè - ne le printemps ;

Ai - - mons, ri - ons, chan - tons sans ces - se, Nous n'a - vons en - cer que vingt ans !

3. Manon's Aria (Act I)

Je suis... en - cor... tout é - tour - di - e... Je suis... en - cor... tout en - gour - di - e...

4. Love Theme (Manon and des Grieux)

5. Des Grieux's Aria

Ma - non, sphynx é - ton - nant, Vé - ri - ta - ble si - rè - ne !...

Werther

Drame lyrique in four acts

Libretto: Édouard Blau, Paul Milliet, and Georges Hartmann, after the novel *Die Leiden des jungen Werthers* (*The Sorrows of Young Werther*) by Johann Wolfgang von Goethe.
Première: 16 February 1892, Vienna (Hofoper).

Characters: Werther (T), The Bailli, a magistrate (Bar), Charlotte, his eldest daughter (Ms), Sophie, her sister (S), Albert (Bar), Schmidt and Johann, friends of the bailli (T, Bar), the six remaining children of the bailli (6 S or children's V); inhabitants of Wetzlar, guests, musicians (chorus).
Setting: Wetzlar, July to December 178…

Synopsis

The sensitive Werther loves Charlotte, who marries Albert out of a sense of duty. Not until Werther shoots himself out of desperation does Charlotte admit her love for him. Werther dies happy.

Act I

The bailli's house. It is the middle of summer and the bailli's children are practicing a Christmas carol with their father. Schmidt and Johann, two hard-drinking friends, arrive to fetch the bailli for an evening at the tavern. Werther, a lonely dreamer, invites Charlotte to a ball.

After the death of her mother, Charlotte has taken over responsibility for the care of her younger brothers and sisters. While her younger sister Sophie stays at home, Charlotte goes off with Werther. Meanwhile, Charlotte's fiancé Albert returns home after a long journey. Charlotte and Werther return at night, and the young man finally dares to confess his love for her. Charlotte returns his feelings, but she must nevertheless refuse him, as she promised her mother on her deathbed that she would marry Albert.

Werther, production photograph with (from left to right) Gabriele Rassmanith, Siegfried Vogel, Oskar Purgstaller, and Carl Schultz, production Harry Kupfer, sets Hans Schavernoch, conductor Gerd Albrecht, Oper Hamburg 1991.
The scene is like a collage, replete with the gestures and relics of the petit bourgeois world. It is a world in which people seem to be little more than puppets in a play, but in fact have intense emotional lives. Massenet was undoubtedly attracted to this 18th-century literary source by the "inner music" of the characters.

Act II

A group of linden trees. On a morning in late summer, Schmidt and Johann are observing people streaming into church, amongst them Charlotte and Albert, who have been married for three months. A distraught Werther waits for her outside the church. Albert speaks to Werther, sympathizing with his situation. Sophie invites Werther to a dance. When Charlotte and Werther are left alone, he once again overwhelms her with declarations of love. Finally she sends him into "exile" until Christmas, so that they can both reconsider their situation. Werther, tormented, flees. His peculiar behavior makes Albert realize that Werther still loves Charlotte.

Act III

On the afternoon of Christmas Eve, Charlotte is rereading Werther's letters, which touch her deeply. In vain, Sophie tries to cheer her up. Charlotte both expects and fears Werther's return. When he arrives they talk about the past. When Charlotte reminds him that he had once wanted to translate Ossian's poems, Werther sees this as a sign that she loves him, and allows his feelings free rein. He tries to persuade her not to suppress her feelings either. For a brief time she lies in his arms, but then her feelings of duty gain the upper hand: Charlotte decides to say goodbye to Werther forever. Returning home, Albert notes his wife's embarrassment and suspects the truth. When a message arrives from Werther saying he is going on a long journey and would like to borrow Albert's pistols, Albert cold-bloodedly sends the weapons to him. Charlotte has premonitions of disaster.

Act IV

Christmas Night. An orchestral interlude describes Charlotte's path to Werther's house. Bursting into the house, Charlotte sees blood on the floor and finds Werther lying gravely wounded on his bed. She wants to fetch help, but Werther insists on spending his last minutes alone with her. Finally she is able to confess her love for him. Their first kiss must also be their last. While the children begin the Christmas carol they had practiced in the summer, Werther dies happily in Charlotte's arms. *P. H.*

Werther, set design (the city in winter) by Alessandro Benois for a production in the Teatro alla Scala, Milan 1950/51. "Deutschland, ein Wintermärchen" ("Germany, a Winter's Tale") was the title Heine gave to the poem he wrote in 1844, 12 years after Goethe's death and almost 50 years before Massenet's opera. In the case of *Werther* this famous title could be taken still further: the winter world sleeps, and only the flame of the sensitive soul – Werther – still flickers.

The French Werther

Massenet's *Werther* unleashed a controversy in Vienna that was motivated by the librettists' very free adaptation of Goethe's epistolary novel. When it was first published, Goethe's *Werther* was responsible for a wave of suicides throughout Europe. Its French adaptation treated this literary classic in a manner that would not have pleased its German readership. As with *Manon* several years earlier, Massenet attempted to place the central events of *Werther* against a colorful and richly detailed background. This time it was the depiction of German domestic life that was not particularly flattering.

The lack of comprehension for Werther's feelings shown by the other characters and the pompous mediocrity of the Biedermeier figures is brilliantly described in music, not least through the opera's framing device – the rehearsal and performance of the Christmas carol. M 6

Werther, production photograph with Keth Ikaia-Purdy and Kathleen Kuhlmann, production Harry Kupfer, sets Hans Schavernoch, conductor Gerd Albrecht, Hamburger Staatsoper 1991.
The director and set designer projected the feelings of the protagonists onto a wild setting of rugged mountains. Here, the otherwise cozy family home is given a ghostly dimension, and a spiritual intimacy develops between the characters left alone in this empty space.

6. Christmas Carol

No - ël!   No - ël!   Jé - sus vient de naî - tre,

Voi - ci no - tre di - vin maî - tre, Rois et ber - gers d'Is - ra - ël!

Werther, the hero of the title

The figure of Werther stands out like a beacon in an intellectually uncomplicated world in which life is regarded simply as the orderly fulfillment of duty. Right at the beginning of the work, his great hymn to nature reveals the importance he attaches to the expression of feeling in all his relationships.  ᴍ₇ Werther is indeed out of place in this petit bourgeois setting, as he is unable to find happiness in simple pleasures nor in a moral code which is burdened by guilt. Werther's death signals the departure of a balanced element from a world whose oppressive pettiness might have been alleviated by his emotional values.

Charlotte's opera?

The treatment of Charlotte in Massenet's opera diverges markedly from Goethe's novel. In the opera, Charlotte is bound to her husband not only by her marriage vows, but also by the oath she swore at her mother's deathbed. In addition, Massenet's Albert is more sinister than Goethe's. At first a sympathetic friend and husband, he changes into a rather negative figure. Against this background, Charlotte takes on certain operatic characteristics, and, in contrast to the rather static figure of the hero, she undergoes a far-reaching dramatic development. The entire opera can be seen as a series of four duets between Charlotte and Werther that trace Charlotte's development in great detail. From girlish innocence she grows to become a true heroine, who acknowledges her real feelings in the last seconds of Werther's life. The turning point, when Werther's feelings resonate in her soul, is the scene in which she reads his letters. ᴍ₈

As she reads, she temporarily suspends her rationale, allowing herself to be swept along by Werther's fervor. At this high point in the story, Massenet's music achieves an ecstatic dimension, which is soon quelled by her cool rejection of Werther. The first three duets having ended in farewell and separation, the lovers are united in Act IV. Happiness is granted to them only in the shadow of death. When Charlotte realizes her tragic mistake she begs for forgiveness, while Werther goes to his death in peace. ᴍ₉   P. H.

Werther, production photograph with Werther and Charlotte, a guest performance by the Sadler's Wells Opera, Vienna 1952.
Just as one would imagine Werther and Charlotte: sensitive, sad – and silent. They are souls who understand each other without having to speak, and who live and act like figures from a sentimental Romantic novel. When they mention to each other such literary names as "Klopstock" or "Ossian," they really mean: "I love you!"

7. Werthers Aria (Act I)

O na - tu - re, plei - ne de grâ - ce Rei - ne du temps et de l'es - pa - ce,

8. Charlotte's Aria (Act III)

Qui m'au - rait dit la pla - ce que dans mon coeur il oc - cu - pe au - jourd'hui?...

9. Love Duet (Charlotte and Werther, Act IV)

Et moi, Werther,... et moi je t'ai - me!...

Menotti, Gian Carlo

b. 7 July 1911 in Cadegliano-Viconago (Italy)

An Italian-American, Menotti studied at the Milan Conservatory from 1923 to 1927, and at the Curtis Institute of Music in Philadelphia under Rosario Scaleri from 1928 to 1933, where he remained until 1955 as a teacher of composition. His interest in European culture led him to visit Austria with his friend Samuel Barber in 1936; it was during this time that his satire on the well-to-do of Vienna, *Amelia al ballo* (*Amelia Goes to the Ball*) was written. In 1958 he founded the Festival of Two Worlds in Spoleto. Essentially a composer for the stage, he achieved international acclaim by combining topical subject matter and conventional staging with modern techniques.

Works: Amelia al ballo (*Amelia Goes to the Ball*) (1937, Philadelphia), *The Old Maid and the Thief* (1941, Philadelphia), *The Medium* (1946, New York), *The Telephone*, or *L'amour à trois* (1947, New York), *The Consul* (1950, Philadelphia), *Amahl and the Night Visitors* (1951, New York), *The Saint of Bleecker Street* (1954, New York), *Maria Golovin* (1958, Brussels), *Le dernier sauvage* (*The Last Savage*) (1963, Paris), *Martin's Lie* (1964, Bristol), *Help! Help! the Globolinks!* (1968, Hamburg), *The Most Important Man* (1971, New York), *Tamu-Tamu* (1973, Chicago), *The Hero* (1976, Philadelphia), *La Loca* (1979, San Diego), *Goya* (1986, Washington), *Giorno da nozze* (*The Wedding*) (1988, Seoul); other operas for television and radio, ballets, piano concerto, violin concerto.

Above
The Consul, Hilde Zadek as Magda Sorel, Vienna 1951.
Menotti's one-act opera *The Telephone* continued the success of *The Medium* (1946). His feeling for effective subject matter and drama brought him international recognition and made him the most performed young composer of his time.

*M*enotti's music contains echoes of Musorgsky, Stravinsky, Puccini, and Debussy. He adapted a historical recitative style and concentrated on powerful dramatic effects.

The Telephone, poster (Amerika Haus, Munich).
Although this was not the first opera to feature a telephone, Menotti's dramatic idea was his own: Ben is unable to have a conversation with Lucy before he sets off on a trip because she is constantly on the telephone. He then leaves her apartment and proposes to her by telephone. The telephone also plays an important role in *The Consul*: because it only rings when events have taken an irrevocable turn, it gives voice to what is an inexpressible tragedy.

The Telephone

Opera buffa in one act

Libretto: Gian Carlo Menotti.
Première: 18 February 1947, New York (Heckscher Theater).

Characters: Lucy (S), Ben (Bar).
Setting: Lucy's apartment, the 20th century

Synopsis

Ben is in love with Lucy and wants to tell her something important before he leaves on a journey. When they enter the apartment, the telephone rings and Lucy proceeds to have a long conversation with a girlfriend. When she hangs up, Ben tenderly begins to sing, but again they are interrupted by the shrill sound of the telephone. Lucy's friend George rebukes her for slandering him; she leaves the room in tears and Ben is tempted to tear out the telephone cable. Horrified, Lucy stops him: she has to ring one of her girlfriends for comfort. Ben has meanwhile left the apartment. He then rings Lucy himself, to ask her if she will be his wife.

S. N.

A fateful telephone call – set to a waltz

When in 1946 Lincoln Kirstein, the organizer of the Ballet Society New York, accepted Menotti's opera *The Medium*, he asked the composer for a short drama to round out the evening. Menotti responded with a two-person drama, which humorously took as its theme the problems of communicating in a technological world. The work's three long telephone conversations are set as arias and sung in a neo-Classical or dramatic Italian manner according to their mood. The conversations with Ben are set as recitative, while the agreement he reaches with Lucy by telephone at the end is marked by a waltz full of harmonious thirds and sixths.

The Consul

Musical drama in three acts (six scenes)

Libretto: Gian Carlo Menotti.
Première: 1 March 1950, Philadelphia (Shubert Theater).
Characters: John Sorel (Bar), Magda Sorel, his wife (S), John's Mother (A), Secret Police Agent (B), Two Detectives (silent), The Consul's Secretary (Ms), Mr Kofner (Bbar), Italian Woman (S), Anna Gomez (S), Vera Boronel (A), Nika Magadoff, a magician (T), Assan, a glass-cutter (Bar), Voice on The Record (S).
Setting: Somewhere in Europe.

Synopsis
Act I
John Sorel and other patriots are fighting against a dictatorial regime. His mother and his wife manage to hide him, but he decides to flee abroad. His wife visits the consulate, hoping to be able to follow him with their child. In the consulate Magda Sorel learns that a lot of people like herself are making futile applications for an exit visa. The consul refuses to speak to anyone before all the forms have been filled out. Although Magda points out the danger of her situation, she is put off until the following week.

Act II
A month has passed, during which several fruitless attempts have been made to obtain a visa. In the meantime, a secret agent is putting Magda under pressure. Her child becomes sick and dies. She hears from a friend that John is hiding in the mountains and is waiting for her. There is a great deal of activity in the consulate, but few of the applicants are given any positive news. In desperation Magda makes a scene with the secretary, who then tries to help her. But when the door to the consul's office opens, the secret agent comes out, proving to Magda the hopelessness of her position.

Act III
Magda tries one last time to speak to the consul. Having heard from a friend that John is planning to return, she warns him in a letter and leaves the consulate. Shortly before the office closes, John seeks refuge in the consulate but is arrested there by the secret police. They agree to his request to be allowed to call Magda. Magda returns home where the telephone is ringing. She pays no attention, turns on the gas, and waits to die. When the telephone rings again, Magda no longer has the strength to lift the receiver.   *S. N.*

Contemporary politics on the stage
Menotti's first long piece was based on a newspaper report of 12 February 1947 about the suicide of a Polish emigrant who had been denied an entry visa to the USA. Remembering the fates of Jewish friends in Austria

The Consul, Hans Braun as John Sorel, Vienna 1951.
After the shattering experience of the mass migrations of the 1940s, the story of *The Consul* was particularly relevant. The situation presented by the opera was one often experienced in reality, and it was precisely the timelessness of this tragedy about fate that made it so well suited to the stage.

and Germany, he chose this story as the theme for his opera. There are unmistakable parallels with Puccini's →*Tosca* of 1900. Menotti revived the techniques of *verismo*, in order to illustrate events in a gripping way: bureaucratic stereotypes are put on display, as are the visions and hallucinations of traditional opera. The enormous international success of the work, which built on the 270 consecutive performances at the Ethel Barrymore Theater in New York, testifies to the quality of the work.   *M. S.*

The Consul, set design by Hans Aeberli for the production by Erich Schumacher, conductor Romanus Hubertus, Vereinigte Städtische Bühnen, Mönchengladbach 1952 (TWS). The New World as a metropolitan labyrinth and a setting representing the impersonal power of bureaucracy.

Messiaen, Olivier

b. 10 December 1908 in Avignon
d. 28 April 1992 in Paris

Messiaen was first and foremost a composer, but he was also a brilliant organist and pianist, a broadly educated and perceptive theorist, and a popular teacher. His pupils include some of the most famous names of European modernism, including Pierre Boulez, →Karlheinz Stockhausen, Iannis Xenakis, and György Kurtág. Messiaen was born in Avignon, the son of Cécile Sauvage, the poet, and Pierre Messiaen, a translator of Shakespeare. From 1919 to 1931 he studied the organ (under Marcel Dupré) and composition (under Paul Dukas) at the Paris Conservatoire, where he himself worked from 1942 as professor of aesthetics, theory, and analysis. In 1955 a course in musical philosophy was established for him. He was the organist at La Trinité in Paris virtually without interruption from 1931. Messiaen created a kind of music that was as indebted to Gregorian chant as it was to the sounds of the Javanese gamelan, that combines the meter of Greek verse with the scales of Indian ragas, and that connects Debussy's and Skryabin's layerings of fourths and fifths with the principles of serial music and with bird songs from around the world. The foundation for all these components is a cosmogony fed by the mysticism of eastern Asia and of European Catholicism. Messiaen presented his aesthetics in a tract published in 1944, *Techniques of My Musical Language*. One of the high points of his career, and a key work of the epoch as a whole, was his *Turangalîla Symphony*, commissioned by the Russian-American conductor Sergey Koussevitzky for the Boston Symphony Orchestra. His opera *Saint François d'Assise* (*St. Francis of Assisi*) was also enormously influential. In it he put an end to the western distinction between the sacred and the profane, restoring to opera its ancient, cultic dimension.

Works: Opera: *Saint François d'Assise* (*St. Francis of Assisi*) (1983); organ works, piano works, orchestral works, choral works, chamber music, including four symphonic meditation pieces for the orchestra: *L'ascension* (*The Ascension*) (1932, organ version 1933), the *Turangalîla-symphonie* (*Turangalîla Symphony*) (1946–48), *Le Réveil des oiseaux* (*Wakening of the Birds*) (for piano and orchestra, 1953), *Oiseaux exotiques* (*Exotic Birds*) (1956), *Chronochromie* (1959–60), *Des canyons aux étoiles* (*The Canyon of the Stars*) (for piano and 40 instruments, 1971–75), and *Éclair sur l'Au-Delà* (*Light on the Beyond*) (1991); choral works, organ works, piano works, and chamber music, including the *Quatuor pour la fin du temps* (*Quartet for the End of Time*) (1941).

St. Francis of Assisi

Saint François d'Assise

Franciscan scenes

Opera in three acts and eight scenes

Libretto: Olivier Messiaen.
Première: 29 November 1983, Paris (Opéra, Salle Garnier).

Characters: St. François/St. Francis (Bar), The Angel (S), The Leper (T), Frère Léon/Brother Leo (Bar), Frère Massée/Brother Masseus (T), Frère Élie/Brother Elias (T), Frère Bernard/Brother Bernard (B), Frère Sylvestre/Brother Sylvester (B), Frère Rufin/Brother Rufinus (B); monks, the voice of Christ (chorus).
Setting: Italy, the 13th century.

Synopsis
Act I

Scene 1: *The Cross.* A street. In dread of death, the friars enquire after the meaning of life. Francis teaches them to live joyfully, which means overcoming fear of death through love of one's fellow men.
Scene 2: *Lauds.* The interior of a monk's cell. Francis praises God's creatures and asks God to give him the ability to love even a leper.
Scene 3: *The Embracing of the Leper.* A hospital. Francis is disgusted by the leper but overcoming his revulsion he kisses and cures him.
(Orchestral interlude: *The Dance of the Leper*)

Act II

Scene 4: *The Traveler Angel.* The mountain of La Verna. An angel requests entry into the monks' quarters. He is turned away at first, but then taken in after teaching them about life after death.
Scene 5: *The Musician Angel.* Francis is profoundly moved by the angel's music and is prepared for death.
Scene 6: *Preaching to the Birds.* Francis preaches to the birds of his home region of Umbria, but also to those at the other end of the world: "All beauty must acquire freedom, the freedom of glory."
(Orchestral interlude: *The Great Concerto of the Birds*)

Act III

Scene 7: *The Stigmata.* Night on La Verna. After a long prayer, Francis is marked by God with the five sacred wounds of Christ, the symbols of perfect charity.
Scene 8: *Death and New Life.* Francis bids farewell to his fellow monks. Dying, he relates the essence of his life and receives God's enlightenment: "Lord! Lord! Music and poetry have led me to you: through image, through symbol, and because I am lacking in truth."

S. N.

Opposite
St. Francis of Assisi, production photograph with José van Dam as Saint Francis, production Peter Sellars, conductor Kent Nagano, Salzburg Festival 1992.
The use of televisions in set design has been relatively common in recent years. Technological furnishings of this kind tend to denote a certain standard of civilization and an associated lifestyle, and represent the flood of visual information in an age of mass reproduction. According to an old saying however "the eye guides man into the world, while the ear guides the world into man."

*M*essiaen was one of the most influential and unusual representatives of French music in the 20th century. His ethically and religiously motivated approach is evident in his work.

A key operatic work

St. Francis of Assisi represents the distillation of Olivier Messiaen's art. The saint's last words are also a confession of faith by the composer. At the same time, the opera is one of the central works of the twentieth century. Rolf Liebermann's suggestion of writing an opera for Paris came as a surprise to Messiaen, and he at first rejected it. Later he recognized the opportunity it represented, and he worked on the opera between 1975 and 1983. The première at the Opéra (under Seiji Ozawa) was considered by the composer to have been true to his intentions. However, with a performance time of 4 hours and 15 minutes, a huge orchestra, and a choir of 150, productions have been few and far between. It has become customary to perform individual scenes, as in Salzburg in 1985 with Dietrich Fischer-Dieskau. There was a concert performance of the entire work at the Opéra Lyon in 1988, with the London Philharmonic Orchestra under Kent Nagano, before Peter Sellar's production was performed to great acclaim at the Salzburg Festival in 1992. In 1997 the work was finally performed on a smaller stage in a production at the Opernhaus in Leipzig, with Jiri Kout and the Gewandhaus Orchestra.

St. Francis of Assisi, photograph from the production by Peter Sellars, Salzburg Festival 1992.
Messiaen's opera *St. Francis of Assisi* demonstrates perfectly the saying "Listen, and your soul will live!" The idea of creation as a song of praise was one of the central messages of the real St. Francis's, as it is of the opera's hero. *St. Francis* is a work that requires no illustration in terms of stage scenery, and this makes it difficult for anyone intending to stage it to find a suitable approach to the work.

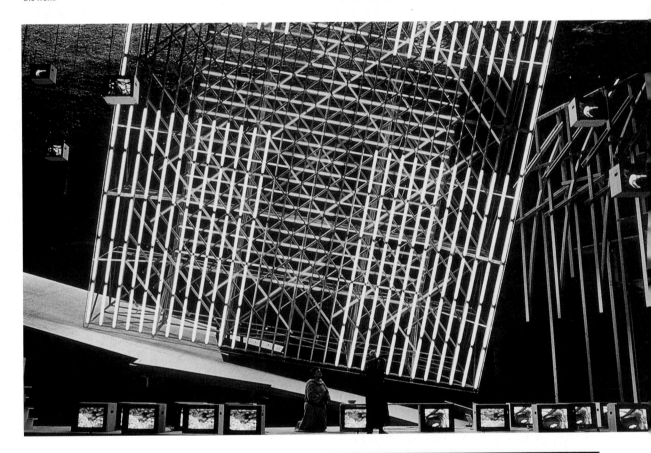

The Birds

St. Francis of Assisi is no piece of esoteric or Catholic hocus-pocus: it is an artwork in which the appearance of the Divine is articulated – under the most trying of circumstances and with the utmost integrity – as an expression of freedom, joy, and fearlessness. Messiaen's music, with its fluctuating rhythm, and chromatically dazzling harmonies, achieves the simultaneous expression of the tangible and the complex. At the center of the opera is the scene in which St. Francis preaches to the birds.

According to Messiaen, birds proclaim God's love and love for God. With their help it is possible to approach divine truth, proceeding step by step through a natural world that is always accessible to our senses.   *S. N.*

Right
St. Francis of Assisi, production photograph with Chris Merritt as the leper, production Peter Sellars, conductor Kent Nagano, Salzburg Festival 1992.
The figure of the leper is a symbol of human suffering, and represents a challenge to do good works. The inspiration for these deeds comes from the biblical proverb about angels having no names but being able to take ours at any time.

Robert the Devil, set design for the original production, after Ciceri, Paris Opéra 1831.

The scene became known for the monastery ruins where Robert acquires the magic branch. In an extended bacchanal, the nuns, rising out of their graves, demonstrate the most dangerous temptations of earthly life: drinking, gambling, and sex. For this scene Ciceri, the most famous set designer of the Paris Opéra, created an imitation of the cloister of the Montfort-l'Amaury monastery, a historic 16th-century building. According to Heinrich Heine's acute observation, the opera's unprecedented success was due to the fact that, after the turning-point in history of the July Revolution of 1830, operagoers saw in Robert a depiction of their own emotions, which wavered between the desire for rebellion and the hope of stability.

Meyerbeer, Giacomo

b. 5 September 1791 in Vogelsdorf (near Berlin)
d. 2 May 1864 in Paris

Born into a wealthy German-Jewish Berlin banking family, he was a child prodigy and studied with Abbé Vogler together with →Carl Maria von Weber. His creative career led from the German *Singspiel* through Italian *opera seria* to French grand opera, becoming the undisputed king of the latter. He created a new genre and brought it to its highest point. His works met with sensational success, unprecedented in operatic history. Although linked most strongly with Paris, he also worked in his native Berlin, particularly during the 1840s, and there became royal musical director.

Works: Robert le diable (*Robert the Devil*) (1831); *Les Huguenots* (*The Huguenots*) (1836); *Le prophète* (*The Prophet*) (1849); *L'étoile du nord* (*The North Star*) (1854); *Dinorah* (1859); *L'Africaine* (*The African Woman*) (1865, unfinished); also *Singspiele*, Italian operas, occasional works and songs.

Grand opera – Europe's greatest opera show

Around 1830, a team of artists was brought together under the direction of Victor Léon, whose members were professionals in the fields of drama, music and set building. The orchestra of the Grand Opéra consisted of more than 70 highly trained musicians. Together with a large number of extras, the chorus was able to bring real crowds of people onto the stage. The ballet, with its long tradition, was considered Europe's finest ensemble. An unprecedented degree of care was now devoted to the stage decor and costumes. The surroundings in which historic events were enacted were to be presented in the most faithful detail. Palaces, churches and similarly impressive locations were given preference and were depicted with amazing attention to accuracy. The librettist Eugène Scribe and the composer Giacomo Meyerbeer had at first planned *Robert the Devil* as an *opéra comique*, but the action was then enriched with visual effects, such as the dice-playing mime in Act I – based on a siciliano, in accordance with the setting ₘ₁ – and the demonic waltz in Act III, when Bertram conjures up the demons. ₘ₂   *P.H.*

1. Robert's Siciliano

O   fortune,   à   ton   ca - pri - ce,   viens,   je li - vre   mon des - tin !

2. Demonic Waltz

Noirs dé - mons, fan - tô - mes, ou - bli - ons les cieux,   des   som - bres roy - au - mes cé - lé - brons les jeux!

*M*eyerbeer was as a composer of opera a precursor of the show-business and film impresarios of the 20th century. He deliberately drew on various national styles to create his own personal style, and influenced many of his contemporaries, even Verdi and Wagner.

Robert the Devil

Robert le diable

Opéra in five acts

Libretto: Eugène Scribe.

Première: 21 November 1831, Paris (Opéra).

Characters: Robert, Duke of Normandy (T), Bertram, his friend (B), Prince of Granada (silent), King of Sicily (silent), Isabelle, Princess of Sicily, his daughter (S), Alice, a Norman peasant girl (S), Raimbaud, her betrothed (T), Alberti, a knight (B), a Herald (T), Majordomo to the King of Sicily (T), a Priest (B), a Lady-in-Waiting to Isabelle (S); knights, courtiers, soldiers, peasants, populace, monks and nuns (chorus).

Setting: In and around Palermo, c.1250.

Synopsis

Robert, Duke of Normandy, who has been banished to Sicily, seeks the hand of Princess Isabelle. In doing so he relies on the help of the devilish Bertram. Alice, Robert's former foster-sister and a faithful servant to his mother, opens his eyes: Bertram is his own father, but at the same time an evil demon, who loves his son but can be united with him only in damnation. With Alice's help, Robert loosens the terrible bonds and wins Isabelle.

Act I

Robert has been banished because of his dissolute way of life and is only reluctantly tolerated in Sicily. A stranger, a knight called Bertram, has befriended him. Robert loves Princess Isabelle and is loved in return by her, and wants to seek her hand at the tournament. The Norman girl Alice brings him his mother's last will and testament, which Robert does not want to read until he is worthy of it. Bertram persuades Robert to take part in a game of dice, in which he loses all his money, and even his weapons.

Act II

Isabelle equips Robert with new weapons so that he can contend for her hand in the tournament. But Bertram foils their plans. He lures Robert into the forest on the pretext of a challenge to a duel from an alleged rival, the Prince of Granada. At the appointed hour Robert does not appear at the tournament; in his place there appears the phantom of the Prince of Granada, created by Bertram, who wins the hand of Isabelle.

Act III

Bertram is hard-pressed by demons: if he has not gained Robert's soul for hell by midnight, he himself will suffer damnation and permanent separation from Robert. Robert still believes in Bertram's faithful friendship, suspecting neither that Bertram is his father, nor that he is a demon. Thus Bertram persuades Robert to acquire a miraculous weapon with which he can vanquish the knight from Granada. He raises from the dead formerly sinful nuns, who take part in a bacchanal during which they induce Robert to acquire the branch of St. Rosalia.

Act IV

Robert uses the magic branch to put Isabelle's court into a motionless trance. He allows Isabelle alone to awaken from the trance and tries to take possession of her by force. She pleads for the mercy of heaven for herself and for him. Robert renounces the powers of evil and breaks the branch. The courtiers awaken and Robert is forced to flee from the wrath of the knights.

Act V

Robert takes refuge in the church from the fury of his pursuers. Here Bertram reveals that he is his father and pleads with him to abandon his soul to hell, as otherwise they will be parted forever. Robert is prepared to do this, but then Alice arrives and gives him his mother's last will and testament, in which she warns him about Bertram. As the earthly representative of his mother, Alice struggles with Bertram for Robert's soul. On the stroke of midnight, Bertram descends into hell. Isabelle and Robert go to the altar together.   *S.N.*

The Huguenots, illustration from the *Opern-Galerie*, 1871.
A father has his own daughter put to death out of religious fanaticism. Could Scribe and Meyerbeer have guessed in 1836 that the situation would be repeated many times over in the century that was to follow?

Emmy Destinn (1878–1930), portrayed in her role as Valentine de Saint-Bris, c.1900.

The Huguenots

Les Huguenots

Opera in five acts

Libretto: Eugène Scribe and Émile Deschamps.
Première: 29 February 1836, Paris (Opéra).
Characters: Marguerite de Valois, Queen of Navarre (S), Raoul de Nangis, Protestant nobleman (T), Marcel, his Protestant servant (B), Valentine de Saint-Bris, a young Catholic noblewoman (S), Count of Saint-Bris, her father (B), Count of Nevers, a Catholic nobleman (B), Urbain, the queen's page (S), Bois-Rosé, a Protestant soldier (T); Catholic nobles: Cossé (T), Tavannes (T), Thoré (B), de Retz (B), Méru (B), Maurevert (B); nobles, ladies of the court, students, soldiers, citizens of Paris, gypsies, monks, Catholic murderers, Protestant women and children (chorus).
Setting: France, August 1572 (before and after the eve of St. Bartholomew).

Synopsis

The Catholic Valentine and the Protestant Raoul love each other, but their union is prevented by personal mistrust and the general enmity between the two Christian religions. Valentine breaks through all the boundaries that restrict her. A noblewoman, she takes to the street in her search of her beloved; a devout Catholic, she declares her devotion to the Protestant faith – and all she achieves is to be united with her beloved in death.

Act I

The Count of Nevers has invited his noble friends to his house, the only Protestant among them being Raoul de Nangis. He wants to set an example of reconciliation between the two religions. But the Catholic noblemen remain sceptical, while Raoul's manservant Marcel offends them with his Protestant brusqueness. Raoul has recently helped an unknown lady out of difficulties in the street, and has fallen in love with her. Now he is forced to observe his beautiful unknown lady meeting Nevers in secret and concludes that she is the Count's mistress. In fact she is Valentine, the daughter of the Count of Saint-Bris, who of his own accord and at the request of Queen Marguerite de Valois releases her from her engagement to Nevers, leaving her free to marry Raoul de Nangis, since she, like the queen, hopes for reconciliation between the hostile parties.

Act II

The queen is satisfied with the result of Valentine's mission. Nevers has agreed to release her from their engagement. She summons Raoul in order to arrange his marriage to Valentine. Raoul recognizes Valentine as the unknown lady, but insults her, believing her to be Nevers' mistress. Her father, Saint-Bris, considers that his honor has been offended. The queen succeeds in preventing open battle between Protestants and Catholics.

Act III

The population of Paris is also divided into Protestants and Catholics, and tension is mounting. The Count of Saint-Bris is planning a murderous attack on Raoul. The latter is warned by Valentine, who still loves him, although she has become the wife of the Count of Nevers. Too late, Raoul recognizes the wrong he has done her.

Act IV

In Nevers' palace, the Catholics are planning to stamp out the Huguenots, led by the Count of Saint-Bris and at the urging of King Charles IX. Nevers refuses to take part and is taken into protective detention. Raoul has secretly visited Valentine in order to ask pardon for his action, and thus learns of the murder plot against his fellow-believers. In vain Valentine tries to restrain him. She even confesses her love to him. After a short moment of happiness, Raoul dashes off in order to warn his Protestant companions.

Act V

The marriage of Marguerite de Valois to Henry IV is being celebrated with great ceremony. Raoul interrupts the proceedings to report the massacre of Huguenots in the streets of Paris.

The hard-pressed Huguenots have fled to a cemetery, among them Raoul and Marcel. Here they are tracked down by Valentine. The Count of Nevers has been killed by his own people. She is free, and Raoul is offered the opportunity to seek the protection of the queen with her. But he stays with his companions in distress, and Valentine adopts the faith of her beloved. Marcel blesses their marriage. Severely wounded, the last of the Huguenots drag themselves through the streets of Paris. Saint-Bris orders them all to be shot. Among them are Raoul, Marcel, and Valentine. Too late, the fanatical Catholic realizes that he has killed his own daughter. Queen Marguerite tries in vain to halt the slaughter.   *S. N.*

The Huguenots, set design for the tragic final scene, by Johann Kautsky, Frankfurt 1880. The triumphant première was followed by performances at other leading European opera houses, where the subject matter, linked as it was to religious conflict, frequently gave directors headaches. In Vienna, Catholics and Protestants were changed to Guelphs and Ghibellines, and in Munich to Anglicans and Puritans. Even in Berlin the piece could not be staged until the death of Emperor Frederick William III in 1842. Nevertheless, in the decades that followed *The Huguenots* became the opera of operas, and was never allowed to be absent from the repertoire. In Paris, in 1903, *The Huguenots* became the first opera to reach the astounding figure of 1,000 performances.

The Huguenots, Wilhelmine Schröder-
Devrient with Eduard Mautius, caricature by
F. Meyer, Berlin 1842.
The great duet of Valentine and Raoul as seen
through the caricaturist's eyes. At the Berlin
première Wilhelmine Schröder-Devrient
(1804–60) is said to have had the more
impressive personality.

Coloratura, bass clarinet, and viola d'amore

A performance of *The Huguenots* requires a few brilliant singers who have a flawless command of the beguiling sound and the effortless virtuosity of Italian bel canto. These demands apply in particular to the role of the queen, with her aria at the beginning of Act I which is full of virtuoso coloratura passages. ₘ₃ The opposite pole is provided by the rough soldier Marcel, who is one of Meyerbeer's most original inventions. The figure of the imperturbable old man, who has dedicated his life to the service of God and the welfare of his earthly master, is often connected with the quotation from the Lutheran chorale, "Ein' feste Burg." It is with this emblematic token of Protestantism that he offends the Catholics (for example, in Act I). ₘ₄ Apart from this melodic quotation, the sound of the lower-toned strings and (in Act IV) the bass clarinet, a new instrument at the time, contributes to the characterization of the earthy figure of Marcel. A similarly bizarre concept in instrumentation consists in making Raoul's Act I aria a dialogue between the singer's voice and the old-fashioned viola d'amore.

Group portraits in black and white

In no other opera by Meyerbeer, earlier or later, do choruses and ensembles play such a pronounced role. Their number is far in excess of the solo items, and lends grandeur to the work. The unrestrained orgy of the Catholics in the first act is contrasted with the frivolous eroticism of the queen's ladies in the second. The plot thickens in the third act to a tension-laden evocation of the streets of Paris. The militant main melody of the septet of male voices could also have come from the pen of the mature Verdi. M 5

This also applies to the central crowd scene in the fourth act, in which the Catholics swear revenge on their enemies. The oath, introduced by Saint-Bris then taken up by the chorus of those assembled, has a menacing authority which expresses the power of evil in unequalled fashion. M 6

The conspiracy is crowned by the entrance of the monks, who promise God's understanding of the planned murders. (It is evidence of the liberality of thought in France at that time that the censors found nothing reprehensible in this portrayal.)

Love duet accompanied by massacre

This somber scene is followed by a love duet, in which the long-awaited reunion of Valentine and Raoul is celebrated. We have the tenor Adolphe Nourrit to thank for the fact that the fourth act closes with this tremendous dialogue, which in its fervor heightens the general air of tension. The dramatic high point, when Raoul learns of the intended plot to murder his fellow-believers, is followed by a quarter of an hour of fluctuation between opposing emotions. Raoul wants to flee, to help, to fight. Valentine restrains him, warning him that he is going to encounter certain ruin. When she runs out of arguments, she makes use of her last ploy: he must stay for her sake, for she loves him. Raoul awakes as if from a nightmare and realizes that he is standing on the threshold of happiness. Intoxicated with joy, he repeats "Tu l'as dit! Oui, tu m'aimes!" ("You've said it! Yes, you love me!"), while Valentine sees her situation much more soberly: "C'est la mort! Voici l'heure!" ("Ah, death, this is the hour"). While the lovers' words contradict each other, the voices merge into a wonderful melody which demonstrates their inseparability. There develops a euphoric, endless dialogue on the same wave of emotion: an extended moment in the shadow of death. M 7

Final act: a chain of catastrophes

It has often been observed that after this high point, the fifth act must inevitably constitute a backward step. Nevertheless, the last act, with the trio of consecration and the supernatural vision, in which the heavens open up above the victims of the massacre, has much that is beautiful to offer. As the choral song of the fleeing Protestants dies away in the roar of the crowd of fanatical murderers, it still has the power to touch the hearts of twentieth-century audiences, inured to everyday spectacles of horror.   P. H.

3. Queen Marguerite's Aria
O beau pa - ys de la Tou - rai - ne! Ri - ants jar - dins, ver - te fon - tai - ne!

4. Chorus of the Huguenots (Marcel)
Sei - gnur, rem - part et seul sou - tien Du fai - ble qui t'a - do - - re!

5. Male-Voice Septet (Act III)
Raoul   Tavannes, Retz   Cossé, Méru   Alle
En mon bon droit j'ai con - fi - an - ce! J'ai con - fi - an - ce! En mon bon droit j'ai con - fi - an - ce! J'ai con - fi - an - ce!

6. Oath of the Catholics
Pour cet - te cau - se sain - te, J'ob - é - i - rai sans crain - te,

7. Love Duet (Valentine and Raoul)
C'est la mort! Voi - ci l'heu - re!
Tu l'as dit! Oui, tu m'ai - mes!

Delay in creation
After the resounding success of *The Huguenots*, the public awaited the next great hit from the partnership of Scribe and Meyerbeer. They had to wait rather a long time. Although Scribe had supplied Meyerbeer with a new libretto as early as 1837 and the composer had set it to music by around 1840, *The Prophet* was put on the back burner because of casting difficulties and disputes with the opera house management. For years, Meyerbeer remained committed to working in his native city of Berlin, where he was musical director, and where he prepared the German national opera *Feldlager in Schlesien* (*The Silesian Encampment*) for performance. It was not until after 1847, when a new management took over at the Paris Opéra, and the celebrated singer Pauline Viardot declared herself ready to take over a leading role, that Meyerbeer's return to Paris could be considered. But the strength of *The Prophet* is once again to be found in the crowd scenes, which could be staged in the most effective manner.

The Prophet, Pauline Viardot as Fidès, Paris. The mezzo-soprano Pauline Viardot (1821–1910) was a member of one of the most important families of singers of the 19th century. (Her father was Manuel García, a famous tenor and teacher of singing, and her sister Maria-Felicia Malibran was a celebrated prima donna.) *The Prophet* is an opera in which the main focus is not on a great love affair; the undisputed star part is that of the mother. The great Viardot sang the role of Fidès at some 200 performances.

The Prophet

Le prophète

Opéra in five acts

Libretto: Eugène Scribe.
Première: 16 April 1849, Paris (Opéra).
Characters: Jean de Leyde/John of Leyden, an innkeeper, later the prophet of the Anabaptists (T), Berthe, betrothed to John (S), Fidès, his mother (Ms), Count Oberthal, a tyrannical landowner (B), Three Anabaptists: Jonas (T), Mathisen (Bar), Zacharie (B); peasant men and women, noblemen and ladies, soldiers, Anabaptists, citizens of Münster (chorus).
Setting: Netherlands and Westphalia, around 1530.

Synopsis

The innkeeper John of Leyden becomes the prophet of the Anabaptists, because he wants to take revenge for past wrongs and prevent new ones. But his righteous anger turns to arbitrary cruelty. The prophet is no longer able to lead the movement, only to keep it within limits. Thus he destroys both friends and enemies, and finally himself.

Act I

John, an innkeeper from Leyden, wishes to marry the poor orphan Berthe, who sets off with his mother Fidès to ask Count Oberthal to give permission for the marriage. Anabaptists are traveling through the country, preaching and calling for resistance to the oppression of those in high places, and are gaining support. But the uprising breaks down in cowardly fashion when one of the oppressors, Count Oberthal, appears. Instead of granting Berthe permission to marry, the Count orders the girl and Fidès to be brought by force to his castle. In view of this new misdeed, the popularity of the Anabaptists increases.

Act II

The Anabaptists believe that they have found in John a useful and much-needed leader for their movement. However, John places more importance on happiness with Berthe than on fame and power. However, he cannot protect Berthe from Oberthal. The latter offers him a choice: to relinquish his bride to him or allow his mother to die. In anguish, John hands over his beloved to Oberthal and agrees to join the Anabaptists.

Act III

John has taken the Anabaptists from one victory to another and is considered to be a prophet. Now winter is on the way. They plan to set up their quarters in Münster and lay siege to the town. Meanwhile, however, the righteous wrath of the Anabaptists has been transformed into vengeful cruelty. This causes a dispute between John and other Anabaptist leaders. When Oberthal falls into the hands of the Anabaptists, he is to be executed, but since the Count feigns remorse, John grants him mercy. He learns from him that Berthe has fled to Münster. John gives orders for the conquest of the town. The attack fails and the Anabaptists blame the prophet. However, by means of his charisma he succeeds in casting his spell over them again.

Act IV

Münster having finally been won, the Anabaptists institute a reign of terror, contrary to John's wishes. Fidès and Berthe are reunited, believing mistakenly that John has been killed by the prophet. Berthe intends to avenge John's death and kill the prophet. In the cathedral of Münster John is crowned as prophet. Fidès recognizes her son, but as the prophet, John must disown his mother, in order to remain true to his goal.

Act V

Behind John's back the Anabaptist leaders negotiate with the emperor, who has come to Münster with superior strength. They are promised exemption from punishment if they surrender the prophet. John now reveals himself to his mother, who is prepared to forgive his bloody deeds if he leaves the Anabaptists. In her search for the prophet, Berthe comes upon the mother and son, and for a brief moment believes herself reunited with her John. When she recognizes him as the prophet, she takes her own life so as not to share in his guilt. John has learned of his betrayal by his fellow-believers. He has secretly prepared to blow up the building in which the negotiations with the emperor's envoys are taking place. When Oberthal enters the room, John gives the signal. Friends and foes die in the ruins, and John expires in the arms of his mother.   *S. N*

Mezzo-soprano arrives: love is neglected

When Pauline Viardot, who had a magnificent mezzo-soprano voice, was engaged for the role of Fidès, both Scribe's libretto and Meyerbeer's music had to be substantially rewritten. This resulted in an opera in which the main focus is not on a great love affair. Indeed, Berthe and John do not have a single love duet. The undisputed star part is that of the mother. John's troubled relationship with her represents the central conflict: her son abandons her and joins the immoral Anabaptists, and at the high point of the story, the coronation scene, he disowns her. But in the last act he returns to her, and both go willingly to their death in order to save the world from uncontrolled power through martyrdom. Meyerbeer had total trust in Viardot's genius and created his most wonderful melodies for her. *M 8*

John, the sect leader

In accordance with the conventions of grand opera, social confrontation is closely bound up with the personal fate of the characters. Scribe drew on historic events, choosing as his raw material the life and career of Jan van Leyden, the so-called King of the Anabaptists, who was hailed as the Messiah and established himself in Münster in 1534, where he announced the coming of the heavenly kingdom. His movement had pre-communist features and fought against worldly and ecclesiastical power. His revolt was bloodily suppressed within two years and he himself died in agony. These events provided a romantic background similar to that of St. Bartholomew's Night in *The Huguenots*. But the basic emotion which guides John on his path is not a nobleman's honor, but religious fanaticism, which increasingly allows him to present himself as a Messiah. He represents the type of the weak hero, who makes the wrong decision and plunges his associates into ruin. His comrades in arms, the Anabaptists, appear as a demonic trio (Jonas, Mathisen, Zacharie). As early as the first act, when they are inciting the people to revolt against their ruler, their leitmotiv rings out, an agitated choral melody – one that was actually composed by Meyerbeer, not borrowed from the repertoire of Protestant melodies as in *The Huguenots*. Franz Liszt based his great Organ Fantasia and Fugue (1850) on this melody. M 9

Stage shocks with noise and silence

The strength of *The Prophet* once again lies in its crowd scenes, which lend themselves to highly effective staging. They predominate in the third act. Here too is the obligatory ballet scene, in which the villagers enjoy themselves on the frozen pond with waltzes, galops, and a skaters' dance. M 10

At the end of this act is John's most impressive entrance: he calms the uproar of his soldiers by means of a prayer, and incites them to fresh battles by means of a march-like triumphal song. M 11

The coronation scene (Act IV) is among Meyerbeer's greatest achievements. This tableau, lasting nearly half an hour, brings together the two threads of the action. John, at the height of his powers, enters the cathedral of Münster in order to be crowned. (The marching music probably influenced Verdi's triumphal march in →*Aida*.) The ceremony is interrupted by the lament of Mother Fidès. After this lyrical interlude, the conflict rises to a climax. John's followers seem to revolt against him. In order to keep them in check, he must perform a miracle. The invocation scene possesses a hypnotic power. Son and mother confront each other, two wills collide, and their dialogue is accompanied only by the mystic sound of the bass clarinets and the heavenly tones of the flutes. *P. H.*

The Prophet, illustration after the set design for the original production, by M. Cambon, Paris 1849.
Within a short time of the première Meyerbeer's crowd scenes were famous. The spectacular stage sets of grand opera were at that time among the sights of Paris, as the city's revue theaters and bars came to be later on.

8. Fidès's Cavatina

O toi qui m'a-ban-don-nes, Mon coeur, mon coeur est dés-ar-mé, Est dés-ar-mé.

9. Chorus of the Anabaptists

Ad nos, ad sa-lu-ta-rem un - - - dam

10. Skaters' Dance

11. John's Song of Triumph

Roi du ciel et des an-ges, Je di-rai tes lou-an-ges Com-me Da-vid ton ser-vi-teur!

The African Woman

L'Africaine

Opéra in five acts

Libretto: Eugène Scribe.
Première: 28 April 1865, Paris (Opéra).

Characters: Vasco da Gama, a Portuguese explorer (T), Inès, daughter of the Grand Admiral, Vasco's beloved (S), Sélica, an African queen (S), Nélusco, an African in Sélica's entourage (Bar), Don Pédro, president of the Royal Council of Portugal, Inès's husband (B), Don Diégo, Grand Admiral, member of the Royal Council, Inès's father (B), Anna, Inès's confidante (Ms), Don Alvaro, a Portuguese nobleman, member of the Royal Council (T), Grand Inquisitor of Lisbon (B), High Priest of Brahma (B); councillors, bishops, ladies of the court, naval officers, sailors, priests, Brahmins, natives (chorus).

Setting: Lisbon, at sea, and in an exotic land, late 15th century.

The African Woman, set design by Johann Kautsky, Wiesbaden 1903 (TWS).
The sea voyage – an unusual setting for an opera. After the great successes of his grand operas, with *The African Woman* Meyerbeer was trying to guide his ship back into the harbor of the Italian opera of his youth, in which individuals still took precedence over the crowd effects. He died more than a year before its first performance.

Synopsis

Vasco da Gama is forbidden to undertake new journeys of discovery; his beloved, Inès, must marry Don Pédro. Only Sélica, the captured African queen, is loyal to him. Don Pédro's expedition is destroyed by the indigenous people. In Africa, Vasco is saved through Sélica's love. But when he meets Inès again, Sélica gives them both their freedom and takes her own life.

Act I

The Grand Admiral plans to marry his daughter Inès to Don Pédro. But she loves Vasco da Gama, the daring sailor who is missing at sea. Vasco, believed dead, appears at a session of the Grand Council, producing two slaves, Sélica and Nélusco, as proof of his discovery of new lands. Nevertheless, the Council rejects his expedition plans. Infuriated, he attacks the Grand Inquisitor and is thrown into prison.

Act II

In prison, Sélica prevents Nélusco from murdering Vasco da Gama, whom she loves. Inès has bought Vasco's freedom at the price of her own hand in marriage. Her husband, Don Pédro, is to lead the new voyages of discovery. Nélusco offers Don Pédro his services and his knowledge of the new lands.

Act III

Don Pédro's ship is steered by Nélusco, who in his thirst for revenge is planning the undoing of the Europeans. Vasco da Gama has followed his rival in another ship, has caught up with him and attempts for Inès's sake to rescue Don Pédro, who, however, angrily rejects Vasco's offer of help. A storm breaks out, and the local people besiege the ship. They massacre the crew, and only Vasco da Gama manages to escape.

Act IV

In her homeland, Sélica is received with ceremony as a queen. She swears to annihilate her enemies without exception. Vasco da Gama admires the splendour of this land and falls into the hands of the sacrificial priests, on the lookout for booty. Sélica saves his life by declaring that Vasco is her husband. Vasco, believing Inès to be dead, resigns himself to his fate.

Act V

Inès has escaped death. The lovers meet. Their tender reunion is interrupted by Sélica. The African queen intends to take revenge for Vasco's betrayal. But then she recognizes that the love between Inès and Vasco is so strong that the man she loves will never be entirely hers, and allows the lovers to return together to Europe. She watches their departure while sitting under the great manzanilla tree, whose blossoms exude a poisonous perfume, so that she dies. Nélusco follows her in death.   *P. H.*

Below right:
The African Woman, photograph from the Kautsky studio, Wiesbaden 1903.
Nine years before the sinking of the *Titanic*, a "ship of disaster" had already been built in Wiesbaden for the May Festival: for the third act of *The African Woman*. Whoever survived the storm at sea was butchered by the natives. Only Vasco da Gama escapes the tumult unscathed. He is to sing again and make further discoveries in the course of the opera.

Toward new shores!

Vasco da Gama is one of a series of weak heroes, like Robert (→*Robert the Devil*) and John (→*The Prophet*). He loves Inès, but when in mortal danger (Act IV) he succumbs almost without hesitation to the African queen Sélica. And when Inès, thought to be dead, reappears, he unscrupulously abandons the African woman in order to flee with Inès. The explanation is that Vasco da Gama's first priority is not requited love. He has other aims: he is a man who subordinates his whole life to an activity which he expects will bring him recognition in the eyes of his fellow humans. This is strikingly similar to the situation of the operatic composer, who, at the mercy of his public's approval, constantly strives after new successes. It is significant that Vasco's only aria in the opera – incidentally the most popular melody that Meyerbeer ever composed – is not dedicated to love, but to a land which he is the first European to enter. He wants to discover new countries and thus attain fame: his name must be immortalized. Fame and immortality: perhaps it is not merely amateur psychology to see in this aim a counterpart to Meyerbeer's personal ambitions. *M 12*   *P. H.*

Above left:
The African Woman, production photograph with Jessye Norman (Sélica) and Gian Giacomo Guelfi (Nélusco), production Franco Enriquez, conductor Riccardo Muti, Maggio Musicale, Florence 1972.
Scene in Act IV, on Sélica's island. The "African woman" is the queen of a distant island, which – according to the libretto – belongs to India. In Meyerbeer's day, the "exotic" meant anything that was not European. However, the role of Sélica is an attractive soprano role in the style of French opera. Jessye Norman, an African American with a wonderful, highly dramatic soprano voice, sang the part at the beginning of her career.

12. Vasco da Gama's Aria

O pa - ra - dis sor - ti de l'on - de,

ciel si bleu, ciel si pur, dont mes yeux sont ra - vis.

Milhaud, Darius

b. 4 September 1892 in Aix-en-Provence
d. 22 June 1974 in Geneva

Milhaud completed his studies at the Paris Conservatoire, was taught by Dukas, Widor, and D'Indy, and joined Dyagilev's circle of artists. However, he left Paris to accompany his friend, the poet and diplomat Paul Claudel, when the latter was posted to Rio de Janeiro. On his return to France in 1918, he became a member of the group known as Les Six, with Honegger, Tailleferre, Poulenc, Auric, and Durey. He was appointed to a professor's chair at Mills College, Oakland, USA, and between 1947 and 1962 divided his time between Paris and Oakland.

Works: Stage works (selection): *Les malheurs d'Orphée* (*The Sorrows of Orpheus*) (1926), *L'enlèvement d'Europe* (*The Rape of Europa*) (1927), *Le pauvre matelot* (*The Poor Sailor*) (1927), *L'abandon d'Ariane* (*Ariadne Forsaken*) (1928), *La délivrance de Thésée* (*Theseus Released*) (1928), *Christophe Colomb* (*Christopher Columbus*) (1930), *Médée* (*Medea*) (1939), *David* (1955), *The Oresteia: Agamemnon, The Choephorae, The Eumenides* (1963, Berlin); ballets, including the successful Surrealist work *Le boeuf sur le toit* (*The Ox on the Roof*) (1919) and *La création du monde* (*The Creation of the World*) (1923); symphonies and other symphonic works, concertos, string quartets and other chamber works, piano works, film music.

The Sorrows of Orpheus

Les malheurs d'Orphée

Opera in three acts

Libretto: Armand Lunel.
Première: 7 May 1926, Brussels (Théâtre de la Monnaie).
Characters: Orphée/Orpheus (Bar), Eurydice/Eurydice (S); manual workers: Smith (T), Waggoner (Bar), Basketmaker (B); animals: Fox (S), Wolf (Ms), Boar (T), Bear (B); gypsies: Eurydice's twin sister (S), her younger sisters, her older sisters (chorus).
Setting: The Camargue, in recent times.

Synopsis

Orpheus, a peasant skilled in the art of healing, has turned away from mankind, but loves and helps animals. His love for the gypsy woman Eurydice meets with disapproval from her family and the villagers. The lovers flee, but Eurydice becomes ill, and Orpheus is powerless to help her. She dies. Orpheus returns to his village, now prepared to help humans as well as animals. Eurydice's sisters hold him responsible for her death and kill him. In a final vision, Orpheus sees himself reunited with Eurydice.

S. N.

The Rape of Europa

L'enlèvement d'Europe

Opéra-minute in eight scenes

Libretto: Henri Etienne Hoppenot.
Première: 17 July 1927, Baden-Baden (Town Hall).
Characters: Agénor/Agenor, King of Thebes (B), Pergamon (Bar), Jupiter/Zeus, as a bull (T), Europe/Europa (S); three serving women and three soldiers (chorus: S, MS, A, T, Bar, B).
Setting: Thebes, in mythical times.

Synopsis

Europa ends her relationship with Pergamon upon discovering her love of animals. The god Zeus transforms himself into a bull. Pergamon tries to kill the animal, but his arrow turns against Pergamon himself. Europa flees on the bull's back. Her liaison with the god is to result in the birth of the monster Minos.

S. N.

The Rape of Europa, costume designs by Hein Heckroth, Essen 1929 (TWS). The visible as an expression of the invisible: this was one of Milhaud's themes. The animal in man interested him, but on this subject he had totally different views from those of German artists (such as Wedekind/Berg → *Lulu*). For the cosmopolitan Frenchman Milhaud, the sexual element was rather one which reconciled and connected humans and animals.

Milhaud composed strikingly concise music with a southern (partly South American) flavor, in which melody was dominant and a distinctive sound was achieved by means of an unconventional use of percussion. He represented French music during the Surrealist era. "Le boeuf sur le toit" came to be his trademark.

Opéras-minutes
The First World War had far-reaching consequences for those returning home. It brought with it, on a massive scale, experiences of the unexpected and the uncontrollable. Time appeared to pass more rapidly; speed and brevity became virtues in themselves. Film and later radio dealt with this by means of cutting techniques. There was a fashion for short and concentrated forms of presentation. This also applied to opera. Material was no longer pleasurably expanded, but concisely presented. Milhaud was a master of this technique. *The Sorrows of Orpheus* lasts 35 minutes. Even shorter is *The Rape of Europa*, a nine-minute work. Milhaud brought the technique of concentration to perfection. *The Poor Sailor*, a realistically tragic story in the form of a "lament," takes 40 minutes in performance, and *Ariadne* is forsaken within just ten minutes. *M. S.*

The Poor Sailor

Le pauvre matelot

Complainte (lament) in three acts

Libretto: Jean Cocteau.
Première: 16 December 1927 Paris (Opéra-Comique).
Characters: The Sailor (T), His Wife (S), His Friend (Bar), His Father-in-Law (B).
Setting: A harbour tavern, time undefined.

Synopsis

After an absence of 15 years, a sailor returns home, is not at first recognized by his wife, doubts her love and provokes his own death. He persuades the wife that he, a stranger, has brought treasures with him, while her husband has remained poor and is pursued by creditors. Not content with this, he tells her that her longed-for husband will soon return, but for himself asks only for a place to sleep for the night, where he is then murdered by the wife. After 15 years' successful battle with her widowed existence, the woman has made herself into a widow; in fleeing from her fate she has brought it upon herself.

Ariadne Forsaken

L'abandon d'Ariane

Opéra-minute in five scenes

Libretto: Henri Etienne Hoppenot.
Première: 20 April 1928, Wiesbaden.
Characters: Ariane/Ariadne (S), Phèdre/Phaedra (S), Thésée/Theseus (T), Dionysos/Dionysus (Bar), Three Stranded Sailors (T, Bar, B), Three Gypsy Bacchantes (S, Ms, A).
Setting: The island of Naxos, in mythical times.

Synopsis

Ariadne no longer loves Theseus; her sister Phaedra, on the other hand, woos him in vain. When both sisters give alms to Dionysus, who is disguised as a beggar, the god shows his gratitude and solves their problems. He makes Theseus drunk and lets him believe that the veiled Phaedra is Ariadne. Theseus leaves the island with Phaedra. Ariadne, abandoned, is happy, and gains her wish – to appear as a constellation in the heavens next to Diana.   *S. N.*

Ariadne Forsaken, stage design by Hein Heckroth, production Karlheinz Gutheim, conductor Hans Mikerey, Städtische Bühnen, Opernhaus Chemnitz 1932 (TWS). Milhaud, a composer who was closely linked with French Surrealism, aimed, as did his artist friends, to question current norms with wit, irony and good humor. In European opera one general theme had emerged over the centuries: the love between man and woman. In *Ariadne Forsaken*, this cliché is deconstructed, and the love between man and woman is replaced by love between woman and the stars. As so often with Milhaud, we are confronted with what is both a joke and a serious discussion.

Moniuszko, Stanisław

b. 5 May 1819 in Ubiel (now Ubel, near Minsk)
d. 4 June 1872 in Warsaw

After beginning his musical education in Minsk and Warsaw, Moniuszko studied in Berlin with C.F. Rungenhagen. From 1840 he worked as an organist in Vilnius, where he made contact with leading figures of the Polish literary world (Kraszewski, Fredro). In 1857 he moved to Warsaw. The première of his opera *Halka* (second version) in Warsaw in 1858 brought him overnight fame. His funeral procession was transformed into a declaration of the Polish desire for freedom and a protest against tsarist oppression.

Works: Operas: *Halka* (1848), *Flis* (*The Raftsman*) (1858), *Hrabina* (*The Countess*) (1860), *Straszny Dwór* (*The Haunted Manor*) (1865), *Paria* (*The Pariah*) (1869); vocal music (seven Masses, a Requiem, secular choral works, 360 songs); instrumental music: *Bajka* (*The Fairy Tale*), overtures, two string quartets.

Moniuszko, like Glinka in Russia, Smetana in Czechoslovakia, and Erkel in Hungary, became known as his country's national composer because he dealt with the urgent problems of his time and was skilled in integrating the folk music of Poland into his compositions.

Halka

Opera in four acts

Libretto: Włodzimierz Wolski.

Première: first version in two acts: concert performance 1 January 1848, Vilnius, staged 28 February 1854, Vilnius; second version in four acts: 1 January 1858, Warsaw (Wielki Theater).

Characters: Stolnik, a landowner and lord high steward to the king (B), Zofia, his daughter (S), Dziemba, Stolnik's estate manager (B), Janusz, a nobleman and landowner (Bar), Halka and Jontek, serfs of Janusz (S, T), A Piper (B), A Peasant (T); nobles, guests, serfs (chorus).

Setting: Near Stolnik's country house outside Kraków, and a mountain village, late 18th century.

Synopsis

The nobleman and landowner Janusz has entered into a liaison with a serf, the peasant girl Halka. She is expecting his child. When he becomes engaged to Zofia, the daughter of the royal lord high steward, he sends the unsuspecting girl back to her native village, with the serf Jontek as an escort. Jontek loves Halka and knows that she has been abandoned by Janusz. But Halka does not believe him. Her fate causes deep dismay among the villagers. When the marriage has taken place, even Halka must recognize Janusz's infidelity and plunges into the river. At the wedding celebrations, the song of the serfs from Halka's village has a menacing undertone.   *S. N.*

The opera as a mirror of the nation
While Frédéric Chopin attained high esteem as a cultural ambassador in France for his oppressed people, his younger colleague Moniuszko was active in his own culture in his native land. He succeeded in combining the characteristics of Italian, French, and German opera with the stylistic qualitites of traditional Polish music. Furthermore, the opera *Halka* became a symbol of national identity because of its patriotic content and its element of social criticism.

Within the limits of what was allowed by the censors, *Halka* provided large sections of Polish society with an opportunity to recognize themselves and their political and cultural situation, and to see it as one that could be altered. Moniuszko did not adapt Polish folk song as sublimely as Chopin, and he smoothed out the folk

Halka, production photograph with Barbara Rusin as Halka (front), production Teresa Kujawa, conductor Tadeusz Kozlowski, guest performance by the Grand Théâtre de Lodz, Opéra National de Lyon 1986.
In the third act Halka acknowledges the betrayal of the landowner Janusz. The peasants become aware of the love story with menacing distress. In Eastern European national operas the sense of national identity was often accompanied by social sensibility.

music of the mountain-dwelling peasants of the Tatra (south of Kraków) rather than using it in its bizarre original form (unlike →Karol Szymanowski in the 1920s). But *Halka* nevertheless became a milestone in nineteenth-century Polish musical history, because in this opera Moniuszko towered above the bland, shallow Romanticism of his contemporaries and laid the foundations for an independent Polish musical culture in the late nineteenth and early twentieth centuries.

Folklore: the ideological shop-window

With dramatic skill Moniuszko combined different folk genres with the traditional forms of Italian and French opera, employing his comprehensive knowledge of the European repertoire and the instinct of the born musical dramatist (an instinct that Chopin lacked). This made *Halka* an important and historic piece of Polish music drama, and also a great success, even outside Poland.

Moniuszko's operas and songs were closely related to questions that were of fundamental importance to contemporary Polish society. In the words of Witold Rudzinski, a musicologist and composer, and the editor of Moniuszko's works, "The ideas contained in his works were common to all parts of the country. Over and above this, Moniuszko represented and generalized a solid technical ability, which was drawn on by the composers of Europe long after his time." This is

precisely the basis of Moniuszko's significance. In his work he created a bridge between traditional Polish music and the music of Chopin.   *H. L.*

Below
Halka, production photograph with Ernst Gutstein (Janusz), Georg Schnapka (Stolnik) and Anni Felbermayer (Zofia), Wiener Volksoper 1966. The landowner Stolnik blesses his daughter Zofia and Janusz before their marriage.

Bottom
Halka, postcard, Warsaw/Moscow 1900. Happy wedding celebrations, with the national costumes forming an outstanding feature. In the national opera of an oppressed people, everything that clearly demonstrated national identity had political significance. The message of such an opera was "We have our own folklore, which can stand proudly beside the greatest musical works."

Akt IV z opery „Halka" Moniuszki.

Monteverdi, Claudio

baptized 15 May 1567 in Cremona
d. 29 November 1643 in Venice

The son of an apothecary, Monteverdi received his education from the choirmaster of the cathedral in Cremona. Here he studied musical theory and composition, played the violin, and sang in the choir. His first musical publication (motets for three voices) appeared when he was 15 (*Sacrae cantiunculae*, 1582). At the age of 20 he published a collection of madrigals for five voices (obligatory at the time for young composers), which was to be followed by eight more. In 1590 he entered the service of Duke Vincenzo Gonzaga I of Mantua, first as a viola player, then as house composer. He accompanied the duke twice on extended trips (to Austria, Hungary, and Flanders). In Mantua he married the singer Claudia Cattaneo. When, in 1612, Duke Francesco, Vincenzo's successor, gave him his notice, he successfully applied for the position of choirmaster at the cathedral of St. Mark's in Venice as successor to Giovanni Gabrieli, who had recently died. Here he lived until his death, a highly esteemed master, composing both sacred and secular works. His creative power retained its freshness and originality until his death at an advanced age.

Works: Surviving full-length stage works: *Orfeo* (*Orpheus*) (1607, Mantua), *Il ritorno d'Ulisse in patria* (*The Return of Ulysses to his Homeland*) (1640, Venice), *L'incoronazione di Poppea* (*The Coronation of Poppea*) (1642–43, Venice); nine volumes of madrigals (1587–1651, the last volume published posthumously), sacred vocal works (including Masses and his major work *Vespro della Beata Vergine* (*Vespers of the Blessed Virgin*) (1610).

Orfeo, production photograph with Reingard Didusch (Eurydice) and Philippe Huttenlocher (Orpheus), production Jean-Pierre Ponnelle, conductor Nikolaus Harnoncourt, Opernhaus Zurich 1975.
With this wild dance (a "moresca") Monteverdi is alluding to the original version of the Orpheus myth, in which the hero meets with an ignominious and brutal death.

*M*onteverdi was one of the first great musical dramatists of all time. He set standards for the operatic genre and synthesized in his works all the stylistic elements of early Italian Baroque music.

Orfeo
Orpheus

Favola in musica

Libretto: Alessandro Striggio the younger.
Première: 24 February 1607, Mantua (Palazzo Ducale).
Characters: La Musica/Music (S), Orfeo/Orpheus (T), Euridice/Eurydice (S), The messenger (S), Caronte/Charon (B), Plutone/Pluto (B), Proserpina (S), Speranza/Hope (S), Echo (T), Apollo (T), Four Shepherds (A, 2T, B), Nymph (S), Two Underworld Spirits (2T); nymphs and shepherds, underworld spirits (chorus); shepherds (ballet).
Setting: Thrace and the underworld.

Synopsis
Prologue
Music praises her powers, and hopes that the listeners will find peace through them, just as Orpheus brought peace to nature with his singing.
Act I
Nymphs and shepherds celebrate the end of Orpheus's unhappiness, now that he is to be married to Eurydice.
Act II
Orpheus expresses his great happiness. Then he receives dreadful news: Eurydice is dead. She was bitten by a snake while picking flowers. The singer sets off for the underworld to win back his wife.
Act III
Led by Hope, Orpheus reaches the gates of the underworld. Here she leaves him. Orpheus must enter the underworld alone. Charon, the ferryman of the dead, refuses to carry him across the river Styx. Orpheus pleads with him in vain; his singing only has the effect of putting Charon to sleep. Orpheus crosses the Styx alone in a boat. The spirits of the underworld are amazed at the powers of this mortal, for whom nothing seems to be impossible.
Act IV
Pluto's wife Proserpina is so moved by Orpheus's lament that she persuades her husband to release Eurydice. Before Eurydice can follow her husband, the ruler of the underworld makes only one condition: Orpheus must not turn to look back. On his way back to the world of light, Orpheus wonders if Eurydice is really following him. He looks back and loses his beloved for ever. The spirits recognize that he has conquered the underworld, but not himself.
Act V
Orpheus is overcome by the pain of his final loss; he vows to renounce all love of women and devote his lyre and his singing to the glorification of his beloved. His father, Apollo, advises him to moderate his grief; his son is to follow him into heaven to eternal life among the gods, where he will be able to see Eurydice's face among the stars. The shepherds pay homage to the deified singer.   S. N.

Recipe for a Baroque hell

"For the portrayal of hell one may proceed as follows, as long as there is a space or a small open courtyard behind the central backcloth. One lights two fires, one opposite the opening of the above-mentioned small courtyard, and the other at such a distance from the first that the persons who have to appear in it can walk or dance through it without suffering any damage. Thus it will appear to everyone as though they were standing in the midst of the flames, since one sees that it is indeed fire, but because of the distance one cannot interpret how it is produced." Niccolò Sabbatini, a stage designer and contemporary of Monteverdi, in his *Practica di fabricare scene* (*Guide to Set Construction*) of 1638 (new edition, Weimar 1926).

Symmetrical structure

Admittedly Jacopo Peri's →*Euridice* preceded Monteverdi's *Orfeo* by only a few years, but the two musical adaptations of the myth differ significantly. Peri's piece consists of a series of recitatives, as though the composer had wished to give a didactic example of monody. In Monteverdi's *Orfeo*, arias and song-like sections alternate with freely recited monologues.

Everything has a natural and spontaneous effect, while the structure of the work has a conscious symmetry. The introductory instrumental toccata corresponds to the closing dance (a moresca), while the two outer acts (I and V) are static (wedding celebrations, and Orpheus's lament followed by Apollo's consolation). In the inner acts (II and IV) we see the repeated loss of Eurydice. The central point is formed by the underworld act (III), in which Orpheus conquers the power of death by means of his art.

High society entertainment

No one knows exactly who first had the strange idea of introducing singing into a dramatic scene. It was all part of the aristocracy's liking for "amusement." The first operatic performances took place within courtly festivals. It was not necessary to dedicate a special place to them; the grand hall of a Renaissance palace would suffice. Good singers and instrumentalists were already part of the court staff. But the audience too – the aristocratic family and its distinguished guests – were musically cultured and often took part in performances. The figures presented included gods and allegorical and mythical figures. People played themselves and stories of current significance were presented, though in mythological disguise. Court chronicles of the time refer to the marriage of Prince Ferdinando de' Medici to Christine of Lorraine. During the celebrations, which lasted for weeks and involved a multiplicity of festival events, theatrical performances were staged. During the intervals, short mythological episodes were presented in the form of song. These mini-operas were called *intermedi* (interludes). Setting: Florence, 1589.

Design for stage machinery for the opera *Germanico sul Reno* (*Germanicus on the Rhine*) by Giovanni Legrenzi (1626–90), pen and wash drawing, artist unknown.
Since natural phenomena and supernatural beings were present on stage from the beginnings of Baroque opera, the art of stage machinery developed rapidly. The framework was disguised by painted clouds and plants, while characters were mounted on the movable parts of the machinery (gods, muses, sirens, cupids, and so on). The entire structure could be moved slowly from the back to the front, or suddenly disappear behind trap doors. The magic of opera was thus completed by skillfully created stage illusions.

Like the ancient Greeks...

The new combination of words and music required a theoretical basis. The ancient Greek tragedies served as models, since it was assumed that words and music had formed a unified whole in them. But apart from a brief choral song from Euripides's tragedy *Orestes*, no sung melodies had survived. And even this was not taken notice of in the "revival" of ancient Greek art. Instead, other sources were relied upon. The musician Vincenzo Galilei (1533–91, the father of the astronomer Galileo Galilei), who was interested in musical history, had already researched and published surviving musical fragments. Another daring Italian, Nicola Vicentino, created an instrument called the *archicembalo*, which could produce what were supposed to be ancient Greek modes. Scholars and artists created a society called the Camerata for the revival of ancient tragedy. The leader of the circle was Count Giovanni Bardi, whose role was later taken over by another aristocrat, Jacopo Corsi. The members included poets such as Ottavio Rinuccini and Gabriello Chiabrera (the first librettists in operatic history) and musicians such as Jacopo Peri, Giulio Caccini, and Emilio de' Cavalieri. Peri and Rinuccini became the progenitors of opera. Between 1594 and 1598 they composed the first full-length opera, *Dafne*, now unfortunately lost. The first surviving opera is based on the myth of Orpheus: *Euridice* (1600), with a libretto by Rinuccini and music by Peri.

Musical sources

The word "opera" (simply meaning "work") was not used for musical drama before 1650; instead, general formulae were employed, such as "dramma per musica" (drama in music), or "favola in musica" (fable in music), since the first narratives in music were not that different from extended madrigals, the most popular musical form and means of expression during the sixteenth and early seventeenth centuries. Among the precursors of the musical drama in several acts were the pastoral plays so popular in Renaissance Italy, above all *Aminta* by Torquato Tasso (1544–95) and *Il pastor fido* (*The Faithful Shepherd*) by Giovanni Battista Guarini (1538–1612). From the beginning, the pastorals included songs and choruses. A whole series of dramatic conventions which later became typical of Baroque opera, such as mistaken identity, the insertion of comic minor characters, and the obligatory happy ending, have their origins here. Another precursor of later operas is found in the Venetian madrigal comedies of the late sixteenth century, particularly those of Orazio Vecchi and Adriano Banchieri. What was special about this genre? There was no musical differentiation between chorus and protagonists; everything was sung by groups of singers. Within the madrigal production of the time an interesting experiment took place. There were three outstanding female singers in Ferrara at the end of the sixteenth century. The composer to the princely court of the d'Este family, Luzzasco Luzzaschi, created solo madrigals for them: pieces for one, two or three voices with chordal accompaniment, mostly played on a keyboard instrument, and underpinned by a bass instrument. Now the time was ripe for a genius who would crystallize the various musical currents into true musical drama: Claudio Monteverdi.

The Return of Ulysses to his Homeland

Il ritorno d'Ulisse in patria

Dramma per musica

Libretto: Giacomo Badoaro, after Homer's *Odyssey*.
Première: 1640, Venice (Teatro di san Cassiano).
Characters: L'Humana Fragilità/Human Frailty (S), Il Tempo/Time (B), La Fortuna/Fortune (S), Amore/Cupid (S), Giove/Jupiter (T), Nettuno/Neptune (B), Minerva (S), Giunone/Juno (S), Ulisse/Ulysses (T), Penelope, his wife (S), Telemaco/Telemachus, their son (T), Antinoo/Antinous, Pisandro/Peisander, Anfinomo/Amphinomus, suitors of Penelope (B, T, A), Melanto, Penelope's maid (S), Eurimaco/Eurymachus, Melanto's lover (T), Eumete/Eumaeus, Ulysses's shepherd (B), Iro/Irus, a foolish sponger among the suitors (T), Ericlea/Eurycleia, Penelope's nurse (Ms); Phaeacians, heavenly beings, sea creatures (chorus).
Setting: Ithaca, in mythical times.

Synopsis
Prologue

Human Frailty blames Time, uncertain Fortune and the power of Cupid for the hard destiny of mankind.

Act I

For many years the chaste Penelope has awaited the return of her husband Ulysses. She complains of her loneliness and the humiliating situation of having to endure the wooing of importunate suitors. Her maid Melanto enjoys the pleasures of love with Eurymachus, and tries to persuade her mistress to enter a new marriage. Neptune, god of the sea, prevents the return of Ulysses, because the latter has killed one of his sons. Now the Phaeacians, with Minerva's help, have brought Ulysses to the shores of Ithaca after much wandering at sea. Neptune transforms Ulysses's ship into a rock, but Minerva prepares the way for her protégé Ulysses. She tells him everything that has happened and transforms him into an infirm old beggar. In this form, with the help of the faithful shepherd Eumaeus, he is to conquer the suitors.

Act II

Minerva reunites father and son. Ulysses makes himself known to Telemachus. In the palace, Penelope's situation is becoming impossible because of the persistent attentions of the suitors. Eumaeus announces the imminent arrival of Ulysses. The hero's name alone puts the suitors into a panic. Before Ulysses's return, they want to extract an acceptance from Penelope and murder Telemachus. Minerva explains her plan to Ulysses. She will inspire Penelope with the right words: she is to suggest a duel between the suitors and the beggar. She herself will then give her support to Ulysses. Ulysses arrives at the palace in the form of the beggar and is recognized by no one. Mocked by Irus, he challenges the parasite to a fight. Penelope presents the impatient suitors with a challenge: whoever can draw Ulysses's bow will become her husband. None of them succeeds in doing so except the beggar, who kills the suitors with his arrows.

Act III

Since he can no longer live at the suitors' expense, Irus commits suicide. Penelope cannot believe that the aged beggar is really Ulysses. Melanto stirs up her doubts. Neither the faithful shepherd Eumaeus nor their son Telemachus is able to convince her of Ulysses's identity. The gods are opposed to human happiness. Minerva and Juno plead with Jupiter to grant peace and repose to the long-suffering Ulysses. The father of the gods obtains mercy from Neptune for the hero, who has been punished by his long wanderings. Eurycleia, Penelope's nurse recognizes an old scar of Ulysses on the beggar's foot. Even this does not convince Penelope of the beggar's true identity. Even when Ulysses stands before her in his own form, she believes herself to have been deceived by the gods. Finally Ulysses reveals himself to her through his knowledge of a secret known only to the two of them: the pattern of the cover of their matrimonial bed. Penelope finally embraces the husband who has returned to her.

S. N.

The Return of Ulysses to his Homeland, production photograph from the prologue with Werner Hollweg and Werner Gröschel, production Jean-Pierre Ponnelle, conductor Nikolaus Harnoncourt, Opernhaus Zurich 1977.
The story of the long wanderings of Ulysses was of particular significance for the city of Venice as a port and center of trade, whose seafaring inhabitants understood all too well the fragility of human life. In the early Venetian operas, the ocean not only played an important role as the scene where events took place, but was also imagined to be a powerful deity. Jean-Pierre Ponnelle evocatively presented the allegory of human fragility in the production forming part of the Monteverdi cycle in Zurich, which has earned an important place in theatrical history.

The Return of Ulysses to his Homeland, production photograph from the film version with Trudeliese Schmidt as Penelope, production Jean-Pierre Ponnelle, 1978.
Penelope and her suitors. The role of Penelope is one of tragic nobility. She has several great declamatory monologues. Her steadfastness served as a model for the wives of Venetian seafarers.

Right
The Return of Ulysses to his Homeland, production photograph,
Württemburgisches Staatstheater, Stuttgart 1995.
Monteverdi's late operas encompass a cosmic world, populated not only by
humans but also by gods, who strive for power and influence, and favor or
punish mortals. In this scene Neptune and Jupiter quarrel over Ulysses.
Neptune kills the Phaeacians, and Jupiter succeeds in rescuing his protégé
with the help of his daughter Minerva.

The Return of Ulysses to his Homeland, set design for Act II by Alfred Siercke,
production Günther Rennert, Hamburgische Staatsoper 1964 (TWS).
Ulysses lies unconscious on the shores of Ithaca; in the background is the ship
of the Phaeacians, transformed into a rock.

The art of song

It was not until the close of the sixteenth century that the concept of "new" music arose – a concept that would have been wholly foreign to composers of the Middle Ages and the Renaissance. A great stir was caused by the public discussion of aesthetic ideas by Italian musicians of the early Baroque, at the center of which was music's relationship to language and poetry. Music was to enhance the poetic content of the text, thereby awakening emotions and passions. "Favellar in musica" – talking in music – was regarded as the most important task of the singer in early Italian music drama, with "singing speech" ("parlar cantando") seeking to capture the rhythms and inflections of spoken Italian.

Singing, particularly solo singing, acquired a new function, with the emphasis on the individual. At this point it becomes legitimate to speak of the birth of Italian bel canto. Three main types of song were distinguished: song with virtuoso coloratura ("cantar passaggiato"), simple, unpretentious song ("cantar sodo"), and an emotional manner of delivery, rich in dynamic light and shade ("cantar d'affetto"). In the sung parts of *Orfeo* Monteverdi made use of all three types of song, for purposes of dramatic expression.

Opera: a matter of taste

Thirty-three years separate Monteverdi's first musical stage work, →*Orfeo*, and his next *dramma in musica* to have survived in its entirety. Monteverdi did not in fact stop creating dramatic music; works which are lost or have survived only in part include *L'Arianna* (1608), *Le nozze di Tetide* (1616), *La finta pazza Licori* (1627), and several dramas in madrigal form such as *Il combattimento di Tancredi e Clorinda* (1624). The opening of the first public opera house in Venice and the lively public interest in opera turned the ageing Monteverdi once again towards the stage. Now he had other challenges to confront than those of three decades earlier. In Venice, one composed not merely for a small aristocratic circle, but for people of varying social status. The audience expected both of the librettist and of the composer an exciting, realistic action with effective scenes, rich in contrast, interesting characters, and spectacular stage effects. Monteverdi's two late operas brilliantly fulfilled these expectations.

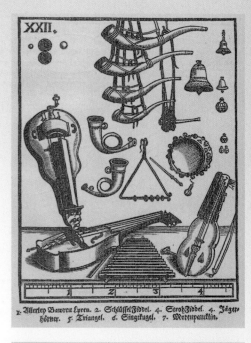

1. Allerley Bawren Lyren. 2. Schlüssel Fiddel. 4. Stroh Fiddel. 4. Jäger Hörner. 5. Triangel. 6. Singeklugel. 7. Morentpancklin.

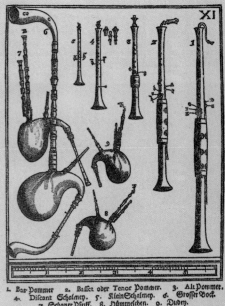

1. Bas Pommer 2. Basset oder Tenor Pommer. 3. Alt Pommer. 4. Discant Schalmey. 5. Klein Schalmey. 6. Grosser Bock. 7. Schaper Pfeiff. 8. Hümmelchen. 9. Dudey.

1. Ein Ar eines Hackebrets/wird aber mit Fingern gegriffen. 2. Eine Sonderbare Laute/ wird nach Art der Harpfen tractiret. 3. Ein gar Alt Italienisch Instrument, davon hinten im Indice, bericht zufinden.

1. Heerpaucken. 2. Soldaten Trummeln. 3. Schweitzer Pfeifflin 4. Amboß

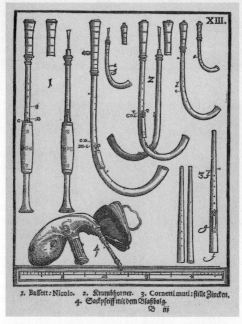

1. Bassett: Nicolo. 2. Krumbhörner. 3. Cornetti muti: stille Zincken.
4. Sackpfeiff mit dem Blaßbalg.

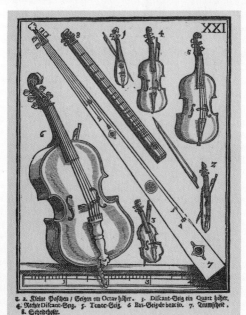

1. 2. Kleine Poschen / Geigen ein Octav höher. 3. Discant-Geig ein Quart höher.
4. Rechte Discant-Geig. 5. Tenor-Geig. 6. Bas-Geig de bracio. 7. Trumscheit.
8. Scholhalter.

The message of instruments

On the title page of the score of *Orfeo*, printed in Venice in 1609, Monteverdi listed various instruments, presumably those that made up the orchestra in the Mantuan performances of 1607. In the score itself there are very few references to the use of particular instruments. This is in accordance with a certain concept of the relationship between notation and performance, which allowed the interpreter much greater freedom than was later to be the case. The notes acted as a reminder for the living development of the music according to the abilities of the musician. The reference to particular instruments does not deny the musician the freedom to determine the number of instruments to be used, and also makes it possible to perform the music according to the instruments and performers available. *Orfeo* can be performed equally effectively by ten or by forty instruments. One should, however, note certain rules of contemporary musical practice in instrumentation: there was a distinction between "fundamental" and "ornamental" instruments, the fundamental ones including keyboard and plucked string instruments (harpsichord, virginals, organ, regal, lute, theorbo, harp), and the ornamental ones (various wind and string instruments, including violas). Monteverdi's indication of the dramatic function of the instruments is interesting. Recorders, strings and plucked instruments provide the basic atmosphere for the pastoral scenes, while the brass instruments (trumpets and trombones), cornetts (a kind of wooden trumpet), and a small, rasping keyboard instrument, the regal, create the tones of the underworld. It is recommended that the figure of Orpheus should be characterized by the refined sounds of the lute, the harp, and the *organo di legno* (wooden organ). The location of the original performance is acknowledged at the beginning of the piece by an introductory fanfare (which Monteverdi entitles "toccata") – the musical coat-of-arms of the Gonzaga family.

Arsenal of instruments

At the time of the birth of opera – as indeed throughout the seventeenth century – there was no standardized operatic orchestra. The French were the leaders in this field, especially Jean-Baptiste Lully (who was, incidentally, of Italian birth). At the time of the *Roi Soleil*, he was already the director of a regular orchestra with a fixed number of musicians. In the Italian Baroque, the term "orchestra" meant a flexible group of instrumentalists, who – like their colleagues of some decades earlier during the Renaissance – possessed an arsenal of instruments. They would select the instruments to be used according to where they were performing and the composition of the group as a whole. The German composer and music scholar Michael Praetorius (1571–1621) produced a lexicon of music in three volumes (*Syntagma musicum*, 1615–20), which constitutes an extremely valuable compendium of the instruments of his time, not least because it alludes to those instruments that gradually disappeared from the orchestra over the course of time.

Illustrations of musical instruments from Michael Praetorius's *Syntagma musicum*, vol. 2 (1615–20).

The wealth and multiplicity of families of musical instruments is striking: there is already a whole series of variants on the viol, the predecessor of today's string instruments (below right). Among the drums (top right), only the kettle drum gained a permanent place in the orchestra. The shawm and pommer (center left) developed into various woodwind instruments. Lutes, bagpipes, crumhorns, hurdy-gurdies, and even recorders were banned from the "modern" eighteenth-century orchestra. J.S. Bach and Handel were familiar with these instruments, but for Mozart they were already relics of a bygone age.

1. Bandoer. 2. Orpheoreon. 3. Penorcon. 4. Italianische Lyra de Gamba.

A new theater in a horseshoe shape

The ground plan of the Teatro Farnese in Parma shows an open arena in the Roman style. The inaugural performance of 21 December 1628 is shown – the *tornero* (music for a tournament) *Mercurio e Marte*, with musical interludes by Monteverdi. The stage and auditorium areas are not strictly separated from each other. This peculiarity later became typical of the Baroque theater. The ground plan for a theater in Venice, converted for operatic performances in 1654 (the Teatro dei SS. Giovanni e Paolo), where Monteverdi's last opera →*The Coronation of Poppea* was first performed in 1642, points clearly to the influence of the Classical amphitheater. Admittedly there are some modifications: the auditorium is arranged in a horseshoe shape, and in place of the amphitheater's rows of seats, democratically equal in status, we find the hierarchically arranged boxes. This became the model for the construction of Italian opera houses. The ownership of a box became a status symbol; they were rented by well-to-do patrician families and often inherited. The front stalls of the early opera houses were used as dance floors at festive balls, and also as standing room at stage performances.

Top right
Drawing of the Teatro dei SS. Giovanni e Paolo in Venice by Carlo Fontana, 1654 (Sir John Soane's Museum, London).

Below left
Ground plan of the Teatro Farnese in Parma by Giovanni Battista Aleotti, 1618–28.

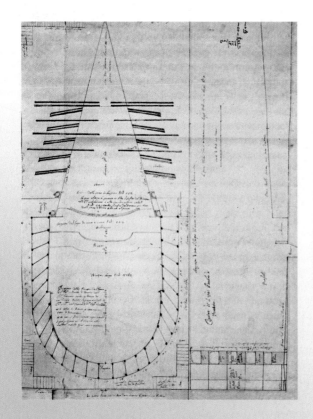

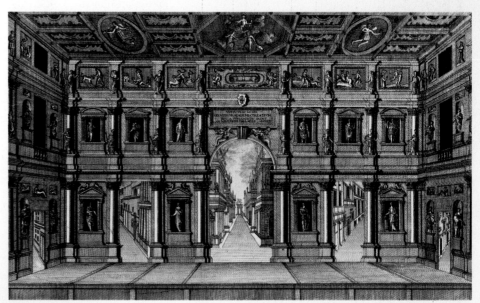

View of the stage backdrop at the Teatro Olimpico in Vicenza, engraving, artist unknown, 1584 (Victoria & Albert Museum, London).
Never originally intended to house opera, the Teatro Olimpico in Vicenza was constructed just prior to opera's emergence as a theatrical genre. Built between 1580 and 1585 it reflects the period revival in classical tragedy more than it does the theatrical style of its successor. The man who envisaged the Teatro Olimpico, now the only surviving renaissance theater, was the architect Andrea Palladio, whose portfolio of work includes numerous other important buildings in and around Vicenza as well as mansion houses along the river Brenta between Venice and Padua. Unfortunately, Palladio did not live to see his theater's inauguration, a performance of Sophocles' *Oedipus Rex*. His reliance on classical-romanticism in architectural design and revival of the elliptical amphitheater, however, formed the blueprint for the construction of subsequent early Italian opera houses.

The first opera house

Opera was first performed to a paying public at the Teatro S. Cassiano in Venice in 1637. The opera in question was imported from Rome – *L'Andromeda*, by Benedetto Ferrari and Francesco Manelli. At the S. Cassiano theater, which sadly no longer exists, a bourgeois public could gain admission through payment, in contrast to the former practice whereby attendance at the opera was a privilege of the nobility. The enterprise proved commercially worthwhile, and over the following decades more than ten opera houses opened in Venice. Thus the city of the lagoon became, with Rome and Naples, one of the most important centers of opera in Italy in the seventeenth and eighteenth centuries. In his late musical-dramatic works Monteverdi was inspired by this rapidly blossoming operatic scene.

The ocean on the Baroque stage

A contemporary of Monteverdi, the stage designer Niccolò Sabbatini, in a book of practical instructions on the art of the stage, described the most frequently appearing objects on the Baroque stage and various ways of representing natural phenomena. There were for example several possibilities for simulating a disturbed ocean surface for the spectators' benefit. The simplest method was considered to be the skillful movement of a blue-painted canvas. A more ambitious solution demanded the construction of wooden panels of waves, which could be cleverly painted and twisted in relation to each other in order to produce the desired effect, from a gently surging sea to a wildly crashing surf.

Historic set design by Giacomo Torelli for the opera *Bellerofonte* (*Bellerophon*) by Francesco Sacrati, Venice 1642 (TWS).
The typical set of a successful Venetian opera: a harbor scene, with St. Mark's Square and the ocean in the background.

The Coronation of Poppea

L'incoronazione di Poppea

Opera musicale

Libretto: Giovanni Francesco Busenello.
Première: 1642 or 1643, Venice (Teatro SS. Giovanni e Paolo).
Character: La Fortuna/Fortune (S), La Virtù/Virtue (S), Amore/Cupid (S), Poppea, a Roman courtesan (S), Nerone/Nero, Emperor of Rome (S), Ottavia/Octavia, Empress of Rome (S), Ottone/Otho, the former lover of Poppea (A), Seneca, a philosopher (B), Drusilla, a lady of the court (S), Nutrice, Octavia's nurse (A), Arnalta, Poppea's nurse (T), Lucano/Lucan, court poet (T), Pallade/Pallas Athene (S), Mercurio/Mercury (B), Venere/Venus (S), A Lictor (B), Liberto, a captain who is a freed man (T), Valletto, a page of the empress (S), Damigella, lady-in-waiting to the empress (S), Two Soldiers (2T); Seneca's friends, consuls, tribunes (chorus or ensemble of soloists).
Setting: Rome, c. AD 62, during the reign of the Emperor Nero.

Synopsis

Prologue

Fortune, Virtue, and Cupid argue about which of them has the greatest influence on humankind.

Act I

Scene 1: Otho, returning home at daybreak, looks forward to seeing his beloved Poppea. However, two soldiers are standing guard in front of his house. Nero himself has taken Otho's place in Poppea's affections.

Scene 2: The soldiers comment critically on the political situation: private interests are placed above public interests. Nero's love for Poppea brings them only hardship and a sleepless night.

Scene 3: Poppea enchants the emperor with her erotic arts. Nero bids her a tender farewell.

Scene 4: Poppea's nurse Arnalta warns her mistress: Nero is a man of unpredictable moods. It is advisable to be on one's guard when dealing with powerful individuals.

Scene 5: The empress Octavia bemoans her fate as a deceived wife. Her nurse advises her to find another man. Octavia rejects this solution.

Scene 6: Seneca tries to comfort Octavia with philosophical observations. The empress pleads with him to defend her rights to Nero and in the Senate. Valletto the page considers the philosopher to be a tactless windbag.

Scenes 7–8: Seneca finds confirmation of his philosophy: even the powerful are pursued by misfortune. Pallas Athene announces to him that he will soon die. He receives her message with dignity.

Scene 9: Seneca challenges his former pupil Nero about his scandalous relationship with Poppea. Nero breaks off their friendship.

Scene 10: Otho, concealed, witnesses the love of Poppea and Nero. The emperor promises Poppea that he will get rid of Seneca.

Scene 11: Poppea mocks Otho, who still loves her. The warm-hearted Arnalta feels pity for the rejected lover.

Scenes 12–13: Otho, who has been injured, considers murdering Poppea, but fears Nero's revenge. He is comforted in his unhappiness by Drusilla, who loves him.

Act II

Scene 1: Mercury, the messenger of the gods, proclaims to Seneca that his death is imminent.

Scene 2: A captain brings Seneca the decree of Nero: death by suicide.

Scene 3: Seneca says farewell to his friends.

Scene 4: Missing from source material.

Scene 5: The page enjoys the company of his beloved.

Scene 6: Nero, with his favorite, Lucan, celebrates the removal of the last obstacle to his union with Poppea: Seneca's reputation and political influence.

Scene 7: Missing from source material.

Scene 8: Otho reproaches himself for his desire to kill Poppea.

Scene 9: The empress forces Otho to make an attempt on Poppea's life. If he is not prepared to do so, she will claim that he has molested the empress.

Scene 10: Drusilla is happy: Poppea, whom she hates, is to die. The page makes comparisons between old and young women and mocks Octavia's nurse.

Scene 11: Otho asks Drusilla to lend him her clothes for his assassination attempt on Poppea.

Scene 12: Poppea already sees herself as empress. Arnalta warns her about excessive ambition and sings her to sleep.

Scenes 13–14: Poppea is guarded in her sleep by Cupid, who thus prevents the murder attempt. Otho, fleeing, is mistaken for Drusilla.

Act III

Scenes 1–2: Drusilla looks forward to Poppea's imminent death and is arrested on suspicion of attempted murder.

Scenes 3–4: For love of Otho, Drusilla takes the blame, but he also confesses and is banished by Nero. Drusilla follows her beloved. Octavia, the instigator of the planned murder, is also sent into exile.

Scene 5: Nothing now stands in the way of Nero's marriage to Poppea.

Scene 6: Octavia bids farewell to Rome.

Scene 7: Arnalta is now the nurse of the future empress and rejoices over her social advancement.

Scene 8: Poppea is crowned empress. Love has conquered.

A. G.

Portrait of Sabina Poppea, unknown master of the Fontainebleau school, 16th century (Musée d'Art et Histoire, Geneva).
The Roman courtesan Poppea, who was crowned as a result of her beauty and her arts of seduction, has enjoyed a certain reputation. Like the unknown painter of the Fontainebleau school, Monteverdi portrayed her as a woman full of erotic powers of attraction.

The Coronation of Poppea, production photograph from the film version with Rachel Yakar as Poppea, production Jean-Pierre Ponnelle, conductor Nikolaus Harnoncourt, 1978.
Poppea has achieved her goal: the courtesan is crowned empress. The strikingly festive atmosphere and the pomp of the marriage ceremony have a grotesque effect which was entirely intentional on Monteverdi's part. Cupid's power actually turned the world upside down. But love contains conflict: Nero loves Poppea, and Poppea loves the throne. Both are fully satisfied.

Monteverdi's world theater

Nero's reign, notorious for its horrific deeds, was described in the *Annals* of the Roman historian Tacitus. Busenello and Monteverdi – unlike later librettists and composers in the history of opera – followed the historical events astonishingly closely, in an astutely realistic manner: the rise of Poppea could equally well have taken place in the Venice of 1642. Was the former world-power Venice, its fame now in decline, not comparable to Nero's Rome? Were there not in both cities courtesans, temperamental rulers, forsaken women, talkative philosophers, worldly-wise nurses, and despised mercenaries? Are these types not to be found at all times and in every society? The work has attracted particular interest since the second half of the twentieth century: *The Coronation of Poppea* is timeless.

Tacitus's and Monteverdi's carousel of society

Before her love affair with Nero, Sabina Poppea had already been twice married. Tacitus's description of the historical Poppea in his *Annals* also applies to Monteverdi's character. "Outwardly she displayed modesty, but in reality she led a life of unrestrained immorality; she went among the people only rarely, and then only with her face partly veiled, in order not to satisfy greedy glances, or because she found it becoming. She never paid any attention to her reputation ... and because she never gave way to any private or foreign passion, she allowed full rein to her sensuality only when it was of service to her to do so." In real life, although not in the opera, Otho, her husband, was at the same time a close friend of Nero's. It was he himself who drew Nero's attention to Poppea's charms. The figure of Nero, the paranoid dictator and matricide, was taken from Tacitus by Monteverdi without substantial alterations, as were those of the philosopher Seneca and the empress Octavia.

New motifs were added, thanks to the obligatory requirement of Baroque opera for intrigue (a man caught between three rival women – Otho, between the empress, Poppea and Drusilla). The Baroque spirit is expressed in the appearance of divine beings, including Pallas Athene as the proclaimer of impending death, and Cupid, who as a *deus ex machina* rescues his protégée Poppea from murder. Busenello and Monteverdi are responsible for the lower-class characters, the two nurses and the page with his sweetheart. It was above all through them that Monteverdi appealed to a broader audience. They represented popular opinion. It was not Seneca but these lower-class characters who drew the real philosophical lessons from the story. After all, Venice was a republic.

Voices

Unlike later operatic composers, Monteverdi did not prescribe specific vocal ranges. In the two manuscripts of the work (from Venice and Naples), there are not even indications of instruments; only the singers' voices and the basso continuo are noted. It was the interpreter's job to complete and execute the sketchy notation according to the rules of the time. He was able to rely on a living performance tradition. This is no longer the case. Following the usage of his day, Poppea and Octavia are to be cast as sopranos (at the original performance, strangely, the role of Octavia rather than that of Poppea was created by the star singer Anna Renzi). The role of Nero was also written for a soprano voice, that is, for a castrato. (Virtuoso castrati conquered the stage in the heyday of Venetian opera,

and dominated it for more than a century: →Handel.) Otho's vocal range suggests that his part was sung by a castrato with a voice in the lower soprano range. For Seneca, as a character of the noble type, the bass range was reserved, but Arnalta was allotted to a tenor, since according to Venetian tradition the "comical old woman" was played by a man. The reverse situation is also found: the page is a breeches role. In stage productions today, many historical traditions are ignored for the sake of credibility, particularly in the case of Nero, who is often played by a tenor on the twentieth-century stage.

The Coronation of Poppea, production photograph from the film version, production Jean-Pierre Ponnelle, conductor Nikolaus Harnoncourt, 1978.
After Seneca has been forced to commit suicide at Nero's command, the emperor orders the court poet Lucan to sing a song in praise of Poppea's sensuality. Two drunkards praise Poppea's charms in a maudlin duet.

Eroticism and authenticity

The 74-year-old Monteverdi portrayed the love of the blood-bespattered tyrant and the power-hungry courtesan with loving sympathy. Poppea and Nero have four scenes on their own, of which three include passionate love duets. Of these three scenes the most impressive is the final duet, in which the two voices merge in an almost endless melody.

For admirers of Monteverdi's music it is almost sacrilegious that music scholars should have raised doubts as to the authenticity of this wonderful duet. Certainly it is not impossible that the ageing Monteverdi ran a sort of workshop with his pupils, as was the practice in the visual arts, and that one of his pupils prepared the duet according to his instructions. But one can be certain that *The Coronation of Poppea* could only have been conceived and executed by a composer of powerful talent for musical drama.

Left
The Coronation of Poppea, production photograph with Rachel Yakar (Poppea) and Eric Tappy (Nero), production Jean-Pierre Ponnelle, part of the Monteverdi cycle at the Opernhaus Zurich, 1977.
It is difficult to accept the hypothesis of music historians that the wonderful final duet by Nero and Poppea, the erotic apotheosis of the whole opera, was not written by Monteverdi himself but by one of his pupils, Francesco Sacrati. Monteverdi fans have been deprived of an illusion, since this hymn to love was formerly considered one of the master's most beautiful works. It may also have been produced by a workshop, similar to those of the Venetian artists. Perhaps one may imagine that the elderly master did on some occasion sing or whistle the wonderful melody of the duet to his pupils …

Il pomo d'oro, Antonio Cesti, showing "The Kingdom of Pluto and Proserpina" (left), "The Feast of the Gods" (right, above), and "Summer" (right, below), colored engravings by Francesco Sbarra after the set design by Lodovico Ottavio Burnacini, Vienna 1668 (TWS).
Three variations on the Baroque stage set with central perspective, the great master of which was Burnacini. The libretto was augmented by 24 large copper engravings. It is astonishing to see how the Baroque set designers were able to magically transform the obligatory stage schemes by means of varied though typical stage properties. The artistic imagination played a decisive role here. Burnacini drew inspiration from important visual artists such as Paolo Veronese and Ferdinando Tocca. *Il pomo d'oro* was in every respect an exceptional opera. Like a great circus, this gigantic piece was played three times a week for a whole year to avid onlookers. At the same time, the work forms an almost encyclopedic compendium of all the elements of Baroque opera.

Cavalli, the prince of court opera

Francesco Cavalli (originally Pietro Francesco Caletti-Bruni, born 14 February 1602 in Crema, died 14 January 1676 in Venice) adopted his new surname in honor of his patron, the Venetian patrician Federigo Cavalli. He was one of the most successful operatic composers of the generation that followed Monteverdi. He began his career at a very young age, as an organist, but as early as the second half of the 1630s he was working at the same time for the first public opera house (Venice's Teatro San Cassiano). Altogether he composed 42 operas, of which only 28 are preserved. His first important work, *La Didone* (*Dido*), composed for the carnival of 1640–41, is notable above all for the arias, with their noble pathos, based on recurring bass motifs (ostinati).

The romantic love story *L'Ormindo* (1644), a *favola regia* (royal fable), is set in Africa, but in the prologue Venice's praises are sung. Cavalli had his most enduring success with the opera *Giasone* (*Jason*, 1649), which, with its characters, both serious and comic, its dream-like elements, and the mixture of traditional folk songs and highly artificial arias, is a classic product of seventeenth-century Venetian opera. In *Serse* (*Xerxes*, 1655), Cavalli went even further in his stress on comedy. This opera also became well known for its ensembles (trios and quartets), which were still unusual at the time. Cavalli was so famous that at the age of almost 60, he received a commission for an opera from Louis XIV in 1660. In the absence of French opera, the Sun King's wedding was celebrated to the tones of Cavalli's *L'Ercole amante* (*Hercules in Love*). Only the ballet music was French; it was by Jean-Baptiste Lully. Cavalli died, a much admired master, in a palazzo on Venice's Grand Canal.

Cesti and his giant apple

Marc Antonio Cesti (baptized 5 August 1623 in Arezzo, d. 14 October 1669 in Florence) was at the same time a Franciscan monk and an opera singer. He began his career as an organist in Volterra, later worked in the service of the Medici family in Florence, and from 1649 composed chiefly operas for Venice. As a celebrated theatrical composer, he was also active in Innsbruck, at the Komödienhaus. He was suspended from his monastic order because of his excessively worldly lifestyle, but was accepted as a singer in the Sistine Chapel, and retained his posts as imperial deputy *Kapellmeister* in both Innsbruck and Vienna, where in 1668 he presented his major work, *Il pomo d'oro* (*The Golden Apple*), the most costly opera of the Baroque era. Cesti was probably poisoned by his enemies. His "giant apple" was originally to have been staged for the wedding of Emperor Leopold I in December 1666, but because of its technical demands its first performance was delayed until July 1668, on the occasion of the birthday celebrations of Empress Margarethe. The prologue glorifies first Austria, then the heir to the throne (although the child had died in the meantime). The opera includes no fewer than 19 scenes and requires 24 complete sets, which depict various places featured in Greco-Roman mythology, from the underworld to the realm of the gods, from Olympus to Athens. The emperor commissioned the greatest theater artist of his time, Lodovico Ottavio Burnacini, to produce the set designs and supervise their construction. The light-hearted and ironic narrative, reminiscent of the action of an adventure novel, is a variation on the well-known story of the Judgment of Paris (T). The story is set in motion by the queen of the underworld, Proserpina (S), who is dissatisfied with her lot. Discord (S), throws an apple to the gods, to be given to the most beautiful of the goddesses. Venus (S), Pallas Athene (S), and Juno (S) lay their claims to this title. The shepherd Paris is asked to pronounce judgment and hands the apple to Venus, because she promises him the most beautiful of all women, Helen (S). War breaks out and storms at sea are unloosed. Finally Jupiter's eagle carries the golden apple out of the mythical sphere into the world of humans and gives it to Empress Margarethe, who unites the courage of Pallas Athene, the power of Juno and the beauty of Venus. The emperor had a theater built specially for this Baroque opera performance. From a musical point of view *Il pomo d'oro* is just as colorful as the mythological scenes and figures presented. Scenes from the under-world and the celestial world alternate with each other and are brought close to the world of humans by means of the comic commentary of the court jester.   J. M.

Mozart, Wolfgang Amadeus

b. 27 January 1756 in Salzburg
d. 5 December 1791 in Vienna

Mozart's musical genius was evident at an early age. His father Leopold was a violinist and composer, the author of an important book on violin technique of the 18th century, and he personally supervised his son's musical education. Concert tours of Europe over many years made Mozart familiar with the most important musical centers and styles: Vienna (1763), Paris, London, Holland, Switzerland (1766), Vienna (1767), Italy (1769–71, including studies in counterpoint with Padre Martini in Bologna, visits to other cities, such as Rome, Milan, Florence, and Naples, and an opera commission), a second journey to Italy (1771), a third journey to Italy (1773, including a further opera commission), Vienna (1773), Munich (1774–75), Mannheim, Paris (1777–79), and Munich (1781, the première of *Idomeneo*). Mozart resigned from his position as honorary orchestral director (since 1769) with the Archbishop of Salzburg and from 1781 lived in Vienna as a freelance composer and piano virtuoso, marrying Constanze Weber in 1782. He drew the attention of Emperor Joseph II, but it was not until after the death of Gluck (1787) that he was taken into the official service of the court as a *Kammermusikus* (chamber musician). Mozart achieved independent success with his operatic masterpieces and instrumental concertos, symphonic works and chamber music. The Prague audiences showed more interest in his art than those in Vienna (the première of *Don Giovanni* took place in Prague in 1787). Mozart adopted as his own both the reform plans of Joseph II and the ideas of the Freemasons (from 1784 he was a member of a Freemasons' lodge). After the death of Joseph II in 1790 he began to experience ever-increasing financial and personal difficulties. His last year was spent in feverish work and in a desperate attempt to establish himself with the new ruler, Leopold II.

Works: Operas, sacred works, symphonies, concertos (particularly piano concertos), string quartets, divertimenti and serenades, violin sonatas, piano trios and other works of chamber music, piano sonatas, songs. The Köchel catalogue records more than 626 works. His last great but incomplete composition is his Requiem. Complete operas: *La finta semplice* (*The Feigned Simpleton*) (1768, K.51 [46a]), *Bastien und Bastienne* (Bastien and Bastienne) (1768, K.50 [46b]), *Mitridate, Re di Ponto* (*Mithridates, King of Pontus*) (1770, K.87 [74a]), *Lucio Silla* (1772, K.135), *La finta giardiniera* (*The Feigned Gardener*) (1775, K.196), *Idomeneo* (1781, K.366), *Die Entführung aus dem Serail* (*The Abduction from the Seraglio*) (1782, K.384), *Der Schauspieldirektor* (*The Impresario*) (1786, K.486), *Le nozze di Figaro* (*The Marriage of Figaro*) (1786, K.492), *Don Giovanni* (1787, K.527), *Così fan tutte* (*All Women Do the Same*) (1790, K.588), *La clemenza di Tito* (*The Clemency of Titus*) (1791, K.621), *Die Zauberflöte* (*The Magic Flute*) (1791, K.620).

Wolfgang Amadeus Mozart, portrait by Barbara Krafft, née Steiner (1764–1825), Gesellschaft der Musikfreunde, Vienna.

*M*ozart's genius had a decisive influence on Viennese classical music. His mastery of composition and his universality remain unsurpassed. In all genres Mozart perfected the art of classical composition.

Dramatically naive, musically brilliant

La finta semplice, with its wealth of musical ideas, is typical of Mozart's precocious talent. If he shows "inexperience" here, then it is not as a musician but as a human being. Admittedly this early work as yet contains none of the great ensembles in which varying emotions are unfolded simultaneously, but Mozart already shows himself to be a master of the true depiction of emotions. Thus, for example, he writes an aria for the protagonist Rosina (no. 9) *M 1* which is amazingly close to the "Rose Aria" in a later masterpiece, →*The*

La finta semplice
The Feigned Simpleton

Opera buffa in three acts – K.51 [46a]

Libretto: Marco Coltellini, after Carlo Goldoni's libretto to the *dramma giocoso* by Salvatore Perillo (Venice 1764).
Première: Presumed 1769, Salzburg (Hoftheater); first documented performance 1921, Karlsruhe.
Characters: Fracasso, captain of Hungarian troops stationed near Cremona (T), Rosina, Fracasso's sister, who pretends to be a simpleton (S), Don Cassandro, a rich landowner from Cremona, a vain and miserly man of honor (B), Don Polidoro, younger brother of Don Cassandro, a vain man of honour (T), Giacinta, sister of Don Cassandro and Don Polidoro (S), Ninetta, Giacinta's chambermaid (S), Simone (T), Sergeant (B).
Setting: A country house near Cremona, 18th century.

Synopsis
Act I

Fracasso and Simone are quartered in the country house of Cassandro and Polidoro. Captain Fracasso is in love with their sister Giacinta, while his subordinate Simone is in love with the chambermaid, Ninetta. However, the two brothers are happy with the status quo, do not want to marry themselves, or to part with their sister. With the help of Fracasso's sister, Rosina, a plot is engineered. Rosina pretends to be a simpleton. Such a woman is not to be feared. The two brothers fall in love with her.

Act II

Giacinta fears a quarrel between the brothers, but Simone looks forward to a fight. The brothers realize that they are rivals, and it comes to a duel. Finally they are deceived by the report that Giacinta has disappeared with all their money.

Act III

The characters pair off: Ninetta and Simone, Giacinta and Fracasso. Rosina finally agrees to marry Cassandro. Only Polidoro is left out in the cold.   *S. N.*

Marriage of Figaro, particularly in the striking dialogue between the oboe and the voice. The passionate aria of Giacinta (no. 24) *M 2* goes far beyond the boundaries of *opera buffa*. This aria may be considered a variation on the third movement of the Symphony in G minor, K.550. *M 3* Mozart was a genius from the very start.

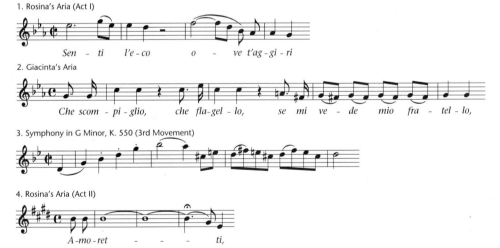

1. Rosina's Aria (Act I)

Sen - ti   l'e - co   o   ve t'ag - gi - ri

2. Giacinta's Aria

Che scom - pi - glio,   che fla - gel - lo,   se mi ve - de   mio   fra - tel - lo,

3. Symphony in G Minor, K. 550 (3rd Movement)

4. Rosina's Aria (Act II)

A - mo - ret   ti,

"Amoretti"

"Cupids, you are hiding here and shooting as you fly; I beg you, do not come to me, do not come to wound this heart" (score no. 15). This is a Rococo image which corresponds not to the coarsely comic but to the touchingly sentimental side of *opera buffa*. Nocturnal mood: a charming young woman is dreaming at the open window; a gentle wind is blowing. A short, undulating motif from the orchestra, like a wafting golden garland. The key is E major, which in Mozart's music usually indicates a solemn mood (such as the farewell trio in the first act of →*Così fan tutte*). M 4

Early operatic experiences

La finta semplice is the work of a 12-year-old. What sort of music was enjoyed by this infant prodigy? During his first journey through western Europe with his father and sister, Mozart took the opportunity, in Paris in 1766–67, to become acquainted with the *tragédies lyriques* of Lully and Rameau, but also with *opéras comiques*, such as those of Philidor and Monsigny. At Versailles Mozart attended a performance of *Bastien and Bastienne* (Favart's version, with Madame Favart in the cast). A few months later, the Mozart family visited both of London's opera houses (the Covent Garden Theater and the

King's Theater). Here *The Beggar's Opera*, by Gay and Pepusch, highly popular after several decades, was still being performed with great success, but Italian opera was also represented, including works by Piccinni, Vento, and Giardini, and above all works by the youngest son of the great Johann Sebastian Bach, Johann Christian, who became Mozart's lifelong friend. In London Mozart also made the acquaintance of the world-famous Italian castrato Giovanni Manzuoli, about whom he was enthusiastic. Manzuoli gave singing lessons to the young genius. From that time on, Mozart composed for the voices of specific singers.

Bastien and Bastienne, production photograph with Dagmar Goldschmidt (Bastienne), Renatus Mészár (Colas) and Lothar Odinius (Bastien), production Petra Müller, conductor Siegmund Weinmeister, costumes Imke Sturm, Staatstheater, Braunschweig 1996.
Mozart's first *Singspiel* could be the story of three young people of today. Bastienne feels that Bastien is not paying enough attention to her and asks a friend for advice.

Bastien and Bastienne

Singspiel in one act – K.50 [46b]

Libretto: Friedrich Wilhelm Weiskern and Johann Heinrich Müller, after a vaudeville (musical comedy) by Marie Justine Benoîte Favart, Charles-Simon Favart, and Harry de Guerville.
Première: Presumed 1768, Vienna; first documented performance 2 October 1890, Berlin.

Characters: Bastienne, a shepherdess (S), Bastien, a shepherd (T), Colas, a supposed magician (B).
Setting: A village, early 19th century.

Synopsis

Bastienne believes herself forsaken by her lover, Bastien, and asks old Colas for advice. He promises to help: Bastienne is to behave as though she loves another. Bastien appears and the girl hides. Colas tells Bastien that Bastienne has another sweetheart. Bastien refuses to believe this. Colas "conjures up" Bastienne. After a short quarrel and their mutual reminders of their former, undisturbed happiness, the lovers are reconciled and praise the magic arts of Colas.

S.N.

French influence

Mozart's first *Singspiel* is influenced by contemporary taste, in which France played a leading role, as it did in the fields of politics, architecture and ladies' fashion. *Bastien and Bastienne* is based on a *Singspiel* by Jean-Jacques Rousseau, whose *Le devin du village* (*The Village Fortune-Teller*) provided a folksy alternative to the solemn *tragédie lyrique* of Lully and Rameau as well as to the popular Italian opera genre. Rousseau's *Singspiel* achieved lasting success: in Paris it kept its place in the repertoire from the first performance in 1753 up to 1829. In the year of its first performance, this very successful work even provoked a parody under the title of *Les amours de Bastien et Bastienne*. The first Bastienne was Madame Favart, a celebrated actress of the time. To the delight of the audience and in defiance of the usual rules, she appeared in a peasant's linen dress, bare-armed and wearing wooden clogs. Mozart attended a performance during his first stay in Paris in 1767. The successful piece was translated and adapted by the Viennese theatrical director Friedrich Wilhelm Weiskern.

Childish game or stroke of genius?

Mozart was 12 years old when he composed his first *Singspiel*. The simplicity of the musical format (most of the arias are song-like) never becomes monotonous, and the typology does not appear stale. The naïveté of a 12-year-old gives the work a particular charm.

Pastorale

This *Singspiel* has a particularly pastoral atmosphere. This is manifested musically both in the frequent use of the key of G major (also used in the overture M 5), which according to the contemporary aesthetic of musical keys represented rural simplicity, and in the preference for triads and naturalistic horn effects.

A village atmosphere is also created by means of dances and dance-like rhythms, ranging from the French musette, imitating the sound of a bagpipe, to the *ländler*, which at that time already served as a musical illustration of the German and Austrian country scene.

Dr. Mesmer makes an appearance

Mozart's juvenile operas were discovered comparatively late by posterity. Little is known of the process of their creation, and it is questionable whether Mozart's *Singspiel* of 1768 was really performed in a pavilion in the garden of the Viennese physician Franz Anton Mesmer. Mozart certainly frequented the doctor's house between 1768 and 1773 and was on friendly terms with him. He thought of him with affection in the first finale of →*Così fan tutte*. Perhaps Mesmer (1734–1815) served as a model for the figure of the magician Colas; after all, he was the inventor of mesmerism, the science of the healing power of magnetism. His method has come to be regarded as the origin of hypnotherapy. In Mozart's *Singspiel*, Colas is a charlatan (or perhaps a skilled psychologist?) whose *buffo* aria consists of magic spells in the form of meaningless chatter. M 6

5. Overture (Pastoral Motif)

6. Aria of the Magician (Colas)

Dig-gi,   dag-gi,   schurry,   mur-ry,   ho-rum,   ha-rum,   li-rum,   la-rum

Bastien and Bastienne, production photograph with Renatus Mészár as Colas, production Petra Müller, conductor Siegmund Weinmeister, costumes Imke Sturm, Staatstheater, Braunschweig 1996. In the role of the pretend magician we can detect the germ of the part of the great impresario of Mozart's later opera, →*Così fan tutte*, Don Alfonso. The young Mozart certainly identified most strongly with the playful personality of his Colas.

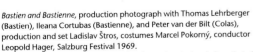

Bastien and Bastienne, production photograph with Thomas Lehrberger (Bastien), Ileana Cortubas (Bastienne), and Peter van der Bilt (Colas), production and set Ladislav Štros, costumes Marcel Pokorný, conductor Leopold Hager, Salzburg Festival 1969.
Up to the 20th century it was considered, even by music scholars, that all the operas which Mozart composed before *The Abduction from the Seraglio* were merely stepping-stones to his later great operatic masterpieces. This valuation, which was unfair to the early works, gradually changed from the late 1960s onward. The Salzburg production of *Bastien* in 1969, in a Rococo-style setting on a small revolving stage, with singers of the highest rank, finally gave convincing proof of the infant prodigy's creative genius.

Mithridates, King of Pontus

Mitridate, Re di Ponto

Dramma per musica in three acts – K.87 [74a]

Libretto: Vittorio Amedeo Cigna-Santi, after the tragedy by Jean Baptiste Racine.
Première: 26 December 1770, Milan (Teatro Regio Ducale).
Characters: Mitridate/Mithridates, King of Pontus (T), Aspasia, his betrothed (S), Sifare/Xiphares, his younger son (S), Farnace/Pharnaces, his elder son (A), Ismene, daughter of the King of Parthia, Farnace's/Pharnaces's betrothed (S), Marzio/Marcius, a Roman tribune, friend of Farnace/Pharnaces (T), Arbate/Arbates, governor of Nymphaeum (S), a Moor (silent), a Roman (silent).
Setting: Pontus, c. 63 BC.

Synopsis
The King of Pontus, Mithridates, has spread the rumor that he is at war with the Romans in order to put his sons Xiphares and Pharnaces, as well as his people, to the test. He is forced to realize that his sons have fallen in love with his betrothed, Aspasia. Even worse, his son Pharnaces seems to have become a friend of the Romans and thus his political rival. Only Xiphares is prepared to fight against the Romans with his father. When Aspasia confesses that she loves Xiphares, Mithridates decides that his sons and betrothed must all die. Xiphares prevents the death of Aspasia and supports his father in a battle with the Romans. But they are defeated, and Mithridates falls on his sword. Dying, he learns that his son Pharnaces has forced the Romans to retreat. He forgives his sons and decides that Aspasia shall marry Xiphares.

S. N.

At the height of *opera seria*
In 1770, the most ambitious operatic genre remained the *opera seria*. The extensive literature on Mozart reiterates that *opera seria* was at that time a defunct genre laden with outdated conventions, which gave the composer no opportunity to create living dramatic figures, functioning only as a framework for bel canto. In fact, Mozart not only enriched *opera seria* but also made use of its stylistic characteristics in his later operas, as may be seen, for example, in the characterization of female roles such as Konstanze, Donna Anna, Fiordiligi and the Queen of the Night. Many of Mozart's concert arias also derive from the standard situations of *opera seria* in terms of mood. Mozart's *opere serie* captivate us with their rich instrumentation (the finest court orchestras were employed to perform them), the multiplicity of feelings they convey, and the virtuosity and expressiveness of the vocal writing.

Above
Mithridates, production photograph from Act III with Christiane Oelze (Xiphares) and Vesselina Kasardua (Pharnaces), production Jonathan Miller, sets Peter J. Davison, costumes Frida Parmeggiani, conductor Roger Norrington, Mozart Festival, Salzburg 1997.
In the Salzburg production, a row of silent figures (extras) performed behind the protagonists, representing courtly and religious life, silent observers in recurring constellations.

Historical playing cards: French court cards, England, c. 1800, Deutsches Spielkarten-Museum, Leinfelden-Echterdingen.

A classic "hand"

Opera seria was traditionally based on five protagonists. These figures had constant dramatic functions and firmly defined vocal ranges. The ruler (god, king, emperor, dictator, general, or prince in Greco-Roman mythology or history) was sung by a tenor. The two rival younger subjects (usually of noble descent) were given castrato parts (*primo uomo* and *secondo uomo*). To these were added two ladies (*prima donna* and *seconda donna*), who usually provided the reason for conflicts between the king and the young men, or between one young man and the other. The "package of singers" was therefore presented to the composer like a pack of playing cards. The rules of the game were also determined by the libretto. The individuality of each of the countless examples of *opera seria* that were produced during the 18th century depended on the musical detail alone.

"Viva il Maestrino!"

How was an opera created in Mozart's day? Soberly and practically. The composer was usually commissioned to set a *scrittura* to music by an aristocrat connected to the theater where the first performance was to take place. The *scrittura* prescribed the subject matter and was usually a complete libretto, which in most cases had already been set to music by other composers. The composer would then begin to work out the recitative, which formed the skeleton, or, as we would say today, the scenario of the opera. It had to be delivered by a certain date to the producer at the theater. Then the singers were engaged and they would make requests for arias and duets (an *opera seria* rarely included larger ensembles). A good composer understood the art of satisfying the demands of singers. This was the situation of the young Mozart in Milan when he was working on

Mithridates. Mozart arrived in Milan on 1 December 1771 and the première took place less than three weeks later. The singers' parts were practically tailor-made for them. The most important thing was to acquire the *prima donna* and the *primo uomo* (usually a famous castrato). The première took place on 26 December 1771 in the Teatro Regio Ducale (La Scala was not yet in existence), with a glittering cast and an orchestra of 56 musicians (a large number at the time), and was a great success. The audience shouted enthusiastically: "Viva il Maestro! Viva il Maestrino!" The composer was given further commissions, and the process started all over again…

Mithridates, production photograph with Felicity Lott, Gardow, Julia Hamari, Yvonne Kenny and Rockwell Blake, production Jean-Pierre Ponnelle, conductor Nikolaus Harnoncourt, Opernhaus, Zürich 1985. The reconciliation scene with the death of the king. In an *opera seria*, the ruler had to be superior to his subjects in the moral sense too. The *opera seria* was a mirror image of court society, and in many cases the actual ruler of the royal residence was seated in the audience.

Lucio Silla

Dramma per musica in three acts – K.135

Libretto: Giovanni de Gamerra.
Première: 26 December 1772, Milan (Teatro Regio Ducale).
Characters: Lucio Silla/Lucius Sulla, a dictator (T), Giunia/Junia, daughter of Caius Marius (S), Cecilio/Cecilius, a respected senator, betrothed to Junia (S), Lucio/Lucius Cinna, a Roman patrician, friend of Cecilius and secret enemy of Sulla (S), Celia, sister of Sulla (S), Aufidius, tribune, friend of Sulla (T); guards, senators, noblemen, soldiers, people, girls (chorus).
Setting: Rome, c. 80 BC.

Synopsis

Cecilius, banished by Lucius Sulla, returns to Rome in secret. His betrothed, Junia, believes him to be dead. Sulla woos Junia in vain; she refuses him. Cecilius and Junia meet, with the help of their friend Lucius Cinna. Sulla intends to marry Junia, even by force. Cinna therefore proposes to Junia that she should kill him in his bed. Junia feels unable to do this, and thus Cinna decides to commit the tyrannicide himself. Junia advises her beloved to flee. In front of the Senate she declares that she would rather kill herself than become the wife of Sulla. Cinna tries, together with Cecilius, to murder Sulla. The attempt fails. Cinna cunningly extracts himself from the trap. Cecilius alone is arrested. Cinna promises marriage to Sulla's sister Celia if she can persuade her brother to renounce Junia. Junia and Cecilius, who has been condemned to death, bid each other farewell. But Celia and Cinna succeed in convincing Sulla that Cecilius's execution will cause an uprising. The dictator reprieves Cecilius and all other banished persons and releases Junia. Cinna marries Celia.   *A. G.*

Left
Lucio Silla, Thomas Moser as Lucius Sulla, Wiener Staatsoper.
In the story of the Roman dictator Lucius Sulla, at first unmerciful, later overcoming his own bad qualities, many passions confront each other: love, steadfastness, loyalty, and readiness for death mingle with force and egoism. Yet the whole is framed by classical dignity. The actions of the state and the conflicts of love are placed in parallel, dark contrasted with light – *chiaroscuro*, as this effect is called in Italian.

Below
Lucio Silla, photograph from the production by Jean-Pierre Ponnelle, conductor Nikolaus Harnoncourt, Opernhaus, Zürich, 1999.

7. Cecilius's Entrance Aria

Il te - ne - ro mo-men-to pre-mio di tan-to a-mo-re, pre - mio di tan-to di tan-to a-mo-re

8. Junia's Bravura Aria

Ah, se il cru-del, se il cru-del ____ pe - ri-glio

9. Cecilius's Farewell Aria

Pu-pil-le a-ma-te te non la-gi-ma-te mo-rir mi fa-te pria di mo-rir, ___ mo-rir mi fa-te pria di mo-rir.

Lucio Silla, photograph from the production by Patrice Chéreau, sets Richard Peduzzi, costumes Jacques Schmidt, conductor Claudio Abbado, Teatro alla Scala, Milan 1983.
Patrice Chéreau's production – in contrast to, for example, Ponnelle's Mozart productions, which attempted to revive the spirit of *opera seria* on a historical basis – demonstrates the timeless political relevance of the piece. The heroes of *Lucio Silla* live and move in the shadow of an inhuman dictatorship. However, the fact that the dictator Lucius Sulla is not finally overthrown is a clear sign that the opera was written before 14 July 1789, the day of the storming of the Bastille. With an altered ending, this subject matter might also have given rise to a rescue opera.

Primo uomo, prima donna

The famous castrato Venanzio Rauzzini (1746–1810) was only a few years older than Mozart, played the piano well, and was also a skillful composer. Mozart had to compose the part of Cecilius for him. His father Leopold Mozart found the first aria in particular incomparably beautiful (no. 2), and thought Rauzzini sang like an angel. (To judge from this aria, Rauzzini's voice must have had an enormous range, from A to a".) The effective orchestral prelude announces a star singer, and yet the singing voice begins with a soft, sustained note, in accordance with the text: "The tender moment, the reward of so great a love, is pictured by my heart in its sweet thoughts." *M 7*

The *prima donna* was no less important: Maria Anna de Amicis (c. 1733–1816). Mozart was supposed to submit the drafts of his arias to her for approval. But he brought her his finished compositions, which she found to be superb. Junia's great aria (no. 11) includes surprisingly difficult passages, which demand half of the bravura range (70 out of 144 bars!). The coloratura passages appear monotonous only on the page; in interpretation they gain in expression and color. Nevertheless, virtuosity dominates, determining even the thematic material. Thus the main theme is based from the outset on a technical formula – an upwardly striving B major triad, completed by a passage which helps the singer to reach the highest note. *M 8*

The *ombra* scene

The central scene of the opera (the end of Act I) is set in a burial vault, a typical scene in Baroque theater: Cecilius, the senator, supposed to be dead, has secretly returned home and meets his betrothed Junia here. The deathly atmosphere is created by monotonous rhythmic movement and mighty orchestral chords from the horns and trombones. Cecilius's monologue, in the form of a *recitativo accompagnato* (accompanied recitative), the mourning chorus (rarely of significance in *opera seria*), and the joyful duet of the lovers in parallel melodies of great virtuosity prove that the young Mozart benefited even from the example of the great operatic reformer Christoph Willibald Gluck. Also reminiscent of Gluck is Cecilius's beautiful though unpretentious aria "Pupille amate, non lagrimate" ("Beloved eyes, do not weep," Act III, no. 21). *M 9*

La finta giardiniera

Dramma giocoso in three acts – K.196

Libretto: First version (Italian) by Giuseppe Petrosellini; second version (German *Singspiel*) by Johann Franz Joseph Stierle.
Première: First version: 13 January 1775, Munich (Opernhaus St. Salvator); second version: May 1780, Augsburg (Komödienstadl).
Characters: Don Anchise, mayor of Lagonero (Schwarzensee) (T), Marchioness Violante Onesti, believed to be dead but disguised as a gardener under the name of Sandrina (S), Count Belfiore, formerly the lover of Violante (T), Arminda, a Milanese noblewoman, formerly the lover of Ramiro, now betrothed to Count Belfiore (S), Ramiro, a knight, Arminda's lover, abandoned by her (S), Serpetta, housekeeper to and in love with Don Anchise (S), Roberto, Violante's servant, passing as her cousin under the name of Nardo, disguised as a gardener, in love with but disregarded by Serpetta (B).
Setting: Schwarzensee, first half of the 18th century.

Synopsis

In a fit of jealousy, Count Belfiore has physically attacked his lover, Violante, and fled, believing he has killed her. Violante, however, survives, and goes in search of Belfiore. Declaring herself to be a gardener, she enters the service of Don Anchise the mayor, for it is in his house that preparations are under way for the wedding of Belfiore and Arminda, the mayor's niece. Arminda also has a tempestuous love affair behind her, with Ramiro, who is invited to the celebrations. When they all meet again, all their old feelings are rekindled, thwarting their new plans. The resulting irritations bring them to the brink of madness. Finally the original couples are reunited: Violante and Belfiore, Arminda and Ramiro.

S. N.

La finta giardiniera, production photograph, Salzburg Marionettentheater, 1975. Are these puppets or living people? Everything follows the recipe of *opera buffa*. Complicated love affairs, despair and hope. In the end everyone finds a partner. Only one person must stay alone (hence the uneven number of characters): Podesta, but presumably not for too long. His ancestors include the *commedia dell'arte* figures of Pantalone and the Doctor. This opera by the 18-year-old Mozart is a comedy sometimes overshadowed by tears. Its immediate model may have been the sentimental *opera buffa La buona figliola* (1760), by Niccolò Piccinni (1728–1800). This scene from the Salzburg Marionettentheater shows Count Belfiore paying court to Arminda.

Catarina Cavalieri

Above
La finta giardiniera, photograph from the production by Karl-Ernst and Ursel Hermann, sets and costumes Karl-Ernst Hermann, conductor Sylvain Cambreling, Théâtre Royal de la Monnaie, Brussels 1986. The Brussels production, which also became part of the program of the Salzburg Festival in 1992, shows the lovers wandering at random in a garden of emotions. *La finta giardiniera* is perhaps Mozart's most misunderstood opera. At first, after only a short time, it disappeared from the operatic stage. The much simpler opera of the same name by Pasquale Anfossi, on the other hand, became a huge success in its day. The Mozart opera was rediscovered only in 1978 with the publication of the work in the complete critical edition.

Right
Catarina Cavalieri, silhouette by Hieronymus Löschenkohl, Vienna 1785. The Viennese singer, who enjoyed a great reputation under the stage name of Catarina Cavalieri (her original name was Kavalier), made her debut in Mozart's *opera buffa* → *La finta giardiniera*. She was the model pupil (and allegedly the mistress) of Mozart's rival Antonio Salieri, and made her career as a leading singer at the Burgtheater. Apart from Sandrina and Konstanze, Catarina Cavalieri sang Madame Silberklang in → *The Impresario* and created the role of Donna Elvira in the Viennese version of → *Don Giovanni*. She is presumed to have been the prima donna for whom Mozart composed the greatest number of roles.

The school of emotions

The initial situation is amusing and sophisticated: the lover encounters his beloved, believed to be dead and disowning her own identity. In this situation, emotions are placed under the microscope. Indeed, we have a school of emotions. Many pieces of the time were given the description *La scuola degli amanti*, or *The School for Lovers* (including, later, →*Così fan tutte*). Mozart himself was still a student in this sense. Violante wants to start a new life as the gardener Sandrina, a life in which love is not the plaything of bored aristocrats, but a force that determines people's fates. The hot-blooded Belfiore attacked his lover out of jealousy (even believing that he had killed her!), and must now learn humility. A highly interesting situation psychologically – a task to which Mozart was well suited.

Love conquers all

Belfiore, carried away by vanity, boasts to the mayor about his family tree. This *buffo* aria (no. 8) seems to anticipate Leporello's "Catalogue Aria" in →*Don Giovanni*. But when Belfiore recognizes Sandrina as his Violante, he gains a tragic dimension (no. 19, a passionate *recitativo accompagnato* and aria). Sandrina has to battle with her own feelings. She still loves her brutal lover (no. 13, an excited, tempestuous aria in G minor, and no. 21, a despairing scene in a wild wooded area), but she is intent on a relationship of equal partners, free from murky passions. In this she succeeds: in the final scene the lovers gaze deeply into each other's hearts. It is almost like a sentimental bourgeois drama.

Idomeneo

Dramma per musica in three acts – K.366

Libretto: Giovanni Battista Varesco after a libretto by Antoine Danchet.

Première: 29 January 1781, Munich (Hoftheater).

Characters: Idomeneo/Idomeneus, King of Crete (T), Idamante/Idamantes, his son (S), Ilia, a Trojan princess, daughter of Priam (S), Elettra/Electra, a princess, daughter of Agamemnon, King of Argos (S), Arbace/Arbaces, confidant of the king (T), High Priest of Neptune (T), Oracle (B); Cretans, Trojans, warriors, sailors, priests (chorus).
Setting: Crete, after the Trojan War.

Synopsis
Before the opera begins
For ten years the king of the island of Crete, Idomeneus, battled against Troy with his warriors, far from home. The city having been finally razed to the ground, and its inhabitants murdered, the victorious Greek army and its allies, including Idomeneus, undertook their homeward journey. For many this journey became a series of wanderings, and victory abroad was transformed into defeat at home. Thus the commander of the Greek army, Agamemnon, met his death in Argos, while his daughter Electra fled to Crete.

Acts I–II
Idamantes, the son of the king of Crete, is passionately in love with Ilia, the Trojan prisoner of war. Ilia returns Idamantes's love, but conceals her feelings, since duty commands her to hate the son of her enemy. For love of Ilia, Idamantes gives the Trojan prisoners their freedom. The Cretans and the Trojan prisoners praise this act of conciliation and peace – all except Electra. She loves Idamantes, and the furies of anger and revenge rage through her heart. Idomeneus's fleet encounters a tempest near the coast of Crete. In mortal danger, the king swears to Neptune that he will sacrifice the first person who comes to meet him on the shores of his home. It is his son Idamantes. Idomeneus keeps silent about his oath to his son and his people, and searches for ways to escape from it. He becomes more and more entangled in his guilt. The god threatens the dilatory king with terrible afflictions to be visited upon the Cretan people. His adviser, Arbaces, recommends that his

Idomenée becomes Idomeneo
One literary source of *Idomeneo* is François Fénelon's novel, in which Idomeneus kills his son. Prosper Jolyot Crébillon added a motive for the deed: rivalry in love. Crébillon's drama of 1705 provided the model for the first musical version, the *tragédie lyrique Idomenée* by Antoine Danchet, with music by André Campra, of 1712. Danchet's libretto was in turn a model for that of Varesco. He got rid of the double love theme (Ilia is now loved only by the heir to the throne), simplified the plot (of three confidants, only Arbaces remained), and reduced the number of deities among the characters.   *S.N.*

Idomeneo, production photograph with Rachel Yakar as Ilia, production Jean-Pierre Ponnelle, conductor Nikolaus Harnoncourt, Opernhaus, Zürich 1980.
No other work has been as frequently produced by Jean-Pierre Ponnelle as *Idomeneo*: 1971 Cologne, 1978 Chicago, 1980 Zürich, 1981 Vienna, 1982 New York (with Pavarotti as Idomeneus), and 1984 Salzburg Festival.

Opposite, below
Idomeneo, photograph from the production by Roberto De Simone, sets Mauro Carosi, costumes Odette Nicoletti, conductor Riccardo Muti, Teatro alla Scala, Milan 1990.
The dramatic material of *Idomeneo* is full of excitement and tension, which is why it fascinated Mozart from the outset. The oath sworn by the returning king and the fateful meeting with his son create a desperate dramatic situation right at the beginning of the piece, which in the course of events develops into a veritable labyrinth in which the protagonists wander about in a state of disorientation. The way out can be found only in the form of a miraculous solution (in the language of 18th-century opera, a *deus ex machina*): Neptune grants his forgiveness.

Inspiring conditions
Idomeneo is a work that was commissioned by the Elector Karl Theodor of Munich. Until this time Mozart had been unable to exercise any influence on the content or form of a commissioned work. He was given that opportunity for the first time in 1780. The librettist Giovanni Battista Varesco could be persuaded to make changes through the good offices of Mozart's father, who acted as a go-between. In Munich, Mozart encountered the famous Mannheim orchestra, which had moved there together with the elector. Its richness of sound and its precise articulation and phrasing influenced the total concept of the opera. Mozart was friendly with the orchestra's leader, Christian Cannabich; the musicianship of the flautist Wendig and the oboeist Camm was praised by many contemporary composers and was influential in the creation of the orchestral parts. Mozart's contemporary Christian Friedrich Daniel Schubart affirmed: "No orchestra in the world has ever surpassed the Mannheim. Its forte is like thunder, its crescendo is a cataract, its dimimuendo a crystal stream babbling far into the distance, its piano a breath of spring" (from Schubart's *Ideen zu einer Ästhetik der Tonkunst – Ideas toward an Aesthetic of Composition –* of 1784). From Mannheim Mozart also knew the two Wendling sisters, Dorothea and Elisabeth, who were to sing the roles of Ilia and Electra.

endangered son should be removed from the island. Together with Electra, he is to embark for Argos. Electra finds new hope. The sea is calm and serene. But Neptune will allow no one to leave the island. He sends storm tides and a monster. The people ask who is guilty of inciting the god's anger. The king offers himself as a sacrifice. But the god will not permit any negotiation. The monster continues to rage.

Act III

Ilia confesses her love for Idamantes to the discreet winds. Idamantes bids farewell to Ilia before leaving to confront the monster. Then Ilia confesses her love to him. The High Priest and the people demand that the king should be loyal to his duty and banish the terror. The king confesses to the oath he made to Neptune. Idamantes is ready for a sacrificial death. Idomeneus lifts the fatal axe, then Ilia offers herself as a sacrifice instead of her beloved Idamantes. A voice is heard, commanding Idomeneus to surrender his governing powers to his son Idamantes and to marry the new king to the Trojan woman. Electra's hopes are now finally destroyed. She turns away from the living and toward the kingdom of the wandering shades. The people pay tribute to Cupid and Juno, the gods of love and marriage.   *S. N.*

Above
Idomeneo, set design for the first production, by Lorenzo Quaglio, Munich 1781 (TSW).
Lorenzo Quaglio was one of the most famous theatrical architects of his time. His sets for the first production of the opera in Munich were accordingly highly praised. The name of Mozart, on the other hand, was not even mentioned: "Production, music, and translation – all come from Salzburg," wrote the *Münchner Zeitung*.

The high point and the limit of a genre

Mozart both used *opera seria* as a model and at the same time subverted its conventions. The plots of *opera seria* are taken from classical mythology, as interpreted in the seventeenth and early eighteenth centuries. They are so constructed that extreme external conditions are juxtaposed: shipwrecks, earthquakes, fiery tempests and epidemics. The libretto places five or seven people in immediate conflict. The extreme external conditions shown on stage are matched by the internal psychological states of the characters: anger and tenderness, revenge and magnanimity, madness and superhuman reason. The polarized effects interpenetrate: Eros begets furies.

Mozart's *Idomeneo* is a late contribution to the *opera seria* repertoire. Figures expressing the spirit of the Enlightenment struggle on the territory of Baroque dramatization. Ilia's aria at the beginning of Act III is part of this Baroque dramatization. It was in accordance with Baroque thinking to ascribe human feelings to nature: the human character complains of his sorrow to the discreet winds. But with the voice of the Oracle, which cuts through the knot of the action, Enlightenment thought already comes into play. The *deus ex machina* is typical of the Baroque era. In *Idomeneo* this force intervening from outside has the effect of a "voice of reason" and thus already belongs to the Enlightenment. Crete is an island. The island-dwellers run towards the sea as if towards a wall. The god in effect lays aside his power, passes it on to the new, "better" ruling couple, but in doing so he ultimately sanctions the *ancien régime*, the old courtly regime. To this extent the mythological parable remains a courtly allegory. But the characters must work out their fates together, for there is no court of appeal that will decide them. On this level the parable gains in dimension in terms of human history. Musically, this is shown in the gradual dissolution of boundaries between musical forms. At the very outset, the overture merges seamlessly into the first recitative, which imperceptibly transforms itself into an aria. In the end, humans need to be informed by humans: how else could the soul become master of the furies?

Idomeneo, production photograph, Teatro alla Scala, Milan 1990.
Idomeneo is the first of Mozart's operas in which the sea plays a dramatic role (the second and last is *Così fan tutte*). In *Idomeneo* it is a hostile element: in its wild rage the sea represents the wrath of Neptune.

10. Idamantes's Solitary Melody (Quartet, Act III)

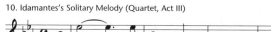

An - drò ____ ra - min - go e so - - - lo.

A quartet of challenged souls

The quartet "Andrò ramingo e solo" ("I shall go alone on my wanderings," E flat major, Act III) is considered to be Mozart's first great ensemble. The four main characters are confronted either with their own death (Idamantes) or the death of a beloved person (Idomeneus fears for his son, Ilia and Electra for their beloved). Each reacts differently according to his or her character, while the music unites the differences into a tone common to all. The emotion flows directly into a melodic structure that avoids the definite development of themes, but still distinguishes the individual emotions from each other. The urgent melodic and harmonic intensifications are constantly revoked until, after a modulation, the tension rises to the point of intolerability. Harmonic indistinctness of the basic key, false endings, and leading-note tensions confirm this situation. At the key word "soffrir" ("suffering"), the basic key breaks off and a yawning chasm opens, which can be crossed only by repeated approaches by all. It is as though the shadow that death throws over life is dispersed by the power of the love that binds these people together, as though death loses his horror when all have looked together into his eyes. But here too there is no definitive ending, no triumph. M 10   S. N.

Below
Idomeneo, production photograph with Peter Schreier (Idomeneus) and Delores Ziegler (Idamantes), production Johannes Schaaf, sets David Fielding, costumes Tobias Hoheisel, conductor Nikolaus Harnoncourt, Wiener Staatsoper 1987.
In the mid-1970s *Idomeneo* was accepted as an important work. The father-son conflict in the opera was seen as reflecting Mozart's own family situation. At the time of the work's composition, shortly after his mother's death, Mozart, now an adult, was trying to loosen the ties that bound him so closely to his father, to which Leopold Mozart reacted with bitterness.

Above
Idomeneo, production photograph, Teatro alla Scala, Milan 1990.
Idomeneus represents a different type of ruler from the familiar one of the courtly *opera seria*. He is a weak hero, and on a lower moral plane than his subjects. Even the solution, the reconciliation with the angry Neptune, is brought about not by him, but by the sincere love of the Trojan princess Ilia.

Idomeneo, set design by Heinz Grete, Städtisches Theater, Nuremberg 1940 (unrealized project) (TWS).
A set design from the time when *Idomeneo* was still seen as a mythological fairy tale complete with a stage dragon. Heinz Grete's design illustrates the prejudice to which Mozart's *opere serie*, with the exception of *La clemenza di Tito*, were subjected throughout the 19th and the first half of the 20th century: namely, that they were naive juvenilia forming part of an outdated operatic genre.

Below
Idomeneo, set design by Max Bignens for the production by Jorge Lavelli, conductor Diego Masson, Théâtre des Champs-Elysées, Paris/Angers 1975 (TWS).
When creating a set for a particular production of a work, designers resort with increasing boldness to forms of expression in accordance with the times, an approach that is entirely justified in the case of *Idomeneo*. Here the sea monster creates a state of panic for which Mozart composed a powerful choral passage of Baroque extravagance. This scene must shock the audience both aurally and visually.

Idomeneo, photograph from the production by Ruth Berghaus, sets Marie-Luise Strandt, conductor Peter Schreier, Staatsoper Unter den Linden, Berlin 1981.
Idamantes (Uta Priew) lies on the sacrificial block, ready for death, but Ilia (Carola Nossek) throws herself between her beloved and the High Priest (Henno Garduhn): to save him, she is ready to die herself.

Choral opera

In most *opera seria* the chorus had merely a walk-on part, celebrating the outcome of the happily disentangled plot. The closing chorus was often no more than a formal counterpart to the joyful fanfare of the overture which opened the opera. In Mozart's *Idomeneo* the chorus plays an important part in the action. The release of the captured Trojans by Idamantes is celebrated by the people as a token of peace, the union of Asia with Europe. In sharp contrast to this hope and optimism, we see the mortal fear of the returning Cretans, who are threatened with defeat in their struggle with the tempestuous force of the sea. Thus Idomeneus's oath is inspired not only by fear for his own life, but also by his responsibility for his warriors. The music of the choruses, and thus the treatment of the people, is sharply profiled and powerfully colored. Thus the almost atmospheric portrayal of the calm serenity of the sea before the intended departure of Idamantes and Electra is contrasted with fear of the sea's turbulence. The most obvious deviation from the conventions of *opera seria* is the *recitativo accompagnato* (accompanied recitative) of Idomeneus, which, contrary to the rules, is followed not by an aria, but by a chorus in which the people burst into a lament. This clear digression has its model in the French *spectacle* (with which Mozart probably became acquainted in Paris), and in the imitation of classical

plays. Euripides' *Iphigenia in Aulis* had influenced the French *spectacle* and, indirectly, Gluck's operas, and it was from this tradition that Mozart gained the inspiration for his great and only choral opera, *Idomeneo*.   *S. N.*

Right
Idomeneo, photograph from the production by Jean-Pierre Ponnelle, conductor Nikolaus Harnoncourt, Opernhaus, Zürich 1980.
Idomeneo is a spectacular opera, with important chorus and ballet scenes on the French model. The extensive declamatory recitatives are also modeled on French taste.

The Abduction from the Seraglio

Die Entführung aus dem Serail

Singspiel in three acts – K.384

Libretto: Johann Gottlieb Stephanie the younger, after a libretto by Christoph Friedrich Bretzner.
Première: 16 July 1782, Vienna (Burgtheater).
Characters: Pasha Selim (spoken), Konstanze (S), Blonde, her maid (S), Belmonte, Konstanze's betrothed (T), Pedrillo, Belmonte's servant and overseer of the Pasha's gardens (T), Osmin, overseer of the Pasha's palace (B), Klaas, a sailor (spoken), A Mute (silent), leader of the guards, Janissaries, retinue of the Pasha (chorus).
Setting: The Pasha's Turkish palace, mid-16th century.

The Abduction from the Seraglio, production photograph with Anneliese Rothenberger (Konstanze) and Michael Heltau (Pasha Selim), Salzburg Festival 1973.
An ideal couple on stage: the celebrated German singer and the famous Austrian actor. In some stage interpretations Selim is shown as either considerably older or distracted and nervous, like an all-powerful dictator. Here he appears as a credible suitor for Konstanze. His tragic situation, that of renunciation of a beautiful captive woman in favor of her distant lover, lends a melancholy aspect to his character.

Synopsis

Previous history

In an attack on the ship of the Spanish nobleman Belmonte, the son of the governor of Oran, Belmonte's betrothed Konstanze and the servants Blonde and Pedrillo fell into the hands of pirates. Sold in the slave market to Pasha Selim, a Spanish renegade, they now live as captives on his country estate in Turkey. Pedrillo has won the confidence of the Pasha and succeeded in conveying news to Belmonte about their whereabouts.

Act I

Belmonte joyfully looks forward to his reunion with his beloved. For the time being, however, he does not know how he is to enter Pasha Selim's palace. Osmin, the overseer, bars him from entry verbally and physically. Only when Pedrillo appears is he able to gain access. Pedrillo has recommended Belmonte to the Pasha as a gifted architect. When the Pasha returns from a pleasure trip, Belmonte is introduced to him.

Act II

Osmin has been given Blonde as a present by the Pasha and has fallen in love with the young Englishwoman. However, he woos her in a crude oriental manner. She gives him a lecture on the correct way to approach a young European woman. Konstanze is consumed by grief; she loves Belmonte, but has also learned to respect the Pasha. She rejects the Pasha's advances. He makes her realize that she is in the hands of a Turkish ruler and that he is in a position to use force. But she fears physical suffering less than mental torment, and is prepared to die. Pedrillo reveals to both women the arrival of Belmonte and the abduction plan, and he begins by putting Osmin to sleep by means of Cypriot wine and a sleep-inducing powder. When the lovers encounter each other, Belmonte's jealousy gets the better of his love, and he questions Konstanze's fidelity to him. Konstanze is in despair: will she really recapture her lost happiness in Belmonte's arms?

Act III

Pedrillo awakens the women at midnight. They are all to escape from the seraglio by means of a ladder. The Mute discovers this and wakes Osmin from his stupor. The escape is foiled and the guilty people arrested. Osmin triumphs: at last the hated Europeans will suffer torture and be hanged on the gallows. The would-be escapees are brought before the Pasha. Belmonte offers ransom money, and thus reveals his origins. He is the son of an arch-enemy of Pasha Selim. Death seems certain for the lovers. But Pasha Selim's noble nature triumphs: he forgives the wrong once done to him, and grants freedom to the son of his enemy, the woman he loves, and their servants. While Osmin alone rages, all pay tribute to the wonderful magnanimity of Pasha Selim.   *S. N.*

Selim, the ideal ruler

It is almost symbolic that Emperor Joseph's famous Edict of Tolerance (total religious freedom) and the restriction of censorship were both introduced in the year in which this opera was created (1781). The ideas of the Enlightenment were illustrated by Mozart and Stephanie mainly through the figure of Pasha Selim. Pasha Selim is not a Turk, but a Christian who has converted to Islam. He is one of the ideal rulers of Enlightenment ideology, whose prototype is to be found in the figure of Sultan Saladin, the "noble heathen" in Gotthold Ephraim Lessing's drama of tolerance *Nathan der Weise* (*Nathan the Wise*) (1777). Stephanie even increased the Pasha's goodness in comparison to Bretzner's text. In the latter, Pasha Selim recognizes Belmonte as his own son, whereas Stephanie and Mozart show him being merciful to the son of his arch-enemy. Does Pasha Selim perhaps represent Joseph II, who represented the new type of ruler for both Mozart and Stephanie?

Joseph II welcomes the *Singspiel*

The *Singspiel* was a manifestation of awakening national feeling. The most successful *Singspiel* before Mozart was *Die Jagd* (*The Chase, 1774*), with a text by Christian Felix Weisse (1732–1804) and music by Johann Adam Hiller (1728–1804). The reforming emperor Joseph II welcomed the *Singspiel*, since he saw in the new genre an opportunity to teach correct German to the multi-ethnic population of Vienna, and to strengthen national feeling, by means of popular stage works. The Burgtheater was raised in 1777 to the status of "royal and imperial national theater," and it functioned as such until 1783 when the Italians reclaimed opera for themselves.

Zaide

In 1779 Mozart was occupying himself with a German *Singspiel*. *Zaide* can be seen as a preliminary study for *The Abduction from the Seraglio*. The Christian Gomatz falls into the power of Sultan Soliman and wins the love of Zaide, whom the Sultan has been wooing in vain. They dare to escape, but are betrayed and brought before the fearsomely enraged Sultan, who refuses all pleas for mercy. The piece was of course to have a happy ending, but we will never know how the problem was to be resolved, since *Zaide* was never completed.

The Abduction from the Seraglio, set design ("The Seraglio") by Otto Müller-Godesberg, Stadttheater, Elberfeld-Barmen 1910 (TWS).
A Turkish setting in the Art Nouveau style. In the early 20th century this included elements of fairytale and orientalism, particularly in Central Europe. An opera such as Mozart's *The Abduction from the Seraglio* seemed positively made for such a stage interpretation.

Why does Pasha Selim not sing?

The romantic interpretation that Mozart had not yet found the appropriate music for Selim is wrong. After *Idomeneo* there were no longer any boundaries to his capacity for expressing feelings in music. So why does Selim not sing? Because in Bretzner's original libretto, his was a speaking part. Moreover, Mozart had no suitable singer at his disposal; the tenor role (the usual register for a ruler in *opera seria*) was taken by Belmonte, and the audience's favorite, Fischer, with his extremely deep bass voice, had to take the part of Osmin. But the main reason was probably that in a *Singspiel* in the manner of the Enlightenment era of Joseph II, great importance was given to the spoken word.

Pasha Selim the unfortunate

Pasha Selim is a man whose soul is difficult to probe, since he does not sing, so that the music cannot reveal his feelings. He could serve as a didactic example of a parable of the noble ruler. But Pasha Selim is an older man (old enough to be Belmonte's father), who has a burning love for Konstanze and finds himself in conflict because of his unrequited love. Why should he renounce this beautiful girl for the sake of an unknown rival? (Only later does it become clear that Belmonte is the son of his arch-enemy – so much the worse!) Is he himself not manly, rich and virtuous enough? To what extent can and should he maintain his loyal attitude toward the young woman?

Right
The Abduction from the Seraglio, production photograph with Akram Tillawi as Pasha Selim, production François Abou Salem, sets Francine Gaspar, conductor Marc Minkowski, Salzburg Festival 1997.
How a Turkish director transforms a German *Singspiel*: the much-discussed Salzburg production placed the piece in a present-day Arab-Turkish setting in the realm of a ruler who is enthusiastically loved by his people. This interpretation set in the modern age even included the machine-gun and the wire fence.

Turks on the operatic stage in the eighteenth century

As early as 1686, during the war with the Turks in the Austro-Hungarian dominions, the first recorded *Singspiel* with a Turkish theme was performed in Hamburg: *Kara Mustafa*, by Johann Wolfgang Franck (text by Lucas von Bostel), whose subject was Kara Mustafa's attack on Vienna. For more than a century, the Turks were an integral part of the operatic stage. The model for Mozart and Johann Gottlieb Stephanie was Christoph Friedrich Bretzner's *Belmont und Constanze oder die Entführung aus dem Serail* (*Belmonte and Constanze, or the Abduction from the Seraglio*) (1781), which had been preceded by the *opera semiseria La schiava liberata* (*The Liberated Slave Girl*), with a text by Gaetano Martinelli, first set to music by Niccolò Jommelli in 1768. The difference between this and Bretzner's *Entführung* is that the liberation of the Westerners is brought about not by force, but by peaceful negotiations with the Sultan. The two Turkish operas by Christoph Willibald Gluck, originally written with French texts, prove that the genre also occurred in France. *Le cadi dupé* (*The Cadi Deceived*) (1761) and particularly *La rencontre imprévue, ou Les Pélerins de Mecque* (*The Unexpected Meeting, or The Pilgrims to Mecca*) (1764) also enjoyed great popularity in Vienna. In 1783, Mozart, in Gluck's presence, improvised, on the basis of a popular *basso buffo* song in the first act of *The Pilgrims to Mecca*, the exquisite piano variations, K.455 ("Unser dummer Pöbel meint").

Osmin

The first Osmin, Johann Ignaz Ludwig Fischer, was a star of the Viennese opera scene. "His voice has the depth of the violoncello and the natural height of the tenor [its range was C-a'], yet neither is its depth grating nor its upper register thin; the voice has lightness, certainty, and attractiveness," wrote Friedrich Reichardt, a critic and composer of the time. Osmin is on the side of evil, yet the means he uses are inappropriate, so that his effect is comic but also uncanny. With him, Mozart extended the boundaries of a *buffo* character. His arias are outbursts of fury in the form of a

Left
The Abduction from the Seraglio, production photograph with Andreas Conrad (Pedrillo) and Franz Hawlata (Osmin), production François Abou Salem, sets Francine Gaspar, conductor Marc Minkowski, Salzburg Festival 1997.

The Abduction from the Seraglio, production photograph with Andreas Grötzinger (actor) and Roland Bracht (singer) as Osmin, production Hans Neuenfels, Staatstheater, Stuttgart 1997.

composition. To Pedrillo's question as to why Osmin might strangle him, he gives the laconic reply: "Because I can't stand the sight of you." The aria that follows is a breathless tirade of abuse. *M 11*

Osmin's furious aria ends in F major, but it is still not over. "I have done nothing to you," pleads Pedrillo. "You have the face of a rogue – that's enough," roars Osmin, swearing an oath by the beard of the Prophet. Mozart added an unexpected part to the aria, which he explained in detail in a letter to his father: "The 'Therefore by the beard of the Prophet' etc. is indeed in the same tempo, but with rapid notes, and as his anger keeps mounting, just when one thinks the aria is already finished, the Allegro assai, in quite a different tempo and a different key, must have a really good effect. A person who finds himself in such a violent rage disregards all order, loses all sense of moderation and aim, he does not know himself any more – and so the music no longer knows itself either. But because the passions, violent or not, must never be expressed to the point of disgust, and the music, even in the most terrifying situation, must never offend the ear, but rather delight it, and must therefore remain music at all times, I have not introduced a key foreign to the basic key of the aria, F, but one which is related to it – not the next one, D minor, but the somewhat more distant A minor." (26 September 1781) *M 12*

The Abduction from the Seraglio, costume design for Osmin by Heinz Grete, Cologne 1914 (TWS).
As a result of the brilliant music written for him, Osmin is equal in stature to the hero. For Mozart he was a comic figure, a *basso buffo*. Osmin embodies the barbaric Turk, while the role of noble foreigner was reserved for Selim. In the productions of the 1980s and 1990s, the figure of Osmin acquired threatening, almost frightening features. This may be connected with the sadistic texts of his arias. But his music secretly laughs at all of this. *M 13*

Turkish music

Mozart knew from the outset that in *The Abduction from the Seraglio* he had to appeal to the Viennese taste for the exotic, the vivid and the amusing: "… the symphony [overture], the chorus in the first act [the Janissaries' chorus] and the final chorus, I will supply with Turkish music," Mozart informed his father by letter two days after receiving the libretto (1 August 1781). M 14

To these were added the famous duet of Pedrillo and Osmin ("Vivat Bacchus!"), which Mozart himself described as a "boozy duet": "per i signori Viennesi [for the Viennese gentlefolk], which consists of nothing but my Turkish tattoo." M 15

The opera's Turkish music ("alla turca") is not in fact authentic, but is nevertheless highly original. In order to create the oriental coloring, Mozart used a particular kind of instrumentation, consisting of various "drums and cymbals" (cymbals, triangles, rattles). Presumably he did not list all the percussion instruments, and indeed it does the piece no harm if the Turkish passages sound somewhat rough and threatening – as was proved by the production and recording under the direction of Nikolaus Harnoncourt.

11. Osmin's Furious Outburst (Aria in F Major)

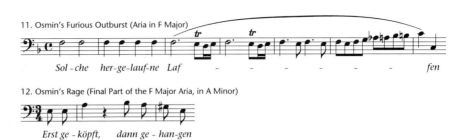

Sol - che her-ge-lauf-ne Laf - - - - - - fen

12. Osmin's Rage (Final Part of the F Major Aria, in A Minor)

Erst ge - köpft, dann ge - han-gen

13. Osmin's Song of Revenge

O, wie will ich tri-um-phie-ren, wenn sie euch zum Richt-platz füh-ren

14. Turkish Music (Overture)

15. Bacchus Duet (Osmin and Pedrillo)

Vi - vat Bac-chus, Bac-chus le-be, Bac-chus war ein bra-ver Mann

The Abduction from the Seraglio, set design by Otto Reigbert for the production by Walter Felsenstein, Städtische Bühnen, Cologne 1932 (TWS).
"Vivat Bacchus, long live Bacchus, Bacchus was a fine fellow!" The philosophy of life attributed to the Turks in the famous "boozy duet" seems not to have caused any bad feeling between the Turks and the Viennese. In reality, however, the Habsburg court was at that time on the verge of a senseless war in the Balkans.

The Abduction from the Seraglio, production photograph with Emanuela von Frankenberg (actress) and Catherine Naglestad (singer) as Konstanze, and Matthias Klink (singer) and Alexander Bogner (actor) as Belmonte, production Hans Neuenfels, sets Christian Schmidt, costumes Bettina Merz, conducted by Lothar Zograsek, Zürttembergisches Staatstheater, Stuttgart 1997.

Before Mozart it was not usual to compose for large ensembles in rather simplistic bourgeois opera. However, Mozart found a quartet to be the ideal analogy for the tense dramatic situation in which the lovers finally meet again after two years.

Left
The Abduction from the Seraglio, production photograph with Eva Mei as Konstanze, Wiener Staatsoper 1990.
"I have slightly sacrificed Konstanze's aria to the fluent throat of Mademoiselle Cavalieri." (Mozart to his father, 26 September 1781) The part of Konstanze remained a challenge for later singers too.

Konstanze, the constant one

The only constant figure in the piece is the appropriately named Konstanze (to whom Mozart felt particularly drawn, not least because of the name she shared with his bride Constanze; their marriage took place at exactly the time he was working on the opera). Konstanze is in love, and love means life to her. This is shown by her three great arias, which express various states of mind (this is the most difficult soprano role in Mozart's operas). In the first, Konstanze confesses that at Belmonte's side she felt happy and secure (no. 6, "Ach, ich liebte," "Ah, I loved," B major) ᴍ 16, in the second she laments the loss of this security (no. 10, "Traurigkeit," "Sadness," G minor) ᴍ 17, and after Selim's threats she triumphs in an almost hysterical bravura aria, because she hopes to be freed from her mental torment by death (no. 11, "Martern aller Arten," "Torments of all kinds," C major). ᴍ 18

Belmonte, the searcher

"Oh, how fearful, oh, how fiery, do you know how it is expressed – and the beating heart full of love is indicated as well – the two violins in octaves. This is the favorite aria of all those they have heard – mine too – and is written entirely for Adamberger's voice ..." (Mozart to his father, 26 September 1781). After studying in Italy and engagements in Munich and London, Valentin Adamberger came to Vienna in 1780. Like Catarina Cavalieri he was a favorite of the emperor, who found him "incomparable." His voice did not have a great range, but his singing was heartfelt and full of sympathy.

Belmonte's key words are fear and happiness. "O wie ängstlich, o wie feurig klopft mein liebevolles Herz" (Oh, how fearful, oh, how fiery, is my heart that beats with love"), he sings in the most beautiful of his four arias (no. 4, A major). ᴍ 19 Belmonte's third aria, "Wenn der Freude Tränen fliessen" ("When the tears of joy are flowing") (no. 15, B major), inspired by his fervently desired reunion with Konstanze, closes (after the extended, lyrically sensitive slow section) rapidly and almost bitterly. The text indeed speaks of the sorrows of separation that have been overcome, but in the background lurk the torments of jealousy, which burst out in the quartet, to disappear finally in the serenity of swaying, enchanted music. Belmonte is happy to have found his beloved again, and he is fearful that she may not have been faithful to him. A conflict arises between the lovers (quartet no. 16, "Ach, Belmonte! Ach, mein Leben!" "Ah, Belmonte! Ah, my life!" D major, Act II), which escalates immediately before the abduction attempt. M 20

After the failure of their flight, the lovers wait for death and are ready to die for each other (duet no. 20). Belmonte has reached his goal (this development is a significant element of the dramatic action of the *Singspiel*). He has attained the same spiritual heights as Konstanze.

16. Konstanze's Memories of Love (Aria in B Major)

Ach ich lieb - te, war so glück - lich, kann-te nicht der Lie-be Schmerz

17. Konstanze's Sadness (Aria in G Minor)

Trau - rig - keit

18. Konstanze's Resoluteness (Aria in C Major)

Mar-tern al - ler Ar-ten, al - ler Ar-ten mö - gen mei - ner war-ten

19. Belmonte's Hopes (Aria in A Major)

O wie ängst-lich, o wie feu-rig klopft mein lie - be-vol - les Herz

20. Reconciliation of the Lovers (Quartet)

The Abduction from the Seraglio, production photograph with Aga Winska (Konstanze) and Hilmar Thate (Pasha Selim), production and sets Karl-Ernst and Ursel Herrmann, conductor Nikolaus Harnoncourt, Vienna Festival 1989. The true abduction takes place in a labyrinth of emotions, as illustrated by Karl-Ernst Herrmann's set.

The Impresario

Der Schauspieldirektor

Comedy with music in one act – K.486

Libretto: Johann Gottlieb Stephanie the younger.
Première: 7 February 1786, Schönbrunn (Orangery).
Characters: Frank, the impresario (spoken), Eiler, a banker (spoken), Buff, an actor (B), Herz, an actor (spoken), Madame Pfeil, Madame Krone and Madame Vogelsang, actresses (3 spoken), Monsieur Vogelsang, a singer (T), Madame Herz and Mademoiselle Silberklang, singers (2 S).
Setting: Rooms of Herr Frank, 18th century.

Synopsis

The impresario Frank (first played by the librettist, Johann Gottlieb Stephanie) is assembling a group of traveling players. Buff (played by Mozart's brother-in-law, Joseph Lange) offers his advice: he should sign up players for low pay, but advertise the performances in a sensational manner, pay less attention to artistic merit than to effectiveness when choosing pieces, and bribe the critics. The financial side is safeguarded by the banker Eiler (played by the then famous Burgtheater actor, Johann Franz Hieronymus Brockmann), who is trying to procure an engagement for his mistress, Madame Pfeil (played by Johanna Sacco, a popular Viennese actress). The various contenders try to prove their talent and outshine each other by presenting a variety of scenes. Particularly acute is the rivalry between the two prima donnas Madame Herz and Mademoiselle Silberklang. (The names, "heart" and "silvery tones", are significant: Mozart created their arias specifically for the two star Viennese singers of the time, his own sister-in-law Aloysia Lange, and Catarina Cavalieri.) Madame Herz's aria is in the Italian style, and that of Mademoiselle Silberklang in the French. The first aria is more sentimental, the second more charming. In the trio ("Ich bin die erste Sängerin," "I am the first singer") the prima donnas continue their competition with ever-mounting aggression, while Monsieur Vogelsang tries in vain to calm the ladies down. (The tenor was the much-admired Valentin Adamberger, whose wife, Maria Anna, played Madame Krone.) When Frank threatens to abandon his plans for a traveling troupe, the artists soon show their understanding and join in a song of praise for the morality of artists.

A. G.

Opera about opera

The Impresario was composed for a court celebration, a cross between a *Singspiel* and a play with overture, two arias, a trio and a strophic ensemble song (vaudeville). Mozart composed brilliant musical interludes for his sister-in-law and former love, Aloysia Lange. Like Mozart, Antonio Salieri had been commissioned to write a work for the occasion, and had composed the opera buffa *Prima la musica e poi le parole* (*First the Music and Then the Words*), to a text by Giovanni Battista Casti. This work also deals with the changing tastes in opera. The conflicts between composer and librettist are depicted with parodistic exaggeration, Casti using the opportunity to satirize his rival Da Ponte. A princely patron of the arts requests the appearance of a certain lady singer. The prima donna (played by the star singer of the Salieri party, Nancy Storace) proves her vocal superiority by singing arias from Giuseppe Arti's opera *Giulio Sabino*, choosing arias composed for a castrato. Storace was parodying the celebrated castrato Marchesi, who had recently performed in Vienna. The emperor wanted to use both works to demonstrate to his guests the multiplicity of Vienna's operatic life. He was happy with the musical carnival joke, and rewarded Salieri with 100 gulden, and Mozart and the other participants in the show with 50. The whole celebration cost him 1000 gulden …

MOZART   *DER SCHAUSPIELDIREKTOR*

WOLFGANG AMADEUS

ANTONIO SALIERI

PRIMA LA MUSICA, POI LE PAROLE

DEUTSCHE STAATSOPER BERLIN

Above
The Impresario, production photograph with (from left to right) Michal Shamir (Madame Herz), Gunda Aurich (Madame Vogelsang), Bengt-Ola Morgny (Herr Vogelsang), Sabine Sinjen (Madame Krone), Thomas Schendel (Buff), Peter Matic (Frank), Maria Hartmann (Madame Pfeil), Christian Berkel (Monsieur Herz), Jane Giering (Mademoiselle Silberklang), and Thomas Wolff (Eiler), production Alfred Kirchner, sets Vincent Callara, conductor Sebastian Lang, Deutsche Oper, Berlin 1991.

The world of Viennese opera

The world of Viennese opera was ruled by the emperor himself. Even in his army encampment at Belgrade during the Turkish war (1787–88) he received regular reports from his "general director of entertainments" Count Orsini Rosenberg about the operatic events in Vienna, including the first performance in Vienna of → *Don Giovanni*. Wars were also conducted in the operatic arena in Vienna. Although not as passionately as in eighteenth-century France, discussions took place about operatic genres – above all in aristocratic circles and in the still comparatively small circle of the educated bourgeoisie. Joseph II had not attained his goal of developing the *Singspiel* into a truly popular genre and establishing a real national *Singspiel* in the Burgtheater on a long-term basis. Only Mozart's *The Abduction from the Seraglio* brought any money into the enterprise. The national *Singspiel* was abandoned in March 1783.

The bourgeois public was not yet ready to support a theater, while the aristocracy showed little interest in the new operatic genre and was pleased when Joseph II once again opened the gates of the court to Italian opera. The house composers in Vienna during Joseph's reign (between 1780 and 1790) were the court composer Salieri and Mozart, who was not actually in the service of the court but enjoyed the sympathy and recognition of the emperor, above all for his instru-

mental work and his virtuoso piano playing. The position of the former court poet Metastasio (1698–1782) was sought by two Italian librettists, Giovanni Battista Casti (1724–1803) and Lorenzo Da Ponte (1749–1838), who settled in Vienna at the same time, around 1782–83. But Casti and Da Ponte had to content themselves with the more modest title of "theater writer." Casti became famous at Salieri's side, Da Ponte at Mozart's, and the latter eventually became immortal. At that time there was no famous castrato living in Vienna; the public had to make do with visiting companies. But there were prima donnas, above all Catarina Cavalieri, who was Salieri's mistress, Aloysia Lange, Mozart's sister-in-law, and Nancy Storace, to whom Mozart was linked by close friendship. After the national *Singspiel* project went bankrupt in 1783, the Italian opera company was reconstituted, and good Italian singers began to come to Vienna.

Lorenzo da Ponte, knight of culture

Lorenzo da Ponte was one of the most fascinating personalities of his day. Coming from an impoverished background and a religious minority (he was a Jew, the fourteenth child of a cobbler, and was originally called Emmanuele Conegliano), he fought his way through all the strata of society as far as the imperial court of

The old Burgtheater, Vienna, colored copper engraving, unknown artist, 18th century, Historisches Museum der Stadt Wien. The old Burgtheater, next to the Burg in Vienna. The Burgtheater saw the first performances of *The Abduction of the Seraglio*, *The Marriage of Figaro*, and the Viennese version of *Don Giovanni*.

Lorenzo da Ponte (1749–1838), oil painting, anonymous, 1786, Columbia University, New York City.
This painting shows da Ponte towards the end of his life, as a poet laureate. A clever, robust, and active man returns our gaze. He had the ability to build a new and creative life for himself in various countries and cultures (Italy, Austria, England, the USA and for a short time Germany).

Vienna. He was constantly in financial difficulties, always enterprising, and obsessed with women, like his friend Giacomo Casanova. Both traveled continually throughout Europe, adventurers with a sharp, critical view of society and above all enlightened citizens, who sought to master their fate by means of their talent and inventiveness. Both were passionate about the theater, and both left behind a notable literary heritage.

Lorenzo da Ponte (he had been given this name by the bishop who baptized him) studied in the priests' seminary in Venice and became a teacher of rhetoric and music in Treviso, where he was dismissed for disseminating the ideas of Rousseau, and finally banned from the republic of Venice. (He should have been thankful not to have been sentenced, like his friend Casanova, to imprisonment in the notorious lead chambers.) He went first to Dresden, then in 1782 to Vienna, where the imperial poet Metastasio became aware of him as a result of one of his poems. In Vienna, at the time of his arrival, da Ponte found a favorable situation for Italian opera, since the national *Singspiel*

demanded by Joseph II had not had the expected success. Thus began da Ponte's career as a librettist. During his nine years in Vienna he wrote a number of librettos, above all for Mozart (→*The Marriage of Figaro*, →*Don Giovanni*, →*Così fan tutte*), but also for Salieri and for other composers of the day.

In 1790, as a result of intrigues, da Ponte was also banned from Vienna. In 1792 he went to London, and in 1805, heavily in debt, he traveled to New York. There he first ran an Italian bookshop, became a professor at the prestigious Columbia University (where he founded the faculty for Italian language and literature), and published his amusing and instructive memoirs. At an advanced age he even attended the American première of *Don Giovanni* and in 1832 the opening of the first New York opera house, which he had helped to found. When he died in New York in 1838, at nearly 90 years old, he was poor in material terms but had retained a remarkable mental alertness.

F. Murray Abraham as Salieri, production photograph from the film *Amadeus* directed by Milos Forman, USA 1984.
Murderer and victim: Salieri and Mozart in Milos Forman's film *Amadeus*. In real life they were merely rivals. In terms of their standing at the imperial court, Mozart had more reason to be jealous of Salieri. As an Italian opera composer, Salieri was much more successful in his lifetime than Mozart. Mozart's operatic masterpieces were incomparably more substantial in musical terms and demanded an unusually high degree of attention from the contemporary audience.

The legend

The relationship between Mozart and Salieri, the two most important Viennese composers during the ten-year autocratic reign of Joseph II, has had a lasting fascination for posterity. The theme of envy, with Salieri as Mozart's murderer, was introduced into the upper reaches of literature by Pushkin, whose tragedy *Envy* (1830) forms the basis of Rimsky-Korsakov's opera *Mozart and Salieri*. The story received further treatment in Peter Shaffer's play *Amadeus* (1979), the film version of which, directed by Milos Forman (1984), proved to be extraordinarily popular. Even those with little interest in Mozart went to see it and as a result became convinced that Mozart had indeed been murdered by Salieri.

The story is convincingly set up in the manner of a thriller: an artist of moderate talent persecutes a genius (of whose brilliance and human weakness he is well aware) to the point of illness and finally death. He commits murder without "poison" and without a "dagger," simply by setting up situations of self-induced anxiety for his rival. What could Mozart have had to fear? Above all, his own father Leopold. Then, poverty. During the second half of the 1780s he found himself in ever-worsening financial difficulties. And not least, he faced the failure of his career, which threatened increasingly with the falling star of Joseph II, and particularly after the emperor's death. Salieri, who in this story represents evil, simply combines these various preoccupations, thereby creating a deathly web of fear for his younger colleague.

The truth

It is always impossible to establish the truth at a distance of 200 years. It is clear, however, that in the case of Mozart and Salieri, the relationship was one of normal rivalry between two spoiled composers. Mozart was not poisoned, although his early, sudden death gave rise, in retrospect, to speculation. (The exact cause of Mozart's death is still not known today, although it is believed to have been some sort of infectious disease.) In addition, in the year of Mozart's death, 1791, Salieri was no longer court operatic composer. (After the death of Joseph II he had asked to be released from his position as court Kapellmeister.) Strangely, after Joseph's death all the important figures of the Viennese operatic scene disappeared, either through death (Mozart), departure (da Ponte) or at least retirement (Salieri). Salieri had been active in Vienna for 20 years and had composed almost 30 operas. The best of these, *Les Danaides*, *Tarare* and *Axur*, enjoyed spectacular success throughout Europe. It is only for a brief period, between 1785 and 1790, that one can speak of a true rivalry between Mozart and Salieri, when they were competing in the field of Italian opera with the same singers for the favors of the Viennese. Salieri's operatic ideal was quite different from that of Mozart; it was directed at the great celebratory operas based on the French pattern. In his major works he was considered a legitimate successor to Gluck – most unusual for an Italian operatic composer. Mozart does comment in his letters on Salieri's "Cabalen" (intrigues), but these were the normal in the world of opera. When Salieri attended a performance of *The Magic Flute* during

Mozart's lifetime, he reacted with sincere enthusiasm to the piece, which was so dissimilar to his own works. Admittedly, Salieri, at least immediately after Mozart's death, did nothing to promote the memory of his colleague, and was of no help to his widow Constanze. But it is also true that he later gave free tuition to Mozart's son Franz Xaver Wolfgang, who was musically talented – as indeed he did for all his pupils, who included Beethoven, Schubert, and Liszt. Salieri was active in Vienna as a teacher almost up to the time of his late death in 1825. This was bad luck, for he lived to experience the cult of Mozart. It was only now that the elderly Salieri became jealous of his former rival, whose earthly remains could not even be identified (Mozart was buried in a communal grave). "He must grow and I must diminish," he is reported to have said, according to a diary entry by his pupil Anselm Hüttenbrenner (a close friend of Franz Schubert). Hüttenbrenner remarked that old Salieri was fond of pointing out alleged errors in Mozart's work. On his sickbed the mentally confused old man pleaded in vain with his pupil Moscheles (the famous pianist): "Malice, all malice, please tell the world, dear Moscheles." Salieri died in 1825.

The legend began to take shape, the avalanche began to roll, and even reached a young genius in faraway Moscow: Alexander Pushkin …

Tom Hulce as Mozart, production photograph from the film *Amadeus* directed by Milos Forman, USA 1984.
No one who has seen the cinematic hit *Amadeus* can forget the boisterous, adolescent, immature laughter of Tom Hulce as Wolfgang Amadeus Mozart. But not even a Mozart was permitted to behave in this way in the presence of a Habsburg emperor. However, his singular relationship with the court society of his day, and his inability to make a "normal" musical career for himself, were made comprehensible by means of this artistic exaggeration.

First reactions
"What is not permitted to be spoken in these times is now sung." (*Wiener Realzeitung*, 11 July 1786)
"Here nothing is spoken of but *Figaro*; nothing played, blown, sung, and whistled but *Figaro*; no opera attended but *Figaro*; and eternally *Figaro* …" (Mozart to his Viennese friend Gottfried von Jacquin from Prague, 14 January 1787)

The Marriage of Figaro

Le nozze di Figaro

Opera buffa in four acts – K.492

Libretto: Lorenzo da Ponte, after the comedy *La folle journée, ou Le mariage de Figaro* by Pierre-Augustin Caron de Beaumarchais.
Première: 1 May 1786, Vienna (Altes Burgtheater).
Characters: Count Almaviva (Bar), Countess Almaviva (S), Susanna, her maid (S), Figaro, the Count's valet, betrothed to Susanna (B), Cherubino, the Count's page (Ms), Bartolo, a doctor from Seville (B), Marcellina, Bartolo's housekeeper (A), Don Basilio, a music master (T), Don Curzio, a magistrate (T), Antonio, a gardener (B), Barbarina, his daughter (S); peasants (chorus).
Setting: Count Almaviva's estate near Seville, mid-18th century.

The Marriage of Figaro, photograph from the production by Jürgen Flimm, Opernhaus, Zürich 1996.
Although the whole of *Figaro* is about love, there is only one love duet, and this occurs in a situation involving pretence: the Count, who is infatuated with Susanna, invites her to a nocturnal rendezvous. Although Susanna only pretends to surrender, this duet crackles with eroticism. Susanna and Figaro are struggling for a life of self-determination in feudal conditions. In the colorful carousel of *Figaro*, behind the breathtaking impetus of the story there lies a psychological theme of "who's who." At any given moment the participants in this game recognize or fail to recognize each other and themselves.

Synopsis
Act I

Figaro is the valet of Count Almaviva, who has officially waived the *droit de seigneur*. Secretly, however, he pursues pretty girls with much success, and is about to try his luck with Susanna, the Countess's maid, who is betrothed to Figaro. The servant couple are in the process of furnishing their own room. Figaro is pleased with its favorable location, not far from the apartments of the Count and Countess. Then Susanna enlightens him: one ring on the bell, and Figaro will be called away; just one step, and the Count will be in their conjugal bed. Figaro declares his defiance of the Count. But the Count has Marcellina and Bartolo on his side. Marcellina has lent money to Figaro on condition that if he cannot

repay it, he must marry her. Bartolo supports Marcellina, in order to take revenge on Figaro, who once helped the Count to abduct Bartolo's ward Rosina (now the Countess). In this way he also hopes to get rid of Marcellina, since the two are the parents of a child that was stolen from them as a baby. The page, Cherubino, has begun a flirtation with Barbarina, the gardener's daughter, which has been detected by the Count, who himself has an eye on Barbarina, and Cherubino has been dismissed. He seeks support from Susanna, but here too he is surprised by the Count, hides behind a chair and becomes an involuntary witness of the Count's attempts to seduce Susanna. When the music teacher Basilio also appears to visit Susanna, the Count in turn hides behind the chair, while Cherubino hides in the chair itself. Don Basilio pleads on behalf of the Count with Susanna, and suggests that the page is probably enjoying the favors of the Countess. At this, the Count leaps enraged from his hiding-place and discovers Cherubino hidden in the chair. Figaro meanwhile has instructed the Count's subjects to scatter flowers in front of him, thanks the Count on their behalf for refusing to exercise the *droit de seigneur*, and urges him to allow Figaro and Susanna to marry soon. The Count achieves a postponement by promising a glittering marriage feast for the couple. Cherubino, however, his rival and a dangerous witness, is to depart immediately to become an officer in a distant regiment.

Act II

The Countess has been let into the plans of Figaro and Susanna, and supports them, as she is anxious to win back the affections of her husband. By means of a secret note, Figaro has let the Count know that his wife has arranged a rendezvous. In this way he hopes to distract the self-confident Count and deter him from his machinations against the wedding. The Count has also been promised a rendezvous with Susanna, but instead of Susanna, Cherubino is to appear in disguise. Cherubino is ready to agree to everything, since he worships the Countess. Then the Count returns from hunting earlier than expected, and angrily invades his wife's apartments. Cherubino is concealed in an adjacent dressing room, while Susanna hides in the room. The Count hears a noise in the dressing room and demands to be allowed to enter. When the Countess refuses to unlock the door, he goes to fetch tools for breaking in. The Countess is obliged to accompany him. The Count locks the door of the room behind him. Meanwhile Susanna slips into the dressing room and Cherubino escapes through the window. Reluctantly the Count is obliged to ask his wife's forgiveness. The women explain that Figaro's note was merely a joke. But all seems to be in vain. The gardener Antonio complains that his flowers have been damaged by someone jumping out of the window, and produces the officer's commission that the page dropped when making his escape. The Count suspects the truth but can prove nothing. The battle seems to be lost. But then Marcellina appears with Figaro's promise of marriage. The Count orders an investigation.

Act III

In order to obtain the money to release Figaro from his promise to Marcellina, Susanna makes a pretense of accepting the Count's advances. But he becomes aware of Susanna's true intentions. Figaro is sentenced either to pay up or to marry Marcellina. In dire straits, Figaro realizes that he needs his parents' permission to marry. To the astonishment of all, it is revealed that he is the long-lost child of Marcellina and Bartolo. Marcellina maternally embraces him. The Countess decides to go to the rendezvous with the Count, wearing Susanna's clothes. She dictates a note to Susanna fixing the time and place. During the wedding ceremony Susanna passes the Count her "little note." As a sign of his agreement he is to send back to her the pin with which the note is fastened. Figaro has not been made a party to the plan. He only notices the Count opening the note and pricking his finger on the pin.

Act IV

Barbarina has lost the pin that she was to return to Susanna. From her, Figaro learns that the letter to the Count was written by Susanna, believes her to be unfaithful and asks his new friends Bartolo and Basilio to wait in the garden at night in order to surprise and punish the faithless bride. Susanna and the Countess appear having exchanged clothing. Marcellina hides in an arbor, where Barbarina is already waiting for Cherubino. Cherubino is looking for Barbarina, but instead finds another lady whom he believes to be Susanna and begins to woo. The Count appears. Cherubino takes refuge in the arbor. The Count begins to court the disguised Countess believing her to be Susanna, and gives her a ring. Figaro meets the supposed Countess, but recognizes Susanna by her voice, and feigns a declaration of love for the Countess. Finally both see through the game, and are reconciled. The Count is searching for "his Susanna." Figaro and Susanna perform a love scene between Figaro and the Countess for his benefit. Enraged, the Count calls his servants. The "guilty couple" beg the Count for forgiveness, but he remains implacable. Then the real Countess reveals herself. The Count must admit defeat and begs his Rosina for forgiveness.

S. N.

The Marriage of Figaro, photograph from the production by Jürgen Flimm, Opernhaus, Zürich 1996.
The Count is defeated – not as a count, but as a man. If he were not a nobleman, his attempted fling with Susanna might perhaps have succeeded, and certainly the matter would not have been placed on a political plane. The great question of the piece, despite the reunion of the couples, remains an open one: how long will their fidelity last?

The Marriage of Figaro, production photograph with Krisztina Laki as Susanna, production Nikolaus Lehnhoff, Deutsche Oper am Rhein, Düsseldorf 1982.
In *Figaro*, much can happen within a short time. Various members of the Count's court gain access to the room of the chambermaid Susanna. Thus, in the first act, a series of tense and comic situations develop.

The predecessor

If one listens carefully to Giovanni Paisiello's *The Barber of Seville* (a piece which is occasionally performed at opera festivals and of which a number of recordings exist), one gains the impression that Paisiello's characters can be regarded to some extent as forerunners of those in Mozart's *Figaro*. Thus, for example, the first aria that Paisiello gives to Figaro, in which he introduces himself to Count Almaviva, makes use of similar melodies to Figaro's cavatina in Mozart's opera (no. 3, "Se vuol ballare," "If you wish to dance"). But what Paisiello invests with dance-like lightness, in Mozart seems more serious and threatening. *M 21, 22*

21. Paisiello, *The Barber of Seville*, Figaro's Aria

Scor - si   giá mol - ti   pa - e - si,

22. Figaro's Cavatina

Se vuol bal - la - re,   si-gnor con - ti - no,

Similarly, Count Almaviva's cavatina in Paisiello's opera (no. 5), which is accompanied on the mandolin, is reminiscent of Cherubino's arietta in *Figaro* in its use of pizzicato effects. *M 23, M 24*

There are also similarities between Paisiello's pure and touching portrayal of Rosina *M 25* and Mozart's Countess, particularly in the latter's E flat major aria in Act III. *M 26* Paisiello's comparable aria (no. 13) is also in E flat major, and in both Paisiello and Mozart this sensitive heroine is accompanied by the clarinet (the favorite instrument of both composers) and the bassoon. With this aria one feels that the *opera buffa* of the time of Paisiello and Mozart was already closely approaching the bourgeois melodrama.

Giovanni Paisiello (1740–1816), oil painting by Elisabeth Vigée-Lebrun, Milan (Museo Teatro alla Scala).
Giovanni Paisiello, an important protagonist of the Neapolitan opera workshop, composed more than 80 operas. His greatest success was *The Barber of Seville*, adapted from the first part of the dramatic trilogy by Beaumarchais (it was first performed in St. Petersburg in 1782). The piece was also performed in Vienna to tempestuous acclaim in the presence of the composer, who had interrupted his journey to Naples to visit the imperial city. Mozart would certainly have attended one of these performances. Paisiello's long life was one of fame and honor. He settled in Naples, where he maintained his leading position in musical life until the end of French rule there in 1815. After the Holy Alliance and the restoration of the monarchy, he lost his exceptional position. In 1816 he also had to witness the reuse of the libretto of *The Barber of Seville* by a young Italian called Rossini. Rossini was not the only composer to reset this libretto, but he was the one who caused most irritation to the old master …

23. Paisiello, *The Barber of Seville*, The Count's Cavatina

Sa - per bra-ma - te,   bel - la, il mio no - me;   ec - co a-scol-ta - te,   ec - co ascol-ta - te,

24. Cherubino's Arietta

Voi, che sa - pe - te   che co-sa è a-mor.

25. Paisiello, *The Barber of Seville*, Rosina's Aria

Giu - sto ciel, che co - no - sce - te   quan - do il cor o - ne - sto   si - ha,

26. The Countess's Cavatina (Act III)

Por - gi a - mor   qual-che ri - sto - ro   al mio   duo - lo, a' miei __ so - spir!

Figaro here, Figaro there

Beaumarchais's *Le mariage de Figaro* was a political time-bomb. The play portrays a count who acts as rival to his servant and loses the game. Napoleon was right when he said years later: "C'était la révolution en action!". *Le mariage de Figaro* was probably completed as early as 1778, but up to 27 April 1784 (the first public performance) it remained a contentious issue in French theatrical circles. Its success was enormous. In 1785 as many as three French editions were published. Beaumarchais and the Comédie Française made enormous sums of money from it.

Figaro in Vienna

In Vienna the debate over *Figaro* was somewhat different in nature from that in France. Emperor Joseph II considered that the play contained "much that is offensive," and prohibited its public performance. But he allowed it to be published, on the basis that Viennese chambermaids and manservants were very fond of going to the theater, but did not read books. Mozart became interested in the material, and asked da Ponte to produce a libretto in Italian. In the mid-1780s it was unusual to choose a contemporary stage play to be set to music, rather than a traditional libretto which had already been set to music several times. But to compose an opera based on a stage play that had been banned by the emperor seemed sheer lunacy.

So why did Joseph II allow *Figaro* to be performed?

Neither da Ponte's plea nor Mozart's talent would have moved the emperor to agreement. It is more likely that Joseph II wanted to teach the nobility the political lesson that a servant can assert his rights against his master. The relationship between emperor and nobility was tense. Joseph II sought absolute power and did away with certain of the nobility's privileges. The

Pierre-Augustin Caron de Beaumarchais (1732–99), oil painting by Jean-Marc Nattier le Jeune, Paris, Comédie Française. Pierre-Augustin Caron, having entered the nobility via a shrewd marriage, added the "de Beaumarchais" to his name and began a career such as was possible only on the eve of the French Revolution. Coming from a poor clockmaker's family, at 21 years of age he had already come up with an invention which he succeeded in defending against an imitator. With the help of music (he was a good harpist, and also played the flute and viola) and his gift for public speaking, he climbed the social ladder and soon became music teacher to the princesses at the French court (after having presented to Madame de Pompadour a ring with a built-in clock). In public life he became best known for his many lawsuits, which he brought to public attention by journalistic means, with bourgeois self-confidence and brilliantly formulated prosecution and defense documents. His major literary work is the Figaro trilogy (*Le barbier de Séville*, written in 1772, first performed in 1775, *Le mariage de Figaro, ou La folle journée*, completed and first performed in 1784, and finally, with far less success, *La mère coupable* of 1792). Here he portrays, with many satirical observations about the late feudal society of the time, the fate of Figaro, who – like himself – comes from the "third estate" and with his fearless bourgeois consciousness asserts himself in the face of all legal and social hindrances.

example of Count Almaviva offered a parallel: that of the bigoted country nobleman who has no understanding of the new tendencies of the age. He seemed – perhaps unconsciously – to share Figaro's opinion: "Foolishness in print is only dangerous when it is suppressed." But Mozart's opera failed to establish itself in Vienna; the first series of performances numbered only nine. The breakthrough was achieved only in Prague, where the spirit of the libretto and the brilliance of the music were properly understood.

The Marriage of Figaro, production photograph from Act II, production Giorgio Strehler, sets Ezio Frigerio, costumes Franca Squarciapino, Teatro alla Scala, Milan 1980. The marriage bed is given symbolic significance in *Figaro*. Although it is never used in the course of the opera, the whole story centers on the problem as to who will first use this cult object of marriage, and with whom? Here we see the marriage bed of the Count and Countess.

The Marriage of Figaro, costume design for
Count Almaviva by Rudolf Heinrich, Munich,
1967/68 (TWS).
Count Almaviva: in Mozart's opera, he is
in the first instance wounded in his manly
vanity. The class difference plays a minor
role here.

Count Almaviva

Once they were friends: the fiery young Count and the all-knowing small-town barber Figaro (→ *The Barber of Seville* by Rossini). It was with Figaro's help that the Count won his beloved, Rosina, who had grown up as an orphan in the house of her uncle, Dr. Bartolo. The Count, with his young wife, moved to his country estate near Seville and took Figaro into his service. For Countess Rosina and Count Almaviva, there now began the typically boring life of the country aristocracy: hunting, garden parties, and court intrigues. The Count continued his secret love affairs with his serfs, with chambermaids and peasant girls. His successes in love permitted him to renounce magnanimously the feudal right of *jus primae noctis* – the right to sleep with any one of his female serfs on her wedding night.

When – perhaps for the first time in his life – he encounters resistance in a love affair, he feels injured, above all in his manly vanity. His intention of reviving the privilege of *jus primae noctis* is merely a weapon in the battle of love and has far less political significance than has been maintained repeatedly since the creation of the drama. The Count desires the pretty, intelligent Susanna, his wife's new maid. This mania for sexual prey is only intensified by the fact that Susanna rejects him and remains true to Figaro.

Figaro

In contrast to the Count, Figaro is more politically conscious in this struggle with his rival. Understandably, his strong political views, which Joseph II found so offensive in Beaumarchais's play, were toned down by da Ponte. Originally, Figaro had a furious monologue in the fifth act, for which 20 years earlier he (and his author) would certainly have had a cell reserved for them in the Bastille. It is extraordinary, and can only be related to the impending revolution, that in the mid-1780s a Count could be addressed in such words, uttered on the open stage: "Nobility, possessions, rank and dignity – oh, how confident they make you! But what have you done to achieve all this? You took the trouble to be born, that's all; otherwise you are a human being no different from a thousand others." Da Ponte cut this monologue. Instead, Figaro, believing himself to be deceived by Susanna, sings an aria of revenge about cuckolded husbands. *M 27*

march-like quality, like that of a chorus. The threateningly muffled orchestral accompaniment (with pizzicato strings) and the sudden leaps in the melody hint at bitter fury and contempt.

The confusing Cherubino

The whole story would not have been worth writing down (two jealous men, a deceived wife and a bride whose wedding night is somewhat delayed), if a young man at the Count's court (a young poor, noble relative), had not plunged everything into confusion. It is Cherubino who creates the magic of this opera; he is the Puck of this midsummer night's dream. Cherubino has something supernatural about him; he is a cherub of love, or more closely observed, a hermaphrodite; a woman sings and plays the role of a boy. In the world of opera this is called a breeches part. Cherubino is a teenager, more of an "it" than a "he" or "she", although he is in love with all the women (except Marcellina). His contemporary in age is the 13-year-old Barbarina, the gardener Antonio's daughter, with whom Cherubino is already playing daring games of love, but his heart is on fire for the Countess (who incidentally is his godmother), while at the same time he likes to steal a kiss from Figaro's future bride. He gets in the way of all the men, particularly the husbands. The Count therefore sends him to the army, where, in the third part of Beaumarchais's trilogy, he is killed in battle. But before his heroic death, he is allowed a few precious hours in the arms of the Countess. She is to bear his child – a child of love, free from politics.

Right
The Marriage of Figaro, costume design for Antonio by Heinrich Lefler, Vienna 1915 (TWS).
In *The Marriage of Figaro* there are no unimportant roles. Even Antonio the gardener, who appears only in the great ensembles at the ends of Acts II and IV, acquires a dramatically essential function at a decisive moment (Finale, Act II). Without him the avalanche of dramatic intrigues could roll no further.

27. Figaro's Aria of Revenge

A - pri - te un po' quegl' oc-chi,   uo - mi ni in-cau-ti e scioc-chi,

His political opinion is not completely suppressed, however. When he hears of the Count's intentions, he sings an impudent plebeian song (no. 3, "Se vuol ballare Signor Contino," "If you wish to dance, My Lord Count" →*M 22*), a dance in triple time but with a

The Marriage of Figaro, production photograph with Andrea Rost as Susanna, production Giorgio Strehler, conductor Ivàn Fischer, Opéra National de Paris 1994. Susannas come and go, but the famous armchair, the hiding-place in Act I, goes on and on.

The world of women in *Figaro*

The great Mozart conductor Otto Klemperer is reported to have said that the characters of *Figaro* are bound to each other by secret erotic threads. For Mozart the most important theme is, once again, love, and – this time – sensuality too. Bedroom, dressing room, summerhouse, gardener's cottage, pavilion – in fact every part of this court can serve as the arena for lovemaking of all kinds. Paradoxically, the two female protagonists, Countess Rosina and the maid Susanna, are loyal and faithful; it is difficult to say who is the prima donna of this piece. Mozart had two outstanding female singers to choose from, both celebrated by the Viennese audiences: Louisa Laschi-Mombelli (the Countess) and Nancy Storace (Susanna). Both were sufficiently important to Mozart for him to attract them both with magnificent roles. The Countess sings two arias ·M 26, M 28 and Susanna only one M 29, but Susanna has more time on stage and takes part in all the ensembles (from duet to nonet). Anyway, the whole story is about her!

Mozart's first Susanna

The great Mozart biographer Alfred Einstein is of the opinion that the only woman of whom Constanze might have had cause to be jealous was Nancy Storace.

28. The Countess's Aria (Act III)

Do - ve so - no i bei mo - men -ti, di dol -cez -za e di _ pia - cer, _

29. Susanna's Rose Aria

Deh vie - ni, non tar - dar, o gio - ia bel - la,

This much admired singer, born in England, the daughter of an Italian double-bass player, came to Vienna in 1783 and immediately became the darling of the public. The temperamental, intelligent and charming figure of Susanna could at the same time be an excellent musical portrait of Nancy Storace. The question as to who is the addressee of the incomparable "Rose Aria" sung by Susanna/Nancy (Figaro is the only other person on stage and it is not certain that Susanna even notices his presence), can have only one answer: Mozart himself.

The art of the ensemble

The Marriage of Figaro is a large-scale, "difficult" opera (as Mozart's father Leopold said of Beaumarchais's drama), but at the same time an intimate chamber-drama for a small ensemble of 11 outstanding singers in all, if one includes the episodic roles of the judge Don Curzio, the gardener Antonio and his daughter Barbarina. Up to the third act, two hostile parties confront each other. Bartolo, Basilio, and Marcellina are on the Count's side, while Figaro, Susanna, and (emotionally at least) Cherubino are on the Countess's. The roles of Antonio, Barbarina and Don Curzio are somewhat neutral. All these charaters are tied to each other through complicated relationships. No one figure is singled out, as in an *opera seria*. All the main characters are granted several opportunities to shine as soloists, with arias and cavatinas. Even Barbarina, played by the 12-year-old Anna Gottlieb, who was later to sing Pamina (→*The Magic Flute*), has a little song to sing. But the inner nature of the characters unfolds in duets, trios, quartets, and so on. Mozart attained an unprecedented density in the ensemble. The enormous finales in the second and fourth acts consist of a chain of ensembles increasing in number (the incomparable second finale extends without a break and without any intervening recitative for more than 940 bars!). A wealth of musical ideas is spread out before us. With *Figaro* Mozart was beating the Italians in Vienna at their own game. The result was a musical "all-round" comedy, with which no contemporary *opera buffa* can compare. It represents a high point in the history of music, and, with →*The Mastersingers of Nuremberg* (Wagner), →*Falstaff* (Verdi), and →*Der Rosenkavalier* (R. Strauss), forms an unsurpassed group of works.

The Marriage of Figaro, set design by Gustav Wunderwald for the production by Georg Hartmann at the opening of the Deutsche Opernhaus in Berlin-Charlottenburg on 16 November 1912 (TWS).
Is the comic opera *Figaro* a drama about marriage? It seems as though the emotional distance between the Count and Countess can be bridged only for a touching moment at the end of the story.

The eroticism of a world in decline

In the operas composed by Mozart to texts by Lorenzo da Ponte (→*The Marriage of Figaro*, →*Don Giovanni*, →*Così fan tutte*), an aura of eroticism is everywhere. These masterpieces preserve the spirit of a world that gradually disappeared after the French Revolution. The decadent, often dissolute lifestyle of the aristocrats of the *ancien régime* is fully depicted here. Da Ponte and Mozart set a carousel spinning, well populated with the typical individuals of a slowly declining society.

Eroticism: a party game

The artistically constructed palaces and parks of the Rococo age are full of symbols of love. The forms of *rocaille* (shell-like decoration) serve as inexhaustible variants of a symbol with which all sorts of associations can be made. In the paintings, frescoes, and statuary

innumerable putti laugh and play. Courtly love and eroticism were inseparable, and love affairs were part of the world of the upper classes. The human body, as both the visual arts and literature testify, was generally regarded as the plaything of amorous pleasures. The reasons for this are to be found in the exalted life of the courtly residences, and also in the social position of their female inhabitants. Women who did not belong to the lowest level of society were mostly brought up in convents and married off by their families, sometimes while still in adolescence. Frequently they did not even know their future husbands, so there was no question whatsoever of love. At a young age they became the consorts of counts, barons, marquises, high officials or army officers. According to the conventions relating to their social position they did not bring up their own children, and were not even allowed to breast-feed them. A self-determined love affair could take place only within social life, and here a sort of body language was employed. All women and men spoke the obvious and yet secret "language of sensuality." Generations of the higher levels of society of the *ancien régime* paid homage in this way to eroticism. A strange, blissful dance of death, to which the guillotine put a sudden end.

Rococo eroticism and bourgeois love

Mozart lived at the time in which Casanova and da Ponte (who were good friends) carried on their love affairs and immortalized them in their detailed and piquant memoirs. But if Diderot's erotic novel *Les bijous indiscrets* (*The Indiscreet Jewels*) and the sexual deviations of the Marquis de Sade caused a considerable stir, so too did a real love story, a novel about bourgeois love and faithfulness, Goethe's *Die Leiden des jungen Werther* (*The Sorrows of Young Werther*), which was responsible for a wave of suicides during the 1780s. Mozart himself composed operas not only about courtly eroticism (→*The Marriage of Figaro*), a dissolute lack of conscience (→*Don Giovanni*), and partner-swapping (→*Così fan tutte*), but also about the faithfulness of lovers (→*The Abduction from the Seraglio*). In his last opera, →*The Magic Flute*, he glorifies monogamy (bourgeois marriage). "Mann und Weib und Weib und Mann reichen an die Gottheit an" ("Man and woman and woman and man attain divinity"), proclaim Pamina and Papageno. They are singing a hymn to marriage. To the amorous world of courtly society, such "virtuous" behavior, based on fidelity, was foreign. But the *Singspiel*, the operatic genre of *The Magic Flute*, appealed to the bourgeois audience, which had different moral ideals. This explains why the bourgeois nineteenth century (starting with Beethoven, who found da Ponte's texts too frivolous) had no use for these works, and why their true rediscovery – particularly in the case of *Così fan tutte* – could take place only in the age of Sigmund Freud and Richard Strauss.

Don Giovanni, production photograph with Irene Theorin as Donna Anna, production Andreas Homoki, conductor Marco Guidarini, sets Hartmut Meyer, costumes Mechthild Seipel, Det Kongelige Teater, Kopenhagen 1996.
It is rarely that Donna Anna emerges from her bedroom in such a desperate state at the beginning of Don Giovanni. Was she injured "only" in her honor by the intruding unknown knight, or was she unable to resist the magical attraction of Don Giovanni? Has she been raped, or did she submit to his advances? Mozart was unmerciful to his operatic hero. The god Eros rules his subjects.

30. Figaro's Aria

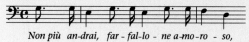

Non più an-drai, far - fal-lo - ne a-mo-ro - so,

Così fan tutte, production photograph with Catherine Naglestad as Fiordiligi, production Klaus Zehelein and Gordon McKechnie, sets Roland Aeschlimann, costumes Dorothee Urmacher, Württembergisches Staatstheater, Stuttgart 1999.
Mozart's most enigmatic and sophisticated opera, *Così fan tutte*, is based on an erotic game. The initial situation, the attempt to put the fidelity of women to the test, is transformed in the course of the story into an erotic adventure on the part of all the protagonists. Does each woman really not realize that her new suitor is her sister's former lover? Game and reality are mingled together in enchanting musical harmony.

Far left
The Marriage of Figaro, production photograph with Maria Ewing (Cherubino) and Margaret Price (the Countess), production Jean-Pierre Ponnelle, Oper Köln 1975.
Cherubino is a "farfallone amoroso," an "amorous butterfly," who flits from woman to woman, as Figaro aptly characterizes him in his famous C major aria at the end of Act I (no. 9). M 30 He appears as a figure representing unrestrained adolescent behavior in the portrayal by Maria Ewing, an outstanding hit by the congenial Mozart director Jean-Pierre Ponnelle.

Left
La petite loge, engraving (detail) by Jean-Michel Moreau le Jeune, Paris 1777/89 (TWS).
During an 18th-century opera performance, another, parallel love duet – or trio – was often taking place in the spectators' box ...
These illustrations were published for the first time in 1777 and are by Jean-Michel Moreau le Jeune (1741–1814), the engraver of the "Cabinet du Roi" at the court of Louis XVI.

Don Giovanni

Il dissoluto punito ossia Il Don Giovanni

Dramma giocoso in two acts – K.527

Libretto: Lorenzo da Ponte.

Première: 29 October 1787, Prague (National Theater).

Characters: Don Giovanni, a young and extremely licentious nobleman (Bar), Commendatore (B), Donna Anna, a noble lady, his daughter (S), Don Ottavio, betrothed to Donna Anna (T), Donna Elvira, a noble lady from Burgos, abandoned by Don Giovanni (S), Leporello, Don Giovanni's servant (B), Zerlina, a peasant girl (S), Masetto, her lover (B); peasants, servants (chorus); musicians.

Setting: Spain, mid-17th century.

Synopsis
Act I

Leporello is yet again waiting for his master, and complains of the troubles of a servant's life. Don Giovanni has crept into the Commendatore's house in order to seduce his daughter. But Donna Anna will not let him have his way with her, and calls for help. Her father challenges the intruder to a duel and is killed by Don Giovanni. The murderer escapes unrecognized. Don Ottavio, Anna's betrothed, arrives too late to help. Donna Anna demands that he avenge her father's murder. Leporello is beginning to find his position too dangerous. He threatens to give his master his notice. Elvira, who has been abandoned by Don Giovanni, is searching for her faithless lover. When she finally confronts him, he flees from her, leaving his servant to deal with her. Leporello shocks the unhappy woman by recounting all his master's successful seductions. The peasant couple Zerlina and Masetto are celebrating their wedding. Don Giovanni is attracted to the bride and invites the wedding party

Don Giovanni, set design by Ludwig Sievert, production Rudolf Hartmann, conductor Clemens Krauss, Bayerische Staatsoper, Munich 1941/42 (TWS).

In terms of the musical world of *Don Giovanni*, it is characteristic that at both the beginning and end of the piece we hear a trio of deep male voices (Don Giovanni, Commendatore, Leporello). These scenes also show dramatic parallels: during the first the Commendatore meets his death, while Don Giovanni perishes in the second. These events are accompanied by the menacing sound of trombones. In the graveyard scene (beginning of Act II), in which Don Giovanni invites the statue to dinner, we also hear trombones, which had been used since the Renaissance to portray celestial (or infernal) powers. The deep, harsh tones suggest a gloomy, hellish mood.

to a feast at his château. While Don Giovanni is wooing Zerlina, Donna Elvira intervenes. Donna Anna and Don Ottavio are seeking an ally and beg their social equal Don Giovanni for help in the search for the Commendatore's murderer. Elvira passionately warns them against Don Giovanni, but he accuses her of hysteria. Only now does Donna Anna recognize Don Giovanni as the unknown intruder who killed her father. She tells her betrothed of her nocturnal experience and demands that he takes revenge upon Don Giovanni. Don Ottavio swears to do so. The wedding guests have come to attend Don Giovanni's festivities. But uninvited guests also appear: Donna Elvira, Donna Anna and Don Ottavio, wearing masks. Don Giovanni sings in praise of freedom. All the guests dance in their own fashion, and the orchestra plays for them. During the dancing, Don Giovanni attempts to seduce Zerlina. Then the masked figures show their true faces and expose Don Giovanni as a murderer. Don Giovanni flees.

Act II

Leporello gives Don Giovanni his notice. His master calms him down with money and kind words. For the sake of a new adventure, master and servant exchange clothing. Don Giovanni has taken a fancy to Donna Elvira's maid, and so tells Leporello to approach Elvira on his behalf. Leporello deceives the poor woman, who forgives the presumed Don Giovanni. The latter drives them away from the scene in order to sing a serenade to the maid. Masetto has armed a band of men and is searching for Don Giovanni. They take Don Giovanni to be Leporello, and he is thus able to escape. Zerlina, rejected by Masetto, pursues her bridegroom and wins his renewed trust. Leporello cannot get rid of Donna Elvira, and is in danger as he is wearing Don Giovanni's clothes. His pursuers are tracking him down. He discards his master's clothing and saves his skin by flight. Don Giovanni and Leporello meet again in the churchyard. Here the statue of the dead Commendatore opens its mouth to defend the peace of the sacred site. Don Giovanni invites the stone statue to dine with him, and the statue accepts. Donna Anna visits her father's tomb. Don Ottavio urges her to marry him. Donna Anna insists that he wait. Don Giovanni's table is laid for the feast. Donna Elvira demands sympathy and repentance from Don Giovanni. Don Giovanni remains unmoved. The stone guest announces his arrival. Elvira flees in horror. The dead Commendatore demands that his fellow nobleman should mend his sinful ways. Don Giovanni's answer is a ninefold refusal. The earth swallows him up. Those who are left behind are virtuous men, lonely women, and a servant without a master. They all approve the just sentence. Leporello must seek a new master, Ottavio urges Donna Anna to marry him, Zerlina and Masetto will be reconciled, and Elvira is to retire to a convent.

S. N

Don Giovanni, production photograph with Thomas Hampson as Don Giovanni, production Franco Zeffirelli, Metropolitan Opera, New York 1990.
How old is Don Giovanni? Although da Ponte refers to him as a young nobleman (the first Don Giovanni, Luigi Bassi, was 21 years old), Don Giovanni can be portrayed equally convincingly by younger and older singers. His eagerness for battle and sexual powers suggest a 20-year-old, while his experience with women makes him appear older. Mozart's music, in any case, makes Don Giovanni appear ageless.

Below
Don Giovanni, production photograph with Johannes Mannov as Don Giovanni, production Andreas Homoki, sets Hartmut Meyer, costumes Mechthild Seipel, conductor Marco Guidarini, Det Kongelige Teater, Copenhagen 1996.
The end of Act I. A strange scene: all except Leporello are in opposition to the hero, and yet he remains invincible; he escapes unscathed even from this situation.

Don Giovanni, production photograph with Ruggero Raimondi as Don Giovanni, production Luc Bondy, sets Erich Wonder, costumes Susanne Raschig, conductor Claudio Abbado, Vienna Festival 1990. The opera begins like a crime thriller: a trespass and murder in the open streets. Although the murderer is being sought throughout the whole story, it is less about sin and punishment than about Don Giovanni's heyday and downfall. The authority of this Mozartian hero is so strong that singers, directors, and aesthetes are constantly posing the question as to whether Don Giovanni is actually of this world. A demonic power is mingled with cunning, rogue-like behavior in Ruggiero Raimondi's interpretation of the character of Don Giovanni.

Don Giovanni: a case of plagiarism?

In 1787, da Ponte simply stole the text of an opera on the subject of Don Juan by Giuseppe Gazzaniga, *Don Giovanni Tenorio ossia Il convitato di pietra* (*Don Giovanni Tenorio, or The Stone Guest*), first performed in Venice in February of that year, and adapted it with a brilliant instinct for dramatic effect. (There had in fact been several adaptations of the same material in recent years, particularly in Venice.) The author of the stolen text, Giovanni Bertati, was not particularly bothered by the theft; indeed, he himself had taken the material from other sources, as was quite normal in the operatic world of the eighteenth century. Gazzaniga's opera was rediscovered in the 1980s, performed at several festivals, and recorded. It is an interesting dramatic mixture, very characteristic of operatic practice at that time, consisting of a prelude and then the Don Juan opera itself. The prelude is a "capriccio drammatico," an episode that takes place practically behind the scenes. An opera troupe is planning to impress a German audience with a novelty, the one-act opera *Don Giovanni Tenorio*. The same characters appear in the opera as in da Ponte's version: Don Giovanni, the Commendatore, Donna Anna, Donna Elvira, the peasant girl (here called Maturina), her betrothed (Biagio), and Leporello (Pasquariello). The mood is more cheerful than in

Mozart's opera: at the dinner there is not only eating and music, but a toast to the city of Venice and its beautiful women. M 31 Here too Don Giovanni goes to hell (portrayed in a rather witty and parodistic rather than terrifying manner). The finale sung by the characters left behind is a humorous, naive song. M 32

Mozart and Prague

The people of Prague are rightly proud of the understanding and enthusiasm with which their ancestors received Mozart's *The Marriage of Figaro*. The result was that the first performance of *Don Giovanni* took place in Prague. Among the members of the art-loving Prague nobility and bourgeoisie were Mozart's friends, Count Thun, František Xaver Dušek (the noted piano teacher and composer), and his wife Josefa (the noted singer). The Italian Pasquale Bondini, the impresario and lessee of the Prague National Theater, also played an important role in Mozart's career in Prague. It was from him that Mozart received the commission for *Don Giovanni*, which he composed partly in Vienna, partly at "Bertramka," the house of the Dušek couple.

Mozart's two visits to Prague in 1787 and the first performance of *Don Giovanni* form an important chapter of his biography. Eduard Mörike's famous

novella of 1855 recounts with poetic imagination the story of his second journey in autumn 1787 and the triumphal first performance. One of the guests at the Prague première was probably the contemporary Don Juan, Giacomo Casanova. He was a close friend of Mozart's librettist, Lorenzo da Ponte, and is believed to have composed a few verses for the libretto.

The Viennese "version"

Today there are more and more references to an independent Viennese "version" of *Don Giovanni*. In fact, as the talents of the Viennese singer who played Don Ottavio were more modest than those of the Prague tenor, and he was very nervous about the plentiful coloraturas of the aria in B major (no. 8, "Il mio tesoro," "My treasure," Act II), Mozart wrote a new aria for him (no. 10b, "Dalla sua pace," "On her happiness," G major, Act I). Today, both arias are usually performed. M 33, M 34

With Aloysia Lange as Donna Anna, Catarina Cavalieri as Donna Elvira, and Luisa Laschi-Mombelli as Zerlina, Vienna had a star cast. To increase the comic situations and flatter Viennese taste, Mozart composed an additional duet (in Act II), in which Zerlina takes Leporello captive, ties him to a chair and threatens him with a knife. Finally Leporello succeeds in escaping through the window, with the chair still attached to his backside. This duet is usually omitted in performances of *Don Giovanni*. All the other Viennese alterations are trifling. There is only one *Don Giovanni*.

31. Gazzaniga, *Don Giovanni Tenorio*, Drinking Song

Fac - cio un brin - di - si di gu - sto a Ve - ne - zia sin - go - lar.

32. Gazzaniga, *Don Giovanni Tenorio*, Finale

Più non fac - cia - si pa - ro - la del ter - ri - bi - le suc - ces - so;

33. Don Ottavio's Aria in B Major (for Prague)

Il mio te - so - ro in - tan - to

34. Don Ottavio's Aria in G Major (for Vienna)

Dal - la sua pa - ce la mia di - pen - de;

Don Giovanni, production photograph from Act I with (from left to right) Lea Nordin (Donna Elvira), Johan Reuter (Masetto), Irene Theorin (Donna Anna), Michael Kristensen (Ottavio), Hanne Fischer (Zerlina), production Andreas Homoki, sets Hartmut Meyer, conductor Marco Guidarini, Det Kongelige Teater, Copenhagen 1996/97. The protagonists except for Don Giovanni and Leporello. All revolve around Don Giovanni, as the planets revolve around the sun. Their whole drama can be described as a "Don Giovanni complex." Their future destinies are overshadowed by their encounter with the eponymous hero.

The title role

If Don Giovanni had been the hero of a Romantic opera or belonged unambiguously to an eighteenth-century operatic genre (*Singspiel, opera seria, opera buffa*), he would have revealed more about himself. In a *dramma giocoso* (the title permits both comic and serious associations), he is enigmatic, revealing nothing about himself. He has no aria in the traditional sense, only two character numbers: the so-called "Champagne Aria," which is more of a song than an aria (no. 11, "Fin ch'han dal vino calda la testa," "So that the wine may go to their heads," Act I) *M 35* and a serenade which Don Giovanni, disguised as Leporello, sings to Donna Elvira's maid (no. 3, Canzonetta, Act II). *M 36*

A portrait of Don Giovanni is given in Leporello's "Catalogue Aria" (no. 4, Act I). *M 37* In this aria, Leporello reveals to Donna Elvira, with a mixture of pride and envy, cheekily and mercilessly, all the erotic genius of his master. Don Giovanni is a fickle, chameleon-like being, who knows how to adapt himself to all sorts of situations and all sorts of women. A Casanova then, although, in contrast to his historical model, he is devoid of any moral sense. The list of his victims is impressive: 640 in Italy, 231 in Germany, 100 in France, 91 in Turkey, and in Spain, so far, 1003 (a total of 2,065!). Leporello also provides some insight into the social strata. His master is totally democratic where love is concerned, and his range includes the peasant girl and the duchess, the young and the old. We do not learn Don Giovanni's age; he is no longer young, but he still possesses powers of attraction and an almost superhuman energy.

Don Giovanni, production photograph with Nicolai Ghiaurov as Don Giovanni, Teatro alla Scala, Milan 1962/63.
Love is mocked in this opera by the exaggerated eroticism of Don Giovanni. It is a bitter story, for all those who remain on stage after the spectacular death of Don Giovanni will carry a spiritual burden for the rest of their lives. An almost unsurpassable cast at the Teatro alla Scala 1962/63 season: Leontyne Price, Nicolai Ghiaurov, Elisabeth Schwarzkopf, and Mirella Freni.

Don Giovanni's downfall

Directors and analysts of *Don Giovanni* would like to solve a problem: what happened in Donna Anna's bedroom? Did she – as in the original material on Don Juan by Tirso da Molina – believe her nocturnal guest to be her lover, Don Ottavio, or did she recognize the masked (or at least disguised) man from the beginning as an unknown intruder? Was she raped by Don Giovanni? Or did he, for the first time in his life, fail in his erotic advances? At any rate, he is chased away by Donna Anna, while she calls for help. Giovanni's downfall begins at this point: he mistakenly attempts to woo his forsaken lover, his courtship of Zerlina is twice forestalled, and he even fails to win Elvira's maid. What remains for him but death?

Eroticism rather than love

Love, the theme that unites all Mozart's operas, is somewhat unusually treated in *Don Giovanni*, in that it remains unfulfilled. There is no pair of lovers in the traditional sense, and no "normal" love duet. Donna Anna and her betrothed Don Ottavio sing only one duet, in which they swear revenge (no. 2, "Fuggi, crudele," "Flee, cruel one," Act I). M 38

Zerlina and Masetto have no duet. On the other hand, Zerlina, affected by Don Giovanni's eroticism, has two arias in which she instructs her bridegroom in the erotic arts of the courtly sort. M 39, M 40

The only love duet takes place between Zerlina and Don Giovanni, but the mood of this delightful song, which has been exceptionally popular since the Romantic period (no. 7, "La ci darem la mano," "There we shall take each other's hand," Act I), is quickly destroyed by the "donna abbandonata" (Donna Elvira). M 41

Who, indeed, is sincerely in love in *Don Giovanni*? An unequivocal answer can be given only in the case of Don Ottavio. This gentle, endearing lover, played by a tenor, has inherited the character of Belmonte in →*The Abduction from the Seraglio*. He is no avenging angel; he would still love Donna Anna if Don Giovanni had usurped his lover's duty in the dark bedroom. But Anna thinks only of revenge and of her dead father. Marriage? Perhaps one day, in happier times, is her enigmatic answer. Donna Elvira, on the other hand, is unhappily in love with Don Giovanni, who has forsaken her and humiliated her more than once. Elvira's obstinacy and, to a certain extent, stupidity (that is, her illusion that Don Giovanni will return to her) have an absurd and therefore comic effect (no. 3, "Ah, chi mi dice mai," "Ah, who will tell me," Act I). M 42

35. Don Giovanni's Champagne Aria

Fin ch'han dal vi - no cal - da la te - sta, u - na gran fe - sta fà pre - pa - rar.

36. Don Giovanni's Serenade

Deh vie - ni al - la fi - ne - stra, o mio _____ te - so - ro,

37. Leporello's Catalogue Aria

Ma - da - mi - na, il ca - ta - lo - go è que - sto

38. Vow of Revenge (Donna Anna and Don Ottavio)

Fug - gi, cru - de - le, fug - gi! la - scia che mora anch' - i - o,

39. Zerlina's Aria (Act I)

Bat - ti, bat - ti, o bel Ma - set - to, la tua po - ve - ra Zer - li - na: sta - rò qui come a - gnel - li - na, le tue bot - te ad a - spet - tar.

40. Zerlina's Aria (Act II)

Ved - rai, ca - ri - no, se sei buo - ni - no, che bel ri - me - di - o ti vo - glio dar.

41. Duet of Unfulfilled Love (Don Giovanni and Zerlina)

Là ci da - rem la ma - no, lá mi di - re - te sì;

42. Elvira's Aria (Act I)

Ah chi mi di - ce ma - i, quel bar - ba - ro dov' è,

Don Giovanni, Luigi Bassi, engraving, Prague 1787 (TWS).
Luigi Bassi (1766–1825), sings Don Giovanni's serenade. Bassi, the first Don Giovanni, began his stage career at the age of 13, and was already a famous singer by the time he sang Don Giovanni for the first time at the age of 21. He had a baritone voice with a light tenor coloration in the upper register. Above all, however, he was a fascinating stage personality, who was praised by his contemporaries and who certainly inspired Mozart in his musical conception of the character of Don Giovanni. Beethoven called Bassi, who remained a presence on the operatic stage for 40 years, a "fiery Italian."

Don Giovanni, production photograph with Johannes Mannov as Don Giovanni, production Andreas Homoki, sets Hartmut Meyer, conductor Marco Guidarini, Det Kongelige Teater, Copenhagen 1996/97. Don Giovanni, as so often, on the run.

What dances, food, drink, and music are enjoyed in *Don Giovanni*?

The finale, with the dinner and the terrifying guest, is found in almost all adaptations of the Don Juan story, including the Gazzaniga opera, the immediate model for da Ponte and Mozart. We do not know the whole menu, but the table is richly decked with various dishes, and Don Giovanni satisfies his enormous hunger ("che barbaro appetito," sighs the hungry Leporello enviously) with a pheasant, among other things. The wine served by Leporello to his master is identified: "Marzimino," an Italian variety, which is still highly prized by connoisseurs. Don Giovanni himself calls this wine "eccellente." The festive food and drink needs to be completed by musical entertainment. For this purpose a "Harmonie" or wind band has been engaged – two each of oboes, clarinets, bassoons, and horns, supported by a double-bass, a chamber-music combination that was usual in Mozart's time and particularly popular with Emperor Joseph II (Mozart wrote wonderful music for this ensemble). At the house of a gentleman such as Don Giovanni the latest operatic hits would of course be played. Mozart first quotes a melody from the opera *La cosa rara* (*The Rarity*) by Vicente Martín y Soler, then one from the opera *Fra i due litiganti il terzo gode* (*When Two Argue, the Third is Pleased*) by Giuseppe Sarti, and finally Figaro's aria from the end of Act I of his own *The Marriage of Figaro*: "Non più andrai, farfallone amoroso" ("You'll go no more, amorous butterfly" → M 30). Given the context, this can be taken as a parodistic comment (Giovanni's love affairs will soon come to an end), but on the other hand it is a witty reminder of the success of *Figaro* in Prague. A. B.

Don Giovanni's ball

The ball scene at the end of Act I is an invention by da Ponte and Mozart. In this impressive scene, the various threads of the action are drawn together: Don Giovanni has invited everyone to the ball. The peasant girl Zerlina dances on the same floor as Donna Anna, the daughter of the (dead) Commendatore of Seville. This "democratic" ball has its roots in the practices of Viennese society in the time of Joseph II. The emperor's reforms included the innovation of making the imperial pleasure gardens and even the masked balls accessible to the people. This explains Don Giovanni's greeting, "Viva la libertà!" (not quite without its dangerous side two years before the French Revolution). The "freedom" in question is the freedom of pleasure (in the sensual sense of the word where Don Giovanni is concerned). The various levels of society are differentiated musically. The guests have three bands playing three different dances to choose from. The masked aristocrats (Donna Elvira, Donna Anna, and Don Ottavio) can take their places in the familiar minuet. M 43

For the bourgeois guests, the master of ceremonies recommends a fashionable *contredanse*, or country dance (Don Giovanni himself takes part in this dance with Zerlina: on the imaginary ladder of social status, he takes one step down and she one up). M 44

Finally, the legs of the peasant girls and lads are not idle: the third band is ready with a ponderous, traditional *ländler*. M 45

Mozart's inimitable stylishness consists in the way in which all three dances are played at the same time during the ball scene.

43. Minuet

44. Contredanse

45. Ländler

Don Giovanni, set design by Ludwig Sievert
for the production by Oscar Wälterlin,
conductor Karl Maria Zwissler, Opernhaus,
Frankfurt 1933/34 (TWS).
Don Giovanni and the stone guest. The set
designer followed the literary model in letting
the Commendatore appear on horseback at
Don Giovanni's dinner. The scene is one of
the most breathtaking ever to have been
composed for the operatic stage. Dark
Baroque splendor and Romantic obsession
with the depths of the human soul
characterize this great scene.

Così fan tutte

Così fan tutte ossia La scuola degli amanti

Opera buffa in two acts – K.588

Libretto: Lorenzo da Ponte.

Première: 26 January 1790, Vienna (Burgtheater).

Characters: Fiordiligi, a lady from Ferrara, living in Naples (S), Dorabella, her sister, also living in Naples (S), Guglielmo, an officer, Fiordiligi's lover (B), Ferrando, an officer, Dorabella's lover (T), Despina, the ladies' chambermaid (S), Don Alfonso, an old philosopher (B); soldiers, servants, sailors, wedding guests (chorus).

Setting: Naples, late 18th century.

Synopsis
Act I
Two young, recently betrothed officers, Guglielmo and Ferrando, are proud of their sweethearts and boast about the constancy of their feelings. Their friend Don Alfonso raises objections, and they agree to a wager to test the fidelity of the two women. The experiment begins. Ferrando and Guglielmo pretend to Fiordiligi and Dorabella that they must go off to the wars. The sorrows of parting: all suspect that things will never be the same again. Alfonso gains an ally, Despina, the servant of the two women. But he tells her only half the truth: that the two officers have to leave and that new suitors have come to court the ladies. Despina plays along; she wants to teach her mistresses the art of survival. The two abandoned women are visited by their sweethearts in disguise, as unknown new suitors. The two suitors claim to live only for love. The women are confused, irritated and moved. The men sense that they are playing with fire and want to stop the experiment, but Alfonso forces them to continue with it.

Act II
Ferrando and Guglielmo are each trying to win the love of the other's bride. Dorabella accepts Guglielmo. Ferrando is in despair, Guglielmo in triumph. Alfonso intervenes to prevent the experiment from breaking down prematurely as a result of Ferrando's disillusionment. Fiordiligi still loves her original betrothed, but is also drawn by her new suitor. She wants to follow Guglielmo into the field of battle, to seek death there. Her new suitor threatens to take his own life. Thus the desperate Ferrando conquers the heart of the desperate Fiordiligi, and Guglielmo's triumph crumbles. Alfonso demands that the marriage of the two new couples should take place. Despina plays notary. But all is revealed: the new husbands are the old sweethearts, and yet not the same. Alfonso has made an error. In the end there is not only disillusionment, but all have learned from experience and must live with what has happened to them.

S. N.

Così fan tutte, photograph from the production by Klaus Zekelein and Gordon McKechnie, costumes Dorothee Urmacher, Württembergisches Staatstheater, Stuttgart 1999.
The wager results in a game that must be played to the end by all taking part. Those who suffer most are Fiordiligi and Ferrando. "And you are wretched too, as wretched as I" – the dawning of a romantic association (from Heinrich Heine's *Buch der Lieder* – (*Book of Songs*)).

Only women

On the theater bill for the first performance is the German translation of the Italian title: *So machen sie's oder Die Schule der Liebhaber* (*Thus They Do It, or The School for Lovers*). The subtitle was an allusion to Salieri's successful piece *La scuola de' gelosi* (*The School for the Jealous*, Venice, 1778). The first German translation of the complete text referred to the original meaning of *Così fan tutte*: *Eine macht's wie die andere* (*One [woman] does it like another*). The Italian title refers exclusively to women. *Così fan tutte* is the most frequently adapted and rewritten of Mozart's operas. More than 30 German versions are recorded. Some titles show that posterity was at a loss over this

piece: *So machen's alle oder Die Mädchen sind von Flandern* (*Thus Do They All, or The Girls are from Flanders*), *Weibertreue* (*Women's Fidelity*), *Mädchentreue* (*Girls' Fidelity*), *Mädchenrache* (*Girls' Revenge*), *Die zwey Tanten aus Mailand oder Die Verkleidungen* (*The Two Aunts from Milan, or The Disguises*), *Die Wette* (*The Wager*), to give but a few examples. The title had already been anticipated in → *The Marriage of Figaro* (Act I), when the Count finds Cherubino hidden in Susanna's room: "Così fan tutte le belle, non c'è alcuna novità" ("That's what all the beautiful girls do, there's nothing new in that"). Così – but how? That is the question in Mozart's most enigmatic opera. *M 46*   M. D.

Così fan tutte, photograph from the production by Luc Bondy, sets Karl-Ernst Herrmann, costumes Jorge Jara, conductor Sir John Pritchard, guest performance by the Opéra National Bruxelles at the Vienna Festival 1986.
Così fan tutte is a chamber piece with six characters and an almost incomprehensible story. A psychodrama in the modern sense: how two men and two women react to an artificially created situation. No trace is found of the theme of swapping lovers in any of the abundant literary models for the libretto (from Ovid to Ariosto). This idea seems to have come from da Ponte. In *Così fan tutte* the changing of partners has the astonishing result that the couples end up in the right grouping: only now does the *primo uomo*, the tenor (Ferrando), pair up with the *prima donna* (Fiordiligi), who was originally the partner of the *primo buffo* or *secondo uomo* (Guglielmo).

Così fan tutte, production photograph with (from left to right) Catherine Naglestad (Fiordiligi) and Claudia Mahnke (Dorabella), production Klaus Zehelein and Gordon McKechnie, sets Roland Aeschlimann, costumes Dorothee Urmacher, Württembergisches Staatstheater, Stuttgart 1999.
The most tragic question in *Così fan tutte* is the question of identity. Can human beings stay true to themselves, or are they helpless, at the mercy of fate and changing circumstances? Will the ability to adapt to a new situation affect their personalities so much that they will not even recognize themselves in the mirror?

46. The Motto

Co - sí fan tut - te!

The search for origins

Strangely, little is known of this opera's beginnings. The first series of performances was broken off after five nights because of the death of Joseph II. After the period of mourning, the opera was performed five more times. Then it disappeared from the Burgtheater's repertory. The opera-mad Count Zinzendorf noted in his journal that Mozart's music was "charmante" and the subject "assez amusant," while the famous German actor Friedrich Ludwig Schröder commented in 1791: "So machen's alle, a Singspiel composed by Mozart, is a wretched thing that belittles all women, cannot possibly please the female spectators and therefore will never succeed." The opinions of an aristocrat and a citizen; Schröder's verdict remained in force for more than a century.

It is constantly being asserted that Joseph II personally recommended the plot of Così fan tutte, with an allusion to a true story current in Vienna at the time, but this is apparently no more than an anecdote. The only evidence of a reference to reality is that the first performers of the roles of Dorabella and Fiordiligi were really sisters and really came from Ferrara. Adriana Gabrieli del Bene – her stage name was "La Ferrarese" – sang the role of Fiordiligi. She was at the time da Ponte's mistress (perhaps it was not by chance that the writer portrayed her in the libretto as chaster than her sister). "Her voice was heavenly, her manner of singing quite new and exceptionally appealing. She did not have a particularly good figure and was not a brilliant actress, but with her very beautiful eyes and her pretty mouth she was unspeakably pleasing in almost all operas," da Ponte rapturously reported in the memoirs he wrote in old age. Mozart created the character of Fiordiligi accordingly; she is stronger, more sturdy than her sister Dorabella, not so lively and supple: "Come scoglio immoto resta" ("As the rock remains firm"), she sings in her first aria (no. 15), which contains melodic

Così fan tutte, production photograph with Cecilia Bartoli as Despina, production Roberto de Simone, costumes Odette Nicoletti, conductor Riccardo Muti, Wiener Staatsoper 1994.
The protagonists of *Così fan tutte* are mainly persons of bourgeois origins (Don Alfonso is perhaps the only aristocrat). The social ranking which was so important in →*The Marriage of Figaro* and →*Don Giovanni* is unimportant here. Except for the chambermaid Despina, all the characters are of equal birth. But even Despina is more of a friend to the ladies than their servant. She is extremely well informed in matters of love, and could in this respect be a tutor to her mistresses.

47. Fiordiligi's Aria (Act I)

Co - me sco - glio   im - mo - to re - sta   con - tra i ven - ti,   e   la tem - pesta, e la tem - pe   sta

leaps that are almost impossible to master. Was the voice of "La Ferrarese" of this nature, or was Mozart maliciously teasing his librettist's mistress? Perhaps he took a fancy to her too … At any rate the aria is a great challenge for any singer. M 47

Così fan tutte, production photograph with Anneliese Rothenberger (Fiordiligi) and Rosalind Elias (Dorabella), production Jean-Pierre Ponnelle, Salzburg Festival 1969.
"Nothing would be gained by an updating, transferring the action to the 20th century," said Jean-Pierre Ponnelle with reference to his Salzburg production of 1969. "The girls of Ferrara were known for their beauty and their easy-going lifestyle. They were considered emancipated …"

The musical miracle

In spite of the parody and irony of da Ponte's masterly libretto, Mozart takes his characters' emotions seriously. *Così fan tutte* is one of tragic beauty. It is difficult to find words for it. Rarely does it give a sense of comedy; the music is transparent, harmonious, perfectly proportioned. Everything has the bittersweet taste of the "last hour," indeed of farewell. *Così fan tutte* contains Mozart's most beautiful scenes of farewell, including the *terzettino* (no. 10) in the unusual key of E major, sung as the women and the falsely sympathetic Don Alfonso wave their adieu to the ships which are supposed to be bearing away their lovers. The muted violins and violas, with the soft accompaniment of bass pizzicatos and the floating sounds of wind instruments, convey a feeling of gentle mourning and melancholy. The wedding hymn in the form of a canon in Act II, with its elegiac melody, lends the situation an air of illusion, as though the moment of the mock-marriage is one of perfect happiness – at least for the two women. *M 48*

48. Wedding Canon

E nel ____ tuo, _ nel mio _ bic - chie - re

49. Homage to Dr. Mesmer (Despina as Doctor)

Que - sto è quel pez - zo di ca - la - mi - ta pie - tra Mes - me - ri - ca,

Così fan tutte, production photograph with (from left to right) Barbara Frittoli (Fiordiligi), Angelika Kirchschlager (Dorabella), Bo Skovhus (Guglielmo), Paul Groves (Ferrando), Monica Bacelli (Despina), and Alessandro Corbelli (Don Alfonso), production Roberto de Simone, sets Mauro Carosi, costumes Odette Nicoletti, conductor Riccardo Muti, Vienna Festival 1997.
Despina's disguises – first as a doctor, later as a notary – follow the tradition of *opera buffa*. With the magnetic stone that Despina uses as a healing remedy in the first of the opera's two finales, Mozart is alluding to his former friend and patron, Dr. Mesmer (→*Bastien and Bastienne*). *M 49*

A labyrinth of emotions

The unique quality of *Così fan tutte* among Mozart's operas is found in the "symmetry" of the libretto, in which the couples and their relationships are arranged as if in a strictly planned French park design. The puppet-like arrangement of the figures even reminds one of the stylized canon of forms of Baroque opera. Symmetry is produced not only through the couples' changing places during the game, but also because Don Alfonso and Despina, while not being a couple, join this symmetrical arrangement. Don Alfonso inclines toward Guglielmo, Despina becomes more intimate with Dorabella, because the personalities of Guglielmo and Dorabella, the new couple, are closer to those of the two disillusioned spirits. This symmetry is overlaid, like an imaginary chessboard, with an interesting asymmetry deriving from the different paths of the two couples. While the relationship between Dorabella and Guglielmo remains within the limits of a playful Rococo-style flirtation, Ferrando and Fiordiligi become entangled in a deeply emotional love affair. A comparison of Guglielmo's first aria (no. 15, "Non siate ritrosi," "Do

not be bashful," or the alternative no. 15a, "Rivolgete a lui lo sguardo," "Turn on him the glance") with that of Ferrando (no. 17 "Un' aura amorosa," "An amorous breeze") clearly brings out the difference. Guglielmo's boastfulness and Ferrando's confession of love are revelations of two contrasting personalities. M 50, M 51, M 52

The two seduction duets are also very different. The sensual Dorabella weakens in an erotic-pastoral duet (no. 23, "Il core vi dono, bell' idolo mio," "I give you my heart, my lovely idol," Act II), while the love duet between Fiordiligi and Ferrando betrays a shattering experience of love (no. 29, "Fra gli amplessi in pochi istanti," "Soon in the embrace," Act II). M 53, M 54

Models: Orlando and Trofonio

The immediate source for the libretto is considered to be the Renaissance epic *Orlando furioso* (*Roland Deranged*) by Ludovico Ariosto (1474–1533). In Canto xxviii we read of two friends who hear of the infidelity of their wives and set off into the world to pay them back in their own coin. The strange "study trip" ends

Così fan tutte, photograph of the production by Klaus Zehelein and Gordon McKechnie, sets Roland Aeschlimann, costumes Dorothee Urmacher, Württembergisches Staatstheater, Stuttgart 1999.
Act II, the wedding scene. The stage arrangement is at the same time symmetrical and asymmetrical. In the center stands Don Alfonso in a triumphant attitude with the marriage contract in his hand (as proof of female inconstancy), while Despina, disguised as a notary, sits at the table. The two couples appear as mirror images of each other: left, Fiordiligi and Ferrando, right Guglielmo and Dorabella; to them the game meant an erotic and amorous adventure.

Così fan tutte, production photograph with Barbara Frittoli (Fiordiligi) and Vera Kasarova (Dorabella), production Roberto de Simone, sets Mauro Carosi, costumes Odette Nicoletti, Vienna Festival 1994.
Are the two sisters, Fiordiligi and Dorabella, interchangeable? Mozart's answer is an unequivocal no. The girls experience a great psychological development.

unexpectedly: other women are not chaste either – they are all the same! The same names are also found in this epic: Fiordiligi, Doralice (!), Fiordespina (!), Guglielmo and Don Alfonso. Even the name "Orlando" is found in an aria for Guglielmo (which was not heard at the first performance), in a parodistic list of other mythological and literary figures (no.15a, "Rivolgete a lui lo sguardo," "Turn on him the glance," Act I). Da Ponte clearly modeled his Fiordiligi on Ariosto's, who dies as a model and symbol of marital fidelity. (In *Così fan tutte*, Fiordiligi declares that she will follow her beloved onto the battlefield.) An initial situation similar to that of *Così fan tutte* is also found in Antonio Salieri's

opera *La grotta di Trofonio* (libretto by Giovanni Battista Casti), which was performed with great success in 1785. Aristone allows his daughters Ofelia and Dori to choose their future husbands. One chooses the unworldly intellectual, the other the life-loving bon vivant. In Aristone's opinion, his daughters should have chosen the other way around, and he advises them to consult the magician Trofonio in order to change their characters (not partners!). After various entanglements, the four young people each revert to the partner of their original choice, which had been dictated by the heart and not by reason. This piece can be considered a direct predecessor of *Così fan tutte*.   *M. D.*

50. Guglielmo's Aria

Non sia - te ri - tro - si, oc - chiet - ti vez - zo - si

51. Guglielmo's Alternative Aria

Ri - vol - ge - te a lui   lo sguar - do   e ve - dre - te   co - me   sta:

52. Ferrando's Aria

Un' au - ra a-mo - ro - sa   del no - stro   te - so - ro

53. Love Duet (Dorabella and Guglielmo)

Il   co - re   vi   do - no,   bell' i - do - lo   mi - o;

54. Love Duet (Fiordiligi and Ferrando)

Fra gli am - ples - si   in po-chi i - stan - ti   giun - ge - rò del fi - do spo - so;

Mozart's late style
Irony is transformed into resignation, and in this way *Così fan tutte* is bound up both with the late instrumental works (the clarinet quintet, the clarinet concerto, the "Prussian" string quartets), and also with the "more serious" late operas, →*La clemenza di Tito* and →*The Magic Flute*. Transparency and simplicity characterize this unique world of sound, which protects the impenetrability of the human soul. A secret that can only be understood – if at all – by hearing and by feeling.

La clemenza di Tito, production photograph,
production and sets Herbert Wernike,
conductor Ulrich Weder, Bremer
Theater 1984.
Vitellia receives yet another unwelcome
message.

Below
La clemenza di Tito, production photograph,
production and sets Herbert Wernike,
conductor Ulrich Weder, Bremer
Theater 1984.
Vitellia has a most difficult part in the drama,
above all because she is the *prima donna*. She
is mistaken several times in the story, makes
several errors, and if the ruler were not so
gracious, she would be destroyed at the end
of the opera. Instead, she reacts to the changing situations in two beautiful and difficult
arias (the second is a rondo with solo basset-
horn accompaniment) and in several ensembles in the *opera seria* style.

La clemenza di Tito

Opera seria in two acts – K.621

Libretto: Caterino Tommaso Mazzolà, after a drama
by Pietro Metastasio.
Première: 6 September 1791, Prague (National
Theater).
Characters: Tito/Titus Flavius Vespasianus, Emperor
of Rome (T), Vitellia, daughter of the deposed
Emperor Vitellius (S), Sesto/Sextus, the friend of
Titus, Vitellia's lover (S), Servilia, sister of Sextus (S),
Annio/Annius, the friend of Sextus, Servilia's lover
(S), Publio/Publius, prefect of the praetorian guard
(B); Romans, senators, patricians, praetorians,
lictors, envoys of the subjugated provinces (chorus).
Setting: Rome, AD 79.

Synopsis
Act I

Vitellia aspires to power via the bed of Emperor Titus.
However, he wants to marry the daughter of the King
of Judea. Vitellia plans revenge. Sextus must kill
Titus. Sextus is Titus's friend, very young and under
the influence of Vitellia. The emperor changes his
mind and sends his foreign bride out of the country.
Vitellia retracts her murderous command. Publius,
the prefect of the praetorian guard, is aware of the
conspiracy and knows the names of those involved.
But Titus refuses to listen. Instead, the emperor
chooses a new bride, Servilia, Sextus's sister. Vitellia
renews the command to murder Titus. But Servilia
confesses to Titus that she loves Annius and does not
seek power. Titus praises her honesty and approves
her marriage to Annius. Finally, Titus decides in favor
of Vitellia. She has achieved her objective and can no
longer cancel the coup. The uprising begins and the
Capitol is in flames. Sextus reports that Titus is dead.

Act II

But Titus is alive. Sextus has murdered someone he
mistook for the emperor. Will Sextus betray Vitellia?
She orders the young man to flee. Sextus is betrayed by
a fellow-conspirator and arrested. If he does not speak,
Vitellia will become empress. She waits. Titus interrogates the boy. Sextus wants to die, and confesses to his
deed. Annius pleads for mercy. The emperor asks for
the reason for his betrayal. But Sextus is silent. The
emperor signs the death sentence, but tears it up
again. Neither of these acts is witnessed by anyone
else. Vitellia believes that Sextus has spoken. She must
now confess voluntarily and speedily. Servilia and
Annius, however, report that Sextus has kept silent
and is to be thrown to the wild beasts, while she is to
be crowned. She must seek mercy for him. If she does
not save him, she will be saved herself. The lion's
stomach or the emperor's bed. The guilt is too much
for her. She confesses and, like Sexus, is allowed to live,
thanks to the emperor's clemency.   S. N.

To rule – but how? Titus on the stage

When the emperor learns of his confidant Sextus's plan to murder him, he first of all attempts (in a great monologue, Scene 8) to assert his rights as a ruler. So he reacts in a traditional manner. But blind emotion is soon replaced by pragmatic considerations. What thoughts led Sextus to wish to kill his friend the emperor? Is the ruler entitled to deliver up his best

friend to the wild beasts in the arena? It is clear that Titus's hidden purpose is to prove Sextus's innocence. It is as though Titus wants what has happened not to have happened. He will try anything to preserve their friendship. This ideal of friendship proves that the ideas of the Enlightenment had again filtered through to Mozart through the medium of Freemasonry. The character of Titus is often criticized because he never takes the initiative. But his passivity inevitably follows from his enlightened state of mind: if passion is replaced by suffering, the meaning of events becomes clear. Titus's noble helplessness results from his position of understanding and acceptance. Thus the eighteenth-century cult of genius had its effect on the type of the enlightened ruler. Titus is one of those great, solitary individuals, who is understood by no one, but whom everyone ought to understand.   *M. D.*

La clemenza di Tito, production photograph, production and sets Herbert Wernike, conductor Ulrich Weder, Bremer Theater 1984.
In *La clémenza di Tito* it is not always easy to tell who belongs to which sex. Sextus (standing in the photograph) is a soprano singing in a breeches part, while Annius is a part for a castrato, thus also in the soprano range. In addition there are the female roles, Vitellia and Servilia (both sopranos). The only deep-voiced singer is Publius. Titus, the tenor, is in the center both vocally and dramatically.

La clemenza di Tito, set design by Giorgio Fuentes, Frankfurt, 1799 (TWS).
The belated child of a dead genre? *Opera seria*, the quintessential Baroque art form, was the last genre to be cultivated throughout Europe before the era of nation-states. At the end of the 18th century *opera seria* moved into the realm of Classicism. It was not by chance that in the first two decades of the 19th century, *La clemenza di Tito* became, after →*The Magic Flute*, the most often performed and most highly appreciated of Mozart's operas. The festive atmosphere of the Baroque courts and the august neo-Classicism of the Napoleonic era were not unrelated to each other. This is evident in large-scale, neo-Classical set designs, such as those of Giorgio Fuentes, who was highly prized by his contemporaries, and his pupil Friedrich Christian Beuther. Goethe praised Beuther's sets for their calm majesty and bright appearance. Classicism was replaced by neo-Classicism.

The libretto – a game of chess?

Pietro Metastasio (whose real name was Trapassi) raised the genre of the libretto to the level of neo-Classical French drama and also furnished it with the latter's rationalism. The fact that the libretto of *La clemenza di Tito* was based on French dramatic models (Racine's *Berenice* and Corneille's *Cinna*) is just as typical of *opera seria* as the fact that the first time it was set to music, it was for a coronation (that of Charles VI in 1734). According to Antonio Caldara, no fewer than 70 composers set this libretto to music, including Hasse, Wagenseil, Gluck, Jommelli, and Traëtta. The series of settings continues to 1816 – that is, to an era which was already dominated by grand opera. *La clemenza di Tito* is an ideal libretto for a coronation, dealing as it does with a Roman emperor who was glorified in his own lifetime as a "benefactor of mankind." But the theme of the parable is not the ruler himself, but the virtue of mercy, as is clear from the title alone.

Musical neo-Classicism

Mozart's genius consisted in bringing to life an out-dated genre, in a style that was coolly elegant and transparent, yet on a grand scale. The compression of the ritornellos of many arias to an introduction of just a few bars did not indicate a relapse into the patterns of the Neapolitan school, for the brevity was to the benefit of the new content. Undoubtedly there are some arias for minor characters that are of less significance from an artistic point of view. But in the arias of Vitellia and Sextus, and also in the ensembles, short melodic phrases are interspersed with smooth, extended cantabile passages. It was therefore a stroke of genius to give the clarinets and basset-horns an outstanding role in the score, above all in the arias of Vitellia and Sextus (nos. 9 and 23). Mozart composed the instrumental part for his friend, the clarinettist Anton Stadler. The chorus (no. 15) has something of the character of a divertimento as a result of the color of the woodwind instruments, dominated by the clarinet. *M 55*

The restrained color and the melancholy of the clarinet family – which reflect the philosophical connections between *La clemenza di Tito* and → *The Magic Flute* – correspond to this "musical neo-Classicism": simplicity, transparency, and restraint. These have their effect on the virtuosity of the vocal writing. *La clemenza di Tito* is not an outdated work. The producer Jean-Pierre Ponnelle referred to Mozart's last opera as forward-looking: "In the score of *La clemenza di Tito* I hear Bellini, and there are even some hints of Verdi. In the choruses, and in the finale of the first act, I cannot help being reminded of the best of Verdi. There are also suggestions of Weber."

La clemenza di Tito, production photograph with Ann Murray (Sextus) and Peter Straka (Titus), production John Dew, sets and costumes Gottfried Pilz, conductor Nikolaus Harnoncourt, Opernhaus, Zürich 1993. Toward the end of the 20th century, important directors increasingly turned to *opera seria*. In John Dew's production Sextus and Titus met in a present-day setting.

Leopold II and his family, painting by Wenzel Werlin, 1773 (Kunsthistorisches Museum, Vienna).
A Habsburg group portrait with a view of Florence: Leopold, still Grand Duke of Tuscany, with his family, under the portrait of his mother, Empress Maria Theresia. Mozart hoped to enjoy under Leopold a continuation of the enlightened policies of Joseph II and perhaps even a position as court composer. But Mozart died three months after the first performance of *La clemenza di Tito*, and three months later Leopold II died in his turn. Thus ended the brief period of the Viennese Enlightenment.

Metastasio and Mozart

Today the courtly Baroque world of Metastasio seems light-years away from Mozart. Yet Mozart was drawn to such texts throughout his life. It was Metastasio who was responsible for the texts of such court pieces as *Il sogno di Scipione* (*The Dream of Scipio*) (1772) and the serenade *Il re pastore* (*The Shepherd King*) (1775), as well as the *azione sacra La Betulia liberata* (*Bethus Liberated*) (1771). Moreover, texts by this king of librettists were indispensable if Mozart wanted to please his singers with concert arias: during his travels in Italy, in Mannheim (Germany), and in Vienna he set to music a total of 20 aria texts by Metastasio. (Mozart had already become familiar with the libretto of *La clemenza di Tito* in 1770 through a version set to music by Hasse.)

Titus and Leopold – rulers with hearts

The choice of text – the libretto was originally written for a coronation – can be seen as appropriate for another reason: the good Roman emperor Titus (AD 79–81) represents the ideal ruler for the age of Joseph II. The emphasis in the adaptation was not solely on the emperor's magnanimity, but also on his renunciation. Titus surrenders hereditary privileges; in choosing a bride he does not follow his heart's inclinations if they are against the interests of the state; and he revokes the sentence of death. In recognizing the priorities of the heart in others, he no longer arrogates to himself the traditional divine attributes of a ruler. This is a decisive step in the direction of the modern ruler who functions as "the first servant of the state." Joseph II and his brother and successor Leopold II represented this type. The libretto of *La clemenza di Tito* was tailor-made for Leopold II. Before his accession to the throne, the Habsburg monarch ruled the Grand Duchy of Tuscany according to Enlightenment ideals. His contemporaries called him "the Solomon of our century" and a "philosopher-ruler." When gallows and instruments of torture were publicly burnt as a result of his new penal code, the nobles of Florence wanted to express their admiration for him with an equestrian statue. But

Leopold refused out of consideration for the common good: the money was used to pay for water mains. This event, which was widely publicized, can be compared with the moment in *La clemenza di Tito* when the emperor determines that the gifts collected in his honor shall be given to the inhabitants of Pompeii, which has been destroyed by a volcanic eruption. And there is another strange parallel between the two rulers: like Titus, Leopold occupied his imperial throne for only two years (1790–92). *M.D.*

55. Titus and His People

(Chor) Ah gra-zie, si ren-da no al som-mo fat- tor,

(Titus) Ah no, sven-tu-ra-to non so-no co-tan-to

The Magic Flute

Die Zauberflöte

Singspiel in two acts – K.620

Libretto: Emanuel Schikaneder.
Première: 30 September 1791, Vienna (Freihaustheater auf der Wieden).
Characters: Sarastro, Priest of the Sun (B), Tamino, a Japanese prince (T), A Speaker (B), Three Priests (B, T and spoken), The Queen of the Night (S), Pamina, her daughter (S), Three Ladies, attendants to the Queen (3S), Three Boys (3S), Papageno, a bird-catcher, employed by the Queen (B), Papagena (S),

The Magic Flute, set design by Leo Pasetti, Munich 1925 (TWS).
The Magic Flute is not only Mozart's most successful operatic composition, but probably the piece most often played in the whole of operatic literature. "The quiet approval" of the première grew, as Mozart himself observed, evening by evening, and thus The Magic Flute finally became an international success. As early as 17 November 1792, a year after the first performance and after Mozart's death, Schikaneder announced the 100th performance, and in October 1795 the 200th performance. This was a miracle in theatrical practice at the time. Goethe, as artistic director in Weimar, had The Magic Flute staged 82 times. He planned to write a sequel to it, but after Mozart's death could no longer find a suitable composer (or at least none who conformed to his taste). The secret of The Magic Flute is that it appeals to all ages and to all levels of society. It is both a fairy tale for children and a universal drama for philosophers.

Monostatos, a Moor, overseer at the Temple (T), Two Armed Men (T, B), Three Slaves (spoken); priests, slaves, retinue of Sarastro (chorus).

Synopsis
Act I

Escaping from a giant serpent, Prince Tamino loses his way, calls for help and faints in exhaustion. Three magical women rescue him and kill the monster. The bird-catcher Papageno boasts to Tamino, who has just regained consciousness, that it was he who killed the serpent. But the three women return, punish the braggart by putting a padlock on his mouth, and reveal themselves to be ladies from the entourage of the Queen of the Night, in whose land the Prince finds himself. The Queen is in distress; her daughter Pamina has been abducted. They give Pamina's portrait to the Prince and the young man falls passionately in love with its subject. The Queen of the Night herself appears and promises Pamina's hand to the Prince if he is able to free the abducted girl from the power of the evil Sarastro. Tamino is prepared to do this. Papageno is to accompany him. To help him in an emergency, Tamino receives a magic flute and Papageno a set of chimes. The padlock is removed from Papageno's mouth and three boys point the way to Sarastro's kingdom. In Sarastro's palace, whose master is away, the overseer Monostatos is trying to force Pamina to let him have his way with her. Meanwhile Papageno has lost contact with Tamino, but by chance finds his way to Pamina alone, and, somewhat involuntarily, saves her from Monostatos. Pamina's joy is great when she hears Papageno's message that Tamino is on his way to save her. In the meantime the Prince has reached the Temple of Wisdom and learns that Sarastro rules here, and therefore cannot be a villain. With his magic flute he calls to Pamina. Papageno's pan-pipes show him the way to his beloved. Pamina and Papageno try to flee, but are intercepted by Monostatos and his slaves. Papageno casts a spell over the guards with the set of chimes: they cannot stop dancing. The escape appears to be succeeding when Sarastro returns from the hunt. He forgives Pamina, punishes the Moor, and has Tamino and Papageno led into the temple to be tested.

Act II

Sarastro declares to his priestly brothers that Tamino and Pamina are destined for each other. This is the reason why he removed Pamina from the influence of her mother. But Tamino must undergo a series of tests before he can be received into the Temple of Wisdom and be worthy of Pamina. Tamino is determined to undergo the tests even at the risk of his own life. Papageno is lured with the promise of a wife, but follows the Prince only with reluctance. The first commandment is absolute silence. The ladies of the Queen of the Night warn the examinees about priestly cunning and mortal danger. But Tamino and Papageno do not allow themselves to be deterred. Monostatos has made his way to the sleeping Pamina. The Queen of the Night is also seeking her daughter and urges Pamina to kill Sarastro and thus win back the sevenfold circle of the sun, the manifestation of greatest power. The Moor steals the dagger given to Pamina by her mother and threatens her with it: love or death. Sarastro rescues Pamina and drives the Moor out of his realm. Pamina confesses to Sarastro her mother's murderous command and pleads for understanding for her. The first test involves obeying the command of silence. Papageno fails. Tamino however remains silent even in the face of Pamina's pleading for a word of love. The girl believes herself to be betrayed by Tamino and is about to take her own life. The three boys take away her dagger and lead her to Tamino. Papageno too wishes to die, since he can no longer hope for the promised reward, a beautiful young wife, but is happy to remain alive when the three boys lead his Papagena to him. Together Pamina and Tamino pass the tests of fire and water. The Queen of the Night and her entourage, led by Monostatos, enter Sarastro's realm, but are destroyed. Pamina and Tamino are united and accepted among the band of the initiated. *S. N.*

Magical instruments

In an opera called *The Magic Flute*, the flute should be the most important instrument. Perhaps it is significant that the first Tamino was a proficient flautist. Speaking of the origin of the magic flute which Tamino receives from the Queen of the Night, Pamina says: "In a magical hour my father cut it from the deepest depths of an oak a thousand years old." The original stage directions tell us that the flute is a symbol of the sun and is gilded. *M 57*

In contrast to Tamino's flute, Papageno's glockenspiel has no symbolic significance. It is a silver toy which can work miracles. The glockenspiel is used three times: first, when Monostatos and the slaves capture Pamina and Papageno, and its magical tones force the guards to sing and dance *M 58;* second, when it accompanies Papageno's song *M 59;* and third, when Papageno conjures up Papagena with its silvery tones. The panpipe is Papageno's own instrument. With its five calling tones and its exotic sound (it is the instrument of Pan, the god of nature, in classical mythology) it expresses Papageno's own nature. *M 56, →M 60*

57. Tamino's Aria with the Magic Flute

Wie stark ist nicht dein Zau-ber-ton, weil, hol - de Flö - te

58. Papageno's Glockenspiel

56. Papageno's Calling Tones

(Panflöte)

The Magic Flute, costume design for Tamino (as a Japanese) by Roland Topor, Essen 1990/91 (TWS).
Schikaneder's description of Tamino as "a Japanese prince" was intended to indicate the hero's distant, fabulous origin. He probably did not have an actual Japanese in mind, but Topor's idea is well founded.

Schikaneder: master of stagecraft

An important part was played in the creation of *The Magic Flute* by the multitalented man of the theater, Emanuel Schikaneder. Mozart had met him in Salzburg, where Schikaneder was making a guest appearance (as Hamlet) with his traveling company. Later they became friends and brother Freemasons in the same lodge. In 1789 Schikaneder became the lessee of the Freihaustheater auf der Wieden (the courtyard of a large building rented out to tenants), where he planned to present decorative pieces with fantastic themes for suburban audiences. It was in this spirit that he wrote the libretto of *The Magic Flute* and directed the production. He reduced the depth of the stage by adding a backcloth behind which he could quickly change the decor while the production was going on. For *The Magic Flute*, he added Baroque theatrical apparatus with a flying mechanism, and presented magic tricks and animals such as monkeys, lions, and snakes. The equipment for the "new mechanical comedy" cost him a fortune: 5000 gulden, about £75,000 by today's values. He himself played Papageno. *M 59, M 60*

The Magic Flute, production photograph showing Mikael Melbye as Papageno with a lion, production Otto Schenk, costumes Yannis Kokkos, conductor Nikolaus Harnoncourt, Wiener Staatsoper 1988.
Otto Schenk's production of *The Magic Flute* was quite in the spirit of the original Viennese production. Papageno is seen here with Sarastro's pet lion.

59. Papageno's Song with the Glockenspiel

Ein   Mädchen o - der   Weib - chen wünscht Pa - pa - ge - no — sich!

60. Papageno's Song with the Panpipe

Der   Vo - gel - fän - ger   bin ich ja, stets lu - stig hei - sa hop - sa - sa!

The exotic as a dramatic-spiritual background

According to the stage directions Tamino is a "Japanese" prince, Pamina lives with Sarastro in a "splendid Egyptian room," and the assembly of priests (Act II) takes place in a palm forest: "18 seats made of leaves, and on each one stands a pyramid and a great black horn set in gold." It was not the first time Mozart made use of Egyptian material. As early as 1773 he had already composed the accompanying music to the drama *Thamos, König in Ägypten* (*Thamos, King of Egypt*) by Tobias Philipp Gebler, which in several respects anticipates the theme of *The Magic Flute*. Egyptian themes were closely bound up with the spiritual world of Freemasonry. A particularly important part was also played by the novel *Séthos* by the Abbé Jean Terasson (1731). *Séthos* can be perceived as the prototype of Sarastro: he is pure, innocent and brave, and rules with 18 initiated priests in a pyramid-shaped temple of wisdom. Here too there is a snake, the symbol of evil, here too trombones sound in the sacred hall, and here, verbatim, is the ancient text of the two armed men, referring to the trials by fire and water: "He who wanders the road, full of troubles …"

The Magic Flute, production photograph with Reinhard Dorn as Papageno with the three boys, production Andreas Homoki, costumes Mechthild Seipel, conductor Georg Fischer, Bühnen der Stadt Köln 1995.
Papageno is given food and wine by the boys. The elevated story of the magic flute is given human characteristics by the figure of Papageno. Papageno is Mozart: the man who loves, enjoys, and plays.

The singers

The casting of the original production reflected a web of personal relationships. Vocally the most difficult role was that taken by Mozart's sister-in-law Josepha Hofer, one of the greatest talents in Schikaneder's company. For over ten years she played the Queen of the Night. The first Tamino was Benedikt Schak, of whom Mozart's father Leopold, a severe critic, wrote: "He sings excellently, has a beautiful voice, a fluent throat, and fine method." Schak was also a good flautist, although it is not recorded whether he actually played the flute himself in *The Magic Flute*. Schak was also considered a house composer to Schikaneder, like Franz Xaver Gerl, the first Sarastro, whose wife Barbara sang Papagena. Gerl was a friend of Mozart's, who wrote for him the famous concert aria with double bass obbligato, "Per questa bella mano" ("For this lovely hand") (K.612). The first Pamina, Anna Gottlieb, had sung Barbarina at the first performance of *The Marriage of Figaro*.

Below
The Magic Flute, photograph from the production by Nikolaus Lehnhoff, sets Susan Pitt, Hessisches Staatstheater, Wiesbaden 1983.

Above
The Magic Flute, photograph from the production by Achim Freyer, Salzburg Festival, 1997/98.
"Man and woman and woman and man attain divinity." This wise saying is sung by Pamina and Papageno, but applies particularly to Tamino and Pamina, who – as the first initiated couple – are, in the cosmos of *The Magic Flute*, able to pass the trials of fire and water and attain the highest state.

The Magic Flute, production photograph with Ai-Lan Zhu as Pamina with the three boys, production Peter Sellars, costumes Dunà Ramicova, Glyndebourne Festival, 1990. It is noteworthy that the motif of suicide, which occurs nowhere else in Mozart's operas with the exception of *Idomeneo*, is found twice in *The Magic Flute*. With Papageno it has a comic effect, but with Pamina there is real danger: she has lost her identity between the realms of Sarastro and her mother. This constellation may be connected with Mozart's experiences in the Freemasons' lodge: you must lose your own ego before you can begin a new life. At the last minute the boys prevent Pamina's suicide attempt.

The Magic Flute, set design by Karl Friedrich Schinkel, Berlin 1816 (TWS).
One of the most famous sets of the 19th century is by Karl Friedrich Schinkel. The triumphal performance on 18 January 1816 at the Opernhaus Unter den Linden in Berlin took place on the occasion of a coronation and peace celebration. A classic example of historicism: grand opera, monumentality and Egyptian-style architecture. At the central point stands the cult image of Osiris with the sunburst and the triangle of the pyramids.

Trials by fire and water

The original stage directions read: "The theater is transformed into two great mountains. In one is a waterfall, which is heard rushing and roaring, while the other spits fire. Each mountain has an entrance through which fire and water can be seen … Two men in black armor lead Tamino inside. Fire burns on their helmets. They read him the transparent writing which appears on a pyramid." M 62

Mozart and Freemasonry

In Mozart's Viennese decade, Freemasonry played an important part, since the Freemasons' ideas were close to the reform policies of Joseph II. The lodges united the best intellectual talents of Vienna: scholars, artists, and enlightened aristocrats formed a private elite. The leading personality of Viennese Freemasonry was Ignaz Born, a noted scientist, who died in the year in which *The Magic Flute* was composed. He could have been the model for Sarastro. Out of the close circle of Mozart's friends and relations, his father Leopold, Joseph Haydn, and Emanuel Schikaneder also belonged to the lodge. Mozart joined it in 1784 and stayed faithful to its principles even after Freemasonry was officially outlawed.

61. Main Theme of the Overture

62. Chorale of the Two Men in Armor

Der, wel-cher wan-dert die - se Stra - ße voll Be-schwer - den

Symbols of Freemasonry in *The Magic Flute*

In *The Magic Flute*, Mozart made use of the principles of Freemasonry and the ideals of Joseph II. One of the greatest miracles of this opera is that the result was not a monumental didactic work, but a true musical drama. The 18 (male) initiates correspond to the lodge brothers, and Sarastro represents the "Master of the Chair." Among the members, there is mutual respect and, in the social sense of the word, equality. The initiates's concern as to whether a prince will be able to endure such severe trials is met by Sarastro with the words: "He is a man; that is more than enough." Tamino begins his career in the nocturnal, starry realm of the Queen of the Night, and ends up as an initiate at Pamina's side in the realm of the sun. He goes from darkness into light, as is prescribed by the initiation ritual of the Freemasons.

Session of the lodge "Zur neugekrönten Hoffnung" ("Newly Crowned Hope"), oil painting, unknown artist (Historisches Museum, Vienna).
The painting depicts a session of the lodge "Zur neugekrönten Hoffnung." The reason for the painting is not clear. The British musicologist H.C. Robbins Landon has identified most of those present, including Mozart, who is seated in the right-hand corner of the picture, chatting with Schikaneder.

The mysterious number three

The number three as a symbol of self-revealing divinity plays an important part in Masonic rites as well as in the fairy-tale world. The overture begins with three powerful chords (the three knocks of the master of the lodge?) and the allegro theme consists of three strokes, repeated. M 61

The "threefold" chord is also heard after the words of Sarastro, when he praises Tamino's three good qualities (virtue, discretion, and beneficence). There are three ladies, three boys, and three magic instruments (flute, glockenspiel, panpipe). Tamino finds three temples at the entrance to Sarastro's realm, and makes three attempts to enter. And, not least, Tamino is put to the test three times.

Female initiates?

Pamina too is subjected to the trials of fire and water. This is all the more remarkable since Masonic lodges consisted exclusively of men. This test of love was more important to Mozart than strict adherence to Masonic convention. Even in the final chorus of the initiates he included female voices. In this interpretation lies all the humanity of *The Magic Flute*, whose new realm includes sisters as well as brothers.

The Magic Flute, set design by Heinrich Leffer and Hugo Baruch (studio), Vienna/ Dresden/ Zürich 1910 (TWS).
It is part of the free and courageous way of thinking of Schikaneder and Mozart that Pamina is also admitted to the trials, but a few derogatory remarks about "women's wiles" are still found in *The Magic Flute.* This set is an Art Nouveau "trial by fire and water."

The Magic Flute, set design by Marc Chagall for the Metropolitan Opera, New York 1965/66.
Set design is an entire artistic field in itself. Working for the stage has held a special attraction for many great artists. One of these is Marc Chagall: a significant part of his work was created for the theater. For Mozart's *The Magic Flute* at the Metropolitan Opera, New York, Chagall painted a vision in lurid colors, a carpet of clouds in yellow, blue, and green as a background, animals with human faces, and the figure of an angel flying and playing music. These characteristic elements of Chagall's painting are at the same time congenial illustrations of Mozart's music.

Right
The Magic Flute, production photograph with
Celina Lindsay as the Queen of the Night,
production Nikolaus Lehnhoff, sets Susan Pitt,
Hessisches Staatstheater, Wiesbaden 1983.

The Magic Flute, costume design for the
Queen of the Night by Pierre-Eugène Lacoste,
Paris 1883 (TWS).
The Queen of the Night, the beautiful
woman with the slenderness of a dancer,
appears with the look of a mythological
goddess.

A family story?

The characters of *The Magic Flute* are genealogically difficult to determine. They appear as in a fairy tale. Once upon a time there was a prince. His name was Tamino and he went out into the world. Papageno does not even know where he was born or who his parents are. We assume that the hostility between the Queen of the Night and Sarastro is based on a family conflict. What was the relationship in the kingdom of the old king (Pamina's father) between the Queen and Sarastro? Nikolaus Harnoncourt presumes that Sarastro lived at the court as a friend of the family. Ingmar Bergman even believes that they are a divorced couple. Is Sarastro perhaps Pamina's father, and the old king merely an invention of "Mother Night," intended to blacken Sarastro in Pamina's eyes? Pamina is the victim of this conflict; she feels that she has been eternally abandoned. Her despairing state of mind leads to an attempted suicide. M 63

Sarastro

The high priest of the initiates is Sarastro, and he is almost always presented as a symbol of humanity. His first aria (in F major, without violins, and with basset-horn) is a kind of priestly prayer. M 64

Further study of Sarastro's personality brings other qualities to light. Originally he was to have returned to his palace from hunting in a triumphal carriage drawn by lions. Also, he is a slave-owner and orders Monostatos to be punished with 77 strokes on the soles of his feet. Yet somewhat later he claims (in his wonderful aria in E major) that "in these hallowed halls" revenge is unknown. M 65

Sarastro has taken possession of Pamina by force. The greatness of Sarastro consists in the fact that he withdraws in favor of his younger rival and takes the lovers under his protection, as a fatherly friend. This is Sarastro's "trial by fire and water." It is thus that he moves in the direction of the pure ideals he proclaims.

The Queen of the Night

At the beginning of the opera the Queen of the Night appears as a suffering mother, whose only daughter has been stolen from her. According to the interpretation of Walter Felsenstein, who initiated a new era in the reception of *The Magic Flute* with his brilliant interpretation at the Komische Oper in Berlin in 1954, this is one of the many tricks she uses to involve Tamino in her struggle for power. M 66 Later in Act II, however, she not only wants to have Sarastro murdered by Pamina, but tries to destroy the whole kingdom of the sun and take over power. M 67
Is the Queen evil by nature, or does she in her desperation become transformed into an avenging angel? These questions are often posed and answered in many different ways by modern directors.

The Magic Flute, photograph from the
production by Robert Wilson, costumes John
Conklin, conductor Armin Jordan, Opéra
National de Paris 1991.
The Queen of the Night and her entourage,
the ladies. The Queen incorporates the
loveless, power-hungry woman. Her
daughter Pamina, on the other hand,
is Mozart's tenderest and purest
female character.

Below
The Magic Flute, production photograph with Amanda Halgrimson (Queen of the Night) and Nina Stemme (Pamina), production Andreas Homoki, sets Hartmut Meyer, conductor Georg Fischer (première Jiri Kout), Oper Köln 1995. The Queen of the Night appears like an avenging angel. She intends to use her daughter Pamina to bring about the murder of Sarastro and so terrorizes her soul.

Above
The Magic Flute, set design with the Queen of the Night by Simon Quaglio, Munich 1818 (TWS).
While Karl Friedrich Schinkel, in the spirit of Goethe, presented *The Magic Flute* as a large-scale neo-Classical work, only two years later Simon Quaglio created a romantic, fairy-tale set, which is well suited to the infernal realm of the Queen of the Night.

63. Pamina in Despair (Aria in G Minor)

Ach, ich fühl's, es ist verschwunden, e - wig hin der Lie-be Glück

64. Sarastro, the Priest (Aria in F Major)

O I - sis und O - si - ris, schen-ket der Weis-heit Geist dem neu-en Paar!

65. Sarastro, the Fatherly Friend (Aria in E Major)

In diesen heil'gen Hal - len kennt man die Ra - che nicht

66. The Queen of the Night as a Suffering Mother (Aria in B Major)

Zum Lei - den bin ich aus-er - ko -ren

67. The Queen of the Night as an Avenging Demon (Aria in D Minor)

Der Höl-le Ra - che kocht in meinem Her-zen

Musorgsky, Modest Petrovich

b. 21 March 1839 in Karevo (in the Pskov administrative district)
d. 28 March 1881 in St. Petersburg

Musorgsky spent his childhood on his noble family's ancestral estate; Russian peasant folklore made a great impression on him at this time. He registered at the Cadet School of Guards in St. Petersburg in 1849, and began a career as a military officer in 1856, but he resigned his commission in 1858 to devote himself to music, although since his family was no longer prosperous he also had to work as a civil servant. Even in his youth, he had been successful as a fine pianist in society salons, and in 1857 he began studying composition with his friend Balakirev, leader of the New Russian School and founder of the group known as the "mighty little heap" or "mighty handful." This group of composers, also called the Russian Five, later included Musorgsky himself, as well as →Borodin, Cui, and →Rimsky-Korsakov. Although he received many invitations, Musorgsky almost never left St. Petersburg, only once going on tour in the Ukraine with the singer Darya Leonova as her piano accompanist in 1879. The première of *Boris Godunov* (1874) was the greatest success of his life; apart from that, his contemporaries viewed his bold musical style with some scepticism. Ignored by the public, he sought refuge in alcohol, and died at the age of 42.

Works: Salambo (*Salammbô*) (1863–66, unfinished), *Zhenit'ba* (*Marriage*) (1868, unfinished), *Boris Godunov* (1874), *Khovanshchina* (*The Khovansky Affair*) (1872–81, unfinished), *Sorochinskaya yarmarka* (*The Fair at Sorochintsi*) (1874–81, unfinished); over 60 songs, choral works with orchestra, orchestral works including *Noch na Lysoy gore* (*A Night on the Bald Mountain*) (1867), piano works including *Kartinki s vïstavki* (*Pictures at an Exhibition*) (1874).

Boris Godunov, Ivan Alexandrovich Melnikov as Boris Godunov.
Ivan Alexandrovich Melnikov (1832–1906) was the creator of the role of Musorgsky's Boris Godunov. He was one of the leading singers of the time in St. Petersburg.

Boris Godunov, photograph from the production by Herbert Wernicke, conductor Claudio Abbado, Salzburg Festival 1994.
Pimen (in historical costume, indicating that religion is outside time) sees himself as a mere chronicler, and does not realize that his account arouses a thirst for power in his young protégé (the usurper Dmitry, here played in modern dress).

Boris Godunov

First version: opera in four parts (seven scenes), 1868–69; second version: opera in a prologue and four acts, 1871–72

Libretto: Modest Musorgsky, after the play of the same name by Alexander Pushkin, and (second version) the *History of the Russian Empire* by Nikolay Karamzin.

Première of second version: 8 February 1874, St. Petersburg (Mariinsky Theater).

Characters: Boris Godunov (Bar), Fyodor and Xenia, his children (Ms and S), Xenia's nurse (Ms), Prince Vasily Ivanovich Shuysky (T), Andrey Shchelkalov, secretary to the Council of Boyars (Bar), Pimen, a chronicler and monk (B), The False Dmitry, a pretender, known as Grigory, a novice and protégé of Pimen (T), Marina Mniszek, daughter of the Sandomierz commander (Ms), Rangoni, a secret Jesuit (B), Missail and Varlaam, runaway monks (B and T), Innkeeper (Ms), A Holy Fool (T), Nikitich, a police officer (B), Mityukha, a peasant (B), Boyar-in-attendance (T), Boyar Khrushchyov (T), Lewicki and Czernikowski, Jesuits (2B); boyars, their children, strel'tsï (militia), guards, police officers, Polish nobles, girls from Sandomierz, itinerant monks, people of Moscow, tramps (chorus), boys (children's chorus).

Setting: Russia and Sandomierz, Poland, 1598–1605.

Synopsis
(Division of acts and scenes from the second, revised version of 1871–72, complemented by the first version of 1868–69)

Prologue
Scene 1: The courtyard of the Novodevichiy Monastery near Moscow. Terror, violence, and famine reign in Russia. The poor people of Moscow are summoned to the monastery, and forced by the police officer, who wields a knout, to sing hymns of supplication. No one knows exactly why or for what until the secretary Shchelkalov tells them: the boyar Boris Godunov has been chosen as the next tsar, but he is unwilling to accept the crown. Pilgrims go to the monastery and beg to be saved from the anarchy now spreading through Russia. They believe a new tsar can help them.
Scene 2: A square in the Kremlin in Moscow. Prince Vasily Shuysky calls for homage to be paid to the new tsar, and the crowd, which has been ordered to come to the Kremlin, acclaim him in song. Boris Godunov, newly crowned, shows himself to the people, bows his knee humbly to God, and invites everyone to the coronation banquet. Now the crowd praise Boris voluntarily and from their hearts.

Act I

Scene 3: Night. A cell in the Chudov Monastery. After an eventful life, the monk Pimen feels called to become a chronicler. He accuses those who hold power of responsibility for all the injustice and suffering in the world. Pimen's pupil, the young novice Grigory, regrets burying himself in the monastic life so young, and asks his mentor about the murder of the Tsarevich Dmitry in Uglich, for Pimen was there at the time. Pimen believes that Boris Godunov murdered Dmitry, who would now have been the same age as Grigory.

Scene 4: A tavern on the border between Russia and Lithuania. The innkeeper is lonely; she longs for love. Three guests arrive: Grigory, who has run away from the monastery, with the two vagabond monks Missail and Varlaam. Grigory plans to escape over the border to Lithuania. The two vagabonds call for wine, and the innkeeper tells Grigory where he can cross the border. A Russian police patrol is making its rounds, and Missail and Varlaam claim to be respectable mendicant monks, saying that Grigory is their companion. The illiterate police officer asks Grigory to read aloud a warrant from the tsar, and from it Grigory realizes that he himself is the wanted man. He changes his own description to the description of Varlaam, but when Varlaam exposes his trick, Grigory escapes by jumping out of the window.

Act II

Scene 1 (1869 version): The tsar's apartments in the Kremlin in Moscow. The tsar's daughter Xenia laments her dead bridegroom. As the future ruler of Russia, Boris's son Fyodor is learning geography. The mighty tsar can do nothing to alleviate his beloved daughter's sorrow, nor has he been able to improve the situation of his people in six years of peaceful rule. His failures trouble him, and weaken his political position. He distrusts the boyars. The powerful Prince Shuysky tests the tsar's strength of will, and finds his ruler weak. The usurper Grigory is a threat to the Russian throne.

Scene 1 (1872 version): The tsar's apartments in the Kremlin in Moscow. The tsar's daughter Xenia laments her dead bridegroom. Her brother and her nurse are unable to comfort her. The tsar cannot alleviate his beloved daughter's sorrow any more than he has been able to improve the situation of his people. He feels guilty about the murder of the Tsarevich Dmitry. His son tells him how the pampered court parrot is tormenting the maidservants. He regards this incident as symbolic, with the parrot standing for popular opinion. Political failures trouble the tsar and weaken his position. He has good reason to distrust the boyars. The powerful Prince Shuysky tests the tsar's strength of will, and finds his ruler weak. The usurper Grigory is a threat to the Russian throne.

Act III

Scene 1: Marina Mniszek's dressing room in Sandomierz Castle. Gold and love do not tempt the ambitious Marina Mniszek; she wants power, and intends to become Tsarina of Russia through an alliance with Grigory, who is claiming to be the Tsarevich Dmitry. The Jesuit Rangoni commands her to enter into such a marriage only if Grigory will promise to impose the Roman Catholic faith on Russia.

Scene 2: Sandomierz Castle, a garden by moonlight, where Marina has a rendezvous with the usurper Grigory. She says she will listen to his declaration of love only when he is tsar, and the enamored Grigory agrees.

Act IV

Scene 1 (1869 version): A square outside St. Basil's Cathedral. Russia is suffering want and misery: the poor assemble outside the cathedral, hoping for alms. News goes around that a ceremony of excommunication of the former monk Grigory is being conducted inside the building. But the starving people believe he is Dmitry returned from the dead, and see him as a savior in their time of need. Children mock the Holy Fool and steal his few coins. The tsar and his retinue leave the cathedral, and the people beg for alms. The Holy Fool addresses the tsar, and the mighty Boris asks the poorest of his subjects to pray for him. But the Fool refuses, saying that no one may pray for a murderer of children.

Scene 1 (1872 version): A great hall in the Kremlin in Moscow. The Council of Boyars condemns the usurper and all his supporters to death. Shuysky is late. He has had the tsar secretly watched, and says that Boris goes in fear and terror of what he believes to be the ghost of the murdered tsarevich; the tsar seems to have gone mad. Boris appears, pulls himself together, and begins the daily business of government. Shuysky has a wise old man brought in. It is Pimen, who tells the boyars of a miraculous cure beside the grave of the murdered tsarevich. This seems to be a judgment on Boris. Feeling that he is near death, the tsar calls for his son, and proclaims him his heir.

Scene 2: A forest clearing near Kromy. Russia is in a state of anarchy. Vagabonds have captured a boyar and intend to kill him. Missail and Varlaam urge the crowd to rebel against the satanic Tsar Boris, and in their wretchedness the people riot. Two Jesuits are to be hanged as their first victims. Then the procession of the False Dmitry approaches. The people welcome the usurper joyfully. As their new tsar, Grigory promises to bring them good fortune, commands them to free the boyar and the two Jesuits, and goes on his way to Moscow, followed by the crowd. Only the Holy Fool remains behind, lamenting Russia's bitter fate.   S. N.

A brilliant self-taught musician and a realistic dramatist, Musorgsky is regarded as the "enfant terrible" of nineteenth-century Russian music. His fragmentary body of work had a great influence on later composers, particularly in France, where he was much admired by Ravel and Debussy.

Right
Boris Godunov, set design by Hein Heckroth suggesting the illusion of freedom behind bars, Essen 1927 (TWS).
The Soviet party ideologists would have liked to interpret the scene in the forest near Kromy as an edifying example of a popular revolution. However, the bitter and realistic message of the scene is just the opposite. The people are being manipulated, and fall into the hands of one ruthless power after another.

Above
Boris Godunov, character photograph from the original production: Marina Mniszek (Yuliya Platonova) and the Jesuit Rangoni (Osip Palachek), 1874.
The first singer to take the part of Marina, Yuliya Fyodorovna Platonova, was influential in obtaining permission for the theatrical management to stage the opera, and made a great contribution to the first production. The photographer employed a clever trick in this studio photograph: the Jesuit Rangoni stands behind the frame of a mirror with no glass in it.

Boris Godunov, character photograph from the original production: Varlaam (Osip Petrov) and Missail (Dushikov), 1874.
The vagabond monks brought a new character type to the operatic stage: people from the lower classes of society who owned nothing and had no settled place in life, anticipating the proletarian operatic protagonists of the 20th century.

Boris Godunov, photograph from the production by Herbert Wernicke, conductor Claudio Abbado, Salzburg Festival 1994.
Herbert Wernicke took Musorgsky's famous dictum about "depicting the present in the past" seriously. When Boris Godunov presents himself to the crowd after his coronation, the figure of Everyman striving for power is visible under his royal garment, and a gallery of his murdered rivals is displayed behind him. Wernicke was also alluding to famous historical photographs and documentary films from the Leninist and Stalinist periods.

Pushkin and Musorgsky: the fathers of *Boris Godunov*

Pushkin made a careful study of Shakespeare's history plays, the works of the Russian historian Karamzin, and the old Russian chronicles. He wished to provide a true version of events in a natural dramatic form. His play *Boris Godunov* was published in 1830, but there was no public performance of the work until Tsar Nicholas II allowed one in 1870, 40 years later and 33 years after Pushkin's death, in the same year as Musorgsky offered the first version of his opera to the management of the Mariinsky Theater in St. Petersburg. Pushkin's drama met with severe criticism. The dangerous democratic statement it made was censored, and it could be staged only with cuts (7 of the 23 scenes were omitted, most of them involving the common people). In Pushkin's interpretation of the story, the greatness of the historical Boris Godunov was unimaginable without his people's support. Musorgsky's *Boris* was rejected by the

theatrical management in 1870, on the grounds that there were too many crowd scenes and that it lacked an important female role – or such, at least, was the official reason given. Musorgsky at first meant to follow Pushkin's original intentions and make the opera a tragedy without any love interest. When he revised the opera in 1871–72, he added the Polish scenes and the love affair between Dmitry and Marina; they enlarge the historical horizon of the work, but are not part of the fundamental mood of the opera, which is dominated by the figure of Boris and by the Russian people. Rimsky-Korsakov suggested to his friend Musorgsky that he could end the opera not with Boris's death but with the scene of revolution in Kromy. It was in this revised form that the opera had its première in 1874.

Above, top of page
Boris Godunov, Fyodor Stravinsky as Varlaam, self-portrait, 1895.
Fyodor Stravinsky immortalized himself in this drawing, in the character of Varlaam as an old mendicant monk. The bass, famous in his own time, was the father of the composer Igor Stravinsky.

Above
Boris Godunov, Fyodor Shalyapin as Varlaam.
In western European opera houses of the 19th century the part of Varlaam was usually given to a buffo bass. However, the deep bass register that Musorgsky intended for the character is capable of robust, rough, and alarming energy, even when Varlaam is singing his famous drinking song in the tavern scene.

Boris Godunov, set design by Eduard Löffler, Mannheim 1928 (TWS).
The mechanical clock in the tsar's palace is historical fact. Musorgsky's inspired idea was to set it moving twice during the opera: first to amuse the tsar's son Fyodor, and again at the end of Act II as a hallucination seen by the suffering Boris. He sees the dynastic developments of the future concentrated into a single moment, as tsars appear and disappear: a tragic realization on the part of the mighty ruler.

Boris Godunov, photograph from the production by Andrey Tarkovsky, conductor Claudio Abbado, sets and costumes Nicolas Dvigoubsky, Wiener Staatsoper 1991. The Russian film director and writer Andrey Tarkovsky directed *Boris Godunov* in 1983 for the Covent Garden Opera House in London. The production, conducted by Claudio Abbado, was sensationally successful. In 1991, five years after Tarkovsky's death and on the initiative of Abbado, his production was revived in the repertory of the Wiener Staatsoper. Tarkovsky's production presented a picture of the power and ultimate frailty of ideologies that depend on violence, prophetically anticipating the collapse of the Soviet empire.

Rimsky-Korsakov's version

Rimsky-Korsakov revised the work in the 1890's, reorchestrating it and making some radical cuts. His revision was criticized, and he produced another version in 1906–08, adding the solemn coronation music and the polonaise.

These insertions are typical of Rimsky-Korsakov's style of revision, nudging Musorgsky's music drama in the direction of grand Romantic opera. That impression is reinforced by his colorful, bright instrumentation, his harmonic and rhythmic refinements and simplifications, and a division into acts and scenes which runs counter to the through-composed flow of Musorgsky's music. At the Paris première in 1908, Shalyapin made Rimsky-Korsakov's version of *Boris Godunov* an outstanding international success, and for decades the opera was known only in this, the most popular version.

Other performing versions and editions

In the 1920s the scene outside St. Basil's Cathedral was added to Rimsky-Korsakov's version, although not in Musorgsky's own orchestration (the contrast with Rimsky-Korsakov would have been too obvious) but in its orchestration by Mikhail Ippolitov-Ivanov. Musorgsky's original score was published in 1928. Performed in Moscow and Leningrad, it was produced with increasing frequency in many different opera houses of western Europe from the 1930s onward. Meanwhile, the work was also staged in other orchestrations (by Emil Melngailis in Riga in 1924, by Dmitry Shostakovich in Leningrad in 1940, and by Karol Rathaus in New York in 1952).

Returning to the original

Rimsky-Korsakov's version is now considered outdated, and a distortion of the original score. But the question of which of the two versions created by Musorgsky himself should be performed remains open. It is not an easy decision. In general, Musorgsky's second version is chosen, with the addition of the scene outside St. Basil's Cathedral from the first version.

The historical facts

The interregnum. Ivan the Terrible left his son Fyodor an unenviable inheritance in 1584. Fyodor himself had been weak-minded from birth, and a regent was appointed to govern for him: Boris Godunov, a minor nobleman of humble origins. When Fyodor died in 1598, Boris ensured that he had the backing of the church and the people of Moscow (through some clever manipulation) and was crowned tsar.

The real Dmitry. Dmitry, the son of Ivan the Terrible's third marriage, not yet of age on his father's death, was brought up in Uglich, far away from Moscow. He died in mysterious circumstances in 1591. The commission of investigation sent to Uglich and led by the powerful boyar Shuysky could establish only that the nine-year-old child, who suffered severely from epilepsy, had probably given himself a mortal wound with his toy dagger. Nonetheless, rumours circulated that Boris had ordered Dmitry's murder in order to get the throne for himself, and the hypothesis is mentioned in Nikolay Karamzin's multi-volume history of Russia, which appeared early in the nineteenth century and was an important historical source for both Pushkin and Musorgsky.

The reign of Boris Godunov. According to contemporary chronicles and other accounts, Boris was a very suitable incumbent of the throne, a good and ambitious tsar. With his many virtues as a ruler, he towered far above the legitimate tsars who had preceded him. But the time and circumstances were against him. Early in 1600 a catastrophic drought caused terrible famine, great fires raged in Moscow, and the peasants and the poor of the city rebelled.

The pseudo-Dimitry. At this point the Polish army crossed the western border intending to set a pretender on the throne – a young man claiming to be Dmitry, the youngest son of Ivan the Terrible. In 1605 and in the middle of this crisis, Boris Godunov suddenly died. There were suspicions that he had been poisoned. The Polish army, with the False Dmitry at its head, entered Moscow. The Poles killed Boris Godunov's son Fyodor, the heir to the throne, and crowned their own "Dmitry" tsar. To seal the alliance between Poland and Russia he immediately married Marina, daughter of the Sandomierz commander Mniszek, who was one of his supporters.

Historical epilogue. In the following years – the "time of troubles" – three other tsars seized the Russian throne, one of them being Vasily Shuysky. Marina Mniszek, apparently no beauty in real life, married two of these tsars in succession after the murder of her first husband, the False Dmitry, and even had a child by the third. The opera seems accurate, at least, in dwelling on her desire to occupy the throne of Russia.   *M.P.*

Boris Godunov, photograph from the production by Andrey Tarkovsky, conductor Claudio Abbado, sets and costumes Nicolas Dvigoubsky, Wiener Staatsoper 1991. Tarkovsky devised a powerful symbol for his conviction that violence cannot be successfully opposed by violence, only by love: the icon of the Virgin Mary. The fragile yet radiant image of the Mother and Child became a central thematic counterpoint to the production, a true ray of light in the dark realm of lies and violence.

Boris Godunov, Ivan Kozlovsky (1900–93) in
the part of the Holy Fool at the Bol'shoy
Theater, Moscow.
The Holy Fool is a recurrent character in
19th-century Russian music and literature,
and he is the only symbolic figure in
Musorgsky's realistic historical music drama.
The weeping fool is also the only person
to see clearly in the political sense, an
embodiment of the misled, terrified, and
oppressed Russian people.

The tsar on the operatic stage

The first Boris was Ivan Melnikov, by special permission
of the censor, since it was usually forbidden to represent members of the tsar's family on stage. However, it
was Fyodor Shalyapin who made the character of the
powerful yet troubled tsar internationally famous when
he sang the part at the Paris première of Rimsky-
Korsakov's second version in 1908. His large-scale and
emotionally theatrical performance determined the
interpretation of the role for decades. In 1952 Boris
Christoff made a recording of the opera, conducted by
Issay Dobrowen, in which he sang three of the bass
parts: Tsar Boris, Varlaam, and Pimen. In the second half
of the twentieth century, with the decline in the tradition of the great Slavonic bass, the brooding and
thoughtful aspect of the character has taken precedence over Boris's stature as a great ruler. Although
Musorgsky, a realist, depicted his heroes impartially, it is
impossible to miss his sympathy for Boris, which is
evident in the tsar's monologue and death scene. M 1, M 2

The people led astray

A critic who attended the première accused Musorgsky
of presenting the people as "unruly, drunkards,
oppressed, and desperate." Nor was that all: he added
that "the composer also depicts them as completely
stupid, superstitious, simple, and good for nothing." It
is true that the people who are commanded to break
into hymns of praise (in the scenes outside the
Novodevichiy Monastery, the Kremlin in Moscow, and
St. Basil's Cathedral) do prove to be simple-minded and
good for very little, while certain other characters, such
as Varlaam and Missail, are unruly drunkards. All this is
in both Pushkin's and Musorgsky's version of the story.
Theirs was a realistic picture, whether the critics praised
or blamed playwright or composer. Under the surface
of the crowd's simple-minded passivity, elemental
powers seethe. They are apparent in the scene outside

St. Basil's Cathedral, and break into open rebellion in
the forest near Kromy. The Russian people are not
depicted in a sympathetic light in this scene, where
they are about to lynch one man and hang two others.
Nonetheless, even here there is a sense of deep pity for
them, since it is obvious that they have been manipulated and led astray, and are understandably fallible.
The Kromy rebels instinctively attack a boyar and the
Jesuits, whom they see as intrusive foreigners, although
they suddenly find themselves on the same side as the
Jesuits in singing the praises of the pretender to the
throne. The Kromy scene has been described as the
"scene of revolution," and it is rather surprising that its
performance was allowed in the former Soviet Union
and the eastern bloc states, since Musorgsky dwells on
the negative rather than the positive features of revolution. However, he did draw distinctions: the poor
people of Moscow are described as the "people"
("narod"), while the rebels of Kromï are called "vagabonds," meaning a rabble or mob ("brodyagi").

The Holy Fool

The figure of the fool is a recurrent type in Russian art,
whether in literature, opera, drama, or the visual arts,
and has been the subject of a number of historical and
sociological studies. According to popular tradition, the
fool wears rags, chains, and a metal cap, and roams the
countryside in summer and winter alike. He is often an
unfortunate madman attracting pity, sometimes a
seeker after the truth revered by the common people.
"Holy Fools", or "Fools-in-God," live on charity, but
must put up with mockery. Their origins are extremely
diverse: they may be from princely families or simple
peasant stock. But they are all related, for their hearts
are pure, their minds naively childish, they are close to
God, and they instinctively have a clear, sharp view of
the world and of humanity. Musorgsky took the character of the fool from Pushkin's play, but it is his music
that makes the figure a symbol of the Russian people. In
the scene outside St. Basil's Cathedral, the sad lament
of the chorus develops from the fool's theme and
returns to it again. M 3

Traditional songs and hymns – sources of inspiration

The pensive melody that opens the opera derives from
the "extended" type of Russian folk song
(*protyashnaya*). Although the theme is Musorgsky's
own invention, it seems to be the quintessence of
traditional Russian melody. M 4

Boris Godunov, production photograph from a guest performance by the
Mariinsky Theater at the Theater Heilbronn, 1996.
One of the most impressive scenes in the opera: Boris Godunov presents
himself to the people as their new tsar and savior. Under the baton of Valery
Gergiyev, the Mariinsky Theater (formally the Kirov Theater) regained its status
as an opera house with very high musical standards.

Boris Godunov, Mark Reisen in 1928 (right), Boris Christoff (below), and Nicolai Ghiaurov (bottom) as Boris Godunov.
A small gallery of the great singers who have sung the part: Mark Reisen, Boris Christoff, and Nicolai Ghiaurov (the last two both of Bulgarian origin). Until recently the figure of Boris was always represented in a very traditional way; not only his royal robes but his emotional gestures were handed on from singer to singer, even when they were not Russians.

Musorgsky also used several genuine folk songs, such as the mocking song in the forest near Kromy. M 5

Another authentic folk song is the basis for the chorus in the coronation scene. Beethoven used the same theme in the second movement of his string quartet op. 59, no. 2 (dedicated to the Russian Prince Razumovsky). The melody was originally a Christmas carol, and was promoted to the status of a general hymn of praise in nineteenth-century Russian opera, also featuring in Anton Rubinstein's *The Merchant Kalashnikov* (1879), Tchaikovsky's →*Mazeppa* (1884), and Rimsky-Korsakov's *The Tsar's Bride* (1899). M 6

The characteristic harmonies of Slavonic church music have also infiltrated Musorgsky's music (for instance in the scene in the Chudov Monastery, and in Boris's death scene). The chorus of blind pilgrims in the prologue combines the polyphony of Russian folk song with the style of Orthodox sacred music. M 7 .   M. P.

1. Boris's Monologue

Тяж - ка дес-ни-ца гроз-но-го су-ди-и, у-жа-сен при-го-вор ду-ше пре-ступ - ной

2. Boris's Death

Се - стру сво-ю, ца-рев-ну, сбе-ре-ги, мой сын, ты ей о - дин хра-ни-тель о-ста -

ешь-ся, на-шей Ксе-ни-и, го-луб - ке чи-стой.

3. Lament of the People

Кор-ми-лец ба - тюш-ка, по-дай Христа ра-ди

4. "Russian" Melody (Prelude)

5. Folk Song in the Forest near Kromy

Не ___ со - кол ле-тит по подне-бесью

6. Theme of the Coronation Chorus

Уж как на не - бе солн - цу крас-но-му сла-ва, сла - ва!

7. Pilgrim's Chorus (Prologue)

Сла-ва те-бе, твор-цу все-выш-не-му, на зем - ли

Khovanshchina

National·music drama in five acts

Libretto: Modest Musorgsky.

Première: In Rimsky-Korsakov's version: 21 February 1886, St. Petersburg (private production in the Kononov hall); with Shostakovich's orchestration: 25 November 1960, Leningrad (Kirov Theater).

Characters: Prince Ivan Khovansky, leader of the *strel'tsï* (militia) (B), Prince Andrey Khovansky, his son (T), Prince Vasily Golitsïn (T), Boyar Shaklovity (Bar), Dosifey, leader of the *raskolniki* or "Old Believers" (B), Marfa, an Old Believer (A), Susanna, an aged Old Believer (S), Scrivener (T), Emma, a girl from the German quarter (S), Pastor (B), Varsonofyev, confidant of Golitsïn (B), Kuzka, one of the *strel'tsï* (T), Two *Strel'tsï* (2 B), Streshnev, a young boyar (T), Accomplice of Golitsïn (T); people of Moscow, new arrivals in the city, *strel'tsï*, Old Believers, maids and Persian slave girls of Ivan Khovansky, Petrovskï (Tsar Peter's bodyguard), crowd (chorus and ballet).

Setting: Moscow and its surroundings in 1682.

Synopsis

Act I

Red Square, Moscow. The *strel'tsï* are lording it over Moscow, boasting of their acts of terrorism. These dangerous times are profitable to the scrivener, since people employ him to write denunciations. The boyar Shaklovity dictates a document telling the tsar of a conspiracy among the *strel'tsï*. A crowd of illiterate people make the scrivener read out a notice listing the names of nobles who have acted against the good of the community. They lament the arbitrary conduct of powerful men. However, they acclaim the arrival of Ivan Khovansky, leader of the *strel'tsï*, who presents himself as the champion of the people. The crowd praise him as a wolf in sheep's clothing. Ivan Khovansky's son Andrey has killed the father of a German girl whose fiancé was forced to go into exile, and now plans to get the unfortunate girl into his power. Ivan Khovansky grudges his son the beautiful Emma, and the two of them quarrel publicly over their victim. The Old Believers oppose the *strel'tsï*. Their spiritual leader Dosifey saves the German Protestant girl from harm, and puts her in the care of Marfa, a young member of the faith, formerly Andrey's lover. Dosifey encourages his followers to live in accordance with the message of the Gospel.

Act II

The palace of Prince Golitsïn, who, as the protégé of the regent Sophia, has broken the power of the boyars and conquered Poland. He fears the sudden vicissitudes of fate. He assists the Germans who have settled in Moscow, including the Lutheran pastor, in so far as it suits him to do so, but, although he is enlightened, Golitsïn is also superstitious. He has summoned Marfa to see him because of her fame as a clairvoyant. She foretells the future, predicting the very fate he himself fears: exile. He gives secret orders to have her murdered. Golitsïn summons the most powerful men in Moscow to his palace: Ivan Khovansky, leader of the *strel'tsï*, and Dosifey, leader of the Old Believers. Golitsïn and Khovansky quarrel over their respective rights. They cannot and will not follow the example of Dosifey, who renounced all his power and titles when he abandoned his former identity as Prince Mïshetsky. Thanks to the help of Tsar Peter's bodyguard, Marfa has escaped the pursuit of Golitsïn's minions. In the tsar's name, Shaklovity announces that the *strel'tsï* accused of rebellion will face justice in a court of law.

Act III

The banks of the Moskva River, in the quarter occupied by the *strel'tsï*. Marfa laments her unhappy love for the undeserving Andrey. The zealot Susanna accuses her of sinful lust, but Dosifey supports her. Shaklovity and Dosifey are concerned for the fate of the nation, but they tread different paths. Unlike Dosifey, Shaklovity does not put his trust in God but in a powerful worldly ruler. There is discontent among the *strel'tsï*, and we hear that the tsar's bodyguard intends to hunt them down. They and their wives seek protection and advice from their leader, Ivan Khovansky, who reassures them and sends them home.

Act IV

Scene 1: In Ivan Khovansky's house. Wishing for entertainment, Khovansky commands his women servants to sing and dance merrily. Golitsïn sends him a message, warning him that the tsar intends to have the *strel'tsï* murdered. The haughty Khovansky regards this warning as an insult, and has Golitsïn's messenger killed. When Shaklovity brings him a summons, he falls into the trap, and is himself killed in the doorway of his own house.

Scene 2: The square outside St. Basil's Cathedral. Golitsïn is on his way into exile, and the people feel sympathy for his fate. Dosifey has discovered from Marfa the tsar's intentions for the Old Believers: they are to be rounded up and murdered. Andrey knows nothing of what is going on; he is searching for Emma, and believes that Marfa has hidden her. The *strel'tsï* who once tyrannized over Moscow are taken away to execution, but Tsar Peter I pardons them and spares their lives at the last minute.

Act V

A hermitage in the forest at night time, where the Old Believers have taken refuge. They are surrounded by the tsar's bodyguards. Dosifey realizes that they are in a hopeless situation, and decides that they should immolate themselves as an act of sacrifice for the salvation of the world. The infatuated Andrey is still in pursuit of Emma, but Marfa comforts him. Dosifey gives the signal for self-immolation. *S. N.*

Khovanshchina, Fyodor Shalyapin as Dosifey, self-portrait, 1911.
Shalyapin sang Dosifey in the first professional production of the work on 12 November 1897, at the Mamontov Theater in Moscow, a private opera house. The role of Dosifey is notable for three great monologues. He features in the opera as a spiritual authority. Even when the new ruler, Tsar Peter I, drives him and his followers to suicide, he remains dominant as a spiritual leader. Shalyapin was one of those singers blessed with the ability to make such a spiritual presence convincing on stage.

Khovanshchina, set design by Ludolfs Liberts, Riga 1927 (TWS).
The ultimate point of suffering reached by the Old Believers in Musorgsky's *Khovanshchina*. In a hopeless situation, pursued by the tsar's adherents, they prepare for self-immolation. The Old Believers are shown in their Orthodox black garments on the right, and on the left in white shrouds prepared for their death by fire.

Khovanshchina, production photograph with Menyelkiyev as Ivan Khovansky, conductor Valery Gergiyev, sets F. F. Fedorovsky, Mariinsky Theater, St. Petersburg 1992. Under Valery Gergiyev, the former high artistic standards of the Mariinsky company were revived, as in this scene where Ivan Khovansky is entertained by his women serfs.

Khovanshchina, Nicolai Ghiaurov in the part of Ivan Khovansky, 1962.
Nicolai Ghiaurov was already singing the barbarically powerful role of Ivan Khovansky even as a young man. Of Bulgarian origin, he has a rather softer voice than most Russian basses. His singing studies in Moscow in the early 1950s were of great significance for his portrayal of Russian operatic roles.

The historical period of *Khovanshchina*

Khovanshchina takes place at the beginning of the reign of Peter I, a restless time of rebellions, schisms in the church, and disputes over the succession. In the opera, Musorgsky condenses the historical events of several years into a few days.

After the death of Tsar Fyodor in 1682, the ten-year-old Peter became tsar, but, under pressure from the *strel'tsï* (militia), then the only armed forces in Russia, he had to share the throne with his half-brother Ivan. It was Princess Sophia, sister of the two boy tsars, who really held power and was behind the *strel'tsï*. The army of *strel'tsï* had been created by Ivan IV (Ivan the Terrible). The *strel'tsï* received wages for their military service, but could also pursue crafts and trades, and lived in special settlements with their families. During Sophia's regency, they terrorized the whole of Moscow. Their leaders, Princes Ivan and Andrey Khovansky, were so powerful that they were a danger even to Sophia herself, and she had them both executed in 1682. Nonetheless Sophia and her favorite, Prince Golitsïn, had to rely on the *strel'tsï* to stabilize her position. In 1689 they plotted to get rid of Peter with the aid of the *strel'tsï*. However, the young tsar had organized the play army of his childhood into an efficient bodyguard, the *Petrovtsï*, which he used to suppress the *strel'tsï*. He then banished Sophia to a convent. The final revolt of the *strel'tsï* came nine years later, in 1698. Peter decided to be rid of them for good, and 2000 *strel'tsï* were beheaded in Red Square. The tsar took part in the executions himself.

A religious war

Before Peter I came to power, around the middle of the seventeenth century, there was a major reform movement in the Russian Orthodox church. The Patriarch Nikon standardized the liturgy, selected the texts of the sacred books, and introduced polyphonic chant. In essence, he was centralizing the church in conformation with the requirements of an absolute monarchy. His reforms led to a split between the clergy and their congregations. The Old Believers (also described as schismatics, or in Russian *raskolniki*) had many adherents, particularly among the peasants. Religious resistance grew into an opposition movement. The Old Believers were mercilessly persecuted by the tsar, but they clung to their faith even at the cost of their lives, choosing either communal death by fire or flight to distant regions rather than submission. Even in the twentiethth century, it was still possible to find some communities of Old Believers in Siberia and certain parts of Europe and America.

The incomplete autograph manuscript

Musorgsky sketched out the scenario with the aid of his friend, the well-known critic and aesthete Vladimir Stasov. He wrote the libretto himself, but work on the composition of the score progressed much more slowly than it had with →*Boris Godunov*. Musorgsky gave the individual scenes plenty of time to mature, and it was often only after years of reflection that he brought himself to put some of them down on paper. The rate at which he worked was determined by the grandeur and novelty of the subject, and his ideas came to diverge increasingly from Stasov's original suggestions. In 1876, while still working on *Khovanshchina*, he began composing a new opera, *The Fair at Sorochintsï*, and he now worked on the two operas simultaneously. In August 1880 he wrote to tell Stasov that *Khovanshchina* was almost finished, but he still had to orchestrate it. However, death brought his work to an end on 28 March 1881.

Retouched by Rimsky-Korsakov

Musorgsky's friend Rimsky-Korsakov orchestrated, abbreviated, and revised the material left by the composer. He cut more than 800 bars from the original score, enough music for an entire act. *Khovanshchina* began its stage career in this revised form in 1886, in a performance by a St. Petersburg amateur company. The first major production was in Savva Mamontov's private theater in Moscow, with Fyodor Shalyapin as Dosifey. Later, Shalyapin directed the productions of 1911 at the Mariinsky Theater in St. Petersburg and the Bol'shoy Theater in Moscow in 1912.

In Paris: Ravel and Stravinsky

Sergey Dyagilev, director of the Ballets Russes, commissioned a new orchestration of the work from Maurice Ravel and Igor Stravinsky for the first Paris performance in 1913. However, Shalyapin was unwilling to sing the part of Dosifey except in Rimsky-Korsakov's version, so the western European public heard a curious hybrid version. Ravel and Stravinsky's orchestration has not been preserved, apart from the finale composed by Stravinsky on the basis of Musorgsky's sketches, and printed in 1914. (In his production for the Wiener Staatsoper in 1989, and in his recording of the work, Claudio Abbado used this version of the finale.)

Back to the original: Shostakovich

As usual at the end of the twentieth century, the Viennese production of 1989 employed the orchestration provided by Dmitry Shostakovich on the basis of Musorgsky's piano score, without cuts or revisions. (Boris Asaf'yev had already orchestrated the original piano score of *Khovanshchina* in 1931, but this version was neither published nor performed.)   *M. P.*

Khovanshchina, costume designs for the Old Believers by Konstantin Korovin, 1911. Korovin's designs for the Old Believers are also typical of his methods. Their black robes are unadorned and close-fitting, marking them off from the outside world. In his musical portrayal of the Old Believers, Musorgsky used authentic hymn tunes. The dominance of male voices emphasizes two emotional extremes: fanaticism is expressed by the high piping sound of the music for the tenors, and calm resignation in the face of death by the deep bass melodies.

Interpretations and misinterpretations

The memorable union of Russia with western Europe imposed by Peter I, who has sometimes been called a royal revolutionary, was achieved by cruel methods and entailed enormous sacrifices. It was only partially successful, yet the military and administrative system he created continued until the end of the twentieth century. The character and reforms of Peter the Great have always been a controversial subject among Russian intellectuals. At the time when Musorgsky was writing *Khovanshchina*, interest in the pros and cons of Peter's reforms was particularly strong, since Russia had celebrated the 200th anniversary of its birth in 1872. Tsar Alexander II, also acclaimed as a royal revolutionary, encouraged the cult of his great predecessor. Even the Russian intelligentsia, which regarded itself as progressive and was critical of dictatorial rule, agreed with the tsar here. It was against this background that Stasov suggested the subject of *Khovanshchina* to Musorgsky. Stasov, the ideologist of the New Russian School, explained on several occasions what the theme meant to him: the clash of a new era with the backward Russia of the old days, the victory of a new world over the reactionary past. Rimsky-Korsakov also saw the "new world" as synonymous with the regime of Peter the Great, and its advent is depicted with great musical beauty in the prelude to the opera, "Dawn over the Moskva River," but it is not clear that Musorgsky would have agreed with this interpretation, and Rimsky-Korsakov gave the theme extra weight in his revision. At the end of the second act, when Marfa describes her rescue by the *Petrovtsï* and Shaklovity announces that the tsar intends to bring the *strel'tsï* to justice, he composed an orchestral postlude on the same theme as the prelude, giving it political significance. M8

The concept of the rise of a new world and the decline of the old continued to flourish in twentieth-century studies of the opera. In the Stalinist period, paradoxical as it may seem, both Peter the Great and Ivan the Terrible (the latter in Sergey Eisenstein's famous film) were presented as models for a ruler of Russia, and Stalin himself liked to be seen in that light. But what were Musorgsky's original intentions? While he let the new political horizons remain rather vague (for Peter the Great never even appears on stage), he placed all the beauty and wealth of his music at the service of the other side, the declining world of a dark, backward, and fanatically bigoted Russia. Was Musorgsky on the wrong side historically?

The view of the world in *Khovanshchina*

In several letters, Musorgsky called *Khovanshchina* a "national music drama," while he described →*Boris Godunov* as a "musical stage work." While the conflict in *Boris Godunov* concerns the clash between the tsar and his people, the ruler does not appear at all in *Khovanshchina*. Instead, the work presents the whole of the rest of the panorama of Russian society, from princes to the poor. Musorgsky paints a picture of the rise of the bureaucratic military and political dictatorship of the late seventeenth century, and the social

8. Dawn over the Moskva River (Prelude)

Khovanshchina, production photograph, production by Harry Kupfer, set by Hans Schavernoch, conducted by Gerd Albrecht, Hamburger Staatsoper 1994.
A production in which ancient history is reminiscent of the recent past, and is also presented with an awareness of the present and anticipation of the near future.

Khovanshchina, photograph from the production by Alfred Kirchner, sets Erich Wonder, costumes Joachim Herzog, conductor Claudio Abbado, Wiener Staatsoper 1989.
Musically, Claudio Abbado's version of the opera for Vienna was a hybrid. He restored episodes that had been cut by Rimsky-Korsakov and even made use of scenes that had been orchestrated by the composer himself, but otherwise used Shostakovich's orchestration, and ended with the finale composed by Igor Stravinsky (the prayer and the self-immolation of the Old Believers). The final scene of this Viennese production was an international sensation: the act of self-immolation was seen as an impressive and dramatically disturbing metaphor. The way in which those preparing to die and the dying raised their arms as if on a sinking ship was interpreted as a desperate cry for help.

upheavals that accompanied the process. The horror that governs the protagonists is mystical and irrational, since there is no good explanation for it in their own times. But Musorgsky had realized that 200 years after the historical events depicted the system would still be largely unchanged, unassailable and alarmingly influential as the result of its rigidity.   *M. P.*

Diversity in musical portraiture

This music drama reflects the diversity of human nature: it contains deeply moral, pure characters, who are conscious of their own responsibilities (Marfa, Dosifey), individuals drawn on a large scale who combine negative, even grotesque characteristics with genuine dignity (Ivan Khovansky, Golitsïn), an intriguer with noble motives (Shaklovity), and a mean-minded, unattractive specimen of humanity with distorted values and no backbone (the scrivener).

Marfa is the composer's most attractive female role. She experiences the events of the opera intensely, in their totality, and, both musically and dramatically, she is radiantly expressive. M 9

Dosifey is both a religious leader and a politician, the factor linking the various opponents of Tsar Peter, and he is trying with all his might to sustain the fragile unity of the rebellion. He is not motivated by lust for power, but follows firm moral and philosophical convictions, and will not compromise on essential principles. To him, the alternative to victory is suicide. The human side of Dosifey appears in his scenes with Marfa and his great monologue at the beginning of Act V. It is obvious that behind his deliberate actions stands a human being aware of the enormous responsibility he bears for them, a man struggling with his own doubts.

In contrast, old Prince Khovansky is unscrupulous and hungry for power. He comes from an ancient princely family, and bases his claim to the throne on his origins. He is leader of the country's crack fighting

force, the *strel'tsï*. The ties between Khovansky and his *strel'tsï* resemble those patriarchal relations that existed in the distant past of the Rus people of Kiev, in the time of the ancient principalities. His farewell to the *strel'tsï* at the end of Act III is affecting: he dismisses his men like a father bidding farewell to his sons.

Prince Golitsïn keeps Ivan Khovansky's despotic inclinations and demands within bounds. He is a reforming politician who wears European clothing and lives in a Baroque palace, but his polished manners conceal an ambivalent personality – "half European, half Asiatic," in Stasov's words. Although he is a reformer, ambition leads him to ally himself with Khovansky, the representative of the old order, and with the Old Believers. His fate is the suffering and exile that Marfa has foretold for him. When her prophecy comes true at the beginning of Act IV, its original melody takes on the nature of a hymn of universal sorrow. Golitsïn's misfortunes are mourned by the sympathetic people. M 10

The ambivalence of Shaklovity's character has very different roots. He appears to be an outright intriguer, and, according to Musorgsky, is "a character role, an archetypal rogue with his fair share of feigned pomposity, but with a certain grand stature despite his bloodthirsty nature." It is worth noting that Musorgsky composed a great aria on patriotism for Shaklovity, which was given by the director of the 1959 Soviet film of *Khovanshchina* to the chorus representing the people. M 11

The grotesquely comic character of the scrivener is the embodiment of human weakness and cowardice. He represents the worst type of bureaucrat, servile to those above him and tyrannical to those lower down the scale.

M. P.

9. Marfa's Aria

Ис - хо - ди - ла мла - дš - шень-ка   все лу - га и бо - ло - та

10. Melody of the Suffering People

11. Schaklovity's Aria

Ах ты, в судь - би - не злосчаст-на-я,   род - на - я Русь

Khovanshchina, photograph from the production conducted by Valery Gergiyev, sets F.F. Fedorovsky, Mariinsky Theater, St. Petersburg 1992. All is ready for the execution of the *strel'tsï*, who are about to suffer the punishment they deserve when the tsar's pardon arrives at the last moment.

The Merry Wives of Windsor, photograph from the production by Robert Herzl, conductor Leopold Hager, sets and costumes Waltraud Engelberg, Wiener Volksoper 1994.
The subject of Falstaff was already familiar on the 18th-century operatic stage, from a setting by Salieri. The story provides material for an original comedy with its roots in the *commedia dell'arte*, and contains a nocturnal scene reminiscent of *A Midsummer Night's Dream*. Nicolai's smoothly elegant music is also timeless, and if the old traditions of its production are revived by new direction on a stage with modern equipment, the work still has great appeal.

Nicolai created his own operatic style from a mixture of Italian and German elements, and was one of the founding fathers of German comic opera.

Nicolai, Otto

b. 9 June 1810 in Königsberg
d. 11 May 1849 in Berlin

From 1826 to 1830 Nicolai studied in Berlin, one of his teachers being Carl Friedrich Zelter. In 1833 he was appointed organist to the chapel of the German embassy in Rome. Here he studied briefly with Giuseppe Baini, and met →Donizetti in Naples. He then became assistant *Kapellmeister* to Conradin Kreutzer at the Kärntnertor Theater in Vienna, but returned to Rome a year later, in 1837, intending to settle there and compose operas. Inspired by the works of →Bellini, he wrote successfully in the Italian operatic tradition. In 1841 he succeeded Kreutzer as principal *Kapellmeister* of the Kärntnertor Theater in Vienna, where he founded the Philharmonic Concerts. In 1847, shortly before his premature death, he returned to Berlin as director of the cathedral choir and *Kapellmeister* of the Royal Opera.

Works: Enrico II (Henry II) (Trieste, 1838), *Il templario (The Templar)* (Turin, 1840), *Odoardo e Gildippe (Odoardo and Gildippe)* (Genoa, 1840), *Il proscritto (The Exile)* (Milan, 1841), *Die lustigen Weiber von Windsor (The Merry Wives of Windsor)* (Berlin, 1849); sacred works, orchestral and chamber music.

The Merry Wives of Windsor

Komische-fantastische Oper in three acts, with dance

Libretto: Salomon Hermann Mosenthal, after the play of the same name by William Shakespeare.
Première: 9 March 1849, Berlin (Königliches Opernhaus).
Characters: Sir John Falstaff (B), Herr Fluth/Ford (B), Herr Reich/Page (B), Fenton (T), Junker Spärlich/Slender (T), Dr. Caius (B), Frau Fluth/Mrs. Ford (S), Frau Reich/Mrs. Page (Ms), Maid Anna Reich/Anne Page (S), Innkeeper and Waiter (spoken), First Citizen (T), Second, Third, and Fourth Citizens (3 spoken), Two Servants of Ford (silent); citizens and women of Windsor, children, masque of elves and spirits (chorus); elves, fairies, midges, wasps, gnomes, goblins, salamanders (ballet); huntsmen, adventurers (extras).
Setting: Windsor in the early 17th century.

Synopsis
Act I

The impoverished knight Falstaff has written identical love letters to the wives of two rich citizens. But the women are friends, and play a trick on Sir John. Mrs. Ford replies to Falstaff, inviting him to a rendezvous, while her friend tells Ford whom his wife is going to meet, and when the meeting is to be.

The difficult birth of a comedy

One of Nicolai's duties as principal *Kapellmeister* of the Kärntnertor Theater was to compose a German opera. In 1842 he advertised unsuccessfully for someone to provide a suitable subject. The suggestion of Shakespeare's comedy *The Merry Wives of Windsor* eventually came from his own circle of friends. Nicolai initially commissioned the writer Jakob Hoffmeister to write texts for two numbers, and being satisfied with the result, sent the author a detailed scenario in 1846. However, Hoffmeister declined the commission. Nicolai finally found his librettist in Mosenthal, the authorized signatory of the Viennese branch of the Rothschilds. The opera was completed in October 1846, which according to the intendant Balocchino was a year too late, and a production in Vienna was now out of the question. Nicolai did have the "Moon Chorus" M1 and the elves' dance M2 performed as a farewell to the Viennese before taking up his new position in Berlin, where he began rehearsing the opera at the request of King Frederick William IV. However, the planned première was prevented by the revolutionary events of the year 1848, and when it finally took place, only two months before Nicolai's death, it was not successful. Neither the public nor the press cared for the work, and Nicolai was never to know how famous his opera would eventually become, several numbers proving to be lasting favorites. M3, M4, M5

Ford turns up at the appointed hour. But his wife has hidden the fat knight in a washing basket, which is carried out of the house by two servants and emptied into the river. The embarrassed Ford is revealed as a jealous domestic tyrant. Page and his wife have plans for their daughter Anne, who is of marriageable age: her mother wants her to marry the Frenchman, Dr. Caius, while her father favors Slender, but Anne herself loves the impoverished Fenton.

Act II

Falstaff is back at the Garter Inn, where he receives another invitation from Mrs. Ford. Flattered, he invites all present to join in a drinking bout. One Sir Brook (Herr Bach in the German libretto) takes part; he is really Ford trying to discover what his wife is up to. He pretends he wants to make a conquest of Mrs. Ford himself, and asks the knight's advice. Sir John boasts of his alleged success, revealing when and where he is to meet Mrs. Ford. Fenton has a secret meeting with Anne, but their billing and cooing is interrupted by Dr. Caius and Slender, each wishing to serenade his beloved. This time, Ford genuinely takes his wife by surprise at her meeting with Falstaff. She disguises the fat knight as her maidservant's aunt, and chases "her" away without arousing Ford's suspicions, for the real old lady has been banned from the house for gossiping too

much. Now sure of victory, Ford invites the neighbors to witness his wife's unfaithfulness – and once again he is put to shame himself.

Act III

The two ladies now tell their husbands the whole secret, and Ford and Page decide to play a trick on the knight. Mrs. Ford invites him to yet another rendezvous, asking him to go to the oak in Windsor Park at midnight dressed as Herne the Hunter. Falstaff duly keeps this appointment, but nothing goes as he had hoped: the citizens, disguised as elves, torment the fat knight. However, they too are fooled, for Anne's parents have given her two different costumes. Her father and mother tell the suitors whom they respectively favor what Anne will be wearing, but she has switched the costumes and sent them to Slender and Caius, asking them to wear those disguises. Each therefore thinks the other is Anne, while she herself, dressed as Titania, marries Fenton in the costume of Oberon the fairy king. Falstaff is humbled by the citizens, and they are all reconciled.

S. N.

The Merry Wives of Windsor, costume designs for Falstaff and the women who teach him a lesson (Mrs. Ford, Mrs. Page, and Anne), the Königliche Schauspiele, Wiesbaden 1902 (TWS).
Around the turn of the century, the opera, which had been received without enthusiasm at its première, was among the most popular in German-speaking countries. There is romantic coloring in Nicolai's work with its themes of forest, moonlight, and the dance of the elves, particularly in the nocturnal scene when Falstaff appears as Herne the Hunter, wearing a pair of antlers on his head. A certain amount of French influence is evident. An important element is the humanity of the characters, almost all of whom have a comic side: the chaste citizen's wife Mrs. Ford, who tricks her simple-minded husband as well as Falstaff; Anne Page, who makes clever use of all the confusion to marry the man she loves against her parents' will; and above all Falstaff himself. The hard-drinking knight with his capacious appetite for love is simultaneously a Don Quixote figure and a domesticated Don Juan.

Intolerance 1960

Azione scenica in two parts

Libretto: Luigi Nono, from an idea by Angelo Maria Ripellino.
Première: 13 April 1961, Venice (Teatro La Fenice).

Characters: A Refugee (T), His Companion (S), A Woman (A), An Algerian (Bar), A Torture Victim (B), Four Policemen (4 spoken); miners, demonstrators, torture victims, prisoners, refugees, Algerians, peasants (chorus).

Setting: A mining village, a city, a police headquarters, a concentration camp, and on the banks of a flooded river, in the present day.

Synopsis

To escape unemployment in the south, the protagonist has come to the mining districts of the north, where he has found work and a woman. In mid-life he wants to go home, and leaves the woman behind. On his way he is confronted by demonstrations, protests, arrests, interrogations, and torture. He finds himself in a concentration camp, escapes, experiences bureaucracy, terror, and fanaticism, and the absurdities and intolerable aspects of a life dominated by fear and hunger. Drawn into these situations, he is subjected to sexual intimidation and blackmail, knows love and solidarity, and is finally halted in his journey on reaching a flooded river: his home is wherever he is needed.

S. N.

Intolerance 1960, photograph from the production by Günter Krämer, sets Andreas Reinhardt, conductor Hans Zander, Hamburgische Staatsoper 1985.
The Hamburg production, with William Cochran and Slavka Taskova as the refugee and his companion, brought recognition that the work was suitable for the general operatic repertory. Dramatically and musically, it was a production of a very high standard.

Points of reference

When Hans Zender, himself a composer of standing, conducted Nono's *Intolerance 1960* in Hamburg in 1985, he said that "elements of introversion and lyrical tenderness are always present in the central passages of Luigi Nono's work." In the 1992 production he conducted in Stuttgart (director Christoph Nel, sets Alfred Hrdlicka) Bernhard Kontarsky emphasized that aspect, and this staging of the work made Nono a classic. However, the première in 1961 had caused a considerable scandal when certain groups, undoubtedly organized and equally clearly neo-fascist, tried to disrupt the performance. This was no coincidence, for while Nono set out from basic human situations, he had linked them to specific circumstances: such phenomena as increasing emigration in search of employment, the growing autocracy of the police, the threat of neo-fascism, and uncontrollable environmental disasters. *Intolerance 1960* depicts mankind existing in the twentieth century in conditions of increasing racial, national, social, and ideological intolerance.

Nono, Luigi

b. 28 January 1924 in Venice
d. 8 May 1990 in Venice

While Nono was a law student in Padua, he began studying composition with Gian Francesco Malipiero at the Venice Conservatory, and later he also studied with Bruno Maderna and Hermann Scherchen. From 1950 to 1959 he regularly took part in the Darmstadt summer courses in new music, and gave a famous lecture there in 1959, stating his own rejection of purely aesthetic experimentation and his support for socially committed music. Since then critics have spoken of the "Nono tradition" in postwar music. →Karl Amadeus Hartmann coined a well-known saying: "Nono utters accusations, and his language is fiery." From 1959 to 1961 Nono was a lecturer at the Dartington summer school. In the 1960s he concentrated intensively on electronic music, working with the Studio di Fonologia of RAI in Milan, and going on many teaching and lecture tours of eastern Europe and Latin America. From 1975 onward Nono lived mainly in Venice, where he became editor of the journal *Laboratori Musicale* in 1979, and after 1980 he began working with the experimental studio of Southwest German Radio in Freiburg. Nono was a Communist as well as a composer, and became a member of the Italian Communist Party in 1952. He was a fascinating character whose friends included the conductor Claudio Abbado, the piano virtuoso Maurizio Pollini, the poet Heiner Müller, the brilliant Russian theatrical director Yury Lyubimov, and a great many contemporary composers, including figures as various as →Alfred Schnittke, Gavin Bryars, and →Paul Dessau. Nono's controversial music aroused much debate. For decades he was accused of putting art to the service of agitation, until the 1979 string quartet *Fragmente – Stille* proved even to his fiercest opponents that, in the words of the poet Hölderlin, "the suffering gives birth to truth" in Nono's music. With this quartet and with *Prometheus*, described by Nono himself as a *tragedia dell'ascolto* (aural tragedy), his work turned in a new direction, leading in 1992 to the production in Stuttgart of his first opera *Intolerance 1960*, which created a great sensation.

Works: Stage works: *Intolleranza 1960* (*Intolerance 1960*) (1961), *Al gran sole carico amore* (*In the Bright Sunshine Heavy with Love*) (1975), *Prometeo* (*Prometheus*) (1984); orchestral works including *Coma una ola de fuerza y luz* (*Like a Wave of Power and Light*) (1972), works for tape (and voices/instruments) including *La fabbrica illuminata* (*The Illuminated Building*) (1964), chamber music including *... soferte onde serena ...* (*... breathing clarity ...*) (1976).

Intolerance 1960, photograph from the production by Christof Nel, sets Alfred Hrdlicka, conductor Bernhard Kontarsky, Württembergisches Staatstheater, Stuttgart 1992.
This Stuttgart production succeeded in making the fate of Nono's Refugee as historically specific as necessary, and as timelessly relevant as possible. The famous Austrian sculptor Alfred Hrdlicka drew inspiration for his interesting spatial use of the stage from his firmly anti-Fascist beliefs.

*N*ono began his composing career as an exponent of what was known as the Darmstadt School, which was influenced by Schoenberg's 12-tone technique, but he did not, like most of his contemporaries, continue along the path to stylistic pluralism and eclecticism. Instead, he found a musical language of his own in which to express extremes: silence and screaming.

The space-sound concept

When writing *Intolerance 1960*, and especially for that work, Nono developed a specific concept of sound and space in which the connections between visual and tonal sources and events are blurred. When the spectator is confronted by faces and figures on stage representing intolerance, he is surrounded by its emanations in terms of sound, both vocal and orchestral. They threaten from behind and attack from the side. When he is surprised and moved by gestures of solidarity on stage, he hears tentative, vibrating voices singing around him, their sounds becoming phonemes, the phonemes then becoming syllables and words intended to form a "canto sospeso," or "suspended singing." Sound must transcend the time and place of performance, literally and figuratively: space must be aurally perceptible in the horizontal as well as the vertical dimension, partly by the arrangement of loudspeakers in the auditorium, and partly by full exploitation of all chromatic possibilities and the technique of syllabic dissection of the text. Opera was to become an aural experience again.

S. N.

Intolerance 1960, photograph from the production by Christoph Nel, sets Alfred Hrdlicka, conductor Bernhard Kontarsky, Württembergisches Staatstheater, Stuttgart 1992.
A production photograph giving a clear signal: the pictorial motif made a cogent statement about the latent identity of eroticism and violence.

In the Bright Sunshine Heavy with Love

Al gran sole carico d'amore

Azione scenica in two parts

Libretto: Luigi Nono and Yury Lyubimov.
Première: First version: 4 April 1975, Milan (Teatro Lirico, company of the Teatro alla Scala); second version: 26 June 1978, Frankfurt am Main (Städtische Bühnen, Oper).
Setting: The Paris Commune of 1871, the Russian Revolutions of 1905 and 1917, and the Latin American liberation movements of the 1950s and 1960s.

Synopsis

Louise Michel, a teacher and heroine of the Paris Commune, encounters Tamara Bunke, Che Guevara's companion in guerrilla warfare. They establish relationships of solidarity with the "Mother" of the Russian Revolution (drawn from Gorky and Brecht) and the figure of Deola, from a story by Pavese. All these women are confronted by violence and the need to counter it. In attempting to withstand it they finally perish as the cycle of violence moves on.   *S. N.*

In the Bright Sunshine Heavy with Love, photographs from the production by Martin Kušej, sets Martin Zehetgruber, costumes Heide Kastler, conductor Lothar Zagrosek, Württembergisches Staatstheater, Stuttgart 1998.
Yury Lyubimov directed the original production of this work, in close collaboration with Nono, as a timeless, abstract requiem for the dead and the victims of many revolutions. Jürgen Flimm produced a second version at the Frankfurt am Main Opera in 1978, conducted by Michael Gielen, which gave concrete historical expression to the situations presented. The Stuttgart production of 1998 aimed for shocking attention to detail.

Not head and mind alone, but heart and hands

At the première of this *azione scenica* (the title is from a line of verse from Arthur Rimbaud's poem *Les mains de Jeanne-Marie*), there were fears of a scandal along the lines of the uproar caused by the première of *Intolerance 1960*, but it did not materialize. Instead, the work was unanimously acclaimed. Nono had worked miracles in persuading Yury Lyubimov, the highly regarded artistic director of the legendary Taganka Theater in Moscow, to visit western Europe. Between them they turned the spotlight on those revolutionary fighters who are ignored by official histories, women used and misused by their enemies and their own revolutionary comrades alike. There is no consecutive action; instead, we encounter historical figures like Louise Michel and Tamara Bunke, and literary characters like the Mother from Maxim Gorky's novel and Brecht's play, and Deola from a story by Cesare Pavese. The music alternates constantly between large or small chorus and the soloists, with four sopranos, an alto, and a tenor conspicuous among them. They sing and act live on stage, but their taped voices are played back over loudspeakers, and they encounter each other many times in various languages, episodes, places, and periods, as if they were spiritual revenants, actors in a story still in progress.

Prometheus

Prometeo

Tragedia dell'ascolto (aural tragedy)

Libretto: Massimo Cacciari.
Première: First version: 25 September 1984, Venice (church of S. Lorenzo); second version: 25 September 1985, Milan (Stabilimento Ansaldo, company of the Teatro alla Scala).

Synopsis

A presentation of the myth of Prometheus, in its various traditions and interpretations by Hesiod, Aeschylus, Pindar, Goethe, Nietzsche, Hölderlin, and Benjamin.

Hearing history the wrong way

Critics have remarked, less than seriously, that it is easy to say what Nono's *Prometheus* is not, much harder to describe what it really is: not an opera, not an *azione scenica*, not even an anti-opera. So what is it? A *tragedia dell'ascolto*, an "aural tragedy," but in what sense?

The texts, from thousands of years of European culture, show Prometheus, who rebelled against the gods, in constant danger of being made a hero and glorified by tradition – in other words, overwhelmed by conformity as opposed to beauty and nobility. The tragedy is that the danger of conformity cannot be averted until the whole truth of the traditions, however uncomfortable, is at least understood. For that reason Nono gave all the performers microphones, instrumentalists as well as singers. The music is performed live, but its tonal side effects such as lip movements and breathing, usually filtered out and suppressed, as well as microtones from the harmonic spectrum of the upper partials, are reinforced by the microphones and perceived by the ear. Recordings of the live sounds are played back, sounding different; mankind and its material, now alienated from it, come together in the space and time of the performance. The non-simultaneous is heard simultaneously. The ideal of this kind of music is "suono mobile," or mobile sound.

Nono issued a total ban on pictures of his *Prometheus*, in an attempt to resist the omnipotent power of artistic consumerism that prettifies the truth, and he thereby brought the old genre of opera to a state of final veracity. It seems appropriate that this happened in Italy with the assistance of a Venetian, since it was from Venice that opera first set out to conquer the world.

S. N.

In the Bright Sunshine Heavy with Love, production photograph with the four sopranos (from left to right) Sarah Leonard, Priti Coles, Sabine Ritterbusch, and Elena Vink; production Travis Preston, sets and costumes Nina Flagstad, conductor Ingo Metzmacher, Hamburger Staatsoper 1999. The Hamburg production of 1999 referred clearly to the collapse of left-wing ideas of revolution, and at the same time explored greater depths. The Angel of History (Ilona König, right) stands beside the four sopranos (left). Nono liked the ninth section of Walter Benjamin's reflections *Über den Begriff der Geschichte* (*On the Concept of History*), which runs: "There is a picture by Paul Klee called *Angelus Novus*. It shows an angel apparently in the act of retreating from whatever it sees before it. Its eyes are wide open, its mouth is open too, its wings are spread. This is what the angel of history must look like, with its countenance turned to the past. Where we see a succession of incidents, the angel recognizes only disaster, and would like to stay where it is, but a storm blowing out of Paradise is caught in its wings. The stormy wind drives it inexorably into the future to which its back is turned, while the piles of rubble before it tower to the sky. What we call progress is that storm."

J. OFFENBACH

Above
Jacques Offenbach, caricature by Amand (TWS).
The musical chronicler of an age of disillusion, Offenbach wrote over 100 stage works between 1839 and 1880. No final catalogue of his works has yet been drawn up – since, as the caricature suggests, both Offenbach himself and posterity were generous in disposing of the manuscripts – but interest is increasingly felt among experts and the general public in forming a complete picture of the composer's extensive body of work, and thus understanding his intentions.

Offenbach, Jacques

b. 20 June 1819 in Cologne
d. 5 October 1880 in Paris

Offenbach's father was a bookbinder and synagogue cantor. His son learned to play the violin first and then the cello. In 1833 the family moved to Paris, where Offenbach continued learning the cello, and studied composition with →Halévy. He earned a living as an orchestral musician at the Opéra-Comique, and composed salon pieces (romances and waltzes). His first attempts to write stage works were not successful. In 1850 he became conductor of the Théâtre Français, and in the year of the Paris World Exhibition (1855) he opened a theater of his own, the Bouffes-Parisiens in the Champs-Elysées. At first his license allowed him to present only pieces called *musiquettes*, with no more than two or three characters. It was with his *opéra bouffon*, Orpheus in the Underworld (1858), that the prototype of the later Offenbach operettas first appeared on stage. At the height of his fame in the 1860s, Henri Meilhac and Ludovic Halévy worked with him as his librettists. After the Franco–Prussian War and the collapse of the Second Empire the mood of society changed, and Offenbach's works became less popular. The Théâtre de la Gaité bankrupted him, and he went on tour in America to revive his fortunes. He died while still working on his *The Tales of Hoffmann*, an *opéra fantastique*, and it was completed by Ernest Guiraud, who distorted it in the process; to this day, despite its popularity, the opera betrays the fact that it was unfinished at the time of the composer's death. Operetta, invented by Offenbach, lived on in the works of →Johann Strauss the younger, Gilbert and Sullivan, Léhar, and other composers in the field, but then declined into the lower reaches of the light music industry. The Offenbach revival that began in the 1920s was largely due to the Viennese essayist Karl Kraus.

Works: Operas: *Die Rheinnixen* (*The Fairies of the Rhine*) (Vienna 1864), *Les contes d'Hoffmann* (*The Tales of Hoffmann*) (Paris, 1881); *operas bouffes, opera bouffons*, and *opérettes bouffes* (selection): *Orphée aux enfers* (*Orpheus in the Underworld*) (1858), *La belle Hélène* (*The Lovely Helen*) (1864), *Barbe-Bleue* (*Bluebeard*) (1866), *La vie parisienne* (*Life in Paris*) (1866), *La Grande-Duchesse de Gérolstein* (*The Grand Duchess of Gerolstein*) (1867).

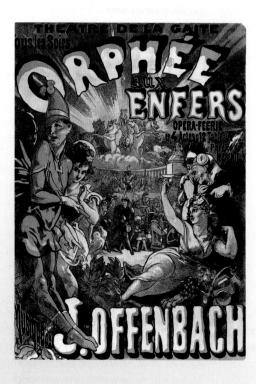

Offenbach was one of the most productive composers for the stage in the history of music. His music "soothes the stress of life, provides refreshment for the mind, and stimulates it to intellectual activity again with a sense of relaxation." (Karl Kraus)

Orpheus in the Underworld, Johann Nepomuk Nestroy as Jupiter and Wilhelm Knaack as Styx, illustration from the first Vienna production at the Carl-Theater in 1860 (TWS). Jupiter, the father of the gods, woos Eurydice in the shape of a fly. He was played in this Viennese production by Johann Nestroy, seen here with Styx, the guardian of the underworld.
Orpheus in the Underworld was Offenbach's first full-length satirical operetta, a cynical account of a depraved and decadent world in which gods and men alike are immoral. Their only honest action is their common indulgence in a great bacchanal in order to forget reality.

Opposite, left
La Périchole, illustration by Faria, Paris (TWS). Offenbach's fine operetta *La Périchole* (*Perichole*) is set in the Peruvian capital of Lima in the 18th century. The story of a street singer (a real character) and the Spanish Viceroy of Peru was a daring one to choose, only a year after the withdrawal of French troops from Mexico. Offenbach toned down the political connotations by emphasizing the work's Spanish coloring.

Opposite, center
Orpheus in the Underworld, poster by Jules Chéret, Paris 1858.
The cheerfully relaxed mood of the piece, combined with classical references and a picture of the opulence of bourgeois society, drew Parisians to the Théâtre de la Gaîté night after night.

Opposite, right
La belle Hélène, title page of first edition, Paris. The title page of the first edition bears a portrait of Anna Judic, who created the part at the première of the work.

The "Mozart of the Champs-Elysées"

At first Offenbach's operettas set out to be no more than the little sisters of grand opera. Operetta remained very closely linked to opera, and indeed parodied opera at first. Offenbach cannot be given sole credit for the invention of this new and irreverent genre (Hervé had preceded him), but it was he who made operetta really popular.

His most successful works were to include *Orpheus in the Underworld* and *La belle Hélène*. At first glance, they appear to deal with tales and heroes of classical mythology; a second look reveals Offenbach's witty allusions to the more grotesque aspects of life during the Second Empire and the Third Republic. Rossini called Offenbach "the Mozart of the Champs-Elysées." The great Russian moralist Leo Tolstoy thought highly of him, and so did the subversive Heinrich Heine, a mocker of conventional morality. Karl Kraus, another sharp-tongued master of the use of language, championed Offenbach's music. As Kraus saw it, operetta was founded on the laws of chaos, and he credited the genre with continuing relevance: "When the healing power of music is united with irresponsible merriment that, amidst all the chaos, brings to mind our real follies, operetta is the one dramatic form really appropriate for the theatrical opportunities available."

The world of the gods in a distorting mirror

Others who were concerned with the "real follies" of the world at the same time as Jacques Offenbach were, rather surprisingly, Richard Wagner and Karl Marx. During the 1850s Wagner was working on his tetralogy (→*The Ring of the Nibelung*), and he foresaw a →*Twilight of the Gods* for mankind, which he saw as driven by avarice and the craving for power. In Offenbach's *opéras bouffes* the gods also indulge their pleasures, but they are dancing on top of the volcano; theirs is a "twilight of the gods" in the light-hearted French manner. Karl Marx, in *Das Kapital*, was another who envisaged a dark ending for the bourgeois world. Music drama, operetta, and political economy all came to the same conclusion: humanity as a whole was on the brink of disaster. While Wagner and Marx both saw that disaster in terms of tragedy, Offenbach, born German but living in France, reacted with cheerful composure. He has been accused of holding up a distorting mirror to the immoral society of his time, and at the same time of "luring it by the witty depiction of its downfall to the theater, where the audience was held spellbound by scantily clad ladies, flirtations, and the eroticism of the cancan." But these are accusations to be leveled at later composers; Offenbach, the "Mozart of the Champs-Elysées," does not deserve them. As the French saying goes, "Honi soit, qui mal y pense" ("Evil be to him who thinks evil"). S. N.

The Tales of Hoffmann

Les contes d'Hoffmann

Opéra fantastique in five acts

Libretto: Jules Barbier, after the play of the same name by Jules Barbier and Michel Carré.

Première: 10 February 1881, Paris (Opéra-Comique).

Characters: Hoffmann (T), Lindorf, also Coppélius, Dr. Miracle, and Captain Dapertutto (B), Andrès, also Cochenille, Frantz, and Pitichinaccio (T), Luther (B), Nathanaël (T), Wolframm (T), Hermann (B), Wilhelm (B), Spalanzani (T), Crespel (T), Peter Schlemil (T), The Muse, also Nicklausse (Ms), Olympia, also Giulietta, Antonia, and Stella (S), A Ghost (Antonia's mother) (Ms); spirits of beer and wine, waiters, students, six lackeys, guests of Spalanzini, guests of Giulietta, servants (chorus).

Setting: Germany and Italy around 1800.

Synopsis
Before the opera begins
The poet Hoffmann and the singer Stella were once passionately in love, but parted when Stella became brilliantly successful, while Hoffmann failed to achieve public acclaim.

Act I
In Luther's tavern, not far from the opera house. Stella has returned to Berlin as a star, and is singing Donna Anna in Mozart's *Don Giovanni*. Hoffmann's Muse fears that her charge will become infatuated with Stella again and neglect his art. She strikes up an alliance with the spirits of beer and wine, and mingles among the young people in the tavern as the student Nicklausse. After seeing Stella on stage as Donna Anna, Hoffmann is deeply distressed, particularly as Counsellor Lindorf has arrived at the tavern, and the poet fears him as a rival. Lindorf has indeed intercepted a letter from Stella to Hoffmann, sending the poet the key to her dressing room.

Hoffmann begins to entertain his student friends with the sad but comic tale of the dwarf Kleinzach, but breaks off as his mind turns once again to thoughts of Stella. He sees Lindorf, and tells his friends that the counsellor has interfered with every one of his love affairs. His friends urge him to tell them the stories of his loves, and as the second act of *Don Giovanni* begins in the opera house, Hoffmann begins to tell his tales.

Act II
A laboratory. The inventor Spalanzani has made an automatic doll, Olympia. He hopes to make money out of the doll, since he has suffered severe financial losses as a result of the failure of his bank. He has ordered lifelike eyes for the doll from the optician

Dr. Coppélius. However, when Coppélius asks for payment Spalanzani gives him a worthless cheque for 500 ducats. Hoffmann has seen Olympia from afar, and has fallen in love with her. Coppélius sells him a pair of spectacles through which the poet sees only what he wants to see – in this case, that the doll Olympia is loving, kind, and alive. Olympia's introduction to the assembled guests is a great success, particularly when she sings a coloratura aria to great effect. Hoffmann declares his love to Olympia, and opens the ball with her, but the automaton runs out of control. Olympia whirls around faster and faster, flinging Hoffmann to the floor, and his spectacles break. Meanwhile Coppélius has discovered that Spalanzani has cheated him, and he destroys the doll in revenge. At last Hoffmann's eyes are opened to Olympia's true nature.

Act III
A room with a harpsichord. Hoffmann has found his former love Antonia, whose mother was a famous singer and whose father is the violin maker Crespel. She and Hoffmann were once engaged, but then she suddenly disappeared. Her father feared that his daughter, who suffered from the same malady as her mother, would die if Hoffmann encouraged her to sing, and Antonia obeyed her father, without knowing his reasons. Hoffmann hears by chance why Antonia abstains from singing on her father's orders, and begs her to be his wife and give up all artistic ambitions. But Dr. Miracle, who attended Antonia's mother and helped to cause her death, tells the daughter that her brilliant talents must not be sacrificed to a bourgeois existence as Hoffmann's wife. He conjures up the voice of her dead mother. Antonia joins in her mother's song, and dies.

Act IV
Scene 1: Venice. The banqueting hall of a palace. Hoffmann seeks oblivion in the arms of the courtesan Giulietta. She is under the influence of Captain Dapertutto, who has already acquired Peter Schlemil's reflection in the mirror through her wiles.
Scene 2: In a garden. Hoffmann kills Schlemil and takes the key to Giulietta's boudoir from the dead man.
Scene 3: A boudoir. Hoffmann gives Giulietta his own reflection. She urges him to flee, since he is being sought for the murder of Schlemil. When Hoffmann realizes that he has lost his reflection but nonetheless has not won Giulietta's love he tries to stab her, but instead kills the deformed Pitichinaccio, the courtesan's real lover.

Act V
Luther's tavern. By the time Hoffmann has finished telling his tales the operatic performance is over. A meeting between Stella and Hoffmann leads to nothing, and Lindorf stakes his claims on the singer.

S. N.

The Tales of Hoffmann, production photograph with Kenneth Riegel as Hoffmann, production Patrice Chéreau, sets Richard Peduzzi, costumes Jacques Schmidt, conductor Jean Perisson, Opéra National de Paris 1978.
It is important to remember that the story of this fantastic opera is told by an old man. *The Tales of Hoffmann* is a late composition by Offenbach, its tone of resignation drawing the line under a life full of illusions and disappointments – it is a work unique in music drama, and full of brilliant and characteristic musical numbers. *M 1 – M 4*

1. Hoffmann's Legend of Kleinzach

(Hoffmann)   *(Chorus)*

Il é - tait u - ne fois à la cour d'Ei-se-nach !   À   la cour d'Ei - se - nach !

(Hoffmann)   *(Chorus)*

Un pe - tit a - vor - ton qui se nommait Klein - zach !   Qui se nom - mait Klein - zach !

2. Olympia's Doll's Song

Les oi - seaux dans la char - mil – – – – – – le,

3. Barcarolle

Bel - le nuit, ô nuit ___ d'amour, Sou - ris ___ à nos i - vres - ses !

4. Hoffmann's Love Theme

O Dieu de quelle i - vresse _ em - bra-ses - tu mon â - me Comme un con-cert di - vin ta voix m'a pé - né - tré !

The Tales of Hoffmann, photograph from the production by Patrice Chéreau, sets Richard Peduzzi, conductor Georges Prêtre, Opéra National de Paris 1974.
The outstanding feature of Patrice Chéreau's production was the deliberate blurring of distinctions between reality and appearance, between waking life and dream, imagination, and fantasy, in line with the saying that our fate is determined not by what we experience, but by the way in which we experience it. Since there is no authentic version of the work, leading directors of various periods, including Walter Felsenstein, Jean-Pierre Ponnelle, Harry Kupfer, and Johannes Schaaf, have taken responsibility for the actual structure of the opera as well as their own interpretations of it.

The opera: a lost reflection

While *The Tales of Hoffmann* is one of the most popular operas in the repertory, it exists only in reworked versions, revisions of those versions, and distortions, and its true essence must remain unknown, for Offenbach used to determine the final form of a work only after its première and the performances that immediately followed. In this case, however, he left an incomplete torso on his death. The première was to have been given at the Théâtre de la Gaité, with recitatives. When that theater went bankrupt, Offenbach granted rights to the première to the Opéra-Comique, where spoken dialogue was the order of the day and a different type of singer predominated. Offenbach began revising the work, but died before he had finished. At the première, which made use of the fragmentary score orchestrated by Ernest Guiraud, the entire Giulietta act (today's Act IV) was omitted, and the famous "Barcarolle" was moved to the Antonia act. The opera was played without the Giulietta act until 1905, and only after it was restored under Hans Gregor at the Komische Oper in Berlin was the work more usually performed with all five acts. Throughout the twentieth century, leading directors have had to try to reconcile their own concepts with the structure of the work as it stands. The reconstruction by Fritz Oeser (1977–78) did not solve the problem, but added further facets. Previously unknown material for the opera is still coming to light, but Offenbach took the secret of its final form to the grave with him.   S. N.

The Tales of Hoffmann, production photograph with Placido Domingo as Hoffmann, production and sets Jean-Pierre Ponnelle, conductor James Levine, Salzburg Festival 1980.
With Placido Domingo as his Hoffmann, Ponnelle told the story with poetic conviction, but in the traditional manner.

Left
The Tales of Hoffmann, costume designs for Lindorf, Coppélius, Dapertutto, and Dr. Miracle by Leonard Fanto, Berlin 1910.
The demonic figures of Coppélius, Dapertutto, and Dr. Miracle (not founded on any character in the works of the real E.T.A. Hoffmann) are different manifestations of Lindorf, just as the three women are all manifestations of Stella.

A thriller featuring a dwarf

The history of the work's construction has continued developing for almost 150 years after Jules Barbier and Michel Carré first wrote their play *Les contes d'Hoffmann*. Until the 1990s it was regarded as the torso of an opera, since no one knew what the complete score would have been like. Then, in 1993, several hundred pages of the original manuscript turned up in a remarkable (and mysterious) find in a château in Burgundy. Some years earlier, the original libretto had been found in the national archives in Paris. The finale of Act IV now assumed a new character: Giulietta no longer disappears in a gondola with Dapertutto, leaving behind the despairing Hoffmann, as she does in the version previously performed. Instead, Hoffmann involuntarily kills Pitichinaccio, and Giulietta's horrified reactions betray the fact that the dwarf was her lover. The new finale of this act had its première in Hamburg on 24 January 1999, an occasion attended by bitter disputes about publication rights.

Above
The Tales of Hoffmann, set design by László
Moholy-Nagy for the production by Ernst
Legal, conductor Alexander von Zemlinsky,
Staatsoper am Platz der Republik, Berlin
1929 (TWS).
Like the French director Patrice Chéreau
at a later date, the Hungarian director
Moholy-Nagy conceived his production of
the opera entirely in the spirit of
E.T.A. Hoffmann himself.

Right
The Tales of Hoffmann, set design by Max
Bignens for the production by Paul Hager,
Volksoper Wien 1964 (TWS).
The world of E.T.A. Hoffmann's fantastic
tales is reflected in Offenbach's opera. It is a
magical piece, with the episodes linked by
some demonic sharp practice. Offenbach's
characters seem to have been conjured
up by a circus illusionist. The wiles of the
charlatans are directed against the hero,
whose hopes are constantly disappointed
and finally wrecked.

Opposite page
The Tales of Hoffmann, photograph from the
première of the newly discovered finale of
Act IV, with Ulrike Schneider (Nicklausse) and
Marcus Haddock (Hoffmann), production
Andreas Baesler, sets Andreas Wilkens,
costumes Susanne Hubrich, conductor
Ingo Metzmacher, Hamburgische
Staatsoper 1999.

Orff, Carl

b. 10 July 1895 in Munich
d. 29 March 1982 in Munich

After studying at the Music Academy in Munich in 1914, Orff became *Kapellmeister* at the Munich Kammerspiele, and from 1918 to 1919 worked at the Nationaltheater, Mannheim, and the Landestheater, Darmstadt. He then returned to Munich, where in 1924 he and Dorothee Günther founded a school for gymnastics, dance, and music. He put his ideas on musical sound into practice by developing a special range of instruments, known as "Orff instruments," which he commissioned from the piano-maker Karl Maendler, and at the same time he set out his ideas on musical education in his *Schulwerk* (*School Work*) of 1935. During this period Orff was also conductor of the Munich Bach Society. Between 1950 and 1960 he taught a master class in composition at the Musikhochschule in Munich. After 1961, he devoted himself to the Orff Institute named after him at the Salzburg Mozarteum.

Works: Stage works: *Carmina burana* (1937), *Der Mond* (*The Moon*) (1939), *Ein Sommernachtstraum* (*A Summer Night's Dream*) (1939/FP 1952), *Die Kluge* (*The Clever Girl*) (1943), *Catulli carmina* (1943), *Die Bernauerin* (*The Bernau Woman*) (1947), *Antigonae* (*Antigone*) (1949), *Astutuli* (*The Tricksters*) (1953), *Trionfo di Afrodite* (*Triumph of Aphrodite*) (1953), *Comoedia de Christi resurrectione* (1957), *Oedipus der Tyrann* (*Oedipus Rex*) (1959), *Ludus de nato infante mirificus* (1960), *Prometheus* (1968), *De temporum fine comoedia* (1973); cantatas, vocal music, music for schools.

The Moon

Kleines Welttheater (little world theater)

Libretto: Carl Orff, after a fairy tale by the Brothers Grimm (Jacob Ludwig Karl and Wilhelm Karl Grimm).
Première: 5 February 1939, Munich (Nationaltheater).
Characters: Narrator (T), Four Young Fellows, who steal the moon (T, 2 Bar, B), A Farmer (Bar), A Village Mayor (spoken), A Landlord (spoken), Another Village Mayor (silent), An Old Man called Petrus, who keeps the sky in order (B), A Small Child, who finds the moon back in the sky (spoken); people drinking in the tavern when the moon is stolen, people glad of the stolen moon who bury the dead thieves, corpses resurrected by the moon (chorus, children's chorus).
Setting: The world and the underworld in the time of fairy tale.

The Moon, set design by Ruodi Barth for the production by Bohumil Herlischka, Deutsche Oper am Rhein, Düsseldorf 1978 (TWS).
The four young fellows carrying out their strange theft. Although the moon is central to the story, the opera is not by any means a nocturne.

Synopsis

Four young fellows on their travels see the moon shining in the branches of an oak. They decide to steal it and take it home to their own dark country. Throughout the rest of their lives they care for the moon so well that each of them is allowed to have a quarter of it buried with him when he dies. The world therefore grows darker and darker. After the death of the last of the four, the moon is reassembled in the underworld. It shines so brightly that the dead are raised, and indulge in a noisy drinking bout. Alarmed by their riotous behavior, Petrus intervenes: first he sends thunder and lightning, then he descends to the underworld himself, and after drinking briefly with the dead he returns them to their rest by removing the cause of all the trouble, the moon itself, and putting it back in the sky. The moon, first seen by a child on earth, is joyfully welcomed by mankind.

M. S.

The Clever Girl

Die Kluge

Tale in 12 scenes

Libretto: Carl Orff, after a fairy tale by the Brothers Grimm.

Première: 20 February 1943, Frankfurt am Main (Städtische Bühnen).

Characters: The King (Bar), The Farmer (B), The Farmer's Daughter (S), The Jailer (B), Man with a Donkey (T), Man with a Mule (Bar), Three Rascals (T, Bar, B).

Setting: A royal castle and its surroundings in the time of fairy tale.

Synopsis

One day a farmer finds a golden mortar in the fields. Ignoring his daughter's warnings, he takes his find to the king. Sure enough, the farmer is not rewarded for his honesty; instead, he is suspected of keeping the pestle that should go with the mortar for himself. Thrown into prison, the farmer laments his fate, and wishes he had taken his daughter's advice. The king is interested to hear of such a clever girl, summons her, and sets her three riddles, all of which she solves. He marries the clever girl. But the new queen is fair-minded as well as clever, and when the king gives the wrong verdict in a legal case, she demands justice. For this offense she is to be thrown out of the castle, but as a favor she may place whatever she loves most in a chest and take it away with her. She tricks the king into falling asleep, and when he wakes next day he is in the chest himself, beneath a tree in blossom.

M. S.

*O*rff created his own inimitable style from a wide diversity of lively rhythms and forceful ostinatos, and used a richly differentiated range of percussion instruments.

The Clever Girl, photograph from the production by Ulrich Rapp, conductor Alexander Winterson, sets Pia Oenel, Deutscher Oper am Rhein, Düsseldorf 1994. The king and the clever girl constantly alternate between erotic attraction to each other and their social difference: Orff's recipe is made up of elements of recitative, rhythmic speech, empathetic delivery, irony, and quotation.

The Clever Girl, set design by Joachim Streubel, Staatsoper Oldenburg 1967 (TWS).
In his stage works, Orff refers back to old European traditions. Both his one-act operas have their roots in the improvised comedy of the Middle Ages. He never wrote an opera in the classic romantic sense; his musical forms and means of expression are linked to older traditions.

Antigone
Antigonae

Tragedy in five acts

Libretto: Friedrich Hölderlin, from the tragedy *Antigone* by Sophocles.
Première: 9 August 1949, Salzburg (Felsenreitschule).
Characters: Antigonae/Antigone (S), Ismene (A), Kreon/Creon (Bar), A Guard (T), Hämon/Haemon (T), Tiresias (T), A Messenger (B), Eurydice (S), Leader of the Chorus (Bar); elders of Thebes (chorus).
Setting: Royal palace of Thebes in mythical times.

Synopsis

The twin brothers Eteocles and Polynices (who, like their sisters Antigone and Ismene, are the offspring of the union between Oedipus and his mother Jocasta) were on different sides at the siege of Thebes and killed each other. King Creon declares Polynices an enemy of the state because he fought for the enemies of Thebes, whereas his brother defended the city. Creon denies Polynices the right to burial. Antigone opposes Creon, and lays her brother to rest with the traditional rites. She is condemned to death for what she has done. Creon's son Haemon, to whom she is betrothed, begs his father for mercy. The seer Tiresias also warns the king of misfortune if he carries out the death sentence. But the pleas of Haemon and the warnings of the seer are in vain. Antigone commits suicide. Creon's wife Eurydice cannot bear such ignominy, and she too takes her own life. The unhappy king is left in isolation.   M. S.

The rebirth of tragedy

Arrangements of works by Monteverdi, and a translation by the poet Hölderlin of the *Antigone* of Sophocles, performed in 1940 in Vienna, gave Orff the idea of a new approach to subjects from classical antiquity. A year later he had developed a concept departing from textual dominance and bringing music to the fore. His individual view of tragedy that has considerable relevance in the 20th century is particularly evident in his musical language, which employs many means of expression, ranging from free cantilenas, *ariosi*, and expressive outbursts to unaccompanied song, and from large fields of sound to the careful use of single instruments, such as the flute to symbolize Eros.

The Tricksters
Astutuli

A Bavarian comedy

Libretto: Carl Orff.
Première: 20 October 1953, Munich (Kammerspiele).

Characters: Two Vagabonds, Two Citizens, Jörg Zaglstecher (the mayor), His Daughters Fundula, Hortula, and Vellicula, Girl Playmates, Three Sponsors, Three Councillors, Wunibald Hirnstössl (the watchman), Unknown Performer, Traveling Woman, Citizens (spoken).

Setting: "The story begins in time immemorial."

Synopsis

The mayor, dignitaries, and people have gathered in an improvised theater to be entertained by the unknown performer. He appears in magician's costume, and conjures up fantastic visions by means of special lighting effects and words and gestures of invocation. Some of the audience doubt him, while others willingly fall under his spell. At the end of this performance, the mayor is to have a new suit of clothes. Reluctantly, he allows himself to be undressed down to his shirt, and then he is supposed to be dressed in his new clothes – but they are invisible. When the people follow the mayor's example, the same thing happens to them. At this point the lights go out and the performer disappears, while the audience waits expectantly for the performance to go on. The young people present take advantage of this opportunity to pair off as lovers, the vagabonds go around picking pockets, while the older citizens feel bored, and wonder if the performer is going to come back at all. Sure enough, both the performer and their clothes are gone. They have all been tricked. Then the performer does come back, but in another costume, announcing the arrival of an alchemist who can turn other metals into gold. When the mayor and the council show their respect for the alchemist, all present bring their money to have it turned into gold. Once again they are cheated. Nonetheless, the people begin to dance, while the two vagabonds make off with the stolen property.   M. S.

The Tricksters, set design by Helmut Jürgens for the Kammerspiele, Munich 1953 (TWS). *Astutuli* (from the Latin "astutus," meaning "cunning") can be regarded as a satyr play in relation to either the tragedy of *Antigone*, or Orff's earlier Bavarian opera *The Bernau Woman* (1942–46). Based on Hans Christian Andersen's fairy tale *The Emperor's New Clothes*, the piece takes as its subject mass suggestion and the human tendency to fall a willing victim to delightful illusions, especially at times of crisis. Orff used a kind of primitive dialect with clear elements of musicality; the melody of speech is dominant.

Carmina burana, costume designs by Hans Aeberli, Essen 1980 (TWS).
Hans Aeberli's costume designs were devised very much in the spirit of the medieval *danse macabre*.

Carmina burana, set design (The Wheel of Fortune) by Hans Aeberli, Städtische Bühnen Essen 1980 (TWS).
"In the midst of life we are in death" was a favorite saying in the Middle Ages. In the *Carmina burana*, however, Orff uses his marked talent for rhythm to represent the opposite viewpoint: in the shadow of death, mankind is alive and kicking. Perhaps the secret of the work's extraordinary popularity lies in this fundamental attitude. *M 1, M 2*

Carmina burana

Cantiones profanae cantoribus et choris cantande comitantibus instrumentis atque imaginibus magicis (secular songs for soloists and chorus, with the accompaniment of instruments and images)

Libretto: Latin and German songs from the *Carmina burana*, a manuscript of c. 1250, selection compiled by Carl Orff.

Première: 8 June 1937, Frankfurt am Main (Opernhaus).

Characters: Soprano, Tenor, Baritone; auxiliary soloists: 2 Tenors, Baritone, 2 Basses; boys' choir, chorus.

Synopsis

A great introductory chorus sings the praises of the fickle goddess of fate, Fortuna. Constantly present in the work by means of passages that recall it, this chorus provides a framework for a logical sequence of events. The songs of the first part ("Primo vere"/"Uf dem Anger") celebrate spring, nature, and the joy of life. The second part ("In taberna") concentrates on earthly pleasures from the point of view of the Abbot of Cockayne, expressed in grotesque solos such as the "Song of the Roasted Swan." The last part ("Cours d'amours"/"Blanziflor et Helena") is devoted to the many and various forms of love. In line with the general structural idea, there are no three-dimensional protagonists in the piece, only prototypes such as adventurers, girls and their companions, gamblers, and loving couples.   *M. S.*

Carmina burana, production photograph with Jacek Strauch and Wolfgang Ablinger-Sperrhocke, production and lighting Werner Michael Esser, sets Kurt Pint, choreography Virgil Stancin, conductor Roman Zeilinger, Landestheater Linz 1995.
The Wheel of Fortune going around full tilt. It raises some up and casts others down, catching bystanders and involving them in the turmoil too.

Catulli carmina

Ludi scenici (scenic games)

Libretto: Poems by Gaius Valerius Catullus, selected by Carl Orff.

Première: 6 November 1943, Leipzig (Städtische Bühnen).

Characters: Catullus, Lesbia, Caelius, Ipsitilla, Ameana, Lovers (dancers); young men, young women, old men (chorus).

Synopsis

The old men pour scorn on the loving vows of young people; it is all nonsense, they say, and nothing on earth lasts forever. For the time being, this conflict of opinion remains undecided. The games that follow will cast more light on the question. Lesbia keeps an appointment with Catullus, who falls asleep in her arms. But she leaves him immediately to delight her other lovers by dancing for them in the tavern. Afraid of missing Lesbia, Catullus sleeps in the street outside her house. As he does so, he dreams of Lesbia making love to Caelius, and abruptly wakes from sleep. Still enamored of Lesbia, Catullus writes Ipsitilla a love letter, but rejects the old whore Ameana. At last he sees Lesbia among her lovers and women friends, and now he brusquely breaks off their affair. She flees, her feelings injured. The conflict between youthful vitality and the experience of age is won by the young, who never learn from the mistakes of their elders, but insist on pursuing their passions: "Eis aiona – forever thine!"

M. S.

Orff's triptych

In 1847 Johann Andreas Schmeller published an edition of the *Carmina burana*, probably the most important collection of medieval Latin and Middle High German lyric poetry from the period 1220–50, and preserved in a manuscript in the monastery of Benediktbeuern. Almost a hundred years later, in 1934, Orff came upon this collection, and was so fascinated by the medieval poems that they immediately gave him the idea of a dramatic cantata. He completed the work in August 1936. To provide a sequence for a full evening's entertainment he wrote a similarly constructed piece, with dancing, based on the poems of Catullus about his love for the patrician Clodia Pulcher (Lesbia). He now had two entirely independent works of music drama, the first to open the evening, the second to form an interlude, and the concluding work was to be on the subject of wedding festivities not set in any particular period. Once again Orff turned to Catullus; he chose several of his poems on weddings, combined them with suitable fragments from Sappho, and concluded with the very effective strophic choral song by Euripides for the appearance of Aphrodite. This third part of the triptych was completed in 1951. Strophic form (without any further development), a strong sense of period, energy, and melodies constructed in small sections are characteristic of the *Carmina burana*. The *Catulli carmina* are much more expressive and subtly sensuous in structure, marked by ecstatic language and much use of percussion instruments, often to startling effect. In the third part, *Triumph of Aphrodite*, the voice dominates the instrumental sound, displaying Orff's new concept of tonality; he gave no clear indication of a key, but simply chose a central tone.

When *Carmina burana* was to be premièred, the work was thought impossible to perform. Its great success was not welcomed by the Nazis, but after the Second World War it became part of the international repertory, either as the opening work of the triptych or on its own, on stage or in the concert hall. The other two parts of the triptych have never achieved the same popularity.   M. S.

Carmina burana, production photograph with Jacek Strauch and Wolfgang Ablinger-Sperrhocke, production and lighting Werner Michael Esser, sets Kurt Pint, conductor Roman Zeilinger, Landestheater Linz 1995.

Triumph of Aphrodite

Trionfo di Afrodite

Concerto scenico (staged concerto)

Libretto: Poems by Gaius Valerius Catullus and Sappho, with the strophic choral song from the *Hippolytus* of Euripides, compiled by Carl Orff.
Première: 14 February 1953, Milan (Teatro alla Scala).
Characters: Bride (S), Bridegroom (T), Three Leaders of the Chorus (T, S, B), Aphrodite (silent); young women, young men, old men, parents, relations, friends, crowd (chorus, dancers).

Synopsis

The archetypal couple, bride and bridegroom, are celebrating their timeless wedding. After nuptial rites and a song of praise to Hymenaeus, the god of marriage, young women lead the bride to the bridal chamber, singing and dancing, while the men sing mocking songs for the bridegroom's benefit. The appearance of the goddess Aphrodite, symbolizing love, completes the ritual.   M. S.

Left
Carmina burana, photograph from the production by Werner Michael Esser, lighting Werner Michael Esser, sets Kurt Pint, conductor Roman Zeilinger, Landestheater Linz 1995.

The Devils of Loudun

Opera in three acts

Libretto: Krzysztof Penderecki, after the novel *The Devils of Loudun* by Aldous Huxley, dramatized by John Robert Whiting.
Première: 20 June 1969, Hamburg (Staatsoper).
Characters: Jeanne, prioress of the Ursuline Order (dramatic S or high Ms), Claire (Ms), Gabrielle and Louise, Ursuline nuns (S and A), Philippe, a young girl (high S), Ninon, a young widow (A), Grandier, priest of St. Peter's (Bar), Father Barré, vicar of Chinon (B), Baron de Laubardemont, the king's commissioner (T), Father Rangier (low B), Father Mignon, confessor of the Ursuline nuns (T), Adam, an apothecary (T), Mannoury, a surgeon (Bar), D'Armagnac, the Mayor (spoken), De Cerisay, the town justice (spoken), Prince Henri de Condé, envoy of the king (Bar), Father Ambrose, an old priest (B), Bontemps, the jailer (Bbar), Court Clerk (spoken); Ursuline nuns, Carmelites, crowd, children, guards, soldiers (chorus).
Setting: The town of Loudun (Vienne) in 1634.

Synopsis
Act I

Jeanne's cell, the streets of Loudun, a bathtub, a church, the confessional, the town walls, the cloisters, the pharmacy. Prioress Jeanne has fallen in love with Father Grandier. She lives out her "sinful love" in her fantasies, hoping for Grandier to become father confessor and adviser to her convent, a post he refuses. The search for evidence of Grandier's dissolute life at first establishes nothing but his political opinions, but then Jeanne confesses her visions of the "diabolical behavior" of Father Grandier to Father Mignon, who orders exorcisms.

Act II

A church, a cell, the convent garden, the town battlements. Accusations against Grandier are mounting – they are unjustified, since he has had no dealings with the nuns. Tiring of such monstrosities, the justice breaks off legal proceedings. Father Mignon suggests new visions to the minds of the nuns, and there are public exorcisms. The nuns and the people are in the grip of madness. Grandier, a man opposed to church and state, is condemned in advance.

Act III

Three cells, a square, St. Peter's church, the convent of St. Ursula, the scene of an auto-da-fé. Although Grandier does not confess, in spite of torture, he is condemned to death and burnt at the stake. After failing to commit suicide, Jeanne falls into a state of insanity.   *M. S*

Penderecki, Krzysztof

b. 23 November 1933 in Debica (Poland)

After completing his studies, Penderecki began teaching composition at the Kraków Conservatory in 1958, and became director there in 1972. From 1966 to 1968 he was lecturer in composition and orchestration at the Folkwang Conservatory in Essen. He became increasingly well known as a conductor, and in 1988 was appointed principal guest conductor of the North German Radio Symphony Orchestra. His outstanding talents won him international recognition, and the stylistic developments of his music have been followed with interest all over the world.

Works: Operas: *Diably z Loudun* (*The Devils of Loudun*) (1969, Hamburg), *Paradise Lost* (1978, Chicago), *Die schwarze Maske* (*The Black Mask*) (1986, Salzburg), *Ubu Rex* (1991, Munich); choral works including *Psalmy Dawida* (*Psalms of David*) (1958), *St. Luke Passion* (1966), the oratorio *Dies irae* (1967), *Te Deum* (1980), and *Polish Requiem* (1984), and orchestral works including *Emanations* for two string orchestras (1959), *Threnos* (1959), *Anaklasis* (1960), and five symphonies.

*A*fter his initial musical experiments, Penderecki developed his own synthesis of avant-garde and historical techniques.

Above
The Devils of Loudun, poster, Geneva 1979.

The Devils of Loudun, photograph from the production by Günter Krämer, sets Carlos Diappi, conductor János Kulka, Deutsche Oper am Rhein, Düsseldorf 1989.
The première in Hamburg, directed by Konrad Swinarski, was conducted by the Pole Henryk Czyz, to whom the opera is dedicated, but it was Günther Rennert's staging of the work at the Staatsoper in Stuttgart two days later, on 22 June 1969, that brought real public success and the acceptance of the opera into the international repertory. János Kulka conducted the work both in Stuttgart in 1969 and in Düsseldorf in 1989.

Timeless fanaticism

Inspired by Whiting's drama, Penderecki was already planning to set it to music in 1964. His plans were realized when, in 1967, Rolf Liebermann commissioned him to write a work for the Staatsoper in Hamburg, for the opening of the 43rd International Music Festival of the ISCM. The subject is based on a real event in France in 1634, when Urbain Grandier was burnt at the stake. Huxley had done historical research for his novel, which Whiting followed quite closely, although his interpretation was different. In his turn, Penderecki sought to suggest a historical dimension transcending period, and presented a stark picture of the cruelty of authoritarian regimes in the auto-da-fé scene: political intrigues and religious fanaticism demand victims and destroy anyone who does not fit in. The musical means are used with restraint in order to provide a faithful illustration of the text. Cluster and glissando techniques, sustained notes, and archaic repetitions suggest the local color of a convent, and also reflect the characters' mental states. Contemplation is one pole, frenzy and possession its opposite. The public had reservations about the work at first, but it then became known all over the world.　M. S.

The Devils of Loudun, production photograph with Trudeliese Schmidt (Jeanne) and Michael Busch (Grandier), production Günter Krämer, sets Carlos Diappi, conductor János Kulka, Deutsche Oper am Rhein, Düsseldorf 1989. Günter Krämer's production brought a new quality to the interpretation of the work, as a plea against any kind of political violence in line with the principles of Amnesty International.

The Black Mask

Opera in one act

Libretto: Krzysztof Penderecki and Harry Kupfer, after Gerhart Hauptmann.
Première: 15 August 1986, Salzburg Festival.
Characters: Silvanus Schuller, the mayor (T), Benigna, his wife (S), Arabella, a young mulatto woman (S), Rosa Sacchi, confidante of Benigna (Ms), Jedidja, a servant in the Schuller household (T), François Tortebat, a Huguenot gardener (B), Daga, a maid (S), Löwel Perl, a merchant (Bar), Robert Dedo, Prince-Abbot of Hohenwaldau (Bbar), Plebanus Wendt, a pastor (B), Hadank, an organist (T), Count Ebbo Hüttenwächter (B), Countess Laura Hüttenwächter (A), Schedel, town councillor (T), Dr. Knoblochzer, town councillor (T), Johnson (spoken), A Voice (A).

Setting: Bolkenhain in Silesia, 1662.

Synopsis

13 people assemble around the rich Mayor Schuller's dining table in Bolkenhain in Silesia at carnival time in 1662, while the plague rages outside. An unknown guest in a black mask arrives, and reminds the company of the past. Benigna, now Schuller's wife, once had an affair with the slave Johnson in Amsterdam. Their daughter Arabella is now living with the Schullers as a maidservant. Johnson forced his mistress to marry the rich slave trader Geldern, and exerted pressure on her until the slave trader died in mysterious circumstances. It is soon revealed that all present have criminal past histories, and Johnson himself is concealed behind the mask of the avenger who brings death.　M. S.

"The material explored has been exhausted." (Penderecki)
In the same way as historical pieces are sometimes quoted at appropriate moments in film scores, Penderecki integrated music of the past such as the *Dies irae* sequence from the medieval Requiem Mass into his total concept of sound. He depicts the unreal by using a subtly nuanced declamatory style, driving energy, and traces of Romanticism, as well as avant-garde techniques. After the première of *The Black Mask* in Salzburg on 15 August 1986, the opera was performed all over Europe, and in 1988 it also had some success in the USA.

Pergolesi, Giovanni Battista

b. 4 January 1710 in Iesi, near Ancona
buried 17 March 1736 in Pozzuoli, near Naples

Pergolesi's family name was originally Draghi, but he was entered in the records of the Naples Conservatory as "Iesi", from the name of his birthplace. He called himself Pergolesi (the form "Pergolese" also occurs in contemporary documents). He lost his mother in 1727 and his father in 1732, and his siblings also died young. He himself was sickly, and walked with a limp. Pergolesi came to music as a choirboy, and then studied violin and composition, for which he showed extraordinary talent. His first major work, a *dramma sacro,* had its première in 1731. He became *maestro di cappella* to the viceroy of Naples in 1732, and his first opera dates from the same year. He had only a few years left in which to compose, for he died of tuberculosis at the age of 26.

Works: Operas: *Salustia* (1732), *Lo frate 'nnamorato* (*The Enamored Friar*) (1732), *Il prigionier superbo* (*The Proud Prisoner*) (1733), *La serva padrona* (*The Maid as Mistress*) (1733), *Adriano in Siria* (*Hadrian in Syria*) (1734), *Livietta e Tracollo,* or *La contadina astuta* (*Livietta and Tracollo,* or *The Cunning Peasant Girl*) (1737), *L'Olimpiade* (*The Olympiad*) (1735), *Il Flaminio* (*Flaminio*) (1735); oratorios, Masses, and other sacred works (including the famous *Stabat mater* of 1736), cantatas, arias, some instrumental pieces.

*P*ergolesi is sometimes called the Italian Mozart, both for his early maturity and for the infectious simplicity, lightness of touch, and beauty of his music.

The Maid as Mistress

La serva padrona

Intermezzo in musica

Libretto: Gennaro Antonio Federico.
Première: 5 September 1733, Naples (Teatro S. Bartolomeo), as an intermezzo performed between the acts of Pergolesi's *opera seria Il prigonier superbo.*
Characters: Uberto, an elderly gentleman (B), Serpina, his maid (S), Vespone, his manservant (silent).
Setting: Italy in the early 18th century.

Synopsis

The maid Serpina (meaning "little snake") runs the household of the rich bachelor Uberto. To escape her imperious moods, he declares his intention of marrying. Serpina says that she herself will be mistress of the house. First she shows Uberto how much he relies on her already. Then she pretends that she is planning to get married herself, and introduces "Captain Tempest," really the servant Vespone in disguise. After meeting the uncouth soldier, Uberto feels sorry for Serpina. When she issues her ultimatum – he must either pay her 4000 talers or marry her himself – Uberto chooses marriage, thereby making his maid mistress of the house. *S. N.*

Laughter permitted

When opera first began, with Jacopo Peri's *Euridice* and Monteverdi's →*Orfeo*, comedy was alien to the genre. Only with the beginnings of public opera in Venice in 1637 did comic figures, many of them plebeian in origin, appear on stage. In the heyday of Venetian opera (Monteverdi, →*The Return of Ulysses to his Homeland*, 1640, and →*The Coronation of Poppaea*, 1642) tragic and comic elements were combined. The Venetian public similarly expected the young Handel to depict emotions alternating between grave sublimity and laughter (→*Agrippina*, 1709). Purely comic opera came into being at a time when the specific characteristics of *opera seria* had been standardized, and its usual place of performance was at aristocratic courts. Opera houses that depended on a paying public, on the other hand, relied on laughter as a magnet to draw audiences. The new development began almost incidentally, in the form of intermezzos, or interludes, to be performed between the acts of an *opera seria*, and the success of these intermezzos encouraged the writing of full-length comic operas.

Musically short-winded

It could not be said that a singer of *opera buffa* needs less breath than a singer of *opera seria*, but the early examples of the genre do consist principally of short motifs, often repeated to the point of becoming ludicrous as a source of comedy. The arias are also shorter. The fluent vocal capacity of the castrato was not needed here; patter-like dialogue was more important, as was the quality of the acting. *Opera buffa* became a chamber genre that relied on sophisticated ensemble playing.

Humor survives everything

Pergolesi did indeed write a small masterpiece, but what exactly was it that turned *The Maid as Mistress* into such an international success in the eighteenth century? The libretto was translated into a number of languages (even Swedish and Russian), and Pergolesi's intermezzo even conquered America in the last decade of the eighteenth century, when it was performed in Baltimore and New York. Its second Paris performance in 1752 set off the famous dispute known as the "Querelle des Bouffons" between the supporters of the courtly French style (→Rameau) and those of the more popular Italian operatic style.

Rousseau and the Encyclopedists, with their adherents, praised Pergolesi's *The Maid as Mistress* as a model of natural, lifelike comedy. His music continued to be highly regarded in the nineteenth and twentieth centuries, even to the point that a number of works by other composers were attributed to him.

Photograph of the composer by Müller Hilsdorf, Munich c. 1930.
The intensity of the statement made in this opera and of its music, tinged with Romantic emotion, led critics to assume that Pfitzner identified with Palestrina, something he always denied.

Palestrina, production photograph with William Cochran (Palestrina) and Wious Slabbert (Cardinal Borromeo), production Nikolaus Lehnhoff, conductor Klaus Wallat, Deutsche Oper am Rhein, Düsseldorf 1999. In both Germany and Austria, productions of *Palestrina* have always been great events. Famous interpreters of the title role include Hans Hotter, Fritz Wunderlich, Julius Patzak, and Peter Schreier.

Palestrina

Musical legend in three acts

Libretto: Hans Pfitzner.
Première: 12 June 1917, Munich (Prinz-regententheater).

Characters: Pope Pius IV (low B), Giovanni Morone and Bernardo Novagerio, cardinal legates of the pope (Bar, T), Cardinal Borromeo (Bar) and other participants in the Council of Trent, Giovanni Pierluigi da Palestrina, *maestro di cappella* at S. Maria Maggiore in Rome (T), Ighino, his son, aged 15 (S), Silla, his pupil, aged 17 (Ms), Five Singers from the Choir of S. Maria Maggiore in Rome (2 T, 2 B, low B), A Young Doctor (A), Apparition of Lucrezia, Palestrina's dead wife (A), Apparitions of Nine Dead Masters of the Art of Music (3 T, 3 Bar, 3 B), Three Angelic Voices (3 high S), Two Papal Nuncios (silent), Giuseppe, Palestrina's old servant (silent); angels, Italian, German, and Spanish servants, participants in the Council, singers of the papal chapel, street folk (chorus); German imperial councillors, cardinals, envoys of the Church, secular princes, ambassadors, patriarchs, archbishops, bishops, heads of religious orders, abbots, canons, spiritual and temporal procurators, theologians, doctors, crowd, soldiers of the city guard (extras).
Setting: Rome and Trent, November to December 1563.

Synopsis
Act I

A room in Palestrina's house in Rome, evening. Silla is singing Palestrina's son Ighino his new madrigal in the style of the Florentine School, and the two boys quarrel, since Ighino prefers the old style of vocal polyphony. Palestrina comes home with Cardinal Borromeo, who does not like Silla's composition. Palestrina defends his pupil's right to his own musical language. Borromeo commissions Palestrina to write a mass in the old polyphonic style for the pope. The question of the style of sacred music has already become a matter of public debate between the pope and the emperor. Palestrina doubts

Pfitzner, Hans

b. 5 May 1869 in Moscow
d. 22 May 1949 in Salzburg

The son of a pianist and violinist, Pfitzner's studied in Frankfurt am Main, and was music director of the theater in Mainz between 1894 and 1896. He taught composition at the Stern Conservatory in Berlin from 1897 to 1907, and in 1903 became *Kapellmeister* at the Theater des Westens there. After a brief period as a conductor in Munich, he took the post of civic music director in Strasbourg in 1908, where he was also director of the Conservatory and the opera house. In 1920 the Berlin Academy of Arts appointed him to give a master class in composition, and he taught at the Munich Academy of Music from 1929 to 1934. Later, he lived in Vienna and Salzburg. He is regarded by music historians as an opponent of modernism. His works were acclaimed by his admirers, but the general public was less enthusiastic.

Works: Der arme Heinrich (*Poor Heinrich*) (1895, Mainz), *Die Rose vom Liebesgarten* (*The Rose from the Garden of Love*) (1901, Elberfeld), *Das Christelflein* (*The Christmas Elf*) (1906, Munich), *Palestrina* (1917, Munich), *Das Herz* (*The Heart*) (1931, Berlin); choral works, songs, orchestral works, chamber music, piano music.

Pfitzner was a passionate advocate of the European tradition. He developed a Romantic style with a strong tendency towards thematic work. His later works show a free approach to dissonance.

whether he can still compose music. Left alone, he sees visions. The old masters of music urge him to complete the great polyphonic tradition, and so does his dead wife Lucrezia. Angels dictate the music to him. Exhausted, he falls asleep. Ighino and Silla find the finished Mass the next morning.

Act II

Trent, the great hall of the prince-bishop's palace. The Council meets in a heated atmosphere. Even as the hall is being prepared for the meeting, the servants of the participating dignitaries quarrel. Cardinal Legate Novagerio tries to make peace. When Cardinal Borromeo tells him of Palestrina's refusal to have his Mass performed, Novagerio speaks of the usefulness of the Inquisition. But Borromeo has already had Palestrina imprisoned. The debate on the style of church music is turbulent. Borromeo plays his trump card: Palestrina's Mass. Nonetheless, there is no agreement. Finally the Council is adjourned. The dignitaries leave the hall in anger, while their servants make for each other with knives drawn.

Act III

A room in Palestrina's house in Rome, towards evening. Ighino had given Borromeo the music for the Mass to save his father from prison. Now Palestrina, his son, and his pupil are waiting to hear the outcome of its performance before the pope. There is loud rejoicing when the door opens, and the singers of the papal chapel describe the extraordinary effect made by the music of the *Missa Papae Marcelli*. The pope himself appears, and appoints Palestrina *maestro di cappella* of the Sistine Chapel. Amidst great rejoicing, the visitors withdraw. Only Borromeo is left behind with Palestrina, and apologizes for his conduct. In spite of everything, Silla decides to go to Florence, and Palestrina understands how he feels. He has found his own peace, beyond praise and blame, and immerses himself in music at his portative organ.

S. N.

Palestrina, set design by Rudolf Hraby (studios) for the production by Hans Pfitzner, conductor Otto Klemperer, Vereinigte Stadttheater, Köln 1919/20 (TWS).
Pfitzner came upon the legend that Palestrina saved church music in August Wilhelm Ambros's history of music. He took his stylistic guidelines from the polyphony of Palestrina's own time, but without attempting an actual historical approach. For period coloring, he studied Palestrina's *Missa Papae Marcelli*, and introduced quotations from the work into his score.

La Gioconda

Gioconda

Dramma lirico in four acts

Libretto: Tobia Gorrio (Arrigo Boito), after a play by Victor Hugo.

Première: First version: 8 April 1876, Milan (Teatro alla Scala); four more versions before 1880.

Characters: La Gioconda, a singer (S), Laura Adorno, a Genoese lady (Ms), Alvise Badoero, one of the leaders of the Venetian Inquisition, husband of Laura (B), La Cieca (the blind woman), Gioconda's mother (A), Enzo Grimaldi, a Genoese prince (T), Barnaba, a street singer (Bar), Zuàne, a sailor in the Regatta (B), A Singer (B), Isèpo, a public scrivener (T), A Pilot (B), Two Distant Voices (T, B); people of all social classes, seamen, senators, ladies and gentlemen, masqueraders, monks, etc. (chorus).
Setting: Venice in the 17th century.

Synopsis

For political reasons, Prince Enzo has been obliged to renounce Laura, the love of his youth. He is betrothed to the singer Gioconda, but he still loves Laura, who has now married Alvise Badoero. His plan to elope with Laura fails. The jealous Gioconda recognizes Laura as the woman who has saved her mother. When Alvise forces his wife to take poison, Gioconda exchanges the potion for a sleeping draft. To allow Laura and Enzo to flee together, she must promise the Inquisition spy Barnaba that she will give herself to him. When Barnaba demands his price, Gioconda stabs herself before his eyes.

Ponchielli, Amilcare

b. 31 August 1834 in Paderno Fasolaro (now Paderno Ponchielli)
d. 16 January 1886 in Milan

Ponchielli received his early musical education from his father, a businessman who played the organ in the village church. From 1843 he studied music theory, composition, and piano at the Milan Conservatory. He began his career as a church organist and music director of the Cremona theater (1854), where his own first opera had its première in 1856. However, Ponchielli's real breakthrough came almost 20 years later, with *La Gioconda* (1876). By then he was already a highly esteemed professor at the Milan Conservatory.

Works: Operas: *I promessi sposi* (*The Betrothed*) (1856), *Bertrando* (1858), *La savoiarda* (*The Savoyard Woman*) (1861), *Roderico, re dei Goti* (*Roderick, King of the Goths*) (1863), *Il parlatore eterno* (*The Eternal Windbag*) (1873), *I lituani* (*The Lithuanians*) (1874), *I mori di Valenza* (*The Moors of Valencia*) (1874), *La Gioconda* (*Gioconda*) (1876), *Il figliuol prodigo* (*The Prodigal Son*) (1880), *Marion Delorme* (1885); ballets, cantatas, church music, songs, orchestral and chamber music, piano works.

From Padua to Venice: Hugo and Boito
Victor Hugo's play of 1835 depicted the atmosphere of terror that reigned during the period of the Council of Ten, with its spying network and its many minor autocratic rulers. Boito took all the main characters from Hugo's play, gave them new names, and moved the scene of the action from Padua to Venice, as a brilliant setting for a grand opera.

*P*onchielli is the most important Italian operatic composer between Verdi and Puccini.

La Gioconda, production photograph with Maria Callas (Gioconda) and Lucia Danieli (Laura), production Mario Frigerio, sets Nicola Benois, Teatro alla Scala, Milan 1950/51.
A rarity among production photographs, showing Maria Callas at the beginning of her career and before her drastic dieting. The great singer of Greek descent had spent some years in America, and founded her European career on the attractive part of La Gioconda at the Arena di Verona. She was internationally famous for her performance in the role.

Before the opera begins

Prince Enzo loved Laura, and was loved in return, but for political reasons she was married to Alvise, one of the leading figures in the Venetian Inquisition. Enzo then became betrothed to the singer Gioconda, who loves him passionately. However, although he is banished from Venice, he cannot forget Laura.

Act I: "The Lion's Jaws"

In the courtyard of the Doge's Palace in Venice, the people are preparing for the Regatta. Barnaba, a street singer and also an Inquisition spy, loves Gioconda. When she brusquely rejects his advances, he hatches a plot. He publicly accuses Gioconda's blind old mother, the deeply religious La Cieca, of being a witch. Only the intervention of the masked Laura prevents the crowd from lynching the old woman. La Cieca gives her rescuer her rosary. Barnaba pretends to be arranging an elopement for Enzo and Laura, but informs Laura's husband Alvise of the time and place of their departure, and gives Gioconda the same information.

Act II: "The Rosary"

The banks of an uninhabited island in the lagoon. The lovers are to escape on board Enzo's ship, but the jealous Gioconda plans to prevent their flight at the last minute. In despair at Enzo's unfaithfulness to her, she wishes to be avenged on her rival, but then, seeing the rosary, she recognizes Laura as her mother's rescuer. In her gratitude, Gioconda now helps Laura, exchanging masks with her. On the arrival of Alvise's armed henchmen, Enzo blows up his ship and escapes death by swimming. Laura returns to her husband, who has been informed of these events by Barnaba.

Act III: "The Ca' d'oro"

Scene 1: Alvise, his masculine pride deeply wounded, determines not to be betrayed again, and orders his unfaithful wife to take poison. Once again the singer Gioconda intervenes to save her rival, exchanging the poison for a draft that will induce a deathlike sleep.

Scene 2: The guests at the masked ball are enjoying themselves, watching a magnificent ballet ("The Dance of the Hours"), while the death bell tolls for Laura. Enzo arrives in haste, and is taken prisoner. With Barnaba's assistance, however, Gioconda plans to reunite Enzo and Laura and enable them to escape. Barnaba's price for his aid is that Gioconda must give herself to him that same night on the Giudecca island.

Act IV: "The Orfano Canal"

Laura, apparently dead, is brought to the Giudecca, where Gioconda awaits her own unhappy fate. Enzo, still thinking Laura dead, means to avenge himself on Gioconda, who is overjoyed at the idea of dying by the hand of the man she loves. At this moment, however, Laura wakes from her deep trance, and Enzo understands what a sacrifice Gioconda has made. Gioconda gives her blessing to the love between Enzo and Laura. Left alone, she is surprised by Barnaba. When the villain demands his reward, Gioconda stabs herself, while Barnaba whispers to the dying woman that he has killed her mother.   *S. N.*

The villain

Boito's most far-reaching changes were to the character of Barnaba. Hugo's villain is an instrument in the author's hands, setting the mechanism of the plot in motion, and he disappears halfway through the play. Boito gave the spy his own subjective motivation: his Barnaba is not just a professional troublemaker but also a rejected lover. The situation leads to the tragic close of the opera and the heroine's suicide. Barnaba dominates the stage from the beginning to the end of the opera, and may be regarded as a preliminary study for Verdi's demonic Iago (→*Otello*).

A rewarding opera for singers

La Gioconda is the quintessential singers' opera, full of catchy melodies and musical numbers such as La Cieca's rosary melody M1, Enzo's romance in Act II M2, Gioconda's famous poison aria at the beginning of Act IV M3, love duets, and electrifying musical genre numbers such as the forlana.   *J. K.*

1. La Cieca's Rosary Melody

A - te que - sto ro - sa - rio che le preghiere a - du - na;

io te lo por - go, ac - cet - ta - lo, ti por - te - rà - for - tu - na;

2. Enzo's Romance

L'angiol mio ver - rà dal cie - lo? l'angiol mio ver - rà dal ma - re?

3. Gioconda's Poison Aria

In que - sti fie - ri mo - men - ti ___ tu sol ___ mi re - sti,

eil cor mi ten - ti

Poulenc, Francis

b. 7 January 1899 in Paris
d. 30 January 1963 in Paris

Poulenc learned the piano from his mother, also studying with Charles Koechlin. The pianist Ricardo Viñes accepted him as a pupil at the age of 15, and introduced him to the musical life of Paris. Meetings with Satie and Auric enriched him intellectually as well as musically, and led him to develop his own individual style. After the First World War, Poulenc, →Honegger, Tailleferre, →Milhaud, Auric, and Durey formed the group known as Les Six, which owed allegiance to no fashionable tendencies but went its own way in writing French music suited to the times. He traveled in Europe with Darius Milhaud, meeting composers of the school of Schoenberg in Vienna, although he did not identify with their artistic ideas. He extended his success as a composer of songs (mainly to texts by Guillaume Apollinaire) and of ballets to the field of opera. Poulenc helped himself without scruples (and with great skill) to the work of Renaissance and Baroque masters; he also imitated the French Romantics, →Verdi, and →Saint-Saëns, took further ideas from Musorgsky, and borrowed from his own contemporaries, including →Stravinsky, Satie, and in particular →Debussy and →Ravel.

Works: Operas: *Les mamelles de Tirésias* (*The Breasts of Tiresias*) (1947, Paris), *Dialogues des Carmélites* (*Dialogues of the Carmelites*) (1957, Milan), *La voix humaine* (*The Human Voice* (1959, Paris); ballets, orchestral works, chamber music, songs.

*P*oulenc had a sure touch with the atmosphere of his time, and was an outstanding and witty stylistic plagiarist.

Dialogues of the Carmelites

Dialogues des Carmélites

Opera in three acts (twelve scenes)

Libretto: Francis Poulenc, after the play by Georges Bernanos.
Première: 26 January 1957, Milan (Teatro alla Scala)

Characters: The Marquis de la Force (Bar), Blanche, his daughter (S), The Chevalier, his son (T), Madame de Croissy, the prioress (A), Madame Lidoine, the new prioress (S), Mother Marie (A), Sister Constance, a novice (S), Mother Jeanne (A), Sister Mathilde (Ms), Father Confessor of the Carmelite convent (T), Two Commissars (T, B), Jailer (B), Javelinot, a physician (Bar), Thierry, a servant (Bar), Two Old Women (spoken), An Old Gentleman (spoken); three old nuns, eight sisters, municipal officials, administrators, prisoners, guards, men and women of the people (chorus).

Setting: Paris and Compiègne, 1789–94, during the French Revolution.

Synopsis
Blanche has suffered from depression since childhood. At her insistence her father, the Marquis de La Force, allows her to enter the convent of the Carmelites. But the prioress considers that Blanche's motives – flight from the world and the fear of death – are inadequate for a true vocation as a nun. However, she grants Blanche refuge, and gives her the ever-cheerful Sister Constance as a companion to help and support her. When the prioress dies, she transfers responsibility for Blanche to the nun Mother Marie. The Revolution is ravaging the land, attacking convents and monasteries with particular ferocity. Blanche's brother tries to persuade her to come home, but she refuses. The convent is dissolved, and the nuns swear to Mother Marie that they will accept martyrdom. Blanche now runs away in panic, dressed as a servant, to her parents' house. But it is in ruins, and her father has been murdered. Mother Marie, also in disguise, offers Blanche a safe hiding place, but she rejects it. Meanwhile the other nuns have been arrested and condemned to death. One by one, they mount the scaffold, bearing witness to their faith in song. Last of all, Constance mounts to her death, and sees Blanche making her way through the crowd. Picking up the last line of the "Veni creator spiritus", Blanche overcomes her fear and dies of her own free will with the others, entrusting her soul to God. *S. N.*

Taking flight in surrealism
In his setting of Guillaume Apollinaire's "drame surréaliste" *Les mamelles de Tirésias* of 1917, Poulenc created the prototype of the surrealist opera that takes the actual insanity of the world to absurd lengths, allowing the release of laughter. At the time of the première in 1947, however, he was criticized for writing such a cheerful piece in the difficult postwar period. The humorous score is full of stylistic parodies: polkas, waltzes, ariettas, and choruses follow one another apparently at random, and extraneous noises emphasize the course of the action. As time went on the work won general recognition.

The Breasts of Tiresias

Les mamelles de Tirésias

Opéra-bouffe in a prologue and two acts

Libretto: Guillaume Apollinaire.
Première: 3 June 1947, Paris (Opéra-Comique).
Characters: Theater Director (Bar), Thérèse, later Tiresias (S), The Husband (Bar), Newspaper Seller (Ms), Elegant Lady (Ms), Fat Lady (Ms), Policeman (Bar), Presto (Bar) Lacouf (T), Journalist (T), Son (T), Bearded Man (B); people of Zanzibar (chorus).
Setting: Zanzibar, an imaginary town between Nice and Monte Carlo, around 1910.

Synopsis
The Theater Director explains that it is the role of dramatic art to raise morale: after the war, the men and women of France must make more babies. Thérèse is tired of being a woman. Her breasts turn into balloons and fly away, and she begins to grow a beard. Now that Thérèse has left him, her husband dresses as a woman and is immediately courted by a policeman. While the women join General Tiresias in the fight for emancipation, the husband announces that bachelors will have babies themselves. The experiment works, and soon countless babies are growing up in readiness for the next war, all of them child prodigies. Overproduction is driving the state to ruin. But nothing can stop the husband except Thérèse/Tiresias. She/he is tired of life without love, and in return for it she is ready to take on all the old laborious business of marriage and child-rearing.

The Human Voice

La voix humaine

Tragédie lyrique in one act

Libretto: Jean Cocteau.
Première: 6 February 1959, Paris (Opéra-Comique).
Character: A Young Woman (S).

Synopsis

A young woman lies on her bed as if dead, coming to life only when the telephone rings. It is her lover, who has left her and is just about to marry another woman. He is calling to say goodbye. At first she feigns composure, then she conjures up their common memories, falls into despair, and finally, at the end of the telephone call, she collapses.   *S. N.*

Dialogues of the Carmelites, set design by Wolfram Munz for the production by Hans Hartleb, conductor Wolfgang Trommer, Stadttheater, Aachen 1969/70 (TWS).
His own feelings of anxiety and a leaning toward Catholicism motivated by philosophical and psychological considerations led Poulenc towards the story of the hesitant Blanche, who finds spiritual peace only in voluntarily choosing to die with the other nuns of her convent. The opera and the play on which it is based are among the few French stage works to present a distinctly negative picture of the French Revolution.

Above
The Human Voice, photograph from the original production with Denise Duval, production and sets Jean Cocteau, Opéra-Comique, Paris 1959.
Jean Cocteau's dramatic monologue of 1930 also inspired Roberto Rossellini to make the film *La voce umana* with Anna Magnani. Cocteau was interested in the phenomenon of "depersonalized communication." The telephone enables people to say goodbye without personal contact, making the final break an easy one for the faithless lover, but hard for the woman he has left.

*P*rokofiev was regarded by his contemporaries as a representative of the art of the grotesque, although in fact he avoided sentimentality of any kind and sought to offer the release of laughter, subtle lyricism, and warmth of feeling.

The Love for Three Oranges, set design by Max Bignens for the production by Arno Assmann, conductor Kurt Eichhorn, Staatstheater am Gärtnerplatz, Munich 1962 (TWS).

In this work Prokofiev clearly turned away from the sultry art of the turn of the century, introducing a kind of revival of *opera buffa*, and avoiding any psychological approach to his protagonists. The rapid change from one scene or situation to another is reminiscent of cinematic techniques, and the consistent use of strongly dissonant and disruptive effects for negative situations suggests the composer's later methods in film scores. He employed extreme vocal techniques and pure triads in a way that made even very innovative effects acceptable to audiences, as is shown by the international popularity of this work.

Prokofiev, Sergey Sergeyevich

b. 23 April 1891 in Sonzovka
d. 5 March 1953 in Moscow

After studying from 1904 to 1914 at the St. Petersburg Conservatory, Prokofiev broadened his education by traveling, and met Dyagilev in London and →Stravinsky in Rome, but he kept returning to the Soviet Union, where he was long respected as an internationally famous composer. When he settled permanently in Russia in 1933, however, he was expected to conform to the principles of Socialist Realism, and could not do so convincingly enough. In 1948 he was censured by the Soviet cultural bureaucracy. Although he promised to tread the Party line, the authorities still found it difficult to see Communist doctrine expressed in his actual works. What appeared inadequate conformity at home seemed in the West to be the ultimate example of political indoctrination.

Works: Maddalena (1912/FP 1979, London), *Igrok* (*The Gambler*) (1929, Brussels), *Lyubov' k tryom apel'sinam* (*The Love for Three Oranges*) (1921, Chicago), *Ognenny angel* (*The Fiery Angel*), (1919, rev.1927/FP 1954, Paris), *Semyon Kotko* (1940, Moscow), *Obrucheniye v monastire* (*Betrothal in a Monastery*) (1940/FP 1946, Leningrad), *Voyna i mir* (*War and Peace*) (1944, Moscow), *Povest' o nastoyashchem cheloveke* (*The Story of a Real Man*) (1948/FP 1960, Moscow); ballets, incidental music, film scores, orchestral works, chamber music, piano music, vocal compositions.

The Love for Three Oranges

Opera in a prologue and four acts (ten scenes)

Libretto: Sergey Prokofiev, after the play *L'amore delle tre melarance* (*The Love for Three Oranges*) by Carlo Gozzi, and the comedy of the same name by Konstantin Vogak, Vsevolod Meyerhold, and Vladimir Solov'yov.
Première: 30 December 1921, Chicago (Auditorium Theater).

Characters: The King of Clubs, king of an imaginary kingdom where everyone dresses as a playing card (B), The Prince, his son (T), Princess Clarice, the king's niece (A), Leander, the prime minister, dressed as the King of Spades (Bar), Truffaldino, a jester (T), Pantalone, the king's confidant (Bar), Celio, a sorcerer and the king's protector (B), Fata Morgana, a witch and Leander's protector (S), Linetta, Nicoletta, and Ninetta, princesses in the oranges (A, Ms, S), Creonta's Cook (B), Farfarello, a devil (B), Smeraldina, an Arab girl (Ms), Master of Ceremonies (T), Herald (B), Trumpeteer (musician playing bass trombone); ten cranks, tragedians, comedians, lyricists, empty heads, imps, doctors, courtiers (chorus); monsters, drunks, gluttons, guards, servants, four soldiers (silent).

Synopsis
Prologue

The supporters of different kinds of drama demand the kind of art that suits them best, and threaten violence in making their claims. The Cranks, representing the theatrical management, send the disputants away, promising to do them all justice in a piece that will satisfy any audience. It bears the curious name of *The Love for Three Oranges*. They then post themselves on two watchtowers by the proscenium arch, to keep an eye on both the opera and the audience.

Act I

A council of doctors diagnoses the prince's sickness as incurable hypochondria. Pantalone tells the king, who is distressed, that according to popular wisdom sickness can be cured by laughter. The king orders entertainments and engages an expert in laughter: the jester Truffaldino. The magicians Celio and Fata

Pre-Socialist surrealism
Prokofiev's opera can be called neo-Classical, or more appropriately surrealistic and absurd. In his avant-garde years, the man who was later to be a master of musical Socialist Realism and the brilliant composer of scores for Eisenstein's films paid homage to a dramatic ideal linked to the aesthetics of Meyerhold, and much closer to the fairy-tale world of Carlo Gozzi than to realistic stage works.

Morgana, who are at odds, express their differences in a game of cards. Celio loses. Fata Morgana's servant Smeraldina tells Prime Minister Leander of the underground power struggle. Celio supports the prince, Fata Morgana is on the side of the prime minister, who is in league with the king's niece Clarice. She is planning to usurp the throne, and therefore does not want the prince to be cured. Celio is weakened, and the imps will not obey him any more. Leander's prospects look promising.

Act II

Truffaldino's attempts to cheer the prince are unsuccessful. Against his will, the hypochondriac is dragged to the festivities, but Truffaldino's art is all in vain. The prince does not even smile. Then Fata Morgana appears, and quarrels with Truffaldino. He collides with the old witch, who stumbles and falls. Now, at last, the prince laughs and is cured. However, he immediately comes under the spell of Fata Morgana's curse: he will fall in love with three oranges. The prince, against his father's will, sets off in search of the oranges. Farfarello blows the prince and his companion Truffaldino off stage with his bellows.

Act III

Now that the sorcerer Celio has lost at cards, Farfarello no longer obeys him. However, Celio succeeds in giving Truffaldino a ribbon. He is to give it to the witch Creonta's cook, who is guarding the three oranges. In Creonta's kitchen, the prince steals the three oranges while Truffaldino distracts the cook's attention with the ribbon, and they both escape with their lives. On the tedious journey home the prince and Truffaldino feel tired and thirsty. While the prince sleeps, and in spite of Celio's warning, Truffaldino opens two of the oranges. Two princesses emerge, demanding water; without it, they are doomed to die of thirst in the desert. With a guilty conscience, Truffaldino steals away. When the prince opens the third orange, Princess Ninetta falls into his arms. But she too would die of thirst if the cranks did not act against all the rules of dramatic propriety and bring a bucket of water on stage. Ninetta sends her prince on ahead to fetch her some suitable clothes. Smeraldina changes the waiting Ninetta into a rat, and takes the princess's place herself. The unhappy prince is forced by his father to take Smeraldina home as his bride.

Act IV

Celio and Fata Morgana accuse each other of fighting unfairly, but Fata Morgana is the stronger. The cranks intervene again, shutting the witch up in one of the towers by the proscenium arch. Now it is up to Truffaldino to bring the story to a happy conclusion. All is ready for the wedding, but there is a rat on the throne, for Celio cannot break the spell. The guards shoot the creature, and Ninetta appears. It is revealed that Leander, Clarice, and Smeraldina were all in league. The king gives orders to hang them, but Fata Morgana escapes with her accomplices through a trapdoor. Nonetheless, there is general rejoicing for the happy couple.   *S.N.*

Above
The Love for Three Oranges, historic playing cards with illustrations by Alfred Rethel: the King of Clubs and the King of Spades, 1852 (Deutsches Spielkarten-Museum Leinfelden-Echterdingen).

The Love for Three Oranges, production photograph with (from left to right) Diana Rehbock (Nicoletta), Donald George (lying front, the prince), Daniel Kirch (Truffaldino), and Caren van Oyen (Linetta), production Andreas Homoki, conductor Mikhail Yurovsky, sets Frank Philipp Schlössmann, costumes Mechthild Seipel, Komische Oper, Berlin 1998.
The thirsty Truffaldino has opened two of the three oranges, although he was forbidden to do so. Instead of juicy fruit, he finds two girls inside. In despair, Truffaldino has to watch the two princesses die of thirst, while the prince sleeps through the tragedy. But the third orange is still intact.

Giacomo Puccini, photograph, 1919.
Like other great operatic composers who had the gift of exploring the depths of the human soul, Puccini was something of a melancholic.

*P*uccini's work is notable for an infallible sense of the theatre, captivating melodic ideas, and musical innovation in the depiction of his scenes. He was the last great composer of the Italian bel canto tradition.

Le villi

The Willis

Opera ballo in two acts

Libretto: Ferdinando Fontana, after the story of the same name by Jean-Baptiste Alphonse Karr.

Première: First version, in one act: 31 May 1884, Milan (Teatro dal Verme); second version, in two acts: 26 December 1884, Turin (Teatro Regio).

Characters: Guglielmo Wulf, a forester (Bar), Anna, his daughter (S), Roberto (T); men and women of the mountains, Villi/Willis (chorus).

Setting: The Black Forest at some undefined time.

Synopsis

The betrothal of Guglielmo Wulf's daughter Anna to Roberto is being celebrated in the forester's house. Roberto has to go to Mainz to receive a legacy, and while there goes to live with a courtesan. Betrayed, Anna dies of grief and becomes one of the Willis, spirits of dead women who have suffered a similar fate. Guglielmo promises his daughter's ghost vengeance. Roberto comes back, now suffering remorse. The Willis draw him into a wild dance, and he finally collapses and dies. *Á. G*

Melancholia

The outstanding and typical feature of Puccini's style is already present in his first opera: a marked tendency to melancholia expressed in misty, shimmering harmonies. The scenes between the lovers are steeped in the "sweet pain" of longing and nostalgia, which is also the basic mood of Anna's love aria: a presentiment of the evanescence of all beauty and happiness, anticipating the emotional climate of →*Manon Lescaut. M 1*

The intermezzo

The intermezzo (or *parte sinfonica*) was composed for the second version, under the title of "L'abbandono" ("Abandonment"), and was acclaimed by contemporary critics. It is a musical description of the seduction of Roberto, who gradually forgets his former lover. The indisputable influence of Wagner on the younger generation of Italian operatic composers is clearly perceptible in this piece. The praise of the critics caused the aged Verdi – who presumably knew Puccini's opera only from hearsay – to comment that: "Opera is opera and symphony is symphony, and I do not think it would be a good idea to make room for a symphony in an

opera simply to allow the orchestra to dance." Such orchestral intermezzos were permissible when they illustrated a certain moment in time (→Mascagni's *Cavalleria rusticana*), but even later Puccini showed a strong inclination to write orchestral pieces of this sort, examples being the intermezzo between Acts II and III of →*Manon Lescaut* and the extensive preludes to the last acts of →*Tosca* and →*Madam Butterfly*.

Puccini, Giacomo

b. 22 December 1858 in Lucca
d. 29 November 1924 in Brussels

Puccini came from a family of musicians. He studied the organ with his father until he was five and after his father's death with Fortunato Magi and later Carlo Angeloni. At the age of ten he became a choirboy at the churches of S. Marino and S. Michele. He continued his musical education in Milan from 1876, studying under →Amilcare Ponchielli and living a bohemian student life. He entered his first opera *Le villi* for a composers' competition; the piece attracted some attention and was performed in 1884. At this time he met the music publisher Giulio Ricordi, who published his works from then on, and set up house with his companion Elvira Bonturi (their son Antonio was born in 1886). In 1891 the family moved into a small house in Torre del Lago, which became Puccini's permanent home. After the première of his hugely successful opera *Manon Lescaut* (1893), he quickly became famous all over the world, yet he always found collaborating with librettists, composing scores, and working on the rehearsals and performances of his operas an arduous task. His works conquered all the major opera houses of the world, and around the turn of the century Puccini was the most popular of all operatic composers.

Works: Operas: *Le villi* (*The Willis*) (1884), *Edgar* (1889), *Manon Lescaut* (1893), *La bohème* (*Bohemian Life*) (1896), *Tosca* (1900), *Madama Butterfly* (*Madam Butterfly*) (1904), *La fanciulla del West* (*The Girl of the Golden West*) (1910), *La rondine* (*The Swallow*) (1917), *Il trittico: Il tabarro, Suor Angelica,* and *Gianni Schicchi* (*The Triptych: The Cloak, Sister Angelica,* and *Gianni Schicchi*) (1918), *Turandot* (1924/FP 1926); works other than operas include songs, choral works (including a *Messa di Gloria* and a Requiem), *Capriccio sinfonico,* and *Crisantemi* (*Chrysanthemums*) for string quartet.

1. Anna's Love Aria

Se co - me vo - i pic - ci - na io fossi, o va - ghi fior,

Edgar, Romilda Pantaleoni, the first Tigrana in Puccini's opera.
Romilda Pantaleoni (1847–1917) was enthusiastically acclaimed in the part of Tigrana at the première of the work. According to contemporary accounts she was not beautiful, but she was a good actress. Her voice was a soprano, not a mezzo-soprano, and the part of Tigrana had to be adapted to suit her vocal register.

Edgar

Dramma lirico in three acts

Libretto: Ferdinando Fontana, from the verse drama *La coupe et les lèvres* (*The Cup and the Lips*) by Alfred de Musset.

Première: First version, in four acts: 21 April 1889, Milan (Teatro alla Scala); new version, in three acts: 28 February 1892, Ferrara (Teatro Comunale).

Characters: Edgar (T), Fidelia (S), Frank, Fidelia's brother (B), Gualterio, their father (B), Tigrana (Ms); peasants, shepherds, women, old people, children, soldiers, servants, monks, citizens (chorus).

Setting: Flanders, 1302.

Synopsis

Edgar and Fidelia are a happy couple until Tigrana wins Edgar's love and rejects her suitor Frank. The new couple live together for a while, but then Edgar tires of Tigrana and longs to return to Fidelia. He joins a troop of soldiers led by Fidelia's brother Frank, and the two men are reconciled. Tigrana has followed Edgar, who disguises himself as a monk and pretends that Edgar has died in battle. The main characters all meet by the coffin of the supposedly dead Edgar. Fidelia mourns him; he then reveals himself and clasps her in his arms, but Tigrana stabs her more fortunate rival. Edgar collapses in complete despair.   *S. N.*

The chorus

By comparison with Puccini's later operas, the chorus features prominently in this early work. Perhaps there are passages where its melodic line and rhythm show clear traces of dependence on Verdi's style, but his is not the only influence. Puccini derived his sense of choral writing and his craftsmanlike technique from his past as a church musician; he had capital of his own to draw on. His early mastery in choral writing is evident in such passages as the fine ensemble that concludes Act I, and the mock Requiem for the supposedly dead Edgar at the beginning of Act III. Dramatically, this piece may have been misconceived: its dimensions are too large, and its striving for effect is based on a deception, but it is still a very imposing musical structure. Arturo Toscanini conducted the piece at Puccini's funeral in 1924. *M 2*

Tigrana

Fontana made two of Musset's female characters into Fidelia ("the faithful") and Tigrana ("the tigress"). Tigrana is also revealed to be a "Moorish foundling," so that she can be related to Mérimée's exoticism and Bizet's gypsy theme (→*Carmen*). In view of Puccini's later work, the dramatic portrayal of a *femme fatale* would not seem to have been the most congenial of subjects for him, and may be regarded more as experimentation with his own potential. Tigrana's vocal register places her in the category of the dramatic mezzo-soprano, obviously modeled on Carmen – a register absent from the mature Puccini's palette. During the revision of the opera a good deal of her part was cut. In the original four-act version she had no less than four arias, later reduced to little more than a single big scene for her in Act I. There is not much music really characteristic of Tigrana left in the revised work; she is given gentle and fluent melodic material in the new duet with Edgar written for Act II. Although her part in the duet expresses her pleading, it hardly suits the musical portrayal of a vamp. In fact, in the first version this melodic material belonged to Fidelia, and Puccini simply transferred it to Tigrana.

Fidelia

In contrast, even in the final version of the opera Fidelia retains three major solo arias (in Acts I and III). Her lyrical, suffering character already displays characteristic features of future Puccini heroines. It is she who provides the true inspiration for Puccini's music. His imaginative force unfolds fully in Fidelia's part and Edgar's tenor role, anticipating future works in his individual use of melody.   *J. K.*

Edgar, set design by Oppo for a production at Milan's La Scala, 1944.
Edgar does not feature in the repertory very often, although Puccini was closer to Verdi in this work than in any of his other operas.

2. Mock Requiem

Re - quiem ae - ter - nam!

Manon Lescaut

Dramma lirico in four acts

Libretto: Leoncavallo, Marco Praga, Domenico Oliva, Luigi Illica, Giuseppe Giacosa, and Giulio Ricordi, after the novel *L'histoire du chevalier des Grieux et de Manon Lescaut* (*The Story of the Chevalier des Grieux and Manon Lescaut*) by Antoine-François Prévost.
Première: 1 February 1893, Turin (Teatro Regio).

Characters: Manon Lescaut (S), Lescaut, her brother, Sergeant of the Royal Guards (Bar), The Chevalier des Grieux (T), Geronte de Ravoir, Treasurer General (B), Edmondo, a student (T), The Innkeeper (B), A Singer (Ms), A Dancing Master (T), A Lamplighter (T), Sergeant of the Royal Archers (B), A Naval Captain (B), A Wigmaker (silent); girls, citizens, crowd, students, musicians, old gentlemen, priests, courtesans, archers, marines, sailors (chorus).
Setting: France and North America in the second half of the 18th century.

Synopsis
Act I
In a square in front of an inn in Amiens, a number of people including the Chevalier des Grieux are waiting for the stagecoach to arrive. Among its passengers are the rich Treasurer General Geronte, Sergeant Lescaut, and his sister Manon. The men go into the building while Manon remains outside, alone. Des Grieux immediately falls in love with the girl. They converse, and she tells the young man that in obedience to her father's wishes she is about to enter a convent. Meanwhile Edmondo, a friend of des Grieux, discovers that Geronte intends to abduct the girl. Des Grieux confesses his love to Manon, and asks her to elope with him. While some students keep Lescaut and Geronte occupied in gambling, des Grieux and Manon elope in the carriage Geronte has ordered.

Act II
Manon is living in Geronte's fine house in Paris, having left des Grieux when his money ran out. Now she feels bored by the chilly magnificence of her surroundings, and longs for the warmth of des Grieux's love again. She hears from her brother that the Chevalier still loves her, and with Lescaut's assistance the lovers meet in Geronte's house, but are surprised by Geronte himself. Des Grieux urges Manon to flee with him. As she gathers her jewels together, the guards, alerted by Geronte, burst in.

Geronte accuses Manon of theft, and she is arrested, taken to prison, tried, and condemned to deportation.

Act III
The efforts made by des Grieux to free her by bribing the guards come to nothing; she must board a ship for America. As the lovers say farewell a sergeant tears Manon brutally from the arms of des Grieux. The ship's captain intervenes and allows des Grieux to come on board too.

Act IV
Manon's desire for luxury has involved des Grieux in crime in New Orleans, and they have had to flee the city. Out in the desert, Manon collapses from exhaustion. Des Grieux searches for water in vain. With her last words, Manon assures him once again of her love, and dies in his arms.   *A. G.*

Manon Lescaut, production photograph with Peter Dvorsky (des Grieux) and Mirella Freni (Manon), production Otto Schenk, conductor Giuseppe Sinopoli, Wiener Volksoper 1986.
The story of an ardent, desperate, doomed but immortal love: Manon and des Grieux can take their place in the pantheon of great lovers beside Romeo and Juliet, Dido and Aeneas, and Tristan and Isolde.

Manon Lescaut, title page of Ricordi's edition of the piano score. The names of the librettists do not feature on the title page of the piano score. In fact no less than five writers worked on the libretto between 1889 and 1892, beginning with Leoncavallo. He was followed by Marco Praga and Domenico Oliva, and finally by Luigi Illica and Giuseppe Giacosa. It was not they but Puccini himself, with his constant demand for alterations, who could claim responsibility for the final version of the libretto of *Manon*, and not surprisingly none of them eventually felt like putting his name to a text of such hybrid origins.

A daring choice of subject

Manon Lescaut was Puccini's first great success, and it came comparatively late in life. By the time it had its première in Turin he was 35 years old. His choice of subject was not without its risks. Jules Massenet's →*Manon* had been a great success in the opera houses of Europe since 1884. In addition, Massenet's masterpiece followed Prévost's novel closely in spirit, atmosphere, and plot. Puccini must have been aware of this, since he knew Massenet's opera, at least in piano score, although it was not produced in any Italian theater until 1893. (Puccini is unlikely to have been familiar with earlier settings of the subject, for instance Auber's version of 1856, although in any case he would have found that Auber treated the story in much the same way as Massenet.)

Many friends of Puccini, including the publisher Ricordi, warned him against competing with Massenet's internationally successful French opera, but in vain. Puccini persisted in his project. "Massenet deals with *Manon* like a Frenchman, with powder and minuets. I shall deal with the subject like an Italian, with desperate passion," was his answer. This was the first manifestation of a curious psychological trait in the composer, one evident later in his choice of material for →*La bohème* (in competition with Leoncavallo) and →*Tosca* (in competition with Franchetti): he became really determined to set a subject only when he knew that other composers were interested in it as well.

An abbé writing on modern love

The Abbé Prévost (Antoine-François Prévost d'Exiles, 1697–1763) became world-famous for his sentimental novel, first published in both Amsterdam and Paris in 1731. Its theme is a scandalous love story between two young people who defy social convention and live according to the dictates of their hearts. Manon is 15 and des Grieux 17 when they meet; she has been sent to Amiens against her will to become a nun, and des Grieux is destined for the Maltese Order. Instead, they elope to Paris and try to build a life together there. Their adventures lead Manon into prostitution, and finally deportation to New Orleans. The couple find no peace anywhere, and in the New World Manon dies in her lover's arms while they are once again fleeing from pursuers. Des Grieux returns to France and tells his story to a certain Monsieur D., hence the full title of the novel: *L'histoire du chevalier des Grieux et de Manon Lescaut, par Monsieur D.* (*The Story of the Chevalier des Grieux and Manon Lescaut, by Monsieur D.*). "Monsieur D." is the writer himself, and one may suspect the presence of autobiographical elements in the love story. Prévost was a seminal figure in modern bourgeois literature, a precursor of Rousseau and Dumas *fils*, and his eventful life might have come straight from a novel. The book was banned immediately after its publication, and no doubt for that very reason became enormously popular.

An important source

In none of his other operas was Puccini so much under the influence of Wagner as in *Manon Lescaut*. In the 1870s and 1880s a wave of enthusiasm for the music of Wagner swept over Italy, where it became fashionable rather later than in the German-speaking countries. Puccini's impressions were also gleaned direct from Bayreuth. At the end of the 1880s and in the early 1890s, he attended performances at the Bayreuth Festival as a representative of the publishing house of Ricordi. His experiences in Bayreuth, particularly the example of Tristan's chromatic music in →*Tristan and Isolde*, left their imprint on the score of *Manon Lescaut*.

French influence

It is hard to imagine Puccini's mature style developing without French influence. Examples of that influence are the musical depiction of the market place in Amiens in Act I and of Manon's Paris salon in Act II: there are no great arias here, only short, song-like interludes (sometimes strophic in structure, as in des Grieux's soliloquy in Act I M 3), and small ariettas and *ariosi* developing from recitatives.

In the account of Manon's boudoir in Paris (Act II) Puccini in fact comes close to the background of "powder and minuets" that he had deplored, deliberately conjuring up the "perfumed atmosphere" of Manon's salon with dance music in the French style and the melody of a minuet. M 4

Much of the music in the opera is borrowed from Puccini's own earlier works: first versions of small chamber compositions, songs, and occasional works written from his schooldays onward. (Such borrowing from himself – a habit he shared with other composers – was part of Puccini's *modus operandi* up to the time of →*Tosca*.) To cite only one coincidence, in its way rather a strange one: the madrigal of greeting that seems so well suited to the Rococo atmosphere of Act II actually comes from a sacred composition written 15 years earlier, the "Agnus Dei" from Puccini's youthful *Messa di Gloria*. M 5

However, the real hit of Act II is the aria Manon sings as she muses, alone, on her yearning for small, straightforward pleasures, despite the luxury of her present surroundings. M 6

Manon

In *Manon Lescaut* Puccini took a step that would effectively determine the whole of his later work: he presented a new type of operatic heroine, one he made very much his own. She is the "little woman in love" ("piccola donna inamorata," as he himself put it later), who also embodies the suffering heroine. This quality relates Manon to Mimi, Cio-Cio-San, and Liù. All her "tragic misdemeanors" are the result of love itself, and in Puccini's philosophy that is why she must endure her sad fate. M 7, M 8

J. K.

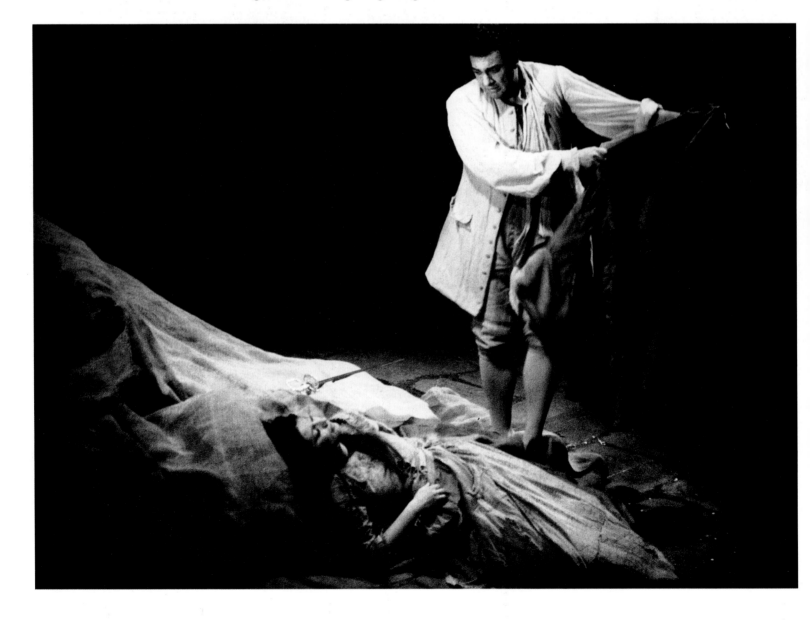

Manon Lescaut, photograph of the production by Pamela McRae, sets Desmond Heeley, conductor Nello Santi, Metropolitan Opera, New York 1990.
An idyllic view of the market square in Amiens: all is hurry and bustle, with students singing and cracking jokes. The stagecoach has arrived from Arras, and the student des Grieux falls in love at first sight with the beautiful girl who has just stepped out of it.

Opposite
Manon Lescaut, production photograph with Sylvia Sass (Manon) and Placido Domingo (des Grieux), production Piero Fagioni, conductor Claudio Abbado, Teatro alla Scala, Milan 1978.
With a few exceptions (who include Minnie and Turandot) Puccini's heroines are doomed to die at the end of his operas. The tragic endings convey no Romantic sense of transfiguration; they occur either suddenly or gradually in a hopeless situation. The composer himself suffered with his characters, for he identified intensely with their fate.

3. Des Grieux's Soliloquy

Don - na non vi - di - ma - i   si - mi - le a que - sta!____

4. Minuet

5. Madrigal

Sul - la vet - ta tu del mon - te er - ri, o Clo - - - ri:____

6. Manon's Aria (Act II)

In   quel -le tri - ne mor -bi - de   nell' al - co - - va do - ra - - ta

7. Manon's Theme (Love Duet between Manon and des Grieux, Act I)

Ma - non ____ Les -caut   mi chia - mo.

8. Love Duet (Manon and des Grieux, Act II)

Ma -non te so - lo   bra - ma, te so - lo bra - ma ____

Manon Lescaut, production photograph with Mirella Freni (Manon) and Peter Dvorsky (des Grieux), production Pamela McRae, sets Desmond Heeley, conductor Nello Santi, Metropolitan Opera, New York 1990.
There is a tragic sense of distance in Manon's love song, performed here by Mirella Freni, making des Grieux feel that physically close as they are, she is very far away.

La bohème, poster from the Komische Oper, Berlin.
In *La bohème* Puccini peopled the operatic stage with heroes and heroines of a new kind, against a previously unfamiliar kind of setting. His protagonists are youthful intellectuals – living in poverty, made sad and happy by everyday problems and joys.

Group photograph (colored later) of (from left to right) Giacomo Puccini and his librettists Giuseppe Giacosa and Luigi Illica. "The Holy Trinity" was the term Puccini used when writing *La bohème* for the team consisting of himself, Luigi Illica (1857–1919), and Giuseppe Giacosa (1847–1906). They were friends, and were bohemian in outlook themselves. However, Puccini was never satisfied with a libretto, and often drove his librettists to despair. Illica and Giacosa nevertheless remained faithful to him, also providing the librettos for →*Tosca* and →*Madam Butterfly*.

La bohème

Scenes from bohemian life in four acts

Libretto: Giuseppe Giacosa and Luigi Illica, after Louis-Henri Murger's novel *Scènes de la vie de bohème*.

Première: 1 February 1896, Turin (Teatro Regio).

Characters: Rodolfo, a poet (T), Mimi, a seamstress (S), Marcello, a painter (Bar), Musetta, a singer (S), Schaunard, a musician (Bar), Colline, a philosopher (B), Benoit, their landlord (B), Parpignol, an itinerant toy vendor (T), Alcindoro, a state councillor (B), A Customs Officer (B); students, seamstresses, milliners, citizens, street vendors and pedlars, soldiers, waiters, children (chorus).

Setting: Paris, around 1830.

Synopsis
Act I
Rodolfo the poet, Marcello the painter, Schaunard the musician, and Colline the philosopher live in lodgings in an attic above the rooftops of Paris. On Christmas Eve they have no money and no firewood. Marcello is so cold that he cannot even hold his brush. Rodolfo sacrifices the manuscript of his play to light a fire. Colline comes home after going out to pawn some of his books, but the pawnshop was closed. Then Schaunard appears with money, firewood, food, and wine, his payment from an English lord. The friends decide to celebrate Christmas at their regular haunt, the Café Momus. Their landlord knocks on the door, demanding his long overdue rent. At last, by flattering him outrageously, they see him on his way. Then the friends leave; only Rodolfo stays behind for a few minutes. There is another knock on the door: their neighbor Mimi's candle has gone out, and she has come to ask for a light. An attack of coughing keeps her there for a while. She loses her key, and has to return. A draft blows out both candles, and as they search for the key in the dark Rodolfo feels the girl's hand. Trust and liking blossom between them. Down in the street, Rodolfo's friends are calling impatiently for him. He and Mimi go down together, arm in arm.

Act II
There is much Christmas merriment in the Latin Quarter. The friends make some purchases; Rodolfo buys Mimi a pink bonnet. He introduces her to his friends, and they fall into conversation on the subject of love. Suddenly an elegant lady appears with a distinguished old gentleman. It is Musetta, Marcello's former mistress. She has already tired of her elderly protector Alcindoro, and deliberately attracts Marcello's attention. Pretending that she needs new shoes, Musetta sends Alcindoro off to buy some, and the former lovers are reunited. The friends follow a passing military band, and when Alcindoro comes back, the waiter presents him with two unpaid bills.

Act III
Musetta and Marcello are staying at an inn at the Enfer customs barrier. Mimi visits Marcello and tells him, despairingly, how Rodolfo has left her because he was jealous. When Rodolfo appears she hides behind a tree, and so learns the true reason for Rodolfo's conduct: it was really his concern for Mimi's health that caused him to leave her. She is severely ill with consumption, and her condition was deteriorating in the attic. Mimi falls into Rodolfo's arms, and they say goodbye. There is a jealous quarrel between Musetta and Marcello, and they too part.

Act IV
Rodolfo and Marcello are back at work in the attic, trying in vain to forget the girls they love. Colline and Schaunard enter, bringing bread and herrings. The friends enjoy a good meal, and then, in high spirits, dance around the room. Schaunard and Colline fight a mock duel with the coal shovel and tongs. Suddenly Musetta appears with the mortally sick Mimi, who longs to see her lover once again. They put the sick girl to bed. Musetta goes to buy Mimi the warm muff she needs, Marcello to call the doctor, Colline to take his coat to the pawnbroker's. Rodolfo and Mimi are left alone, and remember their first evening. The others come back. Mimi is delighted with the muff, believing that it is a present from Rodolfo, and she falls asleep. Musetta prepares the medicine Marcello has brought – but then Schaunard realizes that Mimi has died. Rodolfo collapses in tears over the corpse of his beloved. *A.G.*

Opposite
La bohème, title page of the first edition published by Ricordi.
The Ricordi first edition avoids suggesting the tragic atmosphere of the opera. The title page presents the background to the story of the four bohemians in humorously drawn character sketches: the bustle of Christmas time in Paris (celebrated in noisy public festivities rather than as a quiet family occasion), the atmosphere of the suburbs in winter twilight, and life on the streets and in the attics of Paris. Puccini himself aptly enough described the four sections into which *La bohème* is divided not as acts ("atti"), but as scenes or tableaux ("quadri").

La bohème, costume design for Musetta by Hans Strohbach, Cologne 1931 (TWS). Musetta's costume design is reminiscent of Toulouse-Lautrec. Her famous scene in Act II owes its existence to Puccini's own initiative; he already had the music available, for her famous waltz song uses the music of one of his earlier occasional compositions. In fact, it was originally written for the launching of a ship. M 9

La bohème, production photograph with Caroline Stein as Musetta, production Chris Alexander, conductor Hans Urbanek, Niedersächsische Staatsoper, Hanover 1999.
Musetta is very much a young Parisienne: pretty, flirtatious, and emancipated. She wins back Marcello's love with her sensuous waltz song.

The real bohemians

Henri Murger (1822–61, originally Henry Mürger, the son of an Alsatian immigrant) owes his place in literary history to a single work, his *Scènes de la vie de bohème*. This was a serial novel which first appeared in instalments, was then published in sections in the journal *Corsaire* from 1844, and only later, in 1851, assumed the form of a bound book (*La vie de bohème*). When he first wrote the story the author was 22 years old, and it is clear that he based the material on his own experience. His characters are drawn from the people of the Latin Quarter, young artists and would-be artists with their lovers, who are humble seamstresses and working girls, sad yet cheerful little butterflies living a life of poverty. They all have something lifelike about them, and were obviously modeled on real people. A member of this former bohemian society, Alexandre Schanne ("Schaunard"), did in fact identify many of the figures in his memoirs, written many years later and published in 1887.

La bohème, photograph from the production by Jean-Pierre Ponnelle, sets and costumes Jean-Pierre Ponnelle, conductor Allain Lombard, Strasbourg 1977. No one before Puccini had presented such a realistic picture of the street life of Paris. His music dwells on the scene outside the Café Momus like a film director's camera, focusing alternately on situations, faces, and scenes from ordinary life.

La bohème, Mimi's death scene, production photograph with Mirella Freni (Mimi), Giovanni Raimondi (Rodolfo), and Rolando Panerai (Marcello), production Franco Zeffirelli, Teatro alla Scala, Milan 1963. One of the most touching finales in operatic history. The first to weep over Mimi's death was Puccini himself, when he had just finished composing the score and played the closing scene to a party of his friends. Mimi is the gentlest of all Puccini's female protagonists, making no heroically tragic gestures like Butterfly (→*Madam Butterfly*) or Liù (→*Turandot*). She does nothing out of the ordinary, and her fate is acted out before our eyes: she loves, suffers, and dies.

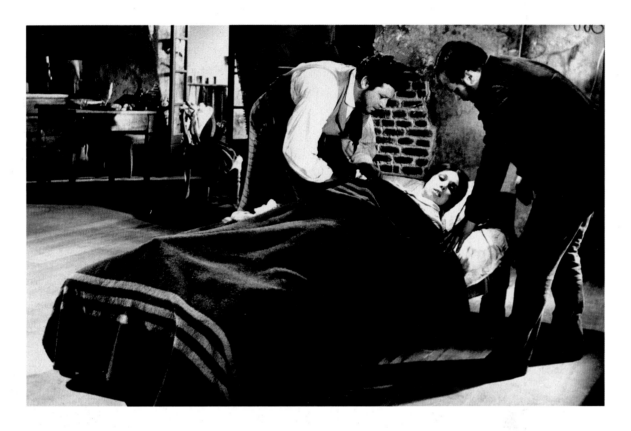

La bohème, set design by Hein Heckroth for the production by Wolf Völker, conductor Alfons Rischner, Städtische Bühnen, Essen 1930/31 (TWS).
La bohème is a dramatic phenomenon, and exceptional even among the body of Puccini's own works: there is almost no plot, and the opera simply presents the atmosphere of life in an attic in the Latin Quarter of Paris.

La bohème – two settings

The origins of the opera can be traced back to the year 1892. The idea came from Ruggiero Leoncavallo, who apparently even offered to write the libretto for Puccini. (Leoncavallo was a librettist as well as a composer, and wrote the texts for all his own operas.) Puccini was not yet familiar with Murger's novel, so he ignored Leoncavallo's offer while he was busy with *Manon Lescaut*. Meanwhile, Leoncavallo had decided that he would like to compose *La bohème* himself. When it turned out in March 1893 that Puccini was working on the same subject, there was heated controversy in the press, and bitter rivalry developed between the two composers, leading to a cooling of their former friendship. Leoncavallo went ahead and composed his own *La bohème*, which had its première at the Teatro La Fenice in Venice in 1897, a year after Puccini's work. The most striking difference between the two operas is that Leoncavallo opens the story in the Café Momus, the setting of Puccini's second act. There are several conflicts in Leoncavallo's version, the arguments are sharper, and the dialogue more passionate; the piece conforms to the contemporary *verismo* style. In contrast, Puccini gives full expression to the ardent lyricism of the bohemian way of life.   J. K

9. Musetta's Waltz Song

Quan - do me'n vo', ___ quando me'n vo' so - let-ta per la via, la gen-te so-sta e mi - ra...

The poetry of small things

"I have a feeling only for small things, and do not want to concern myself with anything else" – this artistic manifesto uttered by Puccini is particularly apt in the case of *La bohème*. It depicts humble people with their small joys, and their often not so small sorrows. The cheerful crackling of a fire in the stove, the dripping of icicles in the wintry setting of Act III, a sunbeam suddenly falling on the dying woman's face – all these are not just events on stage but are also expressed in Puccini's score. His is a "small art" that takes note of such atmospheric minor incidents as the appearance of a toy vendor amidst the hustle and bustle of the Christmas festivities, or the milkmaids coming to the customs barrier at the beginning of Act III, a scene suggestive of a genre painting. Such details make Puccini's "quadri", or tableaux, lively and touching. Perhaps the most popular of them is the philosopher Colline's aria in Act IV, as he determines to pawn his overcoat so that he can buy Mimi some medicine. *M 10 J. K.*

La bohème, photograph from the production by Tom Cairns, sets and costumes Tom Cairns, conductor Oleg Caetani, Württembergisches Staatstheater, Stuttgart 1991.
In Act III, Puccini sets the dialogue of the two pairs of lovers in parallel, but in this case twice two does not make four, since the music never develops into a quartet.

Right
La bohème, production photograph with Gunnel Bohman (Mimi) and Elia Levensky (Rodolfo), production Alfred Kirchner, sets and costumes Andreas Reinhardt, conductor Klaus-Peter Seibel, Oper Frankfurt 1998.
Although the audience learns so much about Mimi and Rodolfo, in some ways the characters remain shadowy. They emerge and disappear into darkness again – eternal prototypes of lovers.

10. Colline's Aria (Act IV)

Vec - chia zi - mar - ra, sen - ti, io resto al pian, tu a - scen - dere il sacro monte or de - vi

La bohème, photograph from the production by Jean-Pierre Ponnelle, sets and costumes Jean-Pierre Ponnelle, conductor Allain Lombard, Württembergisches Staatstheater, Stuttgart 1977.
At the beginning of Act III, Rodolfo tells his friend Marcello that he felt obliged to leave Mimi because of her mortal sickness. The trembling Mimi is listening in the background.

La bohème, production photograph with Mirella Freni (Mimi) and Giovanni Raimondi (Rodolfo), WDR, television recording 1966.
It is probably no exaggeration to say that Mimi and Rodolfo are the most popular pair of lovers in all opera. They are ordinary people, and yet at the same time uniquely operatic figures. Their wonderful melodies transfigure them, proclaiming that by its very nature love can never be an ordinary, everyday affair. There are no love intrigues or villains in this opera. The blows of fate come in the form of sickness, a credible tragedy to all who are moved by the poetry of *La bohème*. M 11 – M 14

11 . Rodolfo (Duet, Act I)

Che ge - li - da ma - ni - na, se la la - sci ri - scal - dar.   Cer - car che gio - va? Al bu - io non si tro - va.

12. Rodolfo's Love Theme (Duet, Act I)

Ta - lor dal mio for - zie - re ___ ruban tutti i gio - iel - li due la - dri: gli oc -chi bel - li.

13. Mimi's Theme (Duet, Act I)

Sì. Mi chia-ma - no Mi - mi, ma il mio no - me è Lu - ci - a ___

14. Mimi's Love Theme (Duet, Act I)

ma quando vien lo sge - lo il primo sole è mi - o, ___ il pri - mo ba-cio del -l'a - pri - le è mi - o! ___

Tosca

Melodramma in three acts

Libretto: Giuseppe Giacosa and Luigi Illica, after the play of the same name by Victorien Sardou.
Première: 14 January 1900, Rome (Teatro Costanzi).
Characters: Floria Tosca, a famous singer (S), Mario Cavaradossi, a painter (T), Baron Scarpia, chief of police (Bar), Cesare Angelotti, a former consul (B), Spoletta, a police agent (T), A Sacristan (B), Sciarrone, a policeman (B), A Jailer (B), A Shepherd (A); singers, choirboys, servers at Mass, crowd (chorus).
Setting: Rome, June 1800.

Tosca, production photograph with Catherine Naglestad as Tosca, production Willy Decker, conductor Lothar Zagrosek, Württembergisches Staatstheater, Stuttgart 1998.
Tosca just before she leaps to her death in the closing moments of the opera. There is no hope of a happy ending and no heroic death, merely the inscrutable fact of death itself: such are the ideas suggested to the audience by the last act.

Synopsis

Act I

Cesare Angelotti, once consul of the former Republic of Rome, has just escaped from imprisonment in the Castel S. Angelo and takes refuge in the church of S. Andrea della Valle. He hides in a chapel where his sister has left women's clothing for him. The Sacristan, going his rounds, watches the painter Cavaradossi at work on a picture of St. Mary, and thinks it looks very like the lady who often comes there to pray, Angelotti's sister the Marchesa Attavanti. However, Cavaradossi has given the subject of his picture the features of his lover, the singer Floria Tosca. When the Sacristan has left a basket of food for Cavaradossi he goes away again, and now Angelotti can venture out of the chapel. He and Cavaradossi recognize one another as old friends, and Cavaradossi promises Angelotti his assistance. When Tosca enters the church, Angelotti has to hide again. The painting arouses Tosca's jealousy, but Cavaradossi succeeds in soothing her. When she has left, Angelotti comes out once more. Cannon fire from the Castel S. Angelo tells them that Angelotti's escape has been discovered, and Cavaradossi says he will take his friend to his country house and hide him there. No sooner have they left than the Sacristan, the young clerics, and the singers of the choir come into the church to celebrate what they have heard is the victory of the *ancien régime* over Napoleon. Looking for Angelotti, Scarpia searches the church with his henchmen, and when Tosca returns to look for Cavaradossi, Scarpia uses a fan found in the chapel in an attempt to prove that the painter has had an assignation with the Marchesa here. The jealous Tosca hurries away, intending to catch the guilty couple in the act at Cavaradossi's house. Scarpia is captivated by the singer's charms, and decides to have his rival followed. He sends spies after Tosca.

Act II

At the Palazzo Farnese, Scarpia is waiting for the report on Angelotti. He has sent Tosca a note telling her to visit him after the concert she is giving, and the singer is bound to comply with the wishes of so powerful a man. Spoletta reports that Angelotti has not been found, but the police have arrested Cavaradossi on suspicion of his involvement in the escape. Cavaradossi is brought in. He denies everything, and tells Tosca to do the same, but when he is taken to the torture chamber Tosca betrays the secret of Angelotti's hiding place in order to save her lover. Cavaradossi curses her. He rejoices when news arrives that Napoleon was not defeated after all, but has won the battle of Marengo, and now he is condemned to death for his libertarian views. Scarpia offers to trade with Tosca: if she will grant him her favors, Cavaradossi's punishment will be only a mock execution. She appears to agree, and Scarpia makes out the safe-conduct she demands for herself and Cavaradossi. But when he approaches her, she stabs him to death.

Act III

On a platform in the Castel S. Angelo, Cavaradossi writes Tosca a letter of farewell. Then the singer herself appears, with the good news that he is free, and there will be only a mock execution. The firing squad is already forming. Cavaradossi stands confidently against the wall, but the guns are loaded with live ammunition. Tosca realizes that Scarpia has betrayed her and Cavaradossi is dead. Her murder of Scarpia has been discovered, and the police can be heard approaching. She leaps to her own death from the platform of the Castel S. Angelo.

A G

Musical scene-setting

When Puccini began composing *Tosca* he became interested in details of local color that would contribute to authenticity and background atmosphere. He asked a Roman acquaintance to let him have the exact variant of the melody of the Gregorian *Te Deum* in the Roman ritual that he wanted for the finale of Act I. Then he inquired about the key to which the great bell of St. Peter's, the "campanone", is tuned. Estimates put it at somewhere around low E, but that was not good enough for Puccini; he went to Rome himself to study the sound of bells ringing for matins in the vicinity of the Castel S. Angelo and St. Peter's. These impressions bore fruit in the introductory music to Act III, where the lyrical description of a summer dawn breaking forms a nostalgic contrast to the tragedy that follows. During the last months of his work on the opera, Puccini also decided to include in this scene a sad folk tune sung by a shepherd boy ("Io de' sospiri, te ne rimanno tanto," "I send you back as many sighs"). He did not ask his librettists to write the text for this song, but turned to a local Roman writer, Luigi Zanasso, to provide him with something in the Campanian dialect that would suggest the genuine folk tradition. M 15

J. K.

Tosca, set design by Ruodi Barth for the production by Bohumil Herlischka, conductor Christian Süss, Deutsche Oper am Rhein, Düsseldorf 1970 (TWS).
Many critics of Puccini's own time regarded his opera as the unhealthy product of an over-heated imagination, a skillfully concocted mixture of sex and sadism, which seemed to them thoroughly implausible. The events of the 20th century have brought out the political significance of the work as well as the love story. Ruodi Barth's sets express such ideas in terms of a severe architectural structure. The monumentality of the architecture, with its strong verticals, is reminiscent of the buildings of the 1930s, and conjures up ideas of the Nazi regime and its terrorist state institutions.

15. Shepherd's Song

Io de' so-spi-ri,＿＿＿ Te ne ri-man-no tan-ti＿＿＿

Making a virtue of necessity

When Maria Jeritza was rehearsing for a revival of *Tosca* in Vienna in 1914, she had a minor accident. At the dress rehearsal, in front of Puccini himself, the famous singer fell and had to sing her aria "Vissi d'arte" ("I have lived for art") in a lying position. Puccini liked the effect so much that he said this very position had been in his mind's eye when he was composing the aria.

The woman we know as Tosca

Puccini's protagonists in *Tosca* are not operatic heroes in the Romantic sense. Cavaradossi has two short arias, Tosca only one, and their duets are fragmentary. It is as if Puccini intended to reduce the work's large-scale lyrical components to a minimum, emphasizing instead the breathtaking course of the action. What lingers in the mind of the operagoer is not Tosca in a series of statuesque scenes, but her whole story: her movements, reactions, and agility. Episodes and situations unreel before our eyes as if in a film: Tosca's appearance in the church as a radiant diva in Act I, her jealous reaction to the model of the painting, her battle of wills with Scarpia in Act II and her tortured lover's cursing of her, her decision to murder Scarpia and the way she then performs the last rites by his body, the "eternal" farewell she takes of Cavaradossi in Act III – all these scenes come together, like a mosaic, to create the figure of the woman audiences have known as Tosca for a century.

A pause for breath – and applause

Remarkably, there is only one aria for the singer of the title role, the second-act aria "Vissi d'arte". This showpiece for a prima donna does hold up the swift course of the action in Act II – a criticism Puccini himself made of it later – but the audience is glad of a chance to applaud the singer. *M 16*   *J. K.*

Left
Tosca, Eva Marton as Tosca, Arena di Verona 1984.
Eva Marton (b. 1944) was a Tosca whom even Scarpia might well fear. A dramatic soprano of Hungarian origin, she has been singing Tosca since 1973 with explosive dynamic force, but her approach is disciplined as she thinks her way through the role. Marton's strong stage presence makes every appearance by her a thrilling theatrical experience.

Opposite, above
Tosca, Maria Callas as Tosca.
The Tosca created by Maria Callas (1923–77) at Covent Garden is still regarded by opera enthusiasts as the supreme interpretation, impossible to surpass. Posterity can glean some idea of her performance in the role, at least in Act II, from a film made at Covent Garden with Tito Gobbi as Scarpia. The production was carefully planned down to the smallest gestures and glances, yet it still seemed spontaneous and captivating, and to interpreters and music historians alike represents a standard that no other production has ever matched.

Tosca, Sarah Bernhardt as Tosca in Victorien Sardou's original play, Paris 1887. A great figure of the turn of the century: Sarah Bernhardt (1844–1923) as Tosca. The successful dramatist Victorien Sardou (1831–1908) wrote several strong dramatic parts (Fédora, Theodora, Tosca) for this famous actress of the Art Nouveau period. Composers and writers including Puccini, Giordano, and Oscar Wilde, were enchanted and inspired by Sarah Bernhardt's personality and dramatic talents.

16 . Tosca's Aria (Act II)

Vis - si d'ar - te, vis - si d'a - mo - re, non fe - ci mai male ad a - ni - ma vi - va!

Above
Tosca, Lotte Lehmann as Tosca.
Lotte Lehmann (1888–1976) in Act I of *Tosca*. Her great musicality and dramatic gifts made her one of the most celebrated prima donnas of the first half of the 20th century. She had an enormous repertory, and was particularly famous for her roles in the operas of Richard Strauss, singing in the premières of several of them. She helped to popularize Puccini's works in the German-speaking countries.

Tosca, Maria Jeritza as Tosca.
Maria Jeritza (1887–1982) was Puccini's ideal Tosca. When he first saw her in the role, the composer set his personal seal of approval on her concept. According to the accounts of those who heard her in her prime, Jeritza had the incomparable dramatic presence of a queen with a volcanic temperament, and possessed a strong, sensuous voice. She was *the* prima donna of her time.

Tosca, title page of the first edition of the piano score, published by Ricordi. "Avanti a lui tremava tutta Roma!" ("And before him all Rome trembled!"), Tosca whispers with horror beside the corpse of Scarpia at the end of Act II. The title page of the first edition immortalizes this moment; the same picture was used as a poster for the première. How did a former shepherd girl (in Sardou's account) come to commit such a murder? The background to the story is that Floria Tosca was brought up by Benedictine nuns and studied singing with the famous maestro Domenico Cimarosa. When the play (and the opera) opens, she is already a celebrated singer in Rome. Her conflict with the authorities arises from her connection with Cavaradossi, and circumstances make her into a tragic heroine, as her emotional theme in the murder scene points out. *M 17*

Tosca, Beniamino Gigli as Cavaradossi.
Beniamino Gigli (1890–1957) in his great role as Cavaradossi. He was regarded as the finest of Puccini tenors, and Cavaradossi was the first Puccini role he sang publicly, in 1915. The part of Cavaradossi is for a lyric tenor, and calls for a soft, velvety voice. His two arias, the picture aria in Act I and the letter aria in Act III, are rather melancholy. Cavaradossi's famous cry in Act III, "Muoio disperato" ("I die in despair"), is Puccini's own idea, and does not occur in Sardou. His outburst in Act II, "Vittoria!" ("Victory!"), on hearing news of the French victory at Marengo, shows him in enthusiastic mood, and as he sings his march-like melody he approaches the preserves of the heroic tenor. *M 18, M 19, M 20*

17. Tosca's Fate Theme

18. Cavaradossi's Picture Aria (Act I)

Re - con - dita ar-mo - ni - a   di bellez - ze di - ver - se!...   È bru - na, Flo - ri - a, l'ar-den - te a-man - te mi - a,

19. Cavaradossi's Letter Aria (Act II)

Oh! dol - ci ba-ci, o languide ca - rez - ze, mentr'io fre - men - te le bel - le   for - me disciogliea   dai ve - li!

20. Cavaradossi's Delusions of Victory (Act II)

L'al - ba   vin - di -ce appar   che fa gli em -pi tremar!   Li - ber - tà sor - ge, crol -lan ti - ran-ni - di! __

Tosca, production photograph from Act II, conductor Semyon Bychkov,
production Luca Ronconi, Teatro alla Scala, Milan 1996/97.
Ronconi's production attempts to show that, by adding aspects of fracture and
distortion to the realistic setting, *Tosca* is a great internal drama about the
workings of fate. Puccini, a composer with a strong feeling for dramatic effect,
left directors very little room for their own interpretations; he planned not only
the emotions to be shown by his characters and the gestures they make, but
also the details of the background against which they move.

Madam Butterfly, poster for the première, Adolfo Hohenstein, 1904.

The première of *Madam Butterfly* was the only fiasco of Puccini's career. The length of Act II, originally intended to last an hour and a half (and to conclude the work), was too much of a strain on Italian audiences. Puccini withdrew the opera to revise it. We owe to that revision one of the most brilliant of all operatic scenes, in which Butterfly waits up all night for Pinkerton. It is very likely that when Puccini first saw a performance of David Belasco's play he was impressed by the episode of Butterfly's "night watch," a silent mime lasting almost a quarter of an hour, which was regarded as sensational at the time and attracted much attention. He introduced this bridging scene into his opera, as a kind of dramatic and musical intermezzo between two acts. He still had to decide on the right place to divide the opera into three acts. The poster shows the loving Butterfly waiting faithfully for her American husband. *M 21*

21. The Humming Chorus

Madam Butterfly

Madama Butterfly

Tragedia giapponese in two acts

Libretto: Giuseppe Giacosa and Luigi Illica, after John Luther Long and David Belasco.

Première: First version, in two acts: 17 February 1904, Milan (Teatro alla Scala); second version, in three acts: 28 May 1904, Brescia (Teatro Grande); final version: 28 December 1906, Paris (Opéra-Comique).

Characters: Cio-Cio-San, known as Madam Butterfly (S), Suzuki, her maid (Ms), Kate Pinkerton (Ms), Benjamin Franklin Pinkerton, lieutenant in the US Navy (T), Sharpless, US consul in Nagasaki (Bar), Goro, a marriage broker (T), Prince Yamadori (T), The Bonze and Yakusidé, Butterfly's uncles (2 B), Imperial Commissioner (B), Official Registrar (B), Butterfly's Mother (Ms), The Aunt (S), The Cousin (S), Dolore ("sorrow"), Butterfly's child (silent), A Cook (silent); Butterfly's friends and relations, servants (chorus).
Setting: Nagasaki, around 1900.

Synopsis
Act I
Lieutenant Pinkerton of the US Navy, who has fallen in love with the 15-year-old Butterfly, a geisha, plans to go through a ceremony of marriage with her – but it will be a marriage he can end at any time. Consul Sharpless warns him against this plan, pointing out that the girl genuinely loves him, but in vain. Butterfly's family agree to the wedding, and the ceremony is performed. When the guests and officials, the consul, the imperial commissioner, and the registrar have left, Butterfly's uncle the Bonze, a priest, arrives, and curses the bride for betraying the religion of her ancestors and converting to Christianity out of love for a foreigner. But Pinkerton comforts his little wife, who now sees him as her only prop and stay.

Act II
Pinkerton has gone home to the United States. Butterfly has heard nothing from him for three years, but she is still waiting patiently and confidently for his return. Sharpless visits her; he has received a letter from Pinkerton saying that he has married an American wife and is to visit Japan with his bride. Sharpless cannot read the letter to Butterfly at once, for she has a visit from Prince Yamadori, who is courting her. However, Butterfly still feels bound to Pinkerton. When the Prince has left, Sharpless is at last able to impart the contents of the letter. Butterfly is shattered. In despair, she shows Sharpless her son by Pinkerton; the consul

had not been aware of the child's existence. Cannon fire from the harbor announces the arrival of Pinkerton's ship. Despite everything, Butterfly hopes he will return to her. She hastily adorns her house with flowers, prepares to receive her lover, and sits up all night waiting for him.

Madam Butterfly, production photograph with Michiè Nakamaru (Butterfly) and Franco Farina (Pinkerton), production Kiju Yoshida, conductor Kent Nagano, Opéra National de Lyon 1995.
The butterfly in full flight … the sad tale of Butterfly is a great love story as well as depicting a tragic clash between cultures.

Act III
Next morning Butterfly is still waiting for her beloved husband, but in vain. Hesitantly, Pinkerton approaches Butterfly's house with the consul. The maid Suzuki sees him first, and is about to tell Butterfly the joyful news when she sees a foreign woman in the background, and learns that this is Pinkerton's wife, who wants to adopt Butterfly's child. Pinkerton cannot find the courage to tell Butterfly the truth, and leaves again. When Butterfly sees the strange woman she understands at last. She is prepared to give the child to his father. She herself takes a dagger inherited from her father, who used it to commit hara-kiri on the emperor's orders. Butterfly reminds herself of the words engraved on it: "Let those who can no longer live with honor die with honor." Then she says goodbye to her son, and commits suicide in the traditional Japanese manner.

A. G.

Madam Butterfly, production photograph with Leontyne Price (Butterfly) and Gabriela Carturan (Suzuki), production Carlo Maestrini, sets and costumes Tsugo Fojita, Teatro alla Scala, Milan 1961.
Butterfly at the moment of her collapse. Until she is forced to face the bitter truth that Pinkerton has a new American wife who wants to adopt her son, she has been strong, steadfast, and full of confidence. She gives way to weakness only briefly, and then takes her leave of the world with the dignity and determination that gives the opera its moving dramatic effect.

Madam Butterfly, Emmy Destinn as Butterfly, 1907.
Emmy Destinn and Enrico Caruso sang in the first London production of the opera at Covent Garden in 1905, and two years later in the composer's presence at the Metropolitan Opera in New York. This photograph, complete with dedication, was taken on the occasion of that first American performance.

In the Japanese style

Puccini had always shown a strong feeling for background color in his operas, but this work was his first chance to use the intriguingly foreign element of exoticism. He did his research very thoroughly, studying original Japanese music and books on Japanese customs, rituals, and architecture. The results of his research are reflected in the score of *Madam Butterfly*. The opera contains some seven authentic Japanese melodies, as well as fragments of others, and the themes include the Japanese imperial hymn. M 22

Furthermore here are a number of motifs that cannot be identified precisely but that still sound exotic, and may be of Puccini's own invention. Even Butterfly's great aria and the "Cherry Blossom" duet with Suzuki in Act II show foreign influence in their melodic phrasing. M 23, M 24

However, the love theme that accompanies the fragile figure of Butterfly from her first entrance, and rings out again like a hymn at the climax of the great love duet in Act I, is entirely Italian in origin. M 25

Pinkerton

The American naval officer Pinkerton is not one of Puccini's most typical tenor heroes. Even Butterfly, who loves this rather undistinguished man with all her heart, identifies him by the American national anthem, which acts as a leitmotiv in the opera. M 26

But the thoughtless young officer we meet in Act I is changed by Butterfly's ardent passion for him. He describes himself in his song-like aria as a "Yankee vagabondo" – a "roving Yankee." M 27

In Act III, however, his farewell to the place where he found brief happiness with his young Japanese wife is not without nostalgia and sorrow. He realizes, too late, that his own love for Butterfly meant more to him after all than a mere temporary marriage. M 28   J. K.

Madam Butterfly, set design by Ludwig Zuckermandel-Bassermann, Lübeck 1932/33 (TWS).
Exoticism in opera, whether of the Middle or Far East, has always represented a challenge to composers and theatrical designers. The sets of Ludwig Zuckermandel-Bassermann, who also designed sets for Verdi's →*Il trovatore* and Weber's →*Der Freischütz*, combine a knowledge of Japanese interiors and art objects with sensitivity to the atmosphere of the opera. The set pictured here conveys a sense of Butterfly yearning for Pinkerton.

22. Japanese Imperial Hymn

23. Butterfly's Great Aria (Act II)

Un bel dí, ve-dre-mo   le-var-si un fil di fu-mo sull' e-stre-mo confin del ma-re.   E poi __ la nave ap-pa-re __

24. Duet (Butterfly and Suzuki, Act II)

Scuo-ti quel-la fron-da di   ci-lie-gio   e m'in-non-da di   fior __

25. Love Duet (Butterfly and Pinkerton, Act I)

Oh! ____ quanti oc-chi fis-si,at-ten __ ti

26. American National Anthem

27. Pinkerton's Entrance Aria (Act I)

Io Yan-kee va-ga-bon-do   si go-de e traf-fi-ca   sprez-zan-do i   ri-schi.

28. Pinkerton's Farewell (Act III)

Ad-di-o fio-ri-to a-sil   di le-ti-zia e d'amor...

Madam Butterfly, Alfred Piccaver as Pinkerton, 1913.
The American naval officer Benjamin Franklin Pinkerton, one of hundreds of Americans in the armed forces who entered into temporary marriages during their lonely months in Japan. Pierre Loti's novel *Madame Chrysanthème* (1887) is one of the sources that give a detailed account of the practice. Loti himself, a Frenchman, had been a naval officer, and enjoyed the pleasures of such a marriage for some months in Nagasaki from the spring to the fall of 1884, although his own experience was not a tragic one. It is on stage, in the play by David Belasco and most of all in Puccini's opera, that the story assumes a tragic aspect.

The origins of Butterfly
David Belasco's one-act play derives from earlier sources. It was drawn in the first place from a novella by John Luther Long (1898). Long himself had never been to Japan, and took the material for his Japanese tales, including *Madam Butterfly*, from accounts of the country by his sister Jennie Correll, wife of a Methodist missionary. Mrs. Correll spent several years in Nagasaki with her husband, and met the real-life model for the story there.

Madam Butterfly, scene from the film by Frédéric Mitterand (1994), with Ying Huan as Butterfly. The fateful gesture when Pinkerton kisses the heroine's hand is symbolic, both joining and dividing man and wife from two different cultures. New and operatic additions to the story include the depiction on stage of Butterfly's arrival and the wedding ceremony; Puccini would not have been true to his genius had he omitted this element of erotic tension. Recently, several Asian singers have taken the part of Butterfly; the young Chinese singer Ying Huan, from Shanghai, sang the role of the delicate Japanese girl in Frédéric Mitterand's film made in Tunisia in 1994 (she was chosen for the part from among 200 candidates).

The Girl of the Golden West

La fanciulla del West

Opera in three acts

Libretto: Guelfo Civinini and Carlo Zangarini, after David Belasco's play *The Girl of the Golden West*.

Première: 10 December 1910, New York (Metropolitan Opera).

Characters: Minnie (S), Jack Rance, Sheriff (Bar), Dick Johnson, alias Ramerrez, a bandit (T), Nick, bartender at the Polka saloon (T), Ashby, Wells Fargo agent (B), Goldminers: Sonora (Bar), Trin (T), Sid (Bar), Bello (Bar), Harry (T), Joe (T), Happy (Bar), Larkens (B); Billy Jackrabbit, an Indian (B), Wowkle, his squaw (Ms), Jake Wallace, a traveling singer (Bar), José Castro, a mestizo in Ramerrez's gang (B), The Pony Express Rider (T); gold miners, men of the camp (chorus).

Setting: California, 1849–50, at the time of the Gold Rush.

Synopsis
Act I

The gold miners spend their evenings in the Polka saloon at the mining camp. Sheriff Jack Rance, who is in love with Minnie, the landlady of the saloon, enters with the agent Ashby; they are both after the bandit Ramerrez. Minnie, the only woman in the camp, is respected by all the men, and takes Bible classes with them. The Pony Express rider arrives with a telegram for Ashby. It is from a Spanish woman offering to reveal the place where Ramerrez is hiding out. Another guest also arrives, giving his name as Johnson from Sacramento. He and Minnie remember meeting on an earlier occasion, and so the miners give the newcomer a friendly welcome. When they leave the saloon Johnson stays behind. He learns from Minnie that the miners have entrusted their gold to her care. Johnson falls in love with Minnie and abandons his original plan of stealing the gold. They agree to meet later that night.

Act II

In her cabin, Minnie prepares for Johnson's visit. She tells him about her past life, and Johnson brings the conversation round to love. They now declare passionate love for each other. As Johnson is about to leave, he is halted by the sound of three shots outside the window. The sheriff and three miners have come to visit Minnie. Johnson hides. The sheriff is concerned for Minnie, suspecting that the stranger is really the wanted bandit Ramerrez. Minnie sends the men away to continue their

The Girl of the Golden West, production photograph of the Polka saloon, production Wolfgang Weber, conductor Leonard Slatkin, Wiener Staatsoper 1988.
A setting previously unknown on the operatic stage: a group of men trying to escape the monotony of their lives through gambling and whisky. Despite their rough-hewn natures, the gold miners are easily moved to tears, but they are also unpredictably impulsive and prepared to hang a man from the nearest tree at any moment for as small an offense as a marked card. The work portrays the romantic Western as seen through Puccini's eyes.

pursuit of the bandit, but she turns Johnson out too. As soon as he steps outside the door he is hit by a bullet. Minnie's love for him revives, and she hides the wounded man in the attic. However, a drop of blood falling from the ceiling betrays Johnson to the sheriff on his return. Minnie suggests a game of poker between herself and the sheriff to decide Johnson's fate. She wins the game with the aid of a counterfeit card.

Act III

In a clearing in the forest, some of the miners are waiting for the others to join them in pursuit of the bandit Ramerrez. A rumor goes around that the wanted man has escaped again. Finally Ashby appears, with Johnson tied to his horse. The noose is just being put around his neck when Minnie gallops up on horseback, takes advantage of the general astonishment, and places herself in front of Johnson with a pistol, threatening to kill first Johnson and then herself if the men do not leave him alone. She reminds the miners how much they all owe her. Gradually the miners are overcome by emotion, and declare themselves ready to pardon Johnson. Minnie and Johnson ride away to begin a new life somewhere else.

A. G.

The Girl of the Golden West, production photograph with Gigliola Frazzoni (Minnie), Giangiacomo Guelfi (Sheriff Jack Rance), and Franco Corelli (Johnson), production Carlo Maestrini, Teatro alla Scala, Milan 1964.

An operatic Western

David Belasco's play *The Girl of the Golden West* was among the earliest examples of the Western genre. Its première (in Philadelphia in 1905) and the period in which it is set were little more than half a century apart. The story takes place during the Californian Gold Rush of 1849–50, and is allegedly based on real events known to the author from family traditions and reminiscences. In his story, which teeters on the brink of kitsch, Belasco dwells on the element of fairy tale rather than the fate of three real people. The improbable figure of the noble bandit, which can offer little in the way of dramatic authenticity apart from the attractions of virility, is among the stereotypes of Romantic robber fiction. The character of the sheriff, a "pocket Scarpia" – always inclined to misuse the power of his office, but eventually forced to obey the unwritten rules of honor among thieves – remains a theatrical villain rather imprecisely drawn. The young saloon proprietor Minnie – the only female character in the setting of Belasco's story, an idol revered by all the rough miners and at the same time the object of their jealousy – is a mixture of very different characteristics: innocence and determination, virtue and severity, dreamy idealism and a strong sense of reality. She is presented as a pistol-packing angel, an expert horsewoman and poker player, just waiting for the man to whom she can give her first kiss, and when the crucial moment in her life comes she fights with great determination for her happiness.

Puccini's Minnie

There are 18 male roles in the opera, but Minnie is the only part for a woman, if we disregard the minor female role of the Indian maidservant Wowkle in the brief episode at the beginning of Act II. This may seem an unusually disproportionate arrangement of the singing parts, but it does not endanger the balance of the score or the drama in the least. Minnie's dramatic importance and the musical strength of her part help to maintain equilibrium. In fact this extreme situation seems to have stimulated Puccini's imagination. He was fascinated by the wealth of emotions he gives to Minnie, and the erotic enchantment of this untouchable Amazon who keeps her distance from all men, with the sole exception of the one to whom she hopes to give her first kiss. After the series of "piccole donne," "little women" predestined to suffer (Manon, Mimi, Butterfly), Puccini presented another model of womanhood in Minnie: while she is full of feminine tenderness and kindness, she is also an energetic, passionate heroine, ready for anything in defense of her happiness. She is a heroine who deserves her place in Puccini's picture gallery of active female characters, together with Tosca and Turandot.

J. K.

The Girl of the Golden West, Tito Gobbi as the sheriff, production Mario Frigerio, costumes Nicola Benois, Teatro Alla Scala, Milan 1955. Jack Rance, the sheriff, loses more than just a poker game; he has to abandon all hope of Minnie's love, and must let his hunted rival go free not once but twice.

A showpiece for the Met

Puccini's "American" opera, *The Girl of the Golden West*, had its première in New York, the first première of a Puccini opera to be given outside Italy, although there was a very strong Italian contingent involved in the production. The two male leads were sung by Enrico Caruso and Pasquale Amati, the conductor was Arturo Toscanini, and the co-director was Tito Ricordi, working with David Belasco and Giulio Gatti-Casazza, general manager of the Met. It was a sensational social occasion and a great success with audiences; the piece remained popular with the public for a long time. After the New York première the opera was staged in Chicago and Boston, and a season later, in May 1911, at Covent Garden in London. The first performance in Italy was not until June 1911, in Rome.

Toscanini and the Metropolitan Opera

Toscanini's first appearance at the Metropolitan Opera, conducting Verdi's →*Aida* (16 November 1908), was not only a sensational success; with this production, the maestro also put an immediate end to artistically stagnant performance practice of the kind that had become established in the old opera houses of Europe during the nineteenth century. Why did Toscanini go to the Met? He hoped to impose his maximalist interpretative standards with the help of a sympathetic management. He was also accompanied by his friend Gatti-Casazza, with whom he got on particularly well because Gatti-Casazza could tolerate his temperamental outbursts. In the turbulent theatrical world of the Met – as Filippo Sacchi, author of a biography of Toscanini, has cogently remarked – they existed side by side like the tortoise (Gatti-Casazza) and the cat (Toscanini), each living in accordance with his own temperament and remaining unscathed. A particular attraction of the Met for Toscanini was the fact that Gustav Mahler had conducted there from 1907. Initially the plan was for Mahler to conduct the German repertory and Toscanini the Italian repertory, but at the very beginning of his New York period Toscanini began working on Wagner: his first venture was with →*The Twilight of the Gods* (which he conducted without a score), and in his second season he was already conducting →*Tristan*. He remained at the Met until 1921, and then returned to La Scala as general music director, staying there until 1929. After becoming involved in a brawl in Bologna with a group of fascists, when he refused to conduct their anthem, he returned to New York, and settled there permanently a few years later.

The Girl of the Golden West, Enrico Caruso as Johnson.
By the time Caruso sang the part of Dick Johnson at the New York première of the opera, he had been a frequent guest at the Metropolitan Opera for seven years, and was paid $10,000 per performance. His first part at the Met was the duke in Verdi's →*Rigoletto* in 1903. In the years that followed he created almost all the major Italian tenor roles here, and if he was in a good mood would agree to sing many baritone heroes as well. Once, when a bass fell sick during a performance of Puccini's →*La bohème,* Caruso even sang Colline's famous overcoat aria "vecchia zimarr, senti."

Above
The auditorium of the Metropolitan Opera, New York.
The Metropolitan Opera has not been the scene of many premières during the 115 years of its history (Puccini's *The Girl of the Golden West* was an exception), but nonetheless the old Met featured among the major opera houses of the world. After the turn of the century the greatest Italian and German singers from Caruso to Leo Slezak gave guest performances here, and in the course of the 20th century the Met came to equal La Scala in importance. To sing at the Met today shows that an artist has reached the pinnacle of the international operatic world. The old Met opened in 1883 with Gounod's →*Faust.* It was destroyed by fire nine years later, and rebuilt. The new theater, designed on the Italian model, was in use until 1965, and was then demolished. A new building was inaugurated the following year, with a production of Samuel Barber's *Antony and Cleopatra.* The new Met in the Lincoln Center was built to plans by the architect Wallace Harrison. The auditorium has over 3,800 seats, and is democratically designed so that the audience can see and hear equally well from every seat in the house.

Group photograph of (from left to right) Giulio Gatti-Casazza, David Belasco, Arturo Toscanini, and Giacomo Puccini, c. 1910.
Giulio Gatti-Casazza (1869–1940) was one of the great theatrical directors of the old school: he had an overall artistic idea of a work, a fine feeling for artistic talent, and, not least, nerves of steel. After studying engineering, he began his career in 1893 at the Teatro Municipale in Ferrara, becoming its director at the age of only 24. He was so successful here that five years later he was appointed director of the greatest opera house in Italy, La Scala. Under his management, such foreign masterpieces as Musorgsky's →*Boris Godunov* and Debussy's →*Pelléas and Mélisande* entered the Italian repertory on the stage of La Scala. He also thought highly of Wagner's music dramas. However, his name is linked most closely with the Metropolitan Opera. He was general manager of that institution twice between 1908 and 1935, and he made the greatest opera house in the United States internationally famous, particularly with Toscanini as music director. Under his management 177 different works were produced at the Met.

Arturo Toscanini (1867–1957)

Thanks to his enormous international reputation as an artist and a man, as well as to sophisticated American recording techniques, Toscanini was filmed conducting many concerts. Even in old age he was a fascinating figure with an incomparable knowledge of the repertory, a fine sense of form, and great personal charisma. Contemporary accounts and later interpretations unanimously agree that he was not only one of the most important conductors of the twentieth century, but the greatest conductor of Italian opera in the world. He played the cello in the orchestra at the première of Verdi's *Otello*, and made his début as an operatic conductor in Rio de Janeiro at the age of 19 with *Aida*. He had a lifelong friendship with Puccini, who was ten years older, and at the age of 29 he conducted the première of *La bohème* at La Scala, Milan. In 1910 he took on the musical direction of *The Girl of the Golden*

West at the Metropolitan Opera in New York, and after Puccini's death he conducted the première of *Turandot* at La Scala. Toscanini's legendary memory, profound knowledge of the works he conducted, and inability to compromise either as a man or as an artist made him the ultimate authority on the faithful interpretation of a work.

Arturo Toscanini at an orchestral rehearsal, undated series of photographs.
Among the tasks of a conductor is to determine and maintain the correct tempo, control the development of orchestral sound, and heighten the intensity of the musicians' feeling. Toscanini's movements while conducting a concert performance were simple and concentrated, but in rehearsal he used to let fly, singing, shouting, protesting, carried away by the masterpiece he was performing.

The Swallow

La rondine

Commedia lirica in three acts

Libretto: Giuseppe Adami.
Première: 27 March 1917, Monte Carlo (Opéra du Casino).

Characters: Magda de Civry (S), Lisette, her maid (S), Ruggero Lastouc, a young man from Montauban (T), Prunier, a poet (T), Rambaldo, a rich Parisian (Bar), Périchaud (B), Gobin (T), Crébillon (B), Rabonnier (Bar), Yvette and Bianca, friends of Magda (2 S), Suzy (Ms), A Butler (B); ladies and gentlemen, seamstresses and grisettes, guests, waiters, servants, curious onlookers, dancing couples (chorus).

Setting: Paris and the Côte d'Azur near Nice during the Second Empire.

La rondine, photograph from the production by Lotfi Mansouri, sets Ralph Funicello, costumes Sam Kirkpatric, conductor Alessandro Siciliani, Lincoln Center State Theater, New York 1993.
The second act in Bullier's restaurant, a fashionable haunt of artists, provides an opportunity to include fashionable dance music. In *La rondine* Puccini aimed to create a work of his own time, not distanced by a historical or exotic setting, something he had already done in →*La bohème*. The conflicts of Act II are reminiscent not only of Verdi's →*La traviata* but also of *La bohème* itself. However, that in itself is the weak point of this later opera by Puccini; reminiscences do not amount to a masterpiece, and the two works are not really comparable. With the two operas of his youth, *La rondine* is the least known of Puccini's stage works.

Synopsis

Magda, a Parisian courtesan, is living under the protection of a rich banker, but still remembers a happy and genuinely loving encounter she once had at Bullier's restaurant. When young Ruggero comes from the provinces to Paris, and is recommended to spend his first evening at Bullier's, Magda's old memories revive. She disguises herself as a servant and steals out of the banker's house. At Bullier's she meets the unsuspecting Ruggero, and tells him her name is Paulette. A deep affection awakens in both. Magda does not return to her golden cage, but spends several happy months of love in Ruggero's company, far from Paris. Only when Ruggero wants to legalize their relationship and marry Magda does she disclose her origins. She then leaves her lover, and returns to Paris and her old life as a courtesan. *S. N.*

The temptation of operetta

In October 1913 Puccini was asked by the two directors of the Carltheater in Vienna, Siegmund Eibenschütz and Heinrich Berté, to write an operetta for the theater. Obviously all they wanted was to acquire a work by a composer whose name was already internationally famous. But what made Puccini accept the commission? Was he tempted by the considerable fee offered? (Originally it was 200,000 Austrian crowns, but according to many accounts it rose to 400,000.) It must also have been tempting to try his hand at operetta, a field into which he had not previously ventured though the genre promised to be highly successful. And all this happened while he was composing his dark one-act opera →Il tabarro.

Lyrical comedy or operetta?

In any case, Puccini was well aware that he had succumbed to temptation, hence his recurrent expressions of discontent with the material and the entire genre during the rather long process of composition, his attempts to back out of the contract at an early stage, and later, as he became more and more involved in the whole affair, his defiant defense of his enterprise. He tried to salvage his integrity by insisting that he was composing not an operetta but a "lyrical comedy," to be clearly distinguished from operetta by the principle of through-composition. However, it cannot be denied that the piece does have a touch of operetta about it. Sentimental, nostalgic operetta – without any tragic reversal of fortune, but without a happy ending either – was one of the new developments of the time in the genre, particularly in the work of Franz Lehár, whom Puccini respected and knew personally. *The Swallow* was composed to a recipe for success: the Viennese waltz is typical of the basic atmosphere, and is joined by various other fashionable dances such as the tango, slow foxtrot, and one-step. The work did indeed prove successful in its time, but in spite of several attempts to revive it (for instance in 1993 at the Lincoln Center State Theater, New York, and in 1994 at La Scala), *La rondine* is something of a rarity on the operatic stage today. *J.K.*

La rondine, photograph from the production by Lotfi Mansouri, sets Ralph Funicello, costumes Sam Kirkpatric, conductor Alessandro Siciliani, Lincoln Center State Theater, New York 1993.
A critical review of *La rondine* called it "the poor man's *La traviata*." The description is accurate, and not just because the première was given in the reduced circumstances of the First World War. The love story of Magda (a typical name in the Austro-Hungarian monarchy) and Ruggero is unmistakably based on the same conflict as that of the Lady of the Camellias, Verdi's →*La traviata*.

Il tabarro

The Cloak

Opera in one act

Libretto: Giuseppe Adami, after Didier Gold's play *La houppelande* (*The Cloak*).

Première: 14 December 1918, New York (Metropolitan Opera) (as no. 1 of *Il trittico*), together with *Suor Angelica* and *Gianni Schicchi*.

Characters: Michele, a barge owner (Bar), Giorgetta, Michele's wife (S), Luigi, a stevedore (T), Tinca ("tench"), a stevedore (T), Talpa ("mole"), a stevedore (B), La Frugola ("ferret"), Talpa's wife (Ms), A Ballad Seller (T), Six *Midinettes* (6 S), A Pair of Lovers (S, T).

Setting: Paris, around 1900.

Synopsis

Michele's barge lies at anchor by the banks of the Seine. The stevedores are just finishing work. Michele watches jealously as his wife Giorgetta turns to young Luigi, ignoring her own husband. A barrel organ is heard. The stevedore Tinca invites Giorgetta to dance, but Luigi pushes him aside. Giorgetta thinks sadly of her earlier happy life on the outskirts of Paris; Luigi himself is from the same area. They declare their love for one another, and Luigi promises to come back as soon as Giorgetta gives him a sign by lighting a match. Michele also dreams of happier times in the past, when he lived in harmony with Giorgetta and their child, who later died. He used to wrap them both in his sailor's cloak. Giorgetta rejects his amorous advances yet again. Sadly, he lights his pipe, and as his match flares Luigi takes it for the agreed signal. Michele hears soft footsteps, and discovers Luigi. In the scuffle that follows, Michele takes Luigi by the throat, forcing him to confess his love for Giorgetta. Then he strangles him and hides the corpse under his cloak. Giorgetta expresses a wish for Michele to wrap her in his cloak again. He raises it, and shows her the corpse of Luigi. When Giorgetta recoils, screaming, he forces her down on the corpse.

A. G.

Il tabarro, set design by Otto Reigbert for the production by Erich Bormann, Städtische Bühnen, Cologne 1934 (TWS).
A gloomily realistic set, designed in the shadow of the great economic crisis and the Nazi dictatorship of the period. *Il tabarro* is a proletarian tragedy.

Il trittico

Soon after 1910 Puccini conceived the idea of a Dante trilogy that would consist of a realistic and naturalistic horror story, a kind of mystery play, and a cheerful *opera buffa*.

In line with Dante's *Divine Comedy*, the first one-act opera, *Il tabarro*, was to represent the Inferno of human misery, the second, →*Suor Angelica*, would stand for Purgatory, and the cheerful third opera, →*Gianni Schicchi*, for Paradise. When the three works had taken their final shape in 1918, a friend of Puccini suggested the term *Il trittico* (*The Triptych*), referring to the winged altars of Gothic art, as an overall title.

A fateful cloak

Didier Gold's play *La houppelande* (*The Cloak*) was a box-office draw early in the second decade of the twentieth century.

This dark drama, written in the spirit of Emile Zola, painted a sensitive picture of proletarian life in a big city. The action lasts from sunset until the middle of the night, and the gradually deepening darkness is not just atmospheric, in line with the general mood of the piece, but also has a symbolic meaning. The cloak itself is an ambivalent symbol: it is the requisite and emblem of family life, a protective covering, but also represents the complete opposite, a cloak that can disguise dark deeds of terror.

I tabarro, photograph from the production by Willy Decker, Oper der Stadt Köln 1995.

Left
Il tabarro, production photograph with (from left to right) Jukka Rasilainen (Michele), Antonio Barasorda (Luigi), and Soya Smolyaninova (Giorgetta), production Udo Samel, sets Bernhard Kleber, Sächsische Staatsoper, Dresden 1998.

The banks of the Seine

Proletarian life outside Paris is finely depicted in the setting of this opera on the banks of the Seine. It is a mixture of tawdry gaiety and hopeless poverty, a picturesque but fateful backdrop for the action. Pairs of lovers stroll along the towpaths, but the suicidally minded are also wandering around in the dark, and the night casts its veil over grim and violent deeds. The river has its own basic tone in Puccini's composition, a note struck even in the introductory music and recurring again and again. The echoes of French Impressionism are unmistakable in the dissolution of the harmonic outlines (Puccini's reminiscence of Debussy's orchestral nocturne *Nuages*, in particular, is clearly perceptible). M 29

The whole atmosphere, even in the ballad seller's strophic song, is sad and desolate. In this song, cheerful images of spring mingle with the flavor of death, and it contains a quotation from Puccini himself in "The Story of Mimi."

There is also a reference to the tragedy that awaits Giorgetta and Luigi: those who have given their lives to love will die for love. M 30   J. K.

Il tabarro, the title page of Ricordi's first edition of 1918.

29. Music of the River Seine

30. The Ballad Seller's Song

Pri - ma - ve - ra, pri - ma - ve - - - ra! Chi ha vis - su - to per a - mo - re, per a - mo - re si mo - rí

Right above
Suor Angelica, Sena Jurinac as Angelica, production Carlo Maestrini, sets Ardengo Soffici, costumes Enzo Rossi, Teatro alla Scala, Milan 1959.
Angelica's only pleasure in life is the convent garden; she lives for the garden, and will die by the plants from it. Is there something of Puccini's favorite sister Iginia, who had herself taken the veil, in this character? The photograph shows the great Austrian singer of Croatian origin, Sena Jurinac, as Angelica.

Suor Angelica

Sister Angelica

Opera in one act

Libretto: Giovacchino Forzano.
Première: 14 December 1918, New York (Metropolitan Opera) (as no. 2 of *Il trittico*, together with *The Cloak* and *Gianni Schicchi*).

Characters: Sister Angelica (S), The Princess, Angelica's aunt (A), The Abbess (Ms), The Monitress (Ms), The Mistress of the Novices (Ms), Sister Genovieffa (S), Sister Osmina (S), Sister Dolcina (S), The Nursing Sister (Ms), Two Alms Sisters (2 S), Two Novices (S, Ms), Two Lay Sisters (S, Ms); nuns, novices, angelic voices (chorus).
Setting: A convent at the end of the 17th century.

Suor Angelica, photograph from the production by Harry Kupfer, sets and costumes Hans Schavernoch, conductor Gerd Albrecht, Hamburgische Staatsoper 1995. The dramatic leitmotiv of Harry Kupfer's production of *Il trittico* is the enclosed stage area. All three one-act operas are performed in a small, restricted space: → *Il tabarro* on and in a barge, *Suor Angelica* in a convent, and → *Gianni Schicchi* in a dead man's bedroom. There is no way of escape from any of these settings.

Right below
Suor Angelica, photograph from the production by Massimo Bogianchino, conductor Claudio Abbado, Teatro alla Scala, Milan 1963.
Puccini's unerring dramatic instinct is to the fore in this tale of convent life. The unfeeling outside world enters the bright, happy, idyllic life of the nuns like a flash of lightning, and clouds darken the sun.

Synopsis

After evening prayers, the nuns go out into the convent garden. Some have small penances imposed on them by the monitress. The nuns pray for their companions who died the year before. Several admit to small wishes of their own; only Sister Angelica claims to have none. The other nuns can hardly believe this. Sister Angelica has been in the convent for seven years, she is apparently from a noble family, and has been longing for years to hear news of her relations. Two alms sisters say that an elegant carriage has drawn up outside the convent gates. Angelica is summoned to the parlor, where she finds her aunt the princess, a distinguished but cold and unapproachable lady. Her aunt has been entrusted with the task of distributing the family inheritance. Angelica's younger sister is getting married, the prin-

cess has done her duty, and has come with papers for Angelica to sign. Angelica asks the name of her sister's bridegroom, and is told he is someone who, out of love, is prepared to overlook the shame Angelica has brought on the family. Angelica answers humbly that she has sacrificed everything else to the Virgin Mary as penance, but the one sacrifice she can never make is to forget her son. Coldly, the princess tells her that the child died of a severe sickness two years ago. Angelica falls to the ground with a cry of grief. When night falls and the convent is quiet, Angelica picks poisonous herbs in the garden and brews a draft from them. No sooner has she taken the poison than she suddenly becomes aware of the great sin of committing suicide, and in despair she calls on the Virgin Mary to save her. The door of the chapel opens, and the Virgin appears with a fair-haired little boy. Angelica reaches out her arms to her son, and dies.   A. G.

An all-female opera

The drama of Sister Angelica unfolds before the back-drop of a careful, detailed picture of convent life. A Tuscan convent at the end of the seventeenth century was a little world to itself. Puccini knew something of the background from personal experience, since one of his sisters, Iginia, was a nun, and became Mother Superior of a convent in Vicepelago.

A marble statue in music

The appearance of Angelica's aunt the princess in the convent comes as a shock. Puccini's portrait of this woman is an artistic masterpiece. She is the only important alto part he ever wrote. For the first time, he gave the basic type of his negative and disruptive male characters female form; Scarpia's threatening baritone is transferred to the dark, imperious alto register. The princess is a static, unmoving figure; indeed, her devastating power lies in her immobility and her rigidly obsessive character. She is like a wall of ice against which any feeling creature will only injure itself mortally. Angelica is bound to lose her desperate struggle against this demonic and pitiless figure. She reveals her heart musically in a short aria sung after she has heard of the death of her child, far away from her. *M 31*   *J. K.*

Suor Angelica, title page of the first edition, published by Ricordi in 1918.

31. Angelica's Aria

O - ra che sei   un   an - ge - lo del cie - lo,   o - ra tu puoi ve - der - la   la   tua   mam - ma,

Suor Angelica, set design by Eduard Löffler, Teatro Municipal, Rio de Janeiro 1942 (TWS).
Puccini was not only familiar with the operatic dimensions of his one act, all-female opera, but also with the real world of nuns. His favorite sister, Iginia, lived in a convent at Vicepelago. When Puccini had finished the opera, he went to see her and played it through to her community, apparently moving them to tears with the tale of the fictional Sister Angelica.

Gianni Schicchi

Opera in one act

Libretto: Giovacchino Forzano, after an episode from Dante Alighieri's *La Divina commedia* (*Divine Comedy*), part 1, "Inferno," Canto xxx.
Première: 14 December 1918, New York (Metropolitan Opera) (as no. 3 of *Il trittico,* together with *The Cloak* and *Suor Angelica*).
Characters: Gianni Schicchi (Bar), Lauretta (S), Zita, Buoso Donati's cousin (A), Rinuccio, Zita's nephew (T), Gherardo, Buoso's nephew (T), Nella, his wife (S), Gherardino, their son (A), Betto di Signa, Buoso's brother-in-law (B), Simone, Buoso's cousin (B), Marco, his son (Bar), La Ciesca, Marco's wife (Ms), Master Spinelloccio, a doctor (B), Ser Amantio di Nicolao, a notary (Bar), Pinellino, a cobbler (B), Guccio, a dyer (B).
Setting: Florence, 1299.

Synopsis

The relations of Buoso Donati are mourning his death with simulated grief. But soon they hear a rumor that Donati has left all his large fortune to a monastery. Simone says that if the will is already with a notary there is nothing to be done, but if it is still in the house ... Feverishly, they start searching for the will, and Rinuccio finds it. Now they wonder what to do next. Rinuccio says he knows someone who can help them: Gianni Schicchi. The other members of the family reject the idea, since Schicchi is an "immigrant," not a native of Florence. Rinuccio points out that the city owes its fame to such immigrants. As if on cue, Gianni Schicchi arrives with his daughter Lauretta, whom Rinuccio wants to marry. Zita refuses her permission, and Gianni Schicchi takes offense and prepares to leave. Only the pleas of Lauretta hold him back. Sure enough, he thinks of a way out of the family's dilemma: if no one except those present knows of Donati's death, then they could make a new will. However, there are harsh penalties for such a fraud: loss of the perpetrator's left hand and exile from the city. When the doctor arrives, Gianni Schicchi imitates Donati's voice, and reassures the doctor through the door, opened just a crack, saying he feels quite well and just wants to sleep. The family sends for the notary and witnesses. Meanwhile each of them whispers information about his or her preferred legacy into Gianni Schicchi's ear. In the notary's presence, wearing the dead man's clothes and lying in his bed, Gianni Schicchi begins dictating "his" will. Donati's relations protest in vain when they hear it, but are reminded of the punishment for fraud that threatens. No sooner have the notary and witnesses left than they all fall on Gianni Schicchi, but he is now master of the house he has "inherited," and drives them all out. Only the happy couple Lauretta and Rinuccio remain behind. Gianni Schicchi turns to the audience: Dante, he says, condemned him to hell for this trick, but he hopes that theirs will be a kinder verdict.   *Á. G.*

Gianni Schicchi, title page of the first edition, published by Ricordi in 1918.

Gianni Schicchi, photograph from the production by Udo Samel, sets Bernhard Kleber, Sächsische Staatsoper, Dresden 1998. Buoso Donati's family illustrates a wide range of human weaknesses. Its members embody greed, hypocrisy, and xenophobia, although they are portrayed as individuals and not allegorical figures. The group of relations offered Puccini a chance to create delightful character sketches through small gestures and musical motifs. From the opening of the piece, he establishes a unique, grotesque, and humorous atmosphere, yet one full of understanding for mankind.

Gianni Schicchi, set design by Eduard Löffler, production and conductor Wolfgang Schubert, Stadttheater, Klagenfurt 1959 (TWS).
This attractive set design in the traditional manner, with its great open loggia, emphasizes the historical and geographical context of *Gianni Schicchi*: the setting is Dante's Florence in the year 1299. The black comedy itself is made timeless by the continuing relevance of human foibles, but both libretto and music relate to the great city of the Italian Renaissance, the capital of Puccini's native Tuscany.

Dante and Puccini

Gianni Schicchi was a historical character, a citizen of Florence and contemporary of Dante, who was related to the Donati family. Schicchi was one of the "contadini," provincials who had emigrated to Florence and were regarded as *nouveaux riches*; they were anathema to the aristocratic Dante, who consequently banished the wily Schicchi to hell. Puccini and his librettist Forzano did not share Dante's opinion.

A variant of the *commedia dell'arte*

The comedy *Gianni Schicchi* belongs to a rich tradition of international literature, and is particularly closely related to the Italian genres of *commedia dell'arte* and *opera buffa*, which were full of satirical treatments of the subject of greed and legacy-hunting. Audiences could enjoy themselves at the expense of victims who had been cheated out of their inheritance. It is not difficult to see traces of the *commedia dell'arte* in *Gianni Schicchi*. Behind Schicchi himself stands Arlecchino (Harlequin), the basic type of all quick-witted jokers, and behind Simone stands Pantalone, while Lauretta and Rinuccio represent the conventional pair of young lovers. The opera also features the characteristic figures of the notary, and the Bolognese "Dottore" in the person of Dr. Spinelloccio ("porcupine"). The "Capitano" (captain) and the Moor get at least a fleeing mention in the text of the libretto.   *J. K.*

32. Lauretta's Aria

Oh! mio bab-bi - no   ca - ro,   mi pia-ce,è bel - lo, bel - lo; vo'an -
da - re in Por - ta Ros - sa   a com-pe-rar   l'a - nel - lo!

Gianni Schicchi, production photograph with Tito Gobbi (Schicchi) and Renata Scotto (Lauretta), production Carlo Maestrini, sets Gianni Vagnetti, costumes Vieri Vagnetti, Teatro alla Scala, Milan 1958/59.
Lauretta softens her father's heart with a song that has become immortal as one of the most popular of all operatic arias: "O mio babbino caro" ("O my beloved father"). *M 32*

Turandot

Dramma lirico in three acts (five scenes)

Libretto: Giuseppe Adami and Renato Simoni, after the play of the same name by Carlo Gozzi and its adaptation by Friedrich von Schiller.
Première: Uncompleted version: 25 April 1926, Milan (Teatro alla Scala); version completed by Franco Alfano, 27 April 1926, Milan (Teatro alla Scala).

Characters: Princess Turandot (S), The Emperor Altoum, her father (T), Timur, dethroned King of Tartary (B), Calaf, his son (T), Liù, a young slave girl (S), Ping, Grand Chancellor (Bar), Pang, General Purveyor (T), Pong, Master of the Kitchens (T), A Mandarin (Bar), The Prince of Persia (T), The Executioner (silent); imperial guard, executioner's henchmen, children, priests, mandarins, dignitaries, eight wise men, Turandot's maids, soldiers, guards, musicians, ghosts of the dead, crowd (chorus).
Setting: Peking in the legendary past.

Turandot, set design by Ludwig Sievert for the production by Lothar Wallerstein, conductor Clemens Krauss, Opernhaus Frankfurt 1927 (TWS).
Together with Verdi's →*Aida*, *Turandot* is perhaps the most spectacular opera on the international stage. The imperial Chinese palace, the crowds, and the many walk-on parts lend the opera a monumental character, tempting directors and set designers to bring this ornately decorative world to life again and again. It presented an intriguing challenge to the famous film director Franco Zeffirelli, who created picturesquely striking tableaux from a wide spectrum of colors and huge crowds of people.

Synopsis
Act I
A mandarin announces Turandot's decree: any man who asks for her hand in marriage must answer three riddles. If he fails to do so he will be executed, a fate that is about to befall the young Prince of Persia. Prince Calaf encounters his father Timur, exiled from his kingdom and now hiding in Peking with the slave girl Liù, who has followed him out of love for Calaf. When the moon rises, the Prince of Persia is led out to execution. The crowd begs Turandot to show mercy, but in vain. She confirms his sentence of death. Calaf is fascinated by Turandot's beauty. Timur, Liù, and the three "masks," the ministers Ping, Pang, and Pong, try to restrain him, but to no avail. He has the gong sounded three times, thus announcing himself as a new suitor for the hand of Turandot.

Act II
The ministers Ping, Pang, and Pong sadly remember the days before Turandot held sway. They fear for the future of China; 13 suitors have already been executed. Loud noise brings the ministers back to reality. The court and the people assemble to watch the unknown new suitor's ordeal. Turandot explains the reasons for her conduct: an ancestress of hers was once raped and murdered by a foreigner, and she has set out to avenge this dreadful deed. Emperor Altoum warns Calaf not to persist, but Calaf three times repeats his wish to submit to the ritual. He successfully answers all three riddles, but Turandot flings herself at her father's feet, begging him not to give her to the stranger. The Emperor says that he will keep his promise. Wishing to win Turandot's love, however, Calaf sets her a riddle of his own: if she can guess his name before sunrise, he will own himself defeated and be prepared to die.

Act III
On Turandot's orders, all the citizens of Peking must spend the night discovering the foreign prince's name. The three ministers question Calaf themselves. Timur and Liù are dragged in, since they have been seen with the stranger. Turandot herself interrogates them. To save the old king, Liù claims that she alone knows the prince's name. She is threatened with torture. Saying farewell to Calaf, she stabs herself, and her body is carried away. Turandot and Calaf are left alone together, and Calaf kisses Turandot, who admits that from the first she both loved and hated him. Calaf places his fate in her hands by telling her his own name. Turandot announces the stranger's name to the people: to her, she says, he is known as Love. A. G

Turandot, poster for the première in 1926.
Puccini died of throat cancer on 29 November 1924, while he was still working on *Turandot*. His friend and musical colleague Franco Alfano (1877–1954) completed the third act from the sketches left by the composer. When the première was given at La Scala the opera had therefore been finished, but Toscanini conducted it only as far as the point where Puccini had been forced to stop work on the score – after the death of Liù.

Why *Turandot*?

The subject of *Turandot* was very different in its nature from any that Puccini had previously tackled. It is not a realistic drama, comparable with the depictions of real life in his earlier operas, but a fairy-tale piece heavy with symbolism and of fresco-like dimensions. Given the date of 1920, Puccini may have felt an urge to compete with another symbolic and spectacular fairy-tale opera, Richard Strauss's →*The Woman Without a Shadow* (1919).

In fact there are over ten settings of *Turandot* in operatic history. Other composers to use the same subject were →Carl Maria von Weber (1809) and →Ferruccio Busoni (1911, 1917). Puccini may even have known Busoni's version.

Turandot, photograph from the production by Franco Zeffirelli, sets Franco Zeffirelli, costumes Anna Anni and Dada Saligieri, conductor Claudio Abbado, Teatro alla Scala, Milan 1983.
Liù, as she appears in the opera, is one of Puccini's most individual creations. From the first she was planned as a contrast to Turandot, the quintessential "little woman in love," a late offshoot of the line that can be traced from Mimi to Butterfly, Giorgetta, and Sister Angelica.

33. Imperial Chinese Anthem

Gozzi

The fairy tale of Turandot originally had nothing to do with China. Most of the folk motifs in the tale suggest a Middle Eastern origin. The Chinese setting did not appear until around the fifteenth to sixteenth centuries in Arabic tales (for instance in the collection of the *Thousand and One Nights*). The first significant Western writer to adapt the subject, Carlo Gozzi, employed *chinoiserie* as an exotic background for his play of 1762. One of the peculiarities of this piece is that Gozzi brings in figures from the Italian *commedia dell'arte* – Truffaldino, Brighella, Tartaglia, and Pantalone – as minor characters against this Chinese background. The idea left its traces on Puccini's own work: characters of impromptu comedy served him as the models for Ping, Pang, and Pong, the three Chinese ministers in the opera.

Schiller

Gozzi's comedy preserved the spirit of rationalism and the Enlightenment, and Friedrich von Schiller intensified these features even further in his stage adaptation of 1802.

The eponymous heroine's emotional development is depicted as a gradual and carefully motivated process – an inner struggle between her pride and her burgeoning love. Turandot's Amazonian nature and her antipathy to the opposite sex are explained as the result of her protest against the status of women, delivered up helplessly to family interests and masculine honor. Turandot's conduct arises from her proud defense of her privilege of choosing her own husband.

The Chinese element

Puccini became acquainted with Chinese melodies on various occasions, one of them being his visit to London in 1920. In fact he used many sources. Analyses have shown that at least six or seven themes of genuine Chinese origin can be identified in the score of *Turandot*. They include an imperial anthem, a melody that Puccini heard played by a Chinese musical box. It is one of the leitmotivs of the opera. M 33

Puccini also conjured up the characteristic sound of the Far East by using an exotic battery of percussion. Chinese gongs, tam-tams, the xylophone, and groups of chimes are used to extend the traditional percussion range. In all there are no fewer than 12 such instruments, a phenomenon without precedent in any of Puccini's previous compositions.

Turandot, photograph from the production by Franco Zeffirelli, costumes Anna Anni and Dada Saligieri, conductor Claudio Abbado, Teatro alla Scala, Milan 1983.
It must have been hard for Puccini to sacrifice his last appealing female character, Liù, to the pitiless logic of dramatic necessity. She is the opposite of Turandot: loving, warm-hearted, sympathetic. She humbly cares for the blind old Tartar king Timur, and her love for Calaf endures even to death. But she cannot fight against the power of love itself, and it is love that destroys her.

Ping, Pang, Pong

In his correspondence, Puccini described the three Chinese ministers as "masks," meaning that they derived from characters of the Italian masquerade or *commedia dell'arte*. He originally saw them as "outsiders" in their fairy-tale Chinese surroundings (and in this he may have been following the example of Strauss's →*Ariadne on Naxos*). He soon dismissed the idea and created genuine Chinese out of the Italian models. But even in the form they finally assumed, these characters retain much of the legacy of the *commedia dell'arte*. In some ways they are still clowns, despite their Chinese costumes. They always move together as a trio on stage, like a self-contained group of puppets, and there is a touch of the grotesque about all their appearances.

J. K.

Turandot, production photograph from Act II, sets and costumes Timothy O'Brien and Tazeena Firth, conductor Lorin Maazel, Wiener Staatsoper 1983.
In this 1983 production, Turandot sang her aria at the top of a stairway reaching to the ceiling of the stage. This interpretation made Turandot's story an account of her gradual descent into the realm of human emotions. When she resigned her dictatorial power to the power of love, the stairway opened up.

Turandot, production photograph with Ghena Dimitrova, production and sets Franco Zeffirelli, costumes Anna Anni and Dada Saligieri, conductor Claudio Abbado, Teatro alla Scala, Milan 1983.
The role of Turandot, although relatively short, is a demanding one, not just because of the part's difficult vocal register but also because the singer must stand motionless at an "unattainable" height, usually wearing a vast costume heavily ornamented with gold. In her great second-act aria, her voice is her sole means of expression.

Right above
Turandot, Lotte Lehmann as Turandot.

Right below
Turandot, Eva Marton as Turandot, Vienna 1983.
At the première, Rosa Raisa sang the difficult part of Turandot. When the opera embarked on its international career, the most famous dramatic sopranos of the time were soon singing the leading role; they included a number of legendary names such as Maria Nemeth, Maria Jeritza, Lotte Lehmann, Eva Turner, and later Maria Callas and Birgit Nilsson. The list could be continued to the present day with such singers as Gwyneth Jones and Ghena Dimitrova. Eva Marton's performance as Turandot was one of the highlights of her operatic career.

The title role

"Who will sing in my opera?" Puccini wondered in 1924, perhaps suspecting that he might not live to see the première himself. "It needs an outstanding heroine and a really good tenor."

What exactly are the demands of the title role? It is not above average length; indeed, Turandot is not heard at all until the middle of the second act. And the legendary "high C" occurs only three times in the whole of her part. However, the frequent changes of register and the almost unrelenting intensity make great demands on the singer's vocal resources, and only a dramatic soprano of quality can master it. M 34

Liù: life or death?

Puccini did not originally envisage the death of Liù. After more than two years working on the score, however, he came to the all but inescapable conclusion that he must condemn her to death. In a letter of November 1922, he told his librettist Adami: "Liù must die. I think there is no way of giving her part the importance it requires unless she dies under torture. And why not? Such a death could have a great effect on changing the cold-hearted Princess's mind." M 35

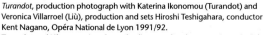

Turandot, production photograph with Katerina Ikonomou (Turandot) and Veronica Villarroel (Liù), production and sets Hiroshi Teshigahara, conductor Kent Nagano, Opéra National de Lyon 1991/92.
Turandot and Liù are not just the embodiments of such contrasting principles as power and love or vengeance and pity, they are also rivals in love, for they love the same man, a fact revealed only by the music. Turandot's words and music have an unconscious dimension of which the outside world – with the exception of Calaf – guesses nothing. When Turandot tries to force Liù to name Calaf, she is really trying to tear Liù's love out of her.

Turandot, production photograph from Act III, production and sets David Hockney, conductor Bruno Bartoletti, Lyric Opera of Chicago 1991/92.
Turandot is the only genuinely choral opera that Puccini ever wrote. From beginning to end, the chorus is on stage almost throughout. That is one reason why the opera is so spectacular, providing stage designers and directors with the opportunity to give their visual imagination free rein – an opportunity they gratefully accept. Lighting effects dominated the production at the Lyric Opera of Chicago.

34. Turandot's Aria (Act II)

Mai nes-sun, nes-sun m'a-vrà! L'orror di chi l'uc-ci-se vi-vo nel cor ___ mi sta!

35. Liù's Aria (Act III)

Tu, che di gel _ sei _ cin-ta, ___ da _ tan-ta fiam-ma

vin-ta ___ l'a-me-ra-i an-che tu! ___

36. Calaf's Aria (Act I)

Non pian-ge-re, Liù! ___ Se in un lon-ta-no gior-no io t'ho sor-ri-so, ___

37. Calaf's Aria (Act III)

Ma il mio mi-stero è chiuso in me, il nome mio nessun sa-prà! No, no, sul-la tua

boc-ca lo-di-rò ___ quando la lu-ce splen-de-rà! ___

How would the story have ended?

In the spring of 1924, six months before his death, Puccini had completed the score up to the scene of Liù's death. This was the nerve center of his opera, and the place where those contradictions he could not resolve came to a head. For the death of Liù is not a factor that will lead to the happy resolution of the plot; it merely confirms, yet again, that Turandot is a cold-hearted murderess. At this point in the action, however, attention turns away from Turandot's conscience and emotions, and focuses on Calaf's feelings instead. Ought not all his passions to die down in the face of such a loving sacrifice as Liù's? How can Calaf's love for the cruel princess flare up again the next moment? This was a problem that Puccini, already mortally ill, took with him to hospital in Brussels on the last journey of his life. Would he ever have found a satisfactory way of solving it?

J. K.

The "Three Tenors" and their victory anthem

Calaf is the most heroic tenor part in Puccini's entire operatic oeuvre. It is not only the high notes Calaf often has to reach that lend the role its particular brilliance, but also its unusual degree of intensity. The music illustrates a state of ardent passion and unremitting will-power that is not displayed so persistently and irresistibly by any of the composer's other characters. Consequently, tenors of international standing such as Mario del Monaco, Giuseppe di Stefano, Placido Domingo, José Carreras, and Luciano Pavarotti have shone in the part. *M 36* Calaf's second aria, "Nessun dorma!" ("Let no one sleep!"), at the beginning of Act III, is one of the most popular tenor arias in operatic history. *M 37*

Psyche

Locke called *Psyche* an English opera. He was a stern defender of English music, which he sought to keep free of foreign influences. *Psyche* contains various musical numbers – a priests' chorus, a *terzetto* of river nymphs, as well as music for a temple procession, a tragic love scene, and a mass suicide. Locke also depicted the god Vulcan and the Cyclops hammering on their anvils, and a gathering of Furies and devils.

John Blow

John Blow's major work was the masque *Venus and Adonis*, in which, contrary to tradition, he set most of the text to music. This work was composed in 1683 for a performance at the royal court. Although it was not the only piece of music he wrote for the theater (he also composed songs and dialogue for five plays between 1680 and 1696), as his only opera it occupies a special position in his oeuvre. The main body of his work consists of settings of the Mass, hymns (of which he produced over 100, including those written for three coronations), 25 odes, songs, music for stringed instruments, and keyboard works (organ and harpsichord).

Blow began his musical career as a chorister in the Chapel Royal and in 1668 became organist at Westminster Abbey, a position he held until 1679. He became a Gentleman of the Chapel Royal in 1674 and organist in 1676. Purcell served an apprenticeship under him during these years. Blow returned to Westminster Abbey as organist in 1695, after Purcell's death.

Portraits of John Blow (Purcell's predecessor and successor as organist at Westminster Abbey) and contemporaries, copperplate engraving by H. Drayton after a design by R. Smirke.

Patriarchs of the English musical stage

Matthew Locke (1621-77) and John Blow (1649-1708), the first composers of the English Baroque, were both of considerable significance for Purcell's development as a composer.

Locke taught Purcell the principles of dramatic style, while Blow provided the model for Purcell's opera →*Dido and Aeneas* with his one-act masque *Venus and Adonis*. Like all English composers, both Locke and Blow enjoyed the patronage of the Crown and the Church.

Matthew Locke

Portrait of Matthew Locke, copperplate engraving by James Caldwell, c. 1770.

During the period of Puritan rule, Locke composed music for the masques *Cupid and Death* (1653), *The Siege of Rhodes* (1656) and *The Cruelty of the Spaniards in Peru* (1658), as well as for the play *The History of Sir Francis Drake* (1659), his contribution consisting of dances, overtures, arias, choruses, and recitatives. Locke's work signaled the arrival of Baroque music on the English stage.

Appointed composer at the Duke's Theater under Charles II, Locke began to write semi-operas, a peculiarly English genre that was later to play an important part in Purcell's oeuvre. The first of these semi-operas were adaptations of Shakespeare's *Macbeth* (1673) and *The Tempest* (1674). Locke's most important semi-opera was *Psyche* (after a text by Thomas Shadwell, 1675): an innovative work, it came close to being a *dramma per musica*.

Venus and Adonis

The librettist of *Venus and Adonis* is unknown, the autograph score containing only a reference to "A Masque for the Entertainment of the King" (Charles II). The part of Venus was sung by Mary Davies, the king's mistress, and Cupid was played by her ten-year-old illegitimate daughter, Lady Mary Tudor. *Venus and*

View of the Dorset Garden Theater in London, copperplate engraving by an unknown artist, 19th century.
The Dorset Garden Theater, London's most splendid Baroque venue, opened in 1671. Both the stage and auditorium were well suited to plays with musical accompaniment (such as adaptations of Shakespeare). In 1689 the theater was renamed the Queen's Theater in reference to Queen Mary. Purcell's stage works – with the exception of *Dido and Aeneas* – were performed here.

Adonis was performed on 17 April 1684 in a Chelsea boarding school run by Josias Priest, where the première of Purcell's *Dido and Aeneas* was to take place five years later.

Baroque love stories

Blow's *Venus and Adonis*, which consists of a French overture, a prologue, and three acts, in many ways anticipates Purcell's *Dido and Aeneas*. The similarities are evident in the division into three acts, in the dramatic function of the choruses and dances, in various melodic details, and in the "love-death" of the finale. In both works, a chorus of lament ("Mourn for thy servant" in *Venus and Adonis*) is one of the most outstanding numbers. Blow, however, was content to limit himself to the use of recitative, ariettas, and choruses, without developing the arias or self-contained scenes of Purcell's later *Dido and Aeneas*. Be that as it may, *Venus and Adonis* is more than a work of mere historical interest, being distinguished by long, arching melodic phrases, carefully wrought structures, and great expressiveness.

P. M.

Purcell, Henry

b. between June and November 1659 in London
d. 21 November 1695 in Westminster, London

Purcell was a chorister in the Chapel Royal until his voice broke in 1673, and in 1677 succeeded his teacher Matthew Locke as composer-in-ordinary for the king's violins. In 1679, aged only 20, he succeeded another of his teachers, John Blow, as organist of Westminster Abbey, and in 1682 became organist of the Chapel Royal. He was given a court appointment in 1683 under Charles II, which was renewed under subsequent monarchs James II (1685) and William III (1689). He left behind a substantial number of compositions, some of which were published in his lifetime. His collected works appeared in 1878 in 25 volumes. Little is known about Purcell's early death at the age of 36, as his contemporaries remained silent on the subject. He is said to have died of a fever contracted after returning home late after a drinking bout and finding himself locked out of his house by his angry wife. Purcell's state funeral in Westminster Abbey was testimony to the great esteem in which the composer was held, as was the title of the first volume of his collected songs, *Orpheus Britannicus*, published in 1698, only three years after his death.

Works: The opera *Dido and Aeneas* (1689); semi-operas: *Dioclesian* (1690), *King Arthur, or The British Worthy* (1691), *The Fairy Queen* (1692), *The Indian Queen* (1695); songs and incidental music for over 40 plays, sacred and secular choral works, songs, fantasias and other pieces for strings, works for harpsichord.

genius for pastoral scenes with the chorus "How blest are shepherds." M1

The fourth scene became famous for the shivering effect of its orchestration, achieved through repeated tremolo chords in the strings. The Cold Genius, called up from the depths of the earth, asks to be allowed to return: "Let me freeze again." M2

The remarkable chromatic coloring intensifies the effect. The fifth scene contains the song of the sirens, "Two daughters of this aged stream are we," followed by one of Purcell's most outstanding compositions, the passacaglia for oboes, strings, soprano, alto, solo bass, and choir, "How happy the lover." M3

In order to conjure up the island in the final scene, a baritone proclaims "Ye blustery brethren" to the accompaniment of a bravura string passage illustrating the raging gales, which then gradually subside. Britannia appears in the calm that follows. The English folk song "Your hay is now mow'd" is one of the final songs of jubilation, as is the famous "Fairest isle, all isles excelling," M4 a patriotic aria whose grandeur challenges that of the elegy at the end of *Dido and Aeneas*.   P.M.

---

*P*urcell is regarded as "Orpheus Britannicus" – the British Orpheus – a brilliant composer who combined the musical movements of his day into an original and personal style of timeless popularity.

Patriotic music

King Arthur became Purcell's most popular work for the stage and was performed throughout the whole of the eighteenth century and well into the nineteenth century. It is the sole example of a semi-opera that did not originate as a masque or a play. The playwright Dryden had wanted to write a patriotic English "dramatick opera" (a play with musical interludes) to celebrate the 25th anniversary of the restoration of the British monarchy (1660–85). King Charles II, who had lived in France during the interregnum, wanted an opera in the French style with singing throughout. Dryden then abandoned his original *King Arthur* project, reworking its prologue into an independent piece for the stage entitled *Albion and Albanius*. The composer was a Frenchman living in London, Louis Grabu, and the work was premièred in 1685. Encouraged by the enormous success of the semi-opera *Dioclesian* in 1690, Dryden returned to *King Arthur*, and revised it specifically for Purcell.

A map set to music

The work is divided into six scenes. The first describes the defeat of the Saxons (Act I), while the second contains the choruses of the quarreling spirits ("Hither this way, this way bend"), which create a truly dramatic moment as Philadel and Grimbald vie with each other to lead Arthur's army in the direction of good and evil respectively. In the third scene Purcell demonstrated his

King Arthur, or The British Worthy

Semi-opera in five acts

Libretto: John Dryden.
Première: May or June 1691, London (Dorset Garden Theater).

Performers: Philadel, an air spirit (S), Grimbald, an earth spirit (Bbar), Shepherd (T), Cupid (S), Cold Genius (B), Aeolus (Bbar), Venus (S); spoken roles.
Setting: The British isles, in mythological times.

Synopsis
Act I

Oswald, the king of the Saxons, threatens the British king, Arthur, with war. They are both rivals for the hand of Emmeline, the blind daughter of the Duke of Cornwall. Oswald would long since have defeated his enemy if Arthur had not been protected by the magician Merlin. Oswald has his own magician, Osmond, and is also assisted by the air spirit Philadel and the earth spirit Grimbald. The two armies eventually clash, and the Saxons are defeated.

Act II

Merlin has succeeded in bringing the air spirit over to Arthur's side. When Grimbald tries to make the

The semi-opera

The semi-opera was invented by Thomas Betterton, an actor and the director of the Dorset Garden Theater. He had become acquainted with the operas of →Jean-Baptiste Lully in France and sought to create an English equivalent. Betterton renovated the Dorset Garden Theater to meet the requirements of opera, thereby paving the way for a form of Restoration drama that was spectacularly staged and included extended musical scenes. The dramatic roles of these scenes were generally those of supernatural beings, their worshipers, and servants. The main action was spoken, although it was the musical component that was responsible for the genre's success.

1. How Blest are Shepherds

How blest are shepherds, how hap-py their lass-es, While drums and trumpets are sound-ing a-larms.

2. The Cold Genius's Aria

What power art thou, who from be-low, Hast made me rise un-will-ing-ly and slow, From beds of ev-er-last-ing snow?

3. How Happy the Lover

How hap-py the lov-er, How ea-sy his chain

4. Fairest Isle

Fair-est isle, all isles ex-cel-ling, Seat of plea-sure and of love.

King Arthur, photograph from the production by Friedrich Meyer-Oertel, sets Heidrun Schmelzer, Gärtnerplatztheater, Munich 1986.
Purcell's semi-opera can be regarded as "the" English national opera, so deeply rooted is the idea of Englishness in both the libretto and the music. The interpretation of the work in the Munich production helped to bridge the gap between a modern audience and the spirit of the English theater of Purcell's day.

British troops lose their way, Philadel guides them back onto the right path.

Act III

With the help of the earth spirit and the magician Osmond, the Saxon king abducts Emmeline. Arthur laments the loss of his love, and the Britons swear to set her free. Oswald courts Emmeline but cannot win her favor, while Philadel restores her sight with the aid of a balm. Osmond, the evil warlock, causes the land and its inhabitants to freeze, but they are restored to life by Cupid's warmth.

Act IV

Osmond now tries to lure Arthur into a wood full of naiads, nymphs, and sirens in order to destroy him. Arthur sees through this ruse, and resists the seductive charms of the two sirens; he destroys the forest and takes Osmond prisoner.

Act V

The two armies engage in battle. There is a duel between Oswald and Arthur, from which Arthur emerges the winner. Magnanimous in victory, he spares the Saxon's life. Emmeline is again reunited with Arthur. Merlin proclaims peace, and all sing in praise of Britannia and her patron saint Saint George.

S. N.

The Fairy Queen, Hans Piesbergen as Bottom, production Wolfgang Hofmann, sets Klaus Teepe, costumes Bettina Ernst, conductor Volker Christ, Theater der Stadt Heidelberg 1995.
Bottom's dream fills him with a dancing spirit. Shakespeare's *A Midsummer Night's Dream* contained a great deal of music, something which was used to advantage in the Elizabethan theater. Since that time many scenes and speeches from the play have become part of the musical repertory, in the works of composers such as Nicolai, Verdi, Britten, and Tippett – echoes can even be heard in the night scene in Wagner's → *The Mastersingers* – while Mendelssohn's unforgettable musical versions of the subject almost form a distinct genre of their own.

An expensive work

The Fairy Queen was Purcell's most extensive work for the stage and the most expensive production of its time. After 200 years of oblivion, the music was rediscovered in 1903, in a manuscript score that had obviously been used for the original production. The first version of the work contained only four musical scenes, the music for the first act being added for the revised version of 1693, so that there would be five musical scenes for the five-act play.

The Fairy Queen

Semi-opera in a prologue and five acts

Libretto: An anonymous adaptation of Shakespeare's *A Midsummer Night's Dream.*

Première: 2 May 1692, London (Dorset Garden Theater); revised version: February 1693, London (Queen's Theater, Dorset Gardens).

Characters: Drunken Poet (Bbar), First and Second Fairies (2 S), Night (S), Mystery (S), Secrecy (counterT), Sleep (B), Coridon (Bbar), Mopsa (S or A), Phoebus (T), Spring (S), Summer (A), Autumn (T), Winter (Bbar), Juno (S), Chinese Man (counterT), Chinese Woman (S), Hymen (B); spoken roles.

Synopsis
Act I
Egeus complains to the duke of Athens about his daughter, Hermia: he wants her to marry Demetrius but she is in love with Lysander. The duke decrees that Hermia's marriage to Demetrius shall take place at the same time as his own.
First musical scene: In a wood near Athens, elves tease three drunken poets, and send them back to the city.
Artisans from Athens have come to the wood to rehearse a play for the forthcoming marriage of the duke. The fairy queen Titania has also come to the wood, to escape the wrath of her jealous husband Oberon.

Act II
Plotting revenge, Oberon orders Puck to prepare a magic potion that when sprinkled on eyelids will induce love for whatever comes in sight. Lysander and Hermia have fled into the wood followed by Demetrius, who, in turn, is being pursued by Helena.
Second musical scene: Titania is entertained by the elves and then retires, attended by her faithful servants the spirits of Night, Mystery, Secrecy, and Sleep.

Act III
Hoping to bring happiness to the Athenian lovers, Oberon directs Puck to apply the magic potion; Oberon himself sprinkles the potion on Titania's eyelids. But Puck makes a mistake that results in both men falling in love with Helena. While rehearsing their play the artisans disturb Puck, who angrily chases them away, placing an ass's head on the weaver. When Titania awakes, the first thing she sees is the donkey-headed weaver, with whom she instantly falls in love.
Third musical scene: The elves entertain Titania's new lover, taking on comic roles such as those of the unhappy couple Coridon and Mopsa.

Act IV

Through Oberon's intervention the lovers are restored to their correct pairings. The fairy king takes pity on Titania and releases her from her illusion.
Fourth musical scene: The sun god Phoebus and the four seasons are called together to celebrate the reconciliation.

Act V

The duke of Athens consents to the marriage of the two couples.
Fifth musical scene: Oberon and Titania invoke the pleasures of love. In a Chinese garden, an oriental Adam and Eve tell of life in paradise. Juno enters with Hymen: love and marriage are praised.   *S. N.*

Shakespeare and Purcell

It was probably Thomas Betterton, the theater director and creator of the semi-opera, who adapted Shakespeare's play for Purcell. The lyrics were not taken from Shakespeare but written specifically for the music. A number of episodes from the original drama were omitted, as were the roles of Hippolyta and Philostrate and the artisans' play *Pyramus and Thisbe* in Act V.   *P. M.*

The Fairy Queen, production photograph, English National Opera, London 1995.
The third musical scene (in Act III) is set in a mythical forest on the banks of a river and in the shade of tall trees. The characters include elves and nymphs, and different kinds of animal; solos, duets, and choruses are heard, followed by the dances of the elves and the haymaker. The words are often erotic.

5. Winter's Song

Next, Win - ter comes slow - ly, pale, mea - ger and   old, _____

An enchanted world with enchanted music

To depict this enchanted world, Purcell used sophisticated effects that were otherwise almost unknown in the theater. There are, for example, musical canons separated by an octave and an octave and a seventh, demanding coloratura passages, a *canzone* set as a fugue, subtle chromatic harmonies, and unique instrumentation (for example, Winter's song *M 5*). The result was superbly crafted music of great imaginative power.

The Fairy Queen, photograph from the production by Wolfgang Hofmann, sets Klaus Teepe, costumes Bettina Ernst, conductor Volker Christ, Theater der Stadt, Heidelberg 1995.
The five musical interludes in song and dance were meant to entertain, and were therefore not strictly bound to the action of the play. Wolfgang Hofmann combined the three ensembles of the Heidelberg theater for his production: singers, actors, and – as seen here – dancers.

Dido and Aeneas

Tragic opera in three acts

Libretto: Nahum Tate, after his own tragedy *Brutus of Alba* and Book iv of Virgil's *Aeneid*.

Première: 11 or 30 April 1689, Chelsea, London (Josias Priest's boarding school for girls).

Characters: Dido, Queen of Carthage (S), Belinda, her confidante (S), Second Woman (S), Aeneas, a Trojan Prince (T), Sorceress (Ms or Bbar), First and Second Witch (2 S), Spirit, in the form of Mercury (Ms), A Sailor (S or T); courtiers, witches, sailors, cupids (chorus, ballet).
Setting: Carthage, in antiquity.

Synopsis
Act I

Dido's palace. Aeneas has escaped from Troy and found refuge in Carthage. Queen Dido falls in love with the Trojan, but is reluctant to acknowledge her feelings.

Act II
Scene 1: A cave. Seeking to bring about Dido's ruin, a sorceress confides her plan to her witches. Disguised as Mercury, she will remind Aeneas of his destiny – to found a new empire in Italy. The sorceress and witches conjure up a storm.
Scene 2: A clearing in a forest. Dido, Aeneas, and a group of courtiers are resting after the hunt. The witches' storm bursts upon them and scatters the party. Aeneas is approached by the false Mercury, who reminds him of the will of the gods. Aeneas accepts his destiny, despite the fact that it pains him deeply.

Act III
Scene 1: On the quay. The sorceress and her witches observe with glee the preparations for the Trojans' departure, and plot further misdeeds: Dido is to die, and Carthage to be scourged with fire, while the Trojans will be lost at sea.
Scene 2: In her palace, Dido laments her fate. When Aeneas declares that he intends defy Jupiter and stay in Carthage, she drives him out and then takes her own life.

S. N.

The English Mozart
Purcell's stage works are especially rich in musical pleasure. He was "the English Mozart:" though he died young he left behind a huge body of work of astonishing perfection.
The last few decades have witnessed a lively interest in Baroque music, which, combined with the ever-growing interest in the English language and English culture, has led to a renaissance for the "British Orpheus."

Dido and Aeneas, set design for the sailors' scene by Hein Heckroth, production Kurt Jooss, conductor Rudolf Schulz-Dornburg, Münster 1926 (TWS).

A milestone – almost missed
Remarkably little is known about the circumstances surrounding the composition and the première of the first English opera. There are no clues as to what may have occasioned the composition (the coronation of William and Mary and the queen's 27th birthday have both been put forward), or who may have performed the male roles of Aeneas (tenor) and the chorus (bass). Neither did the opera contribute anything to Purcell's fame: his breakthrough came with *Dioclesian,* and during his lifetime the songs from his semi-operas were better known than Dido's lament "When I am laid in earth," now regarded as one of the greatest arias in the history of music. M 6

The lament is built over an ostinato consisting of four descending notes in the minor scale. The key is also significant: by Purcell's time G minor had been used by English theater composers as a musical metaphor for death for over two generations. M 7

Before the Trojans cast off, the crew sing a cheerful sailors' song, whose simplicity and vigor have the effect of a folksong. M 8

A political allegory?
In 1689, the year in which the libretto of *Dido and Aeneas* was written, the Catholic king James II was overthrown. In a poem written in 1686, the librettist Nahum Tate had alluded to James II as Aeneas, and in that work the allegory was so constructed as to imply that James had been led down the wrong path by the evil machinations of a witch and her assistants, as a result of which he had abandoned the British people, symbolized by Dido. Witches were often used in the dramas of the day to represent Catholics, but successive generations have argued about what motivated these witches. In Purcell's opera they seem to represent an evil which exists for its own sake, as illustrated by the witches' words "Harm's our delight and mischief all our skill." Yet why should "Catholic" witches want to

eliminate a Catholic king? There is, nevertheless, an historical fact that can be used to support the allegorical interpretation of the story: James II fled to Italy and lived in Rome, just as Aeneas goes to Italy and founds Rome.

P. M.

Dido and Aeneas, set design for the witches' scene by Hein Heckroth, Münster 1926 (TWS).
Though described in 17th-century England as a masque, *Dido and Aeneas* is in fact an opera – if a rather short one – in that it is presented in song throughout. The extreme emotions that Purcell conjures up in this short opera elevate it to the ranks of a great work of art.

6. Dido's Lament

When I am laid, am laid _____ in earth, may my wrongs cre-ate no trou-ble, no trouble in __ thy breast.

7. Ostinato

8. Sailors' Song

Come a-way, fel-low sai-lors, come a-way, Your an-chors be weigh-ing

Aleko

Opera in one act

Libretto: Vladimir Nemirovich-Danchenko, after the poem *Tsygany* (*The Gypsies*) by Alexander Pushkin.
Première: 9 May 1893, Moscow (Bol'shoy Theater).
Characters: Aleko (Bar), A Young Gypsy (T), Zemfira (S), The Old Gypsy, her father (B), An Old Gypsy Woman (A); gypsies (chorus and ballet).
Setting: Russia, in the 19th century.

Synopsis

Weary of quiet bourgeois life, Aleko, a Russian, runs off with a band of itinerant gypsies. He lives with Zemfira, a young gypsy woman, and they have a child together. Although her father warns him not to be possessive over Zemfira, Aleko kills a young man who is in love with her. Rather than sitting in judgment on the murderer, the gypsies disown him and cast him out.

S. N.

Aleko, production photograph with Ferruccio Furlanetto (Aleko) and Elena Zilio (Zemfira), conductor Yury Abramovich, Teatro Regio, Turin 1980. Despite being rejected, Aleko refuses to part from the gypsy girl Zemfira.

1. Aleko's Leitmotiv

Rakhmaninov, Sergey Vasil'yevich

b. 1 April 1873 on the Semyonovo estate (near Oneg, Novgorod)
d. 28 March 1943 in Beverly Hills, Los Angeles

Rakhmaninov was accepted into the St. Petersburg Conservatory at the age of nine, but had to interrupt his studies when his parents could no longer afford to keep him there. With the help of the conductor and pianist Alexander Ziloti he entered the Moscow Conservatory in 1885, where he studied under Sergey Taneyev and Anton Arensky. He completed his piano studies in 1891 at the age of 18, and passed his examinations in composition a year later with *Aleko*. Rakhmaninov worked as a pianist, a composer, and, from the time of his appointment to the legendary Russian Private Opera in Moscow in 1897, a conductor. At about this time he began a lifelong friendship with Fyodor Shalyapin, for whom he was to write three operas. Rakhmaninov's years as a conductor at the Bol'shoy Theater in Moscow (1904–1906) were a period of astonishing musical activity. He became internationally renowned as a pianist, and was highly regarded as a composer, especially on the basis of his Prelude in C sharp minor (op. 3, no. 2) of 1892 and his Second Piano Concerto of 1901. He left Russia in 1917, at the outbreak of the October Revolution. From this point his life and work were characterized by a yearning for his homeland, though in fact he was never to return to Russia. The Russian people similarly remained uppermost in his thoughts, even though performances of his music was for some time forbidden by the authorities, and during the Second World War he donated the profits from many of his legendary concerts to his Russian compatriots. From 1931 to 1939 he created a new home for himself and his family in Switzerland, but moved to the USA before the outbreak of the Second World War, eventually settling there and becoming an American citizen.

Works: Operas: *Aleko* (1893), *Francesca da Rimini* (1906), *Skupoi Rytsar'* (*The Miserly Knight*) (1906), *Monna Vanna* (unfinished, 1907/FP 1984); four piano concertos, the *Rhapsody on a Theme by Paganini* for piano and orchestra op. 43 (1934), piano works, three symphonies, vocal works.

*R*akhmaninov was one of the most outstanding pianists of his day, and a composer whose music was both criticized and loved. It was an art of the emotions in an age that was dominated by the rationalism of New Objectivity. His compositions were either admired as late Romantic works or they were scorned as "film music" (Igor Stravinsky). By drawing his legendary "long musical breath," Rakhmaninov was able to depict the dynamic inner life of the soul and so resist the ephemera of a hectic world obsessed only with sensual pleasure.

Freedom as an inner value

In his first opera, *Aleko*, the 19-year-old composer posed the portentous question of whether we can only be released from our instinctive passions through death. The hero's jealousy, which bursts forth in an act of fateful violence, is anticipated in the introduction to the opera by a leitmotiv: a rapid passage for strings in a dark and somber register, concluded by two intense fff chords from the brass section. M 1

Operas for modest stars

Rakhmaninov's three completed operas are masterful and unusual works. They represent a successful attempt by the composer to follow his own path, independent of music drama and number opera. Characteristic of twentieth-century opera in both form and content, they have remained outsiders to the world of opera, even though they form part of the international repertory. As visions of the human soul, Rakhmaninov's operas demand first class musical interpretations that both enthrall and illuminate. The dense plots, which run for little more than an hour, require total concentration on the part of the artist, and an unconditional renunciation of his or her own personality. Rakhmaninov's friend Fyodor Shalyapin was an artist capable of such renunciation, and it was for him – and others like him – that the three operas were composed.

The Miserly Knight

Skupoi Rytsar'

Opera in one act, three scenes

Libretto: Sergey Rakhmaninov, after the tragedy of the same name by Alexander Pushkin.
Première: 24 January 1906, Moscow (Bol'shoy Theater).
Characters: The Baron (Bar), Albert, his son (T), The Duke (Bar), Jewish Moneylender (T), A Servant (B).
Setting: Tower, cellar, and palace, in the age of chivalry.

Synopsis

Albert, the son of a wealthy but miserly baron, loves tournaments and courtly life. Because he is denied the armor and equipment appropriate to his station, he tries to borrow from a moneylender, who refuses him any further loans until he has paid off his old debts.

Meanwhile the baron is enjoying the spectacle of the treasures he has hoarded in chests in his cellar. His only concern is how to protect this gold from his profligate heirs. Albert has made representations to the duke and requested help; the duke orders the baron to equip his son in a fitting manner. Fearing he will lose his gold, the old man becomes overanxious and dies. To the mortification of the duke, his last thoughts are focused not on his soul but on the preservation of his wealth.   *S. N.*

The Miserly Knight, photograph from the first German production (a co-production with the Mariinsky Theater in St. Petersburg), production Steffen Piontek, sets and costumes Martin Rupprecht, conductor Hans E. Zimmer, Sächsische Staatsoper, Dresden 1993.
The three locations in the opera have a symbolic significance for Rakhmaninov. The son is banished to a tower, his father's favorite haunt is the vault where he hoards his treasure, and it is only the duke who is able to live freely in his castle. The Dresden production gave this symbolism a social interpretation. In the finale, the son stood at the bottom of the stairs, the baron in the middle, and the duke, representing the pinnacle of the social hierarchy, at the top.

Armed with reason, driven by instinct
At a crucial point in his opera *The Miserly Knight* Rakhmaninov abandoned the human voice, describing the union of man and money in a symphonic passage of great metaphorical significance. Deep in his vaults the miserly knight lights a candle and opens his treasure chests, and his gold begins to glint and glitter. At that point the gold theme begins to stir in the orchestra, until it finally radiates in the key of D major. This illumination of the knight's dark cellar appears to be an image of beauty, but is in fact the setting for a sinister and baleful soul.   *S. N.*

Francesca da Rimini

Opera in a prologue, one act, and an epilogue

Libretto: Modest Tchaikovsky, after an episode from Canto V of the *Inferno* of Dante Alighieri's *Divina commedia* (*Divine Comedy*).
Première: 24 January 1906, Moscow (Bol'shoy Theater).
Characters: Dante (T), The Shade of Virgil (Bar), Lanciotto Malatesta, Regent of Rimini (Bar), Francesca, his wife (S), Paolo, his brother (T), Cardinal (silent); tormented spirits (chorus).
Setting: Dante's inferno and Rimini, in the present and a remembered past.

Synopsis
Prologue

The first circle of hell. Dante and his escort, the shade of Virgil, are surrounded by tormented spirits, among them the shades of Francesca da Rimini and Paolo.

Scene 1: Rimini, in Malatesta's palace. The deformed regent, Malatesta, has deceived Francesca into becoming his wife, but is now tormented by the thought that she may be deceiving him with his handsome younger brother, Paolo. Called to war by the pope, Malatesta sets up a trap for Francesca and Paolo.

Scene 2: A room in the palace. Paolo has taken on responsibility for Francesca as requested by his brother. While reading a chivalric romance together they are overwhelmed by their feelings, confess their love for each other, and are surprised and killed by Malatesta.

Epilogue

The first circle of hell. Once again, Dante and the shade of Virgil are surrounded by tormented spirits. The poet is speechless with sympathy for Francesca and Paolo: "The greatest sadness is the recollection of past happiness amidst present sorrow." S. N.

Francesca da Rimini, production photograph with Stanislav Suleymanov (Malatesta) and Rüdiger Oertel (Cardinal), production Sir Peter Ustinov, conductor Mikhail Yurovsky, co-production of the Dresden Music Festival and the Städtisches Theater in Chemnitz, 1993.
Appearances can be deceptive. Malatesta may be kissing the hand of the cardinal but it is the clergyman who seeks help from the warrior.

Above
Francesca da Rimini, production photograph with Svetlana Kachour (Francesca) and Arkady Mishenkin (Paolo), production Sir Peter Ustinov, sets Josef Svoboda, co-production of the Dresden Music Festival and the Städtisches Theater in Chemnitz, 1993.
Francesca and Paolo confess their love for each other without the aid of words.

Hippolytus and Aricia, production photograph with Les Arts Florissants, production Jean-Marie Villégier, conductor William Christie, Opéra Garnier, Paris 1996.
The prologue: a courtly game in which Diana and Cupid battle for preeminence.

*R*ameau was the last important composer for the French court during the Baroque era.

Rameau, Jean-Philippe

baptized 25 September 1683 in Dijon
d. 12 September 1764 in Paris

The son of an organist in Dijon, Rameau studied music first in a Jesuit seminary and later in Milan. Returning to France he became an organist himself, first at Avignon, then at Clermont (1702), and then in Paris (1706), where he published his first harpsichord pieces. In 1709 he succeeded his father at the cathedral Notre-Dame in Dijon. In 1713 he went to Lyon, then returned again to Clermont (1715), where he remained until 1722 or 1723. During this time he composed mainly church music and produced the first volume of his major theoretical work, *Traité de l'harmonie* (1722). He settled in Paris (probably in 1723) where he lived for several years as an independent artist. Having failed to secure a position as organist at the cathedral of St. Paul in Paris, it was only after 1732 that Rameau was able to continue regular work in this sphere, though he wrote several important theoretical texts on music during this time. His desire to compose a work for the stage was finally realized in 1733 with the *tragédie lyrique Hippolytus and Aricia*. Rameau was now 50 and the librettist, the Abbé Simon-Joseph Pellegrin, 70. For 22 years Rameau was the conductor of a private orchestra for the wealthy patron La Pouplinière. He lived with his employer for a period and composed almost 30 works for the stage (operas and ballets). He continued to work on his theoretical writings until his death, these works taking priority over his compositions. He was appointed composer of the king's chamber music in 1745, and was ennobled shortly before his death.

Works: Operas (selection): *Hippolyte et Aricie* (*Hippolytus and Aricia*) (tragédie en musique, 1733), *Castor et Pollux* (*Castor and Pollux*) (tragédie en musique, 1737), *Dardanus* (tragédie en musique, 1739), *Platée* (*Plataea*) (1745), *Naïs* (*Neis*) (opéra pour la paix, 1749), *Zoroastre* (*Zoroaster* or *Zarathustra*) (tragédie en musique, 1749), *Les Boréades* (*The Sons of Boreas*) (1750s); operas-ballets: *Les Indes galantes* (*The Amorous Indies*) (1735), *Les fêtes d'Hébé* (*Hebe's Festivities, or The Lyric Talents*) (1739), *Le temple de la Gloire* (*The Temple of Glory*) (1745), and the *acte de ballet Pigmalion* (*Pygmalion*) (1748); church music, cantatas, several volumes of harpsichord music, chamber music.

Hippolytus and Aricia

Hippolyte et Aricie

Tragédie lyrique in a prologue and five acts

Libretto: Simon-Joseph Pellegrin.

Première: 1 October 1733, Paris (Opéra, Palais Royale).

Characters: Diane/Diana (S), L'Amour/Cupid (S), Jupiter (B), Aricie/Aricia (S), Thésée/Theseus, King of Athens (B), Hippolyte/Hippolytus, Theseus' son by a previous marriage (T), Phèdre/Phaedra, Theseus' wife (S), Oenone, Phaedra's confidante (S), Arcas, Theseus' confidant (T), Tisiphone, a Fury (T), Pluton/Pluto (B), Mercure/Mercury (T), Neptune (B), The High Priestess of Diana (S), Three Fates (counterT, T, B), A Priestess (S), A Sailor (S), A Hunter (B), A Huntress (S), A Shepherdess (S); nymphs of Diana, forest dwellers, followers of Diana and Cupid, priestesses of Diana, underworld gods, hunters and huntresses, shepherds and shepherdesses, Troezenians, sailors, zephyrs (chorus and ballet).
Setting: The Spartan city of Troezen, the underworld, and the forest of Aricia.

Synopsis

Diana wants to prevent Cupid from interfering in her realm but Jupiter insists she allow him free rein for one day. In retaliation she swears to become involved in Cupid's affairs and to support the two lovers Hippolytus and Aricia.

Theseus' wife Phaedra has fallen in love with her stepson Hippolytus, but he is passionately in love with Aricia, who returns his feelings. When Phaedra hears that Theseus has been killed while trying to rescue a friend from the underworld, she confesses her feelings to her stepson. Hearing of his love for Aricia she attempts to stab herself, but Hippolytus wrestles the weapon away from her. Theseus, returning from the underworld, misunderstands the situation, and curses his son. Hippolytus goes into exile with Aricia, but his father's curse reaches him even there. Theseus' own father, the sea god Neptune, takes the youth down to his kingdom. Swearing Hippolytus' innocence, Phaedra takes her own life. Diana saves Hippolytus from Neptune and reunites him with Aricia.   *S. N.*

Settings

In the prologue (the forest of Erymanthus, a mythological landscape) Cupid finds himself in territory
belonging to the virgin goddess Diana. The two have
different conceptions of love, and Jupiter is asked to
judge between them. But even the father of the gods
has to admit the power of Cupid, and free love
triumphs over moral love. The first act is set in Diana's
temple, the second in the underworld, the third in
Theseus' palace at the edge of the sea, and the fourth in
the sacred grove of Diana on the coast (with a hunting
scene and a monster which rises up out of the raging
sea). The fifth act begins in this grove and ends in the
paradise of Diana's kingdom.

An old recipe spiced up

Rameau's *tragédie lyrique Hippolytus and Aricia* was
composed according to a format that had been established by →Lully: a prologue, five acts, a theme from
Greek mythology, and decorative choral and ballet
scenes. But Rameau's depiction of human passions is
warmer and more touching than the musico-dramatic
productions of the reign of the Sun King. For example,
the vision of hell (Act II, Scene 4) is unusually evocative
and Rameau's expressive register extremely daring. The
scenes in Act IV (the hunt, the storm, the abduction of
Hippolytus, and Phaedra's grief and self-accusation)
show the composer as a brilliant dramatist. With a rich
tradition of French orchestral writing behind him,
Rameau was able to treat the orchestra as a highly
versatile expressive tool. Like Lully, Rameau was a

master of orchestral color and greatly accomplished in
his descriptions of nature.   *J. M.*

The last champion of the ancient régime

Rameau's musical tragedies were the last great operatic achievements of the ancien régime. His second version of *Castor and Pollux* marked the defeat of Italian opera in Paris and meant that he and his supporters were finally able to celebrate a triumphant success. *Castor and Pollux* was performed 250 times in Paris before the French Revolution, after which it lay forgotten for a century. In 1903 there was a concert performance organized by the composer Vincent d'Indy. It was not until the 1970s that Rameau was properly rediscovered by the Early Music movement, but there is yet to be a really intensive examination of his work.

Castor and Pollux

Castor et Pollux

Tragédie mise en musique in a prologue and five acts

Libretto: Pierre-Joseph Bernard.

Première: First version: 24 October 1737, Paris (Opéra, Palais Royal); second version: 11 January 1754, Paris (Opéra, Palais Royal).

Characters: Minerve/Minerva (S), Vénus/Venus (S), L'Amour/Cupid (counterT), Mars (B), Télaïre/Telaira, daughter of the Sun (S), Phébé/Phoebe, a Spartan princess (S), Castor, son of Tyndareus and Leda (counterT), Pollux, son of Jupiter and Leda (B), Jupiter (B), A Follower of Hebe (S), A Blessed Spirit (S), The High Priest of Jupiter (T), Two Athletes (counterT, B), A Planet (S), Mercure/Mercury (silent), Hébé/Hebe (dancer); Arts, Pleasures, Graces, Spartans, athletes, priests of Jupiter, Celestial Pleasures, Hebe's attendants, demons, Blessed Spirits, stars (chorus, ballet); people, monsters, planets, gods (extras).

Setting: Sparta and the Elysian fields.

Synopsis
Prologue

The Arts, the Pleasures, Cupid, and Minerva, request Venus' assistance in taming Mars, the god of war, with the bonds of love. Castor has just died in battle, but his half-brother, Pollux, is the son of Jupiter and therefore immortal. Telaira is grieving for her husband Castor. Pollux is in love with her, and for her sake descends into the underworld to redeem his brother. Phoebe tries in vain to keep her husband, Pollux, back. Jupiter lets Pollux know that he will have to pay for his generosity with his own life. Castor refuses to accept Pollux's sacrifice and returns to the world of mortals for one day only. The unhappy Phoebe kills herself. Happily reunited with Telaira in Sparta, Castor intends to return to the underworld against the will of his wife and of the Spartan people. But Jupiter rewards this selfless love by making Castor also immortal. The brothers and their beloved Telaira are given a place in the firmament as constellations.

The settings

Act I

The burial grounds of the Spartan kings (*divertissement*: war-games of the returning soldiers)

Act II

The temple of Jupiter (the pleasures of life denied to Pollux are depicted in dance)

Act III

The entry to the underworld (dance of the demons)

Act IV

The Elysian Fields (dance of the Blessed Spirits)

Act V

Near Sparta (the stars, planets, and moons take part in the joyful festivities)

S. N.

Castor and Pollux, photograph from the production by Pier Luigi Pizzi, sets and costumes Pier Luigi Pizzi, Aix-en-Provence Festival 1991.
Instead of the glorious opening arias of *opera seria* Rameau's *tragédie lyrique* begins with a large choral scene (funeral chorus), which later served as a model for →Gluck's reform operas (*Alcestis, Orpheus and Eurydice*, the two *Iphigenia* operas). The prologue was an allusion to the "preliminary peace" of Vienna in 1735, which brought an end to war by the redistribution of various duchies and cities amongst Europe's royal families.

Castor and Pollux, photographs from the production by Pier Luigi Pizzi, sets and costumes Pier Luigi Pizzi, Aix-en-Provence Festival 1991.
Happy moments in a beautiful landscape near Sparta. The final scene provides dramatic and musical symmetry: the work's formal arch spans the gulf between grief and joy, pain and pleasure.

Partisans of opera

Rameau's first opera →*Hippolytus and Aricia* divided the French operatic world into two camps. The composer was criticized by the guardians of tradition (those who revered the works of Lully), who considered Rameau's operas tedious and "contrary to nature." At later performances, Rameau was forced to shorten his opera – "To speed the story up and not for musical reasons," he admitted. Nevertheless the majority of the public were enthused by his changes.

Later Rameau came under fire from another quarter. The success of a number of performances in Paris of Pergolesi's →*The Maid as Mistress* by an Italian troupe in 1752 resulted in a fierce debate between the defenders of the traditional *tragédie lyrique*, especially the aristocracy, and those who preferred Italian *opera buffa* on account of its simpler, more "natural" forms of expression. The latter were particularly vehement in their criticism of the "exaggerated" weight which Rameau accorded the instrumentation. The most outspoken supporters of *opera buffa* were the French Encyclopedists, especially Jean-Jacques Rousseau, who championed Italian opera and whose *intermède Le devin du village* (*The Village Soothsayer*) is based on the Italian intermezzo. Rameau and Lully thus came to be on the same side of the barricade, and both composers were to fall out of fashion after Rameau's death.   *J. M.*

Ravel, Maurice

b. 7 March 1875 in Ciboure
d. 28 December 1937 in Paris

The son of a Swiss father and a Basque mother, Ravel was brought up in Paris and studied with Fauré and Gédalge at the Conservatoire. He conducted his own orchestral music and performed his own piano works, quickly achieving an international reputation. Ravel accorded a great deal of importance to the conceptual aspects of the creative process, on which he lavished a great deal of effort. The actual execution of his works proceeded quickly by comparison. Ravel was always at pains not to allow himself to be influenced by fashionable trends and to protect the independence of his work. He was subtle in his application of musically innovative developments and did much to contribute to the renewal of musical language.

Works: Operas: *L'heure espagnole* (*The Spanish Hour*) (1911), *L'enfant et les sortilèges* (*The Child and the Spells*) (1925); ballets, including *Daphnis et Chloé* (1912) and *La Valse* (*The Waltz*) (1920), orchestral works, including *Boléro* (1928), piano works, chamber music, including the String Quartet (1903), songs.

*R*avel is, with Debussy, the most important French composer of his generation. His music is characterized by lucid, concentrated forms and sophisticated tonality. "La valse" and "Boléro" virtually became musical signatures of the early 20th century.

L'heure espagnole

The Spanish Hour

Comédie musicale in one act

Libretto: Franc-Nohain (Maurice Ètienne Legrand).
Première: 19 May 1911 (Opéra-Comique).

Characters: Torquemada, a clockmaker (buffo T), Concepción, his wife (S), Gonzalve, a bachelor (T), Ramiro, a muleteer (Bar), Don Inigo Gomez, a banker (buffo B).
Setting: Toledo, in the 18th century.

Synopsis
Every Thursday, at the same hour, the clockmaker Torquemada leaves his house to wind up the city's clocks. This is also the time his wife Concepción (in Spanish, "conception" – a humorous reference to the Catholic dogma of the immaculate conception) receives her lover, Gonzalve. On this occasion, however, proceedings are interrupted by the muleteer Ramiro, who has brought his two grandfather clocks to be repaired. Torquemada asks him to wait until he returns. Concepción sends Ramiro into the bedroom with one of the clocks so that she can be alone with Gonzalve. Just as the two lovers are entangled in each other's arms, Ramiro reappears, and Gonzalve quickly hides in the second clock. The wealthy banker Don Inigo also comes to court the clockmaker's wife. She sends him away and asks the muleteer to swap the clocks around, accompanying him into the bedroom. Left alone in the shop, Don Inigo hides in the empty grandfather clock. Concepción comes out of the bedroom unsatisfied and realizes that Don Inigo is waiting in the clock for her; she asks Ramiro to exchange the clocks once again. But now Don Inigo is unable to satisfy her, for the fat banker is stuck fast in the clock case. Concepción asks Ramiro to carry this clock back into the shop and to accompany her – this time without any timepiece – into the bedroom. Torquemada returns and finds a man in each of Ramiro's two clocks, both of whom claim they had merely wanted to test the internal mechanisms. Don Inigo is still stuck firmly in the casing, and is freed only when Concepción reappears with Ramiro, who rescues the banker from the clock. The muleteer is now Concepción's new lover.

M. S.

L'heure espagnole, set design by Theo Lau for the production by Walter Jacob, Städtische Bühnen, Gelsenkirchen 1958 (TWS). Clocks have dominated productions of this opera since its première, creating a stage set that is visually interesting as well as acoustically effective. The opera begins with a witty musical imitation of a variety of clocks.

A French *commedia dell'arte*

In his *comédie musicale* Ravel rejected the emotional excesses and the hypocrisy of operas such as those by →Massenet and the complex sexuality of Symbolist works such as Debussy's →*Pelléas and Mélisande*. Ravel's play with the concept of time was both witty and original: there is a tightly prescribed period of time in which the clockmaker does his rounds through the city; the seemingly endless time for the lovers who have hidden themselves in the clocks; and the rapidly passing time of the lovers' tryst. Both libretto and music sought to make a connection between the mechanical actions of the clocks and the sexual act. This was a modern French version of the *commedia dell'arte*, which, at the time it was composed, was considered indecent even in France, and was therefore rejected by Albert Carré, the director of the Opéra-Comique.

L'enfant et les sortilèges

The Child and the Spells

Fantaisie lyrique in two parts

Libretto: Colette (Sidonie Gabrielle Colette).
Première: 21 March 1925, Monte Carlo (Grand Théâtre).

Characters: The Child (Ms), Mother (A), The Louis XV Chair (S), The Chinese Cup (Ms), The Fire, also The Princess and The Nightingale (coloratura S), The Tomcat (Bar), The Dragonfly (Ms), The Bat (S), The Owl (S), The Squirrel (Ms), A Shepherdess (S), A Shepherd (A), The Armchair (B), The Grandfather Clock (Bar), The Wedgwood-Teapot (T), The Little Old Man (Arithmetic), also The Frog (T), The Female Cat (Ms), A Tree (B); shepherds, shepherdesses, frogs, animals, trees (chorus, ballet); the settle, the sofa, the ottoman, the wicker chair, the numbers (children's chorus).
Setting: A country house and its garden.

L'enfant et les sortilèges, production photograph with Isabelle Eschenbrenner as the child, production Eric Tappy, sets Christian Rätz, costumes Patrice Caurier, conductor Eric Tappy, Opéra National de Lyon 1989.
The child is tormented by his thoughtless cruelty and hears the voices of the objects and creatures he has mistreated.

Synopsis
Part I

When the child refuses to do his homework, his mother sends him to his room. In a rage he mistreats his furniture, attacks his tame squirrel and the cat, and even his beloved book. But these objects and animals have souls and voices, and accuse the child of his crimes. As darkness falls, this "vision" fades away.

Part II

Because his door has not been kept shut, the child wanders out into the wild and overgrown garden at night. But here the plants and animals he has mistreated also accuse him of cruelty and demand that he be punished. In the general uproar, the squirrel injures itself. Now touched by sympathy the child bandages its wound. This act reconciles the animals, and they call for the child's mother who tenderly enfolds him in her arms.   *M. S.*

Left
L'enfant et les sortilèges, illustration from the magazine *Le théâtre*, Paris, April 1926.
The work contains a series of comical numbers that parody operatic clichés: the duet of the teapot and cup in a ragtime style, the lament of the fairy-tale princess, or the chorus of the numbers. Animal noises and visual effects are also reproduced with astonishing accuracy.

Below
L'enfant et les sortilèges, photograph from the production by Eric Tappy and Didier Puntos, sets Christian Rätz, costumes Patrice Caurier, conductor Eric Tappy, Opéra National de Lyon 1989.
The child is confronted by memories of the adults who have pestered him: relatives, teachers, and nannies.

Enchanted sounds from a cheese grater

Ravel composed his second opera in 1924. The parallels to Lewis Carroll's *Alice in Wonderland* are undeniable, but Ravel's work achieves its originality through its profound pantheism and sophisticated tonal quality. Ravel parodied the style of fashionable dances, and organized the scenes with animals and objects as numbers in a musical revue. New sound effects were achieved through unusual instruments (for example, a cheese grater) and combinations of instruments, the orchestration being in the style of chamber music.   *M. S.*

Reich, Steve

b. 3 October 1936 in New York

Of the various founding fathers of American minimalism (La Monte Young, Terry Riley, Steve Reich, →Philip Glass), Reich is not only the most austere but also the most searching. Reich is a tireless seeker after new acoustic techniques. He studied the piano as a child, and at the age of 14 took up classical percussion under the guidance of Roland Kohlhoff, the timpanist of the New York Philharmonic. In 1957 Reich graduated with honors in philosophy from Cornell University, and began to study composition. He gained his Master of Arts in music in 1963 from Mills College, where his teachers included →Darius Milhaud and →Luciano Berio. A travel scholarship from the Institute for International Education enabled him to visit Ghana in 1970, and from 1973 to 1974 he studied the gamelan under Balinese teachers at the American Society for Eastern Arts in Seattle and Berkeley. He spent time in 1976 and 1977 in New York and Jerusalem, studying the traditional Hebraic forms of recitation, which resulted in 1981 in *Tehillim*. In 1966 he founded an ensemble which at first consisted of three musicians but later expanded to as many as 30. Between 1971 and 1985 he undertook 16 concert tours in Europe and America, giving a total of over 300 concerts to full houses ranging from Carnegie Hall to the Bottom Line Cabaret in New York. His works were quickly taken up by leading orchestras and conductors, and he has received commissions from the larger international music festivals as well as from radio and symphony orchestras and chamber music groups such as the Kronos Quartet. Prominent choreographers, among them Jerome Robbins and Maurice Béjart, have also used Steve Reich's music.

Works: *The Cave* (1993), *It's Gonna Rain* (1965), *Come Out* (1966), *Drumming* (1971), *Tehillim* (1981), *The Desert Music* (1984), *Different Trains* (1988).

The Cave

Video opera in three acts for two sopranos, tenor, baritone, percussion, keyboards, woodwind and strings

Libretto: Steve Reich and Beryl Korot on the basis of interviews and biblical texts.
Video: Beryl Korot.

Première: 15 May 1993, Vienna (Vienna Festival, Exhibition Hall).
Setting: Jerusalem and New York City, 1989–92.

Synopsis

Israelis, Palestinians, and Americans interviewed by Korot and Reich answer questions about the biblical figure of Abraham, his wife Sarah, her slave Hagar, and Abraham's two sons Isaac and Ishmael. The responses are a kaleidoscope of memories, thoughts, verdicts, and witticisms, which bring the biblical stories into the present and serve as an illustration of the current political situation in the Middle East. The interviewees are shown in still and animated video images projected onto five screens in carefully coordinated sequences. These images are supported live by four singers and 13 instrumentalists: a string quartet, woodwind instruments, percussion, and keyboard players, whose performances at their computers also allow them to function as rhythmically tapping typists of data. Passages from Genesis, in the original and translated into three languages, are blended into the performance in sound and vision.   S. N.

The Cave, production photograph with Hugo Munday (baritone), Cheryl Bensman Rowe (soprano), Marlon Beckenstein (soprano), and James Bassl (tenor), production Carey Porloff, sets John Arnone, costumes Donna Zakowska, conductor Paul Hiller, Royal Festival Hall, London 1993.
The four singers in their roles as commentators, narrators, and performers.

*R*eich has been acknowledged as one of the world's most successful living composers. His music has been given a number of labels, such as "minimalist music," "phase music," "trance music," "modular music," and "pulse music." It has a rich traditional background, which includes European music from the 12th to the 18th centuries, the Balinese gamelan, West African music, and American jazz from 1950 to 1965, as well as the work of Stravinsky, Bartók, and Webern.

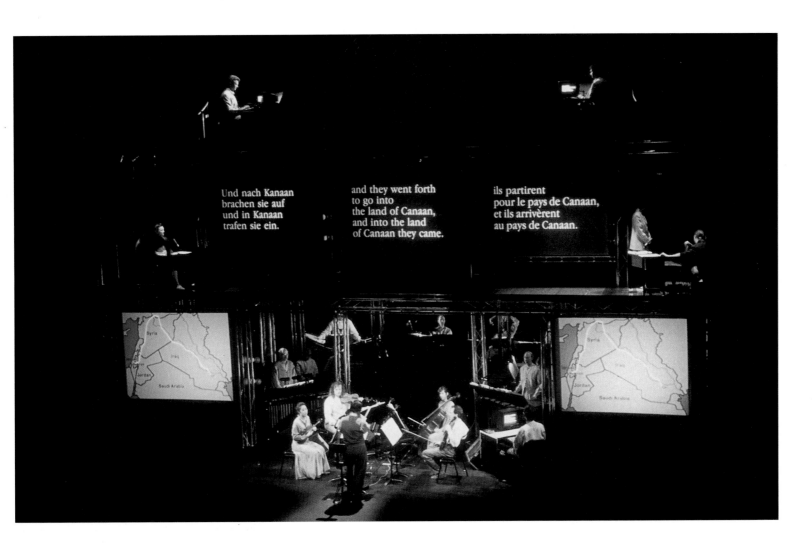

Und nach Kanaan
brachen sie auf
und in Kanaan
trafen sie ein.

and they went forth
to go into
the land of Canaan,
and into the land
of Canaan they came.

ils partirent
pour le pays de Canaan,
et ils arrivèrent
au pays de Canaan.

The inaccessible cave

The Cave refers to the cave of Mechpelah mentioned in Genesis, which lies near the city of Hebron and is reputed to be the burial site of Abraham, his wife Sarah, their descendants Isaac and Jacob, and their wives Rebecca and Leah. It is one of the few sites venerated by both Jews and Moslems. While the Jews trace their descent from Abraham and Sarah through their grand-child Jacob, Moslems establish their kinship with the patriarch through his son Ishmael, the result of a union with Hagar, Sarah's servant. According to an ancient religious tradition, the cave of Mechpelah was also supposed to have contained the entrance to paradise. Today, the interior is no longer accessible. Steve Reich sees this situation as "paradoxical and hopeful at the same time."

For Reich, Abraham was "one of the most radical and visionary figures," for he destroyed the idols of his fathers and established a belief in one almighty and invisible God – a theme that affects Moslems, Jews, and Christians equally. The voices of all three religions are heard in Reich's opera, one act being devoted to each of them. The answers of the interviewees reveal the differences in perspective between their various traditions – as well as the lack of perspective of modern Americans, who can only associate the name Abraham with that of Abraham Lincoln, and the name Ishmael with the novel *Moby Dick*.

Medieval techniques and pop music

Steve Reich requires his singers to sing without vibrato – a style common to the Middle Ages and today's pop music – in order to allow the voices to sound as natural as possible. It was for this reason that Paul Hillier, a specialist in early music, was chosen to conduct the première in Vienna as well as guest performances by the original cast at the Berlin Biennale, the Holland Festival, and other venues in Paris, London, and New York.

An entirely unconventional opera?

Just as he was about to undertake his first work for the musical stage – a commission from the Vienna Festival – Reich admitted that he had no interest in traditional opera. Although at first sight *The Cave* certainly appears to have nothing in common with opera, in that it consists of interviews relayed by video rather than a drama presented in song on stage, the work does make use of the operatic concept of the melodic quality of the speaking voice. In this Steve Reich looked back to →Leoš Janáček: "Spoken melodies are the window onto the human soul, and are of the greatest importance for dramatic music." In *The Cave* Reich uses spoken frag-ments of sentences and linguistic themes, which are echoed on the instruments and whose specific features are acoustically determined. Between these fragments are biblical texts selected for their rigid meter and rhythm, which are sung live and projected onto screens. *S. N.*

The Cave, photograph from the original production, Vienna Festival 1993.
Reich's video opera is a complex stage event. The audience becomes witness to an aural experiment, in which melodies, rhythms, and the entire musical and textual fabric of the work derive from the languages of the people interviewed – Hebrew, Arabic, and English.

The Castle, photograph from the original production with (from left to right) Peter Maus (the teacher), Adrianne Pieczonka (Frieda), and Wolfgang Schöne (K.), production Willy Decker, sets and costumes Wolfgang Gussmann, conductor Michael Boder, Deutsche Oper, Berlin 1992. K.'s living space has been drastically reduced – to the security of being in bed with Frieda. But even this space is threatened by the teacher's visit.

Reimann, Aribert

b. 4 March 1936 in Berlin

Exposed to music at an early age – his father was a university music professor and his mother a singer – Reimann studied piano with Otto Rausch and composition with Boris Blacher at the Berlin Music Academy between 1955 and 1960. By the age of 21 he had established a reputation as a pianist. His professional contact with singers, especially Dietrich Fischer-Dieskau, made him aware of the expressive possibilities of the voice. Avoiding affiliations with any group and working independently as a composer, Reimann accepted a chair in song composition at the Berlin School of Arts in 1983.

Works: Ein Traumspiel (*A Dream Play*) (1965, Kiel), *Melusine* (1971, Schwetzingen), *Lear* (1978, Munich), *Die Gespenstersonate* (*The Ghost Sonata*) (1984, Berlin), *Troades* (1986, Munich), *Das Schloss* (*The Castle*) (1992, Berlin); orchestral music, concertos, chamber music, vocal music, ballets.

Musically brilliant pessimism

Fascinated by subjects from literature, Reimann has followed his interest in the dark side of human existence, be it the insanity of *Lear* or the opaque northern world of *Ein Traumspiel* (*A Dream Play*). There are recurring moments of pessimism brought about by bitter disappointment and unjust suffering. Able to encompass every nuance of these themes with rigorous music, Reimann became one of the most important opera composers of the 20th century with the première of his

*R*eimann is inspired by Berg, Webern, and the music of India. His operas are conceptually rooted in the possibilities of vocal expression.

The Castle

Das Schloss

Opera in two parts (ten scenes with interludes and metamorphoses)

Libretto: Aribert Reimann, after the novel of the same name by Franz Kafka and its dramatization by Max Brod.
Première: 2 September 1992, Berlin (Deutsche Oper).
Characters: K., a stranger aged about 40 (Bar), The Landlord of the "Zur Brücke" Inn (Bar), The Landlady, his wife (dramatic A), Schwarzer, the son of a castle steward (spoken), Arthur and Jeremiah, the assistants (T, Bbar), Barnabas, the castle messenger (T), Olga and Amalia, his sisters (Ms, S), The Landlord of the "Herrenhof" Inn (Bbar), Frieda, a serving girl at the "Herrenhof" (S), The Mayor (B), Mizzi, his wife (silent), The Teacher (T), Bürgel, an undersecretary (spoken), Four Peasants (2 T, 2 B); peasants, servants at the castle (chorus).

Synopsis
Part I

Scenes 1 and 2: In front of and inside the "Zur Brücke" inn. Exhausted, K. reaches the village inn, where he is forced to spend the night in a sleeping bag as there are no spare rooms. Shortly after falling asleep he is woken by Schwarzer, who tells him that if he wants to stay he needs a permit from the castle. K. claims to be the new surveyor, and an enquiry at the castle confirms his details. Two incompetent assistants put themselves at K.'s service. K. wishes to speak with someone in the castle, but finds this is regarded as absurdly presumptuous in a stranger. Barnabas, the messenger, brings him a letter from the official, Klamm: K. is to report to the mayor.
Scene 3: A road and the edge of the forest outside the "Herrenhof" inn. The officials who may be able to provide K. with further information are quartered in the "Herrenhof." K. is not permitted to stay there and is hidden by Klamm's girlfriend, Frieda. He is unable to escape the assistants, however, and they fetch him back.

Lear. The psychological characterization of the vocal parts, which becomes subtler with each opera, reached yet another high point in his version of Kafka's *The Castle*, a commission from the Deutsche Oper in Berlin. The dreadful situation of a person who believes himself to be in the right but stands accused by his peers of an undefined offense – presumably that of his very existence within the system – was given gripping musical expression by Reimann.

M. S.

Scene 4: An attic room in the "Zur Brücke" inn. K. has been living with Frieda for four days in the attic. The landlady, who was once Klamm's lover, declares that a marriage between K. and Frieda is out of the question, in view of his unstable situation. K. goes to see the mayor in order to register for regular employment.

Scene 5: The room of the village mayor. The mayor tells K. that he is only in the village because a file has gone missing. Furthermore, he says, the village does not require a surveyor. K. is outraged.

Part II

Scene 6: An attic room in the "Zur Brücke" inn. The teacher visits K. to tell him that his insubordination to the mayor has been documented. The teacher's offer of a position as the school servant puts K. in a fury. He is urged by Frieda to accept the post, as the landlady has just given them notice.

Scene 7: A lonely village street in the snow. Tired of waiting, K. sets off for the castle followed by the assistants. Barnabas brings Klamm's letter. There is praise for

K.'s work and the prospect of a reward – all of which is clearly false. K. asks to speak to someone in the castle, and beats his assistants so brutally that they flee.

Scene 8: The next day in Barnabas's hut. K. hopes that the messenger has some news for him, but Barnabas is away in the castle. The assistants have left because of K.'s cruelty. Barnabas informs him that the official, Erlanger, will give K. an audience in the "Herrenhof."

Scene 9: A corridor in the "Herrenhof" at night. K. wanders through the "Herrenhof" after an encounter with Frieda, who has become involved with one of the assistants. Files have been distributed to the officials but there is one left over. Watching the sleeping K. a servant takes a piece of paper from it and tears it up.

Metamorphosis: A cemetery with an open grave in the middle and the castle in the distance. All those who have had anything to do with K. are gathered at the graveside. Finally, Barnabas arrives with the message that K. has been given the right to remain. M.S.

The Castle, photograph from the original production with Wolfgang Schöne (K.) and Peter Matič (Bürgel), production Willy Decker, set design and costumes Wolfgang Gussmann, conductor Michael Boder, Deutsche Oper, Berlin 1992.
K. on his way to the grave. Though still struggling he is literally being forced to the very fringes of existence.

Rihm, Wolfgang

b. 13 March 1952 in Karlsruhe

Rihm began studying music theory, piano, and composition at the Music Academy in Karlsruhe at the early age of 16, under Eugen Velte, →Karlheinz Stockhausen, and Klaus Huber, and taught there himself from 1973 to 1978. From 1978 he was a teacher at the Darmstadt summer school, and since 1985 has been professor of composition in Karlsruhe. He is regarded as one of the more important composers of the younger generation and can already lay claim to an extensive oeuvre.

Works: Stage works: *Faust und Yorick* (*Faust and Yorick*) (1977, Mannheim), *Jakob Lenz* (1979, Hamburg), *Oedipus* (1981, Berlin), the ballet *Tutuguri* (1982, Berlin), the dance theater *Medea-Spiel* (*Medea Play*) (1989, Salzburg), *Die Hamletmaschine* (*The Hamlet Machine*) (1987, Mannheim), the music theater *Die Eroberung von Mexiko* (*The Conquest of Mexico*) (1992, Hamburg), the music theater *Séraphin* (1994, Frankfurt); orchestral works, chamber music, songs.

*R*ihm's sources of musical inspiration are derived from a musical tradition that he views positively, as well as from his study of the works of Schoenberg, Varèse, and Stockhausen. He is considered a representative of New Simplicity.

Jakob Lenz, production photograph with Richard Salter as Lenz, production Heinz-Lukas Kindermann, conductor Peter Keuschnig, sets and costumes Dietrich Schoras, Wiener Staatsoper 1988.
Lenz clasps a statue of Goethe. Büchner's theme, an artist brought to ruin by internal forces, allows for the musical depiction of the collapse of a complex personality. The opera's use of traditional forms has boosted its popularity, and it has been performed several times in Europe and the USA.

Jakob Lenz

Chamber opera (13 scenes)

Libretto: Michael Fröhlich, after the novella *Lenz* by Georg Büchner.
Première: 8 March 1979, Hamburg (Staatsoper).
Characters: Lenz (Bar), Oberlin (B), Kaufmann (T), Six Voices (2S, 2A, 2B), Two (four) Children (S, spoken).
Setting: Germany, in the early 19th century.
Synopsis
Lured away from home by inner voices, Lenz reaches Pastor Oberlin's house where, in his delirium, he throws himself into a well. Oberlin rescues him and takes him into his house. At night Lenz is tormented by his desire for Friederike, and another suicide attempt follows. Oberlin again comes to his aid: a walk in the open air is recommended in order to restore his balance. Lenz's voices assume the form of peasants, whose optimistic message induces Lenz to turn to preaching. Kaufmann arrives: he describes the situation in ironic terms and encourages Lenz to return home. Lenz flees again, consoled by his voices, which then begin to prophesy the death of Friederike. He turns back but comes upon the body of a girl laid out for a funeral, which he mistakes for his dead lover. His attempts to revive her fail. Kaufmann once again urges him to return home. Lenz's state finally becomes so grave that he has to be subdued with a straitjacket.   M. S.

The Hamlet Machine

Rihm wrote this five-part work for the Nationaltheater in Mannheim, after the stage play of the same name by Heiner Müller. Although inspired by Shakespeare's *Hamlet*, the work is intended to be autonomous and is not bound to any particular time. Three dimensions of existence – past, present, and an ideal time – are given expression by three performers of the role of Hamlet. The first part, "Family Album," gives voice to Hamlet's own existential sickness, and culminates in his desire to reverse his birth. The second part, "Europe of Woman," takes as its theme Ophelia's suffering and resistance. The third part, "Scherzo," inverts conventional ways of thinking. While Ophelia is doing her striptease, for example, Hamlet dons her clothes and becomes a woman. The fourth part, "Pestilence in Buda, Battle for Greenland," centers on the Hungarian uprising of 1956. Hamlet realizes that he can only register events mechanically, but cannot act. The fifth part, "Deep Sea," shows Ophelia helplessly bound to a wheelchair as a result of all her suffering.

Rihm employed literary quotations in the libretto, and paralleled this in the music by using motifs from the works of Handel, Bach, and Wagner, and a wide range of modern styles including rap. The première on 30 March 1987 was so successful that the production was taken up by the theater in Freiburg in the same year.

The Conquest of Mexico

Rihm created his libretto for *The Conquest of Mexico*, a commission from the opera in Hamburg, from Antonin Artaud's *La conquête de Mexique* (1932) and *Le théâtre de séraphin* (*The Seraphim Theater*) (1936). The opera does not relate a logical sequence of events, but was rather conceived as a series of internal and external states. Historicity and a universal temporal dimension are the two central pillars of the work. Montezuma's acoustic role is female (a dramatic soprano), and his actions serve to define him as an abstract Indian principle embodying nurture, while Cortez's actions are dictated by aggression. The first part, "The Omens," expounds the concepts that are encapsulated in the words "neuter," "male," and "female." In the second part, "Confession," the invading Spanish troops are surprised by the natives. Negotiations between Montezuma and Cortez are hampered by difficulty of communication, and Montezuma is taken prisoner. The third part, "Upheavals," shows the consequences of these fundamental principles: on the one hand the quiet rituals of the Aztecs and on the other the aggressive acts of the Spanish, who mortally injure Montezuma while he is making a speech. "The Abdication" focuses not only on Montezuma's funeral but also on the revenge of the Aztecs. Rihm's musically expressive techniques range from the subtle use of male and female voices to the integration into the performance of prerecorded music – a flexible musical concept which was convincingly demonstrated at the Hamburg première on 9 February 1992. *M. S.*

Jakob Lenz, photograph from the production by Sabrina Hölzer, sets Jean Kalman, costumes Franziska Just, conductor Claire Gibaut, co-production of the Hebbel Theater with the Berlin Philharmonic and Opéra National de Lyon, 1997.
Lenz, tormented by voices and on the verge of madness, kneels by the corpse of an unknown girl whom he takes for Friederike.

Rimsky-Korsakov, Nikolay Andreyevich

b. 18 March 1844 in Tikhvin (district of Novgorod)
d. 21 June 1908 on the estate of Lyubensk (near St. Petersburg)

Born into an aristocratic family, Rimsky-Korsakov was educated at a naval college in St. Petersburg (1856–62) and sailed the world as a naval officer. In 1861 he became acquainted with Mily Balakirev, the spiritual guide of a group of Russian composers of which Rimsky became a member and to which his friends →Borodin, Cui, and →Musorgsky also belonged. At about this time he produced his first compositions. In 1873 he resigned his naval commission and was appointed to the part-time civil post of inspector of naval bands. In 1874 he became Balakirev's successor as director of the Free Music School in St. Petersburg, and it was there that he first began to conduct. From 1882 to 1894 he was assistant director of the imperial chapel, and from 1886 conductor and music director of the concerts initiated by the publisher Mitrofan Belyayev. He enjoyed international success as a conductor, directing an historic series of Russian concerts organized by Sergey Dyagilev in Paris in 1907. He was professor of composition at the St. Petersburg Conservatory, his pupils including →Stravinsky and →Prokofiev. He was considered Russia's musical educator and was a model both for his art and his ethics.

Works: Operas: *Pskovityanka* (*The Maid of Pskov*) (1873), *Boyaryna Vera Sheloga* (*The Noblewoman Vera Sheloga*) (1877/FP 1898), *Mayskaya noch'* (*May Night*) (1880), *Snegurochka* (*The Snow Maiden*) (1882), *Mlada* (1892), *Noch' pered rozhdestvom* (*Christmas Eve*) (1895), *Sadko* (1898), *Mozart i Sal'yeri* (*Mozart and Salieri*) (1898), *Tsarskaya nevesta* (*The Tsar's Bride*) (1899), *Skazka o Tsare Saltane* (*The Tale of Tsar Saltan*) (1900), *Serviliya* (1902), *Kashchei bessmertnyi* (*Kashchei the Immortal*) (1902), *Pan Voyevoda* (*The Commander*) (1904), *Skazaniye o nevidimom grade Kitezhe i deve Fevronii* (*The Legend of the Invisible City of Kitezh and the Maiden Fevroniya*) (1907), *Zolotoy petushok* (*The Golden Cockerel*) (1909); symphonies, symphonic poems and other symphonic works, including *Antar*, *Sheherazade*, *Capriccio espagnol*, *Russian Easter Festival* overture, *Sadko*, chamber music, songs.

Sadko

Opera-bïlina in seven scenes (three or five acts)

Libretto: Nikolay Rimsky-Korsakov, with the assistance of Nikolay Findeyzen, Vladimir Stasov, Vasily Yastrebtsev, Nikolay Shtrup, and Vladimir Bel'sky, after Russian ballads and fairy tales.

Première: 7 January 1898, Moscow (Solodovnikov Theater, Savva Mamontov's Private Russian Opera).

Characters: Sadko, psaltery player and singer in Novgorod (T), Lyubava Buslayevna, his wife (Ms), Nezhata, young psaltery player from Kiev (A), Okean-More, the Sea King (B), Volkhova, his youngest and most beautiful daughter (S), Foma Nazar'ich and Luka Zinov'ich, town fathers of Novgorod (T, B), Duda and Sopel', town entertainers (B, T), Two Entertainers (2 Ms), Two Magicians (2 T), Viking Merchant (B), Hindu Merchant (T), Venetian Merchant (Bar), The Apparition, an ancient heroic warrior in the guise of a pilgrim (Bar); citizens of Novgorod, merchants, sailors, followers of Sadko, minstrel entertainers (merry lads), pilgrims (stern old men), mermaids, pretty maidens, white swans, wonderful sea creatures (chorus); the Sea King's mermaid wife Tsaritsa-Vodyanitsa, her 12 eldest daughters (the rivers, married to the blue seas), her little grandchildren (the small streams), silver and gold fish and other wonderful sea creatures (ballet).
Setting: Novgorod and at sea, in partly legendary and partly historical times.

Synopsis
Scene 1: The rooms of the merchants' guild in Novgorod, where the wealthy merchants are celebrating. Nezhata, the psaltery player, sings the old melodies and is applauded. Entertainers are also being rewarded. The psaltery player Sadko, however, compares the narrow life in the city with a journey on the open seas, for which he is mocked and thrown out.

Scene 2: The banks of Lake Ilmen. Human ears are deaf to the offended musician and so Sadko seeks solace in nature and finds an audience among the mermaids. The Sea King's favorite daughter, Volkhova, presents him with her heart and three golden fish.

Scene 3: Sadko's house, where Lyubava is waiting for her husband. Sadko, however, is deaf to her love and her lament: he can think only of the sea and its princess.

Sadko, production photograph with Vladimir Galouzime (Sadko) and Valentina Sidipova (Volkhova), production Alexey Stepanyuk, conductor Valery Gergiyev, Mariinksy Theater, St. Petersburg 1993.
Sadko's position between his wife and the dream princess does not release any dramatic conflict: the opera is, after all, a legend which ends happily.

Scene 4: The banks of Lake Ilmen. Sadko challenges the merchants: he wagers his life against their fortune that he can harvest golden fish from the lake. He wins, and proceeds to equip and man 30 ships with his newfound wealth. He then sets sail, eager to explore three seas – the North Sea, the Indian Ocean, and the Mediterranean – inspired by the tales he has heard from the three merchants.

Scene 5: On Sadko's ship. Twelve years have passed and Sadko has amassed great wealth. The fleet is hurrying home; only Sadko's ship is becalmed, trapped by invisible forces. When Volkhova calls to Sadko he abandons his ship and it sails off without him. The Sea King draws Sadko down into the depths.

Scene 6: The bottom of the sea. The singer praises the Sea King, and the rivers and lakes celebrate the marriage of Sadko and Volkhova. There is a storm on the surface of the sea as a result of the activity below. The ghost of an ancient warrior appears, and insists that Sadko return home, and that Volkhova be transformed into a river to connect Novgorod with the sea.

Scene 7: Volkhova and Sadko proceed on their nuptial journey to Novgorod in a seashell. On the banks of Lake Ilmen the sea princess takes her leave of Sadko and is transformed into a river. The people of Novgorod extol the river and welcome Sadko as a commander of the elements. Sadko objects, saying that he simply won the favor of the Sea King with his song, and that their thanks are in fact due to the ancient warrior. Sadko's speech is lost in the general rejoicing.

S. N.

Sadko, photograph from the production by Alexey Stepanyuk, sets Vyacheslav Okanyov after Korovin, conductor Valery Gergiyev, Mariinksy Theater, St. Petersburg 1993. The two tableaux set in Novgorod (Scenes 1 and 4) both end in an explosive musical crescendo, and the action of these scenes is similarly arranged to create a sense of rising intensity. Both tableaux reach their climax with the simultaneous use of song and dance, which generates a euphoric and festive atmosphere.

Bīlina **opera**
The *bīlina* is a Russian heroic ballad delivered in a specific vocal style, which enjoyed a revival in the 19th century as a result of the upsurge of nationalism. Concerts by professional singers in St. Petersburg and Moscow featuring *bīlini* they had collected themselves were enthusiastically received by the Russian intelligentsia. These ancient melodies were important sources of inspiration for Russian composers. In his memoirs of 1906 Rimsky himself stressed the importance of the *bīlina* for the opera *Sadko*: "The recitative as used here is derived not from the spoken language but from the melodic lines and manner of performance of the heroic ballads … This recitative runs through the entire opera and lends the work a national and ballad-like character." Lyubava's lament (F minor) and the farewell song of Volkhova (a traditional lullaby) are both in old Russian style. *M 1, M 2*
The atmosphere of the old Russian city of Novgorod blends harmoniously with the characteristic style of the *bīlina* (Scenes 1 and 4), the epic speech-song alternating with folk scenes built up from short, quick repetitions of motifs. *M. P.*

1. Lyubava's Lament

Ох, зна - ю я,   Сад - ко ме-ня не лю - бит, ме - ня   не жаль по - кинуть мужень-ку.

2. Volkhova's Lullaby

Сон по бе-реж - ку хо - дил,   Дре-ма по   лу - гу.

*R*imsky-Korsakov was a master of instrumentation. His sources of inspiration included old Russian ballads, legends, and fairy tales, which he enriched with pantheistic ideas and developed with his tireless powers of imagination.

3. Song of the Mermaids

Сла - ва те - бе, гус - ляр

4. Sadko's Song

Про - бе - га - ли б мо - и бу - сы ко - раб - ли

5. Song of the Viking

О ска - лы гроз - ны - е дро - бят - ся с ре - вом вол - ны

6. Song of the Hindu

Не счесть ал - ма - зов в камен - ных пе - ще - рах, не счесть жем - чу - жин в мо - ре по - лу - ден - ном

7. Song of the Venetian

Го - род пре - крас - ный, го - род счаст - ли - вый, мо - ря ца - ри - ца, Ве - де - нец слав - ный!

8. Volkhova's Metamorphosis

Rimsky and the sea

The Rimsky-Korsakov family had a long association with the sea. A distant ancestor of the composer had been a naval officer under Peter the Great, a Pacific island had been named after his uncle (Korsakov Island), and his older brother, Voin, rose to the position of vice-admiral in the Russian navy. Like Sadko in his song on the banks of Lake Ilmen (Scene 2), Rimsky had dreamed in his youth of long sea voyages. In 1867, aged 22, he composed a symphonic poem called *Sadko*. Three decades later he would lift from this work the musical depiction of the sea, the music for the Sea King, and the turbulent wedding *trepak*. The ocean scenes in *Sadko*, with their lush instrumentation and colorful, often impressionistic harmonies, gave rise to a unique musical world – one in which the influence of Richard Wagner can be detected. The enchanting call of the mermaids as they emerge from the waves is reminiscent of Wagner's flowermaidens (→*Parsifal*), but it also refers to supernatural creatures from earlier operas by Rimsky: the water nymphs in *May Night*, the Bonny Spring in *The Snow Maiden*, and the nymphs in *Mlada*. M 3

The fame of the artist

Sadko's life is a Russian success story. The impoverished artist-singer from Novgorod longs for wealth and fame, and eventually wins both through his art and his adventures at sea before returning home in triumph. The story may refer to the triumph of the middle classes, who, unafraid of taking risks, are able to conquer markets in distant parts. But it may also refer to the triumph of the individual who explores the unknown forces of nature before finally emerging victorious from these self-imposed trials. Both these aspects are present in Rimsky's opera. But the composer, who was more than 50 at the time of its composition, seems to have been especially interested in Sadko's artistic career. Rimsky's Sadko pines neither for material possessions nor for love: he is happy in his hometown and in love with his young wife. Yet he is driven by the curiosity of the artist and by the desire for the fantastic and transcendental, as a result of which he wins fabulous wealth. M 4

Those who talk to Sadko confide in him spontaneously, as seen in the three foreign merchants who tell him of their distant homelands: the Viking from the cold North Sea, the Hindu from the warm southern seas, and the Venetian from the most beautiful city on the Mediterranean. M 5, M 6, M 7

Rimsky's opera does not attempt to explore the psychology of the drama. Sadko's wife, for example, waits nine years for him to return without feeling jealousy or resentment; the inhabitants of Novgorod do not envy Sadko for his sudden wealth; and nor do the two singers, Sadko and Nezhata, enter into competition with each other. Rimsky also avoids placing too great an emphasis on the character of the ancient warrior and his announcement that the power of the Sea King is at an end.

Sadko is not forced to return to the city and to his wife because the empire of the Sea King is pagan and evil, or because his marriage to the king's daughter has led him to commit the sin of bigamy; rather, he returns because he belongs among the people of Novgorod. Enriched by his experiences, the artist's duty is to serve others. Rimsky's Sadko finds himself in a world beyond ordinary human existence, and although he travels a road towards death he is ultimately permitted to return. Sadko's decision means that Volkhova is destined to meet a mortal end, but her metamorphosis into a river helps give Sadko a safe passage back to life and to the land of his fellow men. Of the many attractive female characters in Rimsky's operas, Volkhova is perhaps the most poetic. Her metamorphosis is represented by a beautiful musical description of nature (similar to that in →*The Legend of the Invisible City of Kitezh* when Fevroniya arrives in the invisible city). M8 M.P.

Sadko in the empire of the Sea King, oil painting by Il'ya Repin, St. Petersburg 1876 (Russian State Museum). The opera was greatly inspired by contemporary painting. Indeed, the decorative sets for the première gave the impression of being paintings by prominent artists of the day (such as Leon Bakst), employed by Mamontov as set designers for his private theater. This wonderful picture by Repin may also have played an important part in the genesis of the opera.

The Legend of the Invisible City of Kitezh, set design by Max Bignens for the production by Hans Neugebauer, Bühnen der Stadt Köln, Cologne 1967/68.

Three of the opera's locations belong to the real world, while one is mythical – the invisible city or heavenly realm of Greater Kitezh. Human action takes place in the forest, in the city of Lesser Kitezh, and at the princely seat of Greater Kitezh. The forest is Fevroniya's home, an unspoiled and harmonious place. Lesser Kitezh is the scene of everyday activities and home to everyday people, including Grishka Kuter'ma, a vagrant who willingly serves evil. Greater Kitezh is the fount of all that is good, and symbolizes an idealized fatherland.

Below
The Legend of the Invisible City of Kitezh, production photograph with Miranda van Kralingen (Fevroniya) and Günter Neumann (Grishka), production Harry Kupfer, sets Hans Schavernoch, costumes Reinhard Heinrich, conductor Shao-Chia Lü, coproduction with the Festival of Begrenz, Komische Oper, Berlin 1996.
Good and evil appear in the opera as principles that are both omnipresent and inevitable. In contrast to the dramatic strategies used in Romantic operas, neither Fevroniya nor Grishka is vanquished or destroyed by her/his opponent.

The Legend of the Invisible City of Kitezh and the Maiden Fevroniya

Skazaniye o nevidimom grade Kitezhe i deve Fevronii

Opera in four acts (six scenes)

Libretto: Vladimir Bel'sky, after Russian chronicles, ballads, and tales.

Première: 20 February 1907, St. Petersburg (Mariinsky Theater).

Characters: Fevroniya (S), Grishka Kuter'ma (T), Prince Yury, ruler of Kitezh (B), Prince Vsevolod, his son (T), Fyodor Poyarok (Bar), A Boy, Prince Yury's page (Ms), Two Rich Citizens (T, B), Bard (psaltery player) (B), Bear Trainer (T), Singing Beggar (Bar), Bedyay and Burunday, Mongol warriors (2 B), Sirin and Alkonost, prophetic birds (S, A); the prince's huntsmen, wedding party, domra players, wealthy citizens, beggars, Tartars (chorus, ballet).

Setting: The legendary city of Kitezh and its surroundings, in the 13th century.

Synopsis
Act I

Fevroniya lives alone in the forest, with only the animals for company. Prince Vsevolod loses his way in the forest while hunting and meets Fevroniya. Her purity, joy, and wisdom bewitch him: he falls in love and they agree to marry.

Act II

The people crowd into Lesser Kitezh, among them a bear tamer, psaltery players, jugglers, and beggars. They are expecting the wedding procession that will conduct Fevroniya from her home in the forest to the princely residence. The wealthy citizens of the town persuade the drunken Grishka to mock the bride on account of her lowly birth. Hordes of Tartars attack the town, and take Fevroniya and Grishka prisoner. Under threat of torture, Grishka agrees to show them the way to Greater Kitezh, while Fevroniya prays to God to save it by making it invisible.

Act III

Scene 1: The people of Greater Kitezh learn of the invasion from the army leader Fyodor Poyarok, who has been blinded by the Tartars. Prince Vsevolod leads his men out to fight, leaving behind his father Prince Yury, as well as the women, children, and old men, who pray to God for help. From the tower a boy sees the Tartars approaching. At that moment a thick fog descends and the bells begin to ring of their own accord: Greater Kitezh becomes invisible.

Interlude: *The Battle of Kerzhenets.* Prince Vsevolod and his army are destroyed by the Tartars.

Scene 2: The Tartars camp on the banks of Lake Svetlïy Yar opposite Greater Kitezh. Grishka is bound to a tree while the army shares out its booty. Two leaders argue fiercely over Fevroniya, and one of them is killed. While the enemy army sleeps, Fevroniya is overcome with pity for Grishka and loosens his bonds; they both escape into the woods. At dawn the bells begin to ring and the domes of Greater Kitezh can be seen reflected in the waters of the lake, though the city itself has disappeared. The Tartars flee in panic.

Act IV

Scene 1: Fevroniya and Grishka wander through the wilderness. Tormented by his conscience Grishka loses his mind and runs off. Fevroniya, exhausted, falls asleep. She dreams that flowers are blooming about her and that fantastic birds of paradise are announcing her death and eternal life. Her dead husband appears to lead her to Kitezh.

Interlude: Fevroniya and Vsevolod proceed into the invisible city to the ringing of bells.

Scene 2: In the cathedral of a radiant and idealized Greater Kitezh, Prince Yury is waiting for the young couple. In her happy state Fevroniya thinks of the wretched Grishka, and how much she would like to show him the way back to Kitezh. She sends him an encouraging message while the people of Kitezh celebrate the union of Fevroniya and Vsevolod.   M. P.

The Legend of the Invisible City of Kitezh, production photograph with Peter Rose as Prince Yury, production Harry Kupfer, sets Hans Schavernoch, costumes Reinhard Heinrich, conductor Shao-Chia Lü, Komische Oper, Berlin 1996.
It is hardly surprising that Rimsky's opera is known as "the Slavic →*Parsifal,*" given that this work, like Wagner's, centers on redemption from earthly suffering. Greater Kitezh appears twice, first as the manifestation of an idealized, if isolated, earthly kingdom ruled by Prince Yury, and then as a "divine" place similar to the biblical vision of Jerusalem.

The Legend of the Invisible City of Kitezh,
production photograph with Miranda van
Kralingen (Fevroniya) and Andrzej Dobber
(Fyodor Poyarok), production Harry Kupfer,
sets Hans Schavernoch, costumes Reinhard
Heinrich, conductor Shao-Chia Lü, Komische
Oper, Berlin 1996.
Harry Kupfer was the first internationally
renowned director to set the opera in the
period in which it was composed. Fevroniya is
led by Fyodor Poyarok in a bridal procession
to Greater Kitezh, and is welcomed by the
inhabitants of Lesser Kitezh along the way.

The Legend of the Invisible City of Kitezh,
Marianna Cherkasskaya as Fevroniya in the
original production of 1907.
This Russian mystery opera is characterized by
religious devotion and a child-like naïveté:
Fevroniya is pure and mild, while Grishka is
wild and demonic. Like Wagner's →*Parsifal,*
the opera can be interpreted as a sacred and
ceremonial work.

"The Russian *Parsifal*"

The libretto combines two folk legends: the miraculous salvation of the holy city and the story of the maiden Fevroniya. The "holy fool" of *Kitezh*, who redeems the city through the divine gifts of faith, love, humility, and natural wisdom is, unusually, a woman. The exquisite descending melody that accompanies Fevroniya's prayer for the salvation of the city is the music of redemption (end of Act II). The prayer ceremony in Greater Kitezh is built on this melody, and the miraculous sound of the bells of Kitezh springs from this same theme. M 9

Fevroniya is a child of nature – indeed, almost a part of nature: because she has grown up alone in the forest, she understands the language of the trees, flowers, birds, and animals. Her melodies grow out of the sounds of the forest in the prologue, and this musical depiction of nature is gradually transformed into song. M 10

Fevroniya maintains her inner harmony even during the most dreadful trials, and she has the capacity to share this harmony with her fellow man. While held prisoner by the Tartars, Fevroniya comforts her fellow prisoner, Grishka, even though he has maliciously slandered her by blaming her for his own treachery. She speaks to him of the inner happiness that comes from self-denial and humility, and she does this in a variation of the melody with which she had once sung the praises of her forest home. This music creates a perfect unity in Fevroniya's character. Rimsky was inspired by folk songs in the composition of her melodies, the sole exception being the upwardly striving theme of almost Wagnerian expressiveness with which she proclaims her faith in God. Fevroniya is without doubt the main character of *Kitezh*; her lover Prince Vsevolod (a *heldentenor*)

has a more episodic role. Fevroniya's true partner, and opposite pole, is Grishka (also a tenor, though in this case a Russian character tenor). In his own peculiar way, Grishka is a philosopher: his wretched life has taught him to be egotistical and servile, and to mock those poorer than himself. At a moment of historical gravity this wicked but pathetic rogue betrays his fatherland and slanders the purest of mortals. Yet his slander, like his earlier derision, has no effect on Fevroniya, and it becomes apparent that Grishka only damages himself with his accusations. The pangs of conscience aroused by Fevroniya's gentle humility and compassion are so fierce as to drive him insane. Rimsky depicted Grishka's hallucinations with great ingeniousness: he hears the bells of Kitezh but their mellifluous notes are transformed in his mind into strident dissonances.

Global catastrophe and the Tartars

History breaks in upon the idyll of Kitezh in the form of the Tartar invasion. In philosophical terms, the invasion represents evil in its purest form, or perhaps an act of God. A brief look at Russian history soon explains why in a Russian mystery play the Tartars are chosen to represent evil. In his prologue Bel'sky notes that the Tartar hordes should not be depicted realistically – it was not ethnographic accuracy that was called for here – but rather as they appear in old folk songs. The source of the March of the Tartars is indeed a well-known Russian folk-song. M 11

The terrifying depiction of the Tartar invasion betrays the apocalyptic fears of the Russian intelligentsia at the beginning of the twentieth century. Russian philosophy of religion of this period can also be detected in such scenes. Figures such as Solov'yov, Berdyayev, Florensky, and Mereshkovsky sought a direct experience of God, while Tolstoy was developing his ideas on charity and tolerance. The opera's conclusion is certainly thought provoking: the apotheosis affirms unequivocally that the world is in the hands of evil men, and that the sacred city remains invisible to the masses. As a pantheist, the aging Rimsky had an unorthodox faith, and regarded the world with a sense of profound resignation.

9. Fevroniya's Prayer

Бо - же, со - тво - ри не-ви - дим Ки - тежь-градъ

10. Fevroniya's Nature Theme

Ах, ты лес, мой лес, пус - ты - ня пре-крас -на-я

11. March of the Tartars

Та - кой кра-сы в сте-пи не бу-дет, све - зем в Ор-ду цве-ток бо -лот-ный.

A mystery opera

Rimsky let the idea of a Slavic, religious opera mature for five years around the turn of the century. His original intention had been to bring his dramatic oeuvre to a close with this piece. *Kitezh* is therefore both a confession of faith and a legacy. His stage directions for the première were almost as rigid as Wagner's for →*Parsifal*; he insisted, for example, that special Kitezh bells be made to reproduce their sounds backstage in Act II. After the October Revolution of 1917 *Kitezh* vanished from opera programs: Soviet ideology had no use for a Slavic →*Parsifal*. The opera was nevertheless tolerated, and there was even a recording made in the 1950s (in which the libretto was reworked). But the work did not really begin to come to life on stage again until the performances at the Bol'shoy Theater in Moscow in 1983 and the Mariinsky Theater in St. Petersburg in the 1990s. The interest of the international operatic community has also been reawakened during this time.   *M. P.*

The Legend of the Invisible City of Kitezh, production photograph with Sergey Nayda (Prince Vsevolod), Andzrej Dobber (Fyodor Poyarok), and Christiane Oertel (the boy), production Harry Kupfer, sets Hans Schavernoch, costumes Reinhard Heinrich, conductor Shao-Chia Lü, Komische Oper, Berlin 1996.
Fyodor Poyarok has been blinded by the Tartars during their attack on Lesser Kitezh, and now, led by a boy, he brings news of the disaster to Greater Kitezh. Horrified, Prince Vsevolod learns that his bride Fevroniya has been abducted.

The Golden Cockerel

Zolotoy petushok

Opera in a prologue, three acts, and an epilogue

Libretto: Vladimir Bel'sky, after a tale by Alexander Pushkin.

Première: 7 October 1909, Moscow (Solodovnikov Theater, Sergey Zimin's private opera company).

Characters: Tsar Dodon (B), Princes Gvidon and Afron, his sons (T, Bar), General Polkan (B), Amelfa, the royal housekeeper (A), Astrologer (counterT), Queen of Shemakha (S), The Golden Cockerel (S); boyars, guards, soldiers, canoneers, female slaves, crowd (chorus).

Setting: An imaginary realm.

Synopsis

Prologue

An astrologer introduces himself as the producer of and an actor in the play. He challenges the audience to make sense of the story which is to follow.

Act I

The palace of the tsars. Tsar Dodon was once something of a ruffian, but now he is old and wants a bit of peace and quiet. The boyars and the tsar's two sons are at a complete loss as to how to protect the country from its enemies. The astrologer helps by presenting the tsar with a golden cockerel that will watch over the empire and crow if an enemy threatens. The tsar can rest easy – until the cockerel begins to crow. On the first two occasions Dodon sends his sons against the enemy, but the third time he is forced to take the field himself.

Act II

The battlefield at night. Dodon finds his army defeated. His sons have killed each other, yet the enemy is nowhere to be seen. A beautiful woman appears at dawn and introduces herself as the queen of Shemakha. Dodon offers her his heart and his hand.

Act III

A street in the capital. Dodon returns with his bride. The astrologer demands the queen of Shemakha as payment for the golden cockerel, but Dodon refuses and strikes the astrologer dead. He is then killed himself by a single blow from the golden cockerel's beak. The bird then disappears with the queen. The people are left confused and horrified: how are they to live without a tsar?

Epilogue

The astrologer appears again in front of the curtain as master of ceremonies, claiming that only he and the queen of Shemakha can truly be considered alive: all the other characters he banishes to the kingdom of shadows.   S. N.

The Golden Cockerel, production photograph (Act I) with Michael Guzhov as Dodon, production Dmitry Bertman, sets and costumes Igor Nezhny and Tat'yana Tulubyeva, conductor Lothar Königs, Helikon Opera, Moscow 1999.
In post-socialist Russia the political meanings of the opera were understandably interpreted in light of the immediate past: here, Tsar Dodon appears as party secretary (a reference to the revolutionary leader Lenin) amongst "his" people. *The Golden Cockerel* can be called a biting comedy.

Contemporary caricature of Tsar Dodon.

A caricature of the tsar

Rimsky's interest in Pushkin's fairy-tale poem *The Golden Cockerel* (1834) was aroused by a contemporary caricature of Tsar Dodon. This figure was already a caricature of the tsar in Pushkin's day. The opera's libretto plays directly on events of the early 20th century: Dodon's lament over his two shattered armies, for example, was a reminder of the war against Japan in 1905, which the Russians had disastrously lost as a result of incompetent leadership. The opera exposes the stupidity and narrow-mindedness of the tsarist Empire, much to the irritation of the authorities. Rimsky spent the last months of his life battling with the censors, who refused to allow either a printed edition or a stage production of the opera. He did not live to see the première. *M. P.*

Above
The Golden Cockerel, photograph from the production by Tim Hopkins, sets and costumes Anthony Baker, conductor Wladimir Jurowski, Royal Opera House, London 1998.
Dodon is a caricature of a tsar and is portrayed as an extraordinarily stupid individual. His deep bass voice is the only vestige of the power formerly wielded by the Russian tsars.

The Golden Cockerel, production photograph (Act II) with Marina Andreyeva (queen of Shemakha) and Michael Guzhov (Dodon), production Dmitry Bertman, sets and costumes Igor Nezhny and Tat'yana Tulubyeva, conductor Lothar Königs, Helikon Opera, Moscow 1999.
The queen of Shemakha and her companions, symbols of hypnotic beauty and erotic power, are transformed in the post-socialist generation into women whose love is for sale.

Dodon and his kingdom

Rimsky and his librettist Bel'sky remained faithful to Pushkin's text in their satirical depiction of Tsar Dodon. The composer provided the character of the tsar (the principal bass role) with music that was deliberately simplified, plodding, and naive. The brass passage from the march symbolizing Dodon's power is a caricature of the kinds of songs and marches that are popular with dictators everywhere. *M 12*

Dodon's subjects are a cowardly, demoralized, and faceless bunch, and most of the choruses are correspondingly comical and grotesque. The final chorus, which occurs as the shocked citizens stand beside the corpse of Dodon, is a startling exception. The words "What will happen to us without a tsar?" are deeply ironic, but the music that accompanies them is sympathetic, and conveys Rimsky's feeling for the oppressed people. *M 13*

The queen, the astrologer, and the cockerel

Soviet-Russian scholars of literature and music have often emphasized the peculiarly Russian and folkloric origins of Pushkin's *The Golden Cockerel*. Yet the story has little to do with national folklore; it is rather an adaptation, its most obvious source being the exotic tale *The Legend of the Arabian Astrologer* from the collection *The Alhambra* by the American writer Washington Irving (1783–1859). The connection between the works of Irving and Pushkin was discovered only in 1933 by Anna Akhmatova, who found a French copy of *The Alhambra* in Pushkin's estate. Rimsky and Bel'sky could not have known this, and it is unlikely that they were familiar with Irving's tale. Nevertheless, there does appear to be a link between the works of the American writer and the Russian composer. The oriental element is an integral and organic part of the Arabic milieu in Irving's tales. While this exotic aspect is absent from Pushkin's work it is very much in evidence in the opera. Oriental influences, discernible in Russian music from the time of →Glinka, may be detected in the music written for the fantasy figures of the astrologer and the

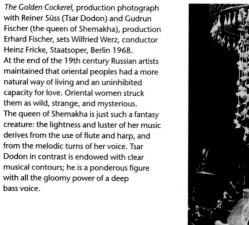

The Golden Cockerel, production photograph with Reiner Süss (Tsar Dodon) and Gudrun Fischer (the queen of Shemakha), production Erhard Fischer, sets Wilfried Werz, conductor Heinz Fricke, Staatsoper, Berlin 1968.
At the end of the 19th century Russian artists maintained that oriental peoples had a more natural way of living and an uninhibited capacity for love. Oriental women struck them as wild, strange, and mysterious. The queen of Shemakha is just such a fantasy creature: the lightness and luster of her music derives from the use of flute and harp, and from the melodic turns of her voice. Tsar Dodon in contrast is endowed with clear musical contours; he is a ponderous figure with all the gloomy power of a deep bass voice.

12. Marching Song in Praise of the Tsar

Царь наш ба - тюш-ка,   у - ра!   У-ра!

13. The People's Lament

14. The Queen of Shemakha Greets the Sun

От-веть мне, зор - ко- е   све - ти - ло,   с вос-то-ка к нам при-хо - дишь   ты

15. Entrance of the Astrologer

Дол - гом вер-но-сти вле-ко - мый

16. Cockerel Motif

Ки-ри-ки,   ки-ри - ку - ку!   Бе-ре-гись, будь на-че - ку!

queen of Shemakha. This music provides a link between *The Golden Cockerel* and the art and fashion of the Art Nouveau movement that was popular at the turn of the century. The queen of Shemakha can be seen as a particular type of Russian femme fatale. The tools of her trade are sensuality and temptation; and, although death follows in her wake, she herself finds death and sin absurd. In spite of this, the queen is the most attractive figure in the opera: she is a child of nature, a goddess of love, and an avenging angel all in one. Bel'sky himself described her as "the demonic temptation of sensual beauty." Her voice is a dramatic, lyrical, and coloratura soprano, and her part is full of poetic beauty, and redolent of the mystical and the exotic – not to mention the erotic. Her music is also particularly colorful, mixing oriental and Russian elements, especially the melodies of Russian folk music. M 14

Compared with the prominent role of the queen, that of the astrologer is small but distinctive. This mysterious oriental character was described by Pushkin as a eunuch, and Rimsky correspondingly wrote the part for a "tenor altino," a high, light tenor voice. The theme of his first aria is taken from the chromatic melody of the queen, his ally in the destruction of Dodon. M 15

While the constantly recurring chromatic melody of the queen is dominated by the soft, deep coloring of the strings and woodwind, the astrologer's part is characterized by the exotic sound of the celesta and that of the golden cockerel by piercing brass phrases (especially on the trumpet), its shrill theme capable of penetrating throughout Dodon's kingdom. Rimsky intended the small part of the cockerel to be performed by a brightly metallic soprano voice. M 16   M. P.

The Golden Cockerel, set design by Ludolfs Lijberts, German Theater, Riga 1928 (TWS). Tsar Dodon meets the queen of Shemakha in front of her tent. In Act II the queen greets the dawn, a symbol of the world of the East that is waiting to be resurrected (the cockerel also belongs to this group of symbols). But the mysterious and exotic figures of the queen and the astrologer are also beings from the East, and both bring destruction; whether this ruin would be permanent was a question the composer himself never resolved.

Tancredi, production photograph with Gloria Scalchi as Tancredi, production Michael Sturminger, Opernhaus Zürich 1996. In recent years the tragic conclusion to Rossini's Ferrara version of the opera has tended to replace the original happy ending.

Below
Tancredi, Giuditta Pasta as Tancredi. Giuditta Pasta (1797–1865), shown here in the role of Tancredi, was a leading personality in the age of bel canto prima donnas. Although she never appeared in any première of Rossini's work, she did give triumphant performances of a number of Rossini heroines that were to inspire Bellini and Donizetti. In the première Tancredi was sung by Adelaide Malanotte-Montresor, though in following years the part was occasionally performed by famous castrati.

Rossini, Gioacchino

b. 29 February 1792 in Pesaro
d. 13 November 1868 in Passy (near Paris)

Rossini received his first music lessons from his father, the horn player and trumpeter Giuseppe Rossini. In 1806 he entered the Bologna Conservatory, where he studied under Padre Stanislao Mattei, and in 1810 received his first commission for an opera. Others quickly followed. He had great success in 1813 with *Tancredi* and *The Italian Girl in Algiers*. In 1815 he went to Naples as musical and artistic director of the Teatro S. Carlo, and during his time there produced a large number of *opere serie* as well as masterpieces of *opera buffa* such as *The Barber of Seville*, *La Cenerentola*, and *The Thieving Magpie*. He married the soprano Isabella Colbran in 1822. After his last opera written for an Italian audience, *Semiramide*, of 1823, he traveled to London, and from 1824 lived in Paris, where he became director of the Théâtre-Italien. His last work for the stage, *William Tell*, was written in 1829. From this point he composed only sacred works, such as the *Stabat Mater* and *Petite messe solennelle*, and short character pieces. Rossini separated from Isabella Colbran in 1837, and in 1846 married Olympe Pélissier. His health began to deteriorate in the early 1850s and he finally died, universally honored, in 1868, in his house near Paris.

Works: 39 operas (including adaptations of his own works), including *Tancredi* (1813), *L'Italiana in Algeri* (*The Italian Girl in Algiers*) (1813), *Il Turco in Italia* (*The Turk in Italy*) (1814), *Il barbiere di Siviglia* (*The Barber of Seville*) (1816), *Otello, ossia Il moro di Venezia* (*Othello, or The Moor of Venice*) (1816), *La Cenerentola, ossia La bontà in trionfo* (*Cinderella, or Goodness Triumphant*) (1817), *Mosè in Egitto* (*Moses in Egypt*) (1818), its French version *Moïse et Pharaon, ou Le passage de la Mer Rouge* (*Moses and Pharaoh, or The Passage through the Red Sea*) (1827), *Guillaume Tell* (*William Tell*) (1829); sacred works, cantatas, songs, the collection of short vocal and instrumental pieces *Péchés de vieillesse* (*Sins of Old Age*) (1857–68).

*R*ossini was a virtuoso among Romantic opera composers. Of his generation he was the composer most influenced by Viennese Classicism (especially by Mozart's operas). He was called, after his birthplace, "the swan of Pesaro."

Tancredi

Melodramma eroico in two acts

Libretto: Gaetano Rossi, after Voltaire's *Tancrède*.
Première: 6 February 1813, Venice (Teatro La Fenice).

Characters: Argirio, King of Syracuse (T), Amenaide, his daughter (S), Tancredi, a Sicilian knight (A), Orbazzano, Duke of Sicily (B), Isaura, Amenaide's confidante (Ms), Roggiero, Tancredi's squire (S); noblemen, knights, shieldbearers, people of Syracuse, Saracens (chorus).
Setting: Syracuse, in the year 1005.

Synopsis
Tancredi and Amenaide are in love, but Tancredi is banished from his home and Amenaide has been promised to another man. The couple are forced to undergo a number of trials, but faithfulness and virtue triumph and they are eventually reunited.

Act I
In Syracuse the reconciliation of the Orbazzano and Argirio families is being celebrated. Together they are to march against the Saracens and their prince Solamir. Argirio promises Orbazzano the hand of his daughter Amenaide. She, however, is in love with Tancredi, to whom she has become secretly engaged. Tancredi returns to Syracuse incognito. Orbazzano intercepts a letter from Amenaide to Tancredi, mistakenly believing that it is intended for Solamir. During the wedding celebrations he accuses Amenaide of high treason and she is thrown into jail.

Act II
Amenaide is condemned to death. Tancredi, still incognito, demands that divine judgment settle the matter, and he challenges the knight to a duel. He defeats Orbazzano and takes the field against the Saracens, whom he also vanquishes. From the dying Solamir he learns that Amenaide is innocent. Victorious, Tancredi returns home to be happily reunited with Amenaide.

(In the revised Ferrara version, Tancredi returns mortally wounded from the battlefield, learns from Argirio that Amenaide is innocent, and then dies in his lover's arms.)

É. P.-L.

A serious Rossini

In Rossini's first *opera seria*, with which he won international recognition (it was performed on many stages and in several languages), his powers of invention and his compositional technique may be seen to have reached maturity. *Tancredi* radiates harmony in the manner of the neo-classical tradition, in which peace, honor, faith, and love are the dominant virtues. This is affirmed by the *lieto fine* (happy ending). Yet Rossini himself appears to have been dissatisfied with the happy ending required by the *opera seria* genre, for within weeks of the première he revised the end of the opera for a production in Ferrara, so that it ended with Tancredi's death. The revision did not please his audiences, however, and he was obliged to restore the original ending, retaining the *lieto fine* for most of his later *opere serie*.

The beating of a youthful heart

It was "the still virginal genius" which, in Stendhal's opinion, made *Tancredi* so enchanting an opera: "[Rossini] found the right degree of richness and luxury with which to adorn beauty without damaging it or overloading it with meaningless ornamentation." Certain of Rossini's formal ideas (such as constructing a scene as an extended musical unit) appear in *Tancredi* for the first time. The wealth of melodic writing in the work is almost overwhelming. The best-known example of an apparently simple and yet emotionally intense piece of vocal writing is Tancredi's entrance aria, "Di tanti palpiti" ("With what beating of my heart"), which became Rossini's first great "hit," said to have been sung by Venetian gondoliers and dignified magistrates alike. Lord Byron's praise of Rossini in *Don*

Juan and Wagner's parody of "Di tanti palpiti" in →*The Mastersingers of Nuremberg* 50 years later testified to the popularity – indeed, the immortality – of this melody by the 21-year-old composer. *M 1*   *É. P.-L.*

Tancredi, production photograph with Tancredi and Amenaide, production and sets Pier Luigi Pizzi, conductor Daniele Gatti, Teatro alla Scala, Milan 1993.
Standardized theatrical gestures to express various kinds of emotion are as much a part of Romantic *opera seria* as a sophisticated vocal style.

1. Tancredi's Entrance Aria

Di tan-ti pal-pi-ti, di— tan-te pe - ne,

Tancredi, production photograph with Giuseppe Scorsin as Orbazzano, production Michael Sturminger, sets Martin Warth, costumes Marquan Dib, conductor Theodor Guschlbauer, Opernhaus Zürich 1996.
Duke Orbazzano is Tancredi's opponent in the opera. This production presented the work as a Mafia story about two rival Sicilian families. It is remarkable how easily familiar characters and situations from certain types of cinema can be adapted to the much older genre of opera: both are dominated by conventions and clichés.

Bottom of page
The Italian Girl in Algiers, photograph from the production by Jean-Pierre Ponnelle, sets and costumes Jean-Pierre Ponnelle, conductor Claudio Abbado, Wiener Staatsoper 1994. The European prisoners arrive at Mustafà's palace and Taddeo shows himself to be unfamiliar with Algerian codes of behavior. In both Rossini's "Turkish" operas the exotic serves as a source of comedy; the music itself never becomes oriental in nature.

The Italian Girl in Algiers, rehearsal photograph with Agnes Baltsa (Isabella) and Claudio Abbado, production, sets, and costumes Jean-Pierre Ponnelle, conductor Claudio Abbado, Wiener Staatsoper 1987. Precise instructions are given during a rehearsal.

The Italian Girl in Algiers

L'Italiana in Algeri

Dramma giocoso per musica in two acts

Libretto: Angelo Anelli.
Première: 22 May 1813, Venice (Teatro di S. Benedetto).

Characters: Mustafà, Bey of Algiers (B), Elvira, his wife (S), Zulma, a slave and Elvira's confidante (Ms), Haly, captain of the Algerian corsairs (B), Lindoro, a young Italian and Mustafà's favorite slave (T), Isabella, an Italian lady (Ms), Taddeo, Isabella's companion (Bar); dignitaries at the court of the Bey, Algerian corsairs, guards, eunuchs, Italian slaves (chorus).
Setting: Algeria in the 17th century.

Synopsis

Captured by pirates, Isabella is sold to the Bey and meets up with her former lover, Lindoro. Isabella succeeds in tricking Mustafà and escaping with her lover.

Act I

Mustafà the Bey is bored with his wife Elvira, and she, in turn, hopes to marry the Italian slave Lindoro. The Bey orders the pirate Haly to bring him an Italian woman, and this is how Isabella, Lindoro's lover, arrives at the Bey's palace, accompanied by her stubborn admirer Taddeo. She quickly realizes what is going on at court, and feigns affection for Mustafà. The unsuspecting Lindoro appears with Elvira, who is forcing her attentions on him, and general confusion results: no one knows just what is happening, or who belongs to whom.

Act II

Isabella and Lindoro plan their escape, including Taddeo in their scheme. In a private ceremony, Isabella bestows the order of "Pappataci" on the lovesick Mustafà, who has made numerous unsuccessful attempts to be alone with her. While Mustafà dutifully fulfills the requirements of his new order – that he should eat, drink, and remain silent – Isabella succeeds in escaping with Lindoro and Taddeo. Outwitted, Mustafà returns to his wife, a chastened man.   É. P.-L.

Samson and Delilah, illustration of a scene
from Act III, Paris 1892.
Samson is led into the temple of Dagon. An
illustration from the first performance in Paris,
which took place 15 years after the première
in Weimar.

A tenor and a mezzo: an unusual couple

The dramatic tension in this work derives not from a triangular relationship, as is so often the case in opera, but from a couple who both harbor unspoken thoughts. Samson struggles with his duties as God's servant, while Delilah is motivated solely by her desire for revenge. An apparently strong but inwardly confused man and an apparently weak but willful woman stand face to face. It is noteworthy that whereas Samson is cast as a conventional heroic tenor, the role of Delilah was composed for a mezzo-soprano and is therefore comparable to such mysterious female characters as Azucena (Verdi, →*Il trovatore*) and Ulrica (Verdi, →*A Masked Ball*). Delilah even has something of the mesmerizing erotic charm of Carmen. The crucial clash between Samson and Delilah occurs in the duet in Act II. A central part of this is Delilah's famous kiss aria,

which, like Don José's "Flower Song" in Bizet's →*Carmen*, is not so much an independent number as another step on the road to a deadly seduction. *M 3*

This magnificent melody winds about itself like a viper, injecting its poison into Samson's veins. Saint-Saëns's dramatic skill shows itself in the way the love duet takes place during a thunderstorm. The weather illustrates God's wrath and symbolizes the moral background to the story – that the loss of Samson's strength is caused by the loss of his purity.

2. Orchestral Motif for Samson's Prayer

3. Delilah's Kiss Aria

Ah !   ré - ponds   à   ma   ten - dres - se !

Mona Lisa

Opera in a prologue, two acts, and an epilogue

Libretto: Beatrice Vay-Dovsky.

Première: 26 September 1915 Stuttgart (Hoftheater).

Characters: A Stranger (Bar), A Woman (S), A Lay Brother (T), Francesco del Giocondo (Bar), Pietro Tumoni (B), Arrigo Oldofredi (T), Alessio Beneventi (T), Sandro da Luzzano (Bar), Masolino Pedruzzi (B), Giovanni de' Salviati (T), Mona Fiordalisa, wife of Francesco (S), Mona Ginevra di Alta Rocca (S), Dianora, Francesco's daughter from his first marriage (S), Piccarda, maid to Mona Fiordalisa (A), Sisto, Francesco's servant (T); people of Florence, nuns from S. Trinità, monks from S. Marco (including Savonarola), servants (chorus, extras).

Setting: The present, and Florence at the end of the 15th century.

Mona Lisa, production photograph, production Gregor Horres, sets Andreas Reinhardt, conductor Ernst Märzendorfer, Wiener Volksoper 1996.

Synopsis
Prologue
In a house of the Carthusian monks. A lay brother is leading a tourist couple through the rooms, telling them of the fate that once befell Mona Lisa there. The woman visitor listens with rapt attention.

Act I
A hall in Francesco's house on Shrove Tuesday. Francesco is married to the beautiful Mona Lisa, but is consumed by jealousy: his wife cannot grace him with the famous smile painted by Leonardo da Vinci. Francesco celebrates the last day of Lent with his guests. His wife has gone to confession, and monks and nuns led by Savonarola preach repentance and contemplation. Giovanni de' Salviati has been commissioned by the pope to purchase a valuable pearl from Francesco, which he promises to deliver up the next day; it has been locked in a large airtight safe with other pearls. Seeing that the lovely Mona Lisa is unhappy, Giovanni tries to persuade her to elope with him. The suspicious Francesco arrives, and Giovanni attempts to hide in the

Schillings, Max von

b. 19 April 1868 in Düren
d. 24 July 1933 in Berlin

After studying with Joseph Brambach and Otto von Königslöw, Schillings studied law, philosophy, and art history at Munich University. From 1892 he was employed as an assistant stage director in Bayreuth. From 1908 to 1918 he was general music director in Stuttgart, and from 1919 to 1925 Intendant at the Preussische Staatsoper in Berlin. He managed the Zoppot Forest Festival from 1926 and in March 1933 became Intendant at the Städtische Oper in Berlin.

Works: Ingewelde (1894, Karlsruhe), *Der Pfeifertag* (*The Day of the Piper*) (1899, Schwerin), *Moloch* (1906, Dresden), *Mona Lisa* (1915, Stuttgart); orchestral works, chamber music, choral works, music for the theater.

From *Lady Godiva* to *Mona Lisa*
In 1911 Schillings met the Viennese actress and playwright Beatrice Vay-Dovsky (1870–1923). He was already at work on a musical setting of her play *Lady Godiva* when she showed him the more recent *Mona Lisa*, which immediately struck him as preferable. It was a wise choice: the topicality of the subject matter – Leonardo da Vinci's painting was stolen in 1911 and turned up again in Florence in 1913 – aroused the interest of opera houses in New York, Vienna, and Berlin.

As a composer Schillings belonged to the Bayreuth circle – he was a successor to Wagner and the teacher of Wilhelm Furtwängler – though he developed his own original style, especially under the influence of Impressionism and "verismo."

safe, which Francesco then locks before throwing the key into the Arno. Lisa collapses, and while unconscious is abused by Francesco.

Act II

A hall in Francesco's house on Ash Wednesday. Mona Lisa wakes and hopes in vain for a sign of life from the safe. Giovanni has suffocated. Dianora, Francesco's daughter from his first marriage, brings her a key found on a boat on the shores of the Arno. Mona Lisa sends the girl off to early morning Mass, but is unable to find the strength to open the safe. She tells Francesco that she has been in possession of the key since the previous evening. When he opens the safe to check it, she pushes him in and turns the lock.

Epilogue

In the house of the Carthusian monks. The woman is deeply moved by the story and gives the lay brother money for a Mass for Mona Lisa's soul. As she leaves she drops a bunch of flowers: they are irises, Mona Lisa's favorite flowers.   S. N.

Opera c. 1911: sex, violence – and jewels

Long before he became general music director in Stuttgart, Schillings was acknowledged as a musical dramatist of considerable skill, his early operas *Ingewelde* and *Moloch* being very well received by the public. Wagner's death left a gaping hole in the world of German opera, and Schillings was one of the composers regarded as a potential successor to the great man, capable of doing justice to the spirit of Bayreuth. Schillings himself – like his most successful German contemporaries →Richard Strauss, →Franz Schreker, and the Austrian →Alexander von Zemlinsky – was looking for more exciting drama, more haunting tunes, more orchestral color, and more eroticism in the subject matter. If there were ever such a thing as an Art Nouveau libretto, then it must surely be Beatrice Vay-Dovsky's text for *Mona Lisa*, with its beautiful and mysterious heroine, sumptuous Renaissance colors, breathtaking jewels, and unbridled eroticism.   M. S.

Mona Lisa, set design by Josef Fenneker for the production by Julius Kapp, Städtische Oper, Berlin 1953 (TWS).
The painting from which the opera takes its name can be seen at the right in an unfinished state.

Schnittke, Alfred Garriyevich

b. 24 November 1934 in Engels (former Soviet Union)
d. 3 August 1998 in Hamburg

The son of a journalist who worked for a time for a Viennese newspaper, Schnittke received his first music lessons in the Austrian capital. In the Soviet Union he attended the Valentinovka Music School near Moscow, became a successful choirmaster and pianist, and finished his studies at the Moscow Conservatory in 1961, having studied composition and counterpoint with Yevgeny Golubov and instrumentation with Nikolay Rakov. Schnittke was open to all stylistic movements: he was inspired by Filip Hershkovich, a pupil of Webern, but equally by →Stravinsky and →Shostakovich. Because his teaching activities at the Conservatory (1961–72) were poorly remunerated, he also wrote film and theater music. He was an independent composer from 1972, and in the 1980s became a member of several European academies. In 1985 he moved to Hamburg, where from 1988 he taught a course in composition at the Conservatory. He was made a German citizen in 1990. Schnittke is among the most famous composers of our age.

Works: Zhizn' s idiotom (Life with an Idiot) (1992, Amsterdam), *Gesualdo* (1994, Vienna), *Historia von D. Johann Fausten* (*The Story of Dr. Johann Faust*) (1995, Hamburg); orchestral music, chamber music, film music, ballets.

Schnittke made the use of a wide range of styles an artistic program. It became a means of making music "both old and new at the same time."

Vova's "Ech"

Ever since Schnittke first encountered Victor Yerofeyev's *Life with an Idiot* in a private reading by the author in 1985 he had been fascinated by the story. At that time his dramatization of the Faust legend *The Story of Dr. Johann Faust* had to take priority (begun 1989), but his publisher and friends constantly urged him to set Yerofeyev's story to music. Finally, Yerofeyev was ready to write the libretto himself, and Mstislav Rostropovich negotiated a commission from the Amsterdam Opera and the Eduard van Beinum Foundation. Now under pressure to meet deadlines, Schnittke broke off work on the Faust project, reduced the libretto by a third and wrote the score. While working on the orchestration for Act I, begun in May 1991, he suffered a stroke which three months later was still preventing him from completing the work. In order to keep to the deadline, the composer Wolfgang Nicklaus and Schnittke's son Andrey wrote the piano score. Pulling out all the musical stops, Schnittke succeeded in creating subtle

Life with an Idiot

Zhizn' s idiotom

Opera in two acts (four scenes)

Libretto: Victor Yerofeyev, after his own short story.

Première: 13 April 1992, Amsterdam (Dutch Opera).

Characters: I, a writer (high Bar), Wife (S), Vova, an idiot (T), Warder (B), Young Madman (T), Marcel Proust (Bar); friends, madmen, homosexuals, voices (chorus).

Setting: Russia, at an undefined time.

Synopsis
Act I
Scene 1: The writer is suffering from a lack of sympathy, a fault that is punished by being obliged to take a madman of his choice into his house. The writer has a "holy fool" in mind, and is congratulated by his friends on receiving such a mild penalty.
Scene 2: The writer looks for his holy fool in the mental asylum, where he hears that the red-haired Vova is said to be completely harmless and a perfect simpleton. A small bribe paid to the warder hurries things along, and soon he is able to take Vova home with him. Vova's only speech is his expressive and highly nuanced sigh, "Ech." The writer's wife, meanwhile, is anything but pleased about this new addition to the family.

Act II
Scene 1: At first communication is impossible with Vova; his "Ech" reveals nothing about his personality or his history. But soon the trouble starts. One day Vova opens the refrigerator and throws the contents into the room. Then he turns to the library, tearing up the wife's beloved edition of Proust. But worse is still to come. When the couple attempt to restrain him, he relieves himself on the carpet, smears the walls, and demolishes the furniture and the telephone. Finally he throws the writer out of the bedroom in order to rape the wife. Vova and the wife both seem to be more content as a result.

gradations of rhythm and pitch in Vova's sigh, his famous "Ech." At the climax of the work there is a great outpouring from the orchestra, which is used throughout with great inventiveness. In spite of its absurd character, the work was initially so well received that performances quickly followed in Vienna (1992), Moscow (1993), and Wuppertal (1993).   *M. S*

Scene 2: Realizing that logical argument with Vova is pointless, the writer replaces the edition of Proust and buys the madman some new clothes. Vova repays him with a posy of violets and begins to help with the housework. But this harmonious state of affairs comes to abrupt end when the wife has an abortion: Vova had been looking forward to having a child. He withdraws from the wife and – much to her disappointment – begins a sexual relationship with the writer. The two men neglect and mistreat the wife and move together into their own room. The wife gives Vova an ultimatum: he must choose which of the two he would like to have contact with. The fool's response is to grab the garden shears, decapitate the wife, and run off. The writer's tolerance level has finally been exceeded and he commits himself to Vova's old asylum. The warder greets him as if he were an old friend.

M. S.

"I have succeeded in writing a shocking text"
Schnittke's librettist, Victor Yerofeyev, is considered modern Russia's most prominent writer. Born in Moscow in 1947, as the son of a diplomat he grew up abroad in an artistically favorable climate but soon encountered difficulties in getting his work published in the Soviet Union. He was expelled from the Russian Writers' Union and his work was banned, a measure which hit him hard as he is only able to write in Russian. During the era of perestroika Yerofeyev was rehabilitated. His novel *The Moscow Beauty* of 1980–82 was published in 1990 to international acclaim. It has since been translated into 20 languages. As in *Life with an Idiot* his theme was the previously taboo topic of sexuality in the Soviet Union. Yerofeyev divides his time between Russia and the USA, where he teaches Slavonic and Romance philology.

S. N.

Life with an Idiot, photograph from the original production with Dale Duesing (I), Teresa Ringholz (wife), and Howard Haskin (Vova), production Boris Pokrovsky, sets Ilya Kabakov, conductor Mstislav Rostropovich, Het Muziektheater, De Nederlandse Opera, Amsterdam 1992.
The basic idea of the opera is the dominance of the irrational over the rational. These two aspects are personified by the articulate writer and the monosyllabic Vova, who is able to utter only the sound "Ech." Vova gains in power while the writer ends up in an asylum in a state of mute insanity.

Schoenberg, Arnold

b. 13 September 1874 in Vienna
d. 13 July 1951 in Los Angeles

Schoenberg was born into a lower-middle-class Jewish family, but like many German-speaking Jews at the turn of the century he was more interested in becoming assimilated into the culture of his country than in pursuing the faith of his forebears. In 1898 he became a member of the Lutheran church. At the beginning of the 1920s, however, his Jewish identity once again became important to him. When as a Jew he was forced to abandon his position in Berlin in 1933 and flee to the USA, he stopped briefly in Paris, where he formally acknowledged his Jewish faith. In musical terms he was primarily an autodidact, and it is perhaps for this reason that he became one of the greatest teachers of the twentieth century. His teaching activities began in 1903 at a private school in Vienna, and from 1904 →Alban Berg and Anton von Webern attended his courses in composition. From 1911 to 1915 and again from 1926 to 1933 Schoenberg taught in Berlin. After emigrating to the USA he continued to teach, first in New York and later in Los Angeles. His first works (such as *Verklärte Nacht* for string sextet) are compositions in the late Romantic style. Soon, however, he began to regard the continuing use of traditional harmony as highly questionable. At the beginning of the 1910s he wrote his most important Expressionist pieces. After experimenting with atonal music he began to search for a new method of composition, and found it in the early 1920s in so-called dodecaphony, or the twelve-note technique. From this point on (with the exception of a few less important compositions) he was to compose only using this technique, which was also adopted by his most gifted pupils, such as Berg and Webern.

Works: Operas: *Erwartung* (*Expectation*) (1909/FP 1924), *Die glückliche Hand* (*The Fateful Hand*) (1913/FP 1924), *Von heute auf morgen* (*From One Day to the Next*) (1930), *Moses und Aron* (*Moses and Aaron*) (1932/FP 1954); the string sextet *Verklärte Nacht* (*Transfigured Night*) (1899), *Gurrelieder* for soloists, choir, and large orchestra (1900–11), *Pelléas und Mélisande* (symphonic poem, 1903), the song cycle *Pierrot Lunaire* (1912), the oratorio *Die Jakobsleiter* (*Jacob's Ladder*) (1917–22), the melodrama *Ein Überlebender aus Warschau* (*A Survivor from Warsaw*) (1947), orchestral works, two chamber symphonies, string quartets, choral works, songs, piano pieces.

Erwartung

Expectation

Monodrama in one act

Libretto: Marie Pappenheim.
Première: 6 June 1924, Prague (Neues Deutsches Theater).
Characters: The Woman (S).
Setting: A forest, in the present.

Synopsis

A woman is wandering through a dark forest. She is terrified and has a premonition that something dreadful is going to happen. She has arranged to meet her lover but finds only his body. At the side of his corpse she experiences the full spectrum of her emotions of jealousy and desperation. Broken and helpless she remains alone.   *S. K.*

Above
Erwartung, photograph from the production by R. Hoffmann, Oper Frankfurt 1994.
According to Schoenberg *Erwartung* was an attempt to portray everything that happens in a single second of intense emotional anguish (an eruption of hate and love) "as seen in slow motion, so to speak, and stretched out to last half an hour."

Erwartung, set design by Arnold Schoenberg (date unknown) (Arnold Schoenberg Center, Vienna).
In 1910 there was the prospect of a performance of *Erwartung* at the Hofoper in Vienna, and Schoenberg asked the painter Max Oppenheim to prepare sketches for the set. He suggested Oskar Kokoschka do the same for a production in Mannheim; neither the production nor the designs came to fruition. Schoenberg himself created several set designs for a projected performance in Berlin in 1930.

A musical seismograph

The libretto for *Erwartung*, which Schoenberg set to music in a fit of fevered inspiration in 1909 (it was not to be premièred until 15 years later), came from the pen of a talented young doctor, Marie Pappenheim. Several of her poems also appeared in Carl Kraus's periodical *Die Fackel* (*The Torch*). The music for *Erwartung* is a perfect example of musical expressionism, a kind of tonal X-ray image, which seeks to chart the internal suffering of a soul as accurately as possible. (The philosopher and music theorist Theodor Wiesengrund Adorno spoke of a "seismographic record of traumatic shock.")

Tonality, themes, and basic motifs in the traditional sense of the word give way to sharp dissonances; what analysts refer to as motivic relationships seem here to be little more than chance resemblance. Piercing fortissimos and scarcely audible pianissimos followed one another in rhapsodic succession. In this piece, Schoenberg took the idea of musical prose – that is, a music devoid of repetition or periods – to an extreme.

Schoenberg was a "conservative revolutionary" (Willi Reich), who, deeply rooted in a German-Austrian musical tradition, pushed the development of Classical and Romantic music to its logical conclusion, evolving a method of composition that entailed using twelve interrelated notes.

The way to the twelve-note technique

Schoenberg saw his development of a compositional method based on the use of all twelve notes of a chromatic scale in historical terms. He maintained that European music had developed continuously throughout its history. The Middle Ages had made use of church modes, and these were followed by an epoch of major and minor keys. When these new possibilities began to show signs of exhaustion, the seven-note diatonic scale was extended chromatically, until in →*Tristan and Isolde* Wagner seemed to have reached the limits of what was possible with tonal relationships. The foundations of this music were still provided by the old system of keys, but chromatic notes were given the same priority as diatonic notes, and this tended to obscure the sense of key. It required but one small step and the entire tonal system would dissolve into atonality – the renunciation of any form of tonal organization. In time, Schoenberg evolved a new principle of organization, the twelve-note technique, which involved using all twelve chromatic notes in such a way that none of them was perceived as tonally significant.   *S. K.*

Erwartung, set design by Alfred Siercke for the production by Günther Rennert, Staatsoper, Hamburg 1954 (TWS).
Schoenberg wanted his one-person drama to be seen as a "frightening dream" although the setting was to be a real forest. Although it is the forest itself that she fears, the woman's path was to be marked out with light in order to depict the progress of her visions.

The Fateful Hand

Die glückliche Hand

Drama with music in one act

Libretto: Arnold Schoenberg.
Première: 14 October 1924, Vienna (Volksoper).
Characters: A Man (Bar), A Woman (silent), A Gentleman (silent); six female voices and six male voices (chorus).
Setting: Anywhere, at any time (symbolic plot).

Synopsis

The work begins with the voice of the subconscious (a small, invisible chorus). The man seems at first to be the victim of a mythical creature – his depression – but this monster soon vanishes. The man perceives that he is a genius – he is capable, after all, of spontaneously bringing forth a beautiful diadem. But what his creative powers bestow on him he is denied by life: happiness. His wife leaves him for an "elegantly and fashionably clad gentleman," the symbol of a rich capitalist, a powerful man – and also the devil. Finally the mythical creature appears again and the man asks himself subconsciously: "Did you have to go through what you've so often gone through before? Did you? Can you not deny yourself? Curb yourself once and for all?"

S. K

The Fateful Hand, set design by Walter Gondolf for the production by Erich Bormann, Bühnen der Stadt, Cologne 1954/55 (TWS).
Set design with a "color score." Schoenberg's *The Fateful Hand* was not the only work of that time to focus on the phenomenon of synesthesia (1913). The late Romantic Russian composer Alexander Skryabin and the painter Vassily Kandinsky experimented with interpretations of color and light, both with and without music. In Bartók's opera →*Bluebeard's Castle* (1911) scenes and human characteristics are also symbolized through color.

An autobiographical tale

Schoenberg composed the piece, which has unmistakable autobiographical elements, in 1913. In 1907 his marriage had undergone a serious crisis when his first wife Mathilde (the sister of his friend, the composer →Alexander von Zemlinsky) had an affair with the painter Richard Gerstl and left her husband and children. Schoenberg's friends (especially Anton von Webern) finally persuaded her to return, but Gerstl committed suicide shortly after.

Colors

Colors play an important role in *The Fateful Hand*, both the full spectrum of visible light as well as the tone colors of the huge orchestra. Schoenberg himself fastidiously worked out the stage lighting. Towards the middle of the piece, for example, there is a "light crescendo" which starts with a weak reddish light and develops through dirty green, dark blue-grey, violet, dark red, blood red, and orange up to a peak of bright yellow. According to the directions in the score, the

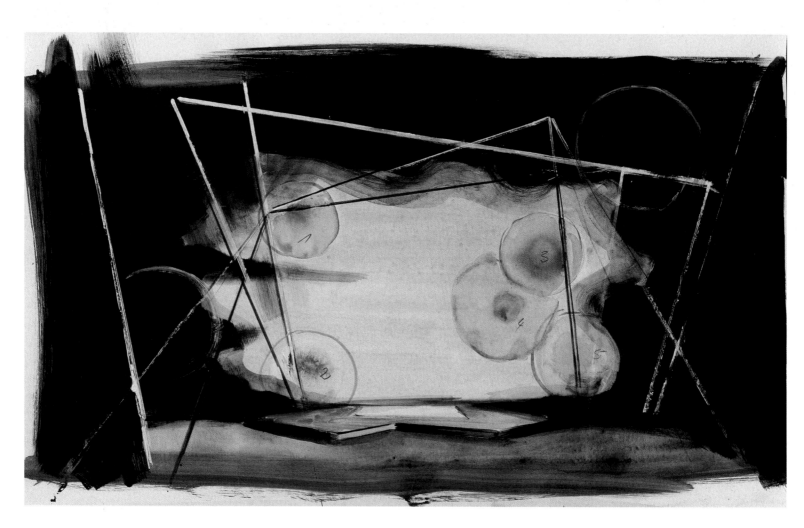

man should act in such a way that this light crescendo (and the accompanying sounds of stormy winds) can be seen to have its origins within him. As might be imagined, the music also has a crescendo at this point.

Schoenberg the painter

Schoenberg used all the tools of artistic expression at his disposal. He was a painter of some talent, although he acquired the skills of the trade at a relatively late stage. His tutor was Richard Gerstl whose studio was in the same building as the apartment of the Schoenberg family: Mathilde Schoenberg often sat for the painter as a model. Some time later, Schoenberg met the Russian painter Vassily Kandinsky, then living in Germany, as well as the artists who belonged to the *Blauer Reiter* (*Blue Rider*) group. Kandinsky was working on a complex theory of color, which he would later teach as a teacher at the Bauhaus. Every color, he maintained, had its own expressive power; yellow, for example, he regarded as the color of activity and energy. Schoenberg seems to have adopted some of these ideas, and this may explain why the eyes of his self-portraits often have a bright yellow shading. The composer created an extensive series of paintings, the core of which is formed by his self-portraits.

Arnold Schoenberg, self-portrait, oil on canvas (date unknown) (Arnold Schoenberg Center, Vienna).
Schoenberg painted a large number of self-portraits in the style of German Expressionism. While he ultimately lacked originality as a painter, his twelve-note technique renewed musical language. But how did this technique function? The composer constructs a series of twelve different notes, known as the note row, which is then used throughout the piece. The row and its derivatives (inversion, retrograde, and retrograde inversion) may also be transposed (that is, it may appear at a different pitch level). This technique was both harshly criticized and praised as a necessary innovation. →M 1

From One Day to the Next

Von heute auf morgen

Opera in one act

Libretto: Max Blonda (Gertrud Kolisch-Schoenberg).
Première: 1 February 1930, Frankfurt (Opernhaus).
Characters: Wife (S), Husband (Bar), Friend (S), Singer (T), Child (spoken).
Setting: A German city, in the present.

Synopsis

After an entertaining evening out, a man and woman return home. The man is unable to get an attractive girlfriend out of his mind and his wife decides to teach him a lesson. She dresses sexily and claims that she is now a "modern" woman, who will no longer put up with the duties expected of a hardworking housewife. In addition she announces that she feels attracted to a singer. The couple argue. By the time the girlfriend and singer really do appear, however, the relationship of the married couple has again stabilized. The man appreciates the advantages of a traditional marriage; he no longer seeks to leave his wife or to live "from one day to the next." The child's question "What does it mean to be modern?" is answered by the falling curtain.   *S. K.*

"The conservative revolutionary"

This was the subtitle given to Willi Reich's Schoenberg monograph of 1968. The inventor of the twelve-note method was without doubt conservative both in his art and in everyday life. As he grew older he became increasingly convinced of the importance of tradition. A year after the death of his first wife he married Gertrud Kolisch, in whom he found an ideal partner who shared his views about morality and tradition. Both regarded "modern" (early twentieth-century) life as immoral and ultimately a threat to society. The similarity of their views is shown by the opera *From One Day to the Next*, for which Gertrud Kolisch-Schoenberg wrote the libretto under the pseudonym Max Blonda. The music is strictly dodecaphonic and demands the utmost concentration and effort from the singers.   *S. K.*

Above
From One Day to the Next, costume design for the wife by Sophia Schroeck for the production by Hans Harleb, Amsterdam 1961 (TWS).
The wife as a modern woman of the demimonde. The central dramatic idea of the work is the metamorphosis of the wife.

From One Day to the Next, production photograph with Else Genter-Fischer (wife), Benno Ziegler (husband), Elisabeth Friedrich (friend), and Anton Maria Topitz (singer), production Herbert Graf, conductor Hans Wilhelm Steinberg, Oper Frankfurt 1930.

Moses and Aaron, poster for a production at the Städtische Oper, Berlin 1960.
Under the musical direction of Hermann Scherchen (production Gustav Rudolf Sellner), Schoenberg's *Moses and Aaron* was staged in Berlin after previous performances in Hamburg and Zürich. This production had a great influence on opera in the 1960s.

Moses and Aaron

Moses und Aron

Opera in three acts (Act III not composed)

Libretto: Arnold Schoenberg.
Première: Concert performance of Acts I and II: 12 March 1954, Hamburg (Musikhalle); stage performance of Acts I and II: 6 June 1957, Zürich (Stadthalle).
Characters: Moses (spoken), Aron/Aaron, his brother (T), A Priest (B), A Young Girl (S), A Sick Woman (A), A Naked Youth (T), An Ephraimite (Bar), A Young Man (Bar), Four Naked Virgins (2 S, 2 A); the voice from the burning bush, naked men, beggars, old men, 70 elders, 12 tribal chieftains, choir (chorus); six solo voices in the orchestra.
Setting: Mount Sinai, c. 1200 BC.

Synopsis
Act I

Scene 1: God reveals himself to Moses as a voice in a burning bush, and challenges him to lead the people of Israel out of captivity in Egypt. God demands that their worship of idols cease and that they acknowledge him as the one true God. Because Moses is able to grasp God's thoughts but not put them into words, Aaron is promised him as an assistant.
Scene 2: Moses and Aaron meet in the desert. Moses wants to proclaim God's Word in its purest form, but Aaron thinks it should be modified to have greater popular appeal.
Scene 3: The news that Moses and Aaron have allied themselves with a "new" God provokes interest as well as hostility among the Israelites.

Scene 4: Moses and Aaron proclaim the message of the one true, invisible, and almighty God. The people respond to Moses' words with skepticism but allow themselves to be persuaded by Aaron.

Act II

Scene 1: Moses remains on the summit of Mount Sinai for 40 days as God reveals His laws. The Israelites are without a leader in the meantime and the first signs of anarchy begin to appear. The 70 elders appeal to Aaron to find a solution for restoring discipline.
Scene 2: The people demand a return to the gods of old and Aaron allows them to set up and worship an image from everyday life – a golden calf.
Scene 3: The golden calf is enthroned; there are dances and bloody rituals.
Scene 4: Moses descends from Mount Sinai with the stone tablets inscribed with God's laws. His divine word destroys the idol.
Scene 5: Moses holds Aaron responsible, but Aaron defends himself. If images are wrong, he says, then so are the tablets, which are nothing more than images of thoughts. At that, Moses destroys the tablets. As the Israelites march behind a pillar of smoke that has changed into a pillar of fire, he remarks with great resignation: "O Wort, du Wort, das mir fehlt" ("O word, word that I lack").

(In Act III, which Schoenberg did not set to music, the conflict between Moses and Aaron continues. Aaron is condemned to death for his offense against the spirit of God's word. But Moses gives him back his freedom, saying, "If you can, you may live." When Aaron steps out of his bonds, he falls down dead.)   s. k.

The complete torso

Schoenberg had initially wanted to write an oratorio, keeping as close to the biblical text as possible. He was prevented from doing so, he thought, by Luther's archaic translation and the contradictions in the Bible concerning the role of Aaron. He therefore decided to adopt a freer approach to the biblical text. The music for Acts I and II was written between May 1930 and March 1932 (before he emigrated to the USA). For Act III, Schoenberg wrote the libretto and sketched several musical scenes in 1937 but did not manage to complete it. When Moses collapses at the end of Act II all the essential elements of the story have been told. Although the work was not finished, it gives the impression of being a closed and completed whole.

Moses and Aaron, photograph from the production by Harry Kupfer, conductor Siegfried Kurz, sets Reinhart Zimmermann, costumes Hartmut Henning, Staatsoper, Dresden 1975.
Harry Kupfer's 1975 production was an outstanding event. Particularly interesting was his conceptual approach: he saw the old biblical story of the ban on images in terms of a contemporary struggle for power.

Moses and Aaron, set design by Paul Haferung for the stage première, production Karl Heinz Krahl, conductor Hans Rosbaud, Stadttheater, Zürich 1957 (TWS).
This production was part of the World Music Festival of the International Society for New Music. It required 50 rehearsals for the orchestra and 350 for the chorus. Although Schoenberg vehemently denied identifying with Moses, he did not deny that the figure bore a certain resemblance to himself. In the conflict between Moses and Aaron, Schoenberg was clearly on Moses' side.

God and the people

The treatment of the chorus in *Moses and Aaron* is quite remarkable. Both God and the Israelites are presented using similar musical means – the peculiar sound of a half-singing, half-speaking chorus. The chosen people are thus – in Schoenberg's view – a mirror image God. In spite of all their misdeeds, they carry the germ of God's perfection within them, while Moses and Aaron are imperfect, because they depend on each other. Moses, the inarticulate man of thought (according to the Bible he even stuttered), expresses himself almost exclusively in speech-song, while the role of Aaron is written in bel canto style.

Alpha and omega

The music of *Moses and Aaron* is pure dodecaphony, in which everything is grounded in a single twelve-note row. The first two chords (the symbol of God) M 2 are formed from the beginning and end of the row, as the "alpha" and "omega." M 1

A dodecaphonic ballet

Schoenberg's polyphony is always brilliant and highly complex. The voices of the chorus are generally rendered as a double inverted canon. The dance around the golden calf became particularly famous. Schoenberg, who otherwise detested the ballet form, attempted with this piece to write an attractive number without abandoning the fundamental principles of dodecaphony.

God on the telephone

The extraordinary idea (perhaps influenced by the fashionable *Zeitoper*, →Krenek) of having God speak over a telephone was proposed by Schoenberg as a solution to a particular problem. God is invisible, which meant that the chorus had to be concealed, with their voices projecting from off stage. Schoenberg feared that they would not be loud enough, and because electronic amplification was still unusual at the time, he proposed installing six telephones on stage, which would then convey the voice of God. This idea was never realized, and was quickly forgotten by the composer himself. S. K.

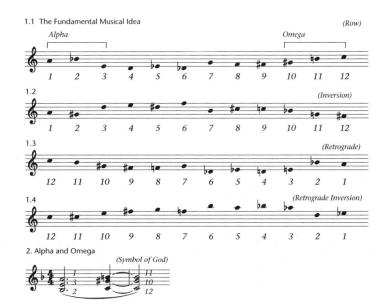

1.1 The Fundamental Musical Idea

2. Alpha and Omega

Schreker, Franz

b. 23 March 1878 in Monaco
d. 21 March 1934 in Berlin

Schreker studied composition in Vienna with Robert Fuchs and Hermann Graedener, and violin under Sigismund Bachrich and Josef Rosé. He was the founder (1908) and later director (1911) of the Vienna Philharmonic Choir, and in 1912 was appointed to a teaching post at the Vienna Music Academy. From 1920 he was the director of the Conservatory in Berlin and in 1932–33 he was given directorship of a course in composition at the Prussian Academy of Arts in Berlin. Schreker was friendly with both →Berg and →Schoenberg, and his pupils included Alois Hába and →Ernst Krenek. He was one of the most popular opera composers of his day, the number of performances of his operas outnumbering even those of →Richard Strauss. In 1933 he was relieved of all his offices by the Nazis.

Works: Operas: *Flammen* (*Flames*) (1902/FP 1985), *Der ferne Klang* (*The Distant Sound*) (1912), *Das Spielwerk und die Prinzessin* (*The Toy and the Princess*) (1913), *Die Gezeichneten* (*The Branded*) (1918), *Der Schatzgräber* (*The Treasure Hunter*) (1920), *Irrelohe* (1924), *Der singende Teufel* (*The Singing Devil*) (1928), *Christophorus* (1929/FP 1978), *Der Schmied von Gent* (*The Smith of Ghent*) (1932); ballets, including *Der Geburtstag der Infantin* (*The Birthday of the Infanta*) (1908), orchestral works, vocal music.

The Distant Sound
Der ferne Klang

Opera in three acts

Libretto: Franz Schreker.

Première: 18 August 1912, Frankfurt (Oper).

Characters: Graumann, a retired minor official (B), His Wife (Ms), Grete, their daughter, also "Greta", a dancer, in Act II, and "Tini" in Act III (S), Fritz, a young artist (T), The Innkeeper at "The Swan" (B), A Strolling Player (Bar), Dr. Vigelius, a shady lawyer (high B), An Old Woman (Ms or high A), a Girl (Ms), Mizi, Milly, Mary, and A Spanish Girl, dancers (S, Ms, S, A), The Count, aged 24, The Baron, aged 50, The Chevalier, aged 30–35, bon viveurs (Bar, B, T), Rudolf, Fritz's close friend and a doctor (high B or Bar), The Actor (Bar), Two Chorus Members (T, B), The Waitress (Ms), An Unsavory Character (T), A Policeman (B), A Servant (spoken); guests, staff of "The Swan," girls, dancers of all nationalities, theater personnel, members of the audience (some masked), serving girls, cab attendants (chorus, ballet).

Setting: A small town, Venice, and a big city, at the beginning of the 20th century.

Synopsis
Act I
Grete and Fritz, a composer, are in love, but Fritz feels drawn to the wider world by the lure of a distant sound, and he takes his leave from his lover. As a joke Dr. Vigelius has advised Grete's drunken father to pawn his daughter to the innkeeper at "The Swan." Grete's father now demands that she marry the innkeeper and no amount of pleading on her part will induce him to change his mind. A mysterious old woman is the only one to show Grete any sympathy. The unhappy girl flees her parents'

*S*chreker was the most popular exponent of a kind of opera that was profoundly influenced by psychoanalysis. He was a master of the expressive use of tonal color, and his work often features symbolically loaded themes exposing the pathos of sexual conflict.

The Distant Sound, production photograph with Catherine Malfitano (Grete) and Thomas Moser (Fritz), production Jürgen Flimm, sets Rolf Glittenberg, conductor Gerd Albrecht, Wiener Staatsoper 1991.
Schreker having once studied in Vienna, the city owed him a revival of his work. Hans Gregor, the director of the court opera, had once rejected *The Distant Sound* on account of what he claimed was an "impossible" libretto. One of the main reasons for the success of the opera when it was revived in 1991 was that Grete and Fritz made such an outstanding dramatic pair on stage. Every production of *The Distant Sound* faces the same problem: how to give the passion inherent in the music tangible form, as seen here in the encounter between Grete and Fritz.

house. When Grete realizes that she will no longer be able to find Fritz, she decides to drown herself in a lake in the forest. But when she perceives the magic of nature she changes her mind, and eventually falls asleep in the forest. The old woman arrives and takes Grete away with her.

Act II

A dance hall in Venice, ten years later. Grete, now "Greta," has become a much sought-after dancer, but is tormented by memories of Fritz. The count and the chevalier compete for her favor. While Grete is considering which of the contenders pleases her most, a boat appears on the sea. Fritz is on board in a miserable state. He has pursued his "distant sound" without ever capturing it; now the sound has brought him to this dance hall. From now on, he says, he wants to remain with Grete. Grete is overjoyed. But when Fritz discovers he is in a brothel, he rejects her and leaves. Grete flees again, this time with the count.

Act III

The garden of a tavern by a theater in a large city, five years later. Dr. Vigelius is reproaching himself for having played the joke on Grete's father that led to her being driven from her home. A new work by Fritz, "The Harp," is being performed at the theater. Grete, who is now making her living as a prostitute, has seen the play and is deeply moved by the music. When, contrary to expectations, the third act fails, Grete wants to offer Fritz her support, and asks Dr. Vigelius to take her to him. Fritz is now gravely ill and living in a secluded spot. He has not heard his "distant sound" for a long time, but when Grete enters it seems to be close by again. Overjoyed, he falls into her arms and dies.

S. N.

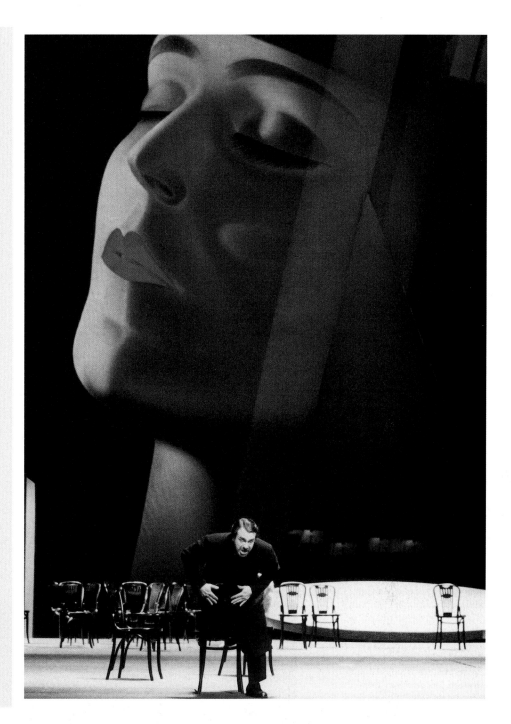

The history of a scandalous success

Around 1900 Schreker was already considering writing an opera in which, in his own words, "the basic concept would not merely require music, but rather is itself music." His only support in elaborating this idea came from the poet Ferdinand Saar. Other friends, including his teacher Robert Fuchs, were not encouraging, considering his ideas too unusual. Schreker did not complete the instrumentation for his first large-scale work for the stage until 1910. The phenomenal success of the première established his reputation as an opera composer, and the work was performed on all the major stages until it was banned by the Nazis. In spite of Schreker's usually Romantic approach to music, this opera is profoundly anti-Romantic. It is not the fate of the artist that is the focus of the work but rather the

misery of those who are left behind. The message of the opera is that the fulfillment of personal happiness and artistic perfection do not lie in some hazy future, but are always at hand in the mundane present. M 1   M. S.

1. The Distant Sound

The Distant Sound, production photograph with Thomas Moser as Fritz, production Jürgen Flimm, sets Rolf Glittenberg, conductor Gerd Albrecht, Wiener Staatsoper 1991.
Dreams, and indeed the world of the subconscious in general, played an important role in the work of Viennese artists at the turn of the century. Schreker's attention focused in particular on what he saw as the (shattered) bridge between dream and reality. Fritz strands himself on the shores of the dream world, his Utopia of perfect art, which, like a siren, lures him to his death.

The Branded, Karl Erb in the role of Alviano Salvago, c. 1918.
The outstanding German tenor Karl Erb (1877–1957) sang the part of Alviano Salvago at the première. The previous year he had taken the title role in the first production of Pfitzner's →*Palestrina*. Erb was a master of the vocal arts, a celebrated singer of Mozart and a highly expressive Evangelist in Bach's Passions.

Style and reception

The music of Franz Schreker's *The Branded* is indebted to Expressionism. It concentrates on a subtle depiction of psychological processes and uses symphonic formal methods to achieve a rigorous and cogent structure. The events of World War I temporarily put a stop to the success of *The Branded* after the warm reception of the première in 1918. By the 1920s, however, the work was once again being performed to great public acclaim. The work was then prohibited by the Nazis, and the post-war generation quickly forgot this formerly celebrated composer. The first uncertain signs of a revival of Schreker's work began to appear in the early 1970s.

The Branded, photograph from the production by Günter Krämer, sets Xenia Hausner, conductor Hans Wallat, Deutsche Oper am Rhein, Düsseldorf 1987.
The key scene of the opera takes place in Carlotta's studio. Her artistic aim of capturing the nobility of an ugly person's soul in paint is misinterpreted by Alviano. A duet develops between tenor and soprano that would ordinarily express mutual love, but in *The Branded* the part of the lover is reserved for the baritone role of Tamare.

The Branded

Die Gezeichneten

Opera in three acts

Libretto: Franz Schreker.

Première: 25 April 1918, Frankfurt (Oper).

Characters: Duke Antoniotto Adorno (high B), Count Andrea Vitellozzo Tamare (Bar), Lovodico Nardi, *podestà* of the city of Genoa (B), His Wife (silent), Carlotta Nardi, his daughter (S), Alviano Salvago, Guidobald Usodimare, Menaldo Negroni, Michelotto Cibo, Gonsalvo Fieschi, Julian Pinelli, and Paolo Calvi, Genoese nobles (3 T, 3 Bar, B), A Maid (Ms), The Chief of Police (B), Ginevra Scotti (S), Martuccia, housekeeper to Salvago (A), Pietro, an assassin (T), A Youth (T), His Friend (B), A Girl (S), Six Senators (2 T, 2 Bar, 2 B), Three Citizens (T, Bar, B), Father (B), Mother (A), Child (S), Three Young People (T, Bar, B), A Huge Man (B), Eight Mummers (silent); people of Genoa, nobles, citizens, soldiers, servants, women, girls, children, fauns, naiads, bacchantes (chorus, ballet, extras).

Setting: Genoa, in the 16th century.

Synopsis
Act I

Alviano has drawn the logical conclusion from his ugliness and avoids the company of women. He has a kind soul, and intends to give his island of Elysium to the people of Genoa. But his noble friends, who without his knowledge have been using the island for their orgies, protest to the duke. One of them, Tamare, has fallen in love with Carlotta, the daughter of the *podestà*. She rejects him, however, because she is drawn to Alviano: she wants to paint his soul.

Act II

Tamare is offended by Carlotta's rebuff and swears to abduct her and turn her into a whore. The duke hears of events on the island, but wants to avoid conflicts and so turns a blind eye. Before she can paint Alviano's soul, Carlotta has to entice it out of him, which she succeeds in doing with her feminine charms. Alviano mistakenly believes that Carlotta is in love with him.

Act III

The astonished Genoese take possession of Alviano's island. Alviano asks the *podestà* for Carlotta's hand, but she rejects him, and falls under the spell of Tamare to whom she gives herself willingly. In the meantime, the duke has started a rumor that Alviano is a seducer and molester of young girls. The outraged crowd forces its way into a secret grotto where Carlotta lies dying. Tamare boasts of his powers of seduction and is stabbed by Alviano. Roused by Tamare's death cries, Carlotta calls for her "loved one" – meaning Tamare – and then dies. Alviano sinks into insanity.   S. N.

The Branded, photograph from the production by Günter Krämer, sets Xenia Hausner, conductor Hans Wallat, Deutsche Oper am Rhein, Düsseldorf 1987. The branded are those who pine for beauty. Beauty – this time in the form of a woman – has a similar function in Schreker's world, as the "distant sound."

The Branded, photograph from the production by Günter Krämer, sets Xenia Hausner, conductor Hans Wallat, Deutsche Oper am Rhein, Düsseldorf 1987. Schreker was fascinated by ugly characters even before he began work on *The Branded*. In 1908 he composed the ballet *Der Geburtstag der Infantin* (*The Birthday of the Infanta*, after the tale by Oscar Wilde), whose suffering hero is a hunchbacked dwarf. Zemlinsky wrote the one-act opera *The Dwarf* using the same material.

The fascination of the hideous

The idea of an ugly but noble man who becomes a murderer through being unhappy in love came from →Alexander von Zemlinsky. He had once been called ugly by his lover, the young Alma Schindler, before she left him for the composer Gustav Mahler. "He was a repulsive gnome. Short, chinless, and toothless, unwashed, and always smelling of the coffee house … and yet endlessly fascinating because of his intellectual acuity and strength," Alma Mahler-Werfel later confessed in her memoirs. After Schreker had completed the libretto of *The Branded* for Zemlinsky he reclaimed the material for himself for a composition that he began in 1911 and completed in 1915.   *M. S.*

The Treasure Hunter

Der Schatzgräber

Opera in a prologue, four acts, and an epilogue

Libretto: Franz Schreker.
Première: 21 January 1920, Frankfurt (Oper).
Characters: The King (high B), The Queen (silent), The Chancellor (T), The Count, also A Herald (Bar), The Master, the king's physician (B), The Fool (T), The Steward (Bar), The Young Nobleman (Bar or high B), Elis, an itinerant singer and scholar (T), The Mayor (B), The Scribe (T), The Innkeeper (B), Els, his daughter (S), Albi, their servant (lyric T), A Mercenary (deep B), Three Townspeople (T, Bar, B), Two Old Spinsters (2 Ms, or 2 A), A Woman (A or Ms), Hangman (silent), Beadle (silent); dukes, counts, knights, nobles and their ladies, mercenaries, monks (chorus, extras).
Setting: A German kingdom, in the Middle Ages.

Synopsis
Prologue

The queen's jewelry has been stolen, and as a result she has lost her beauty and fertility. The fool advises her to enlist the help of Elis, the singer, who is able to find treasure with his magic lute. If Elis finds the jewels, the fool will be granted any woman he chooses.

Act I

On her father's wishes, the innkeeper's daughter Els is to marry a young nobleman, whom she despises. She asks him to procure for her a precious necklace, and then orders the servant Albi to murder him, just as he has murdered her two former suitors. She will then be in possession of the queen's entire collection of jewels, which she has obtained through her suitors. Elis appears at the wedding, having found a necklace in the forest, which he gives to the bride. Elis and Els fall in love. But Albi, who is himself in love with Els, pretends to have found the nobleman's body in the forest, and Elis is accused of murder.

Act II

Elis is awaiting execution. Els begs the fool to help him, and the fool arranges a royal pardon for Elis so that he may recover the queen's jewels. Afraid that Elis will discover that she has the jewels, Els orders Albi to steal Elis's magic lute.

Act III

Els and Elis lie in each other's arms: Els gives the royal jewelry to Elis, on condition that he never ask where she obtained it, and that he always trust her.

Act IV

Elis returns the jewelry to the queen. Albi is arrested, however, and confesses, revealing Els to be an accessory to the murder. The fool reminds the queen of her promise, and so Els is saved from dying at the stake by marrying the fool. Elis abandons Els.

Epilogue

A year later. Els is dying. The fools fetches Elis who sings her one of his most beautiful ballads. She is now able to imagine that everything that has happened has been nothing more than a bad dream, and dies peacefully in Elis's arms.   S. N.

The Treasure Hunter, production photograph with Harald Stamm, Franziska Ponitz, Josef Protschka, and Gabriele Schnaut, production Günter Krämer, conductor Gerd Albrecht, Staatsoper, Hamburg 1989.
This production restored *The Treasure Hunter* to the stage after a long absence.

Else, Elis, Els …

Schreker began work on his ballad-like libretto after a holiday experience in 1915, in which he heard a peasant girl called Else singing old songs to the accompaniment of a lute. In *The Treasure Hunter*, Else became two people: the itinerant singer Elis, who can still sing a beautiful song even in the face of death *M2*, and his beloved Els, the demonic daughter of the tavern owner. Schreker was beset with doubts while working on the opera, and turned to the music critic Paul Bekker for advice. The opera was finally completed in 1918. Schreker developed a unique approach to musical dramaturgy in

The Treasure Hunter – the use of musical "objets trouvés" as acoustic metaphors. These include imitations of old folk songs, lute songs, modal phrases, and quotations, especially the use of the "*Tristan* chord" to signal that redemption is yet to be achieved. *The Treasure Hunter* was to become Schreker's most successful opera, and the last to find wide popularity: there were 44 productions between 1920 and 1925. But censorship under the Nazis and the transition from the overheated emotions of Expressionism to a cooler and more objective style had far-reaching consequences for Schreker's work.   *M. S.*

The Treasure Hunter, set design by Ernst Rufer for the production by Helmuth Götze, Landestheater, Oldenburg 1931 (TWS). The king and the fool. A number of motifs from Schreker's earlier work resurface in this opera: the loving fool, the ideal world of art (alluded to in the four magnificent ballads by the singer Elis), and the leitmotiv of an intoxicated yearning for beauty. During Schreker's own lifetime, *The Treasure Hunter* was his most popular opera.

2. Elis's Final Song

Dort zieh'n wir hin ___ mor-gen zei-tig früh.   *Und wan-dern in   Frie - den   und oh - ne   Hast*

Alfonso and Estrella

Alfonso und Estrella

Synopsis

Mauregato (T) has usurped the throne of King Froila (Bar). Froila lives now in seclusion, studying the forces of nature and acting as adviser to the country people. But his son Alfonso (T) is restless, and drawn by the thought of distant lands. His father gives him the sacred Chain of Eurich, for protection. Meanwhile, Mauregato is encountering a number of difficulties. After a victory over his enemies he had promised his general Adolfo (B) that he would fulfill his every wish. Adolfo now demands the hand of Mauregato's daughter Estrella (S), but she rejects him. Mauregato seeks a way out by referring to an old saying, according to which Estrella may only marry the man who wears the sacred Chain of Eurich. Angered by this refusal Adolfo goes to war against Mauregato. In a remote part of the kingdom, Alfonso meets the fleeing Estrella. They fall in love, and Alfonso gives her the chain he wears. Alfonso defeats Adolfo, and when the royal fathers meet, Froila forgives his old enemy. Mauregato then decides to give up the throne for the sake of both their children.   S. N.

Schubert is the most important exponent of the lied. His operas show him to be a composer of imaginative settings and a creator of subtle inner landscapes.

Schubert, Franz

b. 31 January 1797 in Lichtental (formerly a suburb of Vienna)
d. 19 November 1828 in Vienna

Schubert received musical tuition from an early age, first from his father and then from choir director Michael Holzer. At a choristers' school attached to the imperial court chapel in Vienna he studied with Wenzel Ruzicka, and later privately with Antonio Salieri. His first extant composition dates from 1810 (a four-hand piano fantasy), and his first song, "*Hagars Klage*" ("Hagar's Lament"), was written in 1811. Schubert was given a position as assistant master in his father's school in 1814, but this created difficulties, as a normal working life did not match the demands of an existence entirely shaped by music. Study of Schubert's life makes it clear that he was constantly composing: in the year 1815 alone he wrote 145 songs, including the "*Erlkönig*." He hardly ever moved outside Vienna; only twice (1818 and 1824) did he go to Hungary (Zseliz) as music teacher to the aristocratic Esterházy family. Several of his works were published in his lifetime and he witnessed the unsuccessful premières of two of his stage works, but only a single concert of his music took place before his death – in 1828, the year he died. This outstanding composer was almost totally unknown to his contemporaries, a kind of obscurity that is unparalleled in the history of music. It was only after his death that his work was given the respect it deserved, thanks to prominent musicians such as →Robert Schumann and Franz Liszt.

Works: Stage works (selection): *Des Teufels Lustschloss* (*The Devil's Pleasure Palace*) (c. 1813–15/FP 1949), *Der vierjährige Posten* (*The Four Year Posting*) (1815/FP 1896), *Fernando* (1815), *Die Freunde von Salamanka* (*The Friends from Salamanka*) (1815/FP 1928), *Die Zauberharfe* (*The Magic Harp*) (1820), *Alfonso und Estrella* (1822/FP 1854), *Die Verschworenen* (*The Conspirators*) (1823/FP 1861), *Fierrabras* (1823/FP 1897); over 600 lieder (songs), including the cycles *Die schöne Müllerin* (*The Pretty Miller*) (1823) and *Die Winterreise* (*The Winter's Journey*) (1827), nine symphonies, chamber music, piano works, sacred and secular choral works.

Alfonso and Estrella, production photograph with Olaf Bär (Mauregato) and Thomas Hampson (Froila), production Jürgen Flimm, conductor Nikolaus Harnoncourt, Opernhaus Zürich, Vienna Festival 1997.
Two feuding kings encounter each other on the battlefield: Mauregato, the king of Leon, and Froila, the exiled king of Leon.

Schubert, the opera composer?

As Schubert's achievements in all areas of music were outstanding, it is interesting to ask what his operatic concepts were, given that in spite of his best attempts he failed to meet the expectations of the operatic audiences of his day. Schubert's musico-dramatic ideals were achieved in his two song cycles *Die schöne Müllerin* and *Die Winterreise*, as well as in the operas *Alfonso and Estrella* and *Fierrabras*. His talents as an opera composer were not discovered until the end of the 20th century, though an inventory of his work clearly shows that opera was important to him. He completed ten stage works, most of which were *Singspiele* (German operas with spoken dialogue), but he also composed a romantic opera, *Fierrabras*. None of these were ever performed during Schubert's lifetime. It was Franz Liszt who first drew the public's attention to Schubert's operas with the première of *Alfonso and Estrella* on 24 June 1854 – 26 years after the composer's death.

1.1 Ballad of King Froila

Er folg - te ih - rer Stim - me Ru - fen und stieg ___ den rau - hen Pfad hin - an

1.2 Cycle *Winter's Journey* (Deception)

Ein Licht ___ tanzt freund - lich vor _ mir her, ___ ich folg ___ ihm nach die Kreuz und Quer

Fierrabras, production photograph with László Polgár as Boland, Prince of the Moors, production Ruth Berghaus, conductor Claudio Abbado, Vienna Festival 1988. Schubert used every operatic element currently in use for *Fierrabras*, from the well-crafted ensemble to the simple strophic song. Both music and text seek to make the invisible visible. Elementary desires, hopes, and fears well up within the characters, and the music builds around these emotions to establish fixed points, to create sudden rifts, or even to allow an unexpected weakness to emerge.

Deception and disappointment

It is generally thought that Franz von Schober's libretto is the weak point of *Alfonso and Estrella*. The events of the story as perceived by an audience are essentially only a vehicle for setting emotional states to music, and it is this that makes the work both beautiful and challenging. If the opera is to be fairly judged it should be seen as a parable about how to achieve a life of love that is neither distorted by passions nor consumed by desires. Schubert avoided conventional operatic plots; he was less interested in raging passions than in the gentler feelings of desire, deception, and disappointment. The exiled king Froila, for example, sings a ballad (Act II) that tells the story of a "cloud girl" (a type of siren), who bewitches a youth and lures him into a gorge, only to disappear into a blue haze. This piece is a musical jewel – and a delightful surprise for connoisseurs of Schubert, as it anticipates the song "Täuschung" ("Deception") from the song cycle *Die Winterreise*. The all too human sequence of deception and disappointment inspired Schubert to write the most original and beautiful piece of the opera. *M 1*   *S. N.*

Fierrabras

Synopsis

King Karl (B) sets out to "pacify" the Moors with fire and sword. His daughter Emma (S) is in love with the poor knight Eginhard (T), who hopes to win Karl's trust, and therefore Emma's hand, through bravery. A Moor captured by Karl, Fierrabras (T), also loves Emma. His sister Florinda (S) loves Roland (Bar), one of Karl's knights. Karl sends Roland as an envoy to the Moors to offer them peace by converting to Christianity – or war. The Frankish knights are defeated by Boland, a Moorish prince (B), and are condemned to death. In vain Florinda pleads with her father for mercy. Eginhard, however, manages to free the captives and it is now Boland who is marked for death. At the last minute Fierrabras, the prince's son, appears: he has converted to Christianity. By using both weapons and words he is able to establish peace. Roland is united with Florinda – the Christian with the Moor – and Eginhard with Emma. Fierrabras renounces his claim to Emma.   *S. N.*

Heroic-romantic opera

Schubert described *Fierrabras* as a heroic-romantic opera. The attitude of the young characters is heroic in a very particular sense: unlike their fathers, they do not confront real enemies but rather their inner passions, and these they eventually overcome, as seen in the figure of Fierrabras. But the work is also romantic in that it longs for a reconciliation of the children with their fathers. Josef Kupelwieser's allegedly poor libretto has been held responsible for the fact that the work was never performed, but it is more likely that it was due to the unconventional mood of the opera and its insistence on the renunciation of traditional heroic behavior.

Genoveva

Opera in four acts

Libretto: Robert Schumann and Robert Reinick, after Johann Ludwig Tieck and Christian Friedrich Hebbel.
Première: 25 June 1850, Leipzig (Stadttheater).
Characters: Hidulfus, Bishop of Trier (Bar), Siegfried, Count Palatine (Bar), Genoveva, his wife (S), Golo, a knight (T), Margaretha, a nurse (S), Drago, a steward (B), Balthasar and Caspar, servants in Siegfried's castle (B, Bar), Angelo (silent), Conrad, Siegfried's squire (silent); knights, clergy, squires, maidens, servants, people, apparitions (chorus, extras).
Setting: Strasbourg, AD 730.

Synopsis
Act I

The count palatine, Siegfried, goes to aid Charlemagne in his battle against the Moors, and entrusts his wife to the care of his knight Golo; the servants are placed under the loyal Drago. Golo loves Genoveva and struggles to master his feelings. The nurse Margaretha, who hates Siegfried, encourages Golo to give vent to his passions.

Act II

Golo attempts to court Genoveva, but she rejects and insults him. He then puts about a rumor that Genoveva is deceiving her husband. The outraged servants demand that their mistress be brought to account; they search her rooms and find the innocent Drago, whom they murder on suspicion of being Genoveva's lover. Genoveva is placed under arrest.

Act III

The count lies wounded in Strasbourg. Margaretha makes her way to him quickly. Siegfried soon recovers and Margaretha shows him Genoveva's alleged unfaithfulness in a magic mirror. Enraged, he shatters the mirror and storms off. The ghost of the dead Drago rises up from the shards and warns Margaretha that she should put an end to her malice if she does not wish to end at the stake.

Act IV

The servants lead Genoveva into a rocky and mountainous region. Once again Golo tries to ignite the flame of love in her, but she remains steadfast. Golo produces Siegfried's sword and ring as proof of their master's authority and orders the servants to kill Genoveva, but they cannot bring themselves to murder their mistress. Suddenly, the sound of horns rends the air and the servants flee. Margaretha has confessed the truth to Siegfried and together they have sought out Genoveva in the wilderness. Genoveva is unconditionally prepared to start a new life with Siegfried. The bishop of Trier renews his blessing of their union while the people praise God as the fount of all joy and bringer of mercy. *S. N.*

Schumann, Robert

b. 8 June 1810 in Zwickau
d. 29 July 1856 in Endenich

The son of the owner of a bookshop, Schumann came into contact with literature at an early age. His father died young and his family insisted that he study law, which he did, attending universities in Leipzig and Heidelberg. Yet he soon began to pursue his passion for music, taking piano lessons with the renowned Friedrich Wieck. In 1840 he married Wieck's daughter Clara, a prominent pianist, against her father's wishes. A co-founder of the *Neue Zeitschrift für Musik* (*New Music Journal*) he made a name for himself as a brilliant music critic. In 1843 he accepted a professorship at the Leipzig Conservatory directed by Mendelssohn, and between 1844 and 1850 he worked in Dresden, amongst other things founding the Schumann's Academy of Song. A position as municipal director of music in Düsseldorf, taken up in 1850, had to be abandoned in 1853, owing to his deteriorating mental health. After a suicide attempt he spent the last years of his life in a private asylum in Endenich.

Works: Stage works: *Genoveva* (1850), *Manfred* (incidental music, 1848–49); piano music, songs, symphonies, concertos, chamber music, choral works.

Genoveva, program for a performance of the opera on 29 January 1882 in Dresden (collection of the Robert Schumann House, Zwickau).
There were staged performances of *Genoveva* in the 19th century, though they were rare. Later, because the opera closely resembles an oratorio, it became more usual to give concert performances.

Genoveva, photograph from the production by Katja Czellnik, sets and costumes Heike Scheele, conductor Geoffrey Moull, Stadttheater, Bielefeld 1995/96.
A legend, *Genoveva* tells of the profound spiritual conflicts which underlie everyday life. To stage this requires imagination and a sense of the poetic.

A "German opera"

Schumann's search for a subject capable of meeting his high expectations proved time-consuming and complicated. He scoured the work of writers such as Goethe, Mörike, and Hoffmann, and considered virtually all the themes on which Wagner's operas were later based, before settling on the story of Genoveva. He took the structure of the story and its motifs from Hebbel, while from Tieck he adopted the concept of divine redemption. In his papers, Schumann recorded 1 April 1847 as the day on which he decided what direction the opera was going to take and sketched out the overture. Robert Reinick, a friend of Schumann, wrote the libretto, but the two soon argued and Schumann completed the text himself. In spite of these complications, the opera was written quickly and spontaneously. The première in Leipzig was postponed twice, in favor of Verdi's →Ernani and Meyerbeer's →The Prophet. Although it was a great success, there were only two further performances, and this was a pattern that was to continue for Schumann. Both the musical and poetic qualities of the work are undisputed, but the German theater was and still is unreceptive to Genoveva's peculiar form of introspection. In an attempt to create a "German opera" Schumann abandoned theatrical effects, focusing instead on conveying a strong sense of inner drama. He also used subtly differentiated musical structures in a work dominated by the song form, and in which the orchestra served as both narrative and commentary. Efforts have been made to incorporate this opera into the international repertory, the most successful attempt this century being Gustaf Gründgens' production for the Maggio Musicale in Florence in 1951, under the musical direction of André Cluytens.   M. S.

Genoveva, photograph from the production by Katja Czellnik, sets and costumes Heike Scheele, conductor Geoffrey Moull, Stadttheater, Bielefeld 1995/96.
The mixture of history, chivalry, and Romance with the prosaic and everyday was brought out clearly in the Bielefeld production of *Genoveva*.

Genoveva, excerpt from the *Illustrierte Zeitung* (Leipzig, 13 July 1850) on the occasion of the première ("Schumann's collected newspaper reviews," collection of the Robert Schumann House, Zwickau).
Schumann was himself a newspaper publisher and critic for a time (*Neue Zeitschrift für Musik*, 1834–44). His many expert articles provided readers with information about significant events in the new music of the day.

*S*chumann's poetic style is also evident in his only opera, which he saw as a deliberate attempt to create a "German opera," free of Italian or French influences.

A nose for modern ears

The Nose is a pearl of the Soviet-Russian avant-garde from the 1920s (it was composed between the fall of 1927 and summer 1928). Inspired by Meyerhold's theatrical work, Shostakovich tackled a theme that had much in common with the ideas of the Russian formalist school. The successful première in 1930 was given a great deal of publicity and was followed by 16 further performances. The structure of the work is unique: the gallop, the polka, and the waltz are placed alongside the symphonically conceived interlude; the bawling of the servants is a counterpart to the melodious sentimentality of a high ranking gentleman; and prosaic dialogue is set against a background of sacred music (as in the conversation between the nose and its former owner in the cathedral). The fugue of the percussion section was regarded at the time of its composition as a groundbreaking musical feat. *M 1* Shostakovich alternates highly expressive atonal episodes with others that are playful, neo-Classical or folk inspired, and grotesque elements with masques in a scherzo style. The lyrics may often be prosaic, but are heightened and made to appear strange by unlikely orchestration and unusual rhythms. *The Nose* is a modern opera, and an artwork that exists on a number of levels.

The Nose, costume designs by Ruodi Barth for the scene in the advertising department, including (from left to right) a servant, a gardener, and the chorus of newspaper readers, production Bohumil Herlischka, Staatstheater am Gärtnerplatz, Munich 1971. This scene was destined to become famous: in an eight-voice chorus – a strict double canon with invertible parts – eight different sets of lyrics are sung simultaneously. It is a brilliant piece of organized musical chaos.

Shostakovich, Dmitry Dmitriyevich

b. 25 September 1906 in St. Petersburg
d. 9 August 1975 in Moscow

A child prodigy, Shostakovich graduated early from the St. Petersburg Conservatory in piano, theory, and composition. He became internationally famous with his first symphony (1924–25) and also won great acclaim as a pianist (Chopin Competition, Warsaw 1927). From 1927 he was musical adviser at the Meyerhold Theater in Leningrad, and during the years of Soviet-Russian experimentation in the arts he wrote the operas *The Nose* (1929) and *Lady Macbeth of the Mtsensk District* (1934), which were successful at home and caused a sensation abroad. In 1936 in the course of the formalism campaign by the Stalinist cultural bureaucracy he was branded an enemy of the people. Overnight his works disappeared from the country's opera houses and concert halls. Like his friends General Tukhachevsky and the theatrical genius Meyerhold, he was constantly under threat of arrest and execution. The premières of his 15 symphonies were great social events in Soviet Russia. With his so-called "Leningrad" Symphony (no. 7) of 1942 he confirmed his international standing as a singular composer, but until the death of Stalin in 1953 he was persistently and harshly criticized by party ideologues. Although, as his country's leading composer, he would continue to fulfill his duties in Soviet cultural politics, Shostakovich no longer showed any sign of personal commitment.

Works: Operas: *Nos* (*The Nose*) (1929), *Ledi Makbet Mtsenskogo uyezda* (*Lady Macbeth of the Mtsensk District*) (1934), *Igroki* (*The Gamblers*) (unfinished, 1942); ballets, film music, orchestral music, including 15 symphonies, chamber music, including 15 string quartets.

The Nose

Nos

Opera in three acts and an epilogue

Libretto: Dmitry Shostakovich, Yevgeny Samyatin, Georgy Yonin, and Alexander Preys, after the short story of the same name by Nikolay Gogol.
Première: Concert première: 16 June 1929, Leningrad (Malïy Opernïy Teatr); stage première: 18 January 1930, Leningrad (Malïy Opernïy Teatr).

Characters: Plato Kuzmich Kovalyov, a college inspector (Bar), Ivan Yakovlevich, a barber (B), Praskovya Osipovna, his wife (S), A Captain of the Guard (very high T), Ivan, Kovalyov's servant (T), The Nose (T), Pelageya Grigoryevna Podtochina, a staff officer's widow (Ms), Her Daughter (S), Official from the Advertising Department (B), Doctor (B), Yarishkin (T); 66 episodic roles, including chorus.
Setting: St. Petersburg, c. 1850.

Synopsis
Act I
Inspector Kovalyov is being given a shave. In pleasurable anticipation of his erotic adventures, he scolds the barber for having smelly hands. Later, at home, the barber finds a nose in a freshly baked loaf of bread. His wife chases him out of the house and he tries to get rid of the nose by throwing it into the river Neva. Kovalyov wakes from pleasant dreams to find that his nose is missing. He rushes off to find it, and encounters the offending organ in Kazan Cathedral, dressed as a state councillor. He pleads humbly with his nose to return to his face, but it turns him down flat and disappears.

Act II
Kovalyov tries to find his nose by placing an advertisement in the paper, but they refuse to accept his text for the lost and found column. Kovalyov's servant, Ivan, is unmoved by his master's suffering.

Act III
A police squad is ordered to prevent the nose from leaving the city and stations itself at the coach station. A group of travelers is milling about, and the coach prepares to depart. At the last minute the nose appears and tries to stop the coach, but it only frightens the horses and causes a panic. The nose is suspected of being a robber and is set upon and beaten; it shrinks to its normal size and is captured by the captain of the guard who wraps it in a handkerchief. The captain returns the nose to Kovalyov, who is talked into parting with it with a big tip. But the nose refuses to stay on Kovalyov's face, and even a doctor seems unable to help. Kovalyov suspects a staff officer's widow of stealing the nose, in order to blackmail him into marrying her daughter. He writes, accusing her of this offense, but she denies

his allegations. Meanwhile, the city's inhabitants are crowding into the streets on account of a rumor that Kovalyov's nose can be seen walking about freely. They cause such a disturbance in the Summer Garden that the police and the fire brigade are summoned – but still there is no sign of the nose.

Epilogue

One morning when Kovalyov wakes up he finds the nose back in its normal place on his face. The barber turns up to give him a shave, and once again Kovalyov scolds him for having smelly hands and fantasizes about his amorous adventures. Kovalyov then strolls along the Nevsky Prospekt just as he used to, greeting his acquaintances, flirting with women, and generally enjoying life.   *S. N.*

Shostakovich was a gifted composer who represented the best traditions of the Soviet-Russian avant-garde. He developed an original symphonic style that combined the montage technique of Gustav Mahler with the formal rigor of Bach, also applying this style to opera. He did not "emancipate dissonance," as the western European modernists did, but chose to develop a method of "emancipating musical ambivalence."

1. Percussion: Fugue

The Nose, photograph from the production by Alfred Kirchner, sets Anette Murschetz, costumes Margit Koppendorfer, conductor Mikhail Yurovsky, Opernhaus Leipzig 1999.
Turmoil surrounds the nose. Just before the coach departs, the nose is discovered and captured by a police squad formed especially for this purpose. In spite of the patent absurdity of the events and the comedy of the individual situations, the music is as serious as Gogol was in the story on which the opera was based. When the captain of the guard is instructed to sing loudly and in a high voice, it is not for comic value: his mannerism is realistic, in that "when this person opens his mouth, it is only to shout or give an order:" the captain, in other words, knows only one way of expressing himself.

Lady Macbeth of the Mtsensk District

Ledi Makbet Mtsenskogo uyezda

Opera in four acts, nine scenes

Libretto: Alexander Preys and Dmitry Shostakovich, after the short story of the same name by Nikolay Leskov.

Première: First version: 22 January 1934, Leningrad (Malïy Opernïy Teatr); second version, under the title *Katerina Izmaylova*: 8 January 1963, Moscow (Stanislavsky-Nemirovich-Danchenko Music Theater).

Lady Macbeth of the Mtsensk District, production photograph with Kathryn Harries (Katerina) and Jan Blinkhof (Sergey), production Johannes Schaaf, sets Nina Ritter, costumes Franz Lehr, conductor Ingo Metzmacher, Württembergisches Staatstheater, Stuttgart 1992.
Over the years the inner themes of the opera have emerged ever more clearly. Productions of the work have moved away from the specifically Russian and folkloric aspects of the work to focus on the depiction of social and erotic tensions which express themselves with an elementary power.

Characters: Boris Timofeyevich Izmaylov, a merchant (high B), Zinovy Borisovich Izmaylov, his son, a merchant (T), Katerina L'vovna Izmaylova, Zinovy's wife (S), Sergey, a servant of the Izmaylovs (T), Aksin'ya, cook (S), Shabby Peasant (T), Steward (B), Porter (B), Three Workers (3 T), Millhand (Bar), Coachman (T), Priest (B), Chief of Police (Bar), Policeman (B), Teacher (T), Drunken Guest (T), Officer (B), Sentry (B), Sonetka, a convict (A), Old Convict (B), Woman Convict (S), Apparition of Boris Timofeyevich (B); workers, wedding guests, policemen, convicts (chorus).

Setting: The Russian provinces in the 1860s.

Synopsis
Act I

The merchant's wife, Katerina Izmaylova, is bored: she finds her husband Zinovy repellent and she has no children. When Zinovy is required to leave the house for a few days, Katerina's father-in-law, Boris, humiliates her by forcing her to swear an oath of loyalty to her husband in front of the servants. The cook Aksin'ya suggests a solution: she draws Katerina's attention to a new worker, Sergey, who

was dismissed from his previous position for having an affair with his mistress, and suggests he might be able to relieve Katerina of her boredom. Some of the workers fool about with Aksin'ya, but the situation threatens to get out of hand. Katerina intervenes and is challenged by Sergey to test her strength against his. Katerina decides there is something attractive about his impudence. On the pretext of borrowing some books, Sergey enters Katerina's bedroom and his presence leads to a sexual encounter between the two.

Act II

Plagued by insomnia and dwelling on lust-filled memories, Boris keeps a careful eye on the house and property, especially his daughter-in-law. Just as he is thinking about fulfilling his son's conjugal duties himself, he spies Sergey climbing out of Katerina's window. Sergey falls into the clutches of the old man, who, instead of expending his strength in Katerina's bed, exhausts himself by thrashing Sergey in front of the other servants and the helpless Katerina. He then locks Sergey in the cellar. Feeling hungry, he orders his daughter-in-law to bring him the rest of that day's dish of mushrooms, which she proceeds to garnish with rat poison. While the old man is writhing in agony, she steals his keys and frees Sergey from his temporary prison. Katerina shares her bed with Sergey; when her husband returns that night she and Sergey murder him and dump his body in the cellar.

Act III

Katerina and Sergey are about to be married. As the guests gather in the church a ragged peasant breaks into the Izmaylov's cellar. Instead of finding wine, as he had hoped, he discovers a corpse and immediately runs to the police. The chief of police and his men are feeling slighted, because they have not been invited to the wedding. The peasant's information gives them the excuse they need to present themselves at the festivities. The wedding reception is in full swing when Katerina discovers the broken lock on the cellar door. It is too late to flee, and she and Sergey are arrested.

Act IV

Katerina and Sergey have been sentenced and are on their way to a labor prison in Siberia. In a camp set up for the night along the way, men and women are separated. Katerina bribes the guard to let her see Sergey, who is her only source of comfort and strength. But Sergey reproaches her, blaming her for his misfortune. He has lost interest in her, and is now attracted to a younger prisoner called Sonetka. When Katerina discovers his faithlessness she pushes her rival into the water and jumps in after her. Both women drown, but the relentless march of the prisoners continues.   *S. N.*

Sexual liberation

Lady Macbeth of the Mtsensk District was composed between the fall of 1930 and December 1932, when Shostakovich was still in his mid-20s. Its theme is a most unusual one for an opera: its characters are from the lower class, it is set in one of the innermost Russian provinces, and the motivation for the action is banal: boredom und sexual dissatisfaction. Can music thrive in this kind of atmosphere? *Lady Macbeth* was written at a time when Shostakovich was himself being drawn into the turmoil of love and sexuality: in 1932 he married Nina Varsar, to whom the opera was dedicated. But this was also a time when the principles of sexual liberation were being discussed and put into practice by Soviet youth, even though the official line was still that love and sexuality were to be restricted to the rituals of procreation. The state did everything it could to inculcate the belief that sexual drives should be domesticated and placed at the service of Soviet society. Shostakovich's opera was a reaction against this false creed. His work deals with the untamable nature of sexuality, and with acts of sexual violence and emancipation.

"Muddle instead of music"

Shostakovich was made to pay for his boldness. The première in 1934 was such a success that a second Moscow production followed later the same year. The opera caused quite a stir abroad, too: there was a production in January 1935 in Cleveland, followed by performances in New York, Philadelphia, Stockholm, Prague, and Zürich. But in 1936 the opera was – de facto if not de jure – banned in the Soviet Union. In January the original Leningrad production was performed in Moscow, and was attended by Stalin. The dictator left the theater early to attend a meeting, without expressing an opinion on the work. This was interpreted as a sign of displeasure, and, as is often the case in a totalitarian state, resulted in a hostile press campaign triggered by the infamous "Muddle instead of music" article in Pravda on 28 January 1936. The article attacked Shostakovich for his allegedly false depiction of what was essentially a perfect world. The

Satirical tragedy and satire-tragedy

The mixture of satire and tragedy in the work results in a cornucopia of musical styles: strident sounds taken from everyday life are combined with contrapuntal responses, and naturalistic effects overlay symphonic passages. The music presents situations rather than gesturing towards them, and only the grand and highly expressive orchestral interludes have a commenting function. By increasing and exaggerating the tempo, Shostakovich makes the violence inherent in everyday life evident in his music – a technique he borrowed from the world of the cinema.

Above
Lady Macbeth of the Mtsensk District, Rebecca Blankenship as Katerina, production Christine Mielitz, conductor Donald Runnicles, Wiener Volksoper 1991.
The Russian version of the Lady Macbeth story does not focus on ambition and the desire for power, but on spiritual isolation, inner pain, and eruptions of sexual desire.

work disappeared from the schedules of opera houses throughout the Soviet Union almost overnight. Shostakovich was forced to make changes to *Lady Macbeth*, and this ultimately led to a revision of the piece in 1963 under the title *Katerina Izmaylova*. In this version the conflicts were toned down, and Katerina was presented as a pitiable woman who is tyrannized by a male-dominated society. Not until 1979, four years after Shostakovich's death, was Mstislav Rostropovich able to obtain the score of the original version and allow *Lady Macbeth of the Mtsensk District* to return to the international stage in the form intended by the composer.   *S. N.*

Physical music

If "emotional confusion" is one of the traditional themes of opera, Shostakovich's *Lady Macbeth* tells of the anarchic and mute desires of the body. In order to convey this phenomenon instrumental sounds become metaphors for physical states, and this explains the stumbling, gliding, sliding, grimacing, belching, squeaking, and tumbling noises produced by the instruments. Shostakovich created symbolic sound forms and instrumental color, endowing individual characters with their own aura: the alto flute for Zinovy, the double bassoon for Boris, the cello for Sergey, and the oboe and clarinet for Katerina.

*S*metana, though influenced by Liszt and Wagner, laid the foundations of Czech national opera with the comedy "The Bartered Bride" and the serious masterpiece "Dalibor."

Smetana, Bedřich

b. 2 March 1824 in Litomyšl, eastern Bohemia
d. 12 May 1884 in Prague

After studying at the Josef Proksch music school in Prague, Smetana founded his own music school at the age of 24, which he directed until 1856. He then worked as director of the subscription concerts at the Harmoniska Sällskapet in Göteborg, before returning to Prague in 1861, where he held several official positions. He was forced to give up his post as conductor of the National Theater in 1874, when he became profoundly deaf. His final years were marked by mental illness, which left its mark on his last compositions. Considered the founder of Czech national music, Smetana died in an asylum in 1884.

Works: Operas: *Braniboři v Čechách* (*The Brandenburgers in Bohemia*) (1866, Prague), *Prodaná nevěsta* (*The Bartered Bride*) (1866, Prague), *Dalibor* (1868), *Dvě dvovy* (*The Two Widows*) (1874, Prague), *Hubička* (*The Kiss*) (1876, Prague), *Tajemství* (*The Secret*) (1878, Prague), *Libuše* (1881, Prague), *Čertova Stěna* (*The Devil's Wall*) (1882, Prague), *Viola* (unfinished); symphonic poems, chamber music, sacred choral works.

The birth of Czech national opera

Before turning his attentions to the stage, Smetana expressed great enthusiasm for the symphonic poems of the so-called New German school of composers. The announcement of an opera competition by Count Johann von Harrach in 1861 led him to attempt his first stage work. The theme of the resulting opera, *The Brandenburgers in Bohemia*, adhered closely to the requirements of the competition. The competition organizers sought to create a national style, and the prize-winning opera was to be used for the opening of the Czech Provisional Theater in Prague. Though Smetana made use of the techniques of French and Italian opera in *The Brandenburgers*, he modeled his recitative on the intonation and rhythms of the Czech language, thus making an important contribution to the development of national opera. The opera was first performed in Prague on 30 May 1866. With the composition of *The Bartered Bride* Smetana fulfilled all the criteria for a national opera. The serious tone of his third opera, *Dalibor*, in which the hero pays for his rebellion with his life, seems not to have suited Smetana, for his subsequent operas (*The Two Widows*, *The Kiss*, and *The Secret*) satisfied the popular demand for a happy ending. His penultimate opera, *Libuše*, is patriotic and emotional, composed for the opening of the Prague National Theater. His final opera, *The Devil's Wall*, portrays a comical, Romantic world. Smetana created an operatic style that was in tune with the age.

The Bartered Bride

Prodaná nevěsta

Comic *Singspiel* in three acts

Libretto: Karel Sabina.

Première: First version, in two acts: 30 May 1866; second version: 29 January 1869; third version: 1 June 1869; last version: 25 September 1870 – all at Provisional Theater, Prague.

Characters: Krušina, a peasant (Bar), Ludmila, his wife (S), Mařenka, their daughter (S), Mícha, a landowner (Bar), Háta, his second wife (Ms), Vašek, their son (T), Jeník, Mícha's son from his first marriage (T), Kecal, the village marriage-broker (B), Circus Master (T), Esmerelda, a dancer (S), Muff, a clown (B); villagers, circus artists, children (chorus, ballet, extras).

Setting: A village in Bohemia, in spring, in the mid-19th century.

Synopsis
Act I
Outside the tavern on the village green. The peasants are merrily celebrating the anniversary of the church's consecration. Only Mařenka is unhappy, because she is supposed to marry the stuttering Vašek. Her father Krušina has made an agreement with Vašek's father, the wealthy landowner Mícha,

The Bartered Bride, production photograph with Herwig Pecoraro as Vašek, production Edgar Kelling, sets and costumes Bauer-Eczy, conductor Jan Krenz, Wiener Volksoper 1994. The comedy results from Vašek's stuttering, and is heightened by the presence of a physically and verbally skilled troupe of players.

according to which his daughter will marry one of Mícha's sons. But Mařenka loves the stranger Jeník, who claims that he is from a good family but has been driven from his home by an evil stepmother. At this point the village marriage-broker Kecal intervenes, hoping to make a fat fee, and urges a quick marriage. But Mařenka can think only of Jeník.

Act II

The tavern. Kecal tries to dissuade Jeník from marrying Mařenka. At the same time, Mařenka attempts to frighten Vašek by telling him that if they marry she will only bring him unhappiness. Meanwhile, Kecal has struck his deal: for a large sum Jeník is ready to forego his marriage to Mařenka, on one condition: Mařenka must marry one of Mícha's sons. Everyone is outraged, but Jeník signs the contract.

Act III

Outside the tavern on the village green. A troupe of clowns arrives in the village. Vašek is mesmerized by the dancer, Esmerelda, and pretends to be a bear to please her. Mařenka, meanwhile, is distraught, as she has heard the rumor of the "bartered bride." The problem is soon solved, however: Mícha recognizes Jeník as his son. The agreements made between Krušina and Mícha, and between Kecal and Jeník, can be honored, and Mařenka is finally able to marry Jeník.   *M. S.*

Although based on strictly national aspirations, his work also appealed to international audiences.

A viable national opera

Smetana's idea was to create a Czech national opera that would bear comparison with German opera in the style of Wagner, and he realized this with his second stage work, *The Bartered Bride*. He gave a piano performance of the overture in 1863, and had completed a first version of the opera by 1866. Dissatisfied with its structure, however, Smetana decided to add a third act and also expanded the dance finale of Act I by adding a *furiant*. In January 1869 a second version was ready for the stage, but this was amended still further, so that finally there were four versions. The songs, the balance between dance elements and emotional depth, and, of course, the superb musical portrayal of the characters – all these factors helped the work to achieve international acclaim.   *M. S.*

The Bartered Bride, photograph from the film by Max Ophüls with Liesl Karlstadt and Karl Valentin.
Delightful characters also turn up amongst the clowns in Act III: the circus master, here Karl Valentin, and his wife, Liesl Karlstadt.

Faust, photograph from the production by
Matthias Oldag, sets Heinz Balthes,
conductor Geoffrey Moull, Theater Bielefeld
1993.
Mephistopheles at work. The demonic aspect
of the story is particularly well realized by
Spohr. His music for the scene on the
Blocksberg mountain was echoed several
years later in Mendelssohn's music for
Shakespeare's *A Midsummer Night's Dream*.
The witches' sabbath, and indeed the opera
as a whole, also had a great effect on Weber,
who was working on →*Der Freischütz* at the
time he conducted the première of *Faust*.

Spohr, Louis

b. 5 April 1784 in Braunschweig
d. 22 October 1859 in Kassel

Spohr came from a musical family and received his first violin lessons when he was a child. At the age of 18 he appeared in concert with the outstanding violinist Franz Eck, and soon won such a reputation for virtuosity that he was compared with Paganini. From 1812 to 1815 he was conductor at the Theater an der Wien. After a concert tour of Italy he accepted a position as conductor at the Stadttheater in Frankfurt in 1817. He spent most of his professional life (1822–57) as *Kapellmeister* in Kassel. His reputation as an instrumentalist was due mainly to his legendary interpretations of adagio movements. A romantic individualist, he developed a unique and characteristic style. Spohr's progressiveness as a composer of opera was evident in his structuring of scenes according to dramatic content rather than musical numbers. He also worked with leitmotivs and was responsible for several other ideas for which →Wagner would later take credit.

Works: Die Prüfung (*The Test*) (1806, Gotha), *Alruna, die Eulenkönigin* (*Alruna, the Queen of the Owls*) (1809, Gotha), *Der Zweikampf mit der Geliebten* (*The Duel with the Lover*) (1811, Hamburg), *Faust* (1816, Prague), *Zemire und Azor* (*Zemire and Azor*) (1819, Frankfurt), *Jessonda* (1823, Kassel), *Der Berggeist* (*The Mountain Spirit*) (1825, Kassel), *Pietro von Abano* (1827, Kassel), *Der Alchimist* (*The Alchemist*) (1830, Kassel), *Die Kreuzfahrer* (*The Crusaders*) (1845, Kassel); four oratorios, 10 symphonies, 15 violin concertos, four clarinet concertos, chamber music, over 90 songs.

Zemire and Azor, costume designs by Helga Heckemüller, 1984 (Collection of the International Louis Spohr Society, Kassel).
Costume designers have tended to produce exotic designs for the characters, although Spohr's work is by no means the musical equivalent of the sketches seen here.

Faust

Romantic opera in two acts

Libretto: Josef Karl Bernard.
Première: First version, with prose dialogue: 1 September 1816, Prague (Estates Theater); second version, in Italian, with recitative: 15 July 1852, London (Royal Opera House).
Characters: Faust (Bar), Mephistopheles (Bar), Count Hugo (T), Kunigunde, his betrothed (S), Gulf, a knight (B), Kaylinger (Bar), Wohlhaldt, Wagner, and Moor, Faust's companions (2 T, B), Röschen, a girl (S), Franz, a goldsmith's apprentice (T), Hugo's squire (spoken), Kunigunde's maid (S), A Voice (S), Sycorax, leader of the witches (S), A Guest (spoken); crowd, followers of the count and the knight, women, witches, wedding guests, servants, spirits (chorus, extras); Cupid, Hymen, nymphs, cherubs (ballet).
Setting: Strasbourg and Aachen, in the Middle Ages.

Synopsis
Act I

Faust has regained his youth with the help of Mephistopheles. He has become rich and has won the heart of Röschen, a girl from Strasbourg. To the astonishment of his friends he pledges that henceforth he will do only good. Franz, who also loves Röschen, is jealous and mistrustful. Faust asks Röschen to come to him, but Franz stirs up the townsfolk in order to win back Röschen. Mephistopheles helps Faust and Röschen by taking them off to safety. Faust becomes involved in the affairs of the beautiful Kunigunde, who has been abducted by the knight Gulf. With the aid of Mephistopheles, Faust and Count Hugo, Kunigunde's betrothed, rescue Kunigunde. Faust then falls in love with Kunigunde himself.

Act II

Mephistopheles takes Faust to the witches' sabbath on the Blocksberg mountain, where the lovesick hero is given a magic potion. In Aachen, Kunigunde and Hugo are celebrating their wedding. Amongst the guests are Faust and Mephistopheles; Röschen, who is looking for Faust, is also present, accompanied by Franz. Faust gives Kunigunde some of the magic potion to drink, and its effect is immediately apparent: she falls in love with him. Faust and Kunigunde flee, but are pursued by Hugo. In the ensuing struggle, Faust kills Hugo. Faust and Mephistopheles tire of their escapades. Faust now longs for a quiet life with Röschen, and Mephistopheles wants to return to hell. Kunigunde is still ignorant of Hugo's death, and when she discovers Faust with Röschen, she tries to kill him. Röschen then learns of Faust's liaison with Kunigunde; in her despair she drowns herself. Faust is now entirely alone: Mephistopheles comes to claim him.   *S. N.*

The first Romantic opera?

After several earlier attempts at writing an opera, Spohr, fascinated by the stage machinery at the Theater an der Wien, decided to tackle the Faust theme. He began working on the opera in May 1813, finishing it four months later. Spohr hoped that it would be performed in Vienna, but a conflict with Count Ferdinand Palffy, the director and later the owner of the theater, meant that he had to abandon this idea. The overture to the work was performed in Vienna in 1814 – at the same time as the Congress of Vienna – and the première took place in Prague in September 1816, conducted by →Weber. Had the work been performed slightly earlier, Spohr would probably have gone down in history as the composer of the first Romantic opera instead of E.T.A. Hoffmann (*Undine*, 1816).

A Faust story – but without redemption

The Faust theme was very popular in the early nineteenth century. Spohr's version, however, with its added psychological elements, is quite distinct from comparable folk plays. Though Goethe's *Faust* (first part, 1806) was not yet widely known, Spohr was probably familiar with the work, as he had written music on the theme of Gretchen in 1808–1809. The opera impresses the listener with its nuanced emotions, its melodiousness, and its thrilling drama. Spohr's early use of leitmotivs was crucial to the work's success, and his experimentation with tonal effects was also ahead of its time. Spohr strove to remain at the forefront of musical development through such innovations. The work was performed in Berlin in 1829, and has always been best known in the German-speaking countries. M. S.

Spohr, with Weber, paved the way for German Romantic opera.

Jessonda, Jenny Lutzer as Jessonda, illustration, Vienna 1836 (TWS).
Jessonda, a complicated love story about a beautiful oriental woman, was, with *Faust*, Spohr's most popular opera in the 19th century. In the first act the heroine appears as a widow awaiting death at the stake with great composure. She sings an aria, "Bald bin ich ein Geist geworden" ("Soon I will be but a spirit"), which continues to be one of the most moving moments in early German Romanticism.

The composer and his friendly accompanist

Though a highly accomplished violinist, Spohr was a rather poor pianist. When composing in Vienna he would often visit his friend Meyerbeer, who would sight-read the newly finished pieces with ease while Spohr sang and whistled the vocal parts.

Above
Faust, title page from the first edition of the piano score of the second version of the opera, Vienna 1854 (Collection of the Louis Spohr Society, Kassel).

Jessonda, design for a fresco by Moritz von Schwind, 1854.
Schwind was inspired here by the opera's crucial scene: Jessonda sees Tristan at the well.

La vestale

The Vestal Virgin

Tragédie lyrique in three acts (four scenes)

Libretto: Victor-Joseph Étienne de Jouy.

Première: 15 December 1807, Paris (Opéra, Salle Montansier).

Characters: Licinius, a Roman general (T), Cinna, commander of the legion (T), High Priest (B), Chief Soothsayer (B), A Consul (B), Julia, a young vestal virgin (S), High Priestess of the vestal virgins (Ms); vestal virgins, priests, matrons, young women, senators, consuls, lictors, warriors, gladiators, children, musicians, slaves, prisoners (chorus, extras); young Roman soldiers, people, maenads, Sappho, two women from Lesbos, priests of Venus (ballet, extras).

Setting: Ancient Rome.

Spontini is a representative of the great tradition of pathos in early 19th-century opera.

Synopsis
Act I

The Roman Forum; to the left the Atrium and rooms of the vestal virgins. The general Licinius has returned victorious from his campaign against the Gauls, hoping to win the hand of Julia. In the meantime, Julia has become a priestess of the vestal virgins, in order to comply with the wishes of her late father; this requires her to remain chaste forever, or forfeit her life. Julia is chosen to present the victor's crown to Licinius. During the ceremony he learns that she has to guard the sacred flame of the goddess Vesta alone at night.

Act II

The interior of the temple of the vestal virgins; the sacred fires burn on a great marble altar in the center. Julia's task is to watch over the fire and ensure that it does not go out. Licinius enters and tries to carry her off, but she resists the temptation. While the pair argue, the sacred fire goes out. When the High Priest tries to force Julia to tell him the name of the intruder she refuses to reveal it, and is condemned to death.

Act III

Scene 1: The pyramid tombs on the Porta Collina. Licinius begs in vain for Julia's life, even admitting his part in her guilt. Julia descends into the tomb to be buried alive. As her vestal veil is laid on the altar a storm breaks and a bolt of lightning sets the veil on fire – a sign that Vesta has forgiven Julia.
Scene 2: Temple of Venus of Eryx. Licinius and Julia are married to general rejoicing.   *S. N.*

Spontini, Gaspare

b. 14 November 1774 in Maiolati (Maiolati-Spontini)
d. 24 January 1851 in Maiolati

After studying at the Naples Conservatory, Spontini produced operas for Rome, Venice, Florence, Naples, and Palermo. It was only in Paris (from 1803) and under the patronage of the Empress Joséphine, however, that he began to gain public attention. Even here his successes were matched by great scandals: when his opera *La petite maison* was premièred in 1804, the anti-Italian press caused an uproar which resulted in the performance being canceled. He became acquainted with the work of →Gluck, and modified his style in order to give his operas greater visual and musical appeal. His directorship at the Théâtre-Italien lasted only two years, from 1810 to 1812, owing to Spontini's difficult personality. His last official position, as general music director in Berlin, a position he held from 1820 to 1840, was due to the patronage of King Friedrich Wilhelm III of Prussia.

Works: Operas (selection): *Il puntigli delle donne* (*The Stubbornness of Women*) (1796, Rome), *Le metamorfosi di Pasquale* (*The Metamorphosis of Pasquale*) (1802, Venice), *La finta filosofa* (*The Feigned Philosopher*) (1804, Paris), *Milton* (1804, Paris), *Julie, ou Le pot de fleurs* (*Julie, or The Flowerpot*) (1805, Paris), *La vestale* (*The Vestal Virgin*) (1807, Paris), *Fernand Cortez, ou La conquête du Méxique* (*Fernando Cortez, or The Conquest of Mexico*) (1809, Paris), *Pélague, ou Le roi et la paix* (*Pélague, or The King and Peace*) (1814, Paris), *Olimpie* (*Olympia*) (1819, Paris), *Lalla Rookh* (1821, Berlin), *Nurmahal, oder das Rosenfest von Caschmir* (*Nurmahal, or The Rose Festival of Kashmir*) (1822, Berlin), *Alcidor* (1825, Berlin), *Agnes von Hohenstaufen* (1827, Berlin).

La vestale, photograph from the production by Christine Mielitz, sets and costumes Gerd Friedrich, conductor Robert Duerr, Theater Basel 1994. The temple of the vestal virgins (Act II) translated into the visual language of the late 20th century. The stage resembles the interior of a spaceship, and this lends the scene both a superhuman and an inhuman character.

Forerunner of Romantic opera

Spontini was not the only composer to work with this dramatic material: Bellini was to use it as the basis for his opera →*Norma* over 20 years later. Spontini's dramatic concept, however, is distinctive. True to the sensibilities of the Napoleonic era, he created musical characterization that reaches its peak in the opera's "tableaux" (a kind of acoustic image). He also incorporated spatial effects into the work (a distant chorus and an orchestra placed behind the stage), which were to prove a source of inspiration for →Berlioz. There are also traces of Spontini's musical language in the work of →Rossini, →Meyerbeer, and, especially, →Wagner.

An imported music director

In Berlin the Prussian king Friedrich Wilhelm III appointed Spontini general director of music, gave him a generous salary, and awarded him certain privileges – all of which made the composer a number of enemies. In Germany at that time developments were under way to create a national style, and Spontini's German colleagues resented having an Italian placed over them. To counter such feelings, Spontini arranged to collaborate with E.T.A. Hoffmann on a German version of *Olimpie*, the first performance of which was greeted with skepticism. The Prussian monarch was displeased with what he saw as an unjustified reaction from the critics, and he forbade any negative criticism. The press then changed tack, praising Hoffmann's work out of all proportion to his actual contribution, and giving Weber's →*Der Freischütz* (1821) an ecstatic reception. But Spontini's sensitive style and his talent for structure were finally conceded by even his opponents.   *M. S.*

La vestale, set design by Karl Friedrich Schinkel for the temple of Vesta, reproduced in an engraving by Friedrich Jügel.
The setting for "Spontini's brilliance" – as was said in the 19th century – was genuinely classical. A well-proportioned monumentality matched Napoleon's contemporary attempts at restoring the imperial order. This set design by Karl Friedrich Schinkel (1781–1841) clearly reflects both the classicism and the historicism of the period.

Stockhausen, Karlheinz

b. 22 August 1928 in Mödrath (near Cologne)

Stockhausen studied at Cologne University, at the Conservatory under Frank Martin (1947–51), and later in Paris under →Olivier Messiaen (1952–53); he also worked in the *musique concrète* studio with Pierre Schaeffer. In 1953 he was appointed by Herbert Eimert to a position in the newly established Studio for Electronic Music of West German Radio in Cologne. This studio, under Stockhausen's directorship from 1963, became the most famous international workshop for new music. From 1953 he taught at the Darmstadt summer school, where his influence extended over an entire generation of European composers, including his contemporaries Boulez and →Berio. He became a key figure in modernism in 1956 with his ground-breaking serial composition *Song of the Youths in the Fiery Furnace*, which was originally planned as a Mass for Cologne Cathedral and which later developed into amplified music for the concert hall. Other sound and space experiments followed, including *Groups* for three orchestras (1955–57) and *Carré* for four orchestras (1959–60). At the end of the 1960s he became interested in Eastern philosophy and art, which resulted in a turn to so-called "intuitive music," as demonstrated in his second important spiritual work, *Inori*, of 1974. During the World Exposition in Osaka in 1970 he created and installed the music for the German pavilion. Between 1971 and 1977 he was a professor at the Conservatory in Cologne. Since 1977 he has devoted himself exclusively to composition and to music theory, and has been working on his operatic cycle *Licht* (*Light*), conceived as a heptalogy to be performed across the days of a week and intended as the summation of his life's work.

Works: Opera cycle: *Licht: Die sieben Tage der Woche* (*Light: The Seven Days of the Week*), of which the following have been composed: *Donnerstag aus Licht* (*Thursday from Light*) (1981), *Samstag aus Licht* (*Saturday from Light*) (1984), *Montag aus Licht* (*Monday from Light*) (1988), *Dienstag aus Licht* (*Tuesday from Light*) (1993), *Freitag aus Licht* (*Friday from Light*) (1996); *Studie 1* (*Study 1*) (1953), *Gesang der Jünglinge im Feuerofen* (*Song of the Youths in the Fiery Furnace*) (1955–56), *Gruppen* (*Groups*) for three orchestras (1955–57), *Carré* for four orchestras (1959–60), *Kontakte* (*Contacts*) (1959–60), *Telemusik* (1966), *Mantra* (1970), *Inori* (1974), *Sirius* (1975–77).

Thursday from Light, production photograph, sound projection Karlheinz Stockhausen, producer Michael Bogdanov, sets and costumes Maria Bjørnson, lighting Chris Ellis, conductor Peter Eotvos, Royal Opera House, London 1985.

Light: The Seven Days of the Week

Licht: Die sieben Tage der Woche

Libretto: Karlheinz Stockhausen.

Premières: *Thursday*: 15 March 1981, Milan (Teatro alla Scala); *Saturday*: 25 May 1984, Milan (Teatro alla Scala in the Palazzo dello Sport); *Monday*: 7 May 1988, Milan (Teatro alla Scala); *Tuesday*: 28 May 1993, Leipzig (Opera); *Friday*: 12 September 1996, Leipzig (Opera).

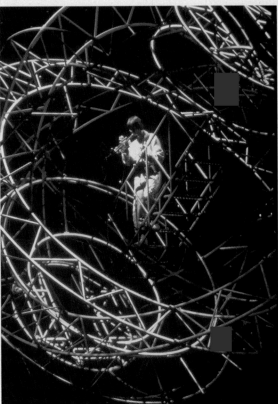

Thursday from Light

Donnerstag aus Licht

Opera in three acts, a greeting, and a farewell

(Michael's day, day of learning, main color blue)

Characters: Michael (T, trumpeter, dancer), Eve, also Mother, Mooneve, and Woman (S, basset-horn player, dancer), Lucifer (B, trombonist, dance-mime), Michael's accompanist in the exam (pianist), Doctor, Orderly, Stretcher Bearer, and Villagers (silent), Pair of Swallows (two clarinettists, the second also a basset-horn player), Penguins at the South Pole (orchestra), Two Boys (two saxophonists), An Artist, Old Woman (actress), Messenger (T); "invisible choruses" (tape); delegates from the Michael Universe (chorus).

Synopsis
Act I

Michael's youth. Michael's mother Eve teaches him singing, joking, and dancing, and his father Lucifer, praying, hunting, shooting, and acting. The mother is consigned to a mental asylum, where she dies, while his father goes off to war and is killed. Michael falls in love with Mooneve, passes a three-stage test, and is accepted into the music school.

Act II

Michael's journey around the world. Michael goes first to the South Pole to see the penguins (musicians), then from Cologne to New York, Japan, Bali, India, Central Africa, and Jerusalem, where the sound of a basset-horn makes him turn his back on society.

Act III

Michael's return home. Eve accompanies her son to his heavenly home. Lucifer tries in vain to distract them. Michael's last words are: "I became a man … to bring the music of heaven to earth and earthly music to heaven, so that people would listen to God and that God would hear his children."

Saturday from Light

Samstag aus Licht

Opera in a greeting and four scenes for 13 performers

(Lucifer's day, Saturday is the day of Saturn, the "day of death and the night of passing over to the light," main colors glossy black and blue-green)

Characters: Lucifer (B, on stilts), Lucifer's dream player (pianist), The Black Cat Katinka (flautist, also piccolo player), The Six Mortal Senses (6 percussionists), An Enormous Human Face (wind orchestra), Michael (piccolo trumpet player), Dancer, Theater Director (actors), A Demonic Hornblower (trombonist), A Wild Black Bird; three groups of 13 monks (chorus); tears (ballet).

Synopsis

Scene 1: *Lucifer's dream, or Piano Piece XIII.* Lucifer dreams the *Piano Piece XIII*, which calls up the five elements; he sinks exhausted into a death-like torpor.

Scene 2: *Katinka's song as Lucifer's requiem.* In memory of all those who seek the eternal light, the cat Katinka rises from the "tomb" of a grand piano and plays wonderful notes on a flute, in order to "lead the souls of the dead to a lucid consciousness through listening." The "six mortal senses" (hearing, sight, smell, taste, touch, and thought) intervene; they "are dismissed by Katinka," who returns to her "tomb."

Scene 3: *Lucifer's dance.* Lucifer is conscious once again, and is able to think and to feel like a human being. There now follow the dances of the eyebrows, the eyes, the cheeks, the nostrils, the upper lip, the tip of the tongue, the chin. Michael objects to the grimacing but is hurled down by Lucifer walking on stilts: the face rests and weeps tears of sympathy.

Scene 4: *Lucifer's farewell.* Monks are celebrating the *Lolli delle virtù* (*Songs in Praise of the Virtues*) by St. Francis of Assisi. A sack full of coconuts falls from the sky. The monks release a wild black bird kept in a cage, and send their best wishes forth into the world, achieved symbolically by smashing fruit to expose its flesh.

S. N.

Stockhausen extends the world of musical experience through the integration of electronic sounds and the strict, almost religious ritual of his musical performances. He differs from all comparable musical figures of his day in his commitment to the idea of music having a Messianic purpose.

Opposite
Thursday from Light, production photograph, sound projection Karlheinz Stockhausen, producer Michael Bogdanov, sets and costumes Maria Bjørnson, lighting Chris Ellis, conductor Peter Eotvos, Royal Opera House, London 1985.
The *Light* cycle will not be complete until the premières of *Wednesday* in May 2000 (Bonn Opera) and *Sunday* in 2003.

Thursday from Light, production photograph, sound projection Karlheinz Stockhausen, producer Michael Bogdanov, sets and costumes Maria Bjørnson, lighting Chris Ellis, conductor Peter Eotvos, Royal Opera House, London 1985.
At a time when Stockhausen's *Light* cycle was being rejected by German opera houses, it was awarded the critics' prize for contemporary music in Bergamo in 1981 and a production was staged at London's Royal Opera House in 1985. The production brought out the universality of the themes of the *Light* cycle, supplementing them with realistic details from modern life.

Monday from Light

Montag aus Licht

Opera in three acts, a greeting, and a farewell

(Eve's day, a musical celebration in honor of the mother, a festival of birth and rebirth, main color bright green)

Characters: Eve (3 S), Lucifer (B), Luzipolyp (B, actor), Three Sailors (3 T), Seven Boys (7 boy S), Cœur de basset (basset-horn player), Three Basset-Horn Players (2 basset-horn players and a voice), Budgie as Pianist (pianist), The Child-catcher (alto flautist with piccolo), Twenty-one Actresses (21 silent); men, women; children's chorus: seven baby animals, seven fairies, girls, children (chorus).

Synopsis
Act I

Eve's first birth. Eve gives the world seven baby animals and seven fairies, but Lucifer is displeased and sends the infants back to Eve's womb: "Start the whole thing over again!"

Act II
Eve's second birth. Eve is impregnated by *Piano Piece XIV* and bears seven boys, who grow up at their mother's breast as if in paradise.

Act III
Eve's magic. The boys become men. A flute player coaxes Eve into performing an erotic duet and then abducts all the subsequent offspring. Eve ages and becomes a mountain around whose peak great white birds circle. In the distance the sounds of baby birds can be heard.

Tuesday from Light

Dienstag aus Licht

Opera in a greeting, two acts, and a farewell
(day of struggle, main color red)

Characters: Michael-Troupe (3 solo trumpets, the first also a flugelhorn, 6 *tutti* trumpets, percussion, synthesizer), Lucifer (B) with Lucifer-Troupe (3 solo trombones, 6 *tutti* trombones, percussion, synthe-

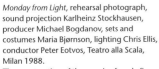

Monday from Light, rehearsal photograph, sound projection Karlheinz Stockhausen, producer Michael Bogdanov, sets and costumes Maria Bjørnson, lighting Chris Ellis, conductor Peter Eotvos, Teatro alla Scala, Milan 1988.
The construction of the massive female figure at the première in Milan. The first day of the week belongs to the primal mother, Eve. She gives birth to animals and humans. She is the "female principle" in the new world mythology of the late 20th century.

sizer), Eve (S), The Passage of The Millennia, The Centuries, The Decades, and The Years (4 dance-mimes), Referee (actor-singer), Three Assistant Referees, also Three Givers of Flowers, also Cook, Lion, and Ape (3 mimes), Small Girl (child actress), A Beautiful Woman (silent), Players for the Passage of the Year (14 musicians), Four Cylinder Clocks (four musical assistants), Synthesizer-Fou (synthesizer player from Lucifer-Troupe); Michael- and Lucifer-ensembles, figures from another world (chorus).

Synopsis
Act I
Course of the year. Archangel Michael competes with his trumpets against the trombones of Lucifer. Michael and Lucifer extend their dispute about life with and without God into a struggle for time itself. The millennia, centuries, decades, and years appear and are brought to a standstill, seduced by Lucifer. Michael persuades them to continue their course and defeats Lucifer.

Act II
Invasion – Explosion with farewell. Musical artillery from the Michael- and Lucifer-troupes fire at one another. Eve, full of compassion, takes in the dead and wounded but cannot stop the raging battle. Lucifer unearths a glass mountain in which figures from another world play with glass machines of war. They depart for more distant transcendental realms.

Friday from Light
Freitag aus Licht
Opera in a greeting, two acts, and a farewell

(day of temptation, main color orange)

Characters: Eve (S), Ludon (B), Kaino (Bar), Ela (basset-horn), Lufa (flute), Synthibird (synthesizer); 12 pairs of dance-mimes: Woman/Man, Cat/Dog, Copying Machine/Typewriter, Car/Racing Car Driver, Slot Machine/Slot Machine Player, Football/Foot, Moon/Rocket, Arm/Syringe with Drugs, Pencil Sharpener/Pencil, Woman's Mouth/Ice-cream Cone, Violin/Bow, Nest/Raven; children's chorus, 12 singers (chorus).

Synopsis
Act I
Friday. Twelve couples have formed. Ludon suggests to Eve a liaison with his son Kaino. Their children play music for and with each other.

Act II
Temptation. Eve enters into a union with Kaino and several of the other couples also swap partners. Hybrid-couples and bastard-children result and they go to war with each other.
Children's war. Eve and the hybrid-couples plead for mercy, which is granted: the hybrid-couples become a great flame which begins to glow: they become light. S. N.

Monday from Light, photograph of Karlheinz Stockhausen at the rehearsals for the première at the Teatro alla Scala, Milan 1988. Stockhausen played a new and complex role in the performance of his works. As composer he defined the material and the structure of the composition; as musical director he controlled the performance from his mixing desk; and as acoustic expert he electronically reshaped the sounds produced by performers.

Music that unites heaven and earth
The idea for the seven-part cycle was developed in 1977. The entire composition is built on a "super formula" sketched out in 1978, which overlays the melodies of the three main figures – Michael, Eve, and Lucifer. The day of reconciliation (*Wednesday*) and the mystical union between Michael and Eve (*Sunday*) were intended for the end of the twentieth century, but their stage productions have yet to be realized. The fundamental idea behind the work is to reaffirm a religious and biologically determined meaning for the days of the week – as opposed to their current pattern of production and consumption – in order to create a connection to God in everyday life. Both old and new forms from European and Asian traditions are extended to create a ritual art form. The music features elements of the Indian Kathakali and the Japanese Gagaku and Noh. Dancers, artists, technicians, and instrumentalists play as important a part as singers. Michael is portrayed by a singer and a trumpeter, while the penguins at the South Pole are played by members of an orchestra in frock coats. Colors, spatial sounds, lighting effects, and props all have their own meaning and their own independent life. The episodes from an individual day in the cycle, like the days themselves, can be presented as autonomous performances. Birds, however, are crucial to each day. As in the music of Stockhausen's teacher →Olivier Messiaen, birds proclaim the love of and love for God. Michael's journey around the earth marks the stations of development in modern music in the last decades of the twentieth century: from the Old to the New World (from →Schoenberg's twelve-tone music to minimalism) and from there to East Asia (to aleatory music, spatial sounds, and new sound generators). With the appearance of the cat Katinka (*Saturday*), Buddhist elements are brought into play, including the belief in six senses (with thought as the sixth sense) and the concept of redemption through the sense of sound, as taught in the Tibetan book of the dead, the *Bardo-Tödol*. This places Stockhausen firmly in an older European and Asian tradition that begins with C.G. Jung's *Bardo-Tödol* studies of the 1920s and extends to Beckett's *Play* of 1963. In spite of initial criticism, evoked by its wealth of unusual and fantastic ideas, *Light* is a truly innovative work that synthesizes the most important compositional techniques of the twentieth century. The old concept of "modulation," which traditionally referred to the change to a different key within a piece of music, became in Stockhausen's hands the change to a different style within a hugely diverse range of cultures and eras. S. N.

Strauss, Johann

b. 25 October 1825 in Vienna
d. 3 June 1899 in Vienna

The son of Johann Strauss the elder (1804–49), he became the most famous member of this Viennese family of composer-conductors, which also included Josef (1827–70) and Eduard (1835–1916). Johann studied music secretly against his father's wishes, and in 1844 received a license to give public concerts. He founded his own ensemble in competition with his father, merging the two orchestras after Johann senior's early death in 1849. His international success was such that he found it necessary to use his two brothers as deputies when his workload became too much and he was forced to rest.

Works: 16 operettas, including: *Der Carneval in Rom* (*Carnival in Rome*) (1873), *Die Fledermaus* (*The Bat*) (1874), *Cagliostro in Wien* (*Cagliostro in Vienna*) (1875), *Prinz Methusalem* (*Prince Methuselah*) (1877), *Blindekuh* (*Blind Man's Buff*) (1878), *Der lustige Krieg* (*The Merry War*) (1881), *Eine Nacht in Venedig* (*A Night in Venice*) (1883), *Der Zigeunerbaron* (*The Gypsy Baron*) (1885), *Simplicius* (1887), *Fürstin Ninetta* (*Princess Ninetta*) (1893), *Jabuka* (1894), *Die Göttin der Vernunft* (*The Goddess of Reason*) (1897); dances (mainly waltzes and polkas), character pieces.

Die Fledermaus

The Bat

Komische Operette in three acts

Libretto: Carl Haffner and Richard Genée, after the play *Le réveillon* (*The Midnight Supper Party*) by Henri Meilhac and Ludovic Halévy.

Première: 5 April 1874, Vienna (Theater an der Wien).

Characters: Gabriel von Eisenstein, a man of private means (T), Rosalinde, his wife (S), Frank, a prison governor (T), Prince Orlofsky (Ms), Alfred, his singing teacher (T), Dr. Falke, a notary (T), Dr. Blind, a lawyer (T), Adele, Rosalinde's maid (S), Ida, her sister (S), Ali-Bey, an Egyptian (T), Ramusin, a diplomatic attaché (T), Murray, an American (B), Marquis Cariconi (B), Frosch, a jailer (spoken), Yvan, the prince's valet (spoken), Melanie, Faustine, Felicita, Minni, and Sidi, party guests (5 S), Hermine, Nathalie, Sabine, and Sylvia, party guests (4 A), Four Servants (4 T), An Usher (silent); dancers, party guests, servants (chorus, extras, ballet).
Setting: A spa town near a large city, 19th century.

*T*he best operetta by "the waltz king" Johann Strauss is a firm favorite of European opera companies.

Die Fledermaus, production photograph, Act II, the soirée at Prince Orlofsky's, Wiener Staatsoper 1993.
Die Fledermaus is very much a Viennese comedy, a work that is more concerned with *Schadenfreude* than cozy entertainment. The festivities at Prince Orlofsky's are a dance on a volcano – but a very Viennese volcano. M T

Synopsis
Before the opera begins

Eisenstein once went to a fancy dress ball as a butterfly accompanied by Falke dressed as a bat. Both men drank too much, and on the way home Eisenstein left his friend to sleep it off in a doorway. The next day Falke woke to the jeers of street urchins, and had to find his way home in broad daylight in bat costume.

Act I

The marriage of Eisenstein and Rosalinde has become a prison, and Eisenstein has been given a real jail sentence for insulting a tax collector. Falke persuades his friend to revolt briefly against the yoke of his marriage and his official punishment: before Eisenstein goes to prison they will both to go to a party hosted by Prince Orlofsky, where there are sure to be plenty of beautiful women. Rosalinde for her part looks forward to eight husband-free days with her admirer, the tenor Alfred; and even the maid Adele rebels against her conditions of service and plans a career for herself as an actress. At that moment Frank, the prison governor, arrives to escort Eisenstein to jail. Mistaking Alfred for Eisenstein he arrests the tenor and leads him off.

Act II

Thanks to Falke's crafty plot, all three rebels meet each other at Prince Orlofsky's. The prince is bored and Falke promises him some entertainment. The "Marquis Renard," alias Eisenstein, flirts with his own wife, who is disguised as a Hungarian countess, and Rosalinde is able to observe at first hand the double lives of her husband and maid. The prison governor Frank, alias "Chevalier Chagrin," becomes friendly with the "Marquis," and pretends to be a patron of young "aspiring actresses" such as Adele and her sister Ida.

Act III

After a merry evening's entertainment, prison governor Frank has new guests: he has caught two butterflies – Adele and her sister Ida – at Orlofsky's party. Eisenstein arrives to serve his eight-day sentence, and is forced to witness his wife making off with her tenor, knowing how she will be amusing herself for the next week. The bat has finally managed to avenge itself. *S. N.*

The waltz dream

The parents of the waltz were the "common people," who found the prudery and stiffness of courtly dancing contrary to their taste. *La valse* conquered the stage of the Grand Opéra in Paris as early as 1800, and soon people were spinning in triple time all across Europe. After the failed revolutions of 1848, the liberating spirit of the waltz, with its illusions of an international brotherhood of man, was transmuted into the pleasure of simply forgetting: "Glücklich ist, wer vergisst, was nicht mehr zu ändern ist" ("Happy the man who can forget that change is impossible"). *M 3*

Vienna is everywhere

The première of *Die Fledermaus* in Vienna in 1874 was a great success, as was the first Berlin performance at the Friedrich Wilhelmstädtisches Theater later the same year. But it was only when Gustav Mahler included *Die Fledermaus* in the program of the Hamburg Opera in 1894 that the work became part of the standard operatic repertory. Several productions of *Die Fledermaus* number among the greatest of all theatrical events, such as Richard Strauss's production at the Hofoper in Berlin in 1899, Max Reinhardt's production at the Deutsches Theater in 1929, and Walter Felsenstein's legendary opening of the Komische Oper in Berlin in 1947. *Die Fledermaus* is a Viennese comedy – but then, Vienna is everywhere. *M 2*   *S. N.*

Die Fledermaus, Otto Schenk as Frosch, Wiener Staatsoper 1993.
Otto Schenk (b. 1930) is one of the most productive and internationally successful opera directors of our time. Here he is pictured in the role of Frosch – a perfect role for topflight actors, and especially for comedians. Schenk's popularity as an actor is not restricted to his native Vienna. His comic abilities recall those of the great Viennese actor, Hans Moser (1880–1964).

Below
Die Fledermaus, Hermann Prey as Eisenstein, production Otto Schenk, conductor Theodor Guschlbauer, Wiener Staatsoper 1993. Eisenstein, a man of private means, dreams of being a marquis for a night, and flirting with all the pretty girls at the ball. Eisenstein was one of this great singer's most celebrated roles.

1. *Fledermaus* Waltz

2. Duidu Waltz

dui -du,   dui -du,   la la la la ___ la,   dui -du,   dui -du,   la la la la ___ la

3. Alfred's Drinking Song

Glücklich ist,   wer vergisst,   was nicht mehr zu än-dern ist!   Glücklich ist,   wer vergisst, was nicht zu än-dern ist!

Pauline de Ahna, 1894.
In the year of the first performance of *Guntram* this promising young singer became the wife of Richard Strauss. She sang the leading female role in the opera. Clearly the composer did not totally identify with the character of Guntram: he was unable to resist the beautiful Freihild. This was the first and last time that Pauline was given a role in one of her husband's operas.

Richard Strauss, 1934.
In front of him is the score of *The Silent Woman*. Strauss was 70, already the grand old man of German music, when Hitler came to power and political events exercised a malign influence on his creative work. In the early years of the Nazi regime he allowed himself to be honored, but after the Zweig affair (over →*The Silent Woman*) he retired from public life, devoting himself untiringly to the works of his last years.

Strauss, Richard

b. 11 June 1864 in Munich
d. 8 September 1949 in Garmisch-Partenkirchen

The son of a famous horn player, Strauss gave early evidence of his musical ability in his juvenile compositions. After studying music and linguistics in Munich, he became *Kapellmeister* in Meiningen, Munich, Weimar, and Berlin, and from 1908 was musical director of the Berlin Philharmonic. He was director of opera in Vienna from 1919 to 1924, and one of the founders and leading personalities of the Salzburg Festival (from 1920). During the Nazi period his political attitude was ambiguous; he was motivated by personal considerations, and was president of the National Socialist Reichs-Musikkammer (State Music Bureau) between 1933 and 1935.

Works: 15 operas: *Guntram* (1894), *Feuersnot* (*Trial by Fire*) (1901), *Salome* (1905), *Elektra* (*Electra*) (1909), *Der Rosenkavalier* (*The Knight of the Rose*) (1911), *Ariadne auf Naxos* (*Ariadne on Naxos*) (1912), *Die Frau ohne Schatten* (*The Woman Without a Shadow*) (1919), *Intermezzo* (1924), *Die ägyptische Helena* (*The Egyptian Helen*) (1928), *Arabella* (1933), *Die schweigsame Frau* (*The Silent Woman*) (1935), *Friedenstag* (*Peace Day*) (1938), *Daphne* (1938), *Die Liebe der Danae* (*The Love of Danae*) (1940/FP 1952), *Capriccio* (1942); symphonic works, including *Macbeth* (1888), *Don Juan* (1888), *Tod und Verklärung* (*Death and Transfiguration*) (1889), *Till Eulenspiegel* (1895), *Also sprach Zarathustra* (*Thus spake Zoroaster*) (1896), *Don Quixote* (1897), *Ein Heldenleben* (*A Hero's Life*) (1898), and *Eine Alpensinfonie* (*An Alpine Symphony*) (1915); chamber music, songs.

Guntram

Handlung in three acts

Libretto: Richard Strauss.

Première: 10 May 1894, Weimar (Hoftheater); revised version: 29 October 1940, Weimar (Nationaltheater).

Characters: The Old Duke (B), Freihild, his daughter (S), Duke Robert, her husband (Bar), Guntram, a singer (T), Friedhold, a singer and member of Guntram's order (B), Fool (T), An Old Woman (A), An Old Man (T), Two Younger Men (2 B), Three Vassals (3 B), A Messenger (Bar), Four Minstels (2 T, 2 B); monks, servants, cavalrymen, poor people, vassals (chorus).

Setting: Germany, in the mid-13th century.

Synopsis

Young Guntram is a member of a medieval order of minstrels, though one who praises Christian rather than sensual love. In a land governed by a tyrant he experiences poverty and brutality. Here he also meets "the mother of the poor." This is Freihild, the generous, unhappy wife of the tyrant. Guntram hopes to convert the ruler with his singing, but fails and kills his opponent in battle. He renounces the love of Freihild, but also turns away from his order to make his peace with God in solitude.

Act I

A forest on Duke Robert's estate. While Guntram gives food to the poor, he becomes aware of his mission: by means of his art, he must convince the tyrant and the people of the restless province of the power of love and peace. The kindly Freihild, who has been forced into marriage with the duke, wants to put an end to her life, but Guntram rescues her. The grateful old duke invites them to a feast.

Act II

At the duke's court. While other singers praise Duke Robert in their songs, Guntram sings of the conflict between peaceful nature and the violent rule of the tyrant. When news arrives of an uprising of the people, Guntram grasps his sword and inflicts a deadly wound on the duke. He is arrested by the old duke. Freihild resolves to free Guntram.

Act III

A prison. Guntram refuses both Freihild's love and the suggestion of his fellow order member Friedhold that he should answer to the order for the killing. He wants to tread his own path towards reconciliation with God.

Guntram, the superman

In the long course of the opera's composition (1887–93), Strauss drafted several versions of the libretto. The original ending of *Guntram* was in accordance with the taste of an old friend of Strauss, an admirer of both Wagner and Liszt. He was the violinist and composer Alexander Ritter. Following Ritter's preferences, Guntram accuses himself of violating the laws of his order. In this early version of the libretto, he already refuses the concept of salvation by a woman (taken from Wagner), but his intention is to do penance for his crime in the Holy Land. During a long journey through Greece and Egypt in 1892, Strauss planned significant alterations. Now his hero turns away not only from his order (the circle around Wagner at Bayreuth?) but also from any protective ideology. In terms of intellectual content, Guntram's great final monologue is strikingly close to the most influential thinker of the turn of the century, Friedrich Nietzsche. "My sorrow is assuaged only by the urge of my heart; my guilt is atoned for only by the penance of my choice; my life is determined only by the law of my soul; my God speaks to me only through myself!"

"Simple and melodic"

Strauss wrote to his parents in 1892, during the composition of *Guntram*, that its music would be "simple and melodic," but a year later he was forced to admit that he could not get rid of a certain nervousness in his writing for the orchestra. The huge orchestra required for *Guntram* (Strauss uses four tenor horns on the stage alone) offers an even broader range of tone-color than Wagner's, and the symphonic inspiration of the scenes and the great monologues already suggests the new dramatic forms of →*Salome* and →*Elektra*. But something of Strauss's intended simplicity was preserved. In the course of the endless symphonic garlands of melody, heartfelt passages of a song-like character sometimes appear (particularly in Guntram's closing monologue). This relationship between the elevated and the simple is what most suggests the later, mature style of Richard Strauss.

Guntram, cast photograph for the original performance with Heinrich Zeller (Guntram, left) and Ferdinand Wiedey (Friedhold), Hoftheater, Weimar 1894.
The monastic clothing, the crucifix worn around the neck, the lyre, and the sword at his belt symbolize the burden of ideas from which Guntram must free himself.

Trial by Fire

Feuersnot

Singgedicht in one act

Libretto: Ernst von Wolzogen.
Première: 21 November 1901, Dresden (Hofoper).
Characters: Schweiker von Gundelfingen, the town governor (T), Ortolf Sentlinger, the mayor (B), Diemut, his daughter (S), Elsbeth, Wigelis, and Margret, her playmates (Ms, A, S), Kunrad, the carpenter (Bar), Jörg Pöschel, the innkeeper (B), Hämerlein, the grocer (Bar), Kofel, the smith (B), Kunz Gilgenstock, the baker and brewer (B), Ortlieb Tulbeck, the master cooper (T), Ursula, his wife (A), Ruger Aspeck, the potter (T), Walpurg, his wife (S); townspeople, servants of the duke, children (chorus).
Setting: Munich, on the day of the midsummer festival, in an indefinite, legendary age.

Synopsis

All Munich is joyfully preparing for the midsummer festival. The young magician Kunrad recklessly kisses Diemut in the street. The proud girl takes her revenge. She invites the infatuated young man to a nocturnal rendezvous, pulls him up in a basket to her balcony, and leaves him hanging halfway up, to the mockery of the crowd. Kunrad then extinguishes all the city's fires and lights. Diemut pulls Kunrad up into her room, and they are united in love. Then the lights go on again, for when "love unites with the magic of genius, then a light must come on even for the worst of Philistines ... ". (Ernst von Wolzogen)

Ein Heldenleben, "The Hero's Adversaries," caricature of Strauss by John Jack Vrieslander, 1902.
In the final decade of the 19th century, Strauss was seen as the hero of the new music. He considered bourgeois conformism and mediocrity to be his adversaries. As early as the symphonic tone poem *Ein Heldenleben* of 1898, the chief protagonist of which is Strauss himself, he portrayed his adversaries in a grotesque and disparaging manner. The "sung poem" *Trial by Fire* is also a work of revenge, for the people of Munich had hissed the first performance of the symphonic poem *Also sprach Zarathustra* in March 1899.

Wolzogen, the librettist

Ernst von Wolzogen (1855–1934) was an interesting figure in German literature at the turn of the century. Like Strauss he came from Munich, and, again like Strauss, had problems with the conservative public of his native city. They met in Munich in late 1898 or early 1899, and were both drawn to Berlin. Strauss became chief conductor at the Hofoper (court opera) there, and Wolzogen founded a literary cabaret on the French model, the "Überbrettl" (1900). A number of important poets and writers of the Jugendstil school, such as Richard Dehmel, Karl von Levetzow, Frank Wedekind, and Otto Julius Bierbaum, worked for this organization. Even the young Arnold Schoenberg earned a wretched crust here for a while, as accompanist and house composer. Strauss and Wolzogen later planned a further one-act piece together (after a novella by Cervantes), but the plan never came to fruition.

A gentle satire

Throughout his life, Strauss quoted from and parodied his own and others' compositions. In the choice of both location and period, a medieval German city at the time of the midsummer festival, the "Subend" (that is, St. John's Eve), the authors were playfully referring to Richard Wagner's →*The Mastersingers*. This also applies to the caricature of the conservative bourgeoisie, which regards with suspicion the representatives of new ideas, Wagner's Walther von Stolzing and Strauss's Kunrad. But the allusions go even deeper. An old magician called Master Reichart (Richard) is conjured up by Kunrad in his hour of need. The young magician represents Strauss himself. The citizens of Munich had treated Wagner very shabbily at the premières of →*Tristan* (1865) and *The Mastersingers* (1868). In his great address to the people of Munich, Kunrad refers unambiguously to this, punning on the name Wagner by using the words "Wagen" (carriage) and "gewagt" (daring), and also on the names Strauss and Wolzogen.

The real Strauss

The text of *Trial by Fire* is full of ambiguous allusions, and Strauss, who had been developing a taste for musical quotations since his autobiographical symphonic poem *Ein Heldenleben*, was in his element. He quotes frequently from Wagner and from himself, always subtly, by suggestion only, and with remarkable virtuosity. The musical style is quite different from that of →*Guntram*. There, we find pathetic, post-Wagnerian music with substantial soprano and tenor roles à la *Tristan and Isolde* or →*Twilight of the Gods*; here, there is a high baritone with spoken, rhetorical declamation. In *Trial by Fire* dramatic events and music are to an extent independent, related to each other only contrapuntally – an approach that Strauss was to continue to use in his operas. Even so, this one-act piece is never dry in its effect. The composer was unable to resist melody, and there is no lack of the grand theatrical effect, without which none of Strauss's later operas could be imagined.

In the finale, as the whole city sparkles with light, the music is full of colors and flashes like fireworks. The eroticism is also striking. Sometimes it is coarsely traditional, even anticlerical, almost "heathen." "All warmth flows forth from woman, all light comes from love." There are erotic allusions in both the text and the music. All this is also found in Strauss's later operas. In *Trial by Fire* the composer took a decisive step in his writing for the stage: away from Richard Wagner and towards a style of his own.

Trial by Fire, set design by Leo Pasetti for the production by Alois Hofmann, conductor Hans Knappertsbusch, Munich 1930 (TWS). Set design by Leo Pasetti with quaint, crooked houses in the Sendlinger Strasse in Munich, showing the magician and even the ominous basket (top right). The story on which the opera is based comes from the highly diverse collection of legends relating to the solstice. Variations of these exist even in non-European legend.

Salome, production photograph with Maria Cebotari (Salome) and Julius Pölzer (Herod), Staatsoper, Berlin 1942.
In this Berlin production Herod was portrayed by an evil, grotesque caricature, a cross between Frankenstein and Count Dracula, while Salome was dressed up as a sophisticated revue artist. This production photograph unambiguously shows that *Salome* was used by the Nazis for propaganda purposes and at the same time regarded as "degenerate art." It was a paradoxical and embarrassing situation, since during those years Strauss was considered a protector of German art.

Salome, Emmy Destinn as Salome, c. 1910. Emmy Destinn in a victorious pose. This image, which today strikes a somewhat ironic note, shows how unfamiliar the figure of Salome was to operatic practice in those days.

Salome

Musikdrama in one act

Libretto: A German translation by Hedwig Lachmann of Oscar Wilde's play.

Première: 9 December 1905, Dresden (Hofoper).

Characters: Herodes/Herod, Tetrarch of Judea (T), Herodias, his wife (Ms), Salome, his stepdaughter (S), Jochanaan/Jokanaan (the prophet John the Baptist) (Bar), Narraboth, captain of the guard (T), The Page of Herodias (A), Five Jews (4 T, B), Two Nazarenes (T, B), Two Soldiers (2 B), A Cappadocian (B), A Slave (S or T).

Setting: A terrace at the fortress of Machaerus, a secondary residence of Herod II Antipas in Peraea, east of the Dead Sea.

Synopsis

Salome, the beautiful stepdaughter of Herod, is fascinated by the imprisoned prophet Jokanaan, who resolutely rejects her. After Salome has danced before Herod according to his wish, she demands as a reward the head of Jokanaan. In this way she possesses the man she desires. Herod has Salome executed.

Scene 1

A festive birthday banquet in Herod's house. The young captain Narraboth has been captivated by Salome's beauty. His friend the page warns him about this passion, but to no effect. Narraboth approaches Salome, who, bored and disgusted by the depraved surroundings of her stepfather's court, has left the banqueting hall and come onto the terrace.

Scene 2

The voice of the imprisoned prophet Jokanaan is heard from his underground cell. He condemns the depravity of Herod and Salome's mother Herodias. Salome wants to see him, but the soldiers refuse to bring him up, having been forbidden to do so on pain of punishment. Only Narraboth is unable to resist the desires of his beloved princess, and leads Jokanaan up to her.

Scene 3

The prophet renews his accusations, and indignantly rejects Salome's erotic approaches. His refusal only provokes her further. Narraboth tries in vain to calm her down, and finally takes his own life.

Scene 4

The ruling couple appear, disturbed by the uproar. Herodias demands the prophet's death. Herod tries to create a diversion. Overwhelmed by Salome's beauty, he asks her to dance for him, promising to fulfill her every wish. Salome dances, and then asks for the head of Jokanaan as her reward. Herod, who believes the prophet to be a holy man, tries to negotiate with Salome, offering her an alternative prize, but in vain. Finally he gives way and has the prophet killed. Salome is presented with the dead man's head on a silver dish, and kisses the mouth passionately. Herod gives orders for her execution.

S. N.

The Salome material in the Bible

In the versions of the story given in the New Testament (in the gospels of Matthew and Mark) Salome takes little interest in the cruel deed. Here is Mark's account (vi, 21–29): "And when a convenient day was come, that Herod on his birthday made a supper to his lords, high captains, and chief estates of Galilee; and when the daughter of the said Herodias came in, and danced, and pleased Herod and them that sat with him, the king said unto the damsel, Ask of me whatsoever thou wilt, and I will give it thee. And he sware unto her, Whatsoever thou shalt ask of me, I will give it thee, unto the half of my kingdom. And she went forth, and said unto her mother, What shall I ask? And she said, The head of John the Baptist. And she came in straightway with haste unto the king, and asked, saying, I will that thou give me by and by in a charger the head of John the Baptist. And the king was exceeding sorry; yet for his oath's sake, and for their sakes which sat with him, he would not reject her."

Heinrich Heine's version

After countless dramatic and heroic representations of Herodias and Salome in the visual arts, the German

Salome, Anja Silja (b. 1940) as Salome. Strauss had to wait for decades for the Salome of his dreams – "16 years old, with the voice of an Isolde." The "revolution" of manners among the young generation of the 1960s also altered the image of Salome. One of the most interesting interpretations was given by Anja Silja, who achieved a compelling effect with her Dance of the Seven Veils.

poet Heinrich Heine made so bold as to offer an alternative interpretation of the motives of Herodias' revenge. In his satirical epic *Atta Troll* (1842) the great sinners of humanity include Herodias, who must ride with the wild hunters until the day of judgement: "In her hands she always carries/That dish with the head/Of John, and she kisses it;/Yes, she kisses the head with fervor./For she once loved John – /The Bible does not speak of it,/But the tale lives on among the people/Of Herodias' bloody love – /Otherwise the lust of this lady/Would be impossible to explain – /Would a woman desire the head/Of a man she does not love?"

The French version

The subject of Herodias or Salome was in the air in France in the second half of the nineteenth century. In 1876 Gustave Moreau exhibited his oil paintings *Salomé dansant devant Hérode* and *L'Apparition*, while Stéphane Mallarmé's dramatic poem *Fragment d'un étude scénique ancienne d'un poème d'Hérodiade* (1869) and Gustave Flaubert's story *Hérodias* (1877) were also in the minds of Parisians. It was only on the operatic stage that there was no sign of the strange Judean family with their house prophet. →Jules Massenet was introduced to the material by his Italian publisher Giulio Ricordi, who in 1878 had a scenario by Angelo Zanardini sent to the composer. Zanardini's libretto was based on Flaubert's story, whose central character is not Salome but her mother.

Scandal over *Salome*

Oscar Wilde, who was well aware of the scandal associated with Massenet's opera *Hérodiade* of 1881, fully expected ten years later that his *Salome* would be banned from the stage in puritanical England. He therefore issued an advance threat to the English theatrical world, censor and all: "If the censor rejects Salome I will leave England and settle in France." To his great disappointment, his mistrust of English society was confirmed: the censor banned the play. Wilde, who had strangely enough written *Salome* in French rather than English, had the play put on in Paris in 1893. But in Paris, too, *Salome* was kept off the stage, and Wilde was not allowed to hear his colorful, sensual sentences spoken by Sarah Bernhardt.

In Germany there was slightly less prudery, in contrast to the Catholic and puritanical countries. *Salome* was performed in Berlin in Max Reinhardt's little theater, with Gertrud Eysoldt in the title role. This performance gave Strauss the idea of an opera about Salome. The first performance of the opera in Dresden took place without a scandal, although the emperor allowed a performance in Berlin only with an optimistic ending: the morning star was to appear in the sky, to indicate the arrival of the three wise men. At the Vienna Hofoper, despite the efforts of Gustav Mahler, *Salome* was not permitted to be performed until the end of the monarchy in 1918; even in New York the première had to be canceled.

The "poor" composer

The following is one of the many anecdotes that circulate around the figure of Strauss, and illustrates the composer's dry sense of humor: "Wilhelm II once said to his artistic director: 'I am very sorry that Strauss has composed this *Salome*; I like him very much, but this will cause him terrible trouble.' This trouble enabled me to build my villa at Garmisch!" (Richard Strauss, *Memoirs of the First Performances of my Operas*, 1942)

Salome and sensuality

While he was writing his play *Salome*, Oscar Wilde formed a friendship with the young diplomat and writer Gomez Carillo from Guatemala, who added certain details to the "birth" of the most scandalous female figure of the turn of the century. Not a day went by in which Wilde did not talk about Salome. During this period the women on the street all looked to him like potential Judean princesses. When walking through the Rue de la Paix he stopped at the jewelers' shops to look for suitable jewelry.

One afternoon he asked young Gomez Carillo: "What do you think – should she be naked? Yes, stark naked, but draped with heavy, jingling necklaces, made of precious stones which shimmer in all colors and are warmed on the breast of her amber-colored body. I do not think of her as an unconscious woman, a dumb tool. No, her lips in Leonardo's painting betray her inner cruelty. Her lust must be immeasurable, her perversion boundless. The pearls must steam on her body."

Sarah Bernhardt as Salome

Sarah Bernhardt, the most famous actress of the fin de siècle, appeared in London for a season in 1892. At a party she asked Oscar Wilde if he would not write a play for her. "I have already done so," Wilde replied to the "serpent of old Nile" (as he called the actress, with impertinent familiarity). Soon afterwards Bernhardt read the play and resolved to play the title role.

Colors

Charles Ricketts, who had been appointed set designer for the planned first performance of Oscar Wilde's *Salome* in London, suggested "a black floor to contrast with Salome's white feet ... The sky should be a strong turquoise green, broken by vertically falling Japanese strips of matting, which form a floating tent above the terrace." Oscar Wilde urged that the Jews should be dressed in yellow, Herod and Herodias in purple, and Jokanaan in white. There was endless discussion about Salome's costume. "Perhaps black as night? Or silver like the moon?" Wilde recommended "green, like an exotic and poisonous lizard." Ricketts wanted to let the moon shine on the terrace, and in such a manner that

Above
Salome, set design by Max Bignens for the production by Wolf Völker, conductor Günter Wich, Düsseldorf 1968 (TWS).
Max Bignens's set design displays an expressive orgy of color, quite in the tradition of Oscar Wilde. The line-work is related to that of Art Nouveau, the predominant style of the period in which *Salome* was created.

Opposite, below
Salome, set design by Max Kruse for the first German production of Wilde's play, Berlin 1903 (TWS).

the source of light should not be seen. Wilde insisted on a "strangely gloomy pattern in the sky." The painter Graham Robertson was also consulted; he recommended that the sky should be violet. "A violet sky," said Wilde, "I had not thought of that. Of course, a violet sky; and then, instead of an orchestra, censers full of incense. Just imagine – the rising clouds of perfume, from time to time wrapping the stage in a veil – a different scent for every sensation."

Max Kruse, the designer for the first performance of the play in Germany in 1903, created a more cautious backdrop, drawing on earlier models. One can imagine this style of scene painting as appropriate for early nineteenth-century neo-classicism and Romanticism. Effects such as those of the light streaming out of the palace gate and the red splashes on the ground were employed soon afterwards by Expressionist designers to heighten dramatic effect.

Right
Salome, set design by Emil Rieck for the Dresden première, 1905 (TWS).

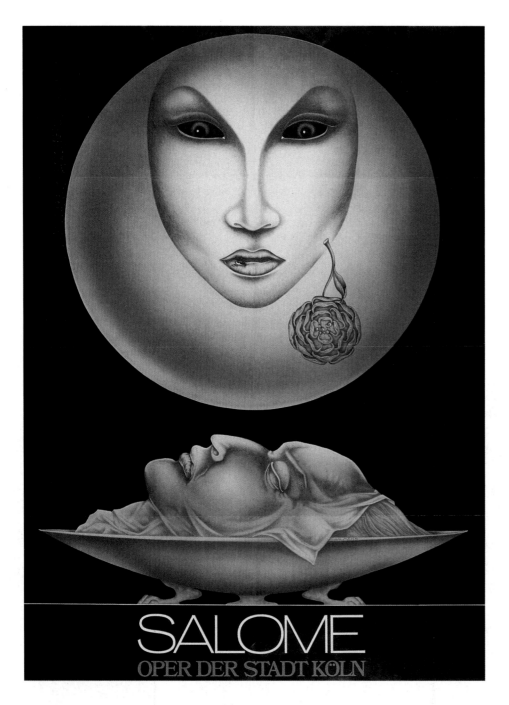

Salome's kiss

Salome, as an experience for the listener, consists of a series of climaxes each surpassing the last in intensity. Salome's dance (the core event in the opera, although composed retrospectively) is the last but one of these climaxes, while the absolute culmination is the kiss and the hurried, brutal murder of Salome. As was standard in popular one-act dramas of the turn of the century, we have a sense of imminent catastrophe from the very beginning of the work (one of the first lines of the play is: "Something terrible is going to happen"). The sight of the bloody head of Jokanaan, which is lifted out of the dungeon by the gigantic black arm of the executioner, may be repellent and frightening. But the music that goes with it is seductively beautiful, and tells of the great passion that is being fulfilled in that moment. It is Salome's *Liebestod*, a paraphrase of Isolde's *Liebestod* in Wagner's →*Tristan and Isolde*. The taste of Jokanaan's lips is bitter to Salome, and the music that accompanies this strange act of love is equally bittersweet. First we hear a chord suggesting the intoxication of love, and then the musical gesture is repeated, but it flows into a contradictory chord: fulfilment and destruction are identical. M 1

1. Salome's Kiss

The moon as a dramatic metaphor

Sarah Bernhardt, the Salome of Oscar Wilde's dreams, expressed her opinion in an interview that the real protagonist of the play was the moon. At the turn of the century, the moon became a much-used metaphor for the sick soul. "See the disc of the moon, how strange it looks. Like a woman rising from the grave," the page warns his friend Narraboth. But the captain, who is in love with Salome, sees something quite different: "She is very strange. Like a little princess whose feet are white doves. It is almost as if she dances." But for Salome the moon is "like a silver flower, cool and chaste. Yes, like the beauty of a virgin, who has stayed pure." The hysteric Herod sees the images of his own fantasy in the moon: "It looks like a crazed woman who seeks lovers everywhere ... like a drunken woman tottering through clouds ..." Only Herodias maintains a sober attitude to the moon: "No, the moon is like the moon, that is all."

Tone-colors

Listening to *Salome*, one has the impression that although the action takes place in a single location, this is a colorful world. But the question of whether everything here is really exotic cannot be answered without reservation. For what does exoticism mean? A foreign coloring? In *Salome* the exotic becomes the distinguishing feature of an atmosphere that dominates the entire opera. This distinguishes it from Romantic exotic operas (such as Saint-Saëns's →*Samson and Delilah*, Goldmark's →*The Queen of Sheba*, or Verdi's →*Aida*). "I always had the same objection to oriental and Jewish operas, that they are lacking in true Eastern coloring and blazing sunlight. The need for this inspired me with truly exotic harmonies, which shimmered particularly in unfamiliar cadences, like shot silk," declared Strauss. Wilde's drama offered him a text that vibrated in orgiastic colors (the "necklace with four rows of pearls," the "most beautiful emerald," the "white peacocks,"

the "yellow and pale red topazes," the "opals, which constantly sparkle, with a fire as cold as ice," and so on). This is the poetry of the Song of Songs, for which Strauss composed luxuriant music, rich in tone-color. Neither did he forget local color. He had no personal experience of the land in which the opera was set, but on his great Egyptian journey of 1892 he had gained similar impressions. The music of *Salome* often sounds oriental. Strauss specifically added a new instrument, whose sound was close to that of the shrill Arabian oboe, the Heckelphone (a kind of bass oboe). The source of light in *Salome* is also of great importance for the atmosphere of the opera. With the exception of the scene of the kiss, the moon is present throughout the piece, whether pale, red, or yellow.

Salome, production photograph with Mara Zampieri as Salome, production Boleslaw Barlog, sets and costumes Jürgen Rose, conductor Peter Schneider, Wiener Staatsoper, 1991.
Salome's monologue after the execution of Jokanaan resounds with a terrible intensity; one almost expects the head to answer her or to return her assurances of love. It is the strangest love duet in operatic history, with one sung and one silent role. The sight is at once repellent and fascinating.

Elektra

Electra

Tragödie in one act (seven scenes)

Libretto: Hugo von Hofmannsthal.
Première: 25 January 1909, Dresden (Hofoper).
Characters: Klytemnästra/Clytemnestra (Ms), Elektra/Electra and Chrysothemis, her daughters (2 S), Orest/Orestes, her son (T), Aegisth/Aegisthus, her lover (T), Orestes' Tutor (B), The Confidante (S), The Trainbearer (S), A Young Servant (T), An Old Servant (B), An Overseer (S), Five Maidservants (A, 2 Ms, 2 S); servants (chorus).
Setting: Mycenae, after the Trojan War.

Synopsis

When Agamemnon led the Greek troops into battle against Troy, the gods demanded the sacrifice of his daughter Iphigenia. Agamemnon obeyed, in spite of the resistance of his wife Clytemnestra. After his victorious return, Agamemnon was killed by Clytemnestra and her lover Aegisthus. These events precede those of the opera. Three children survive: Electra, Chrysothemis, and Orestes. Electra cannot forget her father's murder and longs for revenge. Chrysothemis has forgotten and wants to lead a normal life. Orestes is believed dead, but Electra has had him brought up far away, as a tool of revenge. He returns and kills both Aegisthus and his mother. Electra dies in an ecstatic frenzy of joy.

Scene 1
Electra has been condemned by her mother to live as a maid, since she constantly reproaches her for her past crime. Electra is mocked and insulted by the maids of the court.

Scene 2
Electra, her vision of revenge becoming more passionate, remembers her murdered father.

Scene 3
Electra and Chrysothemis. Chrysothemis wants to lead the life of a normal woman. Electra rejects all compromise, remaining irreconcilable.

Scene 4
Electra and Clytemnestra. The mother is tormented by nightmares and seeks the advice of her rejected daughter. Electra recommends a remedy: she advises Clytemnestra to offer herself to the gods as an expiatory sacrifice.

Scene 5
Electra and Chrysothemis. News arrives of Orestes' death. Now Electra wants to accomplish the act of revenge herself with the help of her sister. Chrysothemis refuses, and Electra decides to act alone.

Scene 6
Orestes is alive. He returns home in secret, recognized by no one, and reveals himself only to Electra. Joyfully she hands over to him the instrument of revenge, the axe.

Scene 7
Electra hears sounds within the palace: Orestes has killed Aegisthus and his mother. She dies in a frenzy of ecstatic triumph.   S. N.

Elektra, production photograph with Hildegard Behrens as Electra, production Otto Schenk, sets Jürgen Rose, conductor James Levine, Metropolitan Opera, New York 1997.
Just as the role of Salome requires, as Strauss put it, a performer with the figure of a 16-year-old and the voice of an Isolde, that of Electra demands a young woman with exceptional dramatic power and the voice of a Brünnhilde. The fact that the work consists of a single act should not be misinterpreted: *Elektra* runs for nearly an hour and a half, and the title role is a great physical and mental challenge, to be mastered only by a singer of considerable ability. Electra dominates the stage from the first moment to the last.

"Blood will tell" – the Atrides

The presumptuous and accursed clan of the Atrides traced its lineage back to the highest god of Olympus, Zeus. The very first of the clan committed an act of sacrilege: King Tantalus slaughtered his son Pelops and served him up as a dish for the gods, in order to test their omniscience. His punishment was to stand up to his chin in water and below a tree laden with fruit, and yet to thirst and hunger eternally. His son Pelops was brought back to life by the gods and produced two sons, Atreus and Thyestes, with whom the mutual eradication of the two branches of the family began. Thyestes violated the marriage of his brother Atreus, and the latter then killed the sons of Thyestes and served their flesh to their father. Thyestes raped his own daughter. Her son Aegisthus killed Atreus.

Above
Elektra, set design by Emil Rieck for the Dresden première, 1909 (TWS).
For the operatic stage the royal court is depicted with images traditionally used to portray Mediterranean exoticism: a dark blue sky, a tree in leaf, a warm, sensual light from within the palace. A high degree of stylization and artificial decorative devices characterized the operatic stage for a long time.

Below
Elektra, set design by Max Kruse, Berlin 1903/4 (TWS).
In Max Kruse's set design for Hofmannsthal's *Elektra*, Mycenae is presented as a strange, unwelcoming Greek landscape, dominated by huge slabs of gray stone. The Lion Gate to the palace of the Atrides resembles the entrance to a prison: low and narrow.

Agamemnon, the son of Atreus, married Clytemnestra, and his brother Menelaus married her sister Helen. The Trojan War began. Iphigenia placed her head under the axe, sacrificed by her father Agamemnon. Clytemnestra shared her bed and power with Aegisthus, and both killed Agamemnon on his return from the war. These are the facts that lie behind the dramas of Aeschylus, Sophocles, Euripides, and the opera by Hofmannsthal and Strauss. Only Electra's ecstatic "dance of death" is not found in the old sources. It was an invention by Hofmannsthal for Strauss, who, following Nietzsche's *Die Geburt der Tragödie aus dem Geiste der Musik* (*The Birth of Tragedy from the Spirit of Music*), highly valued dance as a heightened form of expression and had already used it as such several times (in the symphonic poem *Also sprach Zarathustra* and in the operas →*Trial by Fire* and particularly →*Salome*).

The Electra complex as dramatic nucleus

The Greek world invented by Hofmannsthal and Strauss is far from classical, for neither the setting nor even the mythology is of determining significance. What is important is the human soul. In contrast to → *Salome*, the exotic, the local color, plays no part. Much to the delight of present-day directors, *Elektra* can be staged anywhere: in the slums of a metropolis, on the London Underground, or in a nuclear fallout shelter. Hofmannsthal, always the best interpreter of his own work, saw the essentials of his drama when he wrote: "In Electra the act and the relationship to the act stand at the center. A crime is avenged by a crime, and this revenge is imposed on a being who is doubly ruined because of it: as an individual she believes herself capable, but because of her sex she is incapable of performing the act." This is the reason why Electra – who possesses the greatest dignity of the three female protagonists – is frustrated. Her hesitant relationship with the act reminded Hofmannsthal of *Hamlet*, and indeed the basic situation of his drama bears a number of striking similarities to that of Shakespeare's play. But Electra, the female child, has an even closer subconscious relationship with her father than Hamlet. In

psychiatry, as a parallel to the Oedipus complex, an excessively strong relationship between father and daughter is called an Electra complex. It is a neurotic condition. Electra's first monologue in the opera betrays the pathological dependence of the heroine on her father. A powerful, monumental motif characterizes Agamemnon from Electra's point of view. *M 2* In Electra's emotional world, Agamemnon appears as an affectionate father, which he may not have been objectively. The melodically extended motif betrays a warmth that here, and perhaps to an even greater extent at the end of the opera, is revealed as childish love. *M 3*

After Orestes' double murder of Clytemnestra and Aegisthus, Electra is seized by ecstasy; she dances in a state of rapture and then suddenly falls down dead. Her dance of joy distantly recalls the Ride of the Valkyries from Wagner's → *The Valkyrie*, showing that Electra, like Wotan's Brünnhilde, is a truly heroic daughter. The dance, broken off at its climax by the sudden death of the heroine, is both apotheosis and *Liebestod*, and parallels Salome's kiss and death. At the same time the ending reveals Electra's limits: her life has been fulfilled and so completed by this act of revenge.

2. Agamemnon Motif

3. Electra's Love for Her Father

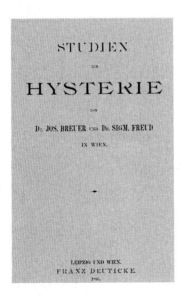

Studies in hysteria?

The *Studien über Hysterie* of Josef Breuer and Sigmund Freud was published six years before the première of Hofmannsthal's tragedy *Elektra*, while Freud's major work *Die Traumdeutung*, or *The Interpretation of Dreams*, appeared six years afterwards. Unlike the relatively phlegmatic Strauss, who did not suffer from crises of creativity or intellect, Hofmannsthal took an interest in psychology. He was thoroughly familiar with Freud's works at a time when they were not widely read, their influence being confined to certain intellectual circles, above all within the Austro-Hungarian monarchy. With *Elektra*, Hofmannsthal was in this respect very much up to date. And Strauss himself had a fine sense of the *Zeitgeist* of these years, recognizing the opportunity to express the depth of the female soul through a mixture of sensitive, nervous, brutal, and lyrical musical moments.

A women's opera

The one-act opera → *Salome* is unusual in the context of the traditional operatic repertory, since it contains no conventional pair of lovers (soprano and tenor). Salome's passionate love is rejected by the ascetic prophet (a baritone in the opera). A character tenor is to be found in Herod, but the absolute ruler of the stage is Salome. In *Elektra* Strauss goes even further in this direction. Electra appears soon after the beginning of the opera and remains on stage until its close. With this role, Richard Strauss created one of the most demanding of all roles for a dramatic soprano. The male parts are decidedly brief and episodic.

Elektra, production photograph with Marie Götze (Clytemnestra) and Thila Plaichinger (Electra), from the first performance at the Schauspielhaus in Berlin, 1909.
The staging was in accordance with the directions of Hugo von Hofmannsthal and was to prove significant for the subsequent history of the interpretation of the opera.

Below
Elektra, production photograph with Brigitte Fassbaender as Clytemnestra, production Harry Kupfer, sets Hans Schavernoch, costumes Reinhard Heinrich, conductor Claudio Abbado, Wiener Staatsoper, 1989. Clytemnestra staggers across the stage in a state of trance, delivering her extraordinary, Expressionistic vocal line. The well-known character player Brigitte Fassbaender created this groaning, screaming, whispering female figure with spectral suggestive power.

Clytemnestra

The mother Clytemnestra appears in the drama as a living corpse: "Her pallid, bloated face, in the lurid light of the torches, appears even paler above her scarlet robe … The queen is covered from head to foot with precious stones and talismans … Her eyelids seem disproportionately large, and it seems to cost her a fearful effort to keep them open." (Hofmannsthal's stage directions)

Clytemnestra is tormented by terrible dreams. She has committed a sin and feels imprisoned in the palace of Mycenae, and is perpetually confronted by her own conscience in the person of Electra, her accuser. Her spiritual disease is doubly motivated – by the fear of unavoidable punishment ("Blut blut zeige," "Blood will tell") and by the obsession that Orestes is not dead and will come one day as an avenger. The whole atmosphere around her is heavy with hysteria. She sings with unnatural slowness, as one sometimes speaks in a dream, and the orchestra becomes noisy when she appears. Her illness is hysteria, which Hofmannsthal describes precisely in her words: "It is not a word, it is not a pain, it does not press upon me, it does not choke me, it is nothing, not even a nightmare, and yet it is so terrible that my soul wishes to be hanged, and every limb of my body screams for death, and yet I am alive and am not even ill … "

Chrysothemis

Chrysothemis is the least popular daughter of Agamemnon and occupies an exceptional position in this accursed family. She is a child of light, a woman who wants happiness in her life. What she would like best is to leave Mycenae: "I am a woman and want a woman's destiny. Better to be dead than to live and not to live!" she cries, weeping, to her sister Electra, who contemptuously ascribes these words to the human weakness and unworthiness of Chrysothemis. The figure of Chrysothemis is highly characteristic of Hofmannsthal's poetic world. He loved the idea of metamorphosis, and in his works often contrasted changeable characters with statue-like heroes (as he did in another collaboration with Strauss, →*Ariadne on Naxos*). Musically, Strauss needed Chrysothemis as a lyrical counterbalance to Electra, although both parts are composed for dramatic sopranos. The two parts nevertheless provide a good example of the difference between "dramatic" and "high dramatic." And finally, in the part of Chrysothemis Strauss gives free rein to his melodic imagination (his most individual musical gift). The cantabile character of this role is enchanting, and there are even waltz-like passages, which for Strauss always meant existing or expected happiness. *M 4*

Elektra, production photograph with Cheryl Studer (Chrysothemis, left) and Eva Marton (Electra), Wiener Staatsoper 1989.
It is typical of the progressiveness of the German operatic world of the beginning of the 20th century that a new opera such as *Elektra* should reach the stage almost simultaneously in both Dresden and Berlin (three weeks apart) with different casts and direction. Strauss gratefully noted the names of the first two interpreters of Electra: Annie Krull (Dresden) and Thila Plaichinger (Berlin).

Left
Elektra, production photograph with Janis Martin (Electra, left) and Livia Budai-Batky (Clytemnestra), production Núria Espert, costumes Franca Squarciapino, conductor Guido Johannes Rumstadt, Oper Frankfurt 1994.

4. Chrysothemis' Yearning for Motherhood

ih - - nen sel - ber __ quillt sü - - sser Trank. __

Der Rosenkavalier, costume design for Octavian by Alfred Roller for the Dresden première, 1911 (TWS)

Der Rosenkavalier, production photograph with Anne-Sofie von Otter (Octavian) and Barbara Bonney (Sophie), production Otto Schenk, costumes Erni Kniepert, conductor Leonard Bernstein, Wiener Staatsoper 1968.

Der Rosenkavalier
The Knight of the Rose

Komödie für Musik in three acts

Libretto: Hugo von Hofmannsthal.
Première: 26 January 1911, Dresden (Hofoper).

Characters: The Feldmarschallin/Marschallin, Marie Thérèse, Princess Werdenberg (S), Octavian, Count Rofrano, called Quinquin, her lover (Ms), Mohammed, her black page (silent), Baron Ochs auf Lerchenau, her cousin (B), Herr von Faninal, a rich gentleman, recently ennobled (Bar), Sophie, his daughter (S), Marianne Leitmetzerin, her duenna (S), Valzacchi, an Italian schemer (T), Annina, his niece and partner (A), A Police Inspector (B), The Marschallin's Majordomo (T), Faninal's Majordomo (T), A Notary (B), An Innkeeper (T), An Italian Singer (T), Three Noble Orphans (S, Ms, A), A Milliner (S), A Vendor of Pets (T), Four Lackeys (2 T, 2 B), Four Waiters (1 T, 3 B), Four Small Children (4 S); A Flautist, A Scholar, A Hairdresser, A Noble Widow, Lerchenau's Valet, A Servant, A Doctor (silent); servants, hired deceivers, guests, musicians, constables, children (chorus).
Setting: Vienna, in the early part of the reign of Maria Theresia.

Synopsis
A beautiful young noblewoman (the Marschallin) sends her young lover Octavian to the nouveau riche Faninal. His mission is to take him a silver rose, to ask for the hand of Faninal's daughter Sophie on behalf of the Marschallin's cousin Baron Ochs. Octavian falls in love with Sophie, the pushy Baron Ochs is made to look a fool, and the Marschallin renounces Octavian so that the young lovers may find happiness.

Act I
Early morning in the Marschallin's bedroom. The embraces of the Marschallin and the young Octavian are interrupted by an unexpected visit: the Marschallin's cousin Baron Ochs has come from the country to seek an intermediary in his courtship of a wealthy young girl. Octavian, who has disguised himself as the chambermaid Mariandel, attracts the baron's attention. The Marschallin appoints Octavian as the baron's go-between. The Marschallin's levee begins: an extraordinary variety of people arrive. When the hurly-burly is over, the Marschallin is left alone. This morning she has a particularly strong sense of the transitory nature of all earthly things, thinking of her own life and love affair. But Octavian, transformed back into a man, cannot understand his mistress's feelings.

Act II
The "Knight of the Rose" is expected at the Faninal household. Octavian delivers the silver rose and is overcome by Sophie's beauty. The baron's coarse behavior repels Sophie; she feels drawn to Octavian and seeks his protection. He takes her part and it leads to a duel with the baron. Faninal orders Octavian to leave his house and his daughter to marry the baron. Then the baron receives an invitation to a rendezvous from "Mariandel," a trick devised by Octavian in order to help Sophie. He falls into the trap and agrees, already dreaming, to the strains of a waltz, of a new love affair.

Act III
The rendezvous is being prepared in an inn. Octavian appears, disguised as "Mariandel," and has difficulty in fending off the baron and concealing his own identity. He has sent a secret message to Faninal, so that the father of the bride may catch the prospective bridegroom red-handed. He has also staged a further comedy: Annina, a professional schemer, accuses the baron of bigamy; he is also to be arrested for the seduction of an innocent girl ("Mariandel"). The baron capitulates. Faninal recognizes the baron's bad character and cancels the wedding. When the Marschallin appears on the scene, she understands the situation and gives Octavian his freedom. The young couple confess their mutual love.   *S. N.*

Der Rosenkavalier, production photograph with Kurt Rydl (Ochs), Trudeliese Schmidt (Octavian), and Heinz Zednik (Valzacchi), production Otto Schenk, sets Rudolf Heinrich, costumes Erni Kniepert, conductor Leonard Bernstein, Wiener Staatsoper 1968. Baron Ochs after the duel, awaiting a glass of Tokay.

Silver sounds

What is the famous sound of the silver rose? It is a subtle blend of sounds consisting of high notes. The melodious major chords are played by three flutes, three violins, harps, and celesta (a small keyboard instrument, whose name, not without justification, means "heavenly"). Strauss uses this sound, which is so typical of the world of *Der Rosenkavalier*, as if it were a separate color, like the painter Gustav Klimt. Thus he translates into music the silvery shimmer and the decoration of the rose in the manner of Art Nouveau, which at the turn of the century played an important role in the performing and applied arts as well as in architecture and even fashion. One might well ask whether Art Nouveau has not left its traces in music too. The most successful musical work of its day, *Der Rosenkavalier* provides evidence of this. *M S*

Ochs versus Rosenkavalier

The common aim of librettist and composer was to write a profitable stage work, but the two had different views on how to achieve this. Strauss inclined more towards a coarsely comic piece, seeing Baron Ochs as the main figure in the opera. Hofmannsthal, on the other hand, saw Viennese comedy as the ideal form of expression. For him the silver rose, its bearer, Octavian, and the Marschallin were all-important. This conflict was mirrored in the tedious process of finding a title. Strauss's first proposal was *Der Ochs von Lerchenau* (*Ochs of Lerchenau*). Later Hofmannsthal's friend and confidant suggested the titles *Der Vetter vom Lande* (*The Country Cousin*) and *Quinquin* (Octavian's nickname). Both were rejected by librettist and composer. After a series of variations, the final title was found at a comparatively late stage, during the preparations for the première. Alfred Roller, the renowned set and costume designer for the original production, asked Strauss on 4 May 1910 if he could use the title suggested faute de mieux by Hofmannsthal, *Der Rosenkavalier*, for his sketches. The composer replied impulsively: "I don't like 'Rosenkavalier' at all, I like 'Ochs'! But what can one do? Hofmannsthal loves the delicate, the ethereal, and my wife demands 'Rosenkavalier.' Let it be 'Rosenkavalier,' then, and to the devil with it!"

Richard Strauss, the avant-gardist

"Truly, I say unto you, the name of our master is Richard Strauss" – the opinion of the 23-year-old →Béla Bartók, who was later to become one of the protagonists of the musical avant-garde, in a letter of 1904. Until the great change in Strauss's musical style took place, effected in 1911 with the composition of *Der Rosenkavalier*, young musicians saw in him the prototype of the progressive composer who had the power to lead European music out of the shadow of the great Romantics into the 20th century. Even the radical →Arnold Schoenberg was among Strauss's supporters, even if only for a short time.

5. Motif of the Silver Rose

Setting: Vienna, c. 1740

For *Der Rosenkavalier*, Hofmannsthal took many names directly from the records of the Viennese nobility. The name of the young Count Rofrano (Octavian's official title) comes from the old family that once owned the Palais Auersperg. His nickname, "Quinquin," is that of a Count Franz Esterházy, a member of the Freemasons' lodge "The Crowned Hope," on the occasion of whose death in 1785 Mozart wrote his Masonic Funeral Music (K.477). Since the second husband of the sister of a Count Rofrano was a field marshal, Marquis Ludwig von Brechainville, she could be seen as the model for the Feldmarschallin. Undoubtedly some characteristics of the empress herself are to be found in this character (it is not without significance that the Marschallin's name, Marie Thérèse, is similar to that of the empress, Maria Theresia). Baron Leupold Anton Ochs auf Lerchenau comes from the Carinthian family of Orsini-Rosenberg, the head of which in Mozart's time was General Director of Entertainments in Vienna and bore the subsidiary name of Freiherr auf Lerchenau. But perhaps the name of the character derives from banker Peter Ochs, who came to Vienna from Switzerland. He was a contemporary of Hofmannsthal, and perhaps personally known to the poet. If he was the model for Baron Ochs, Hofmannsthal seems not to have had a very good opinion of him.

Hofmannsthal enriched the story with a multiplicity of invented details. He used several figures of speech that characterize the dramatic figures but that never really existed as such. The greatest of Hofmannsthal's inventions is the historically credible motif – from the point of view of the Rococo – of the silver rose delivered to the future bride by a "postillon d'amour." A pity that this custom was unknown during the period in question. The empress could have named Hofmannsthal her master of ceremonies at court … The interlude of the aria sung by the Italian singer is usually performed by a famous bel canto tenor. The melody has a strong Italian flavor, but the general impression remains genuinely "Straussian." M 6

6. Aria of the Italian Singer

Di ri - go - ri ar - ma - to il se - no con - tro a - mor mi ri - be - llai, _____

William Hogarth, from the series *Marriage à la Mode*, Scene 4, *The Countess's Levee*, oil painting, 1743 (National Gallery, London). As a source of inspiration for the 18th-century milieu, an oil painting from William Hogarth's series *Marriage à la Mode* played a particularly important part. Hogarth depicted with careful realism and biting sarcasm the social contrasts of early capitalistic society in England during the very decade in which *Der Rosenkavalier* is set. For Act I Hofmannsthal adopted the grouping of figures in the painting *The Countess's Levee*. A lady's levee was a social event. It took place between about eleven and twelve in the morning. The lady was still in her negligee and her hairdresser was summoned to arrange her hair in an artistic manner. There was conversation, love affairs and court intrigues were discussed, petitioners arrived, music was played – all exactly as Hogarth portrays it. It creates a fresh and cheerful polyphony that acted as a spur to Strauss's virtuosity. The melodically enchanting aria of the Italian singer with its inspired flute accompaniment, the mechanically primitive droning of the orphaned beggars, the dry dialogue between the baron and the notary about the "Morgengabe" (the bridegroom's present to the bride), form a colorful acoustic background. The most curious thing about this scene is that, though the effect is that of parody, the music is not neo-Classical. With his individual musical language, Strauss, like Hofmannsthal with his invented figures of speech, achieved a perfect deception.

Time – a strange thing

"Time, what a strange thing it is," philosophizes the Marschallin in front of her mirror at the end of Act I. It would perhaps be too glib a formula to say that *Der Rosenkavalier* is a schizophrenic drama, a comedy and a tragedy at the same time, containing elements of both genres. But the dilemma over the choice of title (*Ochs* or *Rosenkavalier*) already makes us suspect that the authors themselves had difficulty in knowing which aspect of the piece to emphasize in presenting the work to the public. What happens to Baron Ochs in *Der Rosenkavalier* is pure comedy, a game of intrigue, worthy of the *commedia dell'arte* and *opera buffa*. But with the character of the Marschallin, Hofmannsthal and Strauss introduced a semi-tragic, bittersweet mood into the opera. And it is this mood that lends the piece its incomparable, nostalgic atmosphere. For the Marschallin, the root of tragedy is time, growing old. "How can this happen? How does the good Lord do it?" she asks. "And if he must do it in this way, why does he let me see it with such a clear mind?" She decides to anticipate the passage of time and renounce her young lover Octavian of her own free will. "I am in a mood in which I feel the weakness of everything that is governed by time, feel it in my very heart, that one must not hold on to anything, not grasp anything, that everything slips between our fingers, everything we try to hold dissolves, everything passes away like a hazy dream." But the Marschallin is not an old woman, no female version of Hans Sachs, who must renounce love for the benefit of a younger rival. She is in full possession of her charms and her feminine powers of attraction. She is – as Strauss retrospectively described her – "a beautiful young woman of 32 at the most, who one day, when in a bad mood, sees herself as an old woman beside the 17-year-old Octavian. Octavian is neither the first nor the last lover of the Marschallin, who should certainly not play the end of Act I sentimentally, as a tragic farewell to life, but with Viennese grace and lightness, with one eye weeping and one eye dry." A pertinent explanation of the strange "as if" mood of *Der Rosenkavalier*. And in the closing trio (the Marschallin, Sophie, and Octavian), the most beautiful music ever written by Strauss (which was played at his funeral at his own request, under the baton of the young Georg Solti), anyone who does not feel choked will find nothing to appeal to him in *Der Rosenkavalier*. "One simply has to weep ... because it is so beautiful." ("Mariandel" in Act III) M 7

Der Rosenkavalier, studio photograph of Elisabeth Schwarzkopf as the Marschallin, production Rudolf Hartmann, conductor Herbert von Karajan, Wiener Staatsoper 1960.
Aristocratic appearance and angelic voice: Elisabeth Schwarzkopf was one of the greatest singers of the 20th century. Her refined resignation, her slight, often concealed gestures, and her expressive looks made her portrayal of the Marschallin unforgettable. Fortunately, her performance was immortalized on film under the musical direction of Herbert von Karajan.

7. Trio (the Marschallin, Sophie, and Octavian)

Hab' mir's ge - lobt, ihn lieb ___ zu ha - ben   in der rich -ti-gen Weis' ___

A musical anachronism: the waltz

It would be an exaggeration to describe *Der Rosenkavalier* as a waltz opera, but characteristic waltz music is heard three times in the course of the work, each time associated with the figure of Baron Ochs. Historically speaking, the use of a waltz in an opera set in the time of Maria Theresia is a gross anachronism, effectively a falsification. During the mid-eighteenth century the waltz was not danced, particularly in aristocratic circles. The preferred ballroom dance was the courtly minuet in triple time. The rise of the waltz began in the 1820s, when the traditional *ländler* and the German dance were introduced by Viennese composers such as Johann Strauss the elder and Joseph Lanner, first into the inns, and then, elevated by bourgeois elegance, into the ballroom. Soon the waltz conquered the whole of Europe, and up to the outbreak of the First World War it was unchallenged as the most popular of all dances. In Vienna the waltz became so deeply rooted in the social milieu that for Richard Strauss it represented something timeless. Old Vienna manifested itself through the waltz, and even such a well-educated artist as Strauss need not have known how old the waltz really was. For what would *Der Rosenkavalier* be without its waltz? M 8

Der Rosenkavalier, Lotte Lehmann as Octavian, 1920s.
Lotte Lehmann (1888–1976) was Richard Strauss's favorite singer. She sang all the important Strauss roles, some of which she created in the original productions. She made her début in Hamburg in 1909. Between 1914 and 1938 she was a member of the Wiener Staatsoper, after which she emigrated to the USA, where she appeared until 1951, mainly at the Metropolitan Opera. She was the first composer in →*Ariadne on Naxos*, the first dyer's wife in →*The Woman Without a Shadow*, and the first Christine in →*Intermezzo*. She also created the roles of both the Marschallin and Octavian (pictured above) in *Der Rosenkavalier*. She had "a voice full of soul, an excellent articulation of text, and a wonderful stage presence," the elderly composer recalled enthusiastically. (*Memoirs of the First Performances of my Operas*, 1942)

8. Baron Ochs's Waltz

Der Rosenkavalier, production photograph with Lucia Popp (the Marschallin) and Trudeliese Schmidt (Octavian), production Otto Schenk, sets Rudolf Heinrich, costumes Erni Kniepert, conductor Leonard Bernstein, Wiener Staatsoper 1968 (Photo: 1988).
Undoubtedly the musical style of *Der Rosenkavalier* is not as daring as that of →*Elektra*; Strauss, the enfant terrible of the period around 1900, did not pursue any further the path towards atonality. But *Der Rosenkavalier* is not lacking in a scandalous element: it lies in the opera's unconcealed eroticism. The opera begins with an extended bed scene, with the tender reverberation of an intoxicating night of love.

"Secret powers of attraction"

It is not widely known that this waltz is actually a brilliant plagiarism. The melody is in part identical to a waltz by Josef Strauss (the brother of Johann Strauss the younger). Josef Strauss's waltz has an allusive, suggestive title, *Dynamiden: Geheime Anziehungskräfte* (*Dynamiden*: *Secret Powers of Attraction*). But what are these secret powers? Are they perhaps the secret powers of Eros? Science provides the explanation. Josef Strauss, who before beginning his musical career had attended a technical college and worked as a qualified engineer, dedicated the waltz, first performed in 1865, to the union of industrial associations. The melodies of the waltz are the "Dynamiden" (Greek "dynamis," meaning power or force) of *Der Rosenkavalier*: "The music gets into your blood," as Baron Ochs aptly remarks in Act III.

Mozart

According to Strauss's friend and first biographer, Max Steinitzer, during the consultations over the first performance of *Elektra* Strauss remarked: "Next time I will write a Mozart opera." He could have meant this ironically, as the bold musical language, huge orchestra, and difficult vocal parts of *Elektra* were creating considerable problems. But the concept of the "Mozart opera" is extremely important when considering the genesis of *Der Rosenkavalier*. For the listener, the most striking example of déjà vu is found in the final duet between Sophie and Octavian. M 9

The beginning of the duet has the effect of a quotation from →*The Magic Flute* (Pamina and Papageno in the finale of Act II). M 10 But even without this specific link, the duet reminds one of the Viennese Classical style. A further, somewhat ironic relationship also exists between this melody and Franz Schubert's famous song "Das Heidenröslein" ("The Rose on the Heath"). M 11

The melody of the duet is the simplest in the whole opera. As simple as the final solution of the plot: after various emotional complications, two young people come together.

Otherwise very little of Mozart's musical influence is to be found in the opera, although his presence is felt in the dramatic figures and their relationships, above all in the figure of Octavian, whose model is to be found in the figure of Cherubino in Mozart's →*The Marriage of Figaro* (the breeches part, the 17-year-old, the intimate relationship with a mature, elegant woman who has risen in the social scale as a result of her marriage). All these are more than mere coincidence. The sudden flaring up of feelings also reminds one of Mozart's operas, and aroused great interest in the age of psychoanalysis, particularly, of course, Mozart's →*Così fan tutte*. And this very work was one of Strauss's favorite operas. Is it a coincidence that the first performance of *Der Rosenkavalier* took place on the eve of Mozart's birthday and on the same day of the year, 26 January, as the première of *Così fan tutte*?

Der Rosenkavalier, Erna Denera and Elisabeth Böhm von Endert, Berlin 1912. A reminder of Berlin in a studio photograph of *Der Rosenkavalier* (beginning of Act I). The opera's popularity between 1911 and 1914 was equaled only by the most successful operettas of Lehár or Kálman. The public interest was so overwhelming that special *Rosenkavalier* trains to Dresden and Berlin had to be laid on.

9. Final Duet (Sophie and Octavian)

Ist ein Traum, kann nicht wirk - lich sein, ___ dass wir zwei bei - ein - an - der sein

10. Mozart, *The Magic Flute* (Pamina and Papageno)

Könn - te je - der bra - ve Mann sol - che Glöckchen fin - den!

11. Schubert, Das Heidenröslein

Sah ein Knab' ein Rös - lein stehn, Rös - lein auf der Hei - den

Ariadne on Naxos, costume design for the wigmaker by Ernst Stern, Stuttgart, 1912 (TWS).
The wigmaker preserves the world of Molière's comedy *Le bourgeois gentilhomme*, which, though an important source of inspiration for Hofmannsthal and Strauss, was omitted from the second version of the opera. Only the wigmaker survived.

Ariadne on Naxos

Ariadne auf Naxos

Oper in a prologue and one act

Libretto: Hugo von Hofmannsthal.
Première: First version, in one act: 25 October 1912, Stuttgart (Hoftheater, Kleines Haus) (performed after a German version of Molière's *Le bourgeois gentilhomme*); revised version, in a prologue and one act: 4 October 1916, Vienna (Hofoper).

Characters in the prologue: The Composer (S), The Music Master (Bar), The Dancing Master (T), A Wigmaker (Bbar), A Footman (B), An Officer (T), The Majordomo (spoken), The Prima Donna (later Ariadne) (S), The Tenor (later Bacchus) (T), Zerbinetta (S), Harlequin (Bar), Scaramuccio (T), Truffaldino (B), Brighella (T)
Characters in the opera: Ariadne (S), Bacchus (T), Naiad (S), Dryad (A), Echo (S); intermezzo: Zerbinetta (S), Harlequin (Bar), Scaramuccio (T), Truffaldino (B), Brighella (T).
Setting: Vienna, the end of the 17th century.

Synopsis

A rich parvenu gives a party, and for the entertainment of his guests, arranges simultaneous performances of a *commedia dell'arte* play and a tragic opera. Zerbinetta and Ariadne, comedienne and operatic heroine, come to an understanding. The tragedy ends unexpectedly.

Prologue

A large room in the house of a rich parvenu. A young composer is preparing for a performance of his first opera. The master of the house, his patron, gives orders for it to be performed simultaneously with a comedy. Everyone is filled with consternation. Only the comedienne Zerbinetta keeps up her courage and placates the composer with her charm.

The Opera

On a desert island. Ariadne, abandoned by her husband Theseus, bemoans her fate and longs for death. The comedienne Zerbinetta gives the heroine a lecture on how one can forget a man's infidelity by means of a new love. Elemental spirits announce the arrival of a god. Ariadne sinks into the arms of the god whom she believes to be the god of death. But it is Bacchus, who awakens her to new life and new love. *S.N.*

Ariadne on Naxos, set design by Ludwig Sievert, production Carl Hagemann, conductor Wilhelm Furtwängler, Nationaltheater, Mannheim 1916 (TWS).
The beginning of the mystery: the arrival of the god Bacchus. *M 12*
The last half hour of the opera belongs to Ariadne and Bacchus alone. The great duet consists of an enormous musical intensification, which at the moment of ecstatic climax flows into an enchanting melody. Bacchus (a heroic tenor) sings for only 15 minutes, yet this is considered one of the most difficult of the important tenor roles (the first for Strauss since his first opera →*Guntram*).

12. Love Duet (Ariadne and Bacchus)

Dei - ner hab ich um al - - les be - durft! Nun bin — ich ein and - rer,

Divertissement à la Hofmannsthal

As early as 1911, soon after the triumphant première of →*Der Rosenkavalier*, Hofmannsthal had begun to toy with the idea of a new Rococo opera. At this point a book by the French writer Philippe Monnier came into his hands, which described life in Venice at the time of Goldoni, Gozzi, and Casanova. But Hofmannsthal found the germ of his new subject matter in the story of Ariadne, and told the composer about his new idea for a "thirty-minute opera for a small chamber orchestra ... called *Ariadne on Naxos*, which would mingle heroic and mythological figures in eighteenth-century costume ... with figures from the *commedia dell'arte*, Harlequin and Scaramouche, who would provide a *buffo* element that would be interwoven with the heroic element ... " (20 March 1911).

After a few months Hofmannsthal found a comedy that could be used as a framework for *Ariadne*: Molière's *Le bourgeois gentilhomme*, first performed in 1670 at the court of Louis XIV as a *comédie-ballet*, with music by →Jean-Baptiste Lully. "The divertissement *Ariadne on Naxos* will be played after Jourdain's dinner," Hofmannsthal told the composer.

Stuttgart and Vienna versions

Strauss's *Ariadne on Naxos* was first performed in Stuttgart in 1912, under the direction of Max Reinhardt, as a postlude to a performance of a German version of Molière's *Le bourgeois gentilhomme*, which itself used incidental music by Strauss. After the première Strauss decided for practical reasons to dissolve this partnership. He created a new version of the opera, with a prologue, which is the version that is usually performed today. The incidental music to Molière's comedy (1918, Berlin) was transformed into an orchestral suite (1920, Vienna).

Ariadne on Naxos, photograph from the production by Folke Abenius, sets and costumes Søren Fransen, conductor Hans E. Zimmer, Det Kongelige Teater, Copenhagen 1992 (photograph 1999).
What only Mozart succeeded in doing in the 18th century – blending the elements of *opera seria* and *opera buffa* to create a third genre – was easily achieved by Richard Strauss: a character (Ariadne) who has dedicated herself to death, surrounded by comic actors.

Mythology and interpretation

The myth of Ariadne, the daughter of the king of Crete, exists in several versions. With Ariadne's help, Theseus defeated the bull-headed Cretan monster, the Minotaur, thus delivering his native city, Athens, from a bloody tribute. He married Ariadne and they set off for Athens together, but he abandoned her on a desert island. It has been benevolently assumed that Theseus did not want to expose his pregnant wife to the tempests at sea. Another, more sober explanation assumes legal considerations on his part. If Theseus had continued his voyage by sea with Ariadne, they would have lost her impressive Cretan inheritance, particularly her own property. But the most pleasing solution was provided by poetry: the god Bacchus (Dionysus) appeared to Theseus in a dream and claimed Ariadne as his own. Since it was dangerous to contend with a god for a woman, Theseus renounced his place at Ariadne's side in favor of Bacchus.

Hofmannsthal recognized in the encounter between Ariadne and Bacchus a wonderful, mysterious metamorphosis: "We are dealing with a common and yet serious problem: that of fidelity. To hold on to the lost one, to persist eternally, even unto death – or else to live, to live on, to overcome it, to transform oneself, to surrender the unity of the soul, and still to remain oneself after transformation, to remain human, not to sink to the level of the conscienceless beast … Ariadne could be only one man's beloved, be abandoned by only one man. Yet one thing remains, even for her: the miracle, the god. She gives herself to him, for she believes him to be death: but he is death and life at once, he reveals to her the enormous depths of her own nature, makes her into a magician, a sorceress, who transforms poor little Ariadne, conjures up the hereafter in this world, preserves her and transforms her at the same time." (Hofmannsthal in a letter to Strauss, July 1911)

Ariadne on Naxos, set design by Adolph Mahnke for the production by Heinz Arnold, Staatstheater, Braunschweig 1937 (TWS). "Has the performance started, or is the rehearsal still going on?" one wonders as the curtain goes up. The prologue allows us a glimpse behind the scenes.

Ariadne on Naxos, production photograph with (from left to right) Johnny van Hal (tenor/Bacchus), Jørgen Ole Børch (wigmaker), and Andry Stottler (prima donna/Ariadne), production Folke Abenius, sets and costumes Søren Fransen, conductor Hans E. Zimmer, Det Kongelige Teater, Copenhagen 1992 (photograph 1999).
The prologue is a masterpiece of modern theater: a true theatrical capriccio. The artists are able to think themselves into the dramatic characters of the opera that follows. But here too it soon becomes clear that parts are being played: the true face of humanity will be recognized in a few moments.

Right
Ariadne on Naxos, Lotte Lehmann as the composer, Vienna, 1920s.
Hofmannsthal's composer was based on the figure of Mozart. The single lyrical moment in the prologue arises out of the sympathy that develops between the composer and Zerbinetta. In the original Stuttgart production the composer was a speaking role, but in the revised version performed in Vienna in 1916 it was a breeches role for soprano, and sung by Lotte Lehmann.

Ariadne on Naxos, Maria Jeritza as Ariadne, Vienna 1917.
Maria Jeritza sang Ariadne at the première of the Vienna version (the version most often performed today), opposite Bela von Környey's Bacchus. Selma Kurz was Zerbinetta and Lotte Lehmann the composer. The performance was conducted by Franz Schalk, who codirected the Wiener Staatsoper with Strauss from 1919.

Ariadne on Naxos, Edita Gruberová as Zerbinetta, production Filippo Sanjust, conductor Karl Böhm, Wiener Staatsoper 1976.
Zerbinetta is a coloratura role that can be mastered only by singers with a breathtaking upper range and flawless virtuosity. Edita Gruberová (b. 1946) was first cast in this role in the mid-1970s by the great conductor, Karl Böhm, a former friend of the composer.

13. Song of the Comedians

Lie - ben, Has - sen, Hof - fen, Za - gen, al - le Lust _____ und al - le Qual

14. Dance-song of the Comedians

Es gilt, ob Tan - zen, ob Sin - gen tau - ge, von Trä - nen zu trock - nen ein schö - nes Au - ge.

Sad comedians

Apart from a few witty remarks with which they react to Ariadne's eternal lamentations, the *commedia dell'arte* characters hardly create a comic effect. Zerbinetta and her four lovers (Harlequin, Scaramuccio, Truffaldino, and Brighella) come from the world of the great French painter Antoine Watteau (1684–1721). His comedians are distinguished by elevated seriousness rather than exuberance and fun. Admittedly the *commedia dell'arte* figures in *Ariadne* have to dance and sing, quite in accordance with the genre, but they too betray a certain uneasiness. The forsaken island with a weeping, inconsolable woman is a world so foreign to them that they behave in a restrained manner. They sing beautiful, simple songs, appropriate for a calming therapy rather than one of laughter. M 13, M 14

The *Ariadne* orchestra

The main body of the sound is determined by neo-Classical ideals, and this is true of the strings as well as the wind instruments. Yet Strauss's characteristic orchestral colors are also there: two harps, the celesta with its silvery tones, the discreet harmonium, and a variety of percussion instruments. The function of the piano is twofold: in the prologue and in the recitative in the opera Strauss occasionally uses the piano in the manner of a harpsichord, the indispensable instrument of the Baroque age. But, as a child of the nineteenth century, he also mingles the piano with the other instruments of the orchestra. Both the subtle sound of the overture, resembling that of chamber music, and also the great apotheosis with its splendid transformation music – from death to life – beguile us with their instrumental mastery.

The *Ariadne* style

While Richard Strauss is by no means bidding farewell to his late Romantic style in *Ariadne*, the opera's sound-world is more transparent than, for example, that of →*Der Rosenkavalier*, which already marked a change in style in relation to his earlier operas. On the other hand, Strauss also seized the opportunity for pastiche. Thus he wrote a lament for Ariadne in pathetic Baroque style, simple songs for the *buffo* characters, and the great love duet for Ariadne and Bacchus in the Romantic style he had inherited from Wagner. Somewhat curiously, perhaps, Strauss also mingled reminiscences of Bellini and Donizetti. The modernity of *Ariadne on Naxos* does not rest on a new musical language, but on familiarity with the musical past. Today one would call this method of composition "postmodern." Hofmannsthal was quite right to believe in the future rather than the present of this third opera on which he and Strauss collaborated. In his own lifetime, Richard Strauss was named an honorary citizen of the Greek island of Naxos …

Ariadne on Naxos, costume design for Harlequin by Ernst Stern, Stuttgart première, 1912 (TWS).
Harlequin as the sad clown, a favorite figure of the turn of the century.

Zerbinetta

Zerbinetta is the most enigmatic character in the piece. By the standards of the golden age of opera (17th–18th centuries) she should really be the second lady, the *seconda donna*, in other words, the soubrette. From the point of view of her social status – she is an impromptu comedienne – she should be assigned to a lower position in the hierarchy of roles, among the pert, knowing servant girls of *opera buffa*. But with Strauss she outgrows this category. Zerbinetta is one of the most difficult coloratura parts in the whole operatic range (from c' to d'''). She also has a genuine Italian bel canto *scena*. M 15 It is not clear why Strauss wrote such rich and difficult coloratura passages for Zerbinetta, but they certainly contribute to her feminine attractiveness.

Left
Ariadne on Naxos, production photograph with Elisabeth Schwarzkopf (Zerbinetta) and Karl Schmitt-Walter (Harlequin), production Hans Batteux, conductor Artur Rother, Deutsche Oper, Berlin 1940.
Elisabeth Schwarzkopf also sang Zerbinetta in her early years.

15. Zerbinetta's Aria (Cadenza and Rondo Theme)

Als ein Gott kam Je - der ge - gan - gen

The symbolism of the characters

The emperor: The epitome of the closed-off consciousness, not open to foreign natures.
The empress: Her desire to achieve humanity "is the point of the whole work" (Hofmannsthal).
The shadow: The symbol of mortality, humanity.
The nurse: The protectress of the empress on behalf of the world of spirits. Caught up in a world of clinging love, she is unable to follow the empress on her path to sympathy with all beings.
Keikobad: The invisible king of the spirits who tries to guide all beings on the path to sympathy.
The falcon: The messenger of the spirit world, at the same time representing sharp, analytical consciousness.
The dyer: His occupation has a symbolic meaning: he gives color, character, and meaning to everything. He himself incorporates warm feelings. He is the antithesis of the emperor. Among the four protagonists of the piece he is the only one to bear a name (Barak).
The crippled brothers: The imperfect qualities of mankind. They symbolize the inability to recognize and evaluate a situation in life correctly. As the dyer is the antithesis to the emperor, so the crippled brothers are the antithesis to the falcon.
The dyer's wife: She incorporates anarchic forces, which without moral objectives (such as motherhood) can lead to chaos and to the loss of human existence (the shadow).
The voices of the nightwatchmen: They praise love as the only path to harmony between creator and created.
The voices of the unborn children: Symbolizing latent creative possibilities, they await their manifestation.

The Woman Without a Shadow

Die Frau ohne Schatten

Oper in three acts

Libretto: Hugo von Hofmannsthal.
Première: 10 October 1919, Vienna (Staatsoper).
Characters: The Emperor (T), The Empress, Keikobad's daughter (S), The Nurse (Ms), Barak, a dyer (Bar), Barak's Wife (S), The One-Eyed One, The One-Armed One, and The Hunchback, Barak's brothers (2 B-bar, T), A Spirit Messenger (Bar), The Guardian of the Threshold (S), The Apparition of a Youth (T), The Voice of the Falcon (S), A Voice from Above (A), Voices of Unborn Children (3 S, 3 A), Voices of Nightwatchmen (3 B); imperial servants, foreign children, servant spirits, spirit voices (chorus, children's chorus).
Setting:: The place and time of fairy tale.

Synopsis

A mystery play, in which both human beings and spirits participate. Two couples endure trials: emperor and empress (spirit world), the dyer and his wife (human world). Each of them has to change. The empress comes to understand human fate in order to be able to throw a shadow (to become human); the emperor renounces possessive love. Both learn sympathy for others. The physically apathetic dyer develops spiritual sensitivity, and his wife discovers the value of devoted love. Only the nurse who accompanies the empress does not come through the trial, remaining biased in her love for the empress.

The offspring of the king of the spirits, Keikobad, and a human mother, the empress has always longed to become human herself. In the form of a white gazelle she was hunted by the emperor of the Southeastern Isles and appeared to him in the form of a young girl. Thus Keikobad's daughter became the wife of the emperor. But now the emperor has rejected his red falcon, which led him to the white gazelle, and the empress has lost her talisman and with it the power of transformation and the knowledge of her father's command: if she does not become a mother within a year and thus acquire a human shadow, the emperor will turn to stone.

Act I
Scene 1: A terrace above the imperial gardens. Keikobad's messenger warns that in three days time will be up and the emperor will turn to stone. The nurse is triumphant: she hates mankind and would like to return with the empress to the realm of spirits. It is only through the falcon that the empress is reminded of her father's command, which she had forgotten, and despairs. In her great love, the nurse is prepared to procure a shadow for her charge. But the empress must fetch it herself. The two women go down into the human world.

Scene 2: The dyer's house. The nurse has found a woman whose shadow she hopes to possess: the wife of the dyer Barak. She is suffering from poverty and the spiritual limitations of her existence. The dyer, humbly following his trade, does not recognize his wife's nature. This marriage is also childless, and there are constant quarrels. The nurse and the empress enter the service of the dyer's wife as maids.

Act II
Scene 1: The dyer's house. The nurse conjures up the phantom of a youth from a wisp of straw, and persuades the dyer's wife that through him she can experience the fulfilment of her unconscious yearning.
Scene 2: The imperial falconer's cottage in the forest. The emperor is looking for his wife. The red falcon leads him to the falconer's cottage. When the empress and the nurse return late at night, with the "smell of humanity" still clinging to them, the emperor, in his burning jealousy, wants to kill his wife, but is unable to do so, and retreats to a desolate rocky cave.
Scene 3: The dyer's house. The nurse gives Barak a sleeping-draught. The dyer's wife's resistance disappears when the youth is conjured up once again. Tormented by pangs of conscience, she wakes Barak, but is forced to realize that he does not understand her, and runs out of the house in despair. The empress experiences Barak's suffering and feels guilty.
Scene 4: The empress's bedroom in the falconer's cottage. In a vision the empress sees the emperor turning to stone.
Scene 5: Keikobad intervenes. Forces of nature drive the dyer's wife back to her husband. The argument between the two escalates. At this point the empress recognizes her responsibility and refuses the shadow of the dyer's wife, which the nurse has offered her. Elemental forces shake the dyer's house and split it into two. Keikobad issues a summons to judgment.

Act III
Scene 1: Separated from each other, Barak and his wife acknowledge their love. A voice orders them to seek each other out.
Scene 2: The entrance to the temple of the spirits. In a small boat, drawn by mysterious forces, the empress and nurse arrive in an impassable mountain area. Here the empress separates from the nurse to submit to Keikobad's judgment. The nurse is not permitted to reenter the spirit world.
Scene 3: The interior of the temple of the spirits. The empress experiences her hardest trial. In front of the emperor, who has turned to stone almost entirely, she is offered the water of life. If she drinks, she will receive the shadow of the dyer's wife, and the emperor will be allowed to live. She resists temptation. Personal happiness is not to be bought by the suffering of others. Now she receives a shadow of her own from Keikobad, and the emperor awakes to new life.
Scene 4: A scene in the realm of the spirits. Barak and his wife find each other, but are separated by a chasm. The regained shadow forms a bridge between them. *s. n.*

The Woman Without a Shadow, set design by
Leo Pasetti for the production by Kurt Barré,
conductor Hans Knappertsbusch,
Nationaltheater, Munich 1935 (TWS).
The crucial moment when the bridge is
created between the world of spirits and the
world of humans. In the early days of work on
the opera Hofmannsthal noted Goethe's
words: "The human being who is able to
overcome himself can free himself from the
law that binds all creatures." (From the poem
Die Geheimnisse, The Secrets.) This could be
the motto for this opera of mystery.

The unrecognized masterpiece

Strauss and Hofmannsthal wanted to crown their joint
creative achievement with *The Woman Without a
Shadow*. From the outset the opera was planned as a
sort of festival piece, which would be performed only
on great occasions under the best artistic conditions.
The great conductor Karl Böhm formed and trained an
ensemble especially for the performance of *The Woman
Without a Shadow*. His late performances in Vienna and
Salzburg at the end of the 1970s, with Leonie Rysanek,
Birgit Nilsson, James King, and Walter Berry, have
become legendary.

The Woman Without a Shadow is much less well
known today than it deserves. Why has this opera not
proved more accessible? The argument most often put
forward is that the plot is too complicated. But the plot
is not more complicated than those of operas by

Mozart or Handel. The problem is rather the strangeness of the story. →*The Magic Flute*, which in certain
respects could be regarded as a model for *The Woman
Without a Shadow*, presents a series of everyday situations and dialogues, and the non-human initiates and
their strange rites are counterbalanced by a Papageno
who is eager to live life to the full. In *The Woman
Without a Shadow* we are shown pure and abstract
mystery, and the symbolism stands in the way of its
reception. How are we to understand the relationship
of the emperor with his falcon? What do the unborn
children sing while the nurse fries fish in the dyer's
wife's pan? Is the nurse good or evil? What is the
meaning of the imperfect human figures in Barak's
house? And so on. The opera brims with strange,
obscure situations, far removed from everyday life.

The Woman Without a Shadow, Lotte Lehmann as the dyer's wife in the original production, Vienna, 1919.
The punishingly difficult part of the dyer's wife was sung at the Vienna première by Lotte Lehmann.

The Woman Without a Shadow, production photograph with Eva Marton as the dyer, production Nathaniel Merrill and Bruce Donnell, sets and costumes Robert O'Hearn, conductor Erick Leinsdorf, Metropolitan Opera, New York 1981.
The dyer: Eva Marton as successor to Leonie Rysanek at the Metropolitan Opera.

The Woman Without a Shadow, production photograph with Karen Huffstodt as the empress, production Andreas Homoki, sets Wolfgang Gussmann, conductor Armin Jordan, Grand Théâtre de Genève 1997.
The empress is a cosmic role, not only because vocally the role demands almost superhuman qualities, but also in that she moves in the realm of the spirits. Even though she wins her shadow at the end of the opera, she remains a god-like being – similar to Wagner's Brünnhilde.

The masterpiece before its time

As early as a month before the triumphal first performance of *Der Rosenkavalier*, Hofmannsthal was already planning "something big" for Strauss: *The Woman Without a Shadow*, "a fantastical spectacle ... a magical fairy tale, in which two men and two women confront each other." Once again Hofmannsthal drew inspiration from one of Mozart's operas: "The whole ... would stand in relation ... to the →*The Magic Flute* as *Der Rosenkavalier* does to →*Figaro*: that is, in both cases without imitation, but with a certain analogy ... " (Hofmannsthal in a letter to Strauss, 20 March 1911).

The Woman Without a Shadow had the longest gestation period of all Strauss's operas. The score was not completed until 1917 and the first performance took place at the Wiener Staatsoper in 1919 (for the inauguration of Strauss's period as director). Meanwhile the First World War had run its course and Strauss had composed →*Ariadne on Naxos* (1912), the ballet *Josephslegende* (also with Hofmannsthal) (1914), and the bravura piece for orchestra, the →*Alpine Symphony* (1915). The long delay was due not only to conceptual questions. Both authors were aware that this work, which was highly ambitious both musically and in terms of staging, could not be performed in times of war.

Musical genius

In *The Woman Without a Shadow* there are four roles of equal importance, all of them technically very demanding: two dramatic sopranos, a Wagnerian tenor, and a baritone à la Hans Sachs. Yet while the male roles are characterized by the flowing, melodious style we associate with Strauss, the female roles – including the contralto nurse and the soprano voice of the falcon – are more exotic and bizarre.

The Woman Without a Shadow has a delightful sound-world of its own, created above all by the extraordinarily varied instrumentation. Here Strauss amassed the greatest of his operatic orchestras, particularly striking for its mighty arsenal of percussion instruments, including timpani, a glockenspiel, a xylophone, five Chinese gongs, and tam-tams. To these are added two celestas, a glass harmonica, and an organ. This gigantic orchestra can do anything: its raging during the final apotheosis excites even the most phlegmatic of listeners. But it can also divide into chamber music groups. An example of this is the ravishingly beautiful cello solo that accompanies the strange voice of the falcon in the introduction to the emperor's monologue. M 16

The Woman Without a Shadow, set design for the opening scene by Ludwig Sievert, production Rudolf Hartmann, conductor Clemens Krauss, Staatsoper, Munich 1938/39 (TWS).
The spirit messenger brings the command of Keikobad, the king of the spirits, to the nurse.

16. Cello Melody of the Lonely Emperor

The Salzburg Festival

At the time of the first performance of →*The Woman Without a Shadow*, outstanding artists, above all Richard Strauss himself, were already dreaming of the summer festival in Salzburg. The realization of the idea after the First World War is one of the finest achievements of central European culture during the twentieth century. The history of this famous institution covers more than a century, if one includes the years in which it was being planned.

1877–1910: The Mozart Festival, organized by the Mozart Foundation in Salzburg with the participation of the most important conductors of the time, including Hans Richter, Felix Mottl, Richard Strauss, Gustav Mahler, and Felix Weingartner.

1914: Plans are made for a summer festival, but are abandoned at the outbreak of the First World War.

1917: Friedrich Gehmacher and Heinrich Damisch found the Salzburg Festspielhaus (Festival Hall) Committee, and Richard Strauss publishes an appeal for the festival's foundation. In the same year, Max Reinhardt presents a memorandum on the same subject to the board of the Vienna Hofbühnen (court theatres). Although he envisages the festival as located at Hellbrunn, near Salzburg, his artistic program is transferable to Salzburg. He plans two festival houses, one large and one small, for opera and drama respectively, and recommends the foundation of a college of dramatic arts.

1918: Künzelmann, the mayor of Salzburg, adopts Reinhardt's proposals. An artistic committee is formed, including Reinhardt, Strauss, Hofmannsthal, Alfred Roller (set designer), and Franz Schalk (conductor).

1920: The first performance of the mystery play *Jedermann* (*Everyman*) by Hofmannsthal, directed by Max Reinhardt, takes place in the cathedral square (the Domplatz) on 22 August. Since then it has been performed every year.

1922: The first performances of opera: operas by Mozart under the direction of Strauss and Schalk. The

Vienna Philharmonic becomes the festival's regular opera orchestra.

1924: The Felsenreitschule is converted into a theater.

1925: The opening of the Festspielhaus.

1926: The rebuilding of the Festspielhaus (architect Clemens Holzmeister). The first contemporary opera (Strauss's →*Ariadne on Naxos*) is performed in the Felsenreitschule.

1927: The first performance of an opera (Beethoven's *Fidelio*) takes place in the Festspielhaus.

1930s: The first heyday of the Salzburg Festival, with Bruno Walter, Clemens Krauss, Arturo Toscanini, Wilhelm Furtwängler, and Hans Knappertsbusch as regular guest conductors (director Herbert Graf).

post-1945: The repertory is extended to include contemporary operas. The dominating personalities are Wilhelm Furtwängler and Herbert von Karajan (festival director 1956–60 and 1964–89; from 1967 an Easter festival with the Berlin Philharmonic is founded on his initiative).

1990s: The festival is extended to numerous venues: the large and small Festspielhaus, the Felsenreitschule, the Mozarteum, and the Landestheater, as well as the courtyard of the Residenz. The director-general (from 1989) is Gerard Mortier. The artistic program includes the introduction of contemporary art and management revolution (involving a fierce controversy over daring stage interpretations in both opera and spoken plays).

Above
Hans Richter (1843–1916) and Felix Mottl (1856–1911), 1888.
Left, above
Gustav Mahler (1860–1911), portrait by Moriz Nähr, 1907.
Right (top to bottom)
Felix von Weingartner (1863–1942), etching by Johannes Lindner, c. 1905.
Bruno Walter (1876–1962), postcard photograph, c. 1925.
Hans Knappertsbusch (1888–1965), c. 1960.
Wilhelm Furtwängler (1886–1954), portrait by Trude Fleischmann, c. 1927.

The great conductors of the time collaborated on the realization of a unique idea. Their various artistic personalities and styles of conducting contributed decisively to the musical profile that gave the Salzburg Festival its international reputation.

Festival curtain design by the Ferdinand Moser Atelier, Vienna c. 1910 (TWS).
"In times when intellectual property is much rarer than material property, and
in which egoism, envy, hatred, and mistrust appear to rule the world, whoever
supports our proposals will have done a good deed and contributed greatly to
the restoration of brotherliness and neighborly love … " (from Strauss's festival
appeal, the "Salzburger Gründungsaufruf," of 1917). The idea of the festival
was already in the air around 1910, when this festival curtain design was
produced by the Ferdinand Moser Atelier in Vienna.

Rehearsal photograph for a production of Strauss's *Ariadne on Naxos*, Salzburg
Festival, 1926.
1926 was a turning point in the early history of the festival. It was the first year
in which a contemporary opera, Strauss's *Ariadne on Naxos*, was performed.
The conductor was Strauss's protégé, Clemens Krauss, who conducted not
only *Ariadne* but also two concerts by the Vienna Philharmonic, including one
consisting exclusively of works by Strauss (something of a rarity in concert
programs of the time).

Intermezzo, Fritz Fitzau as Baron Lummer, production Max Hofmüller, conductor Hans Knappertsbusch, Munich 1926.
Baron Lummer, the skier, is knocked down by Christine on a musically as well as physically breathtaking toboggan ride (Act I, Scene 2).

New operatic style

Intermezzo is musically much more significant than is generally believed. But both the subject matter and dialogue of this opera are everyday. Since the Baroque era, opera audiences had been used to elevated treatment of plot and language, compared with which this episode from a middle-class marriage with its attractive music and its dialogues that were in part fiendishly difficult to speak and seemed rather baffling. Strauss was aware of this: "This new work opens up a new path ... in its deviation from the long-standing operatic tradition of love affairs and murder." (from the foreword to *Intermezzo*, 1924) *Intermezzo* is the first important *Zeitoper*, or "opera of its time" (→Krenek), if this concept is taken to include the introduction of telegrams, telephones, and newspapers. Paul Hindemith (→*News of the Day*) and Arnold Schoenberg (→*From One Day to the Next*) followed with their contemporary operas, but not until 1929 and 1930 respectively.

Intermezzo

Bürgerliche Komödie mit sinfonischen Zwischenspielen
in two acts

Libretto: Richard Strauss.
Première: 4 November 1924, Dresden (Schauspielhaus).
Characters: Christine (S), Robert Storch, her husband, a conductor (Bar), Franzl, their eight-year-old son (spoken), Anna, their maid (S), Baron Lummer (T), The Notary (Bar), His Wife (S), Stroh, another conductor (T), A Commercial Councillor and A Legal Councillor, Robert's Skat partners (2 Bar), A Singer (B), Fanny, the Storchs' cook (spoken), Marie and Therese, maids (2 spoken), Resi, a young girl (S).
Setting: At the Grundlsee and in Vienna, in the early 1920s.

Synopsis

While the famous conductor and composer Robert Storch is making a guest appearance in Vienna, a letter arrives for him from a woman called Mieze Maier. His wife Christine believes he has been unfaithful to her and wants to file for a divorce immediately. Storch is puzzled, as he does not know anyone called Mieze Maier. She turns out to be the mistress of a Skat playing friend of his called Stroh, also a conductor, and she has made a mistake in the address. After explanations on both sides – Christine has meanwhile indulged in a flirtation with a baron – the couple are reconciled.

Act I

Scene 1: The house of the conductor Robert Storch at the Grundlsee. A turbulent domestic scene before Storch's departure for Vienna. Christine, left on her own, receives a telegram from a girlfriend inviting her to go tobogganing.
Scene 2: At the toboggan-run. Christine knocks down the young Baron Lummer. They introduce themselves.
Scene 3: A ball at the Grundlsee inn. Christine dances and chats with Baron Lummer.
Scene 4: A furnished room in the notary's house. Christine rents a room for the impoverished baron.
Scene 5: At the Storchs' apartment. The baron pays a visit and attempts to gain sympathy.
Scene 6: The baron's room. The baron writes Christine a letter, asking her to lend him 1000 marks.
Scene 7: The dining room at the Storchs'. Christine opens a letter addressed to her husband from Mieze Maier and believes he has been unfaithful to her. She sends her husband a telegram announcing her intention to divorce him.
Scene 8: The child's bedroom. Christine talks to her son Franzl about their future life together without his father.

Act II

Scene 1: Skat session at the house of the Commercial Councillor. During the game Storch receives the telegram from his wife.
Scene 2: The notary's office. Christine wants to start divorce proceedings.
Scene 3: In the Prater. Stormy weather. Storch, desperate, has been followed by his colleague and card-playing friend Stroh. Mieze is Stroh's mistress and has put the wrong address on the letter. Stroh is to leave for the Grundlsee to clear up the misunderstanding.
Scene 4: Christine's dressing-room. Christine cannot believe the explanation of the true state of affairs which Storch has sent her by telegram.
Scene 5: The Storchs' dining room. Stroh tries to explain everything, but without success, as does Storch on his return home. When Christine's little peccadillo the baron appears, the injured woman gives way. Domestic peace is restored.   A. G.

The composer as librettist

The title of the opera is fitting in many ways. It is a tragi-comic interlude in a marriage. But the title can also refer to the temporary break in the collaboration with Hofmannsthal. The idea of a bourgeois conversation piece with music had occurred to Strauss as early as 1916, while he was working on →*The Woman Without a Shadow* (astonishingly early, when one considers that this kind of *Zeitoper*, or "opera of its time," did not come into fashion until the 1920s). Hofmannsthal declined this "completely modern, absolutely realistic opera of character and nerves," and recommended another writer, Hermann Bahr, as librettist. Soon it became clear that this very personal story could only be put into artistic form by Strauss himself. Thus Strauss became his own librettist for the second and last time (almost 30 years after his first opera, →*Guntram*).

Intermezzo, Strauss with the cast of the first Vienna performance, 15 January 1927. Richard Strauss (seated), in "his" villa on the operatic stage, on the occasion of the Viennese première, with (from left to right) Margarethe Kraus (Anna), Karl Ziegler (Baron Lummer), Lotte Lehmann (Christine), Alfred Jerger (Robert Storch), Lothar Wallenstein (director).

Intermezzo, set design by Lothar Schenck von Trapp, production Renato Mordo, conductor Max Rudolf, Hessisches Landestheater, Darmstadt 1929/30 (TWS).
A set design by Schenk von Trapp, typical of the *Zeitoper* of the 1920s. The knave of hearts depicted in the collage (bottom right) is the most important card in the game of Skat – as it is in the Storchs' marital games. In the opera, Strauss set the game (one of his favorite hobbies) for simple chamber music forces (strings and piano).

The Egyptian Helen

Die ägyptische Helena

Oper in two acts

Libretto: Hugo von Hofmannsthal.

Première: 6 June 1928, Dresden (Staatsoper); revised version: 14 August 1933, Salzburg (Festival).

Characters: Helena/Helen (S), Menelas/Menelaus (T), Hermione, their daughter (S), Aithra, a sorceress (S), Altair, an Egyptian prince (Bar), Da-ud, his son (T), Two Servants of Aithra (S, Ms), Three Elves (2 S, A), The Omniscient Sea-Shell (A); servants of Aithra, elves, warriors, slaves, eunuchs (chorus).

The Egyptian Helen, Maria Jeritza as Helen, 1930s.
Maria Jeritza (1887–1982) enchanted opera audiences as Helen. Though she did not sing this great role either at the Dresden première or in the first performance of the reworked Salzburg version (Elisabeth Rethberg and Viorica Ursuleac were the first Helens), Strauss found in Jeritza the ideal Helen.

Setting: Aithra's island, not far from Egypt, and a palm grove at the foot of the Atlas Mountains, after the Trojan War.

Synopsis

Menelaus feels duty bound to kill his unfaithful wife Helen, the cause of the fateful Trojan War, although he loves her as much as ever. Aithra tries to help him by extinguishing his memories of the past with a magic potion and declaring the Trojan Helen to be a phantom. Menelaus begins a new life with the supposedly ideal Egyptian Helen, but former events repeat themselves. Again men fall in love with Helen, and again Menelaus kills a rival. Truth is the only solution. Helen herself gives Menelaus a drink that will restore his memory. Only when love can embrace all aspects of the beloved, even infidelity and inflicted pain, can it survive into the present, changed for the better.

Act I

A chamber in Aithra's palace. Poseidon's beloved, the sorceress Aithra, learns from the omniscient sea-shell that the ship sailing past her island contains Spartans returning from the Trojan War. Menelaus is on the point of killing his wife Helen, the cause of the war in which so many men perished. Aithra sends a storm and the ship sinks. Menelaus and Helen manage to reach the shore and are welcomed by the sorceress. With the help of the elves, Aithra makes Menelaus believe that he has killed his unfaithful wife, in the meantime giving Helen a drink that will restore her youth. Then she convinces the confused man that he has killed only the phantom of Helen, and that the real, true Helen was carried off by the gods and has been waiting faithfully for him in Egypt. She makes him forget all that has happened with a drink that induces oblivion. Menelaus lays down his sword and becomes reconciled to the supposedly "true" Helen. When Aithra wants to send the couple to Sparta, Helen hesitates: will his memory not return when he reaches home? So Aithra removes the couple to an oasis at the foot of the Atlas mountains. But the elves, unhappy about the reconciliation, secretly hide Menelaus' sword and a drink to restore his memory in the travelers' luggage.

Act II

An encampment in a palm grove in the Atlas mountains. Helen believes that she has achieved all she wants, but now Menelaus believes that the Helen who stands before him is a phantom. Altair, the prince of the mountains, pays his respects to the newcomers, accompanied by his son, and both immediately fall in love with Helen. The old game begins anew. Altair sends Menelaus hunting with his son Da-ud, believing that he can seduce Helen while they are away. During the hunt Menelaus and Da-ud quarrel, and Da-ud is killed. Helen is now convinced that she and Menelaus can be saved only by acknowledging the truth about the past, and so gives him the drink that will restore his memory. Menelaus recognizes that he has been with his beloved Helen throughout this time, and that his love can therefore embrace even her infidelity and the suffering she has caused. The ship that brought the couple to Aithra's island rises out of the waves. Menelaus and Helen rejoin their daughter Hermione on board, and the boat sets sail for Sparta.   *S. N.*

The Egyptian Helen, production photograph with Eva Marton (Helen) and Matti Kastu (Menelaus), production Joachim Herz, sets Jörg Zimmermann, costumes Eleonore Kleiber, conductor Wolfgang Sawallisch, Bayerisches Nationaltheater, Munich 1981.
Beneath the mythological surface there lies an everyday marital crisis.

Helen's fate

Hofmannsthal describes the situation of Menelaus with great dramatic sensitivity: "On that night, when the Greeks burst into burning Troy, Menelaus must have found his wife in one of those burning palaces and carried her out between collapsing walls, this woman, the beloved wife who had been stolen away from him, the most beautiful woman in the world, the cause of this war, of those terrible ten years, of this plain full of dead men and this fire, the widow of Paris and the mistress of ten or twelve other sons of Priam, who were now all dead or dying – the widow, then, of these ten or twelve young princes! What a situation for a husband!"

Two Helens?

"So there is the *Helen* of Euripides, the only classical poem that is concerned with this period: Helen and Menelaus returning home from Troy. Here we encounter that motif of a "phantom" of Helen ... that second Helen, not the Trojan but the Egyptian Helen. We are in Egypt, or Pharos, the island belonging to Egypt, near a royal castle. Menelaus appears, alone, returning from Troy. For months his ship has been wandering the seas, driven from shore to shore, always carried off course, away from his home. Helen, the wife he has reclaimed, has been left behind with his warriors in a sheltered bay; he is searching for advice, help, an oracle that will teach him the way home. Then, from the castle's colonnade, there appears Helen, not the beautiful, all too famous Helen whom he left behind on the ship, but another, and yet the same. And she claims to be his wife, claims that the other Helen on the ship is no one, nothing, a phantom, a hallucination, placed in the arms of Paris by Hera long ago, to make fools of the Greeks." (Hofmannsthal, April 1923)

Strauss on Helen

In an interview in the Vienna *Neue Freie Presse*, on 27 May 1928, Strauss spoke about the music of *The Egyptian Helen* with great astuteness: "There is little to be said about the music: it is, I fear, melodious, pleasant to listen to, and unfortunately offers little challenge to the ears of those who have outgrown the 19th century." Was this an ironic dig at the new atonality? *The Egyptian Helen* was at any rate forgotten as quickly as the avant-garde operas of those years. It was not easy to achieve lasting success with a new opera in the 20th century.

Arabella, Viorica Ursuleac (Arabella) and Jaro Prohaska (Mandryka), production Heinz Tietjen, conductor Wilhelm Furtwängler, Staatsoper Unter den Linden, Berlin 1933. "I kiss your hand, Madam" – a typical expression, not only in the royal and imperial Austro-Hungarian monarchy, here taken literally.

Arabella

Lyrische Komödie in three acts

Libretto: Hugo von Hofmannsthal.
Première: 1 July 1933, Dresden (Staatsoper).
Characters: Count Waldner, a retired cavalry officer (B), Adelaide, his wife (Ms), Arabella and Zdenka, their daughters (2 S), Mandryka, a Croatian land-owner (Bar), Matteo, a young officer (T), Count Elemer, Count Dominik, and Count Lamoral, Arabella's suitors (T, Bar, B), The Fiakermilli, belle of the Coachmen's Ball (S), A Fortune-Teller (S), Welko, Djura, and Jankel, Mandryka's servants (spoken), Hotel Porter (spoken), A Chaperone (silent), Three Card Players (3 B), A Doctor (silent), A Waiter (silent); coachmen, hotel residents, ball guests, waiters (chorus).
Setting: Vienna, 1860.

Synopsis

Count Waldner's family is deeply in debt. The elder daughter, Arabella, is being offered to the highest bidder among her suitors, while the younger daughter, Zdenka, has been disowned and has to wear boy's clothes. A tragedy. But as luck would have it, the wealthy suitor really loves the girl on sale, and the disguised girl is able to give up her disguise, because a suitable husband appears for her too. Only one shadow passes across this happiness: a misunderstanding, which awakens jealousy and mistrust. There is a happy ending, but only because Arabella is magnanimous enough to forgive: out of love, or a vision of necessity?

Arabella, Lotte Lehmann as Arabella, Vienna 1933.
Arabella is waiting for the "right man." Her melodious soprano role is one of the most beautiful in Strauss's operas. Arabella is musically related to the female characters of →*Der Rosenkavalier*, the Marschallin and Sophie. *M 17*

Act I

A salon in a hotel in Vienna, the residence of Count Waldner, his wife, and their two daughters, Arabella and Zdenka, the latter in male clothing, as her father cannot afford to introduce her in society. Zdenka is in love with the officer Matteo, who is courting Arabella, and writes letters to him in her sister's name. Arabella is waiting for her great love, love at first sight. Their father has told a wealthy old fellow-officer about their desperate situation, and given him a picture of the beautiful Arabella as bait. And indeed, there is a wealthy fish on the line: the old friend's nephew has fallen in love with the picture, has traveled to Vienna from distant Croatia, and is to be introduced to Arabella at the Coachmen's Ball.

Act II

A public ballroom. At the Coachmen's Ball, Mandryka is introduced to Arabella, as arranged. It is love at first sight. Arabella prematurely leaves the ball in order to say farewell to her maidenly life. Zdenka gives the inconsolable Matteo a key, allegedly to Arabella's room, but actually to her own. Mandryka accidentally witnesses this delivery of the key, concludes that Arabella has already been unfaithful to him, and makes his mind up to leave. Count Waldner only just manages to restrain him.

Act III

An open space in the stairwell of the hotel. Arabella, returning from the ball, meets Matteo, who believes she has just been lying in his arms. Her distant manner upsets him, and they begin a quarrel, which Mandryka, dragged along to the scene by Count Waldner, interprets as a lovers' tiff. Before it comes to a duel and departure, Zdenka explains the situation. Matteo is to marry Zdenka, and Arabella forgives Mandryka, offering him a glass of pure water, a symbol of betrothal according to the custom of Mandryka's Croatian homeland.   *S. N.*

Arabella, Lisa della Casa (Arabella) and Anneliese Rothenberger (Zdenka), production Rudolf Hartmann, sets Stefan Hlawa, costumes Ernie Kniepert, conductor Joseph Keilberth, Salzburg Festival 1958. The two sisters: Arabella is the prima donna, not only in terms of casting but also within her family, while the breeches role and thus the part of the second soprano falls to her younger sister, whom the family cannot afford to dress in the required style.

17. Arabella's Hopes

A - ber der Rich - ti - ge, wenn's ei - nen gibt für mich auf die - ser Welt

Arabella, Richard Strauss (at the piano), Lotte Lehmann (Arabella), Alfred Jerger (Mandryka), and the director Lothar Wallenstein (behind Strauss), after the Vienna première on 21 October 1933.
The 69-year-old Strauss gives instructions after the Vienna première of *Arabella*.

18. Fiakermilli's Yodeling

At the Coachmen's Ball

The first *Fiakerball*, or Coachmen's Ball, took place as early as the reign of Joseph II, in 1787 (the year of Mozart's →*Don Giovanni*, an opera in which another notable ball takes place). It first took place in the suburbs, but across the years moved closer to the city center, finally coming to rest in the *Blumensälen*, or Flower Halls, in an elegant restaurant on the Ringstrasse, always on Ash Wednesday. It reached the peak of its popularity between 1880 and 1900. These balls were attended by all social classes, though

aristocrats came unaccompanied by women. A particular attraction of course was the music: waltzes, songs, *couplets*, marches, and waltzes again, over and over. After 1880 the famous Schrammel Quartet appeared. The absolute star was Emilie Turaczek (1846–89), known as "Fiakermilli," who made such a name for herself as a singer of Viennese songs that in her own time a "Milli cult" grew up in the Austrian capital. Strauss was not very well informed about Fiakermilli. At first he thought she was a yodeler, then a "man-woman in heavy boots" (in fact she did appear wearing high boots, short trousers, and a hussar's hat, and carrying a stick). In →*Arabella* this role demands a coloratura soprano of great virtuosity: her range goes up to high d (d'''). She sings in imitation of yodeling, constantly in the highest soprano range. *M 18*

Vienna again

When they started work together on *Arabella*, Hofmannsthal and Strauss both knew that it would not be easy to create another successful work set in Vienna, almost 20 years after →*Der Rosenkavalier*, and ten years after the war that had ended so disastrously for the Austro-Hungarian Empire. "The important thing is to find the right tone for the whole work, a certain general tone, in which the whole work exists," the poet wrote to the composer on 13 July 1928, after a year of planning the opera together. "The tone of *Arabella* is very different from that of *Der Rosenkavalier*. It is Vienna in both cases – but what a difference between the two – a whole century! Vienna under Maria Theresia – and Vienna of 1860! I dipped the eighteenth-century Vienna into an atmosphere at once ostentatious and intimate (in a language which, by the way, was a total invention of mine), while the atmosphere of *Arabella*, very close to our own time, is more ordinary, natural, vulgar. The three counts carelessly chasing after women and girls, the whole dubious background of this discharged cavalry officer Waldner, has something vulgar about it, a rather vulgar and dangerous Vienna surrounds these figures, against which the independent, brave Arabella and the touchingly unrestrained Zdenka stand out. But above all, for Mandryka this pleasure-seeking, frivolous Vienna of habitual debtors is sheer folly – he is surrounded by the purity of his villages, his oak forests which the axe has never touched, his old folk songs – here the *breadth* of the great half-Slavic Austria enters a Viennese comedy and allows quite a different air to stream in ... "

Arabella, set design for Act III by Otto Reigbert, with costume designs for Arabella and Mandryka, Cologne 1934 (TWS). The most significant encounters within a love affair often occur in unromantic places – in a stairwell, for example.

The Silent Woman

Die schweigsame Frau

Komische Oper in three acts

Libretto: Stefan Zweig, freely adapted by Ben Jonson.
Première: 4 June 1935, Dresden (Staatsoper).
Characters: Sir Morosus, a retired admiral (B), Widow Zimmerlein, his housekeeper (A), Schneiderbart, the barber (Bar), Henry Morosus, the admiral's nephew (T), Aminta, his wife (S), Isotta, Carlotta, Morbio, Vanuzzi, and Farfallo, members of an operatic troupe (2 S, Ms, Bar, 2 B), The Parrot (spoken); actors and neighbors (chorus).
Setting: The drawing-room of Sir Morosus's house in London, c. 1780.

Synopsis

A retired admiral, Sir Morosus, wants to spend his old age in peace and quiet. He is used to giving orders, and – because he is rich – everyone obeys him. Everyone, that is, except his own nephew, who is his heir. He has married a singer and become an actor himself. The old man disinherits him and decides to find himself a silent young wife. But he is outwitted by his nephew, and in the course of the adventure loses much of his hard exterior. In the end Henry gets his inheritance and Morosus his peace and quiet.

Act I
Sir Morosus is extremely sensitive to noise, and his short temper makes life difficult for those around him. Henry, his nephew and heir, makes no allowances for him. He has married a singer and taken to the stage himself, and now wants to lodge in his uncle's house together with a noisy pack of actors. Morosus disinherits him, and orders the barber to find him a young, silent woman immediately: he wants to get married.

Act II
The barber has come to an agreement with Henry: three actresses are presented for Morosus's consideration, and he chooses "Timida," actually Henry's wife Aminta. No sooner has the supposed marriage taken place than the silent woman turns into a noisy virago.

Act III
"Timida" is driving Morosus to desperation with her loud singing and shouting. He longs for peace, and is glad to find that his nephew will take her off his hands. He has learned his lesson and accepts that he is an old man. How beautiful is a life of passion, but how much more beautiful when over.   A. G.

The Silent Woman, Reri Grist as Aminta, Oper der Stadt, Cologne 1975.
The American soprano Reri Grist as Aminta. For her, *The Silent Woman* was a brilliant masterpiece, unencumbered by history.

Destiny separates …

"… if you too abandon me now, I will simply have to lead the life of an unemployed private man, wasting away … I will not give you up, in spite of the fact that we now have an anti-Semitic government." (Strauss to Zweig, 26 February 1935) With these words Strauss demonstrated, for neither the first nor the last time, his creative egoism and political naïveté. The fact is that he was loyal to the Nazi regime: he did not refuse the directorship of the State Music Bureau when Goebbels offered it to him (1933–35), and he conducted at Bayreuth in place of conductors who either refused or were not permitted to appear in Germany during the Third Reich (such as Arturo Toscanini and Bruno Walter). His attitude did not alter until the Dresden première of *The Silent Woman*. Two days before the première Strauss learned that the name of his librettist, who was of Jewish descent, could not appear on the theater posters. Strauss protested vehemently and got his own way. Whether this was good for Zweig was something he did not consider. His artistic status had been injured. But there were more experiences ahead. His letter to Zweig was intercepted by the Gestapo. Strauss, a free citizen, was outraged. In the first flush of his fury he wrote a memorandum to the government (10 July 1935) and at the same time resigned from his post at the State Music Bureau. But in a private note he remarked with resignation that he had actually lost the struggle with those in power: "The work alone has conquered, although Hitler and Goebbels missed the performance (whether deliberately or, as reported, because they were prevented from traveling by a storm) … It is a wretched time when an artist of my standing has to ask a little boy of a minister for permission as to what he may compose and have performed. Well, I too belong to the 'nation of servants and waiters' and almost envy my racially persecuted Stefan Zweig, who now definitively refuses to work for me either openly or in secret, as he has been granted no 'special dispensation' by the Third Reich. I do not understand this Jewish feeling of solidarity and regret the fact that Zweig, as an 'artist,' cannot rise above 'political fashions.' If we do not guard the freedom of artists within ourselves, we cannot demand it from alehouse orators … My life's work seems to have been definitively closed with *The Silent Woman*. Otherwise I might still have created other things which would not have been totally without value." *The Silent Woman* was not performed again in Dresden until after the collapse of the Nazi regime, on 23 November 1946, on which occasion Zweig's name did appear on the posters. But by that time the writer had been dead for four years, having taken his own life in exile in South America.

The Silent Woman in a noisy time

"After the death of Hofmannsthal, that faithful man of genius, I had to accept with resignation that my operatic career was over …" So Strauss recalled the loss of "his" poet in 1928 after a collaboration of over 20 years. He was, however, to encounter another "genius." In 1931, Anton Kippenberg of the publishers Insel Verlag recommended Stefan Zweig as a potential librettist. "If I knew that I would not be wasting an hour of your time, I would gladly permit myself to call on you at some point," wrote Zweig modestly, as early as October of that year. On hearing Zweig's suggestions for a libretto, Strauss, the man of the theater, recognized immediately that in Zweig he had found a worthy successor to Hofmannsthal. Strauss felt strongly drawn to Zweig from the outset. To Hofmannsthal he had been sober, phlegmatic, practical; in his letters to Zweig the 70-year-old was practically gushing. The libretto for *The Silent Woman* appeared to him "more suited to music than either →*Figaro* or →*The Barber of Seville*" (letter to Zweig, 24 June 1932). Zweig too was fascinated by Strauss's skill: "I would never have suspected of him such power of artistic comprehension, such an astonishing degree of dramaturgical knowledge. While one was still relating a plot to him, he was already giving it dramatic form and – what was even more astonishing – adapting it to the limits of his own ability, which he was able to assess with an almost uncanny clarity."

The Silent Woman, set design for Act I by Adolph Mahnke, production Josef Gielen, Dresden 1935 (TWS).
The den of the old sea dog Sir Morosus. A peaceful cabin on the raging ocean of life?

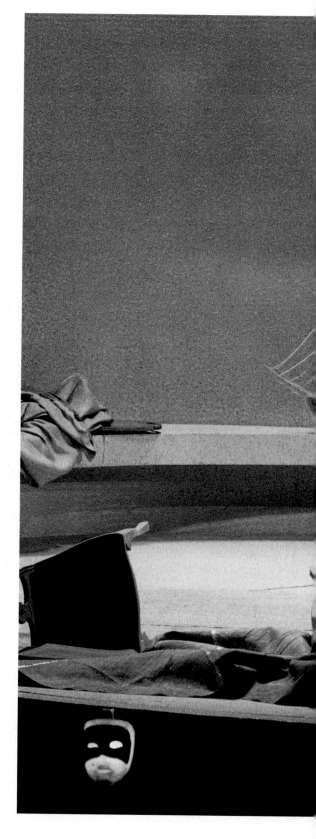

The Silent Woman, production photograph with Kirsten Blanck (Aminta) and Günter von Kannen (Sir Morosus), production and sets Marco Arturo Marelli, conductor Christof Prick, Semperoper, Dresden 1998.
The worst moment of Sir Morosus's marriage: his model boat, the symbol of his identity as a sailor and thus also of freedom, is threatened by his "silent" young wife. It is not merely a joke, but a conflict of generations and of gender. Both suffer bitter consequences, as in Donizetti's comedy of old age, →*Don Pasquale*.

Comedy in old age

Not every composer lives long enough to write a comedy in old age, as Strauss did with *The Silent Woman*. Strauss is nevertheless in good company. Monteverdi composed →*Poppea* at the age of 75, Verdi composed →*Falstaff* at nearly 80, Puccini was 60 when he composed →*Gianni Schicchi*, and Wagner was over 50 when he composed →*The Mastersingers of Nuremberg*. Donizetti's only successful *opera buffa*, →*Don Pasquale*, was written when he was already suffering from the illness that would kill him. Strauss was exactly 70 years old when he composed *The Silent Woman*. He could have concluded his life's work with it. In this work of his old age Strauss employs an extremely melodic style and transparent instrumentation, stylistic parody and musical quotation. The true meaning of *componere*, the putting together of individual musical elements to form a new whole, here becomes apparent. Indeed, Strauss himself spoke of his "happy workshop." He furnished his new opera with many ensembles, in the manner of Mozart. Was this too a sign of old age? Was he replacing the monologic "against the world" singing of the aria with the "listening to each other" or "talking across each other" of the ensemble?

The leitmotiv of Sir Morosus consists of a perfect Classical phrase, actually a slow minuet. ₘ₁₉

At the end of the opera, Morosus finds the appropriate words – and with them the quintessence of this comedy of life: "How beautiful is music, but how much more beautiful when it is over! How wonderful is a young, silent woman, but how much more wonderful when she remains the wife of another! How beautiful is life, but how much more beautiful when one is not a fool, and knows how to live it!"

What is the old man so happy about? Outwardly everything remains the same, but inwardly he has become more compassionate, more broad-minded, and more optimistic.

19. Music of Silence (Act III, finale)

(Bar), Musketeer (B), Bugler (B), Officer (Bar), Front-Line Officer (Bar), A Piedmontese (T), Holsteiner (B), Mayor (T), Prelate (Bar), Woman (S); soldiers, elders, women of the deputation to the commandant, townspeople (chorus).

Setting: The fortress of a besieged city, on 24 October 1648 (the first day of peace after the Thirty Years' War).

Synopsis

After a long siege, the city's inhabitants are exhausted. A deputation headed by the mayor begs the commandant of the fortress to surrender. He asks them to wait until midday, when there will be a signal for the gates of the city to open. The people anticipate a sign of peace, but in reality the commandant is planning to blow up the fortress with himself inside, in accordance with the emperor's orders not to surrender. His wife Maria is moved by her husband's bravery, and the couple renew their loving relationship. At midday the commandant lights the fuse. Then three cannon shots are heard. The commandant extinguishes the fuse, in the belief that the enemy is opening fire and that he can at last go into his final battle. But the bells begin to ring: peace has been declared. The besiegers offer a brotherly embrace, and the people look forward to something they have not known for a long time but that they profoundly long for: peace.   S. N.

Peace Day

Friedenstag

Oper in one act

Libretto: Joseph Gregor, with assistance from Stefan Zweig.
Première: 24 July 1938, Munich (Nationaltheater).

Characters: Commandant (Bar), Maria, his wife (S), Sergeant-Major (B), Private Soldier (T), Corporal

Peace Day – 1938
Peace Day is at once topical and timeless. It is exceptional among Strauss's operas: a large chorus, several prominent parts for men, no refinement or subtlety, everything is powerful, raw, and solid. Occasionally Strauss reverts to Wagnerian pathos (particularly in the declamation of text). The idea for *Peace Day* came from Stefan Zweig. As he no longer wanted or was able to work for Strauss or for a German stage, he had recommended the Viennese theatrical scholar Joseph Gregor (1888–1960) as a new librettist. *Peace Day* deals with a symbolic rather than an historical event. The commandant symbolizes reason, Maria the heart, and the citizens the soul. They are all in opposition, are characterized by suffering and torment, and are driven by a dull longing for happiness. The miracle of peace happens not in a psychologically realistic manner, but as if in a fairy tale. It comes from outside, just as in the saying: "When the need is greatest, help is nearest at hand."

Above left
Peace Day, photograph from the production by Peter Konwitschny, sets and costumes Johannes Leiacker, conductor Stefan Soltesz, Sächsische Staatsoper, Dresden 1999.
Peace Day is not so much an opera as a musical prayer for inner and outer peace, and for this reason is both contemporary and timeless.

Peace Day, set design by Heinz Grete, Nuremberg 1939 (TWS).
Peace Day is based on a painting by Velázquez, *The Surrender of Bredá*, after a drama of the same name by Calderón. At the first performance of Strauss's opera, Ludwig Sievert's monumental set made a strong impression. A year later (the opera was performed a hundred or so times in various German cities), Heinz Grete used Sievert's set as a model for his design for Nuremberg.

Daphne, costume design by Ludwig Sievert, Munich 1941 (TWS).
Daphne at the moment of metamorphosis: her transformation into a laurel tree. The music is no less magical, the instrumental voices and motifs flowing into each other like branches and leaves. The silvery moonlight heightens the effect on stage. M 20

Daphne, production photograph with Zsuzsanna Bazsinka as Daphne, production Peter Konwitschny, sets Johannes Leiacker, Aalto Musiktheater, Essen 1999.
Strauss developed a style described as "claire obscure" especially for Daphne, in order to give Daphne "the twilight she needs to bring to life her fateful involvement with nature and her failure towards humans … " (Strauss to Gregor, 26 January 1936)

20. Daphne's Metamorphosis

Daphne

Bukolische Tragödie in one act

Libretto: Joseph Gregor.
Première: 15 October 1938, Dresden (Staatsoper).
Characters: Peneios (B), Gaea (A), Daphne (S), Leukippos (T), Apollo (T), Four Shepherds (T, Bar, 2 B), Two Maids (2 S); shepherds, maskers, maids (chorus, ballet).
Setting: At Peneios' hut near the river of that name in mythological times.

The transformation
"Can Daphne not be seen as the human embodiment of nature itself, touched by the two deities Apollo and Dionysus ... whom she senses, but does not comprehend, and, having experienced death, rising once again as the symbol of the eternal work of art, the perfect laurel tree?" (Strauss to Gregor, 8 March 1936)

Synopsis
Daphne, the daughter of a river god and Mother Earth, has a totally pure nature, and an affinity with the trees, flowers, and streams. At a festival in honor of Dionysus, the lovely nymph is courted both by her childhood playmate Leukippos and by the god Apollo, but she is incapable of sensual love. Leukippos resorts to cunning, disguising himself as a girl and offering Daphne a Dionysiac drink that will arouse her senses. Apollo exposes his rival and kills him. Daphne, though innocent, regards herself as responsible, and feels alienated from her real self as a result of the drink. Feeling pity for her, Apollo asks Zeus to restore to Daphne her own nature and to give her to him, if not as a wife, as an evergreen laurel tree. The transformation takes place. *S. N.*

Capriccio, Elisabeth Schwarzkopf as the countess, Vienna c. 1960.
All artists seek her favor. The beautiful countess: Elisabeth Schwarzkopf with her enigmatic smile.

Capriccio

Konversationsstück für Musik in one act

Libretto: Clemens Krauss and Richard Strauss.

Première: 28 October 1942, Munich (Nationaltheater).

Characters: Countess Madeleine, a young widow (S), The Count, her brother (Bar), Flamand, a composer (T), Olivier, a poet (Bar), La Roche, a theater director (B), Clairon, an actress (A), Monsieur Taupe, a prompter (T), Two Italian Singers (S, T), The Majordomo (B), Eight Servants (4 T, 4 B), A Young Ballerina (dancer), Three Musicians (violonist, cellist, harpsichordist).

Setting: A chateau near Paris, c. 1775.

Synopsis

An opera about opera. In the salon of an art-loving countess, a party of artists is preparing a birthday celebration. Each of them feels indispensable and particularly valued by the countess. The poet Olivier and the composer Flamand, in particular, compete for the countess's favor. The countess remains undecided. She enjoys the arts, but she cannot favor any one artist, for "if you choose one, you lose the other." Will the opera that she has proposed remain unfinished? If so, then so much the better. Otherwise the ending would certainly be a trivial one.   A. G.

Theatrical capriccio

The idea for *Capriccio* came once again from Stefan Zweig, as with all Strauss's late operas. While they were working together on →*The Silent Woman* in 1934 Zweig showed Strauss a libretto by Giovanni Battista Casti, *Prima la musica, poi le parole*, which had been set to music by Antonio Salieri in 1786 and performed for the first time in Schönbrunn alongside Mozart's →*The Impresario*.

Strauss did nothing about the libretto at the time, but returned to it while he was working on the orchestration of →*The Love of Danae*. At first he was dissatisfied with the development of the plot by Joseph Gregor (Stefan Zweig's successor as Strauss's librettist): "No idea of what I had had in mind: an intellectual dramatic paraphrase of the theme: first the words, then the music (Wagner), or first the music, then the words (Verdi), or only words, no music (Goethe), or only music, no words (Mozart), to mention just a few slogans. Between them of course there are many nuances and variations!" (Strauss to Gregor, 15 May 1939). Then, in the fall of 1939, the renowned conductor Clemens Krauss joined the collaboration. In an exuberant letter full of examples from the musical repertory, he gave the old master a number of important ideas. In 1941 the final title, *Capriccio*, was settled on, an allusion to an eighteenth-century operatic genre of which the best-known representative is Mozart's →*The Impresario*.

Music about music

How can one set to music intellectual conversations about art? It is a capricious idea, which can succeed only if different stylistic parodies are blended to create a unified work. Flamand quickly sets a sonnet to music on his harpsichord. M 22 The countess pensively sings the same melody in the final scene (now accompanied by the harp). With such stylistic bravura, a "real" Italian duet seems to have been a mere finger exercise for Strauss. M 23 And there is dancing (we are in France, after all) – a passepied, a gigue, and a gavotte. M 24

When work on the opera was finished, Clemens Krauss asked Strauss about his plans for further work. The answer took the form of another question, to

21. Chamber Music in the Countess's Salon (Prelude)

22. Flamand's Sonnet

Kein An - dres, das mir so im Her - zen loht, __ nein, Schö - ne, nichts auf die - ser gan - zen Er - de

23. Italian Duet (Soprano and Tenor)

Ad - di - o mia vi - ta, ad - di - o, non __ pian - ge - re il mi-o fa - to

24. Gavotte

which time has supplied the answer "yes": "Is not this D flat major the best ending to my life's work in the theater? One can only leave one's will!" (28 July 1941).

Capriccio, set design by Rochus Gliese for the Munich première of 1942 (TWS). All the action takes place in one room, a salon. At the beginning of the opera we hear enchanting chamber music in Classical style, a string sextet. M 21 The count is reading his sister a sonnet by Olivier: "No other who blazes so in my heart,/No, beautiful one, nothing on this whole earth,/Nothing else that I desire as much as you,/Even if Venus were to offer herself to me."

The Love of Danae, production photograph with Sabine Hass as Danae, production Giancarlo del Monaco, sets and costumes Monika von Zallinger, conductor Wolfgang Sawallisch, Munich Opera Festival, Bayerische Staatsoper, Munich 1988.
Musically, the most original, truly Straussian moment is the musical depiction of the golden rain – the union of Danae and Jupiter. It is conveyed by the sound of the xylophone, celesta, triangle, and flute. M 25

25. The Golden Rain

26. Danae's Love

Wie um-gibst du mich __ mit Frie-den, labst mir im-mer neu __ den Blick

The Love of Danae, photograph from the production by Giancarlo del Monaco, sets and costumes Monika von Zallinger, conductor Wolfgang Sawallisch, Munich Opera Festival, Bayerische Staatsoper, Munich 1988.
The stylized, neo-classical set is reminiscent of the set design by Emil Preetorius for the planned first performance.

The Love of Danae

Die Liebe der Danae

Heitere Mythologie in three acts

Libretto: Joseph Gregor, after a scenario by Hugo von Hofmannsthal.
Première: First public dress rehearsal: 16 August 1944, Salzburg (Festspielhaus); first performance: 14 August 1952, Salzburg (Festspielhaus). (*The Love of Danae* was the last of Strauss's operas to receive its première, although the last but one to be completed.)

Characters: Jupiter (Bar), Merkur/Mercury (T), King Pollux (T), Danae, his daughter (S), Xanthe, Danae's servant (S), Midas (T), Four Kings, nephews of Pollux (2 T, 2 B), Semele, Europa, Alkmene, and Leda, four queens (2 S, Ms, A), Four Guards (4 B); creditors, servants, people (chorus).
Setting: Greece, in mythological times.

Synopsis

In order to pay off his debts, King Pollux offers his daughter Danae to the rich King Midas. Midas actually falls in love with the beautiful Danae, but the god Jupiter intervenes. Against all expectations, Danae decides in favor of the human Midas and against Jupiter, and sticks to her resolve, even when Midas is transformed into a poor donkey-driver. She herself is transformed from a vain, self-loving girl into a woman who bravely defies poverty and hardship. Even Jupiter undergoes a metamorphosis: touched by Danae's love of her husband, resisting all temptation, he turns from a lover to a fatherly friend who dispenses blessings.

Act I

Scene 1: The throneroom of King Pollux. A state crisis: there is no money in the coffers. To soothe his creditors, King Pollux sends his four nephews to King Midas, in the hope of being able to interest Midas in a marriage with his daughter Danae.
Scene 2: Danae's bedroom. Danae dreams of a shower of golden rain, which embraces her like a lover.

Scene 3: A colonnade in the palace. The nephews bring proof of Midas' miraculous ability: he sends Danae a twig which he has turned to gold by the touch of his hand. Midas' ship arrives in port. But the king himself is disguised as a messenger, while Jupiter takes over the form and role of the golden king. Danae then feels a profound sympathy for the real Midas.

Scene 4: The port. Jupiter-Midas is welcomed. Danae recognizes him as the lover who visited her as golden rain, and is uncertain of her feelings.

Act II

A hall in the king's palace. The wives of Pollux's four nephews – Semele, Europa, Alkmene, and Leda – prepare the marriage bed. Each of them has had a liaison with Jupiter. They have recognized the god despite his disguise, and are jealous of their former lover's new favorite. The real Midas puts on royal attire and climbs into the marriage bed with Danae. Jupiter intervenes, and Danae is transformed into a golden statue in Midas' arms. Given the choice of loving the man or the god, she decides in favor of Midas.

Act III

Scene 1: A country road in the East. Once Jupiter gave Midas the gift of being able to transform objects into gold simply by touching them. Now he has withdrawn his favor from his successful rival, and Midas must continue life as a poor donkey-driver. Danae stands by him.

Scene 2: A southern mountain landscape. Jupiter learns from Mercury that the other gods are laughing at him because of his unhappy love of Danae. Pollux and his creditors confront the supposed Midas, and Jupiter escapes only by means of a plentiful downpour of golden rain.

Scene 3: Midas' hut. Jupiter tries his luck with Danae again, but she is happy with Midas. Jupiter blesses their love.   *S. N.*

The ancient German-Greek

Hofmannsthal had already written a scenario for Strauss in April 1920 called *Danae, or The Marriage of Convenience: Little Opera for R. Str.*. Strauss had been interested in Greek mythology since his youth, and in the mid-1930s he returned to Hofmannsthal's material with the intention of composing a kind of mythological operetta à la →Offenbach. In 1944, he remarked to his friend, the scientist Willi Schuh, that the third act was "among the best things I have ever written." In Jupiter, Strauss, who called himself an "ancient German-Greek," created a sort of idealized image of himself in old age, and in Danae he celebrated his ideal woman. *M 26*

The Love of Danae, set design by Emil Preetorius for the planned first performance, Salzburg 1944 (TWS).
The first performance of *The Love of Danae* was planned for the occasion of Strauss's 80th birthday in June 1944 but because of the closure of all theaters after the declaration of "total war" by Hitler and Goebbels it could take place only in the form of a performance camouflaged as a dress rehearsal. Admittedly, it had a star cast: Viorica Ursuleac, Hans Hotter, László Szemere, and the Vienna Philharmonic directed by Clemens Krauss (who was to play an important creative role in Strauss's later opera →*Capriccio*), in a production by Rudolf Hartmann. In 1952, three years after Strauss's death, *The Love of Danae* received its official first performance at the same venue. Annelies Kupper (Danae), László Szemere (Pollux), Paul Schöffler (Jupiter), and Josef Gostic (Midas) sang the principal roles. The work nevertheless failed to establish a place in the international repertory.

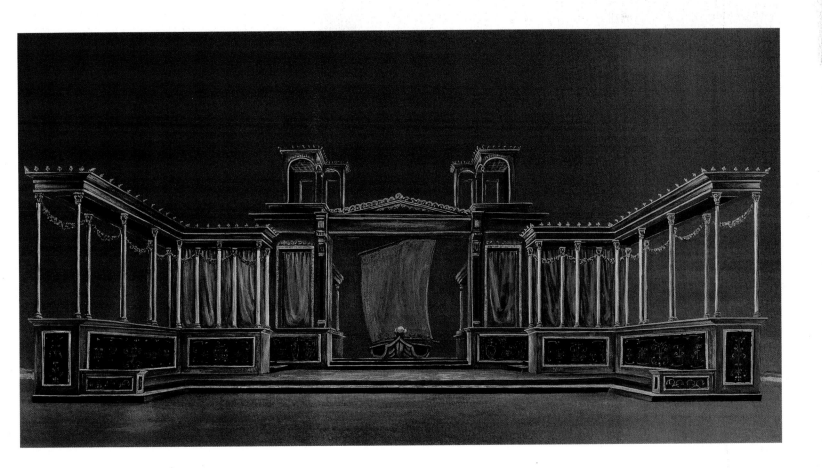

Stravinsky, Igor Fyodorovich

b. 17 June 1882 in Lomonosov (formerly Oranienbaum), Russia
d. 6 April 1971 in New York

As the son of the famous Russian bass Fyodor Stravinsky, he had a great deal of musical experience from his earliest years. He studied composition with →Nikolay Rimsky-Korsakov, and under the latter's influence created the orchestral piece *Feu d'artifice* (*Fireworks*, 1909), which aroused the interest of Sergey Dyagilev, the artistic director and impresario of the Ballets Russes. In 1909 there began a collaboration between the two that made musical and theatrical history, and that led to such masterpieces as *The Firebird*, *Petrushka*, and *The Rite of Spring*. Stravinsky became internationally famous with the epoch-making scandal of the Paris production of *The Rite of Spring* in 1913. He spent the years of the First World War in Switzerland. After the Russian October Revolution (1917) he lived first in Paris (1920–39) and then in the USA (from 1939). He enjoyed the highest artistic and financial recognition to the end of his life.

Works: Operas: *Le rossignol* (*The Nightingale*) (1914), *Mavra* (1922), *Oedipus Rex* (operatic oratorio, 1927), *The Rake's Progress* (1951); other stage works: *Renard* (1915–16), *L'histoire du soldat* (*The Soldier's Tale*) (1918); ballets, including *L'oiseau de feu* (*The Firebird*) (1909–10), *Petrushka* (1910–11), *Le sacre du printemps* (*The Rite of Spring*) (1911–13), and *Pulcinella* (1919–20); sacred music, including the *Symphony of Psalms* (1930), a Mass (1947), *Threni* (1957–58), and the *Requiem Canticles* (1965–66); orchestral works, concertos, chamber music, piano works, songs.

The Nightingale, photograph from the production by A. Petrov, conductor A. Titov, Mariinsky Theater, St. Petersburg, 1995.
Nightingale and emperor, the reconciliation of nature and power. The opera conquered the stages of the world from its first performance in Paris in 1914.

*S*travinsky, a Russian-born cosmopolitan, is the most versatile composer of the 20th century. In this respect he is often compared with Picasso. A leading exponent of musical Fauvism, Expressionism, and neo-Classicism, he nevertheless has his own distinctive stylistic characteristics, which are ever-present and unmistakable.

The Nightingale
Le rossignol

Conte lyrique in three acts

Libretto: Stepan Mitusov and Igor Stravinsky, after Hans Christian Andersen.
Première: 26 May 1914, Paris (Opéra).
Characters: The Nightingale (S), The Fisherman (T), The Cook (S), The Emperor of China (Bar), The Chamberlain (B), The Bonze (B), Three Japanese Envoys (T, 2 B), Death (A); courtiers, chorus of spirits (chorus).
Setting: China, in the time of fairy tale.

Synopsis
Act I
A fisherman is listening to the wonderful song of the nightingale. Courtiers invite the singer to the court of the Chinese emperor. The nightingale gladly accepts the invitation.

Act II
The nightingale sings to the ruler, moving him to tears. Japanese envoys bring an artificial nightingale as a present from their emperor. While the toy is being presented and delights the courtiers, the nightingale, unobserved, flies away.

Act III
The Emperor lies on his deathbed, given up by all, and watched over by death. He calls for music. Only the nightingale hears him. She sings her song to him, and he is restored to health. *S. N.*

Hidden birdsong
Not only the plot but in some respects also the music of this short opera remind one of the fairy-tale operas of →Rimsky-Korsakov, Stravinsky's teacher. Impressionism also left its mark on Stravinsky, particularly the musical language of Debussy. The Chinese March (beginning of Act II), on the other hand, with its gaudy colors, betrays the composer's independent voice. The song of the nightingale is provided by a coloratura soprano positioned in the orchestra; her outward appearance can be freely visualized. The song of the artificial nightingale has a peculiar charm, full of virtuosity but mechanically stiff in character. *M 1*

1.1 The Real Nightingale (Song)

1.2 The Artificial Nightingale (Oboe)

Mavra

Opera buffa in one act

Libretto: Boris Kochno, after the poem *The Little House at Kolomna* by Alexander Pushkin.
Première: 3 June 1922, Paris (Opéra).

Characters: Parasha (S), The Neighbor (Ms), The Mother (A), The Hussar (T).

Synopsis

The young middle-class girl Parasha and a hussar are in love. But how are they to meet? By chance, they find help. The cook has just died, and Parasha engages a new one. Thus her hussar enters the house under the name of Mavra. Her mother is satisfied: Mavra is cheap and diligent. But a man has to shave, and the mother catches him doing so. There is a great scandal and Mavra flees. Parasha looks for her hussar in vain.

S. N.

Mavra, photograph from the production by Y. Alexandrov, conductor A. Paulavichus, Mariinsky Theater, St. Petersburg, 1995. Parasha (right), talking to her mother and the disguised hussar (left). *Mavra* is highly rated by musical connoisseurs. It was staged at the Kroll-Oper in Berlin in 1928 at the instigation of Otto Klemperer, at Milan's La Scala in 1955, in Moscow in 1975 in a production by Dmitry Kitayenko, and in St. Petersburg in 1995.

A Russian folk story with jazz influence

Stravinsky dedicated *Mavra* "to the memory of Pushkin, Glinka, and Tchaikovsky." He explained the motivation for the dedication in his memoirs. The popular, folklore aesthetic of the successful Russian circle of composers known as "The Five" (to which →Rimsky-Korsakov belonged) became less and less congenial to him. →Glinka, →Tchaikovsky, and above all Pushkin, on the other hand, belonged, according to Stravinsky, to that "band of extraordinary personalities who … knew how to merge the Western spirit with specifically Russian elements." As far as the music of the opera is concerned, "Western" spirit should perhaps be understood as "Wild Western" spirit, in that the influence of American jazz is unmistakable. The sound is a hard one, the strings playing a minor role. The orchestral accompaniment of the arias and duets is full of unexpected, "spicy" accents. The melodies frequently remind one of Russian urban folk music – that is, songs that were sung or played not by peasants but by musicians in the city taverns.

S. K.

Mavra, set design by Ewald Dülberg, production and conductor Otto Klemperer, Staatsoper am Platz der Republik, Berlin 1928 (TWS).
A typical Constructivist set, in accordance with the avant-garde reformation of the stage. Only the stove betrays the Russian salon setting. The window is open, suggesting the possibility of a sudden, ominous visit. The hussar would be able to jump in.

Oedipus Rex

Opera-oratorio in two acts

Libretto: Igor Stravinsky and Jean Cocteau, after Sophocles (translated into Latin by Jean Daniélou).
Première: Concert première: 30 May 1927, Paris (Théâtre Sarah Bernhardt); stage première: 23 February 1928, Vienna (Staatsoper).
Characters: Oedipe/Oedipus (T), Jocaste/Jocasta (Ms), Créon/Creon (Bbar), Tirésias/Tiresias (B), A Shepherd (T), A Messenger (Bbar), Narrator (spoken); male chorus.
Setting: Thebes, in mythological times.

Synopsis
Before the opera begins
Laius, the king of Thebes, was killed by an unknown man while out driving. Soon afterwards Oedipus arrived in the city, which was now without a ruler, and through his wisdom saved it from the rage of the murderous Sphinx. Called upon to be the new king, he became the husband of the widowed queen Jocasta.

Act I
In Thebes a plague is raging. The people beg King Oedipus to help them. His brother-in-law Creon has been sent to Delphi, to consult the oracle of Apollo, and on his return announces that the oracle demands atonement for the unavenged murder of King Laius. The murderer is in the city. Oedipus trusts in his own wisdom; he will find the murderer.

He questions the blind seer Tiresias and receives the reply: "The king was murdered by a king." Oedipus accuses the seer of conspiring with Creon against him. The quarrel between the two men summons Jocasta to the scene.

Act II
Jocasta tries to calm them down. She does not believe in oracles, for she has learned that oracles can lie. It had been prophesied to her husband Laius that he would die by the hand of his own son. But was he not killed at the crossroads by an unknown man? Oedipus is gripped by fear: did he not kill an old man twelve years earlier at the same crossroads? As if this were not enough, a messenger brings news of the death of King Polybus. The messenger reveals that Polybus was not Oedipus' father. He was found in the mountains as a child, with pierced feet. Jocasta, suspecting the truth, rushes into the house. Oedipus believes she is ashamed to discover she is the wife of an upstart commoner. He urges the messenger to reveal the secret of his origins and thus learns that he is the son of Laius and Jocasta. Laius, after hearing an ominous utterance by the oracle, had ordered his son to be killed, but Jocasta had secretly arranged for him to be abandoned in the desert. Oedipus is shattered by the truth: "Lux facta est." He goes into the house. A messenger reports to the people that Jocasta has committed suicide. Oedipus has blinded himself and reveals his guilt to the people. In accordance with Apollo's command, he is driven out of Thebes: "You have been loved, Oedipus; farewell."

S. N.

Oedipus Rex, production photograph with chorus from a dance theater production, choreography and production Jan Linkens, conductor Yakov Kreizberg, Komische Oper, Berlin, 1995.
With his peculiar genre definition, "opera-oratorio," Stravinsky intended to clarify an important quality of the work. Even in a stage realization, *Oedipus Rex* is supposed to have a static, oratorio-like effect. The protagonists must stay immobile: King Oedipus should stand in the same place throughout, while Creon and Tiresias must be on stage from the beginning, but without being noticeable. Only light makes them visible to the audience. Jocasta appears when a curtain concealing her is drawn to one side. Only one singer is allowed to move on the stage: this is the messenger who comes from a strange land.

Classical language in modern clothing
In 1925, Stravinsky read a book about St. Francis of Assisi, from which he learned that St. Francis considered colloquial Italian unsuitable for prayer, and that when speaking to God he used French, which he had learned from his mother. Stravinsky began to turn over in his mind this concept of a language that was somehow elevated above the everyday, and thus hit on the idea of writing a stage work with a Latin text. Latin was in a sense elevated, in that it was no longer a living language.

Stravinsky asked his friend Jean Cocteau for a modern version of the Oedipus story, which Cocteau prepared in French and which was then translated into Latin by Cocteau's friend Father Jean Daniélou. Cocteau suggested to Stravinsky the use of a narrator, who would explain the developments of the plot to the audience in the language of the country in which the performance was taking place. The contrast between the dead and living languages gives the work a strange tension.

S. K.

Cocteau and music

Jean Cocteau (1899–1963) had many friends among French musicians and foreign musicians living in France. He was jointly responsible for the scenario for the ballet *Parade*, for which Erik Satie composed the music (1918). In the same year he published a collection of wittily ironic aphorisms, *Le coq et l'arlequin* (*The Cock and the Harlequin*), in which he proclaimed the philosophy of the most recent generation of French composers, which included those who were soon to constitute the group known as "Les Six," among them →Honegger, →Milhaud, and →Poulenc. Somewhat later he created a modern version of *Antigone*, which was set to music by Arthur Honegger, and which Stravinsky liked very much. From the early days Cocteau had a close relationship with Dyagilev's Ballets Russes, and witnessed the controversial first performance of Stravinsky's *The Rite of Spring* (1913). He produced wittily drawn portraits of Satie, Dyagilev, and Stravinsky. He was not so fortunate with the libretto of *Oedipus Rex*. His first attempt displeased the composer. "It was exactly what I did not want," Stravinsky later recalled, "a musical drama in terribly melodious prose." Cocteau readily and patiently reworked the piece several times, until the composer was satisfied. But they did not work together again.

Deep-frozen emotions

"Dignity" – this is the key word for the music of *Oedipus Rex*. Stravinsky himself wrote in his memoirs, the *Chronique de ma vie* of 1936, "The more I steeped myself in it, the more serious the problem of the 'dignity' that a musical work should possess became for me." Without order, no work of art could be created. A composer can create such order if he recalls to life certain formal patterns and creates new connections with traditional elements. This was the intellectual framework for the neo-Classical tendencies that emerged in the 1920s. *Oedipus Rex* is a perfect example of neo-Classicism, its musical numbers creating a clear structure. Jocasta has a great *scena* in the Italian style, which strongly recalls the style of →Donizetti or early →Verdi. *M 2*

The role of Oedipus is particularly rich in coloratura, in accordance with the European musical tradition. Only in his last, brief aria does the style become simpler, as Oedipus divests himself, so to speak, of his royal splendor. The keys and harmonies used in this short scene also have historical significance. The D minor that is heard in the lower parts was regarded as passionate and somber in the eighteenth century, as exemplified by the descent to hell of the eponymous hero of Mozart's →*Don Giovanni*. In the upper parts there glimmers the chord of D major, the key of light: "Lux facta est" ("There was light") are Oedipus' last words. The vocal line at this point is clearly in B minor (allegedly described by Beethoven as the key of suicide). *M 3*

Particularly energetic and powerful is Creon's three-part aria. It begins with a downward triadic motif in C major, accompanied by trumpets. This too can be interpreted in music-historical terms: Creon is conveying the voice of Apollo to the people, so the sound must be clear and majestic. *M 4*

The sound in *Oedipus Rex* mostly tends towards the hard and brilliant. The wind instruments dominate, while the strings play a much less significant role. On the other hand Stravinsky often uses timpani and the deep tones of the piano. There is not a single bar that has a romantic or emotional effect. The passions of the characters are as it were "frozen," hidden inside old musical formulas. *S. K.*

Oedipus Rex, costume design for Jocasta by Ruodi Barth, Paris 1979 (top), and costume design for Oedipus by Lore Haas, Krefeld 1976 (above) (TWS).
Sophocles' *Oedipus* possesses an extraordinary, almost geometric structure. As the action progresses, it draws the protagonists further and further into the past. Cocteau's libretto stresses this aspect of the tragedy. Every figure appearing for the first time take us back one step further.

2. Jocasta's Aria

Ne pro - be - ntur, ___ ne pro - be - ntur o - ra - cu - la

3. Oedipus' Realization

Lux fa - cta est! ___

4. Creon's Aria

Re spon-dit de - us: Lai - um u - lkis-ki, u - lkis-ki, ske - lus ul - kis-ki; Lai - um Lai - um ___

The Rake's Progress

Opera in three acts (nine scenes and an epilogue)

Libretto: W.H. Auden and Chester Kallman, after a series of paintings by William Hogarth.

Première: 11 September 1951, Venice (Teatro La Fenice).

Characters: Trulove (B), Anne, his daughter (S), Tom Rakewell (T), Nick Shadow (Bar), Mother Goose (Ms), Baba the Turk (Ms), Sellem, an auctioneer (T), Keeper of the Madhouse (B); whores and roaring-boys, servants, citizens, madmen (chorus).

Setting: 18th-century England.

Synopsis
Act I
Scene 1: The garden in front of the Trulove family's country house. A spring afternoon. Anne Trulove and Tom Rakewell are rejoicing in their love. Trulove presses his future son-in-law to take up some reliable career. Tom is unwilling to be hemmed in. He wishes for a large amount of money. His wish is immediately fulfilled. An unknown man appears at the gate, and explains to Tom that he is the heir of a recently deceased rich uncle, hitherto unknown to him. The unknown man offers Tom his services: his name is Nick Shadow. His wages can be discussed later, after a year and a day. Tom sets off for London with Nick Shadow, promising Anne that he will soon return.

Scene 2: Mother Goose's brothel (the word "goose" was used in England in the 18th century for syphilis). Whores and their clients praise the love of battle and the battle of love. Nick Shadow introduces Tom to the brothel and goes through the catechism of love with him. Tom is confirmed by Mother Goose herself and loses his innocence.

Scene 3: The Truloves' garden. An autumn night, full moon. Anne has received no news of Tom and fears that he is in trouble. She sets off to find him.

Act II
Scene 1: The morning room of Tom's house in London. Bright morning sunshine. Tom's life follows the course of fashion, but his heart, senses, and understanding seem empty. He wishes for happiness. Nick Shadow knows what must be done. He interprets Tom's melancholy as the result of the lack of freedom, the conformity to what must or should be done. Marriage to a monster, the famous Baba the Turk, would be a meaningless act. Since Tom neither loves nor desires the bearded hermaphrodite, this marriage would be proof of his freedom.

Scene 2: The street in front of Tom's house. Autumn, at twilight. Anne finds Tom at last. But it is too late. Tom's bearded wife, Baba the Turk, the sensation of London, arrives, carried in a sedan chair.

Scene 3: The morning room of Tom's house. Baba has not brought Tom freedom, but slavery through her continual chatter. Tom silences her by pulling a wig over her face. He goes to sleep. Meanwhile Nick Shadow demonstrates to the audience how to make bread out of stones with the help of a crude trick and a machine. Tom awakens and wishes to become a benefactor to mankind. Again Nick Shadow fulfils his wish by presenting him with the wonderful machine.

Act III
Scene 1: The morning room of Tom's house. A spring afternoon. Tom is deeply in debt as a result of the fraudulent machine. The contents of his house are to be sold at auction, including Baba the Turk, now struck dumb and sitting as though lifeless. She revives and returns to the circus. Anne, searching for Tom, is advised by Baba the Turk to look for him in the street and to separate him from Nick Shadow.

Scene 2: A churchyard. A starless night. Tom's time is up. Nick demands his wages: Tom's life and soul. Tom has one last chance: a card game with Nick Shadow with life and death as the stakes. With no wishes or hopes left, Tom guesses at the right cards and recognizes his lost aim in life in the queen of hearts. Nick returns to the land of shadows, but first tears the bond between Tom's soul and his reason.

Scene 3: The madhouse of St. Mary of Bethlehem also known as Bedlam. Tom believes himself to be Adonis and is waiting for his Venus. Anne visits him and gives peace to his wandering spirit. She sings him to sleep. Trulove comes to take his daughter home. Tom awakes, searches in vain for his Venus, and dies in disappointment. But his soul has been saved.

Epilogue: In front of the curtain. Lights on in the auditorium. Baba, Tom, Nick, Anne and Trulove, the men without their wigs, Baba without her beard, point out the moral of the story.

S. N.

The Rake's Progress by William Hogarth (Sir John Soane Museum, London). William Hogarth (1697–1764) is sometimes portrayed as the "English Hieronymus Bosch" of the 18th century. In his stories told in pictures, the great painter and engraver presented the early capitalistic London society of his time with all its contrasts and decadence. The series *The Rake's Progress* was produced in 1732–35 and is one of the painter's satirical, moralizing works. In addition to Stravinsky, Hogarth's paintings inspired Cimarosa (→*The Secret Marriage*) and Richard Strauss (→*Der Rosenkavalier*).

First row, right
I The Rake Taking Possession of His Estate

Opposite
II The Rake's Levee

Second row, left
III The Rake at the Rose Tavern

Second row, right
IV The Arrested, Going to Court

Third row, left
V The Wedding

Third row, right
VI The Rake at a Gaming House

Fourth row, left
VII The Rake in Prison

Fourth row, right
VIII The Madhouse

Inspiration: a socially critical story in pictures

He who leads a life of vice must pay dearly for his actions. This naive moral was used by the English painter and engraver William Hogarth (1697–1764) in several series of paintings intended to instruct the pious citizens of London. In one series Hogarth tells of the fate of a rake. The content of the work, completed in 1733, can be briefly summarized as follows: Tom Rakewell, a virtuous young man, inherits a great fortune after the death of his father. He promises his sweetheart Sarah Young that they will soon be married (I). However, as a rich man he begins to fritter away his money (II). At first his path leads him to the brothel (III). As he incurs large debts, he is forced to steal and is arrested. Sarah stands bail for him (IV). In order to have money again, Tom marries an old, ugly, but wealthy woman. Sarah tries in vain to prevent the marriage (V). Again he begins to squander his money, eventually gambling away his whole fortune (VI). The last stages of his downfall are the prison (VII) and the madhouse (VIII).

Composer and librettist

Stravinsky, who lived in the USA from 1939 onwards, became aware of Hogarth's paintings in 1947, at an exhibition in Chicago. He immediately conceived the idea of an opera on the subject. Following the advice of his Hollywood friend and neighbor T.S. Eliot, he chose W.H. Auden (1907–73) as his librettist. Auden had studied at Oxford, where he belonged to a circle of radical leftwing poets. In 1935 he married Erika, the daughter of Thomas Mann. After fighting against fascism in the Spanish Civil War, he lived in the USA from 1939, served as a pilot during the Second World War. From 1956 he taught poetry at Oxford. He astonished Stravinsky with his poetic virtuosity and gift for improvisation. After a personal encounter in Hollywood (at Stravinsky's invitation) they continued their collaboration by post. Later Stravinsky published part of their correspondence in his book *Memories and Commentaries*.

Their work brought great pleasure to composer and poet alike. They began to transform the story step by step, making out of it an extraordinary blend of the themes of Faust and Don Juan. In this respect, the names are revealing. Anne, for example, is intended to awaken memories of Donna Anna in Mozart's →*Don Giovanni*. Nick Shadow, the devil, does not appear in Hogarth; he is a new figure, half Mephistopheles, half Leporello. It was Auden's suggestion that the inheritance should come not from Tom's father, but from an unknown and therefore somewhat mysterious uncle. Hogarth's ugly old lady became the bearded Baba the Turk, a circus artist. In order to finish the work more quickly, Auden commissioned the help of Chester Kallman, who wrote the auction scene and various other parts of the text.

S. K.

A classical opera?

"The end of a trend," Stravinsky once said of his opera. In *The Rake's Progress* an important line of twentieth-century music was coming to an end. In the 1950s all

The Rake's Progress, photograph from the production by Peter Mussbach, sets Jörg Immendorf, conductor Silvain Cambreling, Salzburg Festival, 1994.
Mother Goose's brothel in London (Act I, Scene 2). Whores and their clients praise the love of battle and the battle of love. Meanwhile, Tom, the village lad, is questioned and confirmed by Mother Goose herself.

young composers were turning away from neo-Classicism. Even the elderly Stravinsky himself caused a sensation with a drastic change of style around this time. However, in *The Rake's Progress* there is no sign of the change. Indeed, it is a masterpiece of neo-Classicism. The short prelude (brass section) resembles the opening toccata from Monteverdi's →*Orfeo*, while some melodies are reminiscent of English Baroque music (→Purcell) and others of the tragic operas of →Gluck. Jazz rhythms are also present, and the music of the brothel scene recalls the jolly chorus of the dwarfs in Walt Disney's *Snow White*. The closest relationship, however, is with several Mozart operas. The great *scena* for Anne in Act I, based on classical forms (recitative, slow aria, short recitative, rapid aria (cabaletta) with a triadic motif in the melody), is consciously constructed according to the Mozartian model. *M 5*

All the scenes are clearly organized into recitative, arias, duets, and so on, quite in the manner of the *opera seria* of the eighteenth century. "Musical drama and opera are two quite different things," commented Stravinsky, "and I personally have dedicated myself all my life to the latter."

The use of keys is also Classical. The first scene is in A major, Mozart's key of love; so are the first bars of the last scene, in which Tom, now in the madhouse, remembers his love. Anne's great scene ends in C major (and with the so-called high C), which is the key associated with purity in Mozart's operas, as it is, for example, in Konstanze's great C major aria (→Mozart, *The Abduction from the Seraglio*, →*M 18*). *M 5*

The instrumentation is masterly and gives the work a particular charm. The rapid repetitions of the trumpet during the triple auction in the auction scene, for example, are quite unique. Lethargic, dismal, and tragic is the deep sound of the strings in the prelude to the churchyard scene that follows. Even the silvery sound of the Baroque/Classical harpsichord turns up repeatedly in the recitatives (the first time being when the devil appears), so as to delineate sections clearly and also to produce a Mozartean atmosphere.

Last stop: Venice

If one takes the boat from Venice to Murano, one passes the little island of San Michele on the way. Perhaps the most beautiful cemetery in the world, it contains the grave of Igor Stravinsky, whether as a result of his last will and testament or at the request of his widow we do not know. But one thing is certain: the composer had a special love of Venice, and the city played an important part in his life. He took part in several festivals there. The choral work *Canticum Sacrum* was composed in 1955 for the cathedral of S. Marco, and it was in Venice that *The Rake's Progress*

was first performed in 1951, with great success. Several great opera houses (including the Metropolitan, the Royal Opera House, and La Scala) had competed for the right to stage the first performance. But Stravinsky's choice fell upon a smaller theater, since he regarded his work as a chamber opera. The splendid Baroque hall of the Teatro La Fenice was ideal for this belated but contemporary work. The première became a great social event, as it would have been in the golden age of opera.

Stravinsky and the devil

Perhaps no other composer has maintained such a close relationship with the devil as Igor Stravinsky. The magician in *Petrushka* already has something demonic about him, and in *The Soldier's Tale* the devil conquers the soul of the soldier. Nick Shadow contents himself with a curse, and the warning (in the epilogue) that the devil never sleeps. Stravinsky portrayed the devil for the last time in *The Flood*. This work, composed in 1962, had originally been conceived for television. Following the Bible, the plot covers the creation of the world, the expulsion from paradise, and the flood. Stravinsky imagined the figure of Satan in a most peculiar manner, as the principle of the visual reversal of bright, white colors into dark, black ones, and vice versa. The idea, however, was never realized. *S. K.*

The Rake's Progress, photograph from the production by Peter Mussbach, sets Jörg Immendorf, conductor Silvain Cambreling, Salzburg Festival, 1994.
Anne Trulove (her name is significant) is one of the most touching figures in operatic literature. She follows her faithless sweetheart, and supports him in times of poverty and death. Anne's search (Act II, Scene 2) is one of the high points of the opera.

5. Anne's Cabaletta

I go, I go to him.   *Love __ can - not fal - ter, Can - not de - sert ___*

Szymanowski, Karol

b. 6 October 1882 in Tymoszówka (Ukraine)
d. 29 March 1937 in Lausanne

Szymanowski came from an artistic aristocratic family. He started to compose in his childhood, but later destroyed his early works, almost without exception. During his student days he joined the group of composers "Young Poland in Music." In 1908 he traveled in Italy, and from then on regarded this country as his second home, drawing artistic inspiration from his many visits there. His masterpiece, the opera *King Roger*, also owes its creation (1918–24) to his Italian experiences. While Szymanowski achieved considerable success in Germany and Austria, where he received several prizes, the circle of leading Polish musicians adopted a somewhat negative attitude to him. As a result, Szymanowski settled in Vienna between 1910 and 1914. The October Revolution of 1917 took him by surprise in his hometown of Tymoszówka. The destruction of the family home forced his family to move first to Jelisavetgrad (Elisabethgrad) and then, after the restoration of the Polish state, to Warsaw in 1919. The composer spent the 1920s partly in Poland, where he gave new impetus to the development of national music through his growing interest in Polish folklore, and partly traveling in Europe and the USA, in order to attend the increasing number of performances of his works. From earliest childhood he had suffered from tuberculosis of the bones, and at the age of 55 he succumbed to this disease in a sanatorium in Lausanne.

Works: Operas: *Hagith* (1913/FP 1922), *Król Roger* (*King Roger*) (1926); orchestral works (including four symphonies and two violin concertos), choral works, chamber music, songs, piano works.

King Roger (The Shepherd)

Król Roger (Pasterz)

Opera in three acts

Libretto: Jarosław Iwaszkiewicz and Karol Szymanowski.
Première: 12 June 1926, Warsaw (Teatr Wielki).

Characters: Roger II, King of Sicily (Bar), Roxana, his wife (S), Edrisi, an Arabian sage (T), Shepherd (T), Archbishop (B), Deaconess (A); priests, monks, nuns, acolytes, courtiers, guards, knights, young men and women, eunuchs, servants, the shepherd's companions (chorus; in Act III the chorus is invisible).
Setting: Sicily, c. 1150.

Synopsis
Act I

In the glow of the setting sun, courtiers and citizens assemble in the cathedral of Palermo to celebrate Mass. The ceremonial High Mass is also attended by King Roger, accompanied by his wife Roxana and his adviser Edrisi. The archbishop and deaconess inform the king that the Church is under threat from the founder of a new religion, a handsome young shepherd who has already gathered many supporters around him. At the king's request, the boy is summoned. The archbishop and deaconess presume him to be a blasphemer and, with encouragement from the excited crowd, demand from the king that he should be sentenced and punished by death. But the shepherd makes an impression on the king and

Drama – without conflicts

Anyone looking for traditional character types in this opera will be disappointed. Also missing is the traditional resolution of conflicts. Why does a king accept the message of a shepherd? Is his wife Roxana in love with the shepherd? And who in fact is the shepherd? Is he a god? A son of God? The leader of a sect? Or only a seducer, an adventurer who succeeds in defying the authority of the Church, in tearing apart iron chains, and in luring his followers into the unknown? Much here is unclear and sketchy. The characters of the drama seem to be bound up in an obscure and above all unresolved chain of events; they appear unexpectedly and disappear in the same manner. But in spite of all this, or perhaps for this very reason, *King Roger* remains an important if still comparatively unknown work. (Hans Werner Henze used the same material and

King Roger, production photograph with Kristine Ciesinski as Roxana, production and sets Peter Mussbach, costumes Florence von Gerkan, conductor Lothar Zagrosek, Württembergisches Staatstheater, Stuttgart 1990.
Roxana: a figure of sensual presence and spirituality.

1. Roxana's Song

queen and their adviser, with his gentleness and humility. The king sets him free, but orders him to attend a trial at his palace.

Act II

In the inner courtyard of the king's palace. The shepherd is expected. The king tells Edrisi of his suffering: Roxana has lost her joy in life and no longer loves him. Roxana admonishes the king to receive the shepherd graciously. The shepherd casts his spell over Roxana and the courtiers. The four minstrels accompanying him play entrancing music, and everyone joins in an intoxicating dance of joy. Only the king attempts to withstand the magic. He orders the shepherd to be put in chains. But the shepherd easily breaks free and calls those present to travel with him to the land of eternal freedom. All follow him, except King Roger and Edrisi. The king gives up his throne and sets off as a pilgrim to search for Roxana and the shepherd.

Act III

In the ruins of the classical theater at Syracuse. After long wanderings, King Roger has arrived here with Edrisi. Roger calls aloud for Roxana. At first she answers him from the distance, then appears before him and praises the cult of the shepherd, who alone is able to help her "ailing life." The shepherd enters the amphitheater in his true form: he is Dionysus, and his companions bacchantes and maenads. They dance ecstatically and then depart with Roxana. Roger remains alone, singing a hymn to the rising sun.   s. N.

constructed a similar complex of themes in his →*The Bassarids*, first performed in 1966.) In *King Roger* Szymanowski attempts to strike a legendary note. With its only loosely connected episodes the work resembles an oratorio. But *King Roger* is very much an opera, for unlike works such as Bartók's →*Bluebeard's Castle*, Honegger's →*Jeanne d'Arc au bûcher*, or Stravinsky's →*Oedipus Rex* it requires scenic realization – because of the colors, the lush splendor of the locations, the dramatically important alternation of light and dark, the symbolism of the setting and rising sun. The action begins in a semidarkened church and ends in the radiant sunshine of a Greek amphitheater. In all three acts there are elements of religious worship: Byzantine, Arab-Oriental, and Greek-pagan. All the mysteries take place within the searching, pondering, tired figure of the king. Is he the alter ego of the composer? Even if so, *King Roger* remains an enigmatic opera.

King Roger, production photograph with Sidwill Hartmann as the shepherd, production and sets Peter Mussbach, costumes Florence von Gerkan, conductor Lothar Zagrosek, Württembergisches Staatstheater, Stuttgart 1990.
The shepherd is in reality the god Dionysus. At his first appearance in Act I the music changes from strict choral writing to solo *ariosi*, rich in variation. Leading conductors have been fascinated time and time again by *King Roger*. Simon Rattle's production of 1998 at the Salzburg Festival was commercially recorded.

Meeting place: Sicily

Szymanowski loved Italy. Not since Mozart had there been another composer north of the Alps for whom *italianità* – in quite a different sense, but comparable in its extent – was so important. Italy was the elixir of life to him. After several journeys to Italy he visited Sicily in 1911 and 1914. "In Sicily the cultures of East and West combined and created a particular climate which has endured until today," he wrote to his friend Jarosław Iwaszkiewicz, who over the next few years was to write an opera libretto based on this not easily expressed experience. In particular, the metopes (reliefs with mythological themes) in the medieval monastery of Selinunte and the abandoned temple at Segesta – "a mixture of Baroque elements and Byzantine mosaics" – exercised a great influence on the composer. He wanted to illustrate the contemporaneity of the remains of vanished cultures and cults both through drama and in musical sounds.

Musical and religious melting pot

In *King Roger* a Dionysian dance demonstrates the transition from Christianity to paganism, from the Middle Ages of the first two acts to the Classical world of the third. (The Dionysian conclusion reminds one of another opera, Richard Strauss's →*Ariadne on Naxos*. Here, too, Dionysus appears at the end – again as a youth with great powers of erotic attraction – to lead Ariadne back from her death-wish to the sensual fever of life.) Roxana's beautiful song at the beginning of Act II, however, belongs, with its Arab-Turkish melodic phrasing, to a third cultural context: that of Islam. It is as if in this opera of 1924 Szymanowski wanted to set up a common monument to all world religions. M 1

*S*zymanowski was the most important Polish composer of the first half of the 20th century. His music, imbued with Slavic spirit, is melodious and characterized by late Romantic opulence, but is also open to contemporary developments (such as neo-Classicism, Expressionism, and Impressionism).

Eugene Onegin, set design by Gustav Wunderwald for the production by Hans Kaufmann, conductor Rudolf Krasselt, Deutsches Opernhaus, Berlin 1913 (TWS).
In Gustav Wunderwald's set design, nature and human loneliness form a bittersweet unity.

Eugene Onegin

Yevgeny Onegin

Lyric scenes in three acts

Libretto: Pyotr Tchaikovsky and Konstantin Shilovsky, after the verse novel by Alexander Pushkin.

Première: 29 March 1879, Moscow (Malïy Theater).

Characters: Larina, a landowner (Ms), Tat'yana/Tatyana and Ol'ga/Olga, her daughters (S, A), Filipp'yevna/Filipyevna, an old nurse (Ms), Yevgeny/Eugene Onegin (Bar), Lensky (T), Prince Gremin (B), A Captain (B), Zaretsky (B), Triquet, a Frenchman (T); peasants, ball guests, landowners, officers (chorus and ballet).

Setting: A country estate and in St. Petersburg, in the 1820s.

*T*chaikovsky is today the most popular of Russian composers. Like Glinka before him, he looked to the West for his formal and harmonic techniques, while retaining a melodic style that in its melancholy and pathos is unmistakably Russian.

Tchaikovsky, Pyotr Il'yich

b. 7 May 1840 in Kamsko-Votkinsk (Ural Region)
d. 6 November 1893 in St. Petersburg

Tchaikovsky began piano lessons at the age of five and soon showed remarkable musical ability. His family moved to St. Petersburg in 1848, where two years later he was sent to the School of Jurisprudence. He was profoundly affected by the death of his mother in 1854, the year in which he produced his first compositions. After a period of employment at the Ministry of Justice from 1859 to 1863 he entered the St. Petersburg Conservatory, where he studied piano and composition with Anton Rubenstein and Nikolay Zaremba, eventually winning the silver medal for his diploma cantata. He moved to Moscow in 1866 to take up a position as professor of harmony at the new conservatory founded by Nikolay Rubenstein (later the Moscow Conservatory). He composed his first opera in 1867 and his first symphony in 1868. He traveled to western Europe, made the acquaintance of various foreign composers, and began a correspondence with the wealthy Nadezhda von Meck, who became his patron. He was briefly and unhappily married to Antonina Milyukova (1877). From 1887 he was active as a conductor, touring Europe and the USA. He died in 1893, though whether from cholera or suicide is still uncertain.

Works: Operas: *Voyevoda* (*The Voyedova*) (1869), *Undina* (*Undine*) (never performed), *Oprichnik* (*The Oprichnik*) (1874), *Yevgeny Onegin* (*Eugene Onegin*) (1879), *Orleanskaya deva* (*The Maid of Orléans*) (1881), *Mazepa* (*Mazeppa*) (1884), *Cherevichky* (*The Tsarina's Boots*) (1887, originally *Kuznets Vakula*, or *Vakula the Smith*, 1876), *Charodeyka* (*The Enchantress*) (1887), *Pikovaya dama* (*The Queen of Spades*) (1890), (*Iolanta*) (1892); ballets: *Swan Lake* (1877), *The Sleeping Beauty* (1890), *The Nutcracker* (1892); orchestral works, including six symphonies, the *Manfred* symphony, the fantasy overture *Romeo and Juliet* (1870), the symphonic fantasy *Francesca da Rimini* (1876), the Serenade for strings, three piano concertos, a violin concerto, and the Variations on a Rococo Theme for cello and orchestra; chamber music, piano works, choral works, songs.

In the country

The first scene is an idyllic portrayal of the country retreat of a wealthy family in nineteenth-century Russia. The daughters of the house sing sweetly melancholic romances, the cooks prepare marmalade on the veranda, and the peasants, weary from the harvest, greet their beloved mistress with undiminished cheerfulness. It could be the beginning of a novel by Turgenev. The only event of importance is that Tatyana meets Onegin. But even this happens, as it were, incidentally. The music flows freely in its depiction of Russian daily life. Although it does include closed numbers, the most important events are expressed in an *arioso* whose melody is derived from the romance. Russian urban folk music was one of Tchaikovsky's most important sources of inspiration. →M 1

Synopsis
Act I

Scene 1: In a garden on the estate of the Larin family. The two young girls, Tatyana and Olga, yearn for love and happiness. Peasants greet their mistress. Only Tatyana listens attentively to them. Lensky, their neighbor, is a poet, engaged to the cheerful Olga. He introduces his friend from St. Petersburg, Eugene Onegin, to the Larin household. While Lensky courts his adored Olga, Onegin entertains the melancholy Tatyana with clever conversation.

Scene 2: Tatyana questions her old nurse about love. She has fallen in love with Onegin, seeing in him the hero of her dreams and of the romantic literature she loves to read. She confesses her love in a letter and sends the nurse to him with it.

Scene 3: Tatyana, excited and uneasy, awaits Onegin. He politely refuses her, saying that he does not seek or need love.

Act II

Scene 1: The nobility of the neighborhood arrive at a name-day ball for Tatyana. The Frenchman Triquet recites some couplets in her honor. Onegin is bored and angry with Lensky for persuading him to attend this ball. To annoy his friend he repeatedly dances with Olga. Lensky is offended and challenges Onegin to a duel.

Scene 2: The following morning the friends confront each other as enemies. Both know that the duel is senseless, but neither has the strength to speak the word that will save them both. Lensky is killed by Onegin.

Act III

Scene 1: After a long sojourn abroad, Onegin returns to St. Petersburg and meets Tatyana again, now Princess Gremina, a beautiful and much admired woman. Onegin falls in love with the woman he once disdained.

Scene 2: Onegin has persuaded Tatyana to meet him and confesses his love to her. Tatyana still loves Onegin, but rejects him, remaining faithful to her husband.

S. N.

Eugene Onegin, photograph from the production by Yury Temirkanov, sets Igor Ivanov, Mariinsky Theater, St. Petersburg 1982.
A ceremonial ball in a nobleman's palace in St. Petersburg. Onegin, who has been living abroad for years, has returned and meets Tatyana, now Princess Gremina. Yury Temirkanov, Valery Gergiyev's predecessor at the Mariinsky Theater, eliminated all the old Soviet slackness both musically and theatrically. Guest appearances made his Tchaikovsky productions internationally famous.

"Superfluous people"

In the character of Eugene Onegin, Pushkin created a type referred to as the "superfluous man," a type also found in Lermontov, Turgenev, Dostoyevsky, Tolstoy, and Chekhov, even in Pasternak himself. His counterpart in Western literature is to be found in Byron (Manfred, Childe Harold).

So who is this superfluous man? A person who in attempting to distance himself from mediocrity becomes alienated from life. The narrow social circle in which Onegin moves induces a feeling of weariness. Tatyana and Lensky also belong to this type. They live less in reality than in their own dreams. Thus their disillusionment is necessary and tragic.

"Lyrical scenes"

In the composition of *Eugene Onegin* Tchaikovsky deliberately diverged from Italian and French operatic conventions. "I don't give a damn about it not being a stageable opera," he wrote to his pupil Sergey Taneyev. "It has been well known for some time that I have no sense of stagecraft ... " In another letter to Taneyev, Tchaikovsky touched on the question of genre: "If opera, as you maintain, is a portrayal of action which is not found in *Onegin*, I am prepared to say that *Onegin* is not an opera, but something different." Finally he settled on the title "Lyrical scenes," diverging from traditional descriptions.

A tragic additional act to the opera

During his work on *Eugene Onegin* a former pupil, Antonina Milyukova, wrote Tchaikovsky a love-letter. Tatyana's letter scene had already been set to music. Tchaikovsky was not only in love with his Tatyana, but identified with her. He then received a second love-letter from Milyukova. Since he did not want to play the part of Onegin (Onegin's behavior was repellent to him), he made a proposal of marriage to the young lady. It was a short marriage, which proved unhappy for both of them. Tchaikovsky was deeply troubled by his homosexuality, and hoped for "normalization" through marriage. After the honeymoon he attempted suicide. Who knows whether this marriage would have taken place at all without Pushkin's *Onegin* and the composer's work on the opera?   *M. P*

Voices

In distributing the vocal parts, Tchaikovsky diverged sharply from tradition. Here the baritone (Onegin) is paired off with the soprano (Tatyana), and the tenor (Lensky) with the contralto (Olga). Only the bass part is conventionally allocated – to the elderly husband. Perhaps the composer wanted to indicate that Tatyana and Lensky belong to a higher spiritual plane by giving them higher voices.

Eugene Onegin, production photograph with Lidiya Chernich (Tatyana) and Irina Bogacheva (nurse), production Stanislav Gaudassinsky, sets and costumes Viachesla Okoniyev, conductor Andrey Anihanov, coproduction of the Musorgsky Opera, St. Petersburg, and the Stadttheater, Heilbronn, 1995.
While Pushkin's verse novel begins with a detailed description of Onegin's childhood, youth, character, and background, it is Tatyana who is musically characterized in the prelude to the opera. The composer placed the musical identification of his best-loved and most important heroine at the beginning of his work. *M 2*
Tatyana's most important musical portrait is the letter scene, in which her meditations during the writing of the letter release a volcanic outburst of emotion. *M 3*

Eugene Onegin set design by Hein Heckroth,
production Hans Hartleb, conductor Sir
Georg Solti, Oper Frankfurt 1957 (TWS).
The fatal duel between Onegin and Lensky
(Act II, Scene 2). A senseless tragedy, which
occurs almost by accident. In an Italian or
French Romantic opera this would be the key
scene with dramatic consequences (revenge,
murder). Here it is merely an episode. The
duel between men who only yesterday were
the best of friends is one of the images of life
in the era of Onegin.

1. Duet (Tatyana and Olga)

Слы-ха-лиль вы за рощей глас ночной пев-ца лю-бви, пев-ца сво-ей пе-ча-ли?

2. Tatyana's Leitmotiv

3. Tatyana's Outburst (Letter Scene)

Во-об-ра-зи: я здесь од-на!

Tatyana

With her rich inner life and strong moral attitude, Tatyana is a typical figure of nineteenth-century Russian literature. In everyday life she is taciturn, shy, and withdrawn, but the emotions that awaken within her are of such extraordinary power that they force her to behave in a way that defies all social conventions: she makes a confession of love. Strong female figures, spiritually similar to Tatyana, are to be found in other operas by Tchaikovsky: Joan of Arc (*The Maid of Orléans*), Nastasia (*The Enchantress*), Maria (→*Mazeppa*), Lisa (→*The Queen of Spades*), and Iolanta (→*Iolanta*). It has sometimes been asked how Tchaikovsky was able to create the beautiful, noble, deeply emotional female characters who populate his operas and who are almost always more important than their male counterparts. But it is clear that he possessed an astonishing power of empathy with the female soul. It is also noteworthy that all his female characters experience unhappiness and considerable disappointment.

Tatyana, both before and after her letter of confession, is surrounded by noisy, talkative people: her mother and nurse, Olga and Lensky, Onegin and the maids. In spite of the conversations going on in the foreground, the music expresses the loneliness, the reveries, and the suffering of Tatyana. It is with Tatyana's ears that we hear the cheerful song of the peasants, the admonitions of her mother and nurse, the glibly instructive words of Onegin, the distant song of the girls picking raspberries. The ballroom scene in Act II is similarly structured. It is introduced by an orchestral prelude, which through the unfolding of the great theme of the letter scene illuminates Tatyana's mental state: what is inexpressible is entrusted to the orchestra. *M 4*

Act II, Scene 2, with Lensky's famous aria and the fatal duel, is the only scene in which Tatyana does not appear. She is nevertheless musically present. The main theme of Lensky's aria is identical to the long, descending melody sung by Tatyana as she waits anxiously for Onegin's answer at the end of Act I. And this melody will reappear when, as Princess Gremina, she again awaits Onegin (Act III, Scene 2). It therefore functions as a kind of destiny motif for both Tatyana and Lensky. *M 5, M 6*

Onegin's great passion, which flares up so suddenly (Act III), was set to music by Tchaikovsky with much less conviction than the vibrations of Tatyana's soul. Although Onegin stands at the center of the first scene of Act III, the most beautiful music, Prince Gremin's aria, is concerned with Tatyana – the new Tatyana, who has been polished up by experience to reveal a precious stone, which gleams outwardly as well as inwardly. *M 7*

In the last scene of the opera Tatyana becomes a true heroine, through her moral attitude and the great strength of soul with which she refuses the pleadings of Onegin. According to the sober reality of everyday life, the story of Tatyana and Onegin ought to continue in the same way as Tolstoy's *Anna Karenina*. With Tatyana's departure and the appearance of her husband, Pushkin's novel mysteriously comes to an end. Tchaikovsky's version lifts Tatyana onto a new moral level: her willpower seals Onegin's fate. *M. P.*

4. Tatyana's Motif Heard Before the Ballroom Scene

5. Tatyana's Monologue (Act I)

Ах! для че-го, сте - на-нью вняв ду - ши боль-ной

6. Lensky's Aria (Act II)

Я лю - блю те-бя, я лю - блю те - бя, как од - на ду - ша по - э - та только любит

7. Gremin's Aria (Act III)

Люб-ви все - воз-ра-сты по - кор-ны, *(Orchester)* е - ё по - ры-вы бла-го - твор-ны

8. Triquet's Couplet

Ка-кой пре - крас-ный э-тот день, ког-да в сей де-ре-вен-ский сень про-сы-паль-ся belle Ta-ti - a - na!

Eugene Onegin, production photograph with Mirella Freni (Tatyana) and Nicolai Ghiaurov (Prince Gremin), Wiener Staatsoper.
It rarely happens that operatic roles correspond so closely to private life: Mirella Freni and Nicolay Ghiaurov are actually married. Prince Gremin's aria is an almost nostalgic, wonderfully beautiful confession of a husband's love for his wife. A musical tribute to the happy state which Tchaikovsky was never able to achieve.

Opposite
Eugene Onegin, photograph from the production by Stanislav Gaudassinsky, sets and costumes Viachesla Okoniev, conductor Andrey Anihanov, coproduction of the Musorgsky Opera, St. Petersburg, and the Stadttheater, Heilbronn, 1995.
In the first scenes of Acts II and III, Tchaikovsky presents the setting. The country party has rather a crude character. Waltzes and marches are played, and Triquet has great success with his couplets. M 8

Mazeppa

Opera in three acts (six scenes)

Libretto: Victor Burenin and Pyotr Tchaikovsky, after Alexander Pushkin's poem *Poltava*.

Première: 15 February 1884, Moscow (Bol'shoy Theater).

Characters: Mazepa/Mazeppa, a Cossack captain (Bar), Kochubey, a Cossack judge (B), Lyubov', his wife (Ms), Mariya, his daughter (S), Andrey, a young Cossack (T), Orlik, confidant of Mazeppa (B), Iskra, a friend of Kochubey (T), A Drunken Cossack (T); Cossacks, guests and servants of Kochubey, soldiers, monks (chorus).

Setting: The Ukraine, at the beginning of the 18th century.

Synopsis
Act I

Scene 1: Mariya is in love with old Mazeppa, and rejects the love of her childhood playmate Andrey. Mazeppa asks his friend Kochubey for his daughter's hand, but is refused on account of the difference in age. Against her parents' wishes, Mariya follows Mazeppa.

Scene 2: Mariya's mother weeps for her lost daughter, while her father swears revenge. He will denounce Mazeppa to Peter the Great for conspiracy. Andrey sets off to see the tsar.

Act II

Scene 1: The tsar has not believed Kochubey's accusations and instead has delivered him into Mazeppa's hands. In Mazeppa's prison Kochubey is tortured, as he adamantly refuses to reveal where his fortune is hidden.

Scene 2: Mazeppa conceals from Mariya what is happening to Kochubey. But her mother seeks her out, tells her the truth, and pleads with her to rescue her father.

Scene 3: The crowd awaits Kochubey's execution. A drunken Cossack makes fun of the authorities and is chased away. Kochubey and his confidant Iskra are led to the place of execution. Mariya and her mother reach the scene at the moment of Kochubey's death.

Incidental music: *The Battle of Poltava*

Act III

Mazeppa has formed an alliance with the Swedes against the tsar, has been defeated, and now seeks refuge at Kochubey's ruined property. Here he encounters Andrey, who fought on the side of the tsar, and raises his sword against the unarmed old man. Here there are alternative suggestions by Tchaikovsky: he is mortally wounded either by Mazeppa himself or by Mazeppa's servant Orlik. Alarmed by the noise, Mariya appears, now demented, and fails to recognize her beloved Mazeppa. Believing Andrey to be a child, she sings the dying man to sleep.   S. N.

Mazeppa, production photograph from Act III with Sergey Moskalkov (Mazeppa) and Yekaterina Vassilenko (Mariya), production Dmitry Bertman, sets and costumes Igor Nezhny and Tat'yana Tulubyeva, conductor Kirill Tikhonov, Helikon Opera, Moscow 1999.
Mariya and Mazeppa in the last scene of the opera. The story reminds one of the legend of Bluebeard, in which a young woman rejects a young suitor and against her parents' wishes goes off with an older man with a bad reputation. But Mariya loses her mind as a result of Mazeppa's schizophrenic behavior – on the one hand he is a loving husband, on the other a brutal soldier, who even takes her father's life.

Mazeppa: hero or villain?
It is still unclear whether the legendary Cossack leader was a hero who fought against the tsar for the freedom of his people, or a cruel villain, a power-hungry political adventurer who had his lover's father killed, stirred up a revolt, and attempted to seize the tsar's power for himself by means of an alliance with Sweden. In Romantic representations of Mazeppa in the visual arts and in music (above all in Liszt's symphonic poem *Mazeppa* of 1854) his character was idealized. For Pushkin, however, he was an evil, ambitious old man, illuminated only by his belated love affair. Pushkin and Tchaikovsky are clearly on the side of Peter the Great, by whom the rebel Cossack leader was defeated. In the orchestral interlude *The Battle of Poltava*, Tchaikovsky uses as the theme of the victory march the same Russian folk song that Musorgsky had used for the hymn of praise in →*Boris Godunov* and Rimsky-Korsakov for the motif of Ivan the Terrible (*The Maid of Pskov*). A musical tribute to the tsar.   M 9

Mazeppa, set design by Fritz Mahnke, Duisberg 1938 (TWS).
Gloom and morbidity characterize Mazeppa's world. During the composition Tchaikovsky suffered from severe depression. The orchestral interlude *The Battle of Poltava* depicts the defeat of the Cossacks. However, Tchaikovsky – who was little interested in the idea of an historical Russian national opera – was far more concerned with the tragedy of human relationships than with historical authenticity.

A final duet of madness

The most moving and poetic moment in the opera is to be found in the finale: the dying Andrey once again confesses his love to Mariya, who, deranged, believes him to be a weary child and sings him a lullaby. M 10

This scene underlines a message that is central to a number of Tchaikovsky's operas: love is based on a misunderstanding between man and woman, and is doomed to perish. *M.P.*

9. Victory March

10. Mariya's March

Спи, мла-де-нец мой пре-крас - ный, спи, мой ми-лый, спи, род-ной!

Ба-юш-ки ба - ю, ба-юш-ки ба - ю!

Mazeppa, production photograph from Act I, production Dmitry Bertman, sets and costumes Igor Nezhny and Tat'yana Tulubyeva, conductor Kirill Tikhonov, Helikon Opera, Moscow 1999.
The girls in wedding dresses represent the "normal" fate of a woman, which Mariya has rejected as a result of Mazeppa's secret power of attraction.

The Queen of Spades, production photograph with Y. Grigozain (Hermann) and A. Filatova (the countess), production Yury Temirkanov, sets Igor Ivanov, Mariinsky Theater, St. Petersburg 1993.
The officer Hermann secretly creeps into the countess's bedroom at night and demands from her the secret of the legendary "three cards." The countess dies of fright.

The Queen of Spades

Pikovaya dama

Opera in three acts (seven scenes)

Libretto: Modest Tchaikovsky, after the story of the same name by Alexander Pushkin.
Première: 19 December 1890, St. Petersburg (Mariinsky Theater).
Characters:: Ghermann/Hermann (T), Count Tomsky (Bar), Prince Yeletsky (Bar), Chekalinsky (T), Surin (B), Chaplitsky (T), Narumov (B), Master of Ceremonies (T), The Countess (Ms), Liza/Lisa, her granddaughter (S), Pauline, Lisa's confidante (A), Governess (Ms), Masha, Lisa's maid (S), Child Commander (boy, spoken); children, nannies, governesses, nurses, strollers, guests, gamblers (chorus).

Characters in the intermezzo (Act II): Prilepa, also Chloë (S), Milovzor, also Daphnis (Pauline) (Ms), Zlatogor, also Plutus (Tomsky) (Bar); Hymen, Cupid, shepherds and shepherdesses (chorus and ballet).

Setting: St. Petersburg, at the end of the 18th century.

Synopsis
Act I
Scene 1: In the Summer Garden at St. Petersburg. The first rays of sunshine tempt the city-dwellers

A love story from an anecdote

Tchaikovsky's brother and modest lifelong collaborator, turned Pushkin's ironic sketch into a romantic melodrama. In his portrayal of Hermann and Lisa the composer's interests were similarly different from the poet's. For Tchaikovsky, Lisa became the embodiment of the ideal Russian woman, who sacrifices her life for her lover. In Pushkin's story she does not die, but marries another man, and in Modest Tchaikovsky's libretto Lisa's fate is left open, in that she simply disappears from the drama after the countess's death. It was Tchaikovsky the composer who introduced the great scene at the quay and the suicide, insisting on its realization even against his brother's wishes. For him *The Queen of Spades* was the tragedy of two people, Hermann and Lisa.   *M. P.*

The Queen of Spades, poster for the Komische Oper, Berlin.
He who treats life as a game of cards can easily be destroyed when he loses. This is the moral of Pushkin's tale.

into the open air. The children of the nobility copy the adults, playing brides and soldiers. Two officers are curious about a friend, the officer Hermann. Every evening he observes the gambling but never takes part himself. Prince Yeletsky introduces his bride Lisa. Hermann recognizes her as the woman he secretly loves. His passion is hopeless, for she is the granddaughter of a rich countess. His friend Tomsky relates the countess's story. As a young beauty she was a reckless gambler, and as a result is said to know the secret of three unbeatable cards. Hermann is fascinated by this and determines to discover the secret for himself.

Scene 2: Lisa's room. The young girls entertain each other by singing. Left alone, Lisa reflects on her secret love for Hermann. Suddenly, he appears before her in person, asking that she decide his fate. She confesses her love to him.

Act II

Scene 1: The great hall in the house of a noble family. Yeletsky senses Lisa's resistance and tries to win her love by his nobility of mind. A pastoral play is to be performed. Lisa slips Hermann the key to her room. When he learns that the way to her room is through that of the countess, he makes up his mind to find out the old lady's secret.

Scene 2: The countess's bedroom. Hermann hides. The countess retires to bed and falls asleep. Hermann threatens the old lady, and she takes fright

and dies. When Lisa discovers his deed, Hermann fails to justify his behavior and flees.

Act III

Scene 1: The barracks. Hermann's room. Lisa has not given up hope of Hermann's love and writes to him to ask him to meet her. The countess's ghost appears to Hermann. He learns the secret of the three cards, without understanding it. He hears only the names of the cards – three, seven, and ace – but not that a condition is attached to them: to make Lisa happy.

Scene 2: The quay in winter. Lisa is waiting for Hermann. For a short moment she manages to awaken Hermann's better nature, but then he is once again possessed by gambling fever. Lisa takes her own life.

Scene 3: A gambling house. Prince Yeletsky has turned to gambling, in an attempt to forget Lisa. Other noblemen similarly try to inject some pleasure into their meaningless lives by gambling. Hermann admits that he too is addicted to this lifestyle. He repeatedly bets on the three, and then on the seven, and wins large amounts of money. No one dares to continue playing with him except the prince, who takes part in the final game. Hermann bets on the ace, but picks up the Queen of Spades, which grins at him with the face of the countess. He stabs himself, begging Yeletsky's forgiveness before he dies.   *S. N.*

A playing card: the Queen of Spades, facsimile of a Russian card of 1817 (Deutsches Spielkarten-Museum, Leinfelden-Echterdingen).
The baleful Queen of Spades is a gloomy joke by the old countess. Perhaps she herself is the Queen of Spades? Her character and the story of her life have blended into a mysterious symbiosis.

The Queen of Spades, photograph from the production by Alexander Galibin, sets Alexander Orlov, conductor Valery Gergiyev, Mariinsky Theater, St. Petersburg 1999.

The Queen of Spades, costume design for the governess by Günter Walbeck, production Nikolaus Sulzberger, Deutsche Oper, Berlin 1977 (TWS).
Who knows what lurks behind the powder and wig of the old governess? As so often in 19th-century Russian literature, it is difficult to tell where reality ends and absurdity begins.

The Queen of Spades, photograph from the production by Yury Temirkanov, sets Igor Ivanov, Mariinsky Theater, St. Petersburg 1993.
Wintry quay in St. Petersburg (Act III, Scene 3). A last rendezvous for the lovers. But Hermann's love for Lisa has fallen victim to his passion for gambling.

Love, passion, and death

To judge from his diaries and letters, Tchaikovsky became thoroughly absorbed in the world of *The Queen of Spades* during composition. When he wrote Lisa's *arioso* (Act III), for which he himself composed the text, he wept, as he did over Hermann's aria of farewell. "Either I am very tired, or this really is very good," he noted in his diary. *M 12*

Other emotions were released by the scene in the countess's bedroom. "In some places – for example, in the fourth scene, which I set to music today – I suddenly experienced such a dreadful fear, such horror and wild panic, that the audience must surely share these feelings when they hear it ... " Here Tchaikovsky eerily quotes an aria from Grétry's opera *Richard the Lion Heart* of 1784, the text of which refers to a nocturnal rendezvous. *M 12*

As early as the great love duet at the end of Act I, whose glowing passion reminds one of Puccini's great love duets, there is something frightening and pathological in the outbursts of Hermann and Lisa. Lisa ascribes this to the passion of love, but Hermann is already gripped by gambling fever, depicted musically by the motif of the three cards.

The noble life – like that in an opera

The Queen of Spades is the most "operatic" of Tchaikovsky's operas. In it Tchaikovsky used various operatic conventions, ranging from those of Mozart through the Italian and French traditions to Bizet. The descriptions of settings are masterly, such as the afternoon promenade in the Summer Garden of St. Petersburg (Act I, Scene 1), the piano music and songs in the salon at home (Act I, Scene 2), and the masked ball, where guests are entertained by choice Rococo music (Act II, Scene 1). The loneliness of the cold, gloomy winter's night (Act III, Scene 2) and the

The Queen of Spades, set design by Eduard Löffler for the production by Alexandre d'Arnals, conductor Issai Dobrowen, Berlin 1924 (TWS).
The night scene between Hermann and the countess (Act II, Scene 2) could be taken from a thriller. Hermann's situation as a poor officer, who can realize his dreams only by gambling and robbery by night, reminds one of the title of a crime novel by Franz Werfel: "Not the murderer but the victim is guilty."

overheated atmosphere of the gambling house (Act III, Scene 3) lead straight from the picture of society to the individual tragedy. Here – as he has already done in *Eugene Onegin* – Tchaikovsky blends the drama of two people into the everyday life of the nobility of the capital city.

Tchaikovsky the neo-Classicist

Ivan Vsevolozhky, the director of the Bol'shoy Theater, with whom the idea of an opera based on *The Queen of Spades* originated, suggested to Tchaikovsky that he should set Pushkin's story of the 1820s in the late eighteenth century. The composer gladly accepted the suggestion, for the Rococo and Classical periods had always been his ideal, as is evident from his works in Classical style (such as the Variations on a Rococo Theme for cello and orchestra, of 1876). Tchaikovsky was one of the first composers who could be described as neo-Classical.

In *The Queen of Spades,* style serves as a musical backdrop: with the chorus and the pastoral play in the ball scene, as well as the song from Grétry's *Richard the Lion Heart* that is hummed by the old countess shortly before her death, a strange old world is being evoked.

In the pastoral play, Tchaikovsky used a melody from the Rococo opera *The Rival Son* by Dmitry Bortnyansky (→Glinka). When he was writing the pastoral play and the ballet divertissement for the ball scene, he wrote in his diary: "I feel as if I were living in the eighteenth century and as though nothing and no one existed after Mozart." *M. P.*

The Queen of Spades, photograph from the production by Alexander Galibin,
sets Alexander Orlov, conductor Valery Gergiyev, Mariinsky Theater,
St. Petersburg 1999.
The genre scenes in The Queen of Spades appear idyllic only at first glance.
In reality they show how tragedies can be played out in the midst of an
indifferent crowd. By means of the abrupt change from a narrative manner
to the musical portrayal of emotions, Tchaikovsky made the soundless
catastrophes of the everyday audible – and thus created situations of truly
ghostly character.

The Queen of Spades, production photograph
from Act I, Scene 1, production Kurt Horres,
sets and costumes Andreas Reinhardt,
conductor Dimitry Kitaenko, Wiener
Staatsoper 1982.
Afternoon promenade in St. Petersburg. The
fatal power of the cards strikes like lightning
into the everyday life of a tired and
conventional society.

11. Lisa's *Arioso*

Ах, ис-то-ми-лась я   го - рем... Но-чью ли, днём,   толь-ко о нём

12. The Countess's Monologue

Je crains de lui par - ler la   nuit

Iolanta, production photograph with (from left to right) Thomas Mäthger (Bertrand), Yelena Yevseyeva (Iolanta), Nikita Storoyev (King René), Georgy Russev Yordanov (Almérich), and Monika Straube (Martha), production Sir Peter Ustinov, sets Josef Svoboda, conductor Mikhail Yurovsky, coproduction by the Dresden Festival and the Städtisches Theater, Chemnitz, 1993.

Iolanta

Iolanta

Lyrical opera in one act

Libretto: Modest Tchaikovsky, after Henrik Hertz's play *Kong Renés Datter* (*King René's Daughter*).

Première: 18 December 1892, St. Petersburg (Mariinsky Theater).

Characters: René, King of Provence (B), Iolanta, his blind daughter (S), Count Vaudémont, a Burgundian knight (T), Ibn-Hakia, a Moorish physician (Bar), Robert, Duke of Burgundy (Bar), Almérich, armour-bearer to King René (T), Bertrand, the castle gate-keeper (B), Martha, his wife and Iolanta's nurse (A), Brigitta and Laura, friends of Iolanta (2 Ms); maids and friends of Iolanta, the king's retinue, the duke's regiment (chorus).

Setting: Provence, in the 15th-century.

Synopsis

The blind girl Iolanta lives in a secluded garden, hidden from the world by her father King René. Those around her keep her blindness a secret from her, so as not to make her unhappy. The girl enjoys the scent of flowers, the sound of the birds, and the singing of her nurse and her friends. She does not feel deprived of anything. When the king asks the famous Moorish physician Ibn-Hakia to cure his daughter, the physician advises that Iolanta should be made aware of her blindness, so that she herself seeks to be cured. The king is afraid to follow the physician's advice.

Robert, Duke of Burgundy, and Count Vaudémont lose their way while hunting and inquisitively climb over the garden wall. Robert has in fact been betrothed to Iolanta since childhood, but now seeks to release himself from the engagement as he has fallen in love with a countess. The two men come across the sleeping Iolanta, and Vaudémont immediately falls in love with her. When the knight realizes that the girl is blind, he tries to explain to her the nature of color and light. King René becomes angry and threatens Vaudémont with execution. He can only be saved if Iolanta is cured of her blindness. As the life of the beloved stranger is at stake, Iolanta wishes to receive her sight, and the cure succeeds. When Vaudémont asks for Iolanta's hand Robert gladly relinquishes it. Nothing now stands in the way of Vaudémont's and Iolanta's happiness.

M. P.

A farewell with a happy ending

Iolanta is Tchaikovsky's last opera, first performed almost exactly eleven months before his sudden death in November 1893. Having seen the composer's resigned, weary face in his late photographs, one cannot help but look for signs of farewell in this beautiful but rarely performed work. In its poetic-philosophical approach, the subject is more akin to a parable than an operatic plot. The miraculous story of Iolanta can be interpreted in various ways. It is impossible to say precisely to what extent Tchaikovsky identified with his heroine and how far he felt related to the blind girl living her isolated life. Is Iolanta a symbol for the artist in general, or a female parallel to Tchaikovsky in particular, who was isolated from "normal" life as a result of his homosexuality? *Iolanta* can also be interpreted in terms of the opposite positions of the king and the physician. The king represents an authoritarian principle: he decides whether or not his daughter shall be told the truth. For the physician, on the other hand, knowledge of the truth is a precondition for Iolanta's cure. In the end the situation is resolved by chance, and love is victorious: a wonderful illusion created by the composer at the end of his own unhappy life, and after the many tragic love relationships of his earlier operas. In the final scene he lifts Iolanta and Vaudémont towards a blissful apotheosis, surrounding them with harp triads as though with a halo. M 13   M. P.

Iolanta, production photograph with Yelena Yevseyeva (Iolanta) and Vyacheslav Pochapsky (Ibn-Hakia), production Sir Peter Ustinov, conductor Mikhail Yurovsky, coproduction by the Dresden Festival and the Städtisches Theater, Chemnitz, 1993. Iolanta and the Moorish physician after the successful eye operation. Only love gives Iolanta the strength to gain her sight. The fairy-tale subject matter and the happy ending may be connected with the fact that Tchaikovsky was planning to have *Iolanta* performed with the ballet *The Nutcracker* in a joint festival performance at the Mariinsky Theater.

13. Duet (Iolanta and Vaudémont)

Им по-знал   я, не-до-стой-ный,   вас, о де   -   ва кра-со-ты

Iolanta, production photograph with (from left to right) Cornelia Strelov (Brigitta), Monika Straube (Martha, standing), Yelena Yevseyeva (Iolanta), and Regine Lehmann-Köbler (Laura), production Sir Peter Ustinov, conductor Mikhail Yurovsky, coproduction by the Dresden Festival and the Städtisches Theater, Chemnitz, 1993. In the first scene, Iolanta's friends sing her to sleep.

Thomas, Ambroise

b. 5 August 1811 in Metz
d. 12 February 1896 in Paris

Thomas studied with Kalkbrenner and Le Sueur at the Paris Conservatoire. From 1837 he wrote about 15 works for the Opéra-Comique, in which he proved himself a successor to →Auber and →Halévy. At the same time he was also influenced by the expressive music of his contemporary Gounod. In 1871 he became director of the Conservatoire, where he instituted a number of reforms while remaining essentially conservative.

Works: The operas *Mignon* (1866) and *Hamlet* (1868), as well as a number of rather ephemeral *opéras comiques*; ballets, instrumental works, songs.

Mignon, poster for the first performance by Jules Chéret, Paris 1866.
Only a few characters and names and a few situations divorced from their original context remind us of Goethe's *Mignon*. Thomas' work is a light opera, in which conventional situations and pleasing musical numbers were intended to inject new life into the mature style of the *opéra comique*.

Right
Mignon, production photograph with Adolf Dallapozza (Wilhelm) and Graciela Araya (Mignon), production Herzl, costumes Toni Businger, conductor Ernst Märzendorfer, Volksoper, Wiener 1988.

*T*homas's style has a dance-like charm, dramatic tension being entirely foreign to him.

Mignon

Opéra comique in three acts

Libretto: Michel Carré and Jules Barbier, after the novel *Wilhelm Meisters Lehrjahre* (*Wilhelm Meister's Apprentice Years*) by Johann Wolfgang von Goethe.
Première: 17 November 1866, Paris (Opéra-Comique).
Characters: Mignon (S or Ms), Wilhelm, a student (T), Philine, an actress (S), Laërte, an actor (T), Lotharil, a traveling singer (B), Jarno, a gypsy (B), Frédérick (T or A); gypsies, actors, courtiers, citizens, peasants (chorus).
Setting:: Germany and Italy, c. 1790.

Synopsis

Wilhelm Meister saves Mignon from the hands of the brutal gypsy Jarno. Drawn to the actress Philine, he does not notice that Mignon is falling in love with him. Only in Italy, after he has cast off all the turbulence of his unstable life, does he recognize his own love for Mignon.

Act I

Sunday entertainments in the marketplace of a small German town. Among the onlookers are the wandering harpist Lotharil, who has lost his memory, and two actors looking for work, Philine and Laërte. Gypsies earn money by entertaining the crowd. Their leader, Jarno, wants to force a little girl to dance. An observer takes her under his protection, buying her freedom from the gypsies. He is Wilhelm Meister, a student. Mignon confesses to her rescuer her unquenchable longing for her lost home in the south. Mignon wants to follow Wilhelm everywhere, dressed as a page. He in turn is drawn to the actress Philine, and follows her to an engagement at a nearby castle.

Act II

Philine and Laërte enjoy the comfort of the castle. There is a flirtation between Philine and Wilhelm, noticed with sorrow by Mignon and Philine's former sweetheart, Frédérick. It almost comes to a duel. When Wilhelm recognizes Mignon's jealousy, he threatens her with separation. Deeply hurt and offended, Mignon wanders off into the castle gardens and meets Lotharil. The two unhappy people pour out their hearts to each other. When the noise of the festive preparations reaches her ears, Mignon expresses a wish that Philine might be struck by lightning. But the actress is celebrating her success as Titania in the performance. Wilhelm regrets his behavior towards Mignon, and goes to look for her. Philine sends the girl into the house for a bunch of flowers. No sooner does she enter the house than it bursts into flames. Misunderstanding Mignon's wish, Lotharil has started a fire. Wilhelm rescues the unconscious Mignon from the burning building.

Act III

Wilhelm has brought Mignon and Lotharil to an Italian castle where he hopes Mignon will recover. Lotharil is guarding Mignon's sleep, while local people celebrate a festival below the window. Wilhelm, who has finally become aware of his love for Mignon, takes over the watch from Lotharil. When Mignon wakes, he confesses his love for her. Before she can reply, Philine's voice is heard in the distance, which startles Mignon. She asks to see Lotharil. The latter appears, this time dressed in splendid clothes. He has recovered his memory: the castle belongs to him, and Mignon is his daughter, who was abducted as a child. The troupe of actors arrives, led by Philine, dancing and singing. Mignon fears that she will lose Wilhelm, but Philine places Wilhelm's hand in Mignon's, while she herself turns back to Frédérick.

P. H.

Hamlet, Ophelia's death, illustration from the original production, Paris 1868.
Ophelia's madness scene, which together with the ballet occupies the whole of the fourth act, is a complex depiction of despair. After a recitative she sings a breathtaking coloratura waltz, and then a ballad, somber in tone, which is in fact Swedish rather than Danish. (The original Swedish melody for this part was inserted as a tribute to Christine Nilsson, one of the first Ophelias.)

THÉATRE IMPÉRIAL DE L'OPÉRA. — *HAMLET*, opéra en cinq actes, paroles de MM. Michel Carré et Jules Barbier, musique de M. Ambroise Thomas. LA PLATE-FORME D'ELSENEUR. – LA MORT D'OPHÉLIE. – Dessin de M. de Neuville. – Voir la Chronique.

Hamlet, Jean-Baptiste Fauré, the first Hamlet, Paris 1868.
The title role of this *grand opéra* is one of the great baritone roles of all time. Up to the fourth act, Hamlet is on stage almost without interruption. Shakespeare's solitary hero preserves his meditative nature, which continually prevents him from carrying out the task that has been assigned to him.

Hamlet

Grand opéra in five acts

Libretto: Michel Carré and Jules Barbier, after the tragedy by William Shakespeare.
Première:: 9 March 1868, Paris (Opéra).
Characters: Hamlet, Prince of Denmark (Bar), Claudius, King of Denmark, Hamlet's uncle (B), Gertrude, Queen of Denmark, Hamlet's mother (S), Polonius, Lord Chamberlain (B), Ophélie/Ophelia, daughter of Polonius (S), Laërte/Laertes, son of Polonius (T), The Ghost of Hamlet's Father (B), Marcellus and Horatio, officers and friends of Hamlet (T, B), Two Gravediggers (T, B); courtiers, soldiers, actors, peasants (chorus).
Setting: Elsinore (Denmark), in medieval times.

Synopsis

Hamlet is visited by the ghost of his father, the former king, who reveals that he was murdered by his brother Claudius, who now rules in his place. Hamlet plans vengeance, and in the meantime rejects his betrothed, Ophelia, who thereupon commits suicide. Hamlet finally murders his uncle and assumes the crown.

P. H.

The Midsummer Marriage

Opera in three acts

Libretto: Michael Tippett.
Première: 27 January 1955, London (Royal Opera House).

Characters: Mark, a young man of unknown parentage (T), Jenifer, his betrothed (S), King Fisher, Jenifer's father, a businessman (Bar), Bella, King Fisher's secretary (S), Jack, Bella's boyfriend, a mechanic (T), Sosostris, a clairvoyant (A), Priest and Priestess of the Temple of the Ancients (B, Ms), A Drunkard (B), A Dancer (T), Strephon (dancer); friends of Mark and Jenifer (chorus); dancers attendant on the Ancients (ballet).
Setting: A ruined temple in a forest, in the present day.

Synopsis
Act I

Mark and Jenifer discover on their wedding morning that they know neither themselves nor each other. They go to the Temple of the Ancients. Jenifer wants to dedicate herself wholly to the spiritual, and disappears heavenwards over a temple staircase. Mark feels drawn to the sensual and sexual, and descends into a temple vault. The Ancients decree that Jenifer and Mark must change places.

Act II

The secretary Bella and the mechanic Jack also want to marry. The Ancients warn them of the dangers of uncontrolled sexuality.

Act III

King Fisher wants to prevent his daughter's marriage to a man without means. Despite warnings from the Ancients he interferes in the initiation rites and meets his death. His sacrifice becomes the pledge of a happy reunion between Mark and Jenifer, who have recognized and accepted their own and each other's wishes and desires. <small>S. N.</small>

Tippett, Michael

b. 2 January 1905 in London
d. 8 January 1998 in London

Tippett studied composition, piano, and conducting at the Royal College of Music, and then worked as a music teacher. In 1933 he became conductor of the Morley College Orchestra in London. As a convinced pacifist he resisted conscription during the Second World War and was imprisoned for a month. From 1951 he was employed by the BBC, and worked as a conductor both at home and abroad. He was knighted in 1966 and from 1969 to 1974 he directed the Bath Festival. At the end of the 1980s he retired from musical life and devoted himself to tree cultivation.

Works: Operas (selection): *Robin Hood* (1934), *The Midsummer Marriage* (1955), *King Priam* (1962), *The Knot Garden* (1970), *The Ice Break* (1977), *New Year* (1989); orchestral music, including four symphonies and a piano concerto; sacred music, including two oratorios; chamber music, including five string quartets; piano music, including four piano sonatas; songs.

A vision
Written between 1946 and 1953, the opera was originally inspired by a vision: the composer had seen a gentle young man being rejected by a cool, hard young woman on a wooded hilltop. According to the teachings of C.G. Jung, collective and magical archetypes – "anima" and "animus" – might have taken over at this point. The girl, inflated by the attentions of the young man, rose up and disappeared into the heavens, while the young man, crushed by the girl's rejection of him, sank down into hell. But it was clear that both would reappear.

Opposite
The Midsummer Marriage, photograph from the production by Graham Vick, conductor Bernard Haitink, Royal Opera House, London 1986.
Tippett's *The Midsummer Marriage* has aroused the interest of numerous top-flight conductors. Paul Sacher took up the concert suite in 1953, while the opera was directed by Colin Davis in 1968, Richard Armstrong in 1976, Mark Elder in 1985, and finally Bernard Haitink in 1986.

Right
The Midsummer Marriage, photograph from the production by Richard Jones, sets Giler Cadle, costumes Nicky Gillibrand, conductor Mark Elder, Bayerische Staatsoper, Munich 1998.
The philosophical and psychological aspects of the libretto (which in itself took the composer two years to complete) provide a broad basis for the stage interpretation of the opera. Its literary and musical sources range from classical literature and Indian philosophy through Shakespeare, William Blake, Mozart, Wagner, Hugo von Hofmannsthal, George Bernard Shaw, T.S. Eliot, and Paul Valéry to C.G. Jung and the anthropologist James George Frazer.

King Priam, production photograph with Andrew Shore as King Priam, production, sets, and costumes Tom Cairns, conductor Paul Daniel, Royal Opera House, London 1995.
The first performance of *King Priam* took place in 1962 on the occasion of the official opening of Coventry Cathedral, which had been rebuilt after its destruction during the war. There were further productions at the Royal Opera House in 1967, 1972, and 1980. The title character became a symbol of the father of a family afflicted by war.

Right
The Knot Garden, photograph from the production by Nicholas Hytner, sets Bob Crowley, conductor Sian Edwards, Royal Opera House, London 1989.
Since the first performance of *The Knot Garden* under Colin Davis in 1970, the Royal Opera House has become the definitive venue for Tippett premières.

Opera as a mirror of the soul

Ballet plays an important part in this opera, in that it provides the transition between the real and the supernatural. It deals with subconscious experiences, according to the composer's theory that human beings must learn to know themselves if they want to master the problems that are created in their personal and social surroundings. After initial difficulties, this opera managed to establish itself, and its success derived in no small part from the expressive power of its extremely lyrical music.

After Benjamin Britten, Tippett was the most important British composer of the 20th century. His music may be described as a highly personal synthesis of a wide variety of musical influences, including English folk song, the music of Sibelius, Stravinsky, and the English Renaissance, and jazz. In the operas, contemporary psychoanalytical preoccupations are presented within a conventional narrative structure.

The Emperor of Atlantis
or The Denial of Death

*Der Kaiser von Alantis
oder Die Todverweigerung*

Spiel in one act

Libretto: Petr Kien.
Première: 16 December 1975, Amsterdam (Bellevue Theater).

Characters: Emperor Überall/Overall (Bar), Loudspeaker (B), Death (B), Pierrot (T), Soldier (T), Girl (S), Drummer (A or Ms).
Setting: Everywhere, at all times.

Synopsis

Pierrot and Death are out in the cold, because humans have forgotten how to laugh and how to die with dignity. Believing himself to be the savior of the world, the emperor of Atlantis proclaims a "holy war" for liberation from the "weed of hatred," and has it openly proclaimed that Death is his ally. Insulted by this, Death demonstrates his power by withholding his services. The emperor is powerless; no one sentenced to death can die, no sick person is released from suffering. Soldiers shoot each other on the battlefield, but go on living. A soldier discovers feminine features in the face of an enemy. Husband and wife recall the forgotten joys of love. "People struggle with life in order to be able to die." Death promises to restore the status quo, but only if the emperor is willing to be the first to die. The emperor allows himself to be led out of the world by Death. *S.N.*

Ullmann, Viktor

b. 1 January 1898 inTeschen (Česky Těšín; northern Moravia)
d. ?18 October 1944 in Auschwitz

Ullmann studied composition from 1918 to 1921 with →Arnold Schoenberg and piano with Eduard Steuermann. Settling in Prague in 1919, he worked as répétiteur and conductor at the Deutsches Theater under →Alexander Zemlinsky, and had his first successes with his own compositions from 1923. In the 1927/28 season he directed the opera program in Aussig to great acclaim. From 1929 to 1931 he was conductor and composer at the Schauspielhaus in Zürich. Under the influence of Rudolf Steiner's anthroposophical teachings, he abandoned all musical activity for two years and ran an anthroposophical bookshop in Stuttgart with his wife. When the Nazis came to power he fled with his wife and one-year-old son to Prague, where he worked as a freelance musician, winning the Hertzka Prize for composition twice and studying quarter-tone composition with Alois Hába. Although banned from performing in public under the Third Reich, he had his second string quartet performed in London in the summer of 1938. On 8 September 1942 Ullmann was deported to the Terezín (Theresienstadt) concentration camp. Here he worked in the music section of the so-called "Freiheitsgestaltung" (leisure activities) project, which had been set up by the Nazis in order to convince international control commissions that prisoners were being properly treated, and which for the inmates represented an opportunity to make a slight improvement in their living conditions. Ullmann's Terezín manuscripts have been preserved. He was taken to Auschwitz on 16 October 1944 as part of a "Liquidationstransport," where he probably died two days later in the gas chamber.

Works: Operas: *Der Sturz des Antichrist* (*The Fall of the Antichrist*) (1935/FP 1995), *Der zerbrochene Krug* (*The Broken Jug*) (1942/FP 1996), *Der Kaiser von Atlantis, oder Die Todverweigerung* (*The Emperor of Atlantis, or The Denial of Death*) (1943/FP 1975); orchestral works, including two symphonies and a symphonic fantasy; chamber music, including string quartets; piano works, songs, incidental music. His most frequently performed compositions are *The Emperor of Atlantis* and the Concerto for Piano and Orchestra, op. 25.

*U*llmann, as a pupil of Schoenberg and Hába, was a master of the most modern techniques of composition, who was able to bring fragile and later transcendental writing into stark contrast with the sphere of worldly sounds.

The Emperor of Atlantis, production photograph with Fred Hoffmann (Pierrot) and Hans-Otto Weiss (Death), production Stephan Kopf, sets Sibylle Schmalbrock, conductor Michael Millard, Staatstheater, Mainz 1993.
The opera begins, according to Petr Kien, with "Pierrot and Death out in the cold." Here Pierrot and Death are reflecting on their situation: in the modern world, their services are no longer required.

The Emperor of Atlantis, production photograph with Birgit Thomas (the girl) and Fred Hoffmann (the soldier), production Stephan Kopf, sets Sibylle Schmalbrock, conductor Michael Millard, Staatstheater, Mainz 1993.
Two enemy soldiers recognize each other as husband and wife. For a short time it is remembered that life can also hold love, tenderness, and happiness.

Music from Terezín

The Emperor of Atlantis was composed in 1942 in Terezín. This was the anteroom to hell, a waiting station for those who were to be transported to Auschwitz. And yet Ullmann noted in his journal: "The only thing that is worth mentioning is … that we did not sit weeping by the rivers of Babylon, but that our will to create was just as strong as our will to live." The opera was banned after the dress rehearsal, but musical material and a libretto were saved.

The first performance in Amsterdam in 1975 was followed in 1977 by the first US performance in San Francisco, and in 1982 by the first Israeli performance in Tel Aviv. It was not until 1985 that the first German performance took place, in Stuttgart, followed by a production by George Tabori at the Kammeroper in Vienna in 1987. In 1988 there was a production in England (at the Bloomsbury Festival in London), and in 1989 in Berlin (the Staatsoper and the Kammeroper Neukölln). Since then the opera has also established a place in the repertory of smaller theaters, an example being its interesting and convincing coupling with the chamber opera *Rothschilds Geige* (*Rothschild's Violin*) by Shostakovich's pupil Venjamin Fleyshman at Neu-Strelitz in 1996. In 1998 there was a further production in the USA, this time in New York.

"Death the gardener" in Auschwitz?

The librettist Petr Kien (1919–44) was primarily a graphic designer, but also a gifted caricaturist, poet, and musician. At the age of 25 he went voluntarily to his death with his parents at Auschwitz. In his libretto for Ullmann, Kien wishes death to be understood not as the medieval figure of the grim Reaper, but as a "gardener." This is an anthroposophic idea and, at the same time, a counter-metaphor to the indiscriminate death of an age characterized by the loss of individuality. As "the gardener Death, I weed out the withered foliage … reap the ripe corn," Death promises in the opera. So he comes at the right time. A timely Death. But in Auschwitz? The piece ends with the words "Do not call vainly upon the great name of Death," sung to the melody of Luther's chorale "Ein feste Burg ist unser Gott" ("A safe stronghold our God is still"), which has itself been misused, or "vainly called upon," by various rulers.

Small in extent, but mighty in content

According to Petr Kien, the opera begins with "Pierrot and Death out in the cold." How could this situation be set to music other than in the manner of →Arnold Schoenberg, →Alban Berg, and Gustav Mahler? Music as the symbol of a music condemned by the Nazis to be "out in the cold." Life without memory, unlived life, is revealed in the figures of the soldier and the girl, defined by the clichés of ballroom dancing and jazz. What is disturbing is that the emperor of Atlantis, unambiguously portrayed as a dictator and tyrant of the most brutal type, and given the revealing name of "Overall," is prepared to go to a sacrificial death, and is given an aria of great beauty and timelessness. Was Petr Kien anticipating his own fate? *The Emperor of Atlantis* is an opera that is small in extent, but mighty in content: death functions as an element that both intensifies the drama and clarifies reality.   *S. N.*

Verdi, Giuseppe

b. 9 or 10 October 1813 in Roncole near Busseto (in the duchy of Parma)
d. 21 January 1901 in Milan

Verdi studied music with Ferdinando Provesi in Roncole near Busseto. In 1831 he met Antonio Barezzi, who took a fatherly interest in him and became his friend and patron. He applied, unsuccessfully, to enter the Milan Conservatory, and then took private lessons from the conductor Vincenzo Lavigna. In 1836, after marrying Margherita Barezzi, he composed his first opera, no longer extant in its original form; he later reworked the music. Both his young children died in the years 1838–39. His first completed opera, *Oberto*, had its première in 1839 at La Scala, Milan. Only a year later his wife died, and his comic opera *King for a Day* was a failure. He was on the point of abandoning composition, but Merelli, impresario of La Scala, persuaded him to compose *Nabucco* (1841). The prima donna Giuseppina Strepponi, who later became Verdi's lifelong companion, starred in the première of the opera, which was hailed as a great success. By 1842 Verdi was regarded as Italy's national composer, and from 1842 to 1849 he wrote a series of rousing operas with a political message, collaborating with the famous librettists Temistocle Solera, Francesco Maria Piave, and Salvatore Cammarano. In 1848 he bought a country estate at Sant' Agata near Busseto. After 1849 Verdi and Giuseppina Strepponi paid frequent visits to Paris. During the 1850s Verdi's works were internationally famous. He became a deputy in Italy's first Republican parliament in Turin in 1860, and a senator in Rome in 1874. He went to Russia several times (visiting St. Petersburg and Moscow in 1861–62), and in Paris in 1862 he met Arrigo Boito, the librettist of his late operas. Verdi founded a retirement home for musicians called the Casa di Riposo, which was built between 1895 and 1899. Giuseppina Strepponi died in 1897, and Verdi was buried beside her in the crypt of the Casa di Riposo four years later.

Works: Between 1839 and 1893, 26 operas (not counting revisions and new versions): *Oberto, conte di San Bonifacio* (*Oberto, Count of San Bonifacio*) (1839), *Un giorno di regno/Il finto Stanislao* (*King for a Day/The False Stanislas*) (1840), *Nabucco* (originally *Nabucodonosor, Nebuchadnezzar*) (1842), *I Lombardi alla prima crociata* (French version *Jérusalem*) (*The Lombards on the First Crusade*) (1843), *Ernani* (1844), *I due Foscari* (*The Two Foscari*) (1844), *Giovanna d'Arco* (*Joan of Arc*) (1845), *Alzira* (1845), *Attila* (1846), *Macbeth* (1847), *I masnadieri* (*The Bandits*) (1847), *Il corsaro* (*The Corsair*) (1848), *La battaglia di Legnano* (*The Battle of Legnano*) (1849), *Luisa Miller* (1849), *Stiffelio* (1850), *Rigoletto* (1851), *Il trovatore* (*The Troubadour*) (1853), *La traviata* (*The Fallen Woman*) (1853), *I vespri siciliani/Les vêpres siciliennes* (*The Sicilian Vespers*) (1855), *Simon Boccanegra* (1857), *Un ballo in maschera* (*A Masked Ball*) (1859), *La forza del destino* (*The Force of Destiny*) (1862), *Don Carlos* (1867), *Aida* (1871), *Otello* (*Othello*) (1887), *Falstaff* (1893); a string quartet (1873), *Messa da Requiem* (1874), *Quattro pezzi sacri* (1898), and several other late works of sacred music.

Giuseppe Verdi, portrait of the composer, wood-engraving from a photograph, 1893.
Fifty-four years lay between Verdi's first opera and his last, a period of operatic history comprising the bel canto era and the great age of Italian music drama. With his astonishing creative powers, Verdi was able to change his musical and dramatic style radically three times in the course of his long life. He composed masterpieces as a young man, a mature composer, and an old man of genius.

*V*erdi is the most important Italian operatic composer of the 19th century. Influenced by French and German trends, he broke the mold of the stereotyped bel canto of his time, and put song to the service of music drama.

Oberto, Count of San Bonifacio

Dramma in two acts

Libretto: Temistocle Solera, after Antonio Piazza's libretto *Rocester*.
Première: 17 November 1839, Milan (Teatro alla Scala).

Characters: Cuniza, sister of Ezzelino da Romano (Ms), Riccardo, Count of Salinguerra (T), Oberto, Count of San Bonifacio (B), Leonora, his daughter (S), Imelda, Cuniza's confidante (Ms); knights, noblewomen, vassals (chorus).

Setting: Ezzelino's castle in Bassano and its vicinity in 1228.

Synopsis

Riccardo, betrothed to Cuniza, seduces Leonora, who is then rejected by her father Count Oberto. When Cuniza learns of Riccardo's infidelity she is prepared to renounce his love to save Leonora's honor. However, Oberto insists on fighting a duel, and dies by Riccardo's sword. Riccardo is repentant, and the despairing Leonora takes her own life.   A. G.

Verdi's first opera

The historical background, only lightly sketched in, is the backdrop for a private drama with many unexpected resemblances to situations in →*Rigoletto* and →*The Force of Destiny*. Those well acquainted with Verdi's later operas will hear his characteristic musical language already present in many passages; it cannot be mistaken for that of any of his predecessors, and has its own energetic and cogent style, revealed more particularly in some of the ensembles and rousing cabalettas. A curiosity for Verdi enthusiasts is the opening theme of a *buffo* duet, M1 which is surprisingly similar to the fanfare in *Aida* written three decades later. →M 94

A comic opera at a time of tragedy
Merelli, impresario of the Teatro alla Scala, needed a comic opera for the 1840/41 season, and commissioned the rising young composer Verdi to write one, but *King for a Day* was a failure. This comic opera was written at a tragic period of Verdi's own life, when he lost his two children and his first wife within a short space of time. The libretto is based on a French comedy by Alexandre Vincent Pineux-Duval, *Le faux Stanislas* (Paris, 1808), itself based on a historical subject, the story of the Polish aristocrat Stanisław Leszczynski. As a political protégé of Louis XV he was king of Poland between 1704 and 1711, and again, with French support, from 1733 to 1736. In 1733 he traveled from France to Warsaw disguised as a coachman in order to make an unexpected appearance. Meanwhile, in this fictional version of the incident, a French chevalier (named Beaufleur in the play and Belfiore in the opera) poses as Stanislas, to induce his enemies to believe that the claimant to the crown of Poland is still in France. The false Stanislas is at the center of the comedy, and stays as an honored guest in Baron Kelbar's house in Brittany, where he helps to unite two young lovers in the face of parental disapproval, and is finally reconciled with the woman he himself loves, who was about to marry another.

King for a Day

The False Stanislas

Un giorno di regno (Il finto Stanislao)

Melodramma giocoso in two acts

Libretto: Felice Romani (revised by Temistocle Solera), after the play *Le faux Stanislas*, by Alexandre-Vincent Pineux-Duval.
Première: 5 September 1840, Milan (Teatro alla Scala).

Characters: Cavaliere di Belfiore, going by the name of Stanislas, King of Poland (Bar), Baron di Kelbar (*buffo* B), Marchesa del Poggio, a young widow and the baron's niece, loved by Belfiore (S), Giulietta di Kelbar, the baron's daughter, loved by Edoardo (Ms), Edoardo di Sanval, a young officer (T), Signor La Rocca, state treasurer of Brittany, Edoardo's uncle (*buffo* B), Count Ivrea, commandant of Brest (T), Delmonte, equerry to King Stanislas (B); valets and chambermaids, vassals of the baron (chorus).

Setting: Near Brest and in Kelbar castle in the first half of the 18th century.

Synopsis

King Stanislas of Poland sends his friend Belfiore to France, to masquerade as the king himself in witnessing a double wedding. But Belfiore loves the Marchesa, one of the brides, and Giulietta too loves not her intended husband but Edoardo. The false king makes Giulietta's lover rich, finds her original bridegroom a well-to-do wife, and wins his own bride.   *Á. G.*

Opposite
Oberto, Count of San Bonifacio, production photograph (Act I, Scene 1), production Gianfranco de Bosio, sets and costumes Maria Antonietta Gambaro, conductor Zoltan Pesko, Teatro Comunale, Bologna 1977.

Opera for a day?

King for a Day did not in fact fall entirely out of the public eye during Verdi's lifetime. Five years after the fiasco of its première in Milan, the piece had several performances in Venice during the 1845/46 season, and – with the prestige Verdi had now acquired behind it – it was also revived in Naples in 1849 at the Teatro S. Carlo. It was not really as bad as its early reception suggested.   *J. K.*

King for a Day, production photograph with Renato Girolami as the Cavaliere di Belfiore, production Helmut Polixa, conductor Asher Fisch, Wiener Volksoper 1995.
What other comic operas might Verdi not have written if his first comedy had been successful with the public?

1. Anticipation of the Fanfare from *Aida* (Buffo duet in *Oberto*)

Dilet -to ge -nero,   a voi ne ven - go;   conten -to ed i -   lare io vi pre -ven - go,

Nabucco

Nabucodonosor

Dramma lirico in four parts

Libretto: Temistocle Solera, after the play *Nabuchodonosor* by Auguste Anicet-Bourgeois and Francis Cornu, and the ballet *Nabucodonosor* by Antonio Cortesi.
Première: 9 March 1842, Milan (Teatro alla Scala).
Characters: Nabucco (Nabucodonosor), King of Babylon (Bar), Ismaele, nephew of King Sedecia of Jerusalem (T), Zaccaria, High Priest of the Hebrews (B), Abigaille, a slave, presumed to be the eldest daughter of Nabucco (S), Fenena, daughter of Nabucco (S), High Priest of Baal (B), Abdallo, an elderly officer of the King of Babylon (T), Anna, Zaccaria's sister (S); Babylonian and Hebrew Soldiers, Jews (Hebrews), Levites, Hebrew maidens, Babylonian women, courtiers, dignitaries, guards and warriors of the Babylonian court, magi, populace (chorus).
Setting: Jerusalem and Babylon, 586–87 BC and the following years.

Synopsis
Part I: "Jerusalem"
Inside the temple of Solomon. The Hebrews pray to Jehovah to save them from the Babylonian army. Their High Priest Zaccaria is holding a hostage: Fenena, daughter of King Nabucco of Babylon. Fenena once freed King Sedecia's nephew Ismaele from captivity in Babylon, and has followed him to Jerusalem. The two young people are in love. Ismaele now intends to render Fenena the same service by setting her free, but Abigaille stands in their way. Thought to be Nabucco's eldest daughter, she too is in love with Ismaele, and has now made her way into the temple with a band of soldiers disguised as Hebrews to find him. When Ismaele rejects her, she swears to take revenge. Nabucco occupies the temple, and Zaccaria threatens to kill Fenena, but Ismaele prevents him. The temple is looted and the Hebrews led away captive. They believe that Ismaele has betrayed his native land.

Part II: "The Impious One"
Scene 1: Apartments in the Babylonian palace. Nabucco has made Fenena regent while he himself continues his campaign against the Hebrews. The priests of Baal see their power threatened by Fenena, who is well disposed toward the Jews, and the High Priest tells Abigaille of a document that shows she is only the child of a slave girl, while Fenena is the rightful heir to the throne. Abigaille allies herself with the priests, who spread false reports that Nabucco has fallen in battle.
Scene 2: A hall in the royal palace. Zaccaria converts Fenena to the Hebrew faith. Ismaele is condemned as a traitor by his tribe, but Fenena's conversion saves him, since it is now a Hebrew woman whom he has helped. Misled by the false news of Nabucco's death, the Babylonians want to see Abigaille crowned queen. She demands the crown from Fenena. Nabucco returns, intervenes, places the crown on his own head, and proclaims himself divine, thus blasphemously defying the gods of Babylon and the God of the Hebrews alike. Lightning strikes him, and he goes mad.

Part III: "The Prophecy"
Scene 1: The hanging gardens of Babylon. Abigaille has herself hailed as queen. The High Priest brings her warrants for the execution of the Hebrews and Fenena. The deranged Nabucco finds his throne occupied, but Abigaille persuades him that she is acting in his own best interests, and makes him sign the death sentences. When Nabucco realizes that his daughter Fenena is among those who are to die he tries to wrest power from Abigaille and reveal the secret of her birth, but Abigaille destroys the incriminating document.
Scene 2: On the banks of the Euphrates. The Hebrews lament their lost freedom and their native land. Zaccaria calls on them to resist, and prophesies the certain destruction of Babylon.

Part IV: "The Fallen Idol"
Scene 1: The royal palace in Babylon. Abigaille has arrested Nabucco, who is tormented by nightmares. Woken by cries and shouting, he believes he is going out to fight the Hebrews. When he realizes that what he hears is his daughter Fenena being led to her execution he prays to Jehovah for forgiveness and aid. His madness leaves him, and with a few soldiers who remain faithful to him he sets out to rescue Fenena.
Scene 2: The hanging gardens. The sacrificial ritual in which the Hebrews will be executed before the image of Baal is about to take place. Nabucco stops the executions and gives orders to destroy the idol. But it collapses of its own accord, and the fetters binding the Hebrews fall away. A temple is to be built to Jehovah. Abigaille dies, asking Fenena and the Hebrews to forgive her.   *S. N.*

Nabucco, production photograph (Act III, Scene1), production Roberto de Simone, sets Mauro Carosi, costumes Odette Nicoletti, conductor Riccardo Muti, Teatro alla Scala, Milan 1986.
The most exciting duet in the opera, between a demented woman and a deranged tyrant, takes place in this scene. In the role of Abigaille – a character made up of hatred, an inferiority complex, and lust for power – Verdi was to a great extent inspired by the singer Giuseppina Strepponi's capacity for dramatic expression.

Nabucco, production photograph (Act IV, Scene 1), production Roberto de Simone, sets Mauro Carosi, costumes Odette Nicoletti, conductor Riccardo Muti, Teatro alla Scala, Milan 1986.
The lion of Babylon recovers his strength: Nabucco draws his sword, and his loyal soldiers strike up a battle song which has been much acclaimed by audiences even in times of peace.

Below
Nabucco, production photograph with Renato Bruson, production Roberto de Simone, sets Mauro Carosi, costumes Odette Nicoletti, conductor Riccardo Muti, Teatro alla Scala, Milan 1986.
Verdi created his first great baritone role in the figure of Nabucco, whose character unites blind lust for power with paternal affection – shatteringly expressed in the mad scene.

The Risorgimento

The father of the Italian reform movement was Giuseppe Mazzini (1805–72). In 1831, in exile in Marseilles, he founded the secret society La Giovine Italia (Young Italy), with the objective of uniting Italy on republican and democratic principles. The Italian freedom fighter Giuseppe Garibaldi (1807–82) met him in 1833 and joined the movement. In 1834 a rebellion they instigated in Piedmont failed, and Garibaldi fled to South America while Mazzini took refuge in London. Towards the end of the 1840s revolutionary risings in Italy gathered pace, and the Austrian troops were driven out of Milan. Charles Albert of Sardinia declared war on Austria and placed himself at the head of the national movement. At the same time Camillo Benso, Count Cavour, founded the journal *Il Risorgimento*, a title that became symbolic of the efforts made from 1815 onward for the resurgence ("risorgimento") of Italy's leading cultural role and political unification under a king. Garibaldi and Mazzini returned from abroad, and in 1849 led the defense of the republic of Rome against the French. However, the French troops broke Italian resistance, and the revolution failed. Italy was not unified until 1860.

Below
Nabucco, photograph from the production by David Pountney, sets Stefanos Lazaridis, Bregenz Festival 1993/94.
The Hebrews represent an oppressed nation, and so deliver Verdi's political message; at the time of the opera's première any Italian patriot could identify with them. The weight given to the choral scenes is striking, and so is the confidence with which Verdi handled the chorus. The choruses of *Nabucco* and the Risorgimento operas that followed are not related so much to Meyerbeer's massed crowds on the grand operatic stage as to the inheritance of →Rossini (*Moses in Egypt*, *William Tell*), expressing the grief and mental turmoil of oppressed peoples.

Above
Giuseppina Strepponi, painting by an unknown artist, 1842 (Museo Teatrale alla Scala, Milan).
In line with Italian operatic practice in general, the most difficult vocal part in *Nabucco* is that of the prima donna. The part of Abigaille calls for a singer in the grand manner, with a wide vocal range (from mezzo to high dramatic soprano) and great expressive ability. The role was sung at the première by a famous star, Giuseppina Strepponi (1815–97). Verdi had met her through a friend, Bartolomeo Merelli, impresario of La Scala, and wrote the part especially for her vocal capacities. In view of the demanding nature of the role it is difficult to believe that, as some of her contemporaries claimed, Giuseppina Strepponi was really past her artistic peak at the time. She did in fact retire from the stage in 1846 to teach singing in Paris. We do not know whether Verdi was already in love with her when he was composing *Nabucco*, but the widowed composer and the prima donna began living together in 1846. Giuseppina Strepponi was a worthy partner for Verdi. She died in 1897, and Verdi survived her by only four years.

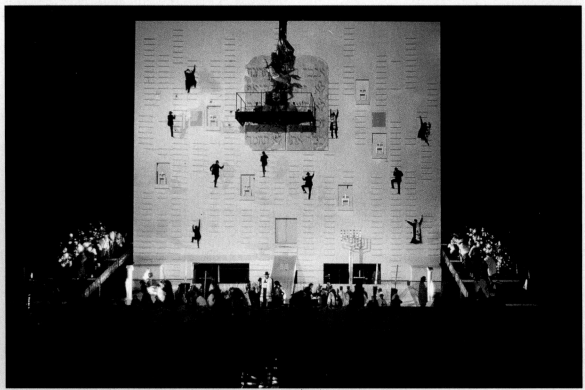

View of the interior of the Teatro alla Scala, Milan, by an unknown artist, 19th-century illustration (TWS).
La Scala has a double meaning. The leading opera house of Italy acquired its name from the church of S. Maria della Scala ("scala" meaning "stairway") that once stood on the site. However, "scala" also has the musical meaning of "scale," as part of the essential daily practice of singers and instrumentalists alike. The Milanese predecessor of La Scala was the Teatro Regio Ducale, where some of the early operas of Mozart and Gluck were performed. After it was destroyed by fire in 1776, the owners of boxes at the theater commissioned the architect Giuseppe Piermarini to design the new Teatro alla Scala. This fine building was inaugurated in 1778 with an opera by Antonio Salieri (*L'Europa riconosciuta*). During the first 150 years of La Scala's existence it gave 350 premières, including those of Verdi's →*Nabucco* (1842), →*Otello* (1887), and →*Falstaff* (1893), Arrigo Boito's *Mephistopheles* (1868), Amilcare Ponchielli's →*La Gioconda* (1876), Alfredo Catalani's →*La Wally* (1892), and Giacomo Puccini's →*Madam Butterfly* (1904). Today La Scala is still a landmark on the international operatic scene. A singer who has taken one of the leading Italian operatic roles in this theater can look forward to a distinguished career.

Life becomes literature

Verdi, usually a man of few words, describes what was probably the most memorable incident of his life with the precision of a professional writer: Merelli had given him the libretto of *Nabucco*, which had been turned down by Otto Nicolai, and Solera's words were transformed into music in his mind: "On the way home I felt a kind of vague discomfort, a great sadness and pain that almost burst my heart. When I arrived, I flung the manuscript down forcefully on the table, and stood there looking at it, lost in thought. As the book fell on the table it opened; my eyes fell, I do not remember how, on the page lying open there before me. And I read: 'Va, pensiero, sull' ali dorate.' I looked through the following lines, and was deeply impressed, the more so because all this was taken almost literally from the Bible, which I had always read with great pleasure. I read one passage; I read two. But then, renewing my resolve to compose no more, I closed the libretto and went to bed. Yet I could not get *Nabucco* out of my mind. It was impossible to sleep; I rose, I read the libretto not just once, no, twice, three times, many times. By morning I may say I knew it all by heart." (autobiographical sketch) *M 2*

"Va, pensiero ... ": Italy's hymn of honor

If the fine and inspiring melody of this chorus had not derived from opera, and from a situation involving imprisonment, and had been given a different, more patriotic text, it might well have become the national anthem of Italy. Verdi was the author of another national hymn. In 1847, writing from exile, Mazzini asked him to provide music for the patriotic poem *Suona la tromba* (*Sound the Trumpet*), by Goffredo Mameli, a young officer in Garibaldi's troops. Verdi sent him the setting in 1848, commenting, "May this hymn soon resound on the plains of Lombardy to the music of the cannon!" Extraordinarily, however, Verdi never became the official composer of an Italian anthem. The song chosen as the national anthem – rather late in the day, and indeed not until after the Second World War – had also been composed in 1847, the year of the Risorgimento, by Michele Novaro (1822–85), and is entitled *Canto degli italiani* (*Song of the Italians*). It sounds like a fiery cabaletta from one of Verdi's own youthful operas. *M 3*

2. Hebrew Chorus

Va, pen-sie-ro, sull'a-li do-ra-te; Va, ti po-sa sui cli-vi, sui col-li, O ve o-
lez-za-no te-pi-de e mol-li L'aure dol-ci del suo-lo na-tal!

3. Italian National Anthem

Fra-tel-li d'I-ta-lia, l'I-ta-lia s'è des-ta

The Lombards on the First Crusade

I Lombardi alla prima crociata

Dramma lirico in four acts

Italian version
Libretto: Temistocle Solera, after the poem by Tommaso Grossi.
Première: 11 February 1843, Milan (Teatro alla Scala).

French version: *Jérusalem*
Libretto: Alphonse Royer and Gustave Vaëz, after Solera's libretto.
Première: 26 November 1847, Paris (Opéra).
Characters: Arvino, leader of the Lombard crusaders (T), and Pagano, later a hermit (B), both sons of Folco, Lord of Rò, Viclinda, Arvino's wife (S), Giselda, their daughter (S), Pirro, Arvino's squire (B), A Milanese Prior (T), Acciano, tyrant of Antioch (B), Oronte, his son (T), Sofia, Acciano's wife, secretly a Christian (S); nuns, priors, hired ruffians, soldiers in Folco's palace, envoys from Persia, Media, Damascus, and Chaldea, crusaders and soldiers, pilgrims, Lombard women, harem women, celestial maidens (chorus).
Setting: Milan, Antioch and its surroundings, and near Jerusalem, around 1096.

The Lombards on the First Crusade, Mme Juliane van Geldern as Giselda, 1847. In Giselda, Verdi created a complex and lifelike feminine portrait. She is the only character drawn with a sense of individual psychology as she struggles with family tradition, trying to shake off the burden of her historical circumstances.

Right
The Lombards on the First Crusade, production photograph with the crusaders, Samuel Ramey as Roger (the equivalent of Pagano in the French version), and the city of Jerusalem in the background, production Robert Carson, Wiener Staatsoper 1995.
Is the Promised Land really Jerusalem, or Milan in Lombardy? The question is never clearly answered in either the original libretto of *The Lombards* or its French version, *Jérusalem*. In any case, at the end of both versions the crusaders and pilgrims gaze in awe at the liberated city of Jerusalem shining in the light of dawn.

Synopsis

The brothers Arvino and Pagano were once rivals for the hand of the fair Viclinda. She married Arvino and bore him a daughter, Giselda. Pagano tried to kill Arvino and was banished for 18 years. Now back from exile, he publicly promises reconciliation, but in secret he is once again planning to murder his brother. However, he kills his father instead, mistaking him for Arvino, and is banished from Milan for ever. Pagano now lives near Antioch as a hermit with a reputation for sanctity. Concealing his true identity, he helps the Lombard crusaders led by Arvino to conquer Antioch, where Arvino discovers Giselda. She has been captured and enslaved, but is loved by Oronte, son of the ruler of Antioch, and converts him to the Christian faith. Giselda recognizes the true, violent nature of the Crusades, and leaves her father. In flight, she comes upon Oronte, who had been reported dead, and they take refuge in their love for each other, renouncing home and family. Pursued by Arvino, Oronte suffers a mortal wound, and is baptized by the hermit in his dying hour. During the conquest of Jerusalem, Pagano is fatally wounded, reveals his identity, and dies reconciled to his brother.

Act I: "The Vendetta"
Scene 1: Milan, the square outside the basilica of S. Ambrogio. The reconciliation between the brothers Arvino and Pagano, formerly divided by rivalry over a woman, is to be confirmed in a church service. Pagano, home from 18 years of exile, pretends to be penitent, but is secretly plotting to murder his brother. Arvino is appointed leader of the army of Lombard crusaders.
Scene 2: Night, near Arvino's house. The nuns of the nearby convent offer up evening prayers for God's blessing and peace, while Pagano is planning murder just outside the convent gates.
Scene 3: In Arvino's house. Arvino's wife Viclinda does not trust Pagano. With her daughter Giselda, she prays to the Virgin Mary for mercy, and promises to make a pilgrimage to the Holy Sepulcher. Pagano and his accomplices set fire to the house. By mistake, however, Pagano kills not his brother but their father. Giselda prevents her father Arvino from taking revenge. Pagano, horrified by his own actions, is banished from the city for ever.

Act II: "The Man of the Cave"
Scene 1: The throneroom of Acciano's palace in Antioch. The crusaders are outside the city, having left a trail of robbery and violence behind them. Acciano resolves to defend his city. Giselda is held prisoner in the palace harem, and Acciano's son Oronte has fallen in love with her. His mother Sofia has already converted to Christianity, and welcomes their relationship.
Scene 2: Outside a cave in the rocks. The exiled Pagano longs for the arrival of the Lombard crusaders so that he can join them. He is doing penance for his crime by living the life of a hermit, and is already regarded as a saint. Arvino himself asks the venerable hermit how he can find his lost daughter and make his way into Antioch. The hermit promises his help.
Scene 3: In the harem of the palace of Antioch. Jealous slave girls mockingly praise Giselda's beauty. Antioch has fallen through treachery, and the crusaders make their way into the palace. Acciano has been killed in the fighting, and so, it seems, has Oronte. Giselda shrinks from her father, saying it cannot be God's will to drench the earth in human blood. Arvino tries to kill his rebellious daughter.

Act III: "The Conversion"

Scene 1: The crusaders' camp in the valley of Jehoshaphat, with Jerusalem in the distance. The pilgrims following the crusaders hail the Holy City. Giselda, in flight from her father's tent, comes upon Oronte, whom she had thought dead. They both renounce all their old ties, and vow to find "a homeland, life, and heaven" in their love alone.

Scene 2: Arvino's tent. Arvino curses his lost daughter. The hermit too has disappeared.

Scene 3: Inside a cave, where Giselda takes refuge with the mortally wounded Oronte. The hermit, who has followed them, baptizes the dying man.

Act IV: "The Holy Sepulcher"

Scene 1: A cave near Jerusalem. Giselda has a vision, in which Oronte appears to her and prophesies that the spring of Siloim will provide water.

Scene 2: The Lombard tents, near the tomb of Rachel. Weak with thirst, the Lombards remember their homeland. Giselda, the hermit, and Arvino bring news of the miracle of the spring. Strengthened again, the Lombards are ready to go on and conquer Jerusalem.

Scene 3: Arvino's tent. The hermit has been mortally wounded in the fighting. Facing death, Pagano reveals his identity, and the two brothers are reconciled. S.N.

The Lombards on the First Crusade, production photograph with Emil Ivanov as Oronte, production Beppe de Tomasi, sets and costumes Ferruccio Villagrossi, conductor Carlo Franci, Stadttheater, St. Gallen 1994.

4. Pilgrims' Chorus

O Si - gno - re, dal tet - to na - ti - o   ci chia-ma - sti con san - ta pro -mes - sa

The libretto and the message

This opera brings to life a period when Milan was an important political power, able to raise an army of its own to conquer distant cities. Italian patriots of the 19th century, in contrast, had to suffer foreign rule. The epic tale of great patriotic leaders, and the libretto by Solera, whose father had once been imprisoned in the infamous Austrian prison of the Spielberg fortress, gave them a sense of their former independence and freedom. No one troubled about the oddities of the libretto, such as when the parched pilgrims on their way to Jerusalem praise the beautiful landscape of their homeland in Lombardy. M 4

The Lombards on the First Crusade, production photograph with Valentin Pivovarov as Pagano, production Beppe de Tomasi, sets and costumes Ferruccio Villagrossi, conductor Carlo Franci, Stadttheater, St. Gallen 1994. The character of Pagano is a curious mixture of good and evil, a type of role that was not typical of Verdi's later work. He is a murderer, but does good as a hermit. Contradictions that are almost impossible to resolve lie between his revenge aria in Act I, the baptism scene in Act III, and his heroic death in Act IV, when the two brothers are finally reconciled.

Ernani

Dramma lirico in four acts

Libretto: Francesco Maria Piave, after the play *Hernani* by Victor Hugo.
Première: 9 March 1844, Venice (Teatro La Fenice).

Characters: Ernani, a bandit (T), Don Carlo, King of Spain (Bar), Don Ruy Gomez de Silva, a Spanish grandee (B), Elvira, his niece and betrothed (S), Giovanna, her nurse (S), Don Riccardo, the king's equerry (T), Jago, Silva's equerry (B); bandits and rebels from the mountains, knights and members of Silva's household, Elvira's maids, the king's knights, Spanish and German nobles and ladies, pages, German soldiers (chorus).

Setting: The Pyrenees, Aix-la-Chapelle, and Saragossa, in 1519.

Ernani, photograph from the production by Luca Ronconi, sets Ezio Frigerio, costumes Franca Squarciapino, conductor Claudio Abbado, Teatro alla Scala, Milan 1982.
Ernani is one of Verdi's Risorgimento operas in terms of the chronology of his compositions, but it has one notable difference from *Nabucco*, *The Lombards*, and *Attila*, with their many choruses. Here the chorus is used less to express patriotic feeling (apart from the chorus of conspirators in Act III) than as a musical backdrop against which the drama of the protagonists is acted out, and to provide appropriate local color at the beginnings of scenes, such as in the robbers' chorus at the beginning of Act I.

Synopsis

Ernani turned rebel when his father was unjustly treated by the king of Spain, and now lives the life of a bandit in the forest with his companions. He is in love with the beautiful Elvira, and plans to rescue her from the clutches of her uncle, Don Ruy de Silva, who intends to marry her himself, against her will. The king, Don Carlo, is also in love with Elvira and abducts her. Ernani and Silva make a pact to rescue her, but on one condition: Ernani must promise to die whenever Silva wishes. Carlo is elected Holy Roman Emperor, a plot to assassinate him is discovered, and only Elvira's pleading saves the conspirators. The king forgives them, and Elvira and Ernani are to be married. But on the wedding night, Silva demands his payment: the death of Ernani, who stabs himself. Elvira falls lifeless to the ground.

Act I: "The Bandit"

Ernani and his followers are planning to abduct Elvira from the castle of Don Ruy Gomez de Silva, who means to force her into marriage. But Don Carlo, King of Spain, also loves Elvira. He pays ardent court to Elvira, but she rejects him. He decides to abduct her, but is confronted by Ernani. Silva intends to avenge himself on both men, but Carlo reveals his royal identity, and with Elvira's aid Ernani escapes.

Act II: "The Guest"

Ernani is believed dead, and Elvira is about to marry Silva. But Ernani, who is really still alive, makes his way to the wedding disguised as a pilgrim and is granted hospitality by Silva. When Don Carlo arrives, having followed the rebel's trail, and demands that he be handed over, Silva refuses. Carlo abducts Elvira. Silva and Ernani make a pact to rescue her, but on one condition: in return for Silva's hospitality, Ernani must die whenever Silva decrees.

Act III: "Clemency"

Don Carlo goes to the ancestral vaults in Aix-la-Chapelle to await the result of the election of the new Holy Roman Emperor. Those conspiring against him, Silva and Ernani among them, also meet there to cast lots for the man who is to assassinate him. The lot falls on Ernani. Three cannon shots are heard, conveying the information that Don Carlo is elected emperor. He has overheard the conspirators, and orders their punishment, but Elvira's pleas induce him to grant clemency. Elvira and Ernani are now to marry.

Act IV: "The Mask"

A black mask casts an ominous shadow over the wedding festivities of Elvira and Ernani. On the wedding night itself, Silva demands Ernani's death. All pleas are in vain. Ernani kills himself, and Elvira falls to the ground unconscious.   S. N.

A drama of individuals

Ernani is not a popular folk opera (although Verdi and Piave included a captivating choral scene in Act III, "Si ridesti il Leon di Castiglia") but a drama in which individual personalities drawn on the grand scale are torn between personal decisions and social principles.

Don Carlo

In his play *Hernani*, Victor Hugo presents Don Carlo in the year 1519, at the turning point of his life (his dates are 1500–58). When the princely young dandy who has led the life of a libertine reflects on his chances of election to the imperial throne, a great future suddenly opens out before him.

his, suggests something of that great dramatic figure Philip II in →*Don Carlos*. (*Don Carlos* is also a sequel to *Ernani* historically, since the Emperor Charles V was the father of Philip II of Spain.)

Melodious passions

The tension of the basic situation constantly heightens the atmosphere. The protagonists sing in the full heat of emotion; in all circumstances, Italian operatic heroes and heroines of the 1840s were duty-bound to be passionate. The emotional exaggerations of the libretto were determined by prescribed and obligatory musical forms; for instance, the text had to provide the motivation for a rapid, rousing cabaletta following the slow section of an aria. M 5

Left
Ernani, production photograph (Act I) with Placido Domingo (Ernani) and Mirella Freni (Elvira), production Luca Ronconi, sets Ezio Frigerio, costumes Franca Squarciapino, conductor Claudio Abbado, Teatro alla Scala, Milan 1982.
Verdi wrote four rewarding roles for *Ernani*. The most original was for bass voice (Silva), but the higher registers also have good parts. *Ernani* is distinguished by its wealth of melody, and in this respect Verdi's fifth opera is a virtuoso success.

Below
Ernani, production photograph with Luciano Pavarotti as Ernani, production Pier Luigi Samaritani, sets Desmond Heeley, Metropolitan Opera, New York 1983.
Ernani is the only opera by Verdi before →*Rigoletto* to offer a tenor role that is popular even with the top operatic stars, including tenors of such different vocal characteristics as Luciano Pavarotti and Placido Domingo.

5. Ernani's Cabaletta

Oh tu, che l'al - ma a - do - ra, vien,   vien, la mia vi - ta in - fio - ra:

per noi d'ogni al - tro   be - ne   il   lo - co amor terrà, a - mor ter - rà.

Ernani

This Spanish Robin Hood figure is of elevated social rank. His father was a Spanish grandee who would not submit to the king, was banished by Philip the Good, and died in exile. His son (still Juan of Aragon at the time) swore vengeance, took the assumed name of Ernani, and tried to overthrow the king at the head of a rebel force of several thousand men.

Silva

Don Ruy Gomez de Silva, unlike Ernani, is from a family that remained loyal to the king. He embodies the "Spanish virtues" of stern virility and the scrupulous observance of personal honor.

Elvira

The woman who affects the lives of three men and almost changes the course of history in this opera has no basis in fact. She was invented by Victor Hugo, who calls her Donna Sol. Piave and Verdi took over Hugo's character: an Italian opera without a prima donna would have been unthinkable in the 1840s.

Ernani and the future

The opera contains certain parallels with later examples of Verdi's operas of passion. Several passages anticipate →*Il trovatore*, such as the trio between Elvira, Ernani, and Don Carlo in Act I, which looks forward to the ensemble of Leonora, Manrico, and Luna the first act of the later opera. Don Carlo himself is the precursor of two later Verdi characters. As a young and thoughtless ruler, he calls to mind Gustavus III of Sweden (→*A Masked Ball*), while the aria accompanied by solo cello in the vaults of Aix-la-Chapelle, in which he assumes the character of a meditative statesman recognizing the loneliness behind the power that will now be

The Two Foscari

I due Foscari

Tragedia lirica in three acts

Libretto: Francesco Maria Piave, after the play *The Two Foscari* by Lord Byron.
Première: 3 November 1844, Rome (Teatro Argentina).

Characters: Francesco Foscari, Doge of Venice (Bar), Jacopo Foscari, his son (T), Lucrezia Contarini, Jacopo's wife (S), Jacopo Loredano, member of the Council of Ten (B), Barbarigo, a senator (T), Pisana, Lucrezia's friend and confidante (S), Officer of the Council of Ten (T), Servant of the Doge (B); members of the Council of Ten and the Senate, Lucrezia's maids, Venetian women, populace, masked figures (chorus).
Setting: Venice, 1457.

Synopsis

Jacopo Foscari, son of the doge of Venice, is accused of murder and banished by the Council of Ten. The man behind the political intrigue is Loredano, who is jealous of the doge. The doge himself is convinced of his son's innocence, but must bow to the verdict of the Council. Jacopo's wife begs for mercy for her husband, but in vain. While the city celebrates a festival, the sentence is carried out, and Jacopo is taken on board the state galley. When the real murderer confesses his guilt, it is too late; Jacopo is already dead. To avert an investigation, Loredano stirs up feeling against the elder Foscari, and the doge, who was elected for life, is forced to retire from his office. An enemy of the family is chosen as the new doge, and Francesco Foscari also dies.

Act I

Scene 1: A hall in the doge's palace in Venice. The Council of Ten and members of the Senate have gathered to discuss a case involving a member of the doge's family. Jacopo, the doge's son, is brought from the state prison, accused of murder.
Scene 2: A hall in the Foscari palace. Jacopo's wife Lucrezia intends to plead before the court on behalf of her husband, who has been condemned to exile.
Scene 3: A hall in the doge's palace. The senators confirm Jacopo's sentence.
Scene 4: The doge's private apartments. Francesco Foscari reflects bitterly on his inability to protect his own son from his accusers' desire for vengeance. Lucrezia begs for her father-in-law's aid. The doge is deeply moved by her courage and love.

Act II

Scene 1: The state prison. Jacopo has a premonition of imminent death, and is haunted by tormenting dreams. He wakes in Lucrezia's arms, and she tells him the verdict of the Council of Ten. His father Francesco has to announce the sentence to him officially, watched in triumph by Loredano, who is one of the Ten and Jacopo's enemy.
Scene 2: A hall in the doge's palace. The sentence passed on Jacopo is confirmed in the council chamber. Jacopo turns to his father for help, but he is powerless to assist him. Lucrezia brings in her two children, hoping for a more merciful sentence, but in vain; the majority of senators support Loredano.

Act III

Scene 1: The Piazzetta of St. Mark's. A cheerful regatta is in progress when the somber state galley appears to take Jacopo away. He takes leave of his wife and children.
Scene 2: The doge's private apartments. Old Francesco Foscari is lamenting the loss of his last son. Unexpectedly, a letter arrives from a man confessing to the murder of which Jacopo was falsely accused. But it is too late: Lucrezia brings the doge news of Jacopo's death. The members of the Council, led by Loredano, demand that the doge resign from his office on the grounds of old age. Lucrezia stands by Francesco Foscari, and leads him away. The great bell of St. Mark's sounds, announcing the appointment of his successor. Old Foscari dies of a broken heart, and Loredano's revenge is complete.   *S. N.*

The Two Foscari, production photograph with (from left to right) June Anderson (Lucrezia), Luciano Pavarotti (Jacopo), and Vladimir Chernov (Francesco), production August Everding, conductor Daniele Gatti, Royal Opera House, London 1995.
In the prison: Lucrezia, Jacopo, and his father, who as doge must inform his own son of his sentence. All three express their sorrow in a moving trio. Few operatic composers have been able to give such profound and at the same time cathartic musical expression to grief as Verdi.

The Two Foscari, production photograph with Renato Bruson, production and sets Pier Luigi Pizzi, Teatro alla Scala, Milan 1988. This production of the opera, largely dispensing with local color, suggested the Venetian setting only in the tolling of the bells and the cheerful regatta scene. That scene also contained the dramatic contrast of the somber state galley arriving to take the innocent victim of injustice into exile.

Lord Byron (1788–1824), portrait by Eduard Schuler, steel engraving (undated). George Gordon, Lord Byron, the author of the play *The Two Foscari* (1821), on which the libretto was based. 19th-century commentators on the arts regarded Lord Byron as the quintessencial Romantic artist.

A study in operatic drama

Francesco Foscari was Verdi's first major role for a father and a ruler. The almost inflexible integrity of the doge, and his acceptance of his lonely destiny as a sovereign, appear to anticipate features of the character of King Philip in →*Don Carlos*. With its chainlike structure and widely arching line, the duet that concludes Act I – for soprano and baritone, Lucrezia and her father-in-law the doge – also looks forward to the great duet between Violetta and Germont in →*La traviata*. The prison scene in Act II, with its sequence running from monologue to duet, trio, and quartet, shows a sense of formal construction and dramatic intensification; the young Verdi employs this rather unusual format for decorative effect. In *The Two Foscari* he experimented (for the first and only time), with leitmotivs for the individual characters. There is a sorrowful minor theme, always associated with the color of a solo clarinet, for Jacopo Foscari, ᴍ6 a rising, agitated string theme for Lucrezia, ᴍ7 and a broad theme of deep string figures for the doge. ᴍ8

J. K.

6. Jacopo Foscari's Theme

7. Lucrezia's Theme

8. The Doge's Theme

Joan of Arc

Giovanna d'Arco

Dramma lirico in a prologue and three acts

Libretto: Temistocle Solera, after Friedrich von Schiller's play *Die Jungfrau von Orleans* (*The Maid of Orléans*).
Première: 15 February 1845, Milan (Teatro alla Scala).

Characters: Carlo VII/Charles VII, King of France (T), Giacomo, a shepherd of Dom-Rémy (Bar), Giovanna/Joan, his daughter (S), Delil, an officer of the king (T), Talbot, commander of the English forces (B); officers of the king, people of Reims, French and English soldiers, good and evil spirits, nobles, heralds, pages, young girls, deputies, villagers, knights, ladies (chorus).

Setting: Dom-Rémy and Reims in the 15th century, during the Hundred Years' War.

Synopsis

King Charles of France has suffered several defeats at the hands of the English, and is discouraged. A vision leads him to the shepherd girl Joan, who yearns to be the savior of France. Joan's father fears that she is tempted by the devil to become the king's mistress, and therefore rejects his daughter. Joan leads the French to victory over the English. The king tells her of his love for her, but her father publicly accuses his daughter of being in league with the devil. The crowd calls for Joan to be handed over to the English. In captivity, she renounces her earthly love for the king, and once more saves France. During a final battle, she places herself at the head of the French army again and brings it victory. Mortally wounded, she dies reconciled with her father, having fulfilled her mission.

Prologue

Scene 1: A great hall in the castle of Dom-Rémy. King Charles tells the villagers and his officers of a dream in which he saw a shrine and was told to dedicate his sword and helmet to the Virgin Mary there. To the villagers, however, this is a place haunted by evil spirits.
Scene 2: A forest. Joan is praying to an image of the Virgin. She imagines herself involved in the struggle between the earthly and heavenly powers of love, and believes she has a vocation to save France. Encouraging the king, she expresses her willingness to follow him. Her father Giacomo, who has overheard the meeting between them, rejects his daughter.

Act I

Scene 1: The English camp near Reims. The English soldiers have heard of Joan's supernatural vocation, and fear the coming battle. Her father Giacomo wants revenge on Charles, supposedly his daughter's seducer, and is ready to give Joan up to the English.
Scene 2: A garden in the royal palace in Reims. After defeating the English in battle, Joan wants only to go home and return to her simple life. Charles confesses his love for her, and asks her to crown him. Joan fears that earthly love may win the victory over heavenly love.

Act II

The square outside Reims Cathedral. While the people praise Joan, Giacomo accuses his daughter of witchcraft and Charles of sacrilege. Believing that she is indeed guilty, Joan does not defend herself. The people call for her to be cast out, and Giacomo delivers her up to the English.

Act III

An English fort, close to the battlefield. Joan, now in prison, prays fervently to be freed and reconciled to the powers of heaven, so that she can stand by the French in battle once again. Giacomo realizes that his daughter is innocent, and sets her free. Joan wins victory for her side and saves Charles, but she herself suffers a deadly wound. All mourn for Joan, who entrusts herself to the care of the Virgin Mary as she did once before in the forest near Dom-Rémy.   S. N.

Joan of Arc, production photograph with June Anderson as Joan, production Philip Prousse, conductor Daniele Gatti, Royal Opera House, London 1996.
One of the least frequently performed of Verdi's operas, and one of the most severely criticized for the alleged weaknesses of its libretto. Efforts have often been made to present it in the same light as →*The Two Foscari* or →*Macbeth*, but to do so distorts perception of this very effective opera and its brilliant title role.

Temistocle Solera (1815–78), portrait photograph.
Solera was Verdi's first librettist, and wrote the texts for his *Oberto, Nabucco, The Lombards, Joan of Arc,* and *Attila.*

An Italianate version of Schiller

Entirely in the tradition of Italian librettos of his time, Solera reduced the number of protagonists in Schiller's original drama to five solo parts, two of them insignificant subsidiary roles, the others the three leading roles of Joan, Charles, and Giacomo. In a straight play, the intervention of supernatural powers in the form of demons and angels and the crucial part played by Giacomo's bigotry appear unusual, but such elements were normal enough in an operatic libretto of the period. Horror effects were welcome on the Romantic operatic stage, and Verdi's work enjoyed a long period of success in its own time. He gave audiences the kind of music they expected of him, and the absence of those dimensions more appropriate to a drama about Joan of Arc did not trouble him. The warlike aspects of Solera's treatment of the theme gave Verdi an opportunity to fill his score with a wealth of martial music, marches, "rattling" choral passages, and rousing cabalettas, in fact with those features that had proved so successful in →*Nabucco* and →*Ernani.* The other numbers, including scenes of prayer, mourning, storm scenes, and choruses of spirits, were mainly drawn from a stock of operatic commonplaces – but commonplaces can be pleasing. Verdi had some difficulty with the ambiguous figure of Joan's father Giacomo, who alternates between her adversary and an affectionate father. *J. K.*

Below
Joan of Arc, production photograph with June Anderson as Joan, production Philip Prousse, conductor Daniele Gatti, Royal Opera House, London 1996. Among the operas of the Risorgimento movement, the story of *Joan of Arc* was the only one that offered Verdi a chance to show the common people in a less than idealized light. The crowd acclaiming Joan in Act II is soon ready to send her to the stake as a witch. However, this ambiguity in the role of the people is not felt in the music itself.

Above left
Joan of Arc, production photograph with June Anderson as Joan, production Philip Prousse, conductor Daniele Gatti, Royal Opera House, London 1996.

Alzira

Tragedia lirica in a prologue and two acts

Libretto: Salvatore Cammarano, after Voltaire's tragedy *Alzire, ou Les Américains* (*Alzira, or The Americans*).
Première: 12 August 1845, Naples (Teatro S. Carlo).

Characters: Alvaro, Governor of Peru (B), Gusmano, his son and successor (Bar), Ovando, a Spanish officer (T), Zamoro and Ataliba, chieftains of a Peruvian tribe (T, B), Alzira, Ataliba's daughter (S), Zuma, her sister (Ms), Otumbo, an Inca warrior (T); Spanish officers and soldiers, Incas, maidservants of the governor (chorus).
Setting: Peru around the middle of the 16th century.

Alzira, production photograph (Act I) with (from left to right) Keiko Fukushima (Alzira) and Giancarlo Pasquetto (Gusmano), production, sets, and costumes Luciano Damiani, conductor Maurizio Benini, Teatro Regio, Parma 1990/91 (Verdi Festival).
In his first official act as governor of Peru, Gusmano sets free the tribal chieftain Ataliba.

Parma's connections with Verdi
Parma is a major musical center, and also the home of the Verdi Institute, the headquarters of international Verdi studies. Furthermore, Toscanini was born in Parma, and studied at the conservatory there. Statues of Verdi and Toscanini stand in the courtyard of the conservatory in memory of these two great Italian musicians. They were close countrymen, for the village of Roncole, where Verdi was born, lies between Parma and Piacenza. Today it is called simply Roncole di Verdi by the local people, and visitors can see the house where Verdi's family lived. Not far away is the little town of Busseto in which the young musician studied, making his first operatic ventures in its small but beautiful opera house. His country estate and villa in Sant' Agata, where he settled in 1849 with Giuseppina Strepponi, are in the same area.

Synopsis

The aging Spanish governor Alvaro is taken prisoner by native Peruvians, but his liberty is restored by the magnanimity of Zamoro, the Inca chieftain. On returning to Lima Alvaro resigns his post and hands his powers over to his son Gusmano. Gusmano also means to rule with generosity, and frees the Inca chieftain Ataliba, who has surrendered to the Spanish, but conflicts arise when his personal and political interests are mingled, for Gusmano loves the Peruvian maiden Alzira, who loves and is loved by Zamoro. Gusmano frees the defeated Zamoro, but claims the right to marry Alzira. Disguised as a Spaniard, Zamoro kills Gusmano during the wedding festivities. The dying Gusmano recognizes that he has done wrong, forgives his murderer, and unites Alzira and Zamoro.

Prologue

Scene 1: A broad plain by the river Rima. The Peruvians, defeated by the Spaniards, have captured the Spanish governor Alvaro and are preparing to kill him. Their chieftain Zamoro, whom they had believed dead, returns to his people and grants old Alvaro his life.

Act I

Scene 1: A square in Lima. Spanish soldiers are marching away to conquer new territory. Alvaro announces his retirement in favor of his son Gusmano. Gusmano's first official action is to free the captive Inca chieftain Ataliba, who has surrendered to the authority of the king of Spain. Gusmano is in love with Ataliba's beautiful daughter Alzira, but she loves Zamoro.
Scene 2: Alzira's bedchamber in the governor's palace. Ataliba tries to convince his daughter of the political necessity of her marriage to Gusmano, but Alzira is still reluctant to agree. A strange and unknown Inca, in reality Zamoro, makes his way into Alzira's apartments. The lovers vow eternal constancy, but are surprised by Gusmano, who condemns his rival to death, thus violating the peace treaty between the Spanish and the Peruvians. His father Alvaro, whose own life Zamoro had spared, begs for mercy, but Gusmano remains implacable. Only a revolt by Incas demanding the release of Zamoro forces him to give way. Spaniard and Peruvian swear to seek each other out on the battlefield and fight to the death.

Act II

Scene 1: Inside the fortifications of Lima. The Spanish soldiers are celebrating their victory over the Incas, and Zamoro and Alzira are in Gusmano's power once again. Zamoro is condemned to death. To save her lover's life, Alzira is now prepared to marry Gusmano.
Scene 2: A rocky cave. The Inca warrior Otumba brings news of Zamoro's release, but when the chieftain learns of the price to be paid for his freedom he vows to prevent Alzira's marriage.
Scene 3: A hall in the governor's palace. On his way to the altar with Alzira, Gusmano is overpowered and mortally wounded by a man in Spanish uniform. It is Zamoro. The dying Gusmano acknowledges his guilt, forgives his murderer, and unites Alzira and Zamoro.   *S. N.*

A little-known preliminary study

Alzira is perhaps the least known of all Verdi's operas. Its première in Naples was acclaimed, but subsequent productions in Italy were less successful, and eventually the piece disappeared from the operatic stage. "It is really bad," was Verdi's own later assessment of this youthful work, yet today the opera is thought to be not so bad after all. The background and setting are unusual, and for a full-blooded Italian opera the work's literary model is even less usual, since it is based on Voltaire's Enlightenment play of 1736, *Alzire, ou Les Américains* (*Alzira, or The Americans*), in which the author propounds his favorite ideas and gives his readers his skeptical view of the true nature of religion. It is the only drama of this kind that ever inspired Verdi to write an opera, although one of his major works, →*The Force of Destiny*, also features a conflict between heartless Christians and a noble savage (in that case a half-breed).

In the area of social customs and racial problems, *Alzira* may also be regarded as a preliminary study for →*Il trovatore*. As a social outsider, the Inca chieftain Zamoro is a variant of Manrico, and he too is temperamental to the point of frenzy, while the tyrannical Gusmano is a predecessor of Count di Luna, and Alzira is in a situation where she has to make a choice similar to Leonora's. It is worth noting that the librettos of both operas were by Salvatore Cammarano, for whom Verdi felt much greater respect than he did for his usual librettist, Piave. Since the 1970s, there have been several successful attempts to revive early operas by Verdi, and with its captivating and ardent music *Alzira* is also worth rediscovery.

Alzira, production photograph (Act II) with Giancarlo Pasquetto (right) as the dying Gusmano, production, sets, and costumes Luciano Damiani, conductor Maurizio Benini, Teatro Regio, Parma 1990/91 (Verdi Festival). A characteristic moment from the closing scene: the young Verdi pleads for the reconciliation of conquered and conquerors, as the Brazilian composer →Gomes had done decades earlier in *The Guarani*.

Attila

Dramma lirico in a prologue and three acts

Libretto: Temistocle Solera, after the tragedy *Attila, König der Hunnen* (*Attila, King of the Huns*) by Zacharias Werner.
Première: 17 March 1846, Venice (Teatro La Fenice).
Characters: Attila, King of the Huns (B), Ezio, a Roman general (Bar), Odabella, daughter of the lord of Aquileia (S), Foresto, a knight of Aquileia (T), Uldino, a young Breton, Attila's slave (T), Leone, an old Roman (B); princes, kings, soldiers, Huns, Gepids, Ostrogoths, Heruls, Thuringians, Quadi, Druids, priestesses, men and women of Aquileia, female warriors of Aquileia, Roman officers and soldiers, Roman maidens and children, hermits, slaves (chorus).
Setting: Aquileia, the Adriatic lagoons, and near Rome, in the middle of the 5th century.

Attila, Ruggero Raimondi as Attila, production Giulio Chazalettes, conductor Giuseppe Sinopoli, Wiener Staatsoper 1990.
"Libo a te, gran Wodano, che invoco" ("I drink to thee, great Wotan, whom I invoke"), the king of the Huns frequently adjures the god Wotan. Where did these references to Germanic mythology come from? In 437 the Romans entered into a military alliance with the Huns against the Burgundians, and although Attila took no part in the fighting himself, his name nonetheless entered Germanic legend, and he was immortalized under the name of Etzel in the *Nibelungenlied*. The story goes that Attila's castle lay on the Danube in present-day Hungary.

Synopsis

Attila, king of the Huns, conquers Aquileia, killing its lord, and intends to use it as a base for his attack on Rome. Odabella, daughter of the lord of Aquileia, impresses Attila with her courage and beauty, and he pays court to her. But the proud Italian woman intends to avenge her father's death. Odabella competes with the Roman general Ezio and her lover Foresto for the privilege of liberating her country from the conquering Hun. Like Judith in the Bible, she finally kills Attila.

Prologue

Scene 1: The main square of Aquileia. Attila and his men are celebrating their victory over the Aquileians. The leader of the captive female warriors of Aquileia, Odabella, makes a great impression on Attila. She is the daughter of the lord of Aquileia whom he has killed. The Roman general and imperial envoy Ezio approaches Attila, but the Hun rejects his suggestion that Attila may rule the rest of the Roman Empire if he will leave Italy in peace.
Scene 2: The Rio Alto in the Adriatic lagoons, where fugitives from Aquileia have settled. Their leader, Foresto, is anxious for the welfare of his beloved Odabella, now in Attila's power.

Act I

Scene 1: A wood near Attila's camp outside Rome, by night. Odabella has joined Attila's army to avenge her father and her lover, whom she believes dead. She has a chance meeting by night with Foresto, who accuses her of treachery. However, she convinces him that her intention is to follow the example of the Biblical heroine Judith and save her people.
Scene 2: Attila's tent. An old man in a dream warns Attila against continuing his campaign to conquer Rome.
Scene 3: Attila's camp. The Hun is not deterred, and summons his troops to march on the city. Then a procession comes toward him, and he recognizes its leader, Pope Leo, as the apparition from his dream. At the same time two figures with flaming swords appear in the sky. The Hun is terror-stricken.

Act II

Scene 1: Ezio's camp near Rome. The Emperor Valentinian wants a truce with Attila, and recalls his general Ezio. Ezio, however, does not obey, but puts his trust in Rome's former greatness and joins forces with Foresto, who is planning to assassinate Attila.
Scene 2: Attila's camp. The king of the Huns is holding a banquet to celebrate the truce. Odabella prevents Foresto's assassination attempt, since she wants to kill the Hun herself. She warns Attila that his goblet is poisoned, and claims the right to punish the guilty Foresto, thus saving him from Attila's wrath. Moved and grateful, the king of the Huns announces his betrothal to Odabella.

Act III

A wood near Attila's camp. Foresto and Ezio are preparing to attack Attila. Believing that Odabella has betrayed him, Foresto is full of indignation and jealousy. However, she has fled from Attila's camp, and assures Foresto of her innocence and constancy. Attila, searching for Odabella, falls into the ambush. Foresto is about to run him through, but Odabella stabs Attila first, thus freeing her people in the manner of the biblical Judith.   S. N.

The Gran Teatro La Fenice in Venice, lithograph by Giovanni Pividor, 1837 (Museo Correr, Venice).

Attila, Gaetano Franschini as Foresto, Venice 1846, portrait print.
The tenor part in this opera is less important than the bass and baritone roles (Attila and Ezio). However, the figure of Foresto was an essential component of an Italian libretto, which always contained a pair of lovers (in this case Foresto and Odabella). Foresto also plays an important part in the prologue, as leader of the fugitives from Aquileia. His cabaletta on the subject of his "beloved homeland" is related to the countless marches of the Italian Risorgimento. M 10

The historical Attila

The mighty king of the Huns was the most successful conqueror of the period of tribal emigrations. He and his army attacked Italy and destroyed Aquileia in the year 452. (The fleeing inhabitants of Aquileia founded the city of Venice among the lagoons.) In the same year, Pope Leo the Great persuaded Attila to withdraw. He died on his wedding night in 453, but the tale that he was murdered by his last wife, a Germanic woman called Hildico, is only a legend, and the assassination scene at the end of the opera is thus pure dramatic fiction.

The political message

Although Verdi had followed up his two popular operas →*Nabucco* and →*The Lombards* by setting librettos of a different nature – two dramas concentrating on the fate of individuals (→*Ernani*, →*The Two Foscari*), a legend with supernatural apparitions (*Joan of Arc*), and an Enlightenment piece based on Voltaire (*Alzira*) – he returned in this work to the idea of music drama with a political message. In subject, although not chronologically, *Attila* is a variation on the Risorgimento theme.

"Resti l'Italia a me!"

It is possible to reconstruct the way in which the Italian public of the time would have interpreted various aspects of the plot. The founding of Venice (the prologue) suggests that Italians have prior, God-given rights to their native land. Odabella compares herself to the biblical figure of Judith (Act I, Scene 1); thus, the Italians are chosen people, like the Hebrews of the Old Testament (→*Nabucco*). In Attila's dream, Pope Leo warns him not to touch the land of the gods (Act I, Scene 2); thus, God will punish the foreign power

oppressing the people. When the emperor Valentinian suggests a truce (Act II, Scene 1), Ezio objects: if the emperor himself is weak, Italy's ancient renown is lost. In the plan to assassinate Attila (Act II, Scene 2), the idea proposed by Ezio and Foresto is that if the tyrant is killed, Italy will be strong again. Attila must die (conclusion of Act III); freedom can be achieved only by (revolutionary) force.

Attila is full of patriotic statements of this sort, and for that very reason was an instant success on the operatic stages of Italy in the 1840s. At its second performance at the Teatro La Fenice, enthusiasm for the duet between Ezio and Attila in the prologue knew no bounds. No one minded the fact that the alliance proposed by the Roman general is in fact dishonorable, when the words he sang were "Avrai tu l'universo, resti l'Italia a me!" – "Let the universe belong to you, but let Italy remain mine!" The audiences in Venice, then under Habsburg rule, understood the true significance of these words. The phrase occurs in the closing line of the strophe, and is repeated 14 times in the final minute of the duet. This verbal suggestion had an enormous effect on the patriotic Venetians. M 9

9. Duet between Ezio and Attila

A - vrai tu l'u - ni - ver - so, resti l'I - ta - lia, re - sti l'I-ta-lia a me.

10. Foresto's Cabaletta

Ca - ra pa - tria, già ma - dre e re - i-na di pos sen - ti mag-na - ni-mi fi - gli

Macbeth

Melodramma in four acts

Libretto: Francesco Maria Piave, after the tragedy by William Shakespeare.
Première: 14 March 1847, Florence (Teatro della Pergola); revised version, in a French translation by Charles Nuitter and Alexandre Beaumont: 21 April 1865, Paris (Théâtre Lyrique).

Characters: Duncano/Duncan, King of Scotland (silent), Macbeth (Bar) and Banco/Banquo (B), generals in Duncan's army, Lady Macbeth, Macbeth's wife (S), Macduff, a Scottish nobleman, Thane of Fife (T), Malcolm, Duncan's son (T), Fleanzio/Fleance, Banquo's son (silent), Lady-in-Waiting to Lady Macbeth (Ms), A Doctor (B), A Servant of Macbeth (B), Sicario and Araldo, murderers (2 B), The Ghost of Banquo (silent), A Herald (B), Hecate, goddess of the night (silent); witches, bards, messengers of the king, English soldiers, Scottish nobles and exiles, aerial spirits, apparitions (chorus).
Setting: Scotland and the Anglo-Scottish border, in the middle of the 11th century.

Synopsis

Macbeth is King Duncan's favorite, and immensely valuable to him as a general. Witches predict that Macbeth himself will be king, but tell his companion Banquo that he will be the father of kings. Macbeth and his wife succumb to temptation, and since the throne is already occupied they murder Duncan, consolidating their criminal hold on power by further murders, including that of Banquo. An atmosphere of chilly isolation gathers around them. Lady Macbeth collapses under the weight of her guilty conscience, goes mad, and dies. Macbeth defies the vengeance of the children and children's children of his murdered subjects, since it has been prophesied that no man born of woman can kill him. He eventually falls victim to Macduff, whose whole family he has murdered, but who was not born of woman, having been cut from his mother's body at birth. Macbeth dies, and the crown passes to the descendants of the murdered Banquo.

Act I

Scene 1: A wood. After victory in battle, the Scottish generals Macbeth and Banquo encounter uncanny figures whom they take to be witches. The witches prophesy that Macbeth, now thane of Glamis, will also become thane of Cawdor, and finally king of Scotland. Banquo, on the other hand, is told that his descendants will be kings. The first part of the prophecy soon proves true: messengers from the king meet Macbeth and greet him as the new thane of Cawdor.
Scene 2: A room in Macbeth's castle. Lady Macbeth receives a letter from her husband telling her of the prophecy. When King Duncan spends the night in Macbeth's castle, husband and wife murder him to gain the throne.

Act II

Scene 1: A hall in Macbeth's castle. Macbeth can take no pleasure in his kingship, for the prophecy that Banquo's heirs will wear the crown weighs on his mind. He and his wife decide to kill Banquo and his son Fleance.
Scene 2: A grove, with Macbeth's castle in the distance. Hired murderers kill Banquo, but Fleance escapes.
Scene 3: A magnificent hall in Macbeth's castle. As the new king of Scotland, Macbeth and his lady are holding a banquet for the nobles of the kingdom.

Macbeth, production photograph with Dietrich Fischer-Dieskau (Macbeth) and Grace Bumbry (Lady Macbeth), production Oscar Fritz Schuh, sets and costumes Teo Otto, conductor Wolfgang Sawallisch, Salzburg Festival 1964.
In Shakespeare's play, Lady Macbeth is the catalyst of Macbeth's evil ambitions; in the operatic version she is the instigator of his crimes as well as a determined participant in them. Her brilliant dramatic soprano role is as important as the title role itself, and it is on this idea that her unusually active part in the drama was based even in Verdi's original conception. In the revision of 1865, Verdi replaced Lady Macbeth's second aria at the beginning of Act II with a new piece that gave the character even greater importance.

Verdi's first setting of a Shakespearean subject

The score of *Macbeth* contains many unusual features that break with convention. Verdi's efforts to do justice to his dramatic original led him along paths he had not taken before, as is obvious both in his formal innovations (with new formal structures embracing entire scenes) and in the musical language itself, with its daring and surprising harmonic changes, the discovery of new timbres, and the handling of keys. A dark underlying tone is characteristic of *Macbeth*. In this opera, Verdi disregarded the aesthetic doctrines of his time (now of course a thing of the past), which criticized the "misuse of minor keys" ("abuso dei minori").   *J. K.*

But the festivities are interrupted when Macbeth learns of Fleance's escape after the murder of Banquo. His guilty conscience shows him the ghost of Banquo, and he speaks to it, striking terror into his guests.

Act III

A dark cavern. Insecure, and alarmed by his own deeds, Macbeth returns to his point of departure and asks the witches for more information about his fate. They tell him that no man born of woman can kill him, and that he will reign until Birnam Wood marches against him, but they also warn him against one of his thanes, Macduff. When he asks about Banquo's descendants, they show him a whole gallery of future kings. Macbeth and his wife, who are childless, feel they have been cheated of their future, and have Macduff's entire family murdered, including the women and children.

Act IV

Scene 1: A desolate place on the border between Scotland and England. Macduff, mourning his family, and Malcolm, the son of the murdered Duncan, have raised an army against Macbeth.

Scene 2: A room in Macbeth's castle. Lady Macbeth's guilty conscience torments her, and she sleepwalks around the castle by night. She can find no peace, and dies of her inner torments.

Scene 3: A hall in the castle. Macbeth falls into a frenzy of rage on learning that Malcolm is marching against him with English aid, and receives the news of his wife's death with indifference.

Scene 4: A wide plain. Macbeth defies the avenging army of Macduff and Malcolm. But now Birnam Wood marches against him, for the enemy soldiers are carrying branches as camouflage. Macbeth is killed by Macduff, who was not born of woman but cut from his mother's body.   *S. N.*

Macbeth, set design by Hans Strobach for his own production, conductor Ernst Cremer, Städtische Bühnen, Cologne 1931.
One of the strangest scenes in all opera: a king and his retinue enter his subject's castle without singing or even speaking a word – they are walk-on parts. The idea that King Duncan will be murdered in this castle is conveyed in silence. A leisurely march accompanies his entry. Verdi specified in the score, "musica villereccia" ("rustic music").

No big tenor part and no love interest

At the première both critics and audience criticized the opera for the absence of a leading tenor role and any love conflict, both of which were expected of the genre at the time. An "opera senz' amore" was not entirely unheard of, but was a great rarity on the nineteenth-century Italian stage. Verdi had boldly ignored tradition by placing not a love story but a study of the psychology of power at the center of this work.

Visions, mental disturbances, and ghosts

The various scenes involving apparitions are among the most exciting and for their time the most modern pages of scoring in operatic history. In itself, Macbeth's monologue before the murder of the king is simply a *recitativo accompagnato* (orchestrally accompanied recitative), a *scena* with extensive *arioso* passages, but this is not a recitative in the usual pattern. It differs from traditional recitative in its unusual length, and in the sensitivity with which the musical formulae accompanying the text reflect every idea and every nuance of mood. A comparison of the libretto with Shakespeare's original (Act II, Scene 1) makes clear the extent to which the authors were faithful to the text: expressions, imagery, and even entire phrases come straight from Shakespeare's play. M 11

The construction of Lady Macbeth's tormented sleepwalking scene in Act IV demanded a new approach from the composer. Neither the form of a conventional aria nor pure recitative would have been adequate. Something between the two had to be found: a freely unfolding *arioso* set within an almost symmetrical framework. Attention is drawn to the special significance of this scene by an extensive orchestral introduction and conclusion. Here Verdi established one of the most important of musical building blocks, a characteristic melody, and it is no chance that the same melody is prominent in the overture, where it points symbolically to guilt and the expiation of guilt. Again, the situation itself is taken almost literally from Shakespeare (Act V, Scene 1), with the doctor and the lady-in-waiting acting as involuntary witnesses of Lady Macbeth's unconscious revelation of her own guilt, and then of her tragic collapse. M 12

The witches

The chorus of witches also belongs to the visionary aspect of the piece. Verdi wrote it for a three-part chorus of women's voices (originally the composer wanted 18 voices, six for each vocal register). Verdi regarded the witches as the "third main role" in his opera, after Macbeth and Lady Macbeth. Even in the original version, the ensemble offered a unique mixture of shrill and grotesque vocal colors. In representing the world of spirits, Verdi – a contemporary of →Berlioz and Liszt – tried to emphasize the demonic dimensions of the music. M 13

Macbeth, set design by Paul Haferung for the Reichs-Gau-Theater, Posen 1944 (TWS). In Verdi's opera the witches are not so much evil beings as elemental spirits; theirs is a world without emotions. Among themselves they are playful and merry. They do not influence the course of the action, but only foretell what the future holds. The concepts of past, present, and future do not exist for them; they live in an eternal time, without beginning or end, and therefore know everything.

The people

The common people hardly feature at all in Shakespeare's play, but in the decade of the Risorgimento Verdi felt it both an internal and an external necessity to include at least one major choral scene in his version of the story. He brought the chorus in at the beginning of Act IV. The enormous success of the choruses in →*Nabucco* and →*The Lombards* may also have induced him to include a chorus that, once again, laments the loss of the exiles' native land in song. The revised version of 1865, however, replaces the 1847 chorus with a different one, leaving the patriotic references of the 1840s behind. The 1865 chorus is concerned with human suffering in a more general sense. This is the language of Verdi's great later works. M 14, M 15 *J. K.*

Macbeth, photograph from the production by Ruth Berghaus, sets Erich Wonder, Württembergisches Staatstheater, Stuttgart 1995.
Shakespeare was a revelation to opera, particularly Italian opera. As early as the 1840s, Verdi was planning to set *Hamlet* and *The Tempest*. For several decades, he also entertained an idea for an opera based on *King Lear*. Around 1850 he even told his French publisher Escudier that he intended to compose operas based on all Shakespeare's major dramas. In the event, he wrote three such operas: *Macbeth*, →*Otello*, and →*Falstaff*, the two last at the very end of his career, while *Macbeth* was composed when he was 33.

11. Macbeth's Monologue

Sulla me-tà del mondo or morta è la na-tu-ra

12. Lady Macbeth's Mad Scene

U-na macchia ...

13. Witches' Dance

14. Exiles' Chorus (1847)

Pa-tria oppres-sa! il dol-ce no-me no, di ma-dre aver non puo-i,

15. Exiles' Chorus (1865)

D'or-fa-nel-li e di pian-gen-ti chi lo spo-so e chi la pro-le

Shakespeare and Schiller, the twin stars in Verdi's literary firmament, in a 19th-century allegorical print.

The Bandits

I masnadieri

Melodramma tragico in four parts

Libretto: Andrea Maffei, after Friedrich von Schiller's play *Die Räuber* (*The Bandits*).
Première: 22 July 1847, London (Her Majesty's Theater).

Characters: Massimiliano, Count Moor (B), Carlo, his son (T), Francesco, Carlo's brother (B), Amalia, an orphan, the count's niece (S), Arminio, the count's treasurer (T), Moser, a pastor (B), Rolla, Carlo's companion (T); bandits, women, boys, servants (chorus).

Setting: Bohemia and Franconia, in the first half of the 18th century.

Synopsis

The intrigues of his jealous brother Francesco have caused Carlo to break with his father Massimiliano and seek his fortune with the bandits. Life among these outcasts from society also disappoints him, but Francesco uses forged letters and misleading news to prevent any reconciliation between Carlo and Massimiliano. He leads Massimiliano and Amalia, whom Carlo loves, to believe that Carlo is dead, and that on his deathbed he expressed his wish that Amalia should marry Francesco. Amalia flees into the Bohemian forests to escape this marriage. Francesco has his father thrown into a dungeon and usurps the inheritance. When Carlo at last sees through his brother's intrigues it is too late: his father has gone mad and is mortally sick, and he has bound himself to the bandits with an oath of loyalty. To save Amalia a life of disgrace he kills her, and then sets out in search of death himself. *S. N.*

Schiller's *Die Räuber* (*The Robbers*) on the Italian operatic stage
Andrea Maffei provided Verdi with the libretto for *The Bandits*. Maffei was a famous poet, the translator of Shakespeare and Schiller into Italian, and the husband of Countess Clara Maffei, a woman who assumed great importance in Verdi's life. Patriotically minded artists and politicians attended the Maffei salon. It was here that Verdi met the most distinguished Italian writer of the time, Alessandro Manzoni. Verdi himself conducted the première of the opera in London, and received tumultuous applause, to a great extent due to the fact that the celebrated prima donna Jenny Lind sang the part of Amalia. However, the opera was not so successful on the continent of Europe. Interestingly, the youthful verve of Schiller's play and its strong vein of social criticism were lost in the operatic version. Intended as it was for Jenny Lind, the part of Amalia is the most difficult to sing, followed by the broadly characterized figure of Carlo's wicked brother Francesco.

Wanted men
The plot of *The Corsair* is remarkably similar to that of *The Bandits*. Corrado and Carlo have both turned to a life of crime after suffering injustice. The two operas are also linked in being based on literary originals by poets who subscribed to the ideals of Romanticism. Originally *The Corsair* had been intended for performance in England (hence the subject from Byron) rather than *The Bandits*, but Verdi found *The Bandits* more interesting, and consequently finished it first.

The Corsair, production photograph with Eduard Tumagian as Seid, production Hans Neugebauer, sets and costumes Hans Brosch, conductor Michelangelo Veltri, Theater im Pfalzbau, Ludwigshafen 1993.
In the 18th century *The Corsair* would have been a typical "Turkish opera," and it does resemble *The Abduction from the Seraglio*, but with a tragic ending. Both the Pasha and Corrado the corsair must die.

The Corsair

Il corsaro

Melodramma tragico in three acts

Libretto: Francesco Maria Piave, after Lord Byron's poem *The Corsair*.
Première: 25 October 1848, Trieste (Teatro Grande).

Characters: Corrado, captain of the corsairs (T), Medora, his beloved (Ms), Seid, Pasha of Coron (Bar), Gulnara, his favorite slave girl (S), Selimo, an Aga (T), Giovanni, a corsair (B), Anselmo, a corsair (silent), A Black Eunuch (T), A Slave (T); corsairs, guards, Turks, slaves, odalisques, Medora's maids (chorus).

Setting: An island in the Aegean and the city of Coron in the Peloponnese, in the early 19th century.

Synopsis

The corsairs enjoy their life of liberty, but their leader Corrado feels a dark fate hanging over him; he can never return to a happy and honorable life. He leads his men on their piratical expeditions with fervent nationalist feeling. During an attack on Pasha Seid of Coron, he is overcome by pity for the slave girls burning to death in the harem and saves their lives. When he is taken prisoner himself he is condemned to death, despite the pleas of the girls he saved. Gulnara, the Pasha's favorite slave, frees Corrado, whom she loves, and stabs the hated and tyrannical Pasha. However, Corrado is faithful to his beloved Medora, who has taken poison on seeing the corsairs return from their Turkish adventure without Corrado. Tired of life, the corsair captain throws himself into the sea. *S. N.*

The Battle of Legnano, photograph from the production by Nicola Benois, Teatro alla Scala, Milan 1961–62.

"There is not, there hardly can be, any music that delights the Italian ear in 1848 other than the music of cannon!" wrote Verdi enthusiastically in a letter to Piave on 21 April 1848. He stayed in Italy to compose the revolutionary battle hymn, and then went to Paris and began work on *The Battle of Legnano*. This last Risorgimento opera has many new features, including the great prayer scene in Act IV, where Verdi combines several musical and dramatic elements into a structure of remarkable complexity: a wide-arching soprano melody (Lida), the chorus on stage (the crowd), and a chorus singing in unison off stage (the Knights of Death).

Operas written out of duty
The Bandits, *The Corsair*, and *The Battle of Legnano* were written at the end of Verdi's "galley years" ("anni di galera"), as the composer himself described his creative period between 1844 and 1850. Verdi was exhausted by the stress of composing without a break, and although he also explored new directions in some of his operas of the late 1840s, these three works are rather conventional in style.

The Battle of Legnano

La battaglia di Legnano

Tragedia lirica in four acts

Libretto: Salvatore Cammarano, after the play *La bataille de Toulouse* (*The Battle of Toulouse*) by François-Joseph Méry.
Première: 27 January 1849, Rome (Teatro Argentina).
Characters: Federico Barbarossa, the German emperor (B), First Consul of Milan (B), Second Consul of Milan (B), Mayor of Como (B), Rolando, a Milanese leader (Bar), Lida, his wife (S), Arrigo, a Veronese soldier (T), Marcovaldo, a German prisoner (Bar), Imelda, Lida's maid (Ms), A Herald (T), Arrigo's Squire (T); the Knights of Death, magistrates and leaders of the people of Como, Lida's maids, people of Milan, senators of Milan, soldiers from Verona, Novara, Piacenza, and Milan, German army (chorus).

Setting: Milan and Como in 1176.

Synopsis

Soldiers and citizens are assembling in Milan to fight for the unity of Italy against the German army under Frederick Barbarossa. Rolando of Milan meets a friend whom he had thought dead, Arrigo of Verona. Despite private tensions – Lida, once loved by Arrigo, is now Rolando's wife – the two are political allies and go to Como together to ask for help for Milan. Since he cannot now enjoy private happiness, Arrigo joins the Knights of Death, a secret society fighting for the unification of Italy under the motto, "Victory or Death." The Lombards finally defeat the German emperor, but Arrigo is mortally wounded, and dies reconciled to Rolando and Lida.

S. N.

A political pamphlet set to music
The Battle of Legnano is a very different kind of work from *The Bandits* and *The Corsair*. It represents Verdi's contribution to Italy's struggles for freedom. At the time of its première the political situation in Rome was so tense that in the middle of January 1849 the pope fled to Gaeta, and from there appealed to foreign powers for help. In this desperate yet not entirely hopeless atmosphere, Verdi's last Risorgimento opera was enthusiastically applauded at its première. The "giuramento" chorus at the beginning of Act I was perfectly suited to the audience's expectations. The subject of the opera was the victory of the Italians, and 12 days after its première, Garibaldi proclaimed the short-lived Roman Republic.

Luisa Miller

Melodramma tragico in three acts

Libretto: Salvatore Cammarano, after Friedrich von Schiller's tragedy *Kabale und Liebe* (*Cabal and Love*).
Première: 8 December 1849, Naples (Teatro S. Carlo).

Characters: Count Walter (B), Rodolfo, his son (T), Federica, Duchess of Ostheim, Walter's niece (A), Wurm, the count's steward (B), Miller, a retired old soldier (Bar), Luisa, his daughter (S), Laura, a peasant girl (Ms), A Peasant (T); Federica's ladies-in-waiting, pages, servants, archers, villagers (chorus).

Setting: The Tyrol, in the first half of the 17th century.

Synopsis

A father obsessed by rank and ambition and his intriguing subordinate try to separate two lovers. Count Walter and his steward Wurm persuade the village maiden Luisa to renounce Rodolfo, whom she loves. The villains of the piece eventually win the day: the count's son, driven to distraction, kills both his beloved Luisa and himself. The lovers feel that they are happily reunited in death. Rodolfo takes Wurm to the grave with him, and leaves his father without an heir.

Act I: "Love"

Scene 1: Outside Miller's house in a pretty village. It is Luisa's birthday, and Rodolfo, who has fallen in love with her, is among the friends who have come to offer good wishes. The castle steward Wurm is a suitor for Luisa's hand, but she does not return his feelings. To eliminate competition, Wurm tells old Miller of Rodolfo's true identity as the son of Count Walter.

Scene 2: A hall in Walter's castle. Wurm has revealed Rodolfo's love affair to the count, who wishes to prevent such a mésalliance and orders his son's marriage to the Duchess of Ostheim, a friend from Rodolfo's childhood. Rodolfo confides his love for Luisa to Federica, but his revelations only arouse her jealousy.

Luisa Miller, production photograph with Daniela Dessì as Luisa, production Daniele Abbado, sets Dante Ferretti, conductor Bruno Bartoletti, Opernhaus Zürich 1999.
In Luisa, Verdi created a female character that would have many successors in his later operas. She is isolated, delivered up to a masculine or male-dominated society, and is the victim of intrigue. In this sense she directly anticipates Gilda in →*Rigoletto*.

Scene 3: Miller's house. Old Miller informs his daughter of Rodolfo's true rank and his approaching marriage. But Rodolfo himself assures Luisa of his love, and they both beg Miller to let them marry. The count, spying on his son, flies into a rage and says he will have Miller and his daughter arrested. Rodolfo then threatens to reveal the sinister machinations that made Walter a count.

Act II: "The Intrigue"
Scene 1: Miller's house. The count has had old Miller thrown into prison. Wurm claims to know a way to save him: on condition of preserving total silence, Luisa must write a letter confessing that she loves him, Wurm, and not Rodolfo. In desperation, she agrees.
Scene 2: A room in Walter's castle. The count is anxious because Rodolfo knows that, with Wurm's assistance, he committed murder to gain his title. The secret can be kept only if Rodolfo gives up Luisa voluntarily. Consequently, Luisa must repeat to the Duchess of Ostheim the declaration of love for Wurm that she has been forced to make.

Scene 3: The castle gardens. Wurm has shown Rodolfo Luisa's letter. In despair, he challenges Wurm to a duel, but Wurm avoids fighting. Walter, pretending paternal concern, says he will allow his son to marry Luisa, but when Rodolfo tells him of Luisa's supposed betrayal, the count advises him to marry the Duchess in an act of revenge of his own.

Act III: "The Poison"
Miller's house. Luisa wants to write Rodolfo a letter confessing that she was blackmailed, but Miller, just released from prison, fears for his liberty. Father and daughter decide to leave the village. While Luisa is deep in a farewell prayer, Rodolfo enters the room unobserved and pours poison into a cup from which he and she both drink. As death approaches, Luisa admits the truth, and the lovers die reconciled. With the last of his strength, Rodolfo stabs the false Wurm. Two fathers are left bereft of their children. *s. n.*

A bourgeois tragedy

This was the subtitle of Schiller's play *Kabale und Liebe* (*Cabal and Love*). Did Verdi turn it into a "bourgeois opera" to compare with the bourgeois setting of →*Stiffelio* (1850) and →*La traviata* (1853)? *Luisa Miller* is bourgeois only in so far as it clearly represents an incursion into the sphere of bourgeois private life. The opera, like the play, presents a tale of individual characters, not a historical and political drama. It introduced many new colors into Verdi's range of dramatic expression, although the operatic adaptation differs in some respects from Schiller's play, which strikes a seditious note. The reasons may be found in the caution felt by both the composer and his librettist, Salvatore Cammarano, in view of the political climate in the kingdom of Naples where the opera was to have its première, as well as in the traditional nature of Verdi's techniques of composition up to this point.

The story of the opera unfolds in a pastoral village setting which has much in common with that of such idyllically sentimental earlier operas as Bellini's →*La sonnambula* and Donizetti's *Linda di Chamounix*. It then describes an intrigue presenting the main features of the action in Schiller's play, but in a rather simplified form. The plot is reduced to the machinations of a local potentate and his accomplice, bound together by a dark deed committed in the past when the count gained his inheritance through a secret act of murder. Yet even in this simplified form, which does not reflect the original, the opera has a certain bourgeois intimacy about it, anticipating the emotional atmosphere of an opera Verdi was soon to write, →*La traviata*. Many critics have thought they detect a connection between the two works, and they are not entirely wrong. A new kind of intimacy does indeed make its appearance here:

the musical characterization of Luisa, the young heroine destined to suffer, creates an expressive effect that was new to Verdi's work. *Luisa Miller* anticipated new perspectives in his depiction of human character. *J. K.*

Above
Luisa Miller, production photograph with Mario Zanessi as Miller, production Margherita Wallmann, sets Attilio Rossi, Teatro alla Scala, Milan 1968.
Miller with the letter that causes the tragedy. In its time Schiller's *Cabal and Love* was a contemporary social drama criticizing the dramatist's own age (and it was the only play of the kind he wrote, among a series of historical works). The opera of Verdi and Cammarano does not entirely reflect the original. The action is moved back to the 17th century, and the scene is changed to a Tyrolean village. Thus the brooding and poisonous atmosphere of a petty principality and the up-to-date social relevance of Schiller's play are eliminated from the opera as a whole.

Luisa Miller, production photograph with Carlos Chausson as Wurm, production Daniele Abbado, conductor Bruno Bartoletti, Opernhaus Zürich 1999.
Wurm is the villain of the piece. He does have some motivation for his intrigues, since he would like to marry Luisa himself, but he acts chiefly out of the sheer love of destructiveness. Of all operatic composers, no one depicted evil as openly and terrifyingly as the two great Romantics Verdi and →Wagner.

Luisa Miller, production photograph with Daniela Dessì as Luisa, production Daniele Abbado, sets Dante Ferretti, Opernhaus Zürich 1999.
Luisa is Verdi's first portrait of a modern woman. It had not previously been usual to show a bourgeois setting on stage. Luisa is so fundamentally ordinary that only extreme events can raise her to the status of a tragic heroine. Her great moment comes in the last act of the opera.

Right
Luisa Miller, production photograph with Lázló Polgár (Count Walter) and Carlos Chausson (Wurm, right), production Daniele Abbado, conductor Bruno Bartoletti, Opernhaus Zürich 1999.
A dialogue between two deep male voices; this situation produces a unique musical and dramatic effect in the encounters between such adversaries as Boccanegra and Fiesco (→Simon Boccanegra), and King Philip and the Grand Inquisitor (→Don Carlos). It makes its first strong dramatic appearance in the meeting between the count and Wurm in Luisa Miller. The two men hate each other, but are bound together by a shared crime.

An overture in the *Freischütz* manner

It may be no coincidence that Verdi's *Luisa Miller* begins with an overture strikingly similar to Weber's overture for →*Der Freischütz*, both in the choice of key (C minor/C major), in style, and now and then in thematic material. The similarity may be the result of the ideas Verdi vaguely associated with "German" dramatic material. In any case, the symphonic generosity of his model in *Der Freischütz* obviously had an encouraging and exemplary effect on Verdi's composition: the overture to *Luisa Miller* was one of his most interesting and successful creations. It is a sonata form Allegro of strict construction, unified in its thematic material and monothematically constructed – evidence of Verdi's thoroughness in his "classical" studies. It may not be among his best-known and most popular overtures (such as those of →*The Sicilian Vespers* and →*The Force of Destiny*), but it is certainly one of his best, and is an early masterpiece, not just in form: its gravity of tone leads unmistakably into the emotional world of tragedy. M 16

The figure of evil

In Act II, the villainous characters of the drama are to the fore: Wurm blackmailing Luisa to write her letter, and Count Walter in his dialogue with Wurm in the following scene. This duet, between two deep bass voices, is a fearful confession, overshadowed by anxiety, of the crimes they committed together in the past, and bears impressive witness to Verdi's skill in characterization. M 17

In the hierarchy of the singers, the count ought to take the dominant role, but Wurm is more interesting as a dramatic character and a model for various other figures in Verdi's later operas. He is the prototype of many arch-villains in Verdi's portrait gallery, for instance Paolo Albiani in →*Simon Boccanegra* and Iago in →*Otello*. Wurm is the perpetrator of wicked deeds, and the power behind the entire mechanism of the intrigue. Is it coincidence that in his musical characterization of this figure Verdi instinctively turned to the same means of expression as he did three and a half decades later with Iago, a diabolical unison trill? It can already be heard here, as Wurm dictates the letter. M 18, M 19

Death and transfiguration

The portrait of the heroine unfolds in its full significance and complexity in Act III, where Verdi's musical description of Luisa most closely approaches the characterization and atmosphere of the great works to come in the 1850s. The instrumental introduction to Act III, in which themes quoted from the overture alternate with motifs from the love duet in the first scene, looks forward to →*La traviata*, where the prelude to Act III also returns to material from the introduction. (As in *La traviata*, again, the musical idea seems to have its source in the overture and not the other way around, as in the so-called potpourri type of overture.) The real highlights of this act are not the situations of high drama in the plot – the agitated passages of recitative between Rodolfo and Luisa

leading to the finale of the drama, and their last despairing duet, which remains within the bounds of convention – but the preceding scenes: the act's opening moments, with its mood of touching sadness (Luisa and her women friends), and the scene that follows between old Miller and his daughter. Luisa's yearning for death, "La tomba è un letto, sparso di fiori" ("Death is a bed strewn with flowers") is a *valse triste* expressing a sense of transfiguration and resignation in the face of death worthy of the atmosphere of the last act of *La traviata*. M 20 In both content and musical form, the duet of father and daughter resembles the duet between Rigoletto and Gilda from Act II of →*Rigoletto*. (Their joint decision to leave the village that has now become a vale of woe also looks forward to *Rigoletto*.) And the sublimity of the opera's conclusion in the final trio introduces audiences to the composer of *The Force of Destiny*. M 21

J. K.

Luisa Miller, production photograph with Juan Pons (Miller) and Daniela Dessì (Luisa), production Daniele Abbado, sets Dante Ferretti, conductor Bruno Bartoletti, Opernhaus Zürich 1999.
Father and daughter: a recurrent situation in Verdi's dramatic oeuvre. It is interesting to note that the theme of an aging man's paternal love for his daughter or another young woman is also prominent in the work of →Wagner (examples include Wotan and Brünnhilde, Hans Sachs and Eva, and King Mark and Isolde, all three cases combining a deep male voice with a soprano). The same pairing of voices had occurred earlier with Sarastro and Pamina in →*The Magic Flute*.

16. Main Theme of the Overture

17. Duet between Walter and Wurm

L'alto re - tag - gio non ho bra-ma - to di mio cu - gi - no, che sol per es - so!

18. Motif of Evil (Wurm)

19. Motif of Evil (Lago in *Otello*)

20. Luisa's Longing for Death

La tomba è un let - to spar - so di fio - ri, in cui del giu - sto la spo - glia dor - me

21. Final Trio (Luisa, Rodolfo, and Miller)

Mi be - ne - di - ci... o pa - dre mi - o... mi be - ne - di - ci...

Who was Stiffelio?

Apparently there were two real people called Stiffelius (or originally Stiffel), both of them Protestant pastors. One lived in the 16th century and was an adherent of Martin Luther, while the other lived in the early 19th century. Both are said to have preached somewhere in Austria, and to have been forced to emigrate to Saxony after persecution. The French authors of the play on which the opera is based moved the scene of the action to Salzburg, still regarded in the early 19th century as a city of religious prejudice and particularly intolerant of Protestantism. Souvestre and Bourgeois drew on both historical figures for the hero of their drama, although they really borrowed little more from history than his name. The plot of the play itself is pure invention by the authors.

Stiffelio, production photograph with Mara Zampieri (Lina), José Carreras (Stiffelio), and Peter Jelosits (Federico), Wiener Staatsoper 1996.
The moment of greatest tension in Act I: Stiffelio hands the fateful book (Klopstock's *Messiah*) to his wife to prove her innocence.

Stiffelio

Dramma lirico in three acts

Libretto: Francesco Maria Piave, after the play *Le pasteur, ou L'évangile et le foyer* (*The Pastor, or The Gospel and the Home*) by Émile Souvestre and Eugène Bourgeois.

Première: 16 November 1850, Trieste (Teatro Grande).

Characters: Stiffelio, an Ahasuerian pastor (T), Lina, his wife (S), Stankar, an old colonel and count of the Empire, Lina's father (Bar), Raffaele von Leuthold, a nobleman (T), Jorg, an old pastor (B), Federico von Frengel, Lina's cousin (T), Dorotea, Lina's cousin (Ms); friends of the count, Ahasuerians (chorus).

Setting: Austria, near the river Salzbach, in the early 19th century.

Later versions:

Guglielmo Wellingrode

A revision by the impresario Mario Lamari for performances in 1851 in Rome (Teatro Apollo) and Florence (Teatro della Pergola). In this version the title figure became a 15th-century statesman.

Aroldo

Première: 16 August 1857, Rimini (Teatro Nuovo). Another adaptation. This time the title role was an English crusader of the 13th century.

Synopsis

Act I

Scene 1: A hall in Count Stankar's castle. The pastor Stiffelio comes home after an absence and tells the company a story: a ferryman gave him a wallet of papers that a man had lost when jumping out of the window after an amorous assignation. Demonstrating his exemplary religious virtue, Stiffelio casts the cloak of Christian charity over the incident and destroys the evidence of wrongdoing. He does not know that it would have revealed his own wife Lina's adultery. Only her father Stankar is suspicious. When he notices Raffaele trying to convey a message to Lina by placing a note in a book, Stankar knows he is right, and urges Lina to keep silent to preserve the family honor.

Scene 2: A reception hall in the castle. The pastor Jorg has also observed the incident of the note in the book, but connects it with Lina's cousin Federico. Stankar gets hold of the paper himself.

Act II

The graveyard of an old church. In despair, Lina has sought refuge by her mother's tomb. Even there, Raffaele pays ardent court to her, but she rejects him, saying that she gave way to him only in a brief moment of weakness. Her father Stankar challenges Raffaele to a duel. The unsuspecting Stiffelio tries to reconcile them in the name of God, but now learns of his wife's adultery, and is prey to conflicting emotions, torn between intense jealousy and the Christian virtue of forgiveness he feels bound to show.

Act III

Scene 1: An anteroom in the castle. Stankar learns that Raffaele intends to elope with Lina. Stiffelio confronts Lina, forcing Raffaele to overhear their conversation unobserved. When the pastor places a document of divorce before his wife, she asks to confess to him as a priest, if he will no longer listen to her as her husband. In her confession, she tells him that she was weak only for a moment, and that her whole heart is still her husband's. Meanwhile, Stankar, mistaking the situation and anxious only to save the family honor, has killed the listening Raffaele.

Scene 2: In church. Despite his distress, Stiffelio still has to minister to the congregation as their pastor. He opens the Bible at random, and is confronted by the story of the woman taken in adultery. Taking it as the text for his sermon, he brings himself to a personal act of forgiveness; he takes back his wife Lina, practising true Christian love of his neighbor in spite of the blow he has suffered.

S. N.

Religion and realism

Verdi thought the subject of *Stiffelio* "good and interesting." It had a modern plot set against a contemporary background, with a moral conflict at its heart, very much in line with the realistic trends in French literature of the time. The play by Émile Souvestre and Eugène Bourgeois, which had its première in Paris in February 1849, dealt with a crisis in the marriage of a Protestant pastor facing a dilemma of conscience: will he avenge himself on his wife's seducer for her adultery and reject her, or will he exercise the forgiveness enjoined on him by his religious office? This was a delicate subject for Catholic Italy in the nineteenth century, where the figure of an Evangelical pastor who was leader of a sect – and a married priest at that – was bound to seem alien, and where the idea of ending a marriage by divorce was scarcely imaginable, if not actually offensive. (This point caused Verdi a good deal of difficulty with the Austro-Italian censorship in Trieste.)

A major score

In this opera Verdi's techniques of composition and sophisticated musical language have already reached the level of the great works to come. In many passages his expressive means are those of the later works, although he was not yet in command of an entirely unified style. Verdi's masterly handling of the ensembles and choruses in this opera has often, and rightly, been emphasized (they include the septet of the introductory scene and the first finale, the quartet in the second finale, and the impressive choral scene of the conclusion). The solo vocal writing also looks to the future. The plain, unornamented line of the leading tenor role made a contemporary critic comment that Verdi's composition had moved far from the bel canto ideal here, so that song could hardly be distinguished from prose. This development announces the advent of the new, smooth, unforced, and purposeful style that was to be the melodic style of the mature Verdi. Another striking feature is the way in which many depictions of atmosphere in *Stiffelio* anticipate certain situations in later masterpieces. The orchestral introduction to Act II, for instance, and the following nocturnal graveyard scene, in which the heroine is tormented by her conscience, are like an early equivalent of Amelia's solo scene at the beginning of Act II of →*A Masked Ball.* M 22   J. K.

Stiffelio, production photograph with José Carreras as Stiffelio, production Elijah Moshinsky, sets Michael Yeargan, conductor Fabio Luisi, Wiener Staatsoper 1996.
Stiffelio is a noble tenor role perfect for the star tenor José Carreras, and is a new type of character, exceptional even among Verdi's tenor heroes. Stiffelio sings in the register of his passionate fellow tenors, but in general is as meditative as a mature bass in a priestly role. The Vienna State Opera production of 1996 rediscovered this Verdi opera for the stage. The director Elijah Moshinsky moved the scene of the action to America in the colonial period.

22.1 Graveyard Scene (Orchestral Introduction, *Stiffelio*)

(Oboe)

22.2 Scene at the Place of Execution (Orchestral Introduction, *A Masked Ball*)

(Cor Anglais)

Rigoletto

Melodramma in three acts

Libretto: Francesco Maria Piave, after Victor Hugo's play *Le roi s'amuse* (*The King's Amusement*).
Première: 11 March 1851, Venice (Teatro La Fenice).

Characters: The Duke of Mantua (T), Rigoletto, his court jester (Bar), Gilda, Rigoletto's daughter (S), Sparafucile, a hired assassin (B), Maddalena, his sister (A), Giovanna, Gilda's confidante (Ms), Count Monterone (B), Marullo, a nobleman (Bar), Matteo Borsa, a courtier (T), Count Ceprano (B), Countess Ceprano (Ms), Court Usher (T), Page (Ms); courtiers, ladies, pages, halberdiers (chorus).

Setting: Mantua and its surroundings in the 16th century.

Synopsis

The duke of Mantua, an absolutist ruler, seduces and dishonors women as he pleases, disposing more or less legally of their husbands or fathers. His court jester is his accomplice and henchman, but believes he can keep his own private life free of taint. As a jester Rigoletto is on equal terms with his master, and mocks the victims of the duke's overbearing conduct. He has a daughter brought up in secret, to whom he shows loving care. But the treatment Rigoletto has meted out to others turns against him. Without knowing it, he acts as an accomplice in the abduction of his own daughter, and finally shares in the guilt for her death. Rigoletto had feared the curse on him uttered by Count Monterone, whom he mocked, but his fate is merely the consequence of his own actions.

Before the opera begins

The duke of Mantua and his hunchbacked court jester Rigoletto have abducted Count Monterone's daughter, and the unfortunate woman has committed suicide.

Act I

Scene 1: A hall in the ducal palace. The duke is boasting of a new adventure: he has seen an unknown young girl, has approached her disguised as an ordinary citizen, and intends to seduce her. Meanwhile, however, his roving eye has fixed upon Countess Ceprano, and he is making unwelcome advances to her even in front of her husband. Rigoletto mocks the couple, helpless in the face of the duke's whims. Almost all the courtiers have already been humiliated by Rigoletto's derision, and when Marullo spreads a rumor to the effect that Rigoletto keeps a mistress in secret, they plan to repay the jester for the disgrace they have suffered at his hands. When Rigoletto mocks the unfortunate Count Monterone, the count curses him.

Scene 2: A blind alley, with Rigoletto's house and garden on one side of the street, and Count Ceprano's palace on the other. Rigoletto has been deeply disturbed by Monterone's curse. A stranger accosts him in the street: it is Sparafucile, a hired assassin, offering his services. Rigoletto notes his name and address. Then he looks for his daughter Gilda, who has grown up shielded from the outside world, knowing nothing of her father's name and profession. In turn, she has not told him that she is in love with an unknown young man whom she has been meeting for months. This man is really the duke, who has told Gilda that he is a student. The courtiers plan to abduct the girl they believe to be Rigoletto's mistress, but Rigoletto comes home unexpectedly, and the courtiers pretend to be plotting the abduction of Countess Ceprano instead. Rigoletto joins in this sinister project, and discovers only too late that he has involuntarily helped them to carry off his own daughter.

Act II

A hall in the ducal palace. The courtiers, believing that Gilda is Rigoletto's mistress, take her to the duke. The court jester has followed his daughter's trail and finds her in the lion's den. The courtiers enjoy the sight of Rigoletto's desperation. He tells his daughter the true identity and nature of the man paying court to her, but it makes no difference to Gilda's feelings: she loves him whether he is a student or a duke. Rigoletto swears to be revenged on the seducer.

Act III

On the banks of the river Mincio; Sparafucile's house. Rigoletto has hired Sparafucile to murder the duke. First, however, he means to cure Gilda of her infatuation by showing proof of the duke's inconstancy. He makes her watch as Sparafucile's accomplice, his beautiful sister Maddalena, flirts with the duke and finally falls victim to his seductive charms herself. Rigoletto tells the confused and despairing Gilda to go to Verona in man's clothing. But Gilda returns to the tavern, and learns of her father's plan to have her lover murdered. Maddalena pleads with her brother to spare the duke and kill the first stranger to come to their door instead. Gilda sacrifices herself by entering the house to meet the deadly blow. Sparafucile hands Rigoletto a sack, which is supposed to contain the corpse of the duke. But then the triumphant Rigoletto hears the voice of the duke in the distance. Opening the sack, he finds his dying daughter. *S. N.*

Rigoletto, production photograph with Catriona Smith (Gilda) and Philip Ens (Sparafucile), production Johannes Schaaf, sets Alexander Lintl, conductor Jun Märkl, Württembergisches Staatstheater, Stuttgart 1994.
Gilda and the assassin Sparafucile. A nocturnal dialogue between two people unknown to each other, and hesitant. The singing voices do not sound together at any point, and the conversation unfolds above an instrumental melody. The orchestration is dark, with no violins at all. Violas, clarinets, and bassoons provide the ominous tone, and the cello and double bass take over the melodic line.

Difficulties over censorship

Rigoletto was not the first or last of Verdi's operas to get him into trouble with the censor. Did the authorities really have grounds for objecting to the delicate theme of libertinage and the lewd story of a bourgeois girl's seduction? When the censorship office gave its blessing to the revised version of *Rigoletto*, those elements were still retained (apart from a single "bedroom scene" from Act III of Hugo's play).

The answer must be sought elsewhere. After the failure of the revolution of 1848–49, Venice was once again under Habsburg rule. The authorities of the Habsburg monarchy obviously could not tolerate Hugo's depiction of a crowned head – King Francis I of France, the seducer in Hugo's play – as an entirely negative character in a moral drama. They probably did not mind much about other aspects of the opera, and were content with changes to the names of the characters and the scene of the action. The action was thus removed from the French court to a small Italian duchy, and the character of Francis I replaced by that of the Duke of Mantua. *J. K.*

Rigoletto, production photograph with Andrea Rost as Gilda, production Sandro Sequi, conductor Simone Young, Wiener Staatsoper 1995.
With the exception of Abigaille (*Nabucco*) and Lady Macbeth (*Macbeth*), Verdi's soprano characters are all pure, angelic beings, casting a shimmering light over the gloomy masculine world. →M 26

Rigoletto, set design by Eduard Löffler, Berlin 1923 (TWS).

Rigoletto stands at a turning point in Verdi's creative development. Bellini had already considered the subject in the 1830s, and abandoned it only because of difficulties over censorship. Verdi had included Victor Hugo's drama in the list of his planned compositions as early as 1844, at the beginning of his career. Hugo took various names and characters from history, including the figure of King Francis I, who ruled France from 1515 to 1547, his mistress Diane de Poitiers, referred to in the play, and her father Count St. Vallier (the equivalent of Verdi's character Count Monterone). The court jester is also a real historical figure; he was modeled on Triboulet, whose features are preserved in a painting by Jean Marot.

Rigoletto

The eponymous hero stands at the center of the opera in all his complexity and inconsistency. Deformed in outward appearance, he nonetheless cherishes a secret that makes up the better half of his nature: his emotions as an anxious, loving father. He is a man with many contradictions in his character and destiny. The original play has passages where the spoken word is inadequate to do justice to his passion, and here the eloquence of song and the intensity of full orchestral sound seem essential. Verdi's "Cortigiani, vil razza dannata" ("Courtiers, vile and damned race") is unsurpassable, like his portrayal of the broken father's suffering and many other passages in this complex depiction of mental conflict. M 23

Rigoletto, production photograph with Roberto Alagna as the duke, production Sandro Sequi, conductor Simone Young, Wiener Staatsoper 1995.
Like the duke's famous aria in Act I M 27, his equally famous Act III song "La donna è mobile" ("A woman is a fickle creature") M 28 is light-hearted in nature. The song in fact derives from Hugo's play, Hugo having taken it in turn from a historical source: according to an inscription in the château of Chambord, the original lines were written by King Francis himself. The song is the duke's musical visiting card, and is heard three times, on the first occasion directly, as a drinking song with banal orchestral accompaniment. It occurs for the second time when the duke is falling asleep in the attic of Sparafucile's house; as he lapses into slumber, and in parallel with his disjointed thoughts, his singing voice falters. Finally, the song is heard again when Rigoletto opens the sack: this time it is like a delusion, a vocal phantom from beyond the grave.

An opera of duets

When Verdi said he had conceived *Rigoletto* "almost entirely without arias and finales, as a series of duets," he was not exaggerating. The opera is notable for such unconventional aspects, including the lack of traditional ensembles in the finales. They are replaced by short, pointed conclusions to the acts. Towards the end of Act I there is a chorus of the courtiers who have come to abduct Gilda, but it is soon over and leads into Gilda's aria, which she sings piano and staccato. The chorus is of the sort employed by Verdi when depicting crowds in a negative light, as a chorus of conspirators. (A peculiarity of the score of *Rigoletto* is that it contains choral passages only for male voices.) M 24 Act II ends with a brief duet of revenge sung by Rigoletto with Gilda's voice taking a subsidiary part; it is the cabaletta in a whole chain of duets. The finale of Act III is another duet between Rigoletto and the dying Gilda, followed by a rapid instrumental conclusion to the tragedy. M 25

J. K.

Rigoletto, costume designs by Otto Reigbert (above), Cologne 1932/33, and Heinrich Lefler (below) (TWS).
Two images of Rigoletto: "For my part," wrote Verdi, "I would like to see the character shown as deformed and ridiculous in outward appearance, but passionate and full of love within. It is for these qualities that I chose the subject."

23. Rigoletto's Emotional Outburst

Cor - ti-gia-ni, vil raz-za dan - na-ta, per qual prezzo ven-de-ste il mio be-ne?

24. The Courtiers' Nocturnal Chorus

Zit - ti, zit - ti mo-via-mo a ven - det -ta,

25. Final Duet between Gilda and Rigoletto

Las - sù ... in cie - lo, vi-ci-na al-la ma-dre ... in e - ter - no per voi ... pre-ghe-rò.

26. Gilda's Aria

Ca - ro no - me che il mio cor fe - sti pri - mo pal - pi - tar

27. The Duke's Aria (Act I)

Questa o quel - la_____ per me pa - ri so - no a quant' al - tre d'in-tor - no_____ d'in tor-no mi ve - do

28. The Duke's Song (Act III)

La don-na è mo-bi-le qual piu-ma al ven - to, mu-ta d'ac-cen - to e di pen - sie - ro.

Polyphonic emotions

The duke's virile attractions are the key to the dramatic situation in the Act III quartet, determining the attitudes of the other participants to him: the teasing, flirtatious Maddalena, the disillusioned and desperate Gilda who still loves him, and Rigoletto thirsting for revenge. The placing on stage of the four singers is interesting, with two of them, Maddalena and the duke, inside Sparafucile's house, while the other two, Gilda and Rigoletto, are spying on them from outside. Each voice in the quartet has its own melody and its own character. M 29

29. Polyphonic Emotions (Quartet)

Gilda: *In - fe - li - ce cor*
Maddalena: *Ah! ah! ri do ben di co-re che tai ba-je cos-tan po-co;*
Herzog: *schia - vo son de' - vez-zi tuo - i*
Rigoletto: *Ch'ei men - ti - va ch'ei*

Il trovatore, Enrico Caruso as Manrico (self-caricature).
There are more difficult tenor roles than Manrico, but hardly any can be more spectacular. Caruso was the first singer whose brilliant career was partly due to his many phonograph recordings. *Il trovatore* is a classic number opera; Verdi intentionally distanced it from the radical innovations of form in →*Rigoletto*. Most of the scenes are constructed on the sequence of cavatina, duet, trio, and finale, also containing double arias, introductory scenes, cabelettas, and rousing ensembles.

Bel canto and the high C
The "high C" is a concept inseparable from the names of the greatest bel canto tenors. A high male voice was already much sought after in the 17th and 18th centuries, the age of the castrati. In the 19th century, their legacy passed on the one hand to prima donnas, and on the other to tenors. The tenor voice is a rare treasure, its attraction consisting of the ability of an unnatural and uncomfortable register to acquire heroic emotional strength through its radiant power and coloring. Good tenor voices are few and far between; there will be ten outstanding basses and twenty good sopranos to a single really great tenor. Tenors are born, not made, and the vocal color of a bel canto tenor differs from that of a Wagnerian tenor. The latter needs staying power and great vocal strength, even a certain musical monumentality. The bel canto tenor, characteristically, has a voice of gentle beauty and natural fluency. The true home of tenors is the south – Italy and Spain – perhaps because of the mild climate of the area, its proximity to the Mediterranean, its pleasing landscape, the warmth of the sun, the mild air, and many other Mediterranean features.

Il trovatore

The Troubadour

Dramma in four parts

Libretto: Salvatore Cammarano, after the play *El trovador* by Antonio García Gutiérrez.
Première: 19 January 1853, Rome (Teatro Apollo).

Characters: Count di Luna, a young Aragonese nobleman (Bar), Leonora, a lady-in-waiting to the princess of Aragon (S), Azucena, a gypsy (Ms), Manrico, an officer in the army of Prince Urgel, the supposed son of Azucena (T), Ferrando, a captain in the count's army (B), Ines, Leonora's confidante (S), Ruiz, a soldier in Manrico's service (T), An Old Gypsy (B), A Messenger (T); nuns, servants and soldiers of the count, gypsies (chorus).
Setting: Biscay and Aragon, in the early 15th century.

Synopsis

Hatred engenders hatred and becomes all-powerful, leaving love no chance. Long before the opera begins, a gypsy woman was accused of bewitching one of the children of the old count, and although innocent she was burnt at the stake. In her death throes she called on her daughter Azucena to avenge her. Azucena herself has been destroyed by her obedience to her mother's command; she stole the child to throw him into the flames, but in a state of frenzy threw her own child on the pyre instead. The other baby survived, and she has brought him up as her own. The country and its people are now at odds in a power struggle, with Prince Urgel opposing the king. Manrico, the gypsy's foster son, is fighting for the prince against the present Count di Luna, who is loyal to the king. Jealousy over their love for the same woman pits Manrico and Luna against each other. Leonora decides in favor of Manrico, and Luna has his rival executed, only to discover that Manrico was really his own brother.

Part I: "The Duel"
Scene 1: An antechamber in the palace of Aliaferia. On guard duty at night, Ferrando entertains his companions with a story from the count's family history: a gypsy woman once bewitched one of the children of the old count, and was condemned to be burnt at the stake. Her daughter stole the child and threw him into the flames of the gypsy's pyre.
Scene 2: The palace gardens by night. Leonora has fallen in love with an unknown knight at a tournament. Now she recognizes her beloved by his voice: he is the troubadour serenading her in the garden. She hastens to meet him. Count di Luna enters; he too loves Leonora. Recognizing his more fortunate rival as a political opponent, he challenges him to a duel.

Part II: "The Gypsy"
Scene 1: A gypsy camp in the mountains of Biscay. Manrico has defeated Luna in the duel, but spared his life. However, Luna lured him to fight again on enemy territory, where Manrico was overcome by superior forces. Azucena the gypsy has nursed the severely wounded man back to life, and now she tells him her story: her mother, although innocent, was burnt at the stake by Luna's father. She herself stole one of the old count's children in revenge, but mistakenly threw her own child into the fire, and has brought up the other baby as hers. Manrico's doubts of his own identity confuse her: she assures him that he is indeed her child, and must avenge his grandmother's death. Manrico is ready to do so, but when he learns that Leonora is to take the veil that very day in grief at his supposed death, he postpones his revenge and makes haste to the convent.
Scene 2: The cloister of a convent near Castellor. Luna has also heard of Leonora's decision to become a nun, and intends to abduct her against her will. Once again, Manrico intervenes. The two lovers flee to the secure fortress of Castellor.

Part III: "The Gypsy's Son"
Scene 1: Luna's military camp outside Castellor. Luna is besieging Prince Urgel's last fortress, which is commanded by Manrico. Azucena is found near the camp and arrested as a spy. When she calls out in her fear for her son Manrico, Luna knows her for the mother of his deadly enemy and orders her execution, while Ferrando recognizes her as the gypsy woman who has been sought so long for stealing Luna's infant brother.
Scene 2: In the fortress of Castellor. Leonora and Manrico are about to be married, but when Manrico hears that Azucena has been taken prisoner, he mobilizes his few troops and, in defiance of common sense, sallies out to fight for his mother.

Part IV: "The Execution"
Scene 1: A wing of the palace of Aliaferia. Luna has won the battle and occupied the fortress of Castellor, taking Manrico prisoner. Leonora has fled. She hears that Manrico and Azucena are to be executed at dawn, and to save her lover she offers herself to Luna. Luna agrees, but Leonora secretly takes poison so that she will not have to keep her promise.
Scene 2: A dark dungeon. Manrico and Azucena are in chains. Leonora urges Manrico to escape, but since she will not go with him he believes she has betrayed him. Only when the poison begins to work does he understand the truth. Leonora is reconciled to him, and dies in his arms. Luna realizes that he has been cheated. He has Manrico executed, forcing Azucena to watch, and now at last she tells him the truth: "He was your brother!"

S. N.

Il trovatore, set design by Ludwig Zuckermandel-Bassermann for the
Stadttheater in Münster, 1936 (TWS).
"Nothing but *Il trovatore* is heard constantly and everywhere, from central
Africa to India," wrote Verdi in 1862 to his friend Count Arrivabene. The opera
became one of Verdi's most popular works even in his own lifetime, and is still
a favorite today. *Il trovatore* is a treasure-house of attractive tunes, notable
among them Manrico's serenade and his cabaletta. The dramatic coloring is
bright and full of contrasts: black, white, and red. *M 30, M 31*

30. Manrico's Serenade

Deser-to sul - la ter - ra, col rio de - sti - no in guer - ra, è sola speme un cor,

è sola spe -me un cor, è sola spe -me un cor, un cor al Tro - va - tor!

31. Manrico's Cabaletta

Di quel -la pi - ra l'or -ren -do fo - co tut -te le fi - bre m'ar - se, av-vam -pò!

Azucena

Azucena is a striking newcomer to Verdi's gallery of feminine portraits, if only for her vocal register. Several of his earlier parts for low female voices, such as Federica in →*Luisa Miller* and Maddalena in →*Rigoletto*, do not come into the same category, since they are subsidiary roles, and of only episodic significance compared with Azucena. Her part, on the other hand, is a leading role *par excellence*. Her vocal register places her at the head of the series of Verdi's later contralto and mezzo-soprano roles, continuing with Ulrica, Eboli, and Amneris. (The terms contralto and mezzo-soprano were not clearly distinguished in Italian practice during the nineteenth century. The description "contralto" never occurs in Verdi's operas, at least not in his solo parts, only mezzo-soprano, as in Azucena's case.) Dramatically, the female characters sung by these lower voices are contradictory in nature, combining both negative and positive features, and the vocal register indicates the character itself. In Verdi's operas, this new kind of female role stands in the same relation to the soprano as does the baritone to the tenor.

Azucena is a woman possessed. Terrible experiences and dreadful deeds have burdened her life. Her mind is torn between conflicting emotions, and she is under the spell of her "idée fixe" – revenge for her mother's dreadful death. It is with revenge in view that she has brought up her supposed son Manrico, although – in a psychologically puzzling contradiction in terms – she also surrounds him with anxious maternal love.

A twilight aura that might be out of a traditional ballad surrounds her. Her first self-revelation in the opening scene of Act II is indeed in the form of a ballad: "Stride la vampa" ("Flames blazing brightly"), a *canzone* (definitely not an aria) in two verses, conjures up a nightmare memory, the short, abrupt motif of the

Left
Il trovatore, production photograph with Rebecca Turner (Leonora) and Corneliu Murgu (Manrico), production Florian-Malte Leibrecht, sets and costumes Markus Lüpertz, conductor Ira Levin, Deutsche Oper am Rhein, Düsseldorf 1996.
Leonora and Manrico in the fortress of Castellor. The news of Azucena's capture forces Manrico to leave his beloved.

Opposite, below
Il trovatore, production photographs with Fiorenza Cossotto as Azucena.
Azucena is one of the most mysterious and complex of Verdi's characters, and
the most important mezzo part in any of his operas. Her inner conflict is
reminiscent of the difficult father and child relationships so prominent in many
of Verdi's operas, from →*Luisa Miller* to →*Don Carlos*. Fiorenza Cossotto is one
of the outstanding singers to have taken the role at La Scala, Milan.

Above
Il trovatore, photograph from the production by Florian-Malte Leibrecht, sets
and costumes Markus Lüpertz, conductor Ira Levin, Deutsche Oper am Rhein,
Düsseldorf 1996.
The sets for this production emphasized the Spanish local color, most obvious
in the gypsy background of *Il trovatore*, by making artistic reference to the
work of Picasso. Figures of such gigantic dimensions have something
threatening about them, corresponding to the musical atmosphere in which
Verdi's operatic characters move.

vocal part and "blazing" trills of the orchestral
accompaniment conveying a vivid image of her
dreadful vision. M 32, M 33 The first scene of Act II belongs
entirely to Azucena. The opening is followed by her
famous narrative – her "racconto" – intended for
Manrico's ears. It conveys the memory of horrors long
past, passing into increased agitation leading almost to
unconsciousness. M 34 In the dungeon scene of Act IV
Azucena seems almost in a trance, on the boundary
between waking and sleeping. Dreadful images of
death by fire alternate with nostalgic and idealistic
pictures of the peaceful mountains for which she longs.
With her fatalistic melody "Ai nostri monti" ("Unto our
mountains"), Azucena moves back into a ballad-like
mode. M 35   J. K.

32. Azucena's *Canzone*

Stri - de la vam - - pa! la   fol - la in - do - - mi - ta

33. Flames Motif (Azucena's Vision)

34. Azucena's Narrative

Con - dot - ta ell' era in cep - pi

35. Azucena's Dream (Dungeon Scene)

Ai no-stri mon - ti   ri - tor - ne - re - mo,   l'an-ti-ca pa - ce   i - vi go - dre - mo,

La traviata

Melodramma in three acts

Libretto: Francesco Maria Piave, after the play *La dame aux camélias* (*The Lady of the Camellias*) by Alexandre Dumas *fils*.
Première: 6 March 1853, Venice (Teatro La Fenice).

Characters: Violetta Valéry, a Parisian courtesan (S), Flora Bervoix, her friend (S), Annina, Violetta's maid (Ms), Alfredo Germont (T), Georgio Germont, his father (Bar), Gaston, Vicomte de Letorières, friend of Alfredo (T), Baron Douphol, Violetta's protector (Bar), Marquese d'Obigny, friend of Flora (B), Doctor Grenvil (B), Giuseppe, Violetta's servant (T), Flora's Servant (Bar), Commissioner (B); friends and servants of Violetta and Flora, masqueraders (chorus).
Setting: Paris and its surroundings, around 1700.

La traviata, production phot with Tiziana Fabbriccini (Violetta) and Roberto Alagna (Alfred), production Liliana Cavani, conductor Riccardo Muti, sets Dante Ferretti, costumes Gabriella Pescucci, Teatro alla Scala, Milan 1991
The only situation in which violence plays any role in *La traviata* is the finale of the second act. Alfred thinks that Violetta has betrayed him. In this scene the torments of the insulted, fatally ill heroine are intensified to the point of unbearability.

Synopsis

A Parisian courtesan and a young man from the provinces discover that there is more to life than the pleasures of society. They rise above egotism when they fall deeply in love. Violetta and Alfredo leave the social life of Paris for the country, but convention catches up with them. Alfredo's father, speaking for his whole family, implores Violetta to give up her love. Violetta puts on an act of indifference for Alfredo's benefit, returns to Paris, and appears to resume her former life as a courtesan. Only on her deathbed does she tell her lover the truth, finding love and happiness in Alfredo's arms.

Act I

A salon in Violetta's house. Violetta Valéry is giving a party to celebrate her return to society after a short but severe attack of tuberculosis. The guests include old acquaintances, and also a young man from the provinces who has fallen genuinely in love with the beautiful Violetta. She uses irony and coquetry in an attempt to suppress the tender emotions she is beginning to feel, but she has already fallen under the magic spell of love. When the guests have left, she thinks she still can hear Alfredo's declaration of his passion for her.

Act II

Scene 1: A country house near Paris. Alfredo and Violetta have retired to the country, to give themselves up to their love for each other. But Alfredo, although a tender lover, is inexperienced in worldly affairs, and discovers only from the maidservant that Violetta is selling her possessions to cover their living expenses. Ashamed, he goes to Paris to raise money. His father, Germont, takes advantage of his absence to visit Violetta, and asks her to give up Alfredo to avoid bringing disgrace on his family. After her first desperate resistance, Violetta agrees to part from Alfredo, and makes the break herself in a farewell letter. Alfredo is shocked and in despair, and his self-esteem is injured. His father's hypocritical words of comfort are no help to him; all he wants is to avenge himself on Violetta.

Scene 2: In Flora's town house. The separation of Violetta and Alfredo is the latest subject of conversation at the masquerade given by Flora, who is delighted to welcome her friend. Violetta arrives with Baron Douphol, whom Alfredo takes to be her new lover. The two men play cards, gambling against each other, and Alfredo's sharp remarks anger the baron. In an attempt to avert a scandal, Violetta appeals to Alfredo. But since she cannot explain why she broke off their relationship, he throws the money he has won at her feet and accuses her of being a mercenary prostitute. The baron challenges him to a duel. The elder Germont finds the party in an uproar, and the innocent Violetta humiliated. He reproaches his son for breaking the rules of social etiquette.

Act III

Violetta's bedroom. Her tuberculosis is now in its final stages, and she does not believe the doctor's assurances of a speedy recovery. Alfredo has wounded the baron in their duel, but was uninjured himself, and has fled abroad. Hearing from his remorseful father of Violetta's selfless sacrifice, Alfredo returns to Paris to ask her forgiveness. The lovers dream of a new life together. But it is too late, and Violetta dies in Alfredo's arms.   *S. N.*

Production photograph with Teresa Stratas from Franco Zeffirelli's film of *La traviata*, Italy 1982.
The Canadian singer, really a lyric soprano, could also take dramatic soprano roles.

La traviata, Maria Callas as Violetta, 1958.
Violetta was a familiar role to Maria Callas. The great prima donna felt particularly drawn to tragic characters, and a singer who gave herself up so entirely to her art may have had personal reasons for that preference.

The Lady of the Camellias

The name of the real Lady of the Camellias was Marie Duplessis. She was only 23 when she died of tuberculosis in 1847 (a year before the publication of the novel by Alexandre Dumas, who calls her Marguérite Gautier). She came to Paris from the provinces at the age of 15, and began work as a midinette (a milliner's assistant). Her unusual beauty and love of adventure soon raised her from this humble sphere, and she became a courtesan in the Paris of the time, kept in great luxury by her rich and aristocratic lovers. She always appeared in public carrying a bouquet of camellias, or with a camellia at her breast. Marie was the same age as young Dumas (son of the famous novelist), and they were both 20 at the time of their liaison, which lasted only a year, from 1844 to 1845. In his novel the cause of their parting is summed up in a tragic turn of phrase: "Dear Marguérite, I am not rich enough to love you as I would wish, but nor am I poor enough to let myself be loved as you envisage."   J. K.

Left
La traviata, Elisabeth Schwarzkopf as Violetta, 1947.
This photograph is a rarity among the pictures of the great Schwarzkopf, undisputed queen of operatic roles by Mozart and Richard Strauss, and supreme as a singer of German lieder. At the beginning of her career she also sang such coloratura parts as Violetta in *La traviata*.

La traviata, Gitta Alpár (Violetta) and Heinrich Schlusnus (Germont), conductor Erich Kleiber, Staatsoper, Berlin 1930.
Gitta Alpár, the daughter of a synagogue cantor, was a famous singer in Germany in the 1920s and early 1930s, particularly in Munich and Berlin, and later made her name in the USA. Her partner, the baritone Heinrich Schlusnus, was regarded as the best German singer of Verdi of his time.

How Marguérite Gautier became Violetta Valéry

The play by Dumas was completed in 1849 and had its première early in 1852, at the Théâtre de la Vaudeville in Paris. In this dramatized version, Dumas abandons the pitiless realism of his novel by presenting a more positive stage heroine, equipped with sympathetic features. "Traviata" is an Italian term that cannot easily be translated in so succinct a form, and means "she who has turned from the right way" – in other words, a "fallen woman." In 1853, the subject of *La traviata* was an extremely suitable one for the Italian operatic stage of the time.

In the whole of his career, Verdi never approached contemporary social and moral problems as closely as he did around 1850, when he was working on →*Luisa Miller*, →*Stiffelio*, and *La traviata*. "I am writing *The Lady of the Camellias* for Venice," he told a friend. "Other composers would not have undertaken it because of the conventions, the period, and a thousand other stupid considerations, but I work on it with the greatest pleasure." He was nevertheless unable to refrain from a certain amount of idealization. All Verdi's great works make it clear that he was a convinced moralist and, contradictory as it may seem, he made a moral work out of the delicate, almost risqué subject of *The Lady of the Camellias*. The operatic treatment has little to do with the realistic depiction of a *demimondaine*, but contents itself with sketching in her social background as a kind of exposition in the first act. The reality of Violetta's past life appears only indistinctly on stage, almost as a kind of introduction to the story, providing the conditions and motivation for the heroine's subsequent tragedy. The true subject of the opera is the story of a moving, ennobling love and its tragic failure – broken by the conventions of society and Violetta's own past.

In constructing his opera, Verdi was able to make particularly effective use of those scenes Dumas had created especially for the dramatization of his novel: the soirée in Act I, Violetta's deathbed scene in Act III, the great dialogue between Violetta and the elder Germont in Violetta's country house, and the party at Flora's house with the scandal of Violetta's humiliation – the moment on which the overwhelming finale of the opera's central act is built.

Salon society: dancing and conversation

Dance music is strikingly prominent in the score of *La traviata*. It might even be said that the prevalent style is that of the waltz (although not the Viennese but the French variety), which sets the tone for the whole piece. Verdi always thought it very important to give each of his works its own distinctive character, and in *La traviata* it is the dance music that provides the opera's unmistakable color. The greater part of Act I, the soirée in Violetta's salon (which is really an extensive introductory scene), is constructed on a series of dance tunes. Fashionable dances such as the polka, the galop, and above all waltzes dominate the music here. As well as providing accompaniment for the actual dances on stage, this series of dances embraces the general cheerful bustle of the guests (played by the chorus), and individual vocal numbers, the most famous being Alfredo and Violetta's drinking song in waltz time. *M 36*

The end of the act, with the conclusion of Violetta's great aria, also surrenders to the whirling rhythm and

La traviata, production photograph with Placido Domingo and Teresa Stratas, from the film by Franco Zeffirelli, Italy 1982.
Zeffirelli is a master of background depiction on the operatic stage as well as in his other films. His settings, carefully studied in every detail, are like photographs of real scenes, although in fact they exist only in his artistic imagination.

La traviata, production photograph with Giusi Devinu (Violetta) and Alfredo Kraus (Alfredo), production Otto Schenk, sets Günther Schneider-Siemssen, costumes Reihs-Gromes, conductor Josef Krips, Wiener Staatsoper 1971 (photograph 1991).
The first encounter in the salon. Violetta and Alfredo perform the famous drinking song, "Libiamo" ("Let's drink"). This duet, with its choral refrain, may be the best-known melody in all opera. Its ardent elegance is in place at any gala evening.

melody of a waltz, suggesting a frenzy in which the temptations of the past live again. M 37 Dances also play a part in Act II, and take on an independent role as interludes for the ballet and chorus at the beginning of the second finale, during the grand evening party in Flora's town house. On this occasion they are dances conveying a Spanish atmosphere, with typical Spanish coloring and accompanied by tambourines: a dance of gypsy girls, a matadors' dance, and finally a *seguidilla*.

The real transfiguration of the dance, however, comes in the great closing ensemble of Act II, and this time with cathartic significance as the result of a tragic turn of events. The slow curve of a broadly developing waltz melody, into which all present are drawn, becomes the apotheosis of the injured Violetta as tragic heroine. With this melody, the composer redeems and transfigures her. M 38

Another function of dance music in *La traviata* is to provide a musical background for a conversational style of singing that is one of the opera's most distinctive features. Examples may be found in Act I, and in the card-playing scene of the Act II finale, where an agitated conversation, conducted in abrupt phrases, takes place over a recurrent orchestral theme. Such a technique was not entirely unprecedented, but it acquires great significance in *La traviata* by setting the tone of social intercourse that marks the piece.   *J. K.*

36. Drinking Song (Alfredo and Violetta)

Li - bia - mo, li - bia-mo ne' lie - ti ca - li-ci che la bel-lez-za in - fio - ra

37. Viletta, the Lady of Society (Aria, Act I)

Sem - pre li - be - ra deg - g'i - o fol - leg - gia - re di gio-ia in gio - ia

38. Violetta, the Heroine (Finale, Act II)

dai ri - mor - si ___ Dio ti sal - vi al-lor ...

The paterfamilias and the courtesan

The crucial turn of the plot in *La traviata*, the scene in which the elder Germont confronts Violetta, is concentrated into a single, extensive duet. It is not static, but develops dramatically. The point at issue is a fateful struggle between two adversaries, ending with Violetta's defeat by Germont's unyielding insistence, and the collapse of all her defenses. In the opening recitative, Violetta is still rejecting Germont's thoughtlessly abrupt opening words with the confident pride of a society lady, but her confidence is soon shaken. Germont responds in more conciliatory tones, but still pursues the same argument. He is concerned for his own daughter's marriage prospects; her respectable bourgeois future is endangered, he says, if the liaison between Violetta and Alfredo continues to compromise his family's reputation. M 39 Violetta's first reaction is surprise and alarm. Her own happiness, the only hope she has in life, is at stake. She does not give up yet, but seeks a way out. She would be prepared to avoid Alfredo for a while, she suggests, but not to renounce him and his love for ever. In any case she has only a short time to live and be happy, and she clings to her love with all her might. M 40 But that is not enough for Germont. He does not believe that Violetta is mortally sick, and behind the apparently smooth tone of a polite conversation he remains unmoved. Violetta, he says,

La traviata, production photograph with Tiziana Fabbriccini (Violetta) and Paolo Coni (Germont), production Liliana Cavani, sets Dante Ferretti, costumes Gabriella Pescucci, conductor Riccardo Muti, Teatro alla Scala, Milan 1991.
La traviata is the only one of Verdi's tragic operas in which physical violence plays no part. The heroine dies of tuberculosis. However, Violetta's decision to sit at her desk and write her lover a farewell letter is as moving as Gilda's self-sacrifice in →*Rigoletto*.

must not think that a liaison such as hers could ever contribute to the family's happiness and social reputation. ₘ₄₁ And Violetta herself knows the rules of the social game. After Germont's insistent words, she whispers, her heart breaking, "It is true, it is true … " Here the scene finally reaches its crucial turning point. Violetta is prepared to sacrifice her own happiness to the interests of others. ₘ₄₂

Her willingness to make that sacrifice arouses Germont's pity, and he searches for words of comfort. What can Violetta do in order to comply with his wishes? He tries to give her practical advice in the penultimate section of recitative, but Violetta herself knows better. She sets the seal on her decision in the closing cabaletta of the duet. ₘ₄₃

In this melody, which resembles a funeral march, Violetta's voice sounds like that of a martyr facing death. It is a moment of drama within the drama, a bravura effect that Verdi repeated only once, decades later, in the act on the banks of the Nile in →*Aida*.   *J. K.*

La traviata, production photograph with Ernst Gutstein (Germont) and Irmgard Arnold (Violetta), production Walter Felsenstein, conductor Kurt Masur, Komische Oper, Berlin 1967.
This production depicted Violetta, without cosmetics or social brilliance, as an ordinary bourgeois woman still hoping for happiness, and Germont as a loving paterfamilias prepared to sacrifice another woman's life for his own daughter's good name.

39. Germont, the Pleading Father

Pu -ra siccome un an - ge -lo   Id-dio mi diè una fi - glia;

se Alfredo ne - ga   rie - de -re in   se - no alla fa - mi - glia

40. Violetta, in the Dialogue with Germont (Duet, Act II)

Non sa - pe - te   quale af - fet - to   vivo, im-men - so m'arda in pet -to?

41. Germont, in the Dialogue with Violetta (Duet, Act II)

Un dì, quan-do   le   ve - ne -ri   il   tem-po a-vrà fu - ga - te,   fia

pre -sto il   te - dio a sor - ge -re …   Che sa -rà al - lor?…   Pen-sa - te …

42. Violetta Makes her Sacrifice for Love (Duet, Act II)

Di - te al-la gio - vi -ne   sì   bel-la e pu - ra,   ch'av-vi u -na vit - ti-ma   del - la. sven-tu - ra,

43. Violetta's Decision (Duet, Act II)

mor - rò!…   la mia   me -mo - ri -a   non fi - a ch'ei ma - le - di - ca,   se

le   mie   pe - ne or - ri - bi -li   vi sia   chi al-men gli   di - ca.

The Sicilian Vespers, production photograph, Teatro alla Scala, Milan 1989.
The Sicilian people and the French soldiers form a great tableau in Act II, in a valley near Palermo with the sea in the background. In spite of the Sicilian setting, this is Verdi's first "French" opera. In it, he looks back to his popular operas of the period before the 1848 revolutions, although not this time for political reasons.

The Sicilian Vespers

I vespri siciliani/Les vêpres siciliennes

Opéra in five acts

Libretto: Eugène Scribe and Charles Duveyrier.
Première: 13 June 1855, Paris (Opéra).
Characters: Montforte/Montfort, Governor of Sicily under Charles d'Anjou, King of Naples (Bar), Le Sire de Béthune (Bar) and Count Vaudemont (B), French officers, Arrigo/Henri, a young Sicilian (T), Giovanni/Jean Procida, a Sicilian doctor (B), Duchess Elena/Hélène, sister of Duke Federigo/Frédéric of Austria (S), Ninetta, her maid (A), Danieli/Daniéli and Manfredo/Mainfroid, two Sicilians (2 T), Tebaldo/Thibault and Roberto/Robert, French soldiers (T, B); Sicilians, French soldiers (chorus).
Setting: In and around Palermo in 1282, when Sicily was occupied by the French.

Synopsis
Act I

The market place of Palermo. Sicily is occupied by the French, and the governor Montforte rules with an iron hand. The oppressed people hope that Duchess Elena, whose own brother was killed by the French, will help them. When Elena comes out of church, a French soldier forces her to sing a song, and she chooses an old Sicilian song of freedom. Montforte enters, and the Sicilians plead with him, except for young Arrigo, who was captured by the French in battle and has now been unexpectedly set free. He and Duchess Elena love each other in secret. He ventures to accuse Montforte. The governor, surprised and impressed, tries to win his friendship, but Arrigo proudly rejects his advances.

Act II

A valley near Palermo. The doctor, Procida, is returning home after long exile. With Elena and Arrigo, he intends to lead the people in their fight for freedom. Arrigo promises Elena to avenge her brother's death. Unexpectedly, Arrigo is summoned to Montforte's palace. He refuses to go, and is dragged there by force. This is the signal for Procida to call on the people to rebel. When the French try to abduct the brides at a Sicilian wedding, popular anger suddenly breaks out. Carried away on this wave of

The Scribe trademark
The libretto has a rather complicated history. It was adapted for Verdi from an earlier work by the French librettist Eugène Scribe (Meyerbeer, → *The Huguenots*). The central character of the original story was the duke of Alba, the infamous Spanish governor of Flanders under King Philip II. In 1838 this libretto, *Le duc d'Albe*, written by Scribe in collaboration with Charles Duveyrier, was offered first to Halévy and then to Donizetti. Donizetti actually began composing a score, but did not complete it. When Verdi politely rejected two earlier outlines for librettos by Scribe in 1852, the writer thought of offering him this still unpublished text, or revising it for him. He met all Verdi's requirements: the title was to be changed, and the plot shifted, as Scribe put it, to "a climate less cold than that of the Netherlands, a climate full of warmth and music, such as Naples or Sicily."   *J. K.*

indignation, the conspirators determine to make their way into the palace in disguise and kill Montforte.

Act III

Scene 1: Montforte's study. Montforte has learned that Arrigo is his own son; just before dying, his wife, who left him after a brief marriage, has revealed their child's existence in a letter. Montforte tells Arrigo that he is the young man's father, but Arrigo can feel no filial love for the oppressor of the Sicilians.

Scene 2: A ballroom in Montforte's palace. Montforte is holding a grand ball. Elena and Procida plan to kill the governor of Sicily, but Arrigo, entangled in conflicting emotions, warns his father. In vain. Montforte defies danger and remains in the ballroom. When Elena tries to stab Montforte, Arrigo throws himself between them and saves his father. The Sicilians are overpowered. Elena and Procida, knowing nothing of Arrigo's crisis of conscience, curse him as a traitor to the cause.

Act IV

A courtyard in the state prison. Arrigo explains his conduct to Elena, and she forgives him. The conspirators are condemned to death, and Arrigo determines to die with them if his father will not pardon them. Montforte makes it a condition of the pardon that Arrigo recognize him as his father and, out of love for Elena, Arrigo agrees. The condemned prisoners are set free, and Montforte plans to settle the differences between France and Sicily by marrying Elena to Arrigo. Procida sees this turn of events as an opportunity to complete his mission of liberation.

Act V

The garden of Montforte's palace. Arrigo and Elena happily entertain the illusion that their marriage will bring reconciliation. But Procida tells Elena his plan: at the sound of the bell for vespers, announcing the wedding, the Sicilians will surprise and attack the French. Elena cannot induce him to change his mind. In the end, and to prevent the bell from ringing, she refuses to go to the altar. Arrigo curses his apparently faithless bride, and Montforte orders the wedding to proceed. The bell rings, and the Sicilians attack Montforte and the French.   *A. G.*

The Sicilian Vespers, poster from the Deutsche Staatsoper, Berlin.
There was in fact a revolt against the French rule of Charles d'Anjou in Sicily in 1282, but in real life it was a long-drawn-out civil war. The whole opera conveys an overheated, warlike atmosphere.

The Sicilian Vespers, production photograph
from the last scene with (from left to right)
Montserrat Caballé (Elena), Sherrill Milnes
(Montforte), and Nicolai Gedda (Arrigo),
Metropolitan Opera, New York 1974.
War or peace: the opera, like nearly all operas
for which Eugène Scribe wrote the libretto,
ends in disaster. The dream cast at the Met,
with Caballé, Gedda, and Milnes, was a
milestone in the performance history of this
opera, not one of Verdi's most popular works.

A demanding overture

It is not surprising that the fine overture of *The Sicilian Vespers* is popular on concert programs to this day. It consists of thematic material from the opera, but not in the free form of a loosely constructed potpourri. Instead, it follows classical principles.

The introduction contains a basic rhythmic formula – the "death motif" – and phrases from a setting of the psalm "De profundis" in the Act IV finale, the main allegro theme of the massacre scene in the last finale, ₘ₄₄ and a theme from the fateful duet between Montforte and his son Arrigo, one of Verdi's most inspired melodic ideas. ₘ₄₅

Verdi's mature compositional skills are revealed not only in his masterly construction of this overture, but throughout the opera: in the sophisticated filigree of the score, in many exquisite combinations of instrumental color in the orchestration, in new nuances and bold features of harmonic language, and above all in the new range and sweep of his melodies. It was Verdi's ambition to measure himself against the criteria of the Parisian operatic stage.

French stylistic elements

The Sicilian Vespers is one of Verdi's longest operas, comparable in extent only with the first, Parisian version of →*Don Carlos*. This is partly because of the long ballet in Act III, itself one of the longest of Verdi's dance interludes, lasting almost half an hour. This ballet divertissement, entitled "The Four Seasons," consists of a series of the fashionable dances of the period: the polka, the mazurka, and the galop. The ballet earned Verdi high praise from the Parisian press at the time. The feature of French opera that most impressed Verdi himself was the grand scale of its productions. He wrote to his friend Countess Clara Maffei in July 1847, when he was spending a few days in Paris for the first time: "I was at the Opéra yesterday evening … the magnificent sets quite dazzled me. They were giving Halévy's →*La*

Juive." Production was a major component of French grand opera, and in line with usual Parisian practice a "mise en scène" with detailed instructions for the staging was worked out for *The Sicilian Vespers*. This method was adopted (as a production book or set of "disposizioni sceniche") for Verdi's future Italian operas. The ideal of grand opera was plenty of diversity: striking sets as the background for large tableaux, solo scenes full of conflict, and tense finales with exciting turns of plot – a composite effect consisting of sets, dramatic action, and musical genre painting. Examples are the fiery tarantella inserted into Act II (chorus and ballet) M 46, and the finale of Act II, where the action leads into a broad genre painting of a sea idyll with barcarolle and chorus. M 47

The famous bolero, Elena's two-strophe *canzone* with choral refrain, which she sings before the interruption of her wedding, is one of the greatest numbers in the whole opera. M 48

Montforte

The figure of Montforte is certainly the most complex and interesting of the characters in *The Sicilian Vespers*, and deserves a place among Verdi's great baritone roles. For all his severity, Montforte often shows warmth and strikes a note of nobility. Significantly, there are phrases in the part reminiscent of Rigoletto's voice, or anticipating King Philip. M 49

J. K.

44. Theme of the Massacre Scene (Overture)

45. Theme of the Duet between Montforte and Arrigo (Overture)

46. Tarantella

47. Sea Idyll (Barcarolle)

Del pia - cer - s'a van - za l'o - ra! Col - le Gra - zie dal tuo cie - lo

48. Elena's *Canzone* (Bolero)

Mer - cè, di - let - te a - mi - che, ___ di quei leg - gia - dri fior

49. Montforte's Aria

In braccio alle do - vi - zie, nel se - no de - gli o - nor

The Sicilian Vespers, costume design for Procida by A. Albert for the première in Paris in 1855.
The freedom fighter Procida ought to represent the positive associations of a liberation movement, with the French governor Montforte, oppressor of the Sicilians, pitted against him as a negative figure. However, Montforte gradually wins more and more of the audience's sympathy and respect. Procida, on the other hand, arouses sympathy only at critical moments in his own story, when threatened by death (in the finales of Acts III and IV). We are left unsure whether the audience ought to be on the side of the "noble" tyrant or the fanatical conspirator.

Simon Boccanegra, production photograph with Mirella Freni (Amelia) and Piero Capuccilli (Boccanegra), production Giorgio Strehler, sets Ezio Frigerio, conductor Claudio Abbado, Teatro alla Scala, Milan 1981.
In Act III Boccanegra sees his daughter for the last time in the doge's palace; he has been granted little time to enjoy the emotions of paternal love. Was Verdi perhaps thinking of his own children, who had died young, when he created the figure of Boccanegra? Of all his dramatic heroes, Boccanegra can most justifiably be regarded as Verdi's alter ego.

Opposite
Simon Boccanegra, production photograph with Carla Baso (Amelia), Phillip Joll (Boccanegra), and James Johnson (Paolo), production Johannes Schaaf, sets Alexander Lintl, costumes Muriel Gerstner, Württembergisches Staatstheater, Stuttgart 1995.
Paolo's poison is taking effect. As a private man, Boccanegra falls victim to his own political persona.

A revised and adapted libretto

Although the original 1857 version of *Simon Boccanegra* is almost unknown today, contemporary accounts give some idea of the reasons why the opera was not a success at the time. The gloomy subject and dark colors of the plot were felt to be depressing. Contemporary critics mentioned the harsh music, its bold treatment of harmony, and the unornamented vocal style. Today, audiences know *Simon Boccanegra* only in its revised and final version of 1880–81. Around 1879–80, when initial discussions for →*Otello* were in progress, Verdi, although initially still hesitant, allowed Giulio Ricordi to persuade him to return to the long-forgotten score of *Simon Boccanegra*. "As it stands, the score is impossible," wrote Verdi in November 1880. "It is too bleak, too sad." It seemed advisable to turn to a dramatist, and Verdi Arrigo Boito was available. Verdi's contact with Boito over the revision also gave him an opportunity to see how well he and the future librettist of →*Otello* could work together.   J. K.

Simon Boccanegra

Melodramma in a prologue and three acts

Original version
Libretto: Francesco Maria Piave, after the play *Simón Bocanegra* by Antonio García Gutiérrez.
Première: 12 March 1857, Venice (Teatro La Fenice).

Final version
Libretto: Revised by Arrigo Boito.
Première: 24 March 1881, Milan (Teatro alla Scala).
Characters in the prologue: Simon Boccanegra, a corsair in the service of the Republic of Genoa (Bar), Jacopo Fiesco, a Genoese nobleman (B), Paolo Albiani, a Genoese goldsmith (Bar), Pietro, a citizen of Genoa, leader of the people's party (Bar).
Characters in the opera: Simon Boccanegra, Doge of Genoa (Bar), Maria Boccanegra, his daughter, going under the name of Amelia Grimaldi (S), Jacopo Fiesco, going under the name of Andrea (B), Gabriele Adorno, a Genoese nobleman (T), Paolo Albiani, the doge's favorite courtier (Bar), Pietro, a courtier (B), Captain of the Archers (T), Amelia's maid (Ms).
Setting: Genoa and its surroundings in the middle of the 14th century.

Synopsis
Prologue

A square in Genoa, with Fiesco's palace. The ambitious Paolo Albiani and Pietro, leader of the people's party, decide to use their influence to have the heroic Simon Boccanegra chosen by the people as their doge. Boccanegra is surprised, but hopes that if he holds such high office he will at last be reunited with his beloved Maria. Her aristocratic father Fiesco is keeping her from him, since he does not want to let her marry a plebeian. Fiesco is prepared to be reconciled if he can have the daughter Maria has borne to Boccanegra and bring her up himself, but the child mysteriously disappeared some time ago. Boccanegra makes his way into Fiesco's palace, only to find his beloved Maria dead. Outside in the square, the people hail Boccanegra as their newly elected doge.

Act I

Scene 1: 25 years later. The garden of the Grimaldi palace. Amelia, the daughter of the noble Grimaldi family banished by the doge, loves Gabriele Adorno, a member of another noble family at odds with Boccanegra. Fiesco and Adorno are plotting a rebellion against the doge. Amelia warns them in vain against violence and hatred; only love, she says, can improve the world. Fiesco tells Gabriele that Amelia was only adopted by the Grimaldi family, and is really of humble birth, but Gabriele still wants to marry her. The doge comes to court Amelia on behalf of his courtier Paolo. She rejects Paolo's offer, pleading her uncertainty about her parentage as the reason. The doge now recognizes Amelia as his own daughter, and they both decide to keep the discovery secret for the time being. But when the doge takes Paolo the news of Amelia's refusal, his former friend turns against him, and plans to have her abducted.

Scene 2: A council chamber in the doge's palace. Boccanegra tries to persuade the councillors not to wage war against the rival Republic of Venice, but his passionate appeal for peace falls on deaf ears. Loud voices are heard outside. Boccanegra appears before the people, and their threatening cries change to shouts of acclamation. The excited crowd drags in Fiesco and Gabriele, who has killed Amelia's would-be abductor, but insists that the man who ordered the abduction is still at liberty. He accuses the doge himself of being that man, and draws a dagger. Amelia throws herself between the two. Boccanegra suspects that Paolo was responsible for the attempted abduction, curses the perpetrator of the crime, and condemns him to exile. He forces Paolo to repeat the curse, and thus to condemn himself.

Act II

A hall in the doge's palace. Paolo plans to bring the doge down in his own ruin, and pours poison into Boccanegra's goblet. Then he has Fiesco and Gabriele summoned from prison. Fate will decide whether the doge dies by poison or a dagger, but Fiesco refuses to commit murder. Paolo then keeps Gabriele back and makes him believe that the doge is planning to dishonor Amelia. The doge drinks the poisoned contents of his goblet, and Amelia prevents Gabriele's assassination attempt. When Gabriele learns that Boccanegra is Amelia's father he begs for forgiveness, and is prepared to fight on the doge's side.

Act III

Inside the doge's palace, with the sea in the background. The doge's party has won a victory. Boccanegra generously grants Fiesco his freedom, but Paolo, who fought on the side of the nobles, is condemned to death. Songs are sung to celebrate the wedding of Amelia and Gabriele. Paolo's poison begins to work, and the dying Boccanegra asks Fiesco to make his peace with him. Fiesco remains hostile, but when Boccanegra reveals that Amelia is his daughter, and thus Fiesco's granddaughter, they are reconciled. Boccanegra names Gabriele as his successor, and dies.

S. N.

The real Boccanegra
The first doge of Genoa, Simon Boccanegra, was not a corsair or even, like his brother Egidio Boccanegra, a seafaring man. (The Spanish dramatist Antonio García Gutiérrez merged two historical figures into a single character in his play.) The real Boccanegra was a member of the merchant and plebeian social classes, and represented their interests against those of the aristocracy. He ruled Genoa in very unstable and difficult times. His first period of power was from 1339 to 1344, when he was forced to resign under pressure from the aristocratic party. He ruled as doge again from 1356 to 1364, and was said to have died of poison. His policies consisted of attempts to settle internal quarrels. In the spirit of the poet Petrarch, who sent letters to the doges of both Venice and Genoa urging preservation of the internal unity of Italy, Boccanegra tried to come to an understanding with the rival seaport city of Venice.

The villainous Paolo

The sublime hymn following Boccanegra's proclamation of peace is followed by a complete contrast: the terrible sound of a curse. At the doge's command Paolo Albiani, as a high dignitary of state, must pronounce a curse on the anonymous abductor of the girl – in point of fact, on himself. This turn of events gives the council chamber scene a conclusion of overwhelming dramatic effect, worthy of Boito's powerful theatrical imagination. While this part of the scene also contributes to the presentation of Boccanegra as a stern and energetic ruler, it belongs first and foremost to Paolo Albiani, a character who was developed fully only by Boito. In Boito's hands, the straightforward villain of the 1857 version became a demonic figure anticipating Iago. Indeed, Paolo inspired Verdi to write music that is reminiscent of Iago – the dark C minor of the curse scene, following the radiant F sharp major of the hymn of peace, fits the character perfectly. M 53

Boccanegra the operatic hero

The character of Boccanegra as a loving father was already present in the 1857 version – a portrait of attractive emotional warmth. It fits into the sequence of paternal roles that constituted a central theme in Verdi's dramatic thinking, running right through his oeuvre from the early example of Francesco Foscari to old Miller and Rigoletto, and finally to King Philip and Amonasro. But none of these characters, often contradictory in nature, is shown in as amiable a light as Boccanegra, whose relationship with his child is loving and unclouded. Overwhelming emotions govern the beautiful duet scene in which father and daughter recognize each other (Act I, Scene 1). In the final version, this duet needed only a few formal adjustments, and a deeper luster in the orchestral coloring and harmony, to produce an even more radiant effect. M 50

However, much of the fully rounded portrait of Boccanegra was still absent from the 1857 version. Verdi had not yet pointed up the difference between the political adventurer and the magnanimous statesman – a dramatic character on the grand scale. He indicated as much in his letter to Boito, showing that he himself was aware of the necessity of a compromise solution: "… my aims are more modest … yet it seems to me that something good might be made of the figures of Fiesco and Simon." Verdi's wish to give his protagonists a more distinct outline was met by the revision of 1880–81, particularly in the new finale to Act I: the council chamber scene, which gives new depth to the character of the statesman, far-sighted politician, and humanist, a ruler with an iron will, as magnanimous in showing mercy as he is unyielding when he metes out punishment.

The new finale begins solemnly, with a discussion of state affairs by the councillors presided over by the doge. The point at issue is peace or war, and it gives the doge the opportunity to state his political creed: the encouragement and maintenance of internal unity between the Italian states. M 51 A large-scale scene of uproar follows: the people have been incited by the aristocracy to rise against Boccanegra. However, the magical power of the doge's authority calms them down. Gabriele Adorno enters the hall at the head of the rebels, intending to hold Boccanegra to account for his supposed abduction of Amelia. After Amelia's own unexpected appearance in the council chamber, to tell her own story of what has happened and thus prove the doge innocent, there is a solemn address by Boccanegra himself: a proclamation of peace, with the other characters joining him in an ensemble. Eventually the people themselves take up the theme, and it becomes a hymn to peace, a great, vaulting musical structure of thrilling vigor. M 52   J. K.

Simon Boccanegra, set design by Hein Heckroth for the production by Rudolf Schulz-Dornburg, conductor Georg Solti, Städtische Bühnen, Opernhaus Essen 1929/30 (TWS).
With its large ensemble scenes, Simon Boccanegra could be described as an Italianate grand opera. However, that is not the whole story: while the protagonists in French grand opera tend to represent a group, and are thus part of the crowd, Verdi presents the populace in contrast to the individual fates of his leading characters. At the point at which Boccanegra the private man suffers the worst imaginable blow of fate in the prologue – his bride dies and his small daughter disappears – he is acclaimed by the people as their new doge.

50. Recognition Scene (Duet between Boccanegra and Amelia)

Figlia! a tal nome io pal - pi-to   qual se m'aprisse i cie - li...   un mondo d'i-nef - fa - bi-li   le - ti - zie a me ri - ve - li

51. Boccanegra's Speech (Council Chamber Scene, Act 1)

Atten - da alle sue   ri - me il cantor   del - la   bion - da Avi -gno -ne - - se.

52. Hymn of Peace (Council Chamber Scene, Act I)

Pian-go su voi,   sul pla - ci-do   rag -gio del vo -stro   cli - vo

53. Curse Motif (Council Chamber Scene, Act I)

Simon Boccanegra, set design by Eduard Löffler, Teatro Municipal, Rio de Janeiro 1941 (TWS).
The council chamber scene is a masterpiece by the mature Verdi. It presents a striking picture of the ease with which the crowd can be manipulated, while the true drama lies in individual relationships. This is a new way of looking at the common people; the young Verdi had sympathized with the crowd as an embodiment of the idea of freedom, but the older composer saw it in a more ambivalent light.

Simon Boccanegra, set design by Josef Fenneker for the production by Rudolf Scheel in the Theater im Admiralspalast, Berlin 1944 (TWS).
Dawn over the sea. Verdi presents Amelia in a natural atmosphere full of promise: in this generally dark opera, she stands for a future free of cares. It was Boito's idea to present the work's musical associations with nature on stage as well, moving the setting of this scene to the seashore just beyond the garden of the Grimaldi palace.

Simon Boccanegra, set design by Josef Fenneker for the production by Rudolf Scheel in the Theater im Admiralspalast, Berlin 1944 (TWS).
The political power struggle casts a dark shadow over Boccanegra's story. As in many of Verdi's other operas, the protagonist has nowhere to go to escape the blows of fate. His heroes are made to wander, of their own volition, in a dark labyrinth.

Below
Simon Boccanegra, production photograph with Mirella Freni and Veriono Lucchetti, guest performance by the Teatro alla Scala in Tokyo, 1981.
Among the unusual features of *Simon Boccanegra* is the fact that the love interest plays only an episodic part. The one love duet in the opera – between Amelia and Gabriele in the garden, against the background of the sea – treats love as more of a philosophical than a dramatic concept, standing for the naive ardors of youth.

Shadows and a dark atmosphere

The tone of the opera is set by three important male roles for the deeper vocal registers: Boccanegra, Paolo, and Fiesco. Fiesco is Boccanegra's reluctant father-in-law and Amelia's grandfather. He stays in the background until almost the end of the opera, but his mysterious figure determines the dark atmosphere. Under the pseudonym "Father Andrea" he leads a shadowy life. The finest hour for the singer of this role comes in Act III, when he emerges from the shadows and once again stands face to face with his archenemy Boccanegra, who is now struggling with death.

When he laid emphasis on Fiesco as well as Boccanegra in his letter to Boito, Verdi was probably hoping for two big male parts of equal importance, both in the lower registers, similar to the pairing of Philip II and the Grand Inquisitor in →*Don Carlos*. The really decisive step in drawing Fiesco's figure more clearly, however, is taken in Verdi's music itself. *M 56*

Opposite
Simon Boccanegra, production photograph with Phillip Joll as Boccanegra, production Johannes Schaaf, sets Alexander Lintl, costumes Muriel Gerstner, Württembergisches Staatstheater, Stuttgart 1995.
The patricians (in wigs) and the plebeians (in hats) engage in hand-to-hand fighting in the council chamber scene (Act I, Scene 2). Boccanegra, whose costume in this production suggested a prophetic figure, overcomes the delicate situation by exerting his own powerful authority.

The sea

Like Verdi's other mature masterpieces, *Simon Boccanegra* has a basic coloring unique to itself (known in Italian operatic practice as "tinta," meaning hue, tint, or color). Here it is the voice and atmosphere of the sea, an appropriate concept for a Genoese subject and a hero whose fate is bound up in many ways with the sea itself. It is interesting that Verdi, who did not usually have much time for the musical depiction of nature, used the method with such clarity here. Even in the original version of *Simon Boccanegra*, Act I begins with a depiction of the waves of the sea. Amelia's cavatina on her first entrance is surrounded by orchestral writing that renders the play of the waves and the breath of the fresh coastal breeze audible, almost visible. *M 54*

The revised score of 1881 made this attractive atmosphere even more striking. In the doge's death scene, the sea sends its last farewell through his open window with the sound of breaking waves, a sound that, for Boccanegra, stands for the whole of his past life. The motif of the sea accompanies the opera almost from the outset in the 1881 version; the introduction to the prelude, an entirely new composition, creates a wave-like tapestry of sound that sets the tone not only for the dialogue of the opening scene, but for the entire opera. *M 55*

J. K.

54. Amelia's Aria

Co - me in que-st'o - ra bru - na sor - ri - don gli a-stri e il ma - re!

Co - me s'u-ni - sce, o lu - na, al - l'on - da il tu - o chia-ror!...

55. Sea Music (Act III)

56. Fiesco's Aria (Act III)

Del - le fa - ci festan - ti al bar - lu - me ci - fre ar-ca - ne, fu - ne - bri ve - dra - i...

Simon Boccanegra, poster for the production at the Teatro alla Scala, Milan 1971.

A Masked Ball

Un ballo in maschera

Melodramma in three acts

Libretto: Antonio Somma, after the libretto *Gustave III, ou Le bal masqué* by Eugène Scribe.
Première: 17 February 1859, Rome (Teatro Apollo).
Characters: (the names in the original version banned by the censors are given in brackets): Riccardo, Count of Warwick, Governor of Boston (Gustavus III of Sweden) (T), Renato, a Creole, his secretary (Count René Anckarstroem, his secretary) (Bar), Amelia, Renato's wife (S), Ulrica (Mam'zelle Arvidson), a fortune-teller (A), Oscar, a page (S), Samuel (Count Ribbing) and Tom (Count Horn), enemies of the count (conspirators against Gustavus) (2 B), Silvano (Christian), a sailor (Bar), A Judge (Armfelt, minister of justice) (T), A Servant (T); deputies (courtiers), officers, conspirators, servants, masked guests (chorus).
Setting: Boston, the end of the 17th century (Stockholm, 1792).

Synopsis (original version)
Act I

Scene 1: An audience chamber in the royal castle. King Gustavus III of Sweden is holding a morning audience, to which petitioners and courtiers are admitted. With their adherents, Count Ribbing and Count Horn, who are planning to assassinate the king, mingle with the crowd. The page Oscar gives the king a guest list for the masked ball that is soon to take place. It includes Amelia, with whom Gustavus is secretly in love, and who is married to his best friend and adviser, Count René Anckarstroem. When Anckarstroem warns the king of a plot against him, Gustavus III is merely relieved that his friend has not guessed at his love for Amelia, and makes light of the warning. A judge lays before him an application for the banishment of the fortune-teller Mam'zelle Arvidson, but the page Oscar defends her. His curiosity aroused, Gustavus decides to visit the fortune-teller himself, with his courtiers. The conspirators see a chance to put their plans into practice.

Scene 2: The fortune-teller's dwelling. Mam'zelle Arvidson is surrounded by a crowd of people, including a seaman who wants to know if he will ever be rewarded for the years of service he has given the king. Gustavus secretly puts money and a commission in his pocket. A noblewoman asks for an interview with Mam'zelle Arvidson. Gustavus, listening, realizes that it is Amelia, who has come to ask Mam'zelle Arvidson for help in struggling to subdue a forbidden love. The fortune-teller recommends a herb that grows in the gallows field, and must be picked with Amelia's own hands by night.

Amelia plans to pluck the herb that very night. Guessing that she means her love for himself, Gustavus decides to follow her. First, however, and disguised as a fisherman, he has his own future told. Mam'zelle Arvidson tells him that he will soon be killed by the next person to take his hand. That person is Anckarstroem, and all present take it as a sign that Mam'zelle Arvidson's prophecies are not infallible. In cheerful mood, the courtiers strike up a song praising the king, and the people join in. Amidst the rejoicing crowd, the king is safe from his would-be assassins. Mam'zelle Arvidson warns him not to make light of her prophecy, but in vain.

Act II

A lonely place at the foot of a hill, the gallows field near Stockholm. It is night. Taking Mam'zelle Arvidson's advice, Amelia has come to look for the herb. Gustavus has followed her in secret; he reveals his love, and wrings from her a confession of her own feelings for him. Anckarstroem in his turn has followed his friend in order to protect him, and warn him of the planned assassination. He exchanges cloaks with Gustavus, who asks him to escort the unknown veiled lady back to the city without asking her identity. The conspirators surround the disguised Anckarstroem, believing that he is the king, and when Amelia intervenes her identity is revealed. The conspirators mock the deceived husband. Furiously jealous, Anckarstroem now invites the conspirators to visit his house next day.

Act III

Scene 1: Anckarstroem's study. Anckarstroem intends to kill his wife, and will not listen to her assurances of her innocence. She gains only a postponement of death, asking to see her child once more. Anckarstroem grants this delay, and then turns his anger against the king. He joins the conspirators, who draw lots to decide who is to kill Gustavus, and the lot falls on Anckarstroem. The page Oscar brings an invitation to the masked ball, and Amelia guesses that the king is to be entrapped that evening.

Scene 2: The king's private apartment in the opera house. Gustavus, torn between his love for Amelia and his loyalty to his friend, decides to send Anckarstroem and his wife to England. Amelia warns him of the plot against him in an anonymous letter, but once again he ignores the warning.

Scene 3: A large and festive ballroom. The ball is in full swing, and the conspirators mingle with the masqueraders. Anckarstroem uses threats to make the page reveal what costume the king is wearing. Amelia tries to persuade Gustavus to leave the ball, but in vain, and Anckarstroem stabs him. Gustavus shows his friend the document sending him to England, swears that nothing unseemly has taken place between himself and Amelia, forgives his murderer, and dies.

S. N.

The victim, Gustavus III (top), and his assassin Johan Jacob Anckarstroem (below).
An assassination attempt was made on King Gustavus III of Sweden at a court ball in Stockholm on the night of 15 March 1792. He died of his wounds a few weeks later. The murder was for purely political reasons: a group of conservative feudal nobles wanted to rid themselves of a ruler who was committed to the principles of enlightened absolutism. Up to the time of his execution, the assassin steadfastly refused to reveal the names of his fellow conspirators.

Opposite page, above
A Masked Ball, production photograph with (from left to right) Magda Nádor (Oscar), Luciano Pavarotti (Gustavus III), and Margaret Price (Amelia), production Gianfranco de Bosio, costumes Santuzza Cali, Wiener Staatsoper 1986.
The most attractive of Verdi's tenor heroes dies for the sake of a mild flirtation – it is the only time one of his male characters initiates the catharsis. The king may not be as immaculate as Verdi's angelic heroines, but he is not genuinely guilty, and is the victim of a misunderstanding. The dramatic effect Scribe intended at this point is reduced to human proportions. Instead of a devastating catastrophe, the audience is offered a sublime and tragic final scene.

Opposite page, below
A Masked Ball, production photograph, production and sets Richard Jones and Antony McDonald, conductor Marcello Viotti, Bregenz Festival 1999.
A new chapter in the history of set design was opened by the two designers of the production of *A Masked Ball* for the Bregenz Festival of 1999. It involved over 300 performers against a spectacular backdrop – an open book measuring 34 x 25 meters floating on Lake Constance. Death, following the course of events, holds the book open in his hands – and is waiting for the King of Sweden at the end of the story.

Difficulties with censorship

To the authorities in Naples, the murder of a European king in the 1790s seemed too close and contemporary a subject not to arouse dangerous associations in the minds of Italians already inflamed by the ideas of the Risorgimento. Verdi was told to revise the piece. He then offered the opera to Rome, but even there he had to make concessions to the censor before he could have his new work produced in February 1859, under its final title of *A Masked Ball*. Some years later, in the new, liberal kingdom of Italy, it would have been possible to restore the historical names and details of Scribe's original libretto, as many productions of the last few decades have done. Verdi, however, chose not to make use of that opportunity.   *J. K.*

A Masked Ball production photograph of Act I, Scene 1, production Franco Zeffirelli, sets Renzo Mongiardino, conductor Claudio Abbado, Teatro alla Scala, Milan 1972. Verdi depicts the atmosphere of the court and the conspiracy theme at the beginning of the opera with simple but concentrated brilliance. Only a few minutes into the prelude, we are already acquainted with the period and the political situation.

Gustavus III

The part of Gustavus III is a major tenor role, but calls for a lyrical, flexible voice rather than a genuine *Heldentenor*. King Gustavus III is a sympathetic, warm-hearted hero, who is ready to give up the love of his life for the sake of friendship. M 58

Oscar

The breeches part of the page Oscar was a new kind of role in Verdi's operas. Oscar is a light soprano, a type familiar on the French musical stage, and a genre character in the French tradition, with strophic songs and a strikingly virtuoso decorative coloratura part. "His" chanson of two verses in the ballroom scene of Act III has become the best-known number in the opera. M 59

Mam'zelle Arvidson

The use of the lower female register for the figure of Mam'zelle Arvidson – a character comparable to Azucena in the earlier →*Il trovatore* – is among Verdi's relatively new methods of suggesting fatalism. There is something mystic and ambiguous about the character: the audience cannot tell whether she is really a superstitious woman who believes herself possessed, or a shrewd and clever manipulator out for profit. M 60

The spirit of the eighteenth century

The basic atmosphere of the opera suggests the courtly elegance of the eighteenth century. The reckless king of Sweden himself fits the image of a light-hearted, courtly society full of zest for life. He is a good, kind-hearted man, a friend to his subjects, and he has warm feelings. In his first aria, sung in his disguise as a fisherman among the crowd at the fortune-teller's house on the harbor, he acts like the ringleader of a cheerful schoolboy prank. M 57

A Masked Ball, production photograph (Act I) with Ludmilla Schmetschu as Mam'zelle Arvidson, production Gianfranco de Bosio, conductor Claudio Abbado, Wiener Staatsoper 1986.
A mood of amusement prevails in Mam'zelle Arvidson's house. Indeed, laughter accompanies the whole action of the piece in an almost uncanny manner. No other opera by Verdi contains so much laughter (there is a laughing aria and a laughing quintet, not to speak of the merriment of the masked ball itself), and nowhere is laughter as deadly as here.

57. Aria Sung by Gustavus Disguised as a Fisherman

Di' tu __ se fe - de - le il flut - to m'a-spet - - ta, se

mol - le di pian - to la don - na di - let - - ta

58. The King's Aria (Act III)

Ma se m'è for - za per - der - ti per-sem - pre, o lu - ce mi - a

59. Oscar's Chanson (Ballroom Scene, Act III)

Sa - per vor - re-ste di che si ve-ste, quan-do l'è co-sa ch'ei vuol na-sco-sa, O - scar lo sa, ma nol di - rà,

tra la la la la la la tra la la la la la la tra la la la la la la la la la la la la la.

Anckarstroem

Anckarstroem is first the king's secretary and devoted friend, and then his bitter enemy. His first aria is a strophic song, м 61 and his second is loosely constructed in three parts, м 62 framing both outbursts of violent emotion and moments of thoughtful reflection.

Amelia

Amelia's solo arias – extensive cavatinas – are elegiac pieces, overshadowed by grief and distress. She is more unfortunate than almost any of Verdi's other heroines, being doomed from the outset, both an unhappy wife and an unhappy, hopeless lover, tormented by feelings of guilt. Her fate is perhaps comparable to that of Queen Elisabeth in →*Don Carlos*, and it is no coincidence that there are similarities in their music. Anticipations of Elisabeth include the dark F minor of Amelia's solo scene at the beginning of Act II, with its elegiac cor anglais obbligato. м 63

60. Mam'zelle Arvidson's Orchestral Motif

61. Anckarstroem's Aria (Act I)

Al - la vi - ta che t'ar - ri - de di spe-ran - ze e gau-dio pie - na

62. Anckarstroem's Aria (Act III)

O dol - cez - ze perdu - te, o me-mo - rie d'un am-ples - so che l'es - se - re in - di - a

63. Amelia's Aria (Act II)

Ma dall' a - ri - do stelo divul - sa come a - vrò di mia mano quell'er - ba, e che

den - tro la mente convul - sa quell' e - te - re-a sem-bian - za mor - rà, _____

The love duet

The requirements of the dramatic development of the situation – an ardent declaration of love, its rejection, and resignation – may explain why Verdi reverted to the most conventional of Italian formal types for the great duet between Amelia and Gustavus in Act II, a duet constructed in two main sections, concluding with a rapid cabaletta. The cabaletta itself is also of tradi- tional construction: the tenor strophe is followed by the soprano, and after a short orchestral interlude the voices join together. M 64

Melodically, however, the duet is innovative, a kind of "Italian Tristan," and indeed *A Masked Ball* was composed at around the same time as Richard Wagner's →*Tristan and Isolde*. M 65

64. Cabaletta from the Duet between Gustavus and Amelia

Ahi, sul fu-ne-reo let - to ov' io so-gna-va spe-gnerlo, gi-gan-te tor-na in pet - to l'a-mor che mi fe - rì!

65. Orchestral Theme of the Declaration of Love (Duet between Gustavus and Amelia)

A Masked Ball, production photograph with Maria Callas as Amelia, production Luchino Visconti, sets and costumes Lila de Nobili, Teatro alla Scala, Milan 1956.
The role of Amelia is not very complex dramatically, but musically it is a big part, since the conflicting emotions she feels as she is torn between married constancy and love provide opportunities for extensive passages of lyricism.

A laughing chorus

The elegance and skillful execution of the big ensemble scenes show Verdi drawing once again from the spark- ling spring of invention that so enriched →*Rigoletto* and →*La traviata*. The famous quintet from the Act I finale is a masterpiece, coming at a moment of general conster- nation when Mam'zelle Arvidson prophesies misfor- tune for the king. The situation is a typical "finale concertato," a moment when the action pauses and the reactions of all present are combined into a poly- phonic ensemble. The position and function of this sort of ensemble was a long-established tradition in Italian operatic finales. However, Verdi's way of approaching it is far from traditional. Each voice retains its character- istic tone, its own means of expression, and its own thematic profile, and there is an abundance of melodies and felicitous inspirations. What could suit the boyish portrait of the king better than his disbelieving laughter (hence the name of "laughing" quintet given to the number)? But there may be some concealed dismay behind his apparent mirth. Mam'zelle Arvidson, who still does not know his identity, reacts with injured defiance, assuring him that her prophecy will indeed come true. M 66

The two leaders of the conspiracy are given an agitated, rapid staccato melody, of the type used for intriguers. M 67 A great arching melody in Oscar's high soprano crowns the whole of this musical structure. M 68

66. Laughing Quintet: Mam'zelle Arvidson

Ah voi, si - gno - ri a que - ste pa - ro - le mie fu - ne - - - ste

67. Laughing Quintet: The Conspirators

La sua pa ro - - la è dar - - do, è ful - - mi - ne lo sguardo

68. Laughing Quintet: Oscar

Ah, _____ e tal _____ fia d'un - queil

The Masked Ball

In the closing scene at the masked ball, Verdi again reverts to patterns and techniques that had proved their worth in the ballroom scenes of →*Rigoletto* and →*La traviata*. Once again the fateful and dramatic moments are accompanied by a dance melody, and once again an atmosphere of civilized social intercourse, with the restrained tone of private conversations, hovers around the graceful dance tune. Concealed by the crowd of dancers at the ball, Amelia makes her way to the disguised king to warn him of the deadly danger facing him, and to tell him of her final renunciation of his love. A group of instrumentalists on stage (playing stringed instruments) strikes up the music for the ball, an ethereally delicate and elegiac mazurka, M 69 up to the point when the orchestral instruments in the pit join in, indicating, by the monotonous repetition of a discordant figure for strings and a death motif, M 70 that all warnings and renunciations have come too late. Disaster is approaching inexorably, and the drama reaches a climax in this dance tune. All that remains is the recognition that there has been a terrible misunderstanding. Remorse, forgiveness, and death belong in the sphere of dramatic resolution and catharsis.

J. K.

69. Minuet-Mazurka (Ballroom Scene)

70. Death Motif

A Masked Ball, production photograph from Act III, Scene 3, production Franco Zeffirelli, sets Renzo Mongiardino, conductor Claudio Abbado, Teatro alla Scala, Milan 1972.
All the characters in this opera wear masks, both literally and figuratively. The courtiers visit Mam'zelle Arvidson in disguise, and on the gallows field Anckarstroem exchanges cloaks with the king, while Amelia veils her face. The true faces of the protagonists are concealed until the last moment. Only Oscar knows anything of what is going on, but he keeps silent.

The Force of Destiny

La forza del destino

Opera in four acts

Libretto: Francesco Maria Piave, after the play *Don Alvaro, o La fuerza del sino* by Angel de Saavedra, with the inclusion of a scene from Schiller's *Wallensteins Lager* (*Wallenstein's Camp*).

Première: 10 November 1862, St. Petersburg (Grand Imperial Theater); revised version, with additional text by Antonio Ghislanzoni: 27 February 1869, Milan (Teatro alla Scala).

Characters: The Marquis of Calatrava (B), Leonora di Vargas, his daughter (S), Don Carlo di Vargas, his son (Bar), Don Alvaro, a half-breed descended from a royal Inca tribe (T), Preziosilla, a young gypsy (Ms), The Padre Guardiano (Father Superior), a Franciscan (B), Fra Melitone (Bar), Curra, Leonora's maid (Ms), An Alcalde (B), Mastro Trabuco, a muleteer, then a pedlar (T), A Surgeon in the Spanish army (T); muleteers, Spanish and Italian country people, Spanish and Italian soldiers of all ranks, orderlies, Italian recruits, Franciscan friars, beggars, vivandières.

Setting: Spain and Italy, in the middle of the 18th century.

Synopsis
Act I

Seville, a hall in the house of the Marquis of Calatrava. Leonora di Vargas is expecting her lover

The Force of Destiny, photograph from the production by Helmut Polixa, sets and costumes Franz Lehr, Theater Bremen 1992. Even in the opening moments of the drama, Leonora is a tragic heroine. She hesitates before an inevitable yet impossible choice between her love for Alvaro and her love for her father. The latter's tragic death has terrible consequences: she is now suspected of being the accomplice of a murderer, must take to flight, is torn from her lover, and suffers the solitude of an exile she herself has chosen. The tragedy of her fate is the central theme of Verdi's musical depiction. The famous destiny motif, which is also the leading motif in the overture, is closely linked to her in the opera itself. →M 76

Don Alvaro, the descendant of an Inca tribe. Since her father has forbidden her marriage to a half-breed, they are planning to elope. Leonora, who loves her father, still hesitates when everything is ready for their flight, and so the Marquis is able to take them by surprise and tries to detain his daughter. Don Alvaro shows his peaceful intentions by throwing down his pistol. It goes off by accident and kills the Marquis.

Act II
Scene 1: The village of Hornachuelos. Leonora and Alvaro escaped but then lost track of each other on that dreadful night. Leonora is now wandering the countryside, homeless, in search of Alvaro, and has disguised herself as a man to avoid the vengeance of her brother Carlo. Down by the harbor, brother and sister suddenly come face to face, and Leonora escapes recognition by Carlo only because the recruitment drive for a new military campaign causes confusion. Carlo tells the curious crowd the story of Leonora and Alvaro, who, he says, has returned to America. Now Leonora feels not only guilty of her father's death, but betrayed and abandoned by Alvaro. She opts for a life of atonement and purification.

Scene 2: The Franciscan monastery of Madonna degli Angeli, near Hornachuelos. Leonora is seeking refuge from her brother's pursuit, and above all release from her own burning desire for her lover. She therefore chooses not refuge in the monastery but the existence of a hermit. The Padre Guardiano knows Leonora's story, and in a solemn ritual she is ushered into a hermitage near the monastery. Anyone who approaches the place to discover the hermit's secret is threatened with damnation.

Act III
Scene 1: Italy. A forest near Velletri. Years have passed; believing that Leonora is dead, Alvaro has joined the Spanish army and made his career under a false name. When he saves an unknown officer's life they become firm friends. The officer is Carlo, also serving under a false name in the Spanish army.

Scene 2: The reception room in the quarters of a high-ranking Spanish officer. Alvaro has been severely wounded. He gives Carlo his possessions, asking him to destroy his documents if he dies. Carlo's suspicions are aroused when his friend mentions the name of Calatrava. His oath forbids him to read the documents, but among the other items he finds a portrait of Leonora, and realizes that his friend is the mortal enemy he has pursued for so long.

Scene 3: Carlo reveals his identity to Alvaro, who has now recovered, and challenges him to a duel. Alvaro tries to make peace with him in the name of their friendship, his own innocence, and Leonora's love, but in vain. Only the guards save Alvaro from the fury of Carlo, who is obsessed with his honor. The world can offer Alvaro neither tolerance nor love, and he decides to seek peace in a monastery. The crowd celebrates the intoxication of war: like alcohol, it offers forgetfulness of the horrors of the world, and those who issue unwelcome reminders of reality, like Fra Melitone, are ignored.

Act IV

Scene 1: The courtyard of the monastery of Madonna degli Angeli. Fra Melitone is distributing alms to the beggars. Carlo has been searching for Alvaro for seven years, and has at last tracked him down at the monastery. Everything else has changed since the dreadful night of the elopement, but Carlo still persists in his search for revenge. Alvaro, now a

monk, tries unsuccessfully to avoid the confrontation.

Scene 2: A valley among inaccessible rocks. Leonora has lived here for years immersed in religious devotions, but without attaining the inner peace she longs for. She still burns with love for Alvaro. Two men burst into her hermitage, looking for a priest. Alvaro has wounded Carlo mortally in a duel. The lovers recognize one another. Dying, Carlo stabs his sister, and Leonora dies in Alvaro's arms, with the Padre Guardiano's blessing. (In the first version, Alvaro then commits suicide by throwing himself over the precipice.)   *S. N.*

Leonora

Verdi drew his musical portrait of Leonora with particular melodic and dramatic power. Her great solo *scena* in Act IV is a monologue that hardly suits the traditional description of it as an aria. Verdi simply called it a "melodia." The monologue is a kind of balance sheet of her existence, lamenting her wasted life, and finally rebelling against her fate. It opens with the invocation of "Pace!" ("Peace!"), but there is no peace in Leonora's troubled soul or in the stormy world around her. Only death can bring peace and calm. It is this presentiment, and her approaching death itself, that make her monologue so moving. *M 71*

Left
The Force of Destiny, production photograph with (from left to right) Julia Varady (Leonora), Giorgio Merighi (Alvaro), and Maria José Brill (Curra, Leonora's maid), production Hans Neuenfels, sets Erich Wonder, conductor Marcello Viotti, Deutsche Oper, Berlin 1998.
Once again, Verdi proves himself to be a master of contrasts, with an opera whose settings range across two countries and embrace both a battlefield and a girl's bedroom.

The Force of Destiny, production photograph with Ilona Tokody (Leonora) and Simon Estes (Padre Guardiano), production Hans Neuenfels, sets Erich Wonder, conductor Marcello Viotti, Deutsche Oper, Berlin 1998. The duet between Leonora and the Padre Guardiano is another artistic high point in the work of Verdi, who may be considered the master of the duet. The sheer extent of this key scene in the opera is impressive: it lasts nearly 20 minutes, what would normally be the length of half an act. Leonora tells the Franciscan of her fate, and her intention of living among the monks unrecognized as a woman. The Padre Guardiano, meeting Leonora for the first time, is won over by the strength and stature of her character; they are two extraordinary people meeting in an extraordinary situation.

71. Leonora's Pace Aria (Act IV)

Cru da-sven - tu - ra m'astringe, ahimè, a lan-guir; co - me il dì pri - mo da tant' an - ni du - ra profon -do il mio sof-frir. Pa - ce, pa - ce, pa-ce, mio Di-o, pa-ce, mio Di - o!

The Force of Destiny, photograph from the production by Helmut Polixa, sets and costumes Franz Lehr, Theater Bremen 1992. The Padre Guardiano and his monks in the finale of Act II. For all the resemblance of this great opera to a novel, Christian thought is a major theme in it. Verdi confronts worldly events – hatred, war, revenge, hypocrisy, and moral decline – with Christian doctrine, and as a dramatist he draws bitter conclusions. The true Christian is the Padre Guardiano, shown here with the symbol of the cross behind his noble figure: he is worthy to act in its name.

Opposite
The Force of Destiny, set design for the last scene by Heinz Grete, Nuremberg and Berlin 1930/31 (TWS).
Leonora wrestles with her destiny in this wild, rocky setting (where she sings her great "pace" aria). Here, beneath the cross, there will be a duel to the death between her lover and her brother. Protagonists and subsidiary roles alike live in the shadow of death in The Force of Destiny. The sense that they are delivered up to their fate gives the opera a special and terrifying tension.

The Padre Guardiano

The character of the Padre Guardiano, prior of the monastery of Madonna degli Angeli, is in stark contrast to the figures of suffering human beings pursued by misfortune. He is among those characters in the drama who determine the fate of the protagonists, crossing Leonora's path at her moment of crisis (Act II, Scene 2), giving refuge and comfort to those who seek it. The depth and gravity of the bass register give his figure great dignity. All Verdi's spiritual characters, from Zaccaria in →Nabucco to the Grand Inquisitor in →Don Carlos and Ramfis in →Aida, could have been chiseled out of marble. They radiate severity and superiority – in this case the superiority conferred by high ethical standards, humane understanding, and kindness. M 72

Alvaro

Even in Saavedra's original play Don Alvaro is a Byronic figure. He has every reason to lament his unjust fate, and is described as "very passionate, but always generous and noble-hearted." From the first, he is destined for a tragic fate. The question of his origin plays a major part in his character: he is a half-breed, a "colored" man. The extensive account in Saavedra's drama provides background information: he is the son of the Spanish viceroy of Peru, a man who married a Peruvian Inca princess and intended to set up an independent kingdom, breaking away from the Spanish crown. Alvaro's scena and romanza (beginning of Act III) give a succinct account of his origin and fate: he says he was born in prison and brought up in a strange land. M 73

Carlo

The pursuer stands beside the two fugitives in importance. Carlo, Leonora's brother, is not only fanatically bent on revenge but also, and above all, a man possessed by ideas of rank. He ruins himself as well as his victims. Don Carlo di Vargas is one of the strangest figures among the negative protagonists Verdi derived from his literary sources. From the first his character is questionable; he is unscrupulous in the means he chooses to pursue his ends, by no means a very perfect gentle knight – yet there is something grand about his persistence. Verdi depicts him as an implacable adversary, but does not deny him a curious kind of magnanimity, even nobility, for instance in the solemn tone and sublime melody of the famous "friendship duet" by the sickbed of the wounded Alvaro. M 74 In complete contrast to this number, the two subsequent duets for Carlo and Alvaro (in Act III and Act IV) are notable for a crescendo of hatred. The last duet is a masterpiece of dramatic intensification, with both text and music constructed on an emotional alternation of ebb and flow. The opening melody of the duet (which is one of the major themes in the overture) is dominated by an elegiac mood of sadness that can never be overcome. There is no victor in this confrontation. M 75   J. K.

72. Duet between the Padre Guardiano and Leonora

Sull' al - ba il piede all' e - re - mo so - lin - ga vol - ge - re - te

73. Alvaro's *Romanza* (Act III)

Del - la na - tal sua ter - ra il pa - dre vol - le spezzar l'e - stranio gio - go

74. The Friendship Duet between Alvaro and Carlo (Act III)

A - mi - co, fi-da - te, fi - da - te nel cie-lo, fi-da-te nel ciel, ___ a-mi-co, fi - da - te nel cielo, fi-da - te.

75. A Settling of Accounts (Duet between Alvaro and Carlo, Act IV)

Le mi - naccie, i fie-ri ac - cen - ti por-tin se - co in pre-da i ven - ti, per-do-

na - te - mi, pie - tà, o fra - tel, pie - tà, pie - tà.

76. Destiny Motif

A framework of genre painting

The continuity of the tragic action is broken several times by genre-like episodes. They are painted in bright, glowing colors that contrast with the dark general tone of the work, and seem to be only loosely connected with the main action, yet they are of essential significance. Against the background of hatred, violence, seduction, intolerance, and mass delusions, the fate of Leonora, Alvaro, and Carlo appears to be only one among many hundreds of similar stories, as the tavern scene of Act II makes clear. Leonora and her pursuer Carlo emerge from the bustling crowd for only a few minutes. But the strophic song sung by Carlo – introducing himself under the false name of Pereda, and telling only half the truth of the story – brings about a complete change in Leonora. Her loneliness is all the more evident because most of the scene is devoted to the others present: travelers, peasants, pilgrims, soldiers, and gypsies, all wandering around like herself, and none of them making any real contact with anyone else.

Trabuco and Preziosilla

Trabuco and Preziosilla seem to be episodic figures, but Verdi by no means treats them as minor roles. On cast lists in contemporary programs, Preziosilla features as a "prima donna mezzosoprano," while Trabuco is described as a "tenore comprimario" and in the Milan cast list of 1869 as a "tenor brillante."

Trabuco appears in the tavern scene as a muleteer whose secret mission is to prepare the way for Leonora's flight. In the scene in the army camp near Velletri he features as a pedlar and market trader – a parallel to the figure of the Croat in Schiller's *Wallensteins Lager* (*Wallenstein's Camp*), and also a descendant of the Jewish pedlar Isacco in Rossini's *The Thieving Magpie*. In his correspondence with Piave, Verdi once refers to Trabuco as an "ebreo" (Hebrew).

The camp scene rounds out Trabuco's portrait into an ironically humorous character sketch, as he offers his wares to the soldiers in song.

·The figure of Preziosilla derives from several sources, not only Saavedra's play but also the generic type of such parts in French opera. Her characteristics as "gypsy girl" or "fortune-teller" are subsidiary attributes deriving from the French model. They are not her essential qualities, but have merely a playful, superficial significance in Verdi's opera. Preziosilla is first and foremost a vivandière, and she even voluntarily assumes the role of female recruiting officer for the army. As early as the tavern scene in Hornachuelos, her two-strophe song on her first appearance encourages men to join up, and we are not surprised to meet her again in the camp outside Velletri (in Italy this time), leading the vivandières accompanying the Spanish troops. She is a woman who has been obliged to live with and by means of war.

Preziosilla's musical showpieces have identifiable predecessors, mainly in the genre scenes of Meyerbeer's →*The Huguenots,* for instance her various strophic songs and dance tunes (including a fiery tarantella with chorus in the army camp scene), and her famous "Rataplan." It is interesting that here the accompaniment is provided not by an instrumental background but by the soldiers' chorus, chanting to the rhythm of the drumbeat. Again, there are parallels in Meyerbeer's opera. In this way Preziosilla becomes the symbol of a woman's fate in wartime – at the opposite pole from Leonora.

War: realism and romanticism

The war is present throughout the whole of Act III. The warlike scenes set the piece in a real historical perspective: an episode from the Austrian Wars of Succession of 1740–48, when the Spanish and Italian troops were allied in the last stages of the campaign and at the battle of Velletri. Much of the depiction of warfare and the military life goes back to Schiller. It is presented in both a realistic and a romantic manner: while it does not hide the misery and tragic consequences of war, it also emphasizes the brightly colored and grotesque elements.

Fra Melitone

The highlight of the army camp scene is Fra Melitone's sermon, structured not as an aria but as a free monologue – a paraphrase of the Capuchin friar's sermon in Schiller's *Wallensteins Lager*. Both the general train of thought in this absurd flood of words, and Schiller's remarkable distortions and plays on words, are skilfully translated or adapted into Italian, thanks to Piave and above all to Andrea Maffei's fine translation of Schiller. Fra Melitone has already appeared in Act II, Scene 2, as the monastery porter accompanying the Padre Guardiano: a curious, surly, grumbling fellow. He seems almost like the comic shadow of the elevated figure of the churchman, a clown in a monastic habit. He returns

The Force of Destiny, photograph from the production by Helmut Polixa, sets and costumes Franz Lehr, Theater Bremen 1992.

at the beginning of Act IV in a comic scene that emphasizes his character even more distinctly; as he dispenses alms to the poor he loses patience, and breaks out into angry jabbering accompanied by gesticulations.

The cast list describes Fra Melitone's part as a "primo baritono brillant," and it is known that Verdi intended the role for a star singer, a fact that illustrates the importance he assigned to the character and the first-rate acting and singing qualities that are necessary to do it justice.

J. K.

Above
The Force of Destiny, photograph from the production by Hans Neuenfels, sets Erich Wonder, costumes Dirk von Bodisco, conductor Paolo Olmi, Deutsche Oper, Berlin 1998.
Nowhere else in Verdi's work do the common people appear in such a poor light as in this opera. They are a mob demoralized by war. In this environment, Fra Melitone's sermon (a translation of the Capuchin's sermon by Schiller) is a ridiculous piece of pomposity.

The Force of Destiny, Giulietta Simionato as Preziosilla and Franco Riccardi as Trabuco, Teatro alla Scala, Milan 1955/56.
As early as the first version of →*Simon Boccanegra,* Verdi aimed to depict people and groups in movement, a feature that, in line with its subject, is particularly striking in *The Force of Destiny*. The opera has something of the quality of a novel, not only in the action and the grouping of episodes in the manner of chapters, but also in the character parts, which contribute to the general narrative.

Don Carlos

Opéra in five acts (Italian version, four acts)

Libretto: Joseph Méry and Camille du Locle, after the play of the same name by Friedrich von Schiller.

Première: French five-act version: 11 March 1867, Paris (Opéra); Italian four-act version, text revised by Camille du Locle, Italian translation by Achille de Lauzières and Angelo Zanardini: 10 January 1884, Milan (Teatro alla Scala).

Characters: Philip II, King of Spain (B), Elisabeth de Valois, his wife (S), Don Carlos, Infante of Spain (T), Princess Eboli, a lady of the court (Ms), Rodrigue, Marquis of Posa (Bar), The Grand Inquisitor (B), The Count of Lerma (T), The Countess of Aremberg (silent), Thibault, the queen's page (S), An Old Monk (B), A Voice from Heaven (S); Flemish deputies, lords and ladies, crowd, pages, guards, monks, officers of the Inquisition, soldiers, condemned heretics (chorus).

Setting: France and Spain, around 1560.

Don Carlos, production photograph with Mara Zampieri (Elisabeth) and Placido Domingo (Carlos), production Pier Luigi Pizzi, conductor Claudio Abbado, Wiener Staatsoper 1989 (photograph 1992). There is a family story at the heart of this grand historical opera – the story of a tragic love that can never be fulfilled, but brings torment to all concerned. Except for the Marquis of Posa and the Grand Inquisitor, all the protagonists in Don Carlos are frustrated in love.

Synopsis

Act I (Prologue in the Italian version)

The forest at Fontainebleau. During the truce of 1559 in the war between Spain and France, envoys from Philip II are visiting the French court. As a pledge of peace, the king of Spain has betrothed his son Don Carlos to Elisabeth de Valois, although the two have not yet seen each other. Elisabeth meets her betrothed only by chance, when she loses her way out hunting, and they immediately fall deeply in love. But their hopes of happiness are dashed when political interests induce Philip to marry Elisabeth himself.

Act II (Act I in the Italian version)

Scene 1: The monastery of San Yuste. Carlos cannot forget his love for Elisabeth. Inconsolable, he flees to the monastery of San Yuste and the tomb of his imperial grandfather Charles V. Here the monks value heavenly peace above worldly power, and here he encounters the marquis of Posa, back from years of absence in the Netherlands, where the Spanish Inquisition is at its height and the Spanish army brutally suppresses all resistance. Posa is aware that Carlos, the friend of his youth, favors peaceful solutions, and hopes to direct the force of Carlos's passions away from Elisabeth and put them instead to the service of the liberation of the Netherlands. Carlos, he says, should ask his father to send him to Flanders.

Scene 2: A pleasant landscape outside the monastery of San Yuste. Posa brings Elisabeth letters from the queen of France, and at the same time asks her to use her influence with Carlos to interest him in moral and political aims. She agrees, granting Carlos an immediate interview, but he is carried away by his unhappy love, and draws a confession of her own disappointed hopes from Elisabeth. Conscious of her position and responsibilities, however, she regains her composure and gives Carlos new courage. The king arrives unexpectedly, finds his wife unaccompanied, and dismisses the lady-in-waiting who ought to have been with her for this breach of etiquette. Elisabeth courageously defies her husband by taking an affectionate leave of the lady-in-waiting. She also makes bitter remarks about Spain. When the king meets Posa and recollects the Marquis's earlier services to the state, he tries to win his support by pardoning his defiance of royal authority, but Posa scorns all personal favors, and asks for mercy for the suffering people of the Netherlands instead. Impressed by his extraordinary courage, Philip wishes to make Posa his friend. He confides his jealousy of his son and his suspicions of Elisabeth to the Marquis, gives him full political powers, and warns him against the Inquisition.

Act III (Act II in the Italian version)

Scene 1: A garden of the palace in Madrid. Elisabeth, not wishing to attend a masquerade, gives her cloak, jewelry, and mask to her confidante Princess Eboli. The princess is passionately in love with Carlos herself, and sends a message luring him into the garden. Carlos thinks he is speaking to the queen, but once they have exchanged words of love the deception is revealed. Carlos has betrayed his secret passion, Eboli feels humiliated, and her love turns to hatred. By chance, Posa has witnessed this development, and would like to kill the princess, whose knowledge makes her dangerous. He then has the idea of making use of the general confusion to sacrifice himself at the appropriate moment. But first, he makes Carlos give him all incriminating documents.

Scene 2: Outside Valladolid Cathedral. The Inquisition is preparing for a public *auto-da-fé*. The crowd has gathered, and the heretics and their executioners come before the king. Philip renews his vow to put down heresy. At this point the deputies from the Netherlands appear, led by Carlos, begging for mercy for their tormented land and people. Carlos asks to be sent to Flanders himself, but the king refuses, and dismisses him. Carlos now draws his sword against his father, and the king punishes this public challenge by having him arrested. When no one else dares ask the Infante to hand over his sword, Posa does so, hoping to limit the damage done by this senseless and emotional act. The burning of the condemned heretics begins. While some of the onlookers show satisfaction, others faint away or feel pity, and a heavenly voice promises peace to the innocent victims of torture.

Act IV (Act III in the Italian version)
Scene 1: The king's study in Madrid. Philip has passed another sleepless night, tormented by jealousy, loneliness, and a sense of impotence. He summons the Grand Inquisitor to ask if it can ever be right for a father to kill his own son. The Grand Inquisitor points to the sacrifice of Jesus, thus turning the Christian idea of redemption into its diabolically inspired opposite, the maintenance of human power. He offers Philip absolution for the murder of Carlos, and in return demands that the king hand over Posa, whose career the Inquisition has long been following. In vain does Philip show his more humane side, pleading that he needs a friend; as a ruler he agrees, for he also needs the Church in order to preserve his power. Elisabeth has discovered the theft of her private jewel case, which the Princess Eboli has had sent to the king. Philip forces it open, discovers a medallion that Carlos once gave Elisabeth in Fontainebleau when they were betrothed, and accuses her of unfaithfulness. Seeing the queen unjustly suspected, Eboli admits her own guilt, and Elisabeth banishes her from the court. Eboli knows that Philip has already made out a death warrant for Carlos, and determines on a bold attempt to rescue him.

Scene 2: A prison. Posa says farewell to Carlos. He has written a letter accusing himself of instigating riots and taking secret documents from Carlos with malicious intent. The vengeance of the disappointed king is swift and violent; a bullet wounds Posa mortally. Dying, he tells Carlos that the queen wishes to see him one last time before he leaves for Flanders. The king comes in person to free his son, believing that he too was betrayed by Posa. Carlos flings the truth in the king's face. The mob led by Princess Eboli demands Carlos's freedom and forces its way into the prison. Only the appearance of the Grand Inquisitor prevents a rebellion.

Act V (Act IV in the Italian version)
The monastery of San Yuste. Posa had named the tomb of Charles V as the place where the Infante and Elisabeth are to meet and say farewell. Elisabeth urges Carlos to be mindful of the freedom of Flanders. Now, at last, Carlos is mature enough to undertake his political mission, but he has hesitated too long, and his confession over his dead friend's body was too revealing. The Inquisition demands its victim. At this point a supernatural power intervenes, as an old monk removes Carlos from human hands. The Grand Inquisitor and Philip both draw back, for the monk speaks with the voice of Charles V, Philip's father, who renounced worldly power for the sake of heavenly peace.   *S. N.*

Don Carlos, production photograph with Placido Domingo as Don Carlos, production Pier Luigi Pizzi, conductor Claudio Abbado, Wiener Staatsoper 1989.
Verdi's Don Carlos diverges considerably from the historical figure. The Spanish Infante was very different in real life from the idealized character later depicted in literature. According to various contemporary accounts he was deformed, hunchbacked, and feeble-minded, and had sadistic inclinations. In 1568 Philip II was obliged to have his son arrested for subversion, and put the case before a committee of Spanish grandees. Don Carlos died in prison while the trial was in preparation.

Don Carlos, production photograph with Agnes Baltsa as Princess Eboli, production Pier Luigi Pizzi, conductor Claudio Abbado, Wiener Staatsoper 1989.
A fiery Spanish lady, Princess Eboli reduces three people to despair in her blind love for Carlos.

Don Carlos, set design by Eduard Löffler for the production by Richard Hein, Nationaltheater, Mannheim 1930 (TWS).
Set for the finale of the *auto-da-fé* scene, with the crowd of onlookers, the heretics, the Flemish deputies, the king, Don Carlos, Posa, and Elisabeth.

History and legend

At the time of the final revision of *Don Carlos* in 1883, Verdi wrote to his publisher Giulio Ricordi: "Brilliant as it is in form and noble sentiments, everything in this drama is false ... The real Don Carlos was feeble-minded, choleric, and unsympathetic. Elisabeth was never in love with Don Carlos. Posa is an imaginary character who could never have existed under the rule of Philip II. And Philip himself says: 'Beware of my Inquisitor,' and 'Who will give me this dead man back?'

The real Philip was not so mild ... In fact, there is nothing really historical about this drama."

The *auto-da-fé*

The great *auto-da-fé* scene is a high point of *Don Carlos*. An *auto-da-fé* (Latin: "actus fidei," Spanish "auto de fe") was the term for an "act of faith" in which those condemned by the spiritual court of the Inquisition were handed over to the secular arm of the law. Public executions, paradoxically, were popular with the spectacle-loving crowd in Spain of the sixteenth and seventeenth centuries. The *auto-da-fé* scene is not in Friedrich von Schiller's play, the basis of the libretto; its many levels of complexity and the massive impact it makes call for the operatic stage. The contemporary production book for the première (the "disposizioni sceniche") shows what huge forces were used: hundreds of chorus members and extras with precisely defined functions had to be positioned on the stage, covering a vast area, and there was also a large brass band on stage to play fanfares. Everything in the production aimed for grand visual and sound effects.

The auto-da-fé finale

The scene opens and closes with passages for chorus and shouts of joy from the crowd that has assembled to witness a terrifying ritual. Amidst these songs of praise, a funeral march in a hollow and threatening minor key is heard as the heretics appear, led to their execution. At the end of the act, when the pyres blaze up, a mystic, heavenly "voice from on high" is heard promising the crown of martyrdom to the dying. In the central part of the scene, the king emerges from the cathedral and makes a speech to the people, proclaiming his inflexible determination to persecute unbelievers and heretics. Then comes the first shock: the entrance of the deputies from Brabant to confront King Philip. The great ensemble of the finale develops from this situation. It is not a neutral presentation of a difficult moment, but clearly illustrates Verdi's own attitude to the positive and negative forces in the drama. Philip's sharply rhythmic solo in the minor key, acknowledging his obsession with power and reasons of state, clashes with the hymn-like melody in the major for the Flemish deputies who have come to support their just cause. The voices of Queen Elisabeth and the sympathetic crowd are associated with the deputies, while the king is supported by the crowd of monks. It is a mighty musical structure, in which the dramatic conflict is powerfully concentrated.   *J. K.*

Opposite, right
Don Carlos, production photograph with
Nicolai Ghiaurov as King Philip, production
Pier Luigi Pizzi, conductor Claudio Abbado,
Wiener Staatsoper 1989.
King Philip II, the most powerful ruler of
the 16th century. His problems as father,
husband, and monarch are a constant theme
running through the whole drama. Verdi
presents him, with extraordinary empathy, as
a powerful man who is nonetheless as much
a victim of fate as the least of his subjects,
although great human authority can be
sensed behind the rigid mask of the
unapproachable sovereign. He is a
monumental dramatic figure.

77. King Philip's Monologue

Dor - mi - rò sol   nel man-to mio re - gal,   quan - do la mia gior -na-ta è giunta a   se - ra

78. Queen Elisabeth's *Romanza*

Non   pian - ger,   mia com - pa - gna, non pian - ger no, le - nis -ci il tuo do - lor.

79. Queen Elisabeth's Aria

s'an-cor si pian-ge in cie   - lo,   pian-gi sul mio do - lo - re,

e   por - ta il pian   - to mi - o al tro - no del Sig -nor

Below
Don Carlos, production photograph with
Mirella Freni as Queen Elisabeth, production
Pier Luigi Pizzi, conductor Claudio Abbado,
Wiener Staatsoper 1989.
The historical model for Elisabeth, Elisabeth
de Valois (1545–68), daughter of King Henri II
of France, was the same age as Don Carlos. At
the age of 15, she became the third wife of
the 33-year-old King Philip II, and she died
when she was only 23. There is no factual
basis at all for an amorous relationship
between Elisabeth and Don Carlos. The
fictional romance was invented a century
after the deaths of those concerned.

80. Veil Song (Princess Eboli)

Nei giar-din del bel - lo _____ sa - racin o - stel - lo _____

81. Princess Eboli's Aria

O _____ mia Re - gi - na, io t'im - mo - la - i   al _____ fol - le er - ror _____   di _____ que - sto cor.

Rhythms from the Escorial

Each of the mature Verdi's operas has its own basic musical color – an aura made up of musical gestures, instrumental colorings, melodic phrasings and characteristic rhythms, differing in every work from →*Rigoletto* to →*Falstaff*. Even singing the most prominent themes or looking at the graphic image of the music presented by the notation reveals differences between these masterpieces. Most of the melodies in *Don Carlos* are dominated by dotted rhythms: short-long, short-long. They illustrate the solemn ceremonial and rigidity of the royal court of Spain in the 16th century. M 84 At the same time a desire for personal and political freedom flashes through them. M 82 In this world, pomp and fanaticism are combined in equal proportions – a musical dimension absent from the solo numbers for the women (Elisabeth and Eboli, →M 78–M 81) and from most of the themes in the duet between Elisabeth and Carlos. M 83 The lyricism of these numbers, marked by extended melodies and supported by a regular rhythm, reveals a world of intimate feeling. And it is only in the king's great monologue, when his gaze is turned inwards to his own heart, that Verdi fails to give him the "short-long" rhythm that conveys his sense of pride and power. →M 77

A discussion of power

The high drama of the dialogue between King Philip and the Grand Inquisitor divides into two sections. In the first, Philip takes the lead. He brings up the idea of whether, as a father, he should surrender his rebellious son to justice, and, if so, whether he could reconcile his execution with his own conscience. This section is tightly constructed on an orchestral motif that recurs at its conclusion. M 84

In the following section the Grand Inquisitor takes the initiative. There are more important matters, he says, than the life of a single rebel. The unity of the Christian faith is at stake, and it is threatened by the subversive activities of a heretical rabble-rouser – the king's friend the marquis of Posa. It is he who must be destroyed. Here the king himself comes under the suspicion of sympathizing with liberal tendencies. In this section the Grand Inquisitor gains the upper hand, and the orchestral accompaniment is dynamic and agitated. M 85 Two deep bass voices and two iron wills clash. At the center of this struggle is the vital question of whether secular or sacred power should take precedence, and which of their leading representatives has priority. In the sixteenth century this would have been an anachronistic question, but in the age of Schiller, and indeed for Verdi around 1867, it was a matter of great importance, bearing on the emancipation of secular powers and the separation of Church and State. The scene reflects problems that were very much of the eighteenth and nineteenth centuries, although of course that does not alter the fact that the depiction of a passionate collision between two forces creates a climax of great musical and dramatic power.

A discussion of politics

Another confrontation between two deep male voices, the duet for King Philip and Posa, is an intimate private conversation. It has been initiated by the king, but his audience with Philip gives Posa the opportunity of revealing the terrible evils of Spanish oppression in Flanders, and trying to persuade the king to make changes. Philip needs Posa, an honest man to whom he can open his heart, someone with whom he can share his human isolation, and to whom he can confide his jealous suspicions of his wife's relationship with his son. He wants Posa to help him.

A discussion of freedom

In the duet between Carlos and Posa (Act II, Italian version Act I), Posa learns of the Infante's secret love for his stepmother Queen Elisabeth. Posa keeps his friend's secret, but from this moment he has an interest in diverting the Infante's depth of feeling into new channels by persuading him to espouse the cause of the Flemish struggle for freedom. The cabaletta at the conclusion of the duet leads into an enthusiastic, march-like dialogue with the two voices strictly in parallel; it is one of the best-known melodies in the entire opera. An idiosyncratic feature of this duet on the subject of friendship and freedom (constructed on the pattern of the traditional Italian duet) is that it is interrupted by a mute scene – the royal couple and a procession of monks cross the stage and enter the monastery – and concludes only after the return of the freedom theme. M 82

A discussion of love

In the final version, Verdi decided on a strange, mystic ending – the salvation of Carlos by an old monk who speaks with the voice of his grandfather Charles V – although he would probably have preferred to conclude the opera with the farewell duet of Elisabeth and Carlos. In its musical content, this wonderful duet (the "duetto d'addio," as the score calls it) is Verdi's last really important artistic statement in the opera. The two lovers have met in the monastery to say a last farewell; they are sad but composed, and resigned to the harsh necessity of renunciation. They remind each other of the dead Marquis Posa, who has left them a task to perform. In the rapid, martial section of the duet, they evoke the heroic aim that is to give meaning to Carlos's future life: his promotion of the cause of Flemish freedom. Then the tempo slows down, and tears flow. The close, in an ethereal "sostenuto, piano" ("sustained and soft"), conveys resignation: the lovers express a hope that one day they will meet again "above," in another, better world. M 83   J. K.

82. Freedom Duet (Carlos and Posa)

Dio, __ che nell' alma in-fon - de-re a-mor __ vo-les-ti e spe - me,

de - sio nel cor ac - cen - de-re tu dèi _____ di li-ber-tà

83. Melody of Resignation (Duet between Elisabeth and Carlos)

In tal dì, ___ che per noi non a-vrà ___ più do-ma-ni

Don Carlos, set design by Eduard Löffler (King Philip and the Grand Inquisitor) for the production by Richard Hein, Nationaltheater, Mannheim 1930 (TWS).
The king consults the Grand Inquisitor: in this nocturnal interview in the king's study at the beginning of Act IV (Italian version Act III), secret and terrible decisions are taken, as in all dictatorships.

84. The King's Orchestral Motif (Duet between King Philip and the Grand Inquisitor)

85. The Grand Inquisitor's Orchestral Motif (Duet between King Philip and the Grand Inquisitor)

Aida

Opéra in four acts

Libretto: Antonio Ghislanzoni, after a scenario by Auguste Mariette.
Première: 24 December 1871, Cairo (Opera House).

Characters: The King of Egypt (B), Amneris, his daughter (Ms), Aida, an Ethiopian slave (S), Radames, captain of the guards (T), Ramfis, the chief priest (B), Amonasro, King of Ethiopia, Aida's father (Bar), The High Priestess (S), A Messenger (T); bodyguards, priests, priestesses, ministers, captains, Egyptian soldiers, dignitaries, Ethiopian slaves and captives, Egyptian people (chorus).
Setting: Memphis and Thebes, during the reign of the Pharaohs.

Aida, production photograph with dancers, production Elijah Moshinsky, conductor Edward Downes, Royal Opera House, London 1994.
In the context of historical reality and artistic verisimilitude, the story of Aida, Amneris, Radames, and Amonasro represents a remarkable symbiosis between historical research (intensive archaeological studies of ancient Egypt were made during the 19th century) and the intellectual approach to history of Verdi's own time. The settings and names of characters are taken from ancient Egypt of between 1500 and 120 BC.

Synopsis
Act I
Scene 1: The royal palace in Memphis. Aida, daughter of the king of Ethiopia, Amonasro, is a slave at the Egyptian court. She has fallen in love with Radames, who returns her feelings (Radames's *romanza* M 86). Amneris, the daughter of the King of Egypt, also loves the brave young warrior (duet: Amneris and Radames). She is uneasy when she observes the depth of sympathy felt by Radames for Aida (trio: Aida, Amneris, and Radames). When war breaks out again between Ethiopia and Egypt, Radames is appointed general. All wish him victory, even Aida, who only later realizes that such a wish makes her disloyal to her father. In despair, she laments her fate in a prayer to the gods of her homeland. She can see no way out of her dilemma: the

necessity of choosing between her father and the man she loves (Aida's *scena* and *romanza* M 87).
Scene 2: Inside the Temple of Vulcan in Memphis. Priests and priestesses invoke the god in song and ritual dance, praying for victory for Radames. Ramfis gives Radames the sacred sword of war.

Act II
Scene 1: Amneris's apartments. The Egyptians, led by Radames, have defeated the Ethiopians. Amneris has herself adorned by her slave girls for the victory celebrations, and tricks Aida into revealing the secret of her love for Radames (*scena* and duet: Aida and Amneris).
Scene 2: Outside one of the gates of Thebes. The returning soldiers are greeted joyfully (grand march and hymn of victory M88, M89). Amneris crowns Radames as the victor, and the king promises to grant him any wish. Radames asks for the freedom of the captive Ethiopians. The king agrees, on condition that Aida and her father remain in Egypt as hostages. He offers Radames the hand of Amneris in marriage, and succession to the throne.

Act III
On the banks of the Nile. The night before her wedding, Amneris goes to the Temple of Isis to pray. Aida is awaiting Radames on the banks of the Nile, where they have a secret rendezvous (Aida's *romanza* M 90). Amonasro takes this opportunity to ask his daughter to make Radames reveal his military plans, reminding her of the sufferings of her people (duet: Aida and Amonasro). Aida persuades Radames to elope with her (duet: Aida and Radames). When Radames tells her the route his army will take in marching on the Ethiopians, Amonasro is triumphant. He emerges from the darkness, revealing himself as king of Ethiopia. Amneris, leaving the temple unexpectedly, witnesses Radames's involuntary betrayal. Aida and Amonasro make their escape, but Radames lets the priests take him prisoner.

Act IV
Scene 1: A hall in the royal palace. Radames has been accused of high treason, and is to answer for his conduct to the priests. Amneris promises to save him if he will renounce Aida. But Radames will let nothing shake his resolve, and is prepared to die (*scena* and duet: Amneris and Radames). The priests condemn him to death.
Scene 2: The Temple of Vulcan, with a vault beneath it where Radames is to be entombed alive. Aida has stolen secretly into the vault to die with her lover. As the priests call on the god, and Amneris prays for eternal peace for Radames, the lovers take their leave of life together (duet: Aida and Radames M 91).   Á. G.

Aerial photograph of the Arena di Verona, 1984.

Since 1913 operatic performances have been given in the Arena di Verona in summer, with 25000 spectators enjoying the show every evening. With its ceremonial crowd scenes and its ballets, intended from the outset for a large stage with magnificently decorative sets, *Aida* is one of the operas most frequently performed in the huge arena of this Renaissance city. While he was composing the work, Verdi hoped not only that it would be performed for the opening of the Suez Canal in 1869, but also that it would have a production at the Opéra in Paris. In fact the opera was finally given its première in Cairo two years after the inauguration of the Canal. The first production in Paris was not until 1880.

Below
Aida, Enrico Caruso as Radames.
His contemporaries said that Caruso became so deeply immersed in his roles that on the day of a performance he would go about with the bearing of "his" hero of the coming evening.

86. Radames's *Romanza*

Ce - le - ste A - i - da, ___ for - ma di - vi - na, ___ mi - sti - co ser - to - di lu - ce e fior

87. Aida's *Romanza* (Act I)

(Klarinette)   e l'a mor mi - o?   (Klarinette)   Dun - que scor - dar pos - s'i - o

88. Entrance of the Victors

Glo - ria all' Egitto, ad   I - si - de   che il sacro suol pro - teg - ge!

89. Hymn of Victory

S'in - trec - ci il lo - to al lau - ro sul crin dei vin - ci - to - ri!

90. Aida's *Romanza* (Act III, Scene on the Banks of the Nile)

O cieli az - zurri, o dolci au - re na - ti - ve do - ve se - re - no il mio mattin bril - lò ...

91. Final Duet (Aida and Radames)

O terra, ad - di - o; addi - o val - le di pian - ti ...

Aida, production photograph with Sylvie Valayre as Aida, production, sets, and costumes Pier Luigi Pizzi, conductor Daniel Oren, Verona 1996.
The opera presents not only the opposition of intriguers and the innocent, but also tragic figures whose actions are logically motivated and ethically justified. This is true of Amneris as well as Aida, and of the representatives of the power of Egypt as well as Amonasro and the Ethiopians.

A tourist spectacle?

Aida is not only a festive but also a festival opera: a popular choice for open-air productions, both a tourist opera and a drama that appeals to discriminating opera enthusiasts. Of the three scenes requiring choreography, the dance of the priestesses in the temple scene (Act I, Scene 2) is not really an independent ballet, but the visual complement to their ritual. The dance of the slaves in Amneris's apartments (Act II, Scene 1) is one of the short interludes that are often found inserted into Verdi's operas as episodes in a complex scene.

The really large-scale ballet – not inserted as an afterthought, but an organic part of the composition – comes in the finale of Act II, and is an attractive and spectacular depiction of the victory procession. Verdi certainly had Parisian models in mind when he wrote this interlude, and he also had his eye on the chances of a production in Paris. It is not known why the opera was not produced there until some time later, in 1880. Verdi was asked to extend the ballet music for the Paris production.

Exoticism

It is curious that the well-documented story of the creation of this work has almost nothing to say about the musical exoticism of *Aida*. At any rate, there are no accounts of Verdi's studying any sources in the fields of ancient or oriental music before writing the score. The Egyptian music may well have been a case of instinctive exoticism on the composer's part, although it is not entirely free from associations with Arab music and reminiscences of Arab melodies. M 92

Certain particular instrumental colorings are also part of the local color of orientalism: "wailing" oboe solos, low flute parts, and in some scenes the striking use of "Egyptian" harps (for instance, in the temple scene, and at the beginning of Act II).

Orchestral coloring

The orchestration of *Aida* is wonderfully colorful. Verdi's experience of contemporary French music led him to make use of many new features derived from the development of modern orchestral techniques, and he made increasing demands on his instrumentalists.

The incomparable atmosphere of the nocturnal scene on the banks of the Nile is the result of magical instrumentation. A violin motif consisting of a single pitch (G) played at four octave levels conjures up associations of water – the river Nile – and a sense of timelessness. It was a bold venture for the time, requiring as it does purity of intonation from 12 violins at once. M 93.1

The motif, like an oscillating spot of color, is supported by the flageolet-like tone of the cellos. M 93.2

A single flute, sounding like a shepherd's song in the distance, gradually brings movement into this static nocturnal scene. M 93.3

Aida, Rudolf Bockelmann as Amonasro at the Staatsoper in Berlin in 1939.
Amonasro, the Lion King of the Ethiopians, is the prototypical heroic baritone role, and in contrast to Radames is a hero seen in defeat. Amonasro really was king of Ethiopia (c. 275–260 BC), and had the two lion figures from the tomb of Tutankhamen moved to his temple as symbols of his power.

Aida, set design by Ludwig Sievert, Munich and Berlin 1937 (TWS). Among the secrets of the immortality of *Aida* – by comparison with the many now forgotten grand operas of the 19th century – are its dramatic content, its sensational sets, and its spectacle.

The *Aida* fanfares

The bombastic brass sound of the Egyptian victory celebrations is in contrast to this music of silence. Besides ordinary brass instruments, Verdi uses others that have entered the history of instrumentation as *Aida* trumpets. In form, they resemble genuine ancient Egyptian trumpets: they are 1.52 meters long, straight, and without valves. Verdi had six trumpets specially made in Milan for the grand march, three in A flat and three in B minor. The three A flat trumpets play the march in unison in E flat major, the B minor trumpets take over the melody in B major. This sudden change of key lends solemnity to the imposing crowd scene. *M 94*   J. K.

The art of singing softly

The recitative passages in which Radames appears as a victorious army commander are accompanied by loud trumpet and trombone signals; the vocal part, according to Verdi's directions, is to be performed "with enthusiasm" ("con entusiasmo"). By way of contrast, his directions for the tenor's famous *romanza* call for an expressive, gentle, and very quiet manner of delivery ("con espressione," "dolce," "sempre dolce," "parlante ppp"). In the four final bars, the singer is required to perform very softly, letting the sound diminish ("pppp," "ppp dim."), and the high B flat, not an easy note to sing, is to be performed quietly and dying away ("pp morendo"). Giuseppe Capponi, the first tenor to consider it impossible to follow these directions, was the founder of a long tradition: Verdi allowed him to sing the repeat of the B flat an octave lower. Encouraged by this compromise, the tenor Ernest Nicolini, the husband of the famous prima donna Adelina Patti, tried transposing the entire *romanza* down a semitone, to A major, but Verdi would have none of it. The *romanza* has remained a nightmare for tenors, not least because Radames has to launch into it almost without introduction at the beginning of the opera. *M 95*   J. K.

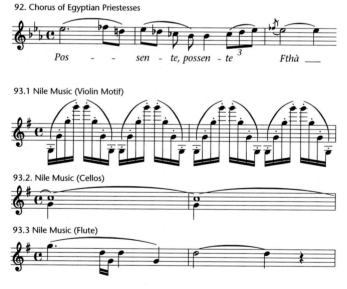

92. Chorus of Egyptian Priestesses

Pos - - sen - te, possen - te   Fthà

93.1 Nile Music (Violin Motif)

93.2 Nile Music (Cellos)

93.3 Nile Music (Flute)

94. Fanfare

95. Conclusion of Radames's *Romanza* (Act I)

un tro - no vici - no al sol,   un tro no-vi-cino al sol

Otello

Othello

Dramma lirico in four acts

Libretto: Arrigo Boito, after the tragedy by William Shakespeare.
Première: 5 February 1887, Milan (Teatro alla Scala).

Otello, production photograph with Kallen Esperian (Desdemona) and Kristian Johannsen (Othello), production Henning Brockhaus, sets Josef Svoboda, costumes Sázka Hejnova, conductor Christian Thielemann, Teatro Communale di Bologna 1993.
It was Boito's brilliant idea to omit Shakespeare's opening scene, set in Venice, and introduce the victorious Othello at the height of his fame in the middle of the storm. From that point on the dramatic arc leads steadily downward, reaching its lowest point in the closing act after Othello's murder of Desdemona.

Characters: Otello/Othello, a Moor, commander of the Venetian fleet and governor of Cyprus (T), Desdemona, his wife (S), Iago, Othello's ensign (T), Emilia, Iago's wife (Ms), Cassio, a captain (T), Roderigo, a Venetian gentleman (T), Lodovico, an ambassador of the Venetian Republic (B), Montano, Othello's predecessor as governor of Cyprus (B), A Herald (B); soldiers and sailors, Venetian ladies and gentlemen, crowd (chorus).
Setting: A maritime city on the island of Cyprus, at the end of the 15th century.

Synopsis
Act I

A square outside the castle, with the harbor and a tavern. During a terrible storm, the people of Cyprus and followers of the Venetian troops fear for the safe return of the commander Othello, who has been victorious in battle against the Turks. Othello's ship comes safely to land, and all greet the conquering hero. Only one man does not join in the rejoicing:

Othello's ensign Iago. He feels slighted by Othello, who has promoted Cassio to the rank of captain over his own head, and is bent on revenge. He chooses the Venetian Roderigo, who is in love with Othello's wife Desdemona, as his tool in an intrigue. After encouraging Cassio to drink, he stages a quarrel between Roderigo and the drunken Cassio. When Montano tries to separate them Cassio wounds him. Just as Iago had planned, Othello hears the uproar and arrives on the scene; holding Cassio responsible for the incident, he demotes him. Desdemona calms Othello's fury. Othello is aware once again of the threats to his love: the union of a black man of obscure origin with a beautiful and rich Venetian noblewoman. He fears for his happiness, but Desdemona herself has no fear, feeling nothing but boundless love.

Act II

A hall in the castle, with a view of the garden. Iago purposefully pursues his intrigue. He advises the despairing Cassio to ask Desdemona to intercede with Othello for him. Iago explains that his petty sense of injury is behind his diabolical plan of revenge. He sees himself as a manipulator of human destinies, for he knows the most vulnerable place in the heart of the strong-willed Othello – his fear of losing Desdemona's love. He presents the relationship of Desdemona and Cassio to Othello in an incriminating light, so that every plea Desdemona makes for Cassio appears to the Moor to be evidence of her infidelity. Iago steals Desdemona's handkerchief, a gift Othello gave her at the time of their wedding, and when Othello demands proof that she is unfaithful, Iago pretends to have seen the handkerchief in Cassio's possession. These slanders, which are made to sound credible, drive Othello to swear a terrible oath renouncing all thoughts of happiness: he will be revenged.

Act III

The great hall of the castle. When Desdemona again asks Othello to pardon Cassio, Othello calls her a whore. Iago prompts Cassio to talk about his mistress Bianca, and manages the conversation so that Othello, listening in secret, is bound to think Cassio is speaking of Desdemona. When he sees the handkerchief lost by Desdemona in Cassio's hands, he is convinced of her infidelity, and decides to kill her. Iago is to dispose of Cassio, and in return will be promoted to captain. Envoys arrive to recall the over-powerful Othello to Venice; Cassio is to take his place in Cyprus. Othello, losing control of himself, publicly humiliates his wife and then collapses. Iago is triumphant.

Act IV

Desdemona's bedroom. She is preparing for the interview with Othello that will decide her fate – life or death – and remembers an old song, which comforts her, as it has comforted many women before her, while simultaneously inducing a mood of fatalism. Othello arrives, and in spite of Desdemona's protestations of innocence, he kills her. Iago's plans for the assassination of Cassio fail, and his wife Emilia exposes his evil machinations. Othello kills himself.   *S. N.*

Arrigo Boito (1842–1918).
The writer and composer provided the librettos for Verdi's *Otello* and *Falstaff*.

Arrigo Boito

The son of a miniaturist and a Polish countess, Boito had a wild youth. He fought a duel (over a quarrel about Rossini and Meyerbeer) with the Sicilian Giovanni Verga, a writer of the *verismo* movement and the author of the play on which →*Cavalleria rusticana* was based. One of the greatest of Italian Wagnerians, Boito was 26 when he composed an opera strongly influenced by Wagner, *Mefistofele* (*Mephistopheles*). He was regarded as the foremost authority on Shakespeare in Italy, and, not least in importance, he was the companion of Eleonora Duse, venerated as one of the greatest actresses of the time. His collaboration with Verdi was the highlight of his career.

Otello, production photograph with Placido Domingo as Othello, production Peter Wood, conductor Zubin Mehta, Wiener Staatsoper 1987.
"Un bacio ... un bacio ... ancora un bacio ... " Othello's murder and suicide, committed as crimes of passion, make his love for Desdemona immortal.

have it said, 'He measured his strength against the giant [i.e. Rossini] and was defeated,' than, 'He tried to hide behind the title *Iago*'."

Iago's first solo is a drinking song of great speed and verve, marked by strange irregularities. The key fluctuates between B minor, D major, and A major, and the musical form is also irregular: as Cassio gradually becomes drunk and can no longer order his thoughts, the musical form itself suggests drunkenness and the lines of the drinking song follow an irregular sequence. Those attributes of Iago that act as leitmotivs, his chromatic slides and diabolical trills, are constantly present in the song. The whole number is like a whirlwind whipped up until it dissolves into chaos – a chaos created by a devil. *M 96*

It was Boito's idea to insert Iago's famous Credo into the work – a confession of godlessness, nihilism, and ill will. The Credo was not written until April 1884, several years after the original concept of the libretto was set down on paper. There is no precise model for this monologue anywhere in Shakespeare's drama. Verdi reacted to Boito's suggestion with immediate enthusiasm, and the result was a brilliant composition, with its series of diabolical trills, terrifying leaps, loud *unisoni*, and foreboding *pianissimi* – and perhaps it is not entirely free of the influence of the "satanic" characters and colors of Boito's own *Mephistopheles*. *M 97*

96. Iago's Drinking Song

I - naf - fia l'u - go - la! _____ trinca, tra-can - na,

pri - - ma _ che _ svam - - pi - no can - to e bic-chier!

97. Iago's Credo

Above left
Otello, costume design for Iago by Alfredo Edel, Milan 1898.
In the character of Iago Verdi created an image of total evil, something he had been attempting – usually in parts for the lower registers of the male voice – since the character of Wurm in →*Luisa Miller*. He had the courage to depict destructive power with all its dramatic consequences. The terrifying thing about this image of evil is that Iago appears in normal human form.

Above right
Otello, production photograph with Renato Bruson as Iago singing his drinking song, production Peter Wood, conductor Zubin Mehta, Wiener Staatsoper 1987.
"Iago is envy. Iago is a villain. Iago is a critic ... He must look attractive and jovial, appearing honest and almost good-natured; he is thought an honorable man by everyone except his wife, who knows him well. If he did not have the considerable charm of a pleasing appearance and apparent honesty, his deceptions could not make him as powerful as he is." (Arrigo Boito)

Iago

Verdi had been working on the characters of his projected opera since 1879. At first it was the figure of Iago that interested him most. In a letter of around 1881 to his friend the Neapolitan painter Domenico Morelli, he wrote: "If I were an actor, and were to play Iago, I would wish for a tall, thin figure with narrow lips, small eyes close to the nose like those of monkeys ... his bearing would be distracted, indifferent to all beyond himself, blasé, skeptical, mocking, like that of a man who speaks both good and ill lightly and with easy superficiality."

It is significant that for quite a long time during the creation of the opera its provisional title was *Iago* (for one reason, to distinguish it from Rossini's still popular opera →*Otello*). Not until 1886 did Verdi finally decide to choose the character of Othello as the title role. "It is true," he wrote, in correspondence with Boito, "that Iago is the demon who sets all in motion, but Othello is the mainspring of the action: he loves, he becomes jealous, he kills, and is killed. For my part I would think it hypocritical not to call the piece *Otello*. I would rather

98. Othello's Entrance

E - sul - ta - te! L'or - go - glio mu - sul - ma - no sepol - to è in mar

99. Othello's Farewell to Fame

O - ra e per sem - pre ad - dio san-te me - mo - rie, ad - dio ___ su - bli - mi in - can - ti del pen - sier!

100. Revenge Duet (Othello and Iago)

Sì, pel ciel ___ mar - mo - reo giu - ro!

Sì, pel ciel ___ mar - mo - reo giu - ro!

Othello

Othello is the greatest and most difficult of Verdi's tenor roles, perhaps the most difficult tenor role in all operatic writing of the nineteenth century. It is comparable only with Tristan. It would be easy to say that all that is required is a *Heldentenor* with a powerful and brilliant voice. But in fact the part of Othello is extremely varied: despair, irony, intimacy, and madness follow each other in rapid succession. As conceived by Verdi and Boito, his basic character is not "eroico" (heroic) but "cupo e terribile" (dark and dreadful). Of course there are famous passages where Othello is either in command of his heroic nature, or looks back to the days when he was. His triumphant entrance in the tempest at the beginning of the opera shows him in all his strength (and presents a great challenge to tenors playing the role). M 98

However, the heroic tone is heard less and less frequently as the opera progresses, until it is felt only indirectly, in the form of self-destructive violence. Once Iago's poison begins to work, he takes his leave of fame with a heroic gesture. M 99

This tone becomes grotesquely effective in his revenge duet with Iago: the victorious commander joins with the villain in pledging himself to the forces of destruction, to wreck his own happiness. M 100   J. K.

Opposite
Otello, costume design for Othello by Alfredo Edel, Milan 1898 (TWS).
Othello is Verdi's last tenor title role. "He has the powerful and upright appearance of a warrior. He is straightforward in his conduct and his bearing, his orders are given with authority, his judgements with composure."
(Arrigo Boito)

Right
Otello, production photograph with Placido Domingo as Othello, production Peter Wood, conductor Zubin Mehta, Wiener Staatsoper 1987.
The greatest Othello of the 1980s and 1990s also sang the title role in Franco Zeffirelli's film of *Otello* (1986). Domingo's depiction of Othello was a high point in his brilliant career, admired all over the world. He was regarded as the quintessential Othello of the last two decades of the 20th century, and was immortalized in the role in Zeffirelli's film. Domingo sang this heroic part, in all its nuances of light and shade, with a combination of dazzling brilliance and sensitivity. His acting abilities are such that his interpretation ranks with those of the greatest Othellos of the spoken theater.

Love feast and Liebestod

An orchestral theme of almost ritual gravity plays a crucial part in the last scene of the opera. It is dark and inexorable, signaling the completion of the tragedy. *M 108* This motif sounds like a variant in the minor key of the love feast motif in Wagner's →*Parsifal*. *Parsifal* had its première five years before *Otello*, but there is no indication that Verdi knew Wagner's last opera. The apparent relationship between the motifs may therefore be pure coincidence. But it is no coincidence that the *Otello* motif appears in Verdi's own →*Don Carlos*. *M 109* Othello's last utterance is one not of grief but of love. Even as he dies, he is consumed by his love for Desdemona.

A role of high ideals

"A strong sense of love, purity, nobility, mildness, innocence, and resignation must radiate from the chaste and harmonious figure of Desdemona. The simpler and more restrained her movements, the more she will move the spectator, and the charm of youth and beauty will complete that impression."
(Arrigo Boito)

Otello, set design by Leo Pasetti, Bayerische Staatsoper, Munich 1931 (TWS). Desdemona, just before her murder. In Act IV of *Otello* murder and suicide merge inexorably into a terrible ritual.

101. Desdemona's Prayer

Pian - gea ___ can - tan - do nel-l'er-ma lan - da, ___ pian-gea la me - sta ___

102. Willow Song (Desdemona)

O Sal - ce! Sal - ce! Sal - ce!

Desdemona

Desdemona is seen in a special light in the opera. She is an angel, not just because of Shakespeare's portrayal of her character, but also and to a great extent through the magic of Verdi's music. In her injured innocence and the general aura of her character, she is related to Queen Elisabeth in →*Don Carlos*, and she is a wonderful fulfillment of Verdi's artistic vision. He gave Desdemona music of beauty and nobility that is almost unparalleled, even in his own works.

The structure of Desdemona's famous scene in Act IV largely corresponds to the other Italian opera on the same subject, Rossini's →*Otello*, written in the early nineteenth century. In both operas, the evening conversation between Desdemona and Emilia moves to the beginning of the last act, in preparation for the climax of the tragedy (instead of taking place in the penultimate scene of the last act, as in Shakespeare). In both Rossini and Verdi a delicate prelude creates the elegiac atmosphere of the scene; Verdi's prelude is pure chamber music for woodwind. And in both operas the scene closes with a "preghiera," or prayer, in Verdi's case a free paraphrase of the text of the *Ave Maria*. There is no prayer in Shakespeare's play. The "preghiera" in Verdi's opera is a characteristic musical interlude, a typical and conventional feature with a long tradition in operatic history. *M 101*

The structural features of Desdemona's "Willow Song" are much the same in both Rossini and Verdi; both composers used a strophic form with "prose" interruptions in the form of recitative. The delicate,

artistic construction of the whole scene – with the song, as it were, quoted in inverted commas, and now and then interrupted by short interchanges of dialogue between Desdemona and Emilia – is drawn from Shakespeare himself. Even the episode when Desdemona, moved by her fearful presentiments, thinks she hears a knock, which Emilia says is only a gust of wind, is presented by both Rossini and Verdi with very effective tone-painting. Shakespeare's poetic idea of interrupting the lines of the song with the recurrent refrain of "Sing willow, willow, willow" becomes the jewel of the scene in Verdi's musical version. The *lamento* motif, "Salce, salce, salce," unaccompanied and outside the general harmonic context, is presented as if in parenthesis, creating a mood that raises the whole passage to transcendental heights. *M 102*

Othello and Desdemona

The love duet that closes Act I represents a surprisingly modern approach to the duet form. The situation itself was freely invented by Boito, with no basis in Shakespeare. The text is a retrospective survey intended to bring into the opera elements of the plot of Shakespeare's opening Venetian act. But as well as having this dramatic function, it becomes an occasion for the lyrical expansiveness essential to opera. Its unexpectedly free phrasing involving changes of key, its harmonic boldness, the delicacy of its instrumentation, which suggests chamber music, all make this duet a kaleidoscope of shimmering colors. It overflows with happiness and musical beauty. *M 103*

The "kiss motif" that appears at the climax of the duet recurs in the final act, first when Othello enters Desdemona's bedroom and then as he lies dying, thus providing a framework for the entire tragedy. In its final appearance it functions as a symbol of love and purification for the dying Othello. *M 104* Othello's only monologue in the opera (in Act III) is a confession of his profound misery, a monotonous murmur on a single note. A brooding bass motif in the orchestra *M 105* and a painful figure for the violins *M 106* supply an oppressive commentary. The final lyrical section of the solo is not the conventional cavatina or cabaletta, but a brief melodic close – a shattering lament. *M 107*   *J. K.*

103. Love Duet (Desdemona and Othello)

Già nel-la not-te den-sa s'e-stingue ogni cla-mor,

già il mio cor fre-me-bon-do s'am-mansa in quest' am-ples-so e si rin-sen-sa.

104. The Dying Othello's Kiss Motif

un ba-cio ...   un ba-cio ...   an-co-ra un ba-cio.

105. Othello's Brooding

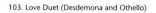

106. Othello's Pain

107. Othello's Lament

Ma, __ o pian-to, o duol! m'han ra-pi-to il mi-rag-gio do-v'io, giu-li-vo, l'a-ni-ma ac-que-to.

108. Tragic Fate Motif (Closing Scene)

109. Predecessor of the Fate Motif (Don Carlos)

Above left
Otello, photograph from the production by Henning Brockhaus, sets Josef Svoboda, costumes Sázka Hejnova, conductor Christian Thielemann, Teatro Communale di Bologna 1993.
Othello at the lowest point of his career (Act III, finale): in his blind jealousy he flings Desdemona to the ground. At this point Verdi's last, shatteringly tragic ensemble finale begins.

Otello, production photograph with Anna Tomowa-Sintow as Desdemona, production Peter Wood, conductor Zubin Mehta, Wiener Staatsoper 1987.

Above right
Otello, Mario del Monaco as Othello, from a television program on the singer, Westdeutscher Rundfunk (West German Radio, WDR), Cologne 1966.

Falstaff

Commedia lirica in three acts

Libretto: Arrigo Boito, after William Shakespeare's plays *The Merry Wives of Windsor* and *King Henry IV*.
Première: 9 February 1893, Milan (Teatro alla Scala).

Characters: Sir John Falstaff (Bar), Fenton (T), Dr. Caius (T), Bardolfo/Bardolph and Pistola/Pistol, followers of Falstaff (T, B), Mrs. Alice Ford (S), Ford, Alice's husband (Bar), Nannetta, their daughter (S), Mistress Quickly (Ms), Mrs. Meg Page (Ms), Landlord of "The Garter" (silent), Robin, Falstaff's page (silent), Ford's Page (silent); citizens of Windsor, Ford's servants, masqueraders (fairies, witches, spirits, and devils).

Setting: Windsor, early in the 15th century during the reign of Henry IV.

Falstaff, production photograph with Giuseppe Taddei as Falstaff and Rudolf Mazzola as Pistol, production Filippo Sanjust, conductor Sir Georg Solti, Wiener Staatsoper 1980 (photograph 1990).
Falstaff is an immortal dramatic character, as vital as Don Juan, as much of a rogue as Till Eulenspiegel, and as inveterate a dreamer and adventurer as Don Quixote. He is a man who feels that life is worth living to the full.

Synopsis

Act I

Scene 1: Inside "The Garter" inn. The fat knight Sir John Falstaff has written identical love letters to the wives of two rich citizens, Alice Ford and Meg Page: he is hoping for a love affair as well as the chance to fill his purse. It is a long time since he paid his followers. Dr. Caius accuses Falstaff's servants of stealing from him, and in response Falstaff throws him out. But when he gives Bardolph and Pistol the letters to deliver, they refuse. Falstaff angrily drives them away, and entrusts the letters to his page.
Scene 2: Ford's garden. Alice and Meg have received and compared Falstaff's letters. With Mistress Quickly's help, they devise a plan to punish the bold knight. Meanwhile, the servants driven away by Falstaff tell Ford of their master's intentions. The jealous Ford decides to visit Falstaff under a false name and find out more. Meanwhile, his wife Alice is planning to invite Falstaff to a rendezvous and make a fool of him.

Act II

Scene 1: "The Garter." Falstaff's servants return, professing penitence. Mistress Quickly brings Falstaff an invitation to a rendezvous with Alice Ford. He is delighted, and his joy knows no bounds when Ford visits him under the name of Fontana, asking him to seduce Alice so that he, Fontana, will be able to make an easier conquest of her. Falstaff boasts that Alice is expecting him that very day, whereupon Ford becomes violently jealous.
Scene 2: Ford's house. Mistress Quickly tells her fellow conspirators that Falstaff is on his way. Alice amuses herself by hearing him pay court to her. Ford comes home unexpectedly, and the women hide Falstaff in a laundry basket. Ford and his friends search the house for Falstaff, but all he finds is his daughter Nannetta in young Fenton's arms. Since he intends to marry Nannetta to Caius, Ford drives Fenton out of the house in a fury. When the men set off in search of Falstaff again, Alice has the laundry basket containing the fat knight emptied out of the window into the river Thames.

Act III

Scene 1: Outside "The Garter." After this misadventure in love, Falstaff accuses the bourgeois world of pettiness and dishonesty. Mistress Quickly brings an invitation from the allegedly inconsolable Alice, arranging another meeting place by Herne's Oak in Windsor Park. Ford and his men overhear the conversation and decide to punish Falstaff. Ford promises Caius the hand of Nannetta, and tells him to go to the park in the costume of a monk. But Alice, who wants to see her daughter marry for love, supports Nannetta's relationship with Fenton.
Scene 2: Windsor Forest. Falstaff appears punctually at midnight. In order to thwart Ford's plan to marry Nannetta to Caius, the women disguise Fenton in a monk's costume. Falstaff's rendezvous with Alice is interrupted by Meg, warning them that the Wild Hunt is coming. The citizens, disguised as elves and spirits, surround Falstaff and beat him soundly. Caius pairs off with a figure he believes to be his bride, but Nannetta appears with the disguised Fenton. Ford, taking him for Caius, gives his blessing to their union. When the masqueraders reveal their identities, Caius and Ford are indignant at finding they have been deceived. Only Falstaff puts a good face on the trickery, particularly since he is invited to the wedding of Nannetta and Fenton. All join in his summing up: "Tutto nel mondo è burla" ("All the world's a jape").

A. G.

An unexpected comedy

Few of Verdi's contemporaries thought the composer, now over 70 years old, would write another opera after →*Otello*, still less that he would write a comedy after 24 successful musical tragedies. *Falstaff* took the musical world of the time by surprise, and was an inestimable gain to the operatic repertory. Rossini, the master of comedy in music, had already predicted that Verdi would never write a comic opera: "Verdi is a composer of a melancholic and grave character; his coloring is dark and tragic, welling profusely and spontaneously from his nature, and for that very reason is to be most highly valued. I have the utmost respect for him, but there can be no doubt that he will never write an *opera semiseria* such as *Linda di Chamounix*, and certainly not an *opera buffa* such as *The Elixir of Love*." (Both operas were written by →Donizeffi.) Unfortunately, Rossini's reflections were published in Ricordi's

Gazetta Musicale in 1879, just at the time when Verdi was feeling more and more strongly inclined to write a comic opera. "I have been looking for a libretto for an *opera buffa* for twenty years, and now that I have found one this article of yours will turn the public against the opera before it is even composed," Verdi complained in a letter to Giulio Ricordi in August 1879. No one could have known of Verdi's plans at the time, and many more years passed before the libretto was written to his satisfaction. "Boito has brushed aside all objections, and provided me with a lyrical comedy that is like no other," Verdi said in 1890 to the Marchese Gino Monaldi, later to be one of his biographers.   *J. K.*

Falstaff, production photograph with John Del Carlo as Falstaff, production Michael Hampe, sets and costumes John Gunter, conductor Fabio Luisi, Deutsche Oper am Rhein, Düsseldorf 1995.
Falstaff sings his famous monologue on honor after his misadventure with the women, wet and chilled, but with a comforting tankard of wine in his hands (beginning of Act III). His philosophy of life is governed by Dionysiac forces.

Falstaff, production photograph with Nancy Gustafson (Alice Ford), Nelly Boschkova (Mistress Quickly), Vesselina Kasarova (Meg Page), and Angela Gheorghiu (Nannetta), production Filippo Sanjust, conductor Sir Georg Solti, Wiener Staatsoper 1980 (photograph 1993).
The quartet of "merry wives," which becomes a nonet in the finale of Act I. The exquisite art of Verdi's ensemble writing, his differentiation between the voices of the various characters, and his skillful polyphony are reminiscent of Mozart's Italian masterpieces (→*The Marriage of Figaro,* →*Don Giovanni,* and →*Così fan tutte*).

An indestructible literary figure

Falstaff was based on the real Sir John Oldcastle, who fought in Scotland around 1400, and later in Wales and France (in 1411). He was accused of heresy in 1413, escaped from the Tower, and was hanged in 1417, not a particularly pleasing biography. Shakespeare paid little attention to these facts. *The Merry Wives of Windsor* is not one of the dramatist's greatest achievements. There is a legend that the play was written in 1599 at the request of Elizabeth I, who wanted to see the fat knight (a familiar figure from Shakespeare's *King Henry IV,* parts 1 and 2) in the comic role of a lover fooled. The name Falstaff is thought to have been Shakespeare's own invention. Whether or not the play was written to royal command, it makes much use of outworn comic models, and is a farce that cannot stand beside the great Shakespearean comedies. To the composers of early operatic versions of the play – and there are about a dozen of them – it was the farcical element that struck them as useful for their purposes. They were thinking in terms of *opera buffa* and *Singspiel.* A few of the better known musical versions are *Die lustigen Weiber und der dicke Hanns* (*The Merry Wives and Fat John*), by →Dittersdorf (1796), *Falstaff,* ossia *Le tre burle* (*Falstaff, or The Three Japes*), by Antonio Salieri (1799), a version by the Irish composer Michael William Balfe (1838), and Otto Nicolai's pleasing and still popular →*The Merry Wives of Windsor* (1849), which Richard Strauss called "a pretty opera."

Commedia lirica

Boito did not make the same mistake as almost every librettist who had adapted the work before him. In keeping to the idea of "three japes" – "tre burle" – they had nothing in mind but an accumulation of burlesque situations. Boito avoided such tautologies as Falstaff's repeated visits to Alice (repetition would inevitably have weakened the effect of what went before), and instead concentrated the action in a single brilliantly devised intrigue (or imbroglio) in the finale of Act II. His libretto is one of exemplary economy, consisting of three well-balanced acts of two scenes each (about 40 minutes for each act, or 20 for each scene). He left out a series of minor figures – amusing as caricatures in a farce, but superfluous and too numerous on the operatic stage. Mistress Quickly is no longer housekeeper to Dr. Caius, but a good-natured neighbor, one of the "merry wives" herself, and Boito gave her a lively sense

110. Love Duet with Quotation from Boccaccio

(Fenton)

Boc-ca ba - cia - ta non per-de ven - tu - ra.

(Nannetta)

An -zi rin - no - va co-me fa la lu - (na)

of humor and qualities more sympathetic than those of her character in the original drama. He also simplified the complications of the plot concerning Nan – Nannetta – and made them easier to disentangle: instead of having three rival suitors she now has only two, Fenton and Dr. Caius, and she has become the daughter of Alice and Ford (not, as in the play, the Pages' child).

But Boito's skill in construction is by no means the only contribution he made to the quality of the opera. He raised the whole piece to a higher intellectual level by complementing the original farcical material with extracts from Shakespeare's *Henry IV*. This was the source of Falstaff's famous monologue on honor, which gives the eponymous protagonist a more rounded character and a certain lordly aura. Boito and Verdi's *Falstaff* is far more than a simple *buffo* figure, and indeed is superior to the farcical figure in Shakespeare's original play. He is not merely a clown who has been fooled, but becomes an affable character of considerable charm, endowed from the outset with those attributes that make him the symbolical figure that confronts us at the end of the opera.

A new way of depicting love also contributes to the higher intellectual level of the opera. The love of Nannetta and Fenton has a poetic character that is not without its playful nuances, but has little in common with the down-to-earth, broadly comic treatment of the theme in the original *Merry Wives*. From the first, Boito felt it essential to emphasize the importance of the love theme to Verdi: "This love between Nannetta and Fenton must appear frequently throughout the whole opera. In all their scenes they are billing and cooing in corners, bold and sly at once, without being discovered, uttering fresh little phrases and short, witty, rapid, mischievous dialogues from beginning to end of the comedy. Theirs ought to be a very merry love, constantly disturbed and interrupted, but always ready to begin again." The result, in the final version, was a series of miniature love duets scattered through the various scenes of the opera. Again, it was Boito's idea to conclude every one of these miniatures with a quotation from Boccaccio's *Decameron*: "Bocca baciata non perde ventura./Anzi rinnova come fa la luna" ("A mouth that is kissed does not lose fortune. It always returns, like the moon.") This refrain gives rise to a musical motif in Verdi's score. M 110

The love theme is painted in tender pastel colors, illuminating the whole opera and raising it to a poetic sphere. It is a happy love, far from all tragedy, if not entirely free of a passing shadow of nostalgia, for Verdi writes here as an old man looking back on youth and love. There is another factor that raises the work of Boito and Verdi to a higher poetic level: the invocation

of the magical and fantastic in the scene in Windsor Forest. What in Shakespeare's *Merry Wives* is simply an episode of farce, in *Falstaff* approaches wonder, conjuring up the fairy-tale atmosphere of Shakespeare's own *A Midsummer Night's Dream*. The music and the libretto create a magical world.   *J. K.*

Falstaff, Dietrich Fischer-Dieskau as Falstaff, production Luchino Visconti, conductor Wolfgang Sawallisch, Bayerische Staatsoper, Munich 1974.
This delightful comedy written in Verdi's old age, and clearly illustrating his attitude to modern music drama, is based on the traditional situations of the *commedia dell'arte*. The figure of Falstaff himself wears a clownish mask. Dietrich Fischer-Dieskau (b. 1925) created a great sensation in the world of opera when, after many serious roles and countless magnificent intepretations of German lieder, he turned to this greatest of all *buffo* parts. He played Falstaff for the first time at the Vienna State Opera in 1966, in a production by Luchino Visconti and conducted by Leonard Bernstein. The occasion marked an important stage in the career of this outstanding artist.

Falstaff, production photograph with John Del Carlo as Falstaff, production Michael Hampe, sets and costumes John Gunter, conductor Fabio Luisi, Deutsche Oper am Rhein, Düsseldorf 1995.
The final fugue, "Tutto nel mondo è burla" ("All the world's a jape"), is inspired by the words of Jaques, "All the world's a stage" in Shakespeare's comedy As You Like It. It gives the character of Falstaff in Verdi's opera much greater depth than he has in Shakespeare's Merry Wives. Falstaff is more than a drunkard here; he grows to the stature of a laughing philosopher.

A chamber work

Falstaff represents Verdi's artistry at its best, and in terms of compositional technique it is his greatest achievement. Its musical riches and artistic complexity are inexhaustible. The scoring of *Falstaff* has the quality of chamber music written for a large orchestra and an ensemble of soloists. The work contains hardly any self-contained numbers, its "arias" consisting rather of a host of small forms arranged side by side in sequence, some of them no more than short melodies. Nor, apart from the title role, are there any major parts: no team of three consisting of prima donna, *Heldentenor*, and baritone. All the figures are really minor roles, but sharply and exquisitely characterized. Verdi's whole artistic development had led him in this direction. For some time "two souls had inhabited his breast," one of which subjected itself to the everyday discipline of the theater, the other being that of an experimenter and innovator. The latter had already signaled its presence in various minor works, including several pieces of sacred choral music, and also appears in major works, as exemplified by the bold "modern" passages found throughout →*Otello*.

Epilogue

Verdi was well aware that Falstaff was his last great dramatic character. Arturo Toscanini found the following lines, written in the 80-year-old Verdi's own hand, in a copy of the score dating from the year 1893:
"Tutto é finito!
Go, go, old John … go your way as long as you can … Delightful old rogue, ever true behind all your different masks, at every time, in every place!!
Go … go … run, run …
Addio!!!"

J. K.

111. Litany for Falstaff

112. Fenton's Sonnet

113. Nannetta's Fairy Song

114. Minuet

115. Violin Theme (Transition to the Fairy World)

116. Final Comic Fugue

The nocturnal magic of Act III

The atmosphere of fantasy and magic took on entirely new colors in Verdi's last opera, colors with no precedent in his earlier works. The comical and the dreamlike mingle felicitously, while the satirical elements have a playful, mocking, scherzo tone, often echoing Verdi's earlier style in the form of parodic self-quotations, with dignified passages quoted in a new comic context. When a mocking litany is sung for the salvation of Falstaff's soul, we hear melodic phrases from the *Requiem* ("Hostias") and from the psalms sung by the priests in *Aida* ("O, che sei d'Osiride") in the scene on the banks of the Nile. M 111

Fenton's sonnet, M 112 Nannetta's fairy song, M 113 and the "enchanted" fantastic sound of midnight striking, with the silvery sound of the minuet accompanying the masked betrothal ceremony towards the end of the second scene of Act III, M 114 also belong to the world of dreams.

However, the approach to a world of dreamy enchantment begins at the end of the first scene of Act III, when Alice distributes the roles for the masquerade among those present. A mystic shimmer inconspicuously infiltrates the mood of the whole scene. As in many other passages of *Falstaff*, this scene is a miracle of transparent instrumentation. "What we needed here," wrote Verdi in September 1891, during the composition of Act III, "was a melody growing softer and softer, and losing itself pianissimo up aloft, preferably with a single violin." That was how he wrote it: a finely chiseled, dancelike theme leads to a transitional passage, and finally dies away with the violins in an improbably high register. M 115

The final comic fugue

One of the first passages of *Falstaff* to be completed, even before Verdi had really begun work on the composition of the opera, was the final fugue. It may originally have been the result of those studies of counterpoint that were usual in Verdi's time, but he surely wrote it subconsciously with the idea of finding a way to approach *Falstaff*. "I amuse myself by writing fugues!" wrote Verdi to his librettist in August 1889. "Sì, signore: a fugue … and a comic fugue at that … one that could well be used in *Falstaff*! What do you mean, you may ask, a comic fugue? Why comic? I don't know why, but a comic fugue it is!" Later, Boito provided the eight lines of verse for the fugue – "Tutto nel mondo è burla"("All the world's a jape"). It was to be the moral drawn at the end of *Falstaff*. M 116

A farewell

The character of Falstaff contains much self-mockery. Confronted by his own comic and ludicrous behavior, exposed to ridicule and "punishment," he has gone through purgatory, but at the end is able to stand up and look his adversaries in the eye, laughing at them: "Son io, che vi fa scaltri. L'arguzia mia crea l'arguzia degli altri." ("I am not only witty in myself, but the cause that wit is in other men.") We may detect in Verdi a similarly ironic attitude to himself, as the great magician of the theater takes leave of the world, at the end of his monumental career, with a peal of laughter. J.K.

Falstaff, production photograph with Giuseppe Taddei (Falstaff) and Bernd Weikl (Ford), production Filippo Sanjust, conductor Sir Georg Solti, Wiener Staatsoper 1980 (photograph 1990).
Few written comments on the figure of Falstaff by Boito and Verdi have been preserved, although in a letter of 1890 Verdi wrote, briefly but cogently: "Falstaff is a rogue who commits all manner of deplorable deeds … but in a comical way. He is a bounder!" It calls for the wisdom of old age to present such a character, and great singers tend to play Falstaff in the closing phases of their careers.

Mein Leben.

Erster Theil:

1813–1842.

Richard Wagner, *My Life*, 3 volumes, 1865–75 (private edition) (Richard Wagner Museum, Bayreuth).
The title page of Wagner's private edition of his three-volume autobiography (1865–75) was illustrated with a picture of a vulture ("Geier" in German); as a schoolboy Wagner was registered at the *Kreuzschule* in Dresden in 1822 under the name Wilhelm Richard Geyer after his stepfather. He later formed a collection of mementos connected with Geyer, and Wagner's affection for his stepfather is also evident in a number of touching letters to him.

RICHARD WAGNER ALS DIRIGENT
Schattenriß von Willi Bithorn

Richard Wagner as a conductor, caricature by Willi Bithorn, Vienna 1910 (TWS).
Richard Wagner gained considerable experience as director of a theater orchestra in Riga. Heinrich Dorn, his former composition teacher and successor as director of music at Riga recalled: "As a conductor, Wagner achieved some quite remarkable things in Riga; he always took great care over rehearsals … and when he stood on the podium his fiery temperament swept along even the oldest members of the orchestra. 'Keep it lively, keep it bright, always keep it a little lively,' were his favorite comments, and they always had the required effect."

Wagner, Richard

b. 22 May 1813 in Leipzig
d. 13 February 1883 in Venice

Wagner studied in Dresden and Leipzig, and then worked as music director at the opera houses of Würzburg, Magdeburg, Königsberg, and Riga (1833–39). After an unsuccessful Parisian sojourn (1839–42) he became court music director in Dresden (1843–49). He played an active part in the Dresden uprisings of May 1849 before fleeing to Switzerland, where he lived in exile in Zürich (1849–58). After periods in Venice, Lucerne, and Paris he worked on a number of important compositions (1858–61) and embarked on a series of concert tours (1861–64). Many of his works were written in Triebschen near Lucerne (1866–72). He instigated the construction of a Festspielhaus (Festival Hall) in Bayreuth where he supervised productions of his own works (1872–83).

Works: 13 complete operas or music dramas: *Die Feen* (*The Fairies*) (1834/FP 1888), *Das Liebesverbot* (*The Ban on Love*) (1836), *Rienzi* (1842), *Der fliegende Holländer* (*The Flying Dutchman*) (1843), *Tannhäuser* (1845), *Lohengrin* (1850), *Tristan und Isolde* (*Tristan and Isolde*) (1865), *Die Meistersinger von Nürnberg* (*The Mastersingers of Nuremberg*) (1868), *Der Ring des Nibelungen* (*The Ring of the Nibelung*); symphonic works, choral pieces, piano music, songs, and numerous writings on aesthetic theory, the most important of which is *Oper und Drama* (*Opera and Drama*) (1851).

Young Wagner and the theater

Wagner probably inherited his passion for the theater and his love of drama from Ludwig Geyer. Of the nine children, four (Albert, Rosalie, Luise, and Klara) took up acting careers. Richard too was a child of the theater: he attended his first opera at the age of five and at ten was swept up in the wave of enthusiasm that greeted the première of Weber's →*Der Freischütz* in Dresden in 1822 – a production conducted by Weber himself. As a seven-year-old Wagner played the young William Tell in a Dresden production of Schiller's play, his sister Klara playing Walter Tell and Ludwig Geyer taking the role of Gesler. As a small child he was captivated by the theatrical wardrobe of his sisters, and throughout his life he was never able to free himself from his obsession with costumes and make-up. His first literary effort was a play, the *Tragedy of Leubald and Adelaide*. But it was the 24-year-old Wilhelmine Schröder-Devrient (1804–60) – probably in the role of Emmy in →Marschner's *The Vampire* in 1829 – who really sealed Wagner's operatic fate. This great singer later enthralled the 21-year-old composer yet again with her dramatic portrayal of Romeo in →Bellini's *The Capulets and the Montagues*.

The Fairies

Grosse romantische Oper in three acts

Libretto: Richard Wagner, after the play *La donna serpente* (*The Snake Woman*) by Carlo Gozzi.
Première: 29 June 1888, Munich (Hoftheater).

Characters: The Fairy King (B), Ada, his daughter, the wife of Arindal (S), Arindal, Prince of Tramond (T), Lora, his sister (S), Morald, commander of the army and Lora's lover (Bar), Drolla, Lora's companion (S), Gernot, Arindal's servant (B), Farzana and Zemina, fairies (2 S), Gunther, from the court of Tramond (T), Harald, Arindal's general (B), Two Children of Ada and Arindal (silent); fairies, Morald's companions, warriors, earth spirits, men of iron, the invisible spirits of Groma (chorus).
Setting: The place and time of fairy tale.

Synopsis

Prince Arindal loses his way while out hunting. A doe lures him into the realm of the fairies, where he lives happily together with Ada, a half-mortal, half-fairy being. For eight years he is instructed not to enquire after his wife's origins, but the temptation finally becomes too great and he poses the fateful question. Banished from the fairy realm, he is followed by the loyal Ada. Arindal's faith proves less resolute and he becomes responsible for his wife being turned into stone. Through self-sacrificing courage and magic, however, Arindal is able to redeem her. He renounces his earthly kingdom and the couple are finally united in the world of the fairies.

Whether Wagner really did see her perform the title role of *Fidelio*, as he maintained in his autobiography, we do not know. What is clear is that her passion made an indelible impression on him, and throughout his life Wagner considered Schröder-Devrient the archetype of a convincing singer-actress.

The search for identity

Throughout his life Wagner struggled to come to terms with his identity. The truth of his origins and the search for a father was a major theme in his life and one that motivated almost all his works. Many of his dramas begin with the death of a father. Tristan, Siegfried, and Parsifal never knew their father; Siegmund grew up with his father but was never to discover his true identity; Tristan and Siegfried had foster fathers; Lohengrin was forced to maintain silence on the subject of his name and descent; in *The Mastersingers* the orphan Walther von Stolzing is asked if he was born honourably; Siegfried urges Mime to tell him who his father is; and Parsifal's mother attempts to keep all knowledge of his father from him. We may never know for certain

Act I

The fairies' garden. The fairies try to prevent a match between the daughter of their king and a mortal, but their efforts are in vain: Prince Arindal and Ada have fallen in love. Because Arindal poses the forbidden question about Ada's origins before the prescribed eight-year period is up, he is cast out of the fairy realm. His earthly kingdom is also in great danger, and Arindal prepares to defend it against his enemies. Ada decides to follow Arindal and become his earthly wife – a step that will require her to forfeit her immortality. Before this can happen, she must put Arindal to the test.

Act II

A palace in the capital of Arindal's kingdom. Arindal proves too weak to withstand Ada's tests (which take the form of terrible visions) and it is she who must pay the price by being turned into stone for a hundred years.

Act III

A ceremonial throne-room in the grand palace of the fairies' underworld kingdom. While the earthly conflict appears to have been resolved – Arindal's sister, Lora, and the leader of the army, Morald, are to rule over the newly liberated lands – Arindal learns of Ada's petrification. Groma, a magician and a friend of the Tramond royal house, gives Arindal a sword, shield, and lyre. With these weapons, Arindal vanquishes the spirits and demons of the underworld; the sounds of the magic lyre free Ada from her stony prison. Arindal attains immortality and is accompanied into the realm of the fairies by his newly awakened bride.   S. N.

who Wagner's father was: the police actuary Carl Friedrich Wilhelm Wagner (1770–1813), a freemason and theater lover, or the painter, poet, and actor Ludwig Geyer (1779–1821), a close family friend of the Wagners and Richard's stepfather from infancy. Richard Wagner himself was never able to resolve to his own satisfaction the question of his uncertain origins.

A valuable record of a young dramatist's development
The poet and composer E.T.A. Hoffmann greatly admired the fairy tale by Carlo Gozzi (1720–1806) and it was he who introduced Wagner to the work. (Adolf Wagner, Richard's uncle and Gozzi's translator, may also have drawn his nephew's attention to it.) Wagner made major changes not only to the title (*La donna serpente*, or *The Snake Woman*) but also to the plot (Ada, for example, is turned into stone rather than into a snake).

The central conflict of the story – and one to which the character Lohengrin would be subjected 12 years later – is the tension between the natural and the supernatural worlds. Like Hoffmann's →*Undine* and

The Fairies, photograph from the production by Friedrich Meyer-Oertel, sets Dieter Flimm, costumes Maria Lucas, conductor Reinhard Schwarz, Staatstheater am Gärtnerplatz, Munich 1989.
The Fairies was never performed in Wagner's own lifetime. The composer gave the score to his patron, King Ludwig II, but even he was never to see the work on stage. To honor the composer of The Ring and Parsifal, The Fairies was finally produced in Munich in 1888, in the face of determined opposition from Wagner's widow, Cosima.

Marschner's →*Hans Heiling* – a work that Wagner discovered only after he began work on his opera in the fall of 1833 – *The Fairies* raises the question of whether a fulfilling love between a mortal and a supernatural being is possible. The theme of Ada's secret origins anticipates →*Lohengrin*, and the sympathy Wagner elicits for the animal shot during Arindal's hunt points to the episode of the murdered swan in →*Parsifal*. The trials the lovers must endure recall →*The Magic Flute*, and Ada's redemption from her deathly petrification parallels the myth of Orpheus.

The musical style is heavily indebted to the contemporary French and German operatic repertory that Wagner had thoroughly studied not only in Dresden and Leipzig but also in Vienna and in Würzburg, where he composed *The Fairies*. Although the nature and sound-world of the opera are not typical of the later Wagner, its mature compositional and dramatic technique as well as the irresistible impetus of the music place it at the forefront of German Romantic opera of its time.

The most dramatically sophisticated – if musically somewhat uninteresting – element of the score is a musical motif that represents yearning for the supernatural world. As if encapsulating the fundamental message of *The Fairies* for the audience, a series of chords is heard that, instead of descending in a natural progression, rises upwards in an unexpected manner. This motif reveals to us, like a secret cypher, that Ada will not lose her immortality and that her husband Arindal, in fulfillment of his mission of redemption through love, will ascend to her fairy realm.   Gy. K.

Richard Wagner, drawing by E.B. Kietz, Paris 1840–42 (Richard Wagner Museum, Bayreuth).

Wagner is the greatest reformer of the stage in the history of opera.

The Ban on Love

or The Novice of Palermo

Grosse komische Oper in two acts

Libretto: Richard Wagner, after William Shakespeare's comedy *Measure for Measure*.
Première: 29 March 1836, Magdeburg (Stadttheater).

Characters: Friedrich, a German and governor of Sicily in the absence of the king (B), Lucio and Claudio, young noblemen (2 T), Antonio and Angelo, their friends (T, B), Isabella, Claudio's sister, now a novice (S), Mariana, a novice (S), Brighella, a police chief (B), Danieli, an innkeeper (B), Dorella, formerly Isabella's maid, and Pontio Pilato, both employees of Danieli (S, T); police, citizens of Palermo, people, maskers (chorus).
Setting: Palermo, in the 16th century.

Synopsis

Friedrich, the stern German governor of Sicily, ruins the annual carnival for the locals by ruling that drinking and extramarital lovemaking are to be punishable by death. The first victim is the young nobleman Claudio. Imprisoned and condemned to death, he appeals for help to his sister Isabella, a novice in a convent, where Mariana, the wife whom Friedrich has abandoned, also resides. Isabella seduces Friedrich and exposes him as a hypocrite, forcing him to acknowledge his wife's existence. After various disguises and cases of mistaken identity, the couples are reunited: Claudio's friend Lucio wins the hand of the beautiful Isabella while Friedrich is reconciled with Mariana. The corrupt and brutal guardian of the law Brighella is transformed into a passionate lover by the lovely Dorella. The carnival can now take place undisturbed.

Act I

Scene 1: The outskirts of Palermo. The German governor's decree outlawing drinking and extramarital lovemaking is announced. Claudio is the first to fall foul of the new law and is arrested.
Scene 2: The convent of the Order of St. Elizabeth. Mariana reveals to Isabella that she is the abandoned wife of Friedrich. Claudio's friend Lucio pleads with Isabella to ask the governor to show mercy for her brother.
Scene 3: The court. While waiting for the governor to appear, Brighella plays at being judge. A petition to rescind the carnival ban is rejected by Friedrich. He condemns Claudio to death. Isabella subsequently offers herself to the governor in exchange for her brother's life.

Act II

Scene 1: The prison garden. Terrified of dying, Claudio agrees to his sister's prostitution. Outraged at his acceptance of her plight, Isabella conceals her real plan from him: Mariana will go to the meeting with Friedrich instead of her.
Scene 2: Friedrich's palace. Friedrich has not kept his word with Isabella: instead of a letter of pardon for Claudio, he has signed the order for his execution.
Scene 3: On the streets. In spite of the ban, people are celebrating the carnival. The chief of police appears to be discharging his duties but quickly disguises himself to pursue a forbidden affair with Dorella. Even Friedrich has donned a mask, but his tryst with Isabella – in reality his own wife Mariana – is interrupted. Isabella summons all the maskers and exposes the upstanding Friedrich as a hypocrite. Friedrich is unable to take revenge: the king of Sicily returns and the governor is immediately relieved of his duties.

S. N.

The Ban on Love, carnival scene (Act II, Scene 3), production Jean-Pierre Ponnelle, sets Jean-Pierre Ponnelle and Pet Halmen, costumes Pet Halmen, conductor Wolfgang Sawallisch, Bayerische Staatsoper, Munich 1983. Wagnerians have never forgiven their great master for this "youthful sin": the composer of *Tristan* and *Parsifal* once had the temerity to try to impress the public with a frivolous carnival piece. It was a futile attempt as it turned out: the première was a disaster and there was not to be another performance during the composer's lifetime. The work was resurrected in 1983 by Jean-Pierre Ponnelle for the Bavarian State Opera. This witty production was influenced by Offenbach, Feydeau and even Ionesco.

An indifferent reception
The Ban on Love was first staged in Magdeburg on 29 March 1836, after only ten days of rehearsals. The tenor had a memory lapse, while the audience found the plot incomprehensible. Wagner later attempted unsuccessfully to stage the opera in Leipzig, Berlin, and Paris.

"Young Germany"

The Ban on Love, the first of Wagner's operas to be staged, was inspired by the ideas of the "Young Germany" movement, which was influential in German thought and literature. "Young Germany" was initiated by German émigrés in France (who included, around 1830, Heinrich Heine and Ludwig Börne), and the cause was quickly taken up by a group of young writers opposed to philistinism and outdated notions of morality. Their ideas were encapsulated in the Utopian novel of 1787, *Ardinghello und die glückseligen Inseln* (*Ardinghello and the Happy Isles*), by Wilhelm Heinse, a writer belonging to the so-called "Storm and Stress" movement. The hero of the novel, Ardinghello, is a Renaissance-like figure. He enjoys life and preaches the uninhibited enjoyment of sensual pleasure. He founds an idealized Utopian state without property, in which all are able to express their individuality. In his trilogy of epistolary novels *Das junge Europa* (*Young Europe*) of 1833–37, Heinrich Laube propounded the ideas and ambitions of the contemporary independence movements alongside critiques of religious and Romantic mysticism and church orthodoxy. The young Wagner was an enthusiastic supporter of the independence movements of his time.

Sources of inspiration

The model for Wagner's *The Ban on Love* was Shakespeare's *Measure for Measure*, which in turn was based on an Italian tale first published in Sicily in 1565 as part of Giambattista Cinzio Giraldi's *Ecatommiti* (*The Hundred Stories*). Unlike his predecessors, however, Wagner's concern was not solely to depict a tale of justice restored but also the triumph of free and open sensuality over puritan hypocrisy. A Mediterranean lust for life is contrasted with the Germanic philistinism of the governor Friedrich. Despite all its intrigues and carnival masks, the opera is a clear indictment of tyranny, censorship, unquestioning obedience, and duplicity. Wagner's "grosse komische Oper" or "grand comic opera" deserves the first epithet not only because of its expansive structure of six scenes, its elaborate use of chorus, ballet, and mime, and its numerous and vivid ensemble passages, but also for its through-composed musical form. Although the light and vivacious musical treatment is reminiscent of French *opera comique*, it is not modeled on that genre. Instead, Wagner followed the Italian tradition of *opera buffa* and its predecessor, the *commedia dell'arte*. The libretto compares Dorella and Brighella to Colombine and Pierrot, and the name of the chief of police, Brighella, is derived from the stories of the *commedia dell'arte*. The figures of Isabella and Mariana are also descendants of two stock female characters from the *commedia dell'arte* – the proud woman and the soft-hearted woman. The brawls in the opening and final scenes, the confusion over the disguises, and the whole parody of the court scene in which a lackey imitates his master (Brighella plays the part of the judge) all belong to the repertory of *opera buffa*. Another direct influence is Act IV of Mozart's →*The Marriage of Figaro*, in which the count, instead of meeting Susanna as intended, encounters his own wife in disguise – just like Friedrich and his wife Mariana in *The Ban on Love*.

In *The Ban on Love* Wagner returned to the dramatic device he had employed in *The Fairies* by using a recurring instrumental motif to represent the central dramatic idea, here that of forbidden love, and by linking it with the character of Friedrich. M 1

Thus Wagner was able to point to the underlying passions responsible for Friedrich's hypocrisy. Similarly, the expansive melody for Isabella – whom Friedrich is unable to forget – is constructed on the same harmonic foundation as the carnival melody. M 2

1. Love Ban Motif

It would perhaps be going too far to draw an analogy between the idea of forbidden love in *The Ban on Love* and the theme of "Power not Love" in →*The Ring of the Nibelung*, or to see Friedrich as a forerunner of Amfortas in →*Parsifal* (both seek to destroy a loathsome "erotic Eden," and both fall victim to their own erotic passions). But it would be justifiable to regard *The Ban*

2. Carnical Theme, Isabella's Theme

on Love as an anticipation of →*Tannhäuser* and to compare Isabella – who rescues Claudio, whose sensual passions have led to his undoing – with Elisabeth. The comparison seems all the more convincing when we consider that a melody from the convent scene in *The Ban on Love* – accompanied by bells and the singing of the "Salve Regina" – was used by Wagner ten years later to symbolize the concept of divine mercy in →*Tannhäuser*. M 3, M 4   *Gy. K.*

3. Salve Regina

Sal-ve Re-gi - na coe - li! Sal - ve!

4. Divine Mercy Motif (*Tannhäuser*)

Rienzi, the Last of the Tribunes

Grosse tragische Oper in five acts

Libretto: Richard Wagner.
Première: 20 October 1842, Dresden (Hoftheater).
Characters: Cola Rienzi, papal notary (T), Irene, his sister (S), Steffano Colonna, head of the Colonna family (B), Adriano, his son (Ms), Paolo Orsini, head of the Orsini family (B), Raimondo, papal legate (B), Baroncelli and Cecco del Vecchio, Roman citizens (T, B), The Messenger of Peace (S), Herald (T); Roman nobles, envoys, priests, monks, soldiers, Roman citizens (chorus).
Setting: Rome, somewhere around the middle of the 14th century.

Rienzi, the Last of the Tribunes, "Rienzi's victory march into Rome," postcard, drawing by Theodor Pixis, Munich 1877/78. A scene reminiscent of Bayreuth. In the background Rienzi marches through the triumphal arch to the cheers of the crowd. Irene and Adriano also share in his joy – in contrast to the patricians in the foreground who turn away in anger.

Richard Wagner-Galerie. II. Theil.

Theodor Pixis pinx.   J. Albert phot.

Rienzi's Siegeseinzug in Rom.
Nr. 15.   (Aus „Rienzi".)   Deponirt 1878.
Verlag von Hanfstaengl's Nachfolger. Berlin.

Synopsis

Adriano Colonna, the son of a patrician family, is in love with Rienzi's sister, Irene. When his father is killed during a popular uprising, Adriano swears to kill the people's tribune and places himself at the head of a group unhappy with Rienzi's political victory; they incite the mob against Rienzi. Irene shares the fate of her brother and decides to die with him on the Capitol. Adriano tries to save her but is killed in the attempt.

Act I

A Roman street in front of Rienzi's house. Supporters of the Orsini family abduct Rienzi's sister Irene, but Adriano Colonna is in love with Irene and rescues her. The two feuding patrician families – Orsini and Colonna – face each other with weapons drawn. Thanks to Rienzi's intervention, an outbreak of violence is prevented. The crowd laud Rienzi as the liberator of Rome and elect him the people's tribune.

Act II

A great hall in the Capitol. The Roman nobility are plotting Rienzi's murder. Rienzi has ordered a banquet of reconciliation to be held at which the nobility are to swear their commitment to concord and lawfulness. At this feast in honor of peace, Orsini attempts to stab Rienzi but the tribune is saved by the armor of his breastplate. The people demand revenge, but Rienzi shows his would-be assassin mercy.

Act III

The great square of the ancient forum. Rienzi leads the armed citizenry against the nobility who have broken their oath. The leaders of the Orsini and Colonna families die in the fighting, and Adriano swears revenge.

Act IV

The great square in front of the Lateran church. Adriano incites the Roman citizenry against Rienzi. As the people's tribune is about to enter the Lateran church with his sister, he is cursed by the papal legate Raimondo: anyone who remains loyal to Rienzi is to be excommunicated. Rienzi is left isolated and without allies; only Irene remains faithful to her brother, rejecting Adriano's advances.

Act V

A hall in the Capitol; a square in front of the Capitol. Rienzi and Irene take their leave of Rome – and of life. The Roman mob sets fire to the Capitol. Adriano returns to rescue his beloved Irene, but at that moment the burning tower collapses, burying Rienzi, Irene, and Adriano beneath it.   A.G.

The day has dawned

"There was pandemonium, a revolution throughout the whole city; I was called to the stage four times and applauded rapturously. People assured me that the success of Meyerbeer's →*The Huguenots* here was nothing compared with that of *Rienzi* ... by the third evening all the seats were sold ... The performance was extraordinarily beautiful – Tichatschek – Devrient – everything – everything was perfect, the like of which has never been seen. A triumph! A triumph! ... The day has dawned ... " (Wagner in Dresden to his sister Cäcilie Geyer and her husband Eduard Avenarius in Paris, 21 October 1842).

Impractical length

In spite of its enormous success, Wagner went on to make several changes to *Rienzi*. The second performance was three-quarters of an hour shorter than the première (which had lasted some six hours).

Wagner also suggested a new version to be spread over two evenings, the first depicting Rienzi's glory (Acts I–III) and the second Rienzi's fall (Acts IV–V). Each of the first three acts is divided into two or three scenes, which pave the way for the gigantic finales. These final scenes are made all the more brilliant by the incorporation of imposing crowd scenes (the people's election of the tribune, the celebration of peace, the ritual of pardon, the pledge of allegiance to the law, the battle scene, the march to war, the prayer scene, the oath of revenge, and the triumphal procession).

The second part has a quite different structure and mood. Act IV begins and ends in a minor key; it is divided into two scenes of equal length and concludes in a slow, ponderous tempo. The first two scenes of Act V solemnly and gravely depict moments of privacy (Rienzi's prayer, the duet for brother and sister), while the third scene serves as an introduction to the finale (the conflagration), which is in the traditionally tragic key of G minor.

Wagner's later practice of spreading a unified dramatic work over several evenings thus has its roots in the impractical length of his first great heroic opera.   *Gy. K.*

Rienzi, the Last of the Tribunes, set design (detail) by Ludwig Sievert, production Hans Meissner, Freilichtbühne am Roten Tor, Augsburg 1934 (TWS).
Ludwig Sievert invested the stage set with the "grim warning" inherent in the story. The isolation of the protagonist is conspicuous by being contrasted with the dramatic crowd scenes.

The historical background

The opera refers to events that occurred between 20 May and 15 December 1347, when the Italian revolutionary Cola di Rienzo (1313–54) established a short-lived Roman republic. In contrast with the opera, Rienzo surrendered to the authority of the Pope, who was allied with the nobility, and he was killed seven years later when yet another attempt was made to found a republic. Against this historical backdrop the opera depicts a conflict of love, freedom, and family honor.

Grand opera for a grandiose theatre

With →*Rienzi* Wagner wanted to create something great for both artistic and political reasons: "From the outset I planned the opera on such a scale that it would be impossible to perform it in a small theater. Moreover, the subject matter meant that it could be done no other way and my work was therefore governed less by intention than by necessity," he wrote in his *Autobiographischen Skizze* (*Autobiographical Sketch*) of 1842. Wagner then tailored his musico-dramatic ideas to the new Semper opera house in Dresden: "The plan to build a magnificent new opera house – it is to be opened on 12 April 1841 – gave me the idea that I might also realize all the practical and technical demands of my opera in a manner corresponding to the possibilities of such a building." (To the general director of the Dresden Hoftheater, Baron August von Lüttichau, 4 December 1840)

Theatrical effects

"My opera will present enormous challenges in both staging and music," Wagner admitted while preparing the chorus master of the Dresden Hoftheater (court theater) for the project ahead. "The offstage choruses, namely the chorus in the Lateran (Act I) and the small chorus 'Vae tibi maledicto' (Act IV), will probably need to be sung by the choir of the Kreuz School ... The chorus of the messengers of peace will certainly not be easy to sing cleanly, and must of course only be attempted by a group selected from the most musical and gifted members of the women's choir ... Another difficulty concerns the great tragic mime in the finale of Act II: in my view the main characters in this scene – Lucretia, Brutus, Tarquinius, and Collatinus – should only be played by proper stage actors accustomed to performing such roles in the theatre" (letter to Wilhelm Fischer, 14 October 1841).

Excerpts from letters dating from the time of the première of →*Rienzi* reveal Wagner's organizational genius. "The envoys must at all costs be played by actors. The costume designer's task is to make the envoys stand out as much as possible by means of their costumes and other insignia; each envoy should be accompanied by a small retinue of heralds etc. and their clothing made as impressive as possible" (letter to Wilhelm Fischer, 8 December 1841).

"I will not sacrifice a single detail of the musical ceremony on stage; it is absolutely critical and can be perfectly well done in Dresden with the help of the army and other military bands. My demands are admittedly unusual: I require an exceptionally good military band, different in composition from the norm; and yet it ought to be possible to assemble one. Please ensure that in Act I the trumpeters and trombonists who accompany Colonna's and Orsini's procession are chosen from cavalry units and are seated on horses: to my mind this must look both splendid and convincing,

Below and opposite above
Exterior and groundplan of the Semper opera house in Dresden, engraving and drawing, c. 1841 (TWS).
The Dresden Hoftheater, or court opera, was designed on the model of horseshoe-shaped Italian opera houses by the architect Gottfried Semper in 1841, shortly before the première of Wagner's →*Rienzi*. Semper's career began early: he was already a professor at the Dresden Academy at the age of 31. In 1849 both he and Wagner were forced into exile for their part in the May uprisings in Dresden. In their Zürich exile they drew up plans together for a theater of the future. The architectural design for the Bayreuth Festspielhaus (Festival Hall) was not Semper's work, however. After his return to Germany he was required to rebuild the Dresden opera house, which burnt down in 1869 (it reopened in 1878). In 1985 the building was again restored and opened for the third time after its destruction in the Second World War. In addition to →*Rienzi*, the opera house gave the premières of →*The Flying Dutchman* (1843) and →*Tannhäuser* (1845). A large number of Richard Strauss's operas were also premièred here: →*Trial by Fire* (1901), →*Salome* (1905), →*Elektra* (1909), →*Der Rosenkavalier* (1911), →*Intermezzo* (1924), →*The Egyptian Helen* (1928), →*The Silent Woman* (1935), and →*Daphne* (1938).

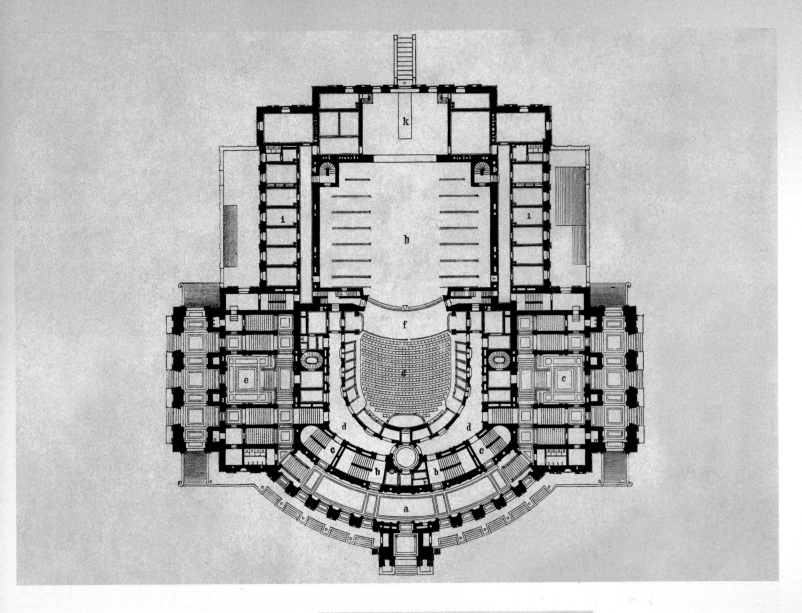

and it should be perfectly possible to achieve on the Dresden stage" (to the director and costume designer of the Dresden Hoftheater, Ferdinand Heine, late January 1842).

"We have had 14 piano rehearsals, and in four weeks ... the performance will take place ... As for Devrient [Wilhelmine Schröder-Devrient, a singer whom Wagner greatly admired, and for whom he created the trouser role of Adriano] I need only say ... she will burst in at the conclusion of the opera on horseback! – Tichatschek ... his voice is tailor-made for my Rienzi and he regards the part as the most brilliant he has ever sung. He will have a suit of armor made of nickel silver, richly decorated with genuine silver which will cost him 400 Thaler" (letter to the painter Ernst Benedikt Kietz, 6 September 1842).

Gy. K.

Joseph Tichatschek (1807–86) as Rienzi (detail), Dresden 1842 (TWS).
The qualities of the type of singer later known as the Wagnerian tenor were described by Wagner himself in a letter to his favorite singer: "Rienzi, a character whom I have conceived myself and striven to give shape to, should be a hero in the fullest sense of the word, a passionate visionary who appeared like a flash of light amongst his wretched, degenerate people, and felt himself called upon to enlighten them and raise them up. It is an historical fact that at the time of his greatest success Rienzi was a young man of about 28 years of age; this, as well as my belief in the manifold character of the tenor voice, moved me to write this part for a tenor, and in doing so to part company – as if the tenor voice were only suited to the character of a lover! – with convention" (to Joseph Tichatschek, 7 September 1841) The Wagnerian tenor, which requires not only considerable power and stamina but also brightness in the upper register, was to become a familiar concept in the world of opera.

Grand opera and "buono stato"

After struggling to make a living in a number of provincial cities that offered only limited artistic opportunities, Wagner's greatest ambition was to see *Rienzi* performed on the stage of an internationally important theater. From around 1810 to 1840 Paris was the center of European opera. To enjoy success there meant that Wagner had to master the distinctive five-act form employed by Meyerbeer (→*Robert the Devil,* →*The Huguenots*), which followed the dramatic precepts of Eugène Scribe. "Grand opera, with all the magnificence of its sets and music, its effects, its grandiose musical passion, stood before me; and my artistic ambition was not merely to imitate it but to surpass all preceding examples of the form with a ruthless skill" (*Eine Mitteilung an meine Freunde, A Message to my Friends,* 1851). Wagner's interest in grand opera had already been aroused by Gasparo Spontini's *Fernand Cortez:* the composer had attended a performance of Spontini's three-act opera in Berlin in the summer of 1836, and, as a direct response, had written a four-act scenario entitled *Die hohe Braut* (*The Noble Bride*), after the novel of the same name by Heinrich König. About a year later

Wagner acquired a German translation of *Rienzi, the Last of the Roman Tribunes*, a three-volume work published in 1835 by the radical English author Edward George Bulwer-Lytton. This book presented in historical form the idea of the good state, or "buono stato" – a topic that fascinated Wagner. A similar idea in Wilhelm Heinse's novel *Ardinghello und die glückseligen Inseln* (*Ardinghello and the Happy Isles*) had earlier inspired him to compose the opera →*The Ban on Love*. That work's theme of freedom of love was now transformed into that of the freedom of the citizen, although the equality of all before the law remained the most important moral and political idea. To these he added the fundamental political idea of the fight against feudal despotism. In the context of the contemporary German political situation, Rienzi became a figure representative of the "Young Germany" movement.

Freedom and prayer

In terms of its music and form, *Rienzi* was an immense success for a composer who was demonstrating his talents with his third opera in six years. It confirmed Wagner's extraordinary appreciation of the sound, function, and character of the chorus (the chorus of joy in C minor in Act III is a particularly effective example) and revealed his flair for composing choral songs and marches. The opera also displayed his remarkable gift for expressive lyricism, particularly in the music for the messenger of peace and in Rienzi's prayer. *M S*   *Gy. K.*

Rienzi, the Last of the Tribunes, production photograph with Gotthelf Pistor (Rienzi) and Else Foerster (Irene), production Walter Felsenstein, sets Alfred Behrend, conductor Fritz Zaun, Oper Köln 1932.
Imploring gestures and the sound of prayer are of fundamental importance for the atmosphere of *Rienzi*. The drama may be warlike but the characters have a deep desire for peace. In that sense the production by the young Walter Felsenstein (1901–75) – the founder and director of the Komische Oper in Berlin – represents an unforgettable moment in what was to prove a fateful year for Germany: 1932.

5. Rienzi's Prayer

Du stärk - test mich, du gabst mir   ho —   he Kraft

Rienzi, the Last of the Tribunes, set design by Bernhard Klein, Berlin 1933 (TWS). The 50th anniversary of Wagner's death in 1933, celebrated in the backdrop for a *Rienzi* production featuring the glories of Rome. At this stage of the opera the Capitol is still intact.

Theodor Lattermann as the Dutchman, illustration by H. Dahm, Berlin 1924.

The Flying Dutchman, set design by Max Brückner, Bayreuth 1880 (TWS). "Eternal destruction, take me in!" The first ships in Bayreuth resemble a Romantic painting from the beginning of the 19th century. Today, images of ships still dominate the sets of *The Flying Dutchman*.

The Flying Dutchman

Romantische Oper in three acts

Libretto: Richard Wagner.

Première: 2 January 1843, Dresden (Hoftheater).

Characters: The Dutchman (Bar), Daland, a Norwegian sailor (B), Senta, his daughter (S), Erik, a huntsman (T), Mary, Senta's nurse (Ms), Daland's helmsman (T); Norwegian sailors, the Dutchman's crew, young women (chorus).

Setting: The Norwegian coast around 1650.

Synopsis

According to an old legend, a Dutch seaman once mocked God out of pride, for which he was condemned to wander the seas for all eternity. Only once in every seven years is he permitted to go ashore, in order to find a woman who would remain true to him until death: she alone will be able to release him from his curse. Senta, the daughter of the sailor Daland, feels herself called to this task, and immediately recognizes the wretched man when he appears at her father's door. She swears everlasting faithfulness to the stranger – to the great joy of her father, who is interested in the Dutchman's riches. Senta must first find the courage to part from the hunter Erik. Witnessing this farewell scene, the Dutchman thinks she has betrayed him and sets sail. Remembering her vow of eternal faithfulness, Senta throws herself into the sea, thus bringing redemption to the Dutchman through her death.

Act I (The coast, steep cliffs)
Scene 1: Daland's ship has sought refuge from a storm and is anchored in a bay near his home. Shortly afterwards the Dutchman's ship arrives.
Scene 2: Seven years have passed. Condemned to wander for all eternity for the crime of blasphemy, the Dutchman goes ashore to search for a woman who can release him from his curse.

Scene 3: Daland is interested in the stranger's treasures and invites the Dutchman to his home, promising him the hand of his daughter, Senta.

Act II (A large room in Daland's house)
Scene 1: Seated at their spinning wheels the young women pass the time in singing. Senta is tired of listening to their songs. She longs for something great that will change her life. She sings the ballad of the Flying Dutchman, whose picture hangs on the wall. During her song she increasingly identifies herself with the figure of the woman who can save the Dutchman from damnation.
Scene 2: The hunter Erik, in love with Senta, has had a dream in which Senta and the Dutchman were united. In vain, he warns her of the ruin she could bring on herself through her obsession.
Scene 3: Daland returns home and introduces the stranger to his daughter as a suitor. Senta recognizes the Dutchman immediately and swears eternal loyalty to him.

Act III (A bay with a rocky shore, Daland's house on one side)
Scene 1: Daland's sailors are boisterously celebrating their return home and invite the Dutchman's crew to join their drinking. An eerie silence reigns on the Dutchman's ship, which is broken by a ghostly presence, terrifying the Norwegian sailors.
Scene 2: Erik tries to change Senta's mind once again by reminding her of the vow of love she made him. The Dutchman accidentally witnesses the scene. Believing Senta to be unfaithful, he immediately sets out to sea. Senta hurls herself into the waves, and the ghostly ship sinks. In the "red glow of the rising sun" the transfigured forms of Senta and the Dutchman can be seen entwined in each other's arms. *S. N.*

The Flying Dutchman, production photograph with Irene Theorin (Senta) and Ronnie Johansen (Dutchman), production Wieland Wagner, conductor Christian Badea, Det Kongelige Teater Kopenhagen 1961/99.

into a very real personal experience when he sailed from Riga to London in a small schooner with a seven-man crew. The four-week passage across the Baltic and North Seas turned into an adventure marked by heavy seas and the craft's eventual distress. The sailors on board recounted the tale of the Flying Dutchman, thus adding veracity and color to the story.

Wagner's encounter with the elemental power of the sea also inspired the music. The motif of the waves in the rising and falling scales of the strings, the unfettered fury of the giant orchestra, the sudden lulls and long crescendos, are all inspired by the composer's direct experience of the forces of nature, of violent storms and howling seas. The opera's overture is especially representative of these elemental forces. *M 6*

Sources of inspiration

The cries of the ship's crew and the ensuing echo inspired the main theme of the sailor's song in Act I and were also the source behind the opera's frequent and characteristic echo effects. *M 7*

Even the imposing desolation and melancholy gloom of the Norwegian fjords witnessed by Wagner aboard the schooner helped to define the musical character of the Dutchman. Pierre-Jean Béranger's dramatic monologue *Le juif errant* (*The Wandering Jew*), in the German translation by Adalbert Chamisso, also proved a source of inspiration. Wagner's later writings equated the Dutchman not only with the legendary figure of Ahasver, the "Wandering Jew," but also with Odysseus.

Wagner's unhappy sojourn in Paris and his disillusionment at the commercialism of musical life there also influenced both the creative process and the final work. *Gy. K.*

The Flying Dutchman, costume design for he Dutchman by Josef Fenneker, Duisburg 1937 (TWS).
The Flying Dutchman is the first of Wagner's operas whose stage directions (preserved in his commentary to a production of 1852) come close to psychological analysis in their detail. This is particularly true of his comments about the difficult leading role: "The performer of this role must be capable of arousing and maintaining the deepest sympathy … His first appearance on stage is to be unusually somber and serious … a certain terrible peace in his external manner even in the most passionate expression of inner pain and anguish … When the first drum roll starts to stir softly, he begins to shake, his fists clenched at his sides as if in a fit, his lip trembling … We must be able to imagine a "fallen angel," who, in the grip of the most frightful torments, proclaims his rage at eternal justice … "

6. Storm Motif

7. Call of the Sailors and its Echo

Hal-lo-jo!

Depicting the forces of nature

The story of *The Flying Dutchman* is derived from literary sources, but its musical and poetic substance is rooted in the composer's own experiences. The most direct literary model was the story *Aus den Memoiren des Herrn von Schnabelewopski* (*From the Memoirs of Herr von Schnabelewopski*) by Heinrich Heine (1834).

Wagner eschewed the ironic and parodic tone of Heine's story and reshaped the tragic tale to make it more suitable for the stage by adding the character of Erik. Wagner's reading of Heine's story was transformed

A ballad

In 1851 Wagner described the ballad sung by Senta as the "thematic heart of all the music" and a "poetic distillation of the entire drama." The ballad comprises two basic motifs: one of redemption *M 8* and one of damnation. *M 9* The horn call with its barren fifths reminiscent of the opening of Beethoven's Ninth Symphony – one of Wagner's seminal musical experiences – suggests an unearthly, ghostly atmosphere, and was used by the composer to symbolize the mythical sailor's damnation. Both motifs were also used in the Dutchman's monologue, in Erik's recounting of his dream, in sections of the duet between the Dutchman and Senta, and in the opera's final scene.

The real world

The two central figures of the Dutchman and Senta – he impelled by a curse and she by her vocation – do not actively shape their destinies but are at the mercy of fate. The most advanced music is reserved for these two characters and for the crew of the ghost-ship.

By contrast, the music of the more lifelike and traditional group of characters – the village girls and the Norwegian sailors – inhabits the sound-world of →Weber's and →Marschner's operas. Standard musical conventions are preserved in the aria sung by the garrulous and greedy Daland, and in the sentimental Erik's romance. *M 10 – M 13*   *Gy. K.*

The Flying Dutchman, set design by Hein Heckroth for the production by Erich Hezel, Städtische Bühnen, Opernhaus Köln 1929 (TWS).
Catastrophe, the elementary forces of nature, and an apotheosis are all captured in a single moment in this set design. From *The Flying Dutchman* onwards, the realm of the miraculous forms an indispensable part of Wagner's musical dramas.

8. Redemption Motif (Senta's Ballad)

Doch, daß der ar-me Mann noch Er-lö-sung fän-de auf Er – den

9. Damnation Motif (Senta's Ballad)

Jo   ho   hoe!   Jo   ho   ho   hoe!

10. Spinning Song

Summ' und brumm', du gu-tes Räd – – chen

11. Sailors' Song

Steuermann! Laß ___ die Wacht!

12. Daland's Aria

Mögst du, mein Kind, den frem-den Mann will-kom-men hei-ßen!

See – mann ist er, gleich mir,   das Gast-recht spricht er an.

13. Erik's Aria

Mein Herz voll Treu-e ___ bis ___ zum Ster-ben

Wilhelmine Schröder-Devrient (1804–60) as Senta.
The performances of Wilhelmine Schröder-Devrient, the foremost diva in German-speaking Europe between 1820 and 1850, were among Wagner's seminal artistic experiences. He probably saw her for the first time in 1829 as Emmy in Marschner's *The Vampire*. She performed in premières of three of Wagner's operas: as Adriano in →*Rienzi*, as Venus in →*Tannhäuser*, and as Senta in *The Flying Dutchman*.

Sentimental naïveté

Wagner wrote of Senta: "Even in her apparent sentimentality she is thoroughly naïve. Only in such a wholly naïve girl, surrounded by the strangeness of the Nordic landscape, could impressions such as the ballad of the Flying Dutchman or the painting of the pallid sailor give rise to an impulse as extraordinarily strong as the desire to save a damned man's soul. All this expresses itself in her as an overpowering madness such as can only take hold of naive souls … "

The Dutchman:
"The soft glowing flame I feel burning here,
Should I, poor wretch, call this love?
Ah, no!
It is the longing for salvation;
Would that it were imparted by such an angel!"

Music as mime

Wagner not only took charge personally, like a director, of all the theatrical components necessary for the première of *The Flying Dutchman*, but also coordinated costumes, sets, the orchestra, and the chorus, and was present at casting. He had done the same at the time of the première of *Rienzi*, but in his next opera he sought as a composer to achieve the complete unity of music and drama. Here, melodrama – music accompanied by gesture in a type of mime – played an important part. Wagner was already familiar with the device from Weber's →*Der Freischütz* and →Marschner's *The Vampire*. *La muette de Portici*, a five-act opera by Auber, held a particular fascination for Wagner; in the final moments of the opera the heroine – like Senta in *The Flying Dutchman* – hurls herself into the sea from a clifftop. Certain aspects of Wagner's style, which reached their culmination in →*The Valkyrie*, have their origins in the score of *The Flying Dutchman*, namely the symphonic conception of the whole work and the careful musical depiction of every movement and gesture of the drama in order to achieve what Wagner called "the most precise correlation of music and action." Examples can be found in the recitative of the Dutchman – a heroic baritone in the Marschner mold – as he steps ashore; and in the mime that occurs when Daland accompanies the Dutchman to his house and they encounter a Senta deathly pale with shock.

Conceived as a one-acter

Wagner originally drew up his scenario in the hope that the directorship of the Grand Opéra in Paris would commission him to set it to music. Previously he had only been charged with providing, jointly with another composer, the music for one act of a ballet.

Wagner's prose sketch for *Le vaisseau fantôme* – the French translation of *The Flying Dutchman* – was designed as a type of one-act curtain-raiser to a full-length ballet.

The directors of the Opéra were satisfied with his work but, because they were bound by a previous obligation to another composer, Wagner was compensated with a payment of 500 francs.

Not until the second version of 1841, written in German verse, did the composer describe *The Flying Dutchman* as a "Romantic opera," in reference to the tradition established by Weber and Marschner.

The number opera is transformed

Wagner still described the individual sections of the new opera as numbers, but on closer inspection they can be seen to be large-scale scenic compositions. The numbers are structured in a completely new way. The Dutchman's aria in Act I is the self-portrait of a demon, in which narrative, prayer, and an outburst of despair are combined. The duet between Senta and the Dutchman is not a dialogue but a double monologue between two souls: in the perception of the other characters they are both silent. There is a remarkable duet between Erik and Senta, in which the huntsman relates his dream to the girl and she experiences the same vision as though she were herself asleep. In the third verse of Senta's ballad the narrative is transformed into reality – Senta suddenly becomes aware of her "evolving from the demands of the dramatic action." vocation, namely to redeem the sufferings of the Dutchman through self-sacrifice.

Gy. K.

Leo Slezak (1873–1946) as a romanticized Tannhäuser (TWS).
Leo Slezak was a born Wagnerian tenor, though he was also gifted in heroic French and Italian tenor roles. He made his début in Brno in 1896 as Lohengrin, became a member of the Vienna Court (later, State) Opera under Mahler and was frequently a guest singer at Bayreuth and at the Metropolitan Opera. Slezak was a gentle and humorous giant of a man. His extensive memoirs provide important insights into the world of opera in the first decades of the 20th century.

Tannhäuser and the Singers' Contest at the Wartburg

Grosse romantische Oper in three acts

Libretto: Richard Wagner.
Première: Dresden version: 19 October 1845, Dresden (Hofheater); revised version: 13 March 1861, Paris (Théâtre Impérial de l'Opéra).
Characters: Tannhäuser, a minstrel (T), Venus (S), Hermann, Landgrave of Thuringia (B), Elisabeth, the landgrave's niece (S), Wolfram von Eschenbach (Bar), Walther von der Vogelweide (T), Biterolf (B), Heinrich der Schreiber (T), Reinmar von Zweter (B), A Young Shepherd (S), Four Noble Pages (2 S, 2 A); knights, counts and nobles, pilgrims, sirens (chorus).
Setting: Thuringia, at the beginning of the 13th century.

Synopsis

The young minstrel Tannhäuser praises sensual love (personified by Venus) as well as a pure, ideal love (represented by Elisabeth), but he is unable to find peace in either. While in the company of Venus he longs for Elisabeth, but when he is back in the everyday world with its restrictive moral code he desires to return to Venus. When he is required to sing the virtues of true love at the singers' contest on the Wartburg, he exalts uninhibited sensual pleasure, thus betraying Elisabeth's pure love. The Pope, God's representative in Rome, denies him absolution for this sin. Elisabeth wastes away while waiting and praying for Tannhäuser to return and eventually she dies. Returning home, the minstrel breathes his last at the side of her bier. Venus's spell is broken and Tannhäuser finds salvation in death.

Act I

Scene 1: Inside the Hörselberg near Eisenach; the grotto of Venus. An ecstatic bacchanal is under way. M 14 Although Tannhäuser sings the praises of Venus and her erotic powers, M 15 he longs to be back in the outside world. He calls out the name of the Virgin Mary and Venus's magic domain vanishes: Tannhäuser finds himself returned to the valley below the Wartburg castle.
Scene 2: The Wartburg valley in springtime. A shepherd's song is followed by a chorus of pilgrims. M-16.2 The landgrave Hermann is returning from a hunt with his minstrels and knights; they recognize in Tannhäuser their long-lost friend, who once belonged to their circle of singers. Wolfram von Eschenbach tells Tannhäuser that Elisabeth has not forgotten him, and that since his disappearance she has not attended any of the song contests. For Elisabeth's sake alone Tannhäuser returns to the Wartburg.

Act II

The Hall of Song in the Wartburg. Elisabeth, in the expectation of meeting Tannhäuser, joyfully greets the hall from which she has been absent for so long. M 17 Wolfram loves Elisabeth, but denies himself for the sake of his friend; he takes Tannhäuser to Elisabeth, and she reveals her feelings for him.

Tannhäuser, set design by Josef Kühn, Wiesbaden 1865 (TWS).
Stage flats were painted in the manner of picture postcards in Wagner's day, as befitted the 19th-century taste for historicism.

The song contest begins. *M 18* The landgrave instructs the singers to compose hymns on the true nature of love. While all the other singers depict an exalted, idealized love, Tannhäuser praises unfettered sensual desire as the real essence of love. *M 15* The crowd becomes increasingly indignant, and Tannhäuser is saved from the wrath of the knights only by Elisabeth. A remorseful Tannhäuser joins a group of pilgrims traveling to Rome.

Act III
The Wartburg valley in the fall. Full of yearning, Elisabeth waits for Tannhäuser. The pilgrims return but without her beloved minstrel. *M 19* Without Tannhäuser, life no longer has any meaning for her. Wolfram is still in love with her, and pours out his melancholy feelings to the evening star. *M 20* Night has fallen and a number of pilgrims approach, amongst whom Wolfram recognizes Tannhäuser. The Pope has denied him absolution, stating that Tannhäuser can never achieve salvation, just as a withered pilgrim's staff could never burst into bloom (Tannhäuser's Narration: Tannhäuser's torment, the Pope's curse *M 21, M 22*). In desperation and rage, Tannhäuser seeks to return to the Venusberg; the goddess of love appears but Wolfram banishes her by calling Elisabeth's name. Venus's spell over Tannhäuser evaporates. At dawn a funeral procession approaches bearing Elisabeth's body. Tannhäuser collapses dead at the side of her bier. Young pilgrims enter bearing a staff that has sprouted fresh green shoots: the visible symbol of Tannhäuser's redemption. *Á. G.*

Tannhäuser, Dietrich Fischer-Dieskau as Wolfram, Bayreuth 1962.
The lovelorn poet Wolfram von Eschenbach. It would be difficult to find a better interpreter of the role of Wolfram von Eschenbach than Dietrich Fischer-Dieskau (b. 1925). Schooled in the poetics of German lieder, his heroic and youthful baritone voice and perfect diction made him the very embodiment of a medieval poet. Fischer-Dieskau did in fact sing the "Hymn to the Evening Star" in the manner of a lied. *M 20*

Wagner's Middle Ages: a blend of legends

There are about a dozen Romantic versions of the legend of Tannhäuser on the Venusberg, and the singers' contest at the Wartburg is also described in ancient chronicles and musical manuscripts. Almost all the prominent poets and writers of the German Romantic era dealt with the subject. Wagner was familiar with a number of these sources, including Novalis's novel *Heinrich von Ofterdingen* (1802); the tales *Der Tannhäuser*, *Der Hörselberg*, *Der getreue Eckhart* (*The Faithful Eckhart*), and *Der Wartburger Krieg* (*The Wartburg Contest*) from Jacob and Wilhelm Grimm's collection of German legends (1816); Ludwig Tieck's novella *Der getreue Eckhart und der Tannenhäuser* (*The Faithful Eckhart and Tannenhäuser*) (1817); E.T.A. Hoffmann's story *Der Kampf der Sänger* (*The Singers' Contest*) (1819); Ludwig Bechstein's *Sagenschatz des Thüringerlandes* (*Legends of Thuringia*) (1835); and, not least, Heine's ironic poem *Der Tannhäuser* (1836–37).

The discovery of Christian Theodor Ludwig Lukas's essay *Der Krieg von Wartburg* (*The Wartburg Contest*) of 1838 was of decisive importance. According to Lukas, the main protagonist of the "Wartburg Contest," Heinrich von Ofterdingen, was none other than the knight and minstrel, Tannhäuser, the hero of the Venusberg legend. This idea opened the way for Wagner to link the two legends. The working out of the relationship between Tannhäuser and Elisabeth was also crucial. In real life Elisabeth was in fact the daughter of the Hungarian king, and was married to the son of Hermann, the landgrave of Thuringia; she eventually became known to history as St. Elizabeth. In Wagner's version of the story she is the landgrave's niece who loves and redeems Tannhäuser. This modification of the story enabled Wagner to reveal dramatically Tannhäuser's schizophrenic state of mind. The composer was also inspired by a romantic experience from his travels: in a Bohemian forest he had come across a shepherd whistling a cheerful dance tune. When Tannhäuser emerges from the spell of Venus into the human world he is greeted by just such a shepherd's melody, although Wagner did not so much quote the original tune as allow himself to be inspired by it. Inspiration was also provided by →Berlioz's *Harold in Italy* (1834), the second movement of which was highly regarded by Wagner and gave him the idea for a chorus of pilgrims.

More of Venus

Two distinct versions of *Tannhäuser* may be identified – a Dresden version and a Paris version. For Wagner, however, there was only ever one version and that was the last that he composed, the Paris version. In the original finale – heard at the first 13 performances in Dresden in 1845 – the Venusberg was suggested by a red glow in the distance, while bells from the Wartburg announced the death of Elisabeth. In revisions made for Dresden two years later, Venus herself appeared at the end of the opera, knights entered carrying the body of Elisabeth on her funeral bier, and Tannhäuser collapsed

dead at the side of his deceased lover. When Wagner came to revise the opera for Paris in late 1860, the music for the opening Venus scene in Venus's grotto was extended and partly reorchestrated. Wagner referred to his advanced orchestral style as a "richness of combinations," and the music of *Tannhäuser* provides ample evidence of his mastery: the distinctive sound of the orchestra; the luminous representation of Venus in the high tremolo of the muted violins; the opaque effect of blended sounds whose various origins

Heine's *Der Tannhäuser* of 1836
Heine adopted a modern, comical approach
to the theme. His poem begins with
the warning:

"Good Christians all be not entrapped
In Satan's cunning snare.
I sing the lay of Tannhäuser,
To bid your souls beware."

Later, Tannhäuser relates his life story to
the Pope:

"I am the noble Tannhäuser,
Who love and lust would win,
These lured me to the Venusberg,
Seven years I bode therein."

"From her hill at last I have escaped,
But through all the live-long day,
Those beautiful eyes still follow me.
'Come back!' they seem to say."

Pope Urban is not touched by
Tannhäuser's fate:

"Sadly the Pope upraised his hand
And sadly began to speak:
'Tannhäuser, most wretched of all men,
This spell thou canst not break.'

The devil called Venus is the worst
Amongst all we name as such.
And nevermore canst thou be redeemed
From the beautiful witch's clutch."

Finally, Tannhäuser returns to Venus who
receives him with joy and understanding:

"Lady Venus awoke from sleep,
And sprang from her bed in haste:
She clasped the knight in her lily-white arms,
And they tenderly embraced."

(First stanza translated by Emma Lazarus, the
remainder by Aaron Kramer in *The Poetry and
Prose of Heinrich Heine*, ed. Frederic Ewen,
Citadel Press, New York, 1948.)

are indiscernible; the rise and fall of ardent string passages creating the impression of orgiastic frenzy and the febrile madness of love. The revisions to the opening scene also had dramatic repercussions.

The scene expresses the contrast between the world of everyday life to which Tannhäuser longs to return and the "paradis artificiel" in which Venus attempts to keep him. Baudelaire's essay *Les paradis artificiels: Opium et haschisch* also appeared in 1860 and Baudelaire was one of the first Frenchmen to study seriously the questions raised by *Tannhäuser*. The scene in Venus's grotto provides the primary source for Wagner's other pieces of sensual music (*The Valkyrie*, Act I; *Tristan and Isolde*, Act II; and the scene between Parsifal and Kundry in Klingsor's magic garden in Act II of *Parsifal*).

Gy. K.

Tannhäuser, set design (Venus's grotto) by Ferdinand Moser, Hofoperntheater, Vienna 1906 (TWS).
The "paradis artificiel" of the opening scene. In this Viennese production from the Art Nouveau period Venus's grotto assumed a tropical luxuriance.

Curse and odyssey

The motif of the curse can be found throughout Wagner's work. Ada is cursed by Arindal in →*The Fairies*; in →*Rienzi* the pronouncement of excommunication has the effect of a curse; and in →*The Flying Dutchman* the doomed sailor is burdened by a curse that can be lifted only by a sacrificial death. Tristan curses the love potion (→*Tristan and Isolde*), Alberich curses love itself (→*The Rhinegold*), and Kundry is condemned to wander throughout the centuries for mocking Christ (→*Parsifal*). From Wagner's very first works, the motif of the curse is closely tied to that of the odyssey. In →*The Fairies* the character who pronounces the curse is himself condemned to wander alone and to traverse the underworld in order to redeem the woman he has cursed. The Dutchman is condemned to sail the seas for eternity, and Tristan journeys back and forth in his odyssey of self-discovery. In →*The Ring of the*

Tannhäuser, set design by Ludwig Sievert for the production by Rudolf Hartmann, conductor Clemens Krauss, Staatsoper, Munich 1933 (TWS).
This illustration is a magnificent example of the German fascination for forests and their moods: pilgrims are depicted in the Thuringian woods with the Wartburg castle in the background. Spring has arrived (Act I). The sublime tranquillity of the woods was of such fundamental importance to Wagner that he began his *Tannhäuser* overture with a melody from the pilgrims' chorus, a piece that combines piety with a celebration of the beauty of the woods. →*M 16.2*

Nibelung the odyssey results from a universal curse, a cosmic journey that only ends with Brünnhilde's suicide. In *Tannhäuser* there are three curses and two odysseys. At the beginning of Act I, Venus curses Tannhäuser when he abandons her, and the singers' contest ends with Tannhäuser's banishment from the Thuringian court (end of Act II). The musical and dramatic focus of Act III is Tannhäuser's Narration, in which the hero relates the words of the Pope: his chances of redemption are the same as those of a withered staff bringing forth new shoots. This curse results in Tannhäuser's second odyssey – his attempt to return to Venus's underworld realm.

Venus, Mary, Elisabeth – Tannhäuser's cries for help

The abrupt shifts in dramatic events so typical of this opera correspond to the hero's character. Far-reaching changes and sudden transformations occur without any transition. Several of these apply only to Tannhäuser's inner development and typify his temperament alone. When he realizes that his hymn to Venus has deeply wounded Elisabeth – "who loved him from the depths of her soul, whose heart he, praising, broke" – he is overcome with remorse, and it is in this state that he hears the pilgrims' chorus ("at the high feast of grace and worship, in humility I confess my sins"). Tannhäuser quickly turns, "his features transformed in the radiance of awakened hope, towards the exit with a cry of 'To Rome!'" Most of these abrupt changes affect the course of the opera's action. Three names seem to have the effect of magic spells: the name of the Virgin Mary brings about the first great change, causing the Venusberg to evaporate. When Wolfram speaks Elisabeth's name, Tannhäuser, "with passion and moved by joy," instantly reverses his decision never to return to the circle of singers. In an exclamation of rapture he sings: "To her! To her! Oh, lead me to her!" After returning from his futile pilgrimage to Rome, however, Tannhäuser seeks to return to Venus and seems to have forgotten Elisabeth altogether. At this moment Elisabeth's name, spoken once again by Wolfram, strikes him like a thunderbolt: "Tannhäuser remains rooted to the spot as if paralyzed." Mention of the goddess of love also causes upheaval at the song contest: "Poor wretches who know not her love – go forth, go forth to the mount of Venus!" Tannhäuser sings in a state of "the greatest rapture," while Elisabeth listens "in growing dread … remaining

upright only with the very greatest expenditure of energy." Later, in Act III, Venus's name causes the magical realm of love to materialize, while Elisabeth's name is used to banish it: "Venus disappears and with her the entire enchanted vision." Wagner's genius is also evident in the way he uses the symmetry of these sudden twists and turns to create a sense of balance in both the pace and the emotion of the work.

Archlike in form: from spring to fall

The story begins in springtime with a spirited bacchanal in E major. The climax of the opera is reached in Act II with the noisy and dramatic clash between Tannhäuser and the singers and Elisabeth's quiet, internal collapse. This is the keystone of the arch, and it is followed by an Adagio ensemble in B major and a polyphonic chorus in the same key, "Mit ihnen sollst du wallen zur Stadt der Gnadenhuld" ("To the city of grace shall you travel as a pilgrim"), with which the act ends. The opera ends in the fall: Act III begins in E flat major as day is turning into night. The tempos that follow are slow (the pilgrims' chorus, prayer, romance, and Tannhäuser's Narration). After the deaths of Elisabeth and Tannhäuser, the opera ends with a melodic fragment in E flat major borrowed from the first E major chorus of pilgrims.   Gy. K.

Tannhäuser, costume designs for Venus (above) by Heinrich Lefler, Berlin 1910, and for Elisabeth (left) by Hugo Baruch, Vienna 1910/11 (TWS).
Art Nouveau representations of Venus and Elisabeth. Elisabeth and Venus are two variations on the principle of the "eternal female" that characterized Wagner's work up to his last female protagonist, Kundry (→*Parsifal*). They represent, respectively, pure and idealized love, the highest goal of the courtly minstrels, and sensual love, the sinking into an eternal night of pleasure. Wagner did not picture Elisabeth exclusively as a pious figure: in Act II she appears as a chaste yet dynamic woman. Her entrance aria *M 19* is expansive and very spirited. An Art Nouveau Venus must have seemed refreshing after the historical tastes of the Bayreuth stage. Venus is an important presence in *Tannhäuser*. Although she is not allocated an aria, her singing points the way to future styles more emphatically than any other character. The entire first scene of Act I is a musical expression of her realm. *M 15*

Lohengrin

Romantische Oper in three acts

Libretto: Richard Wagner.

Première: 28 August 1850, Weimar (Hoftheater).

Characters: Heinrich der Vogler/Henry the Fowler, King of Germany (B), Lohengrin (T), Elsa of Brabant (S), Duke Gottfried, Elsa's brother (silent), Friedrich von Telramund, a count of Brabant (Bar), Ortrud, his wife (Ms), The King's Herald (Bar), Four Noblemen of Brabant (2 T, 2 B); counts and nobles, men and women, servants (chorus).

Setting: Antwerp, in the first half of the 10th century.

Synopsis
Before the opera begins
Before his death the duke of Brabant placed his son Gottfried and daughter Elsa in the care of Count Friedrich von Telramund, promising the count the right to Elsa's hand in marriage. Elsa, however, rejected the count, who then took Ortrud for a wife (Ortrud was a descendant of the pagan Friesian Prince Radbod who ruled Brabant before its conversion to Christianity). It was at this time that Elsa's brother Gottfried disappeared without trace.

The present
The political situation is unstable. The German king, Henry the Fowler, has come to Brabant to rally support against the Hungarians who are threatening war. Brabant, however, is without a leader.

Act I (A meadow on the banks of the river Scheldt near Antwerp)
Scene 1: Telramund accuses Elsa of murdering her brother. A champion for Elsa is called for to fight Telramund.
Scene 2: Elsa beseeches God to come to her aid and in a vision she sees her savior.
Scene 3: The vision comes true: a stranger appears and defeats Telramund. He will stay and become Brabant's new ruler and Elsa's husband on one condition: she must never enquire as to his name or origin.

Act II (The fortress at Antwerp)
Scene 1: Telramund and Ortrud plot how they can regain power.
Scene 2: Ortrud sows doubt in Elsa's heart about the noble origins of her future husband.
Scenes 3–5: The wedding is conducted in ceremonial splendor. Ortrud and Telramund try in vain to expose Lohengrin during the wedding procession to the cathedral.

Act III (The bridal chamber; a meadow on the banks of the Scheldt at daybreak)
Scene 1: Ceremonial entry of the bridal couple.
Scene 2: Elsa and Lohengrin on their wedding night. Elsa asks Lohengrin the forbidden question. Telramund's assassination attempt fails.
Scene 3: Before the king and the assembled people, the stranger gives an answer to Elsa's question: his name is Lohengrin and he is a Knight of the Holy Grail (Lohengrin's Narration). Lohengrin takes his leave; the swan that had originally led him to Brabant is transformed into Gottfried. Elsa collapses and dies.

Á. G.

Wagner and Liszt, caricature by Willi Bithorn, Vienna 1910.
The friendship between the two men was marked by fruitful encounters and bitter disappointments (on Liszt's part). Wagner married Liszt's eldest daughter, Cosima, who was promoted to "First Lady" of the Wagner cult after his death. *Lohengrin* was premièred in Weimar under the direction of Liszt; the autograph version of the score contains several comments from Liszt on matters of interpretation.

Material for a lifetime
Christian Theodor Ludwig Lukas's essay *The Wartburg Contest* (1838) had already inspired Wagner to create *Tannhäuser*. In Lukas's work he was also to discover the anonymous Lohengrin epic with which he was to become thoroughly acquainted through an edition by Joseph Görres (1813) and through Wolfram von Eschenbach's Parsifal poem, which was published in 1841. Wagner also took great pleasure in studying a number of Jacob Grimm's works – *Deutsche Mythologie* (*German Mythology*), *Deutsche Rechtsalterthümer* (*German Antiquities*), and *Weisthümer* (*Words of Wisdom*) – as well as the Grimm Brothers' edition of *Deutschen Sagen* (*German Legends*). He was also drawn to an episode from *The Song of the Nibelungen* (*Nibelung Epic*) – the dispute of the queens – which he reused in the cathedral scene in *Lohengrin*. It could be said then that Wagner had, in one fell swoop, discovered a source of inspiration which was to provide him with material for the rest of his life. This explains the fact that in the 12 weeks following the completion of →*Tannhäuser* Wagner wrote the scenario for →*The Mastersingers of*

Lohengrin, Lohengrin's farewell, postcard, drawing by W. Kaulbach, Bayreuth 1877. Does the opera end without a transfiguration? "The conclusion of a work is everything," Wagner once said. He wrote several versions of the final scene for most of his music dramas and battled to find the right finale. In the case of *Lohengrin*, Elsa's punishment presented the main dramatic problem: "… punishment by separation seems utterly essential, and it cannot be too rigorous because it is the most just and consistent," Wagner wrote to the author Hermann Franck on 30 May 1846.

Lohengrin, Lotte Lehmann (1888–1976) as Elsa. Elsa – dreaming, enraptured – waits for her savior.

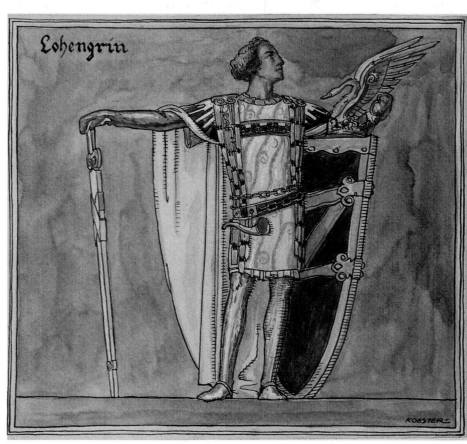

Nuremberg as well as a prose sketch for *Lohengrin*, whose use of the Grail theme already carried within it the germ of the composer's later →*Parsifal*. All these ideas, designs, and plans thus took shape in the two and a half months preceding the première of →*Tannhäuser*. When the score for *Lohengrin* was completed on 28 April 1848, Wagner turned his attention to the idea of a universal tragedy that could be spun from these Germanic legends. In the same year, these reflections led to an interest in the Nibelung legend and inspired him to begin composing the libretto for his first Ring drama: *The Death of Siegfried* (→*The Ring of the Nibelung*).

Gy. K.

Lohengrin, costume design for Lohengrin from the Paul H. Koester studio, Berlin 1905 (TWS). None of Wagner's other heroes, whether gods or men (including Parsifal), is as pure and divine as Lohengrin. Wagner's later works were always concerned with human figures even though they may have resembled gods. But Lohengrin stands before us like a true god, who is lost in the midst of mankind. Could his character be a portrait of Wagner, the Romantic artist?

Wagner in disguise

Lohengrin is connected to →*The Flying Dutchman* by certain "inner threads." The hero in each opera is a mythic outsider driven by a mysterious fate. Both have been sent across the water by supernatural forces, and the women chosen by them are visionaries. Senta and Elsa both imagine the arrival of a lover who does not as yet exist so that his actual appearance seems miraculous. The tragic clash of both pairs of lovers goes to the heart of what it means to love; in this regard Wagner's Elsa is a development of the problematic figure of Tannhäuser. For Wagner, Elsa represents "the woman who can love in this way and this way alone, and who can escape from her rapt worship into the fullness of true love only through the eruption of jealousy … "

The heroes of Wagner's three operas of this period form a self-portrait of the composer. The Dutchman, Tannhäuser, and Lohengrin are symbols of a great man who stands alone against the world. Their dislike of society reflects the disillusionment that Wagner himself had experienced in Riga and in Paris. Measured against such greatness the world at large appears petty, insensitive, unimaginative, and governed by mere convention. Everyday life can no longer sustain the hero or the artist. The new hero appears either as a ghostly apparition from the sea, an opponent of his peers and contemporaries, or he descends from heaven to appear as a savior in a boat drawn by a swan, come to expose the lies and deception of the world. The hero represented by the Dutchman is an abstract figure and cannot be fixed in a social context. His strangeness is bound up with suffering and desire, but the mystic nature of his death causes the outlines of his character to become only more blurred. Tannhäuser is a tangible, living being who seems strange only to his historical contemporaries: in the Romantic era an operagoer might have recognized himself in this figure plagued by inner conflict. In the case of Tannhäuser, a mythic figure becomes a man of flesh and blood, whose feelings and problems are inseparable from the realities of the environment in which he finds himself. It is not his greatness that is illuminated but his challenge to the vacuous conventions of an ossified society. This potential for protest is lacking in the figure of Lohengrin. On the one hand he is a "superman" above mere mortals, but on the other he is emotionally bound to their world. He is a lonely artist, and indeed this is how Wagner interpreted the figure retrospectively in 1851. That date marked the second anniversary of the defeat of the independence movements in Europe. Wagner himself was living in exile at the time.

Transformation from god to man

Lohengrin emanates an aura of exalted isolation. He knows neither the torments of damnation like the Dutchman nor the inner turbulence of Tannhäuser. His aloofness from people and the world gives him a symbolic and somber character. He retains these characteristics until the "sweet sounds" of the well-loved bridal march M 23 have died away, and then reveals himself as a human being for the first time in the bridal chamber with Elsa. This is a true transformation and Wagner implies with a sequence of chords that his crossing of the threshold into the bridal chamber is a miracle.

The love scene has the atmosphere of an enchanting dream: "sweet fragrances delightfully ensnare the senses." The harmonies that introduce the scene express the magic of love rather than its passion. But it is precisely this unorthodox and utterly unique-sounding love music that makes Lohengrin's disillusionment and his human tragedy so convincing. When, after the revelation of his identity (Lohengrin's Narration), he is forced to leave Elsa, it is not as a Knight of the Grail that he has suffered defeat. As an envoy of God he has triumphed – but as a man he has lost.   *Gy. K.*

Birgit Nilsson (b. 1918) as Elsa (top) and Wolfgang Windgassen (1914–74) as Lohengrin, Bayreuth Festival 1954. Birgit Nilsson made her début in 1946 as Agathe (Weber, →*Der Freischütz*). She was one of the greatest Wagnerian sopranos of the 1950s and 1960s. Wolfgang Windgassen was the Bayreuth Wagnerian tenor of the 1950s and 1960s. He sang the mature composer's tenor parts, and his interpretations of Tristan and Lohengrin in particular were legendary. Wieland Wagner is once said to have joked: "When Windgassen can no longer sing, they will have to put a sign on the Bayreuth Festspielhaus: 'Closed today and for the foreseeable future owing to a shortage of tenors' " (Karl Böhm, the conductor of *Tristan* at the 1961 Bayreuth Festival, in his autobiography of 1973.)

Lohengrin, costume design for Ortrud by Heinrich Lefler, Vienna 1907 (TWS). The royal palace is in the grip of evil. The interpretive history of the opera has seen it oscillate between the forces of "darkness" and "light." Embarrassingly, the work enjoyed enormous popularity during the Third Reich.

Opposite
Lohengrin, illustration for the dialogue between Ortrud and Telramund by Hugo L. Braune (TWS).
"Know you this hero brought hither by a swan?" (Act II, Scene 1). For 150 years historians and aesthetic theorists have pondered this same question.

23. Bridal March

Treu - lich be - wacht   blei - bet zu - rück,   wo euch der Se - gen   der Lie - be be - wahr'!

WEISST DU, WER DIESER HELD – DEN HIER EIN SCHWAN GEZOGEN AN DAS LAND?

Lohengrin, set design by Eduard Löffler for the production by Richard Hein, conductor Ernst Cremer, Nationaltheater, Mannheim 1933 (TWS).
"German lands must arm their men, then no one will mock the German empire" (Act I, Scene 1). Never did King Henry's cry seem more threatening than in 1933, the year of the "Thousandth anniversary of victory over the Eastern hordes." For Wagner the words represent a call for the rediscovery of former glory. This concept was popular in the Romantic era in almost all European national dramas, and served to heighten the historical awareness of the audience.

Timbre and dramatic effect

Wagner was consistent in allocating individual characters and states of mind their own distinctive tone colors and timbres. In *Lohengrin* the Grail (A major) is depicted by the rapt and pure sound of the violins playing in their highest register and divided into groups of four and five. The impression of brilliance and translucence is the aural equivalent of the mystic radiance of the Grail. *M 24*

The contrast between the high violin figures and the sounds produced by the lower string and wind instruments corresponds to the difference between the Grail and the world of reality and between various characters in the opera. At the beginning of the second, nocturnal act, the dark timbre of the cellos (largely confined to their lowest string and seldom playing above *piano*) combines with the diminished and augmented intervals of Ortrud's serpentine motif, as if to suggest the very blackness of the night, as well as the black intentions of Ortrud and the deceitful Telramund. *M 25*

Here, as in other scenes, Ortrud and Telramund are characterized by the sound of the bass clarinet and the cor anglais. The dark timbre of both these instruments is designed to emphasize the secretive and mysterious nature of these creatures of the night. Elsa, however, is associated with the oboe, which represents her naïveté and innocence. The sound of the oboe, combined with that of the cor anglais, also expresses grief and sorrow. *M 26*

The trumpet is traditionally the instrument of kings and knights. In *Lohengrin* it is used for the motif heralding the arrival of the eponymous hero. Wagner had a group of special brass instruments designed for the music representing the king: "four long, brass, trumpet-like instruments, of the simplest design, much like those seen in church paintings blown by angels at the Last Judgement." King Henry is always depicted by these four trumpets; they are played in C major and their fanfares are heard throughout the opera, like a "musical costume," and contribute greatly to the opera's historical atmosphere.

Wagner as director

Sounds and images are closely linked in *Lohengrin*, and add greatly to the ceremonial effect. The "old oak," the "simple stone table," the "curved castle wall," the "Byzantine portal of the cathedral," and the "horses entering from the wings" – all these elements were created purely for visual effect. The castle gate, however, is closely linked with a musical symbol – namely, the "two guards who intone the morning song" – and this becomes an integral part of the echo effects employed on stage. The staking out of the dueling area is performed as a musical mime: the seconds pace out the ground in such a way "that after the first eight beats, having taken a step with each beat, they have exchanged positions exactly." This trial by combat is not wholly set as a mime, for it also contains realistic elements, such as "the king beating his sword three times against a shield hanging from an oak tree." The long procession of women in Act II, Scene 4 is precisely coordinated with the tempo and character of the music; the role of the army general also has complex musico-dramatic elements.

A vision of the fatherland

Wagner saw *Lohengrin* staged for the first time at the Vienna Hofoper (court opera) in May 1861. He had not been present at the première in Weimar in 1850, as he had been obliged to flee the previous year to Switzerland: in Saxony he was a wanted man for his part in the Dresden uprising of May 1849. Wagner's contribution to the ideological preparation for the revolution and his participation in the uprising itself, as well as his subsequent writings in exile, find full expression in his massive cycle *The Ring of the Nibelung*; indeed it is only in the Nibelung cycle that the revolutionary aspects of Wagner's character and behavior can be fully discerned. There is, however, a text that belongs to the period of *Lohengrin* that illuminates Wagner's political preoccupations. An article appeared anonymously in a

24. The Grail

25. Ortrud's Motif

26. Elsa's Motif

special supplement to the *Dresdener Anzeiger* (*Dresden Reporter*) of 17 July 1848, entitled "The relationship between republican aspirations and the monarchy." The author, none other than Wagner himself, demanded "social and national reforms at the head of, and throughout the whole body of, society," but he was nevertheless still prepared to consider the king the country's first republican. The artistic expression of this view would appear to be realized in the figure of the good and popular king in *Lohengrin*.

From the aesthetic and dramatic points of view, Wagner had no choice but to work in the genre of the historical drama, especially as the tragic conclusion of his opera was balanced by an actual historical victory. But at the same time the historical drama had personal relevance for Wagner, because within its framework he was able to depict symbolically his views on contemporary social and political issues. *Lohengrin* provides a vision of a unified German fatherland – an alliance between God's emissary, the king, and the people.

And it was with heartfelt sincerity that Wagner composed the music for the good king, the courageous warrior, and the beauties of the homeland. By depicting Germany's past he strove to present a vision of its future. The sound-world Wagner created to evoke this vision is an imaginative rather than an historical one, even though it sounds almost historically

"authentic" to our ears. *Lohengrin*, the last stage work that Wagner described as an opera, is a Romantic construction in the fullest sense of the word. Here, the worlds of myth and history, fairy tale and tragedy become one.   *Gy. K.*

Lohengrin, production photographs with Thomas Moser as Lohengrin and (below) Inga Nielsen as Elsa, production Peter Konwitschny, sets Helmuth Bradel, conductor Ingo Metzmacher, Staatsoper, Hamburg 1998.
In this production the action was set in a classroom, in which pubescent children acted out their fantasies and needs.

Opposite
Costume design for Isolde by Heinrich Lefler,
Vienna 1914 (TWS).
Wagner found the model for his Isolde in two
legends: in the Irish version Tristan's wound is
healed (though his heart must endure a still
greater wound), and in the Breton version
Tristan and Isolde marry. Wagner created his
Isolde, a woman of fatal erotic charms, by
combining these two figures.

Tristan and Isolde, illustration by Franz
Stassen, Berlin 1900 (TWS).
The fateful course of events that leads to the
tragic end of Tristan and Isolde must count as
one of the most bizarre in either historical or
fictional love stories: "… unbewusst, höchste
Lust!" ("… oblivion, the greatest pleasure!")
are the last words of the dying Isolde and
therefore of the opera. This illustration
depicts Tristan and Isolde united in death
(with, below them, the strains of the
Liebestod sounding once again).

Tristan and Isolde

Handlung in three acts

Libretto: Richard Wagner.
Première: 10 June 1865, Munich (Hoftheater).
Characters: Tristan (T), Isolde (S), König Marke/King Mark (B), Kurwenal, Tristan's companion (Bar), Melot, a courtier (T), Brangäne, Isolde's companion (Ms), A Shepherd (T), A Helmsman (Bar), A Young Sailor (T); sailors, knights, squires (chorus).
Setting: At sea, in Cornwall, and in Brittany, during the Middle Ages.

Synopsis
Before the opera begins
The Irish warrior Morold traveled to Cornwall in order to demand the tribute due from King Mark. But Tristan, Mark's nephew and vassal, killed Morold, and in place of the tribute sent Morold's head to Ireland. During the fray, however, Tristan received from the poisoned sword of his opponent a wound that will not heal. The poison had been prepared by Morold's betrothed Isolde, and she alone would be capable of healing the wound. The injured warrior set out for Ireland where, under the name of Tantris, he entrusted himself to the care of Morold's lover. Isolde, however, recognized him as her lover's murderer, as Tantris's sword had a nick in the blade which matched a fragment embedded in Morold's skull. Isolde raised the sword against Tristan to avenge the murder of Morold, but feeling his eyes on her, her hatred turned to love. She therefore nursed him and sent him back to Cornwall cured. Shortly afterwards Tristan returned to the Irish court, now in his real identity, to seek Isolde's hand on behalf of his uncle Mark. In order to effect a reconciliation between the two royal houses, Isolde agreed to the match and embarked on the voyage to Cornwall.

Act I (At sea, on the deck of Tristan's ship)
Scene 1: Tristan is accompanying Isolde, the daughter of the Irish king, to Cornwall, where she is to be married to his uncle, King Mark. Tristan is in love with her, as she is with him, although their feelings remain undeclared. A young helmsman sings a song about an "Irish maid," and Isolde feels she is being ridiculed.
Scene 2: Anxious to talk to Tristan, Isolde calls him to her, but Tristan refuses her invitation.
Scene 3: Deeply offended, Isolde confesses her distress to Brangäne.
Scene 4: Isolde decides to kill herself and Tristan, and she reveals to Brangäne her intention to prepare a poison that they will both drink.
Scene 5: Brangäne exchanges the poison for a love potion that opens the hearts and mouths of Tristan and Isolde, and they reveal their feelings for each other. The ship, which is greeted by Mark, arrives in Cornwall.

Act II (Mark's royal castle in Cornwall at night)
Scene 1: Isolde is now married to Mark, but her longing for Tristan has not diminished. While the king is out hunting, she waits patiently for Tristan.
Scene 2: Tristan and Isolde consummate their love.
Scene 3: The knight Melot, jealous of Tristan, has advised the king to return early to his castle. Mark discovers the lovers. Tristan throws himself on Melot's sword.

Act III (Tristan's castle, Kareol, in Brittany)
Scene 1: Tristan lies dying, waiting for Isolde, who has been summoned by his companion Kurwenal.
Scene 2: Isolde arrives and Tristan dies in her arms.
Scene 3: King Mark arrives in pursuit, accompanied by Melot, who, on entering Tristan's castle, fights with Kurwenal; both are killed. Brangäne confesses to Mark her substitution of the love potion and the king shows forgiveness. With Tristan's demise, Isolde has no further desire to live, and she follows him in death. *S. N.*

Internal and external drama

Wagner described *Tristan and Isolde* as a "Handlung," which is a literal translation of the Greek word "drama." But drama in what sense? The opera is exceptionally poor in external events and Wagner can only have meant the term to refer to internal action. The world in which the external action takes place – the world of duty, morality, and honor, in which Kurwenal, Mark, and Melot exist – is mere illusion to Tristan and Isolde. For them, the "real world" is the interior universe of the soul, where day is transformed into a realm of dreams and night becomes the repository of truth.

The moments of external action, or the actual events of the opera (although they too lack a sense of historical authenticity), are confined to the conclusions of scenes or the ends of acts: Isolde's invitation to Tristan and his refusal as relayed by Kurwenal (Act I, Scene 2); the sudden arrival in Cornwall (end of Act I); Tristan's suicide attempt and his duel with Melot (end of Act II); Isolde's arrival in Kareol followed by that of Mark, and the death of Melot and Kurwenal (final scene of Act III). These simple events take place in objective time: they belong, in other words, to the real world. Subjective time is reserved for events of a different kind: Isolde's dialogue with Brangäne, and Tristan and Isolde's encounter on board the ship and their drinking of the love potion (Act I); their nocturnal love duet and Mark's monologue (Act II); Tristan's internal monologue, his feverish visions, and Isolde's "Liebestod," or "love-death" (Act III, beginning and end). Subjective time means the expansion of a single moment, and it is effected through a labyrinth of internal events and reflection, and through the constant reference to the past by each of the main characters – Tristan, Isolde, and Mark. In this way the past encroaches upon the present, paralyzing whomsoever is held in the grip of memory. A longing for death thus usurps the desire for action. This entire psychological framework is animated by the music, whose medium is the all-knowing orchestra. *Gy. K.*

Tristan and Isolde, set design by Hein Heckroth (Isolde's Liebestod) for the production by Rudolf Schulz-Dornburg, conductor Georg Solti, Städtische Bühnen, Essen 1928 (TWS)
A vision that reveals the inner drama of the opera: a powerful image of the Liebestod.

Tristan and Isolde, production photograph with Wolfgang Schmidt (Tristan) and Jukka Rasilainen (Kurwenal), production and sets Marco Arturo Marelli, costumes Dagmar Niefind-Marelli, conductor Christof Prick, Sächsische Staatsoper, Dresden 1995. Mortally wounded and plagued by visions, Tristan awaits Isolde in a state of feverish ecstasy. Behind him is his loyal servant, Kurwenal. The vocal and acting skills Wagner required from the tenor in Act III have inspired some of the greatest achievements in the history of opera.

The motif of longing

The opera opens with an endless series of ever intensifying waves (cellos, soft, and in unison). Central to this passage is an ascending gesture of yearning (like a sigh), which ends in a chord from the woodwind section. This chord has come to be known as the "*Tristan* chord." The chord's partial resolution signals that a resting point has been momentarily reached. In spite of this, however, the structure remains open-ended and the tension accumulates with magnetic force (like a desire that can never be sated). The same chord is repeated countless times and in infinite variations throughout the opera, until at the very last moment of the drama, Isolde's death, it is finally resolved. In death there is no dissonance. M 27, M 28

A fateful affair

"Since I have never known the real happiness of love in my life, I want to build another monument to this most beautiful of dreams in which love will be properly sated from beginning to end." So wrote Wagner to Liszt in 1854 during his tempestuous love affair with Mathilde Wesendonck (1828–1902), the wife of Wagner's patron, the businessman Otto Wesendonck.

The affair was mirrored in Wagner's creative output: he set Mathilde's *Fünf Gedichte* (*Five Poems*) to music and the relationship influenced his composition of *Tristan and Isolde*.

The *Wesendonck Lieder* are closely related to the music he wrote for *Tristan*. The sketch of Act I, completed at the end of 1857, was prefaced with a dedicatory poem to Mathilde.

The affair finally resulted in a public scandal and Wagner fled in 1858 to Venice, where he orchestrated *Tristan* in the Palazzo Vendramin on the Grand Canal.

27. Motif of Desire (Beginning)

28. Motif of Sated Desire (End)

29. Hymn to the Night (Tristan and Isolde)

O sink' her - nie - der, Nacht der Lie - be

Isolde of the white hand

The Tristan story, with which Wagner had been familiar since his days as music director at Dresden, is part of a cycle of Celtic legends and appears in a number of medieval literary sources. The *Tristan* poem by Chrétien de Troyes (mid-twelfth century), France's most famous "trouvère," or troubadour, has not survived, nor have the verse narratives by Béroul and Thomas d'Angleterre – also from the twelfth century – been preserved intact. The oldest German versions of the story are those by Eilhart von Oberge (*Tristrant*, c. 1190) and Gottfried von Strassburg (*Tristan*, c. 1210). The cobbler poet, Hans Sachs, also treated the Tristan legend in the *Tragedia ... von der strengen Lieb Herrn Tristant mit der schönen Königin Isolden* (*Tragedia ... of the Noble Lord Tristant and the Beautiful Queen Isolde*), of 1553, an ironic reference to which can be found in Act III of →*The Mastersingers of Nuremberg*. In Gottfried von Strassburg's epic poem, edited and published by Hermann Kurtz in 1844, Wagner encountered two separate Isolde figures. Originally he intended that both characters would appear in the opera: Mark's wife, the beautiful Irish Isolde with her magic powers, and the Breton "Isolde of the white hand," whom Tristan marries after he has fled from Mark. Tristan's long wait for Isolde's ship to arrive in Brittany and the use of good and bad omens (ships flying black or white flags, and sad and cheerful shepherd melodies) were probably retained from Wagner's very earliest draft and are derived from the story of the two Isoldes. The idea of the love potion may have been inspired by Donizetti's opera →*The Elixir of Love* , which was a staple of the operatic repertory in Dresden, and by Julius Moses's poem *König Mark und Isolde* (in which the love potion represented fate). A yet more significant contribution to the emotional and intellectual content of *Tristan and Isolde* was made by Friedrich Schlegel's novel *Lucinde* of 1799. This work contains several of the opera's key themes: the poison draught and love potion, the love-death, the magical power of the night, and what Thomas Mann called "passionate sensuality."

Night and dreams

The novel *Lucinde* contains the following dialogue between the lovers: " 'Only in the calm of night,' said Lucinde, 'do longing and love glow and shine full and bright like the radiant sun.' 'And by day,' replied Julius, 'the joy of love shines palely, like the moon's sparing beams.' 'Or it appears and disappears into the sudden darkness,' added Lucinde, 'like those flashes which illuminated our room when the moon was enshrouded.' "

The nocturnal atmosphere of Novalis's poems *Hymnen an die Nacht* (*Hymns to the Night*) may also have influenced Wagner's libretto. Novalis claimed that: "For lovers, death is a wedding night, a secret of sweet mysteries." And in his *Hymnen an die Nacht* he established the relative value of those two distinct elements – light and dark, day and night: "Must the morning always return? Will earthly power never end? Will love's secret sacrifice never burn eternal?" Tristan and Isolde call themselves "devotees of night" – an almost exact echo of a phrase found in Novalis.

Purgatory and delirium

The first act depicts the lovers' efforts to deny their love; the love potion symbolizes the impossibility of resisting true love. The second act concerns the attempt to realize this love in a world of social obligations, marital conventions, and sexual possessiveness. Tristan's wound, which he allows Melot to inflict upon him, symbolizes his defeat by these forces, and it also shows the intensity of his inner conflict. Not until the beginning of the third act is the nature of this wound completely revealed, for at this point Tristan's delirium becomes part of his process of enlightenment. His delirium is both a challenge and a preparation: it is not oblivion he will find in death, but triumph.

Tristan and his fellow sufferers

Wagner was the first in a long line of artists to adapt the legend for its story of tragic love rather than for its theme of adultery. But tragedy in what sense? Is the opera about the impossibility of love under certain social conditions? Or is the tragedy that love always and universally remains unfulfilled? Is this "fearful torment" part of the very nature of love? The essence of Tristan's love and the impossibility of its ever being fulfilled can be explained satisfactorily neither from a socio-political point of view (because it runs counter to the *status quo*) nor from a metaphysical angle (love as fearful torment). Wagner himself emphasized the similarity between Tristan and Siegfried (→ *Twilight of the Gods*) on the one hand, and between Tristan and Amfortas (→*Parsifal*) on the other. In doing so he helped to deepen our understanding of Tristan's tragedy.

Tristan and Isolde, Barbara Kemp as Isolde, drawing by Hanns Haas for a production at the Berlin Staatsoper in 1920.
This illustration transforms the line formed on the page by the musical notation of the motif of desire *M 27* into the figure of a woman – an idea which is virtually impossible to achieve on stage.

Symmetries

The concentration of the external action toward the end of each act can be seen as the culmination of forces that drive the story forward: the effect of the love potion (Act I), Tristan's suicide attempt after his night of love (Act II), Tristan's death in the arms of Isolde (Act III). Joseph Kerman uncovered a further symmetry in the opera's dramatic construction ("Opera as Symphonic Poem," in *Opera as Drama*, New York, 1956). Each act opens with incidental music: the nostalgic song of the sailor (Act I), the sound of distant hunting horns (Act II), and a "shepherd's song played sadly on a shawm" (Act III). A symmetrical construction also characterizes the love duet in Act II as well as Tristan's fevered visions in Act III.

Tristan and Siegfried

"Like Siegfried, Tristan woos the woman destined for him by natural law in the name of another man. He is in the grip of a deception which makes his action involuntary, and he is undone by the misunderstandings that result" (Wagner, 1871). Natural law does not state that love must always mean anguish and want, but rather that one must recognize one's ordained partner, and that this love, once acknowledged, must not be betrayed. Tristan and Siegfried, however, are both traitors to their love.

Tristan and Amfortas

One of the most detailed of the early sketches for the libretto includes the appearance of Parsifal at Tristan's deathbed, during his odyssey in search of the Grail. Though Wagner later abandoned this idea, he originally justified it by saying that "Tristan, suffering from the wound he has received but still unable to die" was identical with the figure of Amfortas in the Grail legend. In 1859, while composing Act III of *Tristan*, he wrote with reference to →*Parsifal*: "Strictly speaking Amfortas is the center and main focus … He is the Tristan of Act III [of *Parsifal*] but an unimaginably intensified version. His spear wound, and probably yet another – in the heart – means that the poor wretch, in his terrible agony, knows no other desire than to die." Seen in this light, Tristan and Amfortas are bound together by their sins.   *Gy. K.*

Tristan and Isolde, production photograph with Wolfgang Windgassen and Birgit Nilsson, Bayreuth 1959.
The hymn to the night →M 29 which Tristan and Isolde sing in the depths of their love (Act II) is an overwhelming piece of music that seems to come from the subconscious. The voices of the two characters merge and the instruments produce an almost narcotic state of suspension that transcends the passage of real time.

Tristan and Isolde, set design by Hans Strohbach for his own production, conductor Eugen Szenkar, Grosse Volksoper, Berlin 1921 (TWS).
This watercolor design by Hans Strohbach is a particularly powerful evocation of the enraptured spiritual world of Tristan and Isolde and the softness of the night that envelops them. In accordance with a typical Romantic concept, the lovers lose themselves in the sublime emotion of the night.

The Mastersingers of Nuremberg

Music drama in three acts

Libretto: Richard Wagner.

Première: 21 June 1868, Munich (Hofoper).

Characters: Mastersingers: Hans Sachs, cobbler (B), Veit Pogner, goldsmith (B), Kunz Vogelgesang, furrier (T), Konrad Nachtigall, tinsmith (B), Sixtus Beckmesser, town clerk (B), Fritz Kothner, baker (B), Balthasar Zorn, pewterer (T), Ulrich Eisslinger, grocer (T), Augustin Moser, tailor (T), Hermann Ortel, soapmaker (B), Hans Schwarz, stocking weaver (B), Hans Foltz, coppersmith (B); Walther von Stolzing, a young Franconian knight (T), David, Sachs's apprentice (T), Eva, Pogner's daughter (S), Magdalene, Eva's nurse (S), A Nightwatchman (B); guildsmen and women, journeymen, apprentices, young women, townspeople (chorus).

Setting: Nuremberg, some time around the middle of the 16th century.

Synopsis
The knight Walther von Stolzing moves to Nuremberg to live as a citizen of the town. At the house of the wealthy goldsmith, Veit Pogner, he meets Veit's daughter Eva and the two fall in love. But in his wish to prove to the world how highly Nuremberg regards the arts, Pogner has promised the hand of his only child to the winner of a song contest. Only members of the guild of mastersingers may take part in the contest and so Walther applies for membership. He is unsuccessful, however, as the jealous Beckmesser, who is also in love with Eva, is appointed "marker" with responsibility for chalking up all the mistakes in Walther's trial song. Although the cobbler Hans Sachs also has an eye on Eva, he decides to help the young lovers and tutors Walther, who is naturally gifted, in the art of song. The knight then wins the contest, defeating the sly Beckmesser. The real victor, however, is Hans Sachs: he has transcended his shortcomings as an artist and a man by giving up his claim to Eva, and by helping Walther to form a new, if still undeveloped, artistic style.

Act I (Inside St. Katharine's Church)
Scene 1: Walther and Eva give each other signs of affection, but Walther learns that the hand of the girl he adores has already been promised to the winner of a song contest.
Scene 2: In order to be able to take part in the contest, Walther has to become a member of the guild of mastersingers. The cobbler's apprentice David introduces Walther to the complex art of the mastersingers.
Scene 3: Walther is auditioned by the masters. Because Beckmesser is in charge of marking, Walther fails the test. Only Sachs recognizes the innovative beauty of Walther's song.

Act II (A street between Sachs's and Pogner's houses)
Scene 1: Evening. Magdalene, David, and the apprentices are looking forward to the approaching midsummer's day festival.
Scene 2: Pogner and Eva. Eva is concerned about the outcome of the song contest.
Scene 3: Sachs reflects upon the innovative quality of Walther's song.
Scene 4: Sachs and Eva. The cobbler notes Eva's interest in Walther.
Scene 5: Late evening. Eva and Walther. In view of their hopeless situation, the two lovers decide to run away from Nuremberg.
Scene 6: Night. Sachs and Beckmesser. Beckmesser sings a serenade to a woman whom he believes to be Eva but who is in fact Magdalene in disguise. Sachs "pronounces judgement" by marking all of Beckmesser's mistakes with his cobbler's hammer. The town clerk's song becomes louder and harsher; it wakes the neighbors who then run out into the street in alarm.
Scene 7: David sees Magdalene at the window and, out of jealousy, begins a fight which degenerates into a brawl and general confusion. Sachs observes the lovers making their escape; he stops them and drags Walther into his house.

Act III (Sachs's workshop; an open meadow outside Nuremberg on midsummer's day)
Scene 1: Early morning. David congratulates Sachs on his name day, the Feast of St. John (midsummer's day). Sachs regards the tumult which took place the previous night as nothing more than a type of midsummer night's dream.
Scene 2: With Sachs's help, Walther decides to write a master song.
Scene 3: Beckmesser finds Hans Sachs's room empty (mime); discovering the manuscript that Walther has written, he is about to make off with it when Sachs returns. The cobbler presents Beckmesser with the manuscript.
Scene 4: Eva visits Sachs in her search for Walther and is treated by Sachs with paternal affection. The girl recognizes Sachs's great humanity. A feeling of divine love fills the room, touching Eva, Magdalene, David, Walther, and Sachs (quintet).
Scene 5: Procession of the guilds. The song contest. Beckmesser's attempt to sing the new song with its unusual words is a fiasco. Walther wins the contest with his characteristic warmth and his new mastery. Sachs is acclaimed by the crowd, and he urges them to honor the "German masters."

S. N.

The Mastersingers of Nuremberg, costume design for Hans Sachs by Josef Flüggen, Bayreuth 1888 (TWS).
Wagner set his "comic opera" in the age of the cobbler-poet Hans Sachs (1494–1576), who wrote 4275 mastersongs, almost 1700 tales, and 208 dramatic works. The term "mastersong" refers to a tradition of medieval German lyric poetry composed from the 14th to the 16th centuries. It was almost exclusively cultivated by artisans and was written according to strict poetic rules.

A German *Midsummer Night's Dream*

A singing contest in Nuremberg: Wagner's plan to write a comic opera after → *Tannhäuser* was realized in a prose sketch in the middle of the summer of 1845 while on holiday in Marienbad. "Just as a merry satyr play would follow a tragedy in ancient Athens, in the course of that pleasure trip the notion of a comic play occurred to me which would in reality be the satyr play to my *Singers' Contest at the Wartburg*. This became *The Mastersingers of Nuremberg* with Hans Sachs the leading figure." (The song contest on the festival meadow in *The Mastersingers* is the pendant to the song contest in the castle in *Tannhäuser*, and the brawl scene a parody of the bacchanal in the Venusberg.)

The "Prize Song"

Walther's "Prize Song" – the greatest melody in the opera – is in the medieval *Bar*-form (AAB, consisting of two stanzas and an *abgesang*). The style of the music, however, is genuinely Wagnerian. *M 30*   *Gy. K.*

30. Walther's Prize Song

Morgenlich leuch-tend in ro - si-gem Schein, von Blüth und Duft geschwellt die Luft, voll al-ler Won - nen, nie er-son-nen, ein Garten lud mich ein, Gast ihm zu sein.

The Mastersingers of Nuremberg, set design from the studio of Franz Gruber, Hamburg 1916 (TWS).
The great brawl and collective insanity of Act II is over. All's quiet in Nuremberg. The nightwatchman can finally sound the "Good Night" on his horn. It is midsummer's eve and the song contest is to take place the following day, on the Feast of St. John. *The Mastersingers of Nuremberg* is replete with references to John ("Johannes" in German). "John" is Sachs's first name (Hans = Johannes), in the church the congregation sings a hymn about John the Baptist, David rehearses a contest song about St. John and congratulates his master on his name-day, and on the eve of the Feast of St. John thousands of glow-worms (known in German as "St. John's worms") glimmer from the lilac bushes of Nuremberg's streets.

Beckmesser: the caricature of a critic

The brunt of Wagner's attack is borne by the character of Beckmesser, the "impassioned" and "crowing" bachelor. In the second and third prose drafts of the libretto, Beckmesser's name was "Veit Hanslich." Eduard Hanslick, an important Viennese critic of conservative taste, was a committed opponent of Wagner. The composer clearly intended the figure of Beckmesser as revenge for the unfavorable criticism he had received from Hanslick.

Beckmesser's serenade

Beckmesser begins his serenade with a mechanical but formless prelude on the lute. For every one of Beckmesser's mistakes Sachs beats his cobbler's last with a hammer. ₘ₃₁

The Mastersingers of Nuremberg, Beckmesser,
illustration by Ferdinand Staeger, Munich
1921 (TWS).
Beckmesser, a caricature of an intellectual,
performs his serenade. His style is contrasted
with the healthy artistic tastes of Hans Sachs:
"Good song keeps time; / And proper rhyme,
/ And lest your pen forget it, / Upon your
shoes I have set it," sings Sachs to Beckmesser
(trans. Frederick Jameson, R. Wagner, *The
Mastersingers of Nuremberg*, Calder, London,
1983). It has often been claimed that Wagner
intended the figure of Beckmesser as an anti-
Semitic caricature, and indeed Beckmesser's
artistic failings are precisely those ascribed to
Jews in Wagner's ominous essay *Das Judentum
in der Musik* (*Judaism in Music*), of 1850.

31.1 Beckmesser's Lute Prelude

31.2 Beckmesser's Serenade

Den Tag seh' ich er - schei -nen, der mir wohl ge -fall'n tut

The Mastersingers of Nuremberg, Eva and Sachs, postcard, drawing by Theodor
Pixis, Bayreuth 1877
Is it really only the shoe that pinches? Considered more closely, the text and
music of *The Mastersingers* – influenced by the world of →*Tristan* – refer to
Sachs's affection for Eva, which he must ultimately renounce: "My child, I
know a sad story of Tristan and Isolde: Hans Sachs was clever and wanted
nothing of Lord Marke's joy" is Sachs's resigned comment to Eva in Act III
(Scene 4). At this point Wagner quoted the motif of longing from →*Tristan and
Isolde*. But the composer, who himself had to renounce his love for a married
woman – Mathilde Wesendonck – later identified with King Mark rather than
with Tristan.

Borrowing from history

"Even the titles of the mastersongs and their melodies are, with the exception of a few invented by me, genuine: on the whole I am amazed by what I was able to make from just a few notes" (letter from Wagner in Karlsruhe to Mathilde Wesendonck during work on the composition, 3 February 1862). Never before had Wagner used an historical source so directly and in such detail as he did Johann Christoph Wagenseil's *Buch von der Meistersinger holdseligen Kunst* (*Book of the Mastersingers' Fair Art*) of 1697, and he would never do so again. The names of 12 old Nuremberg masters, the titles of the songs, the rules for song composition, the list of mistakes and penalties, the various technical expressions, and the melodies themselves are all historically authentic and Wagner borrowed most of them word for word. Even the texts (mostly rhymed doggerel) are historical, and reflect the poetic language of Hans Sachs.

32. Sachs is Greeted by the People

Wach' auf, es na - het gen den Tag; ich

hör' sin - gen im grü - nen Hag ein' won - nigliche

Nach - ti - gall, ihr' Stimm' durchdringet Berg und Tal;

The "applied" Bach

The musical style of *The Mastersingers* is also related to an historical Nuremberg. But in contrast to the text, which retains the character and color of the period, Wagner recreated the musical style not of the sixteenth century but of the eighteenth century, and instead of using the melody with which the historical Hans Sachs's greeted Luther and the Reformation he composed an entirely new one. M 32 He himself described his style as "applied Bach" (Curt von Westernhagen): the procession at the festival meadow with its dotted rhythms recalls a Baroque French overture M 33; the brawl scene is constructed as a fugue, or choral fantasy with introductory fugato (the motif from Beckmesser's lute prelude); M 34 the old formal idea of a passacaglia appears in the reprise of the prelude; and the passages between the long sustained final notes of the chorale "Da zu dir der Heiland kam" ("For to you the Savior comes," Act I, Scene 1) recall Bach's *Christmas Oratorio*. But even in this chorale M 35 Wagner followed his own inclinations rather than borrowing from a Reformation model. The music may thus be described as the concept of "Old Music" realized according to Wagner's own vision. The quintet "Selig, wie die Sonne meines Glückes lacht" ("Blessed, as the sun of my joy laughs" Act III, Scene 4) is another of the Bachian parts of the score; it forms the high point of the drama in combining diverse dramatic strands in a complex but pleasant polyphony (the unfolding of Eva and Walther's love, Sachs's self-denial, the peak of happiness for David and Magdalene). There is a remarkable similarity between the theme of the quintet and that of the *Siegfried Idyll* (→*Siegfried*, Act III, →M 65). M 36

Gy. K.

The Mastersingers of Nuremberg, set design (medieval city scene) from the theatrical studio of Julius Mühldorfer, Munich c. 1880 (TWS).
Nuremberg – a scene from an old German city as a symbol of the past.

33. Festival Theme (Overture)

34. Fugue Theme from the Brawl Scene

35. Chorale (Act 1, Scene 1)

Da   zu   dir   der   Hei -   land kam

36. Quintet (Eva, Magdalene, Walther, Sachs, David)

Se -   lig, wie die   Son -   ne mei - nes   Glü - ckes lacht

Interpretations

No other opera by Wagner has been interpreted so variously as his most popular and realistic work *The Mastersingers of Nuremberg*. The composer himself produced two different interpretations. In his *Programmatischen Erläuterung zum Vorspiel der Oper* (*Programmatic Commentary on the Prelude to the Opera*) (1863), three basic ideas emerge. First, there is his historicist approach, which involves the unearthing of old artistic forms: "the 'leges tabulaturae,' the carefully preserved ancient laws of a poetic form that has long since disappeared." (This idea can be seen as a forerunner of the various stylistic revivals of the twentieth century.) Secondly, there was the idealization of the "genuinely folk-like figure of Hans Sachs," the backwards projection of the Romantic concept of the great artist: "his [Sachs's] own songs resound from the mouths of the populace as a greeting." Finally, there was the examination of the conflicts faced by the artist and a suggestion as to how they might be solved ("the love song resounds to the melodies of the masters,

reconciling pedantry and poetry"). An interpretation of Sachs's inner conflict and notes on the nature of the relationship between Sachs and Eva are the central issues in Wagner's *Erläuterung des Vorspiels zum dritten Akt* (*Commentary on the Prelude to the Third Act*) (1869). Wagner states that Sachs's resignation can already be detected in Act II, in the third stanza of his cobbler's song: "Eva understood this hidden lament and her heart was pierced so deeply by it that she wanted to flee, if only to escape having to listen to his apparently merry song." Indeed, when the cobbler's song is over, Eva, "greatly agitated," says: "The song grieves me, I know not how!"

In his commentary of 1869 Wagner represented the figure of Hans Sachs as the embodiment of poetry. He indicated at this point that, in the prelude to Act III, the strings should "again take up the strains of the real cobbler's song as if the man were looking away from his work, his attention directed upwards, lost in a gentle reverie."

The Mastersingers of Nuremberg, set design by Ludwig Sievert for the production by Rudolf Hartmann, conductor Clemens Krauss, Munich 1943 (TWS).
Festival meadow, c. 1943: the tribunes, the tall flagpoles, and the distant view to the horizon betray the fact that at the time of this production of *The Mastersingers* it was not only "beloved German art" that was worshipped in Germany. These scenic elements could have been taken from the Nazi party's rallies at Nuremberg.

Take heed!

When Wagner came to write Sachs's final address on 28 January 1867 he suddenly had doubts about the dramatic function of this great speech. Ultimately Wagner left the controversial passage of text as it was, even adding an additional stanza: "Take heed! Ill times threaten all; / And if we German folk should fall / And foreigners should rule our land / No king his folk would understand, / And foreign rule and foreign ways / Would darken all our German days; / The good and true were soon forgot, / Did they not live in Masters' art" (trans. Frederick Jameson, R. Wagner, *The Mastersingers of Nuremberg*, Calder, London, 1983). Like Wagner's essays on *Deutsche Kunst und deutsche Politik* (*German Art and German Politics*), of 1867–68, these verses are doubtless expressions of the anxiety and political resignation that were experienced by the middle classes after the failed revolutions of 1848–49. Hugo von Hofmannsthal summed up the historical, nationalistic, and folkloric "Germanness" of *The Mastersingers* in his observations on Nuremberg: "This entire city, which still stood completely intact in the thirties, not merely reflected the German intellectual and emotional world around 1500 but truly lived it in the present, and that was one of the most crucial experiences of the Romantic era … And this gives the opera its sense of indestructible reality – that it brings to life a genuinely closed world which at one time really did exist."   *Gy. K.*

The Mastersingers of Nuremberg, set design from the studio of Franz Gruber, Vienna 1909 (TWS).
Festival meadow, c. 1916: the meadow's edge, the stream, and the tents lend the scene a sense of intimacy.

The Mastersingers of Nuremberg, costume designs for apprentices (final scene) by Heinrich Lefler, Vienna 1909 (TWS).
"Silence! Silence! Make no speech nor murmur!" The great crowd scene gave Wagner the unique opportunity of allowing children's voices to be heard. At no other point in his operas do children appear on stage.

The Rhinegold, set design (detail) for Valhalla by Kurt William Kempin, Darmstadt 1906 (TWS).
The fortress of Valhalla appears situated at an unattainable height. Wagner's excursions into the Alps during his exile in Switzerland almost certainly inspired such visions: the entire →*Rhinegold* was composed during his time in that country.

Overture on a German heroic theme

In June 1837, the *Neue Zeitschrift für Musik* (*New Music Journal*), a periodical founded and at that time edited by Robert Schumann, published an article that emphasized the suitability of German folklore and mythology for presentation on the operatic stage: "Own our folklore speaks to us even more powerfully than the treasures of a foreign people ... and only music will bring forth a miracle ... *Red Riding Hood*, the story of the *Lorelei*, and *Siegfried the Hero* are examples of the poetry that awaits an artist who is capable of reviving them, of making these ancient legendary figures live again in a new form." Then in 1844 the aesthetic theorist Friedrich Theodor Vischer recommended "the Nibelung legend as the basis of a libretto for a great heroic opera" in the periodical *Kritische Gänge* (*Critical Perspectives*). But how was this to be realized? "The Homeric heroes can speak, they are not of that taciturn, compact hardness of the old German ones ... But give these men of iron, these gigantic women a voice, which drama requires ... and they are saved ... Music demands simple motifs, simple action ... *The Song of the Nibelung* was made to be an opera."

Source material: an entire library

Wagner had already studied medieval literature as part of his preparations for writing →*Lohengrin*. The catalogue from his Dresden library shows the great breadth of his mythological, literary, and philological studies concerning the Nibelung legend, there being no fewer than 28 works on the subject in the collection. The most important of them are the Poetic (or Elder) Edda (Icelandic mythology), mythological poems from Scandinavia, the *Heimskringla* (the sagas of Norwegian kings), the *Völsunga Saga*, *Thidreks Saga af Bern*, Jacob Grimm's *Deutsche Mythologie* (*German Mythology*), Wilhelm Grimm's *Die deutschen Heldensage* (*German Heroic Sagas*), *Das deutsche Heldenbuch* (*The German Book of Heroes*) and *Das Nibelungenlied* (*The Song of the Nibelung*) edited by Simrock, and *Der Nibelungen Noth und Klage* (*The Plight and Lament of the Nibelung*) edited by Karl Lachmann. From these various sources Wagner created his own "mythology of mankind."

Creation

The work was written from the end backwards. Wagner first wrote the libretto for *Siegfrieds Tod*, or *The Death of Siegfried*, which was the first version of what became →*Twilight of the Gods* (28 November 1848). Then, after adding a prologue (the Norn scene, Siegfried and Brünnhilde in their cave, →*Twilight of the Gods*, 24 June 1851) he produced the story of the young Siegfried (→*Siegfried*). Five months later he wrote the first prose sketch for →*The Rhinegold*, which was followed immediately by a sketch for →*The Valkyrie*. This chronology is somewhat misleading, however, in that before beginning work on *The Death of Siegfried* Wagner wrote out in prose his conception for the entire cycle, *Der Nibelungen-Mythus* (*The Nibelung Myth*, 20 October 1848). It was almost exactly 26 years later that he wrote under the last bars of the score of →*Twilight of the Gods* the words "I will say nothing more."

The social context and the reform of drama

At the time the cycle was conceived Wagner was a struggling young music director, sickened by the unjust social conditions of the feudal and capitalistic theater business. He was swept up in the revolutions of 1848, took part in the Dresden uprising, and wrote anticlerical and protosocialist articles. After the revolution was crushed he was forced to flee to Switzerland, and was unable to return to Germany until 1860. But he never abandoned his revolutionary ideas during this period in exile: "As the art of the Greeks encapsulated the spirit of a great nation, so too should the art of the future express the spirit of a liberated humanity which goes beyond the limits of nationality," he wrote in an article for *Die Kunst und die Revolution* (*Art and the Revolution*, Zürich, 1849). Throughout his years of work on the *Ring* he remained true to his artistic intentions, as he did to his plans to build a festival hall (Wagner, →Bayreuth: interpretation and ideology). He developed his philosophical and aesthetic ideas in his main theoretical work, *Oper und Drama* (*Opera and Drama*, 1850–51).

Why alter the original conception?

Wagner's original plan was for Siegfried to have the central role in the cycle. This fearless hero was to destroy a society corrupted by gold and power and proclaim a new social order based on love. In time, however, Wagner came to regard this idea as hopelessly utopian. His hero of the future (Siegfried) died with the independence movements, his place being taken by the god Wotan, who represents the old order of the world, striving inexorably toward its own destruction. The figure of Wotan then became the main character in the drama. His sins, based on lovelessness and lust for power, and his tragic recognition that he is powerless to save or prevent the ruin of the world transformed an optimistic heroic drama into an elegy of pessimism and resignation.   S. N.

Twilight of the Gods, set design for the last scene by Max Brückner, Bayreuth 1896 (TWS). *The Ring of the Nibelung* is the greatest artistic undertaking in the history of opera. Seldom has an artist succeeded in putting his ideas of reform into practice, in building his own theater, and in consistently pleasing both his audiences and his patrons. The world he depicted in the opera may indeed have collapsed but the work swept all before it.

Above
The Valkyrie, Birgit Nilsson as Brünnhilde, Bayreuth c. 1960.
Birgit Nilsson was one of the greatest singers at Bayreuth in the post-war era. She also performed the roles of Isolde (→*Tristan and Isolde*) and Elsa (→*Lohengrin*). Her make-up has been used here to emphasis Brünnhilde's human features.

Middle
Ramon Vinay as Siegmund, Bayreuth 1953.

Bottom
Gré Brouwenstijn as Sieglinde, Bayreuth 1956.
Seen here are two suffering yet loving faces from the long history of Wagner productions at the Bayreuth Festival: the brother and sister from the race of the Volsungs are the most human of the cycle's heroes and heroines. Their short and tragic fate favors them with a single night of bliss.

Who's who?

Alberich: A hunchbacked dwarf, a Nibelung (*The Rhinegold*, *Siegfried* II, *Twilight of the Gods* II)

Brünnhilde: A Valkyrie, daughter of Wotan and Erda, Siegfried's wife (*The Valkyrie* II–III, *Siegfried* III, *Twilight of the Gods* Prologue, I–III)

Donner: A god, an elemental power (*The Rhinegold*)

Dragon: A form assumed by Fafner in order to protect the hoard of the Nibelungs (*Siegfried* II)

Erda: The earth goddess, an elemental force (*The Rhinegold*, *Siegfried* III)

Fafner: A giant (*The Rhinegold*; as the Dragon: *Siegfried* II)

Fasolt: A giant (*The Rhinegold*)

Freia: The goddess of love and eternal youth (*The Rhinegold*)

Fricka: A goddess, guardian of wedlock, Wotan's wife (*The Rhinegold*, *The Valkyrie* II)

Froh: A god, the brother of Donner and Freia (*The Rhinegold*)

Gunther: The chief of the Gibichungs, Gutrune's brother (*Twilight of the Gods* I–III)

Gutrune: The sister of the Gibichung chief Gunther (*Twilight of the Gods* I–III)

Hagen: The son of Alberich, half-brother of Gunther and Gutrune (*Twilight of the Gods* I–III)

Hunding: The husband of Sieglinde, descendant of the giants (*The Valkyrie* I–II)

Loge: A demigod, an elemental force, Wotan's adviser, the incarnation of fire (in human form: *The Rhinegold*; as fire: *The Valkyrie* III, *Siegfried* III, *Twilight of the Gods* III)

Mime: A dwarf, a Nibelung, Alberich's brother, master smith, Siegfried's foster-father (*The Rhinegold*, *Siegfried* I–II)

Norns: Fates, daughters of Erda (*Twilight of the Gods* Prologue)

Rhinemaidens (Woglinde, Wellgunde, Flosshilde): Elemental beings (*The Rhinegold*, *Twilight of the Gods* III)

Siegfried: The son of Wotan's children Siegmund and Sieglinde, a fearless hero from the race of the Volsungs, the husband of Brünnhilde and Gutrune (*Siegfried* I–III, *Twilight of the Gods* Prologue, I–III)

Sieglinde: The twin sister and lover of Siegmund, Wotan's daughter, a Volsung, Siegfried's mother (*The Valkyrie* I–III)

Siegmund: The twin brother and lover of Sieglinde, Wotan's son, a Volsung, Siegfried's father (*The Valkyrie* I–II)

Valkyries: (Brünnhilde, Gerhilde, Ortlinde, Waltraute, Schwertleite, Helmwige, Siegrune, Grimgerde, Rossweisse): Daughters of Wotan and Erda (*The Valkyrie* III)

Waltraute: A Valkyrie (*Twilight of the Gods* I)

Wanderer: Wotan as observer (*Siegfried* I–III)

Woodbird: An incarnation of the benign forces of nature, who gives Siegfried important advice (*Siegfried* II)

Wotan: The ruler of the gods, father of Brünnhilde, Siegmund, and Sieglinde, grandfather of Siegfried (*The Rhinegold*, *The Valkyrie* II, III; as the Wanderer: *Siegfried* I–III)

The Valkyrie, Hans Hotter as Wotan, Bayreuth 1953.
Hans Hotter was born for the role of Wotan, and sings the part in the legendary recording made under the direction of Wilhelm Furtwängler, perhaps the most important of all Wagner conductors.

Left
The Rhinegold, the Rhinemaidens (Herta Töpper, Hanna Ludwig, and Erika Zimmermann), Bayreuth 1952.
After the war, musicals were put on in Bayreuth's Festspielhaus for American soldiers. These Rhinemaidens resemble chorus girls in a Broadway musical.

Symbols and attributes

Golden apple tree: It grows in the garden of the gods, tended by Freia. Its fruit brings the gods immortality and eternal youth. (*The Rhinegold*)

Grane: Brünnhilde's steed. It symbolizes Brünnhilde's love of battle and her closeness to nature. (*The Valkyrie, Siegfried, Twilight of the Gods*)

Hammer: The attribute of the god, Donner. An instrument that unleashes the powers of nature. (*The Rhinegold*)

Ravens: Birds of Wotan that herald death. (*Twilight of the Gods* III)

Rhinegold: Originally part of nature, protected by the Rhinemaidens in the depths of the river.

Ring: Symbol of limitless power. Alberich acquires the Rhinegold through theft and the renunciation of love, and from it forges himself a ring. When Wotan steals the ring, Alberich curses its future owners. (In the course of the cycle, the ring passes through the following hands: the Rhinemaidens, Alberich, Wotan, Fafner, Siegfried, Brünnhilde, Siegfried, the Rhinemaidens.)

Spear: Wotan's attribute, both symbol and weapon, made from the World Ash Tree, which guaranteed world order by means of the laws and agreements carved on it. It shatters Siegmund's sword, Nothung (*The Valkyrie* II). It is destroyed by Siegfried's sword, Nothung (*Siegfried* III).

Sword (Nothung): A weapon intended by Wotan for his son Siegmund, which he plunges deep into the trunk of an ash tree. The symbol of the heroic courage of the Volsungs. After Wotan was forced to shatter the sword, the master smith Mime tried in vain to put its pieces back together again. Only Siegfried was capable of forging a new Nothung from the fragments.

Tarnhelm: A magic helmet made by Mime. The owner of the Tarnhelm can make himself invisible and appear in whatever form he chooses. It also symbolizes lies

and deceit. (*The Rhinegold, Siegfried* II, *Twilight of the Gods* I–II)

Valhalla: A castle built by the giants above the clouds for Wotan's tribe, intended as a home for the gods and a symbol of their power.

Significant musical and dramatic episodes

The Rhinegold

On the bed of the Rhine (orchestral prelude)

Wotan's greeting to Valhalla ("Conclude the eternal work!" Scene 2)

Nibelheim forge (Scene 3)

Alberich's curse ("Am I now free?" Scene 4)

Erda's warning ("Give ground, Wotan, give ground!" Scene 4)

Entry of the gods into Valhalla ("Across the bridge to the castle" Scene 4)

Wotan's final song ("In the evening does the sun's eye beam" Scene 4)

The Valkyrie

Siegmund's story ("My father did promise me a sword" Act I, Scene 3)

Love song of Siegmund and Sieglinde (Spring Song: "Winter storms retreat from the blessed moon" Act I, Scene 3)

Annunciation of Death ("Siegmund! Behold me" Act II, Scene 4)

The Ride of the Valkyries ("Hojotoho! Heiaha!" Act III, Scene 1)

Wotan's farewell ("Farewell, you brave, noble child" Act III, Scene 3)

Magic fire music ("Loge, hear me!" Act III, Scene 3)

Siegfried

Song of Siegfried's sword ("Nothung! Nothung! glorious sword!" Act I, Scene 3)

Siegfried's Forging Song ("Hoho! Hoho! Forge, my hammer, a steadfast sword!" Act I, Scene 3)

Forest Murmurs ("That he is not my father" Act II, Scene 2)

Erda's lament ("Since waking I have been in confusion" Act III, Scene 1)

Wotan's song of destiny ("You are not what you imagine yourself to be" Act III, Scene 1)

Brünnhilde's awakening ("Hail, sun! Hail, light!" Act III, Scene 3)

Brünnhilde's greeting of love ("Siegfried! Siegfried! Blessed hero!" Act III, Scene 3)

Twilight of the Gods

Norn scene ("What light shines there!" Prologue)

Dawn and Brünnhilde's song ("To new deeds, great hero" Prologue)

Siegfried's Rhine Journey (Prologue)

Hagen's Watch ("Here I sit on guard" Act I, Scene 2)

Siegfried's death ("Brünnhilde! Sacred bride" Act III, Scene 2)

Funeral March (Siegfried's funeral procession, Act III, Scene 2)

Brünnhilde's final song ("Let great logs be piled on high!" Act III, Scene 3)   S. N.

Left
The Valkyrie, production photograph with Hans-Peter Scheidegger (Wotan) and the Valkyries, production Michael Heinicke, conductor Oleg Caetani, Städtisches Theater, Chemnitz 1997.

Top
The Ring of the Nibelung, Alberich, costume postcard, Bayreuth c. 1900.
Alberich as a repulsive hairy dwarf – just the way he is described by the Rhinemaidens.

Middle
The Valkyrie, Hunding (Ludwig Hofmann), Bayreuth c. 1950.
Hofmann's helmet and facial expression symbolize the threshold between the old and the new at Bayreuth.

Bottom
The Ring of the Nibelung, Alberich (Gustav Neidlinger), Bayreuth 1953.
Alberich as a suffering creature to whom love is denied.

The Ring of the Nibelung

Bühnenfestspiel for a preliminary evening and three days

Preliminary Evening: **The Rhinegold** (Das Rheingold)
In one act

The Rhinegold, production photograph with Catriona Smith (Woglinde), Maria Theresa Ullrich (Wellgunde), and Helene Schneidermann (Flosshilde), production Joachim Schlömer, sets and costumes Jens Kilian, conductor Lothar Zagrosek, Württembergisches Staatstheater, Stuttgart 1999.

Libretto: Richard Wagner.
Première: 22 September 1869, Munich (Hoftheater).

Characters: Gods: Wotan (B), Fricka (S), Freia (S), Erda (A), Donner (B), Froh (T), Loge (T); Nibelungs: Alberich (B), Mime (T); Giants: Fafner (B), Fasolt (B); Rhinemaidens: Woglinde, Wellgunde, Flosshilde (3 S); Nibelungs (chorus).
Setting: Mythological.

Synopsis

The Rhinemaidens frolic in the river, protecting their treasure. The Nibelung, Alberich, woos them but they rebuff and mock him. Alberich curses love and steals the Rhinemaidens' treasure, for whoever possesses the gold and forges a ring from it attains limitless power. In order to gain knowledge and world domination, the god Wotan had once cut a branch from the World Ash Tree to make a spear; on it he carved laws and contractual agreements, thus making himself the defender of order.

Both Alberich and Wotan paid a high price for their thefts: Alberich is denied love, and Wotan loses an eye. Injustice leads to injustice. Wotan has had two giants build him the celestial fortress Valhalla, promising them Freia in payment. But without Freia, the goddess of eternal youth, the gods would inevitably age, and so, following Loge's advice, Wotan offers the giants the gold and ring of the Nibelung.

Alberich's hoard is stolen by a mixture of cunning and force, and the Nibelung lays a curse on the ring. The gold is weighed up against Freia, and Wotan has to add the ring. The giants begin to fight over their treasure and Fafner kills his brother Fasolt: Alberich's curse is beginning to take effect. After a storm, the gods cross a rainbow bridge to Valhalla. Far below, the Rhinemaidens lament the loss of their stolen gold.

Scene 1

At the bottom of the Rhine. The Rhinemaidens watch over their gold. The dwarf Alberich makes advances, and they reject and mock him. Alberich renounces love, and seizes the precious metal.

Scene 2

A mountain height near the Rhine. Wotan and Fricka are arguing about Valhalla, which was built for them by the giants Fafner and Fasolt. The price for the fortress – the goddess Freia – is considered too high. Wotan calls for the assistance of Loge who advises him to offer the giants the hoard of the Nibelung Alberich.

The giants agree to this alternative form of payment, but in the meantime hold Freia as ransom. In order to obtain the gold, Wotan travels to Nibelheim accompanied by Loge.

Scene 3

The subterranean caverns of Nibelheim. The Nibelungs are Alberich's slaves, working for him day and night. His brother, the master smith Mime, fashions for him a ring that bestows limitless power; he also creates a helmet, the Tarnhelm, that bestows invisibility and the power to change one's form. Thus Alberich enjoys both power and guile. Wotan and Loge learn of the ring and the Tarnhelm from the talkative and indiscreet Mime.

Alberich boasts of his treasures and with the help of the Tarnhelm turns himself into a gigantic dragon. Loge then tricks him into turning himself into a toad – a form that makes it possible for the gods to capture him. The gods are now lords of Nibelheim, and they return to the sunlight with the captive Alberich.

Scene 4

A mountain height near the Rhine. Alberich's slaves are forced to drag the Nibelung's entire hoard up to the realm of the gods. Wotan takes Alberich's ring, whereupon the Nibelung curses him and all future owners of the ring. Freia is weighed up against the gold – only the ring is lacking to make up the price demanded by the giants. Wotan at first refuses to part with it, and gives way only when the all-knowing Erda warns that the gods are subject to the ineluctable fate of all living things and that the ring will only hasten their end. Fafner and Fasolt begin to argue over the treasure, and Fafner strikes his brother dead. There is a storm, after which a rainbow may be seen to stretch across the valley to Valhalla. When the lament of the Rhinemaidens rises out of the valley, Wotan dismisses it and leads the gods over the rainbow bridge to the home they have bought so dearly.

S. N.

The primal home

"In the beginning was the water" – so begins Wagner's mythology. According to Wagner the musical inspiration for this primal state came to him during an afternoon nap on 5 September 1853: "I sank into a sort of trance-like state in which I suddenly had the sensation that I was sinking into swiftly flowing water. The rushing of this water began to take on the musical sound of an E flat major chord, the waves of which took the form of a repeated figure … " M 37

37.1 Rhine Motif

37.2 Wave Motif

This musical vision was later bolstered by the addition of a horn (a symbol of nature). Pentatonic coloring accompanies the appearance of the Rhinemaidens. The onomatopoeic language of the maidens, their "Weia! Waga! Woge, du Welle … " ("Weia! Waga! Wave, o wave … "), is also a reference to birth, creation, origins, and a mythic beginning. M 38

The musical images of the gold, which has lain in the depths of the Rhine since time immemorial, are also part of the depiction of awakening nature, M 39 as is the vision of the garden where Freia's golden apples ripen, M 40 the thunderstorm, with Donner, the god of thunder, swinging his hammer, M 41 and the rainbow M 42 that transports Froh over the valley and up to the castle in the evening sun.   Gy. K.

38. Song of the Rhinemaidens

Wei - a! Wa - ga! Wo - ge, du Wel - le, wal - le zur Wie - ge! wa - ga - la wei - a! wal - la - la wei - a - la wei - a!

39. Rhinegold Motif

40. Motif of the Golden Apples

41. Motif of the Thunderstorm

42. Rainbow Motif

Left
The Rhinegold, the Rhinemaidens (from left to right, Joyce Guyer, Jane Turner, and Sarah Fryer), production Alfred Kirchner, conductor James Levine, Bayreuth Festival 1996.
The Rhinemaidens as fisherwomen dressed in the latest fashion.

The Rhinegold, set design by the Franz Moser studio, Innsbruck 1911 (TWS).
A scene from the depths of the Rhine. The Rhinemaidens, still in a state of innocence, take delight in their treasure – the Rhinegold. Alberich (bottom left) watches them with desire.

The Rhinegold, costume portrait of Wotan, Bayreuth c. 1876 (TWS).
According to Sieglinde's narrative this is how Wotan appeared at her wedding to Hunding ("… an old man in a grey cloak; his hat hung low, covering one of his eyes, but the beams from the other struck fear into the hearts of all … "). On that occasion Wotan thrust a sword deep into the trunk of an ash tree so firmly that only his son Siegmund would be able to withdraw it.

The Rhinegold, production photograph with Günter von Kannen as Alberich, production Harry Kupfer, sets Hans Schavernoch, conductor Daniel Barenboim, Bayreuth Festival 1988.
Alberich appeared in this production not as an a priori embodiment of evil, but as a man who has been rejected, mocked, and insulted (by the Rhinemaidens), and then robbed of his ring by Wotan, so that he is finally dominated only by thoughts of hatred and vengeance.

Alberich and Wotan

According to Jacob Grimm, the great nineteenth-century scholar of German mythology and heroic legends, both Alberich and Wotan – the dark spirit and the god of light – are guilty of an egotistical craving for power. This idea inspired Wagner to portray the Nibelung and the god as mirror images of each other. Both of them commit theft in order to obtain the ring and both cling desperately to the power it bestows.

Wagner reinforces these parallel identities by closely relating the ring motif and the Valhalla motif. M 43, M 44

Valhalla's music is in the key of D flat major and that of Nibelheim – the home of Alberich – in B flat minor. B flat minor is the relative minor of D flat major, and there can be no doubt that for Wagner B flat minor represents Valhalla's shadowy opposite. The ruler of Nibelheim is often called "dark Alberich," while Wotan is on one occasion referred to as the "light spirit." The motif of renunciation is essential to an understanding of both characters. At the start of the opera it appears that Wotan is the positive force and Alberich the negative: the god bestows laws on the world and defends order with his spear, while Alberich exploits his people. But we must ask ourselves what it is that Alberich actually wants: he renounces love because nature (symbolized in the Rhinemaidens) denies him satisfaction. His ring is intended to provide him with a surrogate for love: "Erzwäng' ich nicht Liebe, doch listig erzwäng' ich mir Lust?" ("If I could not demand love, might I not with cunning demand pleasure?"). Even in Nibelheim, at the height of his power, he envies the gods their fine lives and their pleasures. Because he cannot eliminate his desire for pleasure he curses the world, wishing love-lessness on it: "Wie ich der Liebe abgesagt, alles, was lebt, soll ihr entsagen: mit Golde gekirrt, nach Gold nur sollt ihr noch gieren" ("Since I have renounced love, so everything that lives must renounce it: tamed by gold, you will lust only after gold").

43. Ring Motif

44. Valhalla Motif

45. Motif of the Nibelungs

Wagner's portrayal of Wotan, on the other hand, shows him to lack this desire for love. Whereas Alberich is unable to forget the love melody of the Rhinemaiden Wellgunde, Wotan would have sacrificed Freia, the goddess of love, in order to attain limitless power, had he not been reined in by the earth goddess Erda. In Wagner's view, Wotan is addicted to power. He is betrayed by his very first words: "Der Wonne seligen Saal bewachen mir Tür und Tor: Mannes Ehre, ewige Macht, ragen zu endlosem Ruhm!" ("The gates of the blessed hall of bliss are guarded by manly honor, eternal power rising to infinite glory!"). As soon as he learns of the ring's powers he wants to possess it, forgetting the Rhinemaidens to whom, as the guardian of universal order, he should return it. Later, in the dispute with Alberich, he mentions the Rhinemaidens only to justify his own theft of the ring. While the giants are weighing up the gold offered them by Wotan, he is absent-mindedly lost in contemplation of the ring. When pressed to add the ring to the hoard promised to the giants, he expresses his innermost thoughts: "Lasst mich in Ruh': den Reif geb' ich nicht!" ("Leave me in peace: I will not give up the ring!"). The other characters beg him to relent, but Wotan turns away from them in anger. This moment is his absolute nadir: his lust for power has become so great that he is prepared to sacrifice the world order he has created in order to attain supreme power.

Nibelheim

The musical vision of Nibelheim is just as powerful as those of the Rhine and Valhalla. At the beginning of the scene a primary note (F) sounds for 60 bars, and the motif of the Nibelung master smith is repeated 24 times, to express the monotony of slave labor in the underground caves. Could this be a depiction of the apocalypse of the working classes? While Wagner was working on *The Ring*, another German exile, Karl Marx, was busy writing his book on the nature of capitalism (*Das Kapital*), the first volume of which appeared in 1867, two years before the première of *The Rhinegold*. Wagner and Marx both died in 1883. *M 45*

The motif of the Nibelungs is accompanied by noises of hammering from the forge – an early and bold example of *musique concrète*. *Gy. K.*

The Rhinegold, Alberich curses the ring, illustration by Franz Stassen, Berlin 1914 (TWS).
In forging the ring, Alberich changed the nature of the gold, and used it to impose his power on the Nibelungs. The source of the ring's power, however, is the curse he places on love. Alberich's renunciation of love is a type of self-damnation, a denial of his own nature, of his humanity. His second curse, after Wotan has stolen the ring from him, is placed on all future owners of the ring. With Alberich's curse the destruction of nature begins (middle). The order of the world is disturbed and the Norns are no longer able to continue spinning the rope of destiny (top). Erda sinks below the World Ash Tree in a deep, cosmic sleep (bottom).

Wotan and Erda

Erda, who rises up from a rocky cleft in a blue light to warn Wotan against holding on to the ring, is an elemental force, and her musical motif is related to water (when she appears the Rhine motif is played in C sharp minor instead of E flat major: M 46, →M 37.1). This might be intended to indicate that she represents Wotan's godliness, which has hitherto been silenced but of which he is now made conscious, or perhaps that she is the expression of his instincts, which bind him to nature. The tonality of C sharp minor is unrelated to E flat major; its tonality is rather associated with Valhalla at night, and with Wotan's illusion and daydream. (It is no coincidence the passage features the distinctive timbre of the so-called Wagner tubas from the Valhalla motif.)

46. Erda's Motif

Erda's original speech is contained in a letter from Wagner to August Röckel (25 January 1854): "A twilight approaches for the gods: your noble race will end in disgrace unless you forsake the ring!" This formulation conceals a promise: if Wotan chooses to give up the ring then the end (twilight) of the gods may still be avoided. At the beginning of 1854 Wagner showed signs of dissatisfaction with Erda's prophecy. He changed the text, thus giving the cycle a completely different direction: "Erda now says: 'All that is, comes to an end: a dark day approaches for the gods: I counsel you, avoid the ring.'" And Wagner added: "We must learn how to die, and that means die in the fullest sense of the word; dread of our own end is the source of all lovelessness, and it arises only where love itself has already expired … The curse attached to the ring is not removed until it is returned to nature by being thrown into the Rhine. For this knowledge Wotan must wait until the very end, the last station of his tragic career: what Loge repeatedly and movingly told him from the outset the power-hungry god totally ignored. At first he learned only – from the example of Fafner – of the power of the curse. It was not until the ring brought about Siegfried's destruction that he understood that restoring the gold to its owners would remedy the wrong: the conditions of his own longed-for destruction were therefore bound up with the removal of this oldest of injustices. Experience is everything."

Loge

"Loge heisst du, doch nenn' ich dich Lüge" ("Loge is your name, but I call you Lie") says Wotan. The god is unable to act or govern without Loge (Lie), who functions as a kind of secretary of state. Loge – also known as Loki – is the Lucifer of Nordic mythology. He embodies Lucifer's power: fierce drives, desires, and burning passions. Loge is the fire of the soul: he brings forth glowing ideas but he can also, when transformed into fire, destroy everything. It is only in *The Rhinegold* that Loge appears as a figure on the stage (as a demigod). In the following three music dramas the audience encounters him as fire. His musical motif is like his nature: restless, flickering, and dazzling, like fire. M 47

The Rhinegold, production photograph with (from left to right) Marian Albert (Froh), Georg Tichy (Alberich), Alan Held (Wotan), Livia Budai-Batky (Fricka), and Ronnie Johansen (Donner), production, sets, and costumes Herbert Wernicke, conductor Sylvain Cambreling, Théâtre Royal de la Monnaie, Brussels 1991.
The Rhinegold as a family saga, with Alberich's famous curse scene shown in an entirely new way. Alberich's arguments, his raging and scolding, have no effect on the Wotan family. They are in a party mood, dressed in top hat and tails and ready to move into Valhalla – a picture of guilt and chutzpah.

Wotan's mind

Wotan leads his wife Fricka into the new home of the gods with the bearing of a nobleman. The sun is shining and a magnificent rainbow bridge leads across to Valhalla. To all intents and purposes this is a happy ending: the fortress has been built, Freia has been returned to the gods, and Alberich has been vanquished. But the ring is somewhere in the world. Hatred and lust for power have poisoned Eden's unspoiled life. The price paid by the gods was too high, a fact of which Wotan is acutely aware. He pauses reflectively on the bridge: "Von Morgen bis Abend, in Müh' und Angst, nicht wonnig ward sie gewonnen! Es naht die nacht: vor ihrem Neid biete sie Bergung nun" ("From morning to night, with sweat and with fear, it was not built with joy! The night nears: may it now offer shelter from her envy"). The father of the gods is then overcome by a thought that is conveyed to us by the orchestra. *M 48*

The thought takes the form of a motif that is associated with the sword Nothung in the second part of the cycle (→*The Valkyrie*). The sword will belong to a hero called Siegmund, Wotan's son, who will act of his own free will but under the direction of his father. Will Siegmund's actions succeed in preventing the end of the world? Wotan is deceiving himself: both he and his race of gods are already marked for destruction when they enter Valhalla (conclusion of *The Rhinegold*). "I am almost ashamed to be among them; how I am tempted to change once again into a licking tongue of flame," Loge comments, expressing the ambivalence of the mood. Later events will prove him right. *Gy. K.*

The Rhinegold, production photograph with (from left to right) Margaret Jane Wray (Freia), Frode Olsen (Fasolt), Alan Held (Wotan), Dieter Schweikart (Fafner), Livia Budai-Batky (Fricka), production, sets and costumes Herbert Wernicke, conductor Sylvain Cambreling, Théâtre de la Monnaie, Brussels 1991.
Wotan haggles over pay with the two giants who built Valhalla. They demand one of the family members: Freia. The sofa, therefore, becomes a fortress that must be defended.

47. Fire Motif (Loge)

48. Sword Motif (Nothung)

The Ring of the Nibelung

Bühnenfestspiel for a preliminary evening and three days

First Day: **The Valkyrie** (Die Walküre)
In three acts

Libretto: Richard Wagner.
Première: 26 June 1870, Munich (Hoftheater).
Characters: Wotan, ruler of the gods (B), Fricka, a goddess, Wotan's wife (S), Siegmund and Sieglinde, twins, children of Wotan and a mortal woman (T, S), Hunding, Sieglinde's husband (B), Brünnhilde, a Valkyrie, Wotan's favorite daughter (S), Ortlinde, Helmwige, Gerhilde, Waltraute, Siegrune, Rossweisse, Schwertleite, Grimgerde, Valkyries, Wotan's daughters, Brünnhilde's sisters (S, A).
Setting: Mythological.

Synopsis
Before the opera begins
Wotan, believing that the gods can only be saved from destruction by a hero who, of his own free will, wins back the ring and returns it to the Rhinemaidens, has begotten the race of the Volsungs through a union with a mortal woman. In the guise of a wolf-man (known as Wälse) Wotan raised the twins Siegmund and Sieglinde in the forest. One day, returning from hunting, the boy and his father found their house burnt to the ground, the mother dead, and no trace of Sieglinde, who had been abducted and was then forced into marriage with Hunding, a member of a hostile tribe. At her wedding a stranger (Wälse/Wotan) had thrust a sword (Nothung) into the trunk of an ash tree. No one has yet proved strong enough to extract the sword.

Act I (Inside Hunding's dwelling)
Scenes 1–3: Pursued by enemies, an exhausted stranger (Siegmund) seeks refuge in Hunding's house following a violent storm. He calls himself Wehwalt ("Woeful") and is offered succor by the woman of the house, Sieglinde; they are brother and sister but do not as yet recognize each other. When Sieglinde's husband Hunding returns home he asks the stranger where he comes from, and it soon becomes clear that the two men are enemies. Hunding offers Siegmund shelter in his house for one night, but the next day he will challenge the stranger to fight to the death. Left alone with Sieglinde, the unarmed Siegmund experiences a miracle: as love awakens between them, the twins begin to realize their identity, and Siegmund succeeds in drawing the sword from the

trunk of the tree. The two rush out into the night in an ecstasy of love and full of hope for the future.

Act II (A wild mountain ridge)
Scenes 1–2: From his heavenly vantage point Wotan observes with pleasure the union of his two children. Wotan knows that if Siegmund emerges the victor in his duel with Hunding then nothing will stand in the way of his plan. To make sure, Wotan sends his favorite daughter Brünnhilde to the place where the fight is to take place, so that she might protect Siegmund. His wife Fricka, however, as the guardian of wedlock, has an altogether different opinion. She warns her husband against supporting acts that are unlawful (such as adultery and incest). Wotan argues that the gods need a hero free from their protection who will do what they cannot do: restore the ring to the Rhinemaidens. Fricka replies that if Wotan supports Siegmund in the coming battle he will not be free from the gods' protection. Wotan acknowledges the justice of her argument and orders Brünnhilde to support Hunding and not Siegmund.
Scenes 3–5: Brünnhilde solemnly proclaims Siegmund's imminent death, but she is overwhelmed by the depth of his love for Sieglinde and so decides to ignore Wotan's command. She promises Siegmund victory over Hunding. Wotan cannot allow such disobedience to go unpunished and intervenes in the contest himself. Nothung, the sword that had been bestowed by Wotan upon his son, is smashed into fragments by Wotan's spear. Siegmund is killed by Hunding, who is then struck down by Wotan. Brünnhilde flees Wotan's wrath, taking Sieglinde and the fragments of the shattered sword with her.

Act III (A rocky mountain peak)
Scenes 1–3: Brünnhilde seeks refuge with the Valkyries, but in vain: Wotan's daughters do not dare to enrage their father further. Brünnhilde parts from Sieglinde. She gives her the shards of Nothung and tells her that she is carrying Siegfried, the most glorious hero in the world. She then awaits her punishment. The vengeful Wotan banishes her from Valhalla, strips her of her divinity, and proclaims his intention of sending her into a deep sleep on a mountain top, prey to the first man who wakes her from this slumber. Brünnhilde begs her father to protect her by surrounding her with a ring of fire that only the bravest of heroes will be able to penetrate. Wotan's heart is softened, and before leaving Brünnhilde he summons Loge, who appears as fire, and commands him to encircle the entire mountain with a sea of flames.

Á. G.

The Valkyrie, Lilli and Marie Lehmann as Helmwige and Ortlinde, photograph by J. Albert (Munich), Bayreuth 1876. Iron helmets and full suits of armor demanded considerable stamina from the Valkyrie during Bayreuth's heroic era.

The Valkyrie, set design by Adolph Mahnke, Königsberg 1942 (TWS).
Two-thirds of The Valkyrie are set on a wild mountain ridge. Here it is portrayed as the empty, gloomy world of gods, who are on the path to destruction. Of all of them, Wotan is the loneliest and guiltiest. On the first day of the cycle he loses his last and most deeply treasured hopes: Siegmund and Brünnhilde. "I trapped myself in my own bonds, I, the least free of all!" he laments in Act II. "I wish for only one thing more: the end." His impending ruin is announced by the birth of Alberich's son, Hagen, whom the lord of Nibelheim had conceived in an act of loveless violence. In The Valkyrie, Wotan's fate is sealed.

Below
The Valkyrie, costume design for the Valkyrie by Karl Emil Doepler, Bayreuth 1876 (TWS). This drawing of a Valkyrie was made for the first performance of the complete cycle in Bayreuth.

Left
The Valkyrie, production photograph with Poul Elming (Sigmund) and Nadine Secunde (Sieglinde), production Harry Kupfer, sets Hans Schavernoch, conductor Daniel Barenboim, Bayreuth Festival 1988.
Siegmund and Sieglinde are both twins and lovers. In the most beautiful musical passage of The Ring they anticipate a single night of bliss – even though they stand in the shadow of death. In this act they enter briefly into a state of harmony with the gods (through the sword Nothung) and with nature (through the season of spring).

An act of love

Within Wagner's *Ring* cycle the first act of *The Valkyrie* is an "act of love," and it concludes as Siegmund and Sieglinde are about to consummate that love. *M 49*

This love scene of more than an hour's duration – interrupted only by a conversation with Hunding – forms a musical highpoint in Wagner's *oeuvre*. There are few composers able to express the emotional and physical effects of love as subtly and thrillingly as Wagner. The "love of the twins" (which refers to the complete union of two people) radiates hope and fulfillment. The musical lyricism of the love between brother and sister, which reveals their mutual affection but not the mysterious origins they have in common, is of quite a different sort from that used for vivid descriptions of nature or the melodic speaking style of the mythological characters in the score of *The Rhinegold*.

The great door of Hunding's house symbolizes the passage from the mythical to the human sphere, as well as the liberation of feelings and Sieglinde's release from a forced marriage. After Sieglinde's tale of the stranger who buried his sword in the trunk of the ash tree, the door to the house springs back "and remains wide open; outside … a glorious spring night; the full moon is shining, casting a bright light on the two figures" (Wagner's stage directions). Thus nature seems to bless the union of Siegmund and Sieglinde. The music also tells us what kind of passion it is that has inflamed their senses and driven them into each other's arms, through long interlocking arches of endless melody and erotically charged harmony. This night scene represents the birth of Wagner's "*Tristan* style." *M 50*

The Valkyrie, set design (magic fire) by Leo Pasetti, Munich 1921 (TWS).
"You shall have a bridal fire, burning as no other bridal fire has burnt! ... For only one man shall take this bride, he who is freer than I, a god!" The magic fire is not merely a decorative stage effect: it is Wotan's purgatory, through which Brünnhilde's righteousness is proved. At this point Wotan ceases to play an active part in the events of the cycle. In →*Siegfried* he appears as the Wanderer, an observer who is no longer capable of action.

49. Motif of the Love of the Volsungs

50. Siegmund's Spring Song

Win - ter-stür - me wi-chen dem Won - ne - mond, __ in mil - dem Lich - te leuch-tet der Lenz; __ auf lau - en Lüf - ten lind und lieb - lich, Wun - der we - bend er sich wiegt; durch Wald und Au - en weht sein A - tem, weit ge - öff - net lacht sein Aug __

The Valkyries

According to Nordic mythology, the Valkyries are the handmaidens of Woden (Wotan). The word "Valkyrie" is derived from the Germanic words "Wal" and "Kür". In Middle High German "Walstatt" meant a battlefield, and "Kür" meant choice. The Valkyries escorted to Valhalla the heroes who had been marked out for death on the battlefield.

The "Ride of the Valkyries" (anticipated in the prelude to Act II and fully developed in the prelude to Act III) is amongst the most popular episodes in the cycle, and it suggests the endless space of a cosmic and supernatural world. It became well known to latter-day audiences through its use in the film *Apocalypse Now* by Francis Ford Coppola, in which a group of American pilots in Vietnam begin their attack to the strains of this piece. How was the awe-inspiring grandeur of this music achieved? Wagner specified a huge brass section for his *Ring* orchestra: eight horns (including two Wagner tubas which were fitted with horn mouthpieces), two tubas, a contrabass tuba, three trumpets, a bass trumpet, three trombones, and a contrabass trombone.

Brünnhilde, the godly renegade

It may seem surprising that the eponymous heroine of the first day of the cycle, the Valkyrie Brünnhilde, does not appear until the second act, but the reasons for this become clear in the course of the drama. With Wotan, she is a key figure in the *Ring*. The audience first encounters her as they do the other Valkyries – riding, in armor, armed, giving out her characteristic cry. *M 51*

51. Brünnhilde's Entry

Ho - jo - to - ho! __ ho - jo - to - ho! __

Nevertheless, as Wotan's favorite child, Brünnhilde occupies a special position among the Valkyries. She embodies Wotan's innermost wishes, his subconscious. Her conflict with her father and her resistance to carrying out Wotan's orders is a reflection of Wotan's inner disharmony. Wotan may have sacrificed Siegmund but he is not left without issue: he knows full well that Sieglinde is pregnant with Siegfried. The thought that he might thus be saved, his third illusion, differs from his earlier attempts at self-preservation in that Wotan can no longer act on his own initiative. He now intervenes only indirectly by employing his hand-maiden Brünnhilde. How does Brünnhilde's metamorphosis begin? Following Wotan's orders she has a conversation with Siegmund in which she announces his imminent death. M 52

Brünnhilde tells Siegmund that those who receive an annunciation of death are prevented from ever

52. Annunciation of Death

returning to the path of life. When Siegmund objects and refers to his magic sword, Brünnhilde answers that the god who made and gave him the sword has now condemned him to death. The news grieves Siegmund deeply, as it means leaving Sieglinde, alone and unprotected. He rails against his father, the god, believing Brünnhilde to be incapable of understanding him because of her similarly godly nature. This triggers Brünnhilde's metamorphosis, opening the way for her to become human. She tells Siegmund that Sieglinde is carrying a child in her womb, and when Siegmund then tries to kill his lover in her sleep, so that she will not be left without a guardian, Brünnhilde restrains him. Her actions are now those of a mortal woman, a response to her feelings. She promises Siegmund that she will stand by him in his battle with Hunding: she – a Valkyrie – will oppose her father – a god – and defend the interests of the Volsungs. Brünnhilde's decision is an independent, human decision; she understands and accepts that Siegmund's sense of morality is of greater value than the reasoning of the gods. She comes to this realization through her emotions and resigns herself to the consequences of her actions, thereby becoming human.

Brünnhilde's sinking into the oblivion of sleep (*The Valkyrie*, Act III) and her awakening to mortality by Siegfried's kiss (*Siegfried*, Act III) are the inevitable results of her inner metamorphosis during her annunciation of Siegmund's death. This moment is of critical importance for the course and the conclusion of the cycle as a whole. *Gy. K.*

The Valkyrie, Siegfried Wagner with harpists and their harps, Bayreuth 1928. Siegfried Wagner (1869–1930) was the talented son (composer, conductor, and director) of Richard Wagner. After his father's death he took over the administration of the festival with his mother, Cosima, and was proud of "his" harps and harpists. "Only" six harps are required in the *Ring*. The seventh is included in case of emergencies.

Below
The Valkyrie, Eva Marton (Brünnhilde) with James Morris (Wotan), production August Everding, sets and costumes John Conklin, conductor Zubin Mehta, Lyric Opera of Chicago 1996.
In the last two decades productions have often turned away from the mythological and concentrated on the historical aspects of the work. The historicist set design and period dress of this *Ring* production at the Lyric Opera of Chicago certainly point in this direction.

The farewell

Brünnhilde, an angel of death in her encounter with Siegmund in Act II, becomes a fallen angel in the conclusion to Act III, when she is banished from Valhalla by her father. To all appearances the Valkyrie bends to Wotan's will: but in fact it is the daughter who instructs the father. She describes to Wotan the shame she felt when confronted with human anguish, love, and the suffering of mortals who defy fate. It is for these reasons that she disobeys the instructions of the god who had planted a love for the Volsung in her own heart. When she reaches this point in her narrative and in her appeal to Wotan, a new theme is presented by the orchestra. It is an expressive motif played on oboes and clarinets, which is in fact a touching variation on the rigid, linear, and mechanically descending trombone motif associated with the spear. *M 53, M 54*

53. Wotan's Spear Motif

54. Brünnhilde's Love for Her Father

55. Wotan's Farewell

Der Au - gen leuch - ten - des Paar, das oft ich lä - chelnd ge - kost

56.1 Spark Motif (Magic Fire)

56.2 Flame Motif (Magic Fire)

The Valkyrie production photograph with Hans-Peter Scheidegger as Wotan, production Michael Heinicke, sets Wolfgang Bellach, costumes Ralf Winkler, conductor Oleg Caetani, Oper Chemnitz 1998. "Whosoever fears the point of my spear shall not enter the fire!" The words with which Wotan draws an impenetrable circle of fire around Brünnhilde, and which bring *The Valkyrie* to a close. This point also marks the end of Wotan's own period of activity: as a prisoner of his own will, he is powerless to influence events further.

Opposite
The Valkyrie, production photograph with Janis Martin (Brünnhilde) and Franz Ferdinand Nentwig (Wotan), production, sets, and costumes Herbert Wernicke, conductor Sylvain Cambreling, Théâtre Royal de la Monnaie, Brussels 1991.
In this production the great game of Germanic mythology (or what was understood as such) seems to have begun quite harmlessly in the living rooms and music rooms of German households – fun for the whole family. The father takes the part of the god, his daughter that of the Valkyrie.

The relationship with the spear motif indicates that hidden behind Wotan's lust for power is a fatherly love; it even reveals the god's plan for a benign world order. Wotan, however, has silenced his better nature, which is represented by Brünnhilde. The last scene of *The Valkyrie* is a test for Wotan, during which he slowly begins to acknowledge the injustice of his actions. Brünnhilde continues to create inner discord in her father. Wotan himself abandons the dream of his youth – his plan for a world order governed wisely by the gods – which has finally become an illusion. His ideas for his own salvation, for the continuation of the gods' dominion, and for a balance in the world order are all abandoned, as he realizes that a new order must come in which the gods will play no part. *M 55*

Magic fire

Wotan's sword-breaking spear becomes a symbol at the end of Act II: although he has slowly come to accept the necessity of renunciation, the ruler of the gods is not yet ready for such a step emotionally. At the end of Act III he still holds the spear in his hand. Its power is now used to call Loge and charge him with casting a ring of fire around the sleeping Brünnhilde, so that she and Siegfried may be united in the future. The magic fire music of this scene is justifiably famous. How does it achieve its effect? A blazing fire is depicted by a rapidly moving motif (piccolo and six harps), which is in turn "encircled" by rapid string passages, while both woodwind and glockenspiel convey the impression of a quickly spreading conflagration. *M 56*   *Gy. K.*

The Ring of the Nibelung

Bühnenfestspiel for a preliminary evening and three days

Second Day: **Siegfried**
In three acts

Libretto: Richard Wagner.
Première: 16 August 1876, Bayreuth (Festspielhaus).
Characters: Siegfried, Wotan's grandson, the son of Siegmund and Sieglinde (T), Brünnhilde, a Valkyrie (S), The Wanderer (Wotan) (B), Alberich, the Nibelung (B), Mime, his brother, Siegfried's foster-father (T), Fafner, a giant in the form of a dragon (B), Erda (A), The Woodbird (S).
Setting: Mythological.

Siegfried, set design for Act II by the Franz Moser studio, Innsbruck, 1911 (TWS). The plot of *Siegfried* is as exciting and colorful as a fairy tale by the Brothers Grimm. There are, moreover, humorous and grotesque situations in it that contrast strongly with the atmosphere of *The Valkyrie*. If, as many scholars claim, the cycle can be conceived of as a dramatic symphony in four movements, then *Siegfried* surely constitutes the Scherzo. The dragon Fafner guards his hoard and the ring. Siegfried approaches in the distance.

Synopsis
Before the opera begins
Having been rescued by Brünnhilde after the battle between Hunding and Siegmund, Sieglinde traveled to a forest in the east for safety, taking with her the fragments of Siegmund's broken sword. There she gave birth to a son, Siegfried, but she herself died. The master smith Mime, a Nibelung, took the orphan into his care, and raised him with the intention of winning back the Nibelung hoard, which is now guarded by the giant Fafner in the form of a huge dragon.

Present action
Siegfried is 18 years old, having been brought up in complete isolation from the world and in ignorance of his origins. He now forces Mime to tell him about his parents, and when he hears about the broken sword sets out to reforge it himself. He kills Fafner with the sword without realizing what he is doing, for he has never learned the meaning of fear. A woodbird teaches him the secrets of the ring and the Tarnhelm, and then directs him to Brünnhilde's rock. Siegfried first kills Mime, who has attempted to poison him, and smashes the spear of his grandfather Wotan, when the god, in the form of the Wanderer, tries to oppose him. Now no one can stop him, and Siegfried passes through the ring of fire to awaken Brünnhilde. At the sight of her Siegfried learns the meaning of both fear and love.

Act I (A cave in the rocks in the forest)
Scene 1: Young Siegfried's strength is so great that his foster-father is unable to forge a sword strong enough to withstand his blows. Siegfried forces Mime to tell him the truth about his origins.

Scene 2: Mime receives a visit from the Wanderer (Wotan) who prophesies his death at the hands of a man who has not learned to feel fear.

Scene 3: Siegfried forges a sword from Nothung's fragments. Mime secretly prepares a poisoned meal. He plans to have Fafner killed by Siegfried and then poison the victor in order to become lord of the ring and of the hoard.

Act II (Deep in the forest)
Scene 1: It is dawn. Alberich is keeping watch outside the cave in which the dragon Fafner is guarding his treasure. He is waiting for his curse to come to fruition once again. From the Wanderer (Wotan) Alberich learns that Mime is seeking to gain mastery over the hoard with Siegfried's help. Wotan is even prepared to help rouse Fafner, but when he and Alberich warn the giant that his mortal enemy is approaching, Fafner refuses to be disturbed.

Scene 2: Mime leads Siegfried to Fafner's cave in order to teach him the meaning of fear. While Siegfried waits under a tree for the terrifying monster that Mime has described, he reflects on his origins, and believes that the forest is speaking to him. He hears the song of a woodbird, and tries in vain to communicate with it by blowing on a flute he has made from a reed. He then blows on his horn, and Fafner emerges from his cave. Siegfried confronts the monster fearlessly, and plunges his sword into its heart. Fafner's blood burns like fire, and when Siegfried puts his hand to his mouth and tastes the blood he finds he is able to understand the language of the woodbird. It advises him to take the ring and Tarnhelm from the cave, and warns him of Mime's cunning.

Scene 3: Like two vultures, Alberich and Mime wait for their prey in front of the cave, neither of them willing to share the gold stolen from the Rhinemaidens. Mime offers Siegfried a poisoned drink to slake his thirst, but Siegfried sees through his ruse and strikes him dead with Nothung. The woodbird tells Siegfried about Brünnhilde.

Act III (The foot of a rocky mountain; on the peak of Brünnhilde's rock)

Scene 1: Wotan is consumed by anxiety, and wakes Erda in order to learn from her how the course of fate may yet be checked. Erda is unable to help him.

Scene 2: As the Wanderer, Wotan attempts to block Siegfried's path to the Valkyrie's resting place, but Siegfried's sword splinters the spear which had once been used to destroy Nothung. Fearless, Siegfried enters the ring of fire and climbs to the top of Brünnhilde's rock.

Scene 3: Siegfried finds the sleeping Brünnhilde and awakens her with a kiss. Brünnhilde returns to consciousness and greets the world as if seeing it for the first time. For love she renounces her divinity and falls joyously into the arms of her hero.   A. G.

Siegfried, production photograph with Siegfried Jerusalem as Siegfried, production Harry Kupfer, sets Hans Schavernoch, conductor Daniel Barenboim, Bayreuth Festival 1988.
In *Herakles* (*Hercules*), Heiner Müller (1929–95) describes how the battle with the dragon begins as a defensive action against an external threat, but finishes as a battle with the hero's own inner drives. Here, Siegfried's struggle with the shadows seems to indicate that he is trying to fend off more than just an external enemy.

Above
Siegfried, set design (Siegfried and the dragon) by the Franz Moser studio, Innsbruck 1911 (TWS).
The fearless hero is about to do battle with the dragon in an enchanted forest. The first production to break with a traditional, mythological interpretation was by Wieland Wagner (1965) – almost 100 years after the work's première. His production explored the various meanings that might be attributed to the fairy tale.

Siegfried, Brünnhilde's awakening, illustration by Hugo L. Braune.
The sight of a woman finally teaches Siegfried to fear ("Burning magic shoots into my heart, fiery fear seizes my eyes, my senses lose their balance! Whom should I call who would come to my aid? Mother! Mother! Think of me!") The moment in which Siegfried's kiss awakens Brünnhilde is the most solemn moment in the entire cycle. Wagner used for it a text from one of the oldest pagan rites of the Edda: the ceremonial saluting of the sunrise ("Hail to you, sun! Hail to you, light! Hail to you, bright day!"). The orchestra at this point recalls Brünnhilde's Annunciation of Death motif (→*The Valkyrie*). Awakening and death are presented as mysteries of life, as riddles about the future. But it is also a moment of redemption, its music being in the key of C major. With it, we reach a "high plain" of hope. We are situated at this point on the roof of the world, and endless distances open up before our eyes – distances that promise more than just a glorious view of Valhalla.

The forest

The forest of Act I is a frightening place, the sort of forest that might have haunted children's imaginations in the nineteenth century. It is characterized musically by the thumping rhythm of the forge, M 57 and by the pairs of thirds associated with the brooding smith, Mime, M 58 which are derived from the chain of thirds in the ring motif. In the form of a dragon Fafner guards the ring, M 59 while Alberich waits for the hero who will slay Fafner so that he may once again seize the ring for himself. The only counterpoise to this treacherous forest world is Siegfried, the real "child of nature." He is symbolized visually and aurally by the horn and its blast. M 60

Wagner devised a unique style for Siegfried's songs – an unusual feature in the score of the cycle. His famous "Forging Song," which he sings while making Nothung, is a great, strophic work song. M 61

57. Forge Motif

58. Mime's Brooding

59. Dragon Motif

60.1 Siegfried's Horn Motif

60.2 Siegfried, the Child of Nature

Hoi - ho! ____ Hau ein! Hau ein!

"Forest Murmurs"

When Siegfried is left alone in front of Fafner's cave (Act II), the music turns from hatred and fear to the gently murmuring melodies of nature. The style of the "Forest Murmurs" is related to the nature imagery of →*The Rhinegold*, and, through its use of trills, to the motif of the blazing fire in →*The Valkyrie*. Just as the sound of water was conveyed in the song of the Rhinemaidens (→*The Rhinegold*, ᴍ 38) so the forest finds a voice in birdsong. ᴍ 62

Gy. K.

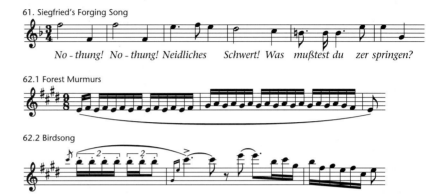

61. Siegfried's Forging Song

No - thung! No - thung! Neidliches Schwert! Was mußtest du zer springen?

62.1 Forest Murmurs

62.2 Birdsong

Below
Siegfried, production photograph with Janis Martin (Brünnhilde) and William Cochran (Siegfried), production, sets, and costumes Herbert Wernicke, conductor Sylvain Cambreling, Théâtre Royal de la Monnaie, Brussels 1991.
The mythology game has moved away from the setting of the living room and the family circle and into the folk realm, signs of which may be seen in the characters and in the buildings. In this scene Siegfried frees Brünnhilde.

The Wanderer

In *Siegfried*, Wotan is known as the Wanderer. The purpose of his itinerant existence is to attain a deeper understanding, of both himself and the world, and to progress from a state of resignation and renunciation to an acceptance of death. "Zu schauen kam ich, nicht zu schaffen" ("I came to observe, not to create"), he says about his own role in the penultimate chapter of the story of his world. He understands the dull indifference of the dragon Fafner (Act II), who, in spite of Alberich's warning, withdraws into his cave. It is with great perception and sympathy that Wotan explains to Alberich: "Alles ist nach seiner Art; an ihr wirst du nichts ändern" ("Everything is according to its nature; this you will not change").

His final proud and solemn words of renunciation transcend the events on stage through a new melody: the abdicating god prophesies the possibility of a new and better world in the form of the love motif of Siegfried and Brünnhilde. *M 63*

"On the peak of the mountain"

No sooner has Siegfried disappeared into the flames than we see him on the peak of the mountain, to which he has been conveyed by a "Jacob's ladder" – a grand melody played on the violins. *M 64*

The *Siegfried Idyll*

The love music for Siegfried and Brünnhilde, with its gently rocking rhythm, is a reference to Brünnhilde's godliness (it is in E major, the key associated with nature in the cycle), as well as to the deep roots of Siegfried's love (Brünnhilde is his lost mother as well as his new found lover). It is one of the most famous passages in the cycle, and came to have a personal significance for Wagner. Having composed the music for Act III in 1869, in December 1870 Wagner arranged for a small ensemble to serenade his wife Cosima with the so-called *Siegfried Idyll*, a chamber orchestra version of the Act III love music that Wagner had written after the birth of their son, Siegfried. *M 65*   Gy. K.

Siegfried production photograph with Victor Braun as the Wanderer, production, sets, and costumes Herbert Wernicke, conductor Sylvain Cambreling, Théâtre Royal de la Monnaie, Brussels 1991.

Siegfried, set design by Ludwig Sievert for the production by Franz Ludwig Hoerth, Stadttheater, Freiburg 1913 (TWS).
Wotan wakes Erda for the last time. This set design illustrates the grandeur and tragedy of this key scene. Man and woman, shadow and light, stand face to face. The parents of the world bid each other a final farewell.

63. Love Motif (Siegfried and Brünnhilde)

Sieg -fried, mein Sohn, das siehst du wohl selbst, dein Le - ben mußt du mir las - sen.

64. Siegfried's Path to the Peak of the Mountain

65. *Siegfried Idyll*

E - wig war ich, e - wig bin ich, e - wig in süß - seh - nen der Won-ne,

The Ring of the Nibelung

Bühnenfestspiel for a preliminary evening and three days

Third Day: ***Twilight of the Gods*** (*Götterdämmerung*)
In a prologue and three acts

Libretto: Richard Wagner.
Première: 17 August 1876, Bayreuth (Festspielhaus).

Characters: Siegfried (T), Brünnhilde, Siegfried's wife, formerly a Valkyrie, Wotan's daughter (S), Gunther, King of the Gibichungs (Bar), Gutrune, Gunther's sister (S), Hagen, son of Alberich, half-brother and adviser of Gunther (B), Alberich, the Nibelung, Hagen's father (B), Waltraute, a Valkyrie, Brünnhilde's sister (Ms), Three Norns, fates (A, Ms, S), Woglinde, Wellgunde, Flosshilde, Rhinemaidens (3 S); vassals, women (chorus).
Setting: Mythological.

Synopsis

The fearless hero Siegfried leaves Brünnhilde's rocky crag and returns to humankind in search of new adventures. He arrives in the kingdom of the Gibichungs, home to Gunther, Gutrune, and Hagen. Hagen has inherited the intense hatred of his father Alberich. He seeks to take revenge on Siegfried for the humiliation suffered by his race, and to win back the ring. Siegfried has given the ring to Brünnhilde as a token of his fidelity. Hagen advises the two royal Gibichungs that Siegfried should be sent to woo Brünnhilde as a bride for Gunther, as a reward for which the hero would be offered Gutrune's hand in marriage. Gutrune gives Siegfried a potion to make him forget Brünnhilde. Siegfried is now ready to enter the ring of fire disguised as Gunther to fetch Brünnhilde for his new friend; he willingly assents to a marriage to Gutrune. Hagen then proceeds to ally himself with the spurned Brünnhilde (from whom Siegfried has snatched the ring), in order to discover how to kill Siegfried. But when Siegfried is dead, Hagen is unable to remove the ring from his finger. The Rhinemaidens explain the truth to Brünnhilde, who ignites Siegfried's funeral pyre and immolates herself in the flames. The fire destroys Valhalla together with the gods. The Rhine breaks its banks and the Rhinemaidens reclaim the stolen ring, dragging Hagen down into the depths with them.

Prologue (The Valkyrie rock at night)

The three Norns are weaving the rope of destiny and discussing the events of the world. The rope suddenly becomes snagged and breaks and the Norns are no longer able to divine the future. *M76* Deeply in love *M77*, Siegfried and Brünnhilde assure each other of their affection, but the restless hero thirsts for action and wishes to return to the world of men for a period. He gives Brünnhilde the ring of the Nibelung and she presents him with her horse, Grane. He then sets out on his journey ("Siegfried's Rhine Journey").

Act I (The hall of the Gibichungs; the Valkyrie rock)

Scene 1: Hagen tells Gunther and Gutrune about Brünnhilde and Siegfried, but his story conceals much of the truth. He awakens desire for Brünnhilde in Gunther, who wishes to have her as his bride, while Gutrune longs to have Siegfried, the greatest hero in the world, for her husband.

Scene 2: Siegfried arrives at the Gibichung court. Following Hagen's plan, Gutrune gives Siegfried a magic potion that makes him forget his past, including his love for Brünnhilde *M78*. Siegfried and Gunther swear blood brotherhood, and Siegfried agrees to woo Brünnhilde in the guise of Gunther with the help of the Tarnhelm. As a reward, he is to marry Gutrune.

Scene 3: Brünnhilde's sister Waltraute tries to persuade her to return the accursed ring to the Rhinemaidens, but Brünnhilde refuses to part with the token of love given her by Siegfried. No sooner has the disappointed Waltraute left than Siegfried's horn is heard. To Brünnhilde's horror it is not her husband who emerges from the flames but a stranger (Siegfried disguised as Gunther), who overpowers hers and steals the ring.

Act II (In front of the Gibichung hall)

Scene 1: Alberich appears to the half-sleeping Hagen. He urges his son to seek revenge and win back the ring.

Scene 2: With the aid of the Tarnhelm, Siegfried returns quickly to the Gibichung court and reports on the success of his journey. Gunther is following with the captive Brünnhilde, and a double wedding is to be celebrated.

Twilight of the Gods, production photograph with the Norns, production Harry Kupfer, sets Hans Schavernoch, costumes Reinhard Heinrich, conductor Daniel Barenboim, Bayreuth 1988–92.
The Norns on the roof of a skyscraper. Instead of a rope, an antenna is now the instrument used by visionaries to explore the future of mankind. But can it still receive a signal?

Twilight of the Gods, Hagen and Alberich, illustration by Hugo L. Braune c. 1905 (TWS)
The darkest scene in Wagner's entire work: Alberich appears to his son Hagen in his sleep: "I raised Hagen to steadfast hatred; he will avenge me and win the ring." Like Wotan, Alberich can no longer influence events directly. In contrast to Siegfried, Hagen comes to know the meaning of the ring – and tries to win it for himself: "So swore I to myself; fears, be silent!"

Scene 3: Hagen summons his vassals to give a fitting greeting to Gunther's future bride.

Scene 4: After arriving in the land of the Gibichungs, Brünnhilde becomes aware of the full extent of the tragedy: Siegfried wears on his finger the ring he stole from her while disguised as Gunther, and no longer recognizes her as his wife. She suspects a trick and announces to all present that she, not Gutrune, is Siegfried's wife. Siegfried is required to prove his innocence and he swears an oath on the point of Hagen's spear; Brünnhilde does the same. One of the two has committed perjury and will have to atone for the crime. Hagen is to assume the duty of punishing the guilty party – which is precisely what he had planned.

Scene 5: Brünnhilde seeks revenge for a disloyalty she cannot comprehend; Hagen continues to strive after the ring; and Gunther suspects Siegfried of having broken their vows of blood brotherhood. Together they conspire against Siegfried. Brünnhilde reveals that there is only one place on Siegfried's body where it is possible to inflict a mortal wound: his back, which he would never turn on an enemy. They plan to have Siegfried killed the next day while out hunting.

Act III (A wooded region on the Rhine; the hall of the Gibichungs)

Scene 1: During the hunt Siegfried loses his way and encounters the Rhinemaidens on the banks of the river. At first he is willing to give them the ring, but when they tell him of the dangers it brings its owners he stubbornly refuses to surrender it.

Scene 2: Pausing for rest, Siegfried tells the hunting party of his youth. Hagen hands him a magic potion that restores his memory and Siegfried begins to recall his past. When he reaches the part where he meets Brünnhilde – thus revealing his supposed perjury – Hagen thrusts his spear into Siegfried's back. A funeral procession brings Siegfried's body back to the hall of the Gibichungs ("Siegfried's Funeral March").

Scene 3: In vain, Hagen attempts to remove the ring from Siegfried's hand. Brünnhilde has learned the truth from the Rhinemaidens and prepares for her own suicide. Her death, undertaken for the sake of love, unleashes a universal catastrophe. Valhalla and the gods are destroyed by fire and the Rhine bursts its banks to flood the flames. The Rhinemaidens retrieve their ring, and when Hagen attempts to seize it from them they drag him down into the depths of the river. *S. N.*

Twilight of the Gods, set design by Otto Müller-Godesberg, Bonn c. 1900 (TWS). Siegfried arrives in the realm of the Gibichungs (the world of mediocrity). It is an important moment and one highly typical of the "paradoxical" dramatic concepts of *Twilight of the Gods*: the first to greet Siegfried on the banks of the Rhine is Hagen, his greatest enemy. The naturalistic yet fairy-tale look of the set design – which includes exotic elements in the foreground – shows that at the turn of the century operas were still considered to be exciting fables.

Siegfried's end

The encounter between Brünnhilde and Siegfried is characterized by both pathos and victory (expressed in the final part of the duet in Act III of →*Siegfried*), and this spirit is maintained in Brünnhilde's joyous greeting of the sun (in *Twilight of the Gods*) with its love motif, as well as in the heroic variation of Siegfried's theme on the French horn. "Siegfried's encounter with Brünnhilde makes him a man. The **E flat** major theme to which he reappears after the marriage night is a vivid depiction of his complete transformation. It is not just the orchestration of his theme that is changed: his entire diction is different" (Wieland Wagner). The lovers exchange tokens of their affection. Brünnhilde gives Siegfried her horse, the symbol of her identity as a Valkyrie, signaling that she has broken with her past, and that of the two of them Siegfried alone is now responsible for action. Siegfried presents her with the ring, knowing nothing of its origins and significance. For him it is little more than a reminder of a heroic deed – "was der Taten je ich schuf, des Tugend schliesst er ein" ("of the deeds I have done, their value it retains") – and a token of his fidelity. Carried away by his youthful energy – which intensifies here into a dithyramb on the free life of men – he marches through the fire and begins his journey. *M 66*

When he arrives at the Gibichung court Siegfried does not find the knightly rituals and games for which his nature and physical prowess hunger, but rather a false and shameful society, driven by self-interest and lust for power, which immediately ensnares him in its lies and turns him into a traitor. The Gibichung hall becomes a second dragon's lair – according to Wieland Wagner's analysis – but one in which Siegfried "no longer hears the voice of nature." Siegfried loses his sensitivity to nature after his experience of sexual love with Brünnhilde. Thus he receives no warning about Gutrune's offering of poison, and the self-confident hero becomes a mere tool, his longing for the companionship of men having turned him into the "creation of the Nibelung's hatred" (Wieland Wagner). *Gy. K.*

66. Siegfried's Heroic Motif

Twilight of the Gods, photograph from the production by Herbert Wernicke, sets and costumes Herbert Wernicke, conductor Sylvain Cambreling, Théâtre Royal de la Monnaie, Brussels 1991.
The play nears its end: the three Norns spin the thread of fate within sight of Valhalla but at a safe distance from it.

Social relevance

Twilight of the Gods was originally conceived in the revolutionary year of 1848 as the drama *The Death of Siegfried*. It is in this work that Wagner's social criticism is most evident. On various occasions Wagner himself interpreted the cycle from a political and social perspective (→*The Ring of the Nibelung*: the genesis of universal drama). Oddly enough it was the Irish dramatist George Bernard Shaw who emphasized this interpretive possibility in his pioneering study, *The Perfect Wagnerite: A Commentary on "The Ring of the Nibelungs"*

(London, 1898). For decades, however, productions showed no interest in it (→Bayreuth: interpretation and ideology). Patrice Chéreau's much-discussed production of *The Ring* on the occasion of the 100th anniversary of its première caused a sensation by setting *Twilight of the Gods* in a late twentieth-century milieu.

Twilight of the Gods, production photograph with Janis Martin as Brünnhilde, production, sets, and costumes Herbert Wernicke, conductor Sylvain Cambreling, Théâtre Royal de la Monnaie, Brussels 1991.
Brünnhilde at the court of the Gibichungs, where Wotan's daughter encounters a widespread apocalyptic mood and a uniformity of thought, action, and appearance.

The cycle is complete

In *Twilight of the Gods*, the cycle comes to an end, questions finally receiving their answers. As Siegfried had previously entered the circle of fire to reach Brünnhilde, so now does she go through the flames to Siegfried. The death which she submits to for her own sake, for Siegfried's, and for that of the gods is not just a redeeming death; the fire which consumes her also expunges the curse of the ring. Brünnhilde's death is a symbol not only of her being reunited with Siegfried but also of birth. Wagner believed that the future of humanity lay in a relationship with a purified nature and in a new world order, and for him this future was symbolized by motherhood. The melody associated with Sieglinde's decision to continue living – when she learns of her pregnancy and Siegfried is given a name – appears for the first time at the end of Act II of →*The Valkyrie*. On that occasion, when Brünnhilde corrected Wotan's error by taking Sieglinde's part on the mountain top, the Valkyrie recognized and experienced maternal courage and sympathy for the first time, and accepted the consequences these would entail for herself. Her death by fire sanctions this compassion, this sympathy that transcends self-interest, raising it to the level of redemption itself. Up to this point Wagner had revealed the principle of redemption and every variation on it through the idea of the "eternal female." At the end of the cycle it receives its ultimate expression as a nature symbol, in the form of global conflagration and flood. With Brünnhilde's last words the Siegfried motif reappears with Sieglinde's motif of motherhood, that "noble miracle." The vision of a catastrophe thus becomes a vision of life. *M 67*

Twilight of the Gods, production photograph with Philip Kang (Hagen) and Günter von Kannen (Alberich), production Harry Kupfer, sets Hans Schavernoch, costumes Reinhard Heinrich, conductor Daniel Barenboim, Bayreuth Festival 1988.
Hagen sits in a watchtower in the middle of a large city. His outfit and posture are familiar from gangster movies and indicate that evil is abroad.

Twilight of the Gods, production photograph with Philip Kang (Hagen) and Deborah Polaski (Brünnhilde), production Harry Kupfer, Bayreuth Festival 1988.

67. Motif of Motherhood

Twilight of the Gods, production photograph with Siegfried Jerusalem as Siegfried, production Harry Kupfer, sets Hans Schavernoch, conductor Daniel Barenboim, Bayreuth Festival 1988.
Myths are poetic reflections of social and historical conflicts. But they also locate man in the cosmos, and this was certainly Wagner's approach to the mythological genre. The last part of the *Ring* cycle refers beyond itself to the social and historical spheres – something that Harry Kupfer brought out in this 1988 production.

Opposite
Twilight of the Gods, production photograph with William Cochran as Siegfried, production, sets, and costumes Herbert Wernicke, conductor Sylvain Cambreling, Théâtre Royal de la Monnaie, Brussels 1991. Trench warfare as the final station of a game that began so harmlessly: Hagen mortally wounds Siegfried.

Of catastrophes and pledges

When Hagen is hauled down to the depths of the river by the Rhine maidens, the motif of the curse also "drowns" and only the stable nature motifs remain. The musical images of earth and sky, river and mountain are united as themes flow into each other: rises and falls, creation and destruction alternate with each other in wave-like movements.

Things assume their original shape and are linked according to their original, natural order. But the beginning and the end are not the same. The gold shines once again in the depths of the waters, but in the memory of mankind the ring does not return completely to a state of nature. It is now more than just gold: it is imbued with the knowledge of its creator, and the causes and consequences of the curse. The nature elements also include the melody of the principle of the "eternal female." Finally, the vision of a global conflagration softens into a "rainbow of harps." Siegfried's motif merges into the motif of motherhood and appears once again in the firmament of Wagner's vision.

This scene corresponds symmetrically with the view of the gods progressing towards Valhalla in the final scene of → *The Rhinegold*. But in contrast to the first part of the cycle there are no lamenting Rhinemaidens or outsiders such as Loge in *Twilight of the Gods*.

The "rainbow" which forms an arch at the end of the last transfiguration of themes is not one of Wotan's visionary images. The "bridge" is the pledge of a new beginning which contains the promise of greater opportunities.

Gy. K.

Parsifal

Bühnenweihfestspiel in three acts

Libretto: Richard Wagner.
Première: 26 July 1882, Bayreuth (Festspielhaus).

Characters: Amfortas, ruler of the kingdom of the Grail (Bar), Titurel, his father (B), Gurnemanz, a knight of the Grail (B), Parsifal (T), Klingsor, a magician (B), Kundry (S or Ms), Klingsor's Flowermaidens (6 S), Two Knights of the Grail (T, B), Four Squires (S, A, 2 T), Voice from Above (A); knights of the Grail, youths and boys, flowermaidens (chorus).
Setting: The Grail castle "Montsalvat" and its environs, the northern mountains of Spain, in mythological times.

Parsifal, Anna Bahr-Mildenburg (Kundry) and Walter von Kirchhoff (Parsifal), Bayreuth 1915.
The sweeping, pathos-laden gestures in Wagner's music are entirely calculated. Everything was designed to have an effect on stage.

Parsifal, poster for a production at the Opernhaus Kiel.
In the world of *Parsifal*, the dove is "the Savior's fair messenger." In the Old Testament the dove brings glad tidings to Noah, and is thus a symbol of peace between God and man. The bird in *Parsifal* has the same function.

Synopsis
Before the opera begins

According to the precepts of the Order of the Grail, only those who are able to renounce sensual love may partake of the miraculous power of the Grail (a chalice that supposedly collected the blood of the dying Christ). Klingsor had not considered himself spiritually capable of this feat and had castrated himself. But the brotherhood of the Grail had still refused to admit him. In revenge he built a magic castle not far from the castle of the Grail and equipped it with a pleasure garden full of enchantingly beautiful maidens. He was thus able to tempt many of the knights of the Grail into breaking their vows of celibacy. Even Amfortas, the ruler of the kingdom of the Grail, fell victim to the seductive beauty of Kundry. Klingsor then robbed him of the sacred spear of the Grail and used it to inflict a wound on him – a wound that will not heal until a "pure fool made wise through compassion" returns the spear.

Act I

Scene 1: The environs of Montsalvat castle, at daybreak. Kundry has been condemned to wander for eternity for having mocked Christ on the cross. Striving for redemption, she serves the knights of the Grail with humility, bringing Amfortas ointments from around the world to heal his wound – but in vain. Gurnemanz tells the squires why Amfortas's wound will not heal and he relates a prophecy that a "pure fool" will one day appear as their savior. An unknown youth enters the castle precincts and shoots down a swan. Taken to task by Gurnemanz, he is told that this is not the "pleasure of the hunt" but murder of a living creature, and the boy breaks his bow. He seems to be both innocent and capable of compassion. Full of hope, Gurnemanz takes him to the castle.

Scene 2: A great hall in the castle of the Grail. Each time the Grail is uncovered, Amfortas's pain increases. But the knights demand their spiritual sustenance and the king must discharge his duties. Parsifal witnesses the ceremony but is unable to describe the significance of what he has seen. Disappointed, Gurnemanz chases him away.

Act II

Klingor's magic castle and garden. While serving the knights of the Grail, Kundry is also obedient to Klingsor; he calls Kundry to him and instructs her to seduce the fool who is approaching the castle. The flowermaidens tease Parsifal in a flirtatious way, but Kundry introduces him to the realm of love with a maternal kiss and calls him by his name: Parsifal. She thus awakens in him knowledge of his origins and of the grief and pain of separation from his mother. Parsifal then experiences pity for all living creatures, comprehends the origins of Amfortas's pain, and is able to resist Kundry. Klingsor hurls the sacred spear at Parsifal. However, it remains hovering above his head. Parsifal makes the sign of the cross with the weapon and the magic domain vanishes.

Act III

Scene 1: The environs of Montsalvat castle, in springtime. Years have passed. Amfortas now refuses to reveal the Grail. Forced to forgo the source of their spiritual strength, the knights of the Grail no longer ride out into the world as bringers of peace, but lead a wretched existence as hermits in the woods. During his long odyssey through the world, Parsifal has discovered his own self as well as empathy for his fellow beings. Now he returns in the armor of a black knight to the land of the Grail in order to redeem Amfortas with the sacred spear ("Good Friday Magic"). For the second time, Gurnemanz leads him into the castle. But first, the aging knight anoints the "redeemed redeemer" as king of the Grail, and Parsifal baptizes Kundry.

Scene 2: In the castle of the Grail. Amfortas's father Titurel has died and the assembled knights demand that the Grail be uncovered. Amfortas, however, refuses to carry out this sacred duty. Parsifal exercises the royal office and heals the long-suffering Amfortas with the sacred spear. Kundry, delivered from her sins, sinks to the ground. *S.N.*

Parsifal, set design by Ludwig Sievert (Act II, final scene), Freiburg 1913/14 (TWS). Unarmed, Parsifal defeats Klingsor's dark power and wins the spear. This incident does not represent a transfiguration, however, because Parsifal's mission is not to destroy Klingsor's kingdom but to redeem the kingdom of the Grail. Many years will pass before he can return to the realm of the Grail, understand the meaning of the mystery of Good Friday, and perform a new deed of redemption.

Mockery and glorification

No other music drama by Wagner has inspired such vehement and contradictory responses as *Parsifal*. Nietzsche, who admired Wagner for the pessimistic philosophy of his *Ring* cycle, considered this operatic "swansong" to be a betrayal. He was not able to forgive Wagner for what he perceived to be a capitulation to Christian belief.

In the Catholic camp, Franz Liszt's companion, the Duchess Carolyne von Wittgenstein, protested against Wagner's supposed desecration and mockery of the Holy Sacrament. The long history of *Parsifal* interpretation has brought forth a number of even more astonishing theories: the community of the Grail as a Nazi elite, or as a homosexual fraternity, the "redeemed redeemer" Parsifal as a "German" Christ, or as a hermaphrodite, and so forth. The opera has also been seen as symbolic of the two poles between which German history has fluctuated – that is, as a portent of war and a harbinger of peace.

Attributes of the Grail

According to tradition the blood of the crucified Christ was collected in a vessel. This chalice emits a red, energy-giving light. Wagner traced the word's etymology in the following way: Sangue reale (royal blood) = San Greal = Sankt Gral = Der heilige Gral (The Holy Grail). The Grail as life-giving chalice is a symbol of the primordial mother. Wagner called the Grail "a spiritual counterpart to the Nibelung hoard." The spear, according to Wagner, was the complementary opposite of the Grail, a symbol of masculinity (akin to Yoni and Lingam in Indian thought). Other instances of Grail symbolism in the nineteenth century are found in the Lutheran-Protestant liturgy, most specifically the "Dresden Amen" (Wagner heard it at his confirmation in Dresden), used by Felix Mendelssohn in the first movement of his fifth symphony, the so-called Reformation Symphony. M 68, M 69

The community of the knights of the Grail is characterized by the faith motif. M 70 The dove that appears in the opera symbolizes the Holy Ghost of Christian faith; it is the same dove that appeared at Christ's baptism in the Jordan by John the Baptist. In the Grail legends the arrival of the dove is an element of great significance, as Lohengrin, the son of Parsifal, attests in his Narration (→Lohengrin): "Alljährlich naht vom Himmel eine Taube, um neu zu stärken seine Wunderkraft" ("Yearly there descends from heaven a dove, come to renew his

68. Grail Motif (Dresden Amen)

69. Mendelssohn, Reformation Symphony, Dresden Amen

70. Faith Motif

71. Story of the Grail (*Lohengrin*)

all - jähr - lich naht   vom Him - mel ei - ne Tau - be

72. Communion Motif

miraculous power"). M 71 The opera begins with the melodious and lofty Communion motif. M 72   *Gy. K.*

Wagner and the "Bühnenweihfestspiel"

Late in life (after 1872) Wagner preferred to refer to all his music dramas composed after →*Lohengrin* as "Bühnenfestspiele," or "stage festival plays." *Parsifal* was

Parsifal, set design by Ludwig Sievert for the production by Paul Legband, Stadttheater, Freiburg 1913 (TWS).
One wonders whether this neo-Romantic set design from Ludwig Sievert's first great period could ever be achieved on stage. The image is a reflection of the heart-felt music Wagner wrote for the world of the Grail and its close relationship with nature (Act I, Scene 1).

described as a "Bühnenweihfestspiel," which is translated both as "festival play for the consecration of a stage" and "sacred stage festival play," the latter perhaps referring to the liturgical Grail scenes in Acts I and III. Wagner died only six months after the première and was unable to and perhaps would not have wanted to prevent the mystification of the work by his admirers. On the contrary, he emphasized the exceptional nature of *Parsifal* among stage works by granting exclusive performance rights to Bayreuth for a period of 30 years and by forbidding applause after the first act, as if his last music drama were a type of ritual or ceremony. However, his strictures could not prevent a "theft" of the Grail: in 1903 *Parsifal* was incorporated into the repertory of the Metropolitan Opera in New York. Although many aspects of the work still puzzle us today, the composer gave several hints in his essay *Religion und Kunst* (*Religion and Art*, 1880) that help to elucidate his enigmatic description of the work. According to Wagner, in times when religion loses its potency as a refuge and expression for the soul, art is able to take over its functions. Through the use of symbols a work of art can make true and credible what in religion is merely stated. Christian as well as Buddhist symbols are at play in *Parsifal*, and Schopenhauerian thought (→*Tristan and Isolde*) was also an important influence. As in the *Ring* cycle, Wagner created his own mythology in *Parsifal* a parable of European civilization threatened with destruction.

Parsifal, production photograph with Toni Krämer (Parsifal) and Matthias Hölle (Gurnemanz), production Götz Friedrich, sets and costumes Günther Uecker, conductor Silvio Varviso, Württembergisches Staatstheater, Stuttgart 1976 (photograph 1993).
Parsifal (from behind) and Gurnemanz. The all-knowing prophet recognizes the redeemer, and in a moving monologue tells him of the miracle of Good Friday. If Parsifal were God or God's son, Gurnemanz's story at this point would be entirely redundant; it is because it has to be recounted that Parsifal is identifiable as a man.

"Good Friday Magic"

What is the meaning of the so-called "Good Friday Magic"? In April 1857, not on Good Friday itself but in a Good Friday spirit, and inspired by a magnificent spring day, Wagner sketched out a drama. This was the first prose draft of *Parsifal*. The composer had been preoccupied with the material since 1845, when he first read Wolfram von Eschenbach's epic poem *Parsifal*. But what motivated him to combine the beauties of nature, Christ's death, and the "redemption of the redeemer"? This same question is asked of Gurnemanz by Parsifal (who has returned in the guise of a black knight), as he beholds the beautiful meadow full of flowers before him: … when all creation, all that blooms, that breathes, lives and lives anew, should only sigh and sorrow". The wise old man answers him: "All creatures rejoice to see the Savior's sign of grace … Himself, the Savior crucified, they see not: and so they raise their eyes to man redeemed, the man set free from sin, set free from terror". These pages of the score are Wagner's greatest musical achievement, full of warmth and intimacy, with delicate, pastel-like instrumentation. It is spring music, composed in the fall of a great life. →*M 77*   *Gy. K*

Parsifal, set design (Act III) by Leo Pasetti, Munich 1924 (TWS).
The name Parsifal is open to quite profound interpretations. In the original French text by Chrétien de Troyes (12th century) the hero's name was "Parceval" ("he who passes through the valley"), in reference to the hero's long wanderings and odysseys. Wolfram von Eschenbach (Wagner's principal source) adopted this form at the beginning of the 13th century with the name "Parzival." Wagner retained this spelling for two decades before settling on "Parsifal" in 1877. The composer had come across a more convincing interpretation of the name for his drama in the work of the prominent philosopher and aesthetic theorist, Joseph Görres: Fal-parsi (Arabic) = the foolish, pure one; Parsi-fal = pure, or holy, fool. The set designer Leo Pasetti depicts Parsifal as "Parceval" in this striking image: his holy fool passes finally through the valley and into the realm of the Grail (at the beginning of Act III). The attractive image also betrays signs of the passage from winter to spring.

Parsifal, Kundry, set design by Ewald Dülberg, Hamburg 1914 (TWS). "Never do I good; I seek peace, ah! but peace. Oh, that no one would wake me!" (Act I).

Kundry

Kundry is one of the most remarkable female figures not only in Wagner's operas but in the entire operatic repertory. She leads a schizophrenic existence, at times behaving like an animal, crawling along the ground, humble in her service of the knights of the Grail, at times obedient to Klingsor, in whose company she appears as a desirable woman, of great erotic allure. The musical motif representing her as the suffering, subservient creature is mysterious, like the gentle rise and fall of a sigh. M 73

Kundry, who had mocked Christ on the way to his crucifixion and was condemned to wander for eternity,

73. Motif of Kundry as a Servant

74. Kiss Motif (Kundry and Parsifal)

is the female counterpart of the Wandering Jew (and thus related to the Flying Dutchman). She seeks rest and yearns for salvation but is ceaselessly driven across the world. As servant of the Grail she represents a type of Eve figure, subordinate to her male masters. As a man-dominating woman of "devilish beauty" she is a variation of the fallen angel. Kundry is all-knowing. She knows about Parsifal's childhood and her seductive powers consist in bringing the young hero to a state of self-knowledge. Through Kundry Parsifal comes to know and understand his hitherto meaningless past. Kundry's kiss is of great importance for him, for in this

Parsifal, Martha Mödl as Kundry, Bayreuth 1953. Martha Mödl was an outstanding Kundry in the "New Bayreuth" era. This photograph conveys the essence of this sleeping, dreaming, and knowing figure, who is nevertheless intent on oblivion. In the period during which Wieland and Wolfgang Wagner held sway at Bayreuth, the faces of the singers – and therefore the souls of the Wagnerian heroes – moved ever further into the foreground.

moment – "made wise through compassion" – he becomes aware of his mission. Wagner expresses the kiss in musical form through the above-mentioned Kundry motif, but here he altered the short sigh to make it a long, ardent, and erotic melody, whose style (like the whole of the Kundry-Parsifal scene) is strongly reminiscent of the music from *Tristan*. M 74

While he was working on the piece Wagner explained the meaning of Kundry's kiss: "The serpent of Paradise and its tempting promise: Adam and Eve gained knowledge. They came to know their own sin. The human race had to atone for this consciousness in misery and shame, until we were redeemed by Christ, who took the sins of humanity upon himself … The inner sense can only be divined by the visionary. Adam and Eve: Christ. What would happen if we were to add to these: Amfortas and Kundry: Parsifal? But with great circumspection!" (7 September 1865).   Gy. K.

Flowermaidens in waltz time

Wagner himself described exactly what sort of creatures Klingsor's maidens are: "Enchanted maidens, blossoms in Klingsor's bewitched garden (tropical), they burst forth in the spring and live until the fall in order to ensnare the heroes of the Grail through their youth and loveliness." In the history of *Parsifal* interpretation, these "enchanted maidens" have come to be known as Wagner's "flowermaidens." These flowermaidens are required to sing and dance in a slow waltz melody in triple time. In the year of the opera's composition the waltz was at the height of its popularity and was considered the embodiment of intoxication and oblivion. Ewald Dülberg's set design (below) captured this neo-Romantic current. M 75

75. Waltz Melody of the Flowermaidens

Komm!   Komm!   Hol -der   Kna - be!

Parsifal, Hans Hotter as Gurnemanz, Bayreuth.
Hans Hotter was as convincing in the role of Gurnemanz as he was in that of Amfortas – bravura achievements of interpretive skill.

Below
Parsifal, Klingsor's flowermaidens, set design by Ewald Dülberg, Hamburg 1914 (TWS). "Are you then flowers?" – an astonished Parsifal asks the flowermaidens. According to Wagner's stage directions, the flowermaidens' faces were to be veiled. They were to form a collective image of sex that is devoid of feeling.

Continuation and completion

After the pessimistic conclusion to →*Twilight of the Gods* (which ends in a catastrophe for mankind), Wagner wanted to demonstrate the possibility of salvation with equally great dramatic power. In this sense, *Parsifal* was a continuation and a completion of his entire *oeuvre*. It is important to bear in mind, however, that Wagner had been refining his thoughts about *Parsifal* since 1845 – that is, since the time of the composition of →*Tannhäuser* and →*Lohengrin*. Fear of a global cataclysm and the hope of finally breaking the power of evil were for decades parallel threads in his creative thought. *Parsifal* is a positive version of →*Tristan* and →*The Ring of the Nibelung*. The links between *Parsifal* and Wagner's other music dramas range from the obvious to the obscure. A number of dramatic motifs, as well as the musical atmosphere in general, indicate a relationship with →*Lohengrin* (the world of the Grail, and the swan motif), while the Grail theme connects it with the journey to Rome in →*Tannhäuser*. Furthermore, the protagonists of *Parsifal* are foreshadowed by figures in earlier operas – Kundry by Venus,

Parsifal by the young Siegfried, and Klingsor by Hagen. Kundry's kiss recalls the kiss with which Siegfried rouses Brünnhilde from her slumbers (→*Siegfried*, Act III), and the suffering, bleeding Amfortas recalls the dying Tristan (→*Tristan and Isolde*, Act III). In the first sketch for his *Parsifal* drama (1857) Wagner intended to have the wandering Parsifal appear at Tristan's sick-bed, and use the magical power of his spear to heal Tristan's wound (his unquenched desire). This would have underlined the fact that both Tristan and Amfortas were heroes who had been brought low by enchanted love and who were therefore forced to suffer the same fate. In the event, however, salvation through Parsifal was reserved for Amfortas alone. In 1879 Wagner made a profound comment to his wife Cosima: he claimed that Siegfried would have had to grow up into a Parsifal figure in order to redeem the suffering Wotan, but that he lacked "a messenger." In other words, no one had ever taught Siegfried about his past (as Kundry taught Parsifal), thereby instilling in him a sense of his own mission. The similarities between Siegfried's and

Parsifal, photograph from the production by Peter Mussbach, conductor Sylvain Cambreling, Théâtre Royal de la Monnaie, Brussels 1989.
The knights of the Grail demand their ritual meal – and the king must perform his duty.

Parsifal, set design by Heinz Grete, Mannheim 1924 (TWS).
Wagner found the artistic motifs for the temple of the Grail in the magnificent cathedral in Siena in 1880. These were then incorporated into the set for the first production. This tradition of set design has proved remarkably durable in productions of *Parsifal*.

Parsifal's origins are striking. Both grow up in the natural world, apart from mankind; both are "fatherless" (the children of nature alone); and both are fearless and lacking in knowledge. Siegfried and Parsifal also make their entrances in much the same way – Siegfried captures a bear and Parsifal kills a swan – and both are characterized by the musical motif of a horn call. However, whereas Siegfried ultimately fails, Parsifal emerges victorious. Made wise through compassion, he is able to overcome his limitations. *M 76* This crucial difference between the two is symbolized by the contrast between the young Siegfried's forging of the sword Nothung and the young Parsifal's destruction of his bow.

Gy. K.

76. Parsifal's Victory Motif

77. Good Friday Magic

Ludwig II, colored photograph, gift from the king to Richard Wagner (Richard-Wagner-Museum, Bayreuth).
Anyone who has visited Ludwig's daring Neuschwanstein Castle in Hohenschwangau (Bavaria) will know to what extent Wagner's operas influenced the world of this highly cultured king. Ludwig II was the first Wagnerian. A personal friend of the composer, he liked to identify with several of Wagner's characters. Built at the same time as the Bayreuth Festspielhaus, Ludwig's castle at Neuschwanstein was constructed in an attempt to recreate the "castle of the Grail." The Hall of Song at Neuschwanstein is an exact copy of the Hall of Song in the castle at Wartburg, and on the pond of the castle's grotto the king liked to glide about in a boat shaped like a swan. Frescoes and paintings depicted scenes from →Tannhäuser, →Lohengrin, and →Parsifal. The young king was declared mentally ill in 1886, three years after Wagner's death, and died in a mysterious suicide in the same year.

The idea for a festival hall

The idea of building a festival hall, a novelty in the theater history of the modern era, was much like those brilliant initial ideas which sparked Wagner's great music dramas in that it took several decades of planning and preparation to achieve. While still in exile in Switzerland in 1850 – the year in which →Lohengrin was first performed – and seemingly without a hope of ever realizing his plans, Wagner had proposed erecting a temporary wooden theatre on a field near Zürich. Here, he would stage three consecutive performances of *The Death of Siegfried* (→*The Ring of the Nibelung*: the genesis of universal drama) before burning the score and demolishing the theatre – a concept similar to the artistic "happenings" of the late twentieth century. Wagner came back to this plan 12 years later, and it was at this time that he settled on the fundamental plan for his music theater of the future. The theater would have a lowered orchestra pit, in which the musicians would be "invisible," and the auditorium would rise in front of the stage like an amphitheater. The first performance in the Bayreuth Festspielhaus took place in 1876, 26 years after Wagner's first thoughts on the subject.

From plans to realization

1859: Wagner meets his most important patron, Ludwig II, who was then 14 years old. Ludwig would become king of Bavaria in 1864.

1864: The king plans the Wagner theater as a monumental structure to be situated close to his residence in Munich.

1864–65: Wagner includes his old Dresden friend Gottfried Semper (→*Rienzi*) in the project. The composer requires the testing of various technical and acoustic aspects in a temporary theater. King Ludwig approves both these developments.

1866–67: At Ludwig's request Semper prepares a model for the king's monumental building, but does not receive his fee.

1868–69: The project proves expensive and therefore politically controversial. After long delays, Semper withdraws. The project is temporarily unable to proceed.

1871: Richard and Cosima find the ideal place for the opera house: Bayreuth. Wagner is offered the eighteenth-century margrave's opera house (built in 1748 by Giuseppe Galli-Bibiena) but decides to build an entirely new structure.

1872: The foundation stone of the Festspielhaus is laid on the "Green Hill" on Wagner's 59th birthday (22 March). The theater is built to a design by Otto Brückwald (1841–1904), making use of ideas by Semper and in consultation with the expert stage technician Karl Brandt (1828–81). The construction takes four years.

1876: The Festspielhaus opens in August with a complete performance of the *Ring* cycle, conducted by Hans Richter, the founding father of the "Bayreuth conductors." Guests include Liszt, Grieg, Bruckner, Tchaikovsky, Saint-Saëns, Nietzsche, Tolstoy, Emperor Wilhelm I, and – of course – Ludwig II of Bavaria.

The Bayreuth Festspielhaus, auditorium. Wagner regarded the following as important prerequisites for his new theater:
• seats were to be all of the same quality with equally good viewing (Ludwig II, however, ordered boxes built for the nobility, though these remained unobtrusive);
• lighting in the auditorium should be of the sort that could be dimmed (a novelty in Wagner's day), in order to encourage the audience to concentrate and focus their attention on events on stage;
• illusions of perspective on the stage should enable the audience to gain a sense of depth and distance;
• the orchestra pit should form a kind of mystical chasm between the stage and the audience; such a gap would mean the attention of the audience could not be distracted by the musicians.

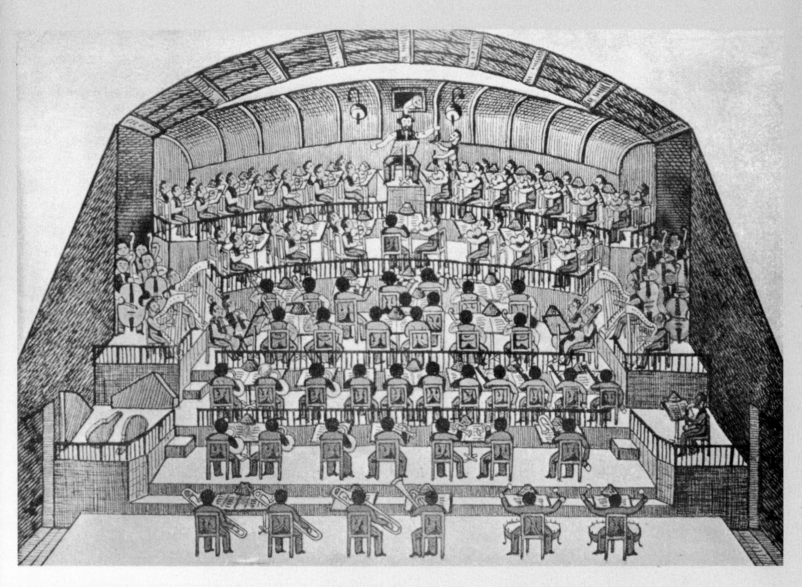

Orchestra pit at Bayreuth, drawing by Heinrich Venzl, 1882.

The orchestra pit

During rehearsals for →*Parsifal* in the Festspielhaus in 1882, first clarinetist Heinrich Venzl produced an extremely valuable document: a drawing of the orchestra pit. Lowering and covering the orchestra meant that its sound was more muted and homogeneous, and that the singers' voices would therefore carry more easily from the stage to the auditorium. The drawing shows the new Wagnerian arrangement of the orchestra. The musicians were now distributed over six podia, with the loudest instruments (trombones, tubas, percussion) positioned at the bottom and the violins at the top. Between them were the trumpets, horns, contrabassoon (second row from the bottom), horns, woodwind (third row from the bottom), cellos and flutes (fourth row), and second violins (fifth row). The harps and double basses were placed at the sides. The sketch also shows Wagner leaning down through a hatch to give instructions to the conductor, Franz Fischer. Franz Strauss, the father of Richard Strauss, is depicted among the horn players (second from the left in the third row from the bottom).

The Bayreuth Festspielhaus, engraving by Otto Brückwald, 1872–76
(Deutsches Theatermuseum, Munich).
The theater of the future was to be functional rather than palatial. Everything should be subordinated to the work on stage. Members of the public were no longer to go to the opera merely to amuse themselves. The new opera house would be a place of pilgrimage, and the performances revelations of genius. Thousands still make this pilgrimage to Bayreuth every year.

The heroic age

Impatient to see *The Ring of the Nibelung* on stage, Ludwig II ordered – against Wagner's wishes – performances of *The Rhinegold* and *The Valkyrie* in Munich in 1869 and 1870 respectively.

The entire *Ring* cycle was performed for the first time at the newly built Bayreuth Festspielhaus in 1876. This Herculean artistic feat ended in financial disaster, as a result of which festival activities were temporarily suspended. The doors of the Festspielhaus reopened for the première of *Parsifal* in 1882. In the meantime the impresario Angelo Neumann had won the right to perform *The Ring* outside Bavaria. He presented the cycle to great acclaim in Leipzig in 1878, in Berlin in 1881 (in Wagner's presence), in London in 1882, and on a tour of several European cities in 1883. In 1889 *The Ring* was first performed to audiences in New York, and by the turn of the century it had conquered the world's stages.

Stage interpretations

The style of the original productions of Wagner's operas, directed by Wagner himself, remained standard at Bayreuth for many years.

Wagner's son Siegfried was the first to begin to modify this tradition in accordance with twentieth-century developments in staging. New interpretations were more easily achieved outside Bayreuth, for instance in Vienna, where, during Gustav Mahler's time, the set designer Alfred Roller was highly successful in putting into practice the reforming ideas of the Swiss theorist, Adolphe Appia. In Bayreuth a new artistic era began under the director Heinz Tietjen and his set designer Emil Preetorius, an era that coincided with the rise of National Socialism.

Wagner's daughter-in-law Winifred, who assumed the direction of the festival after Siegfried's death in 1930, was a close friend of Hitler, and for many years the dictator and his henchmen basked in the glory of the festival.

Hitler himself was not opposed to reforms at Bayreuth. It was at his request that *Parsifal* appeared in a new production with sets by Alfred Roller in 1934 – the first since its première in 1882. Even the rooms in which the Nazi leader stayed during the festival were modernized, traditional ostentation being replaced, according to Wagner's great-granddaughter Nike Wagner, by the "design of power." This period also witnessed the exodus of a number of renowned artists, among them the conductor Arturo Toscanini, who refused to perform before Germany's new fascist rulers.

The history of "New Bayreuth" after the Second World War began in 1951 with a clearing out of the dubious Wagnerian legacy that had been misused by the Nazis. Wagner's grandsons Wieland and Wolfgang Wagner, who had been directing outside Bavaria in the 1930s and 1940s, created a radically new concept in staging. Their interpretations were influenced by psychoanalysis, prominent stylistic elements in their productions being the sloping circular stage and a bold use of lighting.

Wieland Wagner produced *The Ring* in 1951 and 1965, Wolfgang in 1960 and 1970. Outside Bayreuth there were also signs of new directions in staging and musical interpretation, notably in the productions by Günther Rennert (sets Helmut Jürgens) in Hamburg in 1956 and Herbert von Karajan (sets Günther Schneider-Siemssen) in Vienna and Salzburg.

The sculptor Fritz Wotruba created an archaic design for the production by Gustav Rudolf Sellner at the Deutsche Oper in Berlin in 1967 (conductor Lorin Maazel).

Joachim Herz's bold but reasonable idea of incorporating elements of the society of Wagner's day into the mythology of *The Ring* (Leipzig 1973–76, sets Rudolph Heinrich) was followed by Patrice Chéreau's remarkable and controversial production in 1976 for the 100th anniversary of the cycle's première. It was, so to speak, a *Ring* seen from a French perspective: light, witty, relaxed, and lucid in all its depictions of emotion, of joy as well as grief. Critics praised as well as condemned it for its French "demystification" of Wagner.

Chéreau's production began a new chapter in the staging of the work, not least for the "chamber music" concept of conductor Pierre Boulez, which contributed to the process of demystification. Patrice Chéreau rejected the transfiguring view of the central character

Parsifal, production photograph, production and sets Wieland Wagner, Bayreuth Festival 1951–73.

of Siegfried that had been adopted by Wieland Wagner, focusing not on the "child of nature," but on the violent and insensitive character conceived of by Wagner, who only gradually develops a capacity for love and compassion. Every year the modern theater brings forth abstract, modernizing, and historicizing interpretations, to all of which the innovations of set designers make an important contribution. Rudoph Heinrich, for example, portrayed Valhalla as Wall Street in a production at Leipzig, and Chéreau's set designer Richard Peduzzi presented the Rhine as "tamed" by a massive dam. By using a collage technique, Erich Wonder in Munich (production Nikolaus Lenhoff) and

Axel Manthey in Frankfurt (production Ruth Berghaus) set *The Ring* in a context rich in allusive possibilities, one that transcended a specific time or place. Peter Sykora designed a "time tunnel" – a visual evocation of an apocalyptic atmosphere – for the director Götz Friedrich in Berlin.

The most prominent directors (and not only opera directors) are proud of their *Ring* productions: Götz Friedrich, Luca Ronconi, Peter Stein, Peter Hall, Ruth Berghaus, Otto Schenk, Nikolaus Lehnhoff, Harry Kupfer. Everyone wants to sport *The Ring* on his or her finger at least once. Wagner's magical powers, it appears, are undiminished.   S. N. / J. J.

The Valkyrie, set design by Adolphe Appia for a production at the Staatsoper in Munich in 1923 (TWS).
Together with Edward Gordon Craig, Adolphe Appia was one of the most important reformers of theatrical practice at the beginning of the 20th century. His innovations began with set designs and were developed in great detail in his theoretical works. His first revolutionary designs for Bayreuth in 1892 were rejected, and were not revived again until they were adopted by Wieland Wagner. His design for *The Valkyrie* seems to anticipate Fritz Wotruba's design for *The Ring*.

<W>eber was a true master in all areas of music and a genius in the world of theater.

The Freeshooter, set design by Simon Quaglio, Munich 1822 (TWS). Romantic set designs depict the Wolf's Glen in the manner of a painting by the 19th-century German painter Caspar David Friedrich. *The Freeshooter* is a masterpiece, a fairy tale yet also realistic, refined but with a folk quality. The story is taken from the criminal trial of an 18-year-old youth in Bohemia in the year 1710: "That on St. Abdon's Day this boy did, while naked, cast 63 bullets at a crossroads with a huntsman, in the course of which infernal spirits manifested themselves." In 1810 Apel and Laun edited a book of ghost stories, the *Gespensterbuch,* in which this court transcript could be found as *Volkssage vom Freischütz* (*The Legend of the Freeshooter*). Weber read the story that same year.

Weber, Carl Maria von

b. 18 November 1786 in Eutin
d. 5 June 1826 in London

As a boy Weber led an itinerant life with his father's small drama troupe. His teachers during this time included Michael Haydn in Salzburg and Abbé Vogler in Vienna. He was appointed conductor at the theater in Breslau in 1804, and then worked for a short time at Württemberg (1806) and Stuttgart (1807). He became opera director in Prague in 1813, and conductor of the Dresden court theater in 1817. As opera director he made changes to theatrical practice, demanding intensive rehearsals and the training of the chorus. He also sought to establish an operatic repertory. He became the champion of German national opera with the successful première of *Der Freischütz* (1821), which was immediately recognized as a viable alternative to French and Italian opera. With his two following operas – *Euryanthe* and *Oberon* – Weber opened up new horizons for later composers, especially →Richard Wagner.

Works: Stage works: *Peter Schmoll und seine Nachbarn* (*Peter Schmoll and his Neighbors*) (1802), *Silvana* (1810), *Abu Hassan* (1811), *Der Freischütz* (*The Freeshooter*) (1821), *Euryanthe* (1823), *Oberon, or The Elf King's Oath* (1826); orchestral works (symphonies, overtures, concertos), choral works, works for piano, chamber music, songs.

The Freeshooter

Der Freischütz

Romantische Oper in three acts

Libretto: Friedrich Kind.
Première: 18 June 1821, Berlin (Königliches Schauspielhaus).
Characters: Ottokar, a sovereign prince (Bar), Cuno, a hereditary forester (B), Agathe, his daughter (S), Aennchen, her relative (S), Caspar, an assistant forester (B), Max, an assistant forester (T), a Hermit (B), Kilian, a wealthy peasant (Bar), Four Bridesmaids (4 S), Samiel, the Black Huntsman (spoken); hunters, peasants, spirits, bridesmaids, attendants (chorus).
Setting: Bohemia, at the end of the Thirty Years War.

Synopsis

"An old forester in the service of the prince wishes to see his best huntsman, Max, married to his daughter Agathe, and to pass on to him his position as chief forester. The prince agrees to the match, but an ancient law requires that Max must first pass a test of marksmanship. The hunter Caspar also has his eye on Agathe, but he is already in league with the devil. Max, usually an excellent shot, is unable to hit anything in the period leading up to his trial. In desperation, he allows himself to be persuaded by Caspar to cast what are said to be magic bullets. Six of these bullets will hit their targets, but the seventh belongs to the devil. Agathe is to be the target of this seventh shot … Heaven decides otherwise, however, and at the marksmanship trial both Agathe and Caspar fall to the ground – the latter Satan's victim but the former only from fright. Why this happens is explained in the play, and the whole story ends happily." (Weber in a letter to his fiancée.)

Act I

Scene 1: Outside an inn in the Bohemian forest. Agathe, the forester's daughter, has chosen the huntsman Max for her husband, rejecting an older suitor, Caspar. But Max will only be able to win Agathe's hand – and her father's office – if he passes a test of marksmanship. The closer he gets to the day of his trial the less skillful he appears to become, until finally he seems incapable of hitting anything at all. The peasant Kilian beats Max in a competition, and Max is the object of ridicule. Why, the people ask, should this old custom even be necessary any more? Feigning friendship, Caspar offers to help his desperate colleague cast magic bullets. Six of them, he says, will hit their targets without fail, but the seventh belongs to the Evil One, the "Black Huntsman" Samiel. A human life will be the payment demanded by Samiel in return for this seventh and final shot. Caspar himself is getting close to the day when he will have to repay Samiel with his own life. If he can persuade Max to agree to use the magic bullets, the seventh will take Agathe's life and Caspar will be saved. Caspar lends Max his rifle in order to prove to him that the magic bullets work. High up in the clouds, far out of range, a bird is circling. Max fires, and a huge eagle falls to the ground. Max agrees to accompany Caspar to the fearful Wolf's Glen at midnight to cast the magic bullets for his marksmanship trial.

Act II

Scene 1: The forester's house. Agathe has visited a hermit, who gave her white roses and warned her of an unnamed danger. A picture of an ancestor has indeed fallen off the wall on top of her, but although it could have killed her she is only slightly injured. Nevertheless, Agathe is worried. Even her young relative Aennchen's attempts to cheer her up are unsuccessful. Where can Max be, she wonders? Will he bring with him evidence of his skill as a hunter, to give her hope for the approaching trial? When the man she so longs to see finally returns, Agathe is horrified by the dead eagle he brings with him, rather than relieved to find that he has regained his skill as a marksman.

Scene 2: The Wolf's Glen at night. Assisted by Max and in the presence of Samiel, Caspar casts the magic bullets. Around them rages an infernal hunt. Max receives a warning from two apparitions – one of his dead mother, the other of his fiancée Agathe.

Act III

Scene 1: The forest, daytime. Max has used three of the magic bullets in order to demonstrate his skill to Prince Ottokar; he continues to miss every shot with ordinary bullets. He begs Caspar to give him one of his three bullets, but Caspar refuses. Max must save the seventh bullet for the trial.

Scene 2: Agathe's room in the forester's house. Agathe has had a dream in which she saw herself transformed into a white dove. Max fired at her and she fell, but was suddenly changed back to her human shape and saw a great black bird of prey writhing in agony. But this is not the only ill omen of the day. When Agathe opens the box containing her bridal wreath she finds a funeral wreath. The bridesmaids – even the cheeky Aennchen – are horrified, and Agathe is distraught. Courageously, Agathe has the white roses given her by the hermit woven into a new bridal wreath.

Scene 3: The forest. Prince Ottokar gives the sign for Max to begin the trial. The prince points to a white dove and orders Max to fire at it. At that moment Agathe rushes up, crying: "Don't shoot. I am the dove!" But it is too late – Max has already discharged his weapon, and both Agathe and Caspar fall to the ground. But Agathe is accompanied by her protector, the hermit. She lives, and Caspar dies, and Samiel comes to fetch his tribute. Max confesses his misdeeds to the prince, who at first orders exile but then places Max's fate in the hands of the hermit. The hermit decides to allow mercy to prevail over justice: trials of marksmanship are to end, and Max is given permission to marry Agathe after a year. _S. N._

The Freeshooter, photograph from a production by Christof Nel, sets Axel Manthey, Oper Frankfurt 1983.
This is a famous scene from an opera rich in archetypal situations: the bridesmaids (right) want to adorn Agathe (seated) with her bridal wreath; instead, she finds a funeral wreath in the box. Even the impish Aennchen (left) is shocked.

The scene in the Wolf's Glen: both Romantic and modern

In the scene in the Wolf's Glen (Act II, final scene) Weber's bleak vision of the stage (as described in the libretto) is reinforced by the somber tone of the music, which is created through the sustained and unusually deep notes of the clarinets and the tremolo of the strings. After the remarkable dialogue between Caspar (sung) and Samiel (spoken), Max arrives and the casting of the bullets begins. The recipe consists of lead, powdered glass from broken church windows, mercury, three bullets that have already found their targets, the right eye of a hoopoe, and the left eye of a lynx – not to mention an incantation pronounced by Caspar in a short section of melodrama. At the casting of each bullet there is a response: the appearance of a black boar, the sound of dogs barking, a rattling noise, the crack of a whip, the clattering of horses' hooves, and so forth, all of which are depicted by the orchestra in short motifs. The only melody in the traditional sense of the word occurs at the appearance of evil. M2 Weber had the brilliant idea of constructing this scene from only four keys: F sharp minor, C minor, A minor, and E flat major, which derive from Samiel's musical visiting card (the diminished seventh A, C, E flat, F sharp M1). This is his territory and it is his hour.

The Freeshooter, Ludwig Hofmann (1895–1963) as Caspar, 1918.
Here Caspar is played as the incarnation of evil.

Below
The Freeshooter, set design by Ewald Dülberg for the production by Dr. Heyn, conductor Alexander von Zemlinsky, Krolloper Berlin 1928 (TWS).
This design depicts the Wolf's Glen not in a Romantic or illustrative manner but rather as an existential site of danger and decision.

Heaven and hell - polarized in music

The structure of *The Freeshooter* is quite logical. Earth, heaven, and hell are characterized by different keys and thereby contrasted. This idea was based on the old system of key symbolism, in which the minor keys with flats were regarded as dark and gloomy, and the major keys with sharps as bright and pure. Samiel, who represents evil, has no single key: he is characterized by a diminished seventh chord – A, C, E flat, F sharp *M 1* – which was thought highly dissonant in Weber's day. Samiel is provided with a melody, in C minor, only once; this occurs at the climax of the bullet casting, when he is triumphant as the Black Huntsman. *M 2*

The second part of Max's great solo scene, in which he blasphemes and comes close to embracing evil, is also in C minor. *M 3*

Caspar's revenge aria is in D minor, a key that relates him to Samiel, his master. Agathe and Aennchen, on the other hand, sing their charming duet (at the beginning of Act II) in A major. During her evening prayer, Agathe raises her eyes to God, as an expression of which the key changes to E major. *M 4* (Agathe's second prayer in A flat major is a pendant to her first aria. *M 5*)

The most extreme of these heavenly keys – a thanksgiving in B major – is reserved for the hermit, God's representative, when he pronounces judgment on Max. *M 6*

The peasants, huntsmen, Cuno and Kilian, and even Aennchen, *M 7* all have neutral, "everyday" keys: C major, G major, and D major. These characters have their feet firmly on the ground.

1. Samiel's Motif

2. Infernal Hunt

3. Max's Aria

Doch mich um -gar - nen finst - re Mächte

4. Agathe's Prayer

Lei - se, lei - se, from - me Wei - se, schwing dich auf zum Sternen - krei - se!

5. Cavatina of the Praying Agathe

6. Max's Vow

Die Zu - kunft soll __ mein Herz __ be -wäh -ren, stets hei - lig sei __ mir Recht __ und Pflicht.

7. Aennchen's Arietta (Polonaise)

Kommt ein schlanker Bursch ge - gan - gen, blond von Lo - cken o-der braun

The Freeshooter, production photograph with Beatrice Niehoff (Agathe), Barbara Bonney (Aennchen), Gerold Scheder (Caspar), Walter Raffeiner (Max), production Christof Nel, sets Axel Manthey, Oper Frankfurt 1983.
The compromise negotiated in the final scene is presented by a giant hand as if on a plate: Max is given another chance. There was a break with the Romanticizing tradition of *Der Freischütz* productions at the beginning of the 1980s, and it was at this time that Axel Manthey (1945–95) gained a reputation as an important set designer.

A postwar piece

At the time of its première in Berlin in 1821 *The Freeshooter* was politically relevant in a number of ways. The work marked the end of the domination of the German stage by Italian opera, a goal towards which Weber had directed all his musical and literary endeavors. At the same time, *The Freeshooter* is a postwar play, in terms of both its subject matter and the period in which it was composed. The story is set shortly after the Thirty Years War, a conflict in which Caspar had served as a mercenary. The end of the war left him – like so many others – without a livelihood, as a result of which he sold his soul to the devil. He is not so much an evil character as a belated victim of war. *The Freeshooter* was composed just a few years after the Battle of the Nations at Leipzig (1813), which, rather than bringing the freedom that people hoped for, led to renewed feudal sectarianism and strengthened the forces of reaction. Weber was among the many who had hoped for liberty, and had composed patriotic choral works in the battle's wake. A chorus of a similar and yet quite different nature occurs in *The Freeshooter*, sung by the prince's huntsmen. *M 8*

Most of the numbers in this opera became extremely popular: Kilian's mocking song, the chorus of laughing peasants, the *ländler* outside the tavern, *M 9* Caspar's drinking song (given a strident military coloring by a small flute), the song of the bridesmaids, *M 10* as well as Aennchen's polonaise. →*M 7*

The Freeshooter, photograph from the production by Günter Krämer, sets Andreas Reinhardt, conductor Rolf Reuter, Komische Oper, Berlin 1989.
The Wolf's Glen presented in a completely different light – as a place in which the individual is threatened by the demands of his society (here, huntsmen of every type) and the age in which he lives.

Left
The Freeshooter, photograph from the production by Christof Nel, sets Axel Manthey, Oper Frankfurt 1983.
Max finds himself in a hopeless situation: he has fired all his magic bullets and Caspar refuses him any further help. The wall is a metaphor for his desperate plight.

The Freeshooter, Henriette Sontag (1805–54) as Agathe, illustration by N.L. Gosse/S.W. Reynolds, Vienna 1825.

"Delicious" music

Weber's music for *The Freeshooter* constitutes a culinary delight for the ears, serving up dishes of the most varied kinds. Extended sung scenes (such as that for Agathe and Max) are followed by strophic songs (such as the song of mockery, the chorus of laughing peasants, the drinking song, the song of the bridesmaids, and the chorus of hunters). There is a dance (the *ländler*) and a dance-like aria in the polonaise style that was so popular at the beginning of the nineteenth century (Aennchen). The scenes of melodrama (the Wolf's Glen) seem astonishingly modern; indeed, the whole opera sounds fresh and elemental. The orchestra with its instrumental solos is as important as the vocal parts. Ever since *The Freeshooter*, horns have been equated with the German forest, though here the forest is not only an idyllic image but also a projection of the subconscious, of impending anxiety and conflict. *M 11* The sound of the horn is a symbol of the hunt, but also of longing (post horn), an expression of hope, as it is with Agathe. *M 12*

Weber provided the praying figure of Agathe with a solo cello (cavatina), while Max is characterized by the clarinet (Weber's favorite instrument). *M 13*

The musical traits of Aennchen (allegedly a musical portrait of Weber's fiancée, the singer Caroline Brand) are performed by an oboe (polonaise) and viola (romance). The flute is given an important role in the speech by the hermit (finale) representing the victory of human wisdom and divine justice (a reference to Mozart's → *The Magic Flute*).

Opposite
The Freeshooter, production photograph with Günter Neumann (Max) and members of the chorus of the Komische Oper, production by Günter Krämer, sets Andreas Reinhardt, conductor Rolf Reuter, Komische Oper Berlin, 1989.
Max blames dark anonymous forces for his missing his target and losing Agathe. But the staging of this scene reveals the real reason for his distress: the poor huntsman has been driven on by the mob, represented by soldiers from various epochs.

8. Horn Melody (Chorus of Huntsmen)

9. *Ländler*

10. Folk Song

Wir win-den dir den Jung-fern-kranz mit veil-chen-blau-er Sei-de

11. Horn Motif: the Forest (Overture)

12. Melody of Hope (Agathe's Aria)

Him-mel, - nimm des ___ Dan-kes Zäh-ren - für dies Pfand ___ der Hoff-nung an!

13. Max, the Good Huntsman (Aria, Act I)

Euryanthe, Wilhelmine Schröder-Devrient (1804–60) as Euryanthe and Mathias Schuster as Adolar.
The desolate mountain setting of Act III represents the alienation of the lovers. It is, therefore, as much an internal space as an external setting, an aspect of the opera that is mirrored by the music. The sad, lamenting melody for bassoon and flute is one of Weber's most brilliant inventions. *M 14*

Euryanthe

Grosse heroisch-romantische Oper in three acts

Libretto: Helmina von Chézy.
Première: 25 October 1823, Vienna (Kärntnertor-theater).

Characters: King Louis VI of France (B), Adolar, Count of Nevers (T), Euryanthe of Savoy, his betrothed (S), Lysiart, Count of Forest (Bar), Eglantine of Puiset, the daughter of a rebel (Ms), Bertha (S), Rudolf (T); ladies, noblemen, knights, hunters, countryfolk (chorus).
Setting: Préméry and Nevers, c. 1110.

Euryanthe, production photograph with Jürgen Freier (Lysiart) and Magdaléna Hayóssyová (Euryanthe), production Christian Pöppelreiter, sets Wilfried Werz, conductor Siegfried Kurz, Staatsoper Unter den Linden, Berlin 1986.
Lysiart interrupts the festivities at court and accuses Euryanthe of unfaithfulness. Christian Pöppelreiter redeemed the honor of this much-derided libretto by giving it a psychological and historicist interpretation.

Synopsis
Act I
A victory is being celebrated at the king's castle at Préméry. Adolar of Nevers is thinking longingly of his betrothed, Euryanthe. His secret rival is Lysiart, count of Forest, who is bold enough to cast aspersions on Euryanthe's fidelity. He wagers his lands against Adolar's that he can prove her unfaithful. In Nevers, Euryanthe yearns for Adolar. Eglantine, the daughter of a noble rebel, is unable to forget her father's disgrace. She is not as well disposed to Euryanthe as the latter believes, and coaxes a secret from her: when she learned her fiancé had been killed in battle, Adolar's sister Emma had committed suicide by preparing a drink made from poison hidden in a ring. Her spirit now roams eternally, seeking union with her lover, but she will only find it when the tears of an innocent and desperate girl fall on the ring. With the knowledge of this secret, which Euryanthe had vowed not to betray, Eglantine hopes to free herself.

Act II
The castle at Nevers. Lysiart arrives on a mission from the king to accompany Euryanthe to the court. He almost regrets his wager, but his hatred for Adolar gains the upper hand. He discovers Eglantine stealing the ring from Emma's grave and offers her an alliance. Eglantine agrees, but only on condition that Lysiart promises to marry her. At the court, Adolar and Euryanthe are finally reunited. Lysiart, however, accuses her of infidelity, producing the ring as proof of Euryanthe's love for him. Euryanthe is dumbstruck. Adolar considers her faithlessness to be beyond dispute. He renounces her and concedes all his lands to Lysiart.

Act III
A rocky mountain gorge. Adolar is about to kill Euryanthe and she vainly attempts to persuade him of her innocence. When they are both threatened by a snake, Euryanthe throws herself in front of it to protect her lover. Deeply shaken by this act of love, Adolar is no longer capable of killing her, but instead abandons her in the wilderness. The king and his hunting party find Euryanthe, and with her remaining strength she reveals Eglantine's treachery. The king believes her story and promises to help. Outside the castle at Nevers, his former estate, Adolar wanders distraught. He meets some peasants, who tell their former master of Eglantine's intrigues. Adolar approaches the wedding procession of Lysiart and Eglantine, and challenges Lysiart to a duel. The king intervenes, pretending that Euryanthe has died. When Eglantine triumphantly reveals her deed Lysiart stabs her, and is then led off for execution. The royal huntsmen bring in the "dead" Euryanthe. As the lovers embrace, Adolar hears a voice announcing that Emma's spirit has at last found peace.

S. N.

Euryanthe, production photograph with Elisabeth Meyer-Topsoe as Euryanthe, production Wolfgang Quetes, sets Erich Fischer, costumes Ute Frühling, conductor Christian Thielemann, Oper Nürnberg 1991. The innocent Euryanthe is tortured by the voices of her slanderers. Wolfgang Quetes saw parallels between the life of Euryanthe and that of the librettist Helmina von Chézy, who made a courageous stand against injustice in her own day, demanding compensation for war invalids and taking corrupt military officials to court (actions in which she was supported by the writer and lawyer E.T.A. Hoffmann). Quetes explained these parallels in a short self-contained drama performed during the overture.

Jewels from beginning to end

"The music of *Euryanthe* is too little known and appreciated. It is life-blood, and his most noble at that ... A chain of shining jewels from beginning to end." The words of Weber's contemporary Robert Schumann are as true today as they were when written in 1847. Posterity has not been kind to *Euryanthe*, often regarding it merely as a forerunner to Wagner's →*Lohengrin*, without recognizing its originality. It was not until the late 1980s and early 1990s that a number of outstanding productions (Staatsoper Berlin 1986, production Christian Pöppelreiter; Nuremberg 1991, production Wolfgang Quetes; London 1994, conductor Mark Elder) began to make it clear that *Euryanthe* is more than simply good music for a bad libretto. These productions demonstrated that the text refers as much to an inner world as it does an external reality, and that the plot is psychologically credible. For Weber it was important to vary the tone between the chivalrous, the festive, the idyllic, and the demonic. *Euryanthe* employs the principle of musical and theatrical ambiguity in a masterful way. Whenever the characters believe themselves to be happy or secure, the music warns of imminent danger. It was in this sense that the renowned musical aesthete Adolphe Bernhard Marx (1795–1866) called the wedding march of Act III a "stroke of genius."

S. N.

14. Melody of Loneliness (Act III)

Oberon, *or The Elf King's Oath*

Romantische Oper in three acts

Libretto: James Robinson Planché, after Christoph Martin Wieland's poem *Oberon*.
Première: 12 April 1826, London (Covent Garden).

Characters: Oberon, King of the Elves (T), Puck (A), Reiza, daughter of Haroun al Rachid (S), Sir Huon of Bordeaux, Duke of Guienne (T), Sherasmin, his squire (T), Fatima, Reiza's attendant (Ms), Two Mermaids (2 S), Namouna, Fatima's grandmother (spoken), Haroun al Rachid, Caliph of Baghdad (spoken), Babekan, a Saracen prince (spoken), Abdullah, a corsair (spoken), Almanzor, Emir of Tunis (spoken), Roshana, his wife (spoken), A Fairy (spoken), Four Saracen Slaves (spoken), Nadina, a woman from Almanzor's harem (spoken), A Negro Slave (spoken), Mesrous, leader of the harem guards (spoken), A Ship's Captain (spoken), Two Cupids (spoken), Arcon, a Greek slave of the Emir (spoken), Titania, Queen of the Fairies (spoken), Charlemagne, Emperor of the Franks (silent); fairies, ladies, knights, slaves, mermaids (chorus).

Setting: Fairyland, on the banks of the Tigris, Africa and France in medieval times.

Synopsis
Act I
Having argued with his wife Titania, Oberon has sworn to avoid her company until a mortal couple can be found who will remain true to each other through adversity. Puck is unable to find such a couple anywhere in the world, but does report on an interesting case. The knight Huon has murdered a son of Charlemagne in self-defense. The emperor is prepared to commute the death penalty, on condition that Huon kills the man who sits on the left of the caliph of Baghdad, and "kisses the caliph's daughter as his bride" – a mission that is clearly impossible. Oberon is touched by the knight's plight. By means of dreams he makes Huon fall in love with the caliph's daughter Reiza, and she with the Frankish knight. Puck then brings the knight and his squire Sherasmin before Oberon. The elf king offers Huon his support on condition that the knight swears to remain true to Reiza. Huon makes his vow and receives from Oberon a magic horn for use when danger threatens.

Act II
By chance Huon and Sherasmin find themselves at the hut of the old woman Namouna. They learn from her that Reiza has suddenly refused to marry her betrothed, the Saracen prince Babekan, having seen in a dream a European knight whom only she can love. Huon bursts in on the caliph and slays Babekan, who sits at his left-hand side. Sherasmin

renders all present immobile with a blast of the magic horn, and he and Huon make their escape with Reiza, taking with them Reiza's attendant Fatima, who has fallen in love with Sherasmin. Oberon appears and submits Reiza to a vow of loyalty. He then places a ship at their disposal. But Huon and Reiza must endure further trials. Puck orders the spirits of the sea to call up a storm, causing the ship to run aground. In a battle with pirates, Huon is overpowered and separated from Reiza, Sherasmin, and Fatima. Oberon commands Puck to transport the unconscious Huon to Reiza.

Act III
Huon finds himself in the garden of Almanzor, the emir of Tunis, where he is discovered by Sherasmin and Fatima, who have been sold to the emir as slaves. Reiza is being courted by the emir, but remains faithful to Huon. Huon receives flowers from a stranger, which he interprets as a sign of welcome from Reiza. In fact, the flowers are a gift from Roshana, the emir's jealous wife, who hopes to persuade Huon to murder her faithless husband. Huon refuses, unmoved by her attempts to seduce him. Almanzor misinterprets the situation. He orders the execution of Huon and Roshana, and when Reiza begs for mercy for Huon she too is condemned to death. At this moment of great adversity Sherasmin blows the magic horn, at which all the emir's slaves and officials begin to dance, leaving the lovers free to escape. Oberon appears with Titania, and they thank Huon and Reiza for their constancy. The lovers are also welcomed by Charlemagne.

S. N.

Oberon, set design by Otto Reigbert for the production by Walter Felsenstein, conductor Fritz Zawn, Städtische Bühnen, Cologne 1933 (TWS).
The sea evokes a typically English atmosphere – the opera was actually written for England – although the original English language version is unfortunately all too rarely performed. An exception was an excellent production in Lyon in 1985 under the musical direction of John Eliot Gardiner. The ocean – like the forest in →*The Freeshooter* – is both a friendly and a threatening force, and thus gives the work a cosmic dimension.

The year 1826 saw the first performance of *Oberon* and the composition of another piece of German "fairy music" – Felix Mendelssohn's overture for *A Midsummer Night's Dream*, a work in which the dreamlike sound of a horn was linked with the world of fairies. Weber's overture begins with three notes from Oberon's horn – the signal for a fantastic fairy-tale world to appear. *M 15*

The most original passages in the opera are those associated with this musical metaphor, such as when Huon sings of Reiza's charms *M 16* or when Reiza greets Huon from the seashore. *M 17* The horn melody and the three-note motif run throughout the entire work. On the threshold of death himself, the composer expressed a feeling of hope in an inimitable musical fashion.

Oberon, set design by Paul Wolff, Duisburg 1924/25 (TWS). Weber's fondness for oriental subject matter was revealed relatively early, in his opera *Abu Hassan* (1811). He was able to fit the colorful world of his imagination into a well-proportioned musical framework.

Oberon, production photograph with Eberhard Büchner (Oberon) and Friederike Wulff-Apelt (Puck), production Luca Ranconi, conductor Wolfgang Rennert, sets Pier Luigi Pizzi, Deutsche Staatsoper Unter den Linden, Berlin 1976.
At Oberon's command Puck keeps a lookout for Huon so as to be able to come to the knight's rescue when his ship gets into trouble on the high seas. This was almost an Italian version of a German fairy tale. A light-hearted, amusing, and poetic production was created in Berlin using the full range of stage machinery.

15. Oberon's Horn Motif (Overture)

16. Huon's Aria

Jetzt gießt sich aus ein sanf - ter Glanz auf mei - nes __ Le - bens Wo - gen - tanz

17. Reiza's Ocean Aria

Noch seh' ich die Wel - len to - ben

Weill wrote deliberately popular music, influenced by jazz, characterized by memorable melodies and striking rhythms, and at the same time finely crafted and subtly constructed.

The Threepenny Opera, poster, Berlin 1950s/1960s (TWS).
A poster from 1960 for a production at Bertolt Brecht's famous Theater am Schiffbauerdamm, directed by Erich Engel, who had directed the original production of 1928.

The Threepenny Opera

Die Dreigroschenoper

Play with music in a prologue and three acts

Libretto: Bertolt Brecht, after the libretto for *The Beggar's Opera* by John Gay and Johann Christoph Pepusch, individual texts and inspiration taken from François Villon and Karl Kraus.
Première: 31 August 1928, Berlin (Theater am Schiffbauerdamm).
Characters: Jonathan Jeremiah Peachum, head of a band of beggars (Bar), Mrs. Peachum (A), Polly, her daughter (S), Macheath (Mac the Knife), head of a band of street robbers (T), Jenny, a prostitute (S), Brown, London's chief of police (Bar), Lucy, his daughter (S), Macheath's Men (6 T and B), Filch, one of Peachum's beggars (spoken), Smith, first constable (spoken), Moritatensänger (ballad singer) (Bar); beggars, prostitutes, constables (chorus).
Setting: Soho, London.

Synopsis
Prologue

A fair in Soho. The feared and omnipresent king of thieves, Macheath, is celebrated in a ballad.

Act I

Jonathan Peachum runs a business that distributes begging licenses and provides protection to his employees in return for 50 percent of their income. Whoever refuses to cooperate or attempts to leave is punished – like Filch, who had begun to beg independently. Peachum always has plenty of troubles, and this time it's his daughter Polly, who has not returned home for the night. Polly in the meantime is celebrating her marriage to Macheath in a stable furnished with stolen goods. The chief of police, Brown, an old friend of Macheath, attends the wedding. Polly confesses to her parents that she has married Macheath. Peachum, who prefers to operate discreetly, is not pleased to find he has such a famous son-in-law. He resolves to have Macheath arrested.

Act II

Peachum's intervention forces Brown to hunt for Macheath. When Polly warns Macheath, he entrusts her with his business operations and seeks refuge in his old home, a brothel in Soho. The prostitute Jenny, one of his former employees, is bribed by Mrs. Peachum to betray him. Police chief Brown reluctantly takes his friend – a man wanted for multiple murders and theft – into custody. Brown's daughter Lucy causes a scene because Macheath had promised to marry her. When Polly visits her husband, the two women fight, but whereas Polly returns home, Lucy allows Macheath to escape.

Weill, Kurt

b. 2 March 1900 in Dessau
d. 3 April 1950 in New York

Son of the chief cantor at the Dessau synagogue. Weill grew up in a musical environment, and at 17 was already working as répétiteur at the city's Herzogliches Hoftheater on the recommendation of his teacher Albert Bing. He studied at the conservatory in Berlin, at first with →Humperdinck and then from 1920 with →Busoni. Before becoming a successful musical dramatist, he was critic for the journal *Der deutsche Rundfunk* (*German Radio*). In Berlin he met his future wife, the singer Lotte Lenya, and the dramatist Bertolt Brecht. At 28 he had a major international breakthrough with *The Threepenny Opera*. In 1933 he emigrated to France, where he worked with Brecht for the last time on the sung ballet *The Seven Deadly Sins*. In 1935 he began a successful career with Lotte Lenya in the USA, the two becoming US citizens in 1943. With his music for stage and film he achieved great renown. He died of a coronary thrombosis soon after his 50th birthday.

Works: Stage works (selection): *Der Protagonist* (*The Protagonist*) (1926, Dresden), *Royal Palace* (1927, Berlin), *Der Zar lässt sich photographieren* (*The Tsar Has His Picture Taken*) (1928, Leipzig), *Die Dreigroschenoper* (*The Threepenny Opera*) (1928, Berlin), *Aufstieg und Fall der Stadt Mahagonny* (*Rise and Fall of the City of Mahagonny*) (1930, Leipzig), *Die Bürgschaft* (*The Pledge*) (1932, Berlin), *Der Silbersee* (*The Silver Lake*) (1933, Leipzig, Magdeburg, Erfurt), *Johnny Johnson* (1936, New York), *Lady in the Dark* (1941, New York), *One Touch of Venus* (1943, New York), *Street Scene* (1947, New York), *Down in the Valley* (1948, Bloomington), *Lost in the Stars* (1949, New York); film music: *You and Me* (director Fritz Lang, 1938), *Salute to France* (director Jean Renoir, 1944); chamber music, songs.

Act III

Peachum blackmails Brown, threatening to summon his beggars on the day of the coronation. Unless Macheath remains behind lock and key he will make sure these miserable figures spoil the occasion. Macheath is again betrayed by Jenny, caught, and sentenced to be hung. He tries to bribe the guards, but the streets are packed and his money arrives too late. The thieves bid Macheath a last farewell, as does his wife Polly. Macheath is led to the gallows. Suddenly, the king's messenger appears with a royal pardon: Macheath is to receive a pension and a knighthood. *M l*   *S. N.*

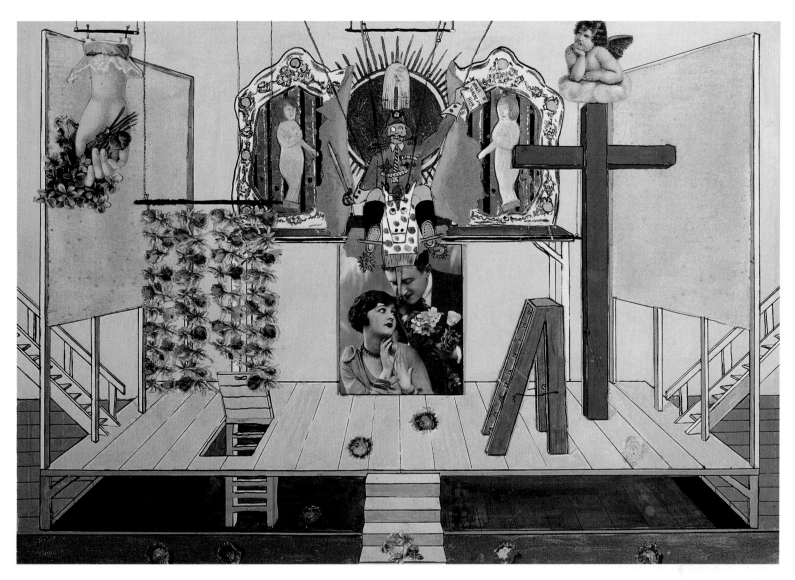

1. The Song of Mac the Knife

Und der Hai - fisch, der hat Zäh - ne, und die trägt er im Ge-sicht,

und Mac-heath der ___ hat ein Mes - ser, doch das Mes - ser sieht man nicht.

The Threepenny Opera, stage design project by Ernst Preusser, Dresden 1929 (TWS). The stage as a montage composed of reliquaries from middle-class life.

Right
The Threepenny Opera, Roma Bahn (Polly) and Harald Paulsen (Macheath) in the original production by Erich Engel, costumes Caspar Neher, conductor Theo Mackeben, Theater am Schiffbauerdamm, Berlin 1928.
When looking for a crowd-pulling play with which to open a new theater in Berlin, the young impresario Ernst Josef Aufricht contacted Bertolt Brecht, who showed him parts of his adaptation of John Gay's *The Beggar's Opera*, which had been revived in London in 1920 and translated by Elisabeth Hauptmann. Aufricht liked the play, although Brecht's idea of using music by Weill was less enthusiastically received.

Anti-romantic, anti-bourgeois

Illusion is rejected, psychology replaced by coolness, aggressiveness, and a calculated lack of tension. The plot and structure of the drama conspicuously preserve and exaggerate old generic conventions: characters marry according to the dictates of morality, and love duets are sung in the appropriate places. While beggars appeal to the piety of passers-by, Mr. Peachum fulfills his Christian duty by singing a hymn. The rejection of illusion should of course make a happy ending impossible. For this reason the plot is brought to a halt and – in accordance with operatic tradition – a *deus ex machina* appears in the form of the king's mounted messenger.

Melodiousness and a refreshing popular tone have secured an unassailable position in operatic history for this work.   *M. S.*

of the desert their car breaks down. They find they can neither go on nor go back to where they came from. They found the city of Mahagonny with the intention of making money out of people. Amongst the new inhabitants are the prostitute Jenny and her girls, and the lumberjacks, Jim, Jack, Bill, and Joe. The lumberjacks have made a great deal of money in Alaska, and they now spend it all in Mahagonny. At the peak of prosperity there is suddenly a crisis: many activities are banned and the inhabitants lapse into boredom. A hurricane approaches the town. Faced with death, Jim finds the solution to Mahagonny's problem: happiness can only be restored if every type of pleasurable activity is permitted.

Rise and Fall of the City of Mahagonny, production photograph with (from left to right) Lenus Carlson (Trinity Moses), Karan Armstrong (Leocadia Begbick), and Robert Wörle (Fatty), production Günter Krämer, sets and costumes Gottfried Pilz and Isabel Ines Glathar, conductor Lawrence Foster, Deutsche Oper, Berlin 1999.

Rise and Fall of the City of Mahagonny

Aufstieg und Fall der Stadt Mahagonny

Opera in three acts

Libretto: Bertolt Brecht.
Première: 9 March 1930, Leipzig (Neues Theater).
Characters: Leocadia Begbick (A or Ms), Fatty, the "bookkeeper" (T), Trinity Moses (Bar), Jenny Hill (S), Tobby Higgins (T), Jim Mahoney (T), Jack O'Brien (T), Bill, alias Bankbook Bill (Bar), Joe, alias Alaska Wolf Joe (B); girls and men of Mahagonny (chorus, extras).
Setting: A fictitious city, in the present.

Synopsis
Act I
Widow Begbick, "bookkeeper" Fatty, and Trinity Moses are on the run from the police. In the middle

Act II
Although the hurricane has made a detour around Mahagonny, the city is destroying itself by following Jim's advice: "Nothing is forbidden, and everything is for sale." Jack dies from the effects of gluttony, and Joe is killed by Trinity Moses in a prize fight. Although Jim loses all the money he has bet on Joe, he still continues to drink to excess. When he has no money left, and his friends Bill and Jenny are no longer willing to help, he is accused of that most serious of crimes – an inability to pay – and thrown into jail.

Act III
The court is in session. Higgins, a murderer, is set free because he has paid a bribe, but Jim is condemned to death. To be without money is a capital crime in Mahagonny, a fundamental human law against which appeal is impossible – as Trinity Moses demonstrates in his play about God in Mahagonny. The commandment to love one's fellow man has no meaning for the inhabitants of Mahagonny. They do not fear hell because they live it every day on earth. Jim is hanged. A war breaks out which pits individual against individual, and no one can help anyone else.   S. N.

Rise and Fall of the City of Mahagonny, Trude Hesterberg (Leocadia) and Lotte Lenya (Jenny), Theater am Kurfürstendamm, Berlin 1931.
Lotte Lenya's Jenny was a highly successful interpretation of the role by an actress. In 1999 Corinna Harfouch recreated Lenya's interpretation in Krämer's Berlin production.

Right
Rise and Fall of the City of Mahagonny, production photograph with Vera Little-Augustithis (Leocadia Begbick), Wolf Appel (Jack O'Brien), and Rolf Kühne (Trinity Moses), production Barbara Karp, sets Allen Charles Klein, conductor Peter Keuschnig, Theater des Westens, Berlin 1985.
Though less than ten years separate the production at the Theater des Westens from that at the Deutsche Oper, the difference between the two productions is striking. Socialism had collapsed in the intervening decade and Krämer portrayed Mahagonny – that is, the new Germany – sinking into an orgy of gluttony and consumption.

Rise and Fall of the City of Mahagonny, production photograph with Dagmar Pecková as Jenny, production Ruth Berghaus, sets Hans-Joachim Schlieker, conductor Markus Stenz, Württembergisches Staatstheater, Stuttgart 1992. Ruth Berghaus was less interested in the excesses that occur under exceptional circumstances than in "everyday capitalism," in which the normal consumer of goods becomes a producer of emotional ruthlessness, and any occasion suffices to stimulate the masses' appetite for entertainment. Here, the chairs are used as a metaphor for this insatiable hunger for new sensations.

The "Songspiel" – a scandal

In 1927 the Festival for German Chamber Music in Baden-Baden commissioned a short opera from Weill. He was initially inclined to turn the offer down, since he was unable to find a suitable subject. In the event, however, he chose five poems from Brecht's *Hauspostille*, and asked the poet to provide a sixth for the finale. The depiction of violence in both the plot and the music predictably led to a scandal when the work was premièred in the Stadthalle in Baden-Baden on 17 July 1927. The performers responded to their outraged audience with a chorus of whistles.

The opera – rebuked

Weill's opera for Baden-Baden dealt with an urban community that was tearing itself apart as a result of the excessive pursuit of pleasure. He now set out to transform this theme into a full-length opera. With Brecht, Weill developed a logic of negative values: a city is founded by criminals, humanity is unreal, love is for sale, and friendship selfish. There is a kind of justice, but it is one in which the poor suffer. If he cannot produce a bribe it is the man without money who is executed rather than the murderer.

Given this concentrated depiction of repugnant forms of human behavior, it is not surprising that the director of the Universal Edition publishing house, Emil Hertzka, had doubts as to whether the work could be performed. Shortly before the première the conductor of the Krolloper in Berlin, Otto Klemperer, rejected *Mahagonny* for being too crass and disconcerting. The next person to express an interest, Gustav Brecher, produced the work at the Neues Theater in Leipzig only after it had been toned down – something with which the authors themselves were partly in agreement. After the première there were further revisions, though a definitive version was never produced as the authors went separate ways in exile.   *M. S.*

Rise and Fall of the City of Mahagonny, poster by Jeruam Naumann, 1961.
Weill's new musical style was evident in this work. Memorable songs, striking tonal harmony, lucid instrumentation, vigorous rhythms, and a popular tone assured this work's success. The subject matter, however, continued to shock audiences into the 1960s.

Street Scene

"An American opera" in two acts

Libretto: Elmer Rice and Langston Hughes, after a play by Elmer Rice.

Première: 9 January 1947, New York (Adelphi Theater).

Musical arrangement: Kurt Weill, with "Wrapped in a Ribbon" and "Moon-faced, Starry-eyed" by Ted Royal.

Characters: Anna Maurrant (S), Frank Maurrant (B), Willie Maurrant (boy S), Rose Maurrant (S), Sam Kaplan (T), Abraham Kaplan (T), Harry Easter (T), Henry Davis (T), Lippo Fiorentino (S), George Jones (T), Carl Olsen (B), Mrs. Fiorentino (S), Mrs. Jones (S or Ms), Mrs. Olsen (A), Daniel Buchanan (T), Jennie Hildebrand (S), Charlie (S or girl S), Mary (S or girl S), Three Schoolgirls (3 girl S), Mrs. Hildebrand (Ms), Mr. Jones (Bar), Two Nannies (2 S), Grace (girl S), Joan (girl S), Joe (boy S), Dick McGann (singer-dancer), Mae Jones (singer-dancer), A Black Woman (S), Two Girls from the Salvation Army (2 S).

Speaking roles: Steve Sankey, Shirley Kaplan, Vincent Jones, Dr. Wilson, Officer Murphy, Marshal James Henry, Fred Cullen, Milkman, Policeman, Ragman, Medical Assistant, Violin Pupil, Ambulance Driver, Man and Woman, Workers, Two Men, Two Furniture-Removers, Shopboys, Girl; crowd, children (chorus).

Setting: New York, June, in the 20th century.

Street Scene, production photograph with Sherri Greenawald (Anna Maurrant) and Lee Merrill (Rose), production Francesca Zambello, conductor Ward Holmquist, Houston Grand Opera 1994.
Rose sees her parents' life together collapsing and offers her mother comfort.

Synopsis

Dog days in the big city. People have been driven onto the streets by the heat. The main topic of conversation is the affair between Mrs. Maurrant and the milkman, who is also married. There are prurient expectations that something is about to happen. All sorts of things happen, but they are not what people expect. The ongoing dispute between Mr. Maurrant, a conservative, and the critical Democrat, Kaplan, becomes unexpectedly heated. A poor widow with three children has a stroke of luck when her daughter receives a scholarship. Rose, the Maurrants' daughter, is surrounded by young men. The young Sam Kaplan wants to be a lawyer; he is interested not only in literature but also in the problems of his fellow men, and is full of understanding – even for Mrs. Maurrant. Rose rejects all her suitors and agrees with Sam that they must live differently from their parents. They make plans to flee the big city and start a new life in the country. The poor widow is evicted and put out on the street. Mr. Maurrant catches his wife with her lover and shoots both of them. The district now has another scandal, and attracts the attention of sensation seekers and the gutter press. Arrested and led away, Maurrant has one final chance to show his daughter that his heart is essentially good, if closed. Rose decides to try living first with her brother, Willie. Only later on, when she is more mature and independent, will she perhaps move in with Sam.   *S. N.*

Left
Street Scene, production photograph with Kay Pascal and Robert McFarland, production Francesca Zambello, conductor James Holmes, sets Adrianne Lobel, Theater des Westens, Berlin 1994.
Anglo-Saxon input at Berlin's Theater des Westens. Francesca Zambello had already directed the work in Houston, and James Holmes had conducted *Street Scene* for the English National Opera in London in 1989 and 1992.

Street Scene, production photograph with Lee Merrill (Rose) and Kip Wilborn (Sam), Houston Grand Opera 1994.
Rose leaves her home intending to build her own life. She wants to be free of ties – even to Sam, who is in love with her.

Made in the USA – the pros and cons

Delighted with American audiences because "they laugh when the music is meant to be funny" and allowed their mood to swing within the space of just a few bars, Weill planned an American opera in which language would naturally flow into music and vice versa. He had in mind a genuinely American story already familiar to him from his time in Berlin: Elmer Rice's Pulitzer Prize winning play *Street Scene*. At first, Rice rejected the idea of turning his play into an opera, but ten years later he collaborated with the poet Langston Hughes to produce the libretto. The love story between Rose and Sam was given more weight, while the discussion surrounding anti-Semitism was moved into the background. In matters of detail, however, it was often only after lengthy discussion that Rice was ready to make concessions.

In *Street Scene*, Weill achieved a synthesis of opera and musical. Leitmotivs provide the work with stability, while spoken scenes serve to portray everyday reality, often with orchestral accompaniment – a technique borrowed from the world of film. The popular Broadway style incorporating dance interludes was combined with older dramatic theories about the unity of time and place.

When the work was tried out in Philadelphia the public stayed away, although the critics' response was extremely favorable. Success came with the première in New York. The performance of the work in Düsseldorf in 1955 caused a sensation, on account of an article written by the philosopher Theodor Adorno. Adorno was highly critical of the American culture industry, and seeing Weill's work as part of this phenomenon accused the composer of having "sold out." Convinced of the primacy of atonality in the twentieth century, musicological scholarship paid little attention to Weill's music before the 1990s.   M. S.

Street Scene, photograph from the production by Francesca Zambello, sets Adrianne Lobel, conductor James Holmes, Theater des Westens, Berlin 1994.
A seemingly happy scene, with neighbors chatting on the street. The summer heat has driven people out of their tiny apartments and onto the streets. But this also means that the tiniest intimacy soon becomes public knowledge – including Mrs. Maurrant's affair. The tragedy begins to take its course.

Shwanda the Bagpiper

Švanda dudák

Opera in two acts (five scenes)

Libretto: Miloš Kareš, after a fairy tale dramatized by Josef Kajetán Tyl.
Première: First version: 27 April 1927, Prague (National Theater); second version: 16 December 1928, Wrocław, Poland (City Theater).
Characters: Shwanda (Bar), Dorota (S), Babinsky (T), Queen (Ms), Magician (B), Judge (T), Executioner (T), Devil (B), The Devil's Familiar (T), Captain of Hell (T), Two Mercenaries (T, B).
Setting: A farm, a castle, and hell, in an indefinite age.

Synopsis
Act I
Scene 1: Shwanda's farm. The thief Babinsky seeks refuge with Dorota, the wife of the bagpiper, and falls in love with her. Shwanda invites the stranger to eat with them, eager for news of the outside world, which he imagines will present marvelous opportunities to someone of his gifts. Shwanda decides to leave his wife and farm and seek his fortune in the land of Queen Iceheart.
Scene 2: The boudoir of Queen Iceheart. The queen has traded her soul for jewelry, but when she hears Shwanda's music she is able to win back the heart she pawned to the magician. She wishes to become the wife of her savior, but the magician prevents the wedding by confronting Shwanda with Dorota. Shwanda recalls his former happiness, rejects the idea of marriage to Queen Iceheart, and is sentenced to death.

Weinberger, Jaromir

b. 8 January 1896 in Prague
d. 8 August 1967 in St. Petersburg, Florida

Though he became an American composer through emigration, Weinberger began his musical education under Jaroslav Kricka and Víteslav Novák in Prague, going on to study with Max Reger in Leipzig. At the age of 26 he was already working as a teacher in Ithaca (NY), and later held teaching positions in Bratislava, Moscow, and Prague. He made a final decision to emigrate to the USA in 1939. Weinberger was active as a teacher of piano and music theory.

Works: Operas: *Švanda dudák* (*Shwanda, the Bagpiper*) (1927, Prague), *Milovany hlas* (*The Loved Voice*) (1931, Munich), *Lidè z Pokerflatu* (*The People of Poker Flat*) (1933, Brünn), *Wallenstein* (1937, Vienna); orchestral works, music for the theater.

Scene 3: A square in front of the city walls in Queen Iceheart's kingdom. The magician acquires Shwanda's bagpipes but Babinsky intervenes: he steals the instrument from the magician and replaces the executioner's axe with a broom. Shwanda begins to play and the crowds that have gathered for the execution begin to dance. Dorota, Shwanda, and Babinsky flee. Shwanda swears faithfulness to Dorota. If he is lying, he says, may the devil take him. No sooner has he uttered these words than the devil appears and Shwanda is taken off to hell. Babinsky imagines that he has finally achieved his objective, but Dorota urges him to fetch Shwanda back.

Act II
Scene 1: Hell. Shwanda refuses to do as the devil asks and provide him with musical entertainment. Babinsky arrives, and beats the devil at cards, winning from him all his treasures, half his kingdom, and Shwanda's soul, even though he had only asked for the last of these. Shwanda is saved and strikes up a tune for the devil and his attendants.
Scene 2: Shwanda's farm. For the last time, Babinsky tries to persuade Dorota to leave Shwanda. He declares that 20 years have passed, and that Dorota is now too old for him. Shwanda approaches his farmstead and sees his wife: young, beautiful, and, above all, ready to make a fresh start.

M. S.

*W*einberger's music is steeped in the traditions of his native country, brilliantly orchestrated, and spiced with musical gags.

Left above
Shwanda the Bagpiper, production photograph with Kostas Paskalis as Shwanda, production Wolfgang Weber, conductor Ivan Pařik, Vienna Volksoper 1986.
Shwanda is led off to his execution (Act I, Scene 2). Babinsky will soon save him, by replacing the executioner's axe with a broom.

Below
Shwanda the Bagpiper, production photograph with Kostas Paskalis (Shwanda) and Jolanta Radek (Dorota), Vienna Volksoper 1986.
Does this opera say anything about the age in which it was written? The folk fairy tale frames the brilliant story of Dorota and Shwanda's marriage. The ending is touching and ironic at the same time: Shwanda joyfully holds Dorota in his arms (Act II, Scene 2).

Opposite above
Shwanda the Bagpiper, production photograph with Kurt Schreibmayer (Babinsky) and Jolanta Radek (Dorota), Vienna Volksoper 1986.
The thief Babinsky tries one final time to seduce the faithful Dorota (Act II, Scene 2) – but in vain.

Opposite below
Shwanda the Bagpiper, set design by Lothar Schenck von Trapp for the production by Renato Mordo, conductor Karl Maria Zwissler, Darmstadt 1929/30 (TWS).
This illustration depicts hell in a constructivist style that was fashionable in the 1920s – a stark contrast to the folk-like quality of the music.

A late folk opera

Weinberger was opposed to avant-garde developments and therefore had no need for sensational operatic subject matter. He made do with two popular characters – a robber and a bagpiper – and a handful of fairy-tale motifs. The relationship between the story and folk culture justified the use of quotations from songs, and these, together with its traditional musical language, guaranteed that the work would be accessible to a wide audience. The tension required for a story with a happy ending was provided by chromatically dense harmony and expressive instrumentation. Irony is expressed through resorting to academic techniques, such as the fugue in the devil's ballet (Act II, Scene 1). The opera's accessibility brought it international renown in the period before the Second World War. Max Brod recommended it to Universal Edition, and it was at their request that Weinberger revised the work, adding two new scenes. The opera enjoyed great success in the USA. Classified as a folk opera, it has most often been produced on small stages since 1945.   M. S.

Wolf, Hugo

b. 13 March 1860 in Slovenj Gradec
d. 22 February 1903 in Vienna

Wolf was born into a wealthy Austrian family. He studied at the Vienna Conservatory from 1875 to 1877, though without gaining a degree. Unsuccessful as a conductor in Salzburg, famous for his music criticism for the *Wiener Salonblatt*, he finally established himself as a composer of lieder in the late 1880s. He composed the opera *The Governer* in 1895. Two years later he suffered a breakdown, and spent the rest of his life in psychiatric care.

Works: A single complete opera, *Der Corregidor* (*The Governor*) (1896, Mannheim), and the incomplete *Manuel Venegas* (1897); lieder cycles, including those to texts by Mörike (1889), Eichendorff (1889), and Goethe (1890), the *Spanisches Liederbuch* (*Spanish Songbook*) (1891), and the *Italienisches Liederbuch* (*Italian Songbook*) (1892, 1896); the symphonic poem *Penthesilea* (1883–85) and a string quartet in D minor (1878–84).

Below
The Governor, production photograph, Berlin 1906.
The miller discovers the governor in a compromising situation in his house (Act III). After Wolf's death, Gustav Mahler's efforts on his behalf led to a series of performances of *The Governor*, of which this Berlin production was one.

Hugo Wolf (1860–1903), photograph. Like Schubert, Wolf was neglected as a composer in his own lifetime.

*W*olf took inspiration from Wagner. His music is distinguished by fine vocal melodies, an uncompromising use of harmony, and subtle dramatic conceptions.

From song to the stage

The story of the opera's birth is closely tied to developments in Wolf's life. An ardent Wagnerian in his youth, in the late 1880s he turned to Mediterranean vitality. While looking for a southern European libretto, he concentrated on lyric poetry, concerned that he might not finish a larger work. When in 1894 Wolf finally accepted the subject matter of Alarcón's tale – he had rejected it in 1889 – and Baron Lippeheide offered him Matzen Castle as a quiet place in which to work, the composer's creative problems ended. He completed the opera in 1895.

The Governor

Der Corregidor

Oper in four acts

Libretto: Rosa Mayreder-Obermayer, after the tale *El sombrero de tres picos* (*The Three-Cornered Hat*) by Pedro Antonio de Alarcón y Arriza.
Première: First version: 7 June 1896, Mannheim (Nationaltheater); second version: 29 April 1898, Strasbourg (Stadttheater).

Characters: Don Eugenio de Zuniga, governor (T), Juan Lopez, mayor (B), Pedro, his secretary (T), Tonuelo, the court messenger (B), Repela, the governor's servant (B), Tio Lukas, a miller (Bar), a Neighbor (T), Donna Mercedes, the governor's wife (S), Frasquita, the miller's wife (Ms), Duenna, a servant of the governor (A), Manuela, the mayor's maid (Ms), Nightwatchman (B), Bishop (silent), Servant (silent); the bishop's retinue, servants of the governor and the mayor (chorus).
Setting: Andalusia, 1804.

Synopsis
Act I

Lukas, a miller, and his wife Frasquita are happily married. The governor pursues the beautiful Frasquita, but the couple simply think him a fool. The governor swears revenge.

Act II

At the instigation of the governor, Lukas is summoned late one night to see the mayor. In the meantime, the governor slips into his house to see Frasquita, but she runs off to fetch her husband. The governor had fallen into water on the way, and so he takes off his clothes to dry and creeps into the miller's bed. A heavy drinking session is under way at the mayor's offices. Lukas drinks all present under the table and makes his way home.

Act III

In the dark, Lukas and Frasquita run past each other. At home the miller finds Don Eugenio undressed in his bed, and seizes the chance for revenge. He puts on the governor's clothes and rushes off to the deceived wife Donna Mercedes. When the governor wakes up he has to put on the miller's clothes. He hurries off to see the mayor, but when he arrives he is mistaken for the miller and given a thrashing.

Act IV

The governor finally arrives home early the next morning, but is barred entry to his house. His servants tell him their master has been in bed for some time, and, believing him to be the drunken miller, give him another thrashing. Donna Mercedes refuses to help her husband, seeing him justly punished for his amorous adventures. Lukas, who in fact remained faithful to his wife, is happily reunited with her. The governor, however, will continue to wonder what went on between his wife and the miller. *S. N.*

The Governor, production photograph, Berlin 1906.
At the governor's instigation the miller is summoned by the mayor – and finds a drinking party in full swing (Act II).

A personal tragedy

At the time of the opera's composition Wolf's health was a cause for concern. His syphilis had entered a terminal stage, though fortunately his mind was not impaired. Two years later Wolf asked his friend the opera director Gustav Mahler to stage *The Governor*. Mahler made his excuses. Shortly afterwards, Wolf began to suffer from the delusion that he was an opera director, and psychiatric help finally became necessary.

Below
The Governor, set design by Heinz Grete, Nuremberg 1942 (TWS).
Wolf's models could not have been more different: Wagner's →*The Mastersingers of Nuremberg* and Bizet's →*Carmen*. *The Governor* combines contrapuntal writing, leitmotivs, and orchestration on a vast scale with lyrical melodies, dance, and situation comedy. Wolf also succeeded in integrating songs such as "In dem Schatten meiner Locken" ("In the shadow of my locks") from his *Spanisches Liederbuch* (*Spanish Songbook*, 1891) – a piece sung by Frasquita – without interfering with the dramatic pace. *M 1*

1. Frasquita's Song

In dem Schat-ten mei-ner Lo-cken schlief mir mein Ge-lieb-ter ein.

The Curious Women

Le donne curiose

Commedia musicale in three acts

Libretto: Luigi Sugana, after the play of the same name by Carlo Goldoni.

Première: 27 November 1903, Munich (Residenztheater).

Characters: Ottavio, a rich Venetian citizen (B), Beatrice, his wife (Ms), Rosaura, their daughter (S), Florindo, Rosaura's betrothed (T), Pantalone, a Venetian merchant (Bar), Lelio (Bar) and Leandro (T), Pantalone's friends, Colombina, the maid of Beatrice and Rosaura (S), Eleonora, Lelio's wife (S), Arlecchino, Pantalone's servant (B), Asdrubale (T), Almoro (T), Alvise (T), Lunardo (B), Momolo (B), Menego (B), Two Gondoliers (T, B), A Servant (silent); servants, gondoliers, people (chorus, extras).

Setting: Venice, the middle of the 18th century.

Wolf-Ferrari, Ermanno

b. 12 January 1876 in Venice
d. 21 January 1948 in Venice

After starting out as a painter, Wolf-Ferrari studied at the Munich Academy of Music (1892–95) under Joseph Rheinberger. His operas quickly achieved popularity. He lived in both Germany and Italy, working as a choral director in Milan, as director of the Conservatorio di Musica Benedetto Marcello in Venice (1902–1909), and as professor at the Salzburg Mozarteum (from 1939). Because he was neither drawn to the cultural politics of the Third Reich nor the avant-garde scene that followed it, he withdrew from public life, spending the last years of his life in his brother's house in Venice.

Works: La Cenerentola (Cinderella) (1900, Venice), *Le donne curiose (The Curious Women)* (1903, Munich), *I quattro rusteghi (The Four Curmudgeons)* (1906, Munich), *Il segreto di Susanna (Susanna's Secret)* (1909, Munich), *I gioielli della Madonna (The Jewels of the Madonna)* (1911, Berlin), *L'amore medico (Love the Physician)* (1913, Dresden), *Gli amanti sposi (The Married Lovers)* (1925, Venice, Dresden), *Das Himmelskleid (Heaven's Mantle)* (1927, Munich), *Sly, ovvero La leggenda del dormiente risvegliato (Sly, or The Legend of the Awakened Sleeper)* (1927, Milan), *La vedova scaltra (The Clever Widow)* (1931, Rome, Berlin), *Il campiello (The Little Square)* (1936, Milan), *La dama boba (The Silly Woman)* (1939, Milan), *Gli dei a Tebe (The Gods at Thebes)* (1943, Hanover); orchestral works, chamber music, vocal music.

The Curious Women, set design by Paul Schönke, Kassel 1927/28 (TWS). Wolf-Ferrari himself thought that posterity would regard *The Curious Women* as nothing more than an "accident." In fact this opera brought him the honorary title of "Mozart redivivus."

Synopsis

Women are not admitted to Pantalone's club. When he organizes a party to celebrate the wedding of a club member, Florindo, the women's curiosity gets the better of them: is it gambling or illicit love that is going on behind the club's closed doors? The women make every attempt to find out, but the men succeed in evading their questions. Even Florindo resists his betrothed, Rosaura, and her threats to break off the engagement prove useless. By pretending to faint, she manages to entice from him the password, "amicizia." Beatrice, Eleonora, and Rosaura procure the keys from their men through trickery, but in spite of their disguises are turned away at the door of the club. Arlecchino lets them peep through a crack in the door. The door suddenly opens and women and men stand face to face. Nothing now stands in the way of a party.   M. S.

The Clever Widow, set design by Max Bignens for the production by Harro Dicks, Darmstadt 1964 (TWS).
This work is a Venetian comedy set to music by a Venetian composer. At a time when the Schoenberg school was already established and film music was beginning to enrich popular culture, Wolf-Ferrari, together with his librettist Mario Ghisalberti, reverted to a story by Goldoni. He wrote this quickly moving and delightful opera in the conviction that "everyone is somehow comical when seen from the outside, but tragic when seen from the inside." He uses the waltz as a connecting element, a characteristic *parlando* to ensure the comprehensibility of the text, and a vital, dance-influenced structure as his musical means of expression, all of them chosen for their suitability to the subject matter.

Right
Sly, production photograph with José Carreras as Sly, production Hans Hollmann, sets Hans Hoffer, costumes Dirk von Bodisco, conductor Rafael Frühbeck de Burgos, Opernhaus Zürich 1998.
Sly is the story of a poor man who becomes the victim of powerful but bored and sensation-hungry people. First performed at La Scala in 1927, it has consistently captured the interest of opera companies and character tenors.

Wolf-Ferrari developed a contemporary style from the opera buffa tradition. The avant-garde schools of his own time did not interest him.

The rebirth of *opera buffa*

Although Wolf-Ferrari's first opera, *Cinderella*, was a fiasco when it opened in Venice, its first performance in Germany, in Bremen in 1902, was an enormous success. Following the advice of the Bremen theater director Friedrich Erdmann-Jesnitzer that he take advantage of the revival of interest in Goldoni's work, Wolf-Ferrari set to music Goldoni's comedy *Le donne curiose*, later having it translated into German. This was a pioneering feat, which initiated a revival of *opera buffa*. Wolf-Ferrari employed accessible melodies and harmonies in turn-of-the-century style, incorporating various stylistic characteristics of music from earlier periods. Opposed to the vast orchestral sound of his day, he used a relatively small orchestra for this burlesque piece, and this guaranteed lucidity. Without feeling it necessary to abandon the advantages of leitmotivic composition, he integrated clearly identifiable arias into a composite structure, thereby creating a type of "through-composed number opera." After the work's première in Munich in 1903 it was swiftly taken up by no fewer than 27 German theaters, while all ten performances of a production in Vienna in 1905 were conducted by Gustav Mahler himself. This enormous success gave Wolf-Ferrari the confidence to continue in his chosen direction. Years later Richard Strauss was to continue in the same vein with his →*Der Rosenkavalier*.   *M. S.*

The Clever Widow

La vedova scaltra

Commedia lirica in three acts

Synopsis

A rich Venetian widow decides to make up for lost time, having been kept out of society by her late husband's last illness. At a ball she meets four admirers, each of whom attempts to win her heart with a gift: an Englishman presents her with a diamond, a Frenchman with a magnificent painting, a Spaniard with his family tree, and an Italian – a "conte" – with a passionate love letter, not entirely free of jealousy and chauvinism. In order to be sure that she is the sole object of their affections, she puts all four suitors to the test. To each of them she appears in disguise during carnival, dressed in the national costume of the man in question: to the Englishman she is a cool companion, to the Frenchman an amusing partner, to the Spaniard a haughty lady, and to the Italian a girl in love. All except the Italian succumb to the charms of what they believe to be their countrywoman. The widow then invites all four to a ball, and confesses her deception. Only the conte has passed the test. After bestowing her hand upon the fortunate man, she opens the ball.   *M. S.*

Zemlinsky, Alexander (von)

b. 14 October 1871 in Vienna
d. 15 March 1942 in Larchmont (New York)

Zemlinsky was educated at the Vienna Conservatory between 1884 and 1892 under Franz Krenn and Robert Fuchs. In 1894 he met Arnold Schoenberg, with whom he became close friends and whom Zemlinsky taught. In 1896 he was introduced to Brahms, who was to come to regard him as his protégé. His first opera *Sarema* was premièred in Munich in 1897. Friendship with Mahler resulted in the performance of his second opera, *Once upon a Time*, at the Vienna Hofoper (court opera), where Mahler was director. In 1901 Zemlinsky married Schoenberg's sister Mathilde. He became conductor at the Volksoper in Vienna in 1904 and at the Hofoper in 1907. He was dismissed by Mahler's successor at the Hofoper, Felix von Weingartner. From 1911 to 1926 he was director of music at the German Theater in Prague, and in 1920 became director of the German Music Academy in the same city. *A Florentine Tragedy* was first performed in Stuttgart in 1917 and *The Dwarf* in Cologne in 1922. Both were well received. From 1927 to 1930 he worked at the Kroll Opera in Berlin, and from 1930 at the Music Academy. He moved to Vienna in 1933 and from there emigrated to America in 1938, by which time when he was already gravely ill. He died alone, in Larchmont, NY, in 1942.

Works: Operas: *Sarema* (1897), *Es war einmal* (*Once upon a Time*) (1900), *Der Traumgörge* (*Görge the Dreamer*) (1906/FP 1980), *Kleider machen Leute* (*Fine Feathers Make Fine Birds*) (1910, rev. 1922), *Eine florentinische Tragödie* (*A Florentine Tragedy*) (1917), *Der Zwerg* (*The Dwarf*) (1922), *Der Kreidekreis* (*The Chalk Circle*) (1933), *Der König Kandaules* (*King Candaules*) (1936; completed by Antony Beaumont, FP 1996); orchestral works, including the Symphony in D minor, the Symphony in B flat major, the Lyric Symphony for soprano, baritone, and orchestra, and the Sinfonietta; chamber music, including four string quartets, a trio (clarinet, cello, and piano), and pieces for wind instruments; three psalm settings for choir and orchestra; song cycles with piano or orchestral accompaniment; piano pieces.

*Z*emlinsky's music dramas all have the search for identity as their central theme. This subject was ultimately the composer's own, as he sought to find a place for himself between the late Romanticism of Brahms, Wagner, and Mahler, and the Schoenberg school. As a gifted composer Zemlinsky felt drawn to the ideals of Schoenberg, but without expressing this interest in his own compositions.

Görge the Dreamer

Der Traumgörge

Oper in two acts and an epilogue

Libretto: Leo Feld.
Première: 11 October 1980, Nuremberg (Opernhaus).
Characters: Görge (T), Grete (S), Miller (B), Pastor (B), Hans (Bar), Princess (S), Gertraud (S), Züngl (T), Kaspar (Bar), Matthes (B), Marei (S), Landlord (T); peasants, youths, children, voices of dreams (chorus).
Setting: Germany, at the time of Napoleon I.

Synopsis
Act I

Görge creates a dream world for himself from books, and experiences the joy of living in a fairy tale. This shields him from the dullness of everyday life in his backward village, but it also alienates him from its inhabitants, including his fiancée, Grete. He has a vision of a princess, and this inspires him to go out into the world. Not even the thought that Hans may steal Grete from him while he is away can hold him back.

Act II

Görge encounters a group of rebellious workers who try to persuade him to be their leader. He becomes friends with Gertraud, a woman who has been wrongly accused of being a witch. The rebels' only aim is to murder and pillage, and they demand that Görge abandon the witch. Görge therefore leaves the rebellion to return to his native village.

Epilogue

Görge attempts to combine reality and utopia by living respectably with Gertraud. Grete, meanwhile, has returned to her former love Hans.   *H. L.*

Görge the Dreamer, photograph from the original production by Gilbert Deflo, sets and costumes Ekkehard Grübler, conductor Hans Gierster, Musiktheater, Nuremberg 1980.
The dreamy Görge is caught up in the chaos of his age, when the workers prepare for an uprising and make Görge their leader (Act II).

Görge the Dreamer, photograph from the original production with Sharon Markovich (Grete) and Karl-Heinz Thiemann (Görge), production Gilbert Deflo, sets and costumes Ekkehard Grübler, conductor Hans Gierster, Musiktheater, Nuremberg 1980.
Grete tries in vain to persuade Görge to stay, but he has packed his bags and wants to be off.

Fine Feathers Make Fine Birds

Kleider machen Leute

Oper in a prologue and three acts; revised version *Musikalische Komödie* in a prologue and two acts

Libretto: Leo Feld, after the novella by Gottfried Keller.
Première: 2 December 1910, Vienna (Volksoper); revised version 20 April 1922, Prague (New German Theater).
Characters: Wenzel Strapinski, journeyman tailor from Seldwyla (T), Councillor (B), Nettchen, his daughter (S), Melchior Böhni, bookkeeper (Bar), Adam Litumlei, notary (Bar), Eulalia, his wife (A), Lieselein, his daughter (S), Polykarpus Federspiel, town clerk (T), Master Tailor (B), The Eldest Son of the House of Häberlein (T), Frau Haberlein (S), The Younger Son of the House of Pütschli-Nivergelt (B), Landlord (B), Landlady (Ms), Boy Waiter (S), Cook (A), Waiter (T), House Servant (T), "A Prologue" (spoken), Two Journeymen Tailors (T and B), Coachman (Bar); men and women from Goldach and Seldwyla (chorus).
Setting: Switzerland, in the 19th century.

Synopsis
Prologue

A country road. Strapinski is taking leave of two friends who are also journeymen tailors. The coachman takes him to Goldach, where he is presented as "His Grace, the duke." The coachman disappears.

Act I

The people of Goldach gather in the tavern to admire the strange "duke" and pay court to him. They are joined by the councillor and his daughter Nettchen, whose jilted admirer Böhni is the only skeptic.

Act II

Strapinski loves Nettchen and does not wish to appear false to her. When he tries to steal away, she holds him back. His rival Böhni unmasks the false duke, but Strapinski strikes back. The people of Goldach, he says, would not have wanted it any other way. He only went along with the ruse out of love, he claims, to be close to Nettchen. When he attempts to leave Goldach once again, Nettchen makes him stay – as her fiancé. "If I can't be a duchess, at least I can be a master tailor's wife!" H.L.

The tailor's theme

Zemlinsky plays brilliantly with the "tailor's theme" (the theme of Strapinski's song "Schneiderlein, was machst denn du?" – "Little tailor, what are you up to?" – which appears for the first time in the prologue) to illustrate the character's ambiguity. The music of the tailor's theme is at first wretched and grotesque, then majestic ("like a count"), before ultimately becoming endearing. The ensemble scenes in the opera – modeled on those of Mozart – are especially remarkable. M 1 H.L.

The Zemlinsky revival

Cancelled during the first rehearsals at the Vienna Hofoper in 1907, *Görge the Dreamer* disappeared for many years before finally being performed at Nuremberg in 1980. The opera had nevertheless enjoyed immense respect in the circles around Schoenberg. Zemlinsky's exaggerated modesty – another sign of his (and Görge's) identity crisis – prevented him from making further efforts to have the work staged during his own lifetime. It is only since the 1980s – when the notion that the avant-garde is continually and linearly progressive collapsed – that Zemlinsky's work has been given the attention it deserves.

1. The Tailor's Song

»Schnei-der-lein, was machst denn du, wachst denn du, gar so flei-ßig heu-te?« Ich näh', ich näh', ich näh' im-mer-zu, wir brau-chen Bür-ger und Stut-zer im Frack

A Florentine Tragedy

Oper in one act

Libretto: The play of the same name by Oscar Wilde, translated by Max Meyerfeld.
Première: 30 January 1917, Stuttgart (Hoftheater).
Characters: Guido Bardi, the son of the duke of Florence (T), Simone, a cloth merchant (Bar), Bianca, his wife (Ms).
Setting: Florence, in the 16th century.

A Florentine Tragedy, production photograph with Wicus Salabbert (Simone) and Kurt Schreibmacher (Guido), production Adolf Dresen, sets and costumes Pal Bardy, conductor Karabtchevsky, Wiener Volksoper 1990.
Simone as the little man victorious. It may be that Simone is the only one of Zemlinsky's heroes to come to terms with his identity crisis (and therefore the composer's) – the only figure to confront and "strike back" at the depressing power structures of his society.

Synopsis

Simone, a cloth merchant, returns from a business trip and finds his wife in a compromising position with Guido Bardi, the son of the duke of Florence. Simone at first pretends to be naive, and flatters Guido, offering him fine cloth and inviting him to dine. His dark and ominous references begin to unnerve his wife's lover. When Simone steps out into the garden for a moment the two lovers embrace, and Simone surprises them once again. A seemingly playful game with swords suddenly becomes serious and bloody; Simone defeats Guido in a duel and then strangles him. Husband and wife sink into each other's arms over the corpse of the dead lover.   *H. L.*

A decadent comedy

A Florentine Tragedy is in fact a cynical comedy rather than a tragedy. Simone knows from the outset what he wants and makes a fool of his rival by playing the servile shopkeeper. At the same time, he makes it clear that he is no longer tied to his wife emotionally, but that she is his possession. The second love scene, which takes place while Simone goes into the garden (the first love scene in Wilde's original manuscript was lost and Zemlinsky replaced it with an extended and colorful

prelude), slows the action before the swift finale with its conclusion – a love duet in the form of a sarcastic aphorism: "Why did you not tell me you were so strong" (Bianca) and "Why did you not tell me you were so beautiful" (Simone).

An opera of its age

Zemlinksy was at the height of his powers when he wrote this one-act opera. He fused Brahms's legacy of contrapuntal chamber music with the late Romantic color of →Strauss and →Schreker, and succeeded in creating a sophisticated portrayal of constantly ambiguous character configurations. In its complex structure, its use of only three voices, and its detailed shading of mood, *A Florentine Tragedy* comes close to musical Expressionism. Typical for the age in which it was composed is the Renaissance setting (Schreker, →*The Branded*, and Schillings, →*Mona Lisa*) and the inversion of values that was so characteristic of the fin de siècle: morality is reduced to a farce, feelings to business, and characters step over corpses to achieve their own ends.

Alexander von Zemlinsky and Harald Paulsen, Berlin 1931.
Zemlinsky put a great deal of energy into interpreting other composers' work. Here, he is seen at a rehearsal of Kurt Weill's *The Threepenny Opera* with the actor Harald Paulsen.

The Dwarf

Der Zwerg

Tragisches Märchen für Musik in one act

Libretto: Georg C. Klaren, after the story *The Birthday of the Infanta* by Oscar Wilde (this title is also occasionally used for Zemlinsky's opera).
Première: 28 May 1922, Cologne (Oper).
Characters: Donna Clara, the Infanta of Spain (S), Ghita, her favorite maid (S), Don Estoban, major-domo (B), Dwarf (T); the Infanta's entourage (play-mates, maids, and ladies) (chorus).
Setting: A Spanish court, in the time of fairy tale.

Synopsis

The Infanta receives a number of presents for her birthday including a misshapen dwarf who knows nothing of his deformity but is celebrated as a singer. The cold Infanta toys with the dwarf, much to the amusement of the court. She makes him sing to her and pay her compliments, and she dances with him and presents him with a white rose, encouraging him to believe she loves him. The maid Ghita wants to end this cruel sport, but cannot bring herself to tell the dwarf the truth about his deformities. While the Infanta and the court celebrate outside in the garden, the dwarf stumbles about in the throne-room and manages to tear down a heavy curtain to reveal a large mirror. He sees his shape for the first time, and collapses with a heartrending cry. The Infanta heartlessly explains that he had only ever been a "toy" to her. While he lies dying of a broken heart, she skips out into the garden to find other diversions.   *H. L.*

The Dwarf, production photograph with Ulrike Steinsky (the Infanta) and Kurt Schreibmayer (dwarf), production Adolf Dresen, sets and costumes Pal Bardy, conductor Karabtchevsky, Vienna Volksoper 1990.
It is perhaps not without justification that people identify the figures of the dwarf – a creature of nature, with genuine feelings – and the Infanta – a child of the upper classes, quite lacking in feeling – with Zemlinsky and his former student and lover Alma Schindler. Alma left Zemlinsky for Gustav Mahler (and then left Mahler for other men). The affairs of this femme fatale were of course known to the composer. But the theme of the opera is ultimately a timeless one, as well as being the theme of Zemlinsky's life: that of identity.

Characters and their musical coloring

The contrasting spheres of the Infanta and her stiff court ceremonial on the one hand and the dwarf and the sympathetic maid Ghita on the other are characterized by unusually sophisticated musical imagery, the former by diatonic melodies and "cold" instruments such as the celesta, the latter by highly expressive chromaticism and voluptuous melodies. Although this one-act work, in contrast to *A Florentine Tragedy*, shows a distinct preference for lyrical and restrained music – complemented by the ironic and grotesque tone of the court's mockery of the clumsy dwarf – the mirror scene is a dissonant explosive *tutti* of breath-taking Expressionist power unique to early twentieth-century opera. *M 2* Yet another impressive feature of the work is the fusion of orchestral movements which fluctuate between late Romanticism and atonality, and ensemble scenes of pretended naïveté. Hidden correspondences in both music and subject matter between *The Dwarf* and *A Florentine Tragedy* encourage the performance of these two one-act operas side by side to fill an entire evening's program.   *H. L.*

Of dwarves and mirrors

Alma Mahler's description of her former lover Zemlinsky as "small, chinless, toothless" is one of many such disrespectful comments about the composer's appearance that caused him a great deal of suffering. This suffering is evident in his one-act opera *The Dwarf*, composed with great feeling in 1922, a small autobiographical story in the guise of a fairy tale. There have been many dwarves in the history of opera, particularly since the Romantic era. The direct predecessor of Zemlinsky's dwarf is the hunchback Alviano in Franz Schreker's opera *The Branded* (1918), who, in spite of his noble soul, loses his beloved on account of his ugliness. When the dwarf in Zemlinsky's opera recognizes his true self he dies of a broken heart. This was also the tragedy of Verdi's →*Rigoletto*, of 1851. Rigoletto plays the part of a jester at the court of the duke of Mantua. It is only as a father whose daughter has been seduced by the duke, and as a man who is mocked and cursed, that he recognizes his real identity: behind the clown's mask there is a loving father, and a sound, noble soul. "Two-facedness" is also the "sickness" of Mime, the Nibelung dwarf in the second part of Wagner's *Ring* cycle (→*Siegfried*, 1876). Mime rears Siegfried in the hope that he will be able to win back the ring by virtue of his fearlessness and strength, and in doing so constantly deceives the heroic youth. When Siegfried learns of Mime's real intentions from the woodbird and confronts the dwarf with his lies, Mime becomes hysterical and this leads to his destruction: he dies at the hands of his strong, handsome, adoptive son.

King Candaules

Der König Kandaules

Oper in three acts

Libretto: Alexander von Zemlinsky, after the German adaptation by Franz Blei of the play *Le roi Candaule* by André Gide.
Première: 6 October 1996, Hamburg (Staatsoper).

Characters: König Kandaules/King Candaules (dramatic T), Gyges (dramatic Bar), Nyssia (dramatic S), Phedros (lyric Bar), Syphax (lyric T), Nicomedes (Bar), Pharnaces (B), Philebos (B), Simias (T), Sebas (T), Archelaos (B), The Cook (B), Trydo (silent); guests (chorus).
Setting: Lydia, in classical antiquity.

Synopsis

Act I

The wealthy king of Lydia, Candaules, invites his favorites to a banquet at which his queen, Nyssia, is to appear unveiled in public for the first time. When a magic ring is found in a fish, the fishermen Gyges is called before the king. At first Gyges shows himself to be indifferent, but when the unfaithfulness of his wife Trydô is revealed to him he strikes her dead in front of the assembled guests. Candaules is fascinated by Gyges and invites him to his castle.

Act II

Candaules wants all his friends to share in his fortune – including his beautiful wife – and so persuades Gyges to use the magic ring to make himself invisible and thereby see Nyssia naked. In so doing he loses Nyssia: in the dark she mistakes Gyges for Candaules and they spend the night together.

Act III

Gyges reveals himself to Nyssia, expecting to be sentenced to death, but she challenges him to murder the lustful king, by whom she feels scandalously betrayed. Gyges does her bidding, but when as the new king he asks Nyssia to resume the veil, she refuses, saying "Candaules has torn it to shreds." *H. L.*

King Candaules, photograph from the original production with (from left to right) Kurt Gysen, Klaus Häger, Mariusž Kwiecień, Ferdinand Seiler, Peter Galliard, James O'Neal, and Simon Yang, production Günther Krämer, sets and costumes Gottfried Pilz, conductor Gerd Albrecht, Oper Hamburg 1996.
King Candaules (James O'Neal) seen in the midst of his friends. The Hamburg productions of *The Florentine Tragedy* (1981) and *The Dwarf* (1983) led to a revival of Zemlinsky's work. The première of *King Candaules* followed in Hamburg in 1996.

King Candaules, photograph from the original production with (from left to right) Mariusž Kwieceň, Kurt Gysen, Peter Galliard, and Ferdinand Seiler, production Günther Krämer, sets and costumes Gottfried Pilz, conductor Gerd Albrecht, Oper Hamburg 1996. Zemlinsky had completed enough of the orchestration for Beaumont to be able to create a unified and coherent reconstruction of the timbres and musical characterization that are so important to Zemlinsky's operas. In this way he was able to rescue this late work for posterity, a fact that the première in Hamburg in 1996 – 54 years after the composer's death – so clearly demonstrated.

A major work finally makes an appearance

By the time he emigrated to the USA Zemlinsky had completed less than half the orchestration for *King Candaules*. Attempts to have the opera performed in New York failed, on account of the bedroom scene in the second act. Fortunately the libretto was finished, and this made it possible for the conductor and Zemlinsky expert Antony Beaumont to bring the work to completion, thereby adding to the repertory another major work of the first half of the twentieth century, to rank alongside Berg's →*Wozzeck* and →*Lulu* and Schoenberg's →*Moses and Aaron*. *King Candaules* is undeniably a major work, and not only for the way it both relates to and transcends its own age. It is a typical "mature work," in that it functions almost as an artistic résumé, with allusions to and stylistic quotations from Zemlinsky's earlier works.

Here, too, one recognizes Zemlinsky's theme – of the search for identity and the crisis of identity – in a configuration of characters that may be constantly reinterpreted, in terms of either Greek mythology, or the political situation of the composer's own time, or the present day. Candaules oscillates between wealth, decadence, and moral liberalism; Gyges is, as the embodiment of "natural man," used and misused by powerful interests; while the conservative moral guar-

dian Nyssia is, as the "dishonored woman," an avenging fundamentalist angel, of whatever variety. The characterization and musical structuring of the three acts are convincingly achieved. The magic ring is signified through soft beats on suspended cymbals, and in Act III, the climactic point of the drama, Zemlinsky repeatedly quotes the motif from the first movement of his Lyric Symphony, where it is accompanied by the words "I cannot find peace."   *H. L.*

Zimmermann, Bernd Alois

b. 20 March 1918 in Bliesheim (now Erftstadt) near Cologne
d. 10 August 1970 in Königsdorf (now Frechen) near Cologne

Zimmermann studied music in Cologne. He was obliged to do social and military service from 1938 to 1945, but then continued his studies in Cologne under Heinrich Lemacher (theory) and Philipp Jarnach (composition). He attended the courses run by Wolfgang Fortner and René Leibowitz at Darmstadt in the years 1948–50, composed music for radio plays for WDR (West German Radio), and had his first performances. From 1956 to 1957 he was president of the German section of the International Society for New Music, and from 1957 professor of composition at the Cologne Music Academy. He was awarded two scholarships by the Villa Massimo in Rome, where he worked on his opera *Die Soldaten*. In 1960 he received the Arts Award from North-Rhine/Westphalia, and in 1966 from the city of Cologne, the year in which he was accepted into the Berlin Academy of the Arts. He committed suicide in 1970.

Works: Stage works: *Die Soldaten* (*The Soldiers*) (1965); ballets, including *Alagoana, Kontraste* (*Contrasts*), *Perspektiven* (*Perspectives*), *Musique pour les soupers du Roi Ubu* (*Music for King Ubu's Supper*); orchestral works, including the Symphony in One Movement, *Photoptosis, Stille und Umkehr* (*Silence and Return*), concertos for violin, viola, cello (2), oboe, trumpet, and two pianos; the *Requiem für einen jungen dichter* (*Requiem for a young poet*), chamber music, piano music, vocal works, electronic music.

*Z*immermann belongs in the broadest sense to the post-war schools of serial music; he described himself jokingly as "the oldest of the young composers." His younger colleagues in turn praised him as "the last man who knew everything."

Die Soldaten

The Soldiers

Oper in four acts

Libretto: Bernd Alois Zimmermann, after the play of the same name by Jakob Michael Reinhold Lenz.
Première: 15 February 1965, Cologne (Städtische Oper).
Characters: Wesener, a fancy-goods merchant in Lille (B), Marie and Charlotte, his daughters (S, Ms), Wesener's old Mother (A), Stolzius, a draper in Armentières (Bar), Stolzius's Mother (A), Obrist, Count of Spannheim (B), Desportes, a young French nobleman (T), Pirzel, a captain (T), Eisenhardt, an army chaplain (Bar), Haudy and Mary, captains (2 Bar), Countess de la Roche (Ms), The Young Count, her son (T); officers and sergeants (chorus).
Setting: French-speaking Flanders, yesterday, today, and tomorrow.

Synopsis
Act I
Scene 1: Wesener's house in Lille. Marie is writing a letter to Madame Stolzius, with whose son she has fallen in love.
Scene 2: Stolzius's house in Armentières. Stolzius is overjoyed when his mother shows him the letter she has received from Marie. His mother disapproves of the liaison and reminds him of his business commitments.
Scene 3: Desportes, an officer and a customer of Wesener, is courting Marie. At first Wesener rejects him, but then advises Marie to keep Stolzius

waiting, as a liaison with Desportes may be socially advantageous.
Scene 4: Chaplain Eisenhardt and several officers discuss theater and morality.
Act II
Scene 5: Wesener does not know to whom he should give his daughter Marie – Desportes or Stolzius. Marie is also uncertain: she loves Stolzius but has ambitions to become the wife of a nobleman.
Scene 6: In the coffee house of Armentières bored officers attempt to amuse themselves. When Stolzius enters they tease him with references to Marie and Desportes.
Scene 7: Marie receives a letter from Stolzius, who reproaches her for her infidelity. Desportes dictates a humiliating response to Marie and then seduces her.
Scene 8: Captain Pirzel and the chaplain discuss the fundamentals of human nature, but without being able to reach an agreement.
Scene 9: Stolzius becomes a soldier in order to get close to Desportes.
Act III
Scene 10: Charlotte reproaches Marie for being a "soldier's girl." After Desportes left her, Marie transferred her affections to his friend Captain Mary.
Scene 11–12: Marie flirts with the young count, but his mother disabuses her of her illusions. Nevertheless, in an attempt to salvage Marie's tattered reputation the countess offers her a position as a housekeeper.
Act IV
Various simultaneous events:
Scene 13: Marie has run away from the countess's service. She is raped by one of Desportes' subordinates.
Scene 14: Stolzius accidentally overhears a conversation between Desportes and Mary in which they make derogatory remarks about Marie. He poisons Desportes and then kills himself.
Scene 15: Marie has become a prostitute; she begs from her father in the street but he no longer recognizes her. In an aural pandemonium meant to encompass a variety of epochs, a number of sounds can be heard: marching feet, parade ground orders given in different languages, and bombs exploding. These noises are interspersed with film projections, showing tanks and a mushroom cloud slowly sinking to earth. *H.L.*

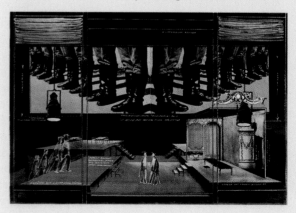

A plurality of idioms

Zimmermann visualized his concept of the simultaneity of different styles – music history as an omnipresent entity – in a symbolic "sphere of time," constructed using the techniques of serialism and integrating quotations and collages. The composer combined this "pluralism" (an inappropriate but frequently used term) with a critique of civilization and culture derived from left-wing Catholic activism. It is this critique that forms the intellectual content of *Die Soldaten*.

Die Soldaten, production photograph with (from left to right) Hans-Joachim Ketelsen (Mary), Regina Schudel (Marie), and Roland Wagenführer (Desportes), production Willy Decker, sets Wolfgang Gussmann, costumes Frauke Schernau and Wolfgang Gussmann, conductor Friedemann Layer, Semperoper, Dresden 1995.
Marie had hoped for social advancement from her love affairs, but she ends as a ruined and broken creature.

Opera as "sphere of time"

Die Soldaten was written in the years 1957–59 and 1962–64 and is a masterpiece of compositional technique. The entire work is based on a single, symmetrically structured series of intervals (→Schoenberg), whose mathematical relationships are transposed to other parameters such as duration, dynamics, density of movement, and meter. Furthermore, each scene is based on a strict musical form: chaconne, ricercar, toccata, and so on. As in Berg's →*Wozzeck* these forms are used solely as a framework within which to place dramatically effective action, and by no means preclude the portrayal of character. Musical genre pictures, quotations from Bach, and jazz (coffee house scene) all have a function within the work's overall musico-dramatic structure. Another feature of *Die Soldaten* is Zimmermann's unusual method of creating a kind of dramatic counterpoint from the simultaneous presentation of different scenes. Zimmermann integrated Lenz's "Storm and Stress" aesthetics into his musico-dramatic conception, taking it further with his idea of the "sphere of time," or the simultaneity and constant availability of past, present, and future (the last portrayed by the threatening closing vision of a nuclear apocalypse). Real action and exemplifying abstraction are thus inextricably linked. The blending of an orchestra, a percussion group, a jazz band, electronic sound, film music, and recorded music was an extremely ambitious undertaking, yet through their logical and consistent patterns of breaking apart and coming together again the various elements form a unified whole. As has been shown by the original production under the musical direction of Michael Gielen and by the many productions that followed, the rejection of the work in 1960 by the Cologne opera director Oscar Fritz Schuh and the general director of music Wolfgang Sawallisch on grounds of unfeasibility constitutes one of the greatest musical scandals of the twentieth century.

H. L.

Zimmermann, Udo

b. 6 October 1943 in Dresden

Udo Zimmermann was a chorister in the Dresden Kreuzchor, one of the most famous boys' choirs in the world. He studied composition, singing, and conducting at the Music Academy in Dresden, and then worked as a producer at the Dresden Staatsoper. He founded the Studio for New Music in Dresden, and became artistic director of the Bonn Workshop Stage in 1985 and director of the Center for Contemporary Music in Dresden in 1986. In 1982 he was appointed professor of composition at the Dresden Music Academy, and from 1988 directed the "musica-viva-ensemble-dresden," before becoming the director of the Leipzig Opera in 1990. Since 1997 he has been the artistic director of Bavarian Radio's well-established "Musica viva" series. As a conductor he has worked internationally with the most renowned orchestras.

Works: Operas: *Weisse Rose* (*White Rose*) (1967, rev. 1986), *Die zweite Entscheidung* (*The Second Decision*) (1970), *Levins Mühle* (*Levin's Mill*) (1973), *Der Schuhu und die fliegende Prinzessin* (*The Owl and the Flying Princess*) (1976), *Die wundersame Schustersfrau* (*The Wonderful Shoemaker's Wife*) (1982), *Gantenbein* (1998); orchestral works, concertos, choral-symphonic works, chamber music, choral music, songs.

The Wonderful Shoemaker's Wife

Die wundersame Schusters frau

Oper in two acts

Libretto: Udo Zimmermann and Eberhard Schmidt, after the play *La zapatera prodigiosa* by Federico García Lorca.
Première: 25 April 1982, Schwetzingen Festival (Schlosstheater).
Characters: Shoemaker's Wife (S), Shoemaker (B-bar), Yellow Neighbor (S), Green Neighbor (S), Violet Neighbor (Ms), Red Neighbor (A), Black Neighbor (A), Two Daughters of the Red Neighbor (2 S), Verger's Wife (Ms), Mayor (B), Don Amsel (T), Lad with a Sash (T), Lad with a Hat (Bar), Youth (Ms).
Setting: Andalusia, in the 20th century.

Synopsis

An old man has married a young woman. But with love things don't always go as they should, and the girl is rude and flirts with other men. The old man runs off, leaving his house and his shoemaker's workshop. Now that his wife is left alone, suitors flood into the house. But she pines for her husband, whose qualities she begins to appreciate now he's gone. In time, the shoemaker returns to his village from foreign parts, disguised as a puppeteer. Seeing his wife's fidelity, he reveals his identity and saves her life: after a duel between two jilted suitors the villagers had been on the point of lynching her. S. N.

Zimmermann created a variegated, pluralistic work in a typically sensitive style heightened by intense outbursts, the expression of a musician whose approach is oriented towards contemplation and silence.

The Wonderful Shoemaker's Wife, production photograph with Beatrice Niehoff (shoemaker's wife) and Peter-Christoph Runge (shoemaker), production Elmar Fulda, sets and costumes Gottfried Pilz, conductor Martin Fratz, Deutsche Oper am Rhein, Duisburg 1995.
The shoemaker returns to his wife in disguise. She doesn't see him but she senses his presence and so discovers her true feelings.

A "farsa violenta"
Udo Zimmermann's fifth opera, *The Wonderful Shoemaker's Wife,* was written between 1978 and 1981 as a commission for the Hamburg Staatsoper at the Schwetzingen Festival. The plot follows Lorca's play of the same name, described as a "farsa violenta" (violent farce). Tadeusz Kantor had opened his legendary theater in Kraków, "Cricot 2," with this piece in 1955. With its floating tonality, Zimmermann's music encompasses tragedy and comedy, a story that mixes reality and fantasy. In this opera, the composer appeals for the "wonderful" in everyone. The title figure is one of the most expressive female characters in 20th-century opera, and this has helped the work to establish a firm place in the contemporary repertory.

White Rose, production photograph with Gabriele Fontana as Sophie Scholl, production Stephan Mettin, sets and costumes Waltraut Engelberg, conductor Stefan Soltesz, Opera Stabile at the Hamburg Staatsoper 1986.
Sophie Scholl in the hours prior to her execution by guillotine. With only two singers and 15 instrumentalists, White Rose seems best suited to a modest production. The work is nevertheless a real challenge for the performers, as it requires their presence throughout. In addition, Zimmermann claimed, there should be a "scenic openness for poetry, dream, and utopia," in which the boundaries between the real and the unreal should always remain fluid.

White Rose

Weisse Rose

Szenen for two singers and 15 instrumentalists

Libretto: Wolfgang Willaschek.
Première: 27 February 1986, Hamburg (Hamburgische Staatsoper, Opera stabile)
Characters: Sophie Scholl (S), Hans Scholl (T or Bar).
Setting: A prison in Munich-Stadelheim, 22 February 1943.

Synopsis

In the hour before their execution, sister and brother Sophie and Hans Scholl recall their life, and the reasons for their resistance to the fascist regime. In the darkest moments of their despair they sense a light in their souls. They begin to question the origins of fascism, and conclude that it took root long before the persecution of any individual: it begins with carelessness and indifference, when people start to retreat into a happiness that is merely personal. Again and again they experience waves of terrible dread at the prospect of their execution and death. But more than their physical extinction they fear the death of the soul.   S. N.

Why only Sophie Scholl and not millions of others?
White Rose, a work composed for the Hamburg Staatsoper in 1984–85, recalls an event from recent German history. In 1943 Sophie and Hans Scholl, two young antifascists from the resistance organization "Weisse Rose," were arrested while distributing flyers. They were tried and executed the same year. On the occasion of the 40th anniversary of their heroic death, many people asked themselves why resistance was considered something normal for the Scholls, when millions of Germans did nothing remotely similar. Michael Verhoeven and Percy Adlon addressed the issue in their films *Die weisse Rose* (The White Rose) and *Fünf letze Tage* (*Five Last Days*), as did the poet Franz Fühmann in his Scholl Prize speech, Christa Wolf in her novella *Kassandra*, and Udo Zimmermann in his opera. Zimmermann had already set the material to music in 1967, but then rejected this first version of the work. He wrote a completely new version for the Hamburg theater, which had only a slightly modified title in common with its predecessor. Wolfgang Willaschek created a montage libretto out of the Scholls' letters and diary entries, but he also drew on biblical verses and his own texts. In recent operatic history there is no other work that has been so readily accepted by both critics and audiences, and spread so quickly to stages throughout the world. In only three years it was performed over 70 times in Europe and beyond.   S. N.

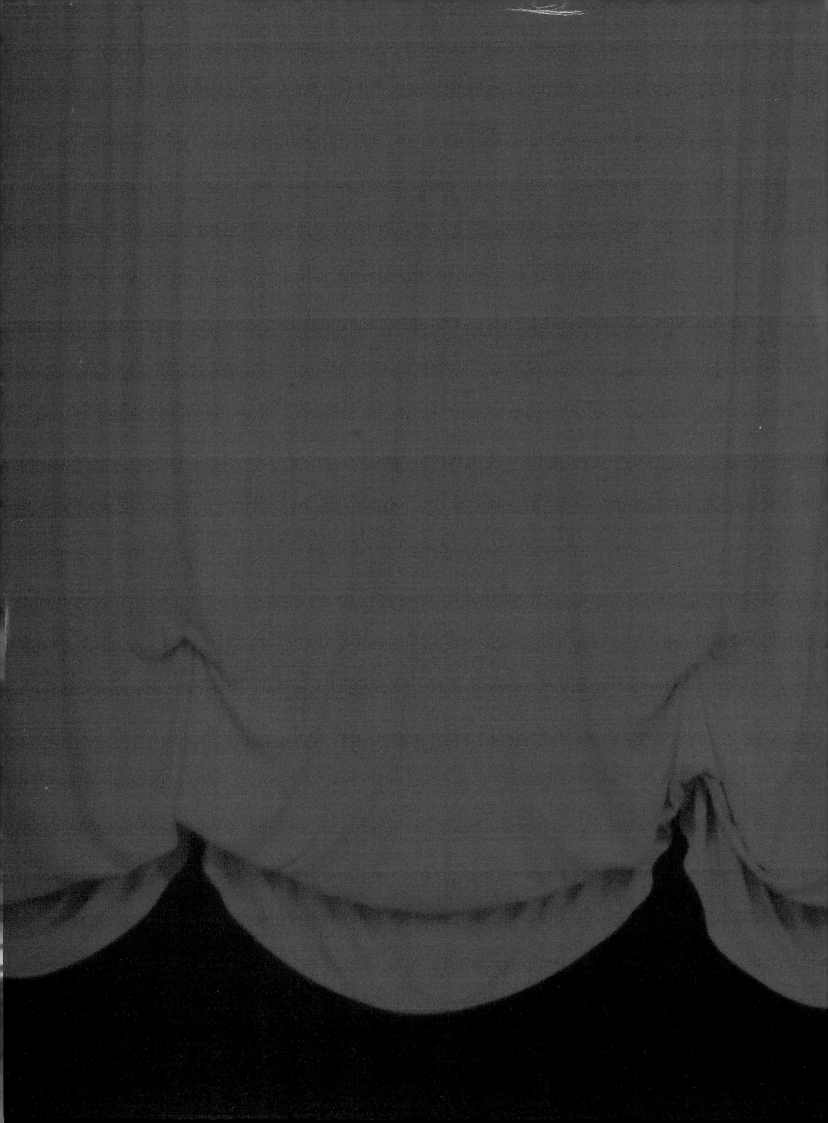

Appendix

Musical Terms

Accordion A portable reed organ, on which notes are produced by the expanding and contracting of the pleated bellows. The piano accordion has a small keyboard rather than buttons. The instrument is used above all in light music and very rarely in opera. The great exception is Alban Berg's *Wozzeck*.

Act One of the main divisions of an opera, derived from the division of Greek dramas into five parts. An act forms a closed unit, in the action as well as in the musical structure.

Acte de ballet (Fr., "danced action") A lavishly produced ballet interlude in an opera at the time of Louis XIV.

Affect An emotion, particularly as expressed in the music of the Baroque period.

Air A French and English term for aria.

Allegro (It., "quick," "lively," "bright") A tempo marking, meaning "to be played at a fast speed and in a cheerful, lively manner." The first movement of a classical symphony or sonata (→sonata form) is usually an Allegro movement.

Alto →contralto, countertenor.

Archicembalo (It.) Musical instrument, invented c. 1570 by the music theorist Nicola Vicentino (1511–76), and based on what were believed to be ancient Greek modes.

Aria (It., "air," "atmosphere," "appearance") A solo song with orchestral accompaniment. A component of opera and of oratorios and cantatas, or an independent concert piece. Originally a song composed of stanzas, the aria developed in the golden age of Baroque opera (c. 1670–1750) into a highly virtuosic solo number. The most popular aria form in this period was the so-called "da capo" aria, which consisted of two sections, after the second of which the singer was instructed to sing "da capo," or "from the top," meaning that they were to sing the first section again, thereby producing the musical form A-B-A. An alternative to the Italian and French aria was offered in the 19th century by the declamatory dramatic monologue (as found, for example, in Wagner's music dramas), but contemporary works also include arias.

Arietta (It.; Fr.: "ariette") A short aria, using a simple form.

Arioso (It., "aria-like") A lyrical style of solo vocal writing; a short passage in this style inserted into a recitative; a short aria.

Atonality The absence of a tonal center. A term coined post-1910, originally derogatory, to denote the music of the composers of the Second Viennese School (Schoenberg, Berg, Webern). (→tonality)

Azione musicale (It., "musical action") A dramatic piece for singers and instrumentalists; also called *azione scenica* ("dramatic action").

Azione sacra (It., "sacred action") A type of oratorio performed at the Viennese court in the 17th and 18th centuries.

Azione scenica →*azione musicale*.

Azione teatrale (It., "theatrical action") A short operatic work for soloists, chorus, and orchestra, and including ballet sequences. Produced with great splendor at princely courts in the 17th and 18th centuries.

Ballad A song with a narrative character. Originally a Romance folk dance-song, it developed from the songs of the French troubadours in the late Middle Ages into a strictly controlled art song with orchestral accompaniment. In the →Romantic era, when the literary ballad came into fashion, its influences are also to be traced in opera. Not only the closed form (alternating solo stanzas and choral refrains) was adopted, but also the narrative form that was so close to Romantic sensibilities. Favorite ballads in the operatic repertory are those of Senta (Wagner, *The Flying Dutchman*) and Warlaam (Musorgsky, *Boris Godunov*), and Nedda's Italian "ballatella" (Leoncavallo, *Pagliacci*).

Ballad opera An English operatic genre consisting of songs and prose dialogue. It flourished in the second half of the 17th and first half of the 18th century. The songs were mostly adaptations of traditional airs and other well-known melodies. The most famous ballad opera was *The Beggar's Opera* by John Gay and Johann Christoph Pepusch (1728).

Ballet (from It. "ballare," to dance) A dance performance to musical accompaniment. Ballet occupies a firm place not only as an independent stage genre but also as an interlude in an opera. Elements of dance were part of opera from the outset. Dance played an important part in French operatic genres up to the 20th century, while its significance was somewhat less great in Italian opera from the end of the 17th century onwards. The composers of Romantic national operas liked to bring traditional elements onto the stage by means of ballet interludes, such as the clog dance in Lortzing's *Tsar und Carpenter*.

Ballet de cour (Fr., "court ballet") A splendidly produced ballet on a mythological subject with musical accompaniment for voices and instruments (also called "ballet héroïque," "heroic ballet"), performed from the late 16th century to the 18th century at the French royal court. The *ballet de cour* is considered an important source for French Baroque opera (→*tragédie lyrique*).

Ballet héroïque →*ballet de cour*.

Baritone (from Gr. "barytonos," full-sounding, resonant) The middle register of the male voice. The most important kinds of baritone voice are the lyric baritone (Germont, Verdi's *La traviata*), the character baritone (Fra Melitone, Verdi's *The Force of Destiny*), and the *buffo* or comic baritone (Gianni Schicchi, in Puccini's opera of that name). The bass-baritone (Hans Sachs, Wagner's *The Mastersingers of Nuremberg*, and Wotan, Wagner's *The Ring of the Nibelung*) lies between the →bass and the baritone.

Baroque (from Port. "barroco," an irregularly shaped pearl) A term used to denote a musical era extending from c. 1600 to c. 1750. A number of important musical genres developed during this era, such as opera, oratorio, and the concerto. The period also saw the establishment of the tonal system, and the introduction of the use of bar lines. The public concert also emerged in the Baroque, as is shown by the construction of the first public opera houses during this period. The most important operatic forms during the Baroque were →*opera seria* and →*tragédie lyrique*. Important Baroque composers include Claudio Monteverdi, Jean-Baptiste Lully, Jean-Philippe Rameau, Henry Purcell, Johann Sebastian Bach, and George Frederick Handel.

Bass (from Lat. "bassus," deep) The lowest type of male voice. Subclasses include the *basso profondo*, or deep bass (Sarastro, Mozart's *The Magic Flute*), the *buffo* or comic bass (Don Basilio, Rossini's *The Barber of Seville*), the character bass (Méphistophélès, Gounod's *Faust*), and the high bass (Caspar, Weber's *Der Freischütz*).

Bass-baritone →baritone.

Basso continuo (It., "continuous bass") (also called "thoroughbass" or "throughbass") A continuous bass line used from the beginning of the 17th century for the accompaniment of singers and later instrumentalists. Figures may be added to the line (figured bass) to indicate what harmony should be played above each note. The basso continuo provided the accompaniment for operatic recitative from the beginnings of opera c. 1600 (Monteverdi's *Orfeo*) to the end of the 18th century.

Bel canto (It., "fine singing") A term used to indicate the elegant Italian vocal style of the 18th and early 19th centuries, the basic characteristics of which are beauty of the tone and refined articulation. The style culminated in the operas of Bellini and Donizetti.

Bïlina (Russ., "event") A Russian heroic ballad delivered in a specific vocal style. In relation to Rimsky-Korsakov's opera *Sadko*, described by the composer as an "opera-bïlina," the term implies an epic story depicted in great static scenes or tableaux.

Brindisi (It., "a toast") A usually cheerful drinking song in strophic form, found in many operas. Famous examples are the "Libiamo" of Alfredo and Violetta in Verdi's *La traviata* and Lady Macbeth's "Si colmi il calice" from Verdi's *Macbeth*.

"Ça ira" (Fr.) A French revolutionary song of 1789. Next to the "Carmagnole" and the "Marseillaise," "Ça ira" is the best-known song of the era of the French Revolution.

Cabaletta (It.) The fast concluding section of an extended aria or duet. (→cavatina)

Cadence (from Lat. "cadere," to fall) A fixed sequence of chords which closes a musical phrase.

Cadenza (as above) A virtuoso passage inserted into an aria, usually just before the end (→coloratura), in which the soloist can demonstrate his or her technical and artistic accomplishment without orchestral accompaniment.

Cakewalk Afro-American dance including pantomimic and grotesque movements. Originating in the USA in 1870, it became popular in Europe c. 1900. The music of the cakewalk is in syncopated two-four time (i.e. with the stress on the second rather than the first beat of the bar), which gives it a slightly jazzy flavor.

Cante jondo (Sp., "deep song") The oldest songs of the →flamenco tradition, from Andalusia in southern Spain.

Canzone (It., "song") A term used in opera to describe a song that actually functions as a song within the drama (e.g. Desdemona's "Willow Song" in Verdi's Otello).

Capriccio (It., "caprice") An eccentric vocal or instrumental composition. A capriccio may be distinguished by formal freedom, exaggerated virtuosity, surprising ideas, or parodic qualities. The theatrical or operatic capriccio (a capriccio drammatico) obeys the internal rules of opera. The theme of operatic capriccios (such as Mozart's The Impresario, Salieri's First the Music and then the Words, and Richard Strauss's Ariadne on Naxos and Capriccio) is the opera itself.

"Carmagnole" A French revolutionary song by an unknown author, named after the town of Carmagnole. It was often sung at executions.

Castrato (from Lat. "castrare," to castrate) A singer castrated as a child in order to prevent the breaking of his voice. The castration of musically gifted boys was practised chiefly from the 16th to the 18th century. In the adult castrato, the combination of the male lungs and resonating cavities and the unbroken voice produced an instrument of astonishing power and agility. Castration was introduced in Spain and Italy so as to be able to use higher voices in church music, in which women were not allowed to take part. The rise of opera saw the beginning of the heyday of the castrati, whose most famous representative was Farinelli (actually Carlo Broschi). In the →Baroque (→opera seria) era the greatest singing stars were castrati. Only French audiences rejected them. When a new ideal of natural performance came into being towards the end of the 18th century, the great age of the castrato came to an end, although castrati were still used in the Sistine Chapel up to the end of the 19th century.

Cavatina (It.) In 18th-century opera, a short aria, without da capo, often an entrance aria. Later examples often conclude with a →cabaletta.

Celesta (from It. "celeste," heavenly) A keyboard made from steel plates, housed in a harmonium-like casing, with the sound produced by hammers and wooden resonators. It has a soft, silvery, bell-like tone. The celesta was first made in Paris in 1886 and soon used in symphonic music (for example by Gustav Mahler) and opera (Leoncavallo, Puccini, Richard Strauss). Probably the most famous operatic scene

that is noted for the "heavenly" sound of the celesta is the delivery of the silver rose in Richard Strauss's Der Rosenkavalier.

Chaconne (Fr.; It.: "ciaconna") A dance of Spanish origin in triple meter and moderate tempo and composed exclusively in the major mode, popular in Spain and Italy in the 17th century. Towards the end of the 17th century, the dance was used in opera (above all by Lully). In the 18th century the chaconne merged with the →passacaglia.

Chanson (Fr., "song") A song with a strong lyrical character. Originally an Old French troubadour song, it came to be a French part-song in the Middle Ages. From 1500, songs of various kinds were called chansons. In the 20th century the term chanson is used mainly in France for a sung poem, usually with political, sentimental, or witty content.

Chiaroscuro (It., "light and dark") In opera, a dramatic technique making use of strong contrasts, and found above all in Mozart.

Chord At least three notes played simultaneously.

Chorus (from Gr. "choros," place for dancing) In opera, either a group of singers with a collective dramatic function (rather than individual roles), or a musical number performed by such a group (always more than one voice to a part). In Italian opera the chorus was at first of minor significance, while in French opera, above all in Gluck, it had an important dramatic function. It was not until the 19th century that the chorus acquired real significance on the operatic stage.

Chromatic (from Gk. "khroma," color) Based on the chromatic scale, which consists of all 12 semitones in the octave (on the piano, the white and black notes from C to the C an octave above), as opposed to the seven-note diatonic scale (the white notes only from C to C).

Church modes Scales used as the basis for composition in the Middle Ages and the Renaissance, derived from the scales used in Byzantine and Greek music. The modes are labeled Ionian, Dorian, Phrygian, Lydian, Mixolydian, and Aeolian. The Ionian mode is the scale that results from playing the white notes of the piano from C to the C an octave above (equivalent to the modern C major scale), the Dorian mode is the white-note scale from D to D, the Phrygian the white-note scale from E to E, and so on. The system of church modes was replaced from the 17th century by the major/minor key system.

Classical (from Lat. "classicus," first-rate, exemplary) The term used to denote a musical era extending from c. 1750 to c. 1820. The ideals of clarity, simplicity, and ready comprehensibility that were promoted by the Enlightenment are the underlying aesthetic principles of the music of this era. Classical music grew out of the attempt to replace the highly ornate and ostentatious music of the →Baroque period with clearly structured, sensitively expressed, and easily comprehended compositions. The dominant musical form at this time was →sonata form. The period from c. 1750 to 1770 is

known as the early Classical period, in which the most important principles were laid down for the period known as Classical, from 1770 to c. 1810, which is represented by the works of Haydn, Mozart, and Beethoven. In the realm of opera, where the change from one style to another took place more slowly than in instrumental music, it was not until the 1770s and 1780s that the Baroque →opera seria form gave way to new forms of musical drama (Gluck's reform operas, →Singspiel, and the operas of Mozart).

Cluster A chord consisting of several adjacent notes, experienced as something between music and noise. The cluster is a popular technique in contemporary music.

Coloratura (from Lat. "colorare," to color) Virtuoso decoration of solo vocal works by means of rapid runs, trills, and the like, which may be either written into the music by the composer or improvised by the singer. The bravura arias of Baroque opera made provision for an improvised →cadenza. Up to the beginning of the 19th century, singers of all voice types had the opportunity to demonstrate their skill by means of coloratura. From the 19th century, coloratura passages are mainly to be found in soprano arias. Famous coloratura arias include the revenge aria of the Queen of the Night in Mozart's The Magic Flute, Lucia's madness aria in Donizetti's Lucia di Lammermoor, and Zerbinetta's aria from Richard Strauss's Ariadne on Naxos.

Comédie-ballet (Fr.) A prose drama with ballet interludes and songs. A genre created in 1663–64 at the instigation of Louis XIV in collaboration with Molière and Lully.

Commedia per musica (in musica) →opera buffa

Concertato (It., from Medieval Latin/It. "concertare," to work together) In opera, an extended ensemble scene in which several protagonists and sometimes also the chorus take part. The term derives from Italian operatic practice of the 19th century. In the works of Bellini, Rossini, Donizetti, and Verdi the concertato is most often found at the end of the act.

Consonance (from Lat. "consonantia," sounding together) The harmonious combination of two or more notes. Within tonal music (→tonality) a consonance constitutes conclusion and repose, unlike →dissonance, which strives for tonal resolution. The attitude to consonance has changed greatly in the course of music history, and also varies between different cultures.

Contralto (It., from Lat. "contratenor altus," high countertenor) The deepest female voice. Sometimes abbreviated to "alto."

Couleur locale (Fr., "local color") An atmospheric musical description of the local characteristics of a place (a town, landscape, etc.).

Countertenor (from Lat. "contratenor," against the tenor) The highest male voice, the counterpart of the female contralto range, also referred to as →alto. The countertenor had an important role in vocal music of the 16th and 17th centuries, especially in England, where the tradition of the countertenor was maintained in ensemble singing. With the growth of the →Early Music movement, the countertenor voice has returned to prominence, for example in the performance of operatic roles originally written for →castratos.

Couplet (Fr.) A strophic song containing witty remarks in the refrain, originating in the 18th century. Particularly popular in *opéra comique* and operetta.

Diatonic (from Gr. "diatonikos," at intervals of a tone) Based on the division of the octave into five whole tones and two semitones. The resulting scales, known as major and minor, form the basis of the tonal system of European music.

Disposizioni sceniche (It., "stage directions") A book of stage directions used in 19th-century Italian opera.

Dissonance (from Lat. "dissonantia," sounding apart) The disharmonious combination of two or more notes, which, in the context of tonal music, strives for harmonious resolution. The opposite of dissonance is →consonance. A dissonance may be more or less intense. The experience of dissonance is relative: it depends on the position of the dissonant →chord within the composition, and also on the cultural context and the period, in that familiarity with initially unfamiliar sounds may be attained.

Divertissement (Fr., "entertainment, distraction") A decorative and entertaining ballet interlude (sometimes with song) used in the French →*comédie-ballet* and *tragédie lyrique* during the →Baroque era.

Dodecaphony →twelve-note music

Dramatic oratorio →oratorio

Dramma buffo →*opera buffa*

Dramma eroico-comico →*opera buffa*

Dramma giocoso →*opera buffa*

Dramma in musica →*opera seria*

Dramma pastorale giocoso (It., "pastoral, light-hearted drama") A light-hearted musical piece, usually with pastoral content.

Dramma per musica →*opera seria*

Dramma tragico →*opera seria*

Duet (from It. "due," two) Music for two solo voices with instrumental accompaniment. Monteverdi's first opera *Orfeo* (1607) closes with a duet. From the 18th century, the duet acquired increasing importance in opera, and in the 19th century a love duet was to be found in almost every opera. The "duetto d'addio" (farewell duet) is a popular variation of the love duet.

Early Music movement A movement that aims at the historically accurate performance of the music of earlier eras. As with the careful restoration of a

painting, the interpreters try to reconstruct the music in an authentic manner. They play on historical instruments in a historical manner that is based to a large extent on old musical sources. Attempts at authentic performances of old music have been made since the early 20th century, but around 1960 interest grew to such an extent that it became possible to speak of an independent school of interpretation. Originally, it was the music of the pre-Classical eras that was seen from a historical point of view, but today the historical approach is extended to all music written before the 20th century.

Endless melody Melody that, in the manner of speech, develops continually through the flowing of one section into another, and that consequently seems never to reach a conclusion. Wagner used this term for the definition of his theory of melody (*Zukunftsmusik, Music of the Future*, 1860). The first suggestions of endless melody are found in the extensive melodies composed by Schubert and Bellini.

Ensemble (Fr., "together") A group of singers or instrumentalists. There are various types of ensemble: →duet (2 singers), trio (3), quartet (4), quintet (5), sextet (6), septet (7), octet (8), and nonet (9). The larger ensembles were rarely found in the Baroque era, where mainly solo arias, duets, and occasionally trios are found. The great age of ensemble scenes begins with Mozart's operas (from →*Idomeneo*). The ensembles of his major operas are an unsurpassed high point in operatic history.

Eroico (It., "heroic") To be performed in a heroic manner.

Exequies (from Lat. "exequiae," funeral procession) Funeral rites in the Christian liturgy. The liturgical texts for funerals were often set to music. The Roman Catholic Mass of the Dead consisting of several movements is called a Requiem Mass.

Exposition (from Lat. "expositio," a setting forth) The presentation of the principal musical themes of a work according to certain formal rules. The term is chiefly used in the sonata and the fugue.

Fanfare A short, signal-like musical phrase, the melody of which is determined by the melodic capacities of the primitive brass instruments on which fanfares would be played in real life. The most famous fanfares in operatic history are to be found in Beethoven's *Fidelio* and Verdi's *Aida*.

Farsa per musica →*opera buffa*

Favola in musica (It., "fable in music") The generic description given to the earliest Italian operas, which were based on mythological fables. Also called "favella in musica." Monteverdi's *Orfeo* is the most famous example of this genre.

Finale The final part of a major musical work. In opera the finale is the closing scene or musical number of an act.

First subject →sonata form

Flageolet (from Fr. "flageoler," to waver or tremble) A small high-pitched flute, used from the 16th century both in dance music and in pastoral scenes in Italian and French opera. Up to the 18th century the flageolet in the operatic orchestra took over the role of the piccolo (as in Mozart's *The Abduction from the Seraglio*). The hollow and piping sounds of the flageolet can also be produced on stringed instruments with a certain light touch of the fingers.

Flamenco (Sp.) A Southern Spanish dance accompanied by singing and guitar playing, of a distinctively passionate character. During the 19th century flamenco was popularized by Andalusian and Old Castilian gypsies. Flamenco is characterized by a plaintive, highly decorated style of singing, whose rhythm is strongly emphasized by castanets, heel-stamping, and hand-clapping. At performances the *bailora* (female dancer) is surrounded by the *tocaores* (guitarists) and *cantaores* (singers).

Folklorism In music, a tendency that consciously imitates the musical styles and characteristics of folk music.

Forte, Fortissimo, Fortefortissimo (It., "loud, very loud, extremely loud") An indication that the music is to be played loudly, very loudly, etc.; abbreviated to f, ff, and fff.

Fourth →interval

Fugue (from Lat. "fuga," flight) A musical composition in which a principal theme and one or more subsidiary themes are developed through imitative counterpoint. The high point of the history of fugue composition was reached between 1650 and 1750.

Gagaku (Jap., "distinguished music") The traditional court music of Japan and its related dances, which has existed almost unchanged since the end of the 8th century (Heian period, 794–1185).

Galop A ballroom dance popular throughout Europe in the 19th century. The galop is structured in three parts, is in duple time, and is characterized by rapid hops.

Gamelan (Indon.) An Indonesian instrumental ensemble, in particular from Java and Bali. It consists mainly of percussion and wind instruments. Since the Paris Exposition of 1889, gamelan music has been a source of inspiration for European composers, including Debussy and Boulez.

General pause A simultaneous pause by all performers in a musical ensemble. The resulting silence is usually an unexpected interruption to the flow of the music. The general pause always has considerable dramatic effect, taking the audience by surprise or heightening the tension.

Genre types In the opera of the 17th to 19th centuries, frequently occurring dramatic figures and situations were allotted certain musical characteristics, which in the course of time became standardized. For example, character types were associated almost invariably with certain vocal registers: the young lover is always a tenor, the comical old woman always a contralto, and so on.

Gigue (Fr., "jig"; It.: "giga") A lively dance of Irish or Scottish origin, often with irregular phrases. In Baroque music, the gigue was also very popular as a movement in a suite. On the operatic stage, the gigue was used above all by Lully and Rameau.

Grand opera A lavish, ornate form of opera, predominant in Paris between 1830 and 1850. Its most important exponents were Auber and Meyerbeer, and its most successful librettist Eugène Scribe. Grand opera was spectacular: it required expensive sets and stage machinery, a large orchestra and choir, and a number of protagonists. Its subjects were almost exclusively drawn from history.

Harmony (from Gk. "harmonia," joining, concord) The formation of →chords and the construction of chord sequences according to certain rules. The German term "Harmoniemusik" denotes a group consisting of woodwind instruments (oboes, clarinets, and bassoons) and horns, which was particularly popular in the time of Mozart.

Impresario (It.) The director of a private opera house or company. The commercial and artistic direction of opera houses or companies developed in the course of the 18th century into an independent professional activity. The most famous impresarios include Domenico Barbaia (Milan, Naples), Giulio Gatti-Casazza (Milan, New York), and, in more recent times, Rudolf Bing (New York), Rolf Liebermann (Hamburg, Paris), and August Everding (Vienna, Munich).

Intermezzo (It., "interlude") An instrumental or sung interlude performed between two scenes or acts of an opera. In the early 18th century, it was customary to perform comic musico-dramatic "intermezzi" between the acts of an →opera seria.

Interval The difference in pitch between two notes sounded simultaneously or one after the other. The smallest intervals in diatonic music are the semitone (minor second) and the tone (major second). The minor third (found in the minor scale) consists of a tone plus a semitone, and the major third (found in the major scale) of two tones. Further intervals within the octave are the fourth, fifth, sixth, seventh, and octave. There are also intervals larger than an octave.

Intonation (from Lat. "intonare," to sound aloud) The tuning of the singing voice or of an instrument to the right pitch.

Introduction An introductory section, usually slow, to the first movement of a symphony. An introduction frequently ends with an imperfect cadence. Numerous introductions are found in Haydn's instrumental works. In the context of opera, the vocal scene that follows the overture is often called the introduction.

Invention (from Lat. "inventio," invention, idea) A composition based on a particular musical idea. The term dates from the 16th century. In the →Baroque period the meaning was extended, "invention" now referring to a musical work whose form is freely

constructed, in which the musical idea is developed further by means of various compositional techniques. The compositional principle of the invention has also been used in the post-Baroque era, for example by Alban Berg in the third act of *Wozzeck*.

Inversion The inverted performance of a series of notes (→twelve-note music, →serialism), whereby the direction of each →interval in the row is reversed (for example, a semitone up becomes a semitone down, a tone down becomes a tone up, and so on).

Key The basic note and →scale on which a musical work is based. Up to the 17th century music made use of →church modes rather than keys. In tonal music (→tonality) the scale (major or minor) and its root note determine the key (for example, the key of A major, A being the basic note on which a major scale is formed). Various keys are regarded as having their own characteristics: major keys, for example, are regarded as clear and brilliant, and minor keys as soft and melancholy.

Lamento (It., "lament") A solo aria in a solemn tempo, in which a character expresses grief. The *lamento* was a favorite type of aria in the 17th and 18th centuries, with a strong emotional effect. Among the most important *lamenti* in the history of opera are Monteverdi's *Lamento d'Arianna* (the only part of his opera *Arianna* to have survived), Dido's lament from Purcell's *Dido and Aeneas*, and Orpheus' lament from Gluck's *Orpheus and Eurydice*.

Largo (It., "broad") A tempo marking, meaning "to be performed very slowly." The term may also denote a musical movement marked "largo." A largo usually has a solemn musical character. The famous "Largo" from Handel's opera *Xerxes* (an aria sung by Xerxes), however, is marked "larghetto" and should therefore be performed in a slightly more lively tempo.

Legato (It., "tied") A direction for performance, meaning that the melodic phrases are to be sung or played smoothly, with each note flowing directly into the next.

Leitmotiv (Ger., "leading motif") A succinct musical →motif which is allocated to and symbolizes a subject, person or idea. The leitmotiv is of central importance in the music dramas of Richard Wagner.

Libretto (It., "little book") A printed book containing the text of an opera. In the 18th century, librettos were often granted more significance than their musical settings, librettists being named before composers. Despite its often considerable literary value, the libretto remains an "open" work, since it is not complete without the music. Influential librettists of their respective times were Pietro Metastasio, Lorenzo da Ponte, Eugène Scribe, Arrigo Boito, and Hugo von Hofmannsthal.

Lieto fine (It., "happy ending") The obligatory happy ending of 17th- and 18th-century Italian opera.

Madrigal (probably from Lat. "cantus matricalis," song in one's mother tongue) A genre of secular song for several unaccompanied voices. Originating in Italy

in the 14th century, it was the most popular form of song between 1530 and 1650. Both the form of the poem on which the madrigal was based and that of the musical composition were quite free and irregular. The madrigal was sung both by small groups of amateurs and by professional singers. In its powerful depiction of text and its development of poetry in music, the madrigal qualifies as an important forerunner of the operatic genre, one of whose creators, Claudio Monteverdi, was also one of the greatest madrigalists.

Maestro (It., "master"; Fr.: "maître") A deferential unofficial form of address to conductors, music teachers, or composers.

Major →key

Major third →interval

"Marseillaise" (Fr.) A French revolutionary song, the national anthem of France since 1889. The officer Claude-Joseph Rouget de Lisle composed this military marching song in 1792 as the "Chant de guerre de l'armée du Rhin" ("War Song of the Rhine Army"). In the 19th century the Marseillaise acquired a symbolic significance as a hymn of freedom and was quoted in this context in many musical works.

Masque (Fr., "mask") A form of entertainment popular at the English court in the 16th and 17th centuries, involving poetry, music, dance, and elaborate sets, and in which masked members of the court would participate.

Mazurka (from Pol. "mazur, mazurek," Mazovian dance) A Polish dance in triple time, with a springy, dotted rhythm. With the polonaise, the mazurka, originating from Mazovia, is the best-known Polish national dance. From 1600 it was widely used in the upper circles of Polish society. Introduced into art music by Chopin in the 19th century, it came to be regarded as a symbol of the Polish national spirit (for example, in the works of Moniuszko).

Melisma (from Gk. "melisma," song) A group of notes sung to a single syllable of text. The term may also be used to refer to the melodic decoration of a song. Melismatic passages are found in Gregorian chant and in folk music, particularly that of the Orient, as well as in opera (→coloratura). Decorated melodies in instrumental music can also be described as "melismatic".

Melodrama (from Gk. "melos," song, and "drama"; It.: "melodramma"; Fr.: "mélodrame") Stage genre in which the spoken word is accompanied and illustrated by instrumental music. Many operas, particularly German *Singspiele*, include melodramatic scenes (such as the prison scene in Beethoven's *Fidelio* and the scene in the Wolf's Glen in Weber's *Der Freischütz*). In Italian and French usage, the term is also used as a synonym for the operatic genre itself.

Meter (from Gk. "metron," measurement, metre) The basic pulse and rhythm of a piece of music, indicated at the beginning of the musical text by a time signature.

Mezzo-soprano (It., "middle soprano") The female voice that lies between the soprano and the contralto. The best-known mezzo role is that of Bizet's Carmen.

Micropolyphony →polyphony

Minimalism A compositional style characterized by the continual, only minimally varied repetition of notes or melodic-rhythmic motifs. Such constant repetition results in the creation of fields of sound that linger within themselves. Minimalist music came into being in the USA in the 1960s as a reaction against the intellectual and speculative →serialism. The effect of Far Eastern philosophical thought, as well as the differentiated sound world of African percussion music, may also be discerned. The most important representatives of this style on the operatic stage are Philip Glass, Steve Reich, and John Adams.

Minor →key

Minor third →interval

Minuet (from Fr. "menu pas," small step) A courtly French dance which became popular in the reign of Louis XIV and remained the most popular court dance for a century. The minuet was an important component of the Baroque suite (a sequence of dances), of the divertimento, and of Classical instrumental forms such as the symphony, the string quartet, and the sonata.

Mirror canon A canon in which the second voice is an →inversion or (less often) a →retrograde of the first.

Mise en scène (Fr., "put on the stage") The production of a stage work.

Modal →church modes

Modulation The transition from one key to another. Modulation is achieved by the use of chords that are common to both keys. Since each key has a different prevailing mood and – at least in Classical and Romantic music – evokes other musical associations, modulations in opera may have a dramatic function.

Monody (from Gk. "monodia," singing alone) Declamatory solo song accompanied by →basso continuo, evolved c. 1600. Musicians and theoreticians believed they could revive the stage practice of classical Greek drama by means of monody. The monodic style, which is an early form of →recitative, was supposed to convey the emotional content of the text. The first operas (by Jacopo Peri and Giulio Caccini) consist chiefly of monody. Monteverdi used monody in his *Orfeo* (1607), interspersed with madrigals and lyrical songs (early arias).

Morendo (It., "dying away") A direction for performance, meaning that the music should become quieter and quieter. On the operatic stage this instruction is used particularly for death scenes.

Moresca (It., from Sp. "morisco," Moor) A crudely comical men's dance, performed since the 14th century as a sword dance, mostly by masked participants, in reference to the battle between Christians and Moors. From the 15th to the 17th century a stylized form of the *moresca* was used in stage works, as, for example, in the finale of Monteverdi's *Orfeo*, probably as a reference to the wild bacchantes by whom the mythological singer was torn to pieces.

Motif The smallest thematically significant component of a musical work. Several motifs form a →theme. In operatic music, a motif, like a sort of musical visiting card, can characterize a person, a natural phenomenon, or an idea (→leitmotiv).

Movement Part of a larger work, musically complete in itself, for example a section of a symphony, sonata, or suite.

Musette (Fr., from Lat. "musum," face) French bagpipe of the 17th and 18th centuries. The instrument was made to produce a sound by means of a blowpipe attached to an airbag, while the melody was played on a pipe with valves. The musette has a characteristic nasal sound, produced without pauses for breath. The name musette is also given to a dance that was originally played on the bagpipes. In French organs there is usually a musette range; the sound of the instrument was imitated in many compositions and on many instruments.

Music drama (from Ger. "Musikdrama") A term used for the operas of Richard Wagner and his German and Italian followers.

Musica villereccia (It., "country music") Country brass band music played in 19th-century Italy. In Verdi's opera *Macbeth* King Duncan enters Macbeth's castle to the accompaniment of "musica villereccia."

Musique concrète (Fr., "concrete music") A type of music in which collages of sound are created by a combination of sounds occurring in real life, which are recorded on tape and modified by electronic or acoustic means. The inventor of this musical procedure was Pierre Schaeffer, who experimented with such collages in Paris from 1948. *Musique concrete* has been used not only in modern art music (including opera) but also in music for film, radio, television, and theater.

Musiquette (Fr.) A short operetta. A term for light music composed for entertainment.

Neo-Classicism The use in the 20th century of formal and stylistic elements of the music of the Classical era (Gluck, Haydn, and Mozart). Neo-Classicism has been motivated both by nostalgia and by a desire to escape from musical Romanticism, which was strongly influenced by emotions and by literary models. The heyday of neo-Classicism was the 1920s and it lasted from about 1918 to 1950. The outstanding figure among neo-Classical composers was Igor Stravinsky.

No (Jap., "skill, art") A form of classical Japanese theater, in which action, the spoken word, song, instrumental music, and dance are blended into a unity as a *Gesamtkunstwerk*, or total art work. The performers in a No play, usually eight in number, are exclusively men. The instrumental accompaniment consists of a small ensemble: *nokan* (flute), two tsuzumis (hourglass drums), and a *shimedaiko* (barrel drum). The chief performer, called Shite, is distinguished by a mask. The figure of Waki is responsible for the progress of the action; in most cases he plays a wanderer.

Note row →twelve-note music, →serialism

Number opera A form of opera consisting of discrete arias, duets, ensembles, and instrumental items. From the end of the 17th century up to the 19th century the number opera was the predominant type of opera, even if the beginnings of a through-composed style is to be found in the →finales of Mozart's operas. Richard Wagner and Giuseppe Verdi abandoned the number opera format, using instead the technique of through-composing, with smooth transitions from one scene to the next. As a result of →neo-Classicism, number operas have been composed as late as the 20th century.

Objet trouvé (Fr., "found object") A method of 20th-century composition, in which musical themes, effects, and phenomena that formerly existed independently are built into a new work as foreign objects.

Oboe d'amore (It., "oboe of love") An oboe in the contralto range with a pear-shaped bell, characterized by a delicate, slightly nasal sound. The oboe d'amore was frequently used in the Baroque period and is said to have been the favorite instrument of Johann Sebastian Bach. Later, composers such as Meyerbeer and Richard Strauss chose the distinctive sound of the oboe d'amore for particular dramatic situations and unusual orchestral color.

Octave →interval

Open string A freely vibrating string on a string instrument (rather than one that has been divided by pressure from the performer's finger).

Opera (It., "work") The most important genre of European musical drama. Between 1600 and 1900 it was preeminent among all musical genres. The term "opera" itself, which came into use in Italy in the late 17th century, underlines the importance and complexity of the genre. Opera came into being as a refined and highly stylized form of expression both of aristocratic court culture and of the lifestyle of the upper ranks of the bourgeoisie. Various political, social, and cultural conditions in the various countries in which it was cultivated led to a differentiation of opera into subgenres. During the 20th century opera lost its leading position, but there was still barely a major composer who was not drawn to it. As always, opera remains the most popular form of serious music.

Opera buffa (It., "comic opera") An Italian operatic genre of the 18th and 19th centuries, whose roots are to be found in improvised comedy (*commedia dell'arte*). Opera buffa began its life as an independent genre in the early 18th century, when comic elements when banished from what then became serious opera (→*opera seria*). Probably the most famous *opera buffa* is Rossini's *The Barber of Seville*.

Opéra comique (Fr., "comic opera") A French operatic genre that emerged in the first half of the 18th century and became the model for the German *Singspiel*. *Opéra comique* consists of spoken dialogue and sung numbers whose content is mostly light-hearted, but sometimes lyrical and moving, or, exceptionally, tragic. The heyday of *opéra comique* was between 1770 and 1870; the last important representative of this genre was Bizet's *Carmen* (1875).

Opera semiseria (It., "semi-serious opera") An Italian operatic genre of the 18th and 19th centuries, which resulted from the combining of serious and comic operatic elements.

Opera seria (It., "serious opera") An Italian operatic genre that emerged in the closing years of the 17th century and early years of the 18th as a musico-dramatic work of an elevated nature. The subject matter of *opera seria* was taken from Greco-Roman mythology or history. Up to about 1770 *opera seria* was considered the most ambitious and important operatic genre. Mozart's opera *La clemenza di Tito* of 1791 is regarded as a relic of an already outdated genre.

Operetta (It., "small work") A light-hearted musico-dramatic genre consisting of spoken dialogue, songs, and dances, which flourished in Paris in the 1850s chiefly in the hands of Jacques Offenbach. Operetta, which provided a parody of serious opera and the world it represented, was always produced with public's appetite for entertainment in mind. The era of operetta lasted from the mid-19th to the mid-20th century. During this period thousands of operettas were created in a number of countries and languages. Of all the operatic genres, operetta is probably most closely related to →*Singspiel* and →*opéra comique*. The basic difference between opera and operetta is operetta's impertinent, satirical, or sweetly sentimental tone. The operettas of Offenbach and Johann Strauss have also won a place on the operatic stage.

Oratorio (from Lat. "oratorium," oratory) A wide-ranging vocal work of sacred or secular content, for solo singers, chorus, and orchestra, with a narrator who is responsible for the progress of the story. The oratorio came into being in Italy in the mid-17th century, at which point it usually served a religious purpose, although it never formed part of the liturgy. The dramatic oratorio, an invention by Handel of the utmost importance for music history, assumed the function of an opera and could in fact be performed as a stage work. A number of 20th-century oratorios, including Stravinsky's *Oedipus Rex* and Honegger's *Jeanne d'Arc au bûcher*, were written expressly for stage performance. Such works are hardly to be distinguished from operas.

Organo di legno (It., "wooden organ") A small portable organ with wooden flute-like pipes. Despite its limited range it was very popular in the 16th and 17th centuries. It was used by Monteverdi in his *Orfeo* to create an atmosphere of sorrow.

Ostinato (It., "obstinate, persistent") A short, constantly repeated motif. The ostinato is mostly found in the bass voice ("basso ostinato"), above which other voices can freely unfold. The ostinato has particular significance in the →basso continuo.

Overture (Fr., "ouverture," opening) An introductory instrumental music for stage works or large-scale vocal works. As early as the 16th century opera composers were supplying instrumental introductions to their operas. These early opera overtures (called "sinfonie") were at this stage very brief. The term "overture" was first used in France at the time of Louis XIV, and referred to a solemn march characterized by a dotted rhythm, which accompanied the entrance of the king. In the 18th century, three-part operatic overtures were cultivated in Naples and Venice. In Mozart's later operas the overture developed into a piece that was related to the opera musically and in terms of atmosphere. In the 19th century the overture assumed further dramatic significance. Its importance for composers can be judged from the fact that Beethoven composed four different overtures for his *Fidelio*. In the music dramas of Wagner and Verdi, the overture was supplanted by the →prelude, which in most cases represents the basic idea of the whole work and, unlike the overture, has no separate musical identity of its own.

Panpipes (relating to Pan, the Greek shepherd-god) A wind instrument common to many early cultures, consisting of several pipes bound together. The pipes, usually made from reed or bamboo, are closed at the ends. Panpipes are very rarely used in serious music. They entered operatic history as Papageno's instrument in Mozart's *The Magic Flute*.

Parlando (It., "speaking") A direction for performance, indicating that the singer is to use a manner close to speech. The instruction *parlando*, also *parlante* (It., "speaking") and *parlar cantando* (It., "speaking in a singing manner"), is used in narrative passages or dialogues in which the meaning of the text is very important. This instruction is found particularly frequently in →*opera buffa*. In instrumental music, *parlando* or *parlante* requires a free, declamatory performance.

Parlante →*parlando*

Parlar cantando →*parlando*

Passacaglia (It., from Sp. "pasar," to walk, and "calle," street) Variations over a repeated four- or eight-bar bass line in slow triple time. Originally a Spanish dance, recorded as early as the late Middle Ages, in the 17th century the passacaglia developed into an independent musical form. Unlike the related →chaconne, the passacaglia is usually in a minor key.

Pasticcio (It., "mess," "hotch-potch") An opera compiled from arias, duets, ensembles, and instrumental pieces from various operas (or other vocal compositions) already in existence, by one or more composers. A typical operatic form of the 18th century, its rise is explained by the great interest in Italian opera (above all →*opera seria*). Since there was no historically developed repertory in the modern sense, this was a way of providing the public with a work with a new libretto but popular, tried and tested arias and ensembles, within a short space of time.

Pastorale (Fr.) A musical work with a pastoral setting and a light-hearted, idyllic character. The earliest operas, Jacopo Peri's *Euridice* and Monteverdi's *Orfeo*, were both pastoral in character, and pastoral subjects continued to be popular in Baroque opera. In French opera of the 17th and 18th centuries, the pastorale, as *pastorale héroïque*, served for the portrayal of nature and of a mythological pastoral idyll.

Pavane (Fr., from It. "Padova," Padua, or Sp. "pavo," peacock; It.: *padovana*) A slow, stately walking dance, particularly popular in the 16th and 17th centuries.

Petite Bande, La (Fr., "the little band") Louis XIV's elite string orchestra, whose leader was Jean-Baptiste Lully.

Phrygian →church modes

Piano, pianissimo (It., "quiet, very quiet") An indication that the music is to be played softly or very softly; abbreviated to p or pp.

Piano score An arrangement for piano of a vocal work (opera, oratorio, etc.) with orchestral accompaniment, particularly important for rehearsing the solo and choral parts of the work.

Polka (from Czech "pulka," half-step) A lively Czech national dance in duple time. The polka, which appeared c. 1830, was, after the →waltz, the most popular European society dance of the 19th century. It was used in Romantic operas on account of its Bohemian folk associations, for example in Smetana's *The Bartered Bride*. In Johann Strauss's *Fledermaus*, the polka also determines the character of some of the vocal numbers.

Polyphony (from Gr. "polyphonia," music of many voices) The use of several voices in a musical work in which the individual voices are rhythmically and melodically independent. Polyphonic music has existed in Europe since the 10th century. It reached its highest point in the 16th century. In opera, polyphony is shown to best advantage in ensemble scenes. The greatest masters of this art of stage polyphony were Mozart and Verdi. In the 20th century, a new development in opera was micropolyphony, in which richly decorated voices form a complex musical web within small sections (above all in the works of Ligeti).

Post-serial style A style which developed as a reaction against →serialism. Post-serialism does not denote a single style, but rather embraces various tendencies that emerged in the work of the younger generation of composers of the second half of the 1950s, which increasingly turned away from speculative serialism.

Preghiera (It., "prayer") A prayer forming the basis of a scene in 18th- and 19th-century Italian opera. A *preghiera* scene can have an intimate, lyrical character, like Desdemona's prayer in Rossini's and Verdi's *Otello*, or may represent a large-scale song of praise or supplication, like the prayers of Moses (Rossini's *Moses in Egypt*), Oroveso (Bellini's *Norma*), and Zaccaria (Verdi's *Nabucco*).

Prelude An orchestral introduction to an opera that

has a close thematic relationship with what follows and that usually leads directly into the first scene, unlike the →overture, which is a self-contained musical composition. The first operatic prelude is that of Wagner's *Lohengrin*, although examples of a close thematic link between overture and opera are to be found in Mozart's later operas.

Prima donna (It., "first lady") The leading female part in opera of the 17th to 19th centuries. The *prima donna* was given the most difficult but also the most effective female role. The *prima donna* role was almost exclusively given to a soprano; if a mezzo-soprano took over the leading role, this was referred to in Italian theatrical practice as the "prima donna mezzo-soprano."

Primo baritono brillante (It., "first brilliant baritone") A baritone who was given a big virtuoso role in Italian operatic practice. Verdi in particular composed important dramatic roles for the →baritone voice, such as Rigoletto, Germont in *La traviata*, and the Marquis of Posa in *Don Carlos*.

Primo buffo (It., "first comic part") The leading male bass part in →*opera buffa*.

Primo uomo (It., "first man") The leading male role in 17th- and 18th-century Italian opera (→*opera seria*). The *primo uomo* role was at first given to a castrato, but in time came increasingly to be allocated to a tenor.

Quartet →ensemble

Querelle des bouffons (Fr., "dispute over the Bouffons [comedians]") A dispute between the supporters of Italian →*opera buffa* and traditional French opera as represented by Lully and Rameau, which arose in the mid-18th century in connection with the performance in Paris of Pergolesi's *The Maid as Mistress* by a troupe called the "Bouffons." The dispute, which continued for years, contributed to the development of the popular genre of →*opéra comique*.

Quintet →ensemble

Ragtime A style of American popular music that developed from the 1860s. Ragtime began as piano music, played by black musicians in bars. It includes elements of dance and marching music, and made an important contribution to the development of jazz. At the turn of the century ragtime became the general musical trademark of the USA. In this context it was used in various compositions by European musicians, for example in Puccini's *The Girl of the Golden West*.

Rappresentazione sacra (It., "sacred drama") The stage performance of an oratorio in the Italian language, cultivated particularly in Florence in the 15th and 16th centuries. The *rappresentazione sacra* was a forerunner of the sacred oratorio and of opera. At the beginning of the 17th century operatic stage works with spiritual, moral content were known as *rappresentazioni*.

Recitative (from It. "recitativo," reciting) A style of vocal writing that attempts to capture the rhythms,

intonation, and irregular movement of speech, usually accompanied instrumentally. The *stile recitativo*, or "reciting style," was developed c. 1600 by the Florentine Camerata, and became one of the chief components of early opera. By the second half of the 17th century, recitative had become a vehicle for conveying the action of an opera through dialogue, while the aria contained the emotional content. Recitative has two forms: *recitativo secco* (It., "dry recitative"), accompanied by →basso continuo alone, which was used for the bulk of the dialogue, and *recitativo accompagnato* (It., "accompanied recitative"), accompanied by orchestra, used for dramatically important moments. French Baroque opera (→*tragédie lyrique*) also makes use of recitative, though it tends to be more lyrical than the recitative of Italian opera. With the replacement of the →number opera by through-composed opera in the 19th century, recitative lost its place in serious opera, though continued to be used in →*opéra comique*. In the 20th century it was used in neo-Classical operas.

Register Part of the range or compass of a voice or instrument. The term may also refer to the characteristic timbre of the voice in the various areas of resonance, for example the "head register" and the "chest register." (The head register in the male voice is known as falsetto.) Classical training in singing aims at a balanced blend of these registers and a seamless transition from one register to another. With the organ, a register includes all the pipes of the same tone color.

Retrograde The performance of a series of notes (→twelve-note music, →serialism) backwards, note for note.

Retrograde inversion The inverted performance of the →retrograde form of the original note row, whereby the direction of each →interval is reversed (for example, a semitone up becomes a semitone down, a tone down becomes a tone up, and so on).

Ricercare (It., "to seek out") A fantasia-like instrumental piece, distinguished by the imitation of snatches of themes and motifs. The *ricercare* was originally an improvised piece for the lute, and enjoyed particular popularity during the Renaissance and the →Baroque period.

Romance A narrative strophic song of Spanish origin. The romance deals with heroic deeds and amorous adventures. In the 18th and 19th centuries the romance became popular in France and Germany, and was successfully introduced into opera (particularly the →*opéra comique* and →*Singspiel*). The Russian traditional song of the 19th century, which was popular in salons and, in a stylized form, on the operatic stage (above all in the operas of Glinka and Tchaikovsky), is a variation of the romance.

Romanticism In music historical terms, a period extending from about 1810/1820 to 1910. The Romantic sensibility – the tendency toward the fantastic, the fabulous, and the mystical, the growing interest in history, and the interest in subjective feeling – formed the basis of Romantic music. The development of national musical schools was one of the most important aspects of the Romantic period (above all in

central and eastern Europe). The strict canon of forms of the →Classical period dissolved in the Romantic era, a multiplicity of forms being characteristic of Romantic music. Artistic subjectivity became an important criterion (which also led to the idealization of the role of the artist). Important Romantic composers who were active in the field of opera include such varied artistic personalities as Giacomo Meyerbeer, Gaetano Donizetti, Gioachino Rossini, Franz Schubert, Vincenzo Bellini, Hector Berlioz, Robert Schumann, Giuseppe Verdi, Richard Wagner, Charles Gounod, Bed_ich Smetana, Modest Musorgsky, Piotr Tchaikovsky, Antonin Dvo_ák and Richard Strauss.

Rondo (It., from Fr. "rondeau," round) A musical piece in which the theme returns regularly like a refrain after brief musical episodes. Unlike the vocal rondeau that developed in late medieval France, the rondo established itself in the →Classical era as a form of instrumental music. The rondo's formal principles, however, were soon transferred to the vocal field. An example of a song composed in rondo form is the "Golden Calf" rondo sung by Méphisto phélès in Gounod's *Faust*.

Saxophone (named after its inventor, Adolphe Sax) A brass instrument with reeds of eight different sizes. Apart from its great importance in jazz and light music, the saxophone, first made in 1840/41, is also used in serious music (for example, by French composers such as Thomas, Bizet, Debussy, and Ravel, and a number of 20th-century composers). Meyerbeer was one of the first to introduce the saxophone into opera.

Scale A fixed sequence of notes within an octave (→key).

Scene (from Gr. "skene," stage wall; It.: "scena") A subdivision of a drama or opera, often marked by the entrance and exit of a character. The term "scena ed aria" (It., "scene and aria") describes a cohesive sequence of →recitatives, →*ariosi*, and a final →aria, often of great virtuosity.

Scherzo (It., "joke") A rapid, lively musical →movement, in triple time. The scherzo, in the 17th century a piece of a light-hearted character, in the →Classical period came to be a movement in a multi-partite musical work as a result of Haydn's string quartets. In the 19th century the scherzo developed into an independent musical work, for example in the works of Chopin. In the 19th-century symphony the scherzo is the third of four movements; in the sonata it frequently replaced the minuet. As a direction for performance, "scherzando" (scherzo-like) indicates a playful, humorous manner.

Score A musical text containing all the instrumental and/or vocal parts of a composition for more than one part, in which the various parts are laid out one below another. It is the text used by conductors in the rehearsal and performance of a work.

Scrittura (It., "writing") The scenario of an opera of the 17th or 18th century. The composer received the *scrittura* from the person commissioning the work, and had a libretto prepared from it.

Second →interval

Second subject →sonata form

Seconda donna (It., "second lady") The most important supporting female role in Italian →opera seria.

Secondo uomo (It., "second man") The most important supporting male role in Italian →opera seria, usually written for a castrato.

Seguidilla (Sp., from "seguir," to follow) A traditional Spanish dance-song in a moderate tempo and uneven beat, with castanet, guitar, or tambourine accompaniment. Bizet introduced the *seguidilla* into opera in his *Carmen*.

Semi-opera An English 17th-century operatic genre. The semi-opera consists of a spoken play with song and dance interludes. The greatest representative of the semi-opera was Henry Purcell (*King Arthur, The Fairy Queen*).

Semitone →interval

Septet →ensemble

Serenata teatrale (It., "theatrical serenade") A courtly festive composition for voice with instrumental accompaniment, of the 17th and 18th centuries. Also a generic description for courtly mini-operas.

Serialism (relating to "series," or "row") A method of composition dating from the years 1950–65, which grew out of the principle of →twelve-note music. In serial music, it is not only the sequence of pitches that is fixed (and here there may be fewer than twelve notes in the row), but also various other musical parameters, such as rhythm, volume, and timbre. This total control of the musical material soon led, however, to the emergence of contrary musical tendencies, namely the total renunciation of all such control and the establishment of chance as the basic principle of composition (aleatory music). Important contributions to serialism were made by Olivier Messiaen, Karlheinz Stockhausen, and Luigi Nono.

Sextet →ensemble

Singspiel (Ger., "song play") A genre of German opera consisting of spoken dialogue interspersed with songs. The *Singspiel* developed in the 18th century (like its French counterpart, the →opéra comique) as an alternative to →opera seria, and found its high point in Mozart's *Singspiele The Abduction from the Seraglio* and *The Magic Flute*. The *Singspiel* moulded the development of German Romantic opera.

Slow foxtrot A popular dance of North American origin that resulted from the combination of →ragtime and one-step. The dance became widespread after the First World War and has remained one of the standard ballroom dances.

Solmization The system of naming notes according to the syllables do, re, mi, fa, sol, la, si, do. Solmization was introduced by Guido d'Arezzo in the 11th century (then with the syllables ut, re, mi, fa, sol, la) as an aid to learning complicated Gregorian melodies. Since the Middle Ages, this method of solmization or sol-fa syllables has been continuously developed; it is still used in music teaching today.

Solo (It., "alone") A piece of music to be performed by a single voice, either alone or with instrumental accompaniment, or by a single instrument.

Sonata (It., from "sonare," to sound) An instrumental composition in several movements for a solo performer or small ensemble. In the 17th century the solo and trio sonata developed out of this (in each case with →basso continuo accompaniment). In the →Classical period the sonata was the favorite genre for chamber music composition, with the first movement in →sonata form.

Sonata form A formal method which predominated in the →Classical period. A sonata form movement consists of a number of sections: exposition, development, recapitulation, and sometimes a coda (to which Beethoven gave particular importance). The exposition introduces the first subject (in the basic key), the second subject (usually in a different but related key), and sometimes also a closing subject. In the development section, the subjects are presented in different keys. In the recapitulation all subjects reappear in the basic key. The coda provides an opportunity for a new reworking of the musical material.

Soprano (It., from "sopra," above) The highest female voice or boy's voice. The soprano can be sub-divided into the following types: coloratura soprano (for example, the Queen of the Night in Mozart's *The Magic Flute*), dramatic soprano (Leonore in Beethoven's *Fidelio*), high dramatic soprano (Isolde in Wagner's *Tristan and Isolde*), lyric soprano (Mimi in Puccini's *La bohème*), juvenile-dramatic soprano (Agathe in Weber's *Der Freischütz*), and soubrette (Blonde in Mozart's *The Abduction from the Seraglio*).

Sostenuto (It., "sustained") A direction for performance, meaning "sustained."

Soubrette →soprano

Staccato (It., "detached") A direction for performance, meaning that the notes are to be detached from each other. The opposite of →legato.

Street ballad A song performed by traveling street singers at fairs from the 17th to 19th centuries. In most cases, texts recounting current events and horror stories were set to well-known tunes.

Suspension The playing of a dissonant note (→dissonance) on the strong beat of a bar. A suspension has the effect of delaying the expected harmonic resolution and thus creates tension.

Synthesizer An electronic instrument for the production of sounds.

Syrinx (Lat., "pipe") Panpipes, made of five, seven, or more pipes of varying length.

Tableau (Fr., "scene") A dramatically closed section (scene) of an opera. The term is used mainly in relation to French opera.

Tambourin (Fr., "little drum") Also called tabor. A small cylindrical drum that is still played in Provençal folk music. In the 18th century the instrument was admitted to the orchestra. The name is also used for a Provençal dance in duple time accompanied by the tambourin.

Tambourine (as above) A small frame drum fitted with bells.

Tango (Sp., from Port. "tanger," to touch, or Sp. "tango," song) A Latin American dance in duple time. The tango developed in Buenos Aires toward the end of the 19th century, mainly from elements of the Cuban habanera and European influences. From 1910 it also became widespread in Europe and developed into a standard ballroom dance. Many composers of the 20th century, such as Stravinsky and Hindemith, used tangos in their compositions.

Tarantella (It., from the town Taranto) A southern Italian folk dance, mostly in triple time. The tarantella was taken up in serious music during the 19th century. With Auber's *La muette de Portici* this unrestrained dance also gained a place in opera.

Tenor (from It. "tenere," to hold) A high male voice. There are various types of operatic tenor: the *tenore di forza* (Othello in Verdi's *Otello*), the heroic tenor or *heldentenor* (Siegfried in Wagner's *The Ring of the Nibelung*), the lyric tenor (Belmonte in Mozart's *The Abduction from the Seraglio*), the *tenore altino* (Pedrillo in the same opera), the *tenore spinto* (the Duke of Mantua in Verdi's *Rigoletto*), the *buffo* tenor (Trabuco in Verdi's *The Force of Destiny*), the character tenor (Herod in Strauss's *Salome*), and the *tenore brillante* (Gustavus III in Verdi's *A Masked Ball*).

Theme (from Gr. "tithemi," to place) A distinctive musical idea, which reappears throughout the course of a work, both in its original form and in variations upon it.

Third →interval

Thorough bass →basso continuo

Toccata (It., from "toccare," to touch) A freely constructed, often virtuoso instrumental work, usually for a keyboard instrument. In the 15th and 16th centuries the term was also used for festive fanfare music for brass and kettledrums. Monteverdi called the introductory music for his *Orfeo* "toccata."

Tonality A system of the relationship of notes to a central note, according to which each note has a function and a place within the hierarchy of notes. In the music of the 17th to 19th centuries the central note is the root note of a major or minor scale. The triads above the first (tonic), fourth (subdominant), and fifth (dominant) steps in the scale form the →cadence. In the tonal system, intervals and chords are differentiated according to their →consonance or →dissonance. In the 20th century the framework of tonality was either extended or abandoned altogether.

In so-called atonal music (→atonality, →twelve-note music), all notes, intervals, and chords are considered to have equal status.

Tragédie lyrique (Fr., "musical tragedy") The most important genre of French court opera of the 17th and 18th centuries. The *tragédie lyrique* was developed by Jean-Baptiste Lully from elements of French tragedy, the →*comédie-ballet*, the →*ballet de cour*, and Italian opera, and was continued by Jean-Philippe Rameau. It consists of a prologue (which usually refers to current court events) and five acts, and its subject matter is drawn from Greco-Roman mythology. Important components are declamatory monologues, short arias ("airs") and duets, and choruses, as well as mime and dance interludes (*divertissements*).

Tragédie (mise) en musique (Fr., "tragedy set to music") An alternative name for →*tragédie lyrique*.

Tremolo (It., "tremulous") The rapid and regular repetition of a single note. The tremolo effect gives the music a restless, turbulent character. In singing, the term indicates variations of intensity in the production of a single note.

Trill The decoration of a note by the rapid, repeated alternation between the basic note and the note immediately above it.

Trio →ensemble

Tutti (It., "all") A term given both to the full complement of a large ensemble and to a musical section in which all members of the ensemble are singing and/or playing at the same time.

Twelve-note music Also known as twelve-tone music or dodecaphony. A method of composition based on a fixed sequence (row) of the twelve chromatic notes of an octave (→interval). No note may be repeated until the other eleven notes have been sounded. The note row can be modified in certain ways (→retrograde, →inversion, or →retrograde inversion). The twelve-note technique was developed as a principle of composition by Arnold Schoenberg c. 1920, and transmitted to his pupils Alban Berg and Anton Webern (the Second Viennese School). Twelve-note music was intended as a strictly rational, well-thought-out principle of composition, in opposition to late Romantic music. Imitation of Anton Webern's strict twelve-note technique led to the creation of →serialism c. 1950.

Unison The simultaneous playing of the same note or notes by several musicians.

Valse triste (Fr., "sad waltz") An instrumental salon piece in slow triple time and a melancholy mood.

Vaudeville (from Fr., "voix de ville," voice of the city) A popular dramatic production with sung interludes, which developed from French improvised performances. The typical round-songs of vaudeville were adopted in the 18th century as finales for →*opéras comiques* and →*Singspiele* (for example, Mozart's *The Abduction from the Seraglio*).

Verismo (from It. "vero," real) An Italian operatic genre with realistic subject matter and treatment. Influenced by literary realism, *verismo* developed between 1890 and 1910 as a counter-movement to Romantic opera. The most important operas of the *verismo* school are Mascagni's *Cavalleria rusticana* and Leoncavallo's *Pagliacci*. The performance style of *verismo* integrated naturalistic expressions of feeling, such as screaming, sighing, or sobbing, into singing. The influence of *verismo* is found in many operas of the period (for example, in Puccini's *Tosca*, Charpentier's *Louise* and d'Albert's *The Lowlands*.

Viola d'amore (It., "viola of love") A popular string instrument of the 17th and 18th centuries, shaped like the present-day viola. In addition to the bowed strings (5–7), the viola d'amore also had 7–14 "sympathetic strings" beneath the fingerboard, which produced a pleasant, muted, nasal sound. The viola d'amore was used in several Romantic operas as an interesting instrumental effect (for example, in works by Meyerbeer and Erkel).

Waltz An Austrian dance for couples in triple time. The waltz developed c. 1770 from the so-called German Dance and the *ländler*. It was introduced into art music by Beethoven and Schubert. At the time of the Congress of Vienna it became widespread throughout Europe. Johann Strauss the elder and Joseph Lanner promoted the waltz as a popular dance. Johann Strauss the younger eventually became the king of the most popular ballroom dance of the 19th century. In 1911, Richard Strauss paid homage to the waltz in his *Der Rosenkavalier*.

Xylophone (from Gr. "xylon," wood, and "phone" voice) A percussion instrument made from wooden bars of various lengths. This instrument was given its name in the 19th century. The xylophone is used in folk music (in Austria and Africa), as well as in art music (for example, by Saint-Saëns, Strauss, Orff, and Puccini).

Zeitoper (Ger., "opera of its time") An operatic genre of the 1920s and early 1930s, in which the plot is placed in a contemporary everyday setting and makes use of modern technological inventions (such as the telephone, telegram, modern methods of transport such as trains and automobiles, and other machines). This comparatively short-lived genre represented an attempt by composers to give new life to the operatic stage.

Index of Works

The index of works lists in alphabetical order the works mentioned in the commentary text. The composer's name appears in brackets. Both the original title and in most cases the English translation are indexed. Page references in bold indicate a synopsis and detailed discussion of the opera.

Carl Orff, *Carmina burana*, costume designs by Hans Aeberli, Essen 1980.

A Journey through Operatic History

Opera chronology

Date	Opera	Composer	Place	Theater
17th century				
24.02.1607	Orfeo	Monteverdi	Mantua	Palazzo Ducale
1640	The Return of Ulysses to his Homeland	Monteverdi	Venice	Teatro S. Cassiano
1642	The Coronation of Poppaea	Monteverdi	Venice	Teatro SS. Giovanni e Paolo
19.01.1674	Alcestis	Lully	Paris	Opéra, Palais Royal
11.04.1689	Dido and Aeneas	Purcell	London	Josias Priest's School for Young Ladies
1691	King Arthur	Purcell	London	Queen's Theater, Dorset Garden
02.05.1692	The Fairy Queen	Purcell	London	Queen's Theater, Dorset Garden
18th century				
26.12.1709	Agrippina	Handel	Venice	Teatro S. Giovanni Grisostomo
24.02.1711	Rinaldo (1st version)	Handel	London	Haymarket Theater
1718	Acis and Galatea	Handel	London	Cannons, Edgware
27.04.1720	Radamisto (1st version)	Handel	London	Haymarket Theater
28.12.1720	Radamisto (2nd version)	Handel	London	Haymarket Theater
20.02.1724	Julius Caesar	Handel	London	Haymarket Theater
13.02.1725	Rodelinda	Handel	London	Haymarket Theater
01.10.1730	Hippolytus and Aricia	Rameau	Paris	Opéra, Palais Royal
06.04.1731	Rinaldo (2nd version)	Handel	London	Haymarket Theater
27.01.1733	Orlando	Handel	London	Haymarket Theater
05.09.1733	The Maid as Mistress	Pergolesi	Naples	Teatro S. Bartolomeo
16.04.1735	Alcina	Handel	London	Covent Garden Theater
16.02.1737	Giustino	Handel	London	Covent Garden Theater
24.10.1737	Castor and Pollux (1st version)	Rameau	Paris	Opéra, Palais Royal
26.04.1738	Xerxes	Handel	London	Haymarket Theater
11.01.1754	Castor and Pollux (2nd version)	Rameau	Paris	Opéra, Palais Royal
05.10.1762	Orpheus and Eurydice (1st version)	Gluck	Vienna	Kaiserliches Hoftheater
26.12.1767	Alcestis (1st version)	Gluck	Vienna	Kaiserliches Hoftheater
1769	La finta semplice	Mozart	Salzburg	Hoftheater
26.12.1770	Mithridates, King of Pontus	Mozart	Milan	Teatro Regio Ducale
26.12.1772	Lucio Silla	Mozart	Milan	Teatro Regio Ducale
19.04.1774	Iphigenia in Aulis	Gluck	Paris	Opéra, Palais Royal
02.08.1774	Orpheus and Eurydice (2nd version)	Gluck	Paris	Académie Royale
13.01.1775	La finta giardiniera (1st version)	Mozart	Munich	Opernhaus St. Salvator
23.04.1776	Alcestis (2nd version)	Gluck	Paris	Académie Royale
18.05.1779	Iphigenia in Tauris	Gluck	Paris	Opéra, Palais Royal
05.1780	La finta giardiniera (2nd version)	Mozart	Augsburg	Komödienstadl
29.01.1781	Idomeneo	Mozart	Munich	Hoftheater
16.07.1782	The Abduction from the Seraglio	Mozart	Vienna	Burgtheater
07.02.1786	The Impresario	Mozart	Schönbrunn	Orangerie
01.05.1786	The Marriage of Figaro	Mozart	Vienna	Altes Burgtheater
29.10.1787	Don Giovanni	Mozart	Prague	Nationaltheater
26.01.1790	Così fan tutte	Mozart	Vienna	Burgtheater
06.09.1791	La clemenza di Tito	Mozart	Prague	Nationaltheater
30.09.1791	The Magic Flute	Mozart	Vienna	Freihaustheater auf der Wieden
19th century				
20.11.1805	Fidelio (1st version)	Beethoven	Vienna	Theater an der Wien
15.12.1807	La vestale	Spontini	Paris	Opéra
06.02.1813	Tancredi	Rossini	Venice	Teatro La Fenice
22.05.1813	The Italian Girl in Algiers	Rossini	Venice	Teatro S. Benedetto
23.05.1814	Fidelio (final version)	Beethoven	Vienna	Kärntnertor Theater
14.08.1814	The Turk in Italy	Rossini	Milan	Teatro alla Scala
20.02.1816	The Barber of Seville	Rossini	Rome	Teatro Argentina
01.09.1816	Faust (1st version)	Spohr	Prague	Ständetheater
04.12.1816	Otello	Rossini	Naples	Teatro del Fondo
25.01.1817	La Cenerentola	Rossini	Rome	Teatro Valle
05.03.1818	Moses in Egypt (1st version, It.)	Rossini	Naples	Teatro S. Carlo
07.03.1819	Moses in Egypt (2nd version, It.)	Rossini	Naples	Teatro S. Carlo
18.11.1821	Der Freischütz	Weber	Berlin	Königliches Schauspielhaus
25.10.1823	Euryanthe	Weber	Vienna	Kärnterhoftheater
10.12.1825	The White Lady	Boieldieu	Paris	Opéra-Comique
12.04.1826	Oberon	Weber	London	Covent Garden
26.03.1827	Moses and Pharaoh (3rd version, Fr.)	Rossini	Paris	Opéra

Date	Opera	Composer	Place	Theater
19th century				
03.08.1829	William Tell	Rossini	Paris	Opéra
28.01.1830	Fra Diavolo	Auber	Paris	Opéra-Comique
06.03.1831	La sonnambula	Bellini	Milan	Teatro Carcano
21.11.1831	Robert the Devil	Meyerbeer	Paris	Opéra
26.12.1831	Norma	Bellini	Milan	Teatro alla Scala
24.05.1833	Hans Heiling	Marschner	Berlin	Königliches Opernhaus
24.01.1835	I puritani	Bellini	Paris	Théâtre-Italien
23.02.1835	La Juive	Halévy	Paris	Opéra
29.02.1836	The Huguenots	Meyerbeer	Paris	Opéra
29.03.1836	The Ban on Love	Wagner	Magdeburg	Stadttheater
09.12.1836	A Life for the Tsar (1st version)	Glinka	St. Petersburg	Grosses Theater
22.12.1837	Tsar and Carpenter	Lortzing	Leipzig	Stadttheater
17.11.1839	Oberto, Count of San Bonifacio	Verdi	Milan	Teatro alla Scala
05.09.1840	King for a Day	Verdi	Milan	Teatro alla Scala
09.03.1842	Nabucco	Verdi	Milan	Teatro alla Scala
20.10.1842	Rienzi, the Last of the Tribunes	Wagner	Dresden	Hoftheater
09.12.1842	Ruslan and Lyudmila	Glinka	St. Petersburg	Grosses Theater
31.12.1842	The Poacher	Lortzing	Leipzig	Stadttheater
22.01.1843	The Flying Dutchman	Wagner	Dresden	Hoftheater
11.02.1843	The Lombards on the First Crusade	Verdi	Milan	Teatro alla Scala
09.03.1844	Ernani	Verdi	Venice	Teatro La Fenice
03.11.1844	The Two Foscari	Verdi	Rome	Teatro Argentina
15.02.1845	Joan of Arc	Verdi	Milan	Teatro alla Scala
13.03.1845	Tannhäuser (Dresden version)	Wagner	Dresden	Hoftheater
21.04.1845	Undine (1st version)	Lortzing	Magdeburg	Stadttheater
12.08.1845	Alzira	Verdi	Naples	Teatro S. Carlo
17.03.1846	Attila	Verdi	Venice	Teatro La Fenice
30.05.1846	The Armorer	Lortzing	Vienna	Theater an der Wien
22.07.1847	The Bandits	Verdi	London	Her Majesty's Theater
20.10.1847	Undine (2nd version)	Lortzing	Vienna	Theater an der Wien
01.01.1848	Halka (1st version, concert)	Moniuszko	Wilna	?
25.10.1848	The Corsair	Verdi	Trieste	Teatro Grande
27.01.1849	The Battle of Legnano	Verdi	Rome	Teatro Argentina
09.03.1849	The Merry Wives of Windsor	Nicolai	Berlin	Königliches Opernhaus
16.04.1849	The Prophet	Meyerbeer	Paris	Opéra
08.12.1849	Luisa Miller	Verdi	Naples	Teatro S. Carlo
28.08.1850	Lohengrin	Wagner	Weimar	Hoftheater
16.11.1850	Stiffelio	Verdi	Trieste	Teatro Grande
11.03.1851	Rigoletto	Verdi	Venice	Teatro La Fenice
15.07.1852	Faust (2nd version, It.)	Spohr	London	Covent Garden
19.01.1853	Il trovatore	Verdi	Rome	Teatro Apollo
06.03.1853	La traviata	Verdi	Venice	Teatro La Fenice
28.02.1854	Halka (1st version, stage)	Moniuszko	Wilna	?
24.06.1854	Alfonso and Estrella	Schubert	Weimar	?
13.06.1855	The Sicilian Vespers	Verdi	Paris	Grand Opéra
12.03.1857	Simon Boccanegra	Verdi	Venice	Teatro La Fenice
01.01.1858	Halka (2nd version)	Moniuszko	Warsaw	?
17.02.1859	A Masked Ball	Verdi	Rome	Teatro Apollo
19.03.1859	Faust	Gounod	Paris	Théâtre-Lyrique
25.06.1859	Genoveva	Schumann	Leipzig	Stadttheater
13.03.1861	Tannhäuser (Paris version)	Wagner	Paris	Théâtre Imperial de l'Opéra
09.08.1862	**Beatrice and Benedick**	Berlioz	**Baden-Baden**	Neues Theater
10.11.1862	The Force of Destiny	Verdi	St. Petersburg	Kaiserliches Grosses Theater
30.09.1863	The Pearl Fishers	Bizet	Paris	Théâtre-Lyrique
04.11.1863	The Trojans (Acts III–V)	Berlioz	Paris	Théâtre-Lyrique
19.03.1864	**Mireille**	Gounod	**Paris**	Théâtre-Lyrique
21.04.1865	Macbeth	Verdi	Paris	Théâtre-Lyrique
28.04.1865	The African Woman	Meyerbeer	Paris	Opéra
10.06.1865	Tristan and Isolde	Wagner	Munich	Hoftheater
30.05.1866	**The Bartered Bride (1st version)**	Smetana	**Prague**	Provisional Theater
17.11.1866	Mignon	Thomas	Paris	Opéra-Comique
11.03.1867	Don Carlos	Verdi	Paris	Opéra
27.04.1867	Romeo and Juliet	Gounod	Paris	Théâtre-Lyrique

Date	Opera	Composer	Place	Theater
19th century				
09.03.1868	Hamlet	Thomas	Paris	Opéra
21.06.1868	The Mastersingers of Nuremberg	Wagner	Munich	Hofoper
29.01.1869	The Bartered Bride (2nd version)	Smetana	Prague	Provisional Theater
01.06.1869	The Bartered Bride (3rd version)	Smetana	Prague	Provisional Theater
22.09.1869	The Ring: The Rhinegold	Wagner	Munich	Hoftheater
19.03.1870	The Guarani	Gomes	Milan	Teatro alla Scala
26.07.1870	The Ring: The Valkyrie	Wagner	Munich	Hoftheater
25.09.1870	The Bartered Bride (4th version)	Smetana	Prague	Provisional Theater
24.12.1871	Aida	Verdi	Cairo	Opera House
08.02.1874	Boris Godunov	Musorgsky	St. Petersburg	Mariinsky Theater
05.04.1874	Die Fledermaus	Strauss, J.	Vienna	Theater an der Wien
03.03.1875	Carmen	Bizet	Paris	Opéra-Comique
10.03.1875	The Queen of Sheba	Goldmark	Vienna	Hofoper
08.04.1876	La Gioconda	Ponchielli	Milan	Teatro alla Scala
16.08.1876	The Ring: Siegfried	Wagner	Bayreuth	Festspielhaus
17.08.1876	The Ring: Twilight of the Gods	Wagner	Bayreuth	Festspielhaus
02.12.1877	Samson and Delilah	Saint-Saëns	Weimar	Hoftheater
29.03.1879	Eugene Onegin	Tchaikovsky	Moscow	Small Theater
07.12.1879	The Trojans (Acts I–II)	Berlioz	Paris	Théâtre du Châtelet
10.02.1881	The Tales of Hoffmann	Offenbach	Paris	Opéra-Comique
26.07.1882	Parsifal	Wagner	Bayreuth	Festspielhaus
17.01.1884	Manon	Massenet	Paris	Opéra-Comique
15.02.1884	Mazeppa	Tchaikovsky	Moscow	Bol'shoy Theater
31.05.1884	Le villi	Puccini	Milan	Teatro dal Verme
05.02.1887	Otello	Verdi	Milan	Teatro alla Scala
29.06.1888	The Fairies	Wagner	Munich	Hoftheater
21.04.1889	Edgar	Puccini	Milan	Teatro alla Scala
17.05.1890	Cavalleria rusticana	Mascagni	Rome	Teatro Costanzi
02.10.1890	Bastien and Bastienne	Mozart	Berlin	?
04.11.1890	Prince Igor	Borodin	St. Petersburg	Mariinsky Theater
05.12.1890	The Trojans (final version)	Berlioz	Karlsruhe	Hoftheater
12.12.1890	The Queen of Spades	Tchaikovsky	St. Petersburg	Mariinsky Theater
16.02.1892	Werther	Massenet	Vienna	Hofoper
21.05.1892	Pagliacci	Leoncavallo	Milan	Teatro dal Verme
01.02.1893	Manon Lescaut	Puccini	Turin	Teatro Regio
09.02.1893	Falstaff	Verdi	Milan	Teatro alla Scala
09.05.1893	Aleko	Rakhmaninov	Moscow	Bol'shoy Theater
23.12.1893	Hansel and Gretel	Humperdinck	Weimar	Hoftheater
10.05.1894	Guntram	Strauss, R.	Weimar	Hoftheater
01.02.1896	La bohème	Puccini	Turin	Teatro Regio
28.03.1896	Andrea Chénier	Giordano	Milan	Teatro alla Scala
07.06.1896	The Governor (1st version)	Wolf	Mannheim	Nationaltheater
07.01.1898	Sadko	Rimsky-Korsakov	Moscow	Solodovnikov Theater
20th century				
14.01.1900	Tosca	Puccini	Rome	Teatro Costanzi
31.03.1901	Rusalka	Dvořák	Prague	Nationaltheater
21.11.1901	Trial by Fire	Strauss, R.	Dresden	Hofoper
30.04.1902	Pelléas and Mélisande	Debussy	Paris	Opéra-Comique
06.11.1902	Adriana Lecouvreur	Cilea	Milan	Teatro Lirico
15.11.1903	The Lowlands (1st version)	d'Albert	Prague	Neues Deutsches Theater
27.11.1903	The Curious Women	Wolf-Ferrari	Munich	Residenztheater
21.01.1904	Jenĕfa	Janáček	Brno	National Theater
17.02.1904	Madame Butterfly	Puccini	Milan	Teatro alla Scala
16.01.1905	The Lowlands (2nd version)	d'Albert	Magdeburg	Stadttheater
09.12 1905	Salome	Strauss, R.	Dresden	Hofoper
24.01.1906	The Miserly Knight	Rakhmaninov	Moscow	Bol'shoy Theater
24.01.1906	Francesca da Rimini	Rakhmaninov	Moscow	Bol'shoy Theater
20.02.1907	The Legend of the Invisible City of Kitezh	Rimsky-Korsakov	St. Petersburg	Mariinsky Theater
25.01.1909	Elektra	Strauss, R.	Dresden	Hofoper
07.10.1909	The Golden Cockerel	Rimsky-Korsakov	Moscow	Solodovnikov Theater
02.12.1910	Fine Feathers Make Fine Birds (1st version)	Zemlinsky	Vienna	?
10.12.1910	The Girl of the Golden West	Puccini	New York	Metropolitan Opera
26.01.1911	Der Rosenkavalier	Strauss, R.	Dresden	Hofoper
19.05.1911	L'heure espagnole	Ravel	Paris	Opéra-Comique
18.08.1912	The Distant Sound	Schreker	Frankfurt/Main	Opernhaus

Date	Opera	Composer	Place	Theater
20th century				
25.10.1912	Ariadne on Naxos	Strauss, R.	Stuttgart	Hoftheater, Kleines Haus
01.04.1913	La vida breve	de Falla	Nice	Théâtre du Casino Municipal
26.05.1914	The Nightingale	Stravinsky	Paris	Opéra
26.09.1915	Mona Lisa	Schillings	Stuttgart	Hoftheater
30.01.1917	A Florentine Tragedy	Zemlinsky	Stuttgart	Hoftheater
27.03.1917	La rondine	Puccini	Monte Carlo	Opéra du Casino
11.05.1917	Harlequin	Busoni	Zürich	Stadttheater
11.05.1917	Turandot	Busoni	Zürich	Stadttheater
12.06.1917	Palestrina	Pfitzner	Munich	Prinzregententheater
25.04.1918	The Branded	Schreker	Frankfurt/Main	Opernhaus
24.05.1918	Bluebeard's Castle	Bartók	Budapest	Opera
14.12.1918	Il tabarro	Puccini	New York	Metropolitan Opera
14.12.1918	Suor Angelica	Puccini	New York	Metropolitan Opera
14.12.1918	Gianni Schicchi	Puccini	New York	Metropolitan Opera
10.10.1919	The Woman Without a Shadow	Strauss, R.	Vienna	Staatsoper
23.04.1920	The Excursions of Mr. Brouček	Janáček	Prague	National Theater
04.12.1920	The City of the Dead	Korngold	Hamburg	Stadttheater
04.12.1920	The City of the Dead	Korngold	Cologne	Opernhaus
21.05.1921	Doktor Faust	Busoni	Bologna	Teatro Comunale
04.06.1921	Murder, Hope of Women	Hindemith	Stuttgart	Württembergisches Landestheater
04.06.1921	The Nusch-Nuschi	Hindemith	Stuttgart	Württembergisches Landestheater
23.11.1921	Kát'a Kabanová	Janáček	Brno	National Theater
30.12.1921	The Love for Three Oranges	Prokofiev	Chicago	Auditorium Theatre
26.03.1922	Sancta Susanna	Hindemith	Frankfurt/Main	Opernhaus
20.04.1922	Fine Feathers Make Fine Birds (2nd version)	Zemlinsky	Prague	New German Theater
28.05.1922	The Dwarf	Zemlinsky	Cologne	Oper
03.06.1922	Mavra	Stravinsky	Paris	Opéra
23.03.1923	Master Peter's Puppet Show (concert)	de Falla	Seville	Teatro S. Fernando
25.06.1923	Master Peter's Puppet Show (stage)	de Falla	Paris	house of the Princesse de Polignac
06.06.1924	Erwartung	Schoenberg	Prague	New German Theater
06.09.1924	The Cunning Little Vixen	Janáček	Brno	National Theater
14.10.1924	The Fateful Hand	Schoenberg	Vienna	Volksoper
04.11.1924	Intermezzo	Strauss, R.	Dresden	Schauspielhaus
21.03.1925	L'enfant et les sortilèges	Ravel	Monte Carlo	Grand Théâtre
21.05.1925	Doktor Faust (German version)	Busoni	Dresden	Opernhaus
11.06.1925	Judith (1st version)	Honegger	Mézières im Waadt	Théâtre du Jorat
14.12.1925	Wozzeck	Berg	Berlin	Staatsoper
13.02.1926	Judith (2nd version)	Honegger	Monte Carlo	Opéra
25.04.1926	Turandot	Puccini	Milan	Teatro alla Scala
07.05.1926	The Sorrows of Orpheus	Milhaud	Brussels	Théâtre de la Monnaie
12.06.1926	King Roger (The Shepherd)	Szymanowski	Warsaw	Teatr Wielki
16.10.1926	Háry János	Kodály	Budapest	Opera
09.11.1926	Cardillac (1st version)	Hindemith	Dresden	Sächsisches Staatstheater/Opernhaus
10.02.1927	Jonny spielt auf	Krenek	Leipzig	Stadttheater
27.04.1927	Shwanda the Bagpiper (1st version)	Weinberger	Prague	National Theater
17.07.1927	The Rape of Europa	Milhaud	Baden-Baden	Stadthalle
16.12.1927	The Poor Sailor	Milhaud	Paris	Opéra-Comique
28.12.1927	Antigone	Honegger	Brussels	Théâtre de la Monnaie
20.04.1928	Ariadne Forsaken	Milhaud	Wiesbaden	?
06.05.1928	The Dictator	Krenek	Wiesbaden	Staatstheater
06.05.1928	The Secret Kingdom	Krenek	Wiesbaden	Staatstheater
06.05.1928	Heavyweight	Krenek	Wiesbaden	Staatstheater
06.06.1928	The Egyptian Helen	Strauss, R.	Dresden	Staatsoper
21.08.1928	The Threepenny Opera	Weill	Berlin	Theater am Schiffbauerdamm
16.12.1928	Shwanda the Bagpiper (2nd version)	Weinberger	Breslau	Stadttheater
21.01.1929	The Treasure Hunter	Schreker	Frankfurt/Main	Opernhaus
08.06.1929	News of the Day (1st version)	Hindemith	Berlin	Krolloper
16.06.1929	The Nose	Shostakovich	Leningrad	Malïy Opernïy Teatr
01.02.1930	From One Day to the Next	Schoenberg	Frankfurt/Main	Oper
09.03.1930	Rise and Fall of the City of Mahagonny	Weill	Leipzig	Neues Theater
12.04.1930	From the House of the Dead	Janáček	Brno	National Theater
14.02.1932	The Magnificent Cuckold	Goldmark	Mannheim	National Theater
01.07.1933	Arabella	Strauss, R.	Dresden	Staatsoper
22.01.1934	Lady Macbeth of the Mtsensk District (1st version)	Shostakovich	Leningrad	Malïy Opernïy Teatr
04.06.1935	The Silent Woman	Strauss, R.	Dresden	Staatsoper
10.10.1935	Porgy and Bess	Gershwin	New York	Alvin Theatre

Date	Opera	Composer	Place	Theater
20th century				
18.12.1936	The Makropulos Case	Janáček	Brno	National Theater
02.06.1937	Lulu (unfinished version)	Berg	Zürich	Stadttheater
08.06.1937	Carmina burana	Orff	Frankfurt/Main	Opernhaus
16.03.1938	Julietta	Martinů	Prague	National Theater
12.05.1938	Joan of Arc at the Stake (concert)	Honegger	Basel	Grosser Musiksaal
28.05.1938	Mathis the Painter	Hindemith	Zürich	Stadttheater
22.06.1938	Charles V	Krenek	Prague	New German Theater
05.02.1939	The Moon	Orff	Munich	Nationaltheater
21.02.1939	A Life for the Tsar (2nd version)	Glinka	Moscow	Bol'shoy Theater
13.06.1942	Joan of Arc at the Stake (stage)	Honegger	Zürich	Stadttheater
20.02.1943	The Clever Girl	Orff	Frankfurt/Main	Städtische Bühnen
06.11.1943	Catulli carmina	Orff	Leipzig	Städtische Bühnen
16.08.1944	The Love of Danae	Strauss, R.	Salzburg	Festspielhaus
07.06.1945	Peter Grimes	Britten	London	Sadler's Wells Theater
12.07.1946	The Rape of Lucretia	Britten	Glyndebourne	Opera House
09.01.1947	Street Scene	Weill	New York	Adelphi Theatre
18.02.1947	The Telephone	Menotti	New York	Heckscher Theatre
03.06.1947	The Breasts of Tiresias	Poulenc	Paris	Opéra-Comique
20.06.1947	Albert Herring	Britten	Glyndebourne	Opera House
06.08.1947	Danton's Death	Einem	Salzburg	?
02.04.1948	Simplicius Simplicissimus (concert)	Hartmann	Munich	Bayrischer Rundfunk
09.08.1949	Antigone	Orff	Salzburg	Felsenreitschule
20.10.1949	Simplicius Simplicissimus (stage)	Hartmann	Cologne	Theater der Stadt, Kammerspiele
01.12.1949	The Prisoner (concert)	Dallapiccola	Turin	Radiotelevisione Italiana
01.03.1950	The Consul	Menotti	Philadelphia	Shubert Theatre
20.05.1950	The Prisoner (stage)	Dallapiccola	Florence	Teatro Comunale
17.03.1951	The Judgment on Lucullus (1st version)	Dessau	Berlin	Deutsche Staatsoper
09.06.1951	Orpheus and Eurydice	Haydn	Florence	Teatro della Pergola
11.09.1951	The Rake's Progress	Stravinsky	Venice	Teatro la Fenice
12.10.1951	The Judgment on Lucullus (2nd version)	Dessau	Berlin	Deutsche Staatsoper
01.12.1951	Billy Budd	Britten	London	Royal Opera House
17.02.1952	Boulevard Solitude	Henze	Hanover	Landestheater
20.06.1952	Cardillac (2nd version)	Hindemith	Zürich	Stadttheater
14.02.1953	Triumph of Aphrodite	Orff	Milan	Teatro alla Scala
17.08.1953	The Trial	Einem	Salzburg	Salzburg Festival
20.10.1953	The Tricksters	Orff	Munich	Kammerspiele
13.03.1954	Moses and Aaron	Schoenberg	Hamburg	Musikhalle
07.04.1954	News of the Day (2nd version)	Hindemith	Naples	Teatro S. Carlo
27.01.1955	The Midsummer Marriage	Tippett	London	Royal Opera House
24.09.1956	The Stag King (abridged version)	Henze	Berlin	Städtische Oper
01.12.1956	Candide	Bernstein	New York	?
26.01.1957	Dialogues of the Carmelites	Poulenc	Milan	Teatro alla Scala
09.07.1957	Simplicius Simplicissimus (new version)	Hartmann	Mannheim	Nationaltheater
25.10.1958	Fate	Janáček	Brno	National Theater
06.02.1959	The Human Voice	Poulenc	Paris	Opéra-Comique
11.06.1960	A Midsummer Night's Dream	Britten	Aldeburgh	Jubilee Hall
25.11.1960	Khovanshchina (Shostakovich version)	Musorgsky	Leningrad	Kirov Theater
13.04.1961	Intolerance 1960	Nono	Venice	Teatro La Fenice
12.06.1961	The Greek Passion	Martinů	Zürich	Stadttheater
08.01.1963	Lady Macbeth of the Mtsensk District (2nd version)	Shostakovich	Moscow	Stanislavsky-Nemirovich-Danchenko Music Theater
10.03.1963	The Stag King (2nd version)	Henze	Kassel	Staatstheater
06.05.1963	Passage	Berio	Milan	Piccola Scala
15.02.1965	The Soldiers	Zimmermann, B.A.	Cologne	Städtische Oper
07.04.1965	The Young Lord	Henze	Berlin	Deutsche Oper
06.08.1966	The Bassarids	Henze	Salzburg	Grosses Festspielhaus
19.10.1966	Aventures/Nouvelles Aventures	Ligeti	Stuttgart	Württembergisches Staatstheater
20.06.1969	The Devils of Loudun	Penderecki	Hamburg	Staatsoper
25.04.1971	State Theater	Kagel	Hamburg	Staatsoper
23.05.1971	The Visit of the Old Lady	Einem	Vienna	Wiener Staatsoper
16.06.1973	Death in Venice	Britten	Snape	The Maltings
04.04.1975	In the Bright Sunshine Heavy with Love (1st version)	Nono	Milan	Teatro Lirico
16.12.1975	The Emperor of Atlantis	Ullmann	Amsterdam	Bellevue-Theater
12.07.1976	We Come to the River	Henze	London	Royal Opera House
25.07.1976	Einstein on the Beach	Glass	Avignon	Théâtre Municipale

Date	Opera	Composer	Place	Theater
20th century				
12.04.1978	Le Grand Macabre	Ligeti	Stockholm	Royal Opera
26.06.1978	In the Bright Sunshine Heavy with Love (2nd version)	Nono	Frankfurt/Main	Städtische Oper
24.02.1979	Lulu (complete version)	Berg	Paris	Opéra
08.03.1979	Jakob Lenz	Rihm	Hamburg	Staatsoper, Opera stabile
05.09.1980	Satyagraha	Glass	Rotterdam	Stadsschouwburg
11.10.1980	Görge the Dreamer	Zemlinsky	Nuremberg	Opernhaus
15.03.1981	Thursday from Light	Stockhausen	Milan	Teatro alla Scala
07.08.1981	Baal	Cerha	Salzburg	Kleines Festspielhaus
09.03.1982	The True Story	Berio	Milan	Teatro alla Scala
25.04.1982	The Wonderful Shoemaker's Wife	Zimmermann, U.	Schwetzingen	Schwetzingen Festival
02.06.1983	The English Cat	Henze	Schwetzingen	Schlosstheater
17.06.1983	A Quiet Place	Bernstein	Houston	Jones Hall
29.11.1983	St. Francis of Assisi	Messiaen	Paris	Opéra
24.03.1984	Akhnaten	Glass	Stuttgart	Württembergisches Staatstheater
25.05.1984	Saturday from Light	Stockhausen	Milan	Teatro alla Scala
07.08.1984	A King Listens	Berio	Salzburg	Kleines Festspielhaus
25.09.1984	Prometheus (1st version)	Nono	Venice	Church of S. Lorenzo
02.04.1985	Doktor Faust (It. version)	Busoni	Bologna	Teatro Comunale
07.05.1985	The Stag King (original version)	Henze	Stuttgart	Württembergisches Staatstheater
25.09.1985	Prometheus (2nd version)	Nono	Milan	Stabilimento Ansaldo
27.02.1986	White Rose	Zimmermann, U.	Hamburg	Opera stabile
15.08.1986	The Black Mask	Penderecki	Salzburg	Salzburg Festival
22.10.1987	Nixon in China	Adams	Houston	Opera House
12.12.1987	Europera	Cage	Frankfurt/Main	Städtische Bühnen
07.05.1988	Monday from Light	Stockhausen	Milan	Teatro alla Scala
18.05.1988	The Fall of the House of Usher	Glass	Cambridge (MA)	?
04.06.1988	Bremen Freedom	Hölszky	Munich	Biennale
29.04.1989	The Governor (2nd version)	Wolf	Strasbourg	Stadttheater
05.05.1990	The Betrayed Sea	Henze	Berlin	Deutsche Oper
19.03.1991	The Death of Klinghoffer	Adams	Brussels	Théâtre Royal de la Monnaie
13.04.1992	Life with an Idiot	Schnittke	Amsterdam	Dutch Opera
02.09.1992	The Castle	Reimann	Berlin	Deutsche Oper
15.05.1993	The Cave	Reich	Vienna	Wiener Festspielhaus
28.05.1993	Tuesday from Light	Stockhausen	Leipzig	Oper
12.09.1996	Friday from Light	Stockhausen	Leipzig	Oper
06.10.1996	King Candaules	Zemlinsky	Hamburg	Staatsoper
11.01.1997	Venus and Adonis	Henze	Munich	Bayerische Staatsoper
28.07.1997	Le Grand Macabre (revised version)	Ligeti	Salzburg	Grosses Festspielhaus

Selective bibliography

Reference works in several volumes

Die Musik in Geschichte und Gegenwart (MGG)
ed. Ludwig Finscher
2nd completely revised edition
Stuttgart, Kassel 1994–2005

Brockhaus-Riemann-Musiklexikon
ed. Carl Dahlhaus and Hans Heinrich
Eggebrecht
Wiesbaden, Mainz 1978–79

*The New Grove Dictionary of Music
and Musicians*
ed. Stanley Sadie
London 1980

Metzler Komponisten Lexikon
ed. Horst Weber
Stuttgart 1992

Pipers Enzyklopädie des Musiktheaters
Oper, Operett, Musical, Ballett
ed. Carl Dahlhaus et al.
Munich 1986ff

General surveys

Anna-Amalie Abert
Geschichte der Oper
Kassel 1994

Manfred Brauneck
Die Welt als Bühne
Geschichte des europäischen Theaters
Stuttgart 1993ff

Donald Jay Grout
A Short History of Opera
New York 1947 (new edition 1965)

Helmut Schmidt-Garre
Oper
Eine Kulturgeschichte
Cologne 1963

Ulrich Schreiber
Opernführer für Fortgeschrittene
Eine Geschichte des Musiktheaters
Kassel etc. 1988–91

Hans Heinz Stuckenschmidt
Oper in dieser Zeit
Europäische Opernereignisse aus vier
Jahrzehnten
Hanover 1964

Robert Fajon
L'opéra du Roi Soleil à Louis de Bien-aimé
Geneva, Paris 1984

Robert Donington
The Rise of Opera
Boston, London 1981

Fully illustrated books including histories of music

Hellmuth Christian Wolff
Oper
Szenen und Darstellung von 1600 bis 1900
(Musikgeschichte in Bildern, iv/1)
Leipzig 1968 (new edition 1985)

Dieter Zöchling
Die Chronik der Oper
Dortmund 1990 (new edition 1996)

Thierry Beauvert
Die schönsten Opernhäuser der Welt
Munich 1995

Works on specific genres and countries

Oper im 20. Jahrhandert
Entwicklungstendenzen und Komponisten
ed. Udo Bermbach
Stuttgart, Weimar 1999

Julian Budden
The Operas of Verdi
London 1973ff (new edition 1992)

Carl Dahlhaus
Vom Musikdrama zur Literaturoper
Munich, Salzburg 1983/Munich 1989

Winton Dean
Essays on Opera
Oxford 1990

Norman Demuth
French Opera
Its Development to the Revolution
Horsham 1963 (new edition 1982)

Sigrid Neef
Handbuch der russischen and sowjetischen Oper
Kassel 1989

Sigrid and Hermann Neef
Deutsche Oper im 20. Jahrhundert
German Democratic Republic 1949–1989
Berlin, Bern etc. 1992

Cameron Northouse
*Twentieth-Century Opera in England and the
United States*
Boston 1976

Nino Pirrotta and Elena Povoledo
Li due Orfei
Turin 1969 (new edition under the title *Music
and Theater from Poliziano to Monteverdi*, New
York 1981)

Für and Wider die Literaturoper
ed. Sigrid Wiesmann
Laaber 1982

Hellmuth Christian Wolff
Geschichte der Komischen Oper
Wilhelmshaven 1981

Volker Klotz
Operette
Porträt and Handbuch einer unerhörten Kunst
Munich, Zurich 1991

Composers

Rowohlt-Monographien (Rowohlt monographs)
inc. L. von Beethoven (1996), R. Strauss (1986),
R. Wagner (1997)
Hamburg

MusikKonzepte
Series on composers
ed. Heinz-Klaus Metzger and Rainer Riehn
Munich 1977ff

*Schriftenreihe "musik konkret" ("Musique
concrete" series)*
ed. Ernst Kuhn
Berlin 1992ff

*The New Grove series of great composers (life
and works in a single volume)*
ed. Stanley Sadie
Stuttgart, various dates

Rudolf Angermüller
Mozart
Die Opern von der Uraufführung bis heute
Frankfurt am Main, Berlin etc. 1988

William Ashbrook
Donizetti and his Operas
New York 1982

Jacques Barzun
Berlioz and the Romantic Century
New York 1969

Philippe Beaussant
Rameau de A à Z
Paris 1983

Volkmar Braunbehrens
Mozart in Wien
Munich 1986

Volkmar Braunbehrens
Salieri
Munich 1989

Mosco Carner
Puccini: A Critical Biography
London 1974

Carl Dahlhaus
Richard Wagners Musikdramen
Velber 1971

Winton Dean
Georges Bizet: His Life and Work
London 1975

Peter Evans
The Music of Benjamin Britten
London, Melbourne etc. 1979

Kurt Honolka
Leos Janacek
Sein Leben, sein Werk, seine Zeit
Stuttgart, Zurich 1982

Krzysztof Meyer
Schostakowitsch
Sein Leben, sein Werk, seine Zeit
Bergisch Gladbach 1995

Stefan Kunze
Mozarts Opern
Stuttgart 1984

Paul Henry Lang
George Frideric Handel
New York 1966

Friedrich Lippmann
*Vincenzo Bellini und die italienische Opera seria
seiner Zeit*
Studien über Libretto, Arienform and Melodik
Cologne, Vienna 1969

Charles Osborn
The Complete Operas of Puccini
New York 1982

Curtis Price
Henry Purcell and the London Stage
Cambridge 1982

Hans F. Redlich
Alban Berg: Versuch einer Würdigung
Vienna 1957

Willi Reich
Alban Berg
Leben und Werk
Zürich 1963

Willi Reich
Schönberg oder Der konservative Revolutionär
Munich 1974

Harvey Sachs
Toscanini
London 1978

Richard Taruskin
Stravinsky and the Russian Tradition
Oxford 1996

Eric Walter White
Benjamin Britten: His Life and Operas
London 1983

Eric Walter White
Stravinsky
The Composer and his Works
London 1976

Herbert Weinstock
Rossini
Adliswil 1981

Subject index

The index of subjects lists alphabetically the topics discussed in the commentaries. Page references in bold refer to a definition of the concept in the glossary.

Picture credits

The publisher has made every effort to trace all owners of reproduction rights. Any persons and institutions wishing to claim rights in connection with illustrations used in this book are requested to contact the publisher.
(tp = top; bm = bottom; rt = right; lf = left; cn = center)

Akademie der Künste (Berlin)
p. 79 tp, lf (Felsenstein-Archiv)
AKG – Archiv für Kunst und Geschichte (Berlin)
p. 200 tp, rt, p. 200 bm, lf, p. 202 cn, lf, p. 286, p. 326, p. 332 cn, rt, p. 340, p. 456, tp, lf, p. 517, p. 616 rt, cn, tp, p. 616 lf, p. 616 rt, tp, p. 616 cn, p. 616 rt, cn, bm, p. 666 bm, lf, p. 679 tp, rt
Amsellem, Gérard (Lyon)
p. 47 tp, rt, p. 95 cn, rt, p. 121 bm, p. 123 bm, p. 154 tp, lf, p. 155 bm, p. 203 tp, lf, p. 205 cn, rt, p. 290 rt, p. 291 tp, p. 322, p. 469 tp, rt, p. 488 cn, lf, p. 503 tp, p. 507 bm, rt, p. 507 tp, cn, p. 513
András Batta Archive (Budapest)
p. 202 bm, rt, p. 330/331
Andrea Rost Archive (Budapest)
p. 122 tp, rt, p. 374 (Operá National de Paris), p. 697 bm, lf (Lelli & Masotti, Milan)
Archiv des Robert Schumann-Hauses (Zwickau)
p. 566 cn, p. 567 bm
Archiv Dr. Zoltán G. Marton (Hamburg/Monaco)
p. 464 bm, lf, p. 596, p. 614 lf, cn (Photo Schaffler, Salzburg), p. 807 bm
Archiv Salzburger Festspiele
p. 381 tp (Ros Ribas), p. 381 bm, lf (Ros Ribas), p. 617 bm (Ellinger)
Archivio Storico del Teatro La Fenice (Venice)
p. 31 bm, lf
Archivio Teatro alla Scala (Milan)
p. 26, p. 28 tp (E. Piccagliani), p. 29 bm (E. Piccagliani), p. 42 (E. Piccagliani), p. 44 bm, lf (Lelli & Masotti), p. 44 bm, lf, p. 58 cn, rt (E. E. Piccagliani), p. 97 (E. Piccagliani), p. 103 cn, rt, p. 107 tp (E. Piccagliani), p. 131 bm (E. Piccagliani), p. 133 bm (Andrea Tamoni), p. 156 tp (Lelli & Masotti), p.164 bm, lf (Lelli & Masotti), p. 276 rt (E. Piccagliani), p. 303, p. 347 (Lelli & Masotti), p. 351 bm (Lelli & Masotti), p. 352 (Lelli & Masotti), p. 352 (Lelli & Masotti), p. 353 tp (Lelli & Masotti), p. 371 bm (Lelli & Masotti), p. 382 bm (E. Piccagliani), p. 444 (E. Piccagliani), p. 453, p. 454 (E. Piccagliani), p. 467, p. 469 bm, rt, p. 473 (E. Piccagliani), p. 473 u (E. Piccagliani), p. 480 tp, rt (E. Piccagliani), p. 480 bm, rt, p. 483 bm, rt, p. 486 cn, lf (Lelli & Masotti), p. 486 bm, rt (Lelli & Masotti), p. 487 bm (Lelli & Masotti), p. 527 (Lelli & Masotti), p. 529 cn, lf, p. 543 (Lelli & Masotti), p. 580 (Lelli & Masotti), p. 581 (Lelli & Masotti), p. 668 (Lelli & Masotti), p. 669 bm (Lelli & Masotti), p. 669 bm (Lelli & Masotti), p. 674 (Lelli & Masotti), p. 675 tp (Lelli & Masotti), p. 677 tp (Lelli & Masotti), p. 689 (E. Piccagliani), p. 691 tp, rt (E. Piccagliani), p. 704 (Lelli & Masotti), p. 708 (Lelli & Masotti), p. 710/711 (Lelli & Masotti), p. 714 (Lelli & Masotti), p. 718 bm, p. 719 tp, rt, p. 722 tp (E. Piccagliani), p. 724 (E. Piccagliani), p. 725 (E. Piccagliani), p. 731 bm, p. 921 (Piccagliani)
Archivio Teatro S. Carlo (Naples)
p. 241 tp, lf, p. 241 cn, bm
Arena di Verona/Ufficio Stampa
p. 739 tp, p. 740 tp
Arnold Schönberg Center (Vienna)
p. 552 bm (© VG Bild-Kunst, Bonn 1999), p. 555 tp (© VG Bild-Kunst, Bonn 1999),p. 555 bm, p. 556 bm
Aumüller, Barbara (Frankfurt/Main)
p. 20 bm, p. 341, p. 460 bm, rt
Baranovsky, Valentin (St. Petersburg)
p. 69 tp, rt, p. 164 bm, lf, p. 167 cn, lf, p. 168 lf, tp, p. 169 tp, rt, p. 413 bm, p. 418 bm, p. 419, p. 514, p. 515, p. 636, p. 637 tp, p. 647, p. 654 tp, lf, p. 655 bm, p. 656 bm, p. 657 tp

Bassewitz, Gert von (Hamburg)
p. 122 tp, lf
Bastian, Peter (Karlsruhe)
p. 66 bm, rt
Baus, Hermann und Clärchen (Cologne)
p. 220, p. 221, p. 564
© Bayreuther Festspiele GmbH
p. 799 cn (Wilhelm Rauh), p. 816 tp, lf (Wilhelm Rauh), p. 820 tp, lf (Wilhelm Rauh), p. 830 bm (Jörg Schulze), p. 832
Bergmann, Wonge (Frankfurt/Main)
p. 279 tp
Betz, Rudolf (Munich)
p. 117 bm
Beu, Thilo (Bonn)
p. 631 lf
bianconero/Franz Schlechter (Heidelberg)
p. 494, p. 495 bm
Bibliothèque Nationale de France (Paris)
p. 30, p. 32 cn, lf, p. 33 bm, lf, p. 46, p. 48, p. 49, p. 51, p. 64 tp, rt, p. 65 bm, p. 93,p. 96 bm, p. 112, p. 189, p. 190, p. 194 tp, lf, p. 288 tp, p. 290 lf, p. 291 rt, bm, p. 316, p. 426 bm, rt, p. 426 cn, bm, p. 447 tp, p. 507 cn, lf, p. 547, p. 661 cn, lf, p. 661 tp, rt, p. 713
Birkigt, Andreas (Leipzig)
p. 16 bm, p. 85 bm, lf, p. 569
Bologna Opera Archive
p. 84 (Lorenzo Capellini)
Bregenzer Festspiele GmbH
p. 8/9 (Benno Hagleiter/Vision Fotostudio AG), p. 89 tp, p. 89 bm (Reinfried Böcher),p. 150 bm, p. 152 cn, lf, p. 153, p. 721 bm (Miro Kuzmanovic)
Brinkhoff/Mögenburg (Geesthacht)
p. 425, p. 562, p. 860, p. 861
Caldwell, Jim
p. 848 tp, p. 849 tp (Courtesy of Houston Grand Opera Archives)
Cande, Daniel (Boulogne)
p. 99, p. 428, p. 429
Cinetext Bildarchiv (Frankfurt)
p. 58 bm, lf, p. 63,p. 203 bm, lf, p. 366, p. 367, p. 572 lf, **p. 573 bm, rt, p. 603, p. 705 rt, tp, p. 706 bm**
Collection Comédie-Francaise (Paris)
p. 371 tp
Columbia University in the City of New York/Office of Art Properties (New York)
p. 365 (Rick Osentoski)
Cooper, Bill (London)
p. 70 tp, rt, p. 71 bm, lf, p. 72 tp, rt
Deutsches Spielkarten-Museum (Leinfelden-Echterdingen)
p. 345 tp, p. 449 tp, rt, p. 449 cn, rt, p. 473 tp, rt, p. 543 bm, p. 655 tp, rt
Döring, Erwin (Dresden)
p. 246 bm, lf, p. 247, p. 479 bm, lf, p. 482 bm, p. 499, p. 630 tp, p. 863
DTM – Deutsches Theatermuseum (Munich)
p. 39 tp, p. 40 bm, p. 41 bm (Archiv Abisag Tüllmann), p. 102 (Archiv Hildegard Steinmetz), p. 114 cn, lf (Archiv Willy Saeger), p. 217 tp, p. 308 (Archiv Abisag Tüllmann), p. 309 cn, rt (Archiv Abisag Tüllmann), p. 309 bm, rt (Archiv Abisag Tüllmann), p. 493 (Archiv Hildegard Steinmetz), p. 539 bm (Archiv Abisag Tüllmann), p. 687 (Archiv Abisag Tüllmann), p. 828 (Archiv Abisag Tüllmann), p. 831 bm, p. 835 (Archiv Abisag Tüllmann), p. 837 (Archiv Abisag Tüllmann), p. 839 tp, lf (Archiv Abisag Tüllmann), p. 847 tp (Archiv Abisag Tüllmann)
EMI ELECTROLA GmbH (Cologne)
p. 464 bm, rt (Houston Rogers), p. 705 cn, rt
Felix, Claus (Nuremberg)
p. 841
Fotoarchiv Theodor Eisner (Salzburg)
p. 363 bm, rt, p. 363 bm, lf
Gehlen, Hannelore (Hamburg)
p. 258
Georg Wenderoth-Verlag/Louis Spohr-Archiv (Kassel)
p. 574 bm, p. 575 bm, lf, p. 575 bm, rt
Giesel, Joachim (Hanover)
p. 458 tp, rt, p. 460 bm, lf

Grand Théâtre de Genève
p. 614 rt (Jaques Straesslé)
© Green, Gordon/The Britten-Pears Library (Aldeburgh)
p. 72 tp, lf
Guy Gravett Picture Index (Hurstpierpoint)
p. 251 cn, rt, p. 251 bm, rt, p. 399 bm
Händel Gesellschaft (Göttingen)
p. 204,p. 205, tp
Helikon Opera (Moscow)
p. 522,p. 523 bm, p. 652,p. 653 bm (Oleg Nachinkin)
Herrmann, Oliver (Berlin)
p. 349 tp, p. 357 bm, p. 358 bm, lf, p. 394
Heysel, Claudia (Dessau)
p. 117 cn, tp
Hiltmann, Joachim (Hamburg)
p. 106
Historisches Museum (Vienna)
p. 364, p. 400 bm
Hoppens, Claudia (Bremen)
p. 86, p. 87 tp, cn
Hösl, Wilfried (Munich)
p. 212 tp, rt, p. 224, p. 229, p. 571 lf, p. 663 tp
Huber, Horst (Stuttgart)
p. 160
© Hulton Getty Picture Collection (London)
p. 40 tp, p. 60 bm, cn (Lafosse), p. 70 bm, cn, p. 75 tp, p. 127 tp, 186 tp, p. 201 tp, p. 490 bm, lf, p. 490 rt bm, p. 491
Hungarian National Library (Budapest)
p. 142 tp, p. 143 tp, rt, p. 143 cn, lf, p. 262, p. 263 cn, p. 263 rt, bm
Hungarian National Museum (Budapest)
p. 216 lf, tp, p. 216 lf, cn, p. 217 rt, bm
Jack, Robbie (London)
p. 495 bm, p. 678, p. 679 tp, lf, p. 679 br, p. 738
Jauk, Thomas Maximilian (Mainz)
p. 19 tp
Kass-Galerie (Szeged)
p. 16 tp, rt, p. 16 tp, lf
Keßler, Astrid (Hamburg)
p. 182
Kiermeyer, Gert (Halle)
p. 208 tp, p. 208 cn
Kilian, Gundel (Wäschenbeuren)
p. 148 tp, p. 149 bm, p. 158 tp, rt, p. 223 bm, p. 227 cn, rt, p. 227 cn, bm, p. 260, p. 270 rt, tp, p. 271 tp, p. 278/279
Kilian, Hannes (Wäschenbeuren)
p. 227 cn, lf
Kirsch, Guido (Freiburg)
p. 688, bm
Kowatsch, Uli (Nuremberg)
p. 226, p. 856, p. 857
kranichphoto (Berlin)
p. 61 bm, p. 107 bm, rt, p. 228 tp, p. 228 bm, p. 234 bm, rt, p. 235 bm, lf, p. 363 tp, p. 510, p. 511, p. 518 bm, p. 519, p. 726, p. 727 tp, lf, p. 727 bm, rt, p. 731 tp, p. 846 bm, p. 846 tp, p. 848 bm, p. 849 bm
Kunsthistorisches Museum (Vienna)
p. 395
Laboratoire Municipal de la Ville Aix-en-Provence
p. 504, p. 505 tp, p. 505 bm
Lagenpusch, Arwid (Berlin)
p. 173 tp, p. 181, p. 520 tp, p. 521, p. 572 tp, rt, p. 638,p. 838 bm, p. 838 tp
Landsberg, Jörg (Bremen)
p. 225, p. 416, p. 430 bm, p. 480 cn, lf, p. 726, p. 728, p. 730, p. 781 bm, p. 781 tp
Lefebvre, Klaus (Ennepetal)
p. 88 lf, cn, p. 231 bm, p. 392 bm, p. 392 tp, p. 393 bm, p. 397 tp, p. 398 bm, p. 403 bm, p. 404 cn, bm, p. 406 bm, rt, p. 438 bm, p. 439, p. 479 tp, rt, p. 552 tp, p. 599 bm, p. 642, p. 643, p. 802, p. 803, p. 808, p. 813, p. 814, p. 818, p. 819, p. 820 bm, p. 925
Les Arts Florissants (Paris)
p. 94, p. 95 bm, lf (Michael Szabo)
Lyric Opera of Chicago
p. 489 (Dan Rest)
Magic Vision/Fratelli Gnani (Bologna)
p. 296, p. 297, p. 666 cn, rt, p. 742, p. 747 tp, lf
Mährisches Museum (Brno)
p. 246 cn, lf

Márta Papp/János Bojti Archive (Budapest)
p. 66 tp, lf, p. 67 tp, rt, p. 67 tp, lf, p. 69 bm, rt,
p. 69 bm, lf, p. 162 bm, p. 163 tp, p. 163 bm,
p. 164 tp, lf, p. 165 tp, p. 166 tp, lf, p. 166 tp, rt,
p. 166 bm, p. 168 bm, lf, p. 169 bm, lf, p. 169 bm,
rt, p. 187, p. 404 cn, lf, p. 407 tp, rt, p. 407 cn, rt,
p. 410 lf, tp, p. 411 cn, lf, p. 411 lf, tp, p. 411 rt,
tp, p. 412, p. 414 tp, p. 414 bm, lf, p. 415, p. 418
tp, lf, p. 520 bm, p. 523 tp, rt, p. 650 bm, lf, p. 650
tp, lf

Matthias, Monica (Lochham)
p. 755 tp

Mentzos, Dominik (Frankfurt/M)
p. 11 tp, p. 158 bm, lf

Metropolitan Opera (New York)
p. 31 cn, lf (Winnie Klotz), p. 198 tp (Winnie Klotz),
p. 199 (Winnie Klotz), p. 379 bm (Winnie Klotz),
p. 401 bm, p. 455 tp (Winnie Klotz), p. 455 bm,
lf (Winnie Klotz), p. 474 cn, lf (Winnie Klotz), p. 474
bm, rt, p. 594 (Winnie Klotz), p. 675 bm, rt (Winnie
Klotz), p. 712 (Louis Mélancon)

Mezey, Béla (Budapest)
p. 541

Michel, Hans Jörg (Mannheim)
p. 133 tp, lf, p. 135 tp

Moatti, Jacques (Paris)
p. 34, p. 44 tp, p. 44 bm, lf (Moatti/Kleinefenn),
p. 45 bm (Moatti/Kleinefenn), p. 45 u (Moatti/
Kleinefenn), p. 96 tp, p. 127 bm, rt, p. 188,p. 397
bm (Moatti/Kleinefenn), p. 402 bm (Moatti/
Kleinefenn)

Müller, Bettina (Wiesbaden)
p. 131 tp, lf, p. 576

Musée dArt et dHistoire (Ville de Genève)
p. 335

Museo Teatrale alla Scala (Milan)
p. 22 cn, rt, p. 370, p. 451 tp, lf, p. 451 bm, lf,
p. 457, p. 466 lf, p. 468, p. 472 tp, lf, p. 485,
p. 534 lf, p. 534 rt, p. 670 tp, p. 670, bm

Mydtskov-Rønne, Martin (Copenhagen)
p. 66 bm, lf, p. 245 rt, p. 376,p. 379 bm,
p. 382 tp, p. 384 bm, p. 607, p. 609 tp, p. 765 tp,
rt

National Gallery Picture Library (London)
p. 103 bm, lf, p. 602

Opernhaus Zürich/Bildarchiv
p. 87 bm, rt (Schlegel & Egle), p. 100 bm,
lf (Schlegel), p. 101 bm, rt (Schlegel),p. 103 tp,
rt (Schlegel), p. 128 rt (Schlegel), p. 129 bm
(Schlegel),p. 167 tp, rt (Schlegel), p. 210/211
(Schlegel), p. 281 bm (Schlegel & Egle)

**Österreichische Nationalbibliothek/Bildarchiv
(Vienna)**
p. 21 tp, p. 21 bm, lf, p. 23 tp, rt, p. 23 bm, lf,
p. 25 tp, p. 27,p. 29 tp, p. 61 cn, lf, p. 82 bm, lf,
p. 98, p. 116,p. 118 tp, lf, p. 118 tp, rt, p. 119 bm,
lf, p. 120, p. 122 bm, rt, p. 124 tp, lf, p. 125 tp,
p. 125 bm, p. 128 lf, p. 131 tp, rt, p. 148 bm,
p. 149 tp, p. 178 tp, lf, p. 178 cn, lf, p. 178 cn,
bm, p. 179, p. 244 cn, bm, p. 245 bm, lf, p. 277 rt,
tp, p. 292, p. 293 tp, p. 293 rt, p. 300, p. 305 p.,
306 tp, rt, p. 307 rt, bm, p. 310, p. 317, p. 362 tp,
p. 406 tp, lf, p. 406 bm, lf, p. 440 cn, lf, p. 440 lf,
bm, p. 465 cn, rt,   465 lf, bm, p. 488 tp, rt,
p. 529 tp, p. 530 tp, p. 536 tp, lf, p. 542, p.
577, p. 589, p. 604 tp, p. 609 bm, cn, p. 609 bm,
rt, p. 614 lf, tp, p. 614 lf, cn, p. 619 tp, p. 620,
p. 622 bm, p. 624, p. 632, p. 667, p. 700 tp, lf,
p. 705 lf, p. 768 bm, lf, p. 777 tp, rt, p. 840 tp

**Österreichischer Bundestheaterverband/Bildarchiv
(Vienna)**
p. 14 bm, p. 20 tp, p. 32,p. 33 tp, p. 36 tp, p. 36
bm, rt, p. 37 tp, p. 37 bm, rt, p. 41 tp, cn, p. 53
bm, p. 55 tp, p. 56/57 (Hannes Gsell), p. 71 tp, lf
(Axel Zeininger), p. 90 cn (Axel Zeininger), p. 91 tp,
p. 108, p. 110, p. 119 tp, p. 121 tp, p. 123 tp,
p. 126 bm, p. 132 tp, lf (Axel Zeininger), p. 133 tp,
lf, p. 136, p. 137, p. 138, p. 140, p. 141 tp, p. 141
bm, p. 157 tp, 157 bm, p. 253, p. 250, p. 254,
p. 264 rt, bm, p. 266, p. 267, p. 268 cn, lf, p. 268
rt, tp, p. 268 bm, p. 269 tp, p. 269 bm, p. 272 cn,
lf (Foto-Fayer, Vienna), p. 272 rt (Foto-Fayer,
Vienna), p. 276 bm, lf, p. 277 lf, p. 277 lf, bm,
p. 282, p. 346 lf, p. 353 bm, p. 360 bm, p. 361,
p. 380, p. 388 tp, lf, p. 389 (Axel Zeininger), p. 398

tp, rt, p. 408, p. 409, p. 417, p. 420, p. 452, p. 472
bm, p. 487 tp, p. 488 bm, rt, p. 512, p. 528 bm,
p. 528 tp, lf, p. 531 cn, rt, p. 532 tp, p. 539 tp, lf,
p. 539 tp, rt, p. 546,p. 548 (Reinhard Werner),
p. 558, p. 559, p. 571 rt, p. 573 tp, p. 582, p. 583
lf, p. 583 rt, p. 593, p. 598 bm, p. 599 tp, p. 600
bm, p. 601, p. 604 bm, p. 610, p. 650 cn, lf,
p. 651, p. 657 bm, rt, p. 660 bm, p. 672 bm,
p. 682, p. 694 (Axel Zeininger),p. 695 (Axel
Zeininger), p. 698 bm, p. 707, p. 721 tp, p. 723,
p. 732 (Axel Zeininger), p. 733, p. 734 tp, lf, p. 734
cn, tp, p. 735, p. 743 bm, p. 744 cn, tp, p. 745,
p. 747 bm, rt (Axel Zeininger), p. 748,p. 750,
p. 753, p. 850 tp, p. 850 bm, p. 851 tp, p. 858 tp,
p. 859

© PAL – Performing Arts Library (London)<P>
p. 28 bm, lf (Clive Barda), p. 79 bm, rt (Clive
Barda), p. 80 tp, rt (Clive Barda), p. 81 (Clive
Barda), p. 242 bm (Clive Barda), p. 508 (Fritz
Curzon), p. 523 tp, lf, p. 544 (Clive Barda), p. 545
(Clive Barda), p. 578 lf (Clive Barda), p. 578 rt
(Clive Barda), p. 579 (Clive Barda), p. 662 (Clive
Barda), p. 663 bm, rt (Clive Barda), p. 663 cn, lf
(Fritz Curzon), p. 676

Palffy (Vienna)
p. 237, p. 323, tp

Paul Sacher-Stiftung (Basel)
p. 43 (Sammlung Luciano Berio)

Peyer, Fritz (Hamburg)
p. 259, p. 441

Pieper, Jaap (Heemstede)
p. 551

Pohlmann, Andreas
p. 532 bm (Théâtre Royal de la Monnaie, Brussels),
p. 533 (Théâtre Royal de la Monnaie, Brussels)

Rabanus, Winfried (Munich)
p. 621,p. 634 bm, p. 634 tp

Ramella & Giannese (Turin)
p. 24, p. 25 bm

Richard, Pierre (Paris)
p. 65 tp, rt, p. 65 bm, lf

Richard Strauss Archive (Garmisch-Partenkirchen)
p. 584 tp, p. 585,p. 586

Richard Wagner Museum (Bayreuth)
p. 754 tp, lf, p. 755 bm, rt, p. 807 tp, (Ramme),
p. 830 tp, lf,

Rittershaus, Monika (Berlin)
p. 174 cn, lf, p. 174/175, p. 218 tp, p. 218 bm,
p. 399 tp, rt, p. 449 bm, p. 785

Robert Marie-Noelle, (Paris)
p. 502,p. 503 bm

Rocholl, Juergen (Berlin)
p. 161 tp, rt, p. 161 bm, lf

Rosegg, Carol (New York)
p. 476,p. 477

Salzburger Marionettentheater
p. 348

Sattmann, Didi (Niederkrenzstetten)
p. 509 (Wiener Festwochen)

Schaefer, A.T. (Stuttgart)
p. 19 bm, p. 222 bm, p. 223 tp, p. 329 tp, p. 358
tp, p. 360 tp, p. 377 bm, p. 386, p. 387 bm, p. 390,
p. 423 tp, p. 423 bm, p. 424 tp, p. 424 bm,
p. 462, p. 570, p. 644, p. 645, p. 696 tp, p. 697 tp,
rt, p. 715, p. 719 bm, p. 798, p. 825 lf, p. 866/867

Schär, Ernst (St. Gallen)
p. 673 lf, p. 673 bm

Schilling, Katrin (Frankfurt/M)
p. 219, p. 236, p. 270 lf, bm, p. 460 tp, lf

Schimert-Ramme, Susan (Zürich)
p. 60 tp, rt, p. 324, p. 325,p. 328 lf, tp, p. 337 lf,
bm, p. 344 lf, p. 345 bm, p. 355 bm

Schnetz, Peter (Basel)
p. 130 tp, rt, p. 145

Schnur, Christian (Basel)
p. 206 bm, lf, p. 211 tp, rt, p. 211 cn, rt, p. 261 tp,
p. 261 bm

Schöne, Marion (Berlin)
147 tp, p. 355 tp, p. 524, p. 840 bm

Schreckenberg, Günter (Darmstadt)
p. 90 tp, p. 91 bm, rt

Schwiertz, Suzanne (Hamburg/Zürich)
p. 167 bm, rt, p. 184, p. 346 rt, p. 368, p. 369 tp,
p. 526 tp, rt, p. 527 bm, p. 690, p. 691 bm, cn, p.
692 bm, rt, p. 692 lf, p. 693, p. 855 bm

Sigmund Freud Museum (Vienna)
p. 597

Sir John Soanes Museum (London)
p. 332, lf, p. 332 tp, rt, p. 640, p. 641

Söllner, Robert (Nuremberg)
p. 11 bm

**Speidel, Elisabeth (Archiv Hamburgische
Staatsoper)**
p. 235 tp, p. 239 bm

Staatstheater Braunschweig
p. 342,p. 343 rt, p. 536 bm, rt, p. 537
(Thomas Ammerpohl)

Stadtarchiv Bonn
p. 183 (Astrid Kessler)

**Stadtarchiv und Landesgeschichtliche Bibliothek
(Bielefeld)**
p. 566 bm, p. 567 bm (Fritz Stockmeier, Bielefeld)

Stadttheater Heilbronn
p. 410 bm, lf, p. 648, p. 650 bm, rt

Stiftung Stadtmuseum (Berlin)
p. 103 cn (Ludwig Binder), p. 114 tp, rt (Eva
Kemlein), p. 146 (Ludwig Binder), p. 843 bm
(Marion Schöne)

Stockmeier, Fritz (Bielefeld)
p. 10, p. 194 bm, p. 195 tp, p. 238, p. 574 tp,

Straub, Eduard (Meerbusch)
p. 126 tp, p. 132 bm, rt, p. 133 tp, rt, p. 172,
p. 251 tp, p. 251 cn, lf, p. 325 bm, rt, p. 328 bm,
p. 336, p. 337 rt, p. 350, p. 369 bm, p. 377 bm, lf,
399 lf, cn, p. 402 tp, rt, p. 430 tp, rt, p. 442 bm,
p. 458 bm, lf, p. 538, p. 560 bm, rt, p. 561 tp,
p. 56, bm, p. 702 tp, p. 703 tp, p. 749, p. 752,
p. 864

Strauss, Bettina (Mainz)
p. 53 tp, rt, p. 664, p. 665

Süddeutscher Verlag Bilderdienst (Munich)
p. 584 (Scherl)

Südostbayerisches Städtetheater (Landshut)
p. 117 tp, rt (Atelier KAPS)

Teatro Communale di Bologna
p. 31 tp, rt (Primo Gnani), p. 84 (Lorenzo Capellini),
p. 540 (Primo Gnani)

Teatro Communale/Maggio Musicale (Florence)
p. 319 lf (Studio Associato PRESS PHOTO)

Teatro Regio di Torino
p. 498

Theater Hof
p. 88 bm (SFF Fotodesign GmbH, Hofmann/Dietz)

Thode, Joachim (Kiel)
p. 134 br, p. 137 b, p. 231 t, p. 302, p. 304,
p. 422, p. 865

**Thorburn, Eric/The Glasgow Picture Library
(Bishopton)**
p. 52, p. 75 bl

**Theaterwissenschaftliche Sammlung der
Universität zu Köln (TWS)**
p. 6/7, p. 1 tp, p. 12 bm, p. 13, p. 14 tp, p. 15,
p. 17, p. 18, p. 21 bm, rt, p. 22 cn, lf, p. 23 tp, lf
(Sammlung Niessen), p. 23 bm, rt (Sammlung
Niessen), p. 33 bm, rt (Sammlung Burggraf), p. 35,
p. 37 bm, lf, p. 38, p. 39 bm, p. 41 tp, p. 47,cn, lf,
p. 49, p. 54, p. 50, p. 55 tp, p. 55 bm, p. 57 rt,
(Sammlung Niessen), p. 58 tp, lf, p. 59, p. 60 tp, lf
(Willi Saeger), p. 62, p. 64 bm (Sammlung
Burggraf), p. 68, p. 72 bm, cn, p. 74, p. 76 cn, lf,
p. 76 cn, rt, p. 77, p. 78, p. 80 bm, lf, p. 82 cn,
p. 83, p. 85 tp, p. 92, p. 100 tp, lf, p. 101 tp, rt,
p. 104 tp, rt, 104 bm, lf, p. 105, bm, lf, p. 109,
p. 110 lf, tp, p. 110 lf, bm, p. 111, p. 113,p. 117
tp, lf, p. 124 bm, p. 129 tp, lf, p. 130 lf
(Sammlung Burggraf), p. 134 cn, lf (Emil Schwab,
Berlin), p. 134 tp, rt (Hildegard Steinmetz),
p. 135 bm, rt, p. 139, p. 144, p. 150 tp, p. 151,
p. 152 cn, rt, p. 154 bm, rt, p. 155 tp, rt, p. 156
bm, p. 171 tp, p. 171 bm, p. 173 bm, p. 176,
p. 177 bm (© Achim Freyer, Berlin), p. 177 u
(© Achim Freyer, Berlin), p. 180, p. 185, p. 186 bm,
p. 192 bm, p. 192 cn, lf, p. 192 cn, bm, p. 193,
p. 195 rt, bm, p. 196 Susan Schimert-Ramme,
Zürich), p. 197 (Paul Leclaire, Cologne), p. 198 cn,
rt, p. 201 bm, p. 203 tp, rt (Sammlung Burggraf),
p. 206 tp, rt (Clive Barda, London), p. 207, p. 209,
p. 211 cn, bm, p. 212 bm, p. 213, p. 214,
p. 215, p. 230, p. 232, p. 233 tp, p. 234 cn, lf,
p. 235 bm, rt, p. 239 tp, p. 240 tp, p. 240 bm

(Salzburger Festspiele), p. 241 tp, rt, p. 242 tp, lf, p. 243 tp, p. 243, bm, p. 248, p. 249, p. 252, p. 255, p. 256, p. 257, p. 264 lf, tp, p. 265 bm, p. 271 bm, p. 273, p. 274 tp, rt, p. 274 bm, p. 275, p. 283, p. 284, p. 285, p. 287, p. 288 bm, p. 289, p. 294, p. 295, p. 298, p. 299, p. 307 bm, lf, p. 307 bm, p. 312 tp, lf, p. 312 cn, bm, p. 313, p. 314, p. 318, p. 319 rt, p. 320, p. 321, p. 323 bm, p. 327, p. 329 bm, p. 333, p. 338, p. 339 rt, tp, p. 338 bm, p. 343 lf (Hildegard Steinmetz), p. 351 tp, p. 354 tp, p. 354 bm, p. 356, p. 357 tp, p. 359, p. 358 rt, bm, p. 362 bm, p. 372, p. 373, p. 375, p. 377 bm, rt, p. 378, p. 381 cn, rt, p. 384 bm (Sammlung Niessen), p. 385, p. 388 bm (Felicitas Timpe, Munich), p. 393 tp, p. 396, p. 398 tp, lf (from Topors theatrical broadcast, © Topor / Kehayoff Verlag, Munich), p. 400 tp, p. 401 tp, p. 402 tp, lf, p. 403 tp, p. 406 tp, rt, p. 407 bm, lf, p. 413 tp, p. 421 tp, rt, p. 421 bm, rt, p. 421 cn, tp, rt, p. 421 cn, bm, rt, p. 426 bm, lf, p. 426 tp, lf, p. 427, p. 430 tp, lf, p. 430 cn, lf, p. 431 bm (Lazlo Moholy-Nagy © VG Bild-Kunst, Bonn 1999), p. 431 bm, p. 432, p. 433 bm (Joachim Streubel © VG Bild-Kunst, Bonn 1999), p. 434, p. 435 tp, rt, p. 435 tp, cn, p. 435 cn, lf, p. 438 lf, p. 440 bm, rt, p. 442 tp, p. 443, p. 447 bm, p. 448, p. 450 tp, lf, p. 456 bm, lf, p. 458 tp, lf, p. 459 tp, p. 459 bm, lf, p. 461 (WDR), p. 463, p. 465 tp, rt (Sammlung Niessen), p. 466 rt, p. 470 bm, p. 470 tp, lf, p. 471 rt, tp, p. 475, p. 474 rt, p. 478, p. 481 bm, p. 483 tp, p. 484, p. 496, p. 497, p. 506, p. 518 tp, p. 525, p. 526 tp, lf (Sammlung Niessen), p. 530 cn, lf (Sammlung Burggraf), p. 535, p. 536 cn, lf, p. 549, p. 553, p. 554, p. 555 cn, rt, p. 556 lf, p. 557, p. 560, tp, lf, p. 563, p. 568, p. 575 tp, cn, p. 587, p. 588 tp, p. 588 bm, p. 590, p. 591 bm, p. 591 tp, p. 592, p. 595 tp, p. 595 bm, p. 598 tp, p. 600 tp, p. 605, p. 606 tp, p. 606 bm, p. 608, p. 611 lf, p. 611 rt, p. 613, p. 615, p. 617 tp, p. 618, p. 618/619, p. 622 tp, p. 623, p. 625, p. 626 (Felicitas Timpe, Munich),

p. 627, p. 630 bm, p. 631 rt, p. 633, p. 635, p. 637 bm, p. 639 cn, rt, p. 639 tp, rt, p. 646, p. 649, p. 653 tp, rt, p. 654 bm, rt, p. 656 tp, rt, p. 656 tp, lf, p. 671, p. 672 tp, lf, p. 677 bm (Sammlung Burggraf), p. 683 tp, p. 683 cn, rt, p. 684 (Felicitas Timpe, Munich), p. 685, p. 686, p. 688 tp, lf (Sammlung Niessen), p. 696 cn, lf, p. 699 cn, lf, p. 699 tp, lf, p. 698 tp, p. 701, p. 702 bm, rt, p. 702 bm, lf, p. 702 cn, bm, lf, p. 702 cn, bm, rt, p. 703 bm (Felicitas Timpe, Munich), p. 706 lf, tp, p. 709, p. 711, bm, rt, p. 716, p. 717, p. 718 tp, lf, p. 718 tp, rt, p. 720 tp, rt, p. 720 cn, rt, p. 722 bm, p. 729, p. 734 bm, p. 737, p. 739 bm, p. 740 cn, rt, p. 741, p. 743 tp, p. 744 lf, tp, p. 744 bm, rt, p. 746, p. 747 tp, rt (WDR), p. 751 (Felicitas Timpe, Munich), p. 754 bm, lf, p. 758, p. 759, p. 760, p. 761 tp, p. 761 bm, (Sammlung Sarnec), p. 762/763, p. 763 rt, p. 764 tp, lf, p. 764 bm, p. 765 cn, rt, p. 766/767, p. 768 tp, p. 769, p. 770 bm, p. 770 bm, lf, p. 771 tp, rt (Rudolf Betz), p. 772/773 cn, p. 774 cn, p.775 lf, p. 775 tp, rt, p. 776 bm, p. 777 tp, rt, (J. Albert), p. 777 bm, p. 778 tp, lf, (Siegfried Lauterwasser, © Bayreuther Festspiele GmbH), p. 778 cn, lf, (Liselotte Strelow VG Bild-Kunst, Bonn 1999), p. 778 rt, p. 779, p. 780, p. 782, p. 783, p. 784, p. 786, (Sammlung Niessen), p. 787 tp, rt, (Walter Kane), p. 787 bm, p. 788, p. 789, p. 790 tp, rt, p. 790 cn, lf, p. 790 bm, (J. Albert), p. 791, p. 792, p. 793 tp, p. 793 bm, p. 794, p. 795, p. 796 cn, rt, (Siegfried Lauterwasser, © Bayreuther Festspiele GmbH), p. 796 tp, lf (Siegfried Lauterwasser, © Bayreuther Festspiele GmbH), p. 796 cn, lf (Liselotte Strelow © VG Bild-Kunst, Bonn 1999), p. 796 bm, lf, (Liselotte Strelow © VG Bild-Kunst, Bonn 1999), p. 796 bm, cn (Liselotte Strelow © VG Bild-Kunst, Bonn 1999), p. 797 tp, rt, (Willy Dose, Bremen), p. 797 cn, rt Atelier Weirich, Eisenach), p. 797 bm, rt, (Liselotte Strelow © VG Bild-Kunst, Bonn 1999), p. 799 bm, p. 800 cn, lf (W. Höffert), p. 801, p. 804 (J. Albert), p. 805 tp, p. 805 bm, rt, p. 806, p. 810, p. 812 tp,

p. 812 bm, p. 815, p. 816 bm, p. 817, p. 822 cn (A. Pieperhoff), p. 822, bm, lf, p. 823, p. 824, p. 825 rt, p. 826 tp, p. 826 bm (Liselotte Strelow © VG Bild-Kunst, Bonn 1999), p. 827 bm, p. 827 tp (Wilhelm Rauh), p. 829, p. 833, p. 834, p. 836 tp, lf, p. 836 bm, p. 839 tp, rt Sammlung Niessen), p. 842, p. 843 tp, p. 844, p. 845 tp, p. 845 bm (Sarneck), p. 846 cn, lf (Willy Saeger), p. 847 bm, p. 851 bm, p. 852, cn, lf, p. 852 cn, rt (Emil Schwalb, Berlin), p. 853 tp, (Emil Schwalb, Berlin), p. 853 bm, p. 854, p. 855 tp, p. 858 bm, p. 862, p. 882

Thode, Joachim (Kiel)<P>
p. 134 bm, rt, p. 147 bm, p. 231 tp, p. 302, p. 304, p. 422, p. 865,

Thorburn, Eric (Bishopton)
p. 52, p. 75 bm, lf

Toepffer, Sabine (Munich)
p. 73, p. 222 tp, p. 233 bm, p. 531 lf, p. 756

Tomasina, Alberto dalla (Parma)
p. 680, p. 681

Trippel, Michael (Berlin)
p. 115 tp, p. 115 bm, p. 628/629

Uhlig, Bernd (Berlin)
p. 344 rt

Unitel Film- und Fernseh-Produktionsgesellschaft mbH & Co (Munich)
p. 800 rt, p. 805 bm, lf, p. 811, p. 820 cn, p. 821

Walz, Ruth (Berlin)
p. 280, p. 281 bm

Wiener Festwochen/Fotoarchiv
p. 387 bm (Théâtre Royal de la Monnaie, Brussels), p. 391, p. 565 (Monika Rittershaus)

© Wood, Roger (Canterbury)
p. 80 tp, lf

Wurst, Peter (Linz)
p. 436, p. 437 tp, rt, p. 437 bm, lf

Wuschanski, Dieter (Chemnitz)
p. 658, p. 659 tp, p. 659 bm, p. 500, p. 501, p. 797   bm, lf, p. 809

List of abbreviations used in the book

A	alto (contralto)
B	bass
Bar	baritone
Bbar	bass-baritone
counterT	countertenor
FP	first performance
Ms	mezzo-soprano
S	soprano
T	tenor
V	voice

Vincenzo Bellini, *La sonnambula*, Maria Callas (Amina) receiving applause at the end of a production at the Teatro alla Scala, Milan, in 1956.

Authors and translators

András Batta (A. B.) Ph.D., Budapest, studied musicology and cello at the Franz Liszt Music Academy in Budapest and received a scholarship to study at the University of Vienna (1978–79). Between 1976 and 1996 he produced numerous musical broadcasts for the Hungarian broadcasting authority and the ORF (Austrian Radio), Vienna (Pasticcio). Since 1979 he has taught music history at the Budapest Music Academy. He has been active as an editor of books on music for the publishers Könemann Music Budapest since 1996. He has produced numerous articles and scholarly publications, program notes, and notes for the recording company Hungaroton. His publications include the first comprehensive illustrated book on Richard Strauss in the Hungarian language (Budapest 1984), and *Träume sind Schäume: Die Operette in der Donaumonarchie* (in German, Budapest 1992).

Miklós Dolinszky (M. D.) Budapest, studied musicology at the Franz Liszt Music Academy in Budapest, and was active as artistic director at the Hungarian State Opera. Since 1993 he has taught in the aesthetics faculty of the Eötvös Loránd University and in the musicology department of the Franz Liszt Music Academy. He has published numerous articles on the aesthetics of music (with the emphasis on Schubert, Mozart, and philological matters), and works as the chief music editor for Könemann Music Budapest. Publications include *Das Mozart-Raumschiff* (collected essays in Hungarian, Budapest 1999).

Ágnes Gádor (Á. G.) Budapest, studied geography and librarianship at the Eötvös Loránd University, Budapest. Since 1971 she has worked in the Central Library of the Franz Liszt Music Academy in Budapest. Her research has focused on Schubert and the history of the Budapest Music Academy. She also works as a translator.

Péter Halász (P. H.) Budapest, studied musicology at the Franz Liszt Music School in Budapest. From 1989 to 1992 he was at the University of Hamburg with a DAAD scholarship and from 1993 to 1994 at the University of Vienna with a Herder scholarship. Since 1995 he has worked at the Institute of Musicology in Budapest. His area of study is twentieth-century Hungarian Music. Halász has edited several volumes of music for Könemann Music Budapest.

Johannes Jansen (J. J.) Cologne, studied musicology and is active as a journalist and writer of books. He is the editor and publisher of the Cologne music journal *Concerto*.

György Kroó (G. K.) Professor, Budapest , studied musicology and violin (1951–56) at the Franz Liszt Music Academy in Budapest, where he has taught music history since 1961 and been director of the musicology department since 1972. A leading editor of popular music programs for Hungarian radio, he was also active for 40 years as a music critic. Kroó has written several books and other publications on music, including some in English, on new Hungarian music, focusing on the work of György Kurtág, in the journal *The New Hungarian Quarterly*. Published books include a concert guide to Bartók (published in several languages), and works on Berlioz, Wagner, Schumann, the rescue opera, Bartók's stage works, and Aladár Rácz (the great Hungarian cimbalom player).

János Kovács (J. K.) Professor, Budapest, studied musicology (1951–56) at the Franz Liszt Music Academy in Budapest, and then worked as music critic on the Hungarian daily newspaper *Magyar Nemzet* (1960–77). In 1963 he became editor and in 1980 artistic director of the concert agency for the Hungarian Philharmonic. Since 1971 he has taught courses on Mozart and Italian opera in the musicology department of the Budapest Music Academy. His research focuses on Mozart, Verdi, and Puccini. He has published a number of scholarly articles.

Sándor Kovács (S. K.) Ph.D., Budapest, studied musicology and piano at the Franz Liszt Music Academy in Budapest, where he has taught music history since 1978. He has produced a number of radio and television broadcasts in Budapest and is also active in Hungarian radio as an editor. Since 1978, Kovács has worked in the Bartók Archives and has edited Béla Bartók's collection of folk songs in several volumes. His areas of research are the music of Béla Bartók, Hungarian folk music, and twentieth-century music.

Hartmut Lück (H. L.) Ph.D., Bremen, studied musicology, Slavonic studies, and German studies in Hamburg, Marburg, and Munich, gaining his doctorate with a comparative study of literary utopias. As a freelance author he writes for newspapers, specialist periodicals, and radio. His special subjects are eastern European music and contemporary music. From 1972 to 1978 he was a lecturer at the universities of Bremen and Oldenburg, from 1979 to 1986 editor of the *Neue Musikzeitung*, and from 1995 to 1996 co-editor of *Musica*. In 1998 he was the first recipient of the "Radio Prize for New Music Media" conferred by the Berlin Academy of Arts.

János Malina (J. M.)   Budapest, studied mathematics at the Eötvös Loránd University and musicology at the Franz Liszt Music Academy in Budapest. He works as an editor for the Hungarian music publisher Editio Musica. A specialist in Renaissance and Baroque music, he gives many concerts as musical director and recorder player with the ensemble Affetti Musicali, which he founded. His research focuses on the chamber vocal music of the seventeenth and eighteenth centuries.

Paul William Merrick (P. M.)   Ph.D., Budapest, born in Leicester, Great Britain, studied at Wadham College, Oxford (B.A., M.A. Oxon.) and at Sheffield University (Ph.D., 1985). He lives in Budapest, where he has taught English music at the Franz Liszt Music Academy since 1982. Publications include *Revolution and Religion in the Music of Liszt* (Cambridge, 1987), and a number of musicological articles, most recently "The Role of Tonality in the Swiss Book of Année de Pèlerinage," in *Studia Musicologica Academiae Scientiarum Hungaricae*, 39, 1998.

Sigrid Neef (S. N.)   Ph.D., Berlin/Herstelle, studied music and theater studies at the Humboldt University in Berlin, worked with Ruth Berghaus from 1979 to 1993 in a number of international opera houses, gave talks, wrote for specialist publications (such as *Musik in Geschichte und Gegenwart* and *Pipers Enzyklopädie des Musiktheaters*), and wrote articles on Russian music (*BMG Classics/Melodiya*). From 1993 to 1995 she taught at the Free University in Berlin. Her books include *Handbuch der russischen und sowjetischen Oper* (Berlin 1985), an illustrated monograph on Ruth Berghaus (Berlin, Frankfurt/Main 1995), *Die Russischen Fünf* (Berlin 1992), and *Deutsche Oper im 20 Jahrhundert* (Bern, Frankfurt/Main 1991).

Alexander E. Osthelder   Düsseldorf, studied musicology in Leeds, Great Britain, and subsequently singing (countertenor) at the Robert Schumann College in Düsseldorf. He is active as a freelance concert soloist. Osthelder translated the contributions of P.M. Merrick from English for the German edition of *Opera*.

Márta Papp (M. P.)   Budapest, studied musicology at the Franz Liszt Music Academy in Budapest. Since 1975 she has worked as an editor for Bavarian Radio. In addition to her work as a journalist, she has published musicological writings on various aspects of Russian music (above all Musorgsky, Rimsky-Korsakov, and Glinka) and on Soviet Russian composers and performers. She is a lecturer at the Budapest Music Academy. Books published include *Musorgsky: Complete Letters and Documents* (in Hungarian, Budapest 1997).

Éva Pintér-Lück (É. P. L.)   Ph.D., Bremen (born in Budapest), studied musicology in Budapest and gained her doctorate in Bremen in 1992 (*Claudio Saracini: Leben und Werk*). Since 1982 she has lived in Bremen, where she works as a freelance music journalist. Since 1989 she has written program notes for the Bremen Philharmonic Orchestra, and since 1999 has been active as a consultant for the encyclopedia *Musik in Geschichte und Gegenwart*. Her research focuses on Renaissance and early Baroque vocal music, and Italian Romantic opera.

Margareta Saary (M. S.)   Ph.D., university professor, Vienna, studied musicology and art history at the University of Vienna, and in 1983 received a research grant from the Vienna Institute for Musicology. She worked as an editor on the *Österreichische Musikzeitschrift*. Since 1986 she has been assistant professor at the Institute for Music Analysis at the University of Music and Performing Arts in Vienna. In 1995 she was appointed to a lectureship at the Institute of Musicology at the University of Graz. Since 1998 she has given classes at the Vienna Institute for Musicology. Her publications include *Persönlichkeit und musikdramatische Kreativität Hugo Wolfs* (Vienna 1984), *Österreichische Komponistinnen der Gegenwart* (CD-ROM,1997–98), *Die Musik der audiovisuellen Medien: Von romantischer Allmacht zu medialer Allgegenwärtigkeit* (Vienna 1999), and *Johann Strauss und das Musiktheater: Opulentes Amusement mit weltweiter Nachfrage* (1999).

Tünde Szitha (T. Sz.)   Budapest, studied musicology at the Franz Liszt Music Academy in Budapest. She has worked as program manager and editor for various Hungarian concert agencies, including the agency for the Hungarian Philharmonic, and also as a writer for radio and printed media. Her research area is new Hungarian music and twentieth-century music.

(The authors are identified in the text by the initials given above.)

The editor has had the privilege of having a "midwife" for this book in the lecturer Sigrid Neef. Without her extensive knowledge, her intimate and intense relationship with opera, and her selfless love of the subject, the book could not have come into being. I am further grateful to the authors for their many stimulating ideas. Special thanks are due to János Álmos of Kottamester BT, Budapest, who is responsible for the fine typesetting of musical excerpts and who gave me countless hours of his time. Dr. Gerald Köhler and Susanne Krischke of the Theatre Studies Institute of the University of Cologne were extremely helpful over the examination and selection of the pictures held there. Pascal Duc provided the French historical illustrative material. The rich scenography of Viennese operatic life was made available by Dagobert Gliencke of the Press Archive of the Vienna State Opera and Dr. Edit Barta of the Press Office of the Vienna Festival. Annie Rado's picture research at the archives of La Scala, Milan, was invaluable, as were the pictures and information supplied by Dr. Zoltán Marton. Special thanks are due to my friend Helmut Zehetner, a member of the Vienna Philharmonic, for shared operatic experiences and conversations about opera. The members of the music editing department at Könemann Music Budapest were invariably ready with advice and assistance: Dr. Éva Arató, István Máriássy, Rita Takács, Tamás Zászkaliczky, and Andrea Sári (editorial assistant). Last but not least, I am grateful to my wife Judit for her sharp-sighted proofreading as well as her confidence and patience in the years during which this book was created.

András Batta

The publisher would like thank all those who have actively contributed to the realization of the present volume. As representatives of all the stage photographers who made their photographs available to us, we thank Gérard Amsellern, Lyon; Klaus Lefebvre, Cologne; A.T. Schaefer, Stuttgart; Eduard Straub, Düsseldorf; and the Performing Arts Library, London. For support in picture research and acquisition, we thank, as representatives, Frau Dr. Bär, Robert Schumann-Haus, Zwickau; Signora Contrini, Museo Teatrale alla Scala, Milan; Signora Fumagalli, Teatro alla Scala, Milan; Andreas Homoki, Cologne; Frau Jäckl, Deutsches Theatermuseum, Munich; Frau Dr. Köger, Spielkarten-Museum, Leinfelden-Echterdingen; Dr. Ulrich Mosch, Paul Sacher-Stiftung, Basel; Andrea Rost and Anna Tóth; Dr. Schirmer, Stiftung Stadtmuseum, Berlin; Michaela Zahirk, ORF Opernredaktion, Vienna. For their help in picture editing we thank Kamilla Kisari, Sylvia Mayer, Nicole Klemme, Pia Oddo, and Dr. Nicolai Thesenwitz.

For their proof correction of the original German edition, we thank Claudia Hammer, Thomas Ristow, and Kirsten Skacel – the last-mentioned also for her work on the extensive indexes. For their active support with layout, correction of musical excerpts, and typesetting we thank Bernd Schreyer, Susanne Happe, Benjamin Knabe, Sonja Niess, Annette Eichler, and Sabine Schwarz; for work on the illustrations, Birgit Beyer and Sabine Emrich.

Giacomo Puccini, *Gianni Schicchi*, stage photograph from the
production by Willy Decker, Oper der Stadt Köln, Cologne 1999.